THE
OXFORD-DUDEN
PICTORIAL
CHINESE & ENGLISH
DICTIONARY

THE
OXFORD-DUDEN
PICTORIAL
CHINESE & ENGLISH
DICTIONARY

HONG KONG
OXFORD UNIVERSITY PRESS
OXFORD · NEW YORK

Oxford University Press, Walton Street, Oxford OX2 6DP
Oxford New York Toronto
Delhi Bombay Calcutta Madras Karachi
Petaling Jaya Singapore Hong Kong Tokyo
Nairobi Dar es Salaam Cape Town
Melbourne Auckland
and associated companies in
Berlin Ibadan

Oxford is a trade mark of Oxford University Press

Published in the United States
by Oxford University Press, New York

© Illustrations: Bibliographisches Institut
Mannheim 1989

© Chinese text: Keys Publishing Company Limited 1989

© English text: Oxford University Press 1989
Limp edition first published 1989

British Library Cataloguing in Publication Data
The Oxford-Duden pictorial Chinese & English dictionary.

1. Chinese language. Chinese English dictionaries
495.1'3'21
ISBN 0-19-584203-0
ISBN 0-19-582786-4 (limp)

Library of Congress Cataloging-in-Publication Data
Main entry under title:
The Oxford-Duden pictorial Chinese & English dictionary.

Includes index.
1. Picture dictionaries, Chinese.
2. Picture dictionaries, English.
I. Title: Oxford-Duden pictorial Chinese & English dictionary.
II. Title: Chinese & English dictionary.
III. Title: Chinese and English dictionary.
PL 1423.094 1988
495.1'321 -- dc 19
ISBN 0-19-584203-0
ISBN 0-19-582786-4 (limp)

Chinese text edited by Keys Publishing Company Limited
and Tung Hua Book Company Limited

English text edited by John Pheby, with the assistance of
Roland Breitsprecher, Michael Clark, Judith Cunningham,
Derek Jordan, and Werner Scholze-Stubenrecht

Illustrations by Jochen Schmidt, Mannheim

Printed in Hong Kong

Foreword

This Chinese & English pictorial dictionary is based on the third, completely revised edition of the German *Bildwörterbuch* published as Volume 3 of the ten-volume *Duden* series of monolingual German dictionaries. The Chinese text was jointly produced by Keys Publishing Company Limited and Tung Hua Book Company Limited while the Chinese index was jointly prepared by Assistant Professor Bu Chun-ying of Hohai University Press and Assistant Professor Li Yu-cai of Nanjing Architecture & Civil Engineering Institute. The English text was produced by the Oxford University Press Dictionary Department, with the assistance of numerous British companies, institutions and technical experts.

There are certain kinds of information which can be conveyed more readily and clearly by pictures than by descriptions and explanations, and an illustration will support the simple translation by helping the reader to visualize the object denoted by a given word. This applies both to technical vocabulary sought by the layman and to everyday objects foreign to the general user.

Each double page contains a plate illustrating the vocabulary of a whole subject, together with the exact Chinese names and their correct English equivalents. The arrangement of the text and the presence of a radical index in Chinese and an alphabetical index in English allow the dictionary to be used either way: as a Chinese-English or an English-Chinese dictionary. This, together with the wide range of vocabulary, which includes a large proportion of specialized words and technical terms, makes the Oxford-Duden Pictorial Dictionary an indispensable supplement to any Chinese-English or English-Chinese dictionary.

序 言

本辞典是根据经彻底修订的德文图解辞典 Bildwörterbuch 第三版编写（该辞典是共有十册的杜登德文辞典中的第三册）。中文部分由启思出版有限公司和东华书局共同编译，英文部分由牛津大学出版社辞典编辑部编译，并得到许多英国公司、机构和专业技术人员的协助。至於按中文部首排的索引则由河海大学出版社副教授卜纯英及南京建筑工程学院副教授李育才协助编纂。

用图示来解释某些词汇，往往较文字的描述更简便和清晰。图示绘出词目所指涉的实物，使读者一目了然。对一般读者来说，本辞典尤其适用於翻查专门术语和认识较陌生的日常用品。

本辞典所收录的词目均以所属范畴分类，以说明同页或邻页的插图。为方便读者翻检，辞典附有英文词目索引及中文词目索引。英文词目索引以字母先后排列，中文词目索引则以部首笔划排列，故本辞典兼具英汉及汉英辞典的双重功能。此外，因词目大部分为学术词汇及专门术语，故牛津–杜登英汉图解辞典实能补充一般辞典的不足，为专业人士案头必备的参考书籍。

Abbreviations used in the text

Am.	American usage	美国用法
c.	castrated (animal)	阉割了的（指动物）
coll.	colloquial	口语
f.	female (animal)	雌的（指动物）
form.	formerly	从前
zoc.	zocular	诙谐语
m.	male (animal)	雄的（指动物）
poet.	poetic	诗中用语
sg.	singular	单数
sim.	similar	类似的
y.	young (animal)	幼小的（指动物）

Contents

The arabic numerals are the numbers of the pictures

Atom, Universe, Earth
Atom I 1
Atom II 2
Astronomy I 3
Astronomy II 4
Astronomy III 5
Moon Landing 6
The Atmosphere 7
Meteorology I 8
Meteorology II and Climatology 9
Meteorological Instruments 10
Physical Geography I 11
Physical Geography II 12
Physical Geography III 13
Map I 14
Map II 15

Man and his Social Environment
Man I 16
Man II 17
Man III 18
Man IV 19
Man V 20
First Aid 21
Doctor I 22
Doctor II 23
Dentist 24
Hospital I 25
Hospital II 26
Hospital III 27
Infant Care and Layette 28
Children's Clothes 29
Ladies' Wear I (Winter Wear) 30
Ladies' Wear II (Summer Wear) 31
Underwear, Nightwear 32
Men's Wear 33
Hairstyles and Beards 34
Headgear 35
Jewellery (*Am.* Jewelry) 36
Types of Dwelling 37
Roof and Boiler Room 38
Kitchen 39
Kitchen Utensils and Appliances 40
Hall 41
Living Room (Lounge) 42
Bedroom 43
Dining Room 44
Tableware and Cutlery 45
Flat (Apartment) 46
Children's Room (Nursery) 47
Kindergarten (Day Nursery) 48
Bathroom and Toilet 49
Household Appliances and Utensils 50

Nature as Environment, Agriculture, and Forestry
Flower Garden 51
Fruit and Vegetable Garden 52
Indoor Plants (Houseplants) 53

目 录

（图示的编号用阿拉伯数字表示）

原子、宇宙、地球
原子 Ⅰ 1
原子 Ⅱ 2
天文学 Ⅰ 3
天文学 Ⅱ 4
天文学 Ⅲ 5
登陆月球 6
大气层 7
气象学 Ⅰ 8
气象学 Ⅱ 和气候学 9
气象仪器 10
自然地理学 Ⅰ 11
自然地理学 Ⅱ 12
自然地理学 Ⅲ 13
地图 Ⅰ 14
地图 Ⅱ 15

人及社会环境
人 Ⅰ 16
人 Ⅱ 17
人 Ⅲ 18
人 Ⅳ 19
人 Ⅴ 20
急救 21
医师 Ⅰ 22
医师 Ⅱ 23
牙医 24
医院 Ⅰ 25
医院 Ⅱ 26
医院 Ⅲ 27
婴儿看护和婴儿用品 28
童装 29
女装 Ⅰ（冬装）30
女装 Ⅱ（夏装）31
内衣、睡衣 32
男装 33
发型和胡须 34
帽子 35
珠宝饰物 36
各种类型的住宅 37
屋顶和锅炉室 38
厨房 39
厨房器皿和用具 40
门厅 41
客厅（起居室）42
寝室 43
饭厅 44
餐具和（西餐用的）刀、叉 45
公寓 46
儿童室（育婴室）47
幼稚园（托儿所）48
浴室和洗手间 49
家用器具 50

自然环境、农业和森林
花园 51
果菜园 52
室内植物 53

Contents   目录

Propagation of Plants 54   植物的繁殖 54

Market Garden (*Am.* Truck Garden, Truck Farm) 55   商品菜园（花园）55

Garden Tools 56   园艺工具 56

Vegetables (Vegetable Plants) 57   蔬菜类（蔬菜作物）57

Soft Fruit and Pomes 58   浆果和梨果 58

Drupes and Nuts 59   核果和坚果 59

Flowers 60   花卉 60

Weeds 61   杂草 61

Farm Buildings (*Am.* Farmstead) 62   农场建筑物（农场及其设施）62

Agriculture (Farming) 63   农业（农事、耕作）63

Agricultural Machinery I 64   农业机械 Ⅰ 64

Agricultural Machinery II 65   农业机械 Ⅱ 65

Agricultural Implements 66   农具 66

Overhead Irrigation 67   喷水灌溉 67

Arable Crops 68   适耕作物 68

Fodder Plants (Forage Plants) 69   饲料植物 69

Breeds of Dog 70   狗的品种 70

Horse I 71   马 Ⅰ 71

Horse II 72   马 Ⅱ 72

Domestic Animals 73   家畜 73

Poultry Farming (Poultry Keeping), Egg Production 74   养鸡场、鸡蛋生产 74

Rearing (*Am.* Raising) of Livestock 75   家畜饲养 75

Dairy 76   乳品厂 76

Bees and Beekeeping (Apiculture) 77   蜜蜂和养蜂 77

Wine growing (Viniculture, Viticulture) 78   葡萄栽培 78

Wine Cellar 79   葡萄酒窖 79

Garden and Field Pests 80   果园和田间害虫 80

House Insects, Food Pests, and Parasites 81   家虫、粮食害虫及寄生虫 81

Forest Pests 82   森林害虫 82

Pest Control 83   害虫防治 83

Forestry I 84   林业 Ⅰ 84

Forestry II 85   林业 Ⅱ 85

Hunting 86   狩猎 86

Hunting Weapons, Hunting Equipment 87   狩猎武器和狩猎装备 87

Game 88   猎物 88

Fish Farming (Fish Culture, Pisciculture) and Angling 89   养鱼和钓鱼 89

Sea Fishing 90   海洋渔业 90

Trades, Crafts, and Industry   **商业、工艺和工业**

Mills 91   磨坊 91

Malting and Brewing I 92   麦芽制造和啤酒酿造 Ⅰ 92

Brewing II 93   啤酒酿造 Ⅱ 93

Slaughterhouse (Abattoir) 94   屠宰场 94

Meat Joints 95   肉的各部分 95

Butcher's Shop 96   肉店 96

Bakery 97   面包店 97

Grocer's Shop (*Am.* Grocery Store) 98   食品杂货店 98

Supermarket 99   超级市场 99

Shoemaker 100   制鞋店 100

Shoes (Footwear) 101   鞋类 101

Needlework 102   手工刺绣 102

Dressmaker 103   裁缝店 103

Tailor 104   裁缝师 104

Ladies' Hairdresser 105   美容院 105

Men's Hairdresser (Barber) 106   男士理发厅 106

Tobacco and Smoking Requisites 107   烟草和烟具 107

Goldsmith, Silversmith 108   金匠、银匠 108

Contents　　目录

Watchmaker, Clockmaker 109	钟表匠 109
Clocks and Watches 110	钟表 110
Optician 111	眼镜店 111
Optical Instruments I 112	光学仪器 Ⅰ 112
Optical Instruments II 113	光学仪器 Ⅱ 113
Photography I 114	摄影 Ⅰ 114
Photography II 115	摄影 Ⅱ 115
Photography III 116	摄影 Ⅲ 116
Cine Film 117	电影摄影机 117
Building Site (Construction Site) I 118	建筑基地（施工基地）Ⅰ 118
Building Site (Construction Site) II 119	建筑基地（施工基地）Ⅱ 119
Carpenter 120	木工（木匠）120
Roof, Timber Joints 121	屋顶、木材接合 121
Roof and Roofer 122	屋顶和屋顶所用材料 122
Floor, Ceiling, Staircase Construction 123	楼层、天花板、楼梯间构造 123
Glazier 124	玻璃匠 124
Plumber 125	铅管工人 125
Plumber, Gas Fitter, Heating Engineer 126	铅管工、瓦斯匠、供暖技师 126
Electrician 127	电工 127
Paperhanger 128	壁纸裱糊工 128
Painter 129	油漆工 129
Cooper and Tank Construction Engineer 130	箍桶工和桶槽建造师 130
Furrier 131	毛皮商，皮货制造工 131
Joiner I 132	细木匠（细木工）Ⅰ 132
Joiner II 133	细木匠（细木工）Ⅱ 133
Do-it-yourself 134	自己动手做所需要的工具 134
Turner (Ivory Carver) 135	车床工（象牙雕刻工）135
Basket Maker 136	编篮工人 136
Blacksmith (Smith) I 137	铁匠（锻工）Ⅰ 137
Blacksmith (Smith) II (Farm Vehicle Engineering) 138	铁匠Ⅱ（农场车辆工程）138
Hammer Forging (Smith Forging) and Drop Forging 139	锤锻和落锤锻 139
Metallworker 140	金工（金属加工）140
Gas Welder 141	气体熔接工 141
Arc Welder 142	电弧熔接工 142
Sections, Bolts and Machine Parts 143	型钢、螺栓和机械零件 143
Coal Mine 144	煤矿 144
Mineral Oil (Oil, Petroleum) 145	矿油（石油）145
Offshore Drilling 146	海上钻探 146
Iron and Steel Works 147	钢铁厂 147
Iron Foundry and Rolling Mill 148	铸铁厂和轧钢厂 148
Machine Tools I 149	工具机 Ⅰ 149
Machine Tools II 150	工具机 Ⅱ 150
Drawing Office 151	制图室 151
Power Plant (Power Station) I 152	发电厂（发电站）Ⅰ 152
Power Plant (Power Station) II 153	发电厂（发电站）Ⅱ 153
Nuclear Energy 154	核能 154
Modern Sources of Energy 155	现代能源 155
Coking Plant 156	焦化厂 156
Sawmill 157	锯木厂 157
Quarry 158	采石场 158
Brickworks (Brickyard, Brickfield) 159	砖厂 159
Cement Works (Cement Factory) 160	水泥工（水泥厂）160
Porcelain and China Manufacture 161	瓷器和陶瓷制造 161
Glass Production 162	玻璃生产 162
Cotton Spinning I 163	棉纺 Ⅰ 163
Cotton Spinning II 164	棉纺 Ⅱ 164
Weaving I 165	机织 Ⅰ 165
Weaving II 166	机织 Ⅱ 166
Knitting 167	针织 167

Contents

目录

Finishing of Textile Fabrics 168

织品最后加工 168

Synthetic (Man-made) Fibres (*Am.* Fibers) I 169

合成（人造）纤维 Ⅰ 169

Synthetic (Man-made) Fibres (*Am.* Fibers) II 170

合成（人造）纤维 Ⅱ 170

Weaves and Knits 171

平织组织和针织组织 171

Papermaking I 172

造纸 Ⅰ 172

Papermaking II 173

造纸 Ⅱ 173

Printing Industry

印刷业

Composing Room (Case Room) I 174

组版房（排字房）Ⅰ 174

Composing Room (Case Room) II 175

组版房（排字房）Ⅱ 175

Composing Room (Case Room) (Phototypesetting, Photocomposition, Photosetting, Filmsetting) III 176

组版房（照相排版，照相组版）Ⅲ 176

Photomechanical Reproduction 177

照相制版 177

Electrotyping and Block Making 178

电铸凸版和铜锌凸版之制造 178

Offset Platemaking 179

平版制版 179

Offset Printing 180

平版印刷 180

Letterpress Printing 181

凸版印刷 181

Photogravure (Gravure Printing, Intaglio Printing) 182

照相凹版印刷（凹版印刷）182

Bookbinding I 183

书籍装订 Ⅰ 183

Bookbinding II 184

书籍装订 Ⅱ 184

Bookbinding III 185

书籍装订 Ⅲ 185

Transport, Communications, and Information Technology

交通、通讯和资讯科技

Horse-drawn Carriages 186

马车 186

Bicycle 187

自行车（脚踏车）187

Motorcycles, Bicycles, Scooters, Mopeds 188

摩托车（机车）、自行车 188

Motorcycle 189

摩托车（机车）189

Internal Combustion Engines 190

内燃机 190

Motor Car (*Am.* Automobile) I 191

小轿车 Ⅰ 191

Motor Car (*Am.* Automobile) II 192

小轿车 Ⅱ 192

Motor Car (*Am.* Automobile) III 193

小轿车 Ⅲ 193

Lorries (*Am.* Trucks), Van, Buses 194

货车、有盖卡车、公共汽车 194

Garage (*Am.* Shop) 195

修车厂 195

Service-Station 196

加油站 196

Tram (*Am.* Street car, Trolley), Interurban Electric Train 197

有轨电车、都市间电动列车 197

Cross-section of a Street 198

街道横剖面 198

Refuse Disposal (*Am.* Garbage Disposition), Street Cleaning 199

垃圾处理、街道清扫 199

Road Construction I (Road Building, Road Making) 200

筑路 Ⅰ（道路施工）200

Road Construction II (Road Building, Road Making) 201

筑路 Ⅱ（道路施工）201

Railway Line (*Am.* Railroad Track) I 202

铁路线（路轨）Ⅰ 202

Railway Line (*Am.* Railroad Track) II (Signalling Equipment) 203

铁路线（信号装置）Ⅱ 203

Station Hall 204

车站大厅 204

Station Platform 205

车站月台 205

Goods Station (Freight Depot) 206

货运站 206

Railway Vehicles (Rolling Stock) I 207

铁路车辆 Ⅰ 207

Railway Vehicles (Rolling Stock) II 208

铁路车辆 Ⅱ 208

Railway Vehicles (Rolling Stock) III 209

铁路车辆 Ⅲ 209

Railway Vehicles (Rolling Stock) IV 210

铁路车辆 Ⅳ 210

Railway Vehicles (Rolling Stock) V 211

铁路车辆 Ⅴ 211

Railway Vehicles (Rolling Stock) VI 212

铁路车辆 Ⅵ 212

Railway Vehicles (Rolling Stock) VII 213

铁路车辆 Ⅶ 213

Contents

Mountain Railways (*Am.* Mountain Railroads) and Cableways) 214
Bridges 215
Rivers and River Engineering 216
Waterway and Hydraulic Engineering 217
Types of Historical Ship 218
Sailing Ship I 219
Sailing Ship II 220
Types of Ship 221
Shipbuilding 222
Motor Ship 223
Navigation 224
Docks, Port, Harbour (*Am.* Harbor) I 225
Docks, Port, Harbour (*Am.* Harbor) II 226
Salvage (Salving) and Towage 227
Life Saving 228
Aircraft I 229
Aircraft II 230
Aircraft III 231
Aircraft IV 232
Airport 233
Space Flight I 234
Space Flight II 235
Post Office I 236
Post Office II (Telephones and Telegraphy) 237
Broadcasting (Radio and Television) I 238
Broadcasting (Radio and Television) II 239
Broadcasting (Television Engineering) III 240
Music Systems (Audio Systems) 241
Teaching Equipment and Information 242
Audiovision (AV) 243
Computer Centre (*Am.* Center) 244

Office, Bank, Stock Exchange
Office I 245
Office II 246
Office III 247
Office IV 248
Office V 249
Bank 250
Stock Exchange 251

Community
Money (Coins and Notes, *Am.* Coins and Bills) 252
Flags 253
Heraldry, Crowns and Coronets 254
Armed Forces I (Army) 255
Armed Forces II (Air Force I) 256
Armed Forces III (Air Force II) 257
Warships I 258
Warships II (Modern Fighting Ships) 259
School I (Primary School) 260
School II (Secondary School) 261
University 262
Election 263
Police 264
Café 265
Restaurant 266
Hotel 267
Town (Town Centre, *Am.* Downtown) 268

目录

登山铁路和缆道 214
桥梁 215
河川和河道工程 216
水道和水力工程 217
历代船舶类型 218
帆船 Ⅰ 219
帆船 Ⅱ 220
船的类型 221
造船 222
内燃机船 223
航海 224
码头、港埠、港 Ⅰ 225
码头、港埠、港 Ⅱ 226
海难救助和曳航（拖船）227
救生 228
飞机 Ⅰ 229
飞机 Ⅱ 230
飞机 Ⅲ 231
飞机 Ⅳ 232
飞机场 233
太空飞行 Ⅰ 234
太空飞行 Ⅱ 235
邮局 Ⅰ 236
邮局 Ⅱ（电话和电报）237
广播（无线电与电视广播）Ⅰ 238
广播（无线电与电视广播）Ⅱ 239
广播（电视工程）Ⅲ 240
音响系统 241
教学设备和资讯技术 242
视听设备 243
电脑中心 244

办公室、银行、证券交易所
办公室 Ⅰ 245
办公室 Ⅱ 246
办公室 Ⅲ 247
办公室 Ⅳ 248
办公室 Ⅴ 249
银行 250
证券交易所 251

社会
货币（硬币和纸币）252
旗帜 253
纹章、王冠和冠饰 254
军备 Ⅰ（陆军）255
军备 Ⅱ（空军 Ⅰ）256
军备 Ⅲ（空军 Ⅱ）257
军舰 Ⅰ（海军）258
军舰 Ⅱ（现代化战舰）259
学校 Ⅰ（小学）260
学校 Ⅱ（初级中学、高级中学）261
大学 262
选举 263
警察 264
咖啡店 265
餐厅 266
旅馆 267
市镇（市中心，〔美〕商业区）268

Contents   目 录

Water Supply 269   给水，供水 269
Fire Service (*Am.* Fire Department) 270   消防队 270
Department Store 271   百货店 271
Park 272   公园 272

Recreation, Games, Sport   **康乐活动、游戏和体育运动**
Children's Playground 273   儿童游乐场 273
Spa 274   温泉 274
Roulette 275   轮盘赌 275
Board Games and Party Game 276   棋类游戏与社交游戏 276
Billiards 277   撞球，弹子 277
Camping and Caravanning (*Am.* Trailering) 278   露营和篷车旅行 278
Surf Riding (Surfing), Skin Diving 279   冲浪运动和潜水运动 279
Bathing Beach 280   海水浴场 280
Swimming Bath (Leisure Centre, *Am.* Center) 281   游泳池（休闲中心）281
Swimming 282   游泳 282
Rowing and Canoeing 283   划船与赛舟 283
Sailing (Yachting) I 284   帆船驾驶（帆船竞赛）I 284
Sailing (Yachting) II 285   帆船驾驶（帆船竞赛）II 285
Motorboats (Powerboats), Water Skiing 286   汽艇（动力艇）和滑水运动 286
Gliding (Soaring) 287   滑翔运动 287
Aerial Sports (Airsports) 288   空中运动 288
Horsemanship, Equestrain Sport 289   骑术（运动）289
Cycle Racing and Motorsports 290   自行车竞赛和摩托车运动 290
Ball Games I (Football, Association Football, Soccer) 291   球类运动 I（足球、英式足球）291
Ball Games II 292   球类运动 II 292
Ball Games III 293   球类运动 III 293
Fencing 294   击剑 294
Free Exercise 295   徒手体操（自由体操）295
Apparatus Gymnastics I 296   器械体操 I 296
Apparatus Gymnastics II (Women's Gymnastics) 297   器械体操 II（女子体操）297
Athletics (Track and Field Events) 298   田径运动（田径赛）298
Weightlifting and Combat Sports 299   举重与运动 299
Mountaineering 300   登山运动 300
Winter Sports I (Skiing) 301   冬季运动 I（滑雪）301
Winter Sports II 302   冬季运动 II 302
Winter Sports III 303   冬季运动 III 303
Countryside in Winter 304   冬季乡间 304
Various Sports 305   其他运动 305

Entertainment, Culture, and Art   **娱乐、文化和艺术**
Carnival 306   狂欢节，嘉年华会 306
Circus 307   马戏团 307
Fair, Fairground 308   市集、市集场地 308
Flea Market 309   廉价市场 309
Films (Motion Pictures) I 310   电影 I 310
Films (Motion Pictures) II 311   电影 II 311
Films (Motion Pictures) III 312   电影 III 312
Films (Motion Pictures) IV 313   电影 IV 313
Ballet 314   芭蕾舞 314
Theatre (*Am.* Theater) I 315   剧场，剧院 I 315
Theatre (*Am.* Theater) II 316   剧场，剧院 II 316
Discotheque 317   唱片伴奏舞厅（的士高）317
Nightclub 318   夜总会 318
Bullfighting, Rodeo 319   斗牛，牛仔竞技 319
Musical Notation I 320   乐谱（音乐记谱法）I 320
Musical Notation II 321   乐谱（音乐记谱法）II 321

Contents

目录

Musical Instruments I 322
Musical Instruments II 323
Musical Instruments III 324
Musical Instruments IV 325
Musical Instruments V 326
Fabulous Creatures (Fabled Beings) 327
Prehistory 328
Chivalry 329
Church I 330
Church II 331
Church III 332
Art I 333
Art II 334
Art III 335
Art IV 336
Art V 337
Artist's Studio 338
Sculptor's Studio 339
Graphic Art 340
Script I 341
Script II 342
Colour (*Am.* Color) 343
Mathematics I 344
Mathematics II 345
Mathematics III (Geometry I) 346
Mathematics IV (Geometry II) 347
Mathematics V (Sets) 348
Chemistry Laboratory I 349
Chemistry Laboratory II 350
Crystals, Crystallography 351
Ethnology I 352
Ethnology II 353
Ethnology III 354
Historical costumes 355

Animals and Plants
Zoo (Zoological Gardens) 356
Invertebrates 357
Articulates 358
Birds I 359
Birds II (European Birds) 360
Birds III (Passerines) 361
Birds IV (Birds of Prey) 362
Birds V (Exotic Birds) 363
Fish, Amphibia, and Reptiles 364
Lepidoptera (Butterflies and Moths) 365
Mammals I 366
Mammals II 367
Mammals III 368
Deep-sea Fauna 369
General Botany 370
Deciduous Trees 371
Conifers 372
Ornamental Shrubs and Trees I 373
Ornamental Shrubs and Trees II 374
Meadow Flowers and Wayside Flowers (Wild Flowers) I 375
Meadow Flowers and Wayside Flowers (Wild Flowers) II 376
Plants of Forest, Marsh, and Heathland 377

乐器 Ⅰ 322
乐器 Ⅱ 323
乐器 Ⅲ 324
乐器 Ⅳ 325
乐器 Ⅴ 326
神话中之动物 327
史前时代史 328
武士制度 329
教堂 Ⅰ 330
教堂 Ⅱ 331
教堂 Ⅲ 332
艺术 Ⅰ 333
艺术 Ⅱ 334
艺术 Ⅲ 335
艺术 Ⅳ 336
艺术 Ⅴ 337
画家的画室 338
雕刻家工作室 339
平面艺术 340
文字 Ⅰ 341
文字 Ⅱ 342
颜色 343
数学 Ⅰ 344
数学 Ⅱ 345
数学 Ⅲ（几何学 Ⅰ）346
数学 Ⅳ（几何学 Ⅱ）347
数学 Ⅴ（集）348
化学实验室 Ⅰ 349
化学实验室 Ⅱ 350
晶体、结晶学 351
人种学 Ⅰ 352
人种学 Ⅱ 353
人种学 Ⅲ 354
历史上的服饰 355

动物和植物
动物园 356
无脊椎动物 357
关节动物 358
鸟类 Ⅰ 359
鸟类 Ⅱ（欧洲鸟类）360
鸟类 Ⅲ（燕雀目）361
鸟类 Ⅳ（猛禽）362
鸟类 Ⅴ（奇特悦人的鸟类）363
鱼类、两栖类和爬虫类 364
鳞翅目（蝶和蛾）365
哺乳动物 Ⅰ 366
哺乳动物 Ⅱ 367
哺乳动物 Ⅲ 368
深海动物相 369
普通植物 370
落叶树 371
针叶树 372
观赏灌木和乔木 Ⅰ 373
观赏灌木和乔木 Ⅱ 374
草地花和路边花（野花）Ⅰ 375
草地花和路边花（野花）Ⅱ 376
森林、沼泽和野生植物 377

Contents

目 录

1-8 atom models
原子模型

1 model of the hydrogen (H) atom
氢原子模型

2 atomic nucleus, a proton
原子核，质子

3 election
电子

4 electron shell
电子自旋

5 model of the helium (HE) atom
氦原子模型

6 electron shell
电子壳层

7 Pauli exclusion principle (exclusion principle, Pauli principle)
庖立不相容原理（排他原理，庖立定理）

8 complete electron shell of the Na atom (sodium atom)
钠原子的（满）电子壳层

9-14 molecular structures (lattice structures)
分子结构（晶格结构）

9 crystal of sodium chloride (of common salt)
氯化钠（食盐）晶体

10 chlorine ion
氯离子

11 sodium ion
钠离子

12 crystal of cristobalite
白矽石（方石英）晶体

13 oxygen atom
氧原子

14 silicon atom
矽原子

15 **energy levels** (possible quantum jumps) of the hydrogen atom
氢原子的能阶（可能的量子迁跃）

16 atomic nucleus (proton)
原子核（质子）

17 electron
电子

18 ground state level
基态能阶

19 excited state
受激状态

20-25 quantum jumps (quantum transitions)
量子跃迁(量子转移）

20 Lyman series
赖曼系

21 Balmer series
巴耳麦系

22 Paschen series
帕申系

23 Brackett serices
布拉克系

24 Pfund series
普芬德系

25 free electron
自由电子

26 Bohr-Sommerfeld model of the H atom
氢原子的波耳-索末菲模型

27 energy levels of the electron
电子的能阶

28 **spontaneous decay** of radioactive material
辐射（放射物）性质的自发衰变

29 atomic nucleus
原子核

30-31 alpha particle (α, alpha radiation, helium nucleus)
阿伐粒子（α阿伐辐射，氦原子核）

30 neutron
中子

31 proton
质子

32 beta particle (β, bata radiation, electron)
贝他粒子（β贝他辐射，电子）

33 gamma radiation (γ, a hard X-radiation)
伽马辐射（γ，强辐射）

34 **nuclear fission**
核分裂

35 heavy atomic nucleus
重原子核

36 neutron bombardment
中子撞击

37-38 fission fragments
分裂碎片

39 released neutron
放出的中子

40 gamma radiation (6)
伽马辐射

41 chain reaction
（连锁反应）链式反应

42 incident neutron
入射中子

43 nucleus prior to fisson
分裂前的原子核

44 fission fragment
分裂碎片

45 released neutron
放出的中子

46 repeated fission
重复分裂

47 fission fragment
分裂碎片

48 **controlled chain reaction in a nuclear reactor**
核反应器内受控制的链式反应

49 atomic nucleus of a fissionable element
可分裂元素的原子核

50 neutron bombardment
中子撞击

51 fission fragment (new atomic nucleus)
分裂碎片（新原子核）

52 released neutron
放出的中子

53 absorbed neutrons
吸收的中子

54 moderator, a retarding layer of graphite
缓和剂，石墨缓和剂

55 extraction of heat (production of energy)
热的萃取（能量的产生）

56 X-radiation
X辐射

57 concrete and lead shield
混凝土和铅屏蔽

58 **bubble chamber** for showing the tracks of high-energy ionizing particles
显示高能游离粒子径迹的气泡计数室

59 light source
光源

60 camera
摄影机

61 expansion line
膨胀线，扩展线

62 path of light rays
光射线路径

63 magnet
磁盘

64 beam entry point
射束（光束）进入点

65 reflector
反射器

66 chamber
气泡室

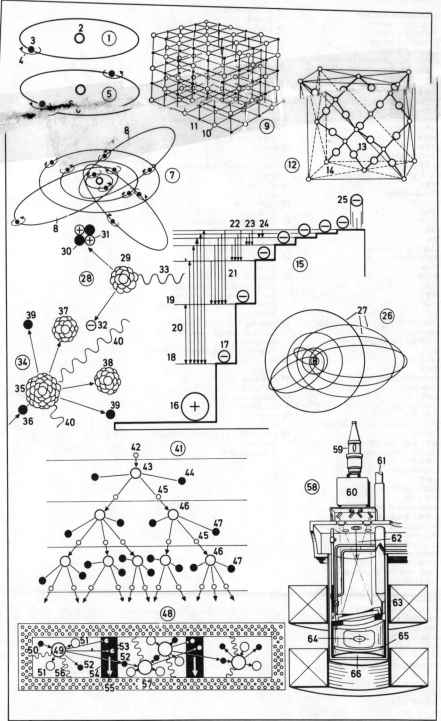

2 Atom II

1-23 radiation detectors
(radiation meters)
辐射探测器（辐射计）
1 radiation monitor
辐射监测器
2 ionization chamber (ion
chamber)
游离室（离子室）
3 central electrode
中心电极
4 measurement range selector
（测）量程选择器
5 instrument housing
仪器外壳（箱）
6 meter
计量器
7 zero adjustment
零点调整（装置），归零（装置）
8-23 dosimeter (dosemeter)
剂量计
8 film dosimeter
软片剂量计
9 filter
滤色器
10 film
软片
11 film-ring dosimeter
环形软片剂量计
12 filter
滤色器
13 film
胶卷
14 cover with filter
带滤色器（纸）的软片套
15 pocket meter (pen meter, pocket
chamber)
小型剂量计（笔型剂量计，小型游离
室）
16 window
游离窗
17 ionization chamber (ion
chamber)
游离室（离子室）
18 clip (pen clip)
夹子，笔夹
19 Geiger counter (Geiger-Müller
counter)
盖革计数器（盖革牟勒计数器）
20 counter tube casing
计数管套
21 counter tube
计数管
22 instrument housing
仪器壳（箱）
23 measurement range selector
（测量）量程选择器
24 Wilson cloud chamber (Wilson
chamber)
威耳生雾室（威耳生室）
25 compression plate
压（缩）板
26 cloud chamber photograph
云雾室照片
27 cloud chamber track of an alpha
particle
阿伐粒子的雾室轨迹（雾迹）
28 telecobalt unit (*coll.* cobalt
bomb)
钴照射设备（亦称：钴弹）
29 pillar stand
立柱
30 support cables
支撑钢索
31 radiation shield (radiation
shielding)
辐射屏蔽（层）

32 sliding shield
滑动屏蔽
33 bladed diaphragm
叶状膜片
34 light-beam positioning device
光束定位装置
35 pendulum device (pendulum)
摆动装置（摆）
36 irradiation table
照射台
37 rail (track)
轨道
38 manipulator with sphere unit
(manipulator)
带球型装置的操作器
39 handle
手柄，把手
40 safety catch (locking lever)
安全把手（锁杆）
41 wrist joint
腕关节
42 master arm
主动臂
43 clamping device (clamp)
夹紧装置（夹钳）
44 tongs
（机械手的）抓手（夹子）
45 slotted board
有槽板
46 radiation shield (protective
shield, protective shielding), a
lead shielding wall [section]
辐射屏蔽（防护屏蔽层），一种铅屏蔽
墙[剖面]
47 grasping arm of a pair of
manipulators (of a master/slave
manipulator)
一双机械手（主动/被动机械手）的抓臂
48 dust shield
防尘护套
49 cyclotron
迴旋加速器
50 danger zone
危险地带（区）
51 magnet
磁体
52 pumps for emptying the vacuum
chamber
真空室抽气用的泵

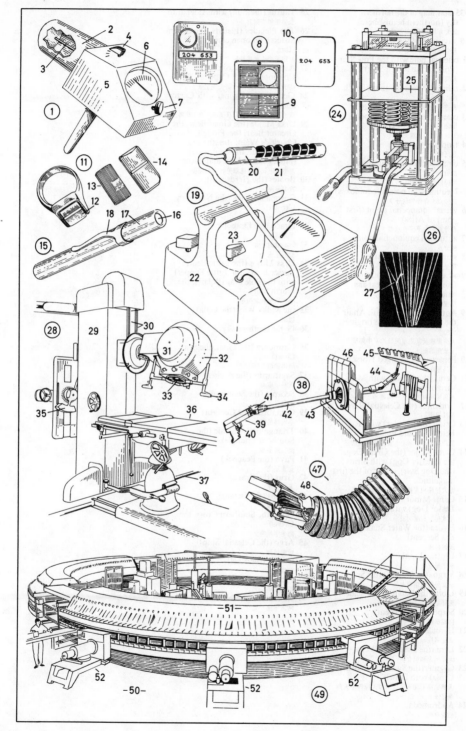

1-35 star map of the northern sky (northern hemisphere)
北天（北半球）的星座

1-8 divisions of the sky
天空的划分（区分）

1 celestial pole with the Pole Star (Polaris, the North Star)
天极和北极星

2 ecliptic (apparent annual path of the sun)
黄道（太阳的视周年轨道，轨迹）

3 celestial equator (equinoctial line)
天球赤道（天球平分线）

4 tropic of Cancer
北回归线

5 circle enclosing circumpolar stars
拱极星的界圈

6-7 equinoctial points (equinoxes)
二分点（春分和秋分）

6 vernal equinoctial point (first point of Aries)
春分点（白羊座的原点）

7 autumnal equinoctial point
秋分点

8 summer solstice (solstice)
夏至

9-48 constellations (grouping of fixed stars into figures) **and names of stars**
星座和星名

9 Aquila (the Eagle) with Altair the principal star (the brightest star)
天鹰星座及其主星河鼓二（牛郎星）（最亮的星）

10 Pegasus (the Winged Horse)
飞马星座

11 Cetus (the Whale) with Mira, a variable star
鲸鱼星座及其变星一蒭藁增二

12 Eridamus (the Celestial River)
波江星座

13 Orion (the Hunter) with Rigel, Betelgeuse and Bellatrix
猎户星座和参宿七，参宿四和参宿五

14 Canis Major (the Great Dog, the Greater Dog) with Sirius (the Dog Star), a star of the first magnitude
大犬星座和天狼星（最高的恒星）

15 Canis Minor (the Little Dog, the Lesser Dog) with Procyon
小犬星座和南河三

16 Hydra (the Water Snake, the Sea Serpent)
长蛇星座

17 Leo(the Lion)
狮子星座

18 Virgo (the Virgin) with Spica
室女星座和角宿大星

19 Libra (the Balance, the Scales)
天秤星座

20 Serpens (the Serpent)
巨蛇星座

21 Hercules
武仙星座

22 Lyra (the Lyre) with Vega
天琴星座和织女星

23 Cygnus (the Swan, the Northern Cross) with Deneb
天鹅星座（北十字星）和天津四（天鹅座之α）

24 Andromeda
仙女星座

25 Taurus (the Bull) with Aldebaran
金牛座和毕宿五

26 The Pleiades (Pleiads, the Seven Sisters), an open cluster of stars
昴宿星团（七姊妹星团），疏散星团

27 Auriga (the Wagoner, the Charioteer) with Capella
御夫星座和五车二（御夫座之α）

28 Gemini (the Twins) with Castor and Pollux
双子星座和北河二（双子座之β）北河三

29 Ursa Major (the Great Bear, the Greater Bear, the Plough, Charles's Wain, *Am.* the Big Dipper) with the double star (binary star) Mizar and Alcor
大熊星座和其目视双星开阳和辅星

30 Bootes (the Herdsman)
牧夫星座

31 Corona Borealis (the Northern Crown)
北冕星座

32 Draco (the Dragon)
天龙星座

33 Cassiopeia
仙后星座

34 Ursa Minor (the Little Bear, Lesser Bear, *Am.* Little Dipper) with the Pole Star (Polaris, the North Star)
小熊星座和北极星

35 the Milky Way (the Galaxy)
银河

36-48 the southern sky
南天

36 Capricorn (the Goat, the Sea Goat)
摩羯星座

37 Sagittarius (the Archer)
人马星座

38 Scorpio (the Scorpion)
天蝎星座

39 Centaurus (the Centaur)
半人马星座

40 Triangulum Australe (the Southern Triangle)
南三角星座

41 Pavo (the Peacock)
孔雀星座

42 Grus (the Crane)
天鹤星座

43 Octans (the Octant)
南极星座

44 Crux (the Southern Cross, the Cross)
南十字星座

45 Argo (the Celestial Ship)
南船星座

46 Carina (the Keel)
船底星座

47 Pictor (the Painter)
绘架星座

48 Reticulum (the Net)
网罟星座

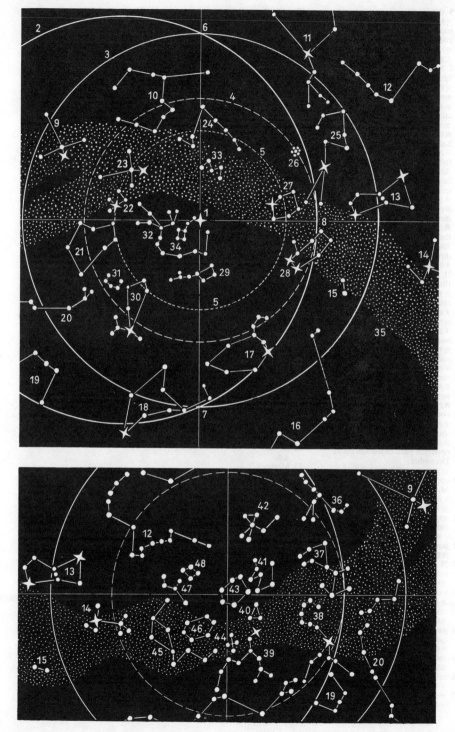

1-9 the moon
月亮，月球
1 moon's path (moon's orbit' round the earth)
月球轨道（月亮绕地球运行的轨道），白道
2-7 lunar phases (moon's phases, lunation)
月相（月的盈亏，变化）
2 new moon
新月
3 crescent (crescent moon, waxing moon)
蛾眉月
4 half-moon (first quarter)
半月（上弦月）
5 full moon
满月
6 half-moon (last quarter, third quarter)
半月（下弦月）
7 crescent (crescent moon, waning moon)
残月
8 the earth (terrestrial globe)
地球
9 direction of the sun's rays
太阳光线的方向
10-21 apparent path of the sun at the beginning of the seasons
各季节开始时太阳的视轨道
10 celestial axis
天球轴，天轴
11 zenith
天顶
12 horizontal plane
地平面
13 nadir
天底
14 east point
东点
15 west point
西点
16 north point
北点
17 south point
南点
18 apparent path of the sun on 21 December
12月21日太阳的视轨道（冬至）
19 apparent path of the sun on 21 March and 23 September
3月21日（春分）和9月23日（秋分）太阳的视轨道
20 apparent path of the sun on 21 June
6月21日（夏至）太阳的视轨道
21 border of the twilight area
曙暮光区域的界限
22-28 rotary motions of the earth's axis
地轴的运动
22 axis of the ecliptic
黄（道）轴
23 celestial sphere
天球
24 path of the celestial pole (precession and nutation)
天极的轨道（岁差和章动）
25 instantaneous axis of rotation
瞬间自转轴
26 celestial pole
天极
27 mean axis of rotation
平均自转轴

28 polhode
地极移动轨迹
29-35 solar and lunar eclipse [not to scale]
日蚀和月蚀[示意图]
29 the sun
太阳
30 the earth
地球
31 the moon
月球，月亮
32 solar eclipse
日蚀
33 area of the earth in which the eclipse appears total
地球上的全蚀带
34-35 lunar eclipse
月蚀
34 penumbra (partial shadow)
半影
35 umbra (total shadow)
本影
36-41 the sun
太阳
36 solar disc (disk) (solar globe, solar sphere)
太阳面（太阳球）
37 sunspots
太阳黑子
38 cyclones in the area of sunspots
太阳黑子附近的气旋
39 corona (solar corona), observable during total solar eclipse or by means of special instruments
当日全蚀时或藉特殊仪器可观察到的日冕
40 prominences (solar prominences)
日珥
41 moon's limb during a total solar eclipse
日全蚀时的月球边缘
42-52 planets (planetary system, solar system) [not to scale] and planet symbols
行星（行星系，太阳系）和行星符号
42 the sun
太阳
43 Mercury
水星
44 Venus
金星
45 Earth, with the moon, a satellite
地球和卫星月球
46 Mars, with two moons (satellites)
火星，带两个卫星
47 asteroids (minor planets)
小行星群
48 Jupiter, with 14 moons (satellites)
木星，带14个卫星
49 Saturn, with 10 moons (satellites)
土星及其10个卫星
50 Uranus, with five moons (satellites)
天王星及其5个卫星
51 Neptune, with two moons (satellites)
海王星及其两个卫星
52 Pluto, with one moon
冥王星，带一个卫星

53-64 signs of the zodiac (zodiacal signs)
黄道十二宫的符号
53 Aries (the Ram)
白羊座
54 Taurus (the Bull)
金牛座
55 Gemini (the Twins)
双子座
56 Cancer (the Crab)
巨蟹座
57 Leo (the Lion)
狮子座
58 Virgo (the Virgin)
室女座
59 Libra (the Balance, the Scales)
天秤座
60 Scorpio (the Scorpion)
天蝎座
61 Sagittarius (the Archer)
人马座
62 Capricorn (the Goat, the Sea Goat)
摩羯座
63 Aquarius (the Water Carrier, the Water Bearer)
宝瓶座
64 Pisces (the Fish)
双鱼座

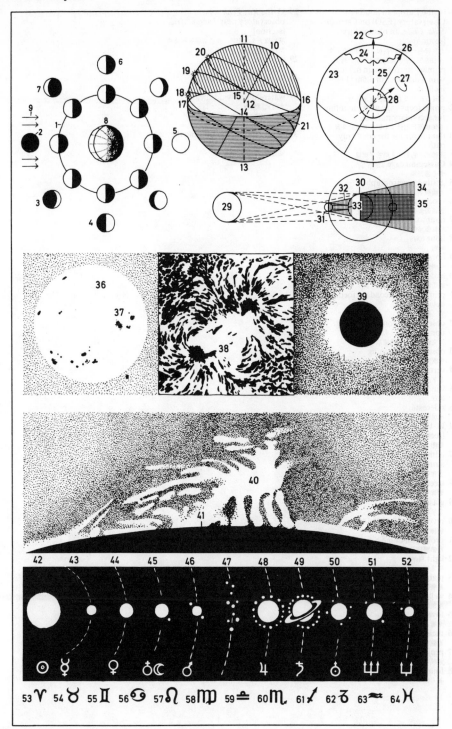

1-16 the European Southern Observatory (ESO) on *Cerro la Silla, Chile,* an observatory [section]
（在智利，塞罗拉西拉）欧洲南方天文台（ESO），望远镜圆顶室（断面图）

1 primary mirror (main mirror) with a diameter of 3.6m (144 inches)
直径 3.6 公尺（144 英吋）的主镜

2 prime focus cage with mounting for secondary mirrors
主聚焦笼和副镜架（固定副镜的装置）

3 flat mirror for the coude ray path
库德式（折轴）光路的平面镜

4 Cassegran cage
卡士格笼架

5 grating spectrograph
光栅摄谱仪

6 spectrographic camera
光谱摄影机

7 hour axis drive
时轴驱动装置

8 hour axis
时轴

9 horseshoe mounting
马蹄形镜架装置

10 hydrostatic bearing
静压轴承

11 primary and secondary focusing devices
主、副聚焦装置

12 observatory dome (revolving dome)
天文台圆顶（迴转圆顶）

13 observation opening
观测窗

14 vertically movable dome shutter
上下活动的圆顶窗板

15 wind screen
风罩

16 siderostat
定星镜

17-28 the *Stuttgart* Planetarium [section]
斯图卡特天文馆[断面图]

17 administration, workshop, and store area
管理处，工作室，储藏室

18 steel scaffold
钢骨支架

19 glass pyramid
金字塔型的玻璃夹层

20 revolving arched ladder
迴转弧型梯子

21 projection dome
投影圆顶

22 light stop
挡光板

23 planetarium projector
星象投影器（星象仪，天象仪）

24 well
星象仪竖井

25 foyer
走廊，休息处

26 theatre (*Am.* theater)
剧院

27 projection booth
放映室

28 foundation pile
基（础）桩

29-33 the *Kitt Peak* solar observatory near *Tucson, Ariz.* [section]
基特峰天文太阳塔，位於美国亚利桑纳州图克森附近（剖面图）

29 heliostat
定日镜

30 sunken observation shaft
倾斜式观测通道

31 water-cooled windshield
水冷式隔热板

32 concave mirror
凹面镜

33 observation room housing the spectrograph
安置摄谱仪的观测室

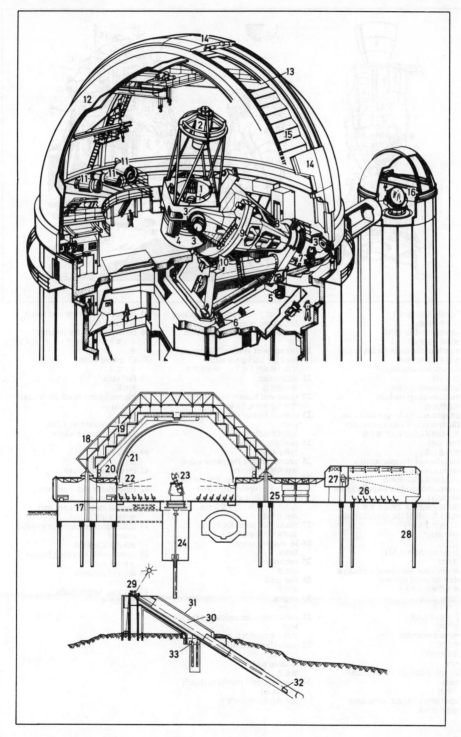

1 Apollo spacecraft
阿波罗太空船
2 service module (SM)
辅助舱，服务舱
3 nozzle of the main rocket engine
火箭主发动机的喷嘴
4 directional antenna
定向天线
5 manoeuvring (*Am.* maneuvering) rockets
机动性火箭
6 oxygen and hydrogen tanks for the spacecraft's energy system
太空船能量系统的氢氧贮槽（箱）
7 fuel tank
燃料槽（箱）
8 radiators of the spacecraft's energy system
太空船能量系统的散热器
9 command module (Apollo space capsule)
指挥舱（阿波罗太空船的太空舱）
10 entry hatch of the space capsule
太空舱的进入舱门
11 astronaut
太空人
12 lunar module (LM)
登月舱
13 moon's surface (lunar surface) a dust-covered surface
覆盖尘埃的月球表面
14 lunar dust
月球尘埃
15 piece of rock
岩石块
16 meteorite crater
陨石坑
17 the earth
地球
18-27 space suit (extra-vehicular suit)
太空衣
18 emergency oxygen apparatus
应急供氧装置

19 sunglass pocket [with sunglasses for use on board]
太阳眼镜袋[於太空船中使用的太阳眼镜]
20 life support system (life support pack), a backpack unit
生命供养系统（包），一种背包装置
21 access flap
存取物品盖
22 space suit helmet with sun filters
带日光滤器的太空头盔
23 control box of the life support pack
生命供养包的控制盒
24 penlight pocket
钢笔手电筒袋
25 access flap for the purge valve
清洗阀用的存取口盖
26 tube and cable connections for the radio, ventilation, and water-cooling systems
与无线电，通风（气）装置和水冷系统连接的管线
27 pocket for pens, tools, etc.
装钢笔、工具等等的袋子
28-36 descent stage
降落级
28 connector
连接器
29 fuel tank
燃料箱
30 engine
发动机
31 mechanism for unfolding the legs
伸开支架用的机械装置
32 main shock absorber
主减震器
33 landing pad
降落垫
34 ingress/egress platform (hatch platform)
进出口台架（舱口台架）

35 ladder to platform and hatch
到舱门与台架的梯子
36 cardan mount for engine
（引擎）发动机的十字（万向）接头装置
37-47 ascent stage
上升装置
37 fuel tank
燃料箱
38 ingress/egress hatch (entry/exit hatch)
进出舱口
39 LM manoeuvring (*Am.* maneuvering) rockets
登月舱机动火箭
40 window
窗
41 crew compartment
太空人室
42 rendezvous radar antenna
太空舱雷达天线
43 inertial measurement unit
惯性测量装置
44 directional antenna for ground control
地面控制定向性天线
45 upper hatch (docking hatch)
上舱口（连接舱口）
46 inflight antenna
飞行天线
47 docking target recess
接合点凹槽

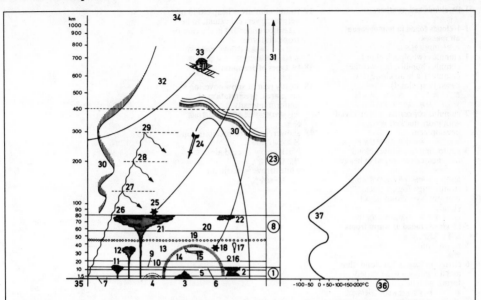

1 **the troposphere**
  对流层
2 thunderclouds
  雷雨云
3 the highest mountain, *Mount Everest* [8,882m]
  埃佛勒斯峰（世界最高峰，8,882 公尺高）
4 rainbow
  虹（霓）
5 jet stream level
  喷射气流带
6 zero level (inversion of vertical air movement)
  大气层温度递减的上限（指空气垂直运动的上限）
7 ground layer (surface boundary layer)
  地面层（地面界层）
8 **the stratosphere**
  平流层
9 tropopause
  对流层顶
10 separating layer (layer of weaker air movement)
  分离层（大气压力只有 50 毫巴）
11 atomic explosion
  原子弹爆炸高度
12 hydrogen bomb explosion
  氢弹爆炸高度
13 ozone layer
  臭氧层
14 range of sound wave propagation
  声波传播范围
15 stratosphere aircraft
  平流层飞机飞行高度
16 manned balloon
  载人气球到达高度
17 sounding balloon
  探空气球到达高度
18 meteor
  陨石（指可以落到地面上成形的）

19 upper limit of ozone layer
  臭氧层上限
20 zero level
  大气层温度递升的上限
21 eruption of Krakatoa
  克拉卡托火山爆发到达高度
22 luminous clouds (noctilucent clouds)
  夜光云
23 **the ionosphere**
  游离层
24 range of research rockets
  研究用火箭范围
25 shooting star
  流星（指虽然看到光辉，但只在大气层中消失的）
26 short wave (high frequency)
  短波（高频）反射高度
27 E-layer (Heaviside-Kennelly Layer)
  E 层（赫维赛德－甘奈利层）
28 F_1-layer
  F_1 层
29 F_2-layer
  F_2 层
30 aurora (polar light)
  极光
31 **the exosphere**
  外气层
32 atom layer
  原子层
33 range of satellite sounding
  卫星探测范围
34 fringe region
  （大气）边缘区
35 altitude scale
  高度标尺
36 temperature scale (thermometric scale)
  温度标尺
37 temperature graph
  温度随高度变化曲线

1-19 clouds and weather
云和天气

1-4 clouds found in homogeneous air masses
均质气团所见到的云

1 cumulus (woolpack cloud, cumulus humilis, fair-weather cumulus), a heap cloud (flat-based heap cloud)
积云（絮状积云，淡积云，晴天积云），一种堆积的云（平底积云）

2 cumulus congestus, a heap cloud with more marked vertical development
浓积云，一种垂直发展更明显堆积的云

3 stratocumulus, a layer cloud (sheet cloud) arranged in heavy masses
层积云，一种排列成大云块的层状云

4 stratus (high fog), a thick, uniform layer cloud (sheet cloud)
层云（浓雾）一种厚而均匀的层状云

5-12 clouds found at warm fronts
暖锋上见到的云

5 warm front
暖锋

6 cirrus, an ice-crystal cloud, thin and assuming a wide variety of forms, with height over 6,000 m
卷云，一种高度超过 6,000 公尺的冰晶云，薄且呈多种形状

7 cirrostratus, an ice-crystal cloud veil
卷层云，一种冰晶云幔

8 altostratus, a layer cloud (sheet cloud) of medium height
高层云，一种中等高度的层状云

9 altostratus praecipitans, a layer cloud (sheet cloud) with precipitation in its upper parts
降水性高层云，一种在其上端有降水的层状云

10 nimbostratus, a rain cloud, a layer cloud (sheet cloud) of very large vertical extent which produces precipitation (rain or snow)
雨层云，一种降雨层状云，一种垂直发展很强，产生降水（雨或雪）的层云

11 fractostratus, a ragged cloud occurring beneath nimbostratus
碎层云，一种出现在雨层云下方的碎云

12 fractocumulus, a ragged cloud like 11 but with billowing shapes
碎积云，和碎层云相似，但呈波浪状

13-17 clouds at cold fronts
冷锋上的云

13 cold front
冷锋

14 cirrocumulus, thin fleecy cloud in the form of globular masses; *covering the sky:* mackerel sky
卷积云，呈球形云块的薄白云；覆盖天空成鱼鳞天

15 altocumulus, a cloud in the form of large globular masses
高积云，呈大型球状云块的云

16 altocumulus castellanus and altocumulus floccus, species of 15
堡状高积云和絮状高积云（15 项的一种）

17 cumulonimbus, a heap cloud of very large vertical extent, to be classified under 1-4 in the case of tropical storms
积雨云，一种垂直范围很广的堆积云，在热带暴风雨的情形下分在第 1-4 项下

18-19 types of precipitation
降水型

18 steady rain or snow covering a large area, precipitation of uniform intensity
大区域的稳定降雨或降雪，强度均的降水

19 shower, scattered precipitation
局部阵雨式的降水
black arrow = cold air
黑箭头＝冷空气
white arrow = warm air
白箭头＝暖空气

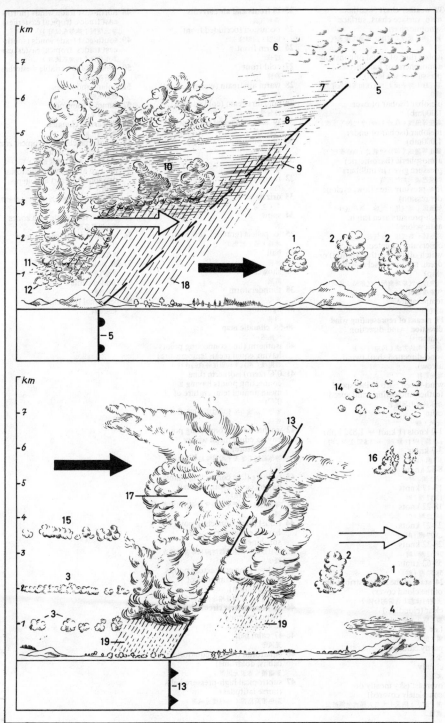

1-39 weather chart (weather map, surface chart, surface synoptic chart)
天气图（地面天气图，地面综观天气图）

1 isobar (line of equal or constant atmospheric or barometric pressure at sea level)
等压线（海平面上，气压相等或恒定的线）

2 pleiobar (isobar of over 1,000mb)
高压等值线（高於1,000毫巴的等压线）

3 meiobar (isobar of under 1,000mb)
低压等值线（等压线低於1,000毫巴）

4 atmospheric (barometric) pressure given in millibars
以毫巴表示的气压值

5 low-pressure area (low, cyclone, depression)
低压区（低气压，气旋，低压区）

6 high-pressure area (high, anticyclone)
高压区（高气压，反气旋）

7 observatory (meteorological watch office, weather station) or ocean station vessel (weather ship)
气象台（气象观测所，气象站）或海洋气象观测船

8 temperature
温度

9-19 means of representing wind direction (wind-direction symbols)
表示方向的方法（风向符号）

9 wind-direction shaft (wind arrow)
风向箭杆

10 wind-speed barb (wind-speed feather) indicating wind speed
指示风速的风速羽

11 calm
无风，静

12 1-2 knots (1 knot = 1.852 kph)
1-2浬/时（1浬/时=1.852公里/时）

13 3-7 knots
3-7浬/时

14 8-12 knots
8-12浬/时

15 13-17 knots
13-17浬/时

16 18-22 knots
18-22浬/时

17 23-27 knots
23-27浬/时

18 28-32 knots
28-32浬/时

19 58-62 knots
58-62浬/时

20-24 state of the sky (distribution of the cloud cover)
天空的状态（云量的分佈）

20 clear (cloudless)
碧（空），晴（无云）

21 fair
晴，好天

22 partly cloudy
少云

23 cloudy
多云

24 overcast (sky mostly or completely covered)
密（云），阴天（天空大部或全部被云遮盖）

25-29 fronts and air currents
锋和气流

25 occlusion (occluded front)
囚锢（囚锢锋）

26 warm front
暖锋

27 cold front
冷锋

28 warm airstream (warm current)
暖气流

29 cold airstream (cold current)
冷气流

30-39 meteorological phenomena
气象现象

30 precipitation area
降水区

31 fog
雾

32 rain
雨

33 drizzle
毛（毛雨）

34 snow
雪

35 ice pellets (graupel, soft hail)
冰珠（霰，软雹）

36 hail
冰雹

37 shower
阵雨

38 thunderstorm
雷雨

39 lightning
闪电

40-58 climatic map
气候图

40 isotherm (line connecting points having equal mean temperature)
等温线（相同平均温度各点的连线）

41 0°C (zero) isotherm (line connecting points having a mean annual temperature of 0°C)
零度等温线（年平均温度为0°C各点的连线）

42 isocheim (line connecting points having equal mean winter temperature)
等冬温线（冬天平均温度相等各点的连线）

43 isothere (line connecting points having equal mean summer temperature)
等夏温线（夏天平均温度相等各点的连线）

44 isohel (line connecting points having equal duration of sunshine)
等日照线（日照持续时间相等各点的连线）

45 isohyet (line connecting points having equal amounts of precipitation)
等雨量线（降雨量相等各点的连线）

46-52 atmospheric circulation (wind systems)
大气环流（风系）

46-47 calm belt
无风带

46 equatorial trough (equatorial calms, doldrums)
赤道槽（赤道无风带）

47 subtropical high-pressure belts (horse latitudes)
副热带高压带（马纬度无风带）

48 north-east trade winds (north-east trades, tropical easterlies)
东北信风（热带东风带）

49 south-east trade winds (south-east trades, tropical easterlies)
东南信风（热带东风带）

50 zones of the variable westerlies
盛行西风带

51 polar wind zones
极地风带

52 summer monsoon
夏季季风

53-58 earth's climates
地球的气候

53 equatorial climate: tropical zone (tropical rain zone)
赤道气候：热带（热带雨区）

54 the two arid zones (equatorial dry zones): desert and steppe zones
两个干燥带（赤道干燥带）：沙漠和草原带

55 the two temperate rain zones
两个温带多雨带

56 boreal climate (snow forest climate)
极北气候（雪林气候）

57-58 polar climates
极地气候

57 tundra climate
苔原气候

58 perpetual frost climate
永冻气候

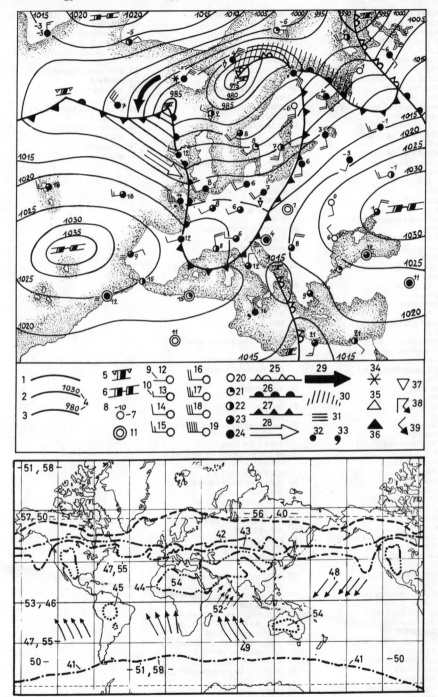

1 mercury barometer, a siphon barometer, a liquid-column barometer
水银气压表，一种虹吸式气压表，液柱气压表

2 mercury column
水银柱

3 millibar scale (millimetre, *Am.* millimetre, scale)
毫巴标尺（毫米标尺）

4 barograph, a self-registering aneroid barometer
气压计，一种自记空盒气压表

5 drum (recording drum)
记录筒

6 bank of aneroid capsules (aneroid boxes)
气压感应盒

7 recording arm
记录杆

8 hygrograph
湿度计

9 hygrometer element (hair element)
湿度表元件（毛发元件）

10 reading adjustment
读数调整

11 amplitude adjustment
振幅调整

12 recording arm
记录杆

13 recording pen
记录笔

14 change gears for the clock work drive
钟表驱动用的变换齿轮装置

15 off switch for the recording arm
记录杆的停止开关

16 drum (recording drum)
记录筒

17 time scale
时间标尺

18 case (housing)
外壳

19 thermograph
自记温度计

20 drum (recording drum)
记录筒

21 recording arm
记录杆

22 sensing element
感应元件

23 silver-disc (silver-disk) pyrheliometer, an instrument for measuring the sun's radiant energy
银盘日射强度表，一种测量太阳辐射能的仪器

24 silver disc (disk)
银盘

25 thermometer
温度计

26 wooden insulating casing
木制绝缘套

27 tube with diaphragm (diaphragmed tube)
装有隔板之受光筒

28 wind gauge (*Am.* gage)
风速表（风速表）

29 wind-speed indicator (wind-speed meter)
风速指示器（风速表）

30 cross arms with hemispherical cups
半球形风杯的横杆

31 wind-direction indicator
风向指示器

32 wind vane
风向标

33 aspiration psychrometer
通风式乾湿球温度表

34 dry bulb thermometer
干球温度表

35 wet bulb thermometer
湿球温度表

36 solar radiation shielding
太阳辐射防护罩

37 suction tube
吸管

38 recording rain gauge (*Am.* gage)
雨量计

39 protective housing (protective casing)
防护外罩（防护外壳）

40 collecting vessel
集水器

41 rain cover
防雨罩

42 recording mechanism
记录机械装置

43 siphon tube
虹吸管

44 precipitation gauge (*Am.* gage)
降水计（雨量计）

45 collecting vessel
收集器

46 storage vessel
储存器

47 measuring glass
量杯

48 insert for measuring snowfall
量雪尺

49 thermometer screen (thermometer shelter)
百叶箱

50 hygrograph
湿度计

51 thermograph
温度计

52 psychrometer (wet and dry bulb thermometer)
干湿表（干湿球温度表）

53-54 thermometers for measuring extremes of temperature
测量温度极值的温度表

53 maximum thermometer
最高温度表

54 minimum thermometer
最低温度表

55 radiosonde assembly
无线电探空装置

56 hydrogen balloon
氢气球

57 parachute
降落伞

58 radar reflector with spacing lines
带距离线的雷达反射器

59 instrument housing with radiosonde (a shor-wave transmitter) and antenna
装有无线电探空装置（短波发射机）（发射）和天线的仪器箱

60 transmissometer, an instrument for measuring visibility
（一种测量能见度的）透射仪

61 recording instrument (recorder)
记录仪（记录器）

62 transmitter
发射机

63 receiver
接收机

64 weather satellite (ITOS satellite)
气象卫星（艾托斯卫星）

65 temperature regulation flaps
温度调节板

66 solar panel
太阳电池板

67 television camera
电视摄影机

68 antenna
天线

69 solar sensor (sun sensor)
太阳感应器

70 telemetry antenna
遥测天线

71 radiometer
辐射仪

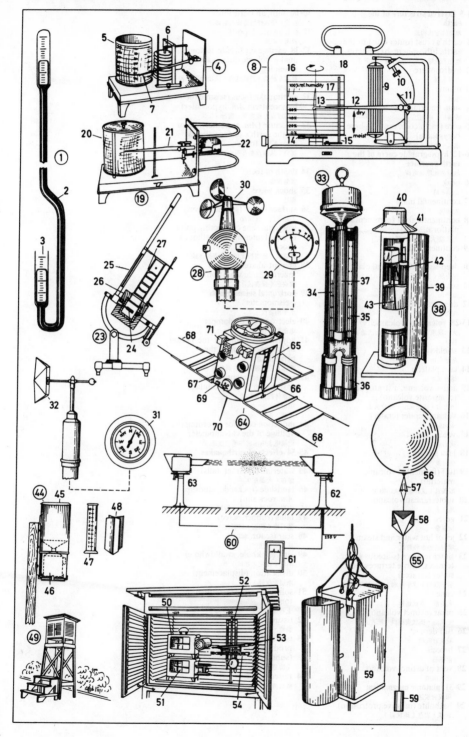

1-5 layered structure of the earth
地球的层状构造

1 earth's crust (outer crust of the earth, lithosphere, oxysphere)
地壳（地球外壳，岩石圈，陆界）

2 hydrosphere
水界水圈

3 mantle
地函

4 sima (intermediate layer)
矽镁层（中间层）

5 core (earth core, centrosphere, barysphere)
地核（地核，核圈，重圈）

6-12 hypsographic curve of the earth's surface
地球表面陆高海深

6 peak
山顶，峰

7 continental mass
大陆块

8 continental shelf (continental platform, shelf)
大陆棚[大陆台地，棚状地层]

9 continental slope
大陆（斜）坡

10 deep-sea floor (abyssal plane)
深海底（深海地面）

11 sea level
海平面

12 deep-sea trench
深海湾

13-28 volcanism (volcanicity)
火山现象，火山作用，火山活动（火山性）

13 shield volcano
盾状火山

14 lava plateau
熔岩高原

15 active volcano, a stratovolcano (composite volcano)
活火山，成层火山（复合火山）

16 volcanic crater (crater)
火山口

17 volcanic vent
火山道

18 lava stream
熔岩流

19 tuff (framented volcanic material)
凝灰岩（成碎块的火山物质）

20 subterranean volcano
地下火山

21 geyer
间歇泉

22 jet of hot water and steam
喷射的热水和蒸汽

23 sinter terraces (siliceous sinter terraces, fiorite terraces, pearl sinter terraces)
泉华阶地（矽华阶地，珍珠矽华阶地）

24 cone
火山锥，锥状地形

25 maar (extinct volcano)
平火山，锅状火山口（死火山）

26 tuff deposit
凝灰岩沉积

27 breccia
角砾石

28 vent of extinct volcano
死火山道

29-31 plutonic magmatism
深成岩浆活动

29 batholite (massive protrusion)
岩基，岩盘（块状岩）

30 lacolith, an intrusion
岩盖（侵入作用造成的岩体）

31 sill, an ore deposit
岩床，矿床

32-38 earthquake (*kinds:* tectonic quake, volanic quake) **and seismology**
地震（种类：造构地震，火山地震）和地震学

32 earthquake focus (seismic focus, hypocentrem *Am.* hypocenter)
地震震源（地震震源，震源）

33 epicentre (*Am.* epicenter), point on the earth's surface directly above the focus
震央（从震源垂直引申到地面上的一点）

34 depth of focus
震源深度

35 shock wave
震波

36 surface waves (seismic waves)
（地震波）表面波

37 isoeismal (line connecting points of equal intensity of earthquake shock)
等震线（地震程度相等各点的连线）

38 epicentral area (area of macroseismic vibration)
震央区（强震区）

39 horizontal seismograph (seismometer)
水平地震仪

40 electromagnetic damper
电磁阻尼器

41 adjustment knob for the period of free oscillation of the pendulum
摆体自由振灢周期的调整钮

42 sprint attachment for the suspension of the pendulum
摇摆体的弹簧装置

43 mass
重锤，摆体

44 induction coils for recording the voltage of the galvanometer
记录电表电压用的感应线圈

45-54 effects of earthquakes
地震效应

45 waterfall (cataract, falls)
瀑布（大瀑布）

46 landslide (rockslide, landslip, *Am.* rock slip)
山崩（岩滑，塌方，滑坡）

47 talus (rubber, scree)
落石堆（积石，碎石波）

48 scar (scaur, scaw)
崖，山崩洼

49 sink (sinkhole, swallowhole)
陷坑（渗穴，吞口）

50 dislocation (displacement)
断层（位移，变位）

51 solifluction lobe (solifluction tongue)
土石缓舌（瓣）状地形

52 fissure
裂缝，裂隙

53 tsunami (seismic sea wave) produced by seaquake (submarine earthquake)
（海底地震所产生的）海啸（地震海浪）

54 raised beach
隆起滩，上升滩

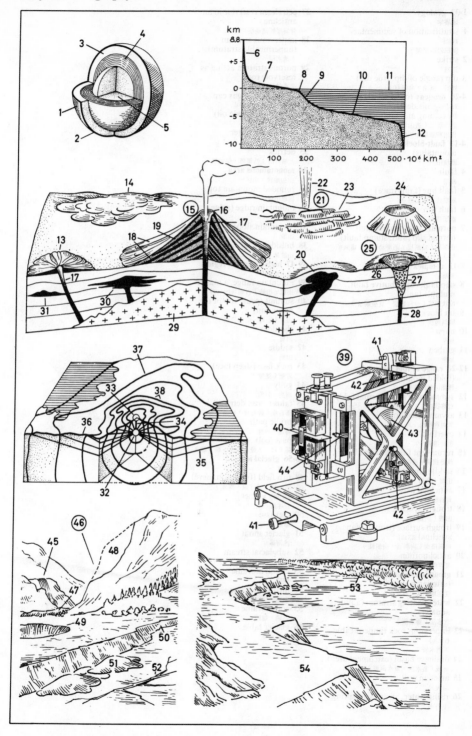

1-33 geology
地质学

1 stratification of sedimentary
rock
沉积岩的层理

2 strike
走向

3 dip (angle of dip, true dip)
倾斜（倾角，真倾斜）

**4-20 orogeny (orogenis,
tectogenis,deformation of rocks
by folding and faulting)**
造山运动（造山运动，造构运动，摺曲
作用和断层作用所引起的岩石变形）

4-11 fault-block mountains (block
mountains)
断块山

4 fault
断层

5 fault line (fault trace)
断层线（断层踪）

6 fault throw
断层落差

7 normal fault (gravity fault,
normal slip fault, slump fault)
正断层（动断层，正滑动断层，塌陷断
层）

8-11 complex faults
复断层

8 step fault (distributive fault,
multiple fault)
阶状断层（分枝断层，复叠断层）

9 tilt block
倾斜地块

10 horst
地垒

11 graben
地堑

12-20 range of fold mountains
(folded mountains)
摺曲山脉的范围

12 symmetrical fold (normal fold)
对称摺曲（正常摺曲）

13 asymmetrical fold
非对称摺曲

14 overfold
倒转摺曲

15 recumbent fold (reclined fold)
伏卧摺曲（横卧摺曲）

16 saddle (anticline)
山鞍（背斜）

17 anticlinal axis
背斜轴

18 trough (syncline)
凹槽（向斜）

19 trough surface (trough plane,
synclinal axis)
向斜槽面（向斜面，向斜轴）

20 anticlinorium
复背斜

21 **groundwater under pressure**
(artesian water)
受压地下水（自流水）

22 water-bearing stratum (aquifer,
aquafer)
含水层（蓄水层）

23 impervious rock (impermeable
rock)
不透水岩

24 drainage basin (catchment area)
流域（集水区，集水面积）

25 artesian well
自流井

26 rising water, an artesian spring
上升水，一种自流泉

27 **petroleum reservoir** in an
anticline
背斜层的储油层

28 impervious stratum
(impermeable stratum)
不透水层

29 porous stratum acting as
reservoir rock
多孔储油岩层

30 natural gas, a gas cap
天然气，一种气帽

31 petroleum (crude oil)
石油（原油）

32 underlying water
下伏水

33 derrick
（油井的）铁架塔，钻油塔

34 **mountainous area**
山岳地区，山区

35 rounded mountain top
圆形山顶

36 mountain ridge (ridge)
山脊

37 mountain slope
山坡

38 hillside spring
山腰泉

39-47 high-mountain region
高山地带

39 mountain range, a massif
山脉，山岭，古地块的一种

40 summit (peak, top of the
mountain)
山顶（山峰，山的顶点）

41 shoulder
山肩

42 saddle
山鞍

43 rock face (steep face)
岩壁（绝壁）

44 gully
雨沟，岩沟

45 talus (scree, detritus)
落石堆（碎石堆，碎屑）

46 bridle path
马道，小路

47 pass (col)
隘（口），垭（口），鞍（部）

48-56 glacial ice
冰河

48 firn field (firn basin, neve)
雪冰原（雪冰原，雪冰）

49 valley glacier
谷冰河

50 crevasse
冰隙

51 glacier snout
冰河鼻

52 subglacial stream
冰下河流

53 lateral moraine
侧碛

54 medial moraine
中碛

55 end moraine
终碛，端碛

56 glacier table
盖石冰桌

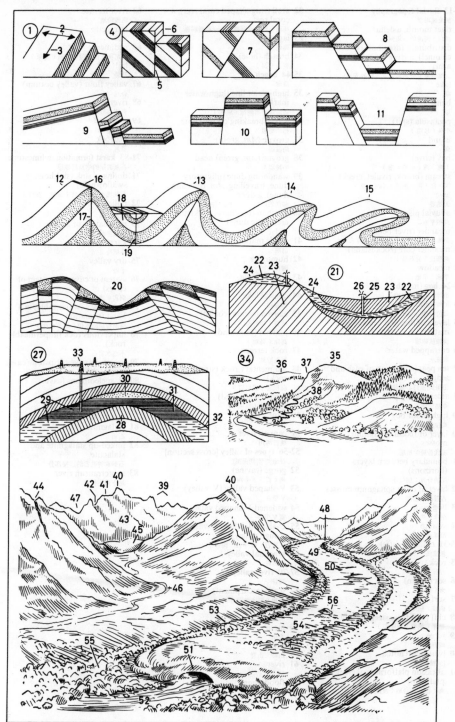

1-13 fluvial topography
河流地形学
1 river mouth, a delta
河口，河流的三角洲
2 distributary (distributary channel), a river branch (river arm)
支流分流（分流河道），河的支流
3 lake
湖
4 bank
岸
5 peninsula (spit)
半岛（沙咀）
6 island
岛
7 bay (cove)
（海）湾（小湾，澳）
8 stream (brook, rivulet, creek)
河，江，川（溪流，小河，溪）
9 levee
天然堤
10 alluvial plain
冲积平原
11 meander (river bend)
曲流（河湾）
12 meander core (rock island)
离堆丘（岩石岛）
13 meadow
草原，草地
14-24 bog (marsh)
沼泽（沼泽、湿地）
14 low-moor bog
低位沼泽
15 layers of decayed vegetable matter
腐蚀植物层
16 entrapped water
截流水
17 fen peat [consisting of rush and sedge]
沼泥炭[由灯心属植物和管茅构成]
18 alder-swamp peat
赤杨沼泽泥炭
19 high-moor bog
高位沼泽
20 layer of recent sphagnum mosses
现代苔藓泥沼层
21 boundary between layers (horizons)
层的分界（层位）
22 layer of older sphagnum mosses
古苔藓泥沼层
23 bog pool
沼泽水坑
24 swamp
沼泽地
25-31 cliffline (cliffs)
悬崖线
25 rock
岩石
26 sea (ocean)
海（洋）
27 surf
矶波，拍岸浪
28 cliff (cliff face, steep rock face)
悬崖（绝壁，断崖面）
29 scree
碎石堆
30 [wave-cut] notch
[波蚀]凹壁
31 abrasion platform (wave-cut platform)
海（浪）蚀台地（波蚀平台）

32 atoll (ring-shaped coral reef), a coral reef
环礁（环状珊瑚礁），一种珊瑚礁
33 lagoon
潟湖
34 breach (hole)
裂口（孔）
35-44 beach
海滩
35 high-water line (high-water mark, tidemark)
高潮线（高潮标，潮标）
36 waves breaking on the shore
拍岸海浪
37 groyne (*Am.* groin)
防坡堤
38 groyne (*Am.* groin) head
防波堤头
39 wandering dune (migratory dune, travelling, *Am.* traveling, dune), a dune
移动的沙丘，沙丘的一种
40 barchan (barchane, barkhan, crescentic dune)
新月丘
41 ripple marks
涟痕
42 hummock
圆丘
43 wind cripple
风损，风残
44 coastal lake
滨海湖
45 canyon (cañon, coulee)
峡谷（熔岩流）
46 plateau (tableland)
高原（高地）
47 rock terrace
岩石阶地
48 sedimentary rock (stratified rock)
沉积岩（成层岩）
49 river terrace (bed)
河流阶地（河床）
50 joint
节理
51 canyon river
峡谷河川
52-56 types of valley [cross section]
谷地类型[剖面图]
52 gorge (ravine)
峡（谷），（沟壑）
53 V-shaped valley (V-valley)
V 型谷
54 widened V-shaped valley
宽 V 型谷
55 U-shaped valley (U-valley, trough valley)
U 型谷（U 字谷，沟谷）
56 synclinal valley
向斜谷
57-70 river valley
河谷
57 scarp (escarpment)
悬崖（崖）
58 slip-off slope
滑走坡
59 mesa
方山
60 ridge
山岭，山脊
61 river
河，川
62 flood plain
泛滥平原

63 river terrace
河流阶地
64 terracette
小阶
65 pediment
山足面，山前侵蚀平原（麓原）
66 hill
丘陵
67 valley floor (valley bottom)
谷底
68 riverbed
河床
69 sediment
沉积物
70 bedrock
基岩
71-83 karst formation in limestone
石灰岩层的喀斯特地形
71 dolina, a sink (sinkhole, swallowhole)
石灰坑，一种陷坑（渗穴，吞口）
72 polje
灰岩盆地
73 percolation of a river
河流渗漏（透）
74 karst spring
喀斯特泉
75 dry valley
干谷
76 system of caverns (system of caves)
洞穴系统
77 water level (water table) in a karst formation
喀斯特层的水位（地下水面）
78 impervious rock (impermeable rock)
不透水岩石
79 limestone cave (dripstone cave)
灰岩洞（滴石洞）
80-81 speleothems (cave formations)
洞穴灰华（洞穴形成）
80 stalactite (dripstone)
钟乳石（滴水石）
81 stalagmite
石笋
82 linked-up stalagmite and stalactite
石笋和钟乳石的连接部分
83 subterranean river
地下河，伏流

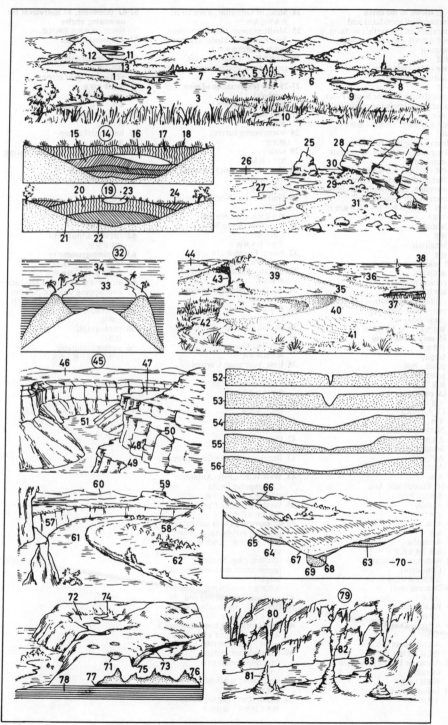

1-7 graticule of the earth
(network of meridians and
parallels on the earth's surface)
地球的经纬线（地球表面的经纬线网）
1 equator
赤道
2 line of latitude (parallel of
latitude, parallel)
纬线
3 pole (North Pole or South Pole)
a terrestrial pole (geographical
pole
极（北极或南极），地极（地理学的
极）
4 line of longitude (meridian of
longitude, meridian, terrestrial
meridian)
经线（子午线，地理经度线）
5 Standard meridian (Prime
meridian, Greenwich meridian,
meridian of Greenwich)
标准子午线（本初子午线，格林威治子
午线）
6 latitude
纬度
7 longitude
经度
8-9 map projections
地图投影法
8 conical (conic) projection
圆锥投影法
9 cylindrical projection (Mercator
projection, Mercator's
projection)
圆柱投影法（麦卡托投影法）
10-45 map of the world
世界地图
10 tropics
回归线，热带
11 polar circles
极圈
12-18 continents
大陆，大洲
12-13 America
美洲
12 North America
北美洲
13 South America
南美洲
14 Africa
非洲
15-16 Europe and Asia
欧洲和亚洲
15 Europe
欧洲
16 Asia
亚洲
17 Australia
澳洲（澳大利亚）
18 Antarctica (Antarctic
Continent)
南极洲（南极大陆）
19-26 ocean (sea)
洋（海）
19 Pacific ocean
太平洋
20 Atlantic Ocean
大西洋
21 Arctic Ocean
北极海（北冰洋）
22 Antarctic Ocean (Southern
Ocean)
南极海（南冰洋）
23 Indian Ocean
印度洋

24 Strait of Gibraltar, a sea strait
直布罗陀海峡
25 Mediterranean (Mediterranean
Sea, European Mediterranean)
地中海（欧洲的地中海）
26 North Sea, a marginal sea
(epeiric sea, epicontinental sea)
北海（缘海，陆缘海）
**27-29 key (explanation of map
symbols)**
图例（地图符号的解释）
27 cold ocean current
寒洋流
28 warm ocean current
暖洋流
29 scale
缩尺（比例尺）
30-45 ocean (oceanic) currents
(ocean drifts)
洋流（漂流）
30 Gulf Stream (North Atlantic
Drift)
墨西哥湾流（北大西洋漂流）
31 Kuroshio (Kuro Siwo, Japan
Current)
黑潮（日本海流）
32 North Equatorial Current
北赤道流
33 Equatorial Countercurrent
赤道逆流
34 South Equatorial Current
南赤道洋流
35 Brazil Current
巴西洋流
36 Somali Current
索马里洋流
37 Agulhas Current
阿古拉斯洋流
38 East Australian Current
东澳大利亚洋流
39 California Current
加里佛尼亚洋流
40 Labrador Current
拉布拉多洋流
41 Canary Current
加那利洋流
42 Peru Current
秘鲁洋流
43 Benguela (Benguella) Current
本吉拉洋流
44 West Wind Drift (Antarctic
Circumpolar Drift)
西风漂流（南极环极洋流）
45 West Australian Current
西澳大利亚洋流
46-62 surveying (land surveying,
geodetic surveying, geodesy)
测量（土地测量，大地测量，大地测
量学）
46 levelling (*Am.* leveling)
(geometrical measurement of
height)
水准测量（几何高度测量）
47 graduated measuring rod
(levelling, *Am.* leveling, staff)
标尺（水准标尺）
48 level (surveying level, surveyor's
level), a surveyor's telescope
水准仪，测量用的望远镜
49 triangulation station
(triangulation point)
三角点
50 supporting scaffold
支撑架
51 signal tower (signal mast)
测标（信号塔，信号柱）

**52-62 theodolite, an instrument for
measuring angles**
经纬仪，测量角度用的仪器
52 micrometer head
测微计钮
53 micrometer eyepiece
测微目镜
54 vertical tangent screw
高低微动螺旋
55 vertical clamp
高低（垂直）制动钮
56 tangent screw
微动螺旋
57 horizontal clamp
水平制动钮
58 adjustment for the illuminating
mirror
照明反光镜的调整装置
59 illuminating mirror
反光镜
60 telescope
望远镜
61 spirit level
气泡水准仪
62 circular adjustment
圆形调整钮
63-66 photogrammetry
(phototopography)
摄影测量（航空摄影测量）
63 air survey camera for producing
overlapping series of pictures
产生图像连续重叠的航测仪（摄影机）
64 stereoscope
立体镜
65 pantograph
缩放仪
66 stereoplanigraph
立体平面绘（测）图仪

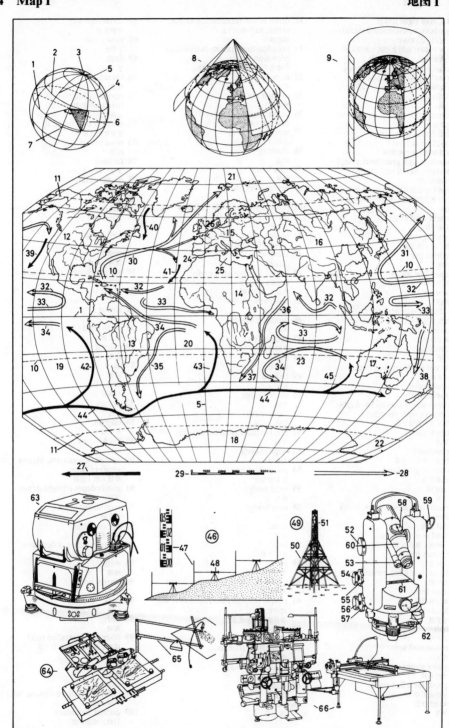

1-114 map signs (map symbols, conventional signs) on a 1:25000 map
（在 1:25000 地图上用的）地图记号
（地图符号，习用地图记号）

1 coniferous wood (coniferous trees)
针叶树林

2 clearing
空地

3 forestry office
林务局

4 deciduous wood (non-coniferous trees)
落叶树林（非针叶树林）

5 heath (rough grassland, rough pasture, heath and moor, bracken)
灌林；丛生的荒野（杂草丛生的草地，杂草丛生的牧地，灌林和沼泽，羊齿蕨）

6 sand (sand hills)
沙地（沙丘）

7 beach grass
海（河）滩草地

8 lighthouse
灯塔

9 mean low water
平均干潮，平均低水位

10 beacon
航标

11 submarine contours
海底等高线

12 train ferry
火车轮渡

13 lightship
灯船

14 mixed wood (mixed trees)
混和树林

15 brushwood
低树林，灌木林

16 motorway with slip road (Am. freeway with on-ramp)
带岔道的高速公路

17 trunk road
干道

18 grassland
牧场，草地，草原

19 marshy grassland
沼泽草地

20 marsh
沼泽

21 main line railway (Am. trunk line)
铁路主线

22 road over railway
上跨道（铁路在下）

23 branch line
铁路支线

24 signal box (Am. switch tower)
信号房

25 local line
地方铁路线

26 level crossing
平交道

27 halt
招呼站

28 residential area
住宅区

29 water gauge (Am. gage)
水位标尺

30 good, metalled road
好的碎石路

31 windmill
风车

32 thorn house (graduation house, salina, salt-works)
制盐场

33 broadcasting station (wireless or television mast)
广播台（无线电或电视天线柱）

34 mine
矿山

35 disused mine
废弃矿山

36 secondary road (B road)
次要（级）道路

37 works
工场

38 chimney
烟囱

39 wire fence
铁栅栏

40 bridge over railway
上跨桥

41 railway station (Am. railroad station)
火车站

42 bridge under railway
（铁路下的）下跨桥

43 footpath
人行道

44 bridge for footpath under railway
铁路下人行路桥

45 navigable river
通航河流

46 pontoon bridge
浮桥

47 vehicle ferry
车辆码头

48 mole
防波堤

49 beacon
航标

50 stone bridge
石桥

51 town (city)
城镇，市镇

52 market place (market square)
市场

53 large church
大教堂

54 public building
公共建筑物

55 road bridge
路桥

56 iron bridge
铁桥

57 canal
运河

58 lock
水门，闸门

59 jetty
突堤码头

60 foot ferry (foot passenger ferry)
人的摆渡

61 chapel (church) without tower or spire
没有尖顶的小教堂

62 contours
等高线

63 monastery (convent)
修道院（女修道院）

64 church landmark
教堂标志

65 vineyard
葡萄园

66 weir
堰

67 aerial ropeway
空中缆索

68 view point
了望台

69 dam
堰

70 tunnel
隧道

71 triangulation station (triangulation point)
三角点

72 remains of a building
建筑物的遗迹

73 wind pump
风泵

74 fortress
要塞（城堡）

75 ox-bow lake
牛轭湖

76 river
河流

77 watermill
风车

78 footbridge
人行桥

79 pond
池塘，水塘

80 stream (brook, rivulet, creek)
小河，溪流

81 water tower
水塔

82 spring
泉

83 main road (A road)
主要道路

84 cutting
路堑

85 cave
岩洞

86 lime kiln
石灰窑

87 quarry
采石场

88 clay pit
粘土坑

89 brickworks
砖厂

90 narrow-gauge (Am. narrow gage) railway
窄规（轨）铁路

91 goods depot (freight depot)
货运站

92 monument
纪念碑

93 site of battle
战场遗迹

94 country estate, a demesne
乡间宅地，庄园

95 wall
城墙

96 stately home
华贵住宅

97 park
公园，私人花园

98 hedge
篱墙

99 poor or unmetalled road
难行之路或尚未铺沙石之路

100 well
井

101 farm
农场

102 unfenced path (unfenced track)
林间小路

103 district boundary
行政区域分界限

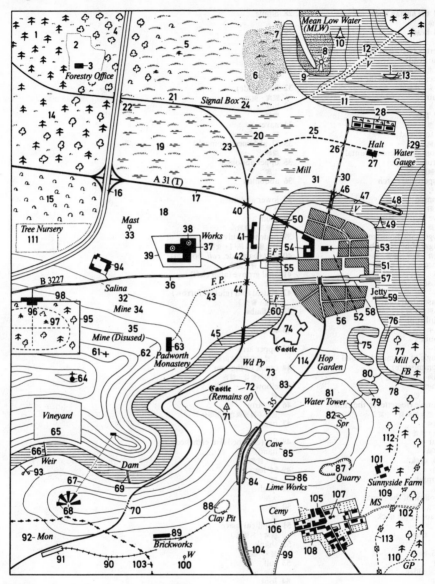

104 embankment
　　堤防
105 village
　　村庄
106 cemetery
　　墓园
107 church (chapel) with spire
　　有尖顶的教堂（小教堂）
108 orchard
　　果树园
109 milestone
　　里程碑
110 guide post
　　路标

111 tree nursery
　　苗圃
112 ride (aisle, lane, section line)
　　小路
113 electricity transmission line
　　输电线
114 hop garden
　　忽布子园，啤酒花种植园

1-54 the human body
人体

1-18 head
头

1 vertex (crown of the head, top of the head)
头顶（头的顶部）

2 occiput (back of the head)
后头，枕骨部

3 hair
头发

4-17 face
脸部

4-5 forehead
前额（头）

4 frontal eminence (frontal protuberance)
前额隆凸部

5 superciliary arch
眉弓

6 temple
太阳穴

7 eye
眼睛

8 zygomatic bone (malar bone, jugal bone, cheekbone)
颧骨（颧骨，轭骨，颊骨）

9 cheek
颊

10 nose
鼻

11 nasolabial fold
鼻唇沟（褶）

12 philtrum
人中

13 mouth
嘴

14 angle of the mouth (labial commissure)
嘴角（唇的接合处）

15 chin
颏，下巴

16 dimple (fossette) in the chin
下巴上的酒窝（小窝）

17 jaw
颚，颌骨

18 ear
耳朵

19-21 neck
颈

19 throat
喉

20 hollow of the throat
颈窝，前颈凹陷处

21 nape of the neck
后颈

22-41 trunk
干，躯干

22-25 back
背

22 shoulder
肩

23 shoulderblade (scapula)
肩胛骨

24 loins
腰，腰部

25 small of the back
腰背部

26 armpit
腋窝

27 armpit hair
腋窝毛，腋下毛

28-30 thorax (chest)
胸廓（胸部）

28-29 breasts (breast, mamma)
乳房

28 nipple
乳头

29 areola
乳头晕

30 bosom
胸

31 waist
腰，腰部

32 flank (side)
腰窝，侧腹

33 hip
臀部

34 navel
脐

35-37 abdomen (stomach)
腹部

35 upper abdomen
上腹

36 abdomen
腹

37 lower abdomen
下腹

38 groin
鼠蹊部，腹股沟

39 pudenda (vulva)
外生殖器（阴门；女阴）

40 seat (backside, *coll.* bottom)
臀部（臀，屁股）

41 anal groove (anal cleft)
肛管

42 gluteal fold (gluteal furrow)
臀褶（臀沟）

43-54 limbs
四肢

43-48 arm
臂

43 upper arm
上臂（肩与肘之间的部分）

44 crook of the arm
前臂弯曲处，臂弯

45 elbow
肘

46 forearm
前臂（肘至腕之间之部分）

47 hand
手

48 fist (clenched fist, clenched hand)
拳（握拳）

49-54 leg
腿

49 thigh
大腿

50 knee
膝

51 popliteal space
腘窝（后膝处）

52 shank
胫，小腿

53 calf
腓

54 foot
足，脚

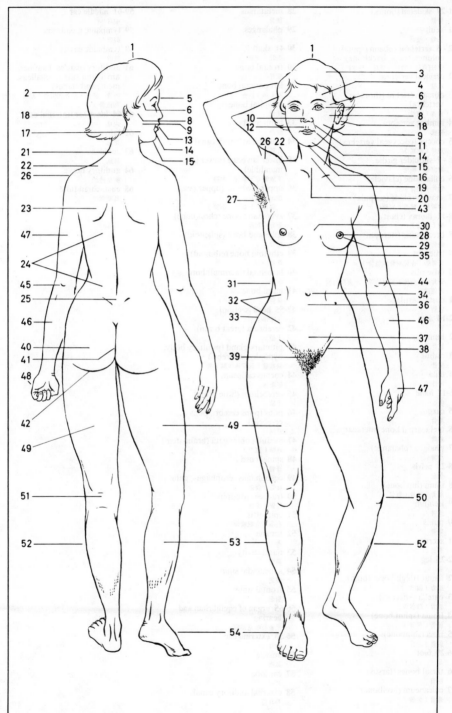

1-29 skeleton (bones)
骨骼
1 skull
头骨，颅骨
2-5 vertebral column (spinal column, spine, backbone)
脊柱[脊柱，脊柱，脊骨（柱）]
2 cervical vertebra
颈椎
3 dorsal vertebra (thoracic vertebra)
背椎（胸椎）
4 lumbar vertebra
腰椎
5 coccyx (coccygeal vertebra)
尾骨（尾椎）
6-7 shoulder girdle
肩带带，胸带
6 collarbone (clavicle)
锁骨（锁骨）
7 shoulderblade (scapula)
肩胛骨，胛骨（肩胛骨）
8-11 thorax (chest)
胸（胸廓）
8 breastbone (sternum)
胸骨
9 true ribs
真肋骨（连於胸骨的肋骨）
10 false ribs
假肋骨（两侧下五对肋骨，不直接与胸骨相接）
11 costal cartilage
软肋
12-14 arm
臂
12 humerus
肱骨
13 radius
桡骨
14 ulna
尺骨
15-17 hand
手
15 carpus
腕骨
16 metacarpal bone (metacarpal)
掌骨
17 phalanx (phalange)
指骨
18-21 pelvis
骨盆
18 ilium (hip bone)
肠骨，胯骨（臀骨）
19 ischium
坐骨
20 pubis
耻骨
21 sacrum
荐骨
22-25 leg
腿
22 femur (thigh bone, thigh)
股骨，腿节
23 patella (kneecap)
膑骨，膝盖骨
24 fibula (splint bone)
腓骨（整骨）
25 tibia (shinbone)
胫骨（胫骨）
26-29 foot
足
26 tarsal bones (tarsus)
跗骨
27 calcaneum (heelbone)
跟骨（肿股）

28 metatarsus
蹠骨
29 phalanges
趾骨
30-41 skull
头骨，颅骨
30 frontal bone
额骨
31 left parietal bone
左（颅）顶骨
32 occipital bone
枕骨
33 temporal bone
颞骨
34 external auditory canal
外耳道
35 lower jawbone (lower jaw, mandible)
下颌骨（下颚骨，大颚）
36 upper jawbone (upper jaw, maxilla)
上颌骨（上颚骨，小颚）
37 zygomatic bone (cheekbone)
颧骨（颊骨）
38 sphenoid bone (sphenoid)
蝶骨
39 ethmoid bone (ethmoid)
筛骨
40 lachrimal (lacrimal) bone
泪骨
41 nasal bone
鼻骨
42-55 head [section]
头[剖面图]
42 cerebrum (great brain)
大脑
43 pituitary gland (pituitary body, hypophysis cerebri)
脑垂腺（脑垂体，脑下腺）
44 corpus callosum
胼胝体
45 cerebellum (little brain)
小脑
46 pons (pons cerebri, pons cerebelli)
桥脑
47 medulla oblongata (brain-stem)
延脑（脑干）
48 spinal cord
脊髓
49 oesophagus (esophagus, gullet)
食管，食道
50 trachea (windpipe)
气管，导管
51 epiglottis
会咽，会咽软骨
52 tongue
舌
53 nasal cavity
鼻腔
54 sphenoidal sinus
蝶窦
55 frontal sinus
额窦
56-65 organ of equilibrium and hearing
平衡和听觉器官
56-58 external ear
外耳
56 auricle
耳廓
57 ear lobe
耳垂
58 external auditory canal
外耳道

59-61 middle ear
中耳
59 tympanic membrane
鼓膜
60 tympanic cavity
鼓腔
61 auditory ossicles: hammer, anvil, and stirrup (malleus, incus, and stapes)
听骨：槌骨，砧骨和镫骨（槌骨，砧骨和镫骨）
62-64 inner ear (internal ear)
内耳
62 labyrinth
迷路
63 cochlea
耳蜗
64 auditory nerve
听觉神经
65 eustachian tube
耳咽管

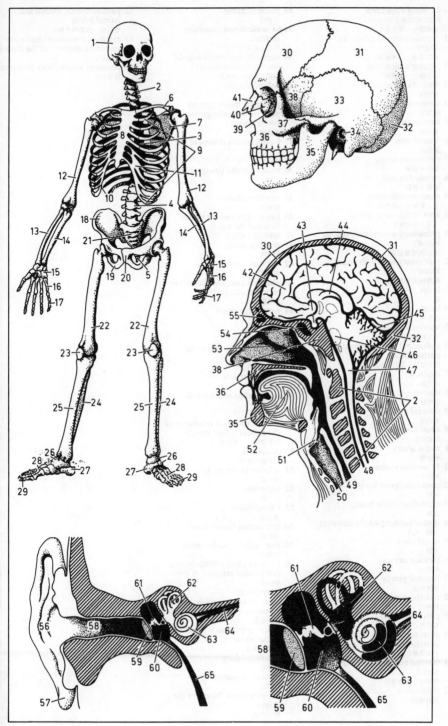

1-21 blood circulation
(circulatory system)
血液循环（循环系统）
1 common carotid artery, an
artery
颈总动脉，一种动脉
2 jugular vein, a vein
颈静脉，一种静脉
3 temporal artery
颞动脉
4 temporal vein
颞静脉
5 frontal artery
额动脉
6 frontal vein
额静脉
7 subclavian artery
锁骨下动脉
8 subclavian vein
锁骨下静脉
9 superior vena cava
上大静脉，上腔静脉
10 arch of the aorta (aorta)
（主）大动脉弓
11 pulmonary artery 'with venous
blood'
肺动脉[带静脉血]
12 pulmonary vein 'with arterial
blood'
肺静脉[带动脉血]
13 lungs
肺
14 heart
心脏
15 inferior vena cava
下大静脉，下腔静脉
16 abdominal aorta (descending
portion of the aorta)
腹大动脉（下行大动脉）
17 iliac artery
胯动脉
18 iliac vein
胯静脉
19 femoral artery
股动脉
20 tibial artery
胫前动脉
21 radial artery
桡动脉

22-33 nervous system
神经系统
22 cerebrum (great brain)
大脑
23 cerebellum (little brain)
小脑
24 medulla oblongata (brain-stem)
延脑（脑干）
25 spinal cord
脊髓
26 thoracic nerves
胸神经
27 brachial plexus
臂神经丛
28 radial nerve
桡神经
29 ulnar nerve
尺骨神经
30 great sciatic nerve 'lying
posteriorly'
大坐骨神经[大腿后部中间]
31 femoral nerve (anterior crural
nerve)
股神经（前股神经）
32 tibial nerve
胫前神经

33 peroneal nerve
腓神经

34-64 musculature (muscular
system)
肌系（肌肉系统）
34 sternocleidomastoid muscle
(sternomastoid muscle)
胸锁乳突肌（胸肌）
35 deltoid muscle
三角肌
36 pectoralis major (greater
pectoralis muscle, greater
pectoralis)
大胸肌
37 biceps brachii (biceps of the
arm)
肱二头肌
38 triceps brachii (triceps of the
arm)
肱三头肌
39 brachioradialis
肱桡肌
40 flexor carpi radialis (radial
flexor of the wrist)
桡侧屈肌（腕屈肌）
41 thenar muscle
拇指肌
42 serratus anterior
前锯肌
43 obliquus externus abdominis
(external oblique)
腹外斜肌
44 rectus abdominis
腹直肌
45 sartorius
缝匠肌
46 vastus lateralis and vastus
medialis
外股肌和内股肌
47 tibialis anterior
胫骨前肌
48 tendo calcaneus (Achilles'
tendon)
跟腱
49 abductor hallucis (abductor of
the hallux), a foot muscle
外展拇肌，一种足肌
50 occipitalis
后头肌（枕肌）
51 splenius of the neck
颈夹肌
52 trapezius
斜方肌
53 infraspinatus
棘下肌
54 teres minor (lesser teres)
小圆肌
55 teres major (greater teres)
大圆肌
56 extensor carpi radialis longus
(long radial extensor of the
wrist)
桡侧伸腕长肌
57 extensor communis digitorum
(common extensor of the digits)
伸指总肌
58 flexor carpi ulnaris (ulnar flexor
of the wrist)
尺侧屈腕肌
59 latissimus dorsi
背阔肌
60 gluteus maximus
大臀肌
61 biceps femoris (biceps of the
thigh)
股二头肌

62 gastrocnemius, medial and
lateral heads
腓肠肌，内侧和外侧头
63 extensor communis digitorum
(common extensor of the digits)
伸趾总肌
64 peroneus longus (long peroneus
腓骨长肌

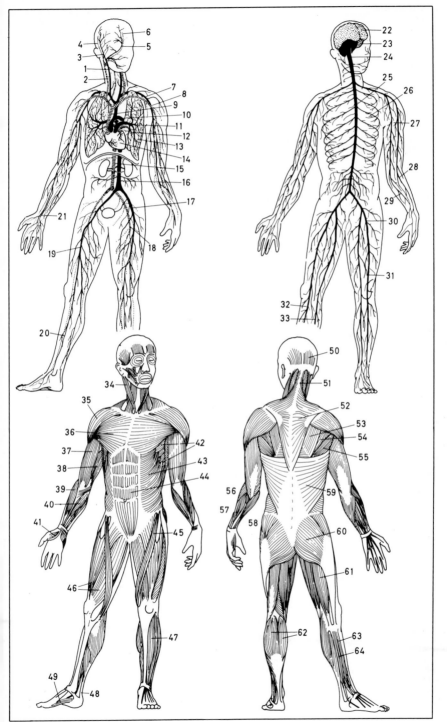

1-13 head and neck
头和颈

1 sternocleidomastoid muscle
胸锁乳突肌

2 occipitalis
后头肌（枕肌）

3 temporalis (temporal, temporal muscle)
颞肌

4 occipito frontalis (frontalis)
额肌

5 orbicularis oculi
眼轮匝肌

6 muscles of facial expression
面部表情肌

7 masseter
嚼肌

8 orbicularis oris
口轮匝肌

9 parotid gland
腮腺（耳下腺）

10 lymph node (submandibular lymph gland)
淋巴结[颌（颈）下淋巴腺]

11 submandibular gland (submaxillary gland)
（颈）颌下腺（颌下腺）

12 muscles of the neck
颈部肌肉

13 Adam's apple (laryngeal prominence) 'in men only'
喉结[唯男人有]

14-37 mouth and throat
口腔和咽喉

14 upper lip
上唇

15 gum
齿龈

16-18 teeth (set of teeth)
齿（牙齿）

16 incisors
门齿

17 canine tooth (canine)
犬齿

18 premolar (bicuspid) and molar teeth (premolars and molars)
前臼齿（二尖齿）和白齿

19 angle of the mouth (labial commissure)
咀角（咀唇接合处）

20 hard palate
硬腭

21 soft palate (velum palati, velum)
软腭

22 uvula
小舌

23 palatine tonsil (tonsil)
扁桃体，扁桃腺

24 pharyngeal opening (pharynx, throat)
咽，喉

25 tongue
舌

26 lower lip
下唇

27 upper jaw (maxilla)
上颚（颌）

28-37 tooth
牙齿

28 periodontal membrane (periodontium, pericementum)
齿根膜，齿骨膜，齿周膜，齿根骨膜

29 cement (dental cementum, crusta petrosa)
白垩质（牙齿的白垩质）

30 enamel
珐琅质

31 dentine (dentin)
齿质

32 dental pulp (tooth pulp, pulp)
齿髓

33 nerves and blood vessels
神经和血管

34 incisor
门齿

35 molar tooth (molar)
白齿

36 root (fang)
齿根

37 crown
齿冠

38-51 eye
眼，目，视官

38 eyebrow (supercilium)
眉，眉毛

39 upper eyelid (upper palpebra)
上眼睑

40 lower eyelid (lower palpebra)
下眼睑

41 eyelash (cilium)
睫毛

42 iris
虹膜

43 pupil
瞳孔

44 eye muscles (ocular muscles)
眼肌

45 eyeball
眼球

46 vitreous body
玻璃体

47 cornea
眼角膜

48 lens
晶状体

49 retina
视网膜

50 blind spot
盲点

51 optic nerve
视神经

52-63 foot
脚，足

52 big toe (great toe, first toe, hallux, digitus I)
大脚趾（第一趾，大拇趾）

53 second toe (digitus II)
第二趾

54 third toe (digitus III)
第三趾

55 fourth toe (digitus IV)
第四趾

56 little toe (digitus minimus, digitus V)
小脚趾（第五趾）

57 toenail
趾甲（脚趾甲）

58 ball of the foot
脚的球状态

59 lateral malleolus (external malleolus, outer malleolus, malleolus fibulae)
外（侧）踝

60 medial malleolus (internal malleolus, inner malleolus, malleolus tibulae, malleolus medialis)
内踝

61 instep (medial longitudinal arch, dorsum of the foot, dorsum pedis)
足背（足弓的背部）

62 sole of the foot
足底，脚底，蹠

63 heel
足跟，踵

64-83 hand
手

64 thumb (pollex, digitus I)
大拇指（拇指，第一指）

65 index finger (forefinger, second finger, digitus II)
食指（第二指）

66 middle finger (third finger, digitus medius, digitus III)
中指（第三指）

67 ring finger (fourth finger, digit anularis, digitus IV)
环指，无名指（第四指）

68 little finger (fifth finger, digitus minimus, digitus V)
小指（第五指，小拇指）

69 radial side of the hand
手的桡骨侧

70 ulnar side of the hand
手的尺骨侧

71 palm of the hand (palma manus)
手掌

72-74 lines of the hand
掌纹，手纹

72 life line (line of life)
生命线

73 head line (line of the head)
智慧线

74 heart line (line of the heart)
感情线

75 ball of the thumb (thenar eminence)
拇指球

76 wrist (carpus)
腕

77 phalanx (phalange)
指骨

78 finger pad
指垫

79 fingertip
指尖

80 fingernail (nail)
指甲

81 lunule (lunula) of the nail
指甲弧影（小月斑）

82 knuckle
手关节

83 back of the hand (dorsum of the hand, dorsum manus)
手背

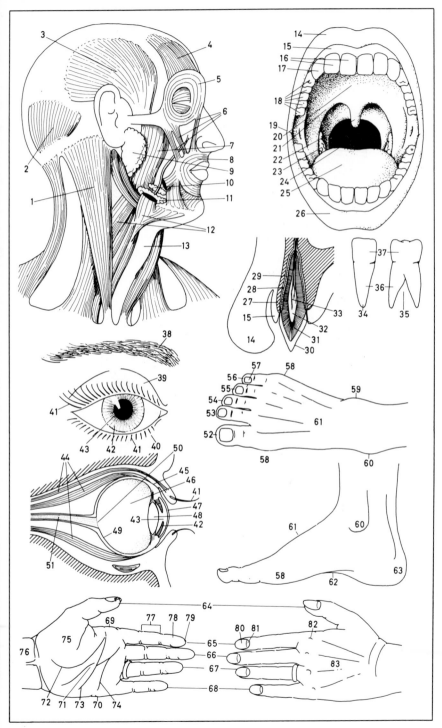

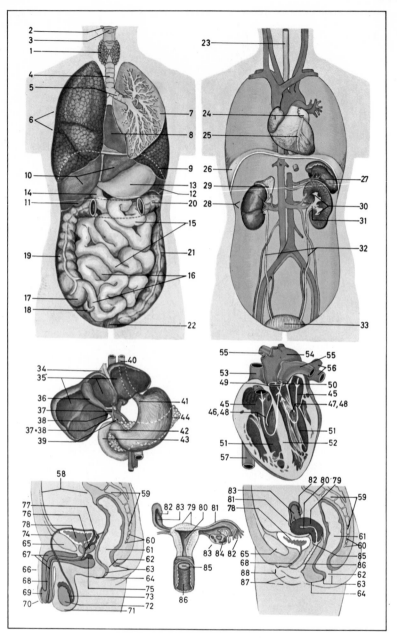

57 internal organs [front view]

内部器官，内脏[前视图]

thyroid gland

甲状腺

3 larynx

喉（头）

hyoid bone (hyoid)

舌骨

thyroid cartilage

甲状软骨

trachea (windpipe)

气管

bronchus

支气管

7 lung

肺

right lung

右肺

upper pulmonary lobe (upper lobe of the lung) [section]

上肺叶（肺的上叶）[剖面图]

heart

心脏

diaphragm

横隔膜

liver

肝（脏）

gall bladder

胆囊

spleen

脾

stomach

胃

22 intestines (bowel)

肠

16 small intestine (intestinum tenue)

小肠

duodenum

十二指肠

jejunum

空肠

ileum

回肠

22 large intestine (intestinum crassum)

大肠

caecum (cecum)

盲肠

appendix (vermiform appendix)

阑尾

ascending colon

升结肠

transverse colon

横结肠

descending colon

降结肠

rectum

直肠

oesophagus (esophagus, gullet)

食道

25 heart

心脏

auricle

心房

anterior longitudinal cardiac sulcus

前纵心沟

diaphragm

隔膜

spleen

脾脏

right kidney

右肾

29 suprarenal gland

肾上腺

30-31 left kidney [longitudinal section]

左肾[纵剖面图]

30 calyx (renal calyx)

肾萼（肾盏）

31 renal pelvis

肾盂

32 ureter

输尿管

33 bladder

膀胱

34-35 liver [from behind]

肝脏[后视图]

34 falciform ligament of the liver

肝的镰状韧带

35 lobe of the liver

肝叶

36 gall bladder

胆囊

37-38 common bile duct

总胆管

37 hepatic duct (common hepatic duct)

肝管（总肝管）

38 cystic duct

胆囊管

39 portal vein (hepatic portal vein)

门静脉（肝门静脉）

40 oesophagus (esophagus, gullet)

食道

41-42 stomach

胃

41 cardiac orifice

贲门孔

42 pylorus

幽门

43 duodenum

十二指肠

44 pancreas

胰脏

45-57 heart [longitudinal section]

心脏[纵剖面图]

45 atrium

心房

46-47 valves of the heart

心瓣

46 tricuspid valve (right atrioventricular valve)

三尖瓣（右心房瓣）

47 bicuspid valve (mitral valve, left atrioventricular valve)

二尖瓣（左心房瓣）

48 cusp

瓣尖

49 aortic valve

大动脉瓣

50 pulmonary valve

肺动脉瓣

51 ventricle

心室

52 ventricular septum (interventricular septum)

心室隔膜

53 superior vena cava

上大静脉

54 aorta

大动脉

55 pulmonary artery

肺动脉

56 pulmonary vein

肺静脉

57 inferior vena cava

下大静脉

58 peritoneum

腹膜

59 sacrum

荐骨

60 coccyx (coccygeal vertebra)

尾骨（尾椎）

61 rectum

直肠

62 anus

肛门

63 anal sphincter

肛门括约肌

64 perineum

会阴

65 pubic symphisis (symphisis pubis)

耻缝，耻骨联合

66-77 male sex organs [longitudinal section]

男性生殖器[纵剖面]

66 penis

阴茎

67 corpus cavernosum and spongiosum of the penis (erectile tissue of the penis)

阴茎海绵体（阴茎的勃起组织）

68 urethra

尿道

69 glans penis

阴茎头，龟头

70 prepuce (foreskin)

包皮

71 scrotum

阴囊

72 right testicle (testis)

右睾丸

73 epididymis

副睾

74 spermatic duct (vas deferens)

输精管

75 Cowper's gland (bulbourethral gland)

考扑氏腺，尿道球腺

76 prostate (prostate gland)

摄护腺，前列腺

77 seminal vesicle

贮精囊

78 bladder

膀胱

79-88 female sex organs [longitudinal section]

女性生殖器[纵剖面图]

79 uterus (matrix, womb)

子宫

80 cavity of the uterus

子宫腔

81 fallopian tube (uterine tube, oviduct)

输卵管

82 fimbria (fimbriated extremity)

输卵管缨

83 ovary

卵巢

84 follicle with ovum (egg)

带卵子的滤泡

85 os uteri externum

子宫外口

86 vagina

阴道

87 lip of the pudendum (lip of the vulva)

阴唇

88 clitoris

阴蒂，阴核

1-13 emergency bandages
紧急缠带法

1 arm bandage
手臂缠带

2 triangular cloth used as a sling
(an arm sling)
用作吊带的三角布（吊腕带）

3 head bandage (capeline)
头部缠带

4 first aid kit
急救包

5 first aid dressing
急救（包扎用的）药品

6 sterile gauze dressing
消毒（无菌）纱布敷料

7 adhesive plaster (sticking
plaster)
绊创膏

8 wound
伤口

9 bandage
缠带

10 emergency splint for a broken
limb (fractured limb)
骨折用的紧急夹板

11 fractured leg (broken leg)
骨折的腿

12 splint
夹板

13 headrest
靠头之物

14-17 measures for stanching the blood flow (tying up of, ligature of, a blood vessel)
止血法（包紧血管）

14 pressure points of the arteries
动脉压迫点

15 emergency tourniquet on the
thigh
大腿紧急止血带

16 walking stick used as a screw
固定用的拐杖

17 compression bandage
压迫缠带

18-23 rescue and transport of an injured person
负伤者的救助和送送

18 Rautek grip (for rescue of victim
of a car accident)
Rautek 氏握法（对车祸伤者的营救）

19 helper
救助者，营救人

20 injured person (casualty)
负伤者（受伤者）

21 chair grip
坐椅握法

22 carrying grip
运送（搬）握法

23 emergency stretcher of sticks
and a jacket
棍棒和夹克做的应急担架

24-27 the positioning of an unconscious person and artificial respiration (resuscitation)
失去知觉人的安放（置）和人工呼吸

24 coma position
昏迷（厥）的姿态

25 unconscious person
失去知觉的人

26 mouth-to-mouth resuscitation
(*variation*: mouth-to-nose
resuscitation)
口对口人工呼吸法（另有：口对鼻人工
呼吸法）

27 resuscitator (respiratory
apparatus, resuscitation
apparatus), a respirator
(artificial breathing device)
人工呼吸器（人工呼吸装置）

28-33 methods of rescue in ice accidents
冰上意外事故的营救法

28 person who has fallen through
the ice
冰上遇难者

29 rescuer
营救者

30 rope
粗绳

31 table (or similar device)
桌子[或类似物]

32 ladder
梯子

33 self-rescue
自救

34-38 rescue of a drowning person
溺水者的营救

34 method of release (release grip,
release) to free rescuer from the
clutch of a drowning person
救助者被溺水者紧抱时的解困法

35 drowning person
溺水者

36 lifesaver
救生员

37 chest grip, a towing grip
胸部抱拖法

38 tired swimmer grip (hip grip)
疲劳泳者的抱拖法（抱腰法）

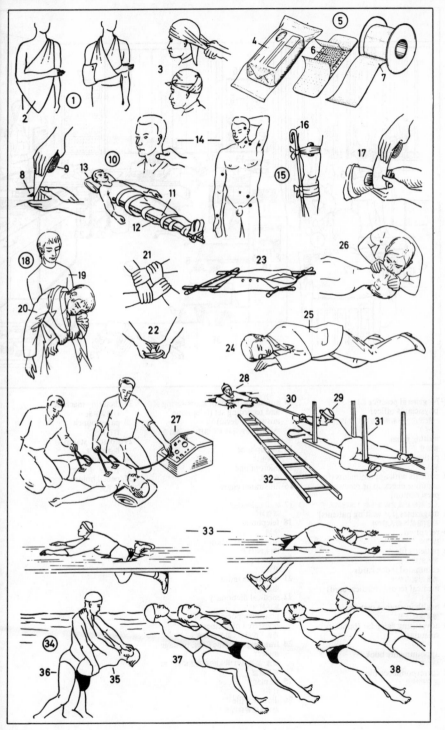

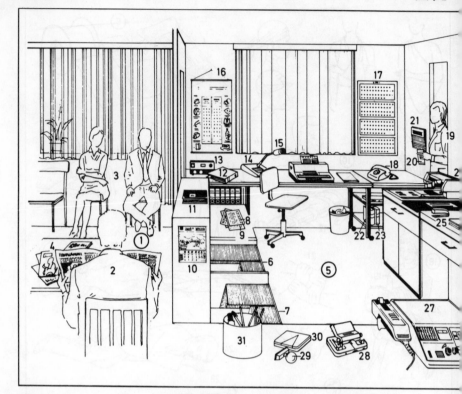

1-74 general practice (*Am.* physician's office)
一般诊疗，一般医疗业务（[美]医生办公室）

1 waiting room
候诊室

2 patient
病人

3 patients with appointments (for aroutine checkup or renewal of prescription)
（定期检查或更换处方的）预约病人

4 magazines [for waiting patients]
杂志[给候诊病人看的]

5 reception
接待室

6 patients file
病人的病历表

7 eliminated index cards
消去的索引卡片

8 medical record (medical card)
病历卡

9 health insurance certificate
健康保险证书

10 advertising calendar (publicity calendar)
广告月历

11 appointments book
预约簿

12 correspondence file
通信档案夹

13 automatic telephone answering and recording set (telephone answering devic)
电话的自动回答和录音组件（电话回答装置）

14 radiophone
无线电话

15 microphone
麦克风

16 illustrated chart
图表

17 wall calendar
墙壁月历

18 telephone
电话

19 [doctor's] assistant
[医生的]助手

20 prescription
处方

21 telephone index
电话簿

22 medical dictionary
医学辞典

23 pharmacopoeia (list of registered medicines)
药典，配药书（註册药物表）

24 franking machine (*Am.* postage meter)
加盖"邮资已付"印记的自动盖印机（邮资秤量器）

25 stapler
订书机

26 diabetics file
糖尿病患者病历卡

27 dictating machine
口述录音机

28 paper punch
打孔器

29 doctor's stamp
医生的图章

30 ink pad
打印台，印色盒

31 pencil holder
铅笔筒

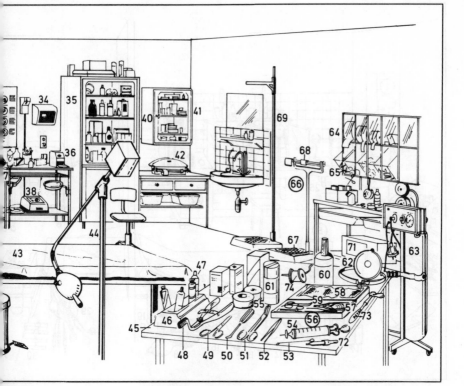

74 surgery
外科手术室

chart of eyegrounds
眼底图表

doctor's bag (doctor's case)
医生的手提箱（包）

intercom
对讲机（内部通话装置）

medicine cupboard
药橱，药柜

swab dispenser
消毒药品定量分配器（拭子分配器）

inflator (Politzer bag)
吹张器（普立兹袋）

electrotome
电刀

steam sterilizer
蒸汽消毒器

cabinet
（存放或陈列用的）小橱

medicine samples
药物样品

baby scales
小型秤盘

examination couch
诊察（疗）牀（台）

directional lamp
定向灯

instrument table
器具桌（台）

tube holder
管架

tube of ointment
药膏（油膏，软膏）管

48-50 instruments for minor surgery
小手术用器具

48 mouth gag
张口器，开口器

49 Kocher's forceps
Kocher 氏钳（动脉钳）

50 scoop (curette)
短勺（刮匙，刮除器）

51 angled scissors
有角剪

52 forceps
镊子

53 olive-pointed (bulb-headed) probe
橄榄头（球头）探针

54 syringe for irrigations of the ear or bladder
耳或膀胱的冲洗注射器

55 adhesive plaster (sticking plaster)
绊创膏

56 surgical suture material
手术缝合器材

57 curved surgical needle
弯曲的手术缝针

58 sterile gauze
消毒纱布

59 needle holder
缝针托盘

60 spray for disinfecting the skin
皮肤消毒的喷雾器

61 thread container
缝线容器

62 ophthalmoscope
检眼镜

63 freezer for cryosurgery
冷冻手术用的冷凝装置

64 dispenser for plasters and small pieces of equipment
胶布和小器具的配给架

65 disposable hypodermic needles and syringes
只用一次的皮下注射针头和注射器

66 scales, sliding-weight scales
磅秤，体重计

67 weighing platform
称重台

68 sliding weight (jockey)
滑动砝码

69 height gauge (*Am.* gage)
身高测量器

70 waste bin (*Am.* trash bin)
垃圾筒

71 hot-air sterilizer
热气消毒器

72 pipette
吸管

73 percussor
听诊器

74 aural speculum (auriscope, aural syringe)
耳镜（耳镜，耳注射器）

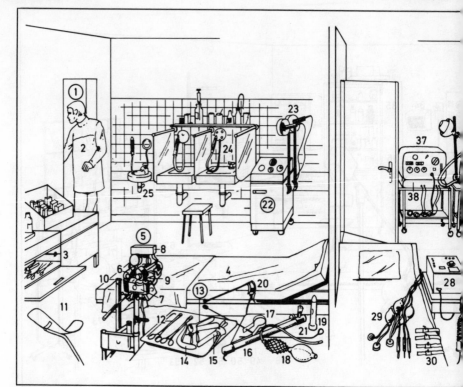

1 consulting room
诊察室
2 general practitioner
一般医师（各科皆看的医师）
3-21 **instruments for gynecological
and proctological examinations**
妇科和直肠检查的器具
3 warming the instruments up to
body temperature
将器具加温至体温的温度
4 examination couch
诊察台（床）
5 colposcope
阴道镜
6 binocular eyepiece
双目镜
7 miniature camera
小型照相机
8 cold light source
冷光源
9 cable release
电缆断路器
10 bracket for the leg support
支脚的腕木托腿架
11 leg support (leg holder)
支脚架（托腿座）
12 holding forceps (sponge holder)
夹持钳（海绵钳）
13 vaginal speculum
阴道窥镜
14 lower blade of the vaginal
speculum
阴道窥镜的下叶板

15 platinum loop (for smears)
白金圈（抹片用）
16 rectoscope
直肠镜
17 biopsy forceps used with the
rectoscope (proctoscope)
和直肠镜联用的活组织检查钳（直肠
镜）
18 insufflator for proctoscopy
(rectoscopy)
直肠镜检查用的吹气器
19 proctoscope (rectal speculum)
直肠镜
20 urethroscope
尿道镜
21 guide for inserting the
proctoscope
直肠镜插入时用的引导子
22 diathermy unit (short-wave
therapy apparatus)
透热疗法设备（短波治疗装置）
23 radiator
辐射器
24 inhaling apparatus (inhalator)
吸入装置（吸人器）
25 basin (for sputum)
痰盂
26-31 **ergometry**
肌力测试，测力试验
26 bicycle ergometer
脚踏测力器

27 monitor (visual display of the
ECG and of pulse and
respiratory rates when
performing work)
监视器（测试时心电图、脉膊和呼吸数
的显示装置）
28 ECG (electrocardiograph)
心电图仪（心动电流描记器）
29 suction electrodes
吸引电极
30 strap-on electrodes for the limb
肢体连接的电极
31 spirometer (for measuring
respiratory functions)
呼吸计，吸气计（量呼吸功能用）
32 measuring the blood pressure
量血压
33 sphygmomanometer
血压计
34 inflatable cuff
量血压用可膨胀的臂带
35 stethoscope
听诊器
36 microwave treatment unit
微波治疗设备
37 faradization unit (application of
low-frequency currents with
different pulse shapes)
感应电疗装置（应用不同形式脉冲的高
频电流）
38 automatic tuner
自动调谐器
39 short-wave therapy apparatus
短波治疗设备

timer
计时器
59 laboratory
实验室，化验室
medical laboratory technician
医学化验技师
capillary tube stand for blood
sedimentation
血液沉淀用的毛细管架
measuring cylinder
量筒
automatic pipette
自动吸管
kidney dish
肾形盘
portable ECG machine for
emergency use
急救用的手提心电图仪（心电描记器）
automatic pipetting device
自动吸管（移）装置
constant temperature water bath
恒温水槽
tap with water jet pump
喷射泵水龙头
staining dish (for staining blood
smears, sediments and other
smears)
染色皿（用於染血抹片，沉淀和其他抹
片）
binocular research microscope
双目检查显微镜
pipette stand for photometry
光度测法用的吸管架

53 computer and analyser for
photometry
光度测法用的电脑和分析器
54 phtotometer
光度计
55 potentiometric recorder
电位（电势）记录仪
56 transforming section
变换部件
57 laboratory apparatus
(laboratory equipment)
化验器材（实验室装置）
58 urine sediment chart
尿沉淀图表
59 centrifuge
离心机

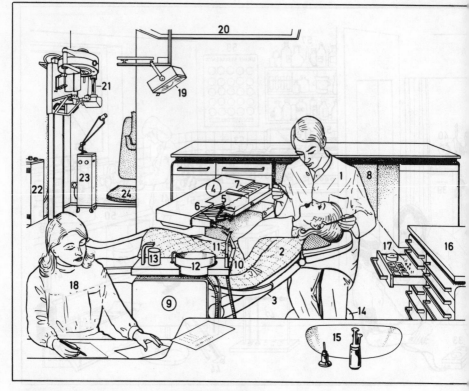

1 dentist (dental surgeon)
牙医师

2 patient
病人，患者

3 dentist's chair
牙科椅子

4 dental instruments
牙科诊疗器具

5 instrument tray
器具盘

6 drills with different handpieces
具不同手柄的牙钻

7 medicine case
药箱

8 storage unit (for dental instruments)
（牙科器具的）贮藏装置

9 assistant's unit
牙科助手的器具柜

10 multi-purpose syringe (for cold and warm water, spray or air)
多功能注射器（水枪）（喷冷水，热水或空气）

11 suction apparatus
吸水装置

12 basin
唾液盆

13 water glass, filled automatically
自动充水的玻璃杯

14 stool
凳子

15 washbasin
洗脸盆，洗手盆

16 instrument cabinet
器具柜

17 drawer for drills
放凿子的抽屉

18 dentist's assistant
牙医助手

19 dentist's lamp
牙科用灯

20 ceiling light
室内照明灯

21 X-ray apparatus for panoramic pictures
X光全像摄影机

22 X-ray generator
X光（射线）发生器

23 microwave treatment unit, a radiation unit
微波医疗装置，一种辐射医疗装置

24 seat
座位

denture (set of false teeth)
假牙（整组假牙）
bridge (dental bridge)
牙桥（齿桥）
prepared stump of the tooth
预备好的牙根
crown (*kinds*: gold crown, jacket crown)
齿冠（种类：金齿冠，甲冠）
porcelain tooth (porcelain pontic)
瓷牙（瓷假牙）
filling
填（补）料
post crown
合钉继续齿冠
facing
镶牙
diaphragm
隔膜
post
牙桩
carborundum disc (disk)
金钢砂盘
grinding wheel
磨（牙）轮
burs
牙钻，圆头钻
flame-shaped finishing bur
火焰形钻子
fissure burs
裂钻
diamond point
钻石刻刀
mouth mirror
口镜（口腔检查器）
mouth lamp
口腔灯
cautery
烧灼器，烙器
platinum-iridium electrode
铂铱电极
tooth scalers
清齿牙器
probe
探针
extraction forceps
拔牙钳
tooth-root elevator
（牙）齿根起子
bone chisel
骨凿
spatula
压舌板
mixer for filling material
填料搅拌器
synchronous timer
同步计时器
hypodermic syringe for injection of local anaesthetic
局部麻醉用的皮下注射器
hypodermic needle
皮下注射针
matrix holder
牙模支持器
impression tray
（牙齿）印模托盘
spirit lamp
酒精灯

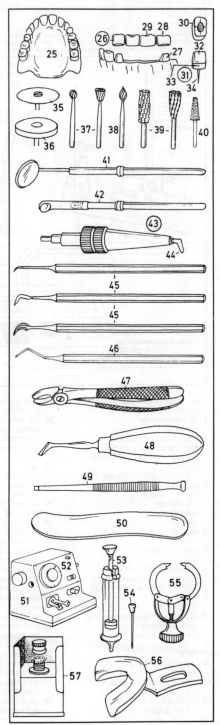

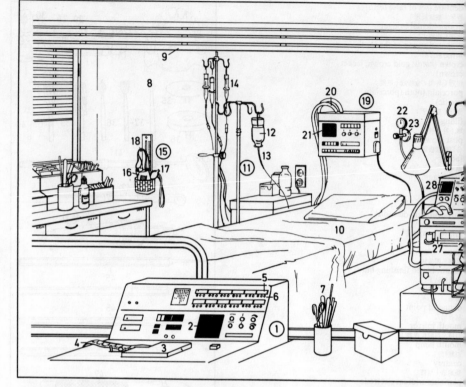

1-30 intensive care unit
加护病房设备
1 - 9 control room
控制室
1 central control unit for monitoring heart rhythm (cardiac rhythm) and blood pressure
监视心律和血压的中心控制装置
2 electrocardiogram monitor (ECG monitor)
心电图监视器
3 recorder
记录器
4 recording paper
记录纸带
5 patient's card
病人卡片
6 indicator lights (with call buttons for each patient)
指示灯（附有每个病人的呼叫按钮）
7 spatula
压舌板，药匙
8 window (observation window, glass partition)
窗（观察窗，玻璃隔板）
9 blind
百叶窗
10 bed (hospital bed)
病床
11 stand for infusion apparatus
点滴（输液）装置的立架
12 infusion bottle
点滴瓶（输液瓶）

13 tube for intravenous drips
静脉注射的点滴注管
14 infusion device for water-soluble medicaments
水溶性药物的输入装置
15 sphygmomanometer
血压计
16 cuff
血压计的臂带
17 inflating bulb
充气小球
18 mercury manometer
水银测压器
19 bed monitor
床头盘视器（装置）
20 connecting lead to the central control unit
连接中心控制设备的导线
21 electrocardiogram monitor (ECG monitor)
心电图监视器
22 manometer for the oxygen supply
氧气供给用的测压计
23 wall connection for oxygen treatment
氧气治疗用的接头部分
24 mobile monitoring unit
移动式的监视装置
25 electrode lead to the short-term pacemaker
短期定调器的电极导线
26 electrodes for shock treatment
休克治疗用的电极

27 ECG recording unit
心电图记录装置
28 electrocardiogram monitor (ECG monitor)
心电图监视器
29 control switches and knobs (controls) for adjusting the monitor
调整监视器用的控制开关和旋钮
30 control buttons for the pacemaker unit
定调装置的控制按钮

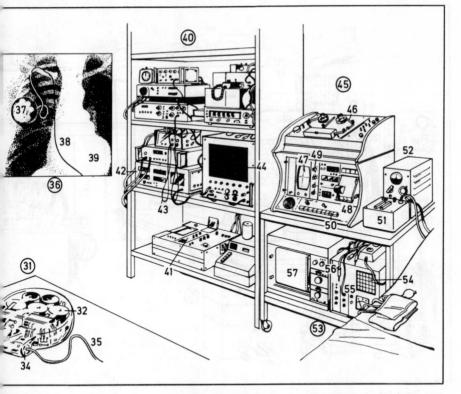

pacemaker (cardiac pacemaker)
（心脏）定调器
mercury battery
水银电池
programmed impulse generator
程序脉冲发生器
electrode exit point
电极出口点
electrode
电极
implantation of the pacemaker
定调器的植入
internal cardiac pacemaker
(internal pacemaker,
pacemaker)
体内心脏定调器（体内定调器，定调
器）
electrode inserted through the
vein
通过静脉插入电极
cardiac silhouette on the X-ray
X光（射线）照射下心脏的影像
pacemaker control unit
定调器控制装置
electrocardiograph (ECG
recorder)
心电图记录器
automatic impulse meter
脉搏自动计测器
ECG lead to the patient
心电图仪与病人连接的导线

44 monitor unit for visual
monitoring of the pacemaker
impulses
脉搏定调器的视觉监视用的监视器（装
置）
45 long-term ECG analyser
长期心电图分析仪
46 magnetic tape for recording the
ECG impulses during analysis
分析心电图脉冲时记录用的磁带
47 ECG monitor
心电图监视器
48 automatic analysis on paper of
the ECG rhythm
心电图节律纸带上的自动分析
49 control knob for the ECG
amplitude
心电图振幅控制旋钮
50 program selector switches for
the ECG analysis
分析心电图用的程式选择开关
51 charger for the pacemaker
batteries
定调器的电池充电器
52 battery tester
电池检查器
53 pressure gauge (*Am.* gage) for
the right cardiac catheter
右心导管用的压力计（血压计）
54 trace monitor
轨迹监视器
55 pressure indicator
血压指示器

56 connecting lead to the paper
recorder
连接纸带记录器的导线
57 paper recorder for pressure
traces
描述血压曲线的纸带记录器

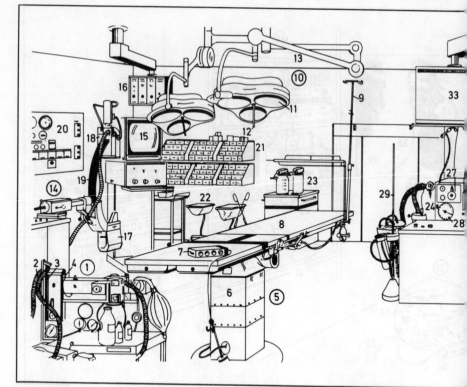

1-54 surgical unit
外科设备

1-33 operating theatre (*Am.* theater)
手术房(室)

1 anaesthesia and breathing apparatus (respiratory machine)
麻醉和呼吸装置(呼吸器)

2 inhalers (inhaling tubes)
吸(人)气管(吸气管)

3 flowmeter for nitrous oxide
氧化亚氮流量计

4 oxygen flow meter
氧气流量计

5 pedestal operating table
基座式手术台

6 table pedestal
手术台基座

7 control device (control unit)
控制装置(设备)

8 adjustable top of the operating table
可调整的手术台台面

9 stand for intravenous drips
静脉注射点滴用的立架

10 swivel-mounted shadow-free operating lamp
装在旋转托架上手术用的无影灯

11 individual lamp
单个灯

12 handle
把手,手柄

13 swivel arm
旋转臂

14 mobile fluoroscope
活动的荧光幕

15 monitor of the image converter
影像转换器的监视器

16 monitor [back]
监视器(背面)

17 tube
拍摄管

18 image converter
影像转换器

19 C-shaped frame
C 型框架

20 control panel for the air-conditioning
空调控制板

21 surgical suture material
外科手术缝合器材

22 mobile waste tray
活动废水盆

23 containers for unsterile (unsterilized) pads
未消毒垫容器

24 anaesthesia and respiratory apparatus
麻醉和人工呼吸装置

25 respirator
人工呼吸器

26 fluothane container (halothane container)
氟烷(吸入全身麻醉药)容器

27 ventilation control knob
通风控制旋钮

28 indicator with pointer for respiratory volume
呼吸量指针式指示器

29 stand with inhalers (inhaling tubes) and pressure gauges (*Am.* gages)
配有吸入管和压力计的立架

30 catheter holder
导管架

31 catheter in sterile packing
无菌密封的导管

32 sphygmograph
脉搏描记器,脉波计

33 monitor
监视器

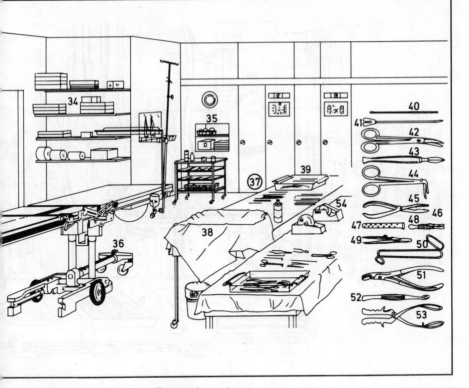

–54 preparation and sterilization room
准备和消毒室
 dressing material
包紮材料
 small sterilizer
小型消毒器
 carriage of the operating table
手术台托架
 mobile instrument table
移动式器具台
 sterile cloth
消毒布
 instrument tray
器具盘
–53 surgical instruments
外科手术器具
 olive-pointed (bulb-headed) probe
橄榄形（球头）探针
 hollow probe
空心探针
 curved scissors
弯剪刀
 scalpel (surgical knife)
解剖刀（手术刀）
 ligature-holding forceps
结紮线支持钳
 sequestrum forceps
死骨镊，腐骨钳
 jaw
钳头（口）
 drainage tube
浅液管，导液管

48 surgeon's tourniquet
外科压脉器
49 artery forceps
动脉钳
50 blunt hook
钝钩
51 bone nippers (bone-cutting forceps)
骨钳（剪骨钳）
52 scoop (curette) for erasion (curettage)
刮除杓（刮匙）
53 obstetrical forceps
分娩钳（产科钳）
54 roll of plaster
绊创膏卷

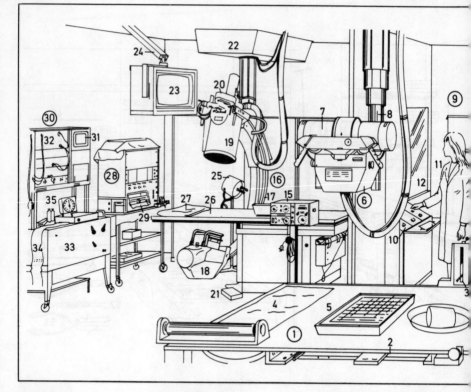

1-35 X-ray unit
X 射线装置

1 X-ray examination table
X 射线检查台

2 support for X-ray cassettes
X 光（射线）胶片盒支架

3 height adjustment of the central
beam for lateral views
侧面摄影用中心束高度调整器

4 compress for pyelography and
cholecystography
肾盂和胆囊摄影用的压迫带

5 instrument basin
器具盆

6 X-ray apparatus for pyelograms
肾盂摄影用的 X 射线装置

7 X-ray tube
X 光（射线）管

8 telescopic X-ray support
伸缩的 X 射线管支架

9 central X-ray control unit
中心 X 射线控制装置

10 control panel (control desk)
控制盘

11 radiographer (X-ray technician)
放射线技师（X 射线技师）

12 window to the angiography
room
血管 X 射线检查室的窗口

13 oxymeter
量氧计

14 pyelogram cassettes
肾盂摄影用胶片盒

15 contrast medium injector
造影剂注入器

16 X-ray image intensifier
X 射线萤光增倍装置

17 C-shaped frame
C 型框架

18 X-ray head with X-ray tube
带 X 射线管的 X 射线头

19 image converter with converter
tube
带变换管的影像变换器

20 film camera
软片摄影机

21 foot switch
脚踏开关

22 mobile mounting
移动式托架

23 monitor
监视器

24 swivel-mounted monitor
support
旋转式监视器支架

25 operating lamp
手术灯

26 angiographic examination table
血管 X 射线检查台

27 pillow
枕头

28 eight-channel recorder
八线记录器

29 recording paper
记录纸

30 catheter gauge (*Am.* gage) unit
for catheterization of the heart
心导管液压计

31 six-channel monitor for pressure
graphs and ECG
血压图和心电图用的六线路监视器

32 slide-in units of the pressure
transducer
血压传感器的滑动装置

33 paper recorder unit with
developer for photographic
recording
摄影记录用的显影纸带记录器（装置）

34 recording paper
记录纸

35 timer
计时器

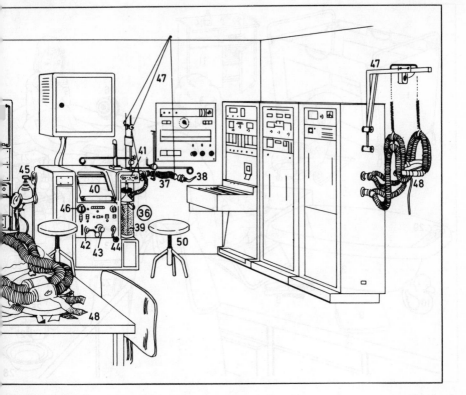

-50 spirometry
肺活量测定法
spirograph for pulmonary
function tests
肺功能检验呼吸描记器
breathing tube
呼吸管
mouthpiece
吹口
soda-lime absorber
碱石灰吸收器
recording paper
记录纸
control knobs for gas supply
供气控制旋钮
O_2-stabilizer
氧稳定器
throttle valve
节流阀
absorber attachment
吸收装置的配件
oxygen cylinder
氧气筒（瓶）
water supply
供水
tube support
管子支撑装置
mask
面罩
CO_2 consumption meter
二氧化碳耗量计
stool for the patient
病人坐凳

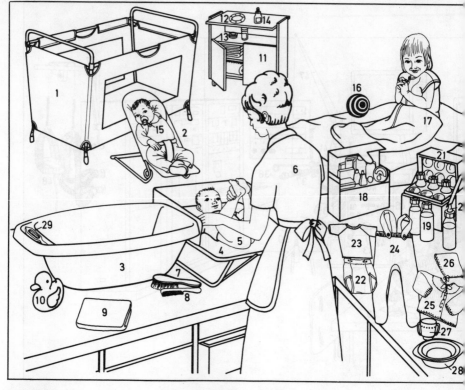

1 collapsible cot 可摺叠的婴儿床	**18** layette box 婴儿全套用品箱
2 bouncing cradle 弹性摇床	**19** feeding bottle 奶瓶
3 baby bath 婴儿浴盆	**20** teat （奶瓶上的）橡皮奶咀
4 changing top 更换篷	**21** bottle warmer 奶瓶保温器
5 baby (new-born baby) 婴儿（新生婴儿）	**22** rubber baby pants for disposable nappies (*Am.* diapers) 使用一次的尿布
6 mother 母亲	
7 hairbrush 发刷	**23** vest 内衣
8 comb 梳子	**24** leggings （小孩）护腿套裤
9 hand towel 手巾	**25** baby's jacket 婴儿上衣
10 toy duck 玩具鸭	**26** hood 兜帽
11 changing unit 更换用品柜	**27** baby's cup 婴儿杯
12 teething ring 出牙环，出牙圈	**28** baby's plate, a stay-warm plate 婴儿盘，一种保温盘
13 cream jar 面霜盒	**29** thermometer 温度计
14 box of baby powder 婴儿粉盒	
15 dummy 奶咀	
16 ball 球	
17 sleeping bag 睡袋	

46 teddy bear
玩具熊（泰迪熊）
47 potty (baby's pot)
小孩便罐
48 carrycot
可携带的婴儿床
49 window
透明窗
50 handles
手提带子

bassinet, a wicker pram
有篷摇篮，柳条婴儿车
set of bassinet covers
全套摇篮盖
canopy
摇篮罩篷
baby's high chair, a folding chair
婴儿用的高脚椅，一种摺叠椅
pram (baby-carriage) [with
windows]
有透明窗的婴儿车
folding hood
摺叠车篷
window
透明窗
pushchair (Am. stroller)
折叠式婴儿车
foot-muff (Am. foot-bag)
暖脚袋
play pen
幼儿用围栏
floor of the play pen
围栏底板
building blocks (building bricks)
积木
small child
幼儿，婴儿
bib
围兜
rattle (baby's rattle)
幼儿摇摇响玩具
bootees
幼儿之轻便短靴

1-12 baby clothes
婴儿服装

1 pram suit
婴儿车装

2 hood
兜帽

3 pram jacket (matinée coat)
婴儿车短上衣

4 pompon (bobble)
绒球；毛球

5 bootees
毛线鞋

6 sleeveless vest
无袖背心

7 envelope-neck vest
无领汗衫

8 wrapover vest
罩衫

9 baby's jacket
婴儿上衣（夹克）

10 rubber baby pants
婴儿橡皮质尿兜裤

11 playsuit
游戏装

12 two-piece suit
两件式套装

13-30 infants' wear
儿童服装

13 child's sundress, a pinafore dress
女孩夏服，一种无袖的便服

14 frilled shoulder strap
有饰边肩带

15 shirred top
可伸缩的上半衫

16 sun hat
遮阳帽

17 one-piece jersey suit
上下连身运动装

18 front zip
前拉链

19 catsuit (playsuit)
游戏装

20 motif (appliqué)
图案（缝饰）

21 romper
背心连裤子的衣服

22 playsuit (romper suit)
小孩的游戏装（玩耍服）

23 coverall (sleeper and strampler)
连身睡衣

24 dressing gown (bath robe)
晨衣（浴袍）

25 children's shorts
儿童短裤，吊带裤

26 braces (*Am.* suspenders)
吊带

27 children's T-shirt
儿童（短袖）圆领汗衫

28 jersey dress (knitted dress)
针织衣服

29 embroidery
刺绣

30 children's ankle socks
儿童的（只到足踝的）短袜

31-47 school children's wear
学童服

31 raincoat (loden coat)
雨衣

32 leather shorts (lederhosen)
皮短裤

33 staghorn button
鹿角钮扣

34 braces (*Am.* suspenders)
吊带

35 flap
飞兜

36 girl's dirndl
女孩紧身连衫裙

37 cross lacing
交叉系带

38 snow suit (quilted suit)
防雪装（以羽毛等填缝的服装）

39 quilt stitching (quilting)
褶缝线

40 dungarees (bib and brace)
粗棉布工作服型的童装（围兜和吊带）

41 bib skirt (bib top pinafore)
围兜裙（围兜无袖便服）

42 tights
紧身裤

43 sweater (jumper)
毛衣（上衣）

44 pile jacket
绒面夹克，软毛上衣

45 leggings
护胫套裤

46 girl's skirt
女孩裙子

47 child's jumper
短袖毛衣（衫）

48-68 teenagers' clothes
青少年服装

48 girl's overblouse (overtop)
下摆外露的女上衣

49 slacks
宽松的裤子

50 girl's skirt suit
少女裙装

51 jacket
夹克衫，短上衣

52 skirt
裙子

53 knee-length socks
长统袜

54 girl's coat
女孩外套

55 tie belt
腰带

56 girl's bag
肩袋

57 woollen (*Am.* woolen) hat
羊毛帽

58 girl's blouse
女用衬衫

59 culottes
裤裙

60 boy's trousers
男孩长裤

61 boy's shirt
男孩衬衫

62 anorak
附有风帽的御寒夹克

63 inset pockets
插（口）袋

64 hood drawstring (drawstring)
兜帽束紧带（拉绳）

65 knitted welt
针织的束紧裤口

66 parka coat (parka)
带有兜帽的皮毛外套

67 drawstring (draw cord)
束紧带，拉绳

68 patch pockets
缝贴在外的口袋

1 mink jacket
貂皮袄

2 cowl neck jumper
大围领套头衫（附有领巾之妇女上衣）

3 cowl collar
宽松的围领

4 knitted overtop
针织套头衫

5 turndown collar
翻领（摺领）

6 turn-up (turnover) sleeve
反摺袖

7 polo neck jumper
套头紧领衫

8 pinafore dress
宽罩型洋装

9 blouse with revers collars
翻领上衣（类似衬衫）

10 shirt-waister dress, a button-through dress
单排扣束腰洋装

11 belt
腰带

12 winter dress
冬季洋装

13 piping
衣服上的管状窄条饰缘，滚边

14 cuff
袖口

15 long sleeve
长袖

16 quilted waistcoat
背心型短袄

17 quilt stitching (quilting)
车缝线

18 leather trimming
皮质滚边

19 winter slacks
冬季便裤

20 striped polo jumper
条纹套头紧领衫

21 boiler suit (dungarees, bib and brace)
衫裤相连的工作装（粗棉布做的工作服，围兜和吊带）

22 patch pocket
贴袋

23 front pocket
胸前袋

24 bib
围兜

25 wrapover dress (wrap-around dress)
无袖长袍裙服

26 shirt
衬衫

27 peasant-style dress
农民式服装

28 floral braid
花边饰带

29 tunic (tunic top, tunic dress)
垂至臀部或低于臀部的宽松外衣

30 ribbed cuff
有线的袖口

31 quilted design
车缝饰纹

32 pleated shirt
百摺裙

33 two-piece knitted dress
针织的两件式套装

34 boat neck, a neckline
船形领，领口

35 turn-up
卷袖或袖口翻边

36 kimono sleeve
连肩袖

37 knitted design
针织图案

38 lumber-jacket
伐木者穿的夹克

39 cable pattern
缆纹图样

40 shirt-blouse
衬衫式上衣

41 loop fastening
环扣

42 embroidery
刺绣，绣花

43 stand-up collar
立领

44 cossack trousers
哥萨克型裤子

45 two-piece combination (shirt top and long skirt)
两件式套装（衬衫和长裙）

46 tie (bow)
束腰带（蝴蝶结）

47 decorative facing
衣领饰边

48 cuff slit
袖口开叉

49 side slit
下摆开叉

50 tabard
无袖外衣

51 inverted pleat skirt
对摺裙

52 godet
女裙开叉处所附三角布片（用以显示摺纹）

53 evening gown
晚礼服

54 pleated bell sleeve
带摺喇叭袖

55 party blouse
宴会礼衫

56 party skirt
宴会裙

57 trouser suit (slack suit)
裤装

58 suede jacket
麂皮袄

59 fur trimming
毛皮饰边

60 fur coat (*kinds*: Persian lamb, broadtail, mink, sable)
毛皮大衣（种类：波斯羔羊皮大衣，粗尾羊皮，貂皮，黑貂皮大衣）

61 winter coat (cloth coat)
冬季大衣

62 fur cuff (fur-trimmed cuff)
毛皮袖口（毛皮装饰袖口）

63 fur collar (fur-trimmed collar)
毛皮领（毛皮装饰领）

64 loden coat
防水大衣

65 cape
披肩

66 toggle fastenings
索环扣

67 loden skirt
防水裙

68 poncho-style coat
斗篷式大衣

69 hood
兜帽，风帽

1 skirt suit
裙装（上衣加裙子的套装）
2 jacket
短上衣，夹克衫
3 skirt
裙子
4 inset pocket
插入式口
5 decorative stitching
装饰缝线
6 dress and jacket combination
礼服和上衣的联合装
7 piping
滚边
8 pinafore dress
围裙式洋装
9 summer dress
无袖夏季洋装
10 belt
腰带
11 two-piece dress
二件式套装
12 belt buckle
腰带扣（装饰扣）
13 wrapover (wrap-around) skirt
单片裙
14 pencil silhouette
铅笔状轮廓，线条
15 shoulder buttons
肩扣
16 batwing sleeve
蝙蝠翼式袖子
17 overdress
外衣
18 kimono yoke
和服式的抵肩
19 tie belt
系腰带
20 summer coat
夏季外衣
21 detachable hood
可分开的风帽
22 summer blouse
夏季短衫
23 lapel
大翻领
24 skirt
裙子
25 front pleat
前摺
26 dirndl (dirndl dress)
紧身连衫裙，阿尔卑斯村女服装（紧胸，摺腰，大裙）
27 puffed sleeve
灯笼袖
28 dirndl necklace
领口花饰
29 dirndl blouse
短衫
30 bodice
紧身胸衣
31 dirndl apron
围裙
32 lace trimming (lace), cotton lace
花边装饰，棉质花边
33 frilled apron
（摺边）饰边围裙
34 frill
饰边，摺边
35 smock overall
工作服，罩衫
36 house frock (house dress)
家居简便洋装
37 poplin jacket
毛葛夹克（短外衣）

38 T-shirt
T 恤，无袖圆领衫
39 ladies' shorts
女士短裤
40 trouser turn-up
裤脚翻折边
41 waistband
腰带，束腰带
42 bomber jacket
轰炸机员式的夹克
43 stretch welt
松紧带镶边
44 Bermuda shorts
百慕达短裤
45 saddle stitching
鞍具式的缝线
46 frill collar
绉褶领
47 knot
装饰花结
48 culotte
裤裙
49 twin set
羊毛外衣与套头绒线衣成套者
50 cardigan
羊毛上衣
51 sweater
毛衣
52 summer (lightweight) slacks
夏季轻便裤
53 jumpsuit
跳伞装
54 turn-up
翻折边
55 zip
拉链
56 patch pocket
贴袋
57 scarf (neckerchief)
领巾，围巾
58 denim suit
斜纹粗布服，牛仔装
59 denim waistcoat
斜纹粗棉布背心，牛仔背心
60 jeans (denims)
牛仔裤
61 overblouse
下摆外露的上衣（不扣于裤内或裙内）
62 turned-up sleeve
卷袖
63 stretch belt
松紧腰带
64 halter top
露背装
65 knitted overtop
针织洋装
66 drawstring waist
束腰绳（带）
67 short-sleeved jumper
短袖运动衫
68 V-neck (vee-neck)
V 型领
69 turndown collar
翻领
70 knitted welt
针织带状镶边
71 shawl
披肩

1-15 ladies' underwear (ladies' underclothes, lingerie)
妇女内衣（贴身衣类）

1 brassière (bra)
乳罩，胸罩

2 pantie-girdle
紧身短内裤

3 pantie-corselette
连胸衣的紧身短内裤

4 longline brassière (longline bra)
长线乳罩

5 stretch girdle
有伸缩性短内裤

6 suspender
吊袜带

7 vest
贴身衣，衬衣

8 pantie briefs
紧身三角裤

9 ladies' knee-high stocking
女用中统袜

10 long-legged (long leg) panties
紧身七分内裤

11 long pants
紧身长内裤

12 tights (pantie-hose)
裤袜

13 slip
连身衬裙

14 waist slip
短衬裙

15 bikini briefs
比基尼三角裤

16-21 ladies' nightwear
妇女睡衣裤

16 nightdress (nightgown, nightie)
睡衣

17 pyjamas (*Am.* pajamas)
宽松睡衣裤

18 pyjama top
睡衣

19 pyjama trousers
睡裤

20 housecoat
家居服，长便袍

21 vest and shorts set [for leisure wear and as nightwear]
背心短裤装[休闲服和当为睡衣]

22-29 men's underwear (men's underclothes)
男士内衣裤

22 string vest
网线汗衫

23 string briefs
网线三角裤

24 front panel
正面遮片

25 sleeveless vest
无袖汗衫，背心

26 briefs
男用三角裤

27 trunks
平口内裤

28 short-sleeved vest
短袖汗衫

29 long johns
长内裤

30 braces (*Am.* suspenders)
吊带

31 braces clip
吊带夹子

32-34 men's socks
男士短袜

32 knee-length sock
中统袜

33 elasticated top
松紧袜口

34 long sock
长短袜

35-37 men's nightwear
男士睡衣裤

35 dressing gown
睡袍

36 pyjamas (*Am.* pajamas)
宽松睡衣裤

37 nightshirt
长睡衫

38-47 men's shirts
男士衬衫

38 casual shirt
便衫

39 belt
腰带

40 cravat
围巾

41 tie
领带

42 knot
领结

43 dress shirt
着为礼服下的衬衫

44 frill (frill front)
（衬衫前装饰用的）绉边

45 cuff
袖口

46 cuff link
袖扣

47 bow-tie
蝴蝶领结

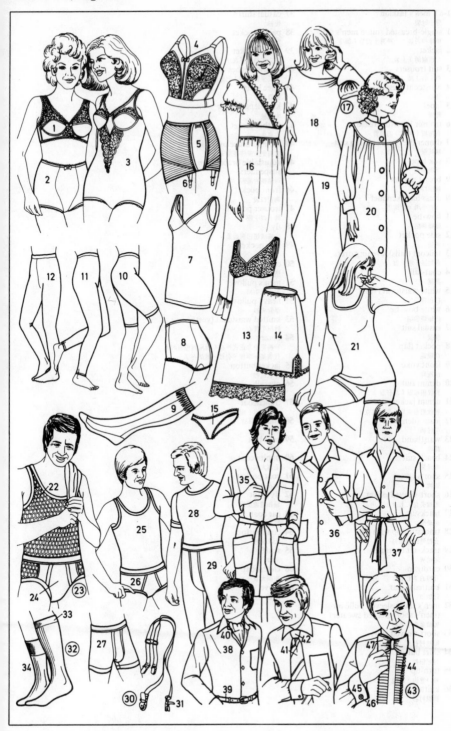

1-67 men's fashion
男士时装

1 single-breasted suit, a men's suit
单排扣西装，一种男士西装（服）

2 jacket
（西服的）上装

3 suit trousers
西（装）裤

4 waistcoat (vest)
背心

5 lapel
翻领

6 trouser leg with crease
有摺痕（裤线）的裤管

7 dinner dress, an evening suit
晚礼服

8 silk lapel
丝绸翻领

9 breast pocket
胸前口袋

10 dress handkerchief
外衣手绢，装饰用

11 bow-tie
蝴蝶领结

12 side pocket
侧袋

13 tailcoat (tails), evening dress
燕尾服，晚礼服

14 coat-tail
燕尾

15 white waistcoat (vest)
白色背心

16 white bow-tie
白蝴蝶领结

17 casual suit
便服

18 pocket flap
口袋盖

19 front yoke
前抵肩

20 denim suit
斜纹粗布服（牛仔服）

21 denim jacket
斜纹粗布夹克（牛仔夹克）

22 jeans (denims)
牛仔裤

23 waistband
腰带

24 beach suit
海滩装

25 shorts
短裤

26 short-sleeved jacket
短袖夹克（上衣）

27 tracksuit
运动服

28 tracksuit top with zip
有拉链的运动衫

29 tracksuit bottoms
运动裤

30 cardigan
开襟的羊毛上衣

31 knitted collar
针织领

32 men's short-sleeved pullover
(men's short-sleeved sweater)
短袖套头羊毛衫

33 short-sleeved shirt
短袖衬衫

34 shirt button
衬衫钮扣

35 turn-up
袖口卷边，滚边

36 knitted shirt
针织衬衫

37 casual shirt
便衫

38 patch pocket
贴袋

39 casual jacket
夹克式的短外衣

40 knee-breeches
（长至膝盖的）七分裤，马裤

41 knee strap
裤管束带

42 knee-length sock
中统袜

43 leather jacket
皮夹克

44 bib and brace overalls
有围兜吊带的连身工作服

45 adjustable braces (Am. suspenders)
可调整的吊带

46 front pocket
胸前口袋

47 trouser pocket
裤（口）袋

48 fly
拉练或钮扣洞遮盖

49 rule pocket
工具袋

50 check shirt
格子衬衫

51 men's pullover
男士套头衫

52 heavy pullover
厚套头衫

53 knitted waistcoat (vest)
针织毛背心

54 blazer
一种宽松非正式外衣（所用颜色有时系代表某一学校、会社、球队等）

55 jacket button
外衣钮扣

56 overall
宽大的罩衫

57 trenchcoat
有带的风（雨）衣

58 coat collar
衣领

59 coat belt
腰带

60 poplin coat
毛葛大衣

61 coat pocket
大衣口袋

62 fly front
钮扣遮盖正面

63 car coat
短大衣

64 coat button
大衣钮扣

65 scarf
围巾

66 cloth coat
布面大衣

67 glove
手套

1-25 men's beards and hairstyles (haircuts)
男士的胡须和发型

1 long hair worn loose
着着披头长发

2 allonge periwig (full-bottomed wig), a wig; *shorter and smoother*: bob wig, toupet
假发（底部尽量张开的假发）；一种较短且较平滑的假发；短辫假发，假发（络）

3 curls
卷发

4 bag wig (purse wig)
囊式假发

5 pigtail wig
辫子式假发；蓄辫假发

6 queue (pigtail)
辫子

7 bow (ribbon)
蝴蝶结（丝带）

8 handlebars (handlebar moustache, *Am.* mustache)
八字胡

9 centre (*Am.* center) parting
中分（头发的分边）

10 goatee (goatee beard), chintuft
山羊胡，下巴上的一撮胡子

11 closely-cropped head of hair (crew cut)
短发（平头）

12 whiskers
腮胡

13 Vandyke beard (stiletto beard, bodkin beard), with waxed moustache (*Am.* mustache)
髭间涂蜡的范大克式髭（剑形髭，锥形须）

14 side parting
侧分

15 full beard (circular beard, round beard)
大胡子（环形胡须）

16 tile beard
瓦形胡须

17 shadow
短髭

18 head of curly hair
卷发头

19 military moustache (*Am.* mustache) (English-style moustache)
军人胡（英式髭）

20 partly bald head
局部秃头

21 bald patch
秃头部分

22 bald head
全秃头

23 stubble beard (stubble, short beard bristles)
残须（短且硬的胡子）

24 side-whiskers (sideboards, sideburns)
鬓

25 clean shave
剃光的面颊

26 Afro look (for men and women)
非洲人的发型（男女通用）

27-38 ladies' hairstyles (coiffures, women's and girls' hairstyles)
女士发型（头发式样，妇女和少女的发型）

27 ponytail
马尾巴

28 swept-back hair (swept-up hair, pinned-up hair)
头发向后紧梳成髻的发型

29 bun (chignon)
假髻

30 plaits (bunches)
编辫子

31 chaplet hairstyle (Gretchen style)
花冠式发型（Gretchen 式发型）

32 chaplet (coiled plaits)
花冠（盘绕的发辫）

33 curled hair
卷发

34 shingle (shingled hair, bobbed hair)
短发

35 pageboy style
娃娃头（西瓜皮式）

36 fringe (*Am.* bangs)
刘海

37 earphones
耳机式发型

38 earphone (coiled plait)
耳机发（盘绕的发辫）

1-21 ladies' hats and caps
女士有边帽和无边帽
1 milliner making a hat
制女帽的人
2 hood
帽兜
3 block
帽模
4 decorative pieces
帽饰
5 sombrero
墨西哥帽，宽边帽
6 mohair hat with feathers
带羽饰的毛帽
7 model hat with fancy appliqué
带花饰的模特儿帽
8 linen cap (jockey cap)
亚麻布帽（骑士帽）
9 hat made of thick candlewick
yarn
粗烛芯纱所编的帽子
10 woollen (*Am.* woolen) hat
(knitted hat)
毛线帽（针织帽）
11 mohair hat
毛帽（安哥拉山羊毛帽）
12 cloche with feathers
带羽毛的钟型帽
13 large men's hat made of sisal
with corded ribbon
由琼麻和丝线制的仿男士帽
14 trilby-style hat with fancy
ribbon
带丝饰的呢帽

15 soft felt hat
软毡（毛）帽
16 Panama hat with scarf
附有领巾的巴拿马帽
17 peaked mink cap
（有帽尖的）貂皮帽（无边）
18 mink hat
貂皮帽（有边）
19 fox hat with leather top
皮顶狐皮帽
20 mink cap
貂皮（无边）帽
21 slouch hat trimmed with flowers
有花饰的垂边软帽

40 men's hats and caps
男士无边和有边帽

trilby hat (trilby)
软呢帽

loden hat (Alpine hat)
粗绒布帽（阿尔卑斯山帽）

felt hat with tassels (Tyrolean hat, Tyrolese hat)
带穗的毡（毛）帽（提洛尔帽）

corduroy cap
楞条花布帽（灯心绒帽）

woollen (Am. woolen) hat
毛线帽

beret
贝雷帽（绒质或羊毛制的扁圆无边帽）

bowler hat
礼帽

peaked cap (yachting cap)
大盘帽（游艇帽）

sou'wester (southwester)
风雨天用的防水帽（后面帽缘较宽）

fox cap with earflaps
有耳盖的狐皮帽

leather cap with fur flaps
有软毛耳盖的皮帽

musquash cap
蟹鼠皮帽

astrakhan cap, a real or imitation astrakhan cap
（苏俄）阿斯特拉罕盖羊皮帽，真品或仿制品

boater
硬草帽

36 (grey, *Am.* gray, or black) top hat made of silk taffeta; *collapsible*: crush hat (opera hat, claque)
高顶丝质礼帽；可摺叠而不致损坏的帽（歌剧帽，捧场员帽）

37 sun hat (lightweight hat) made of cloth with small patch pocket
有小贴袋的布质遮阳帽

38 wide-brimmed hat
宽边帽

39 toboggan cap (skiing cap, ski cap)
雪橇帽（滑雪帽）

40 workman's cap
工作帽

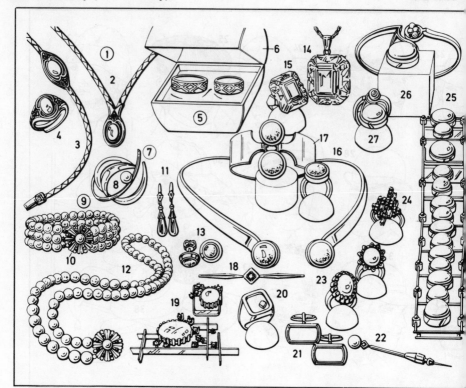

1 set of jewellery (*Am.* jewelry)
一套珠宝饰物
2 necklace
项链
3 bracelet
手镯
4 ring
戒指
5 wedding rings
结婚戒指
6 wedding ring box
结婚戒指盒
7 brooch, a pearl brooch
胸针（领针），一种珍珠胸针
8 pearl
珍珠
9 cultured pearl bracelet
人工养殖珍珠手镯
10 clasp, a white gold clasp
扣子，一种白金扣子
11 pendant earrings (drop earrings)
（垂式）耳坠
12 cultured pearl necklace
人工养殖珍珠项链
13 earrings
耳饰
14 gemstone pendant
宝石坠子
15 gemstone ring
宝石戒指
16 choker (collar, neckband)
项圈（颈圈，颈带）
17 bangle
手镯

18 diamond pin
钻石别针
19 modern-style brooches
时髦饰针
20 man's ring
男士戒指
21 cuff links
袖扣
22 tiepin
领带别针
23 diamond ring with pearl
带有珍珠的钻石戒指
24 modern-style diamond ring
时髦的钻石戒指
25 gemstone bracelet
宝石手镯
26 asymmetrical bangle
不对称的手镯（脚镯）
27 asymmetrical ring
不对称的戒指
28 ivory necklace
象牙项链
29 ivory rose
象牙玫瑰花
30 ivory brooch
象牙胸针
31 jewel box (jewel case)
珠宝盒
32 pearl necklace
珍珠项链
33 bracelet watch
手镯表
34 coral necklace
珊瑚项链

35 charms
饰物（护身符）
36 coin bracelet
钱币手镯
37 gold coin
金币
38 coin setting
硬币镶座
39 link
链子
40 signet ring
徽章戒指
41 engraving (monogram)
雕刻（字母组合的图案）
42-86 cuts and forms
各种形状的琢磨
42-71 faceted stones
多刻面宝石
42-43 standard round cut
标准圆形切割
44 brilliant cut
多角形切割
45 rose cut
玫瑰式切割
46 flat table
平台形
47 table en cabochon
平台凸形宝石（照天然形状琢磨的宝石）
48 standard cut
标准切割
49 standard antique cut
标准传统切割

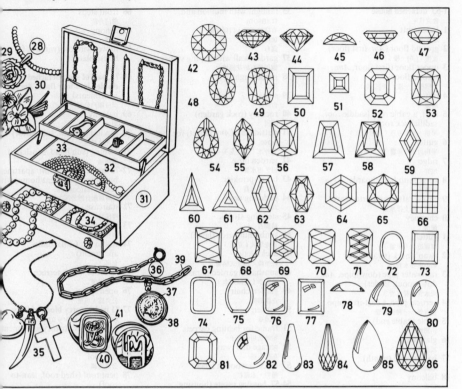

rectangular step-cut
长方阶状切割
square step-cut
正方形状切割
octagonal step-cut
八边形阶状切割
octagonal cross-cut
八边形交叉状切割
standard pear-shape
(pendeloque)
标准梨形
marquise (navette)
两头尖的卵形宝石
standard barrel-shape
标准桶形
trapezium step-cut
梯形阶状切割
trapezium cross-cut
梯形交叉状切割
rhombus step-cut
菱形阶状切割
1 triangular step-cut
三角形阶状切割
hexagonal step-cut
六边形阶状切割
oval hexagonal cross-cut
椭圆六边交叉状切割
round hexagonal step-cut
圆六边形阶状切割
round hexagonal cross-cut
圆六边交叉状切割
chequer-board cut
棋盘状切割

67 triangle cut
　　三角形切割
68-71 fancy cuts
　　华丽精巧的切割
72-77 ring gemstones
　　戒指宝石
72 oval flat table
　　椭圆平台型
73 rectangular flat table
　　长方平台形
74 octagonal flat table
　　八边平台形
75 barrel-shape
　　桶形
76 antique table en cabochon
　　传统平台凸圆形
77 rectangular table en cabochon
　　长方平台凸圆形
78-81 cabochons
　　平底凸圆形宝石
78 round cabochon (simple cabochon)
　　简单凸圆形
79 high dome (high cabochon)
　　高拱圆形（高凸圆形）
80 oval cabochon
　　椭圆凸圆形
81 octagonal cabochon
　　八边凸圆形
82-86 spheres and pear-shapes
　　球形和梨形
82 plain sphere
　　无花饰球形

83 plain pear-shape
　　无花饰梨形
84 faceted pear-shape
　　多刻面梨形
85 plain drop
　　无花饰滴状琢磨
86 faceted briolette
　　三角形多刻面梨形

1-53 detached house
独立住宅

1 basementt
地下室

2 ground floor (*Am.* first floor)
底楼（[美]一楼）

3 upper floor (first floor, *Am.*
second floor)
上层楼（一楼，[美]二楼）

4 loft
阁楼

5 roof, a gable roof (saddle roof,
saddleback roof)
屋顶，山形屋顶（鞍形屋顶）

6 gutter
屋顶边沟（承霤）

7 ridge
屋脊

8 verge with bargeboards
簷缘板

9 eaves, rafter-supported eaves
屋簷，椽支撑屋簷

10 chimney
烟囱

11 gutter
屋顶边沟（承霤）

12 swan's neck (swan-neck)
鹅颈形导水管

13 rainwater pipe (downpipe, *Am.*
downspout, leader)
雨水管（排水管）

14 vertical pipe, a cast-iron pipe
垂直管，一种铸铁管

15 gable (gable end)
山形墙

16 glass wall
玻璃墙

17 base course (plinth)
墙脚

18 balcony
阳台

19 parapet
栏杆

20 flower box
花架

21 French window (French
windows) opening on to the
balcony
开向阳台的落地窗（法式窗）

22 double casement window
双扇门式玻璃窗

23 single casement window
单扇门式玻璃窗

24 window breast with window sill
有槛窗台

25 lintel (window head)
窗楣（梁）

26 reveal
窗框

27 cellar window (basement
window)
地下室窗子

28 rolling shutter
可卷的活动遮板

29 rolling shutter frame
遮板架

30 window shutter (folding shutter)
窗板（摺叠式窗板）

31 shutter catch
窗板搭扣

32 garage with tool shed
附工具棚的车库

33 espalier
树架

34 batten door (ledged door)
木板门（车棚门）

35 fanlight with mullion and
transom
有槛的气窗，门顶气窗

36 terrace
露台

37 garden wall with coping stones
铺压顶石的花园墙

38 garden light
园灯

39 steps
台阶

40 rockery (rock garden)
石园

41 outside tap (*Am.* faucet) for the
hose
室外水（管）龙头

42 garden hose
园艺用水管

43 lawn sprinkler
草皮洒水器

44 paddling pool
戏水池

45 stepping stones
踏脚石

46 sunbathing area (lawn)
日光浴区（草地）

47 deck-chair
轻便椅，摺叠式躺椅

48 sunshade (garden parasol)
遮阳伞（花园阳伞）

49 garden chair
花园靠椅

50 garden table
花园桌

51 frame for beating carpets
拍地毯用的架子

52 garage driveway
车库车道

53 fence, a wooden fence
栅栏，木栅栏

54-57 housing estate (housing
development)
住宅区（住宅开发区）

54 house on a housing estate (on a
housing development)
住宅区的房子

55 pent roof (penthouse roof)
单斜面屋顶

56 dormer (dormer window)
屋顶窗（天窗）

57 garden
花园

58-63 terraced house 'one of a row
of terraced houses', **stepped**
台阶形的排式住宅

58 front garden
宅前花园

59 hedge
灌木树篱

60 pavement (*Am.* sidewalk,
walkway)
人行道

61 street (road)
街道（路）

62 street lamp (street light)
街灯

63 litter bin (*Am.* litter basket)
垃圾箱

64-68 house divided into two flats
(*Am.* house divided into two
apartments, duplex house)
双户公寓（住宅）

64 hip (hipped) roof
四斜面屋顶

65 front door
前门

66 front steps
前门台阶

67 canopy
雨遮

68 flower window (window for
house plants)
花窗

**69-71 pair of semi-detached houses
divided into four flats** (*Am.*
apartments)
双拼四户公寓

69 balcony
阳台

70 sun lounge (*Am.* sun parlor)
日光休息室

71 awning (sun blind, sunshade)
遮阳篷

72-76 block of flats (*Am.* apartment
building, apartment house) with
access balconies
含附属阳台的公寓大楼

72 staircase
楼梯间

73 balcony
阳台

74 studio flat (*Am.* studio
apartment)
套房

75 sun roof, a sun terrace
日光屋顶

76 open space
公共露天场地

77-81 multi-storey block of flats
(*Am.* multistory apartment
building, multistory apartment
house)
多层公寓

77 flat roof
公寓屋顶

78 pent roof (shed roof, lean-to
roof)
单斜面屋顶

79 garage
车库

80 pergola
藤架

81 staircase window
楼梯间窗户

82 high-rise block of flats (*Am.*
high-rise apartment building,
high-rise apartment house)
高楼（层）公寓大厦

83 penthouse
顶楼小屋

84-86 weekend house, a timber
house
渡周末的房子，木头房子

84 horizontal boarding
横钉的木板壁

85 natural stone base course
(natural stone plinth)
天然石墙脚

86 strip windows (ribbon windows)
一个接一个成排的窗户

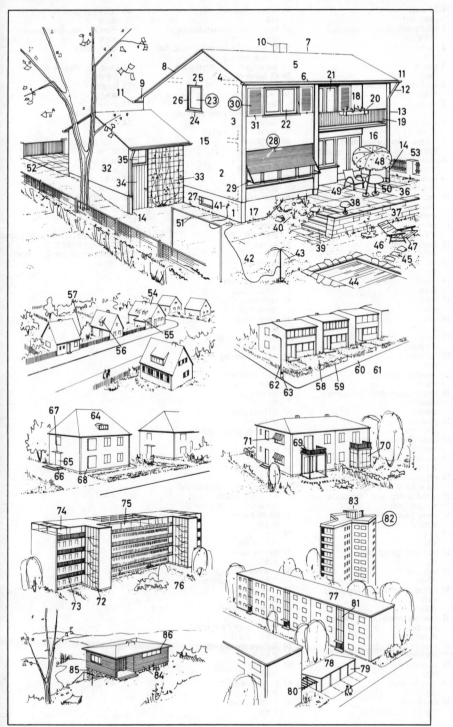

1-29 attic
阁楼，顶楼

1 roof cladding (roof covering)
屋顶复盖层

2 skylight
天窗

3 gangway
通路板

4 cat ladder (roof ladder)
屋顶梯子，爬梯

5 chimney
烟囱

6 roof hook
屋顶钩

7 dormer window (dormer)
阁楼窗户

8 snow guard (roof guard)
防雪板（屋顶防护装置）

9 gutter
屋顶边沟（承雷）

10 rainwater pipe (downpipe, *Am.* downspout, leader)
雨水管（排水管）

11 eaves
屋檐

12 pitched roof
斜屋顶

13 trapdoor
活板门

14 hatch
天花板入口

15 ladder
梯子

16 stile
梯子竖框

17 rung
梯子脚蹬横木

18 loft (attic)
阁楼

19 wooden partition
木板壁

20 lumber room door (boxroom door)
储藏室门

21 padlock
挂锁，扣锁

22 hook [for washing line]
（晒衣绳的）挂钩

23 clothes line (washing line)
晒衣绳

24 expansion tank for boiler
锅炉的膨胀槽

25 wooden steps and balustrade
木梯及扶手栏杆

26 string (*Am.* stringer)
楼梯斜梁

27 step
踏板

28 handrail (guard rail)
扶手

29 baluster
栏杆柱

30 lightning conductor (lightning rod)
避雷针

31 **chimney sweep** (*Am.* chimney sweeper)
烟囱清理者

32 brush with weight
带重锤的刷子

33 shoulder iron
肩铁

34 sack for soot
煤尘收集袋

35 flue brush
（烟囱的）通烟道清洁刷

36 broom (besom)
扫帚

37 broomstick (broom handle)
扫帚柄（扫帚把手）

38-81 hot-water heating system, full central heating
热水暖气系统，完全中央供暖装置

38-43 boiler room
锅炉房

38 coke-fired central heating system
烧焦炭的中央暖气系统

39 ash box door (*Am.* cleanout door)
出灰箱门（美：清灰门）

40 flueblock
暖气通气道

41 poker
火钳，拨火棒

42 rake
拨火耙子

43 coal shovel
煤铲

44-60 oil-fired central heating system
烧油中央暖气系统

44 oil tank
油槽

45 manhole
检修出入孔

46 manhole cover
检修出入孔盖

47 tank inlet
油槽入口，给油口

48 dome cover
圆盖

49 tank bottom valve
油槽底阀

50 fuel oil (heating oil)
燃料油

51 air-bleed duct
通气管

52 air vent cap
排气孔盖

53 oil level pipe
油位管，油量计管

54 oil gauge (*Am.* gage)
油量计

55 suction pipe
吸油管

56 return pipe
回油管

57 central heating furnace (oil heating furnace)
中央暖气炉（烧油暖气炉）

58-60 oil burner
燃油器

58 fan
风扇，送风机

59 electric motor
电动马达

60 covered pilot light
有盖指示灯（点火用的指示灯）

61 charging door
进料门

62 inspection window
检查窗

63 water gauge (*Am.* gage)
水量计，水压计

64 furnace thermometer
炉内温度计

65 bleeder
排水孔

66 furnace bed
炉床（台）

67 control panel
控制板

68 hot water tank (boiler)
热水槽（锅炉）

69 overflow pipe (overflow)
溢流管

70 safety valve
安全阀

71 main distribution pipe
主配管

72 lagging
隔热层

73 valve
阀，气门

74 flow pipe
流入管

75 regulating valve
调节阀

76 radiator
散热器

77 radiator rib
散热片

78 room thermostat
室内温度调节器

79 return pipe (return)
回流管

80 return pipe [in two-pipe system]
[双管系统中的]回流管

81 smoke outlet (smoke extract)
排烟口

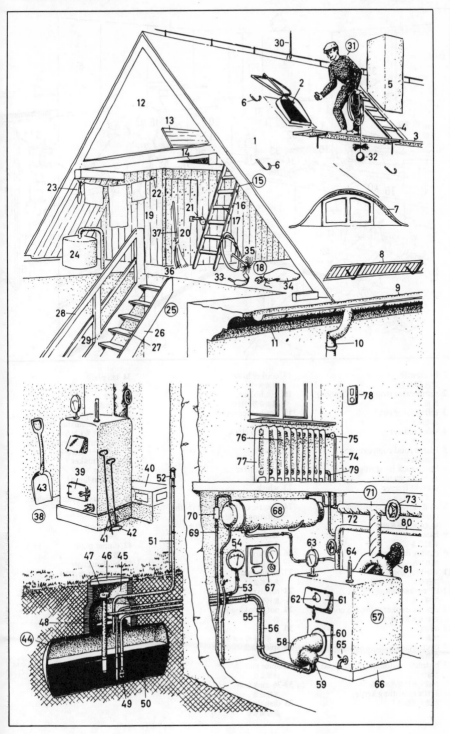

1 housewife 家庭主妇	**17 cooker hood** 排油烟机	**34 tea plate** 茶盘
2 refrigerator (fridge, *Am.* icebox) 冰箱	**18 pot holder** 罐锅壶等的托垫	**35 sink** 洗物槽
3 refrigerator shelf 冰箱搁板（架）	**19 pot holder rack** 托垫挂架	**36 water tap (*Am.* faucet) (mixer tap, *Am.* mixing faucet)** 自来水龙头（混合水龙头）
4 salad drawer 蔬菜抽屉	**20 kitchen clock** 厨房钟	**37 pot plant, a foliage plant** 盆景，一种观赏植物
5 frozen food compartment 食品冷冻室	**21 timer** 定时器	**38 coffee maker** 咖啡（煮）壶
6 bottle rack (in storage door) 瓶架（在贮藏门内）	**22 hand mixer** 手搅拌器	**39 kitchen lamp** 厨房灯
7 upright freezer 立式冷冻库	**23 whisk** （蛋，奶油的）搅拌器	**40 dishwasher (dishwashing machine)** 洗碟机
8 wall cupboard, a kitchen cupboard 壁式碗橱，厨房碗橱	**24 electric coffee grinder (with rotating blades)** 电动咖啡研磨机（带旋转刀片）	**41 dish rack** 盘碟架
9 base unit 底层设备	**25 lead** 电线	**42 dinner plate** 餐盘
10 cutlery drawer 餐具抽屉	**26 wall socket** 墙上插座	**43 kitchen chair** 厨房椅子（靠背椅）
11 working top 工作桌面	**27 corner unit** 角落装置	**44 kitchen table** 厨房桌
12-17 cooker unit 烹调（炊）具	**28 revolving shelf** 旋转架	
12 electric cooker (*also*: gas cooker) 电炉（另有：煤气炉）	**29 pot (cooking pot)** 锅	
13 oven 烤箱	**30 jug** （有把手的）水壶	
14 oven window 烤箱窗	**31 spice rack** 调味品架	
15 hotplate (automatic high-speed plate) 热板（自动高速加热板）	**32 spice jar** 调味品瓶	
16 kettle (whistling kettle) 水壶（鸣笛壶）	**33-36 sink unit** 流理设备	
	33 dish drainer 盘碟滴水架	

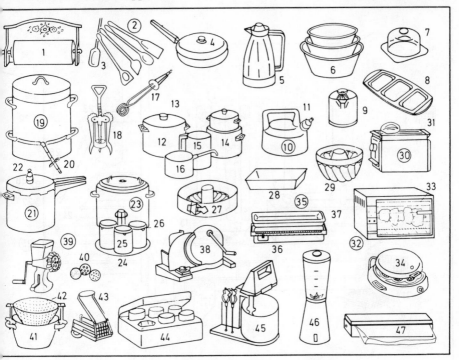

1 general-purpose roll holder
with kitchen roll (paper towels)
　附有厨房卷纸的通用卷纸托架
2 set of wooden spoons
　木匙组
3 mixing spoon
　搅拌匙
4 frying pan
　平底锅
5 thermos jug
　热水瓶
6 set of bowls
　碗组
7 cheese dish with glass cover
　附玻璃盖的乳酪盘
8 three-compartment dish
　三格盘子
9 lemon squeezer
　搾柠檬器
10 whistling kettle
　鸣笛水壶
　whistle
　笛
16 pan set
　锅组
　pot (cooking pot)
　烹饪锅
　lid
　锅盖
　casserole dish
　有盖烤锅
　milk pot
　牛奶罐
　saucepan
　长柄有盖的深锅
　immersion heater
　浸入式加热器

18 corkscrew [with levers]
　（有操纵杆的）拔塞钻
19 juice extractor
　水果、蔬菜等的液汁抽出器
20 tube clamp (tube clip)
　管夹（管钳）
21 pressure cooker
　压力锅（快锅）
22 pressure valve
　压力阀
23 fruit preserver
　水果保存器
24 removable rack
　活动架
25 preserving jar
　保存罐
26 rubber ring
　橡皮圈
27 spring form
　弹性箍
28 cake tin
　饼模（盒型）
29 cake tin
　饼模（盆型）
30 toaster
　烤面包机
31 rack for rolls
　面包卷架
32 rotisserie
　烤肉箱
33 spit
　烤肉叉
34 electric waffle iron
　电气烤饼铁模
35 sliding-weight scales
　滑动砝码秤

36 sliding weight
　滑动砝码
37 scale pan
　秤盘
38 food slicer
　食物切片机
39 mincer (Am. meat chopper)
　绞肉机
40 blades
　绞肉机用的刀片
41 chip pan
　炸马铃薯锅
42 basket
　篮,筐
43 potato chipper
　马铃薯切片器
44 yoghurt maker
　凝态发酵乳制造器
45 mixer
　搅拌器
46 blender
　混合器
47 bag sealer
　塑胶袋封口器

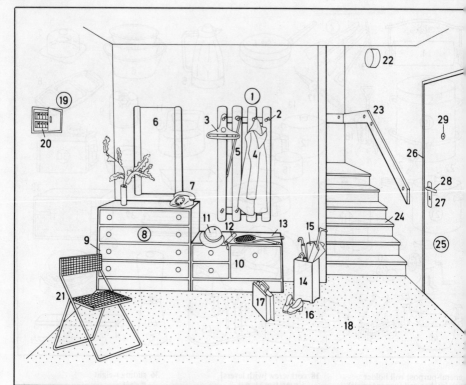

1-29 hall (entrance hall)
门厅（进门厅）
1 coat rack
衣架
2 coat hook
挂衣钩
3 coat hanger
挂衣架
4 rain cape
雨披肩（雨斗篷）
5 walking stick
手杖
6 hall mirror
门厅镜子
7 telephone
电话
8 chest of drawers for shoes, etc.
鞋柜
9 drawer
抽屉
10 seat
坐台
11 ladies' hat
妇女宽边帽
12 telescopic umbrella
折伞
13 tennis rackets (tennis racquets)
网球拍
14 umbrella stand
雨伞架
15 umbrella
雨伞
16 shoes
鞋

17 briefcase
公事包
18 fitted carpet
地毯
19 fuse box
保险丝盒
20 miniature circuit breaker
小型断路器
21 tubular steel chair
钢管靠背椅
22 stair light
楼梯灯
23 handrail
扶手
24 step
阶梯
25 front door
前门
26 door frame
门框
27 door lock
门锁
28 door handle
门把手
29 spyhole
探视孔，猫眼（门上窥视的小孔）

wall units	
各种壁橱柜	
side wall	
侧壁	
bookshelf	
书架	
row of books	
成排的书	
display cabinet unit	
摆饰橱	
cupboard base unit	
橱柜底座部分	
cupboard unit	
橱柜	
television set (TV set)	
电视机	
stereo system (stereo equipment)	
立体音响装置	
speaker (loudspeaker)	
喇叭，扬声器	
pipe rack	
烟斗架	
pipe	
烟斗	
globe	
地球仪	
brass kettle	
铜壶	
telescope	
望远镜	
mantle clock	
有罩的钟	
bust	
半身雕塑	

18 encyclopaedia [in several volumes]
百科全书[多卷本]
19 room divider
室内分隔设计
20 drinks cupboard
饮料柜(酒柜)
21-26 upholstered suite (seating group)
家具组(坐椅组合)
21 armchair
扶手椅
22 arm
扶手
23 seat cushion (cushion)
坐垫
24 settee
有靠背的长椅(中型沙发)
25 back cushion
背垫，靠垫
26 [round] corner section
[圆形]拐角部分
27 scatter cushion
小块的垫子
28 coffee table
咖啡桌
29 ashtray
烟灰缸
30 tray
托盘
31 whisky (whiskey) bottle
威士忌瓶酒
32 sode water bottle (soda bottle)
汽水瓶，苏打水瓶

33-34 dining set
用餐桌椅
33 dining table
餐桌
34 chair
椅子
35 net curtain
网状帘子
36 indoor plants (houseplants)
室内植物

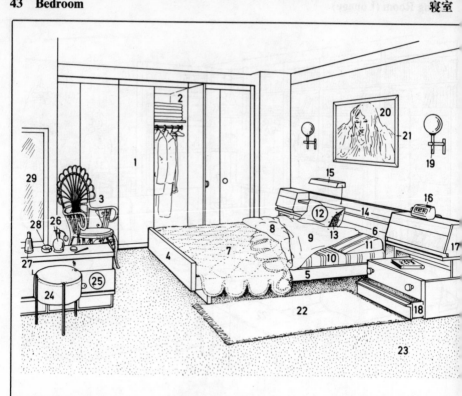

1 wardrobe(*Am.* clothes closet)
   衣柜，衣橱
2 linen shelf
   放置衬衣床单等等的搁板
3 cane chair
   藤椅
4-13 **double bed** (*sim.:* double
   divan)
   双人床（类似：双人睡椅）
4 - 6 **bedstead**
   床架
4 foot of the bed
   床脚板
5 bed frame
   床架（框）
6 headboard
   床头板
7 bedspread
   床罩
8 duvet, a quilted duvet
   羽毛被／棉被
9 sheet, a linen sheet
   被单，一种以亚麻布制成的被单
10 mattress, a foam mattress with
   drill tick
   床垫，一种斜纹布包面的泡沫床垫
11 [wedge-shaped] bolster
   模形垫枕
12-13 **pillow**
   枕头
12 pillowcase (pillowslip)
   枕（头）套
13 tick
   褥套

14 bookshelf [attached to the
   headboard]
   床头板上的书架
15 reading lamp
   阅读灯
16 electric alarm clock
   电子闹钟
17 bedside cabinet
   床头柜
18 drawer
   抽屉
19 bedroom lamp
   寝室灯
20 picture
   画
21 picture frame
   画框
22 bedside rug
   床边小地毯
23 fitted carpet
   地毯
24 dressing stool
   梳妆凳子
25 dressing table
   梳妆柏
26 perfume spray
   香水喷雾器
27 perfume bottle
   香水瓶
28 powder box
   粉盒
29 dressing-table mirror (mirror)
   梳妆台镜

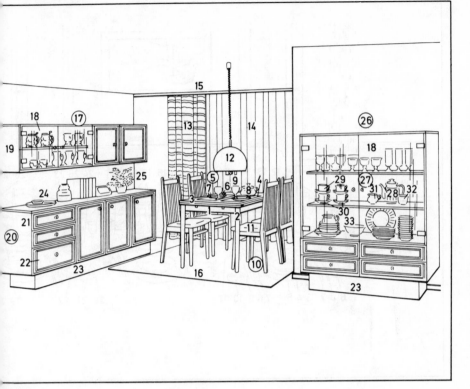

11 dinning set
进餐家具

dining table
餐桌

table leg
桌脚

table top
桌面

place mat
餐具垫

place (place setting, cover)
一人分的一套（副）餐具

soup plate (deep plate)
汤盆（深盆）

dinner plate
西餐盘

soup tureen
有盖汤盆

wineglass
高脚杯，小酒杯

dining chair
餐椅

seat
（椅子的）座部

lamp (pendant lamp)
灯（吊灯）

curtains
窗帘

net curtain
网状窗帘

curtain rail
窗帘轨（窗帘横杆）

carpet
地毯

17 wall unit
墙壁挂橱

18 glass door
玻璃门

19 shelf
板架

20 sideboard
餐具柜

21 cutlery drawer
刀叉（餐具）抽屉

22 linen drawer
餐巾/桌巾抽屉

23 base
柜子底座，基座

24 round tray
圆托盘

25 pot plant
盆栽

26 china cabinet (display cabinet)
瓷器橱（陈列橱）

27 coffee set (coffee service)
咖啡组（整套咖啡用具）

28 coffee pot
咖啡壶

29 coffee cup
咖啡杯

30 saucer
碟

31 milk jug
牛奶壶

32 sugar bowl
（有盖和柄的）糖罐

33 dinner set(dinner service)
成套餐具

1 dining table
餐桌

2 tablecloth, a damask cloth
桌布，一种花缎桌布

3-12 place (place setting, cover)
一副餐具（餐具摆设）

3 bottom plate
底盘（垫盘）

4 dinner plate
餐盘

5 deep plate (soup plate)
深盆（汤盆）

6 dessert plate (dessert bowl)
甜点盘（甜点碗）

7 knife and fork
刀和叉

8 fish knife and fork
吃鱼用的刀和叉

9 serviette (napkin, table napkin)
餐巾

10 serviette ring (napkin ring)
套餐巾的小环

11 knife rest
刀叉台

12 wineglasses
酒杯，玻璃酒杯

13 place card
（宴会等的）席次牌

14 soup ladle
汤杓

15 soup tureen (tureen)
汤盆（有盖的）

16 candelabra
装饰用的支状大炮台

17 sauceboat (gravy boat)
船形调味汁容器

18 sauce ladle (gravy ladle)
调味杓

19 table decoration
餐桌装饰

20 bread basket
面包篮

21 roll
小圆面包

22 slice of bread
面包片

23 salad bowl
沙拉碗

24 salad servers
整套沙拉器具

25 vegetable dish
蔬菜盆

26 meat plate (*Am.* meat platter)
肉盘

27 roast meat (roast)
烤肉

28 fruit dish
水果碟

29 fruit bowl
水果盆

30 fruit (stewed fruit)
水果（泡於糖水中的水果）

31 potato dish
马铃薯盆

32 serving trolley
服务手推车（上菜小柏车）

33 vegetable plate (*Am.* vegetable platter)
蔬菜盘

34 toast
吐司

35 cheeseboard
乳酪板

36 butter dish
奶油碟

37 open sandwich
切开的三明治

38 filling
三明治所夹的食品

39 sandwich
三明治

40 fruit bowl
水果碗

41 almonds (*also:* potato crisps, peanuts)
杏仁（马铃薯片，花生）

42 oil and vinegar bottle
油瓶和醋瓶

43 ketchup (catchup, catsup)
蕃茄酱

44 sideboard
餐具架

45 electric hotplate
电热器

46 corkscrew
拔塞器

47 crown cork bottle-opener (crown cork opener), a bottle-opener
开瓶器

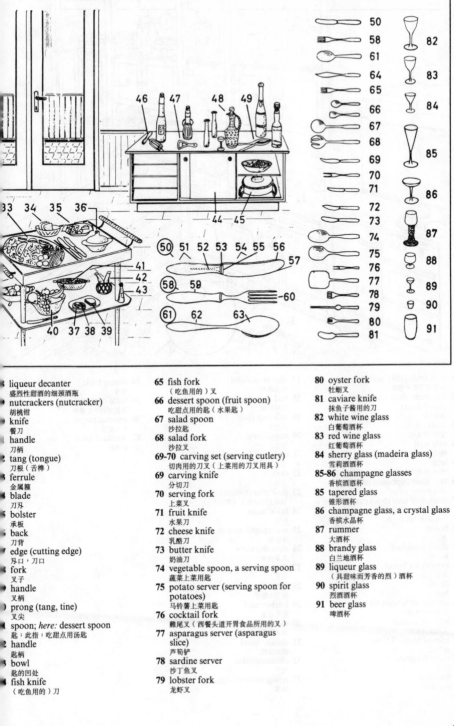

liqueur decanter
盛烈性甜酒的细颈酒瓶
nutcrackers (nutcracker)
胡桃钳
knife
餐刀
handle
刀柄
tang (tongue)
刀根（舌榫）
ferrule
金属箍
blade
刀刃
bolster
承板
back
刀背
edge (cutting edge)
刃口，刀口
fork
叉子
handle
叉柄
prong (tang, tine)
叉尖
spoon; *here:* dessert spoon
匙；此指：吃甜点用汤匙
handle
匙柄
bowl
匙的凹处
fish knife
（吃鱼用的）刀

65 fish fork
（吃鱼用的）叉
66 dessert spoon (fruit spoon)
吃甜点用的匙（水果匙）
67 salad spoon
沙拉匙
68 salad fork
沙拉叉
69-70 carving set (serving cutlery)
切肉用的刀叉（上菜用的刀叉用具）
69 carving knife
分切刀
70 serving fork
上菜叉
71 fruit knife
水果刀
72 cheese knife
乳酪刀
73 butter knife
奶油刀
74 vegetable spoon, a serving spoon
蔬菜上菜用匙
75 potato server (serving spoon for
potatoes)
马铃薯上菜用匙
76 cocktail fork
鸡尾叉（西餐头道开胃食品所用的叉）
77 asparagus server (asparagus
slice)
芦笋铲
78 sardine server
沙丁鱼叉
79 lobster fork
龙虾叉

80 oyster fork
牡蛎叉
81 caviare knife
抹鱼子酱用的刀
82 white wine glass
白葡萄酒杯
83 red wine glass
红葡萄酒杯
84 sherry glass (madeira glass)
雪莉酒酒杯
85-86 champagne glasses
香槟酒酒杯
85 tapered glass
锥形酒杯
86 champagne glass, a crystal glass
香槟水晶杯
87 rummer
大酒杯
88 brandy glass
白兰地酒杯
89 liqueur glass
（具甜味而芳香的烈）酒杯
90 spirit glass
烈酒酒杯
91 beer glass
啤酒杯

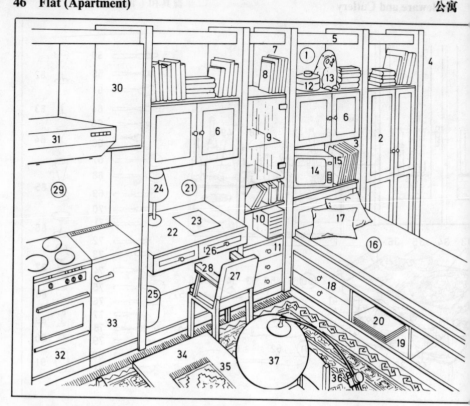

1 **wall units (shelf units)**
壁橱架设置（壁架）
2 **wardrobe door** (*Am.* clothes
closet door)
衣橱门
3 **body**
壁橱/架本体
4 **side wall**
侧墙
5 **trim**
（壁架的）装饰横木
6 **two-door cupboard unit**
双门碗柜
7 **bookshelf unit (bookcase unit)**
[with glass door]
（有玻璃门的）书柜
8 **books**
书
9 **display cabinet**
陈列橱
10 **card index boxes**
索引卡箱（盒）
11 **drawer**
抽屉
12 **decorative biscuit tin**
装饰的饼乾盒
13 **soft toy animal**
软的玩具动物
14 **television set (TV set)**
电视机
15 **records (discs)**
唱片
16 **bed unit**
床、床铺

17 **scatter cushion**
小块软垫
18 **bed unit drawer**
床铺抽屉
19 **bed unit shelf**
床铺架
20 **magazines**
杂志
21 **desk unit (writing unit)**
书桌（写字柜）
22 **desk**
书桌
23 **desk mat (blotter)**
书桌上的衬垫（吸墨纸）
24 **table lamp**
枱灯
25 **wastepaper basket**
废纸篓
26 **desk drawer**
书桌抽屉
27 **desk chair**
椅子
28 **arm**
扶手，靠手
29 **kitchen unit**
厨房设备
30 **wall cupboard**
壁式碗碟柜（橱）
31 **cooker hood**
抽油烟机
32 **electric cooker**
电炉
33 **refrigerator (fridge,** *Am.* **icebox)**
冰箱

34 **dining table**
餐桌
35 **table runner**
装饰用的狭长桌布
36 **oriental carpet**
东方地毯
37 **standard lamp**
落地灯

1 children's bed, a bunk-bed 儿童床（一种附梯子的）双层床	**16** rockers （摇椅、摇篮下装设的）弧状底部
2 storage box 贮存箱	**17** children's book 儿童书
3 mattress 床垫	**18** compendium of games 几种游戏
4 pillow 枕头	**19** ludo 一种骰子游戏
5 ladder 梯子	**20** chessboard 棋盘
6 soft toy elephant, a cuddly toy animal 柔软玩具象，（儿童喜欢抱着睡觉的） 玩具动物	**21** children's cupboard 儿童用的小柜子
7 soft toy dog 软质玩具狗	**22** linen drawer 放置毛巾、床单等的抽屉
8 cushion 垫子	**23** drop-flap writing surface 拆摺写字板
9 fashion doll 洋娃娃	**24** notebook (exercise book) 笔记本（练习簿）
10 doll's pram 玩具娃娃车	**25** school books 教科书
11 sleeping doll 睡觉的洋娃娃	**26** pencil (*also:* crayon, felt tip pen, ballpoint pen) 铅笔（另有：蜡笔，毛笔，原子笔）
12 canopy 车篷	**27** toy shop （扮家家酒用的）玩具店
13 blackboard 黑板	**28** counter 柜台
14 counting beads 算珠	**29** spice rack （玩具）调味品架
15 toy horse for rocking and pulling 摇摆和拖拉用的玩具木马	**30** display 陈列品
	31 assortment of sweets (*Am.* candies) 什锦糖果

32 bag of sweets (*Am.* candies) 糖果袋
33 scales 磅秤
34 cash register 现金出纳机
35 toy telephone 玩具电话
36 shop shelves (goods shelves) 商品架（货物架）
37 wooden train set 木制火车组
38 dump truck, a toy lorry (toy truck) 倾卸车，一种玩具卡车
39 tower crane 塔式起重机玩具
40 concrete mixer 混凝土搅拌机玩具
41 large soft toy dog 大型柔软玩具狗
42 dice cup 骰子杯

1-20 pre-school education
学龄前（儿童）教育（托儿所教育）
1 nursery teacher
幼稚园（托儿所）教师
2 nursery child
幼稚园（托儿所）儿童
3 handicraft
（手工艺品）劳作作品
4 glue
胶水，粘胶
5 watercolour painting (Am. watercolor)
水彩画
6 paintbox
颜料盒
7 paintbrush
画笔
8 glass of water
玻璃水杯
9 jigsaw puzzle (puzzle)
拼图玩具
10 jigsaw puzzle piece
拼图玩具块（片）
11 coloured (Am. colored) pencils (wax crayons)
彩色笔（蜡笔）
12 modelling (Am. modeling) clay (plasticine)
制模粘土（塑像用粘土）
13 clay figures (plasticine figures)
粘土塑像
14 modelling (Am. modeling) board
制模板
15 chalk (blackboard chalk)
粉笔（黑板粉笔）
16 blackboard
黑板

17 counting blocks
计算块
18 felt pen (felt tip pen)
毛笔（毛尖笔）
19 shapes game
造型游戏
20 group of players
一小组游戏者
21-32 toys
玩具
21 building and filling cubes
建造和填塞用的立体方块
22 construction set
积木组件
23 children's books
儿童书
24 doll's pram, a wicker pram
娃娃车，柳条童车
25 baby doll
婴儿娃娃
26 canopy
娃娃车篷
27 building bricks (building blocks)
积木砖（积木块）
28 wooden model building
木制模型建筑物
29 wooden train set
木制火车组
30 rocking teddy bear
摇动玩具熊
31 doll's pushchair
玩具娃娃推车
32 fashion doll
流行玩具娃娃
33 child of nursery school age
幼稚园儿童

34 cloakroom
衣帽间，寄物处

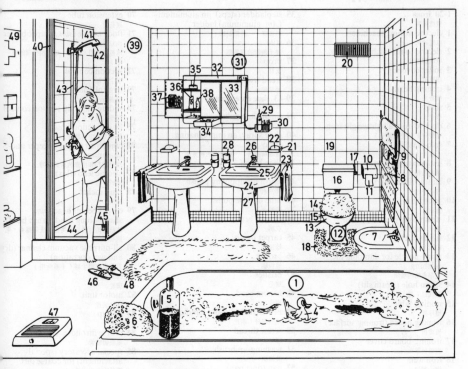

bath
浴缸，澡盆
mixer tap (*Am.* mixing faucet)
for hot and cold water.
冷热水混合的水龙头
foam bath (bubble bath)
泡沫澡水
toy duck
玩具鸭
bath salts
浴盐
bath sponge (sponge)
洗澡海绵
bidet
净身盆
towel rail
毛巾架
terry towel
毛巾
toilet roll holder (*Am.* bathroom
tissue holder)
卫生纸卷架
toilet paper (*coll.* loo paper, *Am.*
bathroom tissue), a roll of crepe
paper
卫生纸，一种绉纹纸卷
toilet (lavatory, W.C., *coll.* loo)
厕所，洗手间
toilet pan (toilet bowl)
抽水马桶
toilet lid with terry cover
铺绒布的马桶盖
toilet seat
马桶坐
cistern
水箱

17 flushing lever
冲水杆
18 pedestal mat
基座垫（脚垫）
19 tile
瓷砖
20 ventilator (extraction vent)
通风孔，换气窗（抽气孔）
21 soap dish
肥皂碟
22 soap
肥皂
23 hand towel
手巾，毛巾
24 washbasin
洗脸盆
25 overflow
溢流口（孔）
26 hot and cold water tap
冷热水龙头
27 washbasin pedestal with trap
(anti-syphon trap)
装有防臭 U 型管的洗脸盆基座
28 tooth glass (tooth mug)
漱口杯
29 electric toothbrush
电动牙刷
30 detachable brush heads
可折卸的牙刷头
31 mirrored bathroom cabinet
洗手间的小镜橱
32 fluorescent lamp
日光灯
33 mirror
镜子
34 drawer
抽屉

35 powder box
粉盒
36 mouthwash
漱口药（剂）
37 electric shaver
电动刮胡刀
38 aftershave lotion
刮脸后用的化妆水
39 shower cubicle
淋浴室（间）
40 shower curtain
淋浴（间）门帘
41 adjustable shower head
可调整的淋浴莲篷头
42 shower nozzle
淋浴喷口
43 shower adjustment rail
淋浴调节杆
44 shower base
淋浴间的地板
45 waste pipe (overflow)
废水管（溢流管）
46 bathroom mule
浴室拖鞋
47 bathroom scales
浴室磅秤
48 bath mat
浴室防滑垫子（踏干脚用）
49 medicine cabinet
药柜

101

50 Household Appliances and Utensils 家用器具

1-20 irons
熨谷用具

1 electric ironing machine
电熨谷机

2 electric foot switch
电动脚踏开关

3 roller covering
滚筒罩

4 ironing head
熨谷头

5 sheet
被单

6 electric iron, a lightweight iron
电熨斗（轻便型熨斗）

7 sole-plate
（熨斗）底板

8 temperature selector
调温选择器

9 handle (iron handle)
熨斗手把

10 pilot light
指示灯

11 steam, spray, and dry iron
蒸汽、喷雾和干烫熨斗

12 filling inlet
注水口

13 spray nozzle for damping the washing
喷湿衣物的喷嘴

14 steam hole (steam slit)
蒸汽口（孔）

15 ironing table
熨斗架

16 ironing board (ironing surface)
熨谷板

17 ironing-board cover
熨谷板罩布

18 iron well
熨斗搁架

19 aluminium (Am. aluminum) frame
铝架

20 sleeve board
烫袖板

21 linen bin
待洗衣物箱

22 dirty linen
脏的衣物

23-34 washing machines and driers
洗衣机和乾衣机

23 washing machine (automatic washing machine)
洗衣机（自动洗衣机）

24 washing drum
洗衣槽

25 safety latch (safety catch)
安全卡梢（安全掣子）

26 program selector control
程序选择控制器

27 front soap dispenser 'with several compartments'
正面洗涤剂分配器[有数格]

28 tumble drier
滚转乾衣机

29 drum
滚槽

30 front door with ventilation slits
设通风细缝的前门

31 work top
工作台面

32 airer
晾衣架

33 clothes line (washing line)
晒衣绳

34 extending airer
摺叠式晾衣架

35 stepladder (steps), an aluminium (Am. aluminum) ladder
四脚梯，一种铝制梯子

36 stile
梯子两侧的直条框

37 prop
支柱

38 tread (rung)
梯架踏板

39-43 shoe care utensils
鞋子的保养工具

39 tin of shoe polish
鞋油盒

40 shoe spray, an impregnating spray
鞋油喷雾器，一种浸润的喷雾器

41 shoe brush
鞋刷

42 brush for applying polish
鞋油刷

43 tube of shoe polish
鞋油膏

44 clothes brush
衣刷

45 carpet brush
地毯刷

46 broom
地板刷

47 bristles
刷毛

48 broom head
刷头

49 broomstick (broom handle)
地板刷杆（刷把）

50 screw thread
螺纹

51 washing-up brush
洗涤刷

52 pan (dust pan)
畚斗（畚箕）

53-86 floor and carpet cleaning
地板和地毯的清扫

53 brush
毛刷

54 bucket (pail)
水桶

55 floor cloth (cleaning rag)
擦地板布（清洗抹布）

56 scrubbing brush
清洁刷子

57 carpet sweeper
地毯清扫器

58 upright vacuum cleaner
立式吸尘器

59 changeover switch
转换开关

60 swivel head
旋转接头

61 bag-full indicator
（吸尘）袋满指示器

62 dust bag container
灰尘袋容器

63 handle
把手

64 tubular handle
管式把手

65 flex hook
电线挂钩

66 wound-up flex
缠绕好的电线

67 all-purpose nozzle
多功能吸嘴（喷嘴）

68 cylinder vacuum cleaner
筒式吸尘器

69 swivel coupling
旋转接头（连接器）

70 extension tube
延长管

71 floor nozzle (sim.: carpet beater nozzle)
地板吸尘咀（类似：地毯拍打器的吸咀）

72 suction control
吸尘控制

73 bag-full indicator
袋满指示器

74 sliding fingertip suction control
指推式吸尘开关

75 hose (suction hose)
软管（吸尘软管）

76 combined carpet sweeper and shampooer
地毯清扫和洗涤两用的机器

77 electric lead (flex)
电线

78 plug socket
插座

79 carpet beater head (sim.: shampooing head, brush head)
地毯的拍打器头（类似：洗涤器头，毛刷头）

80 all-purpose vacuum cleaner (dry and wet operation)
万能真空吸尘器（干湿两用）

81 castor
脚轮

82 motor unit
马达装置

83 lid clip
盖夹

84 coarse dirt hose
粗脏物软管

85 special accessory (special attachment) for coarse dirt
粗脏物专用附件

86 dust container
灰尘容器

87 shopper (shopping trolley)
购物车（购物用的手推车）

1-35 flower garden
花园
1 pergola
绿廊，花架，蔓藤花棚，藤架
2 deck-chair
折叠式躺椅
3 lawn rake (wire-tooth rake)
草耙子（铁丝耙子）
4 garden rake
花园耙子
5 Virginia creeper (American ivy, woodbine, a climbing plant (climber, creeper)
美国藤，五叶地锦（一种生长在北美的爬山虎类植物，忍冬），攀缘植物（匍匐植物）
6 rockey (rock garden)
岩石园（岩石花园）
7 rock plants; *varieties:*
stonecrop (wall pepper), houseleek, dryas, aubretia
岩生植物；种植：景天，石莲花，仙女木属，南庭荠属
8 pampas grass
蒲草
9 garden hedge
绿篱
10 blue spruce
云杉
11 hydrangeas
八仙花，绣球花
12 oak (oak tree)
橡树

13 birch (birch tree)
桦木（白桦树）
14 garden path
花园小路
15 edging
（小路）边饰
16 garden pond
花园池塘
17 flagstone (stone slab)
石板
18 water lily
睡莲
19 tuberous begonias
球根秋海棠
20 dahlias
大丽花，天竺牡丹
21 watering can (*Am.* sprinkling can)
喷水壶（洒水壶）
22 weeding hoe
除草锄
23 lupin
羽扁豆
24 marguerite (oxeye daisies, white oxeye daisies)
茼蒿菊，木春菊（牛眼菊，春白菊）
25 standard rose
嫁接於树干上的玫瑰（花）
26 gerbera
非洲菊，大丁属，大丁草
27 iris
鸢尾属，鸢尾，蝴蝶花

28 gladioli
唐菖蒲，剑兰
29 chrysanthemums
菊花
30 poppy
罂粟花
31 blazing star
矮百合
32 snapdragon (antirrhinum)
金鱼草，龙头花，龙口花
33 lawn
草地
34 dandelion
蒲公英
35 sunflower
向日葵

32 allotment (fruit and
vegetable garden)

2, 16, 17, 29 dwarf fruit trees
(espaliers, espalier fruit trees)
矮干果树（树篱，篱式果树）
quadruple cordon, a wall
espalier
四干形（果树），一种树篱
vertical cordon
直立单干形（果树）
tool shed (garden shed)
工具棚（园内小屋）
water butt (water barrel)
水桶
climbing plant (climber, creeper,
rambler)
攀缘植物（攀缘植物，匍匐植物，蔓生
植物）
compost heap
堆肥
sunflower
向日葵
garden ladder (ladder)
果园梯子
perennial (flowering perennial)
多年生植物（开花的多年生植物）
garden fence (paling fence,
paling)
果菜园栅栏（木栅，园篱）
standard berry tree
嫁接於树干上的浆果树

12 climbing rose (rambling rose) on
the trellis arch
攀缘在拱架上的蔷薇（蔓生蔷薇）
13 bush rose (standard rose tree)
丛生性蔷薇（嫁接於树干上的蔷薇）
14 summerhouse (garden house)
凉亭（园舍）
15 Chinese lantern (paper lantern)
中国式灯笼（纸灯笼）
16 pyramind tree (pyramidal tree,
pyramid), a free-standing
espalier
角锥形树（金字塔形的树），一种独立
式树篱
17 double horizontal cordon
水平双干形（果树）
18 flower bed, a border
花坛，花床
19 berry bush (gooseberry bush,
currant bush)
浆果灌木（醋栗灌木，酸栗灌木）
20 concrete edging
混凝土边饰
21 standard rose (standard rose
tree)
嫁接於树干上的蔷薇（树）
22 border with perennials
多年生植物花坛
23 garden path
果菜园小路
24 allotment holder
家庭果菜园园主

25 asparagus patch (asparagus bed)
芦笋床
26 vegetable patch (vetetable plot)
蔬菜区
27 scarecrow
稻草人
28 runner bean (Am. scarlet
runner), a bean plant on
poles (bean poles)
攀缘豆类（美：红花菜豆），一种攀缘
在支架上的豆类植物
29 horizontal cordon
水平单干果树
30 standard fruit tree
直立式果树
31 tree stake
树木支柱
32 hedge
缘篱

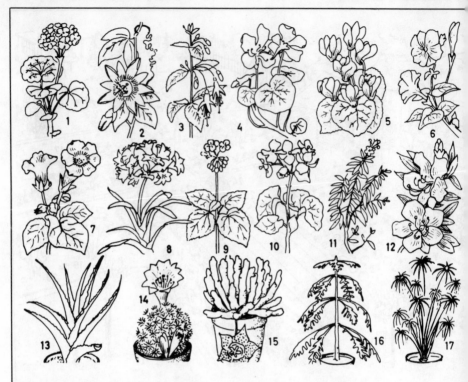

1 pelargonium (crane's bill), a
  geranium
  天竺葵（老鹳草），老鹳草属
2 passion flower (Passiflora), a
  climbing plant (climber, creeper)
  西番莲（西番莲属），攀缘植物
3 fuchsia, an anagraceous plant
  倒挂金钟，吊金钟，灯笼海棠，柳叶菜科
4 nasturtium (Indian cress,
  tropaeolum)
  金莲花，旱金莲（印第安水芹）
5 cyclamen, a primulaceous herb
  仙客来，一种樱桃科植物
6 petunia, a solanaceous herb
  矮牵牛，一种茄科草本植物
7 gloxinia (Sinningia), a
  gesneriaceous plant
  大岩桐（大岩桐属），一种苦苣苔科植物
8 Clivia minata, an amaryllis
  (narcissus)
  君子兰，孤挺花（水仙属）
9 African hemp (Sparmannia), a
  tiliaceous plant, a linden plant
  非洲大麻（一种田麻科植物，椴科植物）
10 begonia
   秋海棠
11 myrtle (common myrtle,
   Myrtus)
   堇宝莲（桃金娘科）
12 azalea, an ericaceous plant
   杜鹃花（一种石南科植物）
13 aloe, a liliaceous plant
   芦荟（百合科植物）
14 globe thistle (Echinops)
   球蓟（单州漏卢属）
15 stapelia (carrion flower), an
   asclepiadaceous plant
   萝藦属（牛尾菜），一种萝藦科植物
16 Norfolk Island Pine (an
   araucaria, grown as an
   ornamental)
   小叶南洋杉（南洋杉属，装饰植物）
17 galingale, a cyperacious plant of
   the sedge family
   香根莎草（莎草科植物之一种）

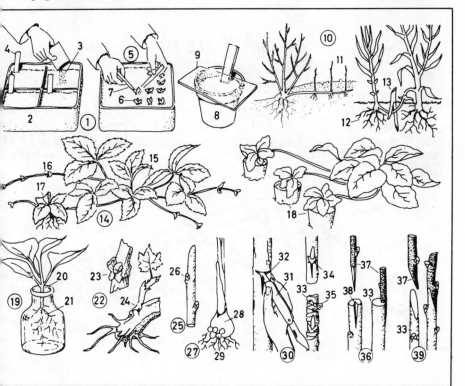

17 small rooted leaf cluster
带细根的叶簇
18 setting in pots
盆中定植
19 cutting in water
水中插枝
20 cutting (slip, set)
插条，插枝
21 root
根
22 bud cutting on vine tendril
藤本上的芽插（芽接）
23 scion bud, a bud
接芽，芽
24 sprouting (shooting) cutting
嫩芽（新梢）插枝
25 stem cutting (hardwood cutting)
茎插（硬木插）
26 bud
芽，萌芽
27 propagation by bulbils (brood bud bulblets)
珠芽繁殖，小鳞茎群（小鳞茎群）繁殖
28 old bulb
老鳞茎
29 bulbil (brood bud bulblet)
小鳞茎（小鳞茎群）
30-39 **grafting** (graftage)
嫁接（嫁接法）
30 budding (shield budding)
芽接（T 字形芽接）
31 budding knife
芽接用刀

seed sowing (sowing)
播种
seed pan
种子箱
seed
种子
label
标签
pricking out (pricking off, transplanting)
移植
seedling (seedling plant)
幼苗（植物幼苗）
dibber (dibble)
点播器（挖穴器）
flower pot (pot)
花盆（花钵）
sheet of glass
玻璃片
propagation by layering
压枝繁殖
layer
压条
layer with roots
带根压条
forked stick used for fastening
固定用的叉状枝
propagation by runners
匍匐茎繁殖
parent (parent plant)
母本，亲本（母本植物）
runner
纤匍枝，匍匐茎

32 T-cut
T 字形切口
33 support (stock, rootstock)
砧木
34 inserted scion bud
插入的接芽
35 raffia layer (bast layer)
莱菲麻层（韧皮层）
36 side grafting
腹接，侧接
37 scion (shoot)
接穗（新梢）
38 wedge-shaped notch
楔形切口
39 splice graft (splice grafting)
搭接法

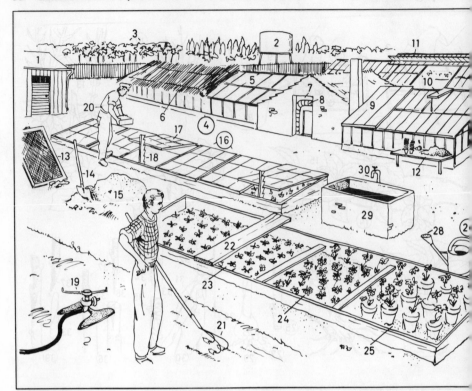

1-51 market garden (*Am.* truck garden, truck farm)
商品菜园（花园）

1 tool shed
工具棚

2 water tower (water tank)
水塔

3 market garden (*Am.* truck garden, truck farm), a tree nursery
树苗圃

4 hothouse (forcing house, warm house)
暖房（人工加速栽培室，温室）

5 glass roof
玻璃屋顶

6 matting, e.g. straw matting, reed matting
覆盖物，如：麦秆、芦苇

7 boiler room (boiler house)
锅炉房

8 heating pipe (pressure pipe)
暖气管，加温管（压力管）

9 shading panel (shutter)
遮光板，遮阳板

10-11 ventilators (vents)
通风口

10 ventilation window (window vent, hinged ventilator)
通风窗（铰接通风窗）

11 ridge vent
屋脊通风口

12 potting table (potting bench)
盆栽桌（盆栽枱）

13 riddle (sieve, garden sieve, upright sieve)
粗筛（筛，园艺筛，立筛）

14 garden shovel (shovel)
园艺铁锹（锹，铲）

15 heap of earth (composted earth, prepared earth, garden mould, *Am.* mold)
土堆（堆肥土，调配土，园用肥土）

16 hotbed (forcing bed, heated frame)
温床（促成栽培的温床，温框）

17 hotbed vent (frame vent)
温床通风口

18 vent prop
通风口支柱

19 sprinkler (sprinkling device)
洒水器（洒水装置）

20 gardener (nursery gardener, grower, commercial grower)
园工（苗圃园工，栽培者，商品生产者）

21 cultivator (hand cultivator, grubber)
耕耘器具，耘锄（手耘锄，除草工具）

22 plank
厚木板

23 pricked-out seedlings (pricked-off seedlings)
移植幼苗

24 forced flowers [forcing]
促成栽培的花

25 potted plants (plants in pots, pot plants)
盆栽植物

26 watering can (*Am.* sprinkling can)
洒水壶（[美]喷水壶）

27 handle
把手

28 rose
喷咀

29 water tank
水池

30 water pipe
水管

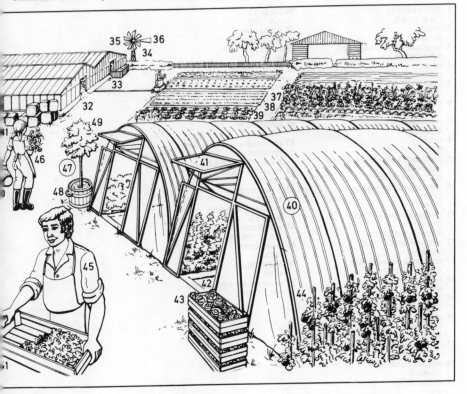

bale of peat
泥炭土包

warm house (heated greenhouse)
暖房（加温的温室）

cold house (unheated greenhouse)
冷房（不加温的温室）

wind generator
风力发电机

wind wheel
风轮

wind vane
风向标

shrub bed, a flower bed
灌木苗床，花坛

hoop edging
围

vegetable plot
蔬菜地，蔬菜区

plastic tunnel (polythene greenhouse)
塑胶棚（聚乙烯暖房）

ventilation flap
通风活板

central path
中央通道

vegetable crate
蔬菜板条箱

tomato plant
番茄植物

nursery hand
苗圃工人

nursery hand
苗圃工人

47 tub plant
盆栽植物，桶栽植物

48 tub
木桶，木盆

49 orange tree
柑橘树

50 wire basket
铁丝篮

51 seedling box
幼苗箱

1 dibber (dibble)
点播器，穴植器

2 spade
铲，铁锹

3 lawn rake (wire-tooth rake)
草耙子（铁丝耙子）

4 rake
耙子

5 ridging hoe
作埂锄

6 trowel
（移植用的）小铲

7 combined hoe and fork
锄耙两用工具

8 sickle
镰刀

9 gardener's knife (pruning knife,
billhook)
园艺刀（剪枝刀，钩刀）

10 asparagus cutter (asparagus
knife)
芦笋割刀

11 tree pruner (long-handled
pruner)
高枝剪（长柄剪枝刀）

12 semi-automatic spade
半自动铲

13 three-pronged cultivator
三齿耘锄，三叉耙

14 tree scraper (bark scraper)
树皮刮刀

15 lawn aerator (aerator)
草地通气器（灌气器）

16 pruning saw (saw for cutting
branches)
修剪锯

17 battery-operated hedge trimmer
电动绿篱修剪机

18 motor cultivator
马达耕耘机

19 electric drill
电钻

20 gear
齿轮

21 cultivator attachment
耕耘机的附件

22 fruit picker
果实采集器

23 tree brush (bark brush)
树皮刷

24 sprayer for pest control
药剂喷雾器

25 lance
喷枪

26 hose reel (reel and carrying cart)
浇水软管卷筒（车）

27 garden hose
花园浇水管

28 motor lawn mower (motor
mower)
机动刈草机

29 grassbox
草箱

30 two-stroke motor
二冲（行）程发动机

31 electric lawn mower (electric
mower)
电动刈（剪）草机

32 electric lead (electric cable)
电线（电缆线）

33 cutting unit
割草部件

34 hand mower
手推刈草机

35 cutting cylinder
切割滚刀

36 blade
刀刃，刀口

37 riding mower
乘车型刈草机

38 brake lock
制动杆

39 electric starter
电起动机

40 brake pedal
制动踏板，脚煞车

41 cutting unit
切割部件

42 tip-up trailer
翻卸拖车

43 revolving sprinkler, a lawn
sprinkler
旋转洒水器，一种草地洒水器

44 revolving nozzle
旋转喷咀

45 hose connector
软管接头

46 oscillating sprinkler
振荡洒水器

47 wheelbarrow
手推车，独轮手车

48 grass shears
剪草剪刀

49 hedge shears
修篱剪刀

50 secateurs (pruning shears)
剪枝刀（修枝铗）

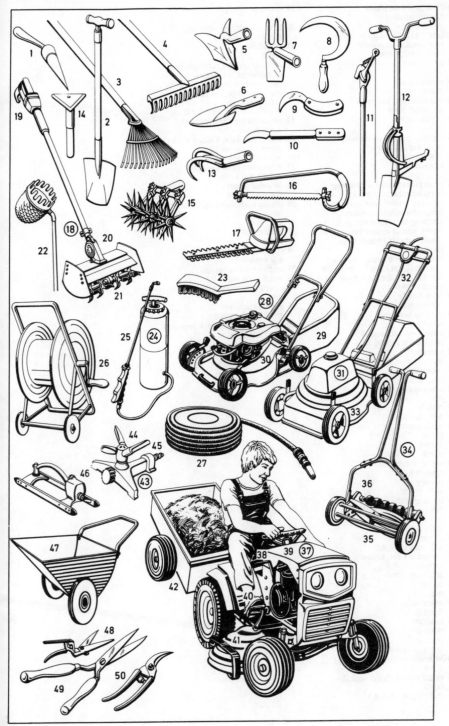

1-11 leguminous plants (Leguminosae)
豆科植物（豆科）

1 pea, a plant with a papilionaceous corolla
豌豆，蝶形花冠植物

2 pea flower
豌豆花

3 pinnate leaf
羽状叶

4 pea tendril, a leaf tendril
豌豆卷须，叶卷须

5 stipule
托叶

6 legume (pod), a seed vessel (pericarp, legume)
豆荚

7 pea [seed]
豌豆〔子〕

8 bean plant (bean), a climbing plant (climber, creeper); *varieties:* broad bean (runner bean, *Am.* scarlet runner), . climbing bean (climber, pole bean), scarlet runner bean; *smaller:* dwarf French bean (bush bean)
豆科植物，一种攀缘植物；变种：蚕豆（扁豆），[美]红花菜豆），攀缘豆（攀缘茎类豆），红花菜豆；株型小的：矮性法国豆（矮性菜豆）

9 bean flower
豆科植物的花

10 twining beanstalk
缠绕豆茎

11 bean [pod with seeds]
菜豆（带有豆实的荚果）

12 tomato
番茄

13 cucumber
胡瓜，黄瓜

14 asparagus
芦笋，石刁柏

15 radish
萝蔔（做生菜用的）

16 white radish
白萝蔔

17 carrot
胡萝蔔

18 stump-rooted carrot
短粗的胡蘿蔔

19 parsley
香芹，洋芫荽

20 horse-radish
辣根（十字花科）

21 leeks
韭蔥（石蒜科）

22 chives
细葱，细香葱（石蒜科）

23 pumpkin (*Am.* squash); *sim.:* melon
南瓜；类似：甜瓜

24 onion
洋蔥

25 onion skin
洋蔥皮

26 kohlrabi
球茎甘蓝

27 celeriac
根芹菜

28-34 brassicas (leaf vegetables)
芸苔属（叶菜类）

28 chard (Swiss chard, seakale beet)
薔菜（牛皮菜，薔莲菜）

29 spinach
菠菜

30 Brussels sprouts (sprouts)
抱子甘蓝（十字花科）

31 cauliflower
花椰菜，菜花

32 cabbage (round cabbage, head of cabbage), a brassica; *cultivated races (cultivars):* green cabbage, red cabbage
甘蓝（包心菜，圆甘蓝），芸苔属的一种；栽培品种：青甘蓝，赤甘蓝

33 savoy (savoy cabbage)
皱叶甘蓝

34 kale (curly kale, kail), a winter green
羽衣甘蓝，一种冬季蔬菜

35 scorsonera (black salsify)
菊牛蒡（黑婆罗门蓼）

36-40 salad plants
生菜（沙拉）植物

36 lettuce (cabbage lettuce, head of lettuce)
萵苣，生菜

37 lettuce leaf
萵苣叶

38 corn salad (lamb's lettuce)
野苣（败酱科）

39 endive (endive leaves)
菊萵苣（生菜食品）

40 chicory (succory, salad chicory)
菊苣

41 globe artichoke
朝鲜蓟（花头可作蔬菜）

42 sweet pepper (Spanish paprika)
甜椒（西班牙辣椒）

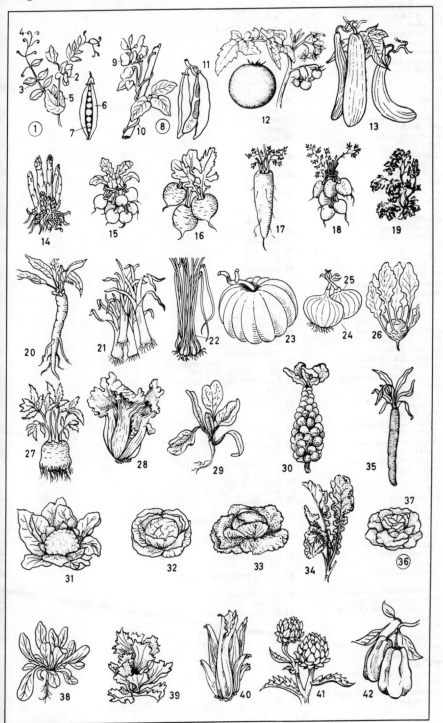

58   Soft Fruit and Pomes

1-30 **soft fruit** (berry bushes)
浆果（浆果灌木）

1-15 **Ribes**
虎耳草科醋栗属的植物

1 gooseberry bush
醋栗矮灌木

2 flowering gooseberry cane
开花的醋栗茎

3 leaf
叶子

4 flower
花

5 magpie moth larva
醋栗尺蠖幼虫

6 gooseberry flower
醋栗花

7 epignynous ovary
上位子房

8 calyx (sepals)
花萼

9 gooseberry, a berry
醋栗，一种浆果

10 currant bush
红醋栗树（灌木）

11 cluster of berries
一串浆果，一串果粒

12 currant
红醋栗

13 stalk
梗（柄）

14 flowering cane of the currant
穗醋栗状花茎

15 raceme
总状花序，串状花

16 strawberry plant; *varieties*: wild
strawberry (woodland
strawberry), garden strawberry,
alpine strawberry
草莓植物；变种：野草莓（森林草
莓），园生草莓，高山草莓

17 flowering and fruit-bearing
plant
开花结果的植物

18 rhizome
根茎，根状茎

19 ternate leaf (trifoliate leaf)
三出叶（三叶轮性）

20 runner (prostrate stem)
纤匐茎（匐茎）

21 strawberry, a pseudocarp
草莓，一种假果

22 epicalyx
副萼

23 achene (seed)
瘦果（种子）

24 flesh (pulp)
果肉

25 raspberry bush
树莓矮灌木（覆盆子矮灌木）

26 raspberry flower
树莓花

27 flower bud (bud)
花蕾

28 fruit (raspberry), an aggregate
fruit (compound fruit)
果实（树莓），一种聚合果（复果）

29 blackberry
黑莓

30 thorny tendril
刺状卷须

31-61 **pomiferous plants**
梨果类植物

31 pear tree; *wild*: wild pear tree
梨树；野梨树

32 flowering branch of the pear tree
开花的梨树枝

33 pear [longitudinal section]
梨[纵切面]

34 pear stalk (stalk)
梨果梗（柄）

35 flesh (pulp)
梨果肉（果肉）

36 core (carpels)
果心（心皮）

37 pear pip (seed), a fruit pip
梨的小种子，果仁

38 pear blossom
梨花

39 ovules
胚珠

40 ovary
子房

41 stigma
柱头

42 style
花柱

43 petal
花瓣

44 sepal
萼片，花萼

45 stamen (anther)
雄蕊（花药）

46 quince tree
榅桲树

47 quince leaf
榅桲树叶

48 stipule
托叶

49 apple-shaped quince
[longitudinal section]
苹果形的榅桲[纵切面]

50 pear-shaped quince
[longitudinal section]
梨形的榅桲[纵切面]

51 apple tree; *wild*: crab apple tree
苹果树；野苹果树：山楂子树

52 flowering branch of the apple
tree
开花的苹果树枝

53 leaf
叶子

54 apple blossom
苹果花

55 withered flower
凋谢的花

56 apple [longitudinal section]
苹果[纵切面]

57 apple skin
苹果皮

58 flesh (pulp)
（苹）果肉

59 core (apple core, carpels)
果心（苹果心，心皮）

60 apple pip, a fruit pip
苹果的小种子，果仁

61 apple stalk (stalk)
苹果梗（柄）

62 codling moth (codlin moth)
苹果卷叶蛾

63 burrow (tunnel)
虫蛀洞穴

64 larva (grub, caterpillar) of a
small moth
一种小蛾的幼虫（幼蛾，蠋）

65 wormhole
虫孔

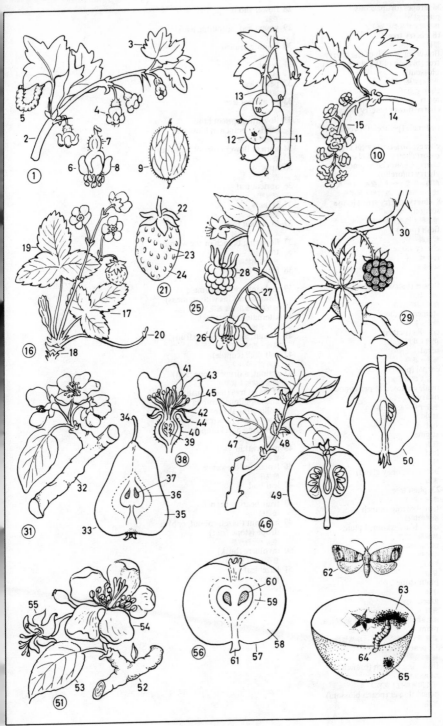

59 Drupes and Nuts

1-36 drupes (drupaceous plants)
核果树（核果类植物）

1-18 cherry tree
樱桃树

1 flowering branch of the cherry tree (branch of the cherry tree in blossom)
开花的樱桃树枝

2 cherry leaf
樱桃叶

3 cherry flower (cherry blossom)
樱桃花

4 peduncle (pedicel, flower stalk)
花梗

5 cherry; *varieties:* sweet cherry (heart cherry), wild cherry (bird cherry), sour cherry, morello cherry (morello)
樱桃；种类：西洋甜樱桃（心形樱桃），野樱桃，酸樱桃，黑樱桃

6-8 cherry (cherry fruit) [cross section]
樱桃树（樱桃）[横剖面]

6 flesh (pulp)
樱桃肉

7 cherry stone
樱桃核

8 seed
种子

9 flower (blossom) [cross section]
樱桃花[横剖面]

10 stamen (anther)
雄蕊（花药）

11 corolla (petals)
花冠（花瓣）

12 sepal
萼片，花萼

13 carpel (pistil)
心皮（雌蕊叶）

14 ovule enclosed in perigynous ovary
包在子房中心内的胚珠

15 style
花柱

16 stigma
柱头

17 leaf
叶子

18 nectary (honey gland)
蜜腺

19-23 plum tree
李树，梅树

19 fruit-bearing branch
结果的树枝

20 oval, black-skinned plum
椭圆形黑皮李子

21 plum leaf
李树叶

22 bud
芽

23 plum stone
李核

24 greengage
青梅

25 mirabelle (transparent gage), a plum
黄李子（透明的李子），李属植物

26-32 peach tree
桃树

26 flowering branch (branch in blossom)
开花的桃树枝（花枝）

27 peach flower (peach blossom)
桃花

28 flower shoot
花枝

29 young leaf (sprouting leaf)
嫩叶

30 fruiting branch
结果枝

31 peach
桃子

32 peach leaf
桃树叶

33-36 apricot tree
杏树

33 flowering apricot branch (apricot branch in blossom)
开花的杏树枝

34 apricot flower (apricot blossom)
杏花

35 apricot
杏子

36 apricot leaf
杏树叶

37-51 nuts
坚果树

37-43 walnut tree
胡桃树，核桃树

37 flowering branch of the walnut tree
开花的胡桃树枝

38 female flower
雌花

39 male inflorescence (male flowers, catkins with stamens)
雄花序（雄花，雄蕊花）

40 alternate pinnate leaf
互生羽状叶

41 walnut, a drupe (stone fruit)
核桃，胡桃（核果）

42 soft shell (cupule)
软外壳（壳斗）

43 walnut, a drupe (stone fruit)
核桃，胡桃（核果）

44-51 hazel tree (hazel bush), an anemophilous shrub (a wind-pollinating shrub)
榛树（矮灌木），风媒灌木

44 flowering hazel branch
开花的榛树枝

45 male catkin
雄荑荑花序

46 female inflorescence
雌花序

47 leaf bud
叶芽

48 fruit-bearing branch
结果枝

49 hazelnut (hazel, cobnut, cob), a drupe (stone fruit)
榛实，一种核果

50 involucre (husk)
总苞（皮，苞叶）

51 hazel leaf
榛树叶

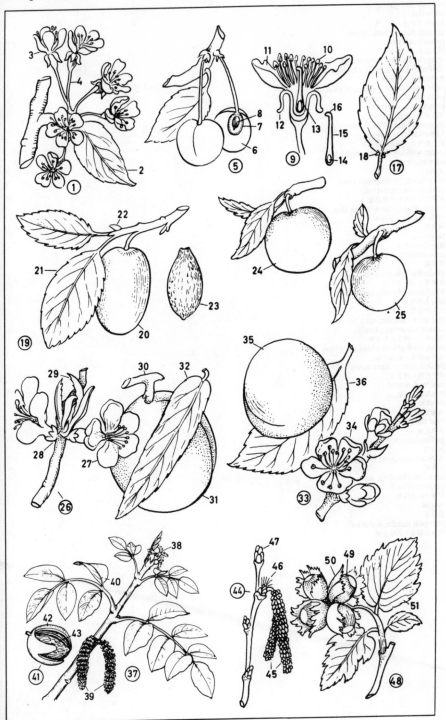

1 snowdrop (spring
  snowflake)
  石蒜科雪花莲 (雪片莲)
2 garden pansy (heartsease
  pansy), a pansy
  园三色堇 (三色堇)
3 trumpet narcissus (trumpet
  daffodil, Lent lily), a narcissus
  喇叭水仙，一种水仙
4 poet's narcissus (pheasant's eye,
  poet's daffodil); *sim.*:
  polyanthus narcissus
  堆眼水仙；类似：多花水仙
5 bleeding heart (lyre flower), a
  fumariaceous flower
  荷包牡丹，一种紫堇科花卉
6 sweet william (bunch pink), a
  carnation
  美洲石竹，洋石竹
7 gillyflower (gilliflower, clove
  pink, clove carnation)
  紫罗兰 (香石竹，康乃馨)
8 yellow flag (yellow water flag,
  yellow iris), an iris
  黄菖蒲
9 tuberose
  晚香玉，夜来香
10 columbine (aquilegia)
  耧斗菜
11 gladiolus (sword lily)
  唐菖蒲 (剑兰)
12 Madonna lily (Annunciation
  lily, Lent lily), a lily
  白色百合花，一种百合
13 larkspur (delphinium), a
  ranunculaceous plant
  飞燕草，一种毛茛科植物
14 moss pink (moss phlox), a phlox
  尖叶福禄考，福禄考属
15 garden rose (China rose)
  园中玫瑰 (月季花)
16 rosebud, a bud
  玫瑰花苞，蓓蕾
17 double rose
  重瓣玫瑰
18 rose thorn, a thorn
  玫瑰花刺
19 gaillardia
  天人菊
20 African marigold (tagetes)
  万寿菊
21 love-lies-bleeding, an
  amaranthine flower
  千穗谷，苋属花
22 zinnia
  百日草
23 pompon dahlia, a dahlia
  绒球大丽花，大丽菊属

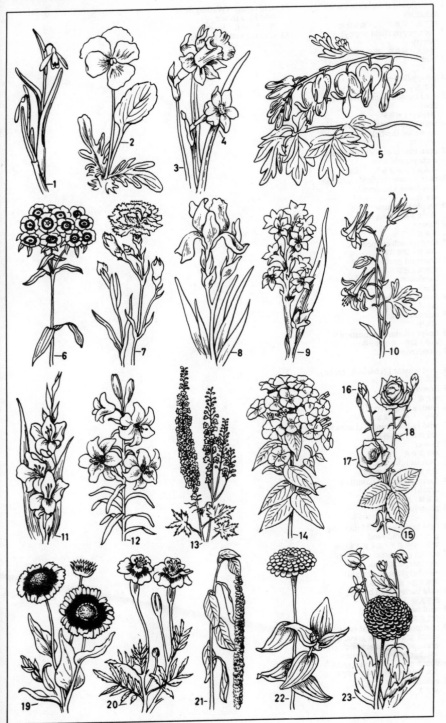

1 corn flower (bluebottle), a centaury
矢车菊（翠蓝），矢车菊属植物

2 corn poppy (field poppy), a poppy
虞美人之丽春花，舞草（罂粟科）

3 bud
芽

4 poppy flower
罂粟花

5 seed capsule containing poppy seeds
含罂粟种子的蒴果

6 corn cockle (corn campion, crown-of-the-field)
麦秆石竹

7 corn marigold (field marigold), a chrysanthemum
孔雀菊（琉球金盏花），菊属

8 corn camomile (field camomile, camomile, chamomile)
黄金菊

9 shepherd's purse
荠，大荠菜（十字花科）

10 flower
荠菜花

11 fruit (pouch-shaped pod)
荠菜果（袋形荚果）

12 common groundsel
麥吾属之杂草

13 dandelion
蒲公英

14 flower head (capitulum)
蒲公英花序（头状花序）

15 infructescence
果实序

16 hedge mustard, a mustard
药用大蒜芥，芥子的一种

17 stonecrop
景天

18 wild mustard (charlock, runch)
野芥子

19 flower
野芥花

20 fruit, a siliqua (pod)
野芥果，长角（荚果）

21 wild radish (jointed charlock)
野生萝卜（有节野芥）

22 flower
野生萝卜花

23 fruit (siliqua, pod)
野生萝卜果（长角荚果）

24 common orache (common orach)
滨藜属

25 goosefoot
藜

26 field bindweed (wild morning glory), a bindweed
旋花（牵牛花），三色旋花属植物

27 scarlet pimpernel (shepherd's weatherglass, poor man's weatherglass, eye-bright)
琉璃繁缕，海绿（报春花科）

28 wild barley (wall barley)
野生大麦

29 wild oat
野生燕麦

30 common couch grass (couch, quack grass, quick grass, quitch grass, scutch grass, twitch grass, witchgrass); sim.: bearded couch grass, sea couch grass
茅草；类似有：有须茅草，海茅草

31 gallant soldier
辣子草

32 field eryngo (Watling Street thistle), a thistle
野刺芹（野蓟），一种蓟

33 stinging nettle, a nettle
刺毛荨麻，荨麻科

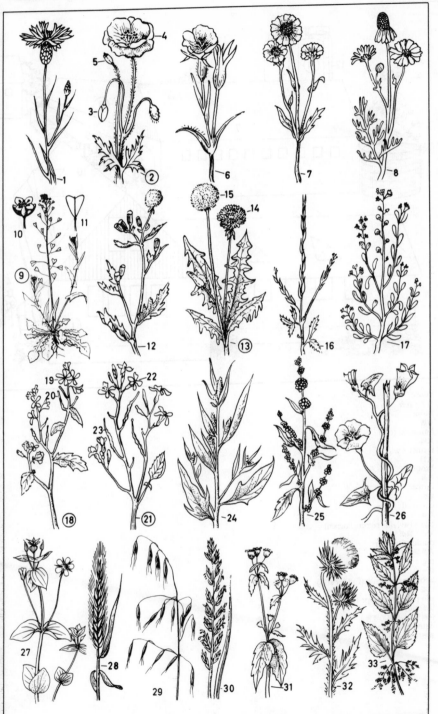

1 house
　房子，农舍
2 stable
　畜厩
3 house cat (cat)
　家猫
4 farmer's wife
　农妇
5 broom
　扫帚
6 farmer
　农夫
7 cowshed
　牛棚
8 pigsty (sty, *Am.* pigpen, hogpen)
　猪栏，猪圈，猪舍
9 outdoor trough
　户外饲槽
10 pig
　猪
11 above-ground silo (fodder silo)
　贮塔（饲料贮塔）
12 silo pipe (standpipe for filling
　the silo)
　饲料管（装饲料的竖管）
13 liquid manure silo
　液底肥池（槽）

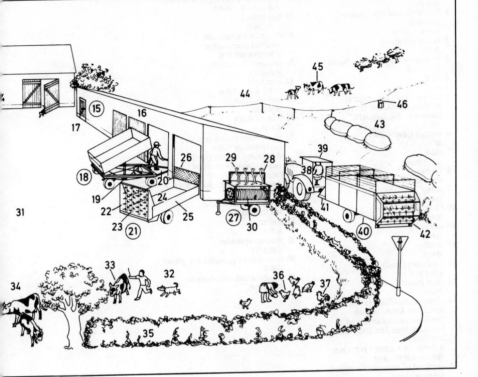

outhouse
外屋，附属的建筑物（与正屋分开，如
谷仓等）

machinery shed
机器房（棚）

sliding door
滑门，拉门

door to the workshop
至工作场的门

three-way tip-cart, a transport vehicle
三面倾卸车，一种运输车辆

tipping cylinder
倾卸气（汽）缸

shafts
车轮轴

manure spreader (fertilizer spreader, manure distributor)
堆肥撒布机（化学肥料撒布机）

spreader unit (distributor unit)
撒布装置（排肥器）

spreader cyclinder (distributor cylinder)
撒肥缸（排肥缸）

movable scraper floor
活动刮板

side planking (side board)
侧板

wire mesh front
金属网挡板

sprinkler stand
洒水车

sprinkler cart
洒水机（立）架

29 sprinkler, a revolving sprinkler
洒水机，旋转式洒水机

30 sprinkler hoses
洒水软管

31 farmyard
农家的中庭

32 watchdog
看门狗

33 calf
小牛，牛犊

34 dairy cow (milch-cow, milker)
乳牛

35 farmyard hedge
场院树篱

36 chicken (hen)
小鸡（母鸡）

37 cock (*Am.* rooster)
公鸡

38 tractor
牵引机，曳引机

39 tractor driver
牵引机司机

40 all-purpose trailer
万用拖车

41 [folded] pickup attachment
[折叠式]拾取附件

42 unloading unit
卸载组件

43 polythene silo, a fodder silo
聚乙烯饲料包，饲料袋

44 meadow
（牧）草地

45 grazing cattle
放牧的牛

46 electrified fence
带电栅栏

1-41 work in the fields
田间工作

1 fallow (fallow field, fallow ground)
休耕地，休闲地

2 boundary stone
界石

3 boundary ridge, a balk (baulk)
界埂，田埂

4 field
田地

5 farmworker (agricultural worker, farmhand, farm labourer, *Am.* laborer)
农场工人

6 plough (*Am.* plow)
犁

7 clod
土块，泥块

8 furrow
犁沟，畦

9 stone
石头，石块

10-12 sowing
播种

10 sower
播种者

11 seedlip
播种袋

12 seed corn (seed)
谷种（种子）

13 field guard
田间守卫者

14 chemical fertilizer, (artificial fertilizer); *kinds*: potash fertilizer, phosphoric acid fertilizer, lime fertilizer, nitrogen fertilizer
化学肥料，（人工肥料）种类：钾肥，磷肥，石灰肥料，氮肥

15 cartload of manure (farmyard manure, dung)
一车肥料（农家肥，粪肥）

16 oxteam (team of oxen, *Am.* span of oxen)
二牛拉车

17 fields (farmland)
农田（耕地）

18 farm track (farm road)
农场小路

19-30 hay harvest (haymaking)
牧草的收获作业

19 rotary mower with swather (swath reaper)
旋转刈幅割草机（刈幅收割机）

20 connecting shaft (connecting rod)
连结轴（连杆）

21 power take-off (power take-off shaft
动力分导装置（动力输出轴）

22 meadow
草地

23 swath (swathe)
刈下的一行草

24 tedder (rotary tedder)
摊草机（旋转摊草机）

25 tedded hay
摊开晒的干草

26 rotary swather
旋转刈幅机

27 trailer with pickup attachment
有拾取附件的拖车

28 fence rack (rickstand), a drying rack for hay
围篱草架，晒草架

29 rickstand, a drying rack for hay
干草（立）架，晒草架

30 hay tripod
干草三脚架

31-41 grain harvest and seedbed preparation
谷物收割和苗床整地

31 combine harvester
联合收获机

32 cornfield
（小）麦田，谷物地

33 stubble field
残株田地

34 bale of straw
藁秆捆

35 straw baler (straw press), a highpressure baler
藁秆打包机，一种高压打包机

36 swath (swathe) of straw (windrow of straw)
刈幅藁秆（刈下后晒乾翻堆成草堆的干草）

37 hydraulic bale loader
液压草捆装载机

38 trailer
拖车

39 manure spreader
肥料撒布机

40 four-furrow plough (*Am.* plow)
四壠犁

41 combination seed-harrow
组合播种耙

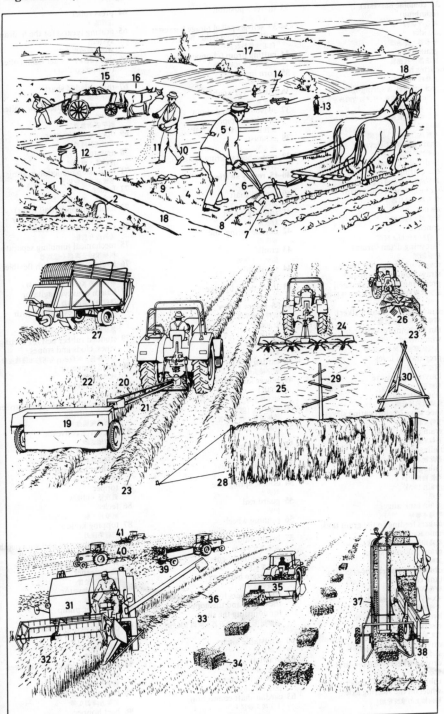

1-33 combine harvester
(combine)
联合收获机

1 divider
分禾器，分茎器

2 grain lifter
扶茎器，扶穗器

3 cutter bar
刀具杆，割刀杆

4 pickup reel, a spring-tine reel
(拾取器的)拾禾轮，有弹簧齿的拔禾轮

5 reel gearing
拾禾轮驱动装置

6 auger
木螺钻

7 chain and slat elevator
链耙式升降器

8 hydraulic cylinder for adjusting the cutting unit
调节切削组件的液压缸

9 stone catcher (stone trap)
集石器（除石器）

10 awner
除芒器，脱芒机

11 concave
（脱粒）凹板，凹面

12 threshing drum (drum)
脱谷圆筒

13 revolving beater [for freeing straw from the drum and preparing it for the shakers]
旋转式搅打机[以圆筒脱谷再送往摆动器（筛）]

14 straw shaker (strawwalker)
稻草筛（稻草摆动器）

15 fan for compressed-air winnowing
压气式簸谷送风机（风扇）

16 preparation level
预加工平面

17 louvred-type sieve
鱼鳞筛

18 sieve extension
鱼鳞筛的延长线

19 shoe sieve (reciprocating sieve)
下筛（振动筛）

20 grain auger
谷粒木螺钻

21 tailings auger
筛除物木螺钻

22 tailings outlet
筛除物排出口

23 grain tank
粮箱

24 grain tank auger
粮箱木螺钻

25 augers feeding to the grain tank unloader
粮箱卸载装置的喂送木螺钻

26 grain unloader spout
卸粮嘴

27 observation ports for checking tank contents
检查箱容量观察口

28 six-cylinder diesel engine
六气缸柴油发动机

29 hydraulic pump with oil reservoir
带贮油器的液压泵

30 driving axle gearing
驱动轴齿轮驱动装置

31 driving wheel tyre (Am. tire)
驱动轮胎

32 rubber-tyred (Am. rubber-tired) wheel on the steering axle
转向轴上的橡胶轮胎

33 driver's position
驾驶员座位

34-39 self-propelled forage harvester
(self-propelled field chopper)
自走式草料收割机

34 cutting drum (chopper drum)
切削圆筒（切碎圆筒）

35 corn head
玉米收割台

36 cab (driver's cab)
驾驶室

37 swivel-mounted spout (discharge pipe)
旋转悬挂式卸载管（排泄管）

38 exhaust
排气管

39 rear-wheel steering system
后轮转向系统

40-45 rotary swather
旋转刈辐机

40 cardan shaft
方向轴

41 running wheel
行驶轮

42 double spring tine
双弹齿

43 crank
曲柄，手摇柄

44 swath rake
集草（铺条）耙

45 three-point linkage
三点连结装置

46-58 rotary tedder
旋转式摊草机

46 tractor
牵引机

47 draw bar
拉杆

48 cardan shaft
十字接头轴

49 power take-off (power take-off shaft)
功率输出轴

50 gearing (gears)
齿轮装置，传动装置

51 frame bar
框杆

52 rotating head
旋转圆盘

53 tine bar
耙齿杆

54 double spring tine
双弹齿

55 guard rail
护轨

56 running wheel
行驶轮

57 height adjustment crank
高度调节手摇柄

58 wheel adjustment
轮调整机构

59-84 potato harvester
马铃薯收获机

59 control levers for the lifters of the digger and the hopper and for adjusting the shaft
调整挖斗，漏斗提升器，和调节轴的控制杆

60 adjustable hitch
可调系扣

61 drawbar
拉杆，牵引杆

62 drawbar support
拉杆支座

63 cardan shaft connection
十字接头轴接头

64 press roller
压榨辊子

65 gearing (gears) for the hydraulic system
液压系统的齿轮装置

66 disc (disk) coulter (Am. colter) (rolling coulter)
圆犁刀

67 three-bladed share
三叶犁头

68 disc (disk) coulter (Am. colter) drive
圆犁驱动装置

69 open-web elevator
开网式升降器

70 agitator
搅拌器，搅动器

71 multi-step reduction gearing
多级减速齿轮装置

72 feeder
进给器，进料器

73 haulm stripper (flail rotor)
茎叶摘除器，截穗机（连枷式转子）

74 rotary elevating drum
旋转提升鼓轮

75 mechanical tumbling separator
机械滚转分离器（选别器）

76 haulm conveyor with flexible haulm strippers
有弹性的茎叶摘除器的输送带

77 haulm conveyor agitator
茎叶输送带搅动器

78 haulm conveyor drive with V-belt
茎叶输送带的三角皮带驱动装置

79 studded rubber belt for sorting vines, clods and stones
分拣藤蔓，泥块和石头用的加强橡皮带

80 trash conveyor
残屑输送器

81 sorting table
分拣台

82 rubber-disc (rubber-disk) rollers for presorting
预拣橡皮圆盘

83 discharge conveyor
卸薯输送器

84 endless-floor hopper
循环活动底板漏斗

85-96 beet harvester
甜菜收获机

85 topper
截顶器，切顶器

86 feeler
测隙片，触

87 topping knife
切甜菜顶刀

88 feeler support wheel with depth adjustment
具有耕深调节装置的测隙片支承轮

89 beet cleaner
甜菜清理器

90 haulm elevator
茎叶升降器

91 hydraulic pump
液压泵

92 compressed-air reservoir
压缩空气（贮气）筒

93 oil tank (oil reservoir)
油箱（油槽）

94 tensioning device for the beet elevator
甜菜升降器的拉紧装置

95 beet elevator belt
甜菜升降器皮带

96 beet hopper
甜菜漏斗

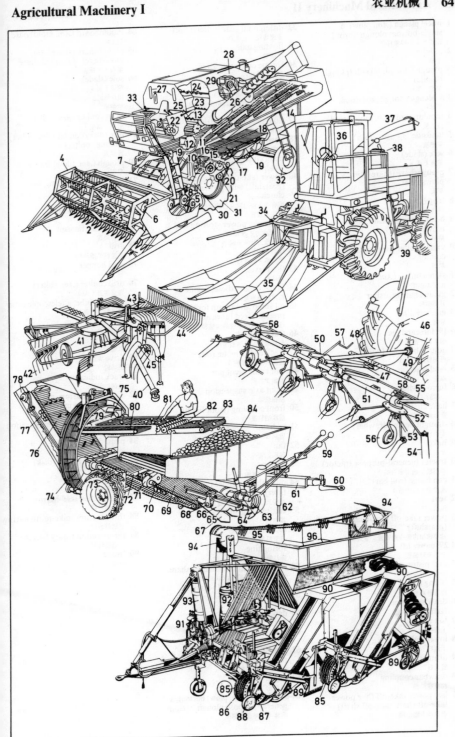

1 **wheel plough** (*Am.* plow), a
single-bottom plough [form.]
轮式犁，一种单杆犁

2 handle
手柄

3 plough (*Am.* plow) stilt (plough
handle)
犁把，犁柄

4-8 **plough** (*Am.* **plow**) **bottom**
犁体

4 mouldboard (*Am.* moldboard)
拨土板

5 landside
犁侧板

6 sole (slade)
犁底（板）

7 ploughshare (share, *Am.*
plowshare)
犁头

8 frog (frame)
犁托

9 beam (plough beam, *Am.*
plowbeam)
犁梁

10 knife coulter (*Am.* colter), a
coulter
犁刀

11 skim coulter (*Am.* colter)
前犁（副犁）

12 guide-chain crossbar
导链横杆

13 guide chain
导链

14-19 **forecarriage**
前车架，前轮架

14 adjustable yoke (yoke)
可调整轭（轭）

15 land wheel
地轮

16 furrow wheel
（犁的）沟轮

17 hake chain
牵引调节扳链

18 draught beam (drawbar)
牵引杆（拉杆）

19 hake
牵引调节板

20 **tractor** (general-purpose tractor)
牵引机（通用牵引机）

21 cab frame (roll bar)
座舱架（轧辊条）

22 seat
座位

23 power take-off gear-change
(gearshift)
功率输出轮变速装置（变速器）

24-29 **power lift**
动力升降装置

24 ram piston
动力油缸活塞

25 lifting rod adjustment
提升杆调整

26 drawbar frame
拉杆架

27 top link
上连杆

28 lower link
下连杆

29 lifting rod
提升杆

30 drawbar coupling
拉杆联结器

31 live power take-off (live power
take-off shaft, take-off shaft)
有效动力输出轴

32 differential gear (differential)
差速齿轮（差速器）

33 floating axle
浮动轴

34 torque converter lever
扭矩变速器杆

35 gear-change (gearshift)
齿轮变速器（齿轮换挡）

36 multi-speed transmission
多速变速箱

37 fluid clutch (fluid drive)
液体离合器（流体驱动）

38 power take-off gear
功率输出齿轮

39 main clutch
主离合器

40 power take-off gear-change
(gearshift) with power take-off
clutch
配有功率输出离合器的有效功率输出齿
轮变速装置

41 hydraulic power steering and
reversing gears
液压动力转向及回动

42 fuel tank
燃料箱，燃油箱

43 float lever
浮动杆

44 four-cylinder diesel engine
四汽缸柴油发动机

45 oil sump and pump for the
pressure-feed lubrication system
压力给油润滑系统的油池和油泵

46 fresh oil tank
新油箱，清洁油箱

47 track rod (*Am.* tie rod)
轮距杆（[美]系杆）

48 front axle pivot pin
前轴支轴销

49 front axle suspension
前轴悬架

50 front coupling (front hitch)
前联结装置

51 radiator
散热器，水箱（汽车）

52 fan
风扇

53 battery
电池组，电池

54 oil bath air cleaner (oil bath air
filter)
油浴式空气清洁器（滤清器）

55 **cultivator** (grubber)
耕耘机

56 sectional frame
分节架

57 spring tine
弹性锄齿，弹齿

58 share, a diamond-shaped share;
sim.: chisel-shaped share
锄铲，菱形锄齿；类似：凿形锄铲

59 depth wheel
限深轮

60 depth adjustment
深度调节器

61 coupling (hitch)
联结装置，联结器（系扣）

62 **reversible plough** (*Am.* plow), a
mounted plough
双向犁，翻转犁

63 depth wheel
限深轮

64-67 **plough** (*Am.* **plow**) **bottom**, a
general-purpose plough bottom
犁体，一种通用犁体

64 mouldboard (*Am.* moldboard)
拨土板

65 ploughshare (share, *Am.*
plowshare), a pointed share
犁头，一种尖犁头

66 sole (slade)
犁底（板）

67 landside
犁侧板

68 skim coulter (*Am.* colter)
前犁（副犁）

69 disc (disk) coulter (*Am.* colter)
(rolling coulter)
圆犁刀

70 plough (*Am.* plow) frame
犁架

71 beam (plough beam, *Am.*
plowbeam)
犁辕

72 three-point linkage
三点连结装置

73 swivel mechanism
旋转装置

74 **drill**
条播机，播种机

75 seed hopper
种子漏斗

76 drill coulter (*Am.* colter)
条播犁刀（头）

77 delivery tube, a telescopic tube
输送管，套筒伸缩管

78 feed mechanism
进给装置

79 gearbox
齿轮箱

80 drive wheel
驱动轮

81 track indicator
轮辙指示器

82 **disc** (**disk**) **harrow**, a
semimounted implement
圆盘耙片，一种半固定式农具

83 discs (disks) in X-configuration
X 形圆盘耙片组

84 plain disc (disk)
普通圆盘耙片

85 serrated-edge disc (disk)
锯齿缘圆盘耙片

86 quick hitch
快速系扣

87 **combination seed-harrow**
组合播种耙

88 three-section spike-tooth harrow
三组钉齿耙

89 three-section rotary harrow
三组旋转耙

90 frame
机架

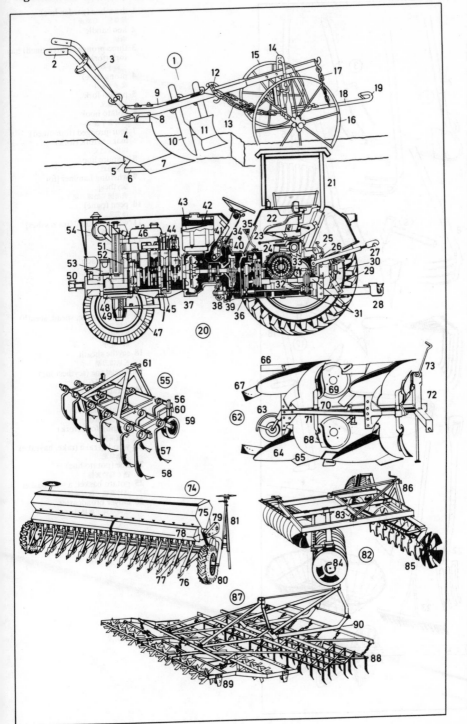

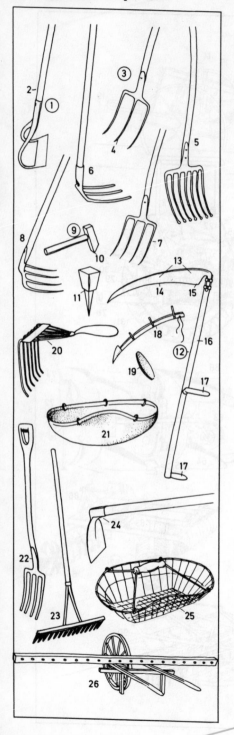

1 draw hoe (garden hoe)
　除草锄（园圃锄）
2 hoe handle
　锄柄
3 three-pronged (three-tined) hay
　fork (fork)
　三齿干草叉
4 prong (tine)
　叉子（齿）
5 potato fork
　马铃薯叉
6 potato hook
　马铃薯手掘叉
7 four-pronged (four-tined)
　manure fork (fork)
　四齿施肥叉
8 manure hoe
　施肥锄耙
9 whetting hammer [for
　scythes]
　磨削锤（磨镰刀用）
10 peen (pane)
　锤尖头
11 whetting anvil [for scythes]
　磨砺（铁）砧
12 scythe
　长柄镰刀
13 scythe blade
　长柄镰刀刀片
14 cutting edge
　切削刃
15 heel
　刀刃根部
16 snath (snathe, snead, sneath)
　大镰刀柄
17 handle
　柄，把手
18 scythe sheath
　长柄镰刀鞘
19 whetstone (scythestone)
　磨石（磨刀石）
20 potato rake
　马铃薯耙
21 potato planter
　马铃薯种植器
22 digging fork (fork)
　挖掘用叉
23 wooden rake (rake, hayrake)
　木制草耙
24 hoe (potato hoe)
　锄（马铃薯锄）
25 potato basket, a wire basket
　马铃薯篮，铁丝提篮
26 clover broadcaster
　三叶草种子撒播机

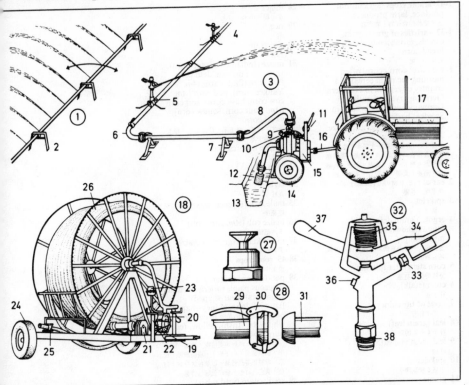

oscillating spray line
摆动式喷管

stand (steel chair)
支架（钢座）

portable irrigation system
可移动式灌溉系统

revolving sprinkler
旋转洒水器

standpipe coupler
立管联结器

elbow with cardan joint (cardan coupling)
带十字接头的肘管

pipe support (trestle)
水管支座（支架）

pump connection
水泵连接器（接头）

delivery valve
输送阀

pressure gauge (*Am.* gage) (manometer)
压力计，压力表（液体压力计）

centrifugal evacuating pump
离心式抽水泵

basket strainer
篮式（过）滤器

channel
水道，沟渠

chassis of the p.t.o.-driven pump (power take-off-driven pump)
功率输出驱动泵的底盘

p.t.o.-driven (power take-off-driven) pump
动力分导装置从动泵

16 cardan shaft
十字接头轴，万向接头轴

17 tractor
牵引机，曳引机

18 long-range irrigation unit
长距离灌溉设备

19 drive connection
驱动连接器

20 turbine
涡轮

21 gearing (gears)
（齿轮）传动装置

22 adjustable support
可调节支座

23 centrifugal evacuating pump
离心式抽水泵

24 wheel
轮

25 pipe support
水管支座

26 polyester pipe
聚酯管

27 sprinkler nozzle
洒水器喷咀

28 quick-fitting pipe connection with cardan joint
带十字接头的速装管连接器

29 M-cardan
M 型万向接头

30 clamp
钳，铁箍，夹子

31 V-cardan
V 型万向接头

32 revolving sprinkler, a field sprinkler
旋转洒水器，一种田地洒水器

33 nozzle
喷咀

34 breaker
打水板

35 breaker spring
打水板弹簧

36 stopper
塞子，阻塞器

37 counterweight
重量平衡器

38 thread
螺纹

1-47 arable crops (agricultural produce, farm produce)
适於耕种的农作物（农产品）

1-37 varieties of grain (grain, cereals, farinaceous plants, bread-corn)
谷类，谷物

1 rye (*also:* corn, 'corn' often meaning the main cereal of a country or region; in Northern Germany; rye; in Southern Germany and Italy: wheat; in Sweden: barley; in Scotland: oats; in North America; maize; in China: rice)
裸麦 [corn] 通常指一个国家和地区的主要粮食作物；德国北部：黑麦；德国南部和意大利：小麦；瑞典：大麦；苏格兰：燕麦；北美：玉蜀黍；中国：稻）

2 ear of rye, a spike (head)
裸麦穗，谷穗

3 spikelet
小穗

4 ergot, a grain deformed by fungus [shown with mycelium]
麦角病，一种由真菌（有菌丝体）引起的谷物病

5 corn stem after tillering
分蘖后的谷物茎

6 culm (stalk)
秆，蓬

7 node of the culm
（茎）秆节

8 leaf (grain leaf)
叶子（谷物的叶子）

9 leaf sheath (sheath)
叶鞘

10 spikelet
小穗（状花序）

11 glume
颖片

12 awn (beard, arista)
芒，谷刺（谷针，刺角芒）

13 seed (grain, kernel, farinaceous grain)
种子（颖果，含淀粉的子实）

14 embryo plant
胚芽植物

15 seed
种子

16 embryo
胚芽

17 root
根

18 root hair
根毛

19 grain leaf
谷叶

20 leaf blade (blade, lamina)
叶片（叶身）

21 leaf sheath
叶鞘

22 ligule (ligula)
叶舌，舌状片

23 wheat
小麦

24 spelt
小麦的一种

25 seed; *unripe:* green spelt, a soup vegetable
种子；未成熟的；青麦，一种汤用植物

26 barley
大麦

27 oat panicle, a panicle
燕麦圆锥花序

28 millet
黍，稷，小米

29 rice
稻

30 rice grain
稻谷

31 maize (Indian corn, *Am.* corn); *varieties:* popcorn, dent corn, flint corn (flint maize, *Am.* Yankee corn), pod corn (*Am.* cow corn, husk corn), soft corn (*Am.* flour corn, squaw corn), sweet corn
玉米；种类：爆玉米，马齿玉米，硬玉米，荚玉米，甜玉米

32 female inflorescence
雌花序

33 husk (shuck)
外壳（外皮）

34 style
花柱

35 male inflorescence (tassel)
雄花序

36 maize cob (*Am.* corn cob)
玉米穗轴

37 maize kernel (grain of maize)
玉米粒（仁）

38-45 root crops
根菜作物

38 potato plant (potato), a tuberous plant; *varieties:* round, roundoval (pear-shaped), flat-oval, long, kidney-shaped potato; *according to colour:* white (*Am.* Irish), yellow, red, purple potato
马铃薯植物，一种块茎植物；种类：圆形，圆椭圆形（梨子形），扁椭圆形，长形，肾脏形马铃薯；以颜色区分有：白色，黄色，红色，紫红色等马铃薯

39 seed potato (seed tuber)
马铃薯种（种块）

40 potato tuber (potato, tuber)
马铃薯块茎

41 potato top (potato haulm)
马铃薯叶

42 flower
马铃薯花

43 poisonous potato berry (potato apple)
有毒的马铃薯浆果

44 sugar beet, a beet
甜菜

45 root (beet)
甜菜根

46 beet top
甜菜顶部

47 beet leaf
甜菜叶

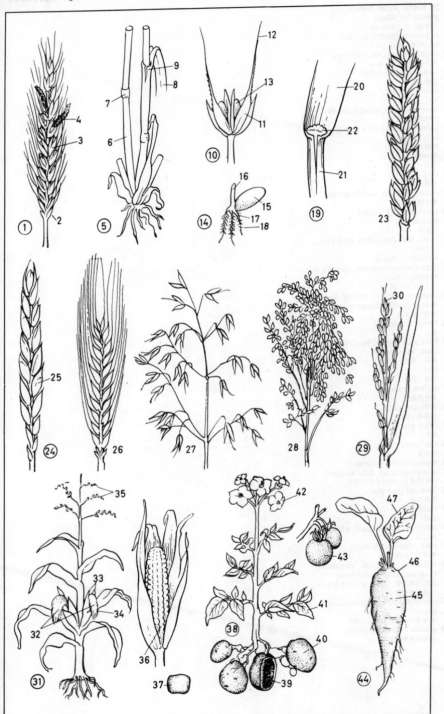

1-28 fodder plants (forage plants) for tillage
（耕地上的）饲料植物

1 red clover (purple clover)
红三叶草（紫红三叶草）

2 white clover (Dutch clover)
白三叶草（荷兰三叶草）

3 alsike clover (alsike)
杂种三叶草

4 crimson clover
深红三叶草

5 four-leaf (four-leaved) clover
四叶苜蓿草

6 kidney vetch (lady's finger, ladyfinger)
野腰子豆

7 flower
花

8 pod
荚蒴，荚果

9 lucerne (lucern, purple medick)
紫苜蓿

10 sainfoin (cock's head, cockshead)
红豆草

11 bird's foot (bird-foot, bird's foot trefoil)
叶或花像鸟足的植物

12 corn spurrey (spurrey, spurry), a spurrey (spurry)
大爪草（石竹科）

13 common comfrey, one of the borage family (Boraginaceae)
雏菊（紫草科）

14 flower (blossom)
花

15 field bean (broad bean, tick bean, horse bean)
蚕豆，扁豆，马豆

16 pod
荚蒴，荚果

17 yellow lupin
黄色羽扇豆

18 common vetch
大巢菜，野豌豆

19 chick-pea
鹰咀豆，小藜豆

20 sunflower
向日葵

21 mangold (mangelwurzel, mangoldwurzel, field mangel)
饲料甜菜（一种饲牛用的甜菜）

22 false oat (oat-grass)
假燕麦草

23 spikelet
小穗

24 meadow fescure grass, a fescue
田边草

25 cock's foot (cocksfoot)
鸭茅草，鸡脚草

26 Italian ryegrass; *sim.:* perennial ryegrass (English ryegrass)
意大利黑麦草；类似：多年生黑麦草（英国黑麦草）

27 meadow foxtail, a paniculate grass
狐尾草，一种有圆锥花序的草

28 greater burnet saxifrage
较大的地榆虎耳草

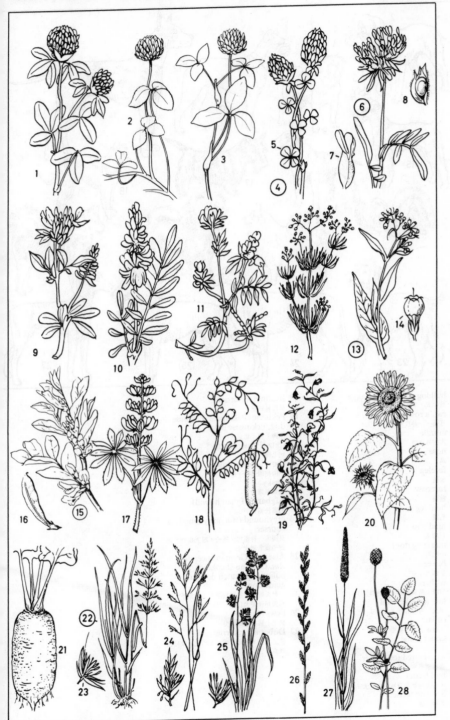

1 bulldog
戏牛犬，牛头犬
2 ear, a rose-ear
耳朵，一种玫瑰耳
3 muzzle
狗的鼻和咀
4 nose
鼻
5 foreleg
前腿
6 forepaw
前脚爪
7 hind leg
后腿
8 hind paw
后脚爪
9 pug (pug dog)
哈巴狗
10 boxer
拳师犬
11 withers
肩隆（两肩骨间隆起的部分）
12 tail, a docked tail
尾巴（剪短的尾）
13 collar
（狗颈上的）项圈
14 Great Dane
大丹狗，丹麦狗
15 wire-haired fox terrier
猎狐刚毛狗（㹴）
16 bull terrier
牛头犬与㹴杂交所生之犬
17 Scottish terrier
苏格兰㹴

18 Bedlington terrier
贝德林顿㹴
19 Pekinese (Pekingese, Pekinese
dog, Pekingese dog)
小狮子狗，北京狗
20 spitz (Pomeranian)
丝毛狗
21 chow (chow-chow)
中国狗的一种，松狮狗
22 husky
爱斯基摩犬
23 Afghan (Afghan hound)
阿富汗猎狗
24 greyhound (*Am.* grayhound), a
courser
灵提（一种躯瘦，腿长，眼光锐利，奔
跑迅速的猎犬）
25 Alsatian (German sheepdog,
Am. German shepherd), a
police dog, watch dog, and
guide dog
一种大狼狗（德国牧羊犬），常予以训
练使担任警犬任务
26 flews (chaps)
猎犬上唇松垂的部分
27 Dobermann terrier
㹴之一种（毛短而润，呈暗色，带棕色
斑点）

43 pointer, a trackhound
短毛大猎犬，一种追踪猎犬

dog brush
狗刷子
dog comb
狗梳子
lead (dog lead, leash); *for hunting:* leash
牵狗的绳或皮带；尤指：拴猎犬的皮带
muzzle
口套，口络
feeding bowl (dog bowl)
狗食钵（碗）
bone
骨头
Newfoundland dog
纽芬兰狗
schnauzer
德国种刚毛梗犬
poodle; *sim. and smaller:* pygmy (pigmy) poodle
贵宾狗；类似且较小的：皮格米种贵宾狗
St. Bernard (St. Bernard dog)
圣伯尔纳犬，雪山救人犬
cocker spaniel
西班牙长耳狗，一种长毛垂耳之犬
dachshund, a terrier
德国种腊肠狗（一种短腿小狗）
German pointer
德国短毛大猎犬
English setter
英国塞特种猎狗，一种长毛猎狗
trackhound
追踪猎犬

1-6 equitation (high school riding, haute école)
骑术，马术（骑马特技，高超的骑术）
1 piaffe
比快步稍慢的步伐
2 walk
慢步行
3 passage
斜行
4 levade (pesade)
马后腿直立前腿上提向后收缩的一种姿势
5 capriole
腾跃
6 courbette (curvet)
腾跃（先举前二蹄，在未着地时举两蹄）
7-25 harness
马具
7-13 bridle
马勒，辔辔
7-11 headstall (headpiece, halter)
络头
7 noseband
鼻羁
8 cheek piece (cheek strap)
颊带（面颊带）
9 browband (front band)
额带（前额带）
10 crownpiece
马两颊之辔绳
11 throatlatch (throatlash)
（马喉下之）辔带
12 curb chain
马衔链，马勒链
13 curb bit
马嚼铁，马衔铁
14 hasp (hook) of the hame (Am. drag hook)
马颈轭搭釦（[美]马颈轭上的牵引钩）
15 pointed collar, a collar
有尖角的马轭
16 trappings (side trappings)
马饰
17 saddle-pad
马鞍褥
18 girth
肚带，系带
19 backband
背带
20 shaft chain (pole chain)
辕杆链
21 pole
辕杆
22 trace
马车之挽辔，挽绳
23 second girth (emergency girth)
辅助肚带（应急肚带）
24 trace
挽辔，挽绳
25 reins (Am. lines)
辔绳
26-36 breast harness
护马具
26 blinker (Am. blinder, winker)
（马的）眼罩
27 breast collar ring
胸轭环
28 breast collar (Dutch collar)
胸轭（荷兰式轭）
29 fork
叉皮，叉形带
30 neck strap
马颈皮带
31 saddle-pad
马鞍褥

32 loin strap
马腰带
33 reins (rein, Am. line)
辔绳
34 crupper (crupper-strap)
兜过马尾下之皮带；马尾鞧
35 trace
挽辔
36 girth (belly-band)
马肚带（马的腹带）
37-49 saddles
马鞍
37-44 stock saddle (Am. western saddle)
放牧马鞍（[美]西部式马鞍）
37 saddle seat
鞍座
38 pommel horn (horn)
鞍头（鞍最前端向上突起的部分）
39 cantle
鞍后的弓形部
40 flap (Am. fender)
鞍的护垫
41 bar
木条（鞍架的一部分）
42 stirrup leather
马镫皮带
43 stirrup (stirrup iron)
马镫（马镫铁）
44 blanket
马鞍毯
45-49 English saddle (cavalry saddle)
英国式马鞍（骑兵马鞍）
45 seat
鞍座
46 cantle
马鞍后之弓形部
47 flap
鞍的护垫
48 roll (knee roll)
鞍卷（膝卷）
49 pad
鞍鞧
50-51 spurs
踢马刺，靴刺
50 box spur (screwed jack spur)
环形靴刺
51 strapped jack spur
用带搭扣螺旋顶靴刺
52 curb bit
马嚼铁，马衔铁
53 gag bit (gag)
箝口具
54 currycomb
马梳
55 horse brush (body brush, dandy brush)
马刷（马体刷，刷马之硬毛刷）

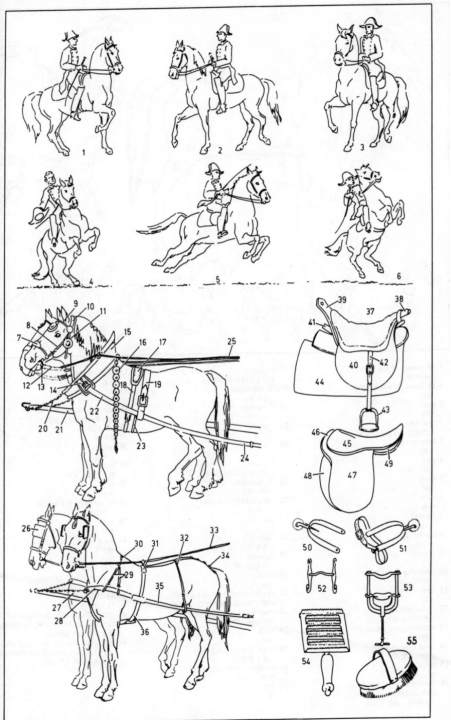

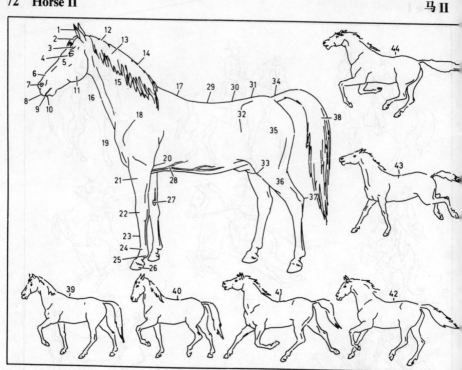

1-38 points of the horse
马的各部分

1-11 head (horse's head)
马头

1 ear
马耳（朵）

2 forelock
马的额毛，马额上的长毛

3 forehead
马额

4 eye
马眼（睛）

5 face
马脸

6 nose
马鼻子

7 nostril
（马）鼻孔

8 upper lip
上咀唇

9 mouth
马咀

10 underlip (lower lip)
下咀唇

11 lower jaw
下颚

12 crest (neck)
马颈脊（头颈）

13 mane (horse's mane)
马的鬃毛

14 crest (horse's crest)
颈脊（马的颈脊）

15 neck
颈

16 throat (*Am.* throatlatch,
throatlash)
马的咽喉，喉头，颈前

17 withers
鬐甲（马两肩骨间的隆起部分）

18-27 forehand
马身的前部

18 shoulder
马的肩胛

19 breast
胸（脯）

20 elbow
肘

21 forearm
前臂（肘至腕间的部分）

22-26 forefoot
前脚，前足

22 knee (carpus, wrist)
膝（腕）

23 cannon
马胫骨

24 fetlock
（生距毛的）肢关节

25 pastern
（马足的）胫

26 hoof
马蹄

27 chestnut (castor), a callosity
蹃蝉，马前腿内部的胼胝，胼胝体

28 spur vein
靴刺静脉

29 back
马背

30 loins (lumbar region)
马腰（腰部）

31 croup (rump, crupper)
臀部（马屁股）

32 hip
髋

33-37 hind leg
后腿

33 stifle (stifle joint)
后膝关节

34 root (dock) of the tail
马尾骨肉部分（不包括尾上的毛）

35 haunch
腰臀部

36 gaskin
下大腿

37 hock
飞，后膝，飞节

38 tail
尾巴

39-44 gaits of the horse
马的步法

39 walk
慢步

40 pace
侧步伐

41 trot
小跑，快步

42 canter (hand gallop)
慢步小跑

43-44 full gallop
马飞奔步法

43 full gallop at the moment of
descent on to the two forefeet
前足下落时的飞奔步法

44 full gallop at the moment when
all four feet are off the ground
四足离地时的飞奔步法

1 cattle
家畜；牲口
cow, a ruminant; *m.* bull; *c.* ox;
f. cow; *y.* calf
母牛，反刍动物；公牛；阉牛；母牛；
小牛
2 horse; *m.* stallion; *c.* gelding; *f.*
mare; *y.* foal
马；未阉的雄马；阉割过的马；母马；
小马（驹）
3 donkey
驴子
4 pack saddle (carrying saddle)
驮鞍（荷鞍）
5 pack (load)
驮载物
6 tufted tail
丛毛尾巴
7 tuft
丛毛
8 mule, a cross between a male
donkey and a mare
骡（子），公驴与母马杂交的混合种
9 pig, a cloven-hoofed animal; *m.*
boar; *f.* sow; *y.* piglet
猪，一种偶蹄家畜；公猪；母猪；小猪
（猪仔）
10 pig's snout (snout)
猪咀（猪的口鼻部）
11 pig's ear
猪耳朵
12 curly tail
卷曲的尾巴
13 sheep; *m.* ram; *c.* wether; *f.* ewe;
y. lamb
羊；绵羊；公羊；阉羊；母羊；小羊
（羔羊）

14 goat
山羊
15 goat's beard
山羊胡须
16 dog, a Leonberger; *m.* dog; *f.*
bitch; *y.* pup (puppy, whelp)
狗，一种利奥贝尔格狗；雄狗；母狗；
小狗（幼犬）
17 cat, an Angora cat (Persian cat);
m. tom (tom cat)
猫，一种安哥拉猫（波斯猫）；雄猫
18-36 small domestic animals
小家畜
18 rabbit; *m.* buck; *f.* doe
兔子；雄兔；雌兔
19-36 poultry (domestic fowl)
家禽
19-26 chicken
鸡
19 hen
母鸡
20 crop (craw)
嗉囊（鸡胃）
21 cock (*Am.* rooster); *c.* capon
公鸡（雄鸡）；阉鸡
22 cockscomb (comb, crest)
鸡冠（雄鸡冠）
23 lap
耳垂（鸡耳朵）
24 wattle (gill, dewlap)
（鸡）肉垂（鸡颈下的垂肉，喉部的垂
肉）
25 falcate (falcated) tail
镰形公鸡尾巴
26 spur
雄鸡肉距

27 guinea fowl
珠鸡
28 turkey; *m.* turkey cock
(gobbler); *f.* turkey hen
火鸡；公火鸡；雌火鸡
29 fan tail
扇形尾（巴）
30 peacock
孔雀
31 peacock's feather
孔雀的羽毛
32 eye (ocellus)
孔雀翎斑（眼状斑）
33 pigeon; *m.* cock pigeon
鸽子；雄鸽子
34 goose; *m.* gander; *y.* gosling
鹅；雄鹅；小鹅（幼鹅）
35 duck; *m.* drake; *y.* duckling
鸭；公鸭；小鸭
**36 web (palmations) of webbed
foot (palmate foot)**
鸭脚蹼（蹼足）

1-27 poultry farming (intensive poultry management)
养鸡场（集约家禽管理）

1-17 straw yard (strawed yard) system
草盖鸡场系统

1 fold unit for growing stock (chick unit)
移动式养鸡遮棚（小鸡棚）

2 chick
小鸡

3 brooder (hover)
孵卵器，伞状育雏器

4 adjustable feeding trough
可调整饲槽

5 pullet fold unit
小母鸡棚

6 drinking trough
饮水槽

7 water pipe
水管

8 litter
垫草，垫褥

9 pullet
小母鸡

10 ventilator
通风设备

11-17 broiler rearing (rearing of broiler chickens)
肉鸡的饲育

11 chicken run (Am. fowl run)
鸡房

12 broiler chicken (broiler)
肉鸡

13 mechanical feeder (self-feeder, feed dispenser)
自动饲器器（饲料分送器）

14 chain
链条

15 feed supply pipe
饲料供给管

16 mechanical drinking bowl (mechanical drinker)
自动饮水钵

17 ventilator
通风设备

18 battery system (cage system)
层架式鸡笼系统

19 battery (laying battery)
育雏笼

20 tiered cage (battery cage, stepped cage)
层架式鸡笼

21 feeding trough
饲槽

22 egg collection by conveyor
以输送器集蛋

23-27 mechanical feeding and dunging (manure removal, droppings removal)
自动饲料和排粪

23 rapid feeding system for battery feeding (mechanical feeder)
层架式鸡笼快速饲养（自动饲器器）

24 feed hopper
漏斗饲槽

25 endless-chain conveyor (chain feeder)
无端链运机（链式饲器器）

26 water pipe (liquid feed pipe)
水管（液状饲料管）

27 dunging chain (dunging conveyor)
排粪链（粪便输送器）

28 [cabinet type] setting and hatching machine
〔橱式〕调节孵蛋机

29 ventilation drum [for the setting compartment]
〔调节室的〕通风滚筒

30 hatching compartment (hatcher)
孵化室（孵化器）

31 metal trolley for hatching trays
孵化盘金属手推车

32 hatching tray
孵化盘

33 ventilation drum motor
通风滚筒马达

34-53 egg production
鸡蛋生产

34 egg collection system (egg collection)
集蛋系统（集蛋）

35 multi-tier transport
多层运输装置

36 collection by pivoted fingers
有轴指耙收集器

37 drive motor
驱动马达

38 sorting machine
分类机，选别机

39 conveyor trolley
输送小车

40 fluorescent screen
萤光幕，萤光屏

41 suction apparatus (suction box) for transporting eggs
运输蛋的吸入装置（吸入箱）

42 shelf for empty and full egg boxes
空箱或装蛋箱架

43 egg weighers
蛋秤

44 grading
分级（产品）

45 egg box
蛋箱

46 fully automatic egg-packing machine
全自动鸡蛋包装机

47 radioscope box
放射线照射装置

48 radioscope table
放射线照射台

49-51 feeder
饲料器

49 suction transporter
吸入运输装置

50 vacuum line
真空管路

51 supply table
供应台

52 automatic counting and grading
自动计数和分级

53 packing box dispenser
包装箱分配器

54 leg ring
足轮，脚环

55 wing tally (identification tally)
翼形计数签（识别标志）

56 bantam
矮脚鸡

57 laying hen
生蛋鸡

58 hen's egg (egg)
鸡蛋

59 eggshell, an egg integument
蛋壳，鸡蛋外壳

60 shell membrane
壳膜

61 air space
气室

62 white [of the egg] (albumen)
蛋白

63 chalaza (*Am.* treadle)
卵带

64 vitelline membrane (yolk sac)
卵黄膜（蛋黄囊）

65 blastodisc (germinal disc, cock tread, cock's treadle)
胚盘（鸡胎）

66 germinal vesicle
胚囊，卵核包

67 white
蛋白

68 yolk
蛋黄

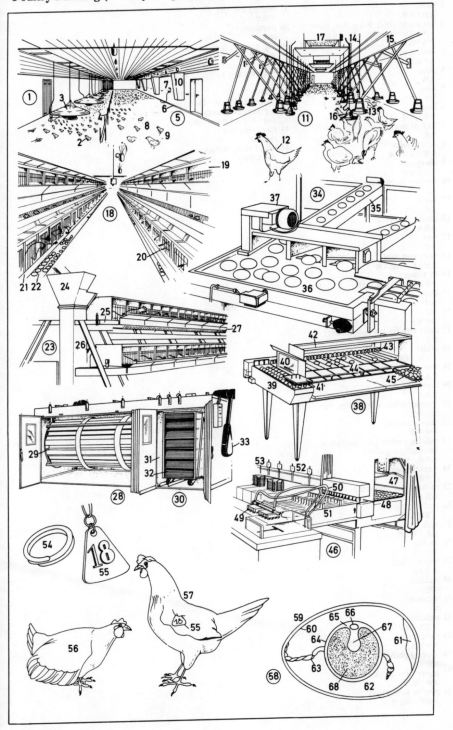

1 **stable**
畜底（马底）

2 **horse stall (stall, horse box, box)**
马底（畜舍内的分隔栏，马栏，马底中
供马活动部分）

3 **feeding passage**
饲养通道

4 **pony**
小马

5 **bars**
栏杆，栅栏

6 **litter**
垫草，垫捣

7 **bale of straw**
草捆

8 **ceiling light**
天窗，天花板窗

9 **sheep pen**
羊栏，羊圈

10 **mother sheep (ewe)**
母羊

11 **lamb**
羔羊，小羊

12 **double hay rack**
双棚条式乾草架

13 **hay**
干草

14 **dairy cow shed**
要把牛拴住的乳牛棚

15-16 **tether**
（拴牲畜用的）系链，系绳

15 **chain**
系链

16 **rail**
围栏横木

17 **dairy cow (milch-cow, milker)**
乳牛

18 **udder**
（牛的）乳房

19 **teat**
乳头，奶头

20 **manure gutter**
粪便沟

21 **manure removal by sliding bars**
滑板排肥

22 **short standing**
简便牛舍

23 **milking parlour (*Am.* parlor), a herringbone parlour**
挤乳间，鱼刺形挤乳

24 **working passage**
工作通道

25 **milker (*Am.* milkman)**
挤乳人

26 **teat cup cluster**
全套挤乳杯

27 **milk pipe**
挤乳（导）管

28 **air line**
空气管线

29 **vacuum line**
真空管路

30 **teat cup**
挤乳杯

31 **window**
窗

32 **pulsator**
脉动泵，真空泵

33 **release phase**
放乳节拍

34 **squeeze phase**
挤压节拍

35 **pigsty (*Am.* pigpen, hogpen)**
猪圈，猪舍

36 **pen for young pigs**
小猪栏，猪仔圈

37 **feeding trough**
饲养槽

38 **partition**
隔板

39 **pig, a young pig**
猪，小猪，乳猪

40 **farrowing and store pen**
分娩围栏（猪栏）

41 **sow**
母猪

42 **piglet (*Am.* shoat, shote) (sow pig [for first 8 weeks])**
小猪（产下八星期后的小猪）

43 **farrowing rails**
分娩护架

44 **liquid manure channel**
液体粪便沟

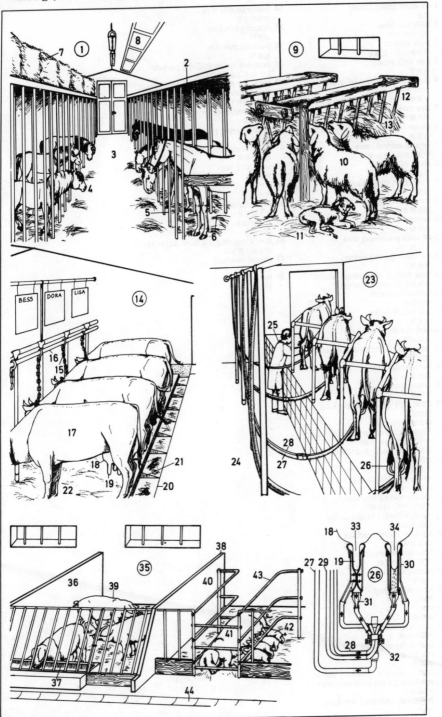

1-48 dairy (dairy plant)
乳品厂

1 milk reception
乳品接收设备

2 milk tanker
乳品搬运车；乳罐车

3 raw milk pump
生乳泵

4 flowmeter, an oval (elliptical) gear meter
流量表（计），一种椭圆形齿轮计量器

5 raw milk storage tank
生乳储存槽

6 gauge (*Am.* gage)
计量表

7 central control room
中央控制室，主控制室

8 chart of the dairy
乳品厂图表

9 flow chart (flow diagram)
流程图

10 storage tank gauges (*Am.* gages)
储存槽表计

11 control panel
控制板

12-48 milk processing area
牛乳加工区

12 sterilizer (homogenizer)
灭菌器

13 milk heater; *sim.*; cream heater
牛乳加热器，类似；乳油加热器

14 cream separator
油分离机

15 fresh milk tanks
鲜乳槽

16 tank for sterilized milk
灭菌乳槽

17 skim milk (skimmed milk) tank
脱脂乳槽

18 buttermilk tank
酪乳槽

19 cream tank
乳油槽

20 fresh milk filling and packing plant
鲜乳装瓶和包装设备

21 filling machine for milk cartons; *sim.*: milk tub filler
乳瓶装箱机，类似；乳盒装箱机

22 milk carton
牛乳纸箱

23 conveyor belt (conveyor)
运送带（输送器）

24 shrink-sealing machine
收缩封口机，缩封机

25 pack of twelve in shrink foil
12 瓶缩箔包装

26 ten-litre filling machine
10 公升填装机

27 heat-sealing machine
热封口机，热封机

28 plastic sheets
塑胶片

29 heat-sealed bag
热封袋

30 crate
条板箱

31 cream maturing vat
奶油熟化桶

32 butter shaping and packing machine
奶油成形包装机

33 butter churn, a creamery butter machine for continuous butter making
牛油搅动机，连续提炼牛油的乳脂机

34 butter supply pipe
牛油供给管

35 shaping machine
成形机

36 packing machine
包装机

37 branded butter in 250 g packets
250 公克包装标示的奶油

38 plant for producing curd cheese (curd cheese machine)
制凝乳酪机（凝乳酪机）

39 curd cheese pump
凝乳酪泵

40 cream supply pump
奶油供应泵

41 curds separator
凝乳分离机

42 sour milk vat
酸乳桶

43 stirrer
搅拌器

44 curd cheese packing machine
凝乳酪包装机

45 packeted curd cheese
凝乳酪包

46 bottle-capping machine (capper)
封盖机，瓶盖机

47 cheese machine
乾酪机

48 rennet vat
制凝乳

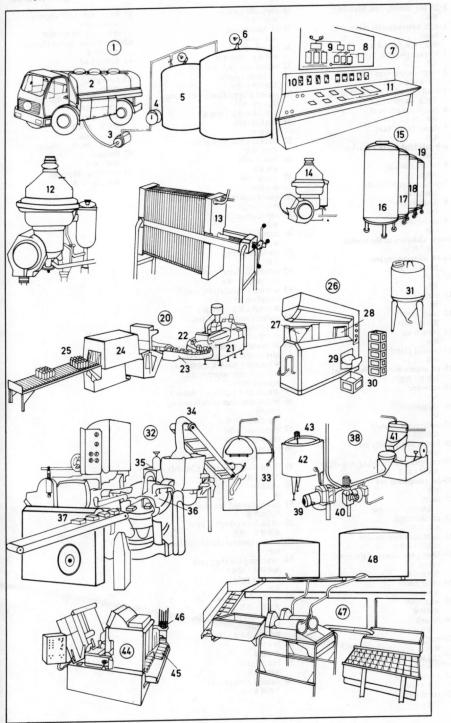

1-25 bee (honey-bee, hive-bee)
蜜蜂

1, 4, 5 castes (social classes) of bees
蜂级（蜜蜂之社会等级）

1 worker (worker bee)
工蜂

2 three simple eyes (ocelli)
三只单眼睛（单眼）

3 load of pollen on the hind leg
采粉足（蜜蜂的后足）

4 queen (queen bee)
雌蜂（蜂王）

5 drone (male bee)
雄蜂

6-9 left hind leg of a worker
工蜂的左后足

6 pollen basket
花粉篮

7 pollen comb (brush)
花粉梳（刷）

8 double claw
双爪

9 suctorial pad
吸盘

10-19 abdomen of the worker
工蜂的腹部

10-14 stinging organs
螫针器官，刺器官

10 barb
倒刺

11 sting
螫针，针

12 sting sheath
螫针鞘，刺鞘

13 poison sac
毒囊

14 poison gland
毒腺

15-19 stomachic-intestinal canal
肠胃管，胃肠管

15 intestine
肠

16 stomach
胃

17 contractile muscle
收缩肌肉

18 honey bag (honey sac)
蜜囊

19 oesophagus (esophagus, gullet)
食物道（食道，食管）

20-24 compound eye
复眼

20 facet
（复眼中的一个）小眼

21 crystal cone
水晶体

22 light-sensitive section
感光区，光敏区

23 fibre (*Am.* fiber) of the optic nerve
视神经纤维

24 optic nerve
视神经

25 wax scale
蜜蜡蜡鳞

26-30 cell
（蜂房的）巢室

26 egg
蜂卵

27 cell with the egg in it
有卵的巢室

28 young larva
幼体，幼虫

29 larva (grub)
幼虫

30 chrysalis (pupa)
蜂蛹（蛹）

31-43 honeycomb
蜂房，蜂巢

31 brood cell
孵卵巢室，育幼巢室

32 sealed (capped) cell with chrysalis (pupa)
有蛹的密封巢室

33 sealed (capped) cell with honey (honey cell)
有蜜的密封巢室（蜂蜜室）

34 worker cells
工蜂巢室

35 storage cells, with pollen
花粉贮存室

36 drone cells
雄蜂巢室

37 queen cell
蜂王巢室

38 queen emerging from her cell
蜂王出巢（房）

39 cap (capping)
蜂罩

40 frame
蜂巢架

41 distance piece
定距片

42 [artificial] honeycomb
[人工]蜜蜂窝，蜂巢

43 septum (foundation, comb foundation)
蜂窝隔膜（巢基，蜂巢基）

44 queen's travelling (*Am.* traveling) box
蜂王移动箱

45-50 beehive, a movable-frame hive (movable-comb hive)
框架式蜂窝（移动框架式蜂窝）

45 super (honey super) with honeycombs
带蜂窝的蜂房上层活动架（蜂房架）

46 brood chamber with breeding combs
带繁殖蜂窝的育蜂室

47 queen-excluder
蜂王隔板，隔王板

48 entrance
入口，巢门

49 flight board (alighting board)
著陆板（降落板），前板

50 window
窗

51 old-fashioned bee shed
旧式的蜂棚

52 straw hive (skep), a hive
稻草蜂巢，蜂巢

53 swarm (swarm cluster) of bees
蜂群

54 swarming net (bag net)
捕蜂群网（袋网）

55 hooked pole
钩杆

56 apiary (bee house)
养蜂场（养蜂房）

57 beekeeper (apiarist, *Am.* beeman)
养蜂家（养蜂者，[美]养蜂人）

58 bee veil
养蜂面罩

59 bee smoker
蜜蜂熏烟器

60 natural honeycomb
天然蜂巢（窝）

61 honey extractor (honey separator)
蜂蜜抽出器（蜂蜜分离器）

62-63 strained honey (honey)
滤过的蜂蜜

62 honey pail
蜂蜜桶

63 honey jar
蜂蜜瓶

64 honey in the comb
在蜂窝中的蜂蜜

65 wax taper
蜜蜡蕊，蜂蜡蕊

66 wax candle
蜜蜡烛，蜂蜡烛

67 beeswax
蜜蜡，蜂蜡

68 bee sting ointment
蜂刺（螫）软膏

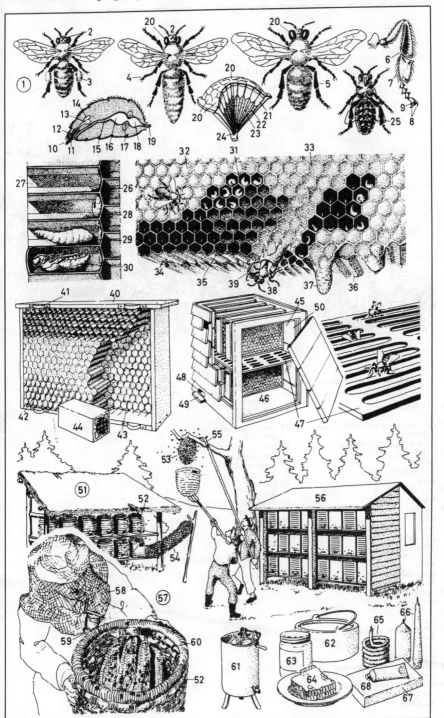

1-21 vineyard area
葡萄园

1 vineyard using wire trellises for training vines
用金属格子架栽培葡萄的葡萄园

2-9 vine (*Am.* grapevine)
葡萄藤

2 vine shoot
葡萄蔓

3 long shoot
长蔓

4 vine leaf
葡萄叶

5 bunch of grapes (cluster of grapes)
一串葡萄

6 vine stem
葡萄茎

7 post (stake)
柱，支柱

8 guy (guy wire)
牵线，牵索

9 wire trellis
金属格子架

10 tub for grape gathering
葡萄采集桶

11 grape gatherer
葡萄采集（者）人

12 secateurs for pruning vines
修剪葡萄用的大剪刀

13 wine grower (viniculturist, viticulturist)
葡萄栽培者

14 dosser carrier
背负葡萄筐的搬运夫

15 dosser (pannier)
背筐，箩筐

16 crushed grape transporter
搾葡萄的运输机

17 grape crusher
葡萄压搾器

18 hopper
漏斗

19 three-sided flap extension
三面板加长部分

20 platform
装卸台，平台

21 vineyard tractor, a narrow-track tractor
葡萄园曳引机，一种窄轨距曳引机

-22 wine cellar (wine vault)
葡萄酒窖（酒窖）
vault
拱形圆屋顶，地窖
wine cask
葡萄酒桶
wine vat, a concrete vat
（供酿造、发酵用的）大桶
stainless steel vat (*also:* vat made
of synthetic material)
不锈钢桶（另有：合成材料制作的大
桶）
propeller-type high-speed mixer
螺旋桨式高速混合机
propeller mixer
螺旋桨式混合机
centrifugal pump
离心泵
stainless steel sediment filter
不锈钢沉积物过滤器
semi-automatic circular bottling
machine
半自动圆形制瓶机
semi-automatic corking machine
半自动制（软木）塞机
bottle rack
酒瓶架
cellarer's assistant
管理酒窖的店员（伙计）
bottle basket
酒瓶篮
wine bottle
葡萄酒瓶

15 **wine jug**
酒壶
16 **wine tasting**
品嚐葡萄酒
17 **head cellarman**
酒窖经理
18 **cellarman**
酒窖店员（酒窖管理员）
19 **wineglass**
酒杯
20 **inspection apparatus** [for
spotchecking samples]
检验器[抽样检验]
21 **horizontal wine press**
水平式葡萄酒压榨机
22 **humidifier**
潮化机，增湿器

1-19　fruit pests
水果害虫，果虫

1 gipsy (gypsy) moth
柿毛虫

2 batch (cluster) of eggs
卵块，一团卵

3 caterpillar
幼虫，毛虫

4 chrysalis (pupa)
蛹

5 small ermine moth, an ermine moth
巢蛾属巢蛾科

6 larva (grub)
幼虫

7 tent
巢网

8 caterpillar skeletonizing a leaf
把树叶吃剩了叶脉的毛虫

9 fruit surface eating tortrix moth (summer fruit tortrix moth)
食心虫，属小卷叶蛾科

10 appleblossom weevil, a weevil
苹果花象鼻虫

11 punctured, withered flower (blossom)
刺穿和凋谢了的花

12 hole for laying eggs
产卵洞，产卵孔

13 lackey moth
苹果蠹蛾

14 caterpillar
幼虫，毛虫

15 eggs
虫卵

16 winter moth, a geometrid
柿星尺蠖，属尺蠖科

17 caterpillar
幼虫，毛虫

18 cherry fruit fly, a borer
樱桃苍蝇

19 larva (grub, maggot)
幼虫，蛆

20-27　vine pests
葡萄害虫

20 downy mildew, a mildew, a disease causing leaf drop
茸毛霉，霉病，圆星性落叶病

21 grape affected with downy mildew
感染霉病的葡萄

22 grape-berry moth
葡萄锈壁虱，茸毛病虱

23 first-generation larva of the grape-berry moth (*Am.* grape worm)
葡萄锈壁虱第一代幼虫（葡萄虫）

24 second-generation larva of the grape-berry moth (*Am.* grape worm)
葡萄锈壁虱第二代幼虫（葡萄虫）

25 chrysalis (pupa)
虫蛹（蛹）

26 root louse, a grape phylloxera
葡萄根蚜虫

27 root gall (knotty swelling of the root, nodosity, tuberosity)
根部虫瘿（树根上的结节）

28 brown-tail moth
枣剌虫

29 caterpillar
幼虫，毛虫

30 batch (cluster) of eggs
卵块

31 hibernation cocoon
越冬茧，冬眠茧

32 woolly apple aphid (American blight), an aphid
苹果毛蚜虫，一种蚜虫

33 gall caused by the woolly apple aphid
由毛蚜虫产生的虫瘿

34 woolly apple aphid colony
苹果毛蚜虫群体

35 San-José scale, a scale insect (scale louse)
圣约瑟虫，一种介壳虫

36 larvae (grubs) [*male* elongated, *female* round]
幼虫[长形雄幼虫，圆形雌幼虫]

37-55　field pests
田间害虫

37 click beetle, a snapping beetle (*Am.* snapping bug)
磕头虫

38 wireworm, larva of the click beetle
铁线虫，磕头虫的幼虫

39 flea beetle
跳甲虫，跳蚤

40 Hessian fly, a gall midge (gall gnat)
麦蝇（似蚊，属瘿虫科）

41 larva (grub)
幼虫，蛆

42 turnip moth, an earth moth
芜菁蛾，土蛾

43 chrysalis (pupa)
蛹

44 cutworm, a caterpillar
糖蛾之幼虫，毛虫

45 beet carrion beetle
食腐烂甜菜的甲虫

46 larva (grub)
幼虫（蛴螬）

47 large cabbage white butterfly
菜粉蝶，菜白蝶，白蝴蝶，白粉蝶

48 caterpillar of the small cabbage white butterfly
（菜粉蝶的幼虫为）青虫，菜虫

49 brown leaf-eating weevil, a weevil
稻象鼻虫

50 feeding site
吃去的部分，被食部分

51 sugar beet eelworm, a nematode (a threadworm, hairworm)
甜菜线虫，线虫类动物

52 Colorado beetle (potato beetle)
科罗拉多甲虫，薯虫

53 mature larva (grub)
成熟的幼虫（蛴螬）

54 young larva (grub)
幼虫（蛴螬）

55 eggs
虫卵

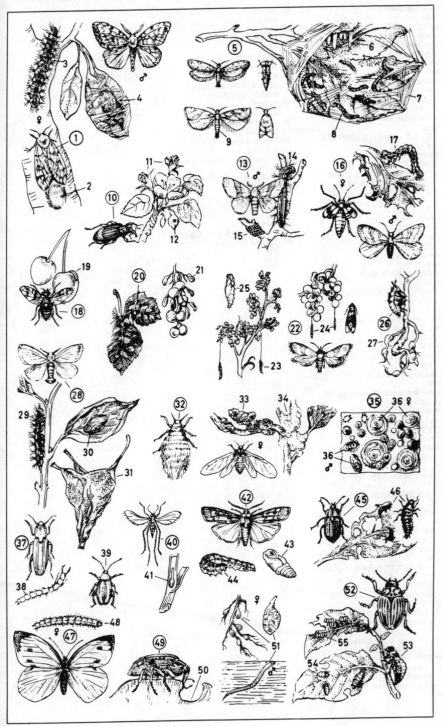

1-14 house insects
家虫

1 lesser housefly
小家蝇

2 common housefly
普通家蝇

3 chrysalis (pupa, coarctate pupa)
蛹

4 stable fly (biting housefly)
厩蝇（叮人的家蝇）

5 trichotomous antenna
三歧触须

6 wood louse (slater, *Am.* sow bug)
土鳖，地鳖（一种小甲虫，居於朽木及湿地）

7 house cricket
家庭蟋蟀

8 wing with stridulating apparatus (stridulating mechanism)
带有鸣叫器官的羽翼

9 house spider
蜘蛛

10 spider's web
蜘蛛网

11 earwig
小蜈蚣，蠼螋

12 caudal pincers
尾螯，尾钳

13 clothes moth, a moth
蠹虫，蠹鱼子

14 silverfish (*Am.* slicker), a bristletail
蠹鱼，无翅昆虫

15-30 food pests (pests to stores)
粮食害虫（仓库害虫）

15 cheesefly
乾酪蝇

16 grain weevil (granary weevil)
谷象鼻虫

17 cockroach (black beetle)
蟑螂

18 meal beetle (meal worm beetle, flour beetle)
食粉甲虫

19 spotted bruchus
绿豆象

20 larva (grub)
幼虫（蛴螬）

21 chrysalis (pupa)
蛹

22 leather beetle (hide beetle)
龟甲虫

23 yellow meal beetle
豆象

24 chrysalis (pupa)
蛹

25 cigarette beetle (tobacco beetle)
烟草甲虫

26 maize billbug (corn weevil)
谷象

27 one of the Cryptolestes, a grain pest
谷类害虫的一种

28 Indian meal moth
玉米螟，属螟蛾科

29 Angoumois grain moth (Angoumois moth)
长毛稻螟

30 Angoumois grain moth caterpillar inside a grain kernel
在谷粒中的稻螟幼虫

31-42 parasites of man
人体内的寄生虫

31 round worm (maw worm)
蛔虫

32 female
雌蛔虫

33 head
蛔虫的头部

34 male
雄蛔虫

35 tapeworm, a flatworm
绦虫

36 head, a suctorial organ
绦虫头部，吸吮器官

37 sucker
吸盘

38 crown of hooks
钩状器官的顶部

39 bug (bed bug, *Am.* chinch)
臭虫（床虱）

40 crab louse (a human louse)
毛

41 clothes louse (body louse, a human louse)
衣虱（附在人体上的虱子）

42 flea (human flea, common flea)
跳蚤

43 tsetse fly
（热带非洲的）采采蝇（传播睡眠病）

44 malaria mosquito
疟蚊

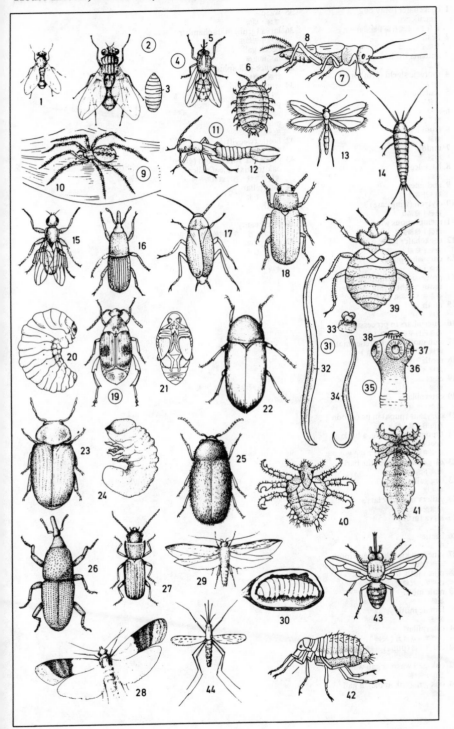

1 cockchafer (May bug), a
  lamellicorn
  金龟子，末端有扁平触须的甲虫
2 head
  金龟子的头部
3 antenna (feeler)
  触须
4 thoracic shield (prothorax)
  前胸
5 scutellum
  盾状甲
6-8 legs
  腿（部）
6 front leg
  前腿
7 middle leg
  中腿
8 back leg
  后腿
9 abdomen
  腹（下腹）
10 elytron (wing case)
  鞘翅（翅鞘）
11 membranous wing
  翅膜（翅膀膜）
12 cockchafer grub, a larva
  金龟子蛴螬，一种幼虫
13 chrysalis (pupa)
  金龟子蛹
14 processionary moth, a nocturnal
  moth (night-flying moth)
  行军虫，夜盗虫，属夜蛾科
15 moth
  飞蛾
16 caterpillars in procession
  前进的行军虫（幼虫）
17 nun moth (black arches moth)
  毒蛾之一种（黑斑纹毒蛾）
18 moth
  舞蛾
19 eggs
  蛾卵
20 caterpillar
  幼虫，毛虫
21 chrysalis (pupa) in its cocoon
  茧内的（蛾）蛹
22 typographer beetle, a bark
  beetle
  印刷甲虫，一种在树皮下钻孔的小甲虫
23-24 galleries under the bark
  树皮下的坑道
23 egg gallery
  卵坑道
24 gallery made by larva
  幼虫挖的坑道
25 larva (grub)
  幼虫
26 beetle
  甲虫
27 pine hawkmoth, a hawkmoth
  松树天蛾，一种天蛾科的蛾
28 pine moth, a geometrid
  松树蛾，尺蠖蛾
29 male moth
  雄蛾
30 female moth
  雌蛾
31 caterpillar
  尺蠖蛾其幼虫为（尺蠖）
32 chrysalis (pupa)
  蛹
33 oak-gall wasp, a gall wasp
  五倍子黄蜂
34 oak gall (oak apple), a gall
  虫瘿

35 wasp
  黄蜂，胡蜂
36 larva (grub) in its chamber
  虫瘿中的幼虫
37 beech gall
  山毛榉虫瘿
38 spruce-gall aphid
  针纵树瘿蚜虫
39 winged aphid
  有翅蚜虫
40 pineapple gall
  凤梨状虫瘿
41 pine weevil
  松木象鼻虫
42 beetle (weevil)
  甲虫（象鼻虫）
43 green oak roller moth (green
  oak tortrix), a leaf roller
  橡树卷叶蛾，卷叶蛾科的一种
44 caterpillar
  幼虫，毛虫
45 moth
  卷叶蛾
46 pine beauty
  夜蛾的一种（食松树的害虫）
47 caterpillar
  幼虫，毛虫
48 moth
  夜蛾

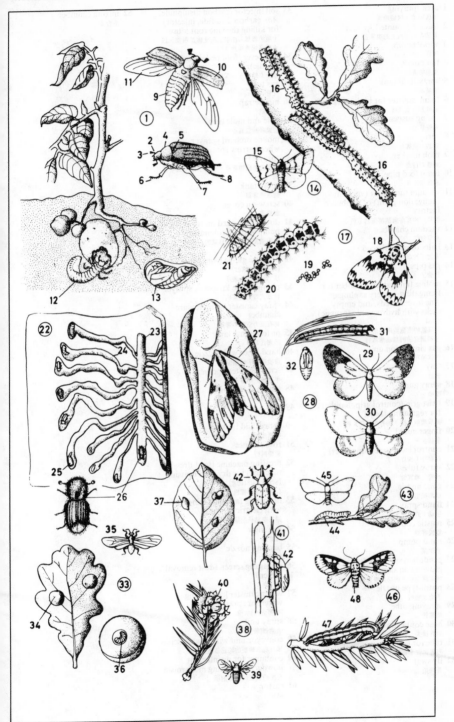

1 area spraying
地区喷雾，区域喷雾

2 tractor-mounted sprayer
安装在牵引机上的喷雾器

3 spray boom
喷杆

4 fan nozzle
扇形喷雾咀

5 spray fluid tank
喷液箱

6 foam canister for blob marking
滴液划行泡沫罐

7 spring suspension
弹簧悬架

8 spray
喷洒，喷雾

9 blob marker
滴液划行器

10 foam feed pipe
泡沫供给管

11 vacuum fumigator (vacuum fumigation plant) of a tobacco factory
烟草厂的真空熏蒸消毒器（机）

12 vacuum chamber
真空室

13 bales of raw tobacco
未加工的烟叶捆

14 gas pipe
气管

15 mobile fumigation chamber for fumigating nursery saplings, vine layers, seeds, and empty sacks with hydrocyanic (prussic) acid
用氢氰酸熏蒸苗床树苗，藤压条和倒空袋的移动熏蒸器

16 gas circulation unit
气体循环装置

17 tray
托盘

18 spray gun
喷枪

19 twist grip (control grip, handle) for regulating the jet
调节喷射（注）的控制手把（柄）

20 finger guard
手指护板

21 control lever (operating lever)
控制杆（操作杆）

22 spray tube
喷管，喷雾管

23 cone nozzle
锥形喷咀

24 hand spray
手动（式）喷雾器

25 plastic container
塑胶容器

26 hand pump
手动泵

27 pendulum spray for hop growing on slopes
增加跳动斜度的摆式喷雾器

28 pistol-type nozzle
手枪式喷咀

29 spraying tube
喷雾管

30 hose connection
软管接头，软管连接（结）

31 tube for laying poisoned bait
布毒饵管，毒饵撒布管

32 fly swat
苍蝇拍

33 soil injector (carbon disulphide, *Am.* carbon disulfide, injector) for killing the vine root louse
土壤消毒器（注射二硫化碳於根部，以杀除藤根寄生虫）

34 foot lever (foot pedal, foot treadle)
踏杆（踏板），深度调整板

35 gas tube
气管

36 mousetrap
捕鼠机

37 vole and mole trap
田鼠和鼹鼠捕捉机

38 mobile orchard sprayer, a wheelbarrow sprayer (carriage sprayer)
移动式果园喷雾机，一种手推车式喷雾机

39 spray tank
药液喷雾箱

40 screw-on cover
螺旋盖

41 direct-connected motor-driven pump with petrol motor
与汽油发动机直接联结的直联式马达驱动泵

42 pressure gauge (*Am.* gage) (manometer)
压力计（压力表）

43 plunger-type knapsack sprayer
柱塞式背负喷雾机

44 spray canister with pressure chamber
具有压力室的喷雾箱

45 piston pump laver
活塞式泵杆

46 hand lance with nozzle
带喷咀的手动喷枪

47 semi-mounted sprayer
半悬挂式喷雾器

48 vineyard tractor
葡萄园用牵引机

49 fan
风扇

50 spray fluid tank
喷洒液箱

51 row of vines
葡萄树行

52 dressing machine (seed-dressing machine) for dry-seed dressing (seed dusting)
乾式种子消毒机

53 dedusting fan (dust removal fan) with electric motor
带有电动机的除尘风扇

54 bag filter
袋滤器

55 bagging nozzle
装袋咀

56 dedusting screen (dust removal screen)
除尘网

57 water canister [containing water for spraying]
[喷雾含水]水箱

58 spray unit
喷洒器[装置]

59 conveyor unit with mixing screw
带有混合螺旋的输送装置

60 container for disinfectant powder with dosing mechanism
有配药装置的消毒剂罐

61 castor
脚轮

62 mixing chamber
混合室

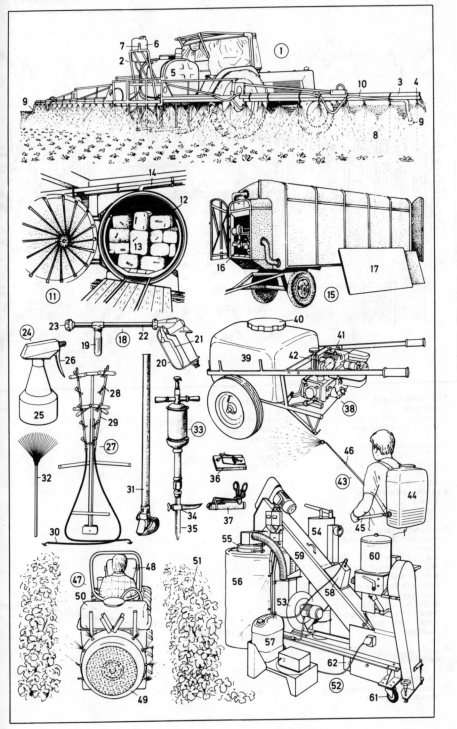

1-34 forest, a wood
森林，林地

1 ride (aisle, lane, section line)
林间车道（森林中两排树间的小径，小
路）

2 compartment (section)
林班（森林区划）

3 wood haulage way, a forest
track
集材道，林中小道

4-14 clear-felling system
皆伐作业

4 standing timber
立木

5 underwood (underbrush,
undergrowth, brushwood, *Am.*
brush)
矮林（生长在大树下的草木，灌木丛）

6 seedling nursery, a tree nursery
播种苗圃，树苗圃

7 deer fence (fence), a wire netting
fence (protective fence for
seedlings); *sim.*: rabbit fence
防鹿篱，一种金属网篱（苗圃中小树的
防护篱）；类似：防兔篱

8 guard rail
护栏

9 seedlings
播种苗，幼苗

10-11 young trees
小树，幼树

10 tree nursery after transplanting
移植苗圃（移植的树苗圃）

11 young plantation
人工幼林

12 young plantation after brashing
整枝后的人工幼林

13 clearing
皆伐

14 tree stump (stump, stub)
树桩（残干）

-37 wood cutting (timber
cutting, tree felling, *Am.*
lumbering)
森林砍伐（林木砍伐，树木砍伐）

timber skidded to the stack
(stacked timber, *Am.* yarded
timber)
堆积的木材（集材）

stack of logs, one cubic metre
(*Am.* meter) of wood
圆木堆，含有一立方公尺体积的木材

post (stake)
桩（支柱）

forest labourer (woodsman, *Am.*
logger, lumberer, lumberjack,
lumberman, timberjack)
turning (*Am.* canting) timber
在翻转木材的林业工人（林业工，[美]
伐木工）

bole (tree trunk, trunk, stem)
树干，树身

feller numbering the logs
给圆木编号的伐木工

steel tree calliper (caliper)
钢制测径尺（卡尺）

power saw (motor saw) cutting a
bole
切割树干的动力锯

safety helmet with visor and ear
pieces
带有面甲和耳罩的安全盔

annual rings
年轮

25 hydraulic felling wedge
液压伐木楔

26 protective clothing [orange top,
green trousers]
防护衣[橙色上衣，绿色裤子]

27 felling with a power saw (motor
saw)
用机力锯伐木

28 undercut (notch, throat, gullet,
mouth, sink, kerf, birdsmouth)
下口，下楂

29 back cut
上口，上楂

30 sheath holding felling wedge
装伐木楔的护套（鞘）

31 log
圆木

32 free-cutting saw for removing
underwood and weeds
清除矮林和杂草的易削锯（高速锯）

33 circular saw (or activated blade)
attachment
圆锯附件（圆锯片）

34 power unit (motor)
动力装置（马达）

35 canister of viscous oil for the
saw chain
锯链用的润滑油桶

36 petrol canister (*Am.* gasoline
canister)
汽油箱

37 felling of small timber (of
smallsized thinnings) (thinning)
小木材的采伐（采伐小径木）

1 axe (*Am.* ax)
斧

2 edge (cutting edge)
斧刃

3 handle (helve)
斧柄

4 felling wedge (falling wedge) with wood insert and ring
带木塞和卡箍的伐木楔块

5 riving hammer (cleaving hammer, splitting hammer)
劈锤

6 lifting hook
吊钩

7 cant hook
搬钩

8 barking iron (bark spud)
剥树皮用的铲（树皮铲）

9 peavy
尖头钩挺

10 slide calliper (caliper) (calliper square)
滑动卡尺

11 billhook, a knife for lopping
钩刀，砍枝用柴刀

12 revolving die hammer (marking hammer, marking iron, *Am.* marker)
旋转烙印铁

13 power saw (motor saw)
机力锯

14 saw chain
锯链

15 safety brake for the saw chain, with finger guard
带手指防护装置锯链的安全制动器

16 saw guide
锯导板

17 accelerator lock
油门销

18 snedding machine (trimming machine, *Am.* knotting machine, limbing machine)
修整机

19 feed rolls
进给辊子

20 flexible blade
柔性刀片

21 hydraulic arm
液压臂

22 trimming blade
修整刀片

23 debarking (barking, bark stripping) of boles
树干剥皮

24 feed roller
进给滚子

25 cyclinder trimmer
圆筒式修木机

26 rotary cutter
锯片机，旋切刀

27 short-haul skidder
短途集材车

28 loading crane
装载起重机

29 log grips
圆木握爪

30 post
车立柱，支柱

31 Ackermann steering system
滚架式折腰转向装置

32 log dump
圆木堆

33 number (identification number)
号印（标志号印）

34 skidder
集材车

35 front blade (front plate)
前护板

36 crush-proof safety bonnet (*Am.* safety hood)
防压碎安全盖帽

37 Ackermann steering system
滚架式折腰转向装置

38 cable winch
缆索绞车

39 cable drum
缆索圆筒

40 rear blade (rear plate)
后护板

41 boles with butt ends held off the ground
粗端离地的树干

42 haulage of timber by road
木材的道路运输（方式）

43 tractor (tractor unit)
曳引机，牵引机

44 loading crane
装载起重机

45 hydraulic jack
液压千斤顶

46 cable winch
缆索绞车

47 post
车立柱，支柱

48 bolster plate
承梁板

49 rear bed (rear bunk)
后挂车底架

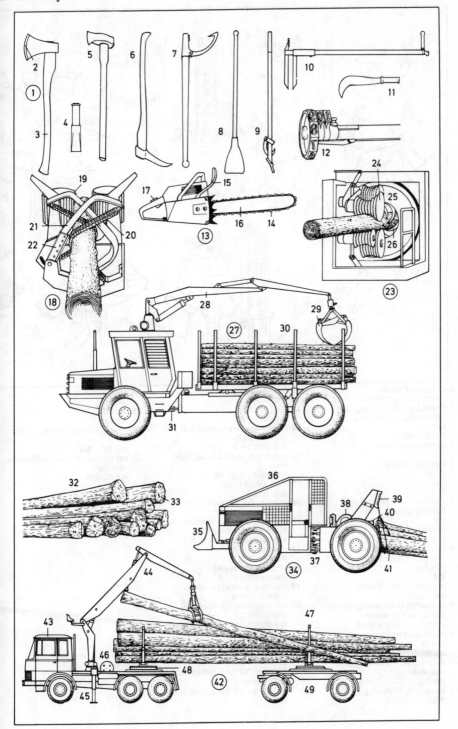

1-52 kinds of hunting
各种狩猎方式，狩猎的种类
1-8 stalking (deer stalking, *Am.*
stillhunting) in the game
preserve
在禁猎地潜随猎物
1 **huntsman** (hunter)
猎人
2 **hunting clothes**
猎人装
3 **knapsack**
背包
4 **sporting gun** (sporting rifle,
hunting rifle)
猎枪
5 **huntsman's hat**
猎帽
6 **field glasses, binoculars**
（小型的）双筒望远镜
7 **gun dog**
猎犬
8 **track** (trail, hoofprints)
踪迹（足迹，足印）
**9-12 hunting in the rutting season
and the pairing season**
在猎物的发情期和交配期狩猎
9 **hunting screen** (screen, *Am.*
blind)
狩猎隐蔽屏（[美]障蔽物）
10 **shooting stick** (shooting seat,
seat stick)
狩猎座杖
11 **blackcock, displaying**
求偶炫耀的黑色公鸡

12 **rutting stag**
发情的牡鹿
13 **hind, grazing**
吃草的红色雌鹿
14-17 hunting from a raised hide
(raised stand)
从高台隐藏处狩猎（高台）
14 **raised hide** (raised stand, high
seat)
高台隐藏处（高台，高架）
15 **herb within range**
射程内的兽群
16 **game path** (*Am.* runway)
猎物跑道
17 **roebuck, hit in the shoulder and
killed by a finishing shot**
肩部中弹受伤而后被击毙的雄鹿
18 **phaeton**
四轮敞篷马车
19-27 types of trapping
设陷阱诱捕野兽的方式
19 **trapping of small predators**
小食肉动物的诱捕
20 **box trap** (trap for small
predators)
箱形捕捉机（小食肉动物的捕捉机）
21 **bait**
诱饵，饵
22 **marten, a small predator**
貂，一种小食肉动物
23 **ferreting** (hunting rabbits out of
their warrens)
用雪貂狩猎（将野兔从兔穴中逐出以捕
捉之）

24 **ferret**
雪貂
25 **ferreter**
捕猎者
26 **burrow** (rabbit burrow, rabbit
hole)
穴（兔穴，兔洞）
27 **net** (rabbit net) over the burrow
opening
张於穴口的网

feeding place for game
(winter feeding place)
放饵处（冬季放饵处），放饵场
poacher
（侵入他人地界）偷猎者
carbine, a short rifle
卡宾枪，一种短来福枪
boar hunt
野猪狩猎区
wild sow (sow, wild boar)
野猪
boarhound (hound, hunting
dog; *collectively*: pack, pack of
hounds)
（猎野猪的）大猎犬（尤指大丹狗，集
合称：群，一群猎犬）
39 beating (driving, hare
hunting)
追赶猎物
aiming position
瞄准姿势
hare, furred game, ground game
野兔，有软毛的猎物，地面上的猎物
retrieving
猎狗寻回猎物
beater
追猎者
bag (kill)
猎物
cart for carrying game
猎物搬运车
waterfowling (wildfowling, duck
shooting, *Am.* duck hunting)
猎水禽（猎水鸟，猎野鸭）

41 flight of wild ducks, winged
game
飞翔的野鸭，展翅飞行的猎物
42-46 falconry (hawking)
鹰猎（放鹰捕猎）
42 falconer
养猎鹰者，鹰猎者
43 reward, a piece of meat
报酬（奖赏），一块肉
44 falcon's hood
鹰的头罩
45 jess
鹰的足带
46 falcon, a hawk, a male hawk
(tiercel) swooping (stooping) on
a heron
猎鹰，猛扑苍鹭的雄鹰
47-52 shooting from a butt
由靶垛射猎
47 tree to which birds are lured
引诱鸟的树，诱鸟树
48 eagle owl, a decoy bird (decoy)
大鸥鸺，一种诱鸟
49 perch
栖木
50 decoyed bird, a crow
被诱鸟，一隻乌鸦
51 butt for shooting crows or eagle
owls
射击乌鸦或大鸥鸺的靶垛
52 gun slit
猎枪的狭缝口

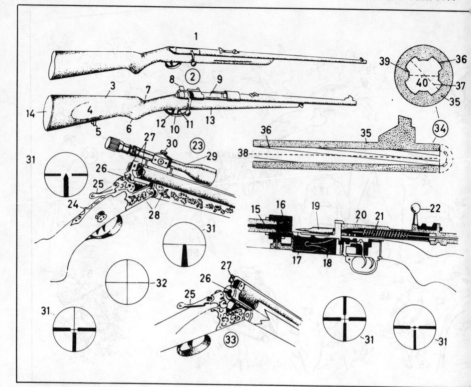

1-40 sporting guns (sporting
rifles, hunting rifles)
猎枪（狩猎来福枪）

1 single-loader (single-loading
rifle)
单发猎枪（单发来福枪）

2 repeating rifle, a small-arm
(fire-arm), a repeater (magazine
rifle, magazine repeater)
连发猎枪，轻武器（火器），连发步枪
（弹匣式枪）

3, 4, 6, 13 stock
枪托

3 butt
枪托

4 cheek [on the left side]
贴腮[左侧面]

5 sling ring
吊环

6 pistol grip
握把

7 small of the butt
枪托的腰部

8 safety catch
保险锁，安全掣子

9 lock
枪机

10 trigger guard
扳机护圈

11 second set trigger (firing trigger)
待击发扳机（射击扳机）

12 hair trigger (set trigger)
微力板机

13 foregrip
前握把

14 butt plate
枪托底板

15 cartridge chamber
弹膛

16 receiver
接收器

17 magazine
（连发枪之）弹匣，弹铗

18 magazine spring
弹匣弹簧

19 ammunition (cartridge)
弹药（枪弹）

20 chamber
弹膛

21 firing pin (striker)
撞针

22 bolt handle (bolt lever)
枪栓柄

23 triple-barrelled (triple-barreled)
rifle, a self-cocking gun
三管枪，自动步枪

24 reversing catch (in various guns:
safety catch)
反向锁扣（在各种枪中：保险锁）

25 sliding safety catch
滑动保险锁

26 rifle barrel (rifled barrel)
来福枪管

27 smooth-bore barrel
滑膛枪管

28 chasing
枪身活板架

29 telescopic sight (riflescope,
telescope sight)
望远镜瞄准器（步枪上的望远镜瞄准
器）

30 graticule adjuster screws
标线片调整具螺丝

31-32 graticule (sight graticule)
标线片（瞄准器的标线片）

31 various graticule systems
复合标线片系统

32 cross wires (Am. cross hairs)
十字瞄准线

33 over-and-under shotgun
重叠式双管猎枪，上下二连管猎枪

34 rifled gun barrel
来福枪管

35 barrel casing
枪管壳

36 rifling
膛线

37 rifling calibre (Am. caliber)
膛线的尺寸（口径）

38 bore axis
枪膛轴

39 land
阳膛线

40 calibre (bore diameter, Am.
caliber)
枪膛口径（枪膛直径，[美]口径）

48 hunting equipment
狩猎装备
double-edged hunting knife
双刃猎刀
[single-edged] hunting knife
[单刃]猎刀
47 calls for luring game (for
calling game)
引诱猎物的号（哨）
roe call
小雌鹿号
hare call
兔号
quail call
鹑笛
stag call
雄鹿号
partridge call
鹌鹑（松鸡）哨
bow trap (bow gin), a jaw trap
弓框捕捉器
small-shot cartridge
散弹药筒
cardboard case
硬纸板弹壳
small-shot charge
散弹
felt wad
填弹塞
smokeless powder (*different
kind:* black powder)
无烟火药（不同种类的：黑色火药）
cartridge
枪弹
full-jacketed cartridge
完整枪弹
soft-lead core
（弹头）软铅芯
powder charge
（一发子弹装的）火药
detonator cap
起爆管
percussion cap
雷管
hunting horn
狩猎号
64 rifle cleaning kit
步枪的擦拭用具
cleaning rod
（枪枝的）通条
cleaning brush
枪刷，擦膛刷
cleaning tow
除尘粗麻屑
pull-through (*Am.* pull-thru)
枪膛清扫绳
sights
瞄准器
notch (sighting notch)
V 字形照门
back sight leaf
表尺
sight scale division
表尺刻度
back sight slide
表尺游标
notch [to hold the spring]
表尺沟（安装弹簧用）
front sight (foresight)
前瞄准器
bead
准星，山形准星
ballistics
弹道学
azimuth
方位，方位角

75 angle of departure
发射角
76 angle of elevation
仰角
77 apex (zenith)
顶点
78 angle of descent
（降）落角
79 ballistic curve
弹道曲线

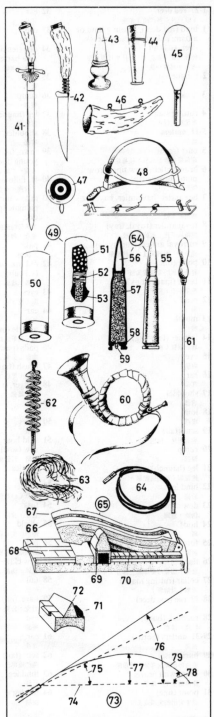

1-27 red deer
（欧洲及亚洲产的）赤鹿

1 hind (red deer), a young hind or a dam; collectively: anterless deer, (y.) calf
雌性马鹿（赤鹿），一种小母鹿，总称：雌性马鹿

2 tongue
舌

3 neck
颈

4 rutting stag
发情期的牡赤鹿

5-11 antlers
鹿角

5 burr (rose)
鹿角根部隆起部分，枝角轮

6 brow antler (brow tine, brow point, brow snag)
额枝角

7 bez antler (bay antler, bay, bez tine)
鹿角的叉枝

8 royal antler (royal, tray)
鹿角从上往下数的第三枝

9 surroyal antlers (surroyals)
鹿角最上面的叉枝（又称冕尖）

10 point (tine)
鹿角突出的尖端或叉齿

11 beam (main trunk)
鹿角主干，角干

12 head
头

13 mouth
嘴

14 larmier (tear bag)
鹿的泪腺（泪囊）

15 eye
眼睛

16 ear
耳朵

17 shoulder
肩部

18 loin
腰部

19 scut (tail)
鹿的短尾（尾巴）

20 rump
臀部

21 leg (haunch)
腰腿部（动物的腰腿）

22 hind leg
后腿

23 dew claw
伪蹄，悬蹄

24 hoof
蹄

25 foreleg
前腿

26 flank
腰窝（肋骨与臀部间之部分）

27 collar (rutting mane)
颈鬃（发情鬃）

28-39 roe (roe deer)
鹿

28 roebuck (buck)
牡鹿，雄鹿

29-31 antlers (horns)
鹿角

29 burr (rose)
鹿角根部隆起部分，枝角轮

30 beam with pearls
鹿角的主干，角干

31 point (tine)
鹿角突出的尖端或叉齿

32 ear
耳朵

33 eye
眼睛

34 doe (female roe), a female fawn or a barren doe
雌鹿，未满一岁的小母鹿

35 loin
腰部

36 rump
臀部

37 leg (haunch)
腰腿部

38 shoulder
肩部

39 fawn, (m.) young buck, (f.) young doe
未满一岁的幼鹿，小雄鹿，小雌鹿

40-41 fallow deer
（欧洲产淡黄色带白斑的）梅花鹿

40 fallow buck, a buck with palmate (palmated) antlers, (f.) doe
淡黄带白斑的雄鹿，一种具有掌状角的雄鹿，雌鹿

41 palm
掌状角

42 red fox, (m.) dog, (f.) vixen, (y.) cub
赤狐，雄狐，雌狐，幼狐

43 eyes
眼（复）

44 ear
耳朵

45 muzzle (mouth)
狐，狗等的口（口鼻部）

46 pads (paws)
肉趾（足掌）

47 brush (tail)
狐尾（尾巴）

48 badger, (f.) sow
獾，雌獾

49 tail
尾巴

50 paws
脚爪

51 wild boar, (m.) boar, (f.) wild sow (sow), (y.) young boar
野猪，野公猪，野母猪，小野猪

52 bristles
鬃毛

53 snout
猪鼻（口鼻部）

54 tusk
长牙，獠牙

55 shield
防护厚皮（肩胛上的厚皮）

56 hide
野猪皮，兽皮

57 dew claw
悬蹄，伪蹄

58 tail
尾巴

59 hare, (m.) buck, (f.) doe
野兔，公兔，母兔

60 eye
眼睛

61 ear
耳朵

62 scut (tail)
兔的短尾巴

63 hind leg
后腿

64 foreleg
前腿

65 rabbit
家兔，兔子

66 blackcock
黑色雄松鸡

67 tail
尾羽

68 falcate (falcated) feathers
镰状尾羽

69 hazel grouse (hazel hen)
黄棕色松鸡

70 partridge
鹧鸪

71 horseshoe (horseshoe marking)
马蹄形斑纹

72 wood grouse (capercaillie)
雷鸟，雷鸡

73 beard
髯毛

74 axillary marking
腋斑

75 tail (fan)
扇形尾羽

76 wing (pinion)
鸟翼（翮）

77 common pheasant, a pheasant, (m.) cock pheasant (pheasant cock), (f.) hen pheasant (pheasant hen)
雉鸡或环颈雉，雄雉，雌雉

78 plumicorn (feathered ear, ear tuft, ear, horn)
耳羽（角状耳羽）

79 wing
翅膀，翼

80 tail
尾羽

81 leg
腿

82 spur
肉距

83 snipe
鹬，沙锥鸟

84 bill (beak)
鸟喙

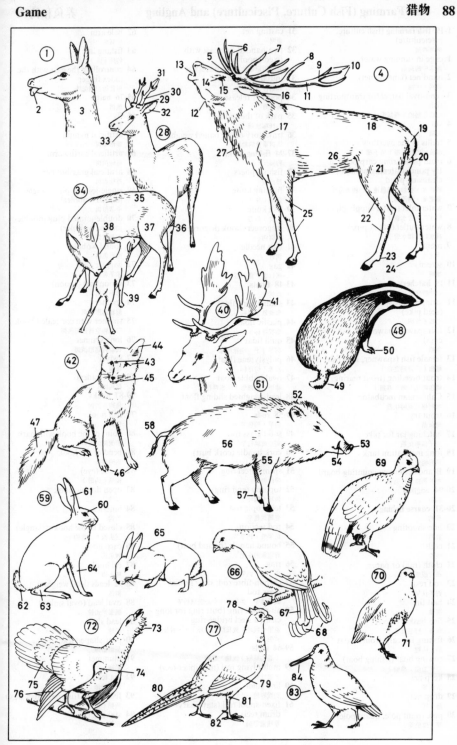

1-19 fish farming (fish culture, pisciculture)
鱼类养殖

1 cage in running water
流水中的网箱

2 hand net (landing net)
袋网，手网

3 semi-oval barrel for transporting fish
运送鱼用的半椭圆形桶

4 vat
大桶

5 trellis in the overflow
溢流中的拦鱼栅（格子栅）

6 trout pond; *sim.*: carp pond, a fry pond, fattening pond, or cleansing pond
鳟鱼池，类似：鲤鱼池，一种鱼苗池，育肥池，清洗池

7 water inlet (water supply pipe)
给水口（给水管）

8 water outlet (outlet pipe)
排水口（排水管）

9 monk
净化池

10 screen
滤网

11-19 hatchery
鱼卵孵化所

11 stripping the spawning pike (seed pike)
挤梭子鱼卵

12 fish spawn (spawn, roe, fish eggs)
鱼卵

13 female fish (spawner, seed fish)
雌鱼（产卵期之鱼）

14 trout breeding (trout rearing)
鳟鱼孵化（鳟鱼养殖）

15 Californian incubator
加利福尼亚孵化器

16 trout fry
鳟鱼苗

17 hatching jar for pike
梭子鱼孵化瓶

18 long incubation tank
长形孵化槽

19 Brandstetter egg-counting board
布兰德斯特计卵板

20-94 angling
钓鱼

20-31 coarse fishing
垂钓

20 line shooting
放钓线

21 coils
线卷

22 cloth (rag) or paper
布片或纸片

23 rod rest
钓竿扶架

24 bait tin
饵罐

25 fish basket (creel)
鱼篓（柳条鱼篮）

26 fishing for carp from a boat
船上钓鲤

27 rowing boat (fishing boat)
划艇渔船（渔船）

28 keep net
活鱼笼

29 drop net
落下网

30 pole (punt pole, quant pole)
篙（撑船篙）

31 casting net
撒网

32 two-handed side cast with fixed-spool reel
具有固定轴的两手操作的侧撒网

33 initial position
起始位置

34 point of release
释放点

35 path of the rod tip
钓杆端端轨迹

36 trajectory of the baited weight
诱饵重量的轨迹

37-94 fishing tackle
钓具

37 fishing pliers
捕鱼钳

38 filleting knife
切鱼（片）刀

39 fish knife
（食）鱼刀

40 disgorger (hook disgorger)
取饵钩

41 bait needle
饵针

42 gag
张口器，撑口器

43-48 floats
浮标

43 sliding cork float
滑动软木浮标

44 plastic float
塑胶浮标

45 quill float
羽茎浮子，翎管浮标

46 polystyrene float
聚苯乙烯浮标

47 oval bubble float
卵形（椭圆形）气泡浮标

48 lead-weighted sliding float
滑动铅锤浮标

49-58 rods
钓竿，钓鱼竿

49 solid glass rod
实心玻璃的竿

50 cork handle (cork butt)
软木把

51 spring-steel ring
弹性钢环

52 top ring (end ring)
顶环（端环）

53 telescopic rod
套筒式鱼竿

54 rod section
鱼竿节，钓竿节

55 bound handle (bound butt)
有包紮的手把

56 ring
鱼竿环，钓竿环

57 carbon-fibre rod; *sim.*: hollow glass rod
碳纤维竿；类似有：空心玻璃钓竿

58 all-round ring (butt ring for long cast), a steel bridge ring
鱼竿引线环（放长线的托环），一种桥式钢环

59-64 reels
（卷钓线的）线轴，卷筒

59 multiplying reel (multiplier reel)
多股绕线轴

60 line guide
钓线导轮

61 fixed-spool reel (stationary-drum reel)
卷线固定轴

62 bale arm
控制柄

63 fishing line
钓丝（线）

64 controlling the cast with the index finger
用食指控制抛线

65-76 baits
鱼饵

65 fly
假蝇

66 artificial nymph
蛹形拟饵

67 artificial earthworm
蚯蚓拟饵

68 artificial grasshopper
蚱蜢拟饵

69 single-jointed plug (single-jointed wobbler)
单节拟饵

70 double-jointed plug (double-jointed wobbler)
双节拟饵

71 round wobbler
圆形鱼饵

72 wiggler
子子鱼饵

73 spoon bait (spoon)
匙形诱饵

74 spinner
旋转匙形诱饵

75 spinner with concealed hook
带隐钩旋转匙形诱饵

76 long spinner
长旋转匙形诱饵

77 swivel
转镮

78 cast (leader)
接钩绳（引线）

79-87 hooks
鱼钩，钓钩

79 fish hook
鱼钩

80 point of the hook with barb
带倒刺的鱼钩尖

81 bend of the hook
钩的弯头

82 spade (eye)
钩柄（钩眼）

83 open double hook
双钩

84 limerick
鱼钩

85 closed treble hook (triangle)
三头钩（三角钩）

86 carp hook
鲤鱼钩

87 eel hook
鳗鱼钩

88-92 leads (lead weights)
铅锤

88 oval lead (oval sinker)
椭圆形铅锤

89 lead shot
铅球

90 pear-shaped lead
梨形铅锤

91 plummet
铅锤

92 sea lead
海上铅锤

93 fish ladder (fish pass, fish way)
鱼梯（鱼道）

94 stake net
张网

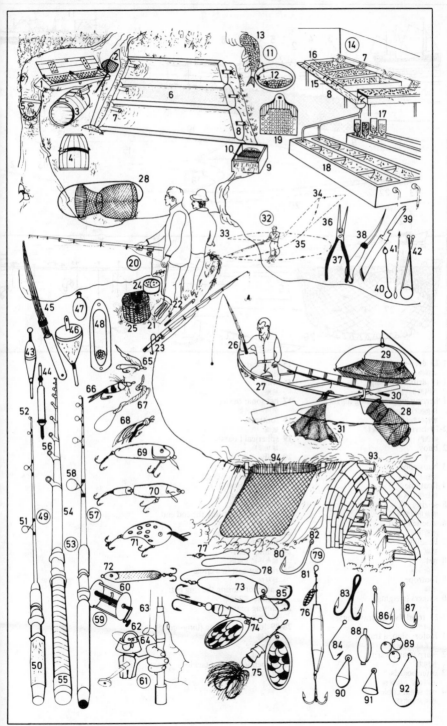

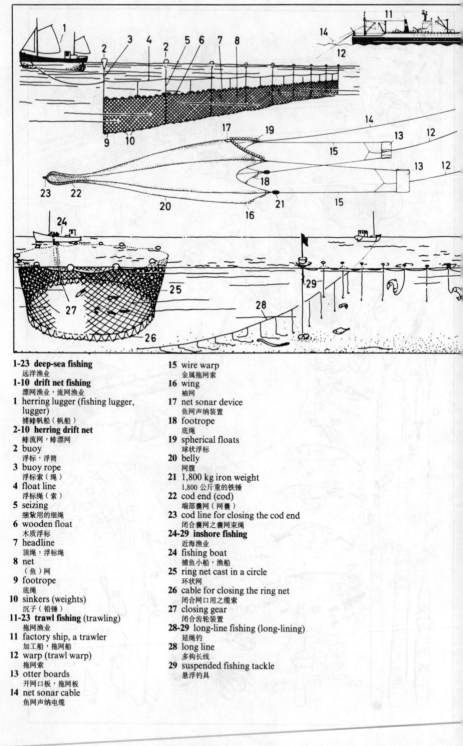

1-23 deep-sea fishing
远洋渔业
1-10 drift net fishing
漂网渔业，流网渔业
1 herring lugger (fishing lugger, lugger)
捕鲱帆船（帆船）
2-10 herring drift net
鲱流网，鲱漂网
2 buoy
浮标，浮筒
3 buoy rope
浮标索（绳）
4 float line
浮标绳（索）
5 seizing
绷紧用的细绳
6 wooden float
木质浮标
7 headline
顶绳，浮标绳
8 net
（鱼）网
9 footrope
底绳
10 sinkers (weights)
沉子（铅锤）
11-23 trawl fishing (trawling)
拖网渔业
11 factory ship, a trawler
加工船，拖网船
12 warp (trawl warp)
拖网索
13 otter boards
开网口板，拖网板
14 net sonar cable
鱼网声纳电缆

15 wire warp
金属拖网索
16 wing
袖网
17 net sonar device
鱼网声纳装置
18 footrope
底绳
19 spherical floats
球状浮标
20 belly
网腹
21 1,800 kg iron weight
1,800 公斤重的铁锤
22 cod end (cod)
端部囊网（网囊）
23 cod line for closing the cod end
闭合囊网之囊网束绳
24-29 inshore fishing
近海渔业
24 fishing boat
捕鱼小船，渔船
25 ring net cast in a circle
环状网
26 cable for closing the ring net
闭合网口用之缆索
27 closing gear
闭合齿轮装置
28-29 long-line fishing (long-lining)
延绳钓
28 long line
多钩长线
29 suspended fishing tackle
悬浮钓具

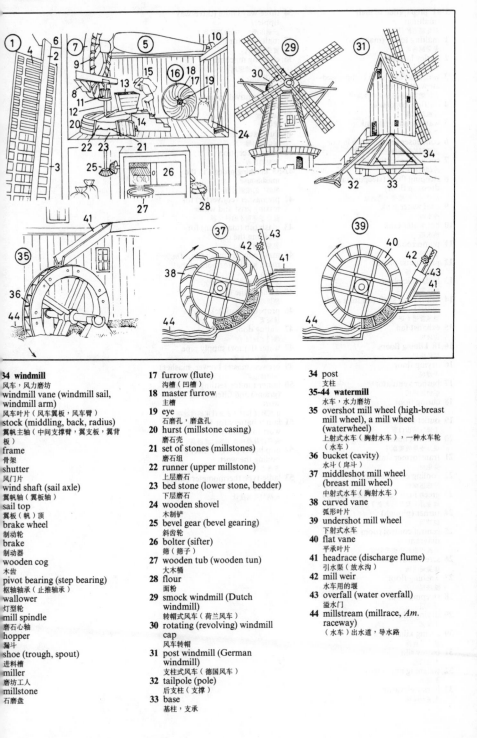

34 windmill
风车，风力磨坊

windmill vane (windmill sail, windmill arm)
风车叶片（风车翼板，风车臂）

stock (middling, back, radius)
翼石主轴（中间支撑臂，翼支板，翼背板）

frame
骨架

shutter
风门片

wind shaft (sail axle)
翼帆轴（翼板轴）

sail top
翼板（帆）顶

brake wheel
制动轮

brake
制动器

wooden cog
木齿

pivot bearing (step bearing)
枢轴轴承（止推轴承）

wallower
灯型轮

mill spindle
磨石心轴

hopper
漏斗

shoe (trough, spout)
进料槽

miller
磨坊工人

millstone
石磨盘

17 furrow (flute)
沟槽（凹槽）

18 master furrow
主槽

19 eye
石磨孔，磨盘孔

20 hurst (millstone casing)
磨石壳

21 set of stones (millstones)
磨石组

22 runner (upper millstone)
上层磨石

23 bed stone (lower stone, bedder)
下层磨石

24 wooden shovel
木制铲

25 bevel gear (bevel gearing)
斜齿轮

26 bolter (sifter)
筛（筛子）

27 wooden tub (wooden tun)
大木桶

28 flour
面粉

29 smock windmill (Dutch windmill)
转帽式风车（荷兰风车）

30 rotating (revolving) windmill cap
风车转帽

31 post windmill (German windmill)
支柱式风车（德国风车）

32 tailpole (pole)
后支柱（支撑）

33 base
基柱，支承

34 post
支柱

35-44 watermill
水车，水力磨坊

35 overshot mill wheel (high-breast mill wheel), a mill wheel (waterwheel)
上射式水车（胸射水车），一种水车轮（水车）

36 bucket (cavity)
水斗（斗斗）

37 middleshot mill wheel (breast mill wheel)
中射式水车（胸射水车）

38 curved vane
弧形叶片

39 undershot mill wheel
下射式水车

40 flat vane
平承叶片

41 headrace (discharge flume)
引水渠（放水沟）

42 mill weir
水车用的堰

43 overfall (water overfall)
溢水门

44 millstream (millrace, Am. raceway)
（水车）出水道，导水路

1-41 preparation of malt (malting)
麦芽制造的设备

1 malting tower (maltings)
麦芽制造塔

2 barley hopper
大麦漏斗

3 washing floor with compressed-air washing unit
有压缩空气洗涤装置的洗涤层

4 outflow condenser
外流凝结器

5 water-collecting tank
集水箱

6 condenser for the steep liquor
浸液用的凝结器

7 coolant-collecting plant
冷却剂收集装置

8 steeping floor (steeping tank, dressing floor)
浸渍层（浸渍槽，清层）

9 cold water tank
冷水箱

10 hot water tank
热水箱

11 pump room
水泵房

12 pneumatic plant
压缩空气场

13 hydraulic plant
液压装置

14 ventilation shaft (air inlet and outlet)
通风管道（进气口和出气口）

15 exhaust fan
排风机

16-18 kilning floors
烘干机层

16 drying floor
干燥层

17 burner ventilator
燃烧送风机

18 curing floor
加工处理层

19 outlet from the kiln
干燥气的出口管

20 finished malt collecting hopper
成品麦芽收集漏斗

21 transformer station
变电所

22 cooling compressors
冷冻压缩机

23 green malt (germinated barley)
绿麦芽（发芽的大麦）

24 turner (plough)
翻拌器

25 central control room with flow diagram
有流程图的中央控制室

26 screw conveyor
螺旋运送机

27 washing floor
洗涤层

28 steeping floor
浸渍层

29 drying kiln
干燥器

30 curing kiln
加工处理器

31 barley silo
大麦储仓

32 weighing apparatus
衡量器

33 barley elevator
大麦升降机

34 three-way chute (three-way tippler)
三通滑槽（三通倾卸装置）

35 malt elevator
麦芽升降机

36 cleaning machine
滤选机（清选机）

37 malt silo
麦芽储仓

38 corn removal by suction
抽除麦粒

39 sacker
装袋器

40 dust extractor
灰尘抽出器

41 barley reception
大麦的接收

42-53 mashing process in the mashhouse
酿酒厂的酿酒过程

42 premasher (converter) for mixing grist and water
混合麦芽和水的转化器

43 mash tub (mash tun) for mashing the malt
麦芽浆槽（桶）

44 mash copper (mash tun, *Am.* mash kettle) for boiling the mash
麦芽浆煮槽锅（桶，壶）

45 dome of the tun
槽顶

46 propeller (paddle)
螺旋桨

47 sliding door
滑门，拉门

48 water (liquor) supply pipe
供（液体）水管

49 brewer (master brewer, masher)
啤酒酿造者

50 lauter tun for settling the draff (grains) and filtering off the wort
沉淀残渣和过滤麦芽汁用的过滤槽

51 lauter battery for testing the wort for quality
麦芽汁品质检查用的过滤器具

52 hop boiler (wort boiler) for boiling the wort
煮沸麦芽汁用的锅炉

53 ladle-type thermometer (scoop thermometer)
长柄勺式温度计

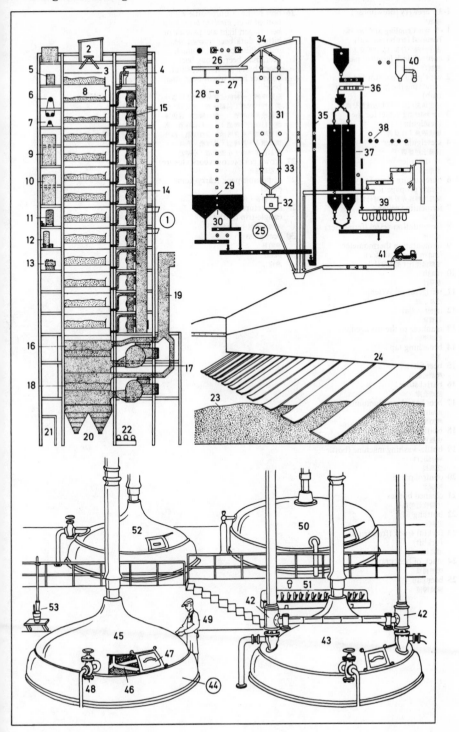

1-31 brewery (brewhouse)
啤酒厂

1 - 5 wort cooling and break removal (trub removal)
麦芽汁的冷却和沉淀物的除去

1 control desk (control panel)
控制台（操纵台）

2 whirlpool separator for removing the hot break (hot trub)
除去高温沉淀物所用的漩涡分离器

3 measuring vessel for the kieselguhr
板状矽藻土计量器

4 kieselguhr filter
硅藻土过滤器

5 wort cooler
麦芽汁冷却器

6 pure culture plant for yeast (yeast propagation plant)
酵母纯粹培养设备（酵母繁殖室）

7 fermenting cellar
发酵室

8 fermentation vessel (fermenter)
发酵槽

9 fermentation thermometer (mash thermometer)
发酵温度计（醪温度计）

10 mash
麦芽汁

11 refrigeration system
冷却系统

12 lager cellar
贮酒室

13 manhole to the storage tank
贮酒槽的人孔

14 broaching tap
龙头

15 beer filter
啤酒过滤器

16 barrel store
酒桶仓库

17 beer barrel, an aluminium (*Am.* aluminum) barrel
啤酒桶，铝桶

18 bottle-washing plant
洗瓶机

19 bottle-washing machine (bottle washer)
洗瓶机

20 control panel
控制盘

21 cleaned bottles
已清洗过的瓶子

22 bottling
装瓶

23 forklift truck (fork truck, forklift)
堆高机

24 stack of beer crates
啤酒箱堆

25 beer can
罐装啤酒

26 beer bottle, a Eurobottle with bottled beer; *kinds of beer:* light beer (lager, light ale, pale ale or bitter), dark beer (brown ale, mild), Pilsener beer, Munich beer, malt beer, strong beer (bock beer), porter, ale, stout, Salvator beer, wheat beer, small beer
瓶装啤酒，一种欧式瓶装啤酒；啤酒种类：淡味啤酒（储藏啤酒，淡麦酒，弱麦酒或苦味啤酒），深色啤酒（棕色啤酒，口味温和啤酒），皮耳森啤酒，慕尼克啤酒，麦芽啤酒，烈性啤酒（烈性黑啤酒），黑啤酒，淡味啤酒，烈啤酒，萨尔瓦多啤酒，小麦啤酒，小啤酒

27 crown cork (crown cork closure)
皇冠形瓶盖

28 disposable pack (carry-home pack)
简便包装（便於携带的包装）

29 non-returnable bottle (single-trip bottle)
不回收的瓶子（单程瓶）

30 beer glass
啤酒杯

31 head
泡沫

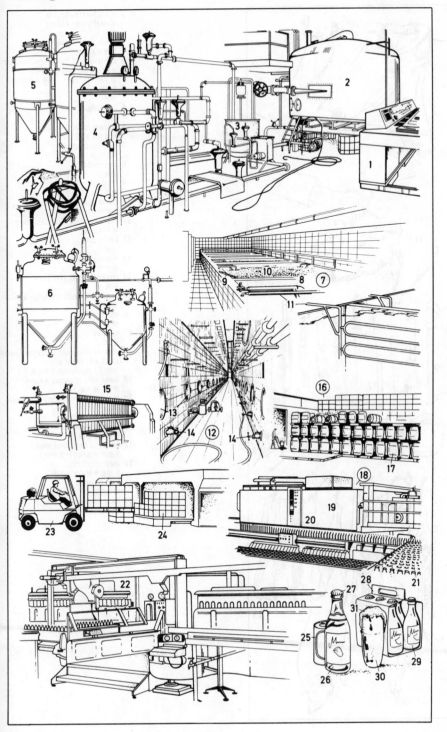

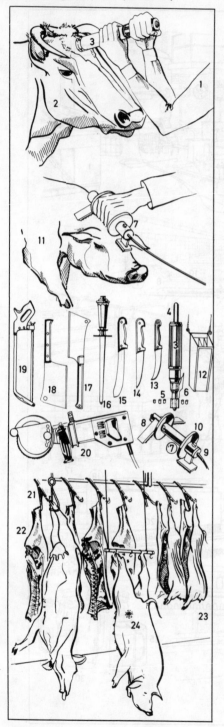

1 slaughterman (*Am.* slaughterer, killer)
  屠夫
2 animal for slaughter, an ox
  要屠宰的动物，牛
3 captive-bolt pistol (pneumatic gun), a stunning device
  屠牛枪（空气枪），一种击昏的器械
4 bolt
  枪栓
5 cartridges
  弹药，子弹
6 release lever (trigger)
  释放杆（板机）
7 electric stunner
  电击昏器
8 electrode
  电极
9 lead
  电线
10 hand guard (insulation)
  手护挡（绝缘体）
11 pig (*Am.* hog) for slaughter
  要屠宰的猪
12 knife case
  刀箱
13 flaying knife
  剥皮刀
14 sticking knife (sticker)
  刺戳刀（尖刀）
15 butcher's knife (butcher knife)
  屠宰刀
16 steel
  磨刀用的钢棒
17 splitter
  劈刀
18 cleaver (butcher's cleaver, meat axe (*Am.* meat ax))
  切肉刀（屠夫的切肉刀，切肉斧）
19 bone saw (butcher's saw)
  骨锯（屠夫锯）
20 meat saw for sawing meat into cuts
  将肉锯成块的肉锯
21-24 cold store (cold room)
  冷冻库（冷藏室）
21 gambrel (gambrel stick)
  马脚状的铁钩（挂肉刺钩）
22 quarter of beef
  包括整条腿的大块牛肉
23 side of pork
  猪体的侧面
24 meat inspector's stamp
  食肉检查员的戳记

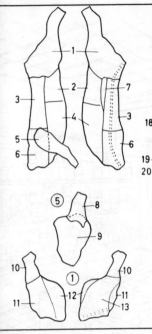

左: meat side 左: 肉侧边;
右: bone side 右: 骨侧边

1-13 animal: calf; meat: veal
动物: 小牛; 肉: 小牛肉
1 leg with hind knuckle
有后关节,(后肘) 的腿肉
2 flank
(小牛腹肉,腰窝肉) 软肋肉
3 loin and rib
腰肉和肋肉
4 breast (breast of veal)
胸肉 (小牛的胸肉)
5 shoulder with fore knuckle
有前关节 (前肘) 的腿肉]前腿肉
6 neck with scray (scrag end)
颈肉
7 best end of loin (of loin of veal)
最好的牛腰肉
8 fore knuckle
前肘 (关节)
9 shoulder
肩膀肉
10 hind knuckle
后肘 (关节)
11 roasting round (oyster round)
圆肉 (适于烤的圆而厚的牛肉)
12 cutlet for frying or braising
用于煎或火炖煮的肉片
13 undercut (fillet)
腰部下侧嫩肉 (里脊)

14-37 animal: ox; meat: beef
动物: 牛; 肉: 牛肉
14 round with rump and shank
包括臀部和小腿的圆而厚的牛肉
15 flank
(牛胁腹肉) 软肋肉
16 thick flank
(厚胁腹肉) 厚软肋肉
thin flank
(薄胁腹肉) 薄软肋肉

17 sirloin
上腰部肉
18 prime rib (fore ribs, prime fore rib)
主肋骨 (前肋骨, 主前肋骨)
19 middle rib and chuck
中肋骨和颈与肩部的肉
20 neck
颈肉
21 flat rib
扁平肋骨
22 leg of mutton piece (bladebone) with shin
有牛胫的 (肩胛骨) 腿肉
23 brisket (brisket of beef)
胸肉 (牛胸肉)
24 fillet (fillet of beef)
牛脊条肉 (里脊肉)
25 hind brisket
后胸肉
26 middle brisket
中胸肉
27 breastbone
胸骨
28 shin
(肩胛骨肉) 牛的前腿肉
29 leg of mutton piece
有肩胛骨的前腿肉
30 bladebone [meat side]
肩胛骨
31 part of top rib
上肋骨的一部分
32 bladebone [bone side]
肩胛骨 (骨侧面)
33 shank
牛小腿肉
34 silverside
最上端牛腿肉
35 rump
臀部肉
36 thick flank
厚软肋肉 (厚胁腹肉)
37 top side
顶边腿肉

38-54 animal: pig; meat: pork
动物: 猪; 肉: 猪肉
38 leg with knuckle and trotter
有肘 (关节) 和蹄的猪腿
39 ventral part of the belly
腹的下部分
40 back fat
背部肥肉
41 belly
腹部
42 bladebone with knuckle and trotter
有肘 (关节) 和蹄的肩胛骨肉
43 head (pig's head)
头 (猪头)
44 fillet (fillet of port)
腰条肉 (猪里脊)
45 leaf fat (pork flare)
腰子附近的 (脂肪层) 肥肉
46 loin (port loin)
腰肉
47 spare rib
排骨肉, 带肉的猪肋骨
48 trotter
猪脚 (蹄)
49 knuckle
(关节) 肘肉
50 butt
51 fore end (ham)
大腿前端肉
52 round end for boiling
可用来炖煮的臀部肉
53 fat end
脂肪部分
54 gammon steak
大腿肉

1-30 butcher's shop
肉店
1 - 4 meat
食用肉
1 ham on the bone
火腿
2 flitch of bacon
醃熏的猪肋肉
3 smoked meat
熏肉
4 piece of loin (piece of sirloin)
一块腰肉（一块牛腰肉）
5 lard
猪油
6-11 sausages
腊肠，香肠
6 price label
价格牌
7 mortadella
煮熟的烟熏香肠
8 scalded sausage; *kinds:* Vienna sausage (Wiener), Frankfurter sausage (Frankfurter)
熟的香肠；种类：维也纳香肠，法兰克福香肠
9 collared pork (*Am.* headcheese)
猪肉卷（[美]肉冻）
10 ring of Lyoner sausage
里昂香肠圈
11 pork sausages; *also:* beef sausages
猪肉香肠，牛肉香肠
12 cold shelves
冷冻架

13 meat salad (diced meat salad)
凉拌肉食（方块凉拌肉食）
14 cold meats (*Am.* cold cuts)
各种冻肉
15 pâté
小馅饼
16 mince (mincemeat, minced meat)
碎肉
17 knuckle of pork
猪肘子
18 basket for special offers
特价品盘
19 price list for special offers
特价品的价格表
20 special offer
特价品
21 freezer
冷藏柜
22 pre-packed joints
预备包装的肉块
23 deep-frozen ready-to-eat meal
低温冷冻的现成餐食
24 chicken
鸡肉
25 canned food
罐头食品
26 can
罐头
27 canned vegetables
蔬菜罐头
28 canned fish
鱼罐头

29 salad cream
沙拉酱
30 soft drinks
不含酒精的饮料（清凉饮料）

9 manufacture of sausages
香肠的制造
37 butcher's knives
各种屠刀
slicer
切片刀
knife blade
刀身
saw teeth
锯齿
knife handle
刀柄
carver (carving knife)
切肉刀
boning knife
去骨刀
butcher's knife (butcher knife)
屠刀
butcher (master butcher)
屠夫，肉贩
butcher's apron
屠夫的围裙
meat-mixing tough
绞肉槽
sausage meat
香肠肉
scraper
刮刀
skimmer
网杓
sausage fork
香肠叉
scalding colander
烫滤器

46 waste bin (*Am.* trash bin)
废物箱，垃圾箱
47 cooker, for cooking with steam or hot air
蒸柜，蒸笼
48 smoke house
烟熏室
49 sausage filler (sausage stuffer)
灌腊肠（香肠）机
50 feed pipe (supply pipe)
输料管
51 containers for vegetables
蔬菜容器
52 mincing machine for sausage meat
香肠肉的绞肉机
53 mincing machine (meat mincer, mincer, *Am.* meat grinder)
绞肉机
54 plates (steel plates)
盘（钢盘）
55 meathook (butcher's hook)
挂肉钩
56 bone saw
骨锯
57 chopping board
砧板
58 butcher, cutting meat
切肉的屠夫
59 piece of meat
一块肉

181

1-54 baker's shop
面包店

1 shop assistant (*Am.* salesgirl, saleslady)
店员（女售货员）

2 bread (loaf of bread, loaf)
面包（一条面包）

3 crumb
面包心

4 crust (bread crust)
面包皮

5 crust (*Am.* heel)
面包端皮

6-12 kinds of bread (breads)
面包的种类

6 round loaf, a wheat and rye bread
圆面包，一种小麦和裸麦做的面包

7 small round loaf
小圆块面包

8 long loaf (bloomer), a wheat and rye bread
长面包（灯笼形面包），一种小麦和裸麦做的面包

9 white loaf
白面包

10 pan loaf, a wholemeal rye bread
全麦面包，一种全裸麦做的面包

11 yeast bread (*Am.* stollen)
发酵面包

12 French loaf (baguette, French stick)
法国面包（长条形面包，法国棒式面包）

13-16 rolls
小圆面包

13 brown roll
全麦小圆面包

14 white roll
白小圆面包

15 finger roll
细长的面包卷

16 rye-bread roll
裸麦小圆面包

17-47 cakes (confectionery)
各种点心（饼干）

17 cream roll
奶油卷

18 vol-au-vent, a puff pastry (*Am.* puff paste)
馅饼，一种压叠成层的和面

19 Swiss roll (*Am.* jelly roll)
瑞士卷（果酱卷）

20 tartlet
小型的果子馅饼

21 slice of cream cake
多层奶油饼（西点）

22-24 flans (*Am.* pies) and gateaux (torten)
派和糕饼

22 fruit flan (*kinds:* strawberry flan, cherry flan, gooseberry flan, peach flan, rhubarb flan)
水果派（种类：草莓派，樱桃派，醋果派，桃子派，大黄派）

23 cheesecake
乳酪蛋糕

24 cream cake (*Am.* cream pie) (*kinds:* butter-cream cake, Bla Forest gateau)
奶油蛋糕（奶油派）（种类：奶油糕，黑森林蛋糕）

25 cake plate
蛋糕盘

26 meringue
由蛋白和砂糖制成的糕饼

27 cream puff
泡芙（奶油松饼）

28 whipped cream
发泡奶油饼

29 doughnut (*Am.* bismarck)
甜甜圈

30 Danish pastry
丹麦糕饼

31 saltstick (saltzstange) (*also:* caraway roll, caraway stick)
盐条（香菜卷，香菜条）

32 croissant (crescent roll, *Am.* crescent)
牛角面包

33 ring cake (gugelhupf)
环形蛋糕（圆形大蛋糕）

34 slab cake with chocolate icing
巧克力糖衣蛋糕

35 streusel cakes
核桃酥饼

36 marshmallow
绵绵糖

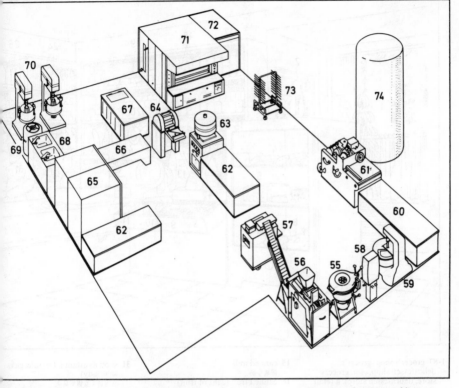

coconut macaroon
蛋白杏仁饼乾
pastry whirl
锅形饼
iced bun
圆形糖衣面包
sweet bread
甜面包
plaited bun (plait)
辫形圆面包
Frankfurter garland cake
花环腊肠饼
slices (*kinds:* streusel slices,
sugared slices, plum slices)
千层派（种类：碎粒饼，糖衣饼，葡萄
乾饼）
pretzel
咸脆饼
wafer(*Am.* waffle)
薄饼（威化饼）；鸡蛋饼
tree cake (baumkuchen)
树形蛋糕
flan case
装派的盒子
0 wrapped bread
包装好的面包
wholemeal bread (*also:*
wheatgerm bread)
全麦面包（麦芽面包）
pumpernickel (wholemeal rye
bread)
粗制裸麦面包（全裸面包）
crispbread
脆面包

51 gingerbread (*Am.* lebkuchen)
姜味面包
52 flour (*kinds:* wheat flour, rye
flour)
面粉（种类：小麦粉，裸麦粉）
53 yeast (baker's yeast)
酵母（发酵粉）
54 rusks (French toast)
干面包（法式吐司）
55-74 bakery (bakehouse)
面包房
55 kneading machine (dough
mixer)
揉面机（揉混机）
56-57 bread unit
面包设备
56 divider
分割机
57 moulder (*Am.* molder)
压模机
58 premixer
预混合机
59 dough mixer
揉混机，揉面机
60 workbench
工作台
61 roll unit
滚压设备
62 workbench
工作台
63 divider and rounder (rounding
machine)
分划器和划圆机

64 crescent-forming machine
新月成型机
65 freezers
冷冻库
66 oven [for baking with fat]
烤箱[带油烘烤]
67-70 confectionery unit
制果糕的设备
67 cooling table
冷却台
68 sink
洗涤槽
69 boiler
锅炉
70 whipping unit [with beater]
搅打装置[带搅打器]
71 reel over (oven)
迴转炉（烤炉）
72 fermentation room
发酵室
73 fermentation trolley
（发酵室用）手推车
74 flour silo
面粉筒仓

1-87 grocer's shop (grocer's, delicatessen shop, *Am.* grocery store, delicatessen store), a retail shop (*Am.* retail store)
杂货店（熟食品商店），一种零售商店

1 window display
橱窗陈列

2 poster (advertisement)
海报（广告）

3 cold shelves
冷藏箱

4 sausages
香肠，腊肠

5 cheese
乳酪

6 roasting chicken (broiler)
烤鸡

7 poulard, a fattened hen
阉母鸡，一种肥母鸡

8-11 baking ingredients
烘烤配料

8 raisins; *sim.:* sultanas
葡萄干，无子葡萄干

9 currants
小粒无子葡萄干

10 candied lemon peel
柠檬果皮蜜饯

11 candied orange peel
橘皮蜜饯

12 computing scale, a rapid scale
计量磅秤，一种快速磅秤

13 shop assistant (*Am.* salesclerk)
店员（售货员）

14 goods shelves (shelves)
货架，商品架

15-20 canned food
罐头食品

15 canned milk
罐装牛奶

16 canned fruit (cans of fruit)
水果罐头

17 canned vegetables
蔬菜罐头

18 fruit juice
果汁

19 sardines in oil, a can of fish
油浸沙丁鱼，一种鱼罐头

20 canned meat (cans of meat)
肉罐头

21 margarine
人造牛油

22 butter
牛油

23 coconut oil, a vegetable oil
椰子油，一种植物油

24 oil; *kinds:* salad oil, olive oil, sunflower oil, wheatgerm oil, ground-nut oil
油，种类：沙拉油，橄榄油，葵花子油，麦芽油，花生油

25 vinegar
醋

26 stock cube
浓缩的汤料块

27 bouillon cube
浓缩的肉汤块

28 mustard
芥末

29 gherkin (pickled gherkin)
小黄瓜（醃渍小黄瓜）

30 soup seasoning
汤的调味料

31 shop assistant (*Am.* salesgirl, saleslady)
女店员（女售货员）

32-34 pastas
面食

32 spaghetti
细通心面（意大利面食）

33 macaroni
通心粉，通心面

34 noodles
面条

35-39 cereal products
谷物制品

35 pearl barley
[小粒，球状的]精白麦

36 semolina
粗粒小麦

37 rolled oats (porridge oats, oat
燕麦（燕麦片）

38 rice
米

39 sago
西谷米

40 salt
食盐

41 grocer (*Am.* groceryman), a shopkeeper (tradesman, retail
Am. storekeeper)
食品杂货商，店主（商人，零售商

42 capers
醃渍续随子花蕾

43 customer
顾客

44 receipt (sales check)
收据

45 shopping bag
购物袋

49 wrapping material
包装材料

wrapping paper
包装纸

adhesive tape
胶带

paper bag
纸袋

cone-shaped paper bag
锥形纸袋

blancmange powder
乳冻点心粉

whole-fruit jam (preserve)
纯果酱

jam
果酱

55 sugar
食糖

cube sugar
方糖

icing sugar (*Am.* confectioner's sugar)
精制细砂糖

refined sugar in crystals
精制结晶糖

59 spirits
酒类

whisky (whiskey)
威士忌酒

rum
甜酒（甘蔗蜜糖酿造）

liqueur
利口酒[具甜味而芳香的烈酒]

brandy (cognac)
白兰地酒

64 wine in bottles (bottled wine)
瓶装葡萄酒

60 white wine
白（葡萄）酒

61 Chianti
意大利产红葡萄酒

62 vermouth
苦艾酒（白葡萄酒的一种）

63 sparkling wine
（起泡葡萄酒）香槟等

64 red wine
红（葡萄）酒

65-68 tea, coffee, etc.
茶，咖啡等

65 coffee (pure coffee)
咖啡（纯咖啡）

66 cocoa
可可

67 coffee
咖啡

68 tea bag
茶袋

69 electric coffee grinder
电动磨咖啡机

70 coffee roaster
咖啡豆烘烤器

71 roasting drum
烘烤鼓轮

72 sample scoop
样品杓，抽样杓

73 price list
价格表

74 freezer
冷藏柜，冰箱

75-86 confectionery (*Am.* candies)
糖果类

75 sweet (*Am.* candy)
糖果

76 drops
水果糖

77 toffees
太妃糖（以糖和奶油做成的糖）

78 bar of chocolate
巧克力棒

79 chocolate box
盒装巧克力

80 chocolate, a sweet
巧克力糖，一种甜食

81 nougat
牛轧糖（奶油杏仁糖）

82 marzipan
蛋白杏仁糖果

83 chocolate liqueur
巧克力酒糖

84 Turkish delight
橡皮糖，胶状糖球

85 croquant
果仁糖，胡桃糖

86 truffle
松露糖

87 soda water
汽水

1-96 **supermarket,** a self-service food store
超级市场，自助式食品店

1 shopping trolley
购物手推车

2 customer
顾客

3 shopping bag
购物袋

4 entrance to the sales area
商场入口

5 barrier
栅栏

6 sign (notice) banning dogs
禁止狗进入的标示

7 dogs tied by their leads
被绳索栓住的狗

8 basket
篮，筐

9 **bread and cake counter** (bread counter, cake counter)
面包和糕饼柜台

10 display counter for bread and cakes
面包和糕饼的陈列柜台

11 kinds of bread (breads)
各式面包

12 rolls
小圆面包

13 croissants (crescent rolls, Am. crescents)
新月形面包，牛角面包

14 round loaf
圆块面包

15 gateau
嘉陀（一种浓味糕饼）

16 pretzel 'made with yeast dough'
脆饼'由发酵的面团做的'

17 shop assistant (Am. salesgirl, saleslady)
店员，[美]女售货员

18 customer
顾客

19 sign listing goods
商品告示牌

20 fruit flan
水果馅饼

21 slab cake
长方块蛋糕

22 ring cake
环形蛋糕

23 **cosmetics gondola,** a gondola (sales shelves)
化妆品陈列架，设於商场中央之陈列架（售货架）

24 canopy
篷子

25 hosiery shelf
袜类、内衣等货品架

26 stockings (nylons)
（尼龙）长袜

27-35 **toiletries** (cosmetics)
化妆品

27 jar of cream (*kinds:* moisturising cream, day cream, night-care cream, hand cream)
瓶装面霜（种类：润肤膏，白日用面霜，夜晚保养用面霜，手部保养霜）

28 packet of cotton wool
脱脂棉包

29 talcum powder
爽身粉

30 packet of cotton wool balls
脱脂棉球包

31 toothpaste
牙膏

32 nail varnish (nail polish)
指甲油

33 shaving cream
刮胡霜

34 bath salts
浴盐

35 sanitry articles
卫生用品（保健用品）

36-37 **pet foods**
宠物食品

36 complete dog food
营养完全的狗食物

37 packet of dog biscuits
狗饼干包

38 bag of cat litter
猫窝袋

39 **cheese counter**
乳酪柜台

40 whole cheese
全脂乳酪

41 Swiss cheese (Emmental cheese with holes
瑞士乳酪，多孔的乳酪

42 Edam cheese, a round cheese
依顿乾酪，一种圆的乳酪

43 gondola for dairy products
乳制品陈列架

44 long-life milk; *also:* pasteurized milk, homogenized milk
保久乳；亦称：杀过菌的牛乳，均质牛乳

45 plastic milk bag
塑胶袋装牛乳

cream
奶油

butter
牛油

margarine
人造牛油

box of cheeses
盒装乳酪

box of eggs
盒装鸡蛋

fresh meat counter (meat
counter)
新鲜肉柜台（肉柜台）

ham on the bone
火腿

meat (meat products)
食用肉（各种肉类）

sausages
香肠

ring of pork sausage
香肠圈（猪肉做的）

ring of blood sausage
香肠圈（猪肉和血做的）

freezer
冷藏室

51 frozen food
冷冻食品

poulard
阉母鸡

turkey leg (drumstick)
火鸡腿

boiling fowl
煮熟的禽肉

frozen vegetables
冷藏蔬菜

62 **gondola for baking ingredients
and cereal products**
烘烤配料和和谷类品的陈列架

63 wheat flour
小麦粉

64 sugar loaf
甜面包

65 packet of noodles
小包面条

66 salad oil
沙拉油

67 packet of spice
调味包

68-70 **tea, coffee, etc.**
茶、咖啡等

68 coffee
咖啡

69 packet of tea
小包茶叶

70 instant coffee
即溶咖啡

71 **drinks gondola**
饮料陈列架

72 soft drinks
不含酒精成份之饮料

73 can of beer (canned beer)
罐装啤酒

74 bottle of fruit juice (bottled fruit
juice)
瓶装果汁

75 can of fruit juice (canned fruit
juice)
罐装果汁

76 bottle of wine
瓶装葡萄酒

77 bottle of Chianti
瓶装红葡萄酒

78 bottle of champagne
瓶装香槟酒

79 emergency exit
紧急出口，安全门

80 **fruit and vegetable counter**
水果和蔬菜柜台

81 vegetable basket
菜篮

82 tomatoes
蕃茄

83 cucumbers
黄瓜

84 cauliflower
花菜

85 pineapple
凤梨

86 apples
苹果

87 pears
梨子

88 scales for weighing fruit
称水果的秤

89 grapes (bunches of grapes)
葡萄（葡萄串）

90 bananas
香蕉

91 can
罐头

92 **checkout**
付款台

93 cash register
现金出纳机，收银机

94 cashier
出纳员

95 chain
链条

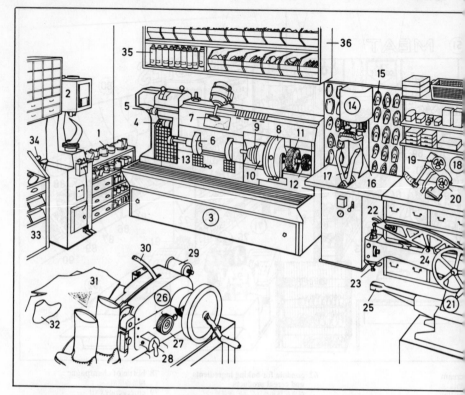

1-68 shoemaker's workshop (bootmaker's workshop)
（皮）鞋匠的工作室
1 finished (repaired) shoes
做好的（修好的）鞋子
2 auto-soling machine
自动装（配）鞋底机
3 finishing machine
完工机（完成最后一道手续的机器）
4 heel trimmer
鞋跟修整机
5 sole trimmer
鞋底修整机
6 scouring wheel
研磨轮
7 naum keag
浮石研磨轮
8 drive unit (drive wheel)
驱动装置（驱动轮）
9 iron
切削压铁
10 buffing wheel
擦光轮
11 polishing brush
擦光刷
12 horsehair brush
马毛刷
13 extractor grid
抽出器的格栅
14 automatic sole press
自动鞋底压型机
15 press attachment
压型机附件

16 pad
缓冲垫，衬垫
17 press bar
压杆
18 stretching machine
伸张（展）机
19 width adjustment
宽度调整
20 length adjustment
长度调整
21 stitching machine
缝合机，缝纫机
22 power regulator (power control)
动力调整器（动力控制）
23 foot
机脚
24 handwheel
手轮，操纵（作）轮
25 arm
腕木，托架，支撑臂
26 sole stitcher (sole-stitching machine)
鞋底缝纫（合）机
27 foot bar lever
脚踏杆
28 feed adjustment (feed setting)
进给调整器（进给设置）
29 bobbin (cotton bobbin)
线轴团（棉线轴）
30 thread guide (yarn guide)
导线杆
31 sole leather
鞋底皮革

32 [wooden] last
（木制）鞋型
33 workbench
工作台
34 last
鞋楦（制鞋用的型）
35 dye spray
染色喷雾器
36 shelves for materials
材料架

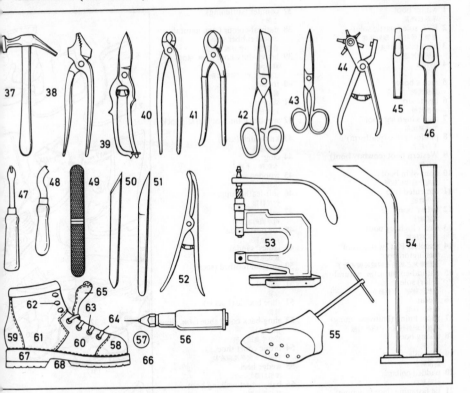

shoemaker's hammer
鞋匠的铁锤（榔头）
shoemaker's pliers (welt pincers)
鞋匠的钳子（镶边钳）
sole-leather shears
鞋底皮革剪
small pincers (nippers)
小铁钳
large pincers (nippers)
大铁钳
upper-leather shears
靴皮剪
scissors
剪刀
revolving punch (rotary punch)
旋转打孔器（钳）
punch
打孔器
punch with handle
有把手（柄）的打孔器
nail puller
拔钉钳
welt cutter
皮革切断器（切削刀）
shoemaker's rasp
鞋锉
cobbler's knife (shoemaker's knife)
（补）鞋匠刀
skiving knife (skife knife, paring knife)
切皮革的刀（薄片刀，削皮刀）
toecap remover
鞋尖拆卸钳

53 eyelet, hook, and press-stud setter
穿带孔，鞋扣和压钮定位器
54 stand with iron lasts
带鞋楦的立架
55 width-setting tree
宽度调整鞋楦
56 nail grip
起钉抓手
57 boot
靴子
58 toecap
鞋尖
59 counter
鞋面后跟部分
60 vamp
靴面
61 quarter
鞋帮的后侧部分
62 hook
鞋扣
63 eyelet
穿带孔
64 lace (shoelace, bootlace)
鞋带
65 tongue
鞋舌
66 sole
鞋底
67 heel
鞋跟
68 shank (waist)
鞋底（鞋跟上不着地的部分）

101 Shoes (Footwear)

1 winter boot
冬季长统靴
2 PVC sole (plastic sole)
聚氯乙烯鞋底（塑胶鞋底）
3 high-pile lining
长绒毛衬里
4 nylon
尼龙
5 men's boot
男长统靴
6 inside zip
内侧拉链
7 men's high leg boot
男式高统靴
8 platform sole (platform)
平台鞋底
9 Western boot (cowboy boot)
牛仔靴
10 pony-skin boot
连毛小马皮长统靴
11 cemented sole
胶合鞋底
12 ladies' boot
女式靴子
13 men's high leg boot
男式高统靴
14 seamless PVC waterproof
wellington boot
无缝聚氯乙烯防水的威灵顿式靴子
15 natural-colour (Am. natural-
color) sole
自然色鞋底，本色鞋底
16 toecap
鞋头，鞋尖
17 tricot lining (knitwear lining)
斜纹毛织品衬里（针织品衬里）
18 hiking boot
健行靴
19 grip sole
防滑鞋底
20 padded collar
衬垫鞋口
21 tie fastening (lace fastening)
鞋带
22 open-toe mule
露趾无后跟女式拖鞋
23 terry upper
厚绒布鞋帮
24 polo outsole
外鞋底
25 mule
无后跟女式拖鞋
26 corduroy upper
灯心绒鞋帮
27 evening sandal (sandal court
shoe)
高跟凉鞋
28 high heel (stiletto heel)
高跟（女子高跟鞋的细鞋跟）
29 court shoe (Am. pump)
（没鞋扣或鞋带的）女轻便高跟鞋
30 moccasin
鹿皮鞋
31 shoe, a tie shoe (laced shoe,
Oxford shoe, Am. Oxford)
牛津鞋（绑带鞋，一种便鞋）
32 tongue
鞋舌
33 high-heeled shoe (shoe with
raisedheel)
高跟鞋
34 casual
便鞋
35 trainer (training shoe)
教练鞋，运动鞋
36 tennis shoe
网球鞋

37 counter (stiffening)
主跟
38 natural-colour (Am. natural-
color) rubber sole
自然色（本色）橡皮鞋底
39 heavy-duty boot (Am. stogy,
stogie)
工作鞋（粗而坚牢的靴）
40 toecap
鞋尖
41 slipper
轻便套鞋
42 woollen (Am. woolen) slip sock
毛织软鞋
43 knit stitch (knit)
编织缝线
44 clog
木底鞋，木屐
45 wooden sole
木鞋底
46 soft-leather upper
软皮鞋帮
47 sabot
粗革面的木底鞋
48 toe post sandal
夹趾凉鞋
49 ladies' sandal
女式凉鞋
50 surgical footbed (sock)
足床
51 sandal
凉鞋
52 shoe buckle (buckle)
鞋扣
53 sling-back court shoe (Am. sling
pump)
后空半高跟女鞋
54 fabric court shoe
轻便的平底半高跟布鞋
55 wedge heel
楔形后跟
56 baby's first walking boot
婴儿学步鞋

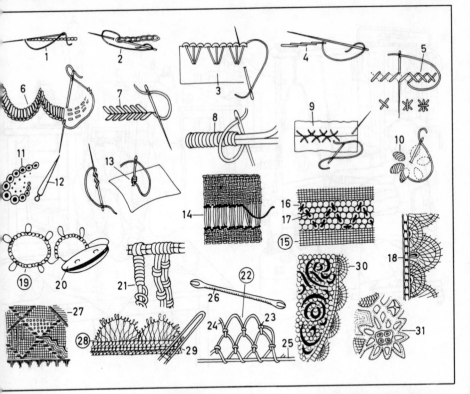

backstitch seam
回针针迹线缝
chain stitch
链缝，链式针（线）迹
ornamental stitch
饰缝，花式线迹
stem stitch
茎干缝，梗形线迹
cross stitch
十字缝，十字形针迹
buttonhole stitch (button stitch)
细孔缝，锁眼针迹
fishbone stitch
鱼骨缝，鱼骨形针迹
overcast stitch
缝边缝法，包边针迹
herringbone stitch (Russian
stitch, Russian cross stitch)
人字形交叉缝（俄罗斯十字线迹）
satin stitch (flat stitch)
缎子缝法，缎纹刺绣针迹
eyelet embroidery (broderie
anglaise)
饰孔刺绣，穿孔刺绣
stiletto
打孔器（锥）
French knot (French dot,
knotted stitch, twisted knot
stitich)
法式结（法国结点，打结针迹，编织的
结缝）
hem stitch work
抽丝后做成花边装饰的刺绣（垂缝刺
绣）

15 tulle work (tulle lace)
网状薄纱刺绣，六角网眼花边刺绣
16 tulle background (net
background)
网状纱底，网布素底（网眼底）
17 darning stitch
补缀缝，织补针迹
18 pillow lace (bobbin lace, bone
lace); *kinds:* Valenciennes,
Brussels lace
梭结花边，枕式花边（种类：瓦朗西
花边，布鲁塞尔花边）
19 tatting
梭织（结）花边
20 tatting shuttle (shuttle)
梭织的绕线轮（梭）
21 knotted work (macrame)
打结花边（丝结的饰缘，流苏花边）
22 filet (netting)
方眼花边网（结网）
23 netting loop
结网圈（环），编网网圈
24 netting thread
结网线，编网丝
25 mesh pin (mesh gauge)
网眼饰针（网眼规）
26 netting needle
结网针
27 open work
透孔织物
28 gimping (hairpin work)
嵌心绣法（发绣）
29 gimping needle (hairpin)
发针

30 needlepoint lace (point lace,
needlepoint); *kinds:* reticella
lace, Venetian lace, Alençon
lace; *sim.* with metal thread:
filigree work
针织花边；种类：针绣挖花花边，威尼
斯式花边，阿朗松式花边，类似：以金
属丝织的，金银丝花边细工
31 braid embroidery (braid work)
编结刺绣（彩饰）（编结织品）

1-27 dressmaker's workroom
裁缝工作室

1 dressmaker
裁缝师

**2 tape measure (measuring tape),
a metre (*Am*. meter) tape
measure**
卷尺,一种公制的卷尺

3 cutting shears
裁剪刀

4 cutting table
裁剪布

5 model dress
衣服的式样

**6 dressmaker's model
(dressmaker's dummy, dress
form)**
服装模特儿(裁缝师的模型,服装模型)

7 model coat
模型女式外套,式样大衣

8 sewing machine
缝纫机

9 drive motor
驱动马达

10 drive belt
驱动带

11 treadle
踏板

**12 sewing machine cotton (sewing
machine thread) [on boobin]**
缝纫机线(线筒)

13 cutting template
裁剪样板(模板)

14 seam binding
滚边材料

15 button box
钮扣盒

16 remnant
碎布,布头

17 movable clothes rack
可移动的衣架

18 hand-iron press
手工熨斗

19 presser (ironer)
熨衣工

20 steam iron
(喷)蒸汽电熨斗

21 water feed pipe
供水管,自来水管

22 water container
水箱,存水桶

23 adjustable-tilt ironing surface
可调整倾斜的熨烫台

24 lift device for the iron
熨斗的升降装置

25 steam extractor
蒸汽排出器

**26 foot switch controlling steam
extraction**
控制蒸汽排出器的脚踏开关

**27 pressed non-woven woollen
(*Am*. woolen) fabric**
熨烫的无纺毛织物

2 tailor's workroom
裁缝师工作室

1 triple mirror
三面镜

2 lengths of material
各种衣料

3 suiting
衣料，西服料

4 fashion journal (fashion
magazine)
时装杂志

5 ashtray
烟灰缸

6 fashion catalogue
时装目录

7 workbench
工作台

8 wall shelves (wall shelf unit)
壁架

9 cotton reel
棉线卷筒

10 small reels of sewing silk
小卷的缝纫丝线

11 hand shears
手工裁剪刀

12 combined electric and treadle
sewing machine
电动和脚踏两用的缝纫机

13 treadle
（脚）踏板

14 dress guard
护衣板

15 band wheel
皮带轮

16 bobbin thread
筒子线

17 sewing machine table
缝纫机台面

18 sewing machine drawer
缝纫机抽屉

19 seam binding
滚边材料

20 pincushion
针垫

21 marking out
划线

22 tailor
裁缝

23 shaping pad
样垫

24 tailor's chalk (French chalk)
裁缝划笔（滑石）

25 workpiece
工作件

26 steam press (steam pressing
unit)
蒸汽熨烫装置

27 swivel arm
旋转臂

28 pressing cushion (pressing pad)
烫平垫

29 iron
熨斗

30 hand-ironing pad
手工熨烫垫

31 clothes brush
衣刷

32 pressing cloth
熨烫布

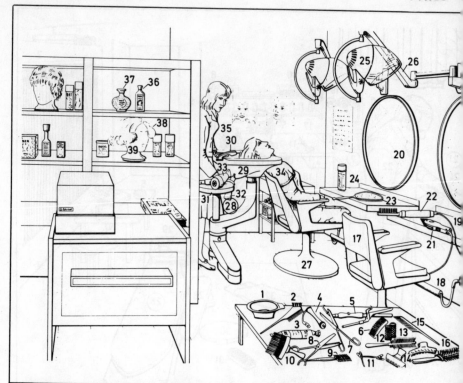

1-39 ladies' hairdressing salon and beauty salon (*Am.* beauty parlor, beauty shop)
女子理发厅和美容院

1-16 hairdresser's tools
理发工具

1 **bowl containing bleach**
装漂白剂的碗

2 **detangling brush**
梳理缠结的发刷

3 **bleach tube**
管装漂白剂

4 **curler** [used in dyeing]
染发用的卷发夹子

5 **curling tongs (curling iron)**
烫发钳

6 **comb (back comb, side comb)**
发梳（后梳，边梳）

7 **haircutting scissors**
理发剪

8 **thinning scissors** (*Am.* thinning shears)
削发剪

9 **thinning razor**
削发剃刀

10 **hairbrush**
发刷，毛刷

11 **hair clip**
发夹

12 **roller**
卷发器

13 **curl brush**
卷发刷

14 **curl clip**
卷发夹

15 **dressing comb**
润饰梳

16 **stiff-bristle brush**
（硬）钢毛刷

17 **adjustable hairdresser's chair**
可调整的理容椅

18 **footrest**
搁脚板

19 **dressing table**
梳妆台

20 **salon mirror (mirror)**
理发厅镜子

21 **electric clippers**
电动理发推子

22 **warm-air comb**
热吹风梳

23 **hand mirror (hand glass)**
手镜

24 **hair spray (hair-fixing spray)**
发喷雾器

25 **drier, a swivel-mounted drier**
干燥器，装于旋臂上的干燥器

26 **swivel arm of the drier**
干燥器的旋臂

27 **round base**
圆型底座

28 **shampoo unit**
洗发设备

29 **shampoo basin**
洗发盆

30 **hand spray (shampoo spray)**
手持喷雾器（洗发喷雾器）

31 **service tray**
工具托盘

32 **shampoo bottle**
瓶装洗发精

33 **hair drier (hand hair drier, hand-held hair drier)**
吹风机（手持型吹风机）

34 **cape (gown)**
披肩

35 **hairdresser**
理容师

36 **perfume bottle**
香水瓶

37 **bottle of toilet water**
瓶装花露水

38 **wig**
假发

39 **wig block**
陈列假发的木头架

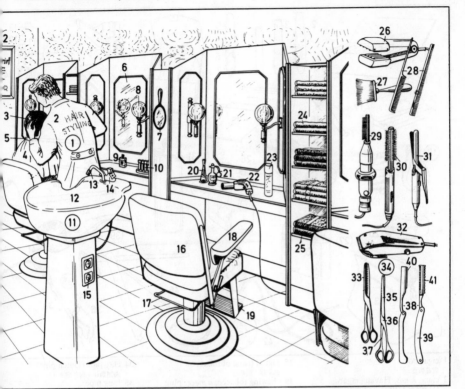

2 men's salon (men's
hairdressing salon, barber's
shop, *Am.* barbershop)
男士理发厅，男士理发店
hairdresser (barber)
理发师
overalls (hairdresser's overalls)
罩衣工作服（理发师工作服）
hairstyle (haircut)
发型（理发）
cape (gown)
肩巾，披肩
paper towel
纸毛巾
salon mirror (mirror)
理发厅镜子
hand mirror (hand glass)
手镜
light
（电）灯
toilet water
化妆水
hair tonic
洗发剂
shampoo unit
洗发设备
shampoo basin
洗发盆
hand spray (shampoo spray)
手持喷雾器（洗发喷雾器）
mixer tap (*Am.* mixing faucet)
（冷热水的）混合龙头
sockets, e.g. for hair drier
插座，例如吹风机用的插座

16 adjustable hairdresser s chair
(barber's chair)
可调整的理发椅
17 height-adjuster bar (height
adjuster)
高度调整杆（高度调整器）
18 armrest
靠椅扶手
19 footrest
搁脚板
20 shampoo
洗发精
21 perfume spray
香水喷雾器
22 hair drier (hand hair drier,
hand-held hair drier)
吹风机（手持吹风机）
23 setting lotion in a spray can
喷罐装的做发化妆水（洗发精）
24 hand towels for drying hair
擦乾头发用的毛巾
25 towels for face compresses
敷脸用的毛巾
26 crimping iron
烫发钳
27 neck brush
颈刷
28 dressing comb
润饰梳
29 warm-air comb
热风梳
30 warm-air brush
热风刷

31 curling tongs (hair curler,
curling iron)
卷发钳
32 electric clippers
电动理发推子
33 thinning scissors (*Am.* thinning
shears)
削发剪
34 haircutting scissors; *sim.:* styling
scissors
理发剪；类似有：各类发型的剪刀
35 scissor-blade
剪刀刃部
36 pivot
枢轴
37 handle
手柄
38 open razor (straight razor)
开式剃刀（直柄剃刀）
39 razor handle
剃刀柄
40 edge (cutting edge, razor's edge,
razor's cutting edge)
刀刃（剃刀刀刃）
41 thinning razor
削发剃刀
42 diploma
执照，营业许可证

1 cigar box
雪茄烟盒
2 cigar; *kinds:* Havana cigar
(Havana), Brazilian cigar,
Sumatra cigar
雪茄；种类：哈瓦那雪茄，巴西雪茄，
苏门答腊雪茄
3 cigarillo
小雪茄烟
4 cheroot
方头雪茄烟
5 wrapper
雪茄烟的外卷叶
6 binder
中卷叶
7 filler
雪茄烟烟心
8 cigar case
雪茄烟盒
9 cigar cutter
雪茄切器
10 cigarette case
香烟盒
11 cigarette packet (*Am.* pack)
一包香烟
12 cigarette, a filter-tipped cigarette
香烟，有滤咀的香烟
13 cigarette tip; *kinds:* cork tip,
gold tip
香烟滤咀；种类：软木滤咀，金箔滤咀
14 Russian cigarette
俄国香烟
15 cigarette roller
卷烟器
16 cigarette holder
香烟烟咀
17 packet of cigarette papers
一盒香烟纸

18 pigtail (twist of tobacco)
撚草烟，烟草卷
19 chewing tobacco; *a piece:* plug
(quid, chew)
咀嚼烟草；一块的称作：嚼烟块
20 snuff box, containing snuff
鼻烟盒
21 matchbox
火柴盒
22 match
火柴
23 head (match head)
火柴头
24 striking surface
擦火柴磷面
25 packet of tobacco; *kinds:* find
cut, shag, navy plug
一包烟草；种类：细切烟丝，板烟，口
嚼烟草块
26 revenue stamp
印花
27 petrol cigarette lighter (petrol
lighter)
汽油香烟打火机（汽油打火机）
28 flint
打火石
29 wick
灯心
30 gas cigarette lighter (gas
lighter), a disposable lighter
瓦斯香烟打火机（瓦斯打火机），可随
意使用的打火机（用完即丢的打火机）
31 flame regulator
火焰调节器
32 chibouk (chibouque)
长烟斗
33 short pipe
短烟斗

34 clay pipe (Dutch pipe)
陶制烟斗（荷兰烟斗）
35 long pipe
长管烟斗
36 pipe bowl (bowl)
烟斗的燃斗
37 bowl lid
烟斗盖
38 pipe stem (stem)
烟斗柄（杆）
39 briar pipe
石南根所制的烟斗
40 mouthpiece
烟咀
41 sand-blast finished or polished
briar grain
喷沙精制或磨光的石南纹烟斗
42 hookah (narghile, narghileh), a
water pipe
水烟筒，一种水烟斗
43 tobacco pouch
烟草袋
44 smoker's companion
吸烟者的用具
45 pipe scraper
烟斗刮刀
46 pipe cleaner
烟管除垢器
47 tobacco presser
烟斗加压器
48 pipe cleaner
烟管除垢杆

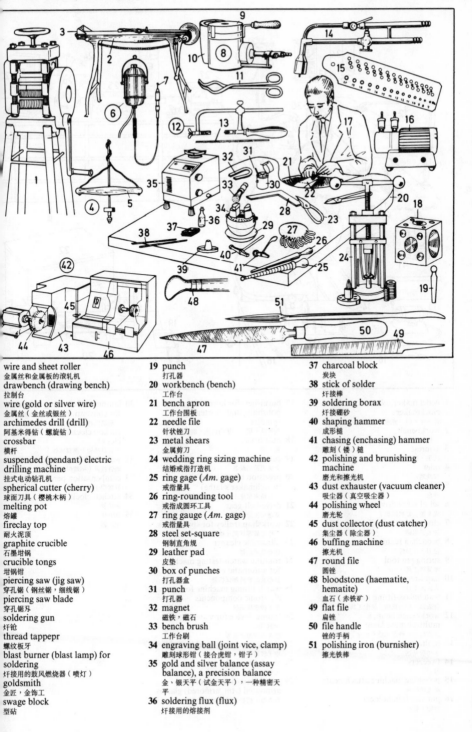

1 wire and sheet roller
金属丝和金属板的滚轧机
2 drawbench (drawing bench)
拉制台
3 wire (gold or silver wire)
金属丝（金丝或银丝）
4 archimedes drill (drill)
阿基米得钻（螺旋钻）
5 crossbar
横杆
6 suspended (pendant) electric
drilling machine
挂式电动钻孔机
7 spherical cutter (cherry)
球面刀具（樱桃木柄）
8 melting pot
熔锅
9 fireclay top
耐火泥顶
10 graphite crucible
石墨坩锅
11 crucible tongs
坩锅钳
12 piercing saw (jig saw)
穿孔锯（钢丝锯，细线锯）
13 piercing saw blade
穿孔锯刃
14 soldering gun
钎铊
15 thread tappepr
螺纹板牙
16 blast burner (blast lamp) for
soldering
钎接用的鼓风燃烧器（喷灯）
17 goldsmith
金匠，金饰工
18 swage block
型砧

19 punch
打孔器
20 workbench (bench)
工作台
21 bench apron
工作台围板
22 needle file
针状锉刀
23 metal shears
金属剪刀
24 wedding ring sizing machine
结婚戒指打造机
25 ring gage (*Am.* gage)
戒指量具
26 ring-rounding tool
戒指成圆环工具
27 ring gauge (*Am.* gage)
戒指量具
28 steel set-square
钢制直角尺
29 leather pad
皮垫
30 box of punches
打孔器盒
31 punch
打孔器
32 magnet
磁铁，磁石
33 bench brush
工作台刷
34 engraving ball (joint vice, clamp)
雕刻球形钳（接合虎钳，钳子）
35 gold and silver balance (assay
balance), a precision balance
金、银天平（试金天平），一种精密天
平
36 soldering flux (flux)
钎接用的熔接剂

37 charcoal block
炭块
38 stick of solder
钎接棒
39 soldering borax
钎接硼砂
40 shaping hammer
成形锤
41 chasing (enchasing) hammer
雕刻（镂）槌
42 polishing and brunishing
machine
磨光和擦光机
43 dust exhauster (vacuum cleaner)
吸尘器（真空吸尘器）
44 polishing wheel
磨光轮
45 dust collector (dust catcher)
集尘器（除尘器）
46 buffing machine
擦光机
47 round file
圆锉
48 bloodstone (haematite,
hematite)
血石（赤铁矿）
49 flat file
扁锉
50 file handle
锉的手柄
51 polishing iron (burnisher)
擦光铁棒

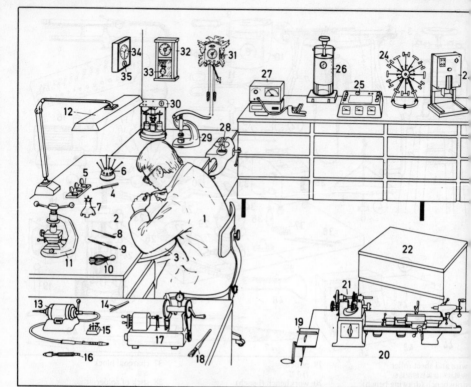

1 watchmaker; *also:* clockmaker
钟表匠，即：修理钟表的人

2 workbench
工作台

3 armrest
扶手，搁手板

4 oiler
加油笔

5 oil stand
油台

6 set of screwdrivers
成（整）套螺丝起子

7 clockmaker's anvil
钟表匠用砧

8 broach, a reamer
拉刀，一种绞刀

9 spring pin tool
弹簧销工具

10 hand-removing tool
表拆卸工具

11 watchglass-fitting tool
钟表皿（护面玻璃）装配工具

12 workbench lamp, a multi-purpose lamp
工作灯，一种多功能（用途）灯

13 multi-purpose motor
多功能马达

14 tweezers
镊子

15 polishing machine attachments
磨光机附件

16 pin vice (pin holder)
针钳（针夹）

17 burnisher, for burnishing, polishing, and shortening of spindles
压光机，用於心轴的压光、磨光和缩短

18 dust brush
灰尘刷

19 cutter for metal watch straps
金属表带切断器

20 precision bench lathe (watchmaker's lathe)
台式精密车床（钟表匠的车床）

21 drive-belt gear
驱动带齿轮装置

22 workshop trolley for spare parts
工作室装零件的手推车

23 ultrasonic cleaner
超音波清洁器

24 rotating watch-testing machine for automatic watches
自动表的旋转测试机

25 watch-timing machine for electronic components
电子表校正仪

26 testing device for waterproof watches
防水表的测试装置

27 electronic timing machine
电子校时器

28 vice (*Am.* vise)
虎钳

29 watchglass-fitting tool for armoured (*Am.* armored) glasses
钟表皿（防护玻璃）的装配工具

30 [automatic] cleaning machine for conventional cleaning
一般清洗钟表用的自动清洗机

31 cuckoo clock (Black Forest clock)
布谷鸟鸣钟（黑森林钟）

32 wall clock (regulator)
墙钟挂钟（标准时钟）

33 compensation pendulum
补整摆子

34 kitchen clock
厨房钟

35 timer
定时器

electronic wristwatch
电子手表
digital readout, a light-emitting
diode (LED) readout; *also:*
liquid crystal readout
数字显示，一种发光二极体的显示；即
液态晶体读出器
hour and minute button
时和分的按钮
date and second button
日期和秒的按钮
strap (watch strap)
表带
tuning fork principle
(principle of the tuning fork
watch)
音叉原理（音叉表原理）
power source (battery cell)
电源（电池）
transformer
变压器
tuning fork element (oscillating
element)
音叉元件（摆动元件）振荡要素
wheel ratchet
棘轮
wheels
轮
minute hand
分针（长针）
hour hand
时针（短针）
principle of the electronic quartz
watch
电子石英表的原理
quartz
石英
integrated circuit
积体电路
oscillation counter
振荡计数器
decoder
解码器
calendar clock (alarm clock)
日历钟（闹钟）
digital display with flip-over
numerals
翻转数字显示器
second indicator
秒指示器
stop button
停止按钮
forward and backward wind
knob
调前或调后的旋钮
grandfather clock
有钟摆的落地大时钟
face
钟面
clock case
钟壳
pendulum
钟摆
striking weight
打点重锤，响槌
time weight
计时动锤
sundial
日晷
hourglass (egg timer)
沙漏，水漏（蛋形计时器）
**43 components of an automatic
watch** (automatic wristwatch)
自动表的零件

32 weight (rotor)
   摆块（转动体）
33 stone (jewel, jewelled bearing), a
   synthetic ruby
   宝石（宝石轴承），一种合成红宝石
34 click
   掣子
35 click wheel
   掣子轮
36 clockwork (clockwork
   mechanism)
   钟表装置（钟表机械装置）
37 bottom train plate
   底部连动板，主夹板
38 spring barrel
   发条盒
39 balance wheel
   平衡轮，摆轮
40 escape wheel
   擒纵轮
41 crown wheel
   冠状轮
42 winding crown
   发条钮
43 drive mechanism
   驱动装置

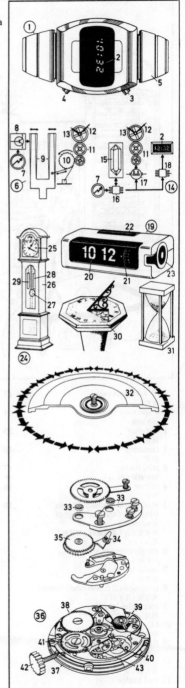

1-19 sales premises
販卖店

1-4 spectacle fitting
试配眼镜

1 optician
眼镜商

2 customer
顾客

3 trial frame
试配镜架（框）

4 mirror
镜子

5 stand with spectacle frames
(display of frames, range of
spectacles)
镜架展示台（镜架陈列，眼镜种类台架）

6 sunglasses (sun spectacles)
太阳眼镜

7 metal frame
金属框

8 tortoiseshell frame (shell frame)
玳瑁框（龟甲框）

9 spectacles (glasses)
眼镜

10-14 spectacle frame
眼镜框

10 fitting (mount) of the frame
眼镜架

11 bridge
鼻（梁）架

12 pad bridge
托叶

13 side
眼镜脚

14 side joint
镜脚与镜片框接合处

15 spectacle lens, a bifocal lens
眼镜镜片，一种双焦镜片

16 hand mirror (hand glass)
手镜

17 binoculars
双筒望远镜

18 monocular telescope (tube)
单筒（眼）望远镜

19 microscope
显微镜

optician's workshop
镜商工作室
orkbench
作台
niversal centring (centering)
pparatus
能定心仪
entring (centering) suction
older
心吸力托盘
cker
盘
ging machine
边机
rmers for the lens edging
achine
片磨边机用的样品（型，模型）
serted former
入模型
tating printer
转磨板
brasive wheel combination
轮组
ontrol unit
制箱（装置）
achine part
械部分
oling water pipe
却水管
eaning fluid
净液，洗涤液
cimeter (vertex
fractionometer)
距测定器（顶点视力检测器）

34 metal-blocking device
   金属压模装置
35 abrasive wheel combination and
   forms of edging
   磨轮组和磨边用的模型
36 roughing wheel for preliminary
   surfacing
   粗磨表面用的粗磨轮
37 fining lap for positive and
   negative lens surfaces
   正负透镜表面的精研磨轮
38 fining lap for special and flat
   lenses
   特殊和平面镜的精研磨轮
39 plano-concave lens with a flat
   surface
   具一个平面的平凹透镜
40 plano-concave lens with a
   special surface
   具特殊表面的平凹透镜
41 concave and convex lens with a
   special surface
   具特殊表面的凹凸透镜
42 convex and concave lens with a
   special surface
   具特殊表面的凸凹透镜
43 ophthalmic test stand
   眼睛测试，验光台
44 phoropter with ophthalmometer
   and optometer (refractometer)
   具眼膜曲率计和验光计（屈光计）的光
   觉计
45 trial lens case
   验光镜箱

46 collimator
   准直仪，准直管，平行光管
47 acuity projector
   敏锐度投影器

1 laboratory and research
microscope, *Leitz system*
实验室和研究用显微镜，列兹系统
2 stand
机架
3 base
底座
4 coarse adjustment
粗调整
5 fine adjustment
微调整
6 illumination beam path
(illumination path)
照明光束路径（照明路线）
7 illumination optics
照明光学部件
8 condenser
聚光器
9 microscope (microscopic,
object) stage
显微镜台
10 mechanical stage
机械台
11 objective turret (revolving
nosepiece)
物镜旋转盘（换镜旋座）
12 binocular head
双目镜头
13 beam-splitting prisms
分光棱镜
14 transmitted-light microscope
with camera and polarizer, *Zeiss
system*
带照相机和起偏振镜的透射光显微镜，
蔡司系统
15 stage base
台架底座
16 aperture-stop slide
孔径光阑滑动片
17 universal stage
万向旋转台
18 lens panel
镜头盘，透镜盘
19 polarizing filter
起偏振滤光器
20 camera
相机
21 focusing screen
调焦屏
22 discussion tube arrangement
检讨（分析）管装置
23 wide-field metallurgical
microscope, a reflected-light
microscope (microscope for
reflected light)
广域冶金显微镜，一种反射光显微镜
24 matt screen (ground glass
screen, projection screen)
无光泽屏（毛玻璃屏，投影屏）
25 large-format camera
大型照相机
26 miniature camera
小型照相机
27 base plate
底座板
28 lamphouse
灯室（箱）
29 mechanical stage
机械台
30 objective turret (revolving
nosepiece)
物镜旋转塔（换镜旋座）
31 surgical microscope
外科（手术的）显微镜
32 pillar stand
柱座

33 field illumination
视场（界）照明
34 photomicroscope
显微照相机
35 miniature film cassette
小型软片盒
36 photomicrographic camera
attachment for large-format or
television camera
供大型相机和电视摄影机用的显微照相
机附件
37 surface-finish microscope
表面修整的显微镜
38 light section tube
光线部分管
39 rack and pinion
齿条和齿轮
40 zoom stereomicroscope
变焦体视显微镜
41 zoom lens
可变焦透镜
42 dust counter
尘量计
43 measurement chamber
测量室
44 data output
数据输出
45 analogue (*Am.* analog) output
相似输出，模拟输出
46 measurement range selector
测定域选择器
47 digital display (digital readout)
数字显示（数字读出）
48 dipping refractometer for
examining food
检验食品用的浸渍折射计
49 microscopic photometer
显微光度计
50 photometric light source
光度计的光源
51 measuring device
(photomultiplier, multiplier
phototube)
测量装置（光电倍加管）
52 light source for survey
illumination
测量照明用的光源
53 remote electronics
遥控电子设备
54 universal wide-field microscope
万能广域显微镜
55 adapter for camera or projector
attachment
照相机或投影机附件用的接合器
56 eyepiece focusing knob
目镜调焦钮
57 filter pick-up
滤色片插口
58 handrest
扶手（板），搁手台
59 lamphouse for incident (vertical)
illumination
入射（垂直）照明灯箱
60 lamphouse connector for
transillumination
透照明灯箱连接器
61 wide-field stereomicroscope
广域体视显微镜
62 interchangeable lenses
(objectives)
可互换的镜头（物镜）
63 incident (vertical) illumination
(incident top lighting)
（垂直）入射照明（顶入射照明）

64 fully automatic microscope
camera, a camera with
photomicro mount adapter
全自动显微照相机，有显微镜座架接头
的照相机
65 film cassette
软片盒
66 universal condenser for research
microscope 1
研究显微镜用的万向聚光器
67 universal-type measuring
machine for photogrammetry
(phototheodolite)
照相测量用的（照相经纬仪）全能测量
机器
68 photogrammetric camera
测量照相机
69 motor-driven level, a
compensator level
马达驱动杆，补整器杆
70 electro-optical
distance-measuring
instrument
电场光学的测距仪器
71 stereometric camera
体视测量照相机
72 horizontal base
水平基座
73 one-second theodolite
一秒纱经纬仪

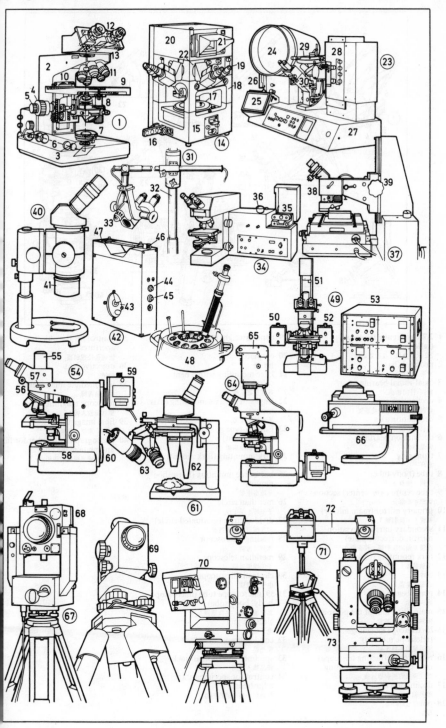

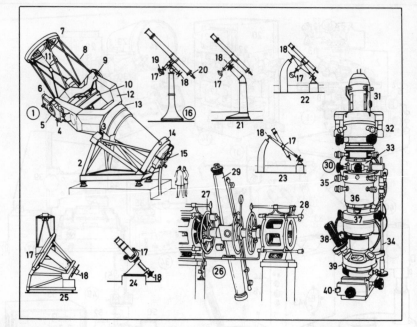

1 **2.2m reflecting telescope (reflector)**
2.2 米（公尺）反射望远镜
2 pedestal (base)
支架（底座）
3 axial-radial bearing
轴向－径向轴承
4 declination gear
倾斜齿轮（偏差转动装置）
5 declination axis
倾斜轴（偏差轴）
6 declination bearing
偏差轴承
7 front ring
前环
8 tube (body tube)
镜筒（筒身）
9 tube centre (*Am.* center) section
镜筒中心部分
10 primary mirror (main mirror)
初镜（主反射镜）
11 secondary mirror (deviation mirror, corrector plate)
次镜（偏向反射镜，校正板）
12 fork mounting (fork)
叉状装置（叉架）
13 cover
遮盖，复盖
14 guide bearing
导向轴承
15 main drive unit of the polar axis
极轴的主驱动装置
16-25 telescope mountings
(telescope mounts)
望远镜的各种座架
16 refractor (refracting telescope) on a German-type mounting
德式座架的折射望远镜
17 declination axis
偏差轴
18 polar axis
极轴

19 counterweight (counterpoise)
平衡锤（对重，配重）
20 eyepiece
接目镜
21 knee mounting with a bent column
弯柱支架（座）
22 English-type axis mounting (axis mount)
英式轴型座架
23 English-type yoke mounting (yoke mount)
英式轭铁型座架
24 fork mounting (fork mount)
叉型座架
25 horseshoe mounting (horseshoe mount)
马蹄型座架
26 meridian circle
子午环，子午仪
27 divided circle (graduated circle)
刻度圆盘（分度圆盘）
28 reading microscope
读数显微镜
29 meridian telescope
子午线望远镜
30 electron microscope
电子显微镜
31-39 microscope tube (microscope body, body tube)
显微镜镜筒（显微镜镜身）
31 electron gun
电子枪
32 condensers
聚光器
33 specimen insertion air lock
样品插入气闸
34 control for specimen stage adjustment
样品台调整用的控制器

35 control for the objective apertures
物镜孔径控制器
36 objective lens
物镜
37 intermediate image screen
中间显像屏
38 telescope magnifier
望远镜放大镜
39 final image tube
最终（末级）显像管
40 photographic chamber for film and plate magazines
软片和感光板用的照相室

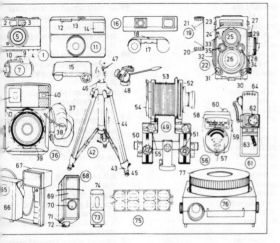

44 tubular leg
管型撑腿
45 rubber foot
橡胶（皮）脚
46 central column
中心柱
47 ball and socket head
球形座头
48 cine camera pan and tilt head
电影照相机可以下左右移动的座头
49 large-format folding camera
大型摺叠照相机
50 optical bench
光具座
51 standard adjustment
标准调整装置
52 lens standard
透镜标准
53 bellows
蛇腹（皮腔）
54 camera back
机背
55 back standard adjustment
机背标准调整装置
56 hand-held exposure meter
(exposure meter)
手提曝光计
57 calculator dial
计算刻度盘
58 scales (indicator scales) with
indicator needle (pointer)
带指针的刻度盘（指示盘）
59 range switch (high / low range
selector)
量程开关（高／低量程选择器）
60 diffuser for incident light
measurement
测量入射光线的漫射体
61 probe exposure meter for large
format cameras
大型照相机用的试探曝光计
62 meter
计量器
63 probe
探针
64 dark slide
底片盒
65 battery-portable electronic flash
(battery-portable electronic
flash unit)
电池供电手提式的电子闪光灯
66 powerpack unit (battery)
动力单元（电池）
67 flash head
闪光灯头
68 single-unit electronic flash
(flashgun)
单一光源电子闪光灯（闪光枪）
69 swivel-mounted reflector
旋钮座反射镜
70 photodiode
光电二极管
71 foot
足部
72 hot-shoe contact
直接接点，直接接触闪光
73 flash cube unit
方形闪光装置
74 flash cube
方形闪光灯
75 flash bar
棒状闪光灯
76 slide projector
幻灯机
77 rotary magazine
旋转式片盒

iniature camera
35mm camera）
小型照相机（35 毫米照相机）
iewfinder eyepiece
景器目镜
meter cell
曝光计电池
ccessory shoe
件插座板
lush lens
入式镜头
ewind handle (rewind, rewind
rank)
片杆（翻片装置，翻片曲柄）
iniature film cassette (135 film
assette, 35 mm cassette)
小型底片壳（135 底片壳，35 毫米底片
）
lm spool
轴
lm with leader
有头的底片
assette slit (cassette exit slot)
片壳夹缝（底片壳出口槽）
artridge-loading camera
式装片照相机
hutter release (shutter release
utton)
门放松器（快门放松器按钮）
ash cube contact
形闪光接点
ectangular viewfinder
形取景器
26 cartridge (instamatic
artridge)
26 底片（插入式）匣式底片
ocket camera (subminiature
amera)
珍照相机（超小型照相机）
10 cartridge (subminiature
artridge)
10 底片（超小型底片）
lm window
片计数窗
20 rollfilm
20 底片
ollfilm spool
片卷简轴
acking paper
纸

22 twin-lens reflex camera
双镜头反射照相机
23 folding viewfinder hood
(focusing hood)
摺叠式取景器遮光罩（聚焦遮光罩）
24 meter cell
曝光计电池
25 viewing lens
取景镜头
26 object lens
物镜
27 spool knob
片轴钮
28 distance setting (focus setting)
距离调整装置（焦点调整装置）
29 exposure meter using
needle-matching system
用指针调准方式的曝光计
30 flash contact
闪光灯接点
31 shutter release
快门放松器
32 film transport (film advance,
film wind)
底片扳送装置（底片前进装置，卷片装
置）
33 flash switch
闪光灯开关
34 aperture-setting control
光圈调整装置
35 shutter speed control
快门速度控制
36 large-format hand camera (press
camera)
大型手提照相机（新闻照相机）
37 grip (handgrip)
柄（手柄）
38 cable release
快门线
39 distance-setting ring (focusing
ring)
距离调整环（调焦环）
40 rangefinder window
测距的观察窗
41 multiple-frame viewfinder
(universal viewfinder)
多框观景窗（通用观景窗）
42 tripod
三脚架
43 tripod leg
三脚架腿

1-105 system camera
照相机系统

1 miniature single-lens reflex camera
小型单镜头反光照相机

2 camera body
机身

3 - 8 lens, a normal lens (standard lens)
镜头，标准镜头

3 lens barrel
镜头筒

4 distance scale in metres and feet
用公尺和英呎的距离标尺

5 aperture ring (aperture-setting ring, aperture control ring)
光圈环（光圈调整环，光圈控制环）

6 front element mount with filter mount
具滤色片（接口）的镜头前镜片座

7 front element
镜头前镜片

8 focusing ring (distance-setting ring)
调焦环[远近（距离）调整环]

9 ring for the carrying strap
携带用的皮带环

10 battery chamber
电池槽

11 screw-in cover
螺丝盖

12 rewind handle (rewind, rewind crank)
退片杆（退片装置，退片曲柄）

13 battery switch
电池开关

14 flash socket for F and X contact
F 和 X 接点用的闪光灯插座

15 self-time lever (setting lever for the self-timer, setting lever for the delayed-action release)
自动拍照杆（自动拍照器用的调整杆，延迟作用放松器用的调整杆）

16 single-stroke film advance lever
单一冲程底片调节杆

17 exposure counter (frame counter)
曝光计数器（框格计数器）

18 shutter release (shutter release button)
快门放松器（快门放松器按钮）

19 shutter speed setting knob (shutter speed control)
快门速度调整钮（快门速度控制）

20 accessory shoe
附件插座

21 hot-shoe flash contact
直接闪光接点

22 viewfinder eyepiece with correcting lens
带校正透镜的观景窗目镜

23 camera back
照相机背

24 pressure plate
压板

25 take-up spool of the rapid-loading system
快速装片的收片盘

26 transport sprocket
输片齿轮

27 rewind release button (reversing clutch)
退片钮（换向离合器）

28 film window
底片计数窗

29 rewind cam
退片凸轮

30 tripod socket (tripod bush)
三角架插座

31 reflex system (mirror reflex system)
反射系统（镜面反射系统）

32 lens
镜头

33 reflex mirror
反射镜

34 film window
底片计数窗

35 path of the image beam
影像束光程（通路）

36 path of the sample beam
样本射束光程（通路）

37 meter cell
计器电池

38 auxiliary mirror
辅助反射镜

39 focusing screen
调焦屏

40 field lens
视场透镜

41 pentaprism
五棱镜

42 eyepiece
接目镜

43-105 system of accessories
附件系统

43 interchangeable lenses
可互换镜头

44 fisheye lens (fisheye)
鱼眼镜头

45 wide-angle lens (short focal length lens)
广角镜头（短焦距镜头）

46 normal lens (standard lens)
标准镜头

47 medium focal length lens
中焦距镜头

48 telephoto lens (long focal length lens)
望远镜头（长焦距镜头）

49 long-focus lens
长焦距镜头

50 mirror lens
反射镜头

51 viewfinder image
观景窗探视器影像

52 signal to switch to manual control
转向手动控制的信号

53 matt collar (ground glass collar)
毛玻璃环

54 microprism collar
显微棱镜环

55 split-image rangefinder (focusing wedges)
分割影像的测距器（调焦光楔）

56 aperture scale
光圈刻度

57 exposure meter needle
曝光计指针

58-66 interchangeable focusing screens
可互换调焦屏

58 all-matt screen (ground glass screen) with microprism spot
具显微棱镜光点的全无泽屏（毛玻璃屏）

59 all-matt screen (ground glass screen) with microprism spot and split-image rangefinder
具显微棱镜和分割影像测距器的全无泽屏（毛玻璃屏）

60 all-matt screen (ground glass screen) without focusing aids
无聚焦辅助设备的全无泽屏（毛玻璃屏）

61 matt screen (ground glass screen) with reticule
具标线行的无泽屏（毛玻璃屏）

62 microprism spot for lenses with a large aperture
大光圈镜头用的显微棱镜光点

63 microprism spot for lenses with an aperture of f = 1 : 3.5 or larger
孔径 f = 1 : 3.5 或更大的镜头显微棱镜光点

64 Fresnel lens with matt collar (ground glass collar) and split-image rangefinder
具无泽环（毛玻璃环）和分割影像测距器的夫瑞奈镜头

65 all-matt screen (ground glass screen) with finely matted central spot and graduated markings
具精密无泽中心光点和刻度线的全无泽屏（毛玻璃屏）

66 matt screen (ground glass screen) with clear spot and double cross hairs
具清晰光点和双十字线（丝）的无泽屏（毛玻璃屏）

67 data recording back for exposing data about shots
记录各镜头曝光数据的装置

68 viewfinder hood (focusing hood)
观景窗（探视器）遮光罩

69 interchangeable pentaprism viewfinder
可互换的五棱镜的观景窗（探视器）

70 pentaprism
五角棱镜

71 right-angle viewfinder
直角（垂直）观景窗（探视器）

72 correction lens
校正镜头

73 eyecup
眼罩

74 focusing telescope
聚焦望远镜

75 battery unit
电池装置

76 combined battery holder and control grip for the motor drive
马达驱动的电池组座和控制手柄

77 rapid-sequence camera
快速照相机（连续照相机）

78 attachable motor drive
可附装的马达驱动装置

79 external (outside) power supply
外接电源

80 ten meter film back (magazine back)
十米底片盒背（片盒背）

81-98 close-up and macro equipment
特写（近距摄影）和放大用装备

81 extension tube
延伸管

82 adapter ring
接口环（圈）

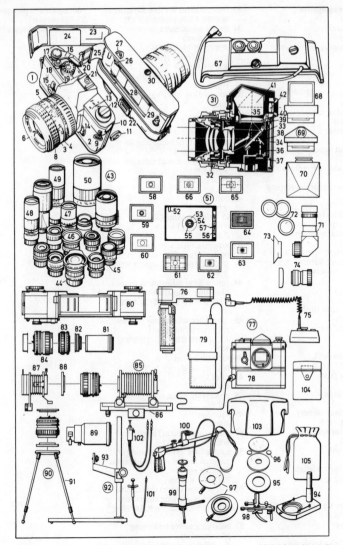

eversing ring
换向环

ens in retrofocus position
焦点位置的镜头

ellows unit (extension bellows,
lose-up bellows attachment)
腹（皮腔）装置（延伸蛇腹，特写蛇
附件）

ocusing stage
焦台

ide-copying attachment
灯片复制附件

ide-copying adapter
灯片复制接合器

icro attachment
photomicroscope adapter)
微附件（显微镜照相机，接合器）

90 copying stand (copy stand,
copypod)
复制台

91 spider legs
三脚架脚

92 copying stand (copy stand)
复制台

93 arm of the copying stand (copy
stand)
复制台悬臂

94 macrophoto stand
放大照相机台

95 stage plates for the macrophoto
stand
放大照相机台的台板

96 insertable disc (disk)
可插入的圆盘

97 Lieberkûhn reflector
来伯古恩反射器

98 mechanical stage
机械台

99 table tripod (table-top tripod)
桌上三角架

100 rifle grip
来福枪式夹

101 cable release
快门线

102 double cable release
双快门线

103 camera case (ever-ready case)
照相机皮套（常备套）

104 lens case
镜头箱

105 soft-leather lens pouch
软皮镜头袋

207

1-60 darkroom equipment
暗房装备（设备）

1 developing tank
显影罐（冲片槽）

2 spiral (developing spiral, tank reel)
卷盘[显影（冲片）卷盘，槽形卷轴]

3 multi-unit developing tank
多单元显影罐（冲片槽）

4 multi-unit tank spiral
多单元槽形卷盘

5 daylight-loading tank
日光下装片显影罐

6 loading chamber
装片室

7 film transport handle
底片扳动手柄

8 developing tank thermometer
显影槽温度计

9 collapsible bottle for developing solution
装显影液用折叠的瓶子

10 chemical bottles for first developer, stop bath, colour developer, bleach-hardener, stabilizer
初次显影剂，停影剂，彩色显影剂，漂白硬化剂，稳定剂等等的化学药剂瓶

11 measuring cylinders
量筒

12 funnel
漏斗

13 tray thermometer (dish thermometer)
托盘温度计（盘子温度计）

14 film clip
底片夹

15 wash tank (washer)
洗涤槽、冲洗槽（洗涤器）

16 water supply pipe
供水管

17 water outlet pipe
排水管

18 laboratory timer (timer)
（实验室）暗房计时器

19 automatic film agitator
底片自动搅拌器

20 developing tank
显影槽

21 darkroom lamp (safelight)
暗房灯（安全灯）

22 filter screen
滤光屏

23 film drier (drying cabinet)
底片干燥器（干燥箱）

24 exposure timer
曝光定时器

25 developing dish (developing tray)
显影盘（显影托盘）

26 enlarger
放大机

27 baseboard
底板，台板

28 angled column
有角度的支柱

29 lamphouse (lamp housing)
放大机的光源（灯室），灯光屏蔽罩

30 negative carrier
底片夹

31 bellows
蛇腹，皮腔

32 lens
镜头

33 friction drive for fine adjustment
精密调整（细调）的磨擦驱动装置

34 height adjustment (scale adjustment)
高度调整器（标尺调整器）

35 masking frame (easel)
遮蔽架（照片架）

36 colour (*Am.* color) analyser
析色器

37 colour (*Am.* color) analyser lamp
析色器灯

38 probe lead
试探具（探针）导线

39 exposure time balancing knob
曝光时间调整旋钮

40 colour (*Am.* color) enlarger
彩色放大机

41 enlarger head
放大机头

42 column
支柱

43-45 colour-mixing (*Am.* color-mixing) knob
色彩调整旋钮

43 magenta filter adjustment (minus green filter adjustment)
紫红色过滤调整装置（减绿过滤调整装置）

44 yellow filter adjustment (minus blue filter adjustment)
黄色过滤调整装置（减蓝过滤调整装置）

45 cyan filter adjustment (minus red filter adjustment)
青色过滤调整装置（减红过滤调整装置）

46 red swing filter
摆动红色过滤器

47 print tongs
晒印夹

48 processing drum
显影筒

49 squeegee
橡胶滚筒

50 range (assortment) of papers
相纸类

51 colour (*Am.* color) printing paper, a packet of photographic printing paper
彩色相纸，整盒相纸

52 colour (*Am.* color) chemicals (colour processing chemicals)
彩色显像用化学药品（彩色显像处理化学药品）

53 enlarging meter (enlarging phototmeter)
放大机测光器（光度计）

54 adjusting knob with paper speed scale
具相纸感光速度标尺的调整旋钮

55 probe
试探具

56 semi-automatic thermostatically controlled developing dish
半自动恒温控制显影盆

57 rapid print drier (heated print drier)
快速晒印干燥器

58 glazing sheet
上光板

59 pressure cloth
压布

60 automatic processor (machine processor)
自动显影机（机械显影机）

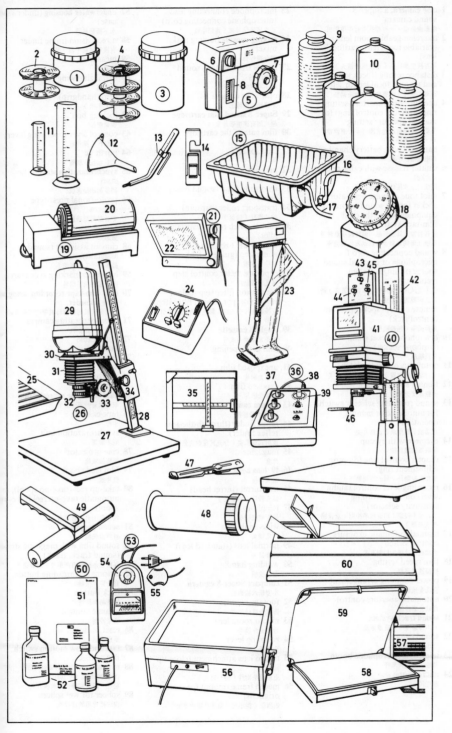

1 **cine camera,** a Super-8
sound camera
电影摄影机，一种超八型有声摄影机
2 interchangeable zoom lens
(variable focus lens, varifocal
lens)
可互换变焦镜头（可变焦距镜头）
3 distance setting (focus setting)
and manual focal length setting
距离（焦点）调整和手动焦距调整
4 aperture ring (aperture-setting
ring, aperture control ring) for
manual aperture setting
手动光圈调整用的光圈环（光圈调整
环，光圈控制环）
5 handgrip with battery chamber
带电池槽的手柄
6 shutter release with cable release
socket
附快门线插座的快门放松器
7 pilot tone or pulse generator
socket for the sound recording
equipment (with the dual
film-tape system)
录音装置（具胶转磁，磁转胶双重转录
系统）用的导频音和脉动发生器插座
8 sound connecting cord for
microphone or external sound
source (in single-system
recording)
供麦克风或外部声源（单音道音）所
用的声源连接电线
9 remote control socket (remote
control jack)
摇控插座（摇控插座）
10 headphone socket (*sim.:*
earphone socket)
耳机插座
11 autofocus override switch
（自动聚焦装置）自动聚焦过越开关
12 filming speed selector
拍摄速度选择器
13 sound recording selector switch
for automatic or manual
operation
自动或手动录音选择开关
14 eyepiece with eyecup
带眼罩的接目镜
15 diopter control ring (dioptric
adjustment ring)
屈光度控制环（屈光度调整环）
16 recording level control (audio
level control, recording
sensitivity selector)
录音水平控制（声音水平控制，录音感
度选择器）
17 manual/automatic exposure
control switch
手动或自动曝光控制开关
18 film speed setting
拍摄速度设定
19 power zooming arrangement
自动变焦装置
20 automatic aperture control
自动光圈控制
21 **sound track system**
（声带系统）录音道系统
22 sound camera
同步录音摄影机
23 telescopic microphone boom
伸缩的麦克风吊杆
24 microphone
麦克风

25 microphone connecting lead
(microphone connecting cord)
麦克风连结导线（连结电线）
26 **mixing console** (mixing desk,
mixer)
混合操作台
27 inputs from various sound
sources
从不同声源的输入
28 output to camera
至摄影机的输出
29 **Super-8 sound film cartridge**
超八型有声胶片盒
30 film gate of the cartridge
片盒的片门
31 feed spool
供片轴
32 take-up spool
收片轴
33 recording head (sound head)
录音头
34 transport roller (capstan)
输片滑杆（绞盘）
35 rubber pinch roller (capstan
idler)
橡皮压片滑杆（绞盘惰轮）
36 guide step (guide notch)
导阶（导槽）
37 exposure meter control step
曝光计控制阶
38 conversion filter step (colour,
Am. color, conversion filter step)
变换滤光片引入阶（彩色变换滤片引
入阶）
39 **single-8 cassette**
单条8毫米卡式带
40 film gate opening
片门孔
41 unexposed film
未曝光影片
42 exposed film
已曝光影片
43 **16 mm camera**
16毫米摄影机
44 reflex finder (through-the-lens
reflex finder)
反射式观景窗（分光式反射观景窗）
45 magazine
片盒
46-49 **lens head**
镜头转座
46 lens turret (turret head)
镜头转塔（转塔头）
47 telephoto lens
远距照相镜头
48 wide-angle lens
广角镜头
49 normal lens (standard lens)
标准镜头
50 winding handle
卷片曲柄
51 **compact Super-8 camera**
小型超八摄影机
52 footage counter
影片长度计数器
53 macro zoom lens
近摄变焦镜头
54 zooming lever
变焦杆
55 macro lens attachment (close-up
lens)
近摄镜头附件（特写镜头）
56 macro frame (mount for small
originals)
近摄架（供小尺寸原底片用的支架）

57 **underwater housing** (underwater
case)
水下摄影机罩
58 direct-vision frame finder
直视观景窗（器）架
59 measuring rod
测量杆
60 stabilizing wing
稳定翼
61 grip (handgrip)
柄（手柄）
62 locking bolt
锁紧螺栓
63 control lever (operating lever)
控制杆（操作杆）
64 porthole
（观察孔）机窗
65 **synchronization start** (sync
start)
同步起动摄影机
66 professional press-type
camera
专业新闻型摄影机
67 cameraman
摄影师
68 camera assistant (sound
assistant)
摄影助手（录音助手）
69 handclap marking sync start
同步起动拍手信号
70 **dual film-tape recording using a
tape recorder**
使用录音机的胶带转磁带的双重录音
71 pulse-generating camera
脉动发生摄影机
72 pulse cable
脉动电线
73 cassette recorder
卡式录音机
74 microphone
麦克风
75 **dual film-tape reproduction**
双重录音的再生装置
76 tape cassette
卡带
77 synchronization unit
同步装置
78 cine projector
电影放映机
79 film feed spool
供片盘
80 take-up reel (take-up spool), an
automatic take-up reel (take-up
spool)
收片盘，自动收片盘
81 **sound projector**
有声放映机
82 sound film with magnetic strip
(sound track, track)
具磁性条纹的有声影片（录音道）
83 automatic-threading button
自动穿片按钮
84 trick button
特殊画面按钮
85 volume control
音量控制
86 reset button
重置按钮
87 fast and slow motion switch
快慢动作开关
88 forward, reverse, and still
projection switch
前进、回转和静止的放映开关
89 splicer for wet splices
湿接接片用的接续机

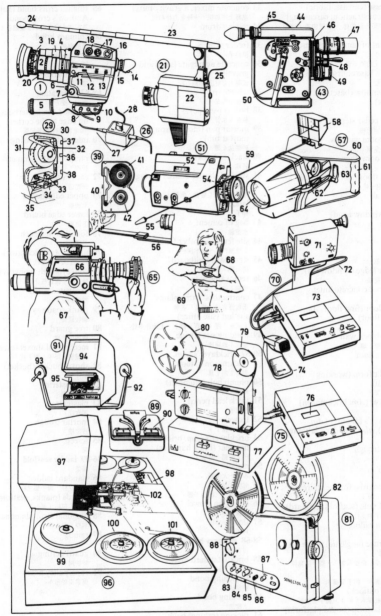

inged clamping plate
双接夹板

ilm viewer (animated viewer
ditor)
看片器（影片编辑机器）

oldaway reel arm
叠式片盘臂

ewind handle (rewinder)
卷柄（回卷机）

iewing screen
幕

lm perforator (film marker)
影片穿孔机（影片标志器）

**96 six-turn-table film and sound
cutting table** (editing table,
cutting bench, animated sound
editor)
六转盘影片和声带的剪辑（接）台（剪
辑台，影片声音剪辑台）

97 monitor
监控器

98 control buttons (control well)
控制钮（控制插孔）

99 film turntable
影片转盘

100 first sound turntable, e.g. for
live sound
实况录音用的初次录音装置

101 second sound turntable for
post-sync sound
后同步录音用的第二次录音装置

**102 film and tape synchronizing
head**
影片和磁带同步头

1-49 carcase (carcass, fabric) [house construction, carcassing]
房架（房架，结构体）[房屋构造，房架的建造]

1 basement of tamped (rammed) concrete
捣固混凝土的地下室

2 concrete base course
混凝土基层

3 cellar window (basement window)
地下室窗户

4 outside cellar steps
户外地下室阶梯

5 utility room window
公用设备室窗

6 utility room door
公用设备室门

7 ground floor (Am. first floor)
底层（[美]一楼）

8 brick wall
砖墙

9 lintel (window head)
楣（窗楣）

10 reveal
窗之侧壁

11 jamb
门窗框边框

12 window ledge (window sill)
窗台板（窗槛）

13 reinforced concrete lintel
混凝土过梁

14 upper floor (first floor, Am. second floor)
二楼

15 hollow-block wall
空心砖（壁）墙

16 concrete floor
水泥地板

17 work platform (working platform)
工作台（架）

18 bricklayer (Am. brickmason)
砌砖工

19 bricklayer's labourer (Am. laborer); also: builder's labourer
小工

20 mortar trough
砂浆槽

21 chimney
烟囱

22 cover (boards) for the staircase
楼梯间盖（板）

23 scaffold pole (scaffold standard)
鹰架，脚手架支柱

24 platform railing
平台栏杆

25 angle brace (angle tie) in the scaffold
鹰架的角撑（角铁条）,脚手架撑

26 ledger
鹰架踏板横木,脚手架横木

27 putlog (putlock)
鹰架踏脚板横木（短）,脚手架踏板

28 plank platform (board platform)
木板平台

29 guard board
护板

30 scaffolding joint with chain or lashing or whip or bond
以链或绳或缠绕绑於鹰架上的接合点

31 builder's hoist
（工用）施工用吊车（吊机）

32 mixer operator
搅拌机操作人，拌和机操作工

33 concrete mixer, a gravity mixer
混凝土拌和机,一种重力拌和机

34 mixing drum
拌和鼓

35 feeder skip
供料吊斗

36 concrete aggregate [sand and gravel]
混凝土骨材[砂和砾石]

37 wheelbarrow
独轮手推车

38 hose (hosepipe)
软管,水管

39 mortar pan (mortar trough, mortar tub)
砂浆盆（槽，桶）

40 stack of bricks
砖堆

41 stacked shutter boards (lining boards)
堆积的衬板（裙板，面板）

42 ladder
梯子

43 bag of cement
水泥袋

44 site fence, a timber fence
工地围栏,一种木围栏

45 signboard (billboard)
揭示牌,告示牌

46 removable gate
可拆下的门

47 contractors' name plates
承包商名牌,营造厂名牌

48 site hut (site office)
（工地小屋）工寮（棚），工地办事处

49 building site latrine
建筑工地厕所

50-57 bricklayer's (Am. brickmason's) **tools**
砌砖工用工具

50 plumb bob (plummet)
垂球,铅锤

51 thick lead pencil
粗铅笔

52 trowel
镘刀（抹子）

53 bricklayer's (Am. brickmason's) hammer (brick hammer)
砖工用锤（砖锤）

54 mallet
木锤,大头锤

55 spirit level
水平器,气泡水平器

56 laying-on trowel
涂抹镘刀（抹子）

57 float
抹子

58-68 masonry bonds
砖石砌法

58 brick (standard brick)
砖（标准砖）

59 stretching bond
顺砌法

60 heading bond
丁砌法

61 racking (raking) back
砌砖时留齿缝（阶梯形）待砌

62 English bond
英国式砌法

63 stretching course
顺砌层

64 heading course
丁砌层

65 English cross bond (Saint Andrew's cross bond)
英国式十字砌法（圣安德鲁十字砌法）

66 chimney bond
烟囱砌法

67 first course
第一层

68 second course
第二层

69-82 excavation
开挖,挖方

69 profile (Am. batterboard) [fixed on edge at the corner]
[固定於墙的]水平标板

70 intersection of strings
水线交叉

71 plumb bob (plummet)
铅锤,垂球

72 excavation side
开挖边

73 upper edge board
上边板

74 lower edge board
下边板

75 foundation trench
基槽

76 navvy (Am. excavator)
挖土工人（挖土机）

77 conveyor belt (conveyor)
输送带（输送机）

78 excavated earth
挖掘的泥土

79 plank roadway
铺板路面

80 tree guard
树的保护栏

81 mechanical shovel (excavator)
机械铲,铲车（挖土机）

82 shovel bucket (bucket)
铲斗

83-91 plastering
涂抹灰泥

83 plasterer
泥水匠

84 mortar trough
砂浆槽

85 screen
筛

86-89 ladder scaffold
梯架

86 standard ladder
梯架立柱,脚手架立柱

87 boards (planks, platform)
木板（厚板，平台）

88 diagonal strut (diagonal brace)
斜撑（斜支柱）

89 railing
栏杆

90 guard netting
防护网

91 rope-pulley hoist
绳索滑轮吊车

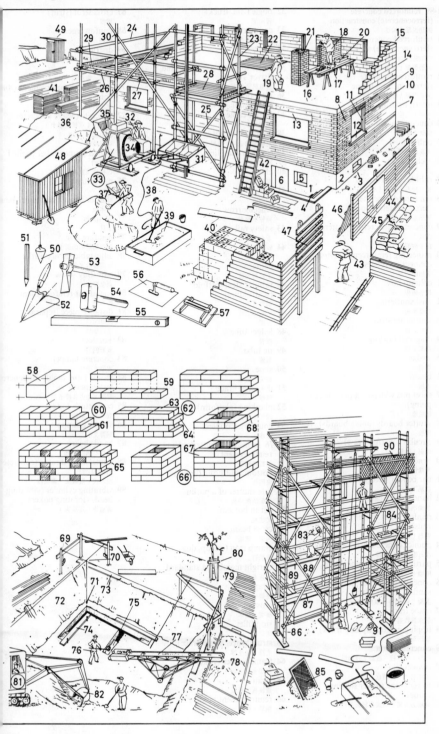

1-89 reinforced concrete (ferroconcrete) construction
钢筋混凝土构造

1 reinforced concrete (ferro-concrete) skeleton construciton
钢筋混凝土骨架结构

2 reinforced concrete (ferroconcrete) frame
钢筋混凝土框架（构架）

3 inferior purlin
下梁（桁梁）

4 concrete purlin
混凝土梁

5 ceiling joist
天花板托梁

6 arch (flank)
拱

7 rubble concrete wall
粗（碎石）混凝土墙

8 reinforced concrete (ferroconcrete) foor
钢筋混凝土楼板

9 concreter (concretor), flattening out
抹平混凝土工

10 projecting reinforcement (*Am.* connection rebars)
突出的钢筋

11 column box
柱子模板

12 joist shuttering
托梁模板

13 shuttering strut
模板支撑

14 diagonal bracing
斜架（撑）

15 wedge
楔块

16 board
木板

17 sheet pile wall (sheet pile, sheet piling)
板桩墙

18 shutter boards (lining boards)
模板

19 circular saw (buzz saw)
圆锯，轮锯

20 bending table
弯曲钢筋的工作台

21 bar bender (steel bender)
钢筋工

22 hand steel shears
手动钢剪

23 reinforcing steel (reinforcement rods)
钢筋（钢筋条）

24 pumice concrete hollow block
浮石混凝土空心块

25 partition wall, a timber wall
隔墙，一种木板墙

26 concrete aggregate [gravel and sand of vaious grades]
混凝土骨料[各种级配的砾石和砂]

27 crane track
起重机轨道

28 tipping wagon (tipping truck)
倾卸车

29 concrete mixer
混凝土搅拌机，混凝土拌和机

30 cement silo
水泥仓，水泥储仓

31 tower crane (tower slewing crane)
高塔起重机（塔式回转起重机）

32 bogie (*Am.* truck)
转向架

33 counterweight
配重，平衡铊

34 tower
塔架

35 crane to driver's cabin (crane driver's cage)
起重机驾驶室

36 jib (boom)
起重臂（吊杆，撑臂）

37 bearer cable
吊索

38 concrete bucket
混凝土输送斗，混凝土吊桶

39 sleepers (*Am.* ties)
轨枕

40 chock
楔形塞块

41 ramp
斜坡道

42 wheelbarrow
独轮手推车

43 safety rail
安全栏杆

44 site hut
工寮

45 canteen
工地福利社

46 tubular steel scaffold (scaffolding)
钢管鹰架

47 standard
支架

48 ledger tube
横管

49 tie tube
系管

50 shoe
桩尖，底座

51 diagonal brace
斜撑

52 planking (platform)
铺板（平台）

53 coupling (coupler)
管接头

54-76 formwork (shuttering) and reinforcement
模板和钢筋

54 bottom shuttering (lining)
底模板

55 side shutter of a purlin
正梁的侧模板

56 cut-in bottom
梁底板

57 cross beam
大梁，横梁

58 cramp iron (cramp, dog)
铁扒钉

59 upright member, a standard
垂直支柱

60 strap
连接板，系板

61 cross piece
横梁，横木

62 stop fillet
固定块

63 strut (brace, angle brace)
支撑（角支撑）

64 frame timber (yoke)
框架木材（轭）

65 strap
连接板，系板

66 reinforcement binding
钢筋，绑扎

67 cross strut (strut)
横撑

68 reinforcement
钢筋

69 distribution steel
分布钢筋

70 stirrup
肋筋，箍筋

71 projecting reinforcement (*Am.* connection rebars)
突出的钢筋

72 concrete (heavy concrete)
混凝土（重质混凝土）

73 column box
柱形模板

74 bolted frame timber (bolted yoke)
以螺栓固定的架材

75 nut (thumb nut)
螺帽

76 shutter board (shuttering boa
厚木板

77-89 tools
工具

77 bending iron
弯曲钢筋用的扳手

78 adjustable service girder
可调整的工作架

79 adjusting screw
调整螺钉

80 round bar reinforcement
圆钢筋

81 distance piece (separator, spacer)
定位垫块

82 Torsteel
异形钢筋

83 concrete tamper
混凝土捣棒

84 mould (*Am.* mold) for concre test cubes
混凝土立方体模子

85 concreter's tongs
混凝土夹钳

86 sheeting support
钢管支承

87 hand shears
手剪（钢筋手剪）

88 immersion vibrator (concrete vibrator)
浸入式（混凝土）震动器

89 vibrating cylinder (vibrating head, vibrating poker)
震动棒（震动头）

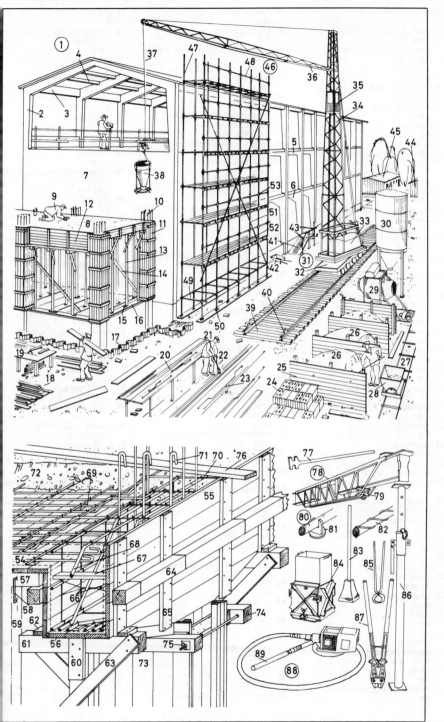

1-59 carpenter's yard
木工场

1 stack of boards (planks)
木板堆

2 long timber (*Am.* lumber)
长圆木（原木）

3 sawing shed
锯木棚（间）

4 carpenter's workshop
木工工作场

5 workshop door
工场门

6 handcart
手推车

7 roof truss
屋架

8 tree [used for topping out ceremony], with wreath
带花环的树[用於上主梁仪式]

9 timber wall
木板墙

10 squared timber (building timber, scantlings)
方木（建筑用木材,制材）

11 drawing floor
划线工作台

12 carpenter
木工

13 safety helmet
安全帽

14 cross-cut saw, a chain saw
横断锯,一种链锯

15 chain guide
导链装置

16 saw chain
锯链

17 mortiser (chain cutter)
凿孔机（链式切割机）

18 trestle (horse)
枪架,支架（马凳）

19 beam mounted on a trestle
置於支架上的梁

20 set of carpenter's tools
一套木工工具

21 electric drill
电钻

22 dowel hole
销钉孔,木钉孔

23 mark for the dowel hole
钻孔的标记（未钻之前）

24 beams
梁

25 post (stile, stud, quarter)
柱（立木,短支柱,间柱）

26 corner brace
角支撑

27 brace (strut)
支撑（支柱）

28 base course (plinth)
底层（基脚,柱脚）

29 house wall (wall)
墙（墙壁）

30 window opening
窗口

31 reveal
窗之侧壁

32 jamb
门窗框边框

33 window ledge (window sill)
窗台板（窗槛）

34 cornice
飞檐

35 roundwood (round timber)
圆木

36 floorboards
楼板

37 hoisting rope
吊索

38 ceiling joist (ceiling beam, main beam)
平顶搁栅（平顶梁,主梁）

39 wall joist
墙梁

40 wall plate
承梁板

41 trimmer (trimmer joist, *Am.* header, header joist)
承梁（搁栅承梁,楣梁）

42 dragon beam (dragon piece)
支承脊楼梁

43 false floor (inserted floor)
假楼板

44 floor filling of breeze, loam, etc.
填煤渣、土等的楼板

45 fillet (cleat)
垫板（楔子）

46 stair well (well)
楼梯井（井）

47 chimney
烟囱

48 framed partition (framed wall)
构架（框墙）,间壁（构架墙）

49 wall plate
承梁板

50 girt
围梁

51 window jamb, a jamb
窗框,边框

52 corner stile (corner strut, corner stud)
角支柱（角立木）

53 principal post
主柱

54 brace (strut) with skew notch
具斜接头的支撑（支柱）

55 nogging piece
压墙槛

56 sill rail
窗台槛

57 window lintel (window head)
窗过梁（窗楣）

58 head (head rail)
楣（框顶）

59 filled-in panel (bay, pan)
砌成之墙板（间格）

60-82 carpenter's tools
木工工具

60 hand saw
手锯

61 bucksaw
架锯

62 saw blade
锯片

63 compass saw (keyhole saw)
圆锯（开孔锯）

64 plane
刨

65 auger (gimlet)
螺旋钻（木钻）

66 screw clamp (cramp, holdfast)
螺旋夹钳（夹钳,夹住器）

67 mallet
木锤,大头锤

68 two-handed saw
双人用锯

69 try square
直角尺,曲尺

70 broad axe (*Am.* broadax)
阔斧

71 chisel
凿

72 mortise axe (mortice axe, *Am.* mortise ax)
榫眼斧

73 axe (*Am.* ax)
斧

74 carpenter's hammer
木工用锤

75 claw head (nail claw)
拔钉爪头（拔钉钳）

76 folding rule
摺尺

77 carpenter's pencil
木工用铅笔

78 iron square
铁直角尺

79 drawknife (drawshave, drawing knife)
拉刀（刮刀）

80 shaving
刨花

81 bevel
斜角规

82 mitre square (*Am.* miter square, miter angle)
斜棱（角）尺

83-96 building timber
建筑用木材

83 undressed timber (*Am.* rough lumber)
原木

84 heartwood (duramen)
心材（木心）

85 sapwood (sap, alburnum)
边材

86 bark (rind)
树皮（树木外皮）

87 baulk (balk)
梁木

88 halved timber
对分材

89 wane (waney edge)
梁木,缺边材

90 quarter baulk (balk)
四等分梁木（四分材）

91 plank (board)
板,板材

92 end-grained timber
纹端向外的木材

93 heartwood plank (heart plank)
木心板

94 unsquared (untrimmed) plank (board)
未修整板材,毛边板材

95 squared (trimmed) board
已修整板材

96 slab (offcut)
板,底板

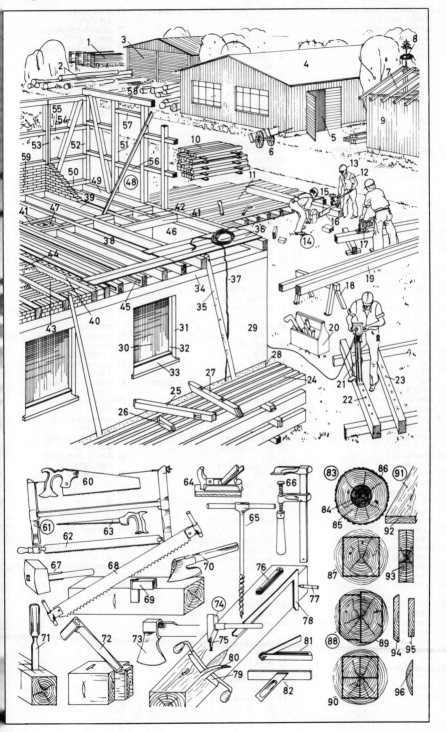

1-26 styles and parts of roofs
屋顶型式及其各部分

1 gable roof (saddle roof, saddleback roof)
山形屋顶（鞍形屋顶）

2 ridge
屋脊

3 verge
山墙簷口

4 eaves
屋簷

5 gable
山墙

6 dormer window (dormer)
屋顶天窗（老虎窗）

7 pent roof (shed roof, lean-to roof)
单坡屋顶（棚顶，坡屋顶）

8 skylight
天窗

9 fire gable
防火山墙

10 hip (hipped) roof
四落水屋顶（四坡屋顶）

11 hip end
端坡，肩脊端

12 hip (arris)
屋脊，角

13 hip (hipped) dormer window
四坡屋顶天窗

14 ridge turret
屋顶小塔

15 valley (roof valley)
屋顶排水沟

16 hipped-gable roof (jerkin head roof)
四坡山墙屋顶（半山头屋顶）

17 partial-hip (partial-hipped) end
小面端坡，小肩脊端

18 mansard roof (*Am.* gambrel roof)
折角屋顶（复斜屋顶）

19 mansard dormer window
折角屋顶天窗

20 sawtooth roof
锯齿式屋顶

21 north light
朝北窗

22 broach roof
塔形屋顶

23 eyebrow
遮阳板

24 conical broach roof
圆锥形屋顶

25 imperial dome (imperial roof)
葱头形圆屋顶

26 weather vane
风信标

27-83 roof structures of timber
木材的屋顶结构

27 rafter roof
椽屋顶

28 rafter
椽

29 roof beam
屋架梁

30 diagonal tie (cross tie, sprocket piece, cocking piece)
斜拉杆（横木小椽）

31 arris fillet (tilting fillet)
簷垫

32 outer wall
外墙

33 beam head
梁头

34 collar beam roof (trussed-rafter roof)
桁架式椽屋顶

35 collar beam (collar)
环梁，系梁

36 rafter
椽

37 strutted collar beam roof structure
支柱式环梁屋顶结构

38 collar beams
环梁，系梁

39 purlin
桁条

40 post (stile, stud)
柱（立柱，短支柱）

41 brace
支撑（斜撑）

42 unstrutted (king pin) roof structure
非支柱式（中枢）屋顶结构

43 ridge purlin
脊桁

44 inferior purlin
次桁条

45 rafter head (rafter end)
椽头

46 purlin roof with queen post and pointing sill
双柱及活闸门槛式屋顶

47 pointing sill
活闸门槛

48 ridge beam (ridge board)
脊梁（脊板）

49 simple tie
单系条

50 double tie
双系条

51 purlin
桁条

52 purlin roof structure with queen post
双柱屋架结构

53 tie beam
系梁

54 joist (ceiling joist)
栏栅（屋顶搁栅）

55 principal rafter
主椽

56 common rafter
普通椽

57 angle brace (angle tie)
角撑（角系条）

58 brace (strut)
支撑（支柱）

59 ties
系条

60 hip (hipped) roof with purlin roof structure
具桁条结构的四坡屋顶

61 jack rafter
小椽

62 hip rafter
角椽

63 jack rafter
小椽

64 valley rafter
沟椽

65 queen truss
偶杆桁架

66 main beam
主梁

67 summer (summer beam)
搁栅梁

68 queen post (truss post)
偶柱（桁架支柱）

69 brace (strut)
支撑（支柱）

70 collar beam (collar)
环梁（系梁）

71 trimmer (*Am.* header)
承梁（顶梁）

72 solid-web girder
实腹版梁

73 lower chord
下弦

74 upper chord
上弦

75 boarding
安装木板

76 purlin
桁条

77 supporting outer wall
支承外墙

78 roof truss
屋架桁架

79 lower chord
下弦

80 upper chord
上弦

81 post
柱

82 brace (strut)
支撑（支柱）

83 support
支承（支座）

84-98 timber joints
木材接合

84 mortise (mortice) and tenon joint
榫眼和榫接

85 forked mortise (mortice) and tenon joint
叉形榫眼和接

86 halving (halved) joint
半缺接合（对搭接）

87 simple scarf joint
单嵌接合

88 oblique scarf joint
斜嵌接合

89 dovetail halving
对分鸠尾榫

90 single skew notch
单缺口斜接头

91 double skew notch
双缺口斜接头

92 wooden nail
木钉

93 pin
梢

94 clout nail (clout)
大帽钉

95 wire nail
铁钉

96 hardwood wedges
硬木楔

97 cramp iron (timber dog, dog)
铁扒钉（木扒钉，扒钉）

98 bolt
螺栓

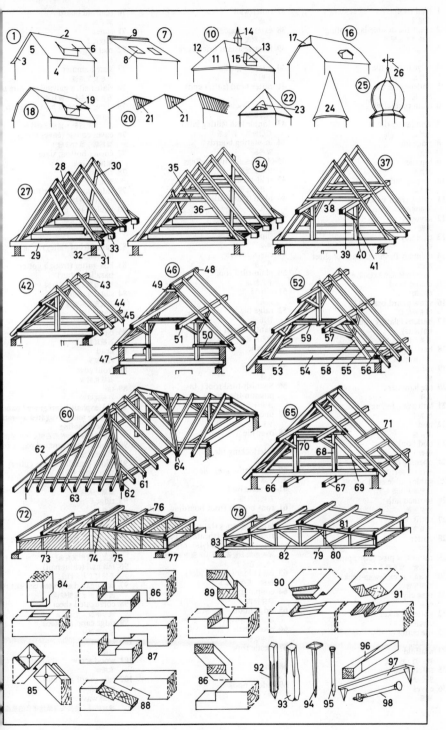

1 tiled roof
瓦屋顶

2 plain-tile double-lap roofing
双搭接平瓦屋顶

3 ridge tile
脊瓦

4 ridge course tile
屋脊瓦，层瓦

5 under-ridge tile
屋簷瓦

6 plain (plane) tile
平瓦

7 ventilating tile
通风瓦，换气瓦

8 ridge tile
脊瓦

9 hip tile
斜脊瓦

10 hipped end
肩脊端

11 valley (roof valley)
屋顶排水沟

12 skylight
天窗

13 chimney
烟囱

14 chimney flashing, made of sheet zinc
（薄锌板做成的）烟囱范水

15 ladder hook
梯头钩

16 snow guard bracket
挡雪板托架

17 battens (slating and tiling battens)
木条（挂瓦木条）

18 batten gauge (Am. gage)
木条量尺（规）

19 rafter
椽

20 tile hammer
瓦锤

21 lath axe (Am. ax)
板条斧

22 hod
灰泥桶

23 hod hook
桶钩

24 opening (hatch)
开口（升降口）

25 gable (gable end)
山形墙（山墙头）

26 toothed lath
齿形板条

27 soffit
挑簷底面

28 gutter
天沟

29 rainwater pipe (downpipe)
雨水管（落水管）

30 swan's neck (swan-neck)
鹅颈弯管

31 pipe clip
管夹

32 gutter bracket
天沟托架

33 tile cutter
切瓦器

34 scaffold
脚手架，施工架

35 safety wall
安全壁

36 eaves
屋簷

37 outer wall
外墙

38 exterior rendering
外墙刷底

39 frost-resistant brickwork
抗冻砖工

40 inferior purlin
下桁条

41 rafter head (rafter end)
椽头

42 eaves fascia
封簷底板

43 double lath (tilting lath)
双层板条（斜板条）

44 insulating boards
隔热板

45-60 tiles and tile roofings
瓦和瓦屋顶

45 split-tiled roof
分开式瓦屋顶

46 plain (plane) tile
平瓦

47 ridge course
屋脊瓦层

48 slip
滑动

49 eaves course
簷瓦层

50 plain-tiled roof
平瓦屋顶

51 nib
瓦尖

52 ridge tile
脊瓦

53 pantiled roof
波形瓦屋顶

54 pantile
波形瓦

55 pointing
勾缝

56 Spanish-tiled roof (Am. mission-tiled roof)
西班牙式瓦屋顶（拱形瓦屋顶）

57 under tile
下瓦

58 over tile
上瓦

59 interlocking tile
联锁瓦

60 flat interlocking tile
平联锁瓦

61-89 slate roof
石板瓦屋顶

61 roof boards (roof boarding, roof sheathing)
屋顶板（屋顶防水衬板）

62 roofing paper (sheathing paper); *also:* roofing felt (Am. rag felt)
屋面油纸（复盖油纸），屋面油毛毡（粗油毛毡）

63 cat ladder (roof ladder)
便梯（屋面用梯）

64 coupling hook
联接挂钩

65 ridge hook
屋脊挂钩

66 roof trestle
屋顶栈桥

67 trestle rope
栈桥绳

68 knot
绳结

69 ladder hook
梯头挂钩

70 scaffold board
脚手板

71 slater
石板瓦工

72 nail bag
钉子袋

73 slate hammer
石板瓦工锤

74 slate nail, a galvanized wire n
石板瓦工用钉，镀锌铁钉

75 slater's shoe, a bast or hemp shoe
石板瓦工用鞋，韧皮或麻底鞋

76 eaves course (eaves joint)
簷瓦层（簷口接缝）

77 corner bottom slate
屋角底石板瓦

78 roof course
屋顶层

79 ridge course (ridge joint)
脊层（屋脊接缝）

80 gable slate
山墙石板瓦

81 tail line
瓦的下边线

82 valley (roof valley)
屋顶排水沟

83 box gutter (trough gutter, parallel gutter)
箱形簷槽（槽，平行沟）

84 slater's iron
石板瓦工用铁件

85 slate
石板瓦

86 back
石板瓦背

87 head
石板瓦头

88 front edge
石板瓦前缘

89 tail
石板瓦尾

90-103 asphalt-impregnated pape roofing and corrugated asbesto cement roofing
柏油纸屋顶和波形石棉水泥板屋顶

90 asphalt-impregnated paper ro
柏油纸屋顶

91 width [parallel to the gutter]
宽度[与簷槽平行]

92 gutter
簷槽，天沟

93 ridge
屋脊

94 join
连接缝

95 width [at right angles to the gutter]
宽度[与簷槽成直角]

96 felt nail (clout nail)
毛毡钉（大头钉）

97 corrugated asbestos cement r
波形石棉水泥板屋顶

98 corrugated sheet
波形薄板

99 ridge capping piece
屋脊盖顶片

100 lap
搭接

101 wood screw
木螺丝

102 rust-proof zinc cup
防锈锌杯

103 lead washer
橡皮垫圈（使接头与螺丝密合的垫圈）

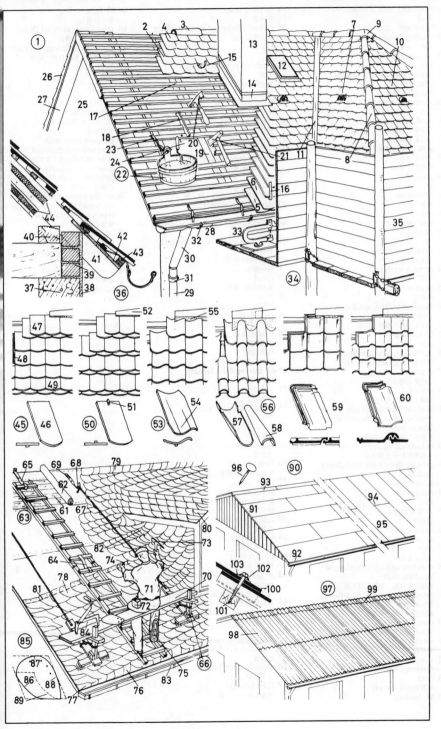

1 basement wall, a concrete wall
地下室墙壁，混凝土墙
2 footing (foundation)
基脚（基础）
3 foundation base
墙基
4 damp course (damp-proof course)
防湿层，防潮层
5 waterproofing
防水工作，防水层
6 rendering coat
涂底层，底涂
7 brick paving
砖铺面，砖铺路面
8 sand bed
砂垫层，砂床
9 ground
地面，粉刷底层
10 shuttering
模板，模
11 peg
木栓，桩，木橛，木钉
12 hardcore
碎石层，硬底层
13 oversite concrete
混凝土面层
14 cement screed
水泥匀（刮）平层
15 brickwork base
砖砌座
16 basement stairs, solid concrete stairs
地下室楼梯，混凝土楼梯
17 block step
台阶
18 curtail step (bottom step)
楼梯最低梯级，起步（梯）级
19 top step
楼梯最高梯级
20 nosing
凸缘，踏步挑头
21 skirting (skirting board, Am. mopboard, washboard, scrub board, base)
壁脚板（壁脚板，护壁板）
22 balustrade of metal bars
金属楼梯栏杆（扶手）
23 ground-floor (Am. first-floor) landing
地面层（一楼）
24 front door
前门
25 foot scraper
脚刮板
26 flagstone paving
板石铺砌，板石铺面
27 mortar bed
水泥砂浆层
28 concrete ceiling, a reinforced concrete slab
混凝土天花板，钢筋混凝土板
29 ground-floor (Am. first-floor) brick wall
地面层（一楼）砖墙
30 ramp
倾斜面，坡道，坡台
31 wedge-shaped step
楔形阶
32 tread
楼梯踏板，级宽
33 riser
楼梯踢脚板，起步板
34-41 landing
平台

34 landing beam
平台梁
35 ribbed reinforced concrete floor
钢筋混凝土层
36 rib
肋
37 steel-bar reinforcement
钢筋
38 subfloor (blind floor)
底层地板
39 level layer
水平层
40 finishing layer
修整层
41 top layer (screed)
顶层（刮板）
42-44 dog-legged staircase, a staircase without a well
人型楼梯，无井楼梯
42 curtail step (bottom step)
楼梯最低梯级，起步（梯）级
43 newel post (newel)
栏杆柱
44 outer string (Am. outer stringer)
外侧斜梁
45 wall string (Am. wall stringer)
贴墙斜梁
46 staircase bolt
楼梯螺栓
47 tread
楼梯踏板，级宽
48 riser
楼梯踢脚板，起步板
49 wreath piece (wreathed string)
（扭曲）弯曲部分（斜梁）
50 balustrade
楼梯栏杆（扶手）
51 baluster
栏杆小柱
52-62 intermediate landing
休息平台
52 wreath
弯曲扶手
53 handrail (guard rail)
扶手（护栏）
54 head post
楼梯端柱
55 landing beam
平台梁
56 lining board
面板，裙板，衬板
57 fillet
嵌条，填角，线角
58 lightweight building board
轻纤维板
59 ceiling plaster
天花板墁灰面
60 wall plaster
墙壁墁灰面
61 false ceiling
假天花板，假平顶
62 strip flooring (overlay flooring, parquet strip)
细条地板（表层地板，镶木地板）
63 skirting board (Am. mopboard, washboard, scrub board, base)
壁脚板（护壁板）
64 beading
串珠状缘饰
65 staircase window
楼梯窗
66 main landing beam
主平台梁
67 fillet (cleat)
嵌条（栓），填角

68-69 false ceiling
假天花板
68 false floor (inserted floor)
假楼板（嵌入楼板）
69 floor filling (plugging, pug)
楼板填料（隔音材料，泥料）
70 laths
板条
71 lathing
板条
72 ceiling plaster
天花板墁灰面
73 subfloor (blind floor)
底层地板
74 parquet floor with tongued-and-grooved blocks
具企口缝（凹凸缝）块的镶木地板
75 quarter-newelled (Am. quarter-neweled) staircase
直角转弯楼梯
76 winding staircase (spiral staircase) with open newels (open-newel staircase)
螺旋式楼梯
77 winding staircase (spiral staircase) with solid newels (solid-newel staircase)
实心中柱式螺旋楼梯
78 newel (solid newel)
楼梯栏杆柱（实心中心柱）
79 handrail
扶手

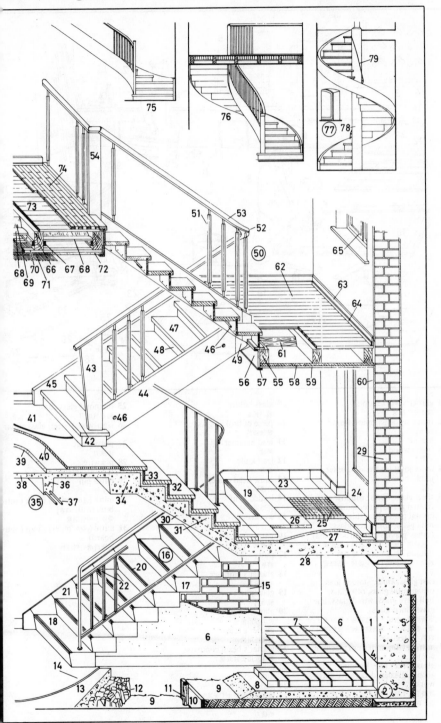

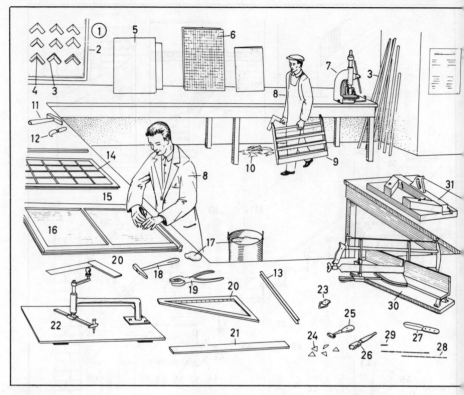

1 glazier's workshop
玻璃匠工作房

2 frame wood samples (frame samples)
框架木样

3 frame wood
框架木

4 mitre joint (mitre, *Am.* miter joint, miter)
斜接

5 sheet glass; *kinds:* window glass, frosted glass, patterned glass, crystal plate glass, thick glass, milk glass, laminated glass (safety glass, shatterproof glass)
平板玻璃；种类：窗户玻璃、毛玻璃、压花玻璃、结晶玻璃板、厚玻璃、乳白玻璃、层压玻璃（安全玻璃、防碎玻璃）

6 cast glass; *kinds:* stained glass, ornamental glass, raw glass, bull's-eye glass, wired glass, line glass (lined glass)
压铸玻璃；种类：有色玻璃，装饰玻璃，粗玻璃，牛眼玻璃，嵌有金丝网的玻璃，有线道玻璃

7 mitring (*Am.* mitering) machine
斜接机

8 glassworker (*e.g.* building glazier, glazier, decorative glass worker)
玻璃工人（例如：建筑玻璃工，玻璃匠，装饰玻璃工）

9 glass holder
玻璃托架

10 piece of broken glass
玻璃碎片

11 lead hammer
铅锤

12 lead knife
铅刀

13 came (lead came)
有槽铅条

14 leaded light
花饰铅条窗

15 workbench
工作台

16 pane of glass
窗玻璃

17 putty
油灰

18 glazier's hammer
玻璃匠用锤

19 glass pliers
玻璃钳

20 glazier's square
玻璃匠用角尺

21 glazier's rule
玻璃匠用尺

22 glazier's beam compass
玻璃匠用长臂圆规

23 eyelet
小环

24 glazing sprig
镶玻璃用的簧片（无头钉）

25-26 glass cutters
玻璃刀

25 diamond glass cutter
钻石玻璃刀

26 steel-wheel (steel) glass cutter
钢砂轮玻璃刀

27 putty knife
油灰刀

28 pin wire
拔无头针用的金属丝

29 panel pin
无头针

30 mitre (*Am.* miter) block (mitre box) [with saw]
带锯子的斜接架

31 mitre (*Am.* miter) shoot (mitre board)
斜接滑槽（斜接板）

etal shears (tinner's snips,
m. tinner's shears)
属剪（洋铁匠剪刀）
bow snips (angle shears)
剪，角剪
b
直板
pping plate
接板
propane soldering apparatus
烷灯接装置
ropane soldering iron, a
atchet iron
烷灯接棒，一种斧形烙铁
ldering stone, a sal-ammoniac
lock
接块（石），硇砂块（石）
oldering fluid (flux)
接剂
eading iron for forming
inforcement beading
成加强灯道用的灯缝铁
ngled reamer
角铰刀（钻孔器）
orkbench (bench)
作台
eam compass (trammel, *Am.*
eam trammel)
臂圆规
ectric hand die
持电动打孔模
ollow punch
心打孔器

14 chamfering hammer
去角锤
15 beading swage (beading hammer)
灯接铁锤
16 abrasive-wheel cutting-off machine
磨轮切割机
17 plumber
铅管工人
18 mallet
大槌
19 mandrel
心轴
20 socket (tinner's socket)
插座
21 block
铁座
22 anvil
砧
23 stake
小铁砧
24 circular saw (buzz saw)
圆锯
25 flanging, swaging, and wiring machine
压（摺）缘，压模，配线机
26 sheet shears (guillotine)
薄板剪（剪板机）
27 screw-cutting machine (thread-cutting machine, die stocks)
螺纹切割机（螺纹模夹把）

28 pipe-bending machine (bending machine, pipe bender)
弯管机（弯曲机，弯管器）
29 welding transformer
电熔接变压器
30 bending machine (rounding machine) for shaping funnels
漏斗形弯曲机

1 gas fitter and plumber
瓦斯匠和铅管工

2 stepladder
摺梯，四脚梯

3 safety chain
安全链条

4 stop valve
停止阀

5 gas meter
瓦斯表

6 bracket
托座

7 service riser
立管

8 distributing pipe
分配管

9 supply pipe
供气管

10 pipe-cutting machine
切管机

11 pipe repair stand
管子修理架

12-25 gas and water appliances
瓦斯和供水设备

12-13 geyser, an instantaneous
water heater
热水器，瞬间热水装置

12 gas water heater
瓦斯热水器

13 electric water heater
电热水器

14 toilet cistern
盥洗室水箱

15 float
浮球，浮筒

16 bell
钟形阀

17 flush pipe
冲洗管

18 water inlet
进水口

19 flushing lever (lever)
冲水杆

20 radiator
放热器，(热)辐射器

21 radiator rib
放热器肋

22 two-pipe system
双管(供热)系统

23 flow pipe
供水管

24 return pipe
回水管

25 gas heater
瓦斯加热炉

26-37 plumbing fixtures
卫生设备

26 trap (anti-syphon trap)
弯管(反虹吸弯管)

27 mixer tap (*Am.* mixing faucet)
for washbasins
洗脸盆(冷热水混合使用)的水龙头

28 hot tap
热水龙头

29 cold tap
冷水龙头

30 extendible shower attachment
可伸长的莲蓬头附件

31 water tap (pillar tap) for
washbasins
洗脸盆用水龙头(柱式龙头)

32 spindle top
心轴顶部

33 shield
护照

34 draw-off tap (*Am.* faucet)
水龙头

35 supatap
双路水龙头

36 swivel tap
旋转龙头

37 flushing valve
冲洗阀

38-52 fittings
零件配件

38 joint with male thread
外螺纹接头

39 reducing socket (reducing
coupler)
异径管节(异径管接头)

40 elbow screw joint (elbow
coupling)
肘管螺纹接头(弯管接头)

41 reducing socket (reducing
coupler) with female thread
带内螺纹的异径管节(异径管接头)

42 screw joint
螺纹接头

43 coupler (socket)
管接头(管节)

44 T-joint (T-junction joint, tee)
T型接头(三通接头，T接头)

45 elbow screw joint with female
thread
带内螺纹的肘管接头

46 bend
弯管接头

47 T-joint (T-junction joint, tee)
with female taper thread
锥形内螺纹T型接头(三通接头，T型
接头)

48 ceiling joint
平顶接头

49 reducing elbow
异径肘管

50 cross
十字接头

51 elbow joint with male thread
带外螺纹的肘管接头

52 elbow joint
肘管接头

53-57 pipe supports
管架

53 saddle clip
鞍形夹

54 spacing bracket
间隔(定位)托架

55 plug
塞栓

56 pipe clips
管夹

57 two-piece spacing clip
双层定位夹

**58-86 plumber's tools, gas fitter's
tools**
铅管工工具，瓦斯匠工具

58 gas pliers
瓦斯钳

59 footprints
瓦斯管螺旋钳

60 combination cutting pliers
钢丝钳

61 pipe wrench
管扳钳

62 flat-nose pliers
扁咀钳，平头钳

63 nipple key
螺纹套管扳手

64 round-nose pliers
圆头钳

65 pincers
尖手钳

66 adjustable S-wrench
可调整S型扳手

67 screw wrench
螺旋(丝)扳手

68 shifting spanner
活动扳手(移位扳手)

69 screwdriver
螺丝起子

70 compass saw (keyhole saw)
圆锯(钥孔锯)

71 hacksaw frame
弓锯架

72 hand saw
手锯

73 soldering iron
烙铁

74 blowlamp (blowtorch) [for
soldering]
钎接时用的喷灯

75 sealing tape
密封带

76 tin-lead solder
锡铅杆料

77 club hammer
手锤(大头锤)

78 hammer
榔头，锤子

79 spirit level
水平仪

80 steel-leg vice (*Am.* vise)
钢管老虎钳

81 pipe vice (*Am.* vise)
管虎钳

82 pipe-bending machine
弯管机

83 former (template)
绕线模(模板)

84 pipe cutter
切管器

85 hand die
手动扳牙

86 screw-cutting machine
(thread-cutting machine)
螺纹切削机

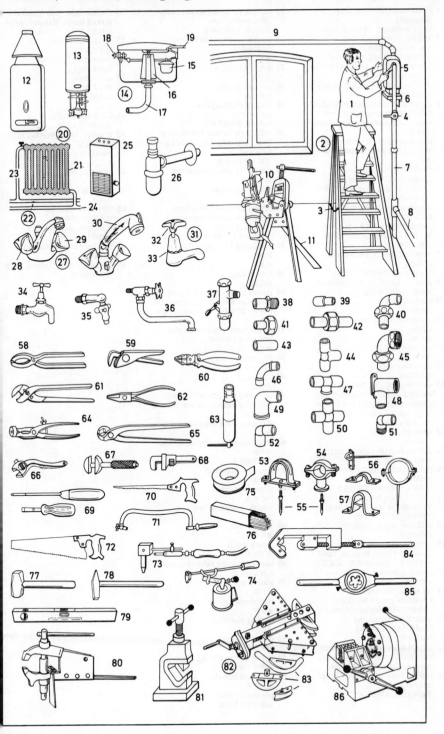

1 electrician (electrical fitter, wireman)
电工（电气装修工，线路检修工）

2 bell push (doorbell) for low-voltage safety current
电铃按钮（门铃）[低压安全电流]

3 house telephone with call button
带呼唤按钮的室内电话

4 [flush-mounted] rocker switch
[嵌装式]摇杆开关

5 [flush-mounted] earthed socket (wall socket, plug point, Am. wall outlet, convenience outlet, outlet)
[嵌装式]接地插座（壁上插座，插塞式插座，[美]壁上插座，便利插座，插座）

6 [surface-mounted] earthed double socket (double wall socket, double plug point, Am. double wall outlet, double convenience outlet, double outlet)
[表面安装式]接地双插座（壁上双插座，双插座，[美]壁上双插座，便利双插座，双插座）

7 switched socket (switch and socket)
开关插座（开关和插座）

8 four-socket (four-way) adapter
四插座（四路）转接器

9 earthed plug
接地插头

10 extension lead (Am. extension cord)
延长线

11 extension plug
延长线插头

12 extension socket
延长线插座

13 surface-mounted three-pole earthed socket [for three-phase conductor]
（三相电路用）表面安装式有中性导体的三极接地插座

14 three-phase plug
三相插头

15 electric bell (electric buzzer)
电铃（电蜂鸣器）

16 pull-switch (cord-operated wall switch)
拉线开关（绳索操纵的墙壁开关）

17 strip of sheet metal [on which wallpaper is laid for cutting]
（裁壁纸用的）薄金属片

18 drill-cast rotary switch
定位式旋转开关

19 miniature circuit breaker (screw-in circuit breaker, fuse)
小型断路器（旋入式断路器，熔断器）

20 resetting button
重接按钮

21 set screw [for fuses and miniature circuit breakers]
[熔断器和小型断路器用的固定螺钉]

22 underfloor mounting (underfloor sockets)
装设于地板下的插座

23 hinged floor socket for power lines and communication lines
电源线和通信线用的铰链地面插座

24 sunken floor socket with hinged lid (snap lid)
带铰链盖凹入地面的插座

25 surface-mounted socket outlet (plug point) box
表面安装式插座出线盒

26 pocket torch, a torch (Am. flashlight)
袖珍手电筒

27 dry cell battery
干电池

28 contact spring
接触弹簧

29 strip of thermoplastic connectors
热塑连接器的插座板

30 steel draw-in wire (draw wire) with threading key, and ring attached
带插入键和环的钢拉线

31 electricity meter cupboard
电表厨

32 electricity meter
电表

33 miniature circuit breakers (miniature circuit breaker consumer unit)
小型断路器（小型断路器消耗装置）

34 insulating tape (Am. friction tape)
绝缘带

35 fuse holder
保险丝座

36 circuit breaker (fuse), a fuse cartridge with fusible element
断路器（熔断器），带易熔元件的保险丝盒

37 colour (Am. color) indicator [showing current rating]
颜色指示器[显示额定电流]

38-39 contact maker
接触装置

40 cable clip
电缆夹

41 universal test meter (multiple meter for measuring current and voltage)
多用途电表（测量电流电压的多用电表）

42 thermoplastic moisture-proof cable
热塑防潮电缆

43 copper conductor
铜导体

44 three-core cable
三心电缆

45 electric soldering iron
电烙铁

46 screwdriver
螺丝起子

47 pipe wrench
管子扳手，管钳

48 shock-resisting safety helmet
抗震安全头盔

49 tool case
工具箱

50 round-nose pliers
圆头钳

51 cutting pliers
剪钳

52 junior hacksaw
轻型弓锯

53 combination cutting pliers
老虎钳，钢丝钳

54 insulated handle
绝缘把手

55 continuity tester
电路连续性测试器

56 electric light bulb (general service lamp, filament lamp)
电灯泡（普通灯，灯丝电灯泡）

57 glass bulb (bulb)
玻璃灯泡（灯泡）

58 coiled-coil filament
绕线式灯丝

59 screw base
螺纹管座

60 lampholder
灯座

61 fluorescent tube
萤光管，日光灯管

62 bracket for fluorescent tubes
日光灯管座

63 electrician's knife
电工刀

64 wire strippers
剥线钳

65 bayonet fitting
卡口座

66 three-pin socket with switch
带开关的三脚插座

67 three-pin plug
三脚插头

68 fuse carrier with fuse wire
带保险丝的保险丝架

69 light bulb with bayonet fitting
带卡口的灯泡

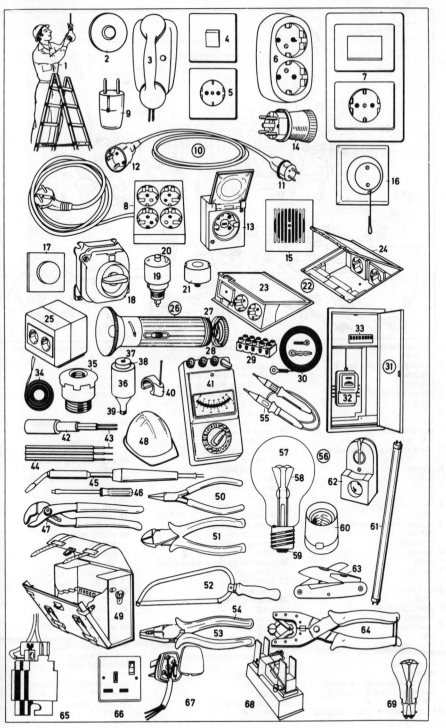

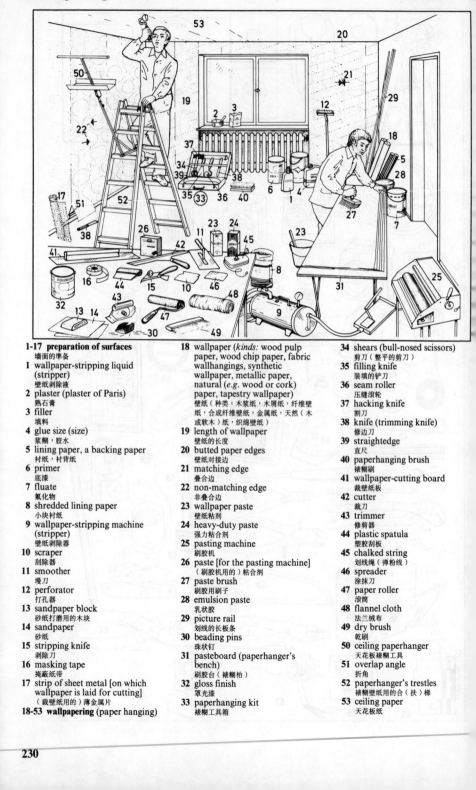

1-17 preparation of surfaces
墙面的准备

1 wallpaper-stripping liquid (stripper)
壁纸剥除液

2 plaster (plaster of Paris)
熟石膏

3 filler
填料

4 glue size (size)
浆糊，胶水

5 lining paper, a backing paper
衬纸，衬背纸

6 primer
底漆

7 fluate
氟化物

8 shredded lining paper
小块衬纸

9 wallpaper-stripping machine (stripper)
壁纸剥除器

10 scraper
刮除器

11 smoother
墁刀

12 perforator
打孔器

13 sandpaper block
砂纸打磨用的木块

14 sandpaper
砂纸

15 stripping knife
剥除刀

16 masking tape
掩蔽纸带

17 strip of sheet metal [on which wallpaper is laid for cutting]
（裁壁纸用的）薄金属片

18-53 wallpapering (paper hanging)

18 wallpaper (*kinds:* wood pulp paper, wood chip paper, fabric wallhangings, synthetic wallpaper, metallic paper, natural (*e.g.* wood or cork) paper, tapestry wallpaper)
壁纸（种类：木浆纸，木屑纸，纤维壁纸，合成纤维壁纸，金属纸，天然（木或软木）纸，织绵壁纸）

19 length of wallpaper
壁纸的长度

20 butted paper edges
壁纸对接边

21 matching edge
叠合边

22 non-matching edge
非叠合边

23 wallpaper paste
壁纸粘剂

24 heavy-duty paste
强力粘合剂

25 pasting machine
刷胶机

26 paste [for the pasting machine]
（刷胶机用的）粘合剂

27 paste brush
刷胶用刷子

28 emulsion paste
乳状胶

29 picture rail
划线的长板条

30 beading pins
珠状钉

31 pasteboard (paperhanger's bench)
刷胶台（裱糊柏）

32 gloss finish
罩光漆

33 paperhanging kit
裱糊工具箱

34 shears (bull-nosed scissors)
剪刀（整平的剪刀）

35 filling knife
装填的铲刀

36 seam roller
压缝滚轮

37 hacking knife
割刀

38 knife (trimming knife)
修边刀

39 straightedge
直尺

40 paperhanging brush
裱糊刷

41 wallpaper-cutting board
裁壁纸板

42 cutter
裁刀

43 trimmer
修剪器

44 plastic spatula
塑胶刮板

45 chalked string
划线绳（弹线线）

46 spreader
涂抹刀

47 paper roller
滚筒

48 flannel cloth
法兰绒布

49 dry brush
乾刷

50 ceiling paperhanger
天花板裱糊工具

51 overlap angle
折角

52 paperhanger's trestles
裱糊壁纸用的合（扶）梯

53 ceiling paper
天花板纸

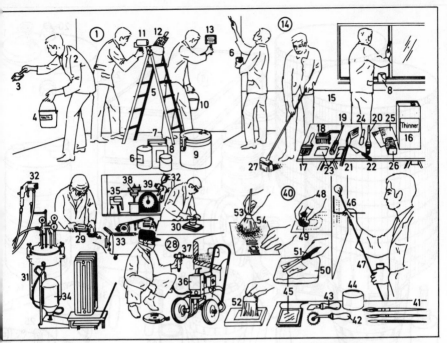

ainting
匚漆
ainter
油漆工
aintbrush
油漆刷
mulsion paint (emulsion)
乳胶漆
tepladder
四脚梯
an (tin) of paint
油漆罐
cans (tins) of paint
各种油漆罐
an (tin) with fixed handle
有固定手柄的油漆罐
aint kettle
油漆桶
drum of paint
大桶油漆
aint bucket
漆桶
aint roller
油漆滚筒
grill [for removing excess paint from the roller]
从滚筒去除过量油漆用的铁格子
tippling roller
点彩滚筒
varnishing
涂漆
oil-painted dado
涂漆的护壁
canister for thinner
稀释用罐
lat brush for larger surfaces (flat wall brush)
较大表面用的扁平刷
tippler
点彩刷

19 fitch
画笔
20 cutting-in brush
削角刷，切入刷
21 radiator brush (flay brush)
暖气炉刷（剥皮刷）
22 paint scraper
油漆刮刀
23 scraper
刮刀
24 putty knife
油灰刀
25 sandpaper
砂纸
26 sandpaper block
砂纸打磨块
27 floor brush
地板刷
28 sanding and spraying
砂打磨和喷漆
29 grinder
研磨器
30 sander
砂磨器
31 pressure pot
压力罐
32 spray gun
喷枪
33 compressor (air compressor)
压缩机（空气压缩机）
34 flow coating machine for flow coating radiators, etc.
用於流动涂层暖气机等的流动涂层机
35 hand spray
人力喷雾（漆）器
36 airless spray unit
无空气喷漆装置
37 airless spray gun
无空气喷（漆）枪

38 efflux viscometer
流出粘度计
39 seconds timer
秒表
40 lettering and gilding
书写和粉饰
41 lettering brush (signwriting brush, pencil)
书写刷（写广告用笔，铅笔）
42 tracing wheel
描绘轮
43 stencil knife
模板镂花刀
44 oil gold size
金油胶
45 gold leaf
金箔
46 outline drawing
轮廓描绘
47 mahlstick
腕木
48 pouncing
以印花粉印花样
49 pounce bag
印花粉袋
50 gilder's cushion
镀金工用的软垫
51 gilder's knife
镀金工用的刀子
52 sizing gold leaf
涂胶於金箔
53 filling in the letters with stipple paint
用点画漆填写文字
54 gilder's mop
涂金用的刷把

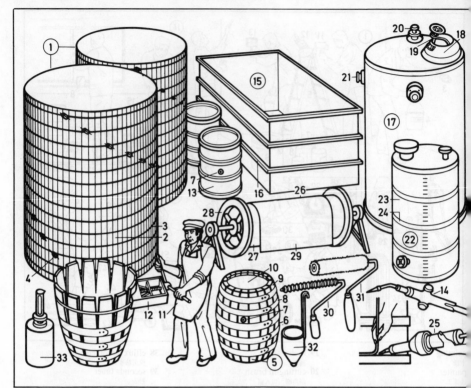

1-33 cooper's and tank construction engineer's workshops
箍桶工与桶槽建造师的工作室

1 tank
大桶，贮槽
2 circumference made of staves (staved circumference)
由木板构成的桶围
3 iron rod
（铁制连杆）铁箍
4 turnbuckle
螺丝扣
5 barrel (cask)
桶（木桶）
6 body of barrel (of cask)
桶身
7 bunghole
（木桶的）塞子
8 band (hoop) of barrel
木桶的箍条
9 barrel stave
木桶板条
10 barrelhead (heading)
桶盖
11 cooper
箍桶工人
12 trusser
箍紧器
13 drum
圆筒（桶）
14 gas welding torch
瓦斯熔接气炬

15 staining vat, made of thermoplastics
由热塑材料造成的染色大桶
16 iron reinforcing bands
加强铁箍
17 storage container, made of glass fibre (*Am.* glass fiber) reinforced polyester resin
玻璃纤维增强聚酯树脂造成的贮储容器
18 manhole
人孔
19 manhole cover with handwheel
带手轮的人孔盖
20 flange mount
凸缘座
21 flange-type stopcock
凸缘型停止旋塞
22 measuring tank
测量桶
23 shell (circumference)
壳（桶围）
24 shrink ring
缩紧环
25 hot-air gun
热气扦枪
26 roller made of glass fibre (*Am.* glass fiber) reinforced synthetic resin
玻璃纤维增强合成树脂制造的滚筒
27 cylinder
圆筒
28 flange
凸缘

29 glass cloth
玻璃布
30 grooved roller
有槽的滚轮
31 lambskin roller
羊皮滚轮
32 ladle for testing viscosity
检验粘度用的长杓子
33 measuring vessel for hardener
硬化剂测量容器

232

furrier's workroom
贩制造工
rrier
皮衣制造工
am spray gun
气喷枪
am iron
气熨斗
ating machine
酸）搅打机
tting machine for letting out
rskins
皮放长切割机
cut furskin
切割之毛皮
out strips (let-out sections)
长皮条（放长切片）
worker
皮工人
-sewing machine
皮缝纫机
wer for letting out
皮放长用的吹风机
furskins
皮
nk skin
皮
r side
面
ther side
革面
furskin
剪下的毛皮

15 lynx skin before letting out
放长前的山猫毛皮
16 let-out lynx skin
放长山猫毛皮
17 fur side
毛面
18 leather side
皮革面
19 let-out mink skin
放长貂皮
20 lynx fur, sewn together (sewn)
缝合的山猫毛皮
21 broadtail
宽尾毛皮
22 fur marker
毛皮标签
23 fur worker
毛皮工人
24 mink coat
貂皮大衣
25 ocelot coat
豹猫皮大衣

1-73 joiner's workshop
细木匠工作室

1-28 joiner's tools
细木匠工具

1 wood rasp
粗木锉

2 wood file
平锉

3 compass saw (keyhole saw)
圆锯（钥孔锯）

4 saw handle
锯柄

5 [square-headed] mallet
[方头]木槌

6 try square
矩尺

7-11 chisels
凿子

7 bevelled-edge chisel (chisel)
斜边凿子

8 mortise (mortice) chisel
榫眼凿

9 gouge
圆凿

10 handle
凿柄

11 framing chisel (cant chisel)
框凿（斜面凿）

12 glue pot in water bath
水槽中的胶罐

13 glue pot (glue well), an insert for joiner's glue
胶罐，放入盛胶罐的热水容器

14 handscrew
手动螺旋（丝）

15-28 planes
刨子

15 smoothing plane
光刨

16 jack plane
粗刨

17 toothing plane
齿刨

18 handle (toat)
手柄

19 wedge
木楔

20 plane iron (cutter)
刨刀

21 mouth
刨咀

22 sole
刨底

23 side
刨侧

24 stock (body)
刨身

25 rebate (rabbet) plane
槽口刨

26 router plane (old woman's tooth)
起槽刨

27 spokeshave
幅刨刀

28 compass plane
圆刨

29-37 woodworker's bench
木工台

29 foot
台脚

30 front vice (Am. vise)
前虎钳（台钳）

31 vice (Am. vise) handle
虎钳手柄

32 vice (Am. vise) screw
虎钳螺丝

33 jaw
钳口

34 bench top
台面板

35 well
工作台上的槽

36 bench stop (bench holdfast)
刨台栓（刨台反转装置）

37 tail vice (Am. vise)
刨台尾部虎钳

38 cabinet maker (joiner)
木工，木匠

39 trying plane
中级刨

40 shavings
刨花

41 wood screw
木螺丝

42 saw set
整锯齿工具

43 mitre (Am. miter) box
斜口锯箱

44 tenon saw
榫锯

45 thicknesser (thicknessing machine)
压刨床（刨成一定厚度的机械）

46 thicknessing table with rollers
带滚筒的压刨台

47 kick-back guard
逆转护板

48 chip-extractor opening
排屑口

49 chain mortising machine (chain mortiser)
链式榫眼机

50 endless mortising chain
环形榫眼铼

51 clamp (work clamp)
夹板，夹子

52 knot hole moulding (Am. molding) machine
造节孔机

53 knot hole cutter
节孔刀具

54 quick-action chuck
快速夹头（卡盘）

55 hand lever
手杆

56 change-gear handle
换齿轮手柄

57 sizing and edging machine
尺度矫正，摺边机（裁割修边机）

58 main switch
主开关（电源开关）

59 circular-saw (buzz saw) blade
圆盘锯锯片

60 height (rise and fall) adjustment wheel
高度（上下）调整轮

61 V-way
V型导轨

62 framing table
构架台

63 extension arm (arm)
延长臂

64 trimming table
修饰台

65 fence
挡板

66 fence adjustment handle
挡板调整手柄

67 clamp lever
夹紧杆

68 board-sawing machine
锯板机

69 swivel motor
旋转马达

70 board support
木板支架

71 saw carriage
锯架

72 pedal for raising the transport rollers
上升运转滚轮用的踏板

73 block board
整块胶合板

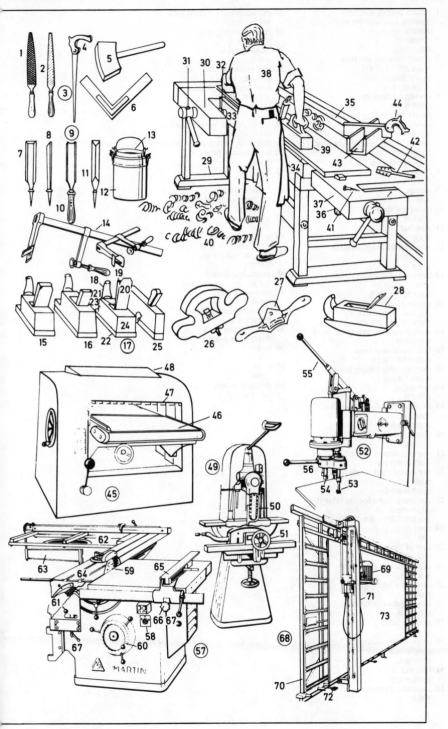

1 veneer-peeling machine
(peeling machine, peeler)
薄板剥皮机（剥皮机）

2 veneer
薄板

3 veneer-splicing machine
薄板编结机（斜切皮机）

4 nylon-thread cop
尼龙线团（圆锥形）

5 sewing mechanism
缝纫机械装置

6 dowel hole boring machine
(dowel hole borer)
定位孔搪床（定位孔搪孔机）

7 boring motor with hollow-shaft
boring bit
具有空心轴搪刀尖块的搪孔马达

8 clamp handle
夹紧手柄

9 clamp
夹钳

10 clamping shoe
夹紧环箍

11 stop bar
停止杆

12 edge sander (edge-sanding
machine)
边缘磨边机

13 tension roller with extension
arm
具延长臂的拉力滚筒

14 sanding belt regulator
(regulating handle)
砂磨带调节器（调整手柄）

15 endless sanding belt (sand belt)
环形砂磨带

16 belt-tensioning lever
砂磨带拉力（紧）杆

17 canting table (tilting table)
倾斜台（倾斜台）

18 belt roller
砂带滚筒

19 angling fence for mitres (*Am.*
miters)
斜接用的角板

20 opening dust hood
开口防尘罩

21 rise adjustment of the table
台面升降调整装置

22 rise adjustment wheel for the
table
台面升降调整轮

23 clamping screw for the table rise
adjustment
台面升降（高度）调整装置的夹紧螺丝

24 console
托架

25 foot of the machine
机脚

26 edge-veneering machine
边缘胶合机

27 sanding wheel
砂磨轮

28 sanding dust extractor
砂磨吸尘器

29 splicing head
编结机头

30 single-belt sanding machine
(single-belt sander)
单带砂磨机

31 belt guard
砂带防护装置

32 bandwheel cover
带轮罩

33 extractor fan (exhaust fan)
抽风机（排风机）

34 frame-sanding pad
框式砂磨垫板

35 sanding table
砂磨台

36 fine adjustment
微动装置

37 fine cutter and jointer
细切断器和刨木机

38 saw carriage
锯架

39 trailing cable hanger (trailing
cable support)
拖曳缆吊架（牵索支架）

40 air extractor pipe
排气管

41 rail
护栏

42 frame-cramping
(frame-clamping) machine
框架夹紧机

43 frame stand
框架座

44 workpiece, a window frame
工件（工作件），窗框

45 compressed-air line
压缩空气管

46 pressure cylinder
压力缸

47 pressure foot
加压脚

48 frame-mounting device
框架固定装置

49 rapid-veneer press
快速胶合板压力机

50 bed
压床

51 press
压力机

52 pressure piston
压力活塞

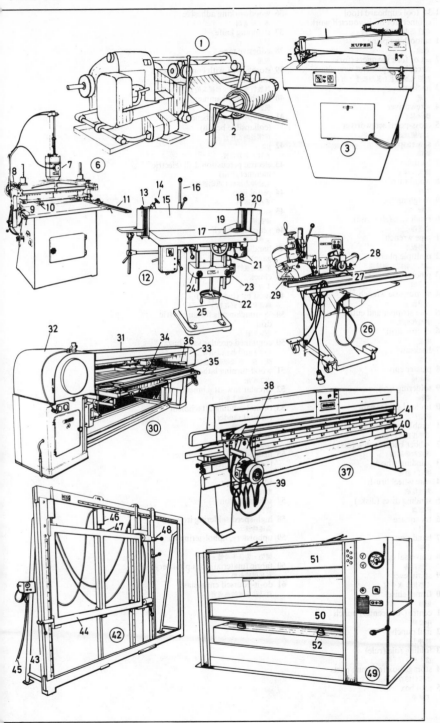

1-34 tool cupboard (tool
cabinet) for do-it-yourself work
自己动手做用的工具橱

1 smoothing plane
光铇

2 set of fork spanners (fork
wrenches, open-end wrenches)
整组叉形扳手（叉形扳手、开口扳手）

3 hacksaw
弓锯

4 screwdriver
螺丝起子

5 cross-point screwdriver
十字螺丝起子

6 saw rasp
锯锉

7 hammer
榔头，锤子

8 wood rasp
木锉

9 roughing file
粗锉

10 small vice (*Am.* vise)
小虎钳

11 pipe wrench
管形扳手

12 multiple pliers
多功用剪钳（钢丝钳）

13 pincers
尖手钳

14 all-purpose wrench
万用扳手

15 wire stripper and cutter
剥线和剪线钳

16 electric drill
电钻

17 hacksaw
弓锯

18 plaster cup
灰泥桶

19 soldering iron
烙铁

20 tin-lead solder wire
锡铅焊丝

21 lamb's wool polishing bonnet
羔羊皮抛光圆盘

22 rubber backing disc (disk)
橡皮衬垫圆盘

23 grinding wheel
磨轮，砂轮

24 wire wheel brush
钢丝轮刷

25 sanding discs (disks)
砂磨盘

26 try square
矩尺

27 hand saw
手锯

28 universal cutter
万能刀具

29 spirit level
（酒精）水平仪

30 firmer chisel
短凿

31 centre (*Am.* center) punch
中心冲

32 nail punch
钉冲头

33 folding rule (rule)
摺（叠）尺

34 storage box for small parts
小零件的存放箱

35 tool box
工具箱

36 woodworking adhesive
木工粘著剂

37 stripping knife
铲刀

38 adhesive tape
胶带

39 storage box with compartments
for nails, screws, and plugs
具放钉子、螺丝和插头的分格存放箱

40 machinist's hammer
机匠榔头（锤）

41 collapsible workbench
(collapsible bench)
可摺叠的工作台

42 jig
夹具，夹紧装置

43 electric percussion drill (electric
hammer drill)
电动冲击钻机（电动锤打钻）

44 pistol grip
手枪式握柄

45 side grip
侧握柄

46 gearshift switch
变速开关

47 handle with depth gauge (*Am.*
gage)
带深度规的手柄

48 chuck
卡盘，夹头

49 twist bit (twist drill)
麻花钻头（麻花钻）

50-55 attachments for an electric
drill
电钻附件

50 combined circular saw (buzz
saw) and bandsaw
圆（盘）锯和带锯组合机

51 wood-turning lathe
木工车床

52 circular saw attachment
圆（盘）锯（附件）

53 orbital sanding attachment
(orbital sander)
轨道式砂磨机

54 drill stand
钻架

55 hedge-trimming attachment
(hedge trimmer)
树篱修剪机

56 soldering gun
电炸枪

57 soldering iron
烙铁

58 high-speed soldering iron
高速烙铁

59 upholstery, upholstering an
armchair
铺垫，为扶手椅铺上布套

60 fabric (material) for upholstery
布套用的布料

61 do-it-yourself enthusiast
自己动手做的热衷者

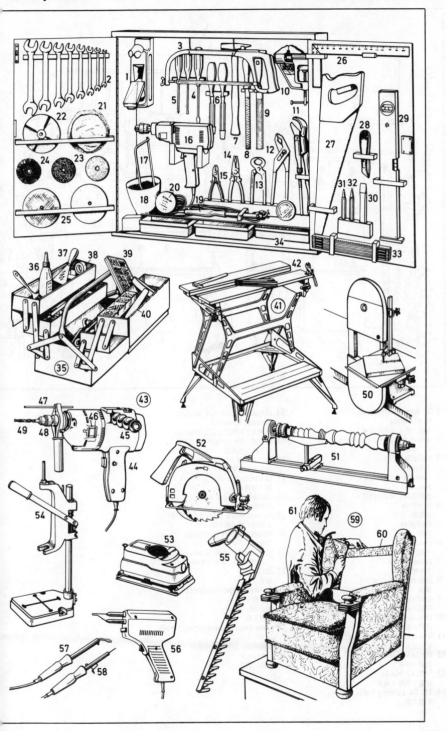

1-26 turnery (turner's
workshop)
车床工厂（车床工作室）
1 wood-turning lathe (lathe)
木工车床
2 lathe bed
车床床台
3 starting resistance (starting
resistor)
起动电阻（起动变阻器）
4 gearbox
齿轮箱
5 tool rest
刀架
6 chuck
卡盘，夹头
7 tailstock
车床尾座
8 centre (*Am.* center)
顶尖
9 driving plate with pin
带销的驱动盘
10 two-jaw chuck
双颚夹头
11 live centre (*Am.* center)
活动顶尖
12 fretsaw
圆锯，线锯
13 fretsaw blade
圆锯（线锯）锯片
14, 15, 24 turning tools
车削刀具

14 thread chaser, for cutting
threads in wood
於木头上切螺纹用的单用螺纹钣刀
15 gouge, for rough turning
粗车削用的圆凿
16 spoon bit (shell bit)
匙头钻（壳形钻）
17 hollowing tool
掏空用的刀具
18 outside calliper (caliper)
外卡钳（卡钳）
19 turned work (turned wood)
车好的工件（旋好的木件）
20 master turner (turner)
车床工
21 [piece of] rough wood
[一段]粗木料（未加工木料）
22 drill
钻子
23 inside calliper (caliper)
内卡钳
24 parting tool
割断工具
25 glass paper (sandpaper, emery
paper)
玻璃砂纸（砂纸，金刚砂纸）
26 shavings
木屑，刨花

basket making (basketry,
asketwork)
篮（篮细工）

weaves (strokes)
织法式样
nding
条编织
randing
条编织
lique
纹编织
nding, a piece of wickerwork
creen work)
帘编织品，一件柳条编织物
eaver
织工
ake
orkboard; *also:* lapboard
作板；亦称：搭膝板
rew block
织用横的突出板
le for holding the block
板定位孔
and
架
ip basket (spale basket)
片条篮子（刨片条篮）
ip (spale)
片条（刨片条）
aking tub
渍盆

14 willow stakes (osier stakes)
柳条，柳枝
15 willow rods (osier rods)
细柳条，细柳枝
16 basket, a piece of wickerwork
(basketwork)
筐，一件柳条编织物
17 border
筐边
18 woven side
编织面
19 round base
圆底
20 woven base
编织底
21 slath
筐底交叉肋
22-24 covering a frame
框架的外扳
22 frame
框架
23 end
末梢（绳头）
24 rib
肋条
25 upsett
骨架，框架
26 grass; *kinds:* esparto grass,
alfalfa grass
禾本科植物草；种类：茅草，苜蓿草
27 rush (bulrush, reed mace)
灯心草（芦苇，香蒲）

28 reed
芦苇
29 raffia (bast)
拉菲亚树的纤维（勒皮，内皮，勒皮纤维）
30 straw
麦秆，稻秆
31 bamboo cane
竹料
32 rattan (ratan) chair cane
藤条料
33 basket maker
编篮工
34 bending tool
弯曲工具
35 cutting point (bodkin)
锥子
36 rapping iron
敲铁
37 pincers
钳子
38 picking knife
刮刀
39 shave
刨刀
40 hacksaw
弓锯

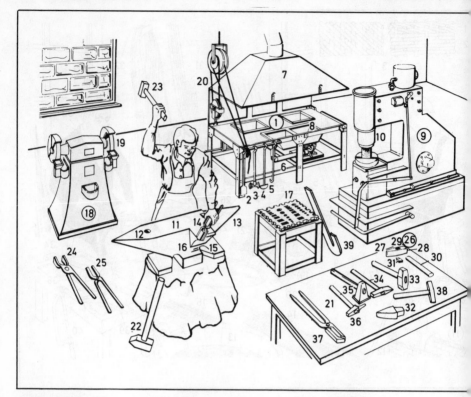

1-8 hearth (forge) with blacksmith's fire
锻工炉
1 hearth (forge)
锻炉
2 shovel (slice)
煤铲
3 swab
水刷
4 raker
炉耙
5 poker
火钩
6 blast pipe (tue iron)
鼓风管（锻炉风咀）
7 chimney (cowl, hood)
烟囱（烟囱罩，烟囱帽）
8 water trough (quenching trough, bosh)
水槽（冷却槽，金属锭冷却槽）
9 power hammer
机力
10 ram (tup)
撞锤（锤头）
11-16 anvil
砧
11 anvil
铁砧
12 flat beak (beck, bick)
铁砧平面端
13 round beak (beck, bick)
铁砧圆角端
14 auxiliary table
辅助工作台

15 foot
砧脚
16 upsetting block
锻粗块
17 swage block
型铁砧，花砧
18 tool-grinding machine (tool grinder)
工具磨床
19 grinding wheel
磨轮
20 block and tackle
滑车组
21 workbench (bench)
工作台
22-39 blacksmith's tools
铁工工具
22 sledge hammer
大锤
23 blacksmith's hand hammer
锻铁锤
24 flat tongs
平口钳
25 round tongs
圆口钳
26 parts of the hammer
锤子的各部分
27 peen (pane, pein)
锤头扁顶端
28 face
锤面
29 eye
锤眼

30 haft
锤柄
31 cotter punch
扁冲头
32 hardy (hardie)
錾
33 set hammer
锻缩锤
34 sett (set, sate)
平头錾
35 flat-face hammer (flatter)
平面锤
36 round punch
圆冲头
37 angle tongs
角钳
38 blacksmith's chisel (scaling hammer, chipping hammer)
铁匠凿锤（去锈锤，凿锤）
39 moving iron (bending iron)
活动铁（弯钢材工具）

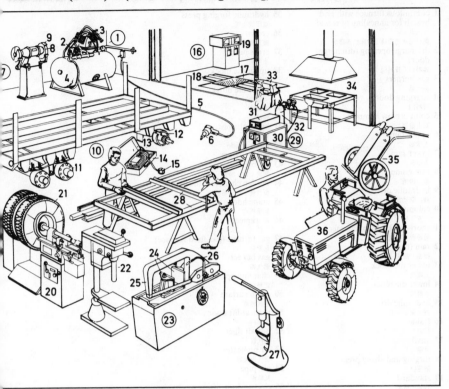

mpressed-air system
宿空气系统
ctric motor
动机，电马达
mpressor
宿机
mpressed-air tank
宿空气槽
mpressed-air line
宿空气管路
rcussion screwdriver
宿螺丝起子
destal grinding machine (floor
nding machine)
座式磨脉
nding wheel
轮，砂轮
ard
户罩
iler
车
ake drum
肢，刹车鼓
ake shoe
块，刹车块
ake lining
车衬
sting kit
验仪器
essure gauge (*Am.* gage)
力计（表）
ake-testing equipment, a
lling road
车试验装置，滚动车道

17 pit
坑（修车坑）
18 braking roller
刹车（掣动）滚子
19 meter (recording meter)
表（记录表）
20 precision lathe for brake drums
刹车鼓的精密车床
21 lorry wheel
载货车轮
22 boring mill
搪床
23 power saw, a hacksaw (power hacksaw)
动力锯，一种弓锯（动力弓锯）
24 vice (*Am.* vise)
虎钳，台钳
25 saw frame
锯框
26 coolant supply pipe
冷却剂供应管
27 riveting machine
铆接机
28 trailer frame (chassis) under construction
建造中的拖车架（车底盘）
29 inert-gas welding equipment
钝气熔接装置
30 rectifier
整流器
31 control unit
控制装置
32 CO₂ cylinder
二氧化碳气瓶

33 anvil
铁砧
34 hearth (forge) with blacksmith's fire
锻匠炉
35 trolley for gas cylinders
瓦斯筒用的手推车
36 vehicle under repair, a tractor
正修理中的车辆，曳引机，牵引机

1 continuous furnace with grid hearth for annealing of round stock
圆材退火用带格子炉床的连续炉

2 discharge opening (discharge door)
排料口（排料门）

3 gas burners
燃气器

4 charging door
进料门

5 counterblow hammer
对击锻锤

6 upper ram
上撞锤

7 lower ram
下撞锤

8 ram guide
撞锤滑槽

9 hydraulic drive
液压驱动装置

10 column
（支）柱

11 short-stroke drop hammer
短冲程落锤机

12 ram (tup)
撞锤（锤头）

13 upper die block
上模块

14 lower die block
下模块

15 hydraulic drive
液压驱动装置

16 frame
构架

17 anvil
铁砧

18 forging and sizing press
锻压机

19 standard
台架，机架

20 table
工作台

21 disc (disk) clutch
圆形离合器

22 compressed-air pipe
压缩空气管

23 solenoid valve
电磁阀

24 air-lift gravity hammer (air-lift drop hammer)
气升式落锤

25 drive motor
驱动马达

26 hammer (tup)
锤（锤头）

27 foot control (foot pedal)
脚踏控制（脚踏板）

28 preshaped (blocked) workpiece
预成形（成块）工件

29 hammer guide
落锤滑槽

30 hammer cylinder
落锤汽缸

31 anvil
铁砧

32 mechanical manipulator to move the workpiece in hammer forging
锤锻时移动工件的机械操作机

33 dogs
牵转具

34 counterweight
配重

35 hydraulic forging press
液压锻压机

36 crown
液压机顶梁

37 cross head
十字头

38 upper die block
上模块

39 lower die block
下模块

40 anvil
铁砧

41 hydraulic piston
液压活塞

42 pillar guide
柱导槽，柱滑槽

43 rollover device
翻转（滚）装置

44 burden chain (chain sling)
负重链（勾环吊链）

45 crane hook
起重机钩

46 workpiece
工件

47 gas furnace (gas-fired furnace)
瓦斯炉

48 gas burner
燃气器

49 charging opening
进料口

50 chain curtain
链式栅幕

51 vertical-lift door
上升门

52 hot-air duct
热气管

53 air preheater
空气预热器

54 gas pipe
瓦斯管

55 electric door-lifting mechanism
电动门机构

56 air blast
鼓风装置

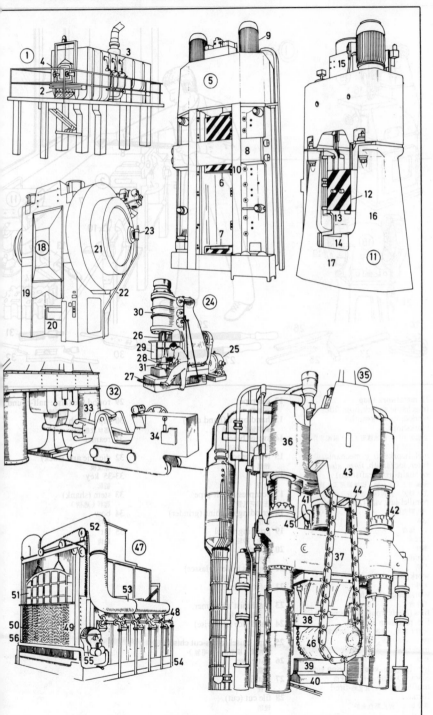

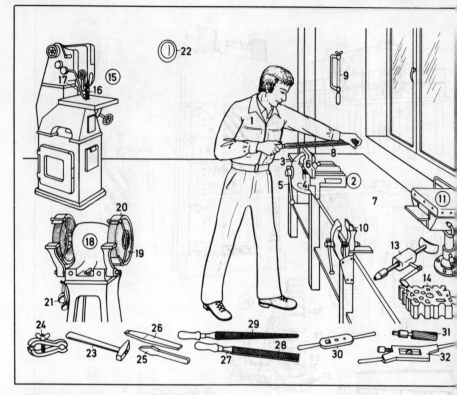

1-22 metalwork shop
(mechanic's workshop, fitter's
workshop, locksmith's
workshop)
金属加工厂（机械修理工厂，装配工
厂，锁匠工厂）

1 metalworker (*e.g.* mechanic,
fitter, locksmith; *form. also:*
wrought-iron craftsman)
金属加工工人（如：机械修理工，装配
工，锁匠；亦包括：锻铁匠）
2 parallel-jaw vice (*Am.* vise)
平行颚虎钳
3 jaw
夹，钳口
4 screw
螺杆
5 handle
手柄
6 workpiece
工件
7 workbench (bench)
工作台
8 files (*kinds:* rough file, smooth
file, precision file)
锉刀（种类：粗锉，细锉，精（密）
锉）
9 hacksaw
弓锯
10 leg vice (*Am.* vise), a spring vice
长脚（老）虎钳，一种弹簧虎钳
11 muffle furnace, a gas-fired
furnace
烙室炉，一种瓦斯点火炉

12 gas pipe
瓦斯管
13 hand brace (hand drill)
曲柄钻（手摇钻）
14 swage block
型铁砧，花砧
15 filing machine
锉机
16 file
锉刀
17 compressed-air pipe
压缩空气管
18 grinding machine (grinder)
磨床
19 grinding wheel
磨轮，砂轮
20 guard
防护罩
21 goggles (safety glasses)
护目镜（安全眼镜）
22 safety helmet
安全帽
23 machinist's hammer
机工锤（榔头）
24 hand vice (*Am.* vise)
手虎钳
25 cape chisel (cross-cut chisel)
起槽凿（横割凿，尖咀錾）
26 flat chisel
扁凿
27 flat file
扁锉
28 file cut (cut)
锉削

29 round file (*also:* half-round file)
圆锉（另有：半圆锉）
30 tap wrench
螺丝攻扳手
31 reamer
绞刀
32 die (die and stock)
螺纹模
33-35 key
钥匙
33 stem (shank)
匙杆（匙柄）
34 bow
匙弓
35 bit
匙齿

door lock, a mortise
ortice) lock
锁，一种榫眼锁
ck plate
门板，背板
ring bolt (latch bolt)
螺栓（弹簧锁）
mbler
的制栓
lt
全
yhole
匙孔
lt guide pin
全销
mbler spring
栓弹簧
llower, with square hole
方孔的从动轮（件）
inder lock (safety lock)
筒锁（安全锁）
inder (plug)
筒

ring

ety key, a flat key
全钥匙，一种扁平钥匙
t-off hinge
绞链
ok-and-ride band
套钩和骑带的铰链
rap hinge
条铰链
rnier calliper (caliper) gauge
m. gage)
标卡尺
eler gauge (Am. gage)
竟规
rnier depth gauge (Am. gage)
标深度尺
rnier

raightedge
尺，标尺
uare
尺
reast drill
压钻
ist bit (twist drill)
花钻头（麻花钻）
rew tap (tap)
丝攻
alves of a screw die
模的两半
rewdriver
丝起子
raper (also: pointed triangle
raper)
刀（即：尖三角刮刀）
ntre (Am. center) punch
心冲
und punch
冲头
at-nose pliers
嘴钳
etachable-jaw cut nippers
分解的颚口剪钳
as pliers
子
ncers
手钳

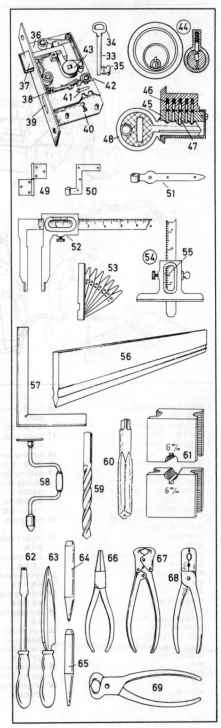

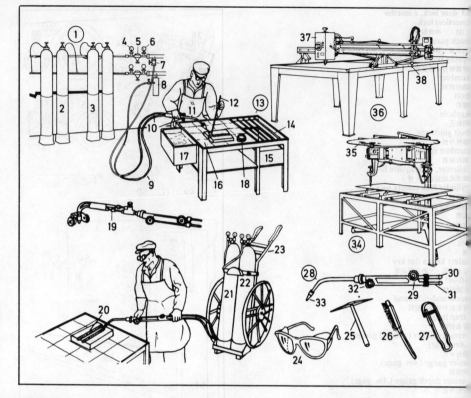

1 gas cylinder manifold 各种贮气瓶	**16** bench covering of chamotte slabs 耐火板复盖的工作台
2 acetylene cylinder 乙炔气瓶	**17** water tank 水槽
3 oxygen cylinder 氧气瓶	**18** welding paste (flux) 熔接剂（钎剂）
4 high-pressure manometer 高压计（高压液压计）	**19** welding torch (blowpipe) with cutting attachment and guide tractor 带切割附件和导向器的熔接气炬（钎枪，吹管）
5 pressure-reducing valve (reducing valve, pressure regulator) 减压阀（降压阀，调压器）	**20** workpiece 工件
6 low-pressure manometer 低压计（低压液压计）	**21** oxygen cylinder 氧气瓶
7 stop valve 停止阀	**22** acetylene cylinder 乙炔气瓶
8 hydraulic back-pressure valve for low-pressure installations 低压装置用的液压止回阀	**23** cylinder trolley 气瓶手推车
9 gas hose 瓦斯管	**24** welding goggles 熔接护目镜
10 oxygen hose 氧气管	**25** chipping hammer 凿锤
11 welding torch (blowpipe) （钎枪）熔接氧炬（吹管）	**26** wire brush 钢丝刷
12 welding rod (filler rod) 熔接条，钎条（填充钎料）	**27** torch lighter (blowpipe lighter) 气炬（钎枪）点火器，吹管点火器
13 welding bench 熔接台	**28** welding torch (blowpipe) 熔接气炬（钎枪），吹管
14 grating 格栅	**29** oxygen control 氧气控制钮
15 scrap box 废料盒（箱）	

30 oxygen connection 氧气接头
31 gas connection (acetylene connection) 瓦斯接头（乙炔接头）
32 gas control (acetylene control) 瓦斯控制钮（乙炔控制钮）
33 welding nozzle 熔接（钎枪）喷咀
34 cutting machine 切割机
35 circular template 圆形模板
36 universal cutting machine 万能切割机
37 tracing head （切割机的）描踪头
38 cutting nozzle 切割喷咀

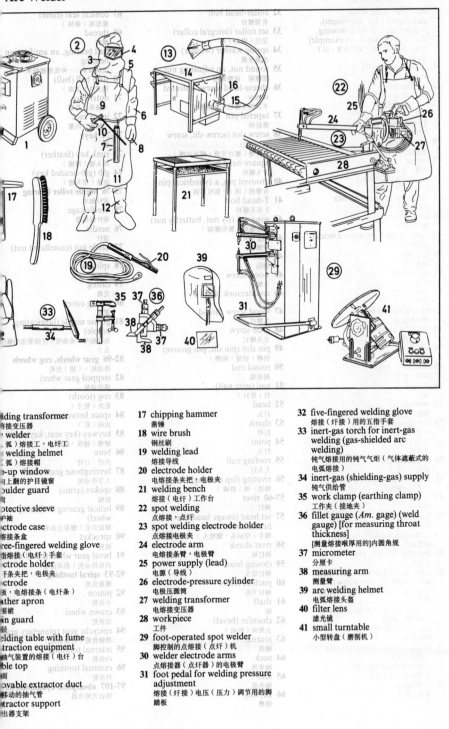

17 chipping hammer
凿锤
18 wire brush
钢丝刷
19 welding lead
熔接导线
20 electrode holder
电熔接条夹把，电极夹
21 welding bench
熔接（电灯）工作台
22 spot welding
点熔接，点灯
23 spot welding electrode holder
点熔接电极夹
24 electrode arm
电熔接条臂，电极臂
25 power supply (lead)
电源（导线）
26 electrode-pressure cylinder
电极压圆筒
27 welding transformer
电熔接变压器
28 workpiece
工件
29 foot-operated spot welder
脚控制的点熔接（点灯）机
30 welder electrode arms
熔接器（点灯器）的电极臂
31 foot pedal for welding pressure adjustment
熔接（灯接）电压（压力）调节用的脚踏板

32 five-fingered welding glove
熔接（灯接）用的五指手套
33 inert-gas torch for inert-gas welding (gas-shielded arc welding)
钝气熔接用的钝气炬（气体遮蔽式的电弧熔接）
34 inert-gas (shielding-gas) supply
钝气供给管
35 work clamp (earthing clamp)
工作夹（接地夹）
36 fillet gauge (Am. gage) (weld gauge) [for measuring throat thickness]
[测量熔接喉厚用的]内圆角规
37 micrometer
分厘卡
38 measuring arm
测量臂
39 arc welding helmet
电弧熔接头盔
40 filter lens
滤光镜
41 small turntable
小型转盘（磨削机）

[material: steel, brass, aluminium (*Am.* aluminum), plastics, etc.; in the following, steel was chosen as an example]
[材料:钢,铜,铝,塑胶等等;以下选钢材为例]

1 angle iron (angle)
角铁（角）

2 leg (flange)
边（凸缘）

3-7 steel girders
钢梁

3 T-iron (tee-iron)
T 型铁

4 vertical leg
垂直边

5 flange
凸缘，缘板

6 H-girder (H-beam)
H 型钢梁（工字钢）

7 E-channel (channel iron)
E 型槽钢（槽铁）

8 round bar
圆杆，圆条

9 square iron (*Am.* square stock)
方铁杆

10 flat bar
扁条

11 strip steel
带钢

12 iron wire
铁丝

13-50 screws and bolts
螺丝和螺栓

13 hexagonal-head bolt
六角头螺栓

14 head
六角头

15 shank
螺柄（杆）

16 thread
螺纹

17 washer
垫圈，垫圈

18 hexagonal nut
六角头螺帽

19 split pin
开尾梢

20 rounded end
圆端

21 width of head (of flats)
六角头的宽度

22 stud
螺椿

23 point (end)
螺栓头（端）

24 castle nut (castellated nut)
堡形螺帽

25 hole for the split pin
开尾螺孔

26 cross-head screw, a sheet-metal screw (self-tapping screw)
十字头螺丝,薄金属板螺丝（自攻螺丝）

27 hexagonal socket head screw
六角承窝头螺丝

28 countersunk-head bolt
埋头螺丝

29 catch
（螺栓）掣子

30 locknut (locking nut)
併紧螺帽（锁紧螺帽）

31 bolt (pin)
螺栓（梢）

32 collar-head bolt
有领螺栓

33 set collar (integral collar)
定位（固定）环

34 spring washer (washer)
弹簧垫圈

35 round nut, an adjusting nut
圆螺帽,调整螺帽

36 cheese-head screw, a slotted screw
平顶圆头螺钉,有槽螺丝

37 tapered pin
推拔销

38 screw slot (screw slit, screw groove)
螺丝槽(螺丝开缝,螺丝沟槽)

39 square-head bolt
方头螺栓

40 grooved pin, a cylindrical pin
有槽销（销）,圆柱形销

41 T-head bolt
T 形头螺栓

42 wing nut (fly nut, butterfly nut)
翼形螺帽（翼形螺帽）

43 rag bolt
棘螺栓

44 barb
倒钩

45 wood screw
木螺丝

46 countersunk head
埋头

47 wood screw thread
木螺纹

48 grub screw
无头螺钉

49 pin slot (pin slit, pin groove)
销槽（销缝,销沟）

50 round end
圆尾端

51 nail (wire nail)
钉（铁钉）

52 head
钉头

53 shank
钉杆

54 point
钉尖

55 roofing nail
大头钉

56 riveting (lap riveting)
铆接,（搭铆）

57-60 rivet
铆钉

57 set head (swage head, die head), a rivet head
铆头（型钻头,螺模头）,一种铆钉头

58 rivet shank
铆钉柄

59 closing head
铆钉结头

60 pitch of rivets
铆钉节距

61 shaft
轴

62 chamfer (bevel)
去角面（斜面）

63 journal
轴颈

64 neck
轴承颈

65 seat
轴承座

66 keyway
键槽

67 conical seat (cone)
锥形座（锥体）

68 thread
螺纹

69 ball bearing, an antifriction bearing
滚珠轴承,一种低摩擦轴承

70 steel ball (ball)
钢滚珠（滚珠）

71 outer race
（轴承）外圈

72 inner race
（轴承）内圈

73-74 keys
键

73 sunk key (feather)
埋头键（滑键）

74 gib (gib-headed key)
嵌头（带头键）

75-76 needle roller bearing
滚针轴承

75 needle cage
滚针保持器

76 needle
滚针

77 castle nut (castellated nut)
堡形螺帽

78 split pin
开尾梢

79 casing
壳箱

80 casing cover
罩盖

81 grease nipple (lubricating nipple)
加油脂咀,黄油咀（注润滑脂的螺纹咀头）

82-96 gear wheels, cog wheels
传动轮,（附）齿轮

82 stepped gear wheel
塔传动轮

83 cog (tooth)
轮齿（轮牙）

84 space between teeth
齿间（距）

85 keyway (key seat, key slot)
键槽（键座,键槽）

86 bore
内径,口径

87 herringbone gear wheel
人字传动轮

88 spokes (arms)
轮辐

89 helical gearing (helical spur wheel)
螺旋齿轮（螺旋正齿轮）

90 sprocket
链轮

91 bevel gear wheel (bevel wheel)
斜齿转动轮（斜面齿轮）

92-93 spiral toothing
螺旋齿轮

92 pinion
小齿轮

93 crown wheel
冠状轮

94 epicyclic gear (planetary gear
周转齿轮（行星齿轮）

95 internal toothing
内齿轮

96 external toothing
外齿轮

97-107 absorption dynamometer
吸收式测功器

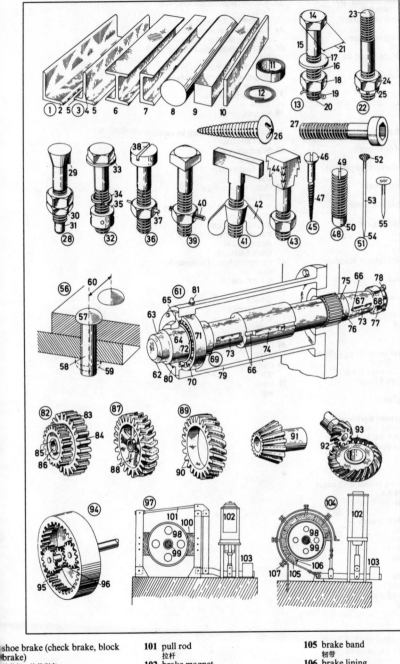

shoe brake (check brake, block brake)
块状钔，块状刹车
brake pulley
钔滑轮，刹车滑轮
brake shaft (brake axle)
钔轴（刹车轴）
brake block (brake shoe)
钔块

101 pull rod
拉杆
102 brake magnet
驱动磁铁
103 brake weight
驱动重量
104 band brake
带钔

105 brake band
钔带
106 brake lining
刹车衬
107 adjusting screw, for even application of the brake
使驱动器平稳用的调节螺丝

1-51 coal mine (colliery, pit)
煤矿（煤矿，采掘场）
1 pithead gear (headgear)
坑口井架
2 winding engine house
卷扬动力机房
3 pithead frame (head frame)
坑口井架
4 pithead building
坑口建筑物
5 processing plant
煤处理（加工）场
6 sawmill
锯木厂
7-11 coking plant
炼焦厂
7 battery of coke ovens
炼焦炉组
8 larry car (larry, charging car)
运煤车
9 coking coal tower
焦煤塔
10 coke-quenching tower
熄焦塔
11 coke-quenching car
熄焦车
12 gasometer
煤气罐（库）
13 power plant (power station)
发电厂
14 water tower
水塔
15 cooling tower
冷却塔
16 mine fan
矿坑换气装置
17 depot
仓库
18 administration building (office building, offices)
行政大楼（办公大楼，办事处）
19 tip heap (spoil heap)
矿渣堆
20 cleaning plant
清洗设备
21-51 underground workings (underground mining)
地下作业（地下采矿）
21 ventilation shaft
通风井
22 fan drift
扇风机风道
23 cage-winding system with cages
运矿笼的升降系统
24 main shaft
主立坑道
25 skip-winding system
吊斗升降系统
26 winding inset
坑底车场装卸处
27 staple shaft
坑内小坑
28 spiral chute
螺旋溜槽（溜道）
29 gallery along seam
沿矿层的坑道
30 lateral
横坑
31 cross-cut
石门
32 tunnelling (Am. tunneling) machine
（坑）隧道开掘机
33-37 longwall faces
长壁工作面

33 horizontal ploughed longwall face
水平控煤长壁工作面（挖掘面）
34 horizontal cut longwall face
水平切割长壁工作面（挖掘面）
35 vertical pneumatic pick longwall face
垂直气压掘起长壁工作面（挖掘面）
36 diagonal ram longwall face
对角长壁工作面
37 goaf (gob, waste)
采掘路
38 air lock
气流闸
39 transportation of men by cars
人员车辆的运输
40 belt conveying
带状运送机
41 raw coal bunker
原煤（粗煤）仓
42 charging conveyor
装煤运送机
43 transportation of supplies by monorail car
单轨车供应品的运输
44 transportation of men by monorail car
单轨车人员的运输
45 transportation of supplies by mine car
煤车供料运输
46 drainage
排水设备
47 sump (sink)
水仓
48 capping
表土
49 [layer of] coal-bearing rock
含煤层
50 coal seam
煤层
51 fault
断层

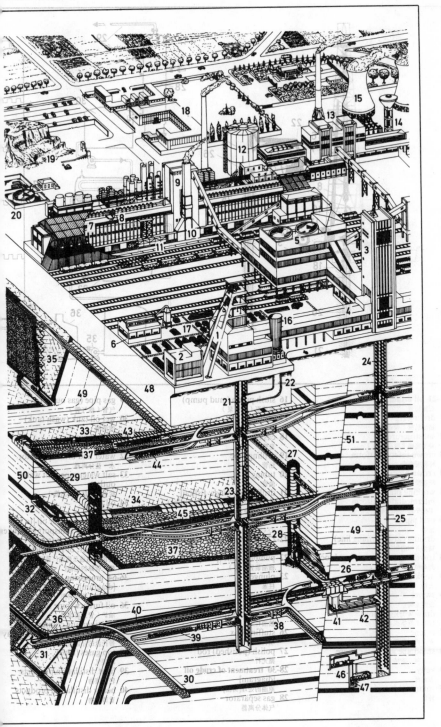

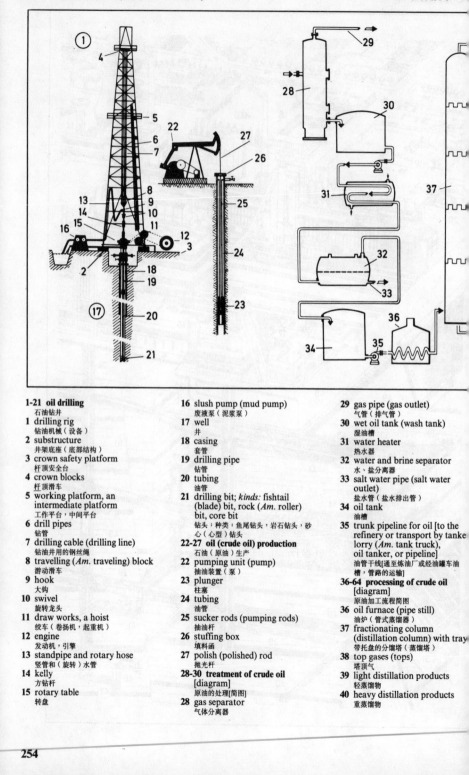

1-21 oil drilling
石油钻井

1 **drilling rig**
钻油机械（设备）

2 **substructure**
井架底座（底部结构）

3 **crown safety platform**
杆顶安全台

4 **crown blocks**
杆顶滑车

5 **working platform, an intermediate platform**
工作平台，中间平台

6 **drill pipes**
钻管

7 **drilling cable (drilling line)**
钻油井用的钢丝绳

8 **travelling (*Am.* traveling) block**
游动滑车

9 **hook**
大钩

10 **swivel**
旋转龙头

11 **draw works, a hoist**
绞车（卷扬机，起重机）

12 **engine**
发动机，引擎

13 **standpipe and rotary hose**
竖管和（旋转）水管

14 **kelly**
方钻杆

15 **rotary table**
转盘

16 **slush pump (mud pump)**
废液泵（泥浆泵）

17 **well**
井

18 **casing**
套管

19 **drilling pipe**
钻管

20 **tubing**
油管

21 **drilling bit;** *kinds:* fishtail (blade) bit, rock (*Am.* roller) bit, core bit
钻头；种类：鱼尾钻头，岩石钻头，砂心（心型）钻头

22-27 oil (crude oil) production
石油（原油）生产

22 **pumping unit (pump)**
抽油装置（泵）

23 **plunger**
柱塞

24 **tubing**
油管

25 **sucker rods (pumping rods)**
抽油杆

26 **stuffing box**
填料函

27 **polish (polished) rod**
抛光杆

28-30 treatment of crude oil [diagram]
原油的处理[简图]

28 **gas separator**
气体分离器

29 **gas pipe (gas outlet)**
气管（排气管）

30 **wet oil tank (wash tank)**
湿油槽

31 **water heater**
热水器

32 **water and brine separator**
水、盐分离器

33 **salt water pipe (salt water outlet)**
盐水管（盐水排出管）

34 **oil tank**
油槽

35 **trunk pipeline for oil [to the refinery or transport by tanker lorry (*Am.* tank truck), oil tanker, or pipeline]**
油管干线[通至炼油厂或经油罐车油槽，管路的运输]

36-64 processing of crude oil [diagram]
原油加工流程简图

36 **oil furnace (pipe still)**
油炉（管式蒸馏器）

37 **fractionating column (distillation column) with trays**
带托盘的分馏塔（蒸馏塔）

38 **top gases (tops)**
塔顶气

39 **light distillation products**
轻蒸馏物

40 **heavy distillation products**
重蒸馏物

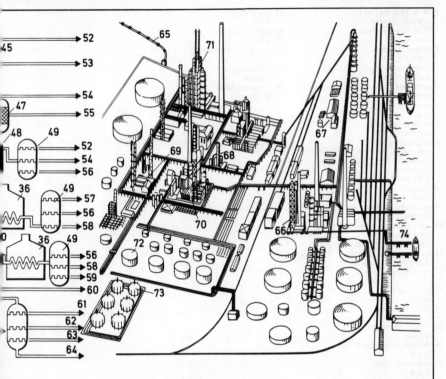

troleum
油，原油

s oil component
油成分

sidue
𣿟，残油

ndenser (cooler)
凝器（冷却器）

mpressor
缩机

sulphurizing
esulphurization, *Am.*
sulfurizing, desulfurization)
ant
硫装置（设备）

ormer (hydroformer,
atformer)
整装置，改质装置（氢重整，铂重
）

talytic cracker (cat cracker)
化裂解装置

istillation column
馏塔

-waxing (wax separation)
蜡（腊分离）

cuum equipment
空设备

oil products
油产品

el gas
料气

uefied petroleum gas (liquid
s)
化石油气（液化气）

54 regular grade petrol (*Am.*
gasoline)
正规汽油，普通汽油

55 super grade petrol (*Am.*
gasoline)
超级汽油

56 diesel oil
柴油

57 aviation fuel
航空燃料

58 light fuel oil
轻燃料油

59 heavy fuel oil
重燃料油

60 paraffin (paraffin oil, kerosene)
石腊（石腊油，煤油）

61 spindle oil
心轴油，锭子油

62 lubrication oil
润滑油

63 cylinder oil
汽缸油

64 bitumen
沥青

65-74 oil refinery
炼油厂

65 pipeline (oil pipeline)
管路（输油管）

66 distillation plants
蒸馏装置

67 lubricating oil refinery
润滑油炼油厂

68 desulphurizing
(desulphurization, *Am.*
desulfurizing, desulfurization)
plant
去硫装置（设备）

69 gas-separating plant
气体分离装置

70 catalytic cracking plant
催化裂解装置

71 catalytic reformer
催化重整装置

72 storage tank
储存槽

73 spherical tank
球面（形）槽

74 tanker terminal
油轮码头

Oil (Oil, Petroleum) 海上钻探

1-39 drilling rig (oil rig)
钻探设备，钻油设备

1-37 drilling platform
钻探平台

1 power station
发电站（发电所）

2 generator exhausts
发电机排气装置

3 revolving crane (pedestal crane)
旋转起重机（托架式起重机）

4 piperack
管架

5 turbine exhausts
涡轮机排气装置

6 materials store
材料仓库

7 helicopter deck (heliport deck, heliport)
直升机降落平台，直升机场甲板

8 elevator
升降机

9 production oil and gas separator
油气分离器

10 test oil and gas separators (test separators)
试验用油气分离器（试验分离器）

11 emergency flare stack
紧急照明弹（闪光）装置

12 derrick
井架

13 diesel tank
柴油槽

14 office building
办公室

15 cement storage tanks
水泥储槽

16 drinking water tank
饮水槽

17 salt water tank
盐水槽

18 jet fuel tanks
喷汽燃料槽

19 lifeboats
救生艇

20 elevator shaft
升降机架

21 compressed-air reservoir
压缩储气筒（罐）

22 pumping station
泵水站

23 air compressor
空气压缩机

24 air lock
气闸

25 seawater desalination plant
海水去盐设备

26 inlet filters for diesel fuel
柴油输入过滤器

27 gas cooler
气体冷却器

28 control panel for the separators
分离器控制盘

29 toilets (lavatories)
盥洗室

30 workshop
工厂

31 pig trap [the 'pig' is used to clean the oil pipeline]
[用来清理油管的]刮管器

32 control room
控制室

33 accommodation modules (accommodation)
居住单位

34 high-pressure cementing pumps
高压水泥泵

35 lower deck
下甲板

36 middle deck
中甲板

37 top deck (main deck)
顶甲板（主甲板）

38 substructure
下部结构

39 mean sea level
海平面

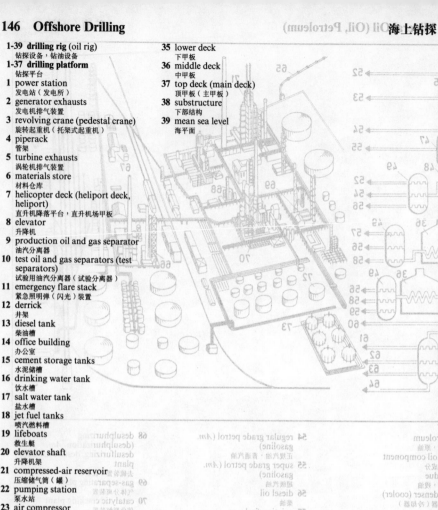

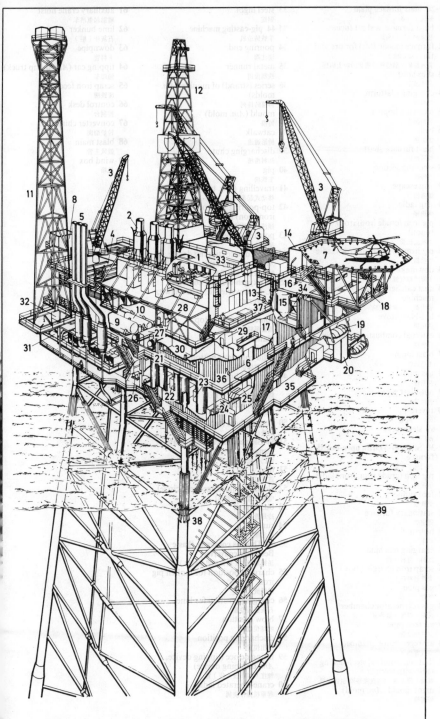

1-20 blast furnace plant
鼓风炉设备

1 blast furnace, a shaft furnace
鼓风炉，一种高炉

2 furnace incline (lift) for ore and flux or coke
装入铁矿、助熔剂或焦炭的炉上斜桥

3 skip hoist
吊斗吊车

4 charging platform
加料台

5 receiving hopper
受料漏斗

6 bell
送矿钟

7 blast furnace shaft
鼓风高炉

8 smelting section
冶炼区

9 slag escape
熔渣出口

10 slag ladle
熔渣桶

11 pig iron (crude iron, iron) runout
生铁溢流管

12 pig iron (crude iron, iron) ladle
生铁桶

13 downtake
下降的排气管

14 dust catcher, a dust-collecting machine
吸尘器，一种集尘机

15 hot-blast stove
热风炉

16 external combustion chamber
外燃室

17 blast main
主送风管

18 gas pipe
瓦斯管

19 hot-blast pipe
热风管

20 tuyère
风口，风咀

21-69 steelworks
钢厂

21-30 Siemens-Martin open-hearth furnace
西门马丁炉

21 pig iron (crude iron, iron) ladle
生铁桶

22 feed runner
受铁槽

23 stationary furnace
固定炉

24 hearth
炉床

25 charging machine
加料（进料）机

26 scrap iron charging box
废铁进料箱（斗）

27 gas pipe
气管

28 gas regenerator chamber
瓦斯（煤气）蓄热室

29 air feed pipe
空气供给管

30 air regenerator chamber
空气蓄热室

31 [bottom-pouring] steel-casting ladle with stopper
具栓（停止器）的[底浇铸模]钢制浇桶

32 ingot mould (*Am.* mold)
铸锭模

33 steel ingot
钢锭

34-44 pig-casting machine
生铁铸造机

34 pouring end
浇注端

35 metal runner
铁制流道

36 series (strand) of moulds (*Am.* molds)
铸模的排列

37 mould (*Am.* mold)
铸模

38 catwalk
桥形通道

39 discharging chute
卸料滑槽

40 pig
生铁块

41 travelling (*Am.* traveling) crane
移动式起重机

42 top-pouring pig iron (crude iron, iron) ladle
倾注式生铁浇桶

43 pouring ladle lip
浇桶注口

44 tilting device (tipping device, *Am.* dumping device)
倾注装置（倾卸装置）

45-50 oxygen-blowing converter (L-D converter, Linz-Donawitz converter)
吹氧转炉

45 conical converter top
圆锥形转炉炉帽

46 mantle
外罩

47 solid converter bottom
转炉整体炉底

48 fireproof lining (refractory lining)
防火炉衬（耐火炉衬）

49 oxygen lance
氧吹管

50 tapping hole (tap hole)
出铁口

51-54 Siemens electric low-shaft furnace
西门子低轴电炉

51 feed
进料口

52 electrodes [arranged in a circle]
电极装置[排成圆形]

53 bustle pipe
冷却管

54 runout
流出槽

55-69 Thomas converter (basic Bessemer converter)
汤姆斯转炉（碱性柏思麦转炉）

55 charging position for molten pig iron
熔铁流入位置

56 charging position for lime
石灰装入位置

57 blow position
吹炼位置

58 discharging position
流出位置

59 tilting device (tipping device, *Am.* dumping device)
倾注（卸）设（装）置

60 crane-operated ladle
起重机操作浇桶

61 auxiliary crane hoist
辅助起重吊车

62 lime bunker
石灰斗（柜）

63 downpipe
下料管

64 tipping car (*Am.* dump truck)
倾卸车

65 scrap iron feed
废铁槽

66 control desk
控制台

67 converter chimney
转炉烟囱

68 blast main
鼓风主管

69 wind box
风箱

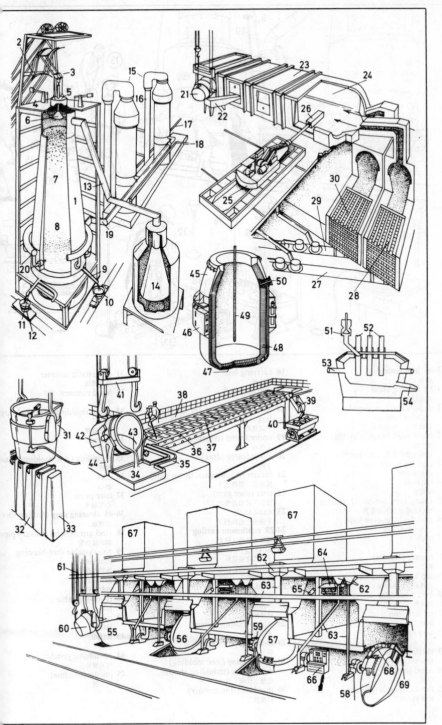

1-45 iron foundry
　　铸铁工厂
1-12 melting plant
　　熔化设备
1 cupola furnace (cupola), a
　melting furnace
　熔铁炉，一种熔化炉
2 blast main (blast inlet, blast
　pipe)
　鼓风主管（鼓风入口，鼓风管）
3 tapping spout
　出铁流出槽
4 spyhole
　窥视孔
5 tilting-type hot-metal receiver
　倾斜式熔化生铁接受器
6 mobile drum-type ladle
　可移动鼓形浇桶
7 melter
　熔工
8 founder (caster)
　铸工
9 tap bar (tapping bar)
　出铁杆（出熔液棍）
10 bott stick (*Am.* bot stick)
　堵塞杆
11 molten iron
　熔铁
12 slag spout
　熔渣流出槽
13 casting team
　浇铸班（组）
14 hand shank
　手柄
15 double handle (crutch)
　双手柄（叉形手柄）

16 carrying bar
　搬运棒
17 skimmer rod
　撇渣杆
18 closed moulding (*Am.* molding)
　box
　闭式模箱
19 upper frame (cope)
　上模箱
20 lower frame (drag)
　下模箱
21 runner (runner gate, down-gate)
　横流道（竖浇道）
22 riser (riser gate)
　冒口（冒口进模口）
23 hand ladle
　手浇桶（长柄杓）
24-29 continuous casting
　连续（浇铸）铸造
24 sinking pouring floor
　下沉式浇铸底板
25 solidifying pig
　凝固生铁
26 solid stage
　固体状态
27 liquid stage
　液体状态
28 water-cooling system
　水冷系统
29 mould (*Am.* mold) wall
　铸型壁
30-37 moulding (*Am.* molding)
　department (moulding shop)
　造模工作间（室）
30 moulder (*Am.* molder)
　砂模技工

31 pneumatic rammer
　气力捣锤
32 hand rammer
　手捣杆
33 open moulding (*Am.* molding)
　box
　开式模箱
34 pattern
　模型
35 moulding (*Am.* molding) sand
　模砂
36 core
　砂心
37 core print
　心型端承
38-45 cleaning shop (fettling shop)
　清理场
38 steel grit or sand delivery pipe
　钢砂输送管
39 rotary-table shot-blasting
　machine
　旋转台珠击机
40 grit guard
　砂粒护板
41 revolving table
　回转台
42 casting
　铸件
43 fettler
　清理工
44 pneumatic grinder
　气力磨轮
45 pneumatic chisel
　气力錾

rolling mill
钢厂

aking pit
热坑炉

aking pit crane
热坑炉起重机

got
锭

got tipper
锭倾倒装置

ooming train (roller path)
块滚子机组（滚子进给路）

orkpiece
件

oom shears
块剪切机

wo-high mill
段轧机

set of rolls (set of rollers)
套辊子

pper roll (upper roller)
辊子

wer roll (lower roller)
辊子

roll stand
子架

ase plate
盘

ousing (frame)
架

oupling spindle
结轴

roove
槽

ll bearing
动轴承

61-65 adjusting equipment
调整装置

61 chock
塞子

62 main screw
主螺丝

63 gear
齿轮，转动装置

64 motor
马达，发动机

65 indicator for rough and fine
adjustment
粗调和微调指示器

**66-75 continuous rolling mill train
for the manufacture of strip**
[diagram]
板条用的连续轧钢机[简图]

66-68 processing of semi-finished
product
半成品的加工（处理）

66 semi-finished product
半成品

67 gas cutting installation
焰割装置

68 stack of finished steel sheets
钢板成品堆

69 continuous reheating furnaces
连续式加热炉

70 blooming train
中块辊轧机组

71 finishing train
完工机组

72 coiler
盘卷器

73 collar bearing for marketing
供贩卖的带钢卷

74 5mm shearing train
5 毫米的剪切机组

75 10mm shearing train
10 毫米的剪切机组

1 **centre** (*Am.* center) **lathe**
顶尖车床

2 **headstock with gear control**
(geared headstock)
带齿轮控制的主轴箱

3 **reduction drive lever**
减速驱动杆

4 **lever for normal and coarse**
threads
标准螺纹和粗牙螺纹手柄

5 **speed change lever**
变速杆

6 **leadscrew reverse-gear lever**
导螺杆逆转齿轮杆

7 **change-gear box**
变换齿轮箱

8 **feed gearbox (Norton tumbler**
gear)
进给齿轮箱（诺顿换向齿轮）

9 **levers for changing the feed and**
thread pitch
变换进给和螺距手杆

10 **feed gear lever (tumbler lever)**
进给齿轮杆

11 **switch lever for right or left**
hand action of main spindle
主轴左右手动作用转换杆

12 **lathe foot (footpiece)**
车床脚座

13 **leadscrew handwheel for**
traversing of saddle
(longitudinal movement of
saddle)
鞍台横向用导螺手轮（鞍台纵向移动）

14 **tumbler reverse lever**
换向逆转杆

15 **feed screw**
进给螺旋

16 **apron (saddle apron, carriage**
apron)
护衬，肖板（鞍台肖板，滑架肖板）

17 **lever for longitudinal and**
transverse motion
纵向横向移动的操作杆

18 **drop (dropping) worm (feed**
trip, feed tripping device) for
engaging feed mechanisms
接合进给机械用的下降螺杆

19 **lever for engaging half nut of**
leadscrew (lever for clasp nut
engagement)
接合主螺杆螺帽用的手杆（夹紧螺帽的
接合手杆）

20 **lathe spindle**
车床轴

21 **tool post**
夹刀柱

22 **top slide (tool slide, tool rest)**
顶滑台（刀具滑台，刀架）

23 **cross slide**
横滑台

24 **bed slide**
床身滑台

25 **coolant supply pipe**
冷却剂供给管

26 **tailstock centre** (*Am.* center)
车床尾座顶尖

27 **barrel (tailstock barrel)**
圆筒（尾座圆筒）

28 **tailstock barrel clamp lever**
尾座筒夹杆

29 **tailstock**
尾座

30 **tailstock barrel adjusting**
handwheel
尾座（架）筒调整手轮

31 **lathe bed**
车床床身

32 **leadscrew**
主螺杆

33 **feed shaft**
进给轴

34 **reverse shaft for right and left**
hand motion and engaging and
disengaging
左右手动作和离合转换轴

35 **four-jaw chuck (four-jaw**
independent chuck)
四爪夹头（四爪独立夹头）

36 **gripping jaw**
夹爪

37 **three-jaw chuck (three-jaw**
self-centring, self-centering,
chuck)
三爪夹头（三爪自定中心夹头）

38 **turret lathe**
转塔式车床

39 **cross slide**
横滑台

40 **turret**
转塔

41 **combination toolholder**
(multiple turning head)
复合刀把，组合刀具支架（多刀转塔）

42 **top slide**
顶滑台

43 **star wheel**
星形轮

44 **coolant tray for collecting**
coolant and swarf
收集冷却剂和切屑的冷却剂盘

45-53 lathe tools
车床工具

45 **tool bit holder (clamp tip tool)**
for adjustable cutting tips
调整截割喷咀用的刀尖块架（夹刀头的
工具）

46 **adjustable cutting tip (clamp tip)**
of cemented carbide or oxide
ceramic
烧结碳化物和氧化陶磁的调整截割喷咀
（刀头）

47 **shapes of adjustable oxide**
ceramic tips
可调氧化陶磁刀头形状

48 **lathe tool with cemented carbide**
cutting edge
具烧结碳化物刀刃的车床工具

49 **tool shank**
刀柄

50 **brazed cemented carbide cutting**
tip (cutting edge)
硬钎烧结碳化物刀刃

51 **internal facing tool (boring tool)**
for corner work
加工角内面刀具（搪孔刀具）

52 **general-purpose lathe tool**
一般用途的车床刀具

53 **parting (parting-off) tool**
割断工具

54 **lathe carrier**
车床牵转具

55 **driving (driver) plate**
驱动盘

56-72 measuring instruments
测定仪器，度量衡仪器

56 **plug gauge** (*Am.* gage)
塞规

57 **'GO' gauging** (*Am.* gaging)
member (end)
"通过"规件（端）

58 **'NOT GO' gauging** (*Am.*
gaging) member (end)
"不通过"规件（端）

59 **calliper (caliper, snap) gauge**
(*Am.* gage)
卡规

60 **'GO' side**
"通过"端

61 **'NOT GO' side**
"不通过"端

62 **micrometer**
分厘卡，测微尺

63 **measuring scale**
测量刻度

64 **graduated thimble**
刻度套管

65 **frame**
骨架，框架

66 **spindle (screwed spindle)**
轴（螺纹轴）

67 **vernier calliper (caliper) gauge**
(*Am.* gage)
游标卡尺

68 **depth gauge** (*Am.* gage)
attachment rule
深度规辅助尺

69 **vernier scale**
游标刻度

70 **outside jaws**
外爪

71 **inside jaws**
内爪

72 **vernier depth gauge** (*Am.* gage)
游标深度规

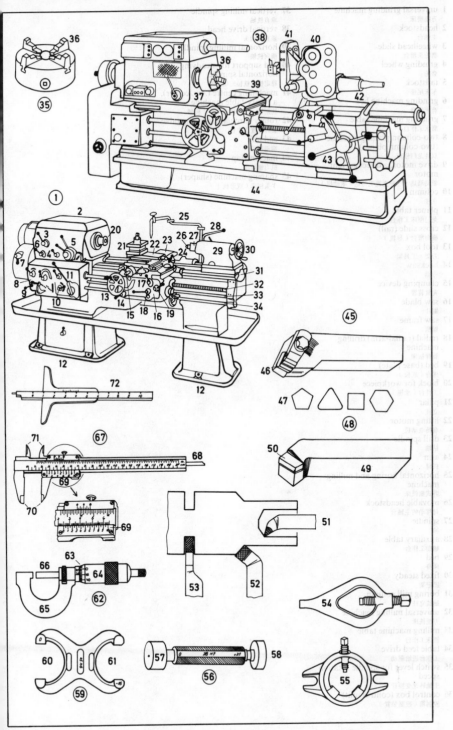

1 universal grinding machine
万能磨床
2 headstock
主轴台
3 wheelhead slide
磨轮头滑台
4 grinding wheel
磨轮
5 tailstock
车床尾座
6 grinding machine bed
磨床床身
7 grinding machine table
磨床工作台
8 two-column planing machine
(two-column planer)
双柱龙门刨床
9 drive motor, a direct current
motor
驱动马达，一种直流电马达（电动机）
10 column
立柱
11 planer table
龙门刨床工作台
12 cross slide (rail)
横向滑台（导轨）
13 tool box
刀架，工具架
14 hacksaw
弓锯
15 clamping device
夹紧装置
16 saw blade
锯片
17 saw frame
锯框
18 radial (radial-arm) drilling
machine
旋臂钻床
19 bed (base plate)
床身（底板）
20 block for workpiece
工件台（承座）
21 pillar
立柱
22 lifting motor
卷扬电动机
23 drill spindle
钻轴
24 arm
机臂
25 horizontal boring and milling
machine
卧式镗铣床
26 movable headstock
可移动的主轴台
27 spindle
轴
28 auxiliary table
辅助工作台
29 bed
床身
30 fixed steady
固定架
31 boring mill column
镗铣立柱
32 universal milling machine
万能铣床
33 milling machine table
铣床工作台
34 table feed drive
工作台进给驱动
35 switch lever for spindle rotation
speed
主轴转速变换杆
36 control box (control unit)
控制箱（控制装置）

37 vertical milling spindle
垂直铣轴
38 vertical drive head
垂直驱动头
39 horizontal milling spindle
横向铣轴
40 end support for steadying
horizontal spindle
稳定横向铣轴的端支座
41 machining centre (Am. center),
a rotary-table machine
切削机，一种转盘（台）机器
42 rotary (circular) indexing table
旋转分度工作台
43 end mill
端面铣刀
44 machine tap
机力螺丝攻
45 shaping machine (shaper)
牛头刨床（成形机）

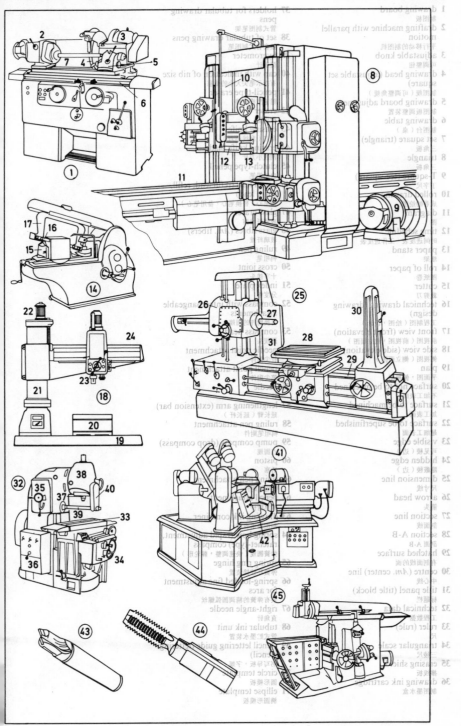

1 drawing board
制图板
2 drafting machine with parallel motion
平行移动的制图机
3 adjustable knob
可调整钮
4 drawing head (adjustable set square)
制图规（可调整角规）
5 drawing board adjustment
制图板调整装置
6 drawing table
制图台（桌）
7 set square (triangle)
三角板
8 triangle
三角板
9 T-square (tee-square)
丁字尺
10 rolled drawing
成卷的绘图
11 diagram
图
12 time schedule
时间进度表，工作进度表
13 paper stand
纸架
14 roll of paper
图纸卷
15 cutter
裁剪刀
16 technical drawing (drawing design)
工程制图（绘图，设计）
17 front view (front elevation)
前视图（前视图，前立面图）
18 side view (side elevation)
侧视图（侧立面图）
19 plan
平面图，俯视图
20 surface not to be machined
不加工表面
21 surface to be machined
加工表面
22 surface to be superfinished
超细工表面
23 visible edge
可见棱（边）
24 hidden edge
隐蔽棱（边）
25 dimension line
尺寸线
26 arrow head
箭头
27 section line
剖面线
28 section A-B
剖面 A-B
29 hatched surface
有剖面线的面
30 centre (*Am.* center) line
中心线
31 title panel (title block)
标题栏
32 technical data
工程数据
33 ruler (rule)
尺
34 triangular scale
三棱尺
35 erasing shield
擦线板
36 drawing ink cartridge
制图墨水盒

37 holders for tubular drawing pens
管式制图笔架
38 set of tubular drawing pens
整套管式制图笔
39 hygrometer
湿度计
40 cap with indication of nib size
有指示笔尖大小的插塞
41 pencil-type eraser
铅笔型橡皮擦
42 eraser
橡皮擦
43 erasing knife
刮刀（刮线小刀）
44 erasing knife blade
刮线小刀片
45 clutch-type pencil
自动铅笔
46 pencil lead (refill lead, refill, spare lead)
铅笔心（替换笔心，备用笔心）
47 glass eraser
玻璃纤维擦
48 glass fibres (*Am.* fibers)
玻璃纤维
49 ruling pen
鸭咀笔
50 cross joint
十字接头
51 index plate
分度板
52 compass with interchangeable attachments
可换附件的圆规
53 compass head
圆规头
54 needle point attachment
针尖附件
55 pencil point attachment
笔尖附件
56 needle
针
57 lengthening arm (extension bar)
延长臂（延长杆）
58 ruling pen attachment
鸭咀笔附件
59 pump compass (drop compass)
点圆规
60 piston
活塞
61 ruling pen attachment
鸭咀笔附件
62 pencil attachment
铅笔附件
63 drawing ink container
制图墨水容器
64 spring bow (rapid adjustment, ratchet-type) compass
弹簧圆规（快速调整，棘轮形）
65 spring ring hinge
弹簧环铰接装置
66 spring-loaded fine adjustment for arcs
装有弹簧的精调圆弧螺丝
67 right-angle needle
直角针
68 tubular ink unit
管式贮墨水装置
69 stencil lettering guide (lettering stencil)
书写导板，字规
70 circle template
圆形模板
71 ellipse template
椭圆形模板

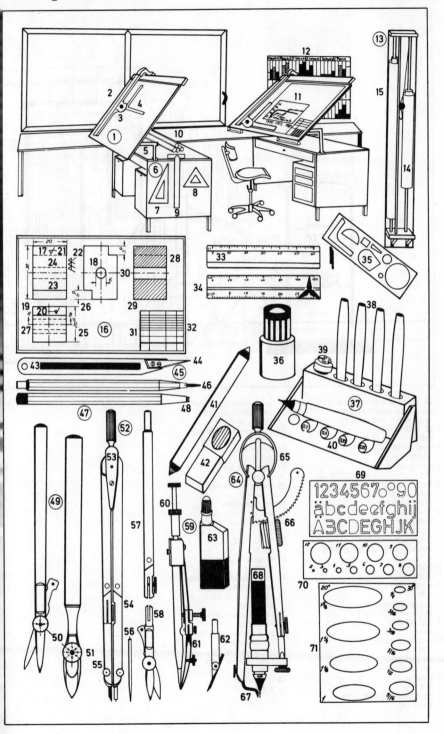

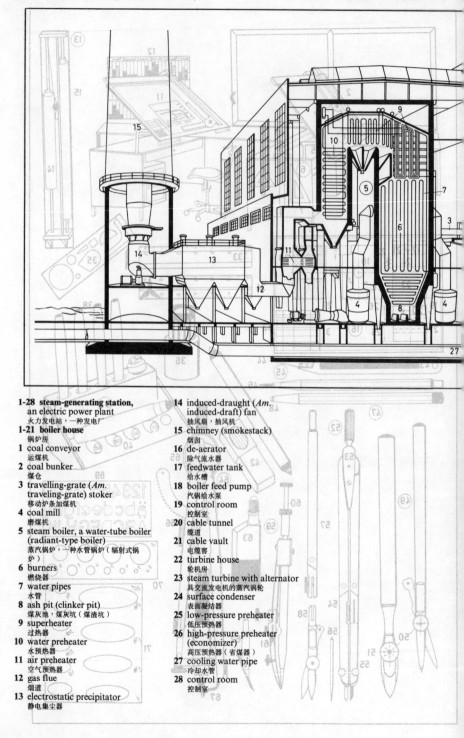

1-28 steam-generating station,
an electric power plant
火力发电站，一种发电厂

1-21 boiler house
锅炉房

1 coal conveyor
运煤机

2 coal bunker
煤仓

3 travelling-grate (*Am.*
traveling-grate) stoker
移动炉条加煤机

4 coal mill
磨煤机

5 steam boiler, a water-tube boiler
(radiant-type boiler)
蒸汽锅炉，一种水管锅炉（辐射式锅炉）

6 burners
燃烧器

7 water pipes
水管

8 ash pit (clinker pit)
煤灰池，煤灰坑（煤渣坑）

9 superheater
过热器

10 water preheater
水预热器

11 air preheater
空气预热器

12 gas flue
烟道

13 electrostatic precipitator
静电集尘器

14 induced-draught (*Am.*
induced-draft) fan
抽风扇，抽风机

15 chimney (smokestack)
烟囱

16 de-aerator
除气流水器

17 feedwater tank
给水槽

18 boiler feed pump
汽锅给水泵

19 control room
控制室

20 cable tunnel
缆道

21 cable vault
电缆窨

22 turbine house
轮机房

23 steam turbine with alternator
具交流发电机的蒸汽涡轮

24 surface condenser
表面凝结器

25 low-pressure preheater
低压预热器

26 high-pressure preheater
(economizer)
高压预热器（省煤器）

27 cooling water pipe
冷却水管

28 control room
控制室

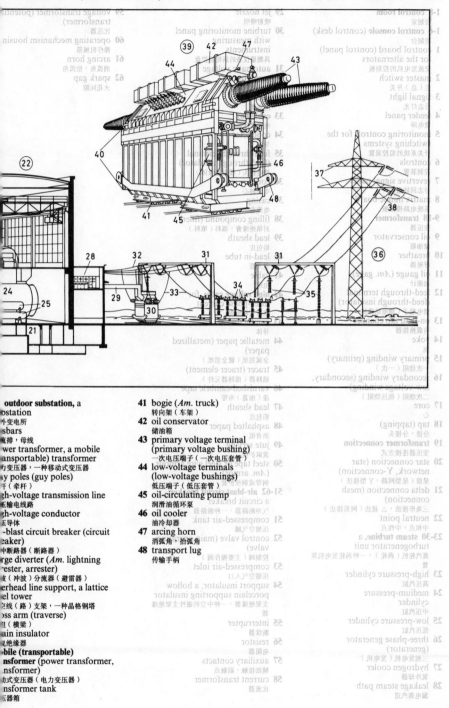

outdoor substation, a
bstation
外变电所
sbars
排、母线
wer transformer, a mobile
ansportable) transformer
力变压器，一种移动式变压器
y poles (guy poles)
（牵杆）
gh-voltage transmission line
压输电线路
gh-voltage conductor
压导体
-blast circuit breaker (circuit
eaker)
断路器（断路器）
rge diverter (Am. lightning
rester, arrester)
波（冲波）分流器（避雷器）
erhead line support, a lattice
el tower
线（路）支架，一种晶格钢塔
oss arm (traverse)
目（横梁）
ain insulator
链绝缘子
bile (transportable)
nsformer (power transformer,
nsformer)
力式变压器（电力变压器）
nsformer tank
器箱

41 bogie (*Am.* truck)
转向架（车架）
42 oil conservator
储油箱
43 primary voltage terminal
(primary voltage bushing)
一次电压端子（一次电压套管）
44 low-voltage terminals
(low-voltage bushings)
低压端子（低压套管）
45 oil-circulating pump
润滑油循环泵
46 oil cooler
油冷却器
47 arcing horn
消弧角，抬弧角
48 transport lug
传输手柄

1-8 control room
控制室

1-6 control console (control desk)
控制台

1 control board (control panel)
for the alternators
交流发电机的控制板

2 master switch
主（总）开关

3 signal light
号志灯光

4 feeder panel
馈电屏

5 monitoring controls for the
switching systems
开关系统的监控装置

6 controls
控制装置

7 revertive signal panel
号志回转盘

8 matrix mimic board
系统电路模拟板

9-18 transformer
变压器

9 oil conservator
储油箱

10 breather
呼吸器

11 oil gauge (*Am.* gage)
油面计

12 feed-through terminal
(feed-through insulator)
馈电端子（馈电绝缘体）

13 on-load tap changer
有载换接器

14 yoke
轭

15 primary winding (primary)
一次绕阻（一次）

16 secondary winding (secondary,
low-voltage winding)
二次绕阻（低压绕阻）

17 core
心

18 tap (tapping)
分接，分接头

19 transformer connection
变压器连接方式

20 star connection (star
network, Y-connection)
星接（星型网络，Y型接法）

21 delta connection (mesh
connection)
三角形接法，△接法（网形接法）

22 neutral point
中和点，中性点

23-30 steam turbine, a
turbogenerator unit
蒸汽轮机（涡轮），一种涡轮发电机装
置

23 high-pressure cylinder
高压汽缸

24 medium-pressure
cylinder
中压汽缸

25 low-pressure cylinder
低压汽缸

26 three-phase generator
(generator)
三相发电机（发电机）

27 hydrogen cooler
氢冷却器

28 leakage steam path
漏电蒸汽道

29 jet nozzle
喷射喷咀

30 turbine monitoring panel
with measuring
instruments
具测量仪表的涡轮监控盘

31 automatic voltage
regulator
自动电压调整器

32 synchro
同步器

33 cable box
电缆接线箱

34 conductor
导体

35 feed-through terminal
(feed-through insulator)
馈电接头（馈电绝缘体）

36 core
电缆轴心

37 casing
电缆套

38 filling compound (filler)
封填绝缘膏，填料（填料）

39 lead sheath
铅包皮

40 lead-in tube
引入管

41 cable
电缆

42 high voltage cable, for
three-phase current
高压三相电缆

43 conductor
导体

44 metallic paper (metallized
paper)
金属箔纸（镀金箔纸）

45 tracer (tracer element)
描踪器（描踪器元件）

46 varnished-cambric tape
漆（细葛）布带

47 lead sheath
铅包皮

48 asphalted paper
沥青纸

49 jute serving
黄麻护线

50 steel tape or steel wire armour
(*Am.* armor)
钢带或钢丝护套

51-62 air-blast circuit breaker,
a circuit breaker
气冲断路器，一种断路器

51 compressed-air tank
压缩空气罐

52 control valve (main operating
valve)
控制阀（主要操作阀）

53 compressed-air inlet
压缩空气入口

54 support insulator, a hollow
porcelain supporting insulator
支架绝缘器，一种中空的磁性支架绝缘
器

55 interrupter
断续器

56 resistor
电阻器

57 auxiliary contacts
辅助接触，副触点

58 current transformer
比流器

59 voltage transformer (potential
transformer)
比压器

60 operating mechanism housing
操作机械箱

61 arcing horn
消弧角，抬弧角

62 spark gap
火花间隙

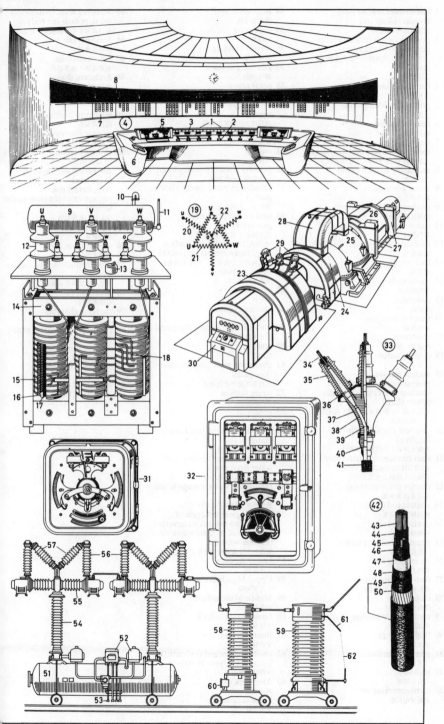

1 **fast-breeder reactor** (fast breeder) [diagram]
快速增殖反应器[简图]

2 primary circuit (primary loop, primary sodium system)
一次电路（一次环路，一次钠系统）

3 reactor
反应器

4 fuel rods (fuel pins)
燃料棒

5 primary sodium pump
一次钠泵

6 heat exchanger
热交换器

7 secondary circuit (secondary loop, secondary sodium system)
二次电路（二次环路，二次钠系统）

8 secondary sodium pump
二次钠泵

9 steam generator
蒸汽产生器

10 cooling water flow circuit
冷却水流动回路

11 steam line
蒸汽管线

12 feedwater line
给水管线

13 feed pump
给水泵

14 steam turbine
蒸汽涡轮机

15 generator
发电机

16 transmission line
输电线路

17 condenser
冷凝器，凝结器

18 cooling water
冷却水

19 **nuclear reactor**, a pressurized-water reactor (nuclear power plant, atomic power plant)
核反应器，一种压水反应器（核能发电厂，原子发电厂）

20 concrete shield (reactor building)
混凝土屏蔽（反应器建筑物）

21 steel containment (steel shell) with air extraction vent
具抽气孔的钢安全壳（钢壳）

22 reactor pressure vessel
反应器压力容器

23 control rod drive
控制棒驱动装置

24 control rods
控制棒

25 primary coolant pump
一次冷却泵

26 steam generator
蒸汽产生器

27 fuel-handling hoists
燃料输送吊车（起重机）

28 fuel storage
燃料仓

29 coolant flow passage
冷却剂流道管

30 feedwater line
供水管线

31 prime steam line
主蒸汽管道

32 manway
人员专用道

33 turbogenerator set
涡轮发电机组

34 turbogenerator
涡轮发电机

35 condenser
冷凝器

36 service building
服务大楼

37 exhaust gas stack
排气烟囱

38 polar crane
极性起重机

39 cooling tower, a dry cooling tower
冷却塔，一种乾冷冷却塔

40 pressurized-water system
压水系统

41 reactor
反应器

42 primary circuit (primary loop)
一次电路（一次环路）

43 circulation pump (recirculation pump)
循环泵（再循环泵）

44 heat exchanger (steam generator)
热交换器（水蒸汽产生器）

45 secondary circuit (secondary loop, feedwater steam circuit)
二次电路（二次环路，给水蒸汽电路）

46 steam turbine
蒸汽涡轮机

47 generator
发电机

48 cooling system
冷却系统

49 boiling water system [diagram]
沸水系统[简图]

50 reactor
反应器

51 steam and recirculation water flow paths
蒸汽和再循环水流通道

52 steam turbine
蒸汽涡轮机

53 generator
发电机

54 circulation pump (recirculation pump)
循环泵（再循环泵）

55 coolant system (cooling with water from river)
冷却系统（以河水冷却）

56 **radioactive waste storage in salt mine**
放射性废料储放於盐矿中

57-68 geological structure of abandoned salt mine converted for disposal of radioactive waste (nuclear waste)
置放放射性废料的废盐矿之地质结构

57 Lower Keuper
下考依发

58 Upper Muschelkalk
上壳灰岩层

59 Middle Muschelkalk
中壳灰岩层

60 Lower Muschelkalk
下壳灰岩层

61 Bunter downthrow
斑砂岩降侧

62 residue of leached (lixiviated) Zechstein (Upper Permian)
淋溶镁灰残留物

63 Aller rock salt
阿莱岩盐

64 Leine rock salt
莱茵岩盐

65 Stassfurt seam (potash salt seam, potash salt bed)
斯塔斯弗矿层（钾盐层，钾盐床）

66 Stassfurt salt
斯塔斯弗盐

67 grenzanhydrite
限界流体，越界流体

68 Zechstein shale
镁灰油页岩

69 shaft
矿井

70 minehead buildings
坑口建筑物

71 storage chamber
贮藏室

72 storage of medium-active waste in salt mine
盐矿中的中放射性废料的贮藏

73 511m level
511 公尺的水平坑道

74 protective screen (anti-radiation screen)
保护壁（抗辐射屏）

75 lead glass window
铅玻璃窗

76 storage chamber
贮藏室

77 drum containing radioactive waste
装放射性废料的金属桶

78 television camera
电视摄影机

79 charging chamber
进料室

80 control desk (control panel)
控制盘

81 upward ventilator
向上通风装置

82 shielded container
遮蔽容器

83 490m level
490 公尺的水平坑道

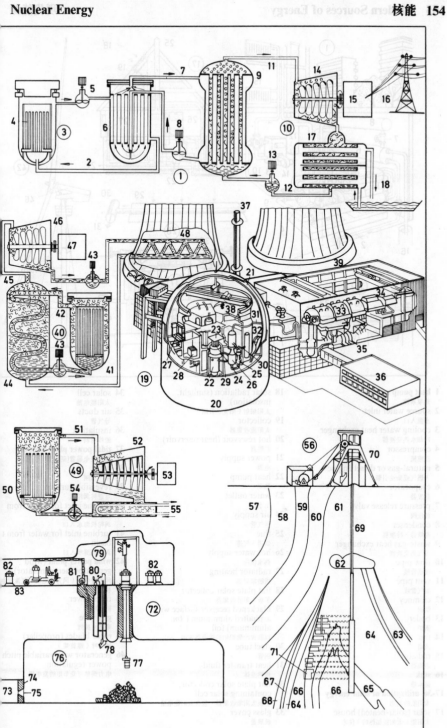

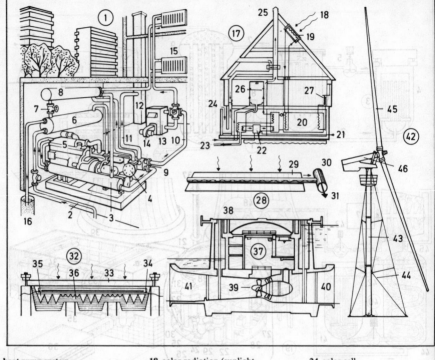

1 heat pump system
  热泵系统
2 source water inlet
  水源入口
3 cooling water heat exchanger
  冷却水热交换器
4 compressor
  压缩机
5 natural-gas or diesel engine
  天燃气或柴油引擎
6 evaporator
  蒸发器
7 pressure release valve
  放压阀
8 condenser
  凝结器，冷凝器
9 waste-gas heat exchanger
  废气热交换器
10 flow pipe
  流送管线
11 vent pipe
  通气管线
12 chimney
  烟囱
13 boiler
  锅炉
14 fan
  风扇
15 radiator
  散热器
16 sink
  排水槽
17-36 utilization of solar energy
  太阳能的利用
17 solar (solar-heated) house
  太阳能（太阳能加热的）住宅

18 solar radiation (sunlight,
  insolation)
  太阳辐射（阳光，日晒）
19 collector
  太阳能收集器
20 hot reservoir (heat reservoir)
  贮热器
21 power supply
  电源
22 heat pump
  热泵
23 water outlet
  出水口
24 air supply
  供气管
25 flue
  烟道，气道
26 hot water supply
  热水供应
27 radiator heating
  供暖辐射器
28 flat plate solar collector
  平板太阳能收集器
29 blackened receiver surface with
  asphalted aluminium (*Am.*
  aluminium) foil
  以沥青涂黑铝铂的接受器表面
30 steel tube
  钢管
31 heat transfer fluid
  传热流体
32 flat plate solar collector,
  containing solar cell
  平板太阳能收集器，包含太阳能电池
33 glass cover
  玻璃盖

34 solar cell
  太阳能电池
35 air ducts
  导气管
36 insulation
  绝缘材料
37 tidal power plant [section]
  潮汐发电装置[剖面图]
38 dam
  坝，水闸
39 reversible turbine
  可逆转涡轮机
40 turbine inlet for water from
  the sea
  涡轮机海水入口
41 turbine inlet for water from th
  basin
  涡轮机海水入口
42 wind power plant (wind
  generator, aerogenerator)
  风力发电厂（风力发电机，气流发电
  机）
43 truss tower
  桁架塔
44 guy wire
  牵线，拔线
45 rotor blades (propeller)
  转子叶（螺旋桨）
46 generator with variable pitch
  power regulation
  电力调整可变节矩的发电机

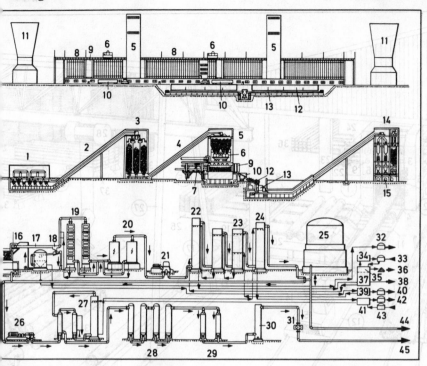

coking plant
厂

nping of coking coal
工的倾卸

conveyor
运送机

vice bunker

l tower conveyor
运送机

al tower

ry car (larry, charging car)
车（运煤车）

sher ram

tery of coke ovens
炉电池组

ce guide
导路

enching car, with engine
击的淬火车

enching tower
火塔

ke loaking bay (coke wharf)
台

ke side bench
台

eening of lump coal and culm
煤和屑煤的筛分

ke loading
装载

coke-oven gas processing
焦炉煤气的处理

charge (release) of gas from
coke ovens
焦炉释放出的煤气

17 gas-collecting main
煤气主管

18 coal tar extraction
焦油的分离

19 gas cooler
煤气冷却器

20 electrostatic precipitator
静电集尘器

21 gas extractor
煤气抽出器

22 hydrogen sulphide (*Am.*
hydrogen sulfide) scrubber
(hydrogen sulphide wet
collector)
硫化氢清洁器（硫化氢湿式收集器）

23 ammonia scrubber (ammonia
wet collector)
氨（气）清洁器（氨气湿式收集器）

24 benzene (benzol) scrubber
苯清洁器

25 gas holder
贮气罐

26 gas compressor
煤气压缩机

27 debenzoling by cooler and heat
exchanger
冷却器和换热器脱苯

28 desulphurization (*Am.*
desulfurization) of pressure gas
加压煤气的去硫

29 gas cooling
煤气冷却

30 gas drying
煤气干燥

31 gas meter
煤气表

32 crude tar tank
粗焦油槽

33 sulphuric acid (*Am.* sulfuric
acid) supply
硫酸供应（入）

34 production of sulphuric acid
(*Am.* sulfuric acid)
硫酸的生产

35 production of ammonium
sulphate (*Am.* ammonium
sulfate)
硫酸铵产品

36 ammonium sulphate (*Am.*
ammonium sulfate)
硫酸铵

37 recovery plant for recovering the
scrubbing agents
回收洗油的回收装置

38 waste water discharge
废水排出

39 phenol extraction from the gas
water
从煤气水中抽取

40 crude phenol tank
粗酚槽

41 production of crude benzol
(crude benzene)
粗苯产品

42 crude benzol (crude benzene)
tank
粗苯槽

43 scrubbing oil tank
洗涤油槽

44 low-pressure gas main
低压煤气总（主）管

45 high-pressure gas main
高压煤气总（主）管

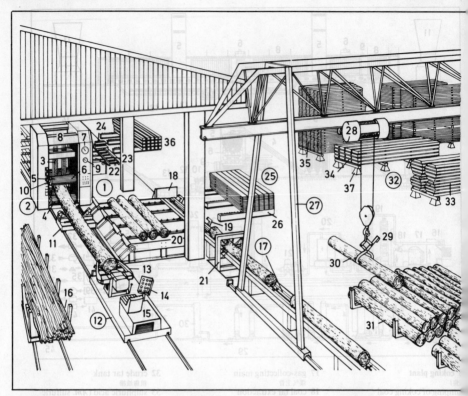

1 sawmill
锯木厂
2 vertical frame saw (*Am.* gang mill)
立式框锯（排锯）
3 saw blades
锯条
4 feed roller
进料滚子
5 guide roller
导向滚子
6 fluting (grooving, grooves)
开槽
7 oil pressure gauge (*Am.* gage)
油压表
8 saw frame
锯框
9 feed indicator
进料指示器
10 log capacity scale
原木体积标尺
11 auxiliary carriage
辅助托车
12 carriage
送料车
13 log grips
圆木卡钩
14 remote control panel
遥控板
15 carriage motor
进料车马达
16 truck for splinters (splints)
木板输送车

17 endless log chain (*Am.* jack chain)
无端原木链（原木运输链）
18 stop plate
止板
19 log-kicker arms
推木臂
20 cross conveyor
横向运送机
21 washer (washing machine)
洗涤机，冲洗机
22 cross chain conveyor for sawn timber
锯成木材后的横向链式运送机
23 roller table
滚台
24 undercut swing saw
过切摆动圆锯，落地式摆锯
25 piling
木板堆
26 roller trestles
滚子支架
27 gantry crane
高架移动起重机
28 crane motor
起重机马达
29 pivoted log grips
枢轴原木卡钩
30 roundwood (round timber)
圆木（圆木材）
31 log dump
圆木堆
32 squared timber store
方形木材堆积场

33 sawn logs
已锯开的圆木
34 planks
厚木板
35 boards (planks)
薄木板
36 squared timber
方形木材
37 stack bearer
木材堆支座

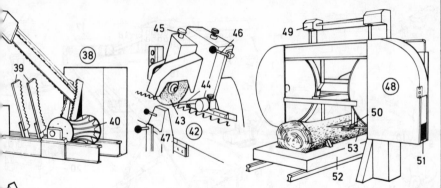

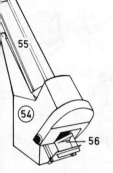
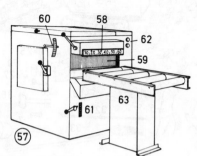
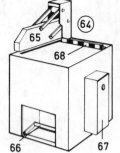

automatic cross-cut chain saw
动横割链锯
grips
木卡钩
d roller
料滚子
ain-tensioning device
连装置
w-sharpening machine
锯机
nding wheel (teeth grinder)
轮（锯齿磨轮）
d pawl
给掣子
pth adjustment for the teeth
nder
齿磨轮高度调整钮
er (lever) for the grinder
uck
杀夹头升降杆（控制杆）
lding device for the saw blade
条的夹紧（固定）装置
rizontal bandsaw for sawing
圆木用的水平带锯
ght adjustment
度调整装置
ip remover
屑去除机
ip extractor
屑抽除装置
rriage
架

53 **bandsaw blade**
带锯条
54 **automatic blocking saw**
自动切块锯
55 **feed channel**
进料导槽
56 **discharge opening**
卸料口
57 **twin edger (double edger)**
双刃截边锯
58 **breadth scale (width scale)**
宽度标尺
59 **kick-back guard**
逆转护板
60 **height scale**
高度标尺
61 **in-feed scale**
进料标尺
62 **indicator lamps**
指示灯
63 **feed table**
进料台
64 **undercut swing saw**
过切摆动圆锯，落地式摆锯
65 **automatic hold-down with protective hood**
具保护罩的全自动压紧装置
66 **foot switch**
脚踏开关
67 **distribution board (panelboard)**
配电板（仪表板）
68 **length stop**
长度调整装置

1 **quarry,** an open-cast
   working
   采石场，露天开采
2 overburden
   表土，被复岩
3 working face
   开采面，已开采或正在开采的采石场
4 loose rock pile (blasted rock)
   松散岩石堆（已炸开之岩石）
5 quarryman (quarrier), a quarry
   worker
   采石工人
6 sledge hammer
   大锤
7 wedge
   楔
8 block of stone
   石块
9 driller
   钻工
10 safety helmet
   安全帽
11 hammer drill (hard-rock drill)
   锤打钻（硬岩钻）
12 borehole
   钻孔
13 universal excavator
   万能掘凿机（挖掘机）
14 large-capacity truck
   大容量的卡车
15 rock face
   岩石采掘面
16 inclined hoist
   倾斜起重机

17 primary crusher
   初次轧碎机
18 stone-crushing plant
   碎石设备
19 coarse rotary (gyratory) crusher;
   sim.: fine rotary (gyratory)
   crusher
   旋转式粗碎石机；类似有：旋转式细碎
   石机
20 hammer crusher (impact
   crusher)
   锤碎机（冲击轧碎机）
21 vibrating screen
   振动筛
22 screenings (fine dust)
   筛屑（细砂）
23 stone chippings
   石屑，石片
24 crushed stone
   碎石
25 shot firer
   （点火）引爆工人
26 measuring rod
   量杆
27 blasting cartridge
   弹药包
28 fuse (blasting fuse)
   信管（雷管）
29 plugging sand (stemming sand)
   bucket
   填塞砂桶（封口用砂）
30 dressed stone
   修整过的块石

31 pick
   镐
32 crowbar (pinch bar)
   撬棍
33 fork
   叉
34 stonemason
   石匠，石工
35-38 **stonemason's tools**
   石匠工具
35 stonemason's hammer
   石匠用的榔头（锤子）
36 mallet
   大锤
37 drove chisel (drove, boaster,
   broad chisel)
   粗削凿（宽凿）
38 dressing axe (*Am.* ax)
   修整斧

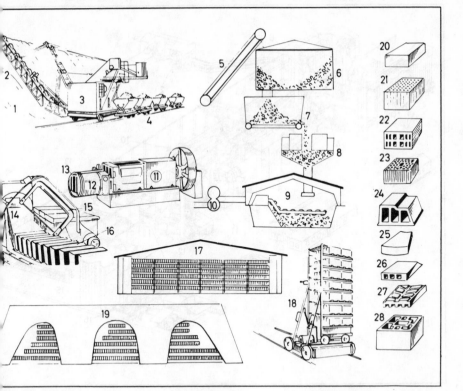

1 ...y pit
...坑（采掘场）
2 ...m, an impure clay (raw clay)
...土，一种不纯粘土（生粘土）
...rburden excavator, a
...ge-scale excavator
...型挖掘机，一种大型挖掘机
...rrow-gauge (Am.
...rrow-gage) track system
...（窄）轨铁道系统
...lined hoist
...科起重机
...uring chambers
...化室（泥料陈腐室）
...x feeder (feeder)
...形进料器
...ge runner mill (edge mill, pan
...nding mill)
...辗机（轮辗机，盘式磨粉机）
...ling plant
...砖设备（工场）
...uble-shaft trough mixer
...ixer)
...轴槽形搅拌机
...rusion press (brick-pressing
...achine)
...压机（压砖机）
...cuum chamber
...空室
...e
...压）模
...ay column
...土条

15 cutter (brick cutter)
切砖机
16 unfired brick (green brick)
未锻烧的砖（生坯）
17 drying shed
干燥棚
18 mechanical finger car (stacker
truck)
机械操作手车（堆叠车）
19 circular kiln (brick kiln)
砖窑
20 solid brick (building brick)
硬砖（建筑用砖）
21-22 perforated bricks and hollow
blocks
有孔砖和空心砖块
21 perforated brick with vertical
perforations
具垂直孔的有孔砖
22 hollow clay block with
horizontal perforations
具平行孔的空心粘土砖块
23 hollow clay block with vertical
perforations
具直孔的空心粘土砖块
24 floor brick
地板砖
25 compass brick (radial brick,
radiating brick)
弧形砖（扇形砖，辐射线形砖）
26 hollow flooring block
空心地板砖
27 paving brick
铺地砖

28 cellular brick [for fireplaces]
(chimney brick)
格形砖[壁炉用的]（烟囱砖）

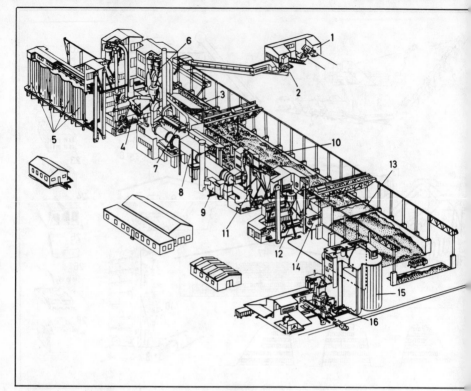

1 raw materials (limestone,
clay, and marl)
原料（石灰石，粘土，泥灰）

2 hammer crusher (hammer mill)
锤碎机

3 raw material store
原料库

4 raw mill for simultaneously
grinding and drying the raw
materials with exhaust gas from
the heat exchanger
碾磨并同时用热交换器排气来干燥原料
的粗磨机

5 raw meal silos
生料（原料）粉槽

6 heat exchanger (cyclone heat
exchanger)
热交换器（旋风热交换器）

7 dust collector (an electrostatic
precipitator) for the heat
exchanger exhaust from the raw
mill
从粗磨机热交换器排出灰尘的收集器
（静电集尘器）

8 rotary kiln
回转窑

9 clinker cooler
水泥熟料冷却器

10 clinker store
水泥熟料库

11 primary air blower
一次鼓风机

12 cement-grinding mill
水泥碾磨机

13 gypsum store
石膏库

14 gypsum crusher
石膏碾碎机

15 cement silo
水泥槽（水泥仓）

16 cement-packing plant
水泥包装厂（设备）

nding cylinder (ball mill)
r the preparation of the raw
aterial in water
料和水混合的磨料筒（球磨机）
mple sagger (saggar, seggar),
th aperture for observing the
ing process
开口观察燃烧过程用的样品水泥箱
ttle kiln (beehive kiln)
agram]
状窑（蜂窝式窑）[简图]
ing mould (Am. mold)
烧模
nnel kiln
道窑
ger cone (pyrometric cone,
n. Orton cone) for measuring
h temperatures
准用以测量高温
-airing pug mill (de-airing pug
ess), an extrusion press
空搅拌机，一种挤制机
ay column
土条
rower throwing a ball (bat) of
ay
制粘土坯的拉坯工人
ug of clay
土块
rntable; *sim.*: potter's wheel
台；类似：陶车
ter press
滤机

13 filter cake
滤块
14 jiggering, with a profiling tool;
sim.: jollying
具成形工具的旋坯；类似：辘轳
15 plaster mould (*Am.* mold) for
slip casting
注浆用的石膏模
16 turntable glazing machine
转台上釉机
17 porcelain painter (china painter)
瓷器画工（陶器画工）
18 hand-painted vase
手绘花瓶
19 repairer
修理工
20 pallet (modelling, *Am.*
modeling, tool)
托板（制造模形的工具）
21 shards (sherds, potsherds)
陶瓷器的碎片

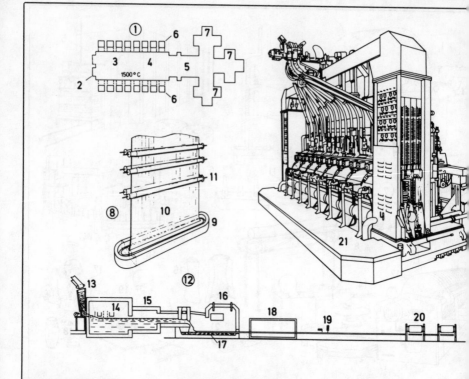

1-20 sheet glass production
(flat glass production)
玻璃片的制造（平板玻璃的制造）

1 glass furnace (tank furnace) for
the Fourcault process [diagram]
制玻璃炉（富可法制玻璃熔炉[简图]

2 filling end, for feeding in the
batch (frit)
填料端；分批进料（玻璃原料）

3 melting bath
电解槽，熔化槽

4 refining bath (fining bath)
精炼槽

5 working baths (working area)
作业槽

6 burners
燃烧器

7 drawing machines
拉制机

8 Fourcault glass-drawing
machine
富可法玻璃拉制机

9 slot
沟，槽

10 glass ribbon (ribbon of glass,
sheet of glass) being drawn
upwards
将玻璃带引上（玻璃带，玻璃板带）

11 rollers (drawing rolls)
滚子（引伸滚子）

12 float glass process
浮式玻璃制造法

13 batch (frit) feeder (funnel)
玻璃原料进给装置

14 melting bath
熔化槽

15 cooling tank
冷却槽

16 float bath in a protective
inert-gas atmosphere
在惰性气体保护下的浮槽

17 molten tin
熔化的锡

18 annealing lehr
退火炉

19 automatic cutter
自动切割机

20 stacking machines
堆积机

21 IS (individual-section) machine,
a bottle-making machine
IS 机，一种制瓶机

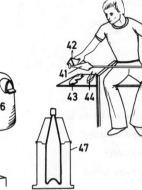

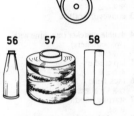

blowing processes
制法
ow-and-blow process
制过程
troduction of the gob of
olten glass
解玻璃原料的滴入
st blowing
一次吹制
ction
吸
ansfer from the parison mould
m. mold) to the blow mould
m. mold)
玻璃瓶模转换到吹制模
heating
加热
owing (suction, final shaping)
制（抽吸，最后成型）
elivery of the completed vessel
品瓶的输送
ress-and-blow process
吹制法
troduction of the gob of
olten glass
解玻璃原料的滴入
lunger
塞
ressing
压
ansfer from the press mould
m. mold) to the blow mould
m. mold)
挤压模转换到吹制模

35 **reheating**
再加热
36 **blowing** (suction, final shaping)
吹制（抽吸，最后成型）
37 **delivery of the completed vessel**
成品容器的输送
38-47 **glassmaking** (glassblowing,
glassblowing by hand, glass
forming)
玻璃吹制造（玻璃吹制，人工吹制玻璃，
玻璃成形）
38 **glassmaker** (glassblower)
玻璃工人（玻璃吹制工）
39 **blowing iron**
吹管
40 **gob**
熔解的玻璃原料
41 **hand-blown goblet**
人工吹制（高）有脚玻璃杯
42 **clappers for shaping the base
(foot) of the goblet**
高脚玻璃杯成形用的拍板
43 **trimming tool**
修剪工具
44 **tongs**
夹钳
45 **glassmaker's chair** (gaffer's
chair)
玻璃工人坐椅
46 **covered glasshouse pot**
有盖的熔化玻璃罐
47 **mould** (*Am.* mold), into which
the parison is blown
已成形长颈瓶的吹模

48-55 **production of glass fibre** (*Am.*
glass fiber)
玻璃纤维的生产
48 **continuous filament process**
连续玻璃纤维丝的生产过程
49 **glass furnace**
玻璃熔炉
50 **bushing containing molten glass**
装熔化玻璃的套筒
51 **bushing tips**
套筒端
52 **glass filaments**
玻璃纤维丝
53 **sizing**
尺度矫正
54 **strand** (thread)
绳股
55 **spool**
卷线轴
56-58 **glass fibre** (*Am.* **glass fiber**)
products
玻璃纤维产品
56 **glass yarn** (glass thread)
玻璃丝
57 **sleeved glass yarn** (glass thread)
卷筒玻璃丝（玻璃线）
58 **glass wool**
玻璃绒

1-13 supply of cotton
棉花的供给

1 ripe cotton boll
成熟的棉花铃

2 full cop (cop wound with weft yarn)
满管线纱

3 compressed cotton bale
压实的棉花包

4 jute wrapping
黄麻包装布

5 steel band
打包铁皮

6 identification mark of the bale
棉花捆包商标

7 bale opener (bale breaker)
拆包机

8 cotton-feeding brattice
给棉口

9 cotton feed
棉花供给

10 dust extraction fan
吸尘扇

11 duct to the dust-collecting chamber
通至集尘室的管道

12 drive motor
驱动马达

13 conveyor brattice
输棉口

14 double scutcher (machine with two scutchers)
双座打棉机

15 lap cradle
棉卷支架

16 rack head
齿条头，减磨齿杆头

17 starting handle
起动杆

18 handwheel, for raising and lowering the rack head
升降齿条头用的手轮（升降减磨齿杆用的手轮）

19 movable lap-turner
活动的卷棉器

20 calender rollers
滚压机

21 cover for the perforated cylinders
有孔滚筒的盖子

22 dust escape flue (dust discharge flue)
排尘风道

23 drive motors (beater drive motors)
驱动马达（搅打驱动马达）

24 beater driving shaft
搅打驱动轴

25 three-blade beater (Kirschner beater)
三叶搅打机

26 grid [for impurities to drop]
格子[落尘用的]

27 pedal roller (pedal cylinder)
踏板滚子

28 control lever for the pedal roller, a pedal lever
踏板滚子的控制杆，一种脚踏杆

29 variable change-speed gear
变速齿轮箱

30 cone drum box
锥形鼓轮箱

31 stop and start levers for the hopper
棉箱的开关杆

32 wooden hopper delivery roller
木制棉箱传送滚轮

33 hopper feeder
棉箱给棉机

34 carding machine (card, carding engine)
梳棉机

35 card can (carding can), for receiving the coiled sliver
接受卷成长棉条的梳棉箱

36 can holder
梳棉罐支柱

37 calender rollers
滚压机

38 carded sliver (card sliver)
梳棉机棉条

39 vibrating doffer comb
振动式集棉滚筒梳

40 start-stop lever
开关杆

41 grinding-roller bearing
磨滚子承轴

42 doffer
集棉滚筒

43 cylinder
滚筒

44 flat clearer
盖板清洁辊滚子

45 flats
盖板

46 supporting pulleys for the flats
盖板支承滑轮

47 scutcher lap (carded lap)
打棉卷棉机

48 scutcher lap holder
卷棉架

49 drive motor with flat belt
具平带的驱动马达

50 main drive pulley (fast-and-loose drive pulley)
主要驱动滑轮（松紧驱动滑轮）

51 principle of the card (of the carding engine)
梳棉机（引擎）的原理

52 fluted feed roller
沟槽给棉滚轮

53 licker-in (taker-in, licker-in roller)
取棉刺滚子

54 licker-in undercasing
刺滚子漏底

55 cylinder undercasing
滚筒漏底

56 combing machine (comber)
精梳机

57 drive gearbox (driving gear)
驱动齿轮箱

58 laps ready for combing
精梳备用卷棉

59 calender rollers
滚压机

60 comber draw box
梳棉机的拉箱

61 counter
计数器

62 coiler top
卷轴顶部

63 principle of the comber
精梳机的原理

64 lap
卷棉

65 bottom nipper
下钳板

66 top nipper
上钳板

67 top comb
顶梳

68 combing cylinder
梳棉滚筒

69 plain part of the cylinder
滚筒的无针部分

70 needled part of the cylinder
滚筒的梳针部分

71 detaching rollers
分支滚轮

72 carded and combed sliver
精梳棉条

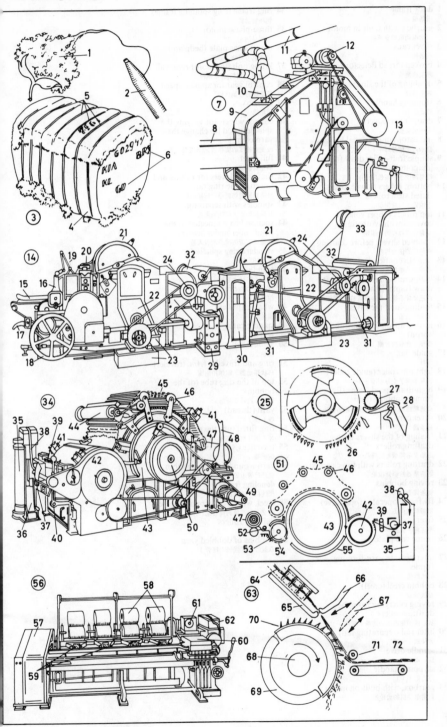

1 **draw frame**
併条机

2 gearbox with built-in motor
自附电动机的变速箱

3 sliver cans
棉条筒

4 broken thread detector roller
断条检测滚子

5 doubling of the slivers
棉条併合

6 stopping handle
停止把手

7 draw frame cover
併条机盖板

8 indicator lamps (signal lights)
指示灯（信号灯）

9 simple four-roller draw frame
[diagram]
简易四滚子併条机[简图]

10 bottom rollers (lower rollers),
fluted steel rollers
下滚轮，沟纹钢轮

11 top rollers (upper rollers)
covered with synthetic
复着合成橡皮的上滚轮

12 doubled slivers before drafting
牵伸前的併合棉条

13 thin sliver after drafting
牵伸后的细棉条

14 high-draft system (high-draft
draw frame) [diagram]
高速牵伸系统（高速併条机）〔简图〕

15 feeding-in of the sliver
棉条的进给

16 leather apron (composition
apron)
皮圈（合成的胶圈）

17 guide bar
导杆

18 light top roller (guide roller)
轻质上滚子（导引滚子）

19 high-draft speed frame (fly
frame, slubbing frame)
高速粗纺机（粗纺机，头道粗纺机）

20 sliver cans
棉条筒

21 feeding of the slivers to the
drafting rollers
进给至牵伸滚轮的棉条

22 drafting rollers with top clearers
附清洁器的牵伸滚轮

23 roving bobbins
幼条筒管

24 fly frame operator (operative)
粗纺机操作工

25 flyer
整捻轮，锭翼

26 frame end plate
机尾板

27 intermediate yarn-forming
frame
间纺纱机

28 bobbin creel (creel)
卷线轴架

29 roving emerging from the
drafting rollers
从牵伸滚轮出来的幼条（粗纱）

30 lifter rail (separating rail)
升降轨（分离轨）

31 spindle drive
锭驱动

32 stopping handle
停止把手

33 gearbox, with built-on motor
自附电动机的齿轮箱

34 **ring frame** (ring spinning frame)
钢环精纺机

35 three-phase motor
三相马达

36 motor base plate (bedplate)
电动机（马达）底座

37 lifting bolt [for motor removal]
[马达移动用的]起重螺栓

38 control gear for spindle speed
锭速度的控制齿轮

39 gearbox
齿轮箱

40 change wheels for varying the
spindle speed [to change the
yarn count]
改变锭速度的变换齿轮[改变纱线数]

41 full creel
满卷线轴架

42 shafts and levers for raising and
lowering the ring rail
升降钢环精纺机用的转轴槓杆

43 spindles with separators
具隔片的锭，幼锤隔离板

44 suction box connected to the
front roller underclearers
连接前下清洁滚子的吸入箱

45 **standard ring spindle**
标准环形锭子

46 spindle shaft
锭子（纺锤）羽轴（纺锤）

47 roller bearing
滚轴轴承

48 wharve (pulley)
滑轮

49 spindle catch
锭钩

50 spindle rail
锭轨

51 ring and traveller (*Am.* traveler)
环状移动器，钢领和钢圈

52 top of the ring tube (of the
bobbin)
纱管（筒管）顶部

53 yarn (thread)
纱（线）

54 ring fitted into the ring rail
装入钢环轨的钢环

55 traveller (*Am.* traveler)
钢丝圈

56 yarn wound onto the bobbin
绕於筒管上的纱

57 **doubling frame**
撚线机，捻线机

58 creel, with cross-wound cheeses
装交叉卷线筒的筒管架

59 delivery rollers
输送滚轮

60 bobbins of doubled yarn
双股纱线的线轴（筒管）

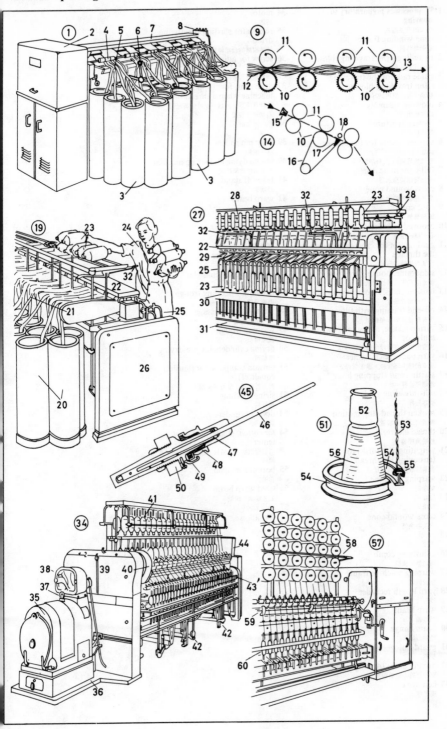

1-57 processes preparatory to weaving
织布的准备过程

1 cone-winding frame
锥形绕纱机

2 travelling (*Am.* traveling) blower
移动式鼓风机

3 guide rail, for the travelling (*Am.* traveling) blower
移动式鼓风机用的导轨

4 blowing assembly
鼓风机组件

5 blower aperture
鼓风机的吹口

6 superstructure for the blower rail
鼓风机导轨的上部结构

7 full-cone indicator
圆锥筒满筒指示器

8 cross-wound cone
交叉卷绕的锥形筒

9 cone creel
锥形筒架

10 grooved cylinder
有凹槽的滚筒

11 guiding slot for cross-winding the threads
交叉卷绕的线导槽

12 side frame, housing the motor
装（电动机）马达的侧架

13 tension and slub-catching device
张力和清纱装置

14 off-end framing with filter
带有过滤器的车尾机架

15 yarn package, a ring tube or mule cop
成束的纱（环管纱，锥形管纱）

16 yarn package container
成束的纱（环管纱，锥形管纱）

17 starting and stopping lever
起动停止杆

18 self-threading guide
引纱导杆

19 broken thread stop motion
断线自动停止装置

20 thread clearer
纱线清理装置

21 weighting disc (disk) for tensioning the thread
调节纱线张力的重量盘

22 warping machine
整经机

23 fan
风扇

24 cross-wound cone
交叉卷绕筒

25 creel
筒架

26 adjustable comb
可调整的梳机

27 warping machine frame
整经机架

28 yarn length recorder
纱线计长器

29 warp beam
经纱轴

30 beam flange
经轴凸缘

31 guard rail
护栏

32 driving drum (driving cylinder)
驱动鼓轮（驱动滚筒）

33 belt drive
皮带驱动

34 motor
马达

35 release for starting the driving drum
转动滚筒的自动释压踏板

36 screw for adjusting the comb setting
调整梳机装置的螺钉

37 drop pins, for stopping the machine when a thread breaks
断纱自停落针，当一支纱线折断时自动停止装置

38 guide bar
导棒

39 drop pin rollers
落针滚轮

40 indigo dying and sizing machine
靛蓝染色和浆纱机

41 take-off stand
经轴架

42 warp beam
经纱轴

43 warp
经纱

44 wetting trough
润湿槽

45 immersion roller
浸入滚轮

46 squeeze roller (mangle)
压挤滚轮

47 dye liquor padding trough
染液浸槽

48 air oxidation passage
空气氧化通道

49 washing trough
洗涤槽

50 drying cylinders for pre-drying
预烘筒

51 tension compensator (tension equalizer)
张力补偿器（张力平衡器）

52 sizing machine
浆纱机

53 drying cylinders
烘筒

54 *for cotton:* stenter; *for wool:* tenter
用於棉织物：开辐机；用於毛织物：拉辐机

55 beaming machine
卷轴机

56 sized warp beam
上浆经轴，织轴

57 rollers
导纱滚轮

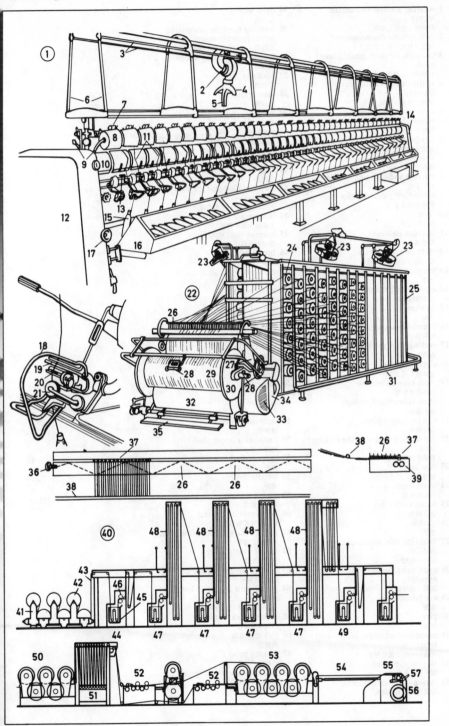

1 **weaving machine** (automatic loom)
织布机（自动织布机）
2 pick counter (tachometer)
转速计数指示器（转速计）
3 shaft (heald shaft, heald frame) guide
转轴导件（综梁，综轴）
4 shafts (heald shafts, heald frames)
转轴（综梁，综轴）
5 rotary battery for weft replenishment
纬纱补充旋转台
6 sley (slay) cap
扣盖
7 weft pirn
纬纱纺锭
8 starting and stopping handle
开关手柄
9 shuttle box, with shuttles
织梭箱和梭子
10 reed
扣，钢扣
11 selvedge (selvage)
布的织边
12 cloth (woven fabric)
布，织成品（编织纤维）
13 temple (cloth temple)
边撑
14 electric weft feeler
电动纬线触杆
15 flywheel
飞轮
16 breast beam board
胸梁板
17 picking stick (pick stick)
投梭棒
18 electric motor
电动机（马达）
19 cloth take-up motion
织物卷紧装置
20 cloth roller (fabric roller)
卷布滚轮
21 can for empty pirns
空纺锭箱
22 lug strap, for moving the picking stick
移动投梭棒用的凸带
23 fuse box
保险丝盒
24 loom framing
织布框架
25 metal shuttle tip
金属梭尖
26 shuttle
梭子
27 heald (heddle, wire heald, wire heddle)
综丝，综线
28 eye (eyelet, heald eyelet, heddle eyelet)
综眼，综丝眼
29 eye (shuttle eye)
梭眼
30 pirn
纺锭
31 metal contact sleeve for the weft feeler
纬线触杆的金属接触套
32 slot for the feeler
探针孔，触杆口
33 spring-clip pirn holder
纺锭固定用的弹簧夹

34 drop wire
引入线
35 weaving machine (automatic loom) [side elevation]
织布机（自动织布机）[侧视图]
36 heald shaft guiding wheels
综轴导轮
37 backrest
后扶架
38 lease rods
分纱棒
39 warp (warp thread)
经纱
40 shed
梭口，梭道
41 sley (slay)
扣座
42 race board
走梭板
43 stop rod blade for the stop motion
停机用的停止杆，停机撞头
44 bumper steel
（保险）缓冲钢板
45 bumper steel stop rod
缓冲钢板停止
46 breast beam
胸梁
47 cloth take-up roller
织物卷紧滚轮
48 warp beam
经纱梁
49 beam flange
经轴凸缘
50 crankshaft
曲轴
51 crankshaft wheel
曲轴轮
52 connector
连接器
53 sley (slay)
扣座
54 lam rods
拉综杆
55 camshaft wheel
锤轴轮
56 camshaft (tappet shaft)
锤轴（挺杆轴）
57 tappet (shedding tappet)
挺杆（挺杆盖）
58 treadle lever
踏杆
59 let-off motion
经纱放出器
60 beam motion control
织轴运动控制装置
61 rope of the warp let-off motion
经纱放出器索
62 let-off weight lever
秤杆放出器
63 control weight [for the treadle]
[踏式]控制秤杆
64 picker with leather or bakelite pad
带皮革或电木衬垫的弹棉机
65 picking stick buffer
投梭棒缓冲器
66 picking cam
投梭盘
67 picking bowl
投梭转子
68 picking stick return spring
投梭棒回动弹簧

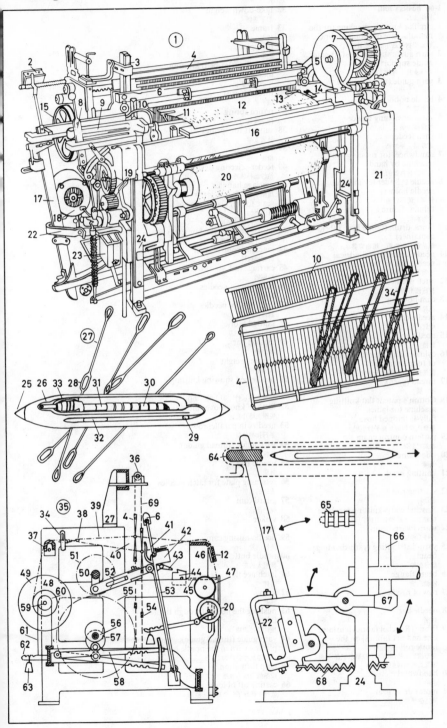

1-66 hosiery mill
针织工厂

1 circular knitting machine for the manufacture of tubular fabric
管形织物制造用的圆形针织机

2 yarn guide support post (thread guide support post)
导纱支柱（导线支柱）

3 yarn guide (thread guide)
导纱（导线）

4 bottle bobbin
瓶形筒管

5 yarn-tensioning device
纱线张力装置

6 yarn feeder
进纱器，导纱器

7 handwheel for rotating the machine by hand
用手旋转机器的手轮

8 needle cylinder (cylindrical needle holder)
针筒（筒形针架）

9 tubular fabric
管形织物

10 fabric drum (fabric box, fabric container)
织品筒（织物箱，织物容器）

11 needle cylinder (cylindrical needle holder) [section]
针筒（筒形针架）[断面图]

12 latch needles arranged in a circle
排成圆形的舌针

13 cam housing
凸轮箱

14 needle cams
织针凸轮

15 needle trick
针槽

16 cylinder diameter (also diameter of tubular fabric)
圆筒直径（即圆筒形织物的直径）

17 thread (yarn)
纱，线

18 Cotton's patent flat knitting machine for ladies' fully-fashioned hose
哥登氏专利的女袜平针织机

19 pattern control chain
款式控制链

20 side frame
侧架

21 knitting head
针座

22 starting rod
起动杆

23 Raschel warp-knitting machine
拉歇尔式，经纱针织机

24 warp (warp beam)
经纱（经轴）

25 yarn-distributing (yarn-dividing) beam
纱分配轴

26 beam flange
经轴凸缘

27 row of needles
针列

28 needle bar
针座

29 fabric (Raschel fabric) [curtain lace and net fabrics] on the fabric roll
卷布滚轮上的织品，（拉歇尔织品）[窗帘花边和网眼织品]

30 handwheel
手轮

31 motor drive gear
马达驱动齿轮

32 take-down weight
取下重锤

33 frame
机架

34 base plate
底座

35 hand flat (flat-bed) knitting machine
手动平针织机

36 thread (yarn)
线（纱）

37 return spring
回动弹簧

38 support for springs
弹簧支架

39 carriage
滑架（座）

40 feeder-selecting device
给纱选择装置

41 carriage handles
滑座（架）把手

42 scale for regulating size of stitches
调节织针尺寸标尺

43 course counter (tachometer)
横列计数器（转速表）

44 machine control lever
机械操纵杆

45 carriage rail
滑座轨

46 back row of needles
后排针

47 front row of needles
前排针

48 knitted fabric
已织成的针织品

49 tension bar
张力棒

50 tension weight
张力重锤

51 needle bed showing knitting action
针床上显示针（编）织的动作

52 teeth of knock-over bit
脱圈沉降片片齿

53 needles in parallel rows
平行排列的针

54 yarn guide (thread guide)
导纱导线

55 needle bed
针床

56 retaining plate for latch needles
舌针的扣板

57 guard cam
保护凸轮

58 sinker
铅锤

59 needle-raising cam
提针凸轮

60 needle butt
针粗大的部分

61 latch needle
舌针

62 loop
线圈

63 pushing the needle through the fabric
推针穿过织物

64 yarn guide (thread guide) placing yarn in the needle hook
导纱器放纱於针钩上

65 loop formation
线圈的形成（成圈）

66 casting off of loop
收针（织好了一个环），脱圈

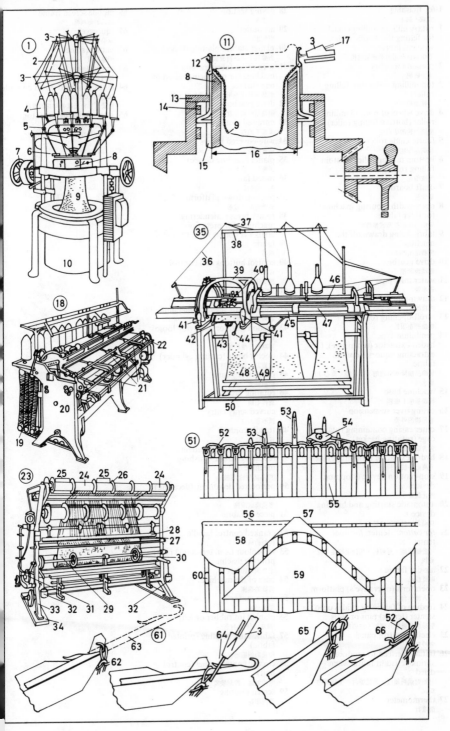

1-65 finishing
完成，加工

1 rotary milling (fulling) machine for felting the woollen (*Am.* woolen) fabric
毛织品毡合用的迴转缩绒机

2 pressure weights
压力砝码

3 top milling roller (top fulling roller)
上铣滚轮

4 drive wheel of bottom milling roller (bottom fulling roller)
底铣滚轮的驱动轮

5 fabric guide roller
导纱滚轮

6 bottom milling roller (bottom fulling roller)
底铣滚轮

7 draft board
牵伸板

8 open-width scouring machine for finer fabrics
细织品用的扩布式精炼机

9 fabric being drawn off the machine
机器送出的织品

10 drive gearbox
驱动齿轮箱

11 water inlet pipe
进水管

12 drawing-in roller
内拉滚轮

13 scroll-opening roller
螺旋开布滚轮

14 pendulum-type hydro-extractor (centrifuge), for extracting liquors from the fabric
从织品抽除水分用的，摆子型（离心）脱水机

15 machine base
机器基座（底座）

16 casing over suspension
悬吊物的外壳

17 outer casing containing rotating cage (rotating basket)
包含旋转笼（篮）的外壳（罩）

18 hydro-extractor (centrifuge) lid
（离心）脱水机盖

19 stop-motion device (stopping device)
停止装置

20 automatic starting and braking device
自动起动机和制动装置

21 *for cotton:* stenter; *for wool:* tenter
用於棉织品：开幅机；用於毛织品：拉幅机

22 air-dry fabric
晾乾织品

23 operator's (operative's) platform
工人操作台

24 feeding of fabric by guides onto stenter (tenter) pins or clips
引导织品进给开幅机（拉幅机）

25 electric control panel
电控制盘

26 initial overfeed to produce shrink-resistant fabric when dried
开始时供料超过，当乾燥时产生防缩的织品

27 thermometer
温度计

28 drying section
干燥室

29 air outlet
空气出口

30 plaiter (fabric-plaiting device)
折叠机（织品折叠装置）

31 wire-roller fabric-raising machine for producing raised or nap surface
织品表面起毛用的钢丝滚轮起毛机

32 drive gearbox
驱动齿轮箱（盒）

33 unraised cloth
未起毛的布

34 wire-covered rollers
钢丝滚轮

35 plaiter (cuttling device)
折叠机（折叠装置）

36 raised fabric
起毛的织品

37 plaiting-down platform
折叠织品之置板

38 rotary press (calendering machine), for press finishing
旋转压平机（滚压机），压平完工用

39 fabric
织品

40 control buttons and control wheels
控制按钮和控制轮

41 heated press bowl
热压滚子

42 rotary cloth-shearing machine
迴转式剪布机

43 suction slot, for removing loose fibres (*Am.* fibers)
排除松纤维的抽吸口

44 doctor blade (cutting cylinder)
螺旋刀（剪毛圆筒）

45 protective guard
防护装置

46 rotating brush
旋转毛刷

47 curved scray entry
弧形布入口

48 treadle control
控制踏板

49 [non-shrinking] decatizing (decating) fabric-finishing machine
[织品防缩的]蒸绒机

50 perforated decatizing (decating) cylinder
多孔蒸绒滚筒

51 piece of fabric
织品

52 cranked control handle
控制曲柄

53 ten-colour (*Am.* ten-color) roller printing machine
十色滚轮印花机

54 base of the machine
机器的底座

55 drive motor
驱动马达

56 blanket [of rubber or felt]
[橡皮或毡的]衬布

57 fabric after printing (printed fabric)
印花后的织品

58 electric control panel (control unit)
电控制盘（控制装置）

59 screen printing
筛网印花

60 mobile screen frame
活动的筛网框

61 squeegee
涂染料滚轮

62 pattern stencil
图案模板

63 screen table
筛网台

64 fabric gummed down on table ready for printing
贴於工作台上准备印花的织品

65 screen printing operator (operative)
筛网印花操作工人

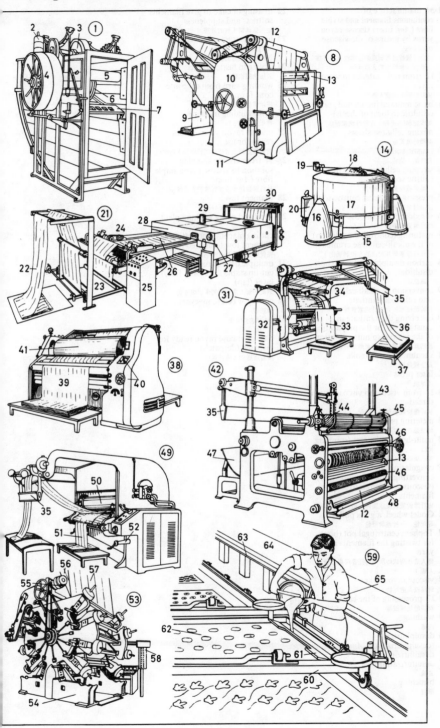

1-34 manufacture of
continuous filament and staple fibre (*Am.* fiber) **viscose rayon yarns** by means of the viscose process
经由纤维胶过程制造的连续细丝，纤维人造丝，和纤维胶人造丝纱

1-12 from raw material to viscose rayon
从原料到纤维胶人造丝

1 basic material [beech and spruce cellulose in form of sheets]
基本原料[山毛榉，赤松纤维素板]

2 mixing cellulose sheets
混和纤维素板

3 caustic soda
苛性钠，烧硷

4 steeping cellulose sheets in caustic soda
纤维素板浸於苛性钠中

5 pressing out excess caustic soda
压出过量的苛性钠

6 shredding the cellulose sheets
将纤维素板粉碎

7 maturing (controlled oxidation) of the alkali-cellulose crumbs
硷性纤维素碎片的成熟（控制氧化）

8 carbon disulphide (*Am.* carbon disulfide)
二硫化碳

9 conversion of alkali-cellulose into cellulose xanthate
把硷纤维素转化成纤维素黄酸

10 dissolving the xanthate in caustic soda for the preparation of the viscose spinning solution
胶丝溶液溶准备的黄酸溶於苛性钠中

11 vacuum ripening tanks
真空成熟槽

12 filter press
压滤机

13-27 from viscose to viscose rayon thread
从纤维胶液至粘胶人造丝

13 metering pump
计量泵

14 multi-holed spinneret (spinning jet)
多孔纺纱头（吐丝头）

15 coagulating (spinning) bath for converting (coagulating) viscose (viscous solution) into solid filaments
由纤维胶液转变成固体人造丝的凝固槽

16 Godet wheel, a glass pulley
导丝轮，一种玻璃滑轮

17 Topham centrifugal pot (box) for twisting the filaments into yarn
将人造丝绕成纱所用的托普汉离心壶（罐）

18 viscose rayon cake
纤维胶人造丝饼

19-27 processing of the cake
丝饼的处理过程

19 washing
洗涤

20 desulphurizing (desulphurization, *Am.* desulfurizing, desulfurization)
去硫

21 bleaching
漂白

22 treating of cake to give filaments softness and suppleness
使人造丝饼柔软的处理

23 hydro-extraction to remove surplus moisture
去除过剩水分的脱水机

24 drying in heated room
於加热间烘乾

25 winding yarn from cake into cone form
将丝饼绕成锥形丝筒

26 cone-winding machine
锥形绕线机

27 viscose rayon yarn on cone ready for use
卷於锥形筒上可使用的纤维胶人造丝纱

28-34 from viscose spinning solution to viscose rayon staple fibre (*Am.* fiber)
从纤维胶纺丝液至纤维胶人造丝

28 filament tow
拖拉出来的细丝（纤维）

29 overhead spray washing plant
架空喷洗设备

30 cutting machine for cutting filament tow to desired length
将丝切成理想长度的切割机

31 multiple drying machine for cut-up staple fibre (*Am.* fiber) layer (lap)
烘乾切断人造丝用的多层烘乾机

32 conveyor belt (conveyor)
输送带

33 baling press
压力打包机

34 bale of viscose rayon ready for dispatch (despatch)
准备运送的人造丝丝包

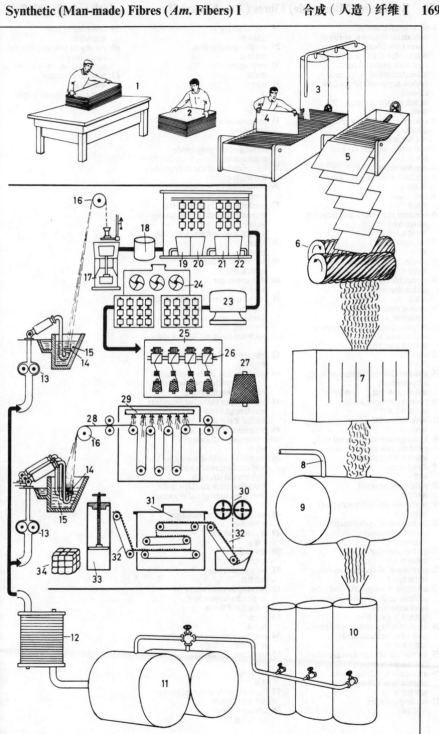

1-62 manufacture of
polyamide (nylon 6, perlon)
fibres (*Am* fibers)
聚醯胺纤维（尼龙6，贝纶）的制造

1 coal [raw material for
manufacture of polyamide
(nylon 6, perlon) fibres (*Am.*
fibers)]
煤[制造聚醯胺纤维（尼龙6，贝纶）的
原料]

2 coking plant for dry coal
distillation
煤干燥蒸馏用的焦化设备

3 extraction of coal tar and
phenol
焦油和酚的提取

4 gradual distillation of tar
焦油的分馏

5 condenser
冷凝器

6 benzene extraction and dispatch
(despatch)
苯的提取和输送

7 chlorine
氯

8 benzene chlorination
苯的氯化

9 monochlorobenzene
(chlorobenzene)
一氯苯

10 caustic soda solution
苛性钠溶液

11 evaporation of chlorobenzene
and caustic soda
氯苯和苛性钠的蒸发

12 autoclave
热压釜

13 sodium chloride (common salt),
a by-product
氯化钠（一般食盐），一种副产品

14 phenol (carbolic acid)
酚（液体石碳酸）

15 hydrogen inlet
氢气入口

16 hydrogenation of phenol to
produce raw cyclohexanol
酚的氢化产生粗环己醇

17 distillation
蒸馏

18 pure cyclohexanol
纯环己醇

19 oxidation (dehydrogenation)
氧化（去氢）

20 formation of cyclohexanone
(pimehinketone)
环己酮的形成

21 hydroxylamine inlet
盐酸羟胺入口

22 formation of cyclohexanoxime
环己酮的形成

23 addition of sulphuric acid (*Am.*
sulfuric acid) to effect molecular
rearrangement
加硫酸使分子从新排列

24 ammonia to neutralize sulphuric
acid (*Am.* sulfuric acid)
加氢中和硫酸

25 formation of caprolactam oil
己醯环胺油的形成

26 ammonium sulphate (*Am.*
ammonium sulfate) solution
硫酸铵溶液

27 cooling cylinder
冷却滚筒

28 caprolactam
己醯环胺

29 weighing apparatus
秤重装置

30 melting pot
熔化罐

31 pump
泵

32 filter
过滤器

33 polymerization in the
autoclave
在热压釜内聚合

34 cooling of the polyamide
聚醯胺的冷却

35 solidification of the polyamide
聚醯胺的固化

36 vertical lift (*Am.* elevator)
升降机

37 extractor for separating the
polyamide from the remaining
lactam oil
从内醯胺油中分离聚醯胺用的抽出器

38 drier
干燥机

39 dry polyamide chips
干燥的聚醯胺片

40 chip container
胺片容器

41 top of spinneret for melting the
polyamide and forcing it
through spinneret holes
(spinning jets)
熔化聚醯胺和从喷丝孔压挤出来的喷丝
头

42 spinneret holes (spinning jets)
喷丝孔

43 solidification of the polyamide
filaments in the cooling tower
於冷却塔中聚醯胺丝的固化

44 collection of extruded filaments
into thread form
将挤压出来的丝条集合成丝束

45 preliminary stretching
(preliminary drawing)
预拉伸

46 stretching (cold-drawing) of the
polyamide thread to achieve
high tensile strength
聚醯胺丝线的拉伸至达到高抗拉强度

47 final stretching (final drawing)
最后拉伸

48 washing of yarn packages
丝件的洗涤

49 drying chamber
干燥室

50 rewinding
复卷筒

51 polyamide cone
聚醯胺筒

52 polyamide cone ready for
dispatch (despatch)
准备运送的聚醯胺筒

53 mixer
混合器

54 polymerization under vacua
真空下的聚合（作用）

55 stretching (drawing)
拉伸

56 washing
洗涤

57 finishing of tow for spinning
纺纱用拖线的整理

58 drying of tow
拖线的干燥

59 crimping of tow
拖线的卷缩

60 cutting of tow into normal
staple lengths
拖线切割成一般（标准）纤维长度

61 polyamide staple
聚醯胺纤维

62 bale of polyamide staple
聚醯胺纤维包

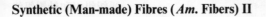

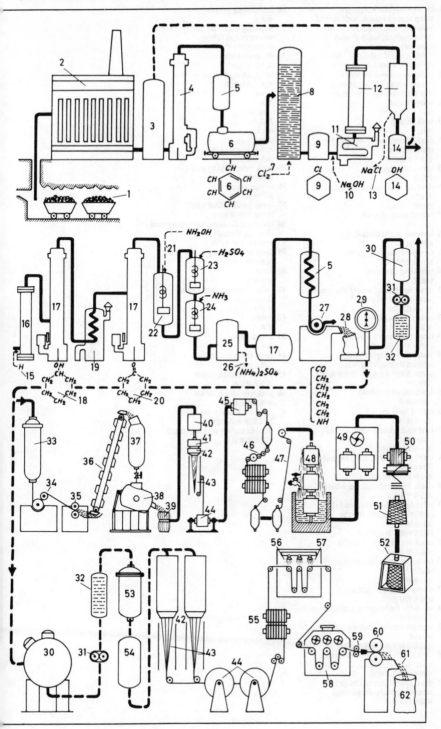

1-29 weaves [black squares:
warp thread raised, weft thread
lowered; white squares: weft
thread raised, warp thread
lowered]
平织组织[黑方块：经纱升起，纬纱下
沉；白方块：纬纱升起，经纱下沉]

1 plain weave (tabby weave)
[weave viewed from above]
平织（有波纹的织品）[从上观看织纹]

2 warp thread
经纱

3 weft thread
纬纱

4 draft (point paper design) for
plain weave
平织用的编织图案

5 threading draft
穿轴图

6 denting draft (reed-threading
draft)
穿扣图

7 raised warp thread
经纱升起

8 lowered warp thread
经纱下沉

9 tie-up of shafts in pairs
轴片成对的穿吊

10 treadling diagram
跳线图

11 draft for basket weave (hopsack
weave, matt weave)
柳条织品图案

12 pattern repeat
重复花样

13 draft for warp rib weave
以经纱为稜织品的图案

14 section of warp rib fabric, a
section through the warp
以经纱为稜织品的断面，部分断面经过
经纱

15 lowered weft thread
下沉的纬纱

16 raised weft thread
上升的纬纱

17 first and second warp threads
[raised]
第一和第二经纱[上升的]

18 third and fourth warp threads
[lowered]
第三和第四经纱[下沉的]

19 draft for combined rib weave
混合稜平织图案

20 selvedge (selvage) thread draft
(additional shafts for the
selvedge)
织边穿轴图（织边附加轴）

21 draft for the fabric shafts
织品穿轴图

22 tie-up of selvedge (selvage)
shafts
织边轴的穿吊

23 tie-up of fabric shafts
织品轴的穿吊

24 selvedge (selvage) in plain weave
平织的轴片

25 section through combination rib
weave
经过混合稜平织的断面图

26 thread interlacing of reversible
warp-faced cord
双面经线纹面交织图

27 draft (point paper design) for
reversible warp-faced cord
双面经线纹面图

28 interlacing points
交织点

29 weaving draft for honeycomb
weave in the fabric
蜂巢织品的平织图

30-48 basic knits
基本针织组织

30 loop, an open loop
线圈，开口线圈

31 head
圈头

32 side
圈边

33 neck
圈颈

34 head interlocking point
圈头连接点

35 neck interlocking point
圈颈连接点

36 closed loop
闭口线圈

37 mesh [with inlaid yarn]
网状组织[带镶嵌的]

38 diagonal floating yarn (diagonal
floating thread)
对角浮纱（对角浮线）

39 loop interlocking at the head
线圈在圈头交织

40 float
浮线组织

41 loose floating yarn (loose
floating thread)
松散浮纱（松散浮线）

42 course
针路

43 inlaid yarn
镶嵌纱

44 tuck and miss stitch
集圈浮线组织

45 pulled-up tuck stitch
套穿集圈组织

46 staggered tuck stitch
交错集圈组织

47 2 × 2 tuck and miss stitch
2 × 2 集圈和浮线组织

48 double pulled-up tuck stitch
双套穿集圈组织

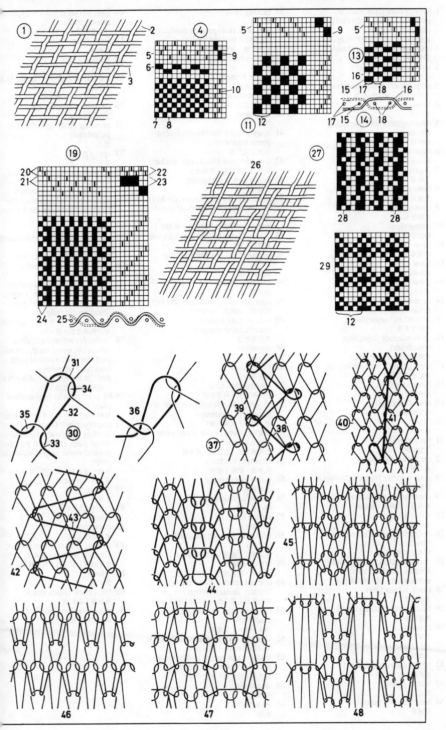

1-52 sulphate (*Am.* sulfate)
pulp mill (kraft pulp mill) [in
diagram form]
硫酸纸浆厂（牛皮纸浆厂）[图示]

1 chippers with dust extractor
带吸尘器的削片机

2 rotary screen (riffler)
回转筛

3 chip packer (chip distributor)
木片包装机（木片分配器）

4 blower
鼓风机

5 disintegrator (crusher, chip
crusher)
粉碎机（轧碎机，木片轧碎机）

6 dust-settling chamber
灰尘沉淀室（降尘室）

7 digester
蒸解釜

8 liquor preheater
溶液预热器

9 control tap
控制龙头

10 swing pipe
摆动管

11 blow tank (diffuser)
通风槽（扩散器）

12 blow valve
通风阀

13 blow pit (diffuser)
通风坑（扩散器）

14 turpentine separator
松节油分离器

15 centralized separator
集中分离器

16 jet condenser (injection
condenser)
喷射凝结器（注射凝结器）

17 storage tank for condensate
凝液贮存槽

18 hot water tank
热水槽

19 heat exchanger
热交换器

20 filter
过滤器

21 presorter
预选别机

22 centrifugal screen
离心筛

23 rotary sorter (rotary strainer)
旋转选别机（旋转滤器）

24 concentrator (thickener, decker)
浓缩器（调稠器，增稠器）

25 vat (chest)
槽（浆槽）

26 collecting tank for backwater
(low box)
回水收集槽（低箱）

27 conical refiner (cone refiner,
Jordan, Jordan refiner)
锥形精制（浆）机（约旦精制机）

28 black liquor filter
黑液滤器

29 black liquor storage tank
黑液贮槽

30 condenser
冷凝器

31 separators
分离器

32 heater (heating element)
加热器（加热元件）

33 liquor pump
液泵

34 heavy liquor pump
浓液泵

35 mixing tank
混合槽

36 salt cake storage tank (sodium
sulphate storage tank)
盐饼贮槽（硫酸钠贮槽）

37 dissolving tank (dissolver)
溶解槽

38 steam heater
蒸汽加热器

39 electrostatic precipitator
静电集尘器

40 air pump
气泵

41 storage tank for the uncleared
green liquor
未清绿液贮槽

42 concentrator (thickener, decker)
浓缩器（调稠器，增稠器）

43 green liquor preheater
绿液预热器

44 concentrator (thickener, decker)
for the weak wash liquor (wash
water)
稀洗液用的浓缩器（调稠器，增稠器）

45 storage tank for the weak liquor
稀释液贮槽

46 storage tank for the cooking
liquor
蒸煮液贮槽

47 agitator (stirrer)
搅拌器

48 concentrator (thickener, decker)
浓缩器（调稠器，增稠器）

49 causticizing agitators
(causticizing stirrers)
苛化搅拌器

50 classifier
类析器

51 lime slaker
化灰器

52 reconverted lime
再转换石灰，再生石灰

53-65 groundwood mill (mechanical
pulp mill) [diagram]
磨木浆厂（机械纸浆厂）[简图]

53 continuous grinder (continuous
chain grinder)
连续磨木机（连续链式磨木机）

54 strainer (knotter)
粗滤器，滤筛（结障）

55 pulp water pump
纸浆水泵

56 centrifugal screen
离心筛

57 screen (sorter)
筛（选别机）

58 secondary screen (secondary
sorter)
（二次）二道筛（二道选别机）

59 rejects chest
筛渣槽，废料池

60 conical refiner (cone refiner,
Jordan, Jordan refiner)
锥形精制（浆）机（约旦精制机）

61 pulp-drying machine (pulp
machine)
纸浆干燥机（纸浆机）

62 concentrator (thickener, decker)
浓缩器（调稠器，增稠器）

63 waste water pump (white water
pump, pulp water pump)
废水泵（白水泵，纸浆水泵）

64 steam pipe
蒸汽管

65 water pipe
水管

66 continuous grinder (continuou[s]
chain grinder)
连续磨木机（连续链式磨木机）

67 feed chain
给料链

68 groundwood
磨木浆

69 reduction gear for the feed ch[ain]
drive
进料链驱动的减速齿轮

70 stone-dressing device
磨石刻石装置

71 grinding stone (grindstone,
pulpstone)
磨石

72 spray pipe
喷管

73 conical refiner (cone refiner,
Jordan, Jordan refiner)
锥形精制（浆）机（约旦精制机）

74 handwheel for adjusting the
clearance between the knives
(blades)
调整刀片间隙用的手轮

75 rotating bladed cone (rotatin[g]
bladed plug)
旋转刀片的锥部（旋转刀片插座）

76 stationary bladed shell
固定刀片壳

77 inlet for unrefined cellulose
(chemical wood pulp, chemic[al]
pulp) or groundwood pulp
(mechanical pulp)
未精制纤维素（化学木浆）或磨木浆
浆（机械纸浆）的入口

78 outlet for refined cellulose
(chemical wood pulp, chemic[al]
pulp) or groundwood pulp
(mechanical pulp)
精制纤维素（化学纸浆）或磨木纸浆
（机械纸浆）的出口

79-86 stuff (stock) preparation
plant [diagram]
原料，材料（存料）准备设备[简图]

79 conveyor belt (conveyor) for
loading cellulose (chemical
wood pulp, chemical pulp) o[r]
groundwood pulp (mechanic[al]
pulp)
装载纤维素（化学木浆）或磨木浆（机
械纸浆）的运送带

80 pulper
散浆机

81 dump chest
卸料槽

82 cone breaker
锥形轧碎机

83 conical refiner (cone refiner,
Jordan, Jordan refiner)
锥形精制（浆）机（约旦精制机）

84 refiner
精浆机

85 stuff chest (stock chest)
纸料槽（存料槽）

86 machine chest (stuff chest)
原料贮槽（纸料槽）

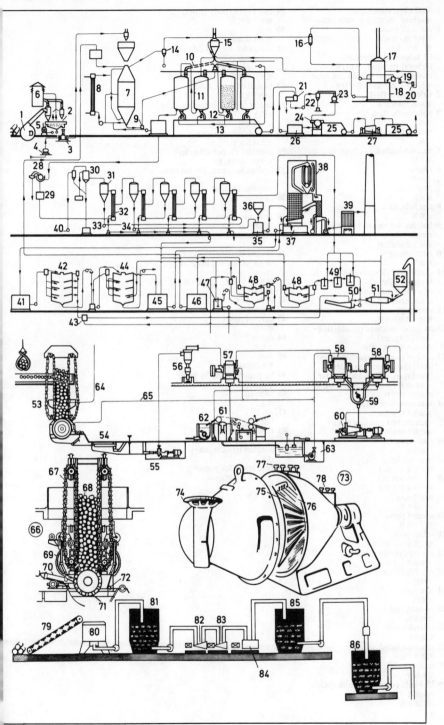

1 stuff chest (stock chest, machine chest), a mixing chest for stuff (stock)
原料贮槽（存料槽），原料的一种混合槽

2-10 laboratory apparatus (laboratory equipment) for analysing stuff (stock) and paper
分析原料和纸张用的实验室仪器

2 Erlenmeyer flask
锥形瓶，锥形烧瓶

3 volumetric flask
量瓶

4 measuring cylinder
量筒

5 Bunsen burner
本生灯

6 tripod
三脚架

7 petri dish
佩垂皿

8 test tube rack
试管架

9 balance for measuring basis weight
测量纸张定量的秤

10 micrometer
测微计

11 centrifugal cleaners ahead of the breastbox (headbox, stuff box) of a paper machine
造纸机网前箱的离心除渣器

12 standpipe
竖管，圆筒形水塔

13-28 paper machine (production line) [diagram]
造纸机（生产线）[简图]

13 feed-in from the machine chest (stuff chest) with sand table (sand trap, riffler) and knotter
从带砂滤器（砂阱，沉沙器）和结筛器的原料贮槽进料

14 wire (machine wire)
金属线（机械电线）

15 vacuum box (suction box)
真空箱（吸取箱）

16 suction roll
吸水滚轮

17 first wet felt
第一湿毛布（毡）

18 second wet felt
第二湿毛布（毡）

19 first press
第一压榨机

20 second press
第二压榨机

21 offset press
偏位压榨机（副压榨机）

22 drying cylinder (drier)
干燥滚筒（干燥器）

23 dry felt (drier felt)
干燥毡

24 size press
压榨机

25 cooling roll
冷却滚轮

26 calender rolls
轧光滚轮

27 machine hood
机器罩（盖）

28 delivery reel
卷取纸轴

29-35 blade coating machine (blade coater)
刮刀涂布机

29 raw paper (body paper)
粗纸（纸坯）

30 web
整卷印刷用纸

31 coater for the top side
顶面涂布器

32 infrared drier
红外线干燥器

33 heated drying cylinder
加热干燥滚筒

34 coater for the underside (wire side)
下边涂布器（网面）

35 reel of coated paper
涂布的卷筒纸

36 calender (Super-calender)
轧光机（超级轧光机）

37 hydraulic system for the press rolls
压榨滚轮的液压系统

38 calender roll
轧光滚轮

39 unwind station
退纸操作台

40 lift platform
上升台

41 rewind station(rewinder, re-reeler, reeling machine, re-reeling machine)
回卷台（回卷机，复卷筒，摇纱机，复摇纱机）

42 roll cutter
滚轮切纸机

43 control panel
控制盘

44 cutter
切纸机

45 web
整卷的印刷用纸

46-51 papermaking by hand
手工造纸

46 vatman
捞工

47 vat
纸浆槽

48 mould (*Am.* mold)
模

49 coucher (couchman)
伏工

50 post ready for pressing
为压制作准备的工作

51 felt
毡（毛布）

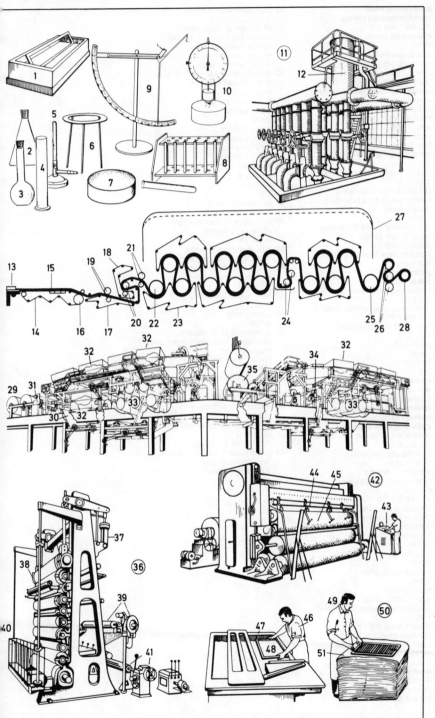

1 **hand-setting room**
(handcomposing room)
手工排字（排版）房
2 composing frame
排字架
3 case (typecase)
活字盘（铅字盘）
4 case cabinet (case rack)
字盘柜（字盘架）
5 hand compositor (compositor,
typesetter, maker-up)
排版工人（排字工，铅字工，手民）
6 manuscript (typescript)
原稿（打字稿）
7 sorts, types (type characters,
characters)
杂类活字符号，整套铅字（铅字，活
字）
8 rack (case) for furniture (spacing
material)
活版填料架（铅字隔条、空铅等）
9 standing type rack (standing
matter rack)
存版架
10 storage shelf (shelf for storing
formes, *Am.* forms)
保存架（印版储存架）
11 standing type (standing matter)
存版（印件）
12 galley
活版盘，铅字盘
13 composing stick (setting stick)
检字手盘
14 composing rule (setting rule)
排字量规（组字规）
15 type (type matter, matter)
铅字，活字
16 page cord
捆版绳
17 bodkin
锥子
18 tweezers
镊子
19 **Linotype line-composing (line-
casting, slug-composing, slug-
casting)machine, a
multi-magazine machine**
林诺铸版机（整行铸字机），一种万能
铸版铸字排字机
20 distributing mechanism
(distributor)
配字模装置（配字器）
21 type magazines with matrices
(matrixes)
具有字模的活字库
22 elevator carrier for distributing
the matrices (matrixes)
配字模的升降牵转具（托架）
23 assembler
配字器
24 spacebands
齐行楔
25 casting mechanism
铸版机
26 metal feeder
金属供给装置（供铅器）
27 machine-set matter (cast lines,
slugs)
机械排字条（铸字条，铅字条）
28 matrices (matrixes) for
handsetting (sorts)
手工排字（排版）之字模
29 Linotype matrix
整行排铸字模
30 teeth for the distributing
mechanism (distributor)
配字模装置用齿

31 face (type face, matrix)
字面（铅字面，字模）
32–45 **monotype single-unit
composing (typesetting) and
casting machine (monotype
single-unit composition caster)**
单字排字机和单字铸版机
32 monotype standard composing
(typesetting) machine
(keyboard)
标准单字排字机（键盘式）
33 paper tower
纸带架
34 paper ribbon
纸质打字机色带
35 justifying scale
整版尺（齐行标尺）
36 unit indicator
单位指示器
37 keyboard
键盘
38 compressed-air hose
压缩空气软管
39 monotype casting machine
(monotype caster)
单字铸字机
40 automatic metal feeder
自动金属供应装置（供铅器）
41 pump compression spring
(pump pressure spring)
泵压缩弹簧
42 matrix case (die case)
字模盒
43 paper tower
纸带架
44 galley with types (letters,
characters, cast single types, cast
single letters)
有活字（字母、符号、单字铸件）的铅
字盘
45 electric heater (electric heating
unit)
电热器（电热装置）
46 matrix case (die case)
字模盒
47 type matrices (matrixes) (letter
matrices)
（铅）活字字模（字母字模）
48 guide block for engaging with
the cross-slide guide
衔接横向滑件导座的导块

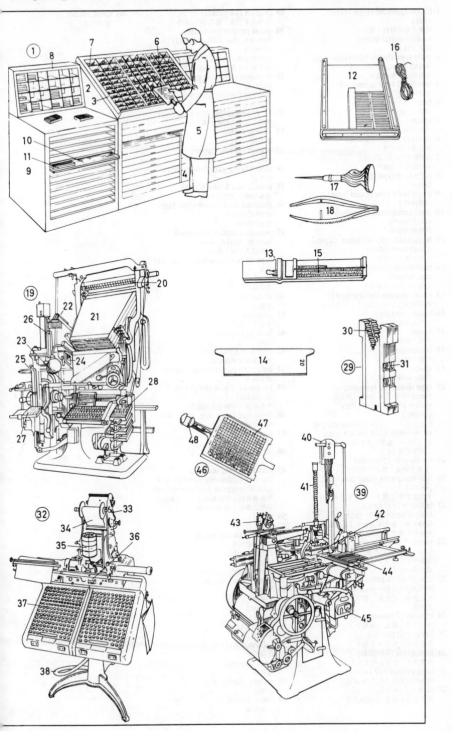

1-17 composition (type matter, type)
组版（铅字材料，铅字）
1 initial (initial letter)
起首字母
2 bold type (bold, boldfaced type, heavy type, boldface)
粗体铅字，黑体铅字
3 semibold type (semibold)
中黑体铅字
4 line
字行
5 space
字行间隔，行间，行距
6 ligature (double letter)
复合字（双字母）
7 italic type (italics)
斜体铅字（斜体字）
8 light face type (light face)
细体铅字
9 extra bold type (extra bold)
特黑体铅字
10 bold condensed type (bold condensed)
黑体凝缩活字
11 majuscule (capital letter, capital, upper case letter)
大写字体（大写字母）
12 minuscule (small letter, lower case letter)
小写字体（小写字母）
13 letter spacing (interspacing)
调节间隔法（中间空间），字母间隔
14 small capitals
小号大写字母
15 break
中止（段落）
16 indention
行首空白（缩进）
17 space
空铅，间隔，字间
18 type sizes [one typographic point = 0.376 mm (Didot system), 0.351 mm (Pica system)]
铅字大小（尺寸）[（欧洲制法国活字规格）一个印刷点 = 0.376 毫米（迪多点制），0.351 毫米（派卡制）（12 点大之活字规格）]
19 six-to-pica (2 points)
½ 派卡字体（英文 2 点铅字）
20 half nonpareil (four-to-pica) (3 points)
半无上字体 ⅓ 派卡（英文 3 点铅字）
21 brilliant (4 points); *sim.*: diamond (4½ points)
显明字体（英文 4 点铅字）；类似：钻石字体（英文 4½ 点铅字）
22 pearl (5 points); *sim.*: ruby (*Am.* agate) (5½ points)
珍珠字体（英文 5 点铅字）；类似：玛瑙字体（5½ 点）
23 nonpareil (6 points); *sim.*: minionette (6½ points)
无上字体（英文 6 点铅字）；类似：6 ½ 点字体
24 minion (7 points)
宠仆字体（英文 7 点铅字）
25 brevier (8 points)
短字体（英文 8 点铅字）
26 bourgeois (9 points)
布鲁泽依司字体（英文 9 点铅字）
27 long primer (10 points)
过高初阶字体（英文 10 点铅字）
28 pica (12 points)
派卡字体（英文 12 点铅字）

29 English (14 points)
古体英文字体（英文 14 点铅字）
30 great primer (two-line brevier, *Am.* Columbian) (16 points)
大宰相字体（两行短字字体，[美]哥伦布式字体）（英文 16 点铅字）
31 paragon (two-line primer) (20 points)
模范字体（两行过高初阶字体，英文 20 点字体）
32-37 typefounding (type casting)
活字（铅字）制造（铸造）
32 punch cutter
雕刻师
33 graver (burin, cutter)
雕刻刀
34 magnifying glass (magnifier)
放大镜
35 punch blank (die blank)
钢模坯体（空白之钢模）
36 finished steel punch (finished steel die)
刻好的钢模
37 punched matrix (stamped matrix, strike, drive)
冲压成之字模（钢模）
38 type (type character, character)
铅字
39 head
铅字头
40 shoulder
字肩
41 counter
字谷（字地）
42 face (type face)
字面
43 type line (bodyline)
铅字廓线（字体廓线）
44 height to paper (type height)
铅字高度
45 height of shank (height of shoulder)
字身高度（字脚至字肩高度）
46 body size (type size, point size)
铅字尺寸（铅字大小，点的大小）
47 nick
铅字缺刻
48 set (width)
铅字宽度
49 matrix-boring machine (matrix-engraving machine), a special-purpose boring machine
字模搪孔机（字模雕刻机），一种特定目的之搪孔（雕刻）机器
50 stand
机架（台）
51 cutter (cutting head)
刀具（切割头）
52 cutting table
切割台
53 pantograph carriage
比例尺之滑座（轨运器）
54 V-way
V 型槽
55 pattern
字模版
56 pattern table
字模台
57 follower
从动装置
58 pantograph
缩放器
59 matrix clamp
字模夹
60 cutter spindle
刀具主轴

61 drive motor
驱动马达

Alfred **John Dodsley,** essayist and journalist, was born in Wenlock on the 5th August 1841 and died on the 4th October 1920 in Birmingham. His father was a journeyman thatcher and as a boy Dodsley was sent to work in the fields as a bird-scarer. Having taught himself to read and write fluently – for many years the only books he possessed were a Bible and a volume of Tillotson's sermons – he went to Shrewsbury to study. Living in extreme poverty he began to write for the EAST HEREFORDSHIRE GAZETTE and a collection of his essays together with some poems on country life was published in 1868 under the title *"Rural Thoughts".* Among his most popular works were *"The Diary of a Derbyshire Shepherd"* (1872), *"Rural Verses"* (1879), *"Leaves from a Countryman's Notebook"* (1893) and *"Memoirs of Nineteenth Century Shropshire",* published posthumously. Dodsley also contributed many articles on country life to London papers and championed the cause of the agricultural worker during the depression of the 1880's. The latter years of his life were embittered by controversy raised by his protests against the unemployment caused by mechanised farming.

16— He was for many years president of the **Society for the Protection of the Liberties of the Farm-worker.**

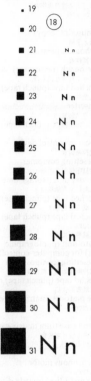

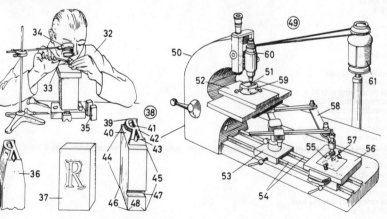

1 keyboard console (keyboard unit) for phototypesetting
照相打字之键盘操作台

2 keyboard
键盘

3 manuscript (copy)
原稿，手稿

4 keyboard operator
键盘操作者

5 tape punch (perforator)
纸带穿（打）孔机（器）

6 punched tape (punch tape)
穿孔纸带

7 filmsetter
软片卷动装置

8 punched tape (punch tape)
穿孔纸带

9 exposure control device
曝光控制装置

10 typesetting computer
照相打字组版之电脑

11 memory unit (storage unit)
记忆单位（存储单位）

12 punched tape (punch tape)
穿孔纸带（孔带）

13 punched tape (punch tape) reader
穿孔纸带阅读机

14 photo-unit (photographic unit) for computer-controlled typesetting (composition)
电脑控制排版用之照相装置

15 punchd tape (punch tape) reader
穿孔纸带阅读机

16 type matrices (matrixes) (letter matrices)
字模

17 matrix case (film matrix case)
字模盒（软片字模盒）

18 guide block
导块

19 synchronous motor
同步马达

20 type disc (disk) (matrix disc)
铅字盘（字模盘）

21 mirror assembly
反射镜组件

22 optical wedge
光楔

23 lens
透镜

24 mirror system
反射镜系统

25 film
软片（胶卷）

26 flash tubes
闪光管

27 matrix drum
字模筒

28 automatic film copier
软片自动复制机

29 central processing unit of a photocomposition system (photosetting system) for newspaper typesetting
报纸照相排版系统之资料处理机（新闻排版用照相排字机之中央处理装置）

30 punched tape (punch tape) input (input unit)
穿孔纸带输入（输入装置）

31 keyboard send-receive teleprinter (Teletype)
键盘式电传打字机

32 on-line disc (disk) storage unit
线上磁碟储存装置

33 alphanumeric (alphameric) disc (disk) store (alphanumeric disc file)
字母数字磁碟储存器（字母数字磁碟档）

34 disc (disk) stack (disc pack)
磁碟储存架

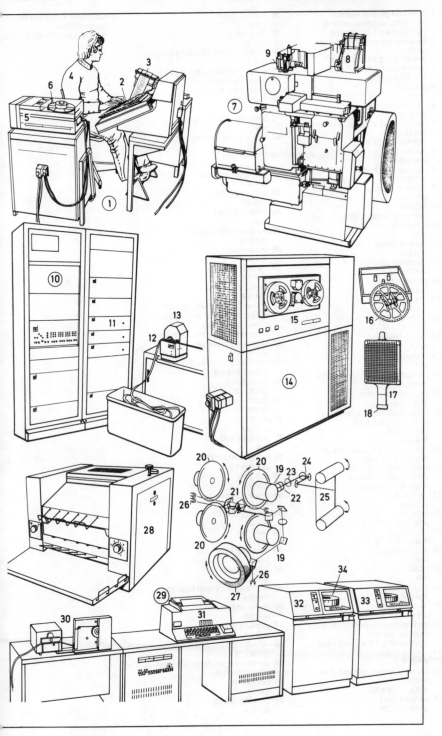

1 overhead process camera
(overhead copying camera)
吊式制版照相机（吊式复制相机）

2 focusing screen (ground glass
screen)
聚焦幕（检影玻璃板或毛玻璃板）

3 hinged screen holder
铰接聚焦幕托架

4 graticule
格子线

5 control console
操作控制台

6 hinged bracket-mounted control
panel
铰接的托架式控制板

7 percentage focusing charts
调焦率图表

8 vacuum film holder
真空软片吸气板

9 screen magazine
网目屏箱

10 bellows
相机之暗匣（蛇腹，暗箱）

11 standard
机架

12 register device
定位装置

13 overhead gantry
吊式门架

14 copyboard
原稿板架

15 copyholder
原稿夹框

16 lamp bracket
灯的托架

17 xenon lamp
氙气灯

18 copy (original)
原稿

19 retouching and stripping desk
修版和揭膜桌

20 illuminated screen
照明毛玻璃屏

21 height and angle adjustment
桌子高度和角度之调整器

22 copyboard
原稿板架

23 linen tester, a magnifying glass
布纹检验器，放大镜之一种

24 universal process and
reproduction camera
万能制版用之复制相机

25 camera body
相机机身

26 bellows
蛇腹，暗箱

27 lens carrier
透镜移动装置（镜头架）

28 angled mirror
角镜

29 stand
支架

30 copyboard
原稿板架

31 halogen lamp
卤素灯

32 vertical process camera, a
compact camera
立式制版照相机（简单小型式摄影机）

33 camera body
相机机身

34 focusing screen (ground glass
screen)
调焦屏（毛玻璃屏）

35 vacuum back
真空软片吸盖版

36 control panel
控制盘

37 flash lamp
闪光灯

38 mirror for right-reading images
正相镜

39 scanner (colour, *Am.* color,
correction unit)
扫描器（影色修正机）

40 base frame
基座

41 lamp compartment
灯室

42 xenon lamp housing
氙灯罩

43 feed motors
进给马达

44 transparency arm
透明臂

45 scanning drum
扫描滚筒

46 scanning head
扫描头

47 mask-scanning head
修色扫描头

48 mask drum
修色滚筒

49 recording space
记录间隔

50 daylight cassette
明室暗箱

51 colour (*Am.* color) computer
with control unit and selective
colour correction
装有控制装置与选色校色之彩色电脑

52 engraving machine
雕刻机

53 seamless engraving adjustment
无缝雕刻调整装置

54 drive clutch
驱动离合器

55 clutch flange
离合器凸缘

56 drive unit
驱动装置

57 machine bed
机座

58 equipment carrier
部件移动装置

59 bed slide
刀架滑座（板）

60 control panel
控制盘

61 bearing block
轴承座

62 tailstock
尾座

63 scanning head
扫描头

64 copy cylinder
原稿圆筒

65 centre (*Am.* center) bearing
中间轴承

66 engraving system
雕刻装置

67 printing cylinder
印刷滚筒

68 cylinder arm
圆筒臂（柄）

69 electronics (electronic) cabinet
电子设备柜（电箱）

70 computers
电脑

71 program input
程式输入

72 automatic film processor fo
scanner films
软片扫描用的软片自动显影（处理

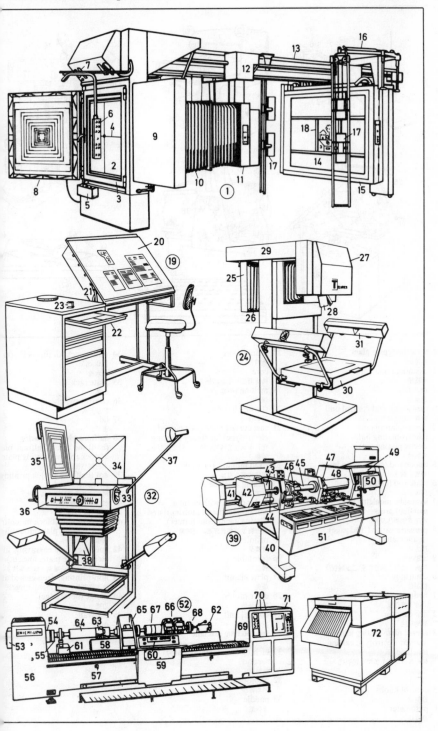

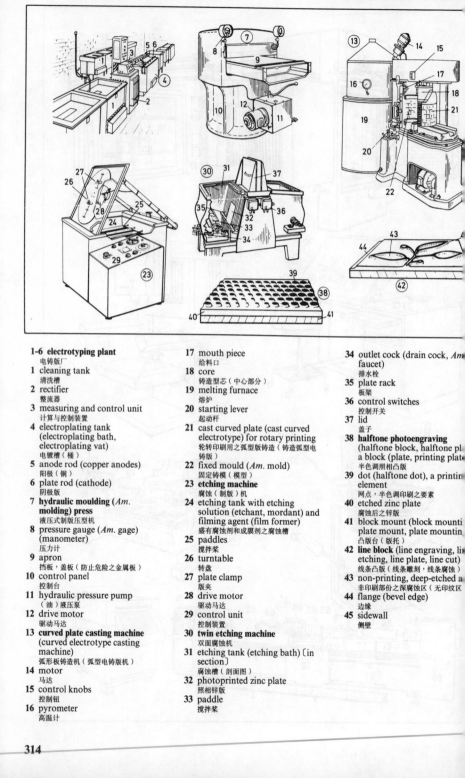

1-6 electrotyping plant
电铸版厂
1 cleaning tank
清洗槽
2 rectifier
整流器
3 measuring and control unit
计算与控制装置
4 electroplating tank
(electroplating bath,
electroplating vat)
电镀槽（桶）
5 anode rod (copper anodes)
阳极（铜）
6 plate rod (cathode)
阴极版
7 hydraulic moulding (*Am.*
molding) press
液压式制版压型机
8 pressure gauge (*Am.* gage)
(manometer)
压力计
9 apron
挡板，盖片（防止危险之金属板）
10 control panel
控制台
11 hydraulic pressure pump
（油）液压泵
12 drive motor
驱动马达
13 **curved plate casting machine**
(curved electrotype casting
machine)
弧形板铸造机（弧型电铸版机）
14 motor
马达
15 control knobs
控制钮
16 pyrometer
高温计

17 mouth piece
给料口
18 core
铸造型芯（中心部分）
19 melting furnace
熔炉
20 starting lever
起动杆
21 cast curved plate (cast curved
electrotype) for rotary printing
轮转印刷用之弧型版铸造（铸造弧型电
铸版）
22 fixed mould (*Am.* mold)
固定铸模（模型）
23 **etching machine**
腐蚀（制版）机
24 etching tank with etching
solution (etchant, mordant) and
filming agent (film former)
盛有腐蚀剂和成膜剂之腐蚀槽
25 paddles
搅拌桨
26 turntable
转盘
27 plate clamp
版夹
28 drive motor
驱动马达
29 control unit
控制装置
30 **twin etching machine**
双面腐蚀机
31 etching tank (etching bath) [in
section]
腐蚀槽（剖面图）
32 photoprinted zinc plate
照相锌版
33 paddle
搅拌桨

34 outlet cock (drain cock, *Am.*
faucet)
排水栓
35 plate rack
板架
36 control switches
控制开关
37 lid
盖子
38 **halftone photoengraving**
(halftone block, halftone pl[ate],
a block (plate, printing plate))
半色调照相凸版
39 dot (halftone dot), a printin[g]
element
网点，半色调印刷之要素
40 etched zinc plate
腐蚀之锌版
41 block mount (block mounti[ng],
plate mount, plate mountin[g])
凸版台（版托）
42 **line block** (line engraving, li[ne]
etching, line plate, line cut)
线条凸版（线条雕刻，线条腐蚀）
43 non-printing, deep-etched a[rea]
非印刷部份之深腐蚀区（无印纹区）
44 flange (bevel edge)
边缘
45 sidewall
侧壁

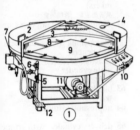

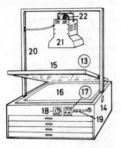

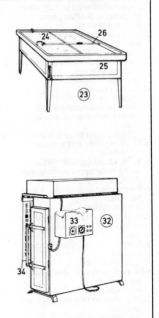

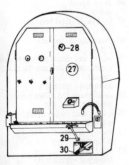

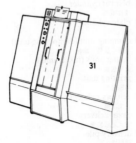

ate whirler (whirler,
atecoating machine) for
ating offset plates
布感光液用之平版烘版机
ding lid
动盖, 活动盖
ectric heater
热器
mperature gauge (*Am.* gage)
度计
ater connection for the spray
nit
雾装置的给水接头
ray unit
雾装置
nd spray
按喷雾器
late clamps
夹
nc plate (*also*: magnesium
ate, copper plate)
板 (另有：镁板，铜板）
ontrol panel
制台
rive motor
动马达
rake pedal
车踏板
acuum printing frame (vacuum
ame, printing-down frame)
空烘（晒）版架
ase of the vacuum printing
ame (vacuum frame,
rinting-down frame)
空烘（晒）版架之基座
late glass frame
璃版架
ated offset plate
布感光液之平板

17 control panel
控制盘
18 exposure timer
曝光计时器
19 vacuum pump switch
真空泵开关
20 support
支架
21 point light exposure lamp, a
quartz-halogen lamp
点光源，曝光灯，一种石英卤素灯
22 fan blower
吹风机
23 stripping table (make-up table)
for stripping films
揭膜用之拼版台
24 crystal glass screen
水晶玻璃网
25 light box
灯光箱（光度一样时作胶卷薄膜检查之
箱子）
26 straightedge rules
直尺（划直线用尺）
27 vertical plate-drying cabinet
垂直版之干燥箱
28 hygrometer
湿度计，垂直版
29 speed control
速度控制
30 brake pedal
刹车踏板
31 processing machine for
presensitized plates
p.s版（预制感光板）显影机
32 burning-in oven for glueenamel
plates (diazo plates)
上胶用之烘版箱（重氨基板，偶氮盐
版）
33 control box (control unit)
控制箱（控制装置）

34 diazo plate
重氮基版（偶氮盐版）

180 Offset Printing　平版印刷

1 four-colour (*Am.* four-color) rotary offset press (rotary offset machine, web-offset press)
四色平版轮转印刷机
2 roll of unprinted paper (blank paper)
未印的卷筒纸（空白纸卷）
3 reel stand (carrier for the roll of unprinted paper)
卷筒纸架（未印刷卷筒支架）
4 forwarding rolls
前进滚轮（输纸轮）
5 side margin control (margin control, side control, side lay control)
卷筒纸左右控制装置
6-13 inking units (inker units)
印版著墨装置
6, 8, 10, 12 inking units (inker units) in the upper printing unit
印刷机上部之著墨装置
6-7 perfecting unit (double unit) for yellow
黄色双面印刷装置
7, 9, 11, 13 inking units (inker units) in the lower printing unit
印刷机下部之著墨装置
8-9 perfecting unit (double unit) for cyan
青色双面印刷装置
10-11 perfecting unit (double unit) for magenta
紫红色双面印刷装置
12-13 perfecting unit (double unit) for black
黑色双面印刷装置
14 drier
干燥器
15 folder (folder unit)
折页装置
16 control desk
控制柏
17 sheet
单张，纸页
18 four-colour (*Am.* four-color) rotary offset press (rotary offset machine, web-offset press) [diagram]
四色平版轮转印刷机[简图]
19 reel stand
卷筒纸支架
20 side margin control (margin control, side control, side lay control)
左右控制装置
21 inking rollers (ink rollers, inkers)
著墨滚轮
22 ink duct (ink fountain)
油墨输送管（墨槽）
23 damping rollers (dampening rollers, dampers, dampeners)
润版滚
24 blanket cylinder
橡皮滚筒
25 plate cylinder
印版滚筒
26 route of the paper (of the web)
行纸路线
27 drier
干燥器
28 chilling rolls (cooling rollers, chill rollers)
冷却滚
29 folder (folder unit)
折页装置
30 four-colour (*Am.* four-color) sheet-fed offset machine (offset press) [diagram]
四色单张纸平版印刷机[简图]
31 sheet feeder (feeder)
（给）馈纸装置
32 feed table (feed board)
给纸桌（给纸台）
33 route of the sheets through swing-grippers to the feed drum
由输纸咬爪至给纸滚筒之给纸路线
34 feed drum
给纸滚筒
35 impression cylinder
压力滚筒
36 transfer drums (transfer cylinders)
传递滚筒
37 blanket cylinder
橡皮滚筒
38 plate cylinder
印版滚筒
39 damping unit (dampening unit)
润版（装置）单位
40 inking units (inker units)
著墨装置
41 printing unit
印刷装置
42 delivery cylinder
递纸滚筒
43 chain delivery
链式递纸装置
44 delivery pile
递纸堆
45 delivery unit (delivery mechanism)
收纸单位
46 single-colour (*Am.* single-color) offset press (offset machine)
单色平版印刷机
47 pile of paper (sheets, printing paper)
纸堆（堆纸，印刷用纸）
48 sheet feeder (feeder), an automatic pile feeder
给纸机（自动给纸机）
49 feed table (feed board)
给纸桌（给纸台）
50 inking rollers (ink rollers, inkers)
著墨滚轮
51 inking units (inker units)
著墨装置
52 damping rollers (dampening rollers, dampers, dampeners)
湿版滚
53 plate cylinder, a zinc plate
印版滚筒，一种锌版
54 blanket cylinder, a steel cylinder with rubber blanket
橡皮滚筒，一种包有橡皮布的钢滚筒
55 pile delivery unit for the printed sheets
已印刷过之单张纸的收纸装置
56 gripper bar, a chain gripper
咬纸杆，一种链式之夹纸装置
57 pile of printed paper (printed sheets)
印刷过之纸堆（印张）
58 guard for the V-belt (vee-belt) drive
V 型带转动之护板
59 single-colour (*Am.* single-color) offset press (offset machine) [diagram]
单色平版印刷机[简图]
60 inking unit (inker unit) with inking rollers (ink rollers, inkers)
具着墨滚轮之着墨装置
61 damping unit (dampening u with damping rollers (dampening rollers, dampers dampeners)
具润版滚之润版装置
62 plate cylinder
印版滚筒
63 blanket cylinder
橡皮滚筒
64 impression cylinder
压力滚筒
65 delivery cylinders with gripp
具咬纸夹之递纸滚筒
66 drive wheel
驱动轮
67 feed table (feed board)
给纸台（板）
68 sheet feeder (feeder)
给纸机
69 pile of unprinted paper (blan paper, unprinted sheets, blan sheets)
未印刷纸堆（空白纸堆）
70 small sheet-fed offset press
小型单张纸平版印刷机
71 inking unit (inker unit)
著墨装置
72 suction feeder
吸式给纸机
73 pile feeder
自动堆纸机，自动续纸器
74 instrument panel (control pa with counter, pressure gauge (*Am.* gage), air regulator, an control switch for the sheet feeder (feeder)
装有计数器，压力计，空气调节器和纸器控制开关之仪表盘（控制盘）
75 flat-bed offset press (offset machine) ('Mailänder' proofi press, proof press)
平台平版印刷机（打样机）
76 inking unit (inker unit)
著墨装置
77 inking rollers (ink rollers, inkers)
著墨滚轮
78 bed (press bed, type bed, forr bed, *Am.* form bed)
台（印版台）
79 cylinder with rubber blanket
具橡皮布之滚筒
80 starting and stopping lever fo the printing unit
印刷装置的起动杆与停止杆
81 impression-setting wheel (impression-adjusting wheel)
印刷调节轮，压力调节轮

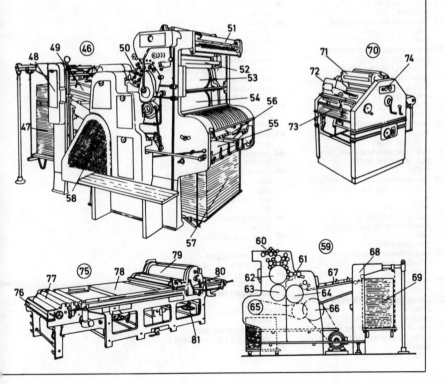

1-65 presses (machines) for letterpress printing (letterpress printing machines)
凸版印刷机

1 **two-revolution flat-bed cylinder press**
二迴转凸版平台印刷机

2 impression cylinder
压印滚筒

3 lever for raising or lowering the cylinder
滚筒之升降杆（手柄）

4 feed table (feed board)
给纸台（板）

5 automatic sheet feeder (feeder) [operated by vacuum and air blasts]
单张自动给纸机[利用真空与吹气操作的]

6 air pump for the feeder and delivery
给收纸用之气泵

7 inking unit (inker unit) with distributing rollers (distributor rollers, distributors) and forme rollers (*Am.* form rollers)
装有散墨滚（分配滚）与触版墨滚（水滚）之着墨装置

8 ink slab (ink plate) inking unit (inker unit)
著墨装置台（板）

9 delivery pile for printed paper
已印刷好之收纸堆

10 sprayer (anti set-off apparatus, anti set-off spray) for dusting the printed sheets
印刷纸张喷粉器[防反（转）印装置,防反印喷粉]

11 interleaving device
夹入间隔纸之装备

12 foot pedal for starting and stopping the press
印刷机之起动与停止踏板

13 **platen press** (platen machine, platen) [in section]
平压印刷机（剖面图,俗称圆盘机）

14 paper feed and delivery (paper feeding and delivery unit)
给纸与收纸装置

15 platen
压印板

16 toggle action (toggle-joint action)
肘节（曲柄）机构

17 bed (type bed, press bed, forme bed, *Am.* form bed)
印版台

18 forme rollers (*Am.* form rollers) (forme-inking, *Am.* forminking, rollers)
触版墨滚（水滚）

19 inking unit (inker unit) for distributing the ink (printing ink)
散墨用的著墨装置

20 **stop-cylinder press** (stop-cylinder machine)
停迴转印刷机

21 feed table (feed board)
给纸台（板）

22 feeder mechanism (feeding apparatus, feeder)
给纸机械（给纸装备,给纸机）

23 pile of unprinted paper (blank paper, unprinted sheets, blank sheets)
未印刷之纸堆,空白纸堆

24 guard for the sheet feeder (feeder)
给纸机护板

25 pile of printed paper (printed sheets)
已印好之纸堆

26 control mechanism
控制装置

27 forme rollers (*Am.* form rollers) (forme-inking, *Am.* forminking, rollers)
触版墨滚（水滚）

28 inking unit (inker unit)
着墨装置

29 **[Heidelberg] platen press** (platen machine, platen)
海德堡圆盘机

30 feed table (feed board) with pile of unprinted paper (blank paper, unprinted sheets, blank sheets)
具未印刷纸堆的给纸台

31 delivery table
收纸台

32 starting and stopping lever
起动杆（手柄）与停止杆

33 delivery blower
收纸吹风器

34 spray gun (sprayer)
喷枪

35 air pump for vacuum and air blasts
真空和吹气用之气泵

36 **locked-up forme** (*Am.* form)
装版（组版）装妥待印之活版印刷版

37 type (type matter, matter)
铅字（铅字材料）

38 chase
排版框

39 quoin
紧版楔子

40 length of furniture
活版填料之长度

41 **rotary letterpress press** (rotary letterpress machine, web-fed letterpress machine) for newspapers of up to 16 pages
适用於 16 页报纸用之凸版轮转印刷机

42 slitters for dividing the width of the web
卷筒纸之宽度分切器

43 web
卷筒纸（滚筒纸）

44 impression cylinder
压印滚筒

45 jockey roller (compensating roller, compensator, tension roller)
操作滚轮（补偿滚轮,补偿器,张力滚轮）

46 roll of paper
卷筒纸

47 automatic brake
自动制动器

48 first printing unit
正面印刷装置（第一面印刷装置）

49 perfecting unit
双面印刷装置

50 inking unit (inker unit)
著墨装置

51 plate cylinder
印版滚筒

52 second printing unit
反面印刷装置（第二面印刷装置）

53 former
折页三角板

54 tachometer with sheet count
具计纸器之转速器

55 folder (folder unit)
折页机

56 folded newspaper
已折叠好之报纸

57 **inking unit** (inker unit) for the rotary press (web-fed press) [section]
轮转（卷筒纸）印刷机之著墨装置[图]

58 web
卷筒纸

59 impression cylinder
压印滚筒

60 plate cylinder
印版滚筒

61 forme rollers (*Am.* form rollers) (forme-inking, *Am.* forminking, rollers)
触版墨滚（着墨滚）

62 distributing rollers (distributing rollers, distributors)
散墨滚（分布滚,匀墨滚）

63 lifter roller (ductor, ductor roller)
升墨滚（给水滚,给墨滚）

64 duct roller (fountain roller, fountain roller)
墨槽导滚（给水滚或给墨滚）

65 ink duct (ink fountain)
油墨槽,墨斗

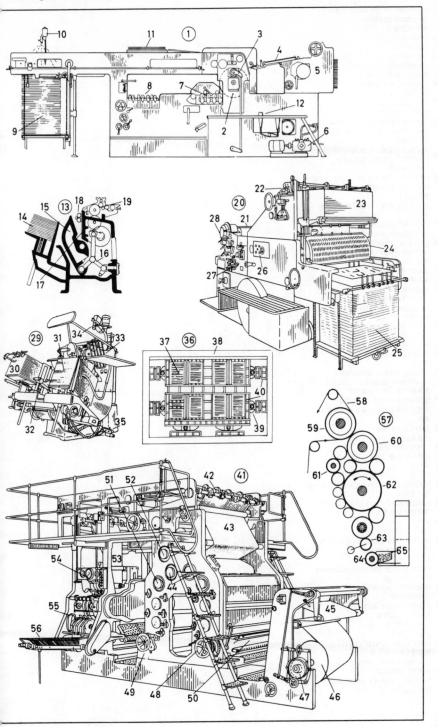

182 Photogravure (Gravure Printing, Intaglio Printing)

1 exposure of the carbon tissue
(pigment paper)
碳素纸之曝光（颜料纸）

2 vacuum frame
真空晒版框

3 exposing lamp, a bank of
quartzhalogen lamps
曝光灯，石英卤素排灯

4 point source lamp
点光源灯

5 heat extractor
抽热器，散热器

6 carbon tissue transfer machine
(laydown machine, laying
machine)
碳素纸之转版机（过版机）凹版过版机

7 polished copper cylinder
抛光的铜滚筒

8 rubber roller for pressing on the
printed carbon tissue (pigment
paper)
压在印过碳素纸上之橡皮滚轮（颜料
纸）

9 cylinder-processing machine
滚筒式显影机（滚筒式版面冲洗机）

10 gravure cylinder coated with
carbon tissue (pigment paper)
著碳素纸之凹印滚筒

11 developing tank
显影槽

12 staging
护膜处理或分段腐蚀

13 developed cylinder
显影滚筒

14 retoucher painting out (stopping
out)
修版（局部描胶，局部涂保护剂）

15 etching machine
腐蚀机

16 etching tank with etching
solution (etchant, mordant)
装有腐蚀液（剂）之腐蚀槽

17 printed gravure cylinder
印过之凹版滚筒（已具线划之凹版滚
筒）

18 gravure etcher
凹版腐蚀工

19 calculator dial
计算器标度盘

20 timer
计时器

21 revising (correcting) the cylinder
修正滚筒架

22 etched gravure cylinder
腐蚀过之凹版滚筒

23 ledge
台板

24 multicolour (Am. multicolor)
rotogravure press
彩色轮转凹版印刷机

25 exhaust pipe for solvent fumes
溶剂气体排出管

26 reversible printing unit
反转印刷单位

27 folder (folder unit)
折页机（折页装置）

28 control desk
控制台，操纵台

29 newspaper delivery unit
报纸递（收）纸装置

30 conveyor belt (conveyor)
输纸带（输纸装置）

31 bundled stack of newspapers
捆好之报纸堆

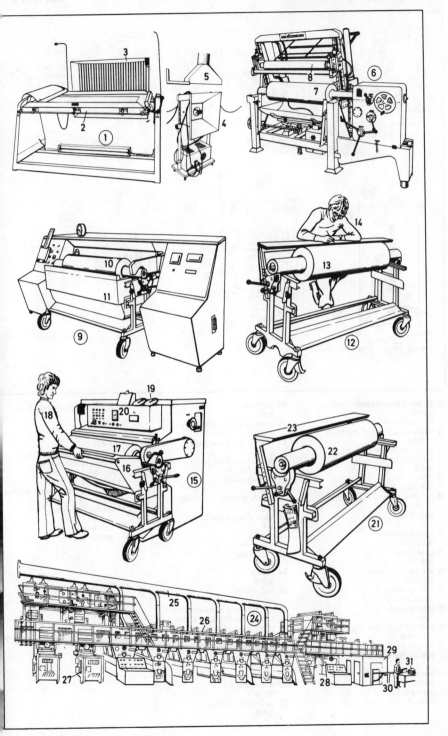

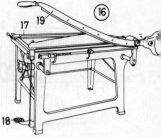

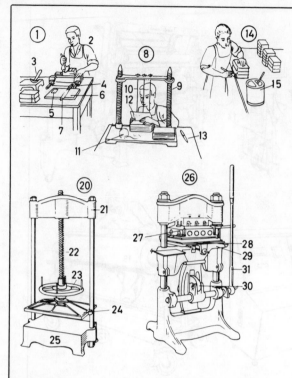

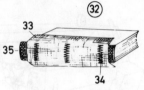

1-35 hand bookbindery (hand bindery)
手工书籍装订所

1 gilding the spine of the book
书背烫金

2 gold finisher (gilder), a bookbinder
烫金工，装订工

3 fillet
饰线用之工具

4 holding press (finishing press)
烫金机（加工机）

5 gold leaf
金箔

6 gold cushion
金箔之垫板

7 gold knife
金箔之切割刀

8 sewing (stitching)
绳线订书

9 sewing frame
手工绳线装订架

10 sewing cord
订书线

11 ball of thread (sewing thread)
订书之线球

12 section (signature)
折叠目，书帖（折叠记号，印好折叠号码待装订之纸张）

13 bookbinder's knife
装订用刀

14 gluing the spine
书背上胶

15 glue pot
胶桶

16 board cutter (guillotine)
纸板裁切机（裁断机）

17 back gauge (*Am.* gage)
后量规

18 clamp with foot pedal
脚踏式之压纸柄

19 cutting blade
切刀

20 standing press, a nipping press
固定机（加压机）

21 head piece (head beam)
顶梁

22 spindle
主轴，导杆

23 handwheel
操纵轮

24 platen
加压盘

25 bed (base)
基座

26 gilding (gold blocking) and embossing press, a hand-lever press; *sim.*: toggle-joint press (toggle-lever press)
烫金压花机，手动式杠杆压力机；类似：肘节压力机

27 heating box
加热箱

28 sliding plate
滑动板

29 embossing platen
压花板

30 toggle action (toggle-joint action)
肘节部分

31 hand lever
手动杆

32 book sewn on gauze (mull, scrim) (unbound book)
缝上纱布之书籍（未装订之书）

33 gauze (mull, scrim)
纱布（书背用布，平纹布，绵织品或织品）

34 sewing (stitching)
线订部分（线装）

35 headband
绑带头，堵头布

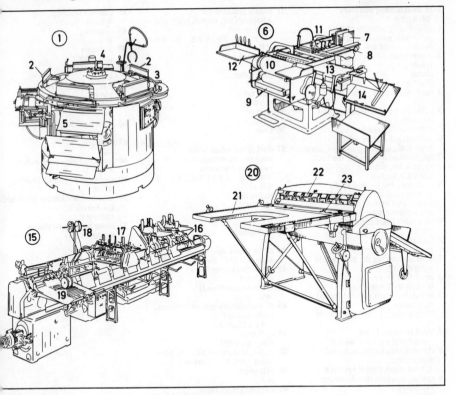

bookbinding machines
籍装订机

hesive binder (perfect binder)
or short runs
版胶装机

anual feed station
工供料台

atoff knife and roughing
ation
刀与铣背机

uing mechanism
胶装置

elivery (book delivery)
书口

ase maker (case-making
achine)
套制作机

oard feed hopper
纸板装置

ckup sucker
纸器

ue tank
水槽

over cylinder
壳滚筒

cker head
纸头

ed table for covering materials
nen, paper, leather]
面材料之供应台〔亚麻布，纸，皮〕

ressing mechanism
压装置

elivery table
书台

15 **gang stitcher** (gathering and
wire-stitching machine, gatherer
and wire stitcher)
穿线装订机（配页铁丝订书机）

16 **sheet feeder** (sheet-feeding
station)
给纸装置

17 **folder-feeding station**
摺页之给纸装置

18 **stitching wire feed mechanism**
订书铁丝之供应装置

19 **delivery table**
收书台

20 **rotary board cutter** (rotary
board-cutting machine)
轮转纸版切割机

21 **feed table with cut-out section**
带裁刀之给纸台

22 **rotary cutter**
旋转切刀

23 **feed guide**
给纸导规

1-35 bookbinding machines
书籍装订机械

1 guillotine (guillotine cutter,
automatic guillotine cutter)
裁纸机（自动裁纸机）

2 control panel
控制盘

3 clamp
压纸装置

4 back gauge (*Am.* gage)
后量规

5 calibrated pressure adjustment
[to clamp]
校准压力调节器"对夹具"

6 illuminated cutting scale
带照明装置之裁切标尺

7 single-hand control for the back
gauge (*Am.* gage)
后量规之单手控制器

8 combined buckle and knife
folding machine (combined
buckle and knife folder)
带扣与刀混和之摺叠机

9 feed table (feed board)
给纸台

10 fold plates
折页板

11 stop for making the buckle fold
使带扣摺叠之停止装置

12 cross fold knives
横向摺叠刀，直角摺叠用之刀

13 belt delivery for parallel-folded
signatures
平行摺叠记号之带式递送装置（纵向摺
叠）

14 third cross fold unit
三次横折装置，第三直角摺叠装置

15 delivery tray for cross-folded
signatures
直角折叠记号用之递送盘（横向摺叠）

16 sewing machine (book-sewing
machine)
绳线装订机

17 spool holder
线轴架

18 thread cop (thread spool)
圆锥型线团（线轴）

19 gauze roll holder (mull roll
holder, scrim roll holder)
纱布卷架（平纹布卷架书背用布）

20 gauze (mull, scrim)
纱布（书背用布，平纹布）

21 needle cylinder with sewing
needles
带缝纫针之针滚筒

22 sewn book
缝好纱布之书芯

23 delivery
收书之装置

24 reciprocating saddle
往复移动之骑马钉鞍座

25 sheet feeder (feeder)
给纸器

26 feed hopper
给纸装置

27 casing-in machine
装套机（上封机）

28 joint and side pasting
attachment
压槽与书脊侧上胶附件

29 blade
刮刀

30 preheater unit
预热装置

31 gluing machine for
wholesurface, stencil, edge, and
strip gluing
（上胶机）全书面，压花板，切口及书
带粘合用之上胶机

32 glue tank
胶水筒

33 glue roller
胶水滚轮

34 feed table
给书装置

35 delivery
收书台

36 **book**
书

37 dust jacket (dust cover,
bookjacket, wrapper), a
publisher's wrapper
书皮（书套，封套）出版社之封套（包
装纸）

38 jacket flap
书套耳页

39 blurb
印於书套耳页之广告

40-42 binding
装订

40 cover (book cover, case)
封面（书籍封面，书壳）

41 spine (backbone, back)
书背，书脊

42 tailband (footband)
书背之装订线

43-47 preliminary matter (prelims,
front matter)
书籍正文前之附页

43 half-title
简略书名（标题）

44 half-title (bastard title, fly title)
半标题，简略书名（简略标题）

45 title page
扉页

46 full title (main title)
全书名（主标题）

47 subtitle
副标题

48 publisher's imprint (imprint)
出版社之印记

49 fly leaf (endpaper, endleaf)
衬页，糊贴页（书籍卷首或卷尾之空白
页）

50 handwritten dedication
手写题辞

51 bookplate (ex libris)
藏书者之印记，藏书签名，书本标签

52 open book
翻开之书

53 page
页

54 fold
折合处

55-58 margin
页边空白处

55 back margin (inside margin,
gutter)
书脊边空白处，订口

56 head margin (upper margin)
（页数上端）空白处上边空白

57 fore edge margin (outside
margin, fore edge)
（页数前端）空白处，前边空白

58 tail margin (foot margin, tail,
foot)
（页数下端）空白处，下边空白

59 type area
版面

60 chapter heading
章节标题

61 asterisk
星号

62 footnote
注脚，脚注

63 page number
页数

64 double-column page
双栏页

65 column
栏

66 running title (running head)
栏外标题

67 caption
标题

68 marginal note (side note)
旁注

69 signature (signatue code)
摺叠符号

70 attached bookmark (attached
bookmarker)
贴付於书上之书签

71 loose bookmark (loose
bookmarker)
活书签

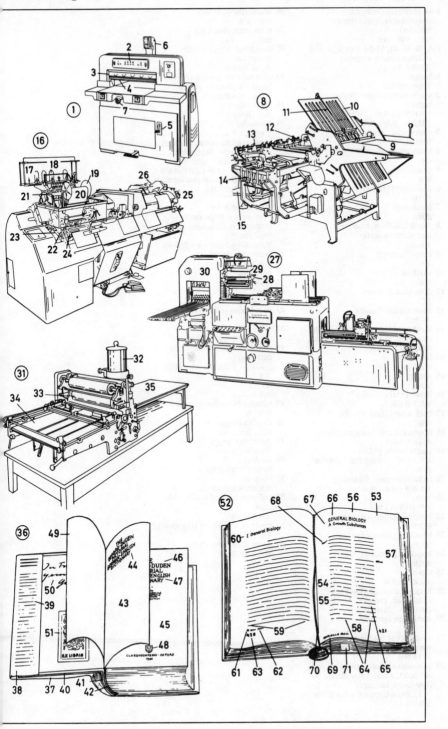

1-54 carriages (vehicles, conveyances, horse-drawn vehicles)
马车（车辆，马车）

1-3, 26-39, 45, 51-54 carriages and coaches (coach wagons)
马车及轿式大马车

1 berlin
有篷的四轮马车

2 waggonette (*larger*: brake, break)
（有相等两排纵座的）四轮游览马车
（较大的：四轮大马车）

3 coupé; *sim.*: brougham
双座轿式四轮马车

4 front wheel
前轮

5 coach body
车身

6 dashboard (splashboard)
挡泥板

7 footboard
踏脚板

8 coach box (box, coachman's seat, driver's seat)
车夫座位

9 lamp (lantern)
车灯

10 window
车窗

11 door (coach door)
车门

12 door handle (handle)
车门把手

13 footboard (carriage step, coach step, step, footpiece)
踏脚板（上下车踏板）

14 fixed top
固定车顶（车篷）

15 spring
弹簧

16 brake (brake block)
刹车（刹车块）

17 back wheel (rear wheel)
后轮

18 dogcart, a one-horse carriage
单马双轮小马车

19 shafts (thills, poles)
车杠，车辕（马车的杠和辕，马车的辕杆）

20 lackey (lacquey, footman)
男仆跟班（侍者，随从）

21 livery
（男仆所穿的）制服

22 braided (gallooned) collar
镶边衣领

23 braided (gallooned) coat
镶边外套

24 braided (gallooned) sleeve
镶边袖口

25 top hat
大礼帽，高顶帽

26 hackney carriage (hackney coach, cab, growler, *Am.* hack)
出租马车，二马四轮马车

27 stableman (groom)
马夫

28 coach horse (carriage horse, cab horse, thill horse, thiller)
拉马车的马

29 hansom cab (hansom), a cabriolet, a one-horse chaise (one-horse carriage)
一马二轮双座有盖小马车（车夫座位为车篷后方）

30 shafts (thills, poles)
车杠，车辕

31 reins (rein, *Am.* line)
缰绳

32 coachman (driver) with inverness
著长披肩的车夫

33 covered char-a-banc (brake, break), a pleasure vehicle
有车篷的长形游览马车

34 gig (chaise)
单马二轮马车

35 barouche
一种四轮大马车

36 landau, a two-horse carriage; *sim.*: landaulet, landaulette
四轮有顶篷的马车；类似：小型之 landau 马车（二人乘坐之四轮马车）

37 omnibus (horse-drawn omnibus)
公共马车（马拉交通车）

38 phaeton
轻快的四轮敞篷马车

39 Continental stagecoach (mailcoach, diligence); *also*: road coach
欧式公共马车（邮政马车，公共马车）

40 mailcoach driver
邮政马车夫

41 posthorn
马车喇叭

42 hood
可摺叠车篷

43 post horses (relay horses, relays)
驿马

44 tilbury
双轮轻便马车（供二人乘坐）

45 troika (Russian three-horse carriage)
三头马车，三马并拉的马车（俄国三马马车）

46 leader
先导马

47 wheeler (wheelhorse, pole horse)
后马，辕马

48 English buggy
英式二轮单座马车

49 American buggy
美式四轮单座马车

50 tandem
两马前后纵驾的两轮马车

51 vis-a-vis
有面对面座位的马车

52 collapsible hood (collapsible top)
可摺叠的车篷

53 mailcoach (English stagecoach)
邮政马车（英国公共马车）

54 covered (closed) chaise
箱式四轮轻便马车

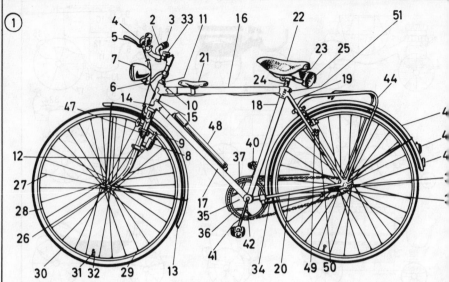

1 bicycle (cycle, *coll.* bike, *Am.* wheel), a gent's bicycle, a touring bicycle (touring cycle, roadster)
脚踏车，自行车
2 handlebar (handlebars), a touring cycle handlebar
车把（手），旅行自行车车把
3 handlebar grip (handgrip, grip)
车把（手）握套
4 bicycle bell
车铃
5 hand brake (front brake), a rim brake
手刹车（前刹车），轮缘刹车
6 lamp bracket
灯架
7 headlamp (bicycle lamp)
前灯（脚踏车灯）
8 dynamo
磨电机
9 pulley
磨电机滑轮
10-12 front forks
前叉
10 handlebar stem
车把（轴）主干
11 steering head
转向头
12 fork blades (fork ends)
前叉脚（叉端头）
13 front mudguard (*Am.* front fender)
前挡泥板
14-20 bicycle frame
车架
14 steering tube (fork column)
转向管（前叉立柱）
15 head badge
车头标记
16 crossbar (top tube)
车架横杆
17 down tube
下管

18 seat tube
座管
19 seat stays
座垫支柱管，立叉
20 chain stays
链条支柱管，平叉
21 child's seat (child carrier seat)
小孩的座位
22 bicycle saddle
鞍座
23 saddle springs
鞍座弹簧
24 seat pillar
鞍座支柱
25 saddle bag (tool bag)
鞍座袋（工具袋）
26-32 wheel (front wheel)
前轮
26 hub
轮毂
27 spoke
轮辐（辐条）
28 rim (wheel rim)
胎环，钢圈
29 spoke nipple (spoke flange, spoke end)
轮辐螺纹套管（轮辐凸缘，轮辐端）
30 tyres (*Am.* tires) (tyre, pneumatic tyre, high-pressure tyre); *inside*: tube (inner tube), *outside*: tyre (outer case, cover)
轮胎（打气轮胎，高压轮胎）；内：内胎；外：外胎
31 valve a tube valve with valve tube or a patent valve with ball
气门，带气门管的管阀或带浮球的特制气门阀
32 valve sealing cap
气门封帽
33 bicycle speedometer with milometer
带计转器自行车速率计
34 kick stand (prop stand)
偏支车架（支柱架）

35-42 bicycle drive (chain drive)
自行车转动装置（链条转动装置）
35-39 chain transmission
链条转动
35 chain wheel
链轮
36 chain, a roller chain
链条，滚轮链条
37 chain guard
链罩（盖）
38 sprocket wheel (sprocket)
链轮
39 wing nut (fly nut, butterfly nut)
翼形螺帽
40 pedal
踏板
41 crank
（踏板）曲柄
42 bottom bracket bearing
底托架轴承，中轴
43 rear mudguard (*Am.* rear fender)
后挡泥板
44 luggage carrier (carrier)
（载）带物架
45 reflector
反光镜
46 rear light (rear lamp)
后灯
47 footrest
搁脚板
48 bicycle pump
自行车气筒
49 bicycle lock, a wheel lock
车锁
50 patent key
专用钥匙
51 cycle serial number (factory number, frame number)
自行车号码（工厂号码，车架号码）

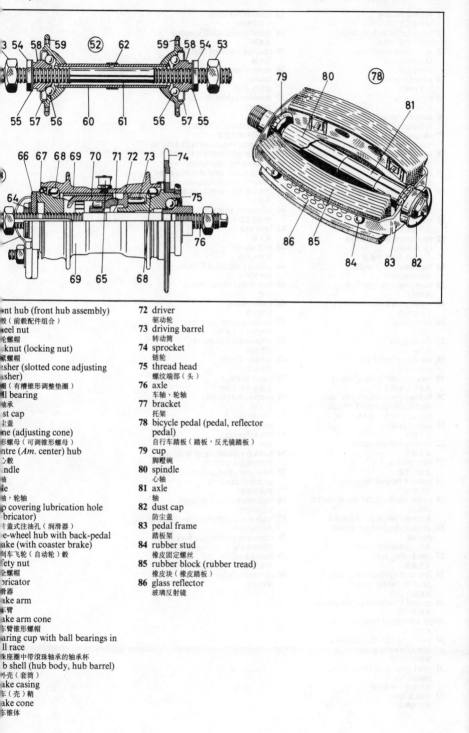

nt hub (front hub assembly)
毂（前毂配件组合）
eel nut
轮螺帽
knut (locking nut)
紧螺帽
sher (slotted cone adjusting
asher)
圈（有槽锥形调整垫圈）
l bearing
轴承
t cap
上盖
ne (adjusting cone)
形螺母（可调锥形螺母）
ntre (*Am.* center) hub
心毂
ndle
轴
le
轴、轮轴
p covering lubrication hole
bricator)
片盖式注油孔（润滑器）
e-wheel hub with back-pedal
ake (with coaster brake)
刹车飞轮（自动闸）毂
fety nut
全螺帽
oricator
滑器
ake arm
车臂
ake arm cone
车臂锥形螺帽
aring cup with ball bearings in
ll race
珠座圈中带滚珠轴承的轴承杯
b shell (hub body, hub barrel)
外壳（套筒）
ake casing
车（壳）鞘
ake cone
车锥体

72 driver
   驱动轮
73 driving barrel
   转动筒
74 sprocket
   链轮
75 thread head
   螺纹端部（头）
76 axle
   车轴、轮轴
77 bracket
   托架
78 bicycle pedal (pedal, reflector
   pedal)
   自行车踏板（踏板，反光镜踏板）
79 cup
   脚蹬碗
80 spindle
   心轴
81 axle
   轴
82 dust cap
   防尘盖
83 pedal frame
   踏板架
84 rubber stud
   橡皮固定螺丝
85 rubber block (rubber tread)
   橡皮块（橡皮踏板）
86 glass reflector
   玻璃反射镜

1 folding bicycle
可摺自行车
2 hinge (*also*: locking lever)
铰接(亦称:锁杆)
3 adjustable handlebar (handlebars)
可调整把手
4 adjustable saddle
可调整鞍座
5 stabilizers
稳定轮
6 motor-assisted bicycle
马达助动的自行车,摩托车
7 air-cooled two-stroke engine
气冷式二冲程发动机(引擎)
8 telescopic forks
可伸缩的筒式前叉
9 tubular frame
圆管车架
10 fuel tank (petrol tank, *Am.* gasoline tank)
燃料槽(油槽)油箱
11 semi-rise handlebars
半升式车把
12 two-speed gear-change (gearshift)
二速换档(齿轮变速器)
13 high-back polo saddle
高背马球型鞍座
14 swinging-arm rear fork
摆动后叉
15 upswept exhaust
上斜排气管
16 heat shield
遮热板
17 drive chain
传动链
18 crash bar (roll bar)
护杆(滚条)
19 speedometer (*coll.* speedo)
速率计(里程表)
20 battery-powered moped, an electrically-powered vehicle
电池动力的摩拖车电动车的一种
21 swivel saddle
活动鞍座
22 battery compartment
蓄电池箱
23 wire basket
金属丝货篮
24 touring moped (moped)
旅行摩拖车
25 pedal crank (pedal drive, starter pedal)
踏板曲柄(脚蹬驱动,起动踏板)
26 single-cylinder two-stroke engine
单缸二冲程发动机(引擎)
27 spark-plug cap
火星塞盖
28 fuel tank (petrol tank, *Am.* gasoline tank)
燃料箱,油箱
29 moped headlamp (front lamp)
摩托车前灯
30-35 handlebar fittings
车把配件
30 twist grip throttle control (throttle twist grip)
握转油门控制
31 twist grip (gear-change, gearshift)
换档握把(变换齿轮)
32 clutch lever
离合器握柄

33 hand brake lever
手刹车握柄
34 speedometer (*coll.* speedo)
速率器
35 rear-view mirror (mirror)
后视镜
36 front wheel drum brake (drum brake)
前轮鼓式刹车
37 Bowden cables (brake cables)
包登式刹车索
38 stop and tail light unit
刹车灯和尾灯装置
39 light motorcycle with kickstarter
带脚蹬起动器的轻型摩托车
40 housing for instruments with speedometer and electronic rev counter (revolution counter)
带速率器和电子转速计(转速表)的仪表盘
41 telescopic shock absorber
伸缩式避震器
42 twin seat
双人座
43 kickstarter
脚蹬起动器
44 pillion footrest, a footrest
后座搁脚板
45 handlebar (handlebars)
车把
46 chain guard
护链装置
47 motor scooter (scooter)
小轮摩托车(速克达)
48 removable side panel
可拆侧板
49 tubular frame
管制车架
50 metal fairings
金属整流罩(减阻物)
51 prop stand (stand)
支车架
52 foot brake
脚刹车
53 horn (hooter)
喇叭
54 hook for handbag or briefcase
手提包或公文包的挂钩
55 foot gear-change control (foot gearshift control)
脚换档控制
56 high-riser; *sim.*: Chopper
高把自行车
57 high-rise handlebar (handlebars)
高把自行车的把手
58 imitation motorcycle fork
模仿摩托车前叉
59 banana saddle
香蕉型鞍座
60 chrome bracket
镀铬托架

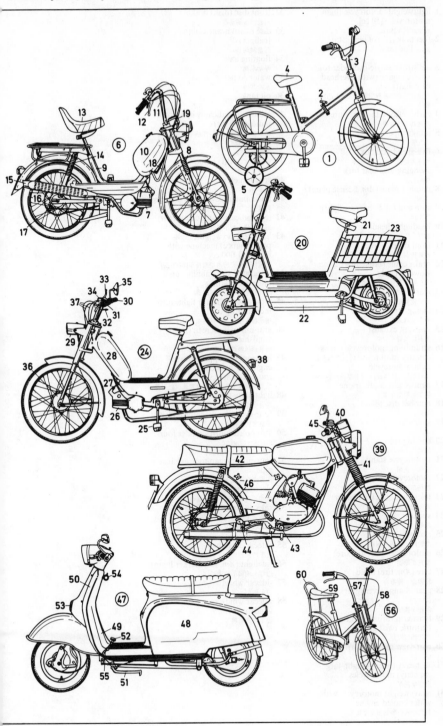

1 lightweight motorcycle (light motorcycle) [50 cc]
轻型摩托车[50 cc]

2 fuel tank (petrol tank, *Am.* gasoline tank)
油箱

3 air-stroke single-cyclinder four-stroke engine (with overhead camshaft)
气冷式单缸四冲程引擎（带顶上凸轮轴）

4 carburettor (*Am.* carbouretor)
汽化器（化油器）

5 intake pipe
进气管

6 five-speed gearbox
五速齿轮箱

7 swinging-arm rear fork
摆动后叉

8 number plate (*Am.* license plate)
牌照

9 stop and tail light (rear light)
停车尾灯

10 headlight (headlamp)
前灯

11 front drum brake
前鼓轮刹车

12 brake cable (brake line), a Bowden cable
刹车线，包登式刹车线

13 rear drum brake
后鼓轮刹车

14 racing-style twin seat
赛车型双人座

15 upswept exhaust
上斜排气管

16 scrambling motorcycle (cross-country motorcycle) [125 cc], a light motorcycle
越野摩托车[125 cc]，轻型摩托车的一种

17 lightweight cradle frame
轻型炮架型车架

18 number disc (disk)
号码盘

19 solo seat
单人座

20 cooling robs
散热片，冷却肋

21 motorcycle stand
摩托车支架

22 motorcycle shain
摩托车链条

23 telescopic shock absorber
伸缩避震器

24 spokes
轮辐

25 rim (wheel rim)
（轮网，轮圈）钢圈

26 motorcycle tyre (*Am.* tire)
摩托车轮胎

27 tyre (*Am.* tire) tread
轮胎面，轮箍面

28 gear-change lever (gearshift lever)
齿轮变换杆

29 twist grip throttle control (throttle twist grip)
握转油门控制

30 rear-view mirror (mirror)
后视镜

31-58 heavy (heavyweight, large-capacity) motorcycles
重型摩托车

31 heavyweight motorcycle with water-cooled engine
具水冷式引擎的重型摩托车

32 front disc (disk) brake
前轮圆盘制动器

33 disc (disk) brake calliper (caliper)
圆盘制动卡

34 floating axle
浮动车轴

35 water cooler
水冷却器

36 oil tank
油箱

37 indicator (indicator light, turn indicator light)
指示器（指示灯，转向指示灯）

38 kickstarter
脚蹬起动器

39 water-cooled engine
水冷式引擎

40 speedometer
速率计

41 rev counter (revolution counter)
转速表

42 rear indicator (indicator light)
后方向灯（指示灯）

43 heavy (heavyweight, high-performance) machine with fairing [1 000 cc]
带流线形外壳的重型摩托车[1 000 cc]

44 integrated streamlining, an integrated fairing
流线型车罩，整体减阻罩

45 indicator (indicator light, turn indicator light)
指示器（指示灯，转向指示灯）

46 anti-mist windscreen (*Am.* windshield)
防雾挡风玻璃

47 horizontally-opposed twin engine with cardan transmission
带方向转动装置的水平对置式双缸引擎

48 light alloy wheel
轻合金车轮

49 four-cyclinder machine [400 cc]
四缸摩托车[400 cc]

50 air-cooled four-cyclinder four-stroke engine
气冷式四缸四冲程引擎

51 four-pipe megaphone exhaust pipe
四管喇叭筒式排气管

52 electric starter button
电动发动器按钮，起动器电钮

53 sidecar machine
带侧边车的摩托车

54 sidecar body
边车车身

55 sidecar crash bar
边车防护杆

56 sidelight (*Am.* sidemarker lamp)
边灯（侧面车种表示灯）

57 sidecar wheel
边车轮

58 sidecar windscreen (*Am.* windshield)
边车挡风玻璃

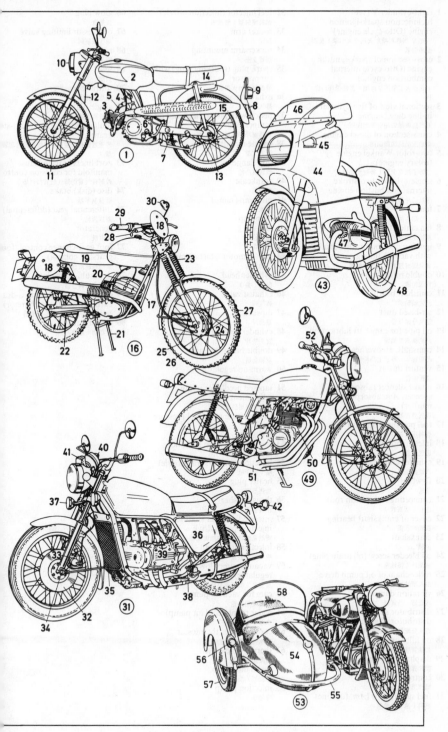

1 eight-cylinder V (vee)
fuelinjection spark-ignition
engine (Otto-cycle engine)
八缸 V 型燃料喷射火花点火擎（奥图
循环引擎）

2 cross-section of spark-ignition
engine (Otto-cycle internal
combustion engine)
火花点火引擎的剖面图（奥图循环内燃
机）

3 sectional view of five-cylinder
in-line diesel engine
五汽缸单排柴油引擎剖面图

4 cross-section of diesel engine
柴油发动机的剖面图

5 two-rotor Wankel engine
(rotary engine)
二转子汪克引擎（旋风发动机）

6 single-cylinder two-stroke
internal combustion engine
单缸二冲程内燃机

7 fan
（冷却）风扇

8 fan clutch for viscous drive
粘性驱动用的风扇离合器

9 ignition distributor (distributor)
with vacuum timing control
真空定时控制的点火分配器

10 double roller chain
双滚轮链

11 camshaft bearing
凸轮轴轴承

12 air-bleed duct
空气分供导管

13 oil pipe for camshaft lubrication
凸轮轴润滑油管

14 camshaft, an overhead camshaft
凸轮轴，一种顶上凸轮轴

15 venturi throat
文氏喉管

16 intake silencer (absorption
silencer, *Am.* absorption
muffler)
吸气消音器

17 fuel pressure regulator
燃料压力调节器

18 inlet manifold
进气歧管

19 cylinder crankcase
汽缸曲轴箱

20 flywheel
飞轮

21 connecting rod (piston rod)
连杆（活塞杆）

22 cover of crankshaft bearing
曲轴轴承盖

23 crankshaft
曲轴

24 oil bleeder screw (oil drain plug)
放油栓（排油塞）

25 roller chain of oil pump drive
油泵驱动的滚轮链

26 vibration damper
减震器，消震器

27 distributor shaft for the ignition
distributor (distributor)
点火分配器用的分配器轴

28 oil filler neck
加油管嘴，油填注颈

29 diaphragm spring
膜片弹簧

30 control linkage
操作用的连杆组

31 fuel supply pipe (*Am.* fuel line)
燃料（油）供给管

32 fuel injector (injection nozzle)
燃料喷射器（喷油咀）

33 rocker arm
摇臂

34 rocker arm mounting
摇臂支座

35 spark plug (sparking plug) with
suppressor
带控制器的火星塞

36 exhaust manifold
排气歧管

37 piston with piston rings and oil
scraper ring
带活塞环和刮油环的活塞

38 engine mounting
引擎支架

39 dog flange (dog)
牵转具凸轮

40 crankcase
曲轴箱

41 oil sump (sump)
油池

42 oil pump
油泵

43 oil filter
滤油器

44 starter motor (starting motor)
起动马达

45 cylinder head
缸盖（头）

46 exhaust valve
排气阀

47 dipstick
量油尺

48 cylinder head gasket
缸头垫片

49 double bushing chain
双轴套链

50 warm-up regulator
温车运转调整器

51 tapered needle for idling
adjustment
空转调整用的锥形针

52 fuel pressure pipe (fuel pressure
line)
燃料压力管

53 fuel leak line (drip fuel line)
漏油管（滴油管）

54 injection nozzle (spray nozzle)
喷（油）咀

55 heater plug
加热器塞

56 thrust washer
止推垫圈

57 intermediate gear shaft for the
injection pump drive
喷油泵驱动用的中间齿轮轴

58 injection timer unit
喷油定时装置

59 vacuum pump (low-pressure
regulator)
真空泵（低压调整器）

60 cam for vacuum pump
真空泵用凸轮

61 water pump (coolant pump)
水泵（冷却剂泵）

62 cooling water thermostat
冷水恒温器

63 thermo time switch
温度定时开关

64 fuel hand pump
手动燃（油）料泵

65 injection pump
喷油泵

66 glow plug
预热塞

67 oil pressur limiting valve
油压限制阀

68 rotor
转子

69 seal
封垫

70 torque converter
扭矩变速器

71 single-plate clutch
单片离合器

72 multi-speed gearing (multi-step
gearing)
多速齿轮转动装置（多级齿轮转动装
置）

73 port liners in the exhaust
manifold for emission control
控制排气量的排气歧管口衬垫

74 disc (disk) brake
圆盘刹车器

75 differential gear (differential)
差速齿轮

76 generator
发电机

77 foot gear-change control (foot
gearshift control)
换档控制踏板

78 dry multi-plate clutch
乾式多片离合器

79 cross-draught (*Am.* cross-draft)
carburettor (*Am.* carburetor)
交叉通气式的汽化器（化油器）

80 cooling ribs
冷却肋，散热片

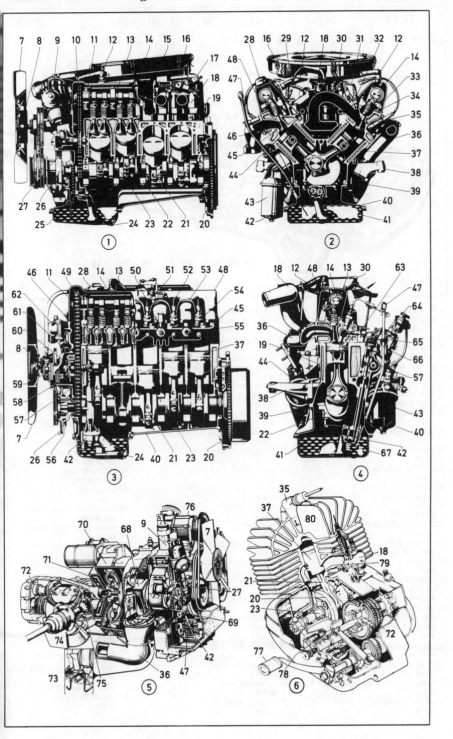

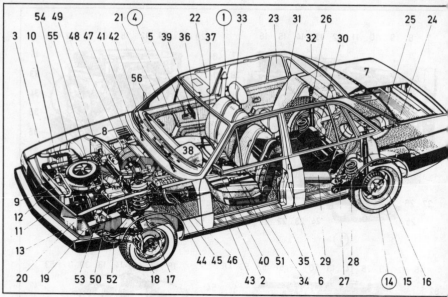

1-56 motor car (car, *Am.* automobile, auto), a passenger vehicle
小轿车，一种客车
1 monocoque body (unitary body)
单壳车体（单位车体）
2 chassis, the understructure of the body
底盘，车身底架
3 front wing (*Am.* front fender)
前翼（前挡板）
4 car door
车门
5 door handle
车门把手
6 door lock
车门锁
7 boot lid (*Am.* trunk lid)
行李箱盖
8 bonnet (*Am.* hood)
引擎盖（发动机盖）
9 radiator
散热器（水箱）
10 cooling water pipe
冷却水管
11 radiator grill
散热器护栅，水箱饰筐
12 badging
标记
13 rubber-covered front bumper (*Am.* front fender)
用塑胶橡皮包住的前保险杆[前档板]
14 car wheel, a disc (disk) wheel
车轮，圆盘式车轮
15 car tyre (*Am.* automobile tire)
车胎
16 rim (wheel rim)
轮辋，钢圈
17-18 disc (disk) brake
制动盘（盘式刹车）
17 brake disc (disk) (braking disc)
制动盘，刹车盘
18 calliper (caliper)
刹车夹

19 front indicator light (front turn indicator light)
前指示灯（前转向指示灯）
20 headlight (headlamp) with main beam (high beam), dipped beam (low beam), sidelight (side lamp, *Am.* sidemarker lamp)
有强光，弱光，边灯的前灯（大灯）
21 windscreen (*Am.* windshield), a panoramic windscreen
挡风玻璃，一种广角挡风玻璃
22 crank-operated car window
摇把（曲轴）操纵的车窗
23 quarter light (quarter vent)
三角窗（边窗）
24 boot(*Am.* trunk)
行李箱
25 spare wheel
备用车轮
26 damper (shock absorber)
减震器
27 trailing arm
从动臂
28 coil spring
螺旋弹簧
29 silencer (*Am.* muffler)
消音器
30 automatic ventilation system
自动通风系统
31 rear seats
后座
32 rear window
后窗
33 adjustable headrest (head restraint)
可调式座椅头枕
34 driver's seat, a reclining seat
驾驶员座位，倾斜式座位
35 reclining backrest
倾斜靠背
36 passenger seat
乘客座位
37 steering wheel
方向盘

38 centre (*Am.* center) console containing speedometer (*coll.* speedo), revolution counter (rev counter, tachometer), clo fuel gauge (*Am.* gage), water temperature gauge, oil temperature gauge
中心仪表台，包括：速率表（里程表），转速表，钟，油量表，水温表，油温表
39 inside rear-view mirror
车内后视镜
40 left-hand wing mirror
左侧翼后视镜
41 windscreen wiper (*Am.* windshield wiper)
挡风玻璃的雨刷
42 defroster vents
除霜器通气孔
43 carpeting
车垫
44 clutch pedal (*coll.* clutch)
离合器踏板
45 brake pedal (*coll.* brake)
刹车踏板
46 accelerator pedal (*coll.* accelerator)
油门踏板
47 inlet vent
进气口，通风口
48 blower fan
风扇
49 brake fluid reservoir
刹车油贮存器
50 battery
蓄电瓶
51 exhaust pipe
排气管
52 front running gear with front wheel drive
以前轮驱动的前行齿轮
53 engine mounting
引擎架

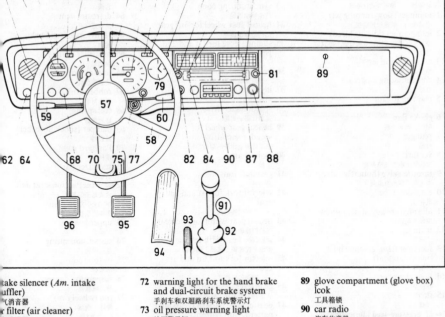

...ake silencer (*Am.* intake
...uffler)
气消音器
... filter (air cleaner)
气滤清器
...ght-hand wing mirror
...侧后视镜
... dashboard (fascia panel)
...表板
...ntrolled-collapse steering
...lumn
...伸缩转向柱
...eering wheel spoke
...向盘轮辐
...dicator and dimming switch
...向指示灯和前灯减光开关
...per/washer switch and horn
...刷/冲洗器开关和喇叭按钮
...le window blower
...窗送风装置
...delight, headlight, and parking
...ght switch
...灯、大灯和停车灯开关
...g lamp warning light
...灯警示灯
...g headlamp and rear lamp
...witch
...雾灯和后雾灯开关
...el gauge (*Am.* gage)
...油表，油量表
...ater tempertaure gauge (*Am.*
...age)
...温表
...arning light for rear fog lamp
...雾灯警示灯号
...azard flasher switch
...故或危险闪光灯开关
...ain beam warning light
...光灯警示灯号
...ectric rev counter (revolution
...ounter)
...动转数表
...el warning light
...量警示灯

72 warning light for the hand brake
and dual-circuit brake system
手刹车和双迴路刹车系统警示灯
73 oil pressure warning light
油压警示灯
74 speedometer (*coll.* speedo) with
trip mileage recorder
带行驶里程记录的速率表
75 starter and steering look
起动器和转向角限制器
76 warning lights for turn
indicators and hazard flashers
转向指示灯和危险闪光灯的警示灯号
77 switch for the courtesy light and
reset button for the trip mileage
recorder
(车门打开后即自动开灯的)车箱开关和
里程纪录器归零按钮
78 ammeter
电流表
79 electric clock
电钟
80 warning light for heated rear
window
后窗加温警示灯
81 switch for the leg space
ventilation
下部通风开关
82 rear window heating switch
后窗加温开关
83 ventilation switch
通风开关
84 temperature regulator
温度调节器
85 fresh-air inlet and control
新鲜空气入口及控制
86 fresh-air regulator
新鲜空气调节器
87 warm-air regulator
暖气调节器
88 cigar lighter
香烟点火器

89 glove compartment (glove box)
lcok
工具箱锁
90 car radio
汽车收音机
91 gear lever (gearshift lever,
floor-type gear-change)
变速杆(排档杆，落地式变速杆)
92 leather gaiter
防尘皮套
93 hand brake lever
手刹车杆
94 accelerator pedal
油门踏板
95 brake pedal
刹车踏板
96 clutch pedal
离合器踏板

1-15 carburettor (*Am.* carburetor), a down-draught (*Am.* downdraft) carburettor
化油器，一种下吸式化油器

1 idling jet (slow-running jet)
空转喷咀（低速运转喷咀）

2 idling air jet (idle air bleed)
空转空气喷咀（空转空气分供，排放装置）

3 air correction jet
空气调节喷咀

4 compensating airstream
补偿气流

5 main airstream
主气流

6 choke flap
阻气（挡风）板

7 plunger
柱塞

8 venturi
文氏管，喉管，窄颈管

9 throttle valve (butterfly valve)
节流阀（蝶形节流阀）

10 emulsion tube
乳化管

11 idle mixture adjustment screw
空转调整螺丝

12 main jet
主喷咀

13 fuel inlet (*Am.* gasoline inlet) (inlet manifold)
进油孔（进油歧管）

14 float chamber
浮筒室

15 float
浮筒

16-27 pressure-feed lubricating system
压力输送润滑系统

16 oil pump
油泵

17 oil sump
油池，油槽

18 sump filter
油池过滤器

19 oil cooler
油冷却器

20 oil filter
油过滤器

21 main oil gallery (drilled gallery)
主油道

22 crankshaft drilling (crankshaft tributary, crankshaft bleed)
曲轴道（曲轴支管）

23 crankshaft bearing (main bearing)
曲轴轴承（主轴承）

24 camshaft bearing
凸轮轴轴承

25 connecting-rod bearing
连杆轴承

26 gudgeon pin (piston pin)
活塞销

27 bleed
浅放口，排放口

28-47 four-speed synchromesh gearbox
四速同步啮合齿轮箱

28 clutch pedal
离合器踏板

29 crankshaft
曲轴

30 drive shaft (propeller shaft)
驱动轴（驱动轴螺旋浆轴）

31 starting gear ring
起动齿轮圈

32 sliding sleeve for 3rd and 4th gear
三、四档的滑动套筒

33 synchronizing cone
同步驱动锥室

34 helical gear wheel for 3rd gear
三档的螺旋齿轮

35 sliding sleeve for 1st and 2nd gear
一、二档的滑动套筒

36 helical gear wheel for 1st gear
一档的螺旋齿轮

37 lay shaft
副轴

38 speedometer drive
速率计驱动齿轮

39 helical gear wheel for speedometer drive
速率计驱动齿轮的螺旋齿轮

40 main shaft
主轴

41 gearshift rods
换档杆

42 selector fork for 1st and 2nd gear
一、二档的换档叉

43 helical gear wheel for 2nd gear
二档的螺旋齿轮

44 selector head with reverse gear
带倒车齿轮的（选择）换档器头

45 selector fork for 3rd and 4th gear
三、四档的换档叉

46 gear lever (gearshift lever)
变速杆（变速杆，换档杆）

47 gear-change pattern (gearshift pattern, shift pattern)
档位

48-55 disc (disk) brake [assembly]
盘式刹车（制动器）[组件]

48 brake disc (disk) (braking disc)
刹车盘

49 calliper (caliper), a fixed calliper with friction pads
刹车夹，具摩擦垫的固定刹车夹

50 servo cylinder (servo unit)
倍力汽缸（倍力装置）

51 brake shoes
刹车片

52 brake lining
刹车衬

53 outlet to brake line
通向刹车系统出口

54 wheel cylinder
刹车分泵

55 return spring
复位弹簧

56-59 steering gear (worm-and-nut steering gear)
转向齿轮（螺杆螺帽式转向齿轮）

56 steering column
转向机柱

57 worm gear sector
螺杆扇形齿轮

58 steering drop arm
转向垂臂

59 worm
螺杆

60-64 water-controlled heater
水控加热器

60 air intake
进气口

61 heat exchanger (heater box)
热交换器（加热器箱）

62 blower fan
风扇

63 flap valve
舌阀

64 defroster vent
除霜通气孔

65-71 live axle (rigid axle)
动轴（固定轴）

65 propeller shaft
驱动轴

66 trailing arm
前置定位臂

67 rubber bush
橡皮衬套

68 coil spring
螺旋弹簧

69 damper (shock absorber)
减震器

70 Panhard rod
横杆

71 stabilizer bar
稳定杆

72-84 MacPherson strut unit
烛式悬架装置

72 body-fixing plate
车体固定板

73 upper bearing
上轴承

74 suspension spring
悬吊弹簧

75 piston rod
活塞杆

76 suspension damper
悬吊减震器

77 rim (wheel rim)
轮缘，钢圈

78 stub axle
转（向）轴

79 steering arm
转向臂

80 track-rod ball-joint
横杆球关节

81 trailing link arm
前置定位斜臂

82 bump rubber (rubber bondin
缓冲橡胶块（橡胶连接）

83 lower bearing
下轴承

84 lower suspension arm
下悬吊臂

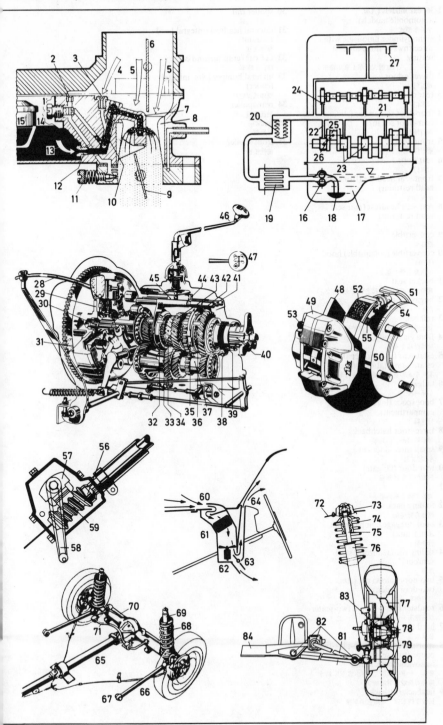

1-36　car models (*Am.* automobile models)
小轿车型式

1 eight-cylinder limousine with three rows of three-abreast seating
三列三座八汽缸的大轿车（豪华轿车）

2 driver's door
司机门

3 rear door
后车门

4 four-door saloon car (*Am.* four-door sedan)
四门轿车

5 front door
前车门

6 rear door
后车门

7 front seat headrest (front seat head restraint)
前座头枕

8 rear seat headrest (rear seat head restraint)
后座头枕

9 convertible
摺篷车

10 convertible (collapsible) hood (top)
可摺叠车顶（篷）

11 bucket seat
箕形座（座板可翻起之座位）

12 buggy (dune buggy)
汽车，小客车（砂土车）

13 roll bar
安全铁杆（架），翻车保护杆

14 fibre glass body
玻璃纤维车身

15 estate car (shooting brake, estate, *Am.* station wagon)
实用车，客货两用轿车（旅行车）

16 tailgate
车尾闸板

17 boot space (luggage compartment)
行李箱

18 three-door hatchback
带后舱口的三门轿车

19 small three-door car
小型三门轿车

20 rear door (tailgate)
后车门（车尾闸板）

21 sill
梁（车体底框的梁）

22 folding back seat
摺叠靠背座椅

23 boot (luggage compartment, *Am.* trunk)
行李箱

24 sliding roof (sunroof, steel sunroof)
滑顶

25 two-door saloon car (*Am.* two-door sedan)
二门轿车

26 roadster (hard-top), a two-seater
双座跑车（金属顶盖）

27 hard top
金属顶盖

28 sporting coupé, a two-plus-two coupé (two-seater with removable back seats)
赛车，一种"二加二"座小客车（两个座位可折成靠背座椅）

29 fastback (liftback)
长坡度的车顶，可掀起的车顶

30 spoiler rim
扰流板边缘

31 integral headrest (integral head restraint)
整体头枕

32 GT car (gran turismo car)
GT 小轿车

33 integral bumper (*Am.* integral fender)
整体式保险杆

34 rear spoiler
后扰流板

35 back
车后部

36 front spoiler
前扰流板

1 light cross-country lorry
(light truck, pickup truck) with
all-wheel drive (four-wheel
drive)
（全）四轮驱动的轻型越野卡车
2 cab (driver's cab)
驾驶座
3 loading platform (body)
载货台（装载台）
4 spare tyre (*Am.* spare tire), a
cross-country tyre
备用轮胎，越野轮胎
5 light lorry (light truck, pickup
truck)
轻型货车（轻型卡车轻便卡车）
6 platform truck
平台卡车
7 medium van
中型有盖卡车
8 sliding side door [for loading
and unloading]
〔装卸货物用的〕滑动侧门
9 minibus
小型公车
10 folding top (sliding roof)
摺叠式车顶（滑顶）
11 rear door
后车门
12 hinged side door
铰链侧门
13 luggage compartment
行李箱
14 passenger seat
乘客座位
15 cab (driver's cab)
驾驶座
16 air inlet
进气口
17 motor coach (coach, bus)
长途客车
18 luggage locker
行李锁柜
19 hand luggage (suitcase, case)
手提行李（皮箱）
20 heavy lorry (heavy truck, heavy
motor truck)
重型卡车
21 tractive unit (tractor, towing
vehicle)
牵引装置（拖车）
22 trailer (drawbar trailer)
拖车（拉杆拖车）
23 swop platform (body)
交换（易）台
24 three-way tipper (three-way
dump truck)
三向倾卸卡车
25 tipping body (dump body)
倾卸车体
26 hydraulic cylinder
液压汽缸
27 supported container platform
支承货柜平台
28 articulated vehicle, a vehicle
tanker
连结车，一种油罐车辆
29 tractive unit (tractor, towing
vehicle)
牵引装置（拖车）
30-33 semi-trailer (skeletal)
半拖车（骨架）
30 tank
油罐
31 turntable
转盘
32 undercarriage
车盘底盘
33 spare wheel
备用车轮
34 midi bus [for short-route town
operations]
中型公车〔短距离市内运输用〕
35 outward-opening doors
向外开的门
36 double-deck bus (double-
decker bus)
双层公共汽车
37 lower deck (lower saloon)
下层
38 upper deck (upper saloon)
上层
39 boarding platform
上车台
40 trolley bus
电车（无轨电车）
41 current collector
集电器
42 trolley (trolley shoe)
触轮
43 overhead wires
架空电线
44 trolley bus trailer
无轨电车拖车
45 pneumatically sprung rubber
connection
气动弹力橡胶连结部分

1-55 agent's garage
(distributor's garage, *Am.*
specialty shop)
代理商修车厂

1-23 diagnostic test bay
诊断试车台，测试场

1 computer
电脑

2 main computer plug
主机插头

3 computer harness (computer cable)
电脑电线

4 switch from automatic to manual
从自动到手动开关

5 slot for program cards
程式卡片插入孔

6 print-out machine (printer)
列表机

7 condition report (data print-out)
条件报告（打出数据）

8 master selector (hand control)
主选择开关（手控）

9 light read-out [green: OK; red: not OK]
灯光显示〔绿：正确；红：错误〕

10 rack for program cards
程式卡片架

11 mains button
电源按钮，主按钮

12 switch for fast readout
快速显示开关

13 firing sequence insert
启动程序输入

14 shelf for used cards
用过的卡片架

15 cable boom
电线吊架

16 oil temperature sensor
油温感应器

17 test equipment for wheel and steering alignment
车轮和转向调整试验设备

18 right-hand optic plate
右边镜片

19 actuating transistors
致动电晶体设备

20 projector switch
聚光灯开关

21 check light for wheel alignment, a row of photocells
车轮定位检查灯，一排光电池

22 check light for steering alignment, a row of photocells
转向调整检查灯，一排光电池

23 power screwdriver
电动螺丝起子

24 beam setter
光束调节器

25 hydraulic lift
液压提升装置

26 adjustable arm of hydraulic lift
液压提升装置的调整臂

27 hydraulic lift pad
液压提升装置台

28 excavation
坑道

29 pressure gauge (*Am.* gage)
压力计

30 grease gun
注油枪

31 odds-and-ends box
零星物品箱

32 wall chart [of spare parts]
〔组零件〕一览表

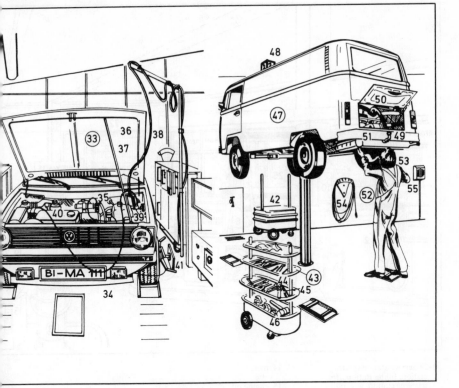

-matic computer test
自动检查
or car (car, *Am.* automobile,
)), a passenger vehicle
车，客车
ne compartment
机（引擎）箱
net (*Am.* hood)
机（引擎）罩
net support (*Am.* hood
port)
机（引擎）罩支柱
puter harness (computer
ne)
电线
n computer socket; *also*:
ti-outlet socket
插座；多出口插座
emperature sensor
感应器
el mirror for visual wheel
steering alignment
车轮定位转向对准用的车轮镜
trolley
推车
ls

act wrench
板手
que wrench
板手
y hammer (roughing-out
mer)
用锤（粗车锤）

47 vehicle under repair, a minibus
修理中心的汽车，小型巴士
48 car location number
车位号码
49 rear engine
后发动机（引擎）
50 tailgate
车尾闸板
51 exhaust system
排气系统
52 exhaust repair
排气系统修理
53 motor car mechanic (motor
vehicle mechanic, *Am.*
automotive mechanic)
汽车修理工人
54 air hose
充气软管
55 intercom
内部通话装置

1-29 service station (petrol station, filling station, *Am.* gasoline station, gas station), a selfservice station
加油站，一种自助加油站

1 petrol (*Am.* gasoline) pump (blending pump) for regular and premium grade petrol (*Am.* gasoline (*sim.:* for derv)
用於普通和高级汽油的油泵（混合泵）

2 hose (petrol pump, *Am.* gasoline pump, hose)
软管（油泵的软管）

3 nozzle
喷咀

4 cash readout
现金数目显示（器）

5 volume read-out
容量显示（器）

6 price display
价格显示

7 indicator light
指示灯

8 driver using self-service petrol pump (*Am.* gasoline pump)
使用自助油泵的驾驶人

9 fire extinguisher
灭火器

10 paper-towel dispenser
擦手纸分配器

11 paper towel
擦手纸

12 litter receptacle
废物箱，垃圾箱

13 two-stroke blending pump
二冲程混合泵

14 meter
量器

15 engine oil
机油

16 oil can
油壶

17 tyre pressure gauge (*Am.* tire pressure gage)
轮胎压力计

18 air hose
空气软管

19 static air tank
固定贮气槽（罐）

20 pressure gauge (*Am.* gage) (manometer)
压力计

21 air filler neck
充气咀

22 repair bay (repair shop)
修理间

23 car-wash hose, a hose (hosepipe)
洗车软管

24 accessory shop
附属修理间

25 petrol can (*Am.* gasoline can)
油罐

26 rain cape
雨篷

27 car tyres (*Am.* automobile tires)
汽车轮胎

28 car accessories
汽车附件

29 cash desk (console)
付款台

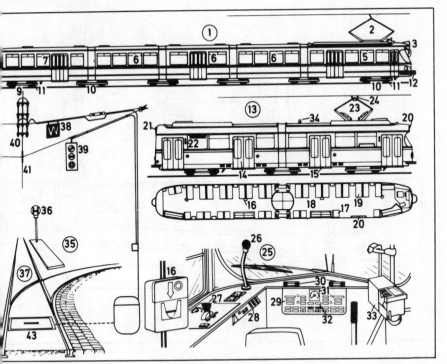

15	step
	车梯
16	ticket-cancelling machine
	轧票机
17	single seat
	一人座位
18	standing room portion
	立位部分
19	double seat
	双人座位
20	route (number) and destination sign
	行车路线（号码）和终点站标志
21	route sign (number sign)
	路线标志（号码标志）
22	indicator (indicator light)
	指示器（指示灯）
23	pantograph (current collector)
	缩放机（集电器）
24	carbon or aluminium (*Am.* aluminum) alloy trolley shoes
	碳素或铝合金的触轮滑块
25	driver's position
	驾驶室
26	microphone
	麦克风
27	controller
	控制器，操纵器
28	radio equipment (radio communication set)
	无线电装置（无线电通信装置）
29	dashboard
	仪表（板）盘
30	dashboard lighting
	仪表盘照明

31 speedometer
速率计
32 buttons controlling doors, windscreen wipers, internal and external lighting
车门，风挡雨刷，内外照明的控制按钮
33 ticket counter with change machine
其零钱兑换机的售票计算器
34 radio antenna
无线电天线
35 tram stop (*Am.* streetcar stop, trolley stop)
有轨电车停靠站
36 tram stop sign (*Am.* streetcar stop sign, trolley stop sign)
有轨电车停靠标志
37 electric change points
电动转辙机（道岔）
38 points signal (switch signal)
转辙信号
39 points change indicator
转辙指示器
40 trolley wire contact point
架空线接触点
41 trolley wire (overhead contact wire)
架空线（架空接触线）
42 overhead cross wire
架空交叉线
43 electric (*also*: electrohydraulic, electromechanical) points mechanism
电动（亦称：电动液压，电动机械）转辙机构

**ve-axle articulated railcar
interurban rail service**
间铁路的十二车轴有轨电车
rent collector
器
d of the railcar
电车车头
: of the railcar
电车车尾
riage A containing the motor
电动机（马达）的第一节车厢
riage B (*also*: carriages C and
节车厢（同样：第三及第四节

riage E containing the motor
动机（马达）的第五节车厢
r controller
操纵器
gie
架
rying bogie 转向架
eel guard
板
mper (*Am.* fender)
槽，缓冲器
axle articulated railcar
annheim] type) for tram
n. streetcar, trolley) and
an rail services
有轨电车和铁路的六轴有轨电车
罕型，西德南部城市）
rance and exit door, a double
ding door
车门，双折层车门

15 step
车梯

1-5 road layers
路层

1 anti-frost layer
不冻层

2 bituminous sub-base course
沥青底基层

3 base course
基层

4 binder course
结合层

5 bituminous surface
沥青路面

6 kerb (curb)
路缘，镶边石

7 kerbstone (curbstone)
缘石

8 paving (pavement)
铺砌层

9 pavement (*Am.* sidewalk, walkway)
人行道（人行道，走道）

10 gutter
排水沟

11 pedestrian crosssing (zebra crossing, *Am.* crosswalk)
人行道（斑马线）

12 street corner
街角

13 street
街道

14 electricity cables
电缆

15 telephone cables
电话电缆

16 telephone cable pipeline
电话电缆管线

17 cable manhole with cover (with manhole cover)
带人孔盖的电缆人孔

18 lamp post with lamp
路灯柱和路灯

19 electricity cables for technical installations
设备用电缆

20 subscribers' (*Am.* customers') telephone lines
用户电话线

21 gas main
总气管，瓦斯总管

22 water main
总水管

23 drain
下水道

24 drain cover
下水道盖

25 drain pipe
下水管

26 waste pipe
废水管

27 combined sewer
总下水

28 district heating main
区域供热总管

29 underground tunnel
地下隧道

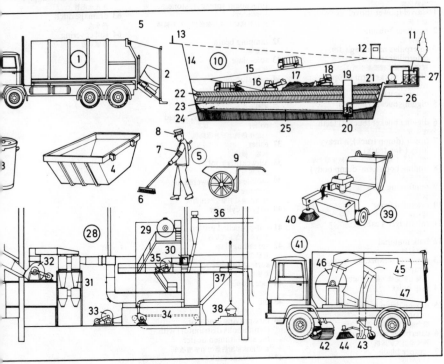

1 ~~use collection vehicle~~
m. garbage truck)
圾车

~~stbin-tipping device (*Am.*~~
~~rbage can dumping device), a~~
~~st-free emptying system~~
圾桶倾倒装置，垃圾清除装置

~~stbin (*Am.* garbage can, trash~~
n)
圾箱

~~use container (*Am.* garbage~~
ntainer)
圾容器

~~ad sweeper (*Am.* street~~
eeper)
道夫

~~om~~
帚

~~orescent armband~~
光臂章

~~p with fluorescent band~~
荧光带的帽子

~~ad sweeper's (*Am.* street~~
eeper's) barrow
道夫手推车

~~ntrolled tip (*Am.* sanitary~~
ndfill, sanitary fill)
管理的垃圾场

~~reen~~

~~eigh office~~
磅处

~~nce~~
栏

~~bankment~~
坝

15 access ramp
入口坡道（倾斜路面）
16 bulldozer
推土机
17 refuse (*Am.* garbage)
垃圾
18 bulldozer for dumping and compacting
倾倒和压缩用的推土机
19 pump shaft
泵井
20 waste water pump
废水泵
21 porous cover
多孔复盖层
22 compacted and decomposed refuse
已压缩和分解腐烂的垃圾
23 gravel filter layer
碎石（砂砾）过滤层
24 morainic filter layer
碛石层
25 drainage layer
排水层
26 drain pipe
排水管
27 water tank
水槽
28 refuse (*Am.* garbage) incineration unit
垃圾焚烧装置
29 furnace
焚烧炉
30 oil-firing system
燃油装置

31 separation plant
分离用的设备
32 extraction fan
排气风扇
33 low-pressure fan for the grate
炉篦的低压风扇
34 continuous feed grate
连续供料炉篦
35 fan for the oil-firing system
燃油装置所用的风扇
36 conveyor for separately incinerated material
分离焚烧的材料运送装置
37 coal feed conveyor
供煤运送装置
38 truck for carrying fuller's earth
运送漂土的手推车
39 mechanical sweeper
清扫机
40 circular broom
圆形帚
41 road-sweeping lorry (street-cleaning lorry, street cleaner)
路面清扫车
42 cylinder broom
圆筒形帚
43 suction port
吸尘口
44 feeder broom
进给扫帚
45 air flow
空气流
46 fan
鼓风机
47 dust collector
集尘器

349

1-54 road-building machinery
筑路机械

1 shovel (power shovel, excavator)
挖土机

2 machine housing
机器外壳

3 caterpillar mounting (*Am.* caterpillar tractor)
履带式装置（履带牵引机）

4 digging bucket arm (dipper stick)
挖斗臂（挖斗操纵杆）

5 digging bucket (bucket)
挖斗

6 digging bucket (bucket) teeth
挖斗齿

7 tipper (dump truck), a heavy lorry (*Am.* truck)
倾卸卡车（倾卸卡车），一种重型卡车

8 tipping body (*Am.* dump body)
倾卸车体

9 reinforcing rib
加强肋

10 extended front
延长端

11 cab (driver's cab)
驾驶室

12 bulk material
散装材料

13 concrete scraper, an aggregate scraper
混凝土铲运机，砂石铲运机

14 skip hoist
吊斗吊车

15 mixing drum (mixer drum), a mixing machine
混合筒（混合机）

16 caterpillar hauling scraper
履带牵引式铲运机

17 scraper blade
铲运刮板

18 levelling (*Am.* leveling) blade (smoothing blade)
整平刮板

19 grader (motor grader)
平土机（马达平土机）

20 scarifier (ripper, road ripper, rooter)
松土机、翻掘机

21 grader levelling (*Am.* leveling) blade (grader ploughshare, *Am.* plowshare)
平土机整平刮板，平土机犁头

22 blade-slewing gear (slew turntable)
刮刀转动齿轮，转动盘

23 light railway (narrow-gauge, *Am.* narrow-gage, railway)
轻便铁路（窄轨铁路）

24 light railway (narrow-gauge, *Am.* narrow-gage) diesel locomotive
轻便铁路（窄轨铁路）柴油火车

25 trailer wagon (wagon truck, skip)
拖（货）车（货车，吊斗）

26 tamper (rammer); *heavier*: frog
捣紧机（撞锤，捣具）；较重型的：蛙形捣具

27 guide rods
导向杆

28 bulldozer
推土机

29 bulldozer blade
推土机刮板

30 pushing frame
推进架

31 road-metal spreading machine (macadam spreader, stone spreader)
碎石撒播机（碎石撒播机，石头撒播机）

32 tamping beam
捣紧梁

33 sole-plate
底板

34 side stop
侧挡板

35 side of storage bin
贮料仓侧板

36 three-wheeled roller, a road roller
三轮压路机，一种碾路机

37 roller
滚轮，碾轮

38 all-weather roof
全天候顶篷

39 mobile diesel-powered air compressor
移动式柴油引擎空气压缩机

40 oxygen cylinder
氧气筒

41 self-propelled gritter
（自动）自走式复砂机

42 spreading flap
复砂活板

43 surface finisher
整面机

44 side stop
侧挡板

45 bin
料仓，料斗

46 tar-spraying machine (bituminous distributor) with tar and bitumen heater
自带柏油和加热器的柏油喷洒车

47 tar storage tank
柏油贮槽

48 fully automatic asphalt drying and mixing plant
全自动柏油混合和乾燥装置

49 bucket elevator (elevating conveyor)
箕斗升运机（上升送机）

50 asphalt-mixing drum (asphalt mixer drum)
柏油混合筒

51 filler hoist
填料器

52 filler opening
填料口

53 binder injector
粘结料注入器

54 mixed asphalt outlet
混合沥青出口

55 typical cross-section of a bituminous road
柏油路的典型横断面

56 grass verge
草皮路边缘

57 crossfall
横向坡度（斜度）

58 asphalt surface (bituminous layer, bituminous coating)
柏油路面（沥青复盖层）

59 base (base course)
基层（路基）

60 gravel sub-base course (hardcore sub-base course, Telford base), an anti-frost layer
碎石底基层，一种防冻层

61 sub-drainage
地下排水道

62 perforated cement pipe
多孔水泥管

63 drainage ditch
排水沟

64 soil covering
土壤复盖

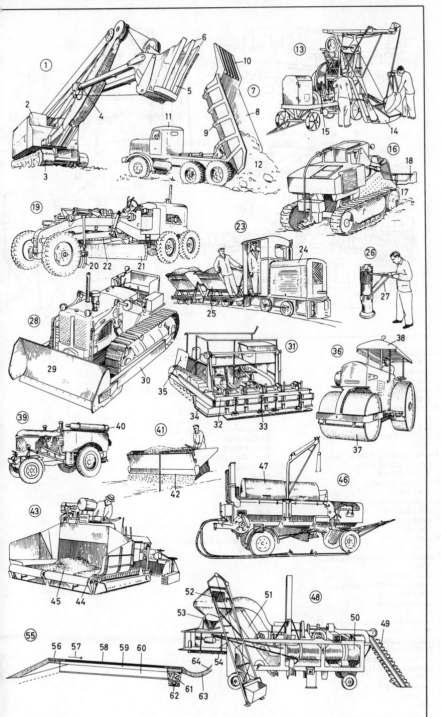

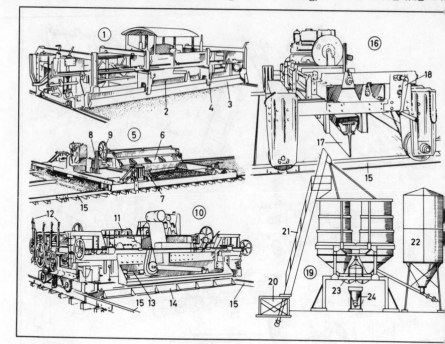

1-24 **concrete road construction** (highway construction)
混凝土路的铺筑（公路的铺筑）
1 subgrade grader
路基整平机
2 tamping beam (consolidating beam)
捣实梁
3 levelling (*Am.* leveling) beam
整平梁
4 roller guides for the levelling (*Am.* leveling) beam
整平梁的滚轮导槽
5 concrete spreader
混凝土撒播机
6 concrete spreader box
混凝土撒播机箱
7 cable guides
缆绳导轮
8 control levers
控制杆；操纵杆
9 handwheel for emptying the boxes
混凝土箱的倾倒手轮
10 concrete-vibrating compactor
混凝土振动压实机
11 gearing (gears)
齿轮装置
12 control levers (operating levers)
控制杆（操纵杆）
13 axle drive shaft to vibrators (tampers) of vibrating beam
驱动振动梁振动器的驱动轴
14 screeding board (screeding beam)
匀泥板（整平梁）
15 road form
路型

16 joint cutter
切缝机
17 joint-cutting blade
切缝刀片
18 crank for propelling machine
推进机器的曲柄
19 concrete-mixing plant, a stationary central mixing plant, an automatic batching and mixing plant
混凝土搅拌装置，固定式中央搅拌装置，自动配料搅拌装置
20 collecting bin
集料箱
21 bucket elevator
箕斗升运机
22 cement store
水泥贮筒
23 concrete mixer
混凝土搅拌器
24 concrete pump hopper
混凝土泵漏斗

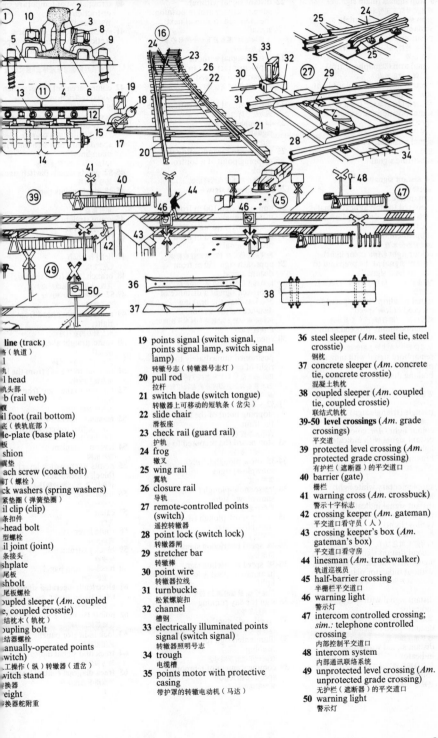

line (track)
路（轨道）
l
轨
l head
轨头部
b (rail web)
腹
il foot (rail bottom)
底（铁轨底部）
le-plate (base plate)
板
shion
震垫
ach screw (coach bolt)
钉（螺栓）
ck washers (spring washers)
紧垫圈（弹簧垫圈）
il clip (clip)
条扣件
-head bolt
型螺栓
il joint (joint)
条接头
shplate
尾板
shbolt
尾板螺栓
oupled sleeper (*Am.* coupled
e, coupled crosstie)
结枕木（轨枕）
pupling bolt
结螺栓
anually-operated points
witch)
工操作（纵）转辙器（道岔）
witch stand
换器
eight
换器舱附重

19 points signal (switch signal,
points signal lamp, switch signal
lamp)
转辙号志（转辙器号志灯）
20 pull rod
拉杆
21 switch blade (switch tongue)
转辙器上可移动的短轨条（岔尖）
22 slide chair
滑板座
23 check rail (guard rail)
护轨
24 frog
辙叉
25 wing rail
翼轨
26 closure rail
导轨
27 remote-controlled points
(switch)
遥控转辙器
28 point lock (switch lock)
转辙器闸
29 stretcher bar
转辙棒
30 point wire
转辙器拉线
31 turnbuckle
松紧螺旋扣
32 channel
槽钢
33 electrically illuminated points
signal (switch signal)
转辙器照明号志
34 trough
电缆槽
35 points motor with protective
casing
带护罩的转辙电动机（马达）

36 steel sleeper (*Am.* steel tie, steel
crosstie)
钢枕
37 concrete sleeper (*Am.* concrete
tie, concrete crosstie)
混凝土轨枕
38 coupled sleeper (*Am.* coupled
tie, coupled crosstie)
联结式轨枕
39-50 **level crossings** (*Am.* grade
crossings)
平交道
39 protected level crossing (*Am.*
protected grade crossing)
有栏杆（遮断器）的平交道口
40 barrier (gate)
栅栏
41 warning cross (*Am.* crossbuck)
警示十字标志
42 crossing keeper (*Am.* gateman)
平交道口看守员（人）
43 crossing keeper's box (*Am.*
gateman's box)
平交道口看守房
44 linesman (*Am.* trackwalker)
轨道巡视员
45 half-barrier crossing
半栅栏平交道口
46 warning light
警示灯
47 intercom controlled crossing;
sim.: telephone controlled
crossing
内部控制平交道口
48 intercom system
内部通讯联络系统
49 unprotected level crossing (*Am.*
unprotected grade crossing)
无护栏（遮断器）的平交道口
50 warning light
警示灯

1-6 stop signals (main signals)
停止信号灯（主号志机）

1 stop signal (main signal), a
semaphore signal in 'stop'
position
停车信号灯（主号志机），臂形号志在
停车位置

2 signal arm (semaphore arm)
信号臂（臂形号志）

3 electric stop signal (colour light,
Am. color light, signal) at 'stop'
显示停止信号的电动色灯停止信号

4 signal position: 'proceed at low
speed'
信号位置：'慢行'（减速信号）

5 signal position: 'proceed'
信号位置：'行进'

6 substitute signal
代用信号灯

7-24 distant signals
远处号号

7 semaphore signal at 'be
prepared to stop at next signal'
"准备於下一个信号机处停车"的臂形
信号灯

8 supplementary semaphore arm
辅助臂形号志臂

9 colour light (*Am.* color light)
distant signal at 'be prepared to
stop at next signal'
"准备於下一个信号灯处停车"的远方色
灯信号

10 signal position: 'be prepared to
proceed at low speed'
信号位置："准备慢行"（准备减速）

11 signal position: 'proceed main
signal ahead'
信号位置："在主号志机前继续行进

12 semaphore signal with indicator
plate showing a reduction in
braking distance of more than
5%
带显示不大於 5% 刹车距离显示板的臂
形号志

13 triangle (triangle sign)
三角号志

14 colour light (*Am.* color light)
distant signal with indicator
light for showing reduced
braking distance
带显示减少的刹车距离指示灯的远方色
灯

15 supplementary white light
辅助白灯

16 distant signal indicating 'be
prepared to stop at next signal'
(yellow light)
指示"准备於下一个信号灯停车"的远方
信号灯（黄色灯）

17 second distant signal (distant
signal with supplementary light,
without indicator plate)
第二个远方信号灯（带辅助信号灯无指示板的
远方信号灯）

18 distant signal with speed
indicator
带速度指示器的远方信号灯

19 distant speed indicator
远方速度指示器

20 distant signal with route
indicator
带进路指示器的远方信号灯

21 route indicator
进路指示器

22 distant signal without
supplementary arm in position:
'be prepared to stop at next
signal'
不带辅助臂"准备於下一个信号停车"
的远方信号灯

23 distant signal without
supplementary arm in 'be
prepared to proceed' position
不带辅助臂"准备继续行进"的远方信
号灯

24 distant signal identification plate
远方信号灯的识别板

**25-44 supplementary
signals**
辅助信号

25 stop board for indicating the
stopping point at a control
point
指示停止於指定点的停止板

26-29 approach signs
接近标志

26 approach sign 100 m from
distant signal
距离远方信号灯 100 米的接近标志

27 approach sign 175 m from
distant signal
距离远方信号灯 175 米的接近标志

28 approach sign 250 m from
distant signal
距离远方信号灯 250 米的接近标志

29 approach sign at a distance of
5% less than the braking
distance on the section
区间距离少於 5% 制动（刹车）距离时
的接近标志

30 chequered sign indicating stop
signals (main signals) not
positioned immediately to the
right of or over the line (track)
指示停止信号（主号志机）的方格号
志，并不表示立即停止於右边位置或超
越位置

**31-32 stop boards to indicate the
stopping point of the front of
the train**
指示火车前方停止点的停止板

33 stop board (be prepared to stop)
停止板（准备停车）

**34-35 snow plough (*Am.*
snowplow) signs**
雪犁号志

34 'raise snow-plough (*Am.*
snowplow)' sign
雪犁升起号志

35 'lower snow-plough (*Am.*
snowplow)' sign
雪犁放下号志

36-44 speed restriction signs
限速号志

36-38 speed restriction sign
[maximum speed 3 × 10 = 30
kph]
限速号志〔最高时速 30 公里〕

36 sign for day running
白天行车号志

37 speed code number
速度号号

38 illuminated sign for night
running
夜间行车用的照明号志

39 commencement of temporary
speed restriction
暂时限速的起点

40 termination of temporary spe
restriction
暂时限速的终点

41 speed restriction sign for a
section with a permanent spe
restriction [maximum speed
× 10 = 50 kph]
区间长时限速的限速号志〔最高时速
公里〕

42 commencement of permanen
speed restriction
长时限速的起点

43 speed restriction warning sig
[only on main lines]
〔只於干线上的〕限速警示标志

44 speed restriction sign [only o
main lines]
〔只於干线上的〕限速号志

45-52 points signals (switch sign
转辙器信号

45-48 single points (single
switches)
单转辙器

45 route straight ahead (main li
直行进路（干线）

46 [right] branch
〔右〕支线

47 [left] branch
〔左〕支线

48 branch [seen from the frog]
支线（由辙叉可见该标志）

49-52 double crossover
交叉渡线

49 route straight ahead from lef
right
由左而右的直行进路

50 route straight ahead from rig
to left
由右而左的直行进路

51 turnout to the left from the le
由左转左的号志

52 turnout to the right from the
right
由右转右的号志

53 manually-operated signal box
(*Am.* signal tower, switch tow
手操作的号志箱

54 lever mechanism
握杆机构

55 points lever (switch lever)
[blue], a lock lever
转辙杆[蓝色]，一种锁杆

56 signal lever [red]
信号杆[红色]

57 catch
轮档

58 route lever
进路握杆

59 block instruments
闭塞器

60 block section panel
闭塞区间盘

61 electrically-operated signal bo
(*Am.* signal tower, switch tow
电动操作信号

62 points (switch) and signal kno
转辙器和信号钮

63 lock indicator panel
锁闭指示盘

64 track and signal indicator
轨道和信号指示器

65 track diagram control layout
带线路图的控制台

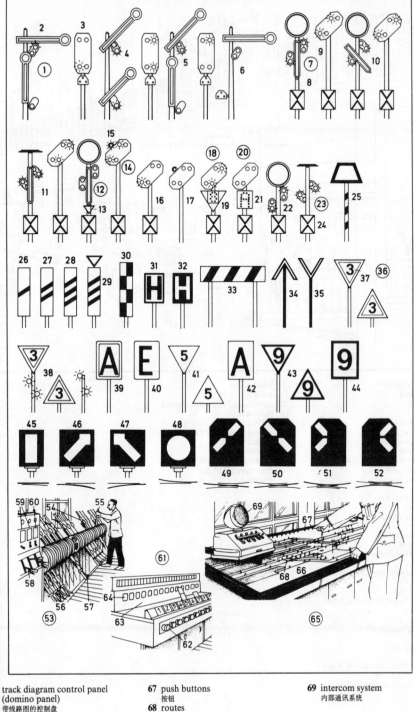

track diagram control panel
(domino panel)
带线路图的控制盘

67 push buttons
按钮

68 routes
路线

69 intercom system
内部通讯系统

1 parcels office
   包裹处理室
2 parcels
   包裹
3 basket [with lock]
   [带锁的]篮子
4 luggage counter
   行李过磅处
5 platform scale with dial
   具刻度盘的磅秤
6 suitcase (case)
   手提箱
7 luggage sticker
   行李标签
8 luggage receipt
   行李收据
9 luggage clerk
   行李（办事）员
10 poster (advertisement)
   海报公告（广告）
11 station post box (*Am.* station
   mailbox)
   车站内的邮筒
12 notice board indicating train
   delays
   列车误点通知栏
13 station restaurant
   车站餐厅
14 waiting room
   候车室
15 map of the town (street map)
   市区地图[街道地图]
16 timetable (*Am.* schedule)
   时间表

17 hotel porter
   旅馆搬运工，门僮
18 arrivals and departures board
   (timetable)
   列车到站与开车时间（刻）表（板）
19 arrival timetable (*Am.* arrival
   schedule)
   到站时间表
20 departure timetable (*Am.*
   departure schedule)
   开车时间表

TO THE TRAINS

TICKETS

CHANGE

ft luggage lockers
李寄存柜

hange machine
李钱兑换机

unnel to the platforms
向站台的地下道

assengers
客

eps to the platforms
向站台的阶梯

tation bookstall (*Am.* station
ookstand)
站书报摊

ft luggage office (left luggage)
李寄存处

ravel centre (*Am.* center); *also*:
ccommodation bureau
游中心；即：订位处

nformation office (*Am.*
nformation bureau)
问处

tation clock
站时钟

ank branch with foreign
xchange counter
办外汇业务的银行分行

ndicator board showing
xchange rates
示汇率的指示板

ailway map (*Am.* railroad map)
路交通（路线）图

cket office
票处

35 ticket counter
售票柜台

36 ticket (railway ticket, *Am.*
railroad ticket)
车票（火车票）

37 revolving tray
转盘

38 grill
窗口

39 ticket clerk (*Am.* ticket agent)
售票员

40 ticket-printing machine
(ticket-stamping machine)
车票日期印刷机

41 hand-operated ticket printer
手操作车票印刷机

42 pocket timetable (*Am.* pocket
train schedule)
火车时刻简表

43 luggage rest
行李台

44 first aid station
急救站

45 Travellers' (*Am.* Travelers') Aid
旅客救护处

46 telephone box (telephone booth,
telephone kiosk, call box)
公用电话亭

47 cigarettes and tobacco kiosk
售烟亭

48 flower stand
花台

49 railway information clerk
铁路询问服务员

50 official timetable (official
railway guide, *Am.* train
schedule)
公务时刻表（公务铁路手册，火车行车
时刻表，公家印制）

1 platform 月台	**16** news trolley 售报手推车	**32** barrow 手推车
2 steps to the platform 通向月台的台阶（月台台阶）	**17** news vendor (*Am.* news dealer) 售报小贩	**33** drinking fountain 饮水器
3 bridge to the platforms 月台天桥	**18** reading matter for the journey 旅行读物	**34** electric Trans-Europe Expre *also:* Intercity train 贯通欧洲的高速电气火车，亦称市际 车
4 platform number 月台号码	**19** edge of the platform 月台边	
5 platform roofing 月台顶篷	**20** railway policeman (*Am.* railroad policeman) 铁路警察	**35** electric locomotive, an expre locomotive 电气火车头
6 passengers 旅客	**21** destination board 终点站牌	**36** collector bow (sliding bow) 弓形集电器
7-12 luggage 行李	**22** destination indicator 终点站指示牌	**37** secretarial compartment 秘书厢
7 suitcase (case) 手提箱	**23** departure time indicator 开车时间指示牌	**38** destination board 终点站牌
8 luggage label 行李标签	**24** delay indicator 误点指示牌	**39** wheel tapper 检修员
9 hotel sticker 旅馆标签	**25** suburban train, a railcar 郊区列车	**40** wheel-tapping hammer 检车锤
10 travelling (*Am.* traveling) bag 旅行袋	**26** special compartment 专用车	**41** station foreman 车站领班
11 hat box 帽形盒	**27** platform loudspeaker 月台扩音器	**42** signal 信号牌
12 umbrella, a walking-stick umbrella 雨伞，一种手杖雨伞	**28** station sign 站牌	**43** red cap 搬运工人
13 main building; *also:* offices 办公室	**29** electric trolley (electric truck) 电动推车（电动卡车）	**44** inspector 检查员
14 platform 月台	**30** loading foreman 搬货工头（领班）	**45** pocket timetable (*Am.* pocke train schedule) 袖珍时刻表（袖珍列车时刻表）
15 crossing 路口	**31** porter (*Am.* redcap) 搬运工	

1 ramp (vehicle ramp); *sim.:*
livestock ramp
斜坡（车辆坡道）；类似：家畜车坡道

2 electric truck
电动卡车

3 trailer
拖车

4 part loads (*Am.* package freight,
less-than-carload freight); *in
general traffic:* general goods in
general consignments (in mixed
consignments)
散货（包装货物，未满一车的货
物）；在一般运输中有：一般托运的
（各种混装托运的）一般货物

5 crate
条板箱

6 goods van (*Am.* freight car)
货车车厢

7 goods shed (*Am.* freight house)
货车车棚

8 loading strip
装载条板

9 loading dock
装载台

10 bale of peat
泥炭包

11 bale of linen (of linen cloth)
麻布捆

12 fastening (cord)
扣接绳

13 wicker bottle (wickered bottle,
demijohn)
带有柳条筐的坛子

14 trolley
手推车

15 goods lorry (*Am.* freight truck)
货运卡车

16 forklift truck (fork truck,
forklift)
叉式起重机

17 loading siding
装载线

18 bulky goods
大批货物

19 small railway-owned (*Am.*
railroad-owned) container
铁路专用小型装载箱

20 showman's caravan (*sim.:* circus
caravan)
供表演团体用的大篷车

21 flat wagon (*Am.* flat freight car)
平板货车

22 loading gauge (*Am.* gage)
货物装载规

23 bale of straw
稻草捆

24 flat wagon (*Am.* flatcar) with
side stakes
带侧柱的平板货车

25 fleet of lorries (*Am.* trucks)
运货车队

26-39 **goods shed** (*Am.* freight
house)
货仓

26 goods office (forwarding office,
Am. freight office)
货物装载处

27 part-load goods (*Am.* package
freight)
散装货物

28 forwarding agent (*Am.* freight
agent, shipper)
运输业者，运输行

29 loading foreman
装载领班

30 consignment note (waybill)
货运单（运货单）

31 weighing machine
磅秤

32 pallet
拖板

33 porter
搬运工

34 electric cart (electric truck)
电动卡车

35 trailer
拖车

36 loading supervisor
装载督察

37 goods shed door (*Am.* freight
house door)
货仓门

38 rail (slide rail)
滑轨

39 roller
滚轮

40 weighbridge office
地磅房

41 weighbridge
地磅，秤桥

42 marshalling yard (*Am.*
classification yard, switch yard)
调车场

43 shunting engine (shunting
locomotive, shunter, *Am.* switch
engine, switcher)
调车机车

44 marshalling yard signal box
(*Am.* classification yard switch
tower)
调车场信号箱

45 yardmaster
调车场长

46 hump
调车场

47 sorting siding (classification
siding, classification track)
分类线（编组线）

48 rail brake (retarder)
铁轨制动器（减速器）

49 slipper brake (slipper)
制动器，制动滑块

50 storage siding (siding)
存车线

51 buffer (buffers, *Am.* bumper)
缓冲器

52 wagon load (*Am.* carload)
满载的货车

53 warehouse
仓库

54 container station
货柜场

55 gantry crane
高架起重机

56 lifting gear (hoisting gear)
升降装置

57 container
货柜

58 container wagon (*Am.* container
car)
货柜车

59 semi-trailer
半拖车

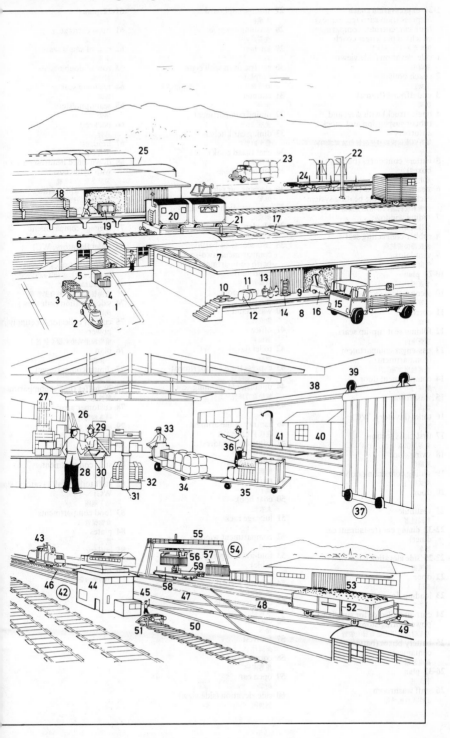

1-21 express train coach
(express train carriage, express train car, corridor compartment coach), a passenger coach
快车车厢，一种客车

1 side elevation (side view)
侧面图

2 coach body
车身

3 underframe (frame)
底架

4 bogie (truck) with steel and rubber suspension and shock absorbers
带有钢质和橡胶悬挂装置和减震器的转向架

5 battery containers (battery boxes)
蓄电池箱

6 steam and electric heat exchanger for the heating system
供暖系统的蒸汽和电热交换器

7 sliding window
滑移式窗户

8 rubber connecting seal
橡胶连接密封圈

9 ventilator
气窗，通风口

10-21 plan
平面图

10 second-class section
二等车剖面图

11 corridor
走廊

12 folding seat (tip-up seat)
摺叠座椅

13 passenger compartment (compartment)
旅客包房车厢

14 compartment door
隔间门

15 washroom
盥洗室

16 toilet (lavatory, WC)
厕所

17 first-class section
头等车剖面

18 swing door
避旋门

19 sliding connecting door
滑式拉门

20 door
门

21 vestibule
车间过道

22-32 dining car (restaurant car, diner)
餐车

22-25 side elevation (side view)
侧视图

22 door
车门

23 loading door
装货车

24 current collector for supplying power during stops
停车时给电用之集电器（装置）

25 battery boxes (battery containers)
蓄电池箱

26-32 plan
平面图

26 staff washroom
工作人员盥洗室

27 storage cupboard
贮藏柜

28 washing-up area
洗餐具间

29 kitchen
厨房

30 electric oven with eight hotplates
具八热板的电炉（八灶式餐用电炉）

31 counter
柜台

32 dining compartment
餐室

33 dining car kitchen
餐车厨房

34 chef (head cook)
厨师领班

35 kitchen cabinet
厨房柜子

36 sleeping car (sleeper)
卧车

37 side elevation (side view)
侧视图

38-42 plan
平面图

38 two-seat twin-berth compartment (two-seat two-berth compartment, *Am.* bedroom)
双座双铺室

39 folding doors
摺叠车门

40 washstand
盥洗台

41 office
值班室

42 toilet (lavatory, WC)
厕所

43 express train compartment
快车车厢隔间

44 upholstered reclining seat
软垫靠背座椅

45 armrest
扶手

46 ashtray in the armrest
在扶手上的烟灰盒

47 adjustable headrest
可调整的枕套

48 antimacassar
椅套

49 mirror
镜子

50 coat hook
大衣钩

51 luggage rack
行李架

52 compartment window
车窗

53 fold-away table (pull-down table)
可摺叠茶几

54 heating regulator
暖气调节器

55 litter receptacle
废物箱

56 curtain
窗帘

57 footrest
搁脚台

58 corner seat
角落座位

59 open car
敞车

60 side elevation (side view)
侧视图

61-72 plan
平面图

61 open carriage
连通车厢

62 row of single seats
单排座

63 row of double seats
双排座

64 reclining seat
靠椅

65 seat upholstery
座垫

66 backrest
靠背

67 headrest
头靠（枕）

68 down-filled headrest cushion with nylon cover
带尼龙套下凹头枕

69 armrest with ashtray
有烟灰盒的扶手

70 cloakroom
行李寄放处

71 luggage compartment
行李间

72 toilet (lavatory, WC)
厕所

73 buffet car (quick-service buffet car), a self-service restaurant car
自助餐车厢，一种自助餐车

74 side elevation (side view)
侧视图

75 current collector for supplying power
给电源用的集电器（装置）

76 plan
平面图

77 dining compartment
餐室

78-79 buffet (buffet compartme
餐饮部

78 customer area
顾客购物区

79 serving area
服务区

80 kitchen
厨房

81 staff compartment
值班室

82 staff toilet (staff lavatory, sta
WC)
员工厕所

83 food compartments
食物保管室

84 plates
盘子

85 cutlery
餐具

86 till (cash register)
柜台的收银抽屉

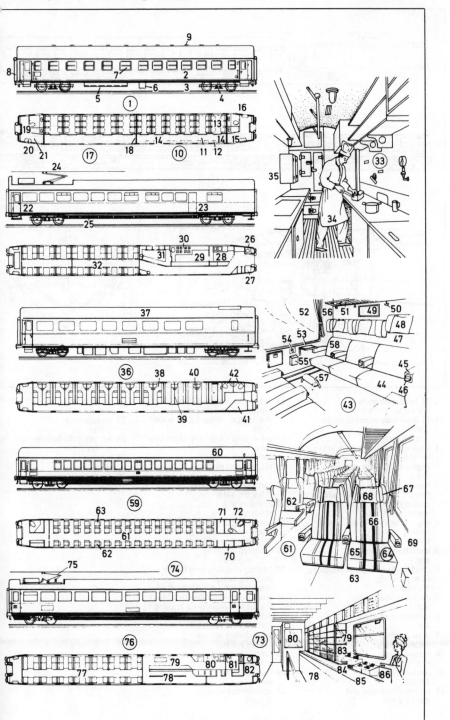

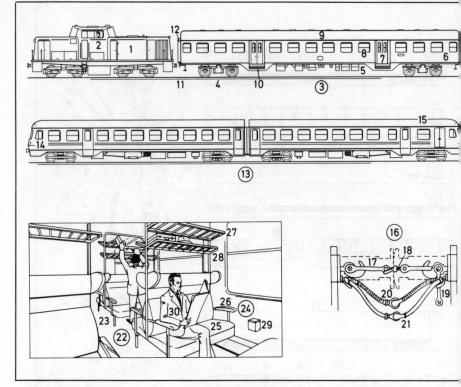

1-30 **local train service**
区间（普通）列车服务

1-12 **local train** (short-distance train)
区间列车（短程列车）

1 **single-engine diesel locomotive**
单（引擎）发动机柴油火车头

2 **engine driver** (*Am.* engineer)
司机

3 **four-axled coach (four-axled car) for short-distance routes, a passenger coach (passenger car)**
短程的四轴客车，客车

4 **bogie (truck) [with disc (disk) brakes]**
转向架（车架）〔带圆盘刹车〕

5 **underframe (frame)**
底架

6 **coach body with metal panelling** (*Am.* paneling)
带金属镶板的车

7 **double folding doors**
双摺门

8 **compartment window**
车窗

9 **open carriage**
中央通路式的客车

10 **entrance**
入口

11 **connecting corridor**
连接通道

12 **rubber connecting seal**
橡胶连结密封圈

13 **light railcar, a short-distance railcar, a diesel railcar**
轻便轨道列车，短程轨道列车，柴油轨道列车

14 **cab** (driver's cab, *Am.* engineer's cab)
驾驶室

15 **luggage compartment**
行李间

16 **connecting hoses and coupling**
连接软管和连接器

17 **coupling link**
连接器连杆

18 **tensioning device (coupling screw with tensioning lever)**
拉力装置（具拉杆的连接螺钉）

19 **unlinked coupling**
未连接的连接器

20 **heating coupling hose (steam coupling hose)**
供暖连接器软管（蒸气连接器软管）

21 **coupling hose (connecting hose) for the compressed-air braking system**
压缩空气制动系统连接软管

22 **second-class section**
二等客车的区划

23 **central gangway**
中央通路

24 **compartment**
隔间

25 **upholstered seat**
软垫座位

26 **armrest**
扶手

27 **luggage rack**
行李架

28 **hat and light luggage rack**
帽和轻型行李架

29 **ashtray**
烟灰缸

30 **passenger**
旅客，乘客

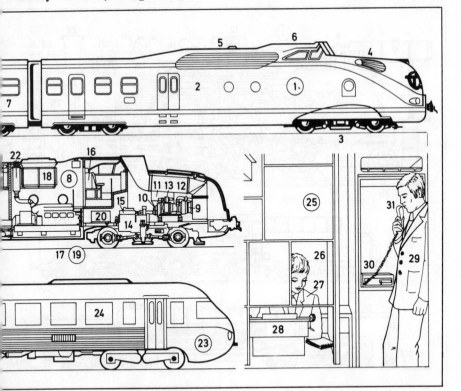

Trans-Europe Express
穿欧洲的快车
erman Federal Railway
ainset, a diesel trainset or gas
rbine trainset
意志联邦铁路列车，一种柴油列车或
气轮机列车
iving unit
动装置
ive wheel unit
动轮装置
ain engine
发动机（引擎）
esel generator unit
油发电机装置
b (driver's cab, *Am.* engineer's
b)
映室
cond coach
等车
s turbine driving unit
iagram]
气机驱动装置〔简图〕
s turbine
气轮机
rbine transmission
机传动装置
r intake
气管
haust with silencers (*Am.*
ufflers)
消音器的排气管
ynastarter
力起动器

14 **Voith transmission**
付特（液体）传动装置
15 **heat exchanger for the
transmission oil**
传动装置油的热交换器
16 **gas turbine controller**
燃气轮机控制器
17 **gas turbine fuel tank**
燃气轮机燃料槽
18 **oil-to-air cooling unit for
transmission and turbine**
传动装置和气轮机用的"油—汽"冷却
装置
19 **auxiliary diesel engine**
辅助柴油发动机（引擎）
20 **fuel tank**
燃料箱
21 **cooling unit**
冷却装置
22 **exhaust with silencers (*Am.*
mufflers)**
带消音器的排气装置
23 **Société Nationale des Chemins
de Fer Français (SNCF)**
**experimental trainset with
six-cylinder underfloor diesel
engine and twin-shaft gas
turbine**
法国国营铁路公司，具有六缸底架柴油
发动机（引擎）和双轴燃气轮机的
SNCF 试验列车
24 **turbine unit with silencers (*Am.*
mufflers)**
带消音器的轮机装置

25 **secretarial compartment**
秘书室
26 **typing compartment**
打字室
27 **secretary**
秘书
28 **typewriter**
打字机
29 **travelling (*Am.* traveling)
salesman**
旅行的推销员，做商业旅行的商人
30 **dictating machine**
录音机
31 **microphone**
扩音器，麦克风

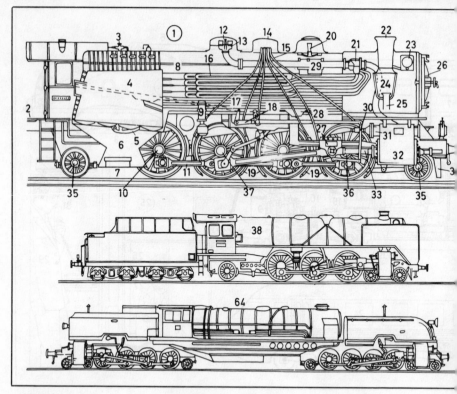

1-69 steam locomotives
蒸汽（火车头）机车
2-37 locomotive boiler and driving gear
机车锅炉和驱动装置
2 tender platform with coupling
带连接器的煤水（补给）平台
3 safety valve for excess boiler pressure
防止锅炉过压的安全阀
4 firebox
火箱
5 drop grate
倾卸炉篦
6 ashpan with damper doors
带风门的灰盘
7 bottom door of the ashpan
灰盘底门
8 smoke tubes (flue tubes)
烟管
9 feed pump
给水泵
10 axle bearing
车轴轴承
11 connecting rod
连（接）杆
12 steam dome
汽包
13 regulator valve (regulator main valve)
调节器阀（调节器主阀）
14 sand dome
砂包

15 sand pipes (sand tubes)
砂管
16 boiler (boiler barrel)
锅炉（锅胴）
17 fire tubes or steam tubes
火管或蒸汽管
18 reversing gear (steam reversing gear)
回动机构（蒸汽回动机构）
19 sand pipes
砂管
20 feed valve
进给阀
21 steam collector
集汽器
22 chimney (smokestack, smoke outlet and waste steam exhaust)
烟窗（烟和废汽排出口）
23 feedwater preheater (feedwater heater, economizer)
给水预热器（给水加热器，节热器）
24 spark arrester
防止火花器
25 blast pipe
排气管
26 smokebox door
烟箱门
27 cross head
十字头
28 mud drum
清泥器
29 top feedwater tray
顶部给水盘

30 combination lever
组合杆
31 steam chest
蒸汽室
32 cylinder
汽缸
33 piston rod with stuffing box (packing box)
带填料函的活塞杆
34 guard iron (rail guard, *Am.* pilot, cowcatcher)
排障器
35 carrying axle (running axle, dead axle)
从轮轴（导轮轴，静车轴）
36 coupled axle
连动轴
37 driving axle
驱动轴
38 express locomotive with tend
带煤水车的高速机车

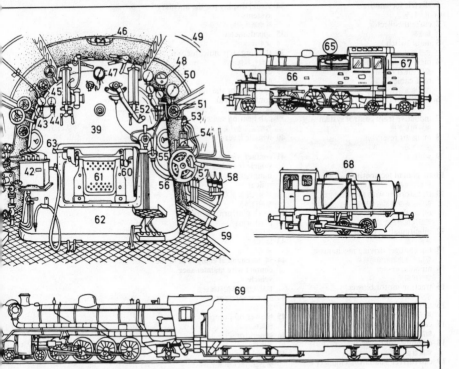

cab (driver's cab, *Am.* gineer's cab)
驶室，司机室
eman's seat
炉的位置
op grate lever
卸炉篦杆
e steam injector
络蒸汽喷射器
tomatic lubricant pump
utomatic lubricator)
动润滑泵（自动润滑器）
eheater pressure gauge (*Am.* ge)
热器压力计
rriage heating pressure gauge
m. gage)
厢加热压力计
ater gauge (*Am.* gage)
位计
ht
灯
iler pressure gauge (*Am.* ge)
炉压力计
stant-reading temperature
auge (*Am.* gage)
测温度计
b (driver's cab, *Am.* engineer's
ab)
驶室
ake pressure gauge (*Am.* gage)
动压力计

51 whistle valve handle
（汽）笛阀手柄
52 diver's timetable (*Am.* engineer's schedule)
驾驶时刻表
53 driver's brake valve (*Am.* engineer's brake valve)
驾驶制动阀
54 speed recorder (tachograph)
速率记录器（转速记录仪）
55 sanding valve
撒砂阀
56 reversing wheel
倒车手轮
57 emergency brake valve
紧急制动阀（刹车阀）
58 release valve
放汽阀
59 driver's seat (*Am.* engineer's seat)
（司机）驾驶的位置
60 firehole shield
炉口盖（罩）
61 firehole door
炉门
62 vertical boiler
立式锅炉
63 firedoor handle handgrip
炉门握把
64 articulated locomotive (Garratt locomotive)
活节火车头
65 tank locomotive
带水柜的火车头

66 water tank
水箱（柜）
67 fuel tender
燃料补给车
68 steam storage locomotive (fireless locomotive)
蒸汽储压火车头（贮汽火车头）
69 condensing locomotive (locomotive with condensing tender)
凝结式火车头（带凝结补给的火车头）

1 **electric locomotive**
电力机车

2 current collector
集电器

3 main switch
总开关

4 high-tension transformer
高压变压器

5 roof cable
篷顶电缆

6 traction motor
牵引马达

7 inductive train control system
感应列车系统

8 main air reservoir
主贮气器

9 whistle
汽笛

10-18 **plan of locomotive**
机车平面图

10 transformer with tap changer
带分接头变换器的变压器

11 oil cooler with blower
带鼓风机的油冷却器

12 oil-circulating pump
油循环泵

13 tap changer driving mechanism
分接头变换器的驱动机构

14 air compressor
空气压缩机

15 traction motor blower
牵引马达鼓风机

16 terminal box
端子箱

17 capacitors for auxiliary motors
辅助马达用的电容器

18 commutator cover
整流器盖（罩）

19 cab (driver's cab, *Am.* engineer's cab)
司机室

20 controller handwheel
驾驶盘

21 dead man's handle
事故刹车手柄装置

22 driver's brake valve (*Am.* engineer's brake valve)
驾驶制动阀

23 ancillary brake valve (auxiliary brake valve)
辅助制动阀

24 pressure gauge (*Am.* gage)
压力计

25 bypass switch for the dead man's handle
事故刹车手柄的旁通开关

26 tractive effort indicator
牵引力指示器

27 train heating voltage indicator
列车供暖电压指示器

28 contact wire voltage indicator (overhead wire voltage indicator)
接触线电压指示器（架空线电压指示器）

29 high-tension voltage indicator
高电压指示器

30 on/off switch for the current collector
集电器开关

31 main switch
主开关

32 sander switch (sander control)
撒砂器开关

33 anti-skid brake switch
防滑制动开关

34 visual display for the ancillary systems
补助系统用的可见显示

35 speedometer
速率计

36 running step indicator
连续行程指示器

37 clock
时钟

38 controls for the inductive train control system
感应列车系统用的控制器

39 cab heating switch
驾驶室供暖开关

40 whistle lever
汽笛杆

41 **contact wire maintenance vehicle** (overhead wire maintenance vehicle), a diesel railcar
接触线维修车（架空线维修车），一种柴油轨道车

42 work platform (working platform)
工作台

43 ladder
梯子

44-54 **mechanical equipment of the contact wire maintenance vehicle**
接触线维修车的机械设备

44 air compressor
空气压缩机

45 blower oil pump
鼓风机油泵

46 generator
发电机

47 diesel engine
柴油发动机（引擎）

48 injection pump
喷射泵

49 silencer (*Am.* muffler)
消音器

50 change-speed gear
变速齿轮，变换齿轮

51 cardan shaft
万向轴

52 wheel flange lubricator
轮凸缘润滑器

53 reversing gear
回动机构

54 torque converter bearing
扭矩变速器轴承

55 **accumulator railcar** (battery railcar)
蓄电池轨道车

56 battery box (battery container)
电池箱

57 cab (driver's cab, *Am.* engineer's cab)
驾驶室

58 second-class seating arrangement
二等座位配置

59 toilet (lavatory, WC)
厕所

60 **fast electric multiple-unit train**
高速电动多机牵引列车

61 front railcar
前端轨道车

62 driving trailer car
拖车车厢

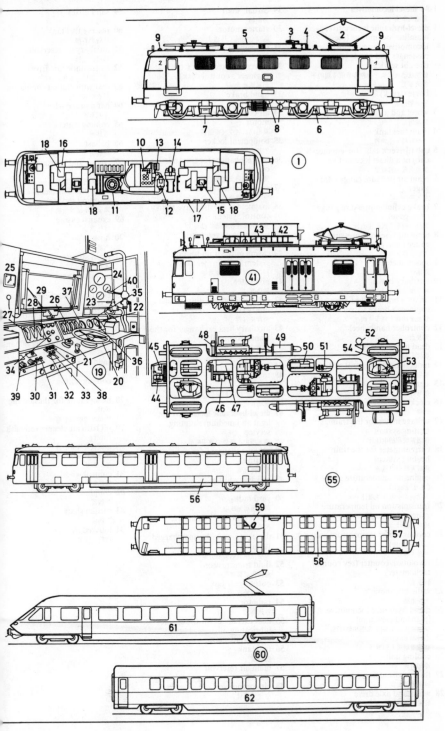

1-84 diesel locomotives
柴油火车头

1 diesel-hydraulic locomotive, a
mainline locomotive (diesel
locomotive) for medium
passenger and goods service
(freight service)
柴油液动火车头，一种客货服务用的干
线火车头

2 bogie (truck)
转向架

3 wheel and axle set
轮轴组

4 main fuel tank
主燃料槽（主油箱）

5 cab (driver's cab, *Am.* engineer's
cab) of a diesel locomotive
柴油火车头驾驶室

6 main air pressure gauge (*Am.*
gage)
主气压计

7 brake cylinder pressure gauge
(*Am.* gage)
制动（刹车）汽缸压力计

8 main air reservoir pressure
gauge (*Am.* gage)
主贮气器压力计

9 speedometer
速率计

10 auxiliary brake
辅助制动器

11 driver's brake valve (*Am.*
engineer's brake valve)
驾驶驱动器（刹车）阀

12 controller handwheel
驾驶盘

13 dead man's handle
事故（刹车）手柄

14 inductive train control system
感应列车系统

15 signal lights
信号灯

16 clock
时钟

17 voltage meter for the train
heating system
供暖系统用的电压计

18 current meter for the train
heating system
供暖系统用的电流表

19 engine oil temperature gauge
(*Am.* gage)
发动机（引擎）油温计

20 transmission oil temperature
gauge (*Am.* gage)
传动油温计

21 cooling water temperature gauge
(*Am.* gage)
冷却水温计

22 revolution counter (rev counter,
tachometer)
转速表

23 radio telephone
无线电话

24 diesel-hydraulic locomotive
[plan and elevation]
柴油液压火车头[平面图和侧视图]

25 diesel engine
柴油发动机（引擎）

26 cooling unit
冷却装置

27 fluid transmission
液压传动装置

28 wheel and axle drive
轮轴传动机构

29 cardan shaft
方向轴

30 starter motor
起动电动机（马达）

31 instrument panel
工具盘

32 driver's control desk (*Am.*
engineer's control desk)
司机驾驶台

33 hand brake
手刹车

34 air compressor with electric
motor
具电动机的空气压缩机

35 equipment locker
工具柜

36 heat exchanger for transmission
oil
传动油的热交换器

37 engine room ventilator
引擎室的通风口

38 magnet for the inductive train
control system
感应列车控制系统的磁石

39 train heating generator
列车供暖发生器

40 casing of the train heating
system transformer
列车供暖系统变压器罩

41 preheater
预热器

42 exhaust silencer (*Am.* exhaust
muffler)
消音排气器

43 auxiliary heat exchanger for the
transmission oil
传动油用的辅助热交换器

44 hydraulic brake
液压制动器

45 tool box
工具箱

46 starter battery
起动蓄电池

47 **diesel-hydraulic locomotive** for
light and medium shunting
service
调车用中小型柴油液压机车

48 exhaust silencer (*Am.* exhaust
muffler)
消音排气管

49 bell and whistle
车钟和汽笛

50 yard radio
调车场用无线电

51-67 elevation of locomotive
机车正视图

51 diesel engine with supercharged
turbine
带压气轮机的柴油引擎

52 fluid transmission
流体传送装置

53 output gear box
输出齿轮箱

54 radiator
散热器

55 heat exchanger for the engine
lubricating oil
引擎润滑油热交换器

56 fuel tank
燃料槽

57 main air reservoir
主贮气器

58 air compressor
空气压缩机

59 sand boxes
砂箱

60 reserve fuel tank
储备燃料槽

61 auxiliary air reservoir
辅助贮气器

62 hydrostatic fan drive
液压扇驱动装置

63 seat with clothes compartme
带衣柜的座位

64 hand brake wheel
手刹车轮

65 cooling water
冷却水

66 ballast
压载物

67 engine and transmission con
wheel
引擎和传动控制轮

68 **small diesel locomotive** for
shunting service
调车用小型柴油机车

69 exhaust casing
排气罩

70 horn
汽笛

71 main air reservoir
主贮气器

72 air compressor
空气压缩机

73 eight-cylinder diesel engine
八缸柴油引擎

74 Voith transmission with
reversing gear
具回动机构的付特液体传动装置

75 heating oil tank (fuel oil tank
供热油槽（燃料油槽）

76 sand box
砂箱

77 cooling unit
冷却装置

78 header tank for the cooling
water
冷却水用的集水箱

79 oil bath air cleaner (oil bath
filter)
油池式空气清洁器

80 hand brake wheel
手刹车轮

81 control wheel
操纵轮

82 coupling
连接器

83 cardan shaft
万向轴

84 louvred shutter
散热百叶窗

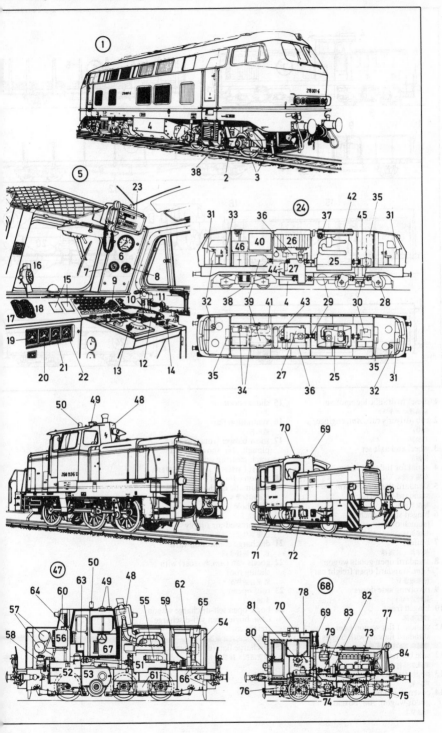

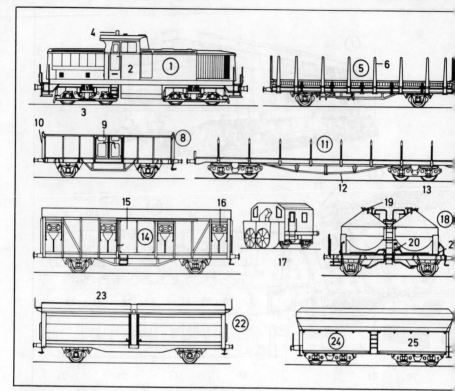

1 diesel-hydraulic locomotive
    柴油液动火车头
2 cab (driver's cab, *Am.* engineer's
    cab)
    驾驶室
3 wheel and axle set
    轮轴组
4 aerial for the yard radio
    车场无线电天线
5 standard flat wagon (*Am.*
    standard flatcar)
    标准平板车
6 hinged steel stanchion
    (stanchion)
    铰接钢柱
7 buffers
    缓冲器，减震器
8 standard open goods wagon
    (*Am.* standard open freight car)
    标准敞货车
9 revolving side doors
    旋转式侧门
10 hinged front
    铰接端部
11 standard flat wagon (*Am.*
    standard flatcar) with bogies
    带转向架的标准平板车
12 sole bar reinforcement
    底条加强材
13 bogie (truck)
    转向架
14 covered goods van (covered
    goods wagon, *Am.* boxcar)
    有篷货车

15 sliding door
    滑门，拉门
16 ventilation flap
    通风舌门
17 snow blower (rotary snow
    plough, *Am.* snowplow), a
    track-clearing vehicle
    扫雪机（旋转雪犁），一种轨式清扫机
18 wagon (*Am.* car) with
    pneumatic discharge
    气动卸货车
19 filler hole
    填料口
20 compressed-air supply
    压缩空气供给装置
21 discharge connection valve
    放气（连接）阀
22 goods van (*Am.* boxcar) with
    sliding roof
    滑顶有盖货车
23 roof opening
    车顶开口
24 bogie open self-discharge wagon
    (*Am.* bogie open self-discharge
    freight car)
    带转向架的自卸敞篷车
25 discharge flap (discharge door)
    卸货活板（卸货门）

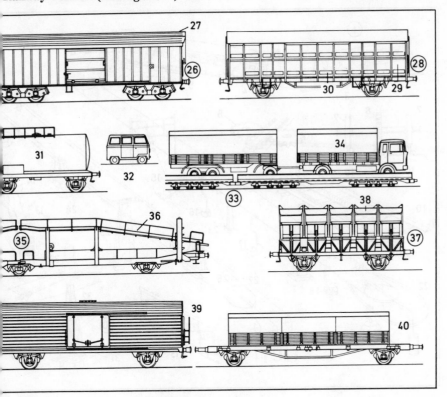

ie wagon with swivelling
. swiveling) roof
车顶的转向架车
velling (*Am.* swiveling) roof
车顶
e-capacity wagon (*Am.*
e-capacity car) for small
stock
小牲畜的大容量货车
·wall with ventilation flaps
tted wall)
风舌门的侧壁（板条壁）
tilation flap
舌门
k wagon (*Am.* tank car)
车
k inspection railcar
检查车
n special wagons (*Am.* open
cial freight cars)
无盖货车
ry (*Am.* truck) with trailer
车的货车
-tier car carrier (double-deck
carrier)
汽车的双层运载车
ged upper deck
上层
er wagon (*Am.* dump car)
h skips
斗的倾卸车
p

39 general-purpose refrigerator
wagon (refrigerator van, *Am.*
refrigerator car)
通用冷藏车
40 interchangeable bodies for flat
wagons (*Am.* flatcars)
可在平板车上装拆的车体

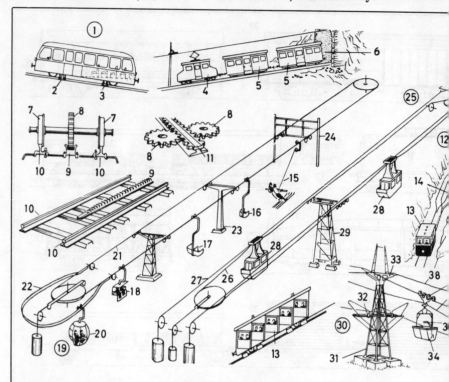

1-14 mountain railways (*Am.* mountain railroads)
登山铁路
1 adhesion railcar
粘著力轨道车
2 drive
驱动装置
3 emergency brake
紧急刹车（制动器）
4-5 rack mountain railway (rack-and-pinion railway, cog railway, *Am.* cog railroad, rack railroad)
齿条登山铁路（齿条与齿轮铁路，镶齿铁路，齿轨铁路）
4 electric rack railway locomotive (*Am.* electric rack railroad locomotive)
齿轨铁路电动机车
5 rack railway coach (rack railway trailer, *Am.* rack railroad car)
齿轨铁路客车（齿轨铁路拖车）
6 tunnel
隧道
7-11 rack railways (rack-and-pinion railways, *Am.* rack railroads) [systems]
齿轨铁路系统
7 running wheel (carrying wheel)
转动轮（运送轮）
8 driving pinion
驱动小齿轮

9 rack [with teeth machined on top edge]
齿形轨条〔顶部有齿牙〕
10 rail
轨
11 rack [with teeth on both outer edges]
齿形轨条〔两侧有齿牙〕
12 funicular railway (funicular, cable railway)
缆索铁道
13 funicular railway car
登山缆车，电缆车
14 haulage cable
拖索
15-38 cableways (ropeways, cable suspension lines)
缆道（索道，缆索挂线）
15-24 single-cable ropeways (single-cable suspension lines), endless ropeways
单缆索道，无端（循环）索道
15 drag lift
牵引缆车
16-18 chair lift
有座架缆车
16 lift chair, a single chair
缆车座，单人座
17 double lift chair, a two-seater chair
缆车双座，双人座
18 double chair (two-seater chair) with coupling
带连接器的双人座

19 gondola cableway, an endle[ss] cableway
有边车缆道，一种（循环）无端缆[道]
20 gondola (cabin)
有边车（座舱）
21 endless cable, a suspension (supporting) and haulage ca[ble]
（循环）无端缆索，一种具吊牵引[缆]（缆）
22 U-rail
U 型轨道
23 single-pylon support
单柱支架
24 gantry support
门型支架
25 double-cable ropeway (dou[ble] cable suspension line), a suspension line with balanc[ed] cabins
双缆索道，一种有平衡舱的架空索[道]
26 haulage cable
牵引缆
27 suspension cable (supporting cable)
悬吊缆索（支撑索）
28 cabin
座舱
29 intermediate support
中间支架
30 cableway (ropeway, suspen[sion] line), a double-cable ropewa[y] (double-cable suspension li[ne])
缆道（索道，悬吊索），一种双缆[道]（双缆悬吊线）

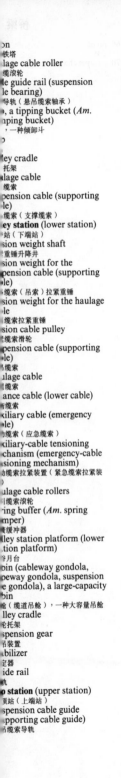

on
铁塔
lage cable roller
缆滚轮
e guide rail (suspension
le bearing)
导轨（悬吊缆索轴承）
o, a tipping bucket (*Am.*
ping bucket)
，一种倾卸斗
o

ey cradle
托架
ulage cable
缆索
pension cable (supporting
le)
缆索（支撑缆索）
ey station (lower station)
站（下端站）
sion weight shaft
重锤升降井
sion weight for the
pension cable (supporting
le)
缆索（吊索）拉紧重锤
sion weight for the haulage
le
缆索拉紧重锤
sion cable pulley
缆索滑轮
pension cable (supporting
le)
缆索
ulage cable
缆索
ance cable (lower cable)
缆索
xiliary cable (emergency
le)
缆索（应急缆索）
xiliary-cable tensioning
chanism (emergency-cable
sioning mechanism)
缆索拉紧装置（紧急缆索拉紧装
ulage cable rollers
缆索滚轮
ring buffer (*Am.* spring
mper)
缓冲器
lley station platform (lower
tion platform)
停月台
bin (cableway gondola,
eway gondola, suspension
e gondola), a large-capacity
bin
舱（缆道吊舱），一种大容量吊舱
lley cradle
轮托架
spension gear
吊装置
abilizer
定器
ide rail
轨
o station (upper station)
顶站（上端站）
spension cable guide
pporting cable guide)
吊缆索导轨

59 suspension cable anchorage
(supporting cable anchorage)
悬吊缆索停泊点（架空索锚固点）
60 haulage cable rollers
牵引缆索滚轮
61 haulage cable guide wheel
牵引缆索导轮
62 haulage cable driving pulley
牵引缆索驱动滑轮
63 main drive
主驱动装置
64 standby drive
备用驱动装置
65 control room
控制室
66 **cabin pulley cradle**
吊舱滑轮托架
67 main pulley cradle
主滑轮托架
68 double cradle
双托架
69 two-wheel cradle
双轮托架
70 running wheels
转动轮
71 suspension cable brake
(supporting cable brake), an
emergency brake in case of
haulage cable failure
悬吊缆索制动器（刹车），一种牵引缆
索失效时的紧急制动器（刹车）
72 suspension gear bolt
悬吊齿轮
73 haulage cable sleeve
牵引缆索套管
74 balance cable sleeve (lower cable
sleeve)
平衡缆索套管
75 derailment guard
防止脱轨装置
76 **cable supports** (ropeway
supports, suspension line
supports, intermediate supports)
缆索支承架
77 pylon, a framework support
铁塔，构架的支架
78 tubular steel pylon, a tubular
steel support
钢管铁塔，一种钢管式支架
79 suspension cable guide rail
(supporting cable guide rail,
support guide rail)
悬吊缆索导轨（支承导轨）
80 support truss, a frame for work
on the cable
支承构架，於缆索上工作的构架
81 base of the support
支架的基部

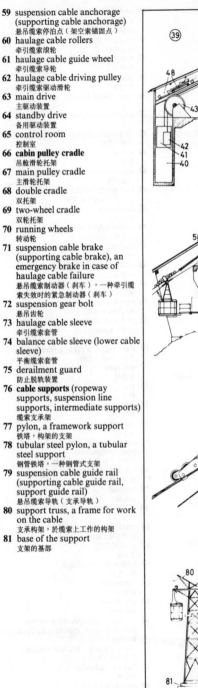

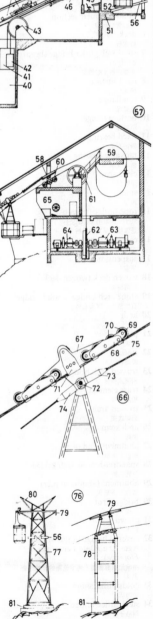

1 cross-section of a bridge
桥梁横断面

2 orthotropic roadway
(orthotropic deck)
钢桥面车道（钢面板）

3 truss (bracing)
桁架（支撑）

4 diagonal brace (diagonal strut)
斜支撑（斜支柱）

5 hollow tubular section
空心管型断面

6 deck slab
桥面板

7 solid-web girder bridge (beam
bridge)
实腹梁桥（梁桥）

8 road surface
路面

9 top flange
上翼缘

10 bottom flange
下翼缘

11 fixed bearing
固定支承

12 movable bearing
活动支承

13 clear span
淨跨径

14 span
跨径

15 rope bridge (primitive
suspension bridge)
悬索桥（早期的吊桥）

16 carrying rope
主索

17 suspension rope
吊索

18 woven deck (woven decking)
织网桥面

19 stone arch bridge, a solid bridge
石拱桥，一种实心桥

20 arch
拱

21 pier
桥墩

22 statue
雕饰物

23 trussed arch bridge
桁架式拱桥

24 truss element
桁架构件

25 trussed arch
桁架式拱

26 arch span
拱跨

27 abutment (end pier)
桥台（岸墩）

28 spandrel-braced arch bridge
空腹拱桥

29 abutment (abutment pier)
桥台（桥墩）

30 bridge strut
桥撑

31 crown
拱顶

32 covered bridge of the Middle
Ages (the *Ponte Vecchio* in
Florence)
中世纪的有盖桥（佛罗伦斯的庞特维奇
奥）

33 goldsmiths' shops
金饰店

34 steel lattice bridge
钢格子桥

35 counterbrace (crossbrace,
diagonal member)
反杆撑（对角构件）

36 vertical member
垂直桁材

37 truss joint
桁架节点

38 portal frame
桥门架

39 suspension bridge
吊桥

40 suspension cable
主索

41 suspender (hanger)
吊索（吊杆）

42 tower
桥塔

43 suspension cable anchorage
主索锚座

44 tied beam [with roadway]
连车道（路面）的系梁

45 abutment
桥台

46 cable-stayed bridge
斜索桥（斜张桥）

47 inclined tension cable
斜拉索

48 inclined cable anchorage
斜索锚座

49 reinforced concrete bridge
钢筋混凝土桥

50 reinforced concrete arch
钢筋混凝土桥拱

51 inclined cable system (multiple
cable system)
（倾）斜（缆）索系统

52 flat bridge, a plate girder bridge
平桥，一种钣梁桥

53 stiffener
加劲杆

54 pier
桥墩

55 bridge bearing
桥梁支承

56 cutwater
分水角

57 straits bridge, a bridge built of
precast elements
狭桥，一种预铸构造的桥

58 precast construction unit
预铸构件

59 viaduct
高架桥

60 valley bottom
谷底

61 reinforced concrete pier
钢筋混凝土桥墩

62 scaffolding
工作架

63 lattice swing bridge
格子旋桥

64 turntable
转盘

65 pivot pier
旋转桥墩

66 pivoting half (pivoting section,
pivoting span, movable half) of
bridge
桥的半迴旋部分（迴旋部分，迴旋跨径
可移动之半部分）

67 flat swing bridge
平旋桥

68 middle section
中间部分

69 pivot
旋轴

70 parapet (handrailing)
栏杆

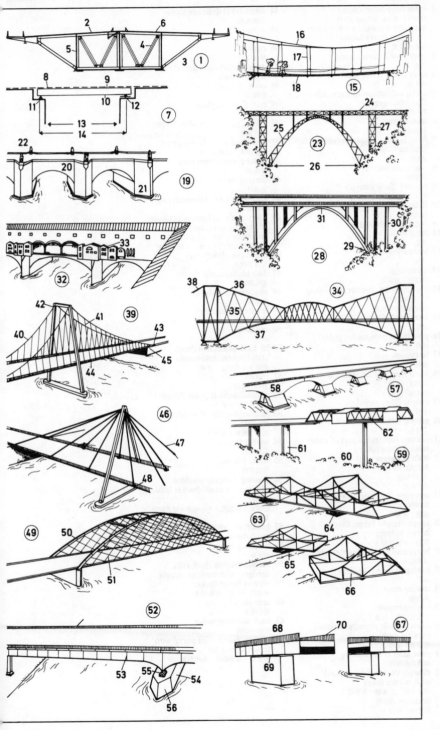

1 **cable ferry** (*also: chain ferry*), a passenger ferry
缆索渡船（链索渡船），一种旅客渡船

2 ferry rope (ferry cable)
渡船用缆索

3 river branch (river arm)
支流

4 river island (river islet)
河中岛

5 collapsed section of riverbank, flood damage
河岸塌陷部分，洪水冲损处

6 **motor ferry**
电动渡船

7 ferry landing stage (motorboat landing stage)
渡船码头

8 pile foundations
桩基础

9 current (flow, course)
水流

10 **flying ferry** (river ferry), a car ferry
高速渡船，一种汽车渡船

11 ferry boat
渡船

12 buoy (float)
浮标

13 anchorage
停泊处，抛锚处

14 harbour (*Am.* harbor) for laying up river craft
停泊河船的碇泊场

15 **ferry boat** (punt)
渡船

16 pole (punt pole, quant pole)
撑篙

17 ferryman
渡船夫

18 blind river branch (blind river arm)
盲支流

19 groyne (*Am.* groin)
丁坝

20 groyne (*Am.* groin) head
丁坝头

21 fairway (navigable part of river)
航道（河中可通航部分）

22 **train of barges**
牵引式驳船

23 river tug
河中拖船

24 tow rope (tow line, towing hawser)
拖缆，拖绳

25 barge (freight barge, cargo barge, lighter)
驳船（运货船）

26 bargeman (bargee, lighterman)
驳船船夫

27 **towing** (hauling, haulage)
牵引

28 towing mast
牵引桅

29 towing engine
牵引发动机（引擎）

30 towing track; *form.:* tow path (towing path)
拖船道（牵道）

31 river after river training
疏浚后的河川

32 **dike** (dyke, main dike, flood wall, winter dike)
堤（主堤，洪水壁，冬季堤）

33 drainage ditch
排水沟（明沟）

34 dike (dyke) drainage sluice
堤排水闸

35 wing wall
翼墙

36 outfall
排水口

37 drain (infiltration drain)
排水沟（暗沟）

38 berm (berme)
护坡道

39 top of dike (dyke)
堤顶

40 dike (dyke) batter (dike slope)
堤防斜坡

41 flood bed (inundation area)
洪水河床（泛滥区）

42 flood containment area
蓄洪区

43 current meter
流速计

44 kilometre (*Am.* kilometer) sign
里程标

45 dikereeve's (dykereeve's) house (dikereeve's cottage); *also:* ferryman's house (cottage)
堤防管理人住屋；亦称：渡船夫住屋

46 dikereeve (dykereeve)
堤防管理人

47 dike (dyke) ramp
堤防坡道

48 summer dike (dyke)
夏季堤

49 levee (embankment)
堤防（河堤）

50 sandbags
砂袋

51-55 **bank protection** (bank stabilization, revetment)
护岸（岸坡稳定，护坡）

51 riprap
抛石，堆石

52 alluvial deposit (sand deposit)
冲积层（砂沉积）

53 fascine (bundle of wooden sticks)
沉梢（梢捆，束柴）

54 wicker fences
编枝栅拦

55 stone pitching
石砌护坡

56 **floating dredging machine** (dredger), a multi-bucket ladder dredge
挖泥船（挖泥机），一种多斗梯式挖泥船

57 bucket elevator chain
挖斗升降机链

58 dredging bucket
挖泥斗

59 **suction dredger** (hydraulic dredger) with trailing suction pipe or barge sucker
吸泥机（吸扬式控泥船）

60 centrifugal pump
离心抽水机，离心泵

61 back scouring valve
后部冲刷阀

62 suction pump, a jet pump with scouring nozzles
抽水泵，带冲刷喷咀的喷射泵

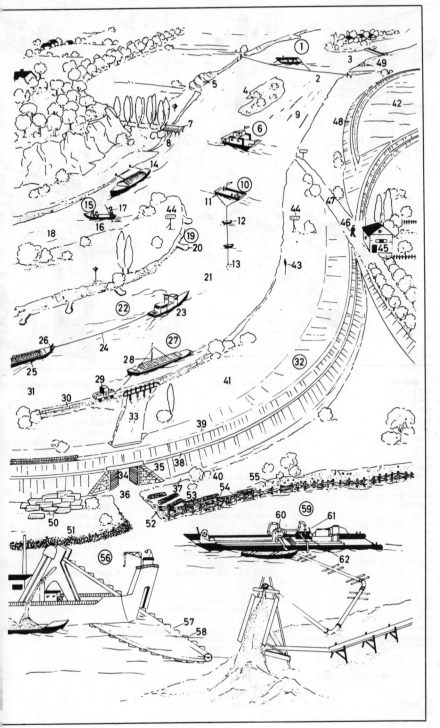

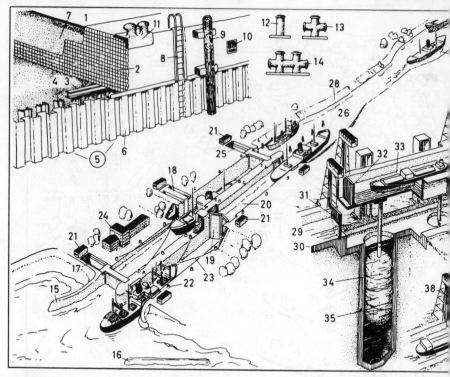

1-14 quay wall
岸壁，码头
1 road surface
路面
2 body of wall
墙体
3 steel sleeper
钢轨枕
4 steel pile
钢桩
5 sheet pile wall (sheet pile bulkhead, sheetpiling)
板桩墙（板桩隔壁，钢板桩）
6 box pile
箱形桩
7 backfilling (filling)
回填，回填土
8 ladder
梯子
9 fender (fender pile)
护舷木（护舷桩）
10 recessed bollard
凹状系船柱
11 double bollard
双系船柱
12 bollard
系船柱
13 cross-shaped bollard (cross-shaped mooring bitt)
十字型系船柱
14 double cross-shaped bollard (double cross-shaped mooring bitt)
双十字型系船柱
15-28 canal
运河

15-16 canal entrance
运河入口
15 mole
防波堤，突堤
16 breakwater
防波堤
17-25 staircase of locks
阶梯式船闸
17 lower level
下游水位
18 lock gate, a sliding gate
船闸门，滑动闸门
19 mitre (*Am.* miter) gate
人字闸门
20 lock (lock chamber)
船闸室
21 power house
发电厂
22 warping capstan (hauling capstan), a capstan
卷绞盘（牵引绞盘），一种绞盘
23 warp
拖船索
24 offices (e.g. canal administration, river police, customs)
办公处（例如：运河管理处，河上警察局，海关）
25 upper level (head)
上游水位
26 lock approach
船闸引道
27 lay-by
河道中停泊驳船处
28 bank slope
岸坡

29-38 boat lift (*Am.* boat elevat
船之升降
29 lower pound (lower reaach)
下游区间，下游通行河道（下游河间
30 canal bed
运河床
31 pound lock gate, a vertical g
河道闸门，一种垂直闸门
32 lock gate
船闸门
33 boat tank (caisson)
船槽
34 float
浮筒
35 float shaft
浮筒升降井
36 lifting spindle
提升转轴
37 upper pound (upper reach)
上游区间，上游通行河道（上游河间
38 vertical gate
垂直闸门

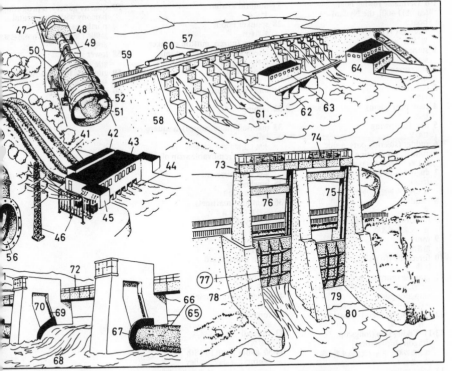

pumping plant and reservoir
水站和水库
rebay
电
ge tank
压塔（取水室，水室）
essure pipeline
力管道
lve house (valve control
ouse)
室（阀控制室）
rbine house (pumping station)
轮机室（抽水站）
scharge structure (outlet
ructure)
水构造物
ntrol station
制室
ansformer station
电站

axial-flow pump (propeller
ump)
流式抽水机（推进抽水机）
rive motor
动马达
ear
齿轮）传动装置
rive shaft
动主轴
ressure pipe
力管，压送管
uction head
水头
npeller wheel
叶轮
6 sluice valve (sluice gate)
水阀（泄水闸门）

53 crank drive
曲柄传动装置
54 valve housing
阀室
55 sliding valve (sliding gate)
滑动阀（滑动闸门）
56 discharge opening
排水口
57-64 dam (barrage)
坝（堰）
57 reservoir (storage reservoir,
impounding reservoir,
impounded reservoir)
水库（蓄水库）
58 masonry dam
砌工坝
59 crest of dam
坝顶
60 spillway (overflow spillway)
溢洪道
61 stilling basin (stilling box,
stilling pool)
静水池
62 scouring tunnel (outlet tunnel,
waste water outlet)
冲刷隧道（排水隧道，废水排水道）
63 valve house (valve control
house)
阀室（阀控制室）
64 power station
发电厂
65-72 rolling dam (weir), a barrage;
other system: shutter weir
滚坝（堰），一种拦水坝（堰）；另一
种型式是：橢堰
65 roller, a barrier
滚轴，一种栅栏

66 roller top
滚轴顶部
67 flange
[滚轴]凸缘
68 submersible roller
过水滚轴
69 rack track
齿形轨
70 recess
轨槽，凹槽
71 hoisting gear cabin
起重传动装置室
72 service bridge (walkway)
工作桥（人行道）
73-80 sluice dam
泄水坝
73 hoisting gear bridge
起重传动装置（升降装置）
74 hoisting gear (winding gear)
吊重齿轮（卷扬机构）
75 guide groove
导槽
76 counterweight (counterpoise)
泄水平衡锤（平衡重）
77 sluice gate (floodgate)
泄水闸门（防洪闸门）
78 reinforcing rib
加强肋
79 dam sill (weir sill)
坝槛（堰槛）
80 wing wall
翼墙

1-6 Germanic rowing boat
[ca. AD 400], the Nydam
boat
德国划船（西元400年），一种"奈德
姆"划船

1 stern post
舳柱
2 steersman
舵手
3 oarsman
刘桨手
4 stem post (stem)
艏柱
5 oar, for rowing
刘船桨
6 rudder (steering oar), a side
rudder, for steering
舵（橹），控制方向的侧舵
7 **dugout,** a hollowed-out tree
trunk
独木舟，一种挖空的树干
8 paddle
桨

9-12 trireme, a Roman warship
有三层桨座的战船，罗马战船
9 ram
船首撞角
10 forecastle (fo'c'sle)
艏楼
11 grapple (grapnel, grappling
iron), for fastening the enemy
ship alongside
爪钩，钩杆（用以钩住并排敌船）
12 three banks (tiers) of oars
三排（层）桨

13-17 Viking ship (longship,
dragon ship) [Norse]
维京海盗船（中古时代北欧单帆多桨长
船，龙船）
13 helm (tiller)
舵柄
14 awning crutch with carved
horses' heads
带雕刻马头的船篷支架
15 awning
船篷
16 dragon figurehead
龙形船头
17 shield
盾

18-26 cog (Hansa cog, Hansa ship)
小船，附属於大船的供应船（汉瑟船）
18 anchor cable (anchor rope,
anchor hawser)
锚缆，锚索
19 forecastle (fo'c'sle)
艏楼
20 bowsprit
艏斜桅
21 furled (brailed-up) square sail
卷起的横帆
22 town banner (city banner)
城市旗帜
23 aftercastle (sterncastle)
艉楼
24 rudder, a stem rudder
舵，一种艏舵
25 elliptical stern (round stern)
椭圆舳（圆舳）
26 wooden fender
木碰垫

27-43 caravel (carvel) ['Santa
Maria' 1492]
轻快帆船（圣玛琍亚号1492年）

27 admiral's cabin
船长室
28 spanker boom
后纵帆杆
29 mizzen (mizen, mutton spanker,
lateen spanker), a lateen sail
后帆，大三角帆
30 lateen yard
三角帆桁
31 mizzen (mizen) mast
后帆桅
32 lashing
捆索系索
33 mainsail (main course), a square
sail
主帆（主桅主帆）、横帆的一种
34 bonnet, a removable strip of
canvas
小帆，可拆卸的帆布片
35 bowline
艏缆（张帆索）
36 bunt line (martinet)
帆脚索（纹帆索）
37 main yard
主帆桁
38 main topsail
中桅主帆
39 main topsail yard
中桅主帆桁
40 mainmast
主桅
41 foresail (fore course)
前帆
42 foremast
前桅
43 spritsail
斜杠帆

44-50 galley [15th to 18th
century], a slave galley
两排桨的帆船（15-18世纪），一种奴
隶船
44 lantern
灯笼，信号灯
45 cabin
船舱
46 central gangway
中间过道
47 slave driver with whip
持鞭子的奴隶监督
48 galley slaves
划船的奴隶
49 covered platform in the forepart
of the ship
船首隐蔽平台
50 gun
火炮

51-60 ship of the line (line-of-battle
ship) [18th to 19th century],
a three-decker
战舰（18-19世纪），三层甲板船
51 jib boom
艏帆斜桅
52 fore topgallant sail
前上桅帆
53 main topgallant sail
主上桅帆
54 mizzen (mizen) topgallant sail
后上桅帆
55-57 gilded stern
镀金船尾
55 upper stern
船尾上部
56 stern gallery
船尾了望台

57 quarter gallery, a projecting
balcony with ornamental
portholes
船侧尾了望台，一种具有装饰舷窗
出望台（露台）
58 lower stern
船尾下部
59 gunports for broadside fire
舷侧炮火用炮门
60 gunport shutter
炮门挡板

1-72 rigging (rig, tackle) and
sails of a bark (barque)
多桅帆船的帆缆（船具，滑车辘轳）

1-9 masts
桅

1 bowsprit with jib boom
带艏帆的斜桅的艏斜桅

2-4 foremast
前桅

2 lower foremast
下前桅

3 fore topmast
前中桅

4 fore topgallant mast
前上桅

5-7 mainmast
主桅

5 lower mainmast
下主桅

6 main topmast
主中桅

7 main topgallant mast
主上桅

8-9 mizzen (mizen) mast
后桅

8 lower mizzen (lower mizen)
下后桅

9 mizzen (mizen) topmast

10-19 standing rigging
静索

10 stay
牵索，支索

11 topmast stay
中桅支索

12 topgallant stay
上桅支索

13 royal stay
顶桅支索

14 jib stay
艏帆支索

15 bobstay
首斜桅支索

16 shrouds
桅牵索

17 fore topmast rigging (main
topmast rigging, mizzen (mizen)
topmast rigging)
前中桅索具（主中桅索具，后中桅索
具）

18 fore topgallant rigging (main
topgallant rigging)
前上桅索具（主上桅帆索具）

19 backstays
后支索

20-31 fore-and-aft sails
船首及船尾帆

20 fore topmast staysail
前中桅支索帆

21 inner jib
内艏帆

22 outer jib
外艏帆

23 flying jib
艏三角帆

24 main topmast staysail
主中桅支索帆

25 main topgallant staysail
主上桅支索帆

26 main royal staysail
主顶桅支索帆

27 mizzen (mizen) staysail
后桅支索帆

28 mizzen (mizen) topmast staysail
后中桅支索帆

29 mizzen (mizen) topgallant
staysail
后上桅支索帆

30 mizzen (mizen, spanker, driver)
后桅（后纵帆）

31 gaff topsail
纵帆斜桁顶帆

32-45 spars
帆、桅、桁

32 foreyard
前桅桁

33 lower fore topsail yard
前中桅下帆桁

34 uppper fore topsail yard
前中桅上帆桁

35 lower fore topgallant yard
前上桅下帆桁

36 upper fore topgallant yard
前上桅上帆桁

37 fore royal yard
前顶桅帆桁

38 main yard
主帆桁

39 lower main topsail yard
主中桅下帆桁

40 upper main topsail yard
主中桅上帆桁

41 lower main topgallant yard
主上桅低帆桁

42 upper main topgallant yard
主上桅上帆桁

43 main royal yard
主顶桅帆桁

44 spanker boom
后纵帆杠（杆）

45 spanker gaff
后纵帆斜桁

46 footrope
根缆

47 lifts
吊索（帆桁吊索）

48 spanker boom topping lift
后纵帆杠（杆）端吊索

49 spanker peak halyard
后纵帆杠（杆）顶吊索

50 foretop
前桅楼

51 fore topmast crosstrees
前中桅桅顶横杆

52 maintop
主桅楼

53 main topmast crosstrees
主中桅桅顶横杆

54 mizzen (mizen) top
后桅楼

55-56 square sails
横帆，方帆

55 foresail (fore course)
前帆（前桅帆）

56 lower fore topsail
前中桅下帆

57 upper fore topsail
前中桅上帆

58 lower fore topgallant sail
前上桅下帆

59 upper fore topgallant sail
前上桅上帆

60 fore royal
前顶帆

61 mainsail (main course)
主帆（主桅帆）

62 lower main topsail
主中桅下帆

63 upper main topsail
主中桅上帆

64 lower main topgallant sail
主上桅下帆

65 upper main topgallant sail
主上桅上帆

66 main royal sail
主顶帆

67-71 running rigging
转动（活动）索具

67 braces
操桁索

68 sheets
帆脚索

69 spanker sheet
后纵帆帆脚索

70 spanker vangs
后纵帆斜桁支索

71 bunt line
绞帆索

72 reef
卷帆部分，缩帆索，卷帆索

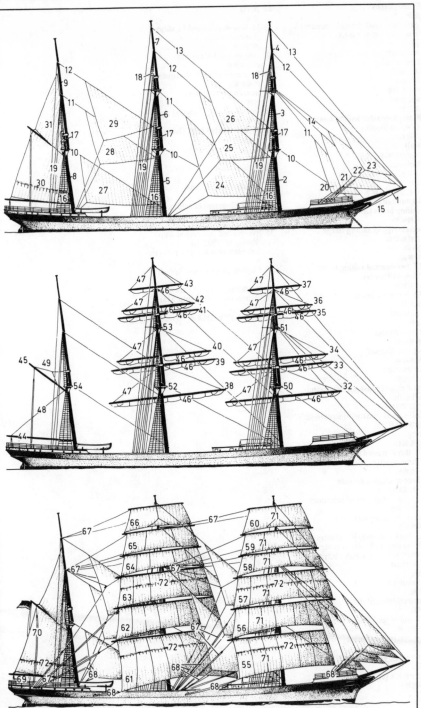

1-5 sail shapes
帆的类型

1 gaffsail (*small:* trysail, spencer)
斜帆（前桅之纵帆，斜桁帆）

2 jib
船首三角帆

3 lateen sail
大三角帆

4 lugsail
斜桁用横帆

5 spritsail
斜杠帆

6-8 single-masted sailing boats
(*Am.* sailboats)
单桅帆船

6 tjalk
荷兰单桅帆船（小船）

7 leeboard
下风板

8 cutter
独桅快艇（小艇）

9-10 mizzen (mizen) masted sailing boats (*Am.*** sailboats)**
后桅帆船

9 ketch-rigged sailing barge
双桅帆驳船

10 yawl
小帆船

11-17 two-masted sailing boats
(*Am.* sailboats)
双桅帆船

11-13 topsail schooner
顶帆船

11 mainsail
主帆

12 boom foresail
前桅帆桁

13 square foresail
前桅横帆

14 brigantine
双桅帆船

15 half-rigged mast with fore-and-aft sails
半边带纵帆的桅

16 full-rigged mast with square sails
全部为横帆的桅

17 brig
双桅帆船

18-27 three-masted sailing vessels
(three-masters)
三桅帆船

18 three-masted schooner
三桅纵帆船

19 three-masted topsail schooner
三桅顶帆船

20 bark (barque) schooner
多桅帆船

21-23 bark (barque) [cf. illustration of rigging and sails in plate 219]
多桅帆船〔看图 219，帆具及帆的说明〕

21 foremast
前桅

22 mainmast
主桅

23 mizzen (mizen) mast
后桅

24-27 full-rigged ship
全帆帆船

24 mizzen (mizen) mast
后桅

25 crossjack yard (crojack yard)
后桅下桁横帆

26 crossjack (crojack)
后桅横帆

27 ports
舷窗

28-31 four-masted sailing ships
(four-masters)
四桅帆船

28 four-masted schooner
四桅纵帆船

29 four-masted bark (barque)
四桅帆船

30 mizzen (mizen) mast
后桅

31 four-masted full-rigged ship
四桅全帆帆船

32-34 five-masted bark (barque)
五桅帆船

32 skysail
顶帆上的小方帆

33 middle mast
中桅

34 mizzen (mizen) mast
后桅

35-37 development of sailing ships
over 400 years
四百年间帆船的发展

35 five-masted full-rigged ship 'Preussen' 1902-10
五桅全帆帆船"普鲁士号"（1902-1910年）

36 English clipper ship 'Spindrift' 1867
英国快速帆船"浪花号"（1867年）

37 caravel (carvel) 'Santa Maria' 1492
多桅小帆船"圣玛琍亚号"（1492年）

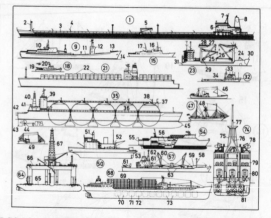

51 steaming light mast
蒸汽灯桅
52 helicopter hangar
直升机库
53 stern towing point, for gripp
the bow of ships in tow
船尾拖曳点，扣住船首以拖行
54 **roll-on-roll-off (ro-ro) trailer
ferry**
（开上开下）拖车渡轮
55 stern port (stern opening) w
ramp
带坡道的艄门
56 heavy vehicle lifts (*Am.* heav
vehicle elevators)
重型车辆升降机
57 **multi-purpose freighter**
多用途货船
58 ventilator-type samson
(sampson) post (ventilator-t
king post)
通风管式吊杆柱（通风管式主柱
59 derrick boom (cargo boom,
cargo gear, cargo-handling g
吊杆，起重杆（货物装卸装置）
60 derrick mast
吊杆桅
61 deck crane
甲板起重机
62 jumbo derrick boom (heavy-
derrick boom)
重型吊杆
63 cargo hatchway
货舱口
64 **semisubmersible drilling
vessel**
半潜式钻探船
65 floating vessel with machine
带机器的浮船
66 drilling platform
钻探平台
67 derrick
钻塔
68 **cattleship** (cattle vessel)
家畜（运输）船
69 superstructure for transport
livestock
运输家畜的上层建筑
70 fresh water tanks
新鲜（淡）水槽
71 fuel tank
燃料槽
72 dung tank
粪便槽
73 fodder tanks
饲料（草料）槽
74 **train ferry** [cross section]
火车渡轮
75 funnel
烟窗
76 exhaust pipes
排气管
77 mast
桅
78 ship's lifeboat hanging at the
davit
吊于吊架上的救生艇
79 car deck
汽车甲板
80 main deck (train deck)
主甲板（火车甲板）
81 main engines
主发动机（引擎）

1 **ULCC** (ultra large crude
carrier) of the [all-aft' type
机型超大型油轮
2 foremast
前桅
3 catwalk with the pipes
有管的窄道
4 fire gun (fire nozzle)
灭火枪，灭火喷咀
5 deck crane
甲板起重机
6 deckhouse with the bridge
甲板房舱和船桥（楼）
7 aft signal (signalling) and radar
mast
船尾信号和雷达桅
8 funnel
烟囱
9 **nuclear research ship** 'Otto
Hahn', a bulk carrier
"奥托汉"核能研究轮，一种散装货轮
10 aft superstructure (engine room)
艉上层建筑（机舱）
11 cargo hatchway for bulk goods
(bulk cargoes)
散装货物舱口
12 bridge
楼（船桥）
13 forecastle (fo'c'sle)
艏楼
14 stem
船首
15 **seaside pleasure boat**
海滨游艇
16 dummy funnel
假烟囱
17 exhaust mast
排气桅
18 **rescue cruiser**
救难巡洋舰
19 helicopter platform (working
deck)
直升机平台（工作甲板）
20 rescue helicopter
救难直升机
21 **all-container ship**
全货柜轮
22 containers stowed on deck
装置于甲板上的货柜
23 **cargo ship**
货船
24-29 cargo gear (cargo-handling
gear)
货物装卸装置
24 bipod mast
双脚桅

25 jumbo derrick boom (heavy-lift
derrick boom)
重型吊杆（起重杆）
26 derrick boom (cargo boom)
吊杆，起重杆
27 tackle
滑轮组
28 block
滑车
29 thrust bearing
推力轴承
30 bow doors
艏门
31 stern loading door
船尾装货门
32 **offshore drilling rig supply
vessel**
海上钻探补给船
33 compact superstructure
紧凑的上层建筑
34 loading deck (working deck)
载货甲板（工作甲板）
35 **liquefied-gas tanker**
液化气运输船
36 spherical tank
球型罐
37 navigational television receiver
mast
航海电视接收机桅杆
38 vent mast
通气（风）管桅
39 deckhouse
甲板房舱
40 funnel
烟囱
41 ventilator
通风机
42 transom stern (transom)
船尾梁
43 rudder blade (rudder)
舵叶（面）
44 ship's propeller (ship's screw)
船的推进器（船的螺浆）
45 bulbous bow
球形艏
46 steam trawler
蒸汽拖网渔船
47 **lightship** (light vessel)
灯塔船
48 lantern (characteristic light)
信号灯
49 smack
（设有养鱼槽的）渔帆船
50 ice breaker
破冰船

ssenger liner (liner, ocean
er)
朗客轮（定期越洋轮）
em
首
nnel with lattice casing
格子套的烟窗
g dressing (rainbow dressing,
ing of flags extending over
astheads, e.g., on the
aiden voyage)
彩装饰（遍布于各桅顶间的彩旗
，如：首次航行）
awler, a factory ship
网渔船，一种工厂船
llows
架，滑车架台
ern ramp
尾倾斜台
ntainer ship
箱船
ading bridge (loading
atform)
卸桥（装卸平台）
a ladder (jacob's ladder, rope
dder)
上用梯（绳梯，软梯）
rge and push tug assembly
船和推拖船组合体
sh tug
推拖船
g-pushed dumb barge (tug-
shed lighter)
船推进的无动力驳船
ot boat
水船
mbined cargo and passenger
er
朗客货轮

97 passengers disembarking by
   boat
   经由小船上岸的旅客
98 accommodation ladder
   舷梯
99 coaster (coasting vessel)
   沿海船，近海船
100 customs *or* police launch
   海关或水警汽艇
101-128 excursion steamer
   (pleasure steamer)
   旅游汽船
101-106 lifeboat launching gear
   救生艇下水装置
101 davit
   吊架
102 wire rope span
   顶跨钢索
103 lifeline
   救生索
104 tackle
   滑车组
105 block
   滑车
106 fall
   吊索
107 ship's lifeboat (ship's boat)
   covered with tarpaulin
   复盖防水布罩的船载救生艇
108 stem
   船首
109 passenger
   旅客
110 steward
   服务员
111 deck-chair
   甲板座椅
112 deck hand
   甲板人员

113 deck bucket
   甲板水桶
114 boatswain (bo's'n, bo'sun,
   bosun)
   水手长
115 tunic
   短上衣
116 awning
   （甲板上的）遮篷
117 stanchion
   支柱
118 ridge rope (jackstay)
   遮篷索
119 lashing
   系索，绑索
120 bulwark
   舷墙
121 guard rail
   导轨
122 handrail (top rail)
   扶手栏杆
123 companion ladder
   (companionway)
   升降梯（口）
124 lifebelt (lifebuoy)
   救生带（救生圈）
125 lifebuoy light (lifebelt light,
   signal light)
   救生圈灯（救生带灯，信号灯）
126 officer of the watch
   (watchkeeper)
   值班人员
127 reefer (*Am.* pea jacket)
   双排扣厚呢上衣
128 binoculars
   双眼望远镜

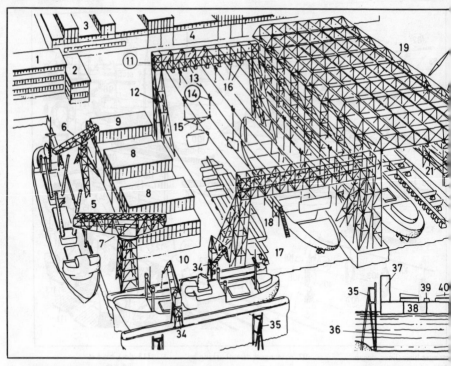

1-43 shipyard (shipbuilding yard, dockyard, *Am.* navy yard)
造船厂
1 administrative offices
管理办公室
2 ship-drawing office
船舶制图室（绘图室）
3-4 shipbuilding sheds
造船工场
3 mould (*Am.* mold) loft
放样间
4 erection shop
建造工场
5-9 fitting-out quay
装配码头
5 quay
码头
6 tripod crane
三脚架起重机
7 hammer-headed crane
锤型起重机
8 engineering workshop
轮机工作间
9 boiler shop
锅炉工场
10 repair quay
修理码头
11-26 slipways (slips, building berths, building slips, stocks)
船台（造船台）
11-18 cable crane berth, a slipway (building berth)
缆索起重机，一种船台（造船台）
11 slipway portal
船台门架
12 bridge support
桥支架

13 crane cable
起重机缆索
14 crab (jenny)
活动吊车（悬链导车）
15 cross piece
横梁
16 crane driver's cabin (crane driver's cage)
起重机驾驶室
17 slipway floor
船台底板
18 staging, a scaffold
搭架，一种台架
19-21 frame slipway
构架式船台
19 slipway frame
船台构架
20 overhead travelling (*Am.* traveling) crane (gantry crane)
高架式移动起重机
21 slewing crab
转动起重机
22 keel in position
放於定位上的龙骨
23 luffing jib crane, a slipway crane
悬臂式起重机，一种船台起重机
24 crane rails (crane track)
吊车轨道，起重机轨道
25 gantry crane
高架起重机
26 gantry (bridge)
门式起重机机架
27 trestles (supports)
架柱（支柱）
28 crab (jenny)
活动吊车，悬链导车

29 hull frames in position
於定位上的船体构架
30 ship under construction
建造中的船
31-33 dry dock
乾船坞
31 dock floor (dock bottom)
船坞底板
32 dock gates (caisson)
坞门
33 pumping station (power hou
泵室（动力室）
34-43 floating dock (pontoon de
浮坞（浮箱，驳船坞）
34 dock crane (dockside crane),
jib crane
船坞起重机，悬臂式起重机
35 fender pile
碰垫桩，护舷桩
36-43 working of docks
船坞的作业
36 dock basin
船渠
37-38 dock structure
船坞结构
37 side tank (side wall)
侧舱（侧壁）
38 bottom tank (bottom pontoo
底舱（下浮箱）
39 keel block
龙骨墩
40 bilge block (bilge shore, side
support)
舭部坞墩（舭部墩柱，边墩柱）
41-43 docking a ship
进坞的船隻

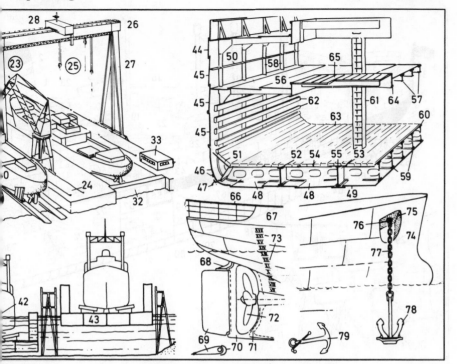

...oded floating dock
水浮坞，注水式浮坞

g towing the ship
曳船

ptied (pumped-out) dock
空水的船坞

structural parts of the ship
的结构（构造）部分

longitudinal structure
向结构

shell (shell plating, skin)
壳（船壳板，船表壳）

er strake
侧厚板列

le strake
板列

ge stake
板列

ge keel
龙骨

ttom plating
底外板

at plate keel (keel plate)
板龙骨（龙骨板）

ringer (side stringer)
材，舷缘板（侧纵材）

nk margin plate
缘板

ngitudinal side girder
纵梁

ntre (Am. center) plate girder
ntre girder, kelson, keelson,
rtical keel)
心板纵梁（中心纵梁，内龙骨，垂直
骨）

54 tank top plating (tank top, inner bottom plating)
重底顶板，柜舱顶板（舱顶，内舱底板）

55 centre (*Am.* center) strake
中心板列

56 deck plating
钢甲板

57 deck beam
甲板梁

58 frame (rib)
肋骨架

59 floor plate
底板

60 cellular double bottom
格子[二]重底

61 hold pillar (pillar)
舱柱

62, 63 dunnage
垫料

62 side battens (side ceiling, spar ceiling)
舱侧条（舱侧垫材，间距垫材）

63 ceiling (floor ceiling)
舱底板，垫材（舱底垫材）

64-65 hatchway
舱口，货舱口

64 hatch coaming
舱口缘围

65 hatch cover (hatchboard)
舱口盖板

66-72 stern
船尾

66 guard rail
护栏

67 bulwark
舷墙

68 rudder stock
舵杆

69-70 Oertz rudder
欧兹舵（流线型舵）

69 rudder blade (rudder)
舵面

70-71 stern frame
船尾架

70 rudder post
舵柱

71 propeller post (screw post)
推进器柱（螺桨柱）

72 ship's propeller (ship's screw)
推进器，螺旋桨

73 draught (draft) marks
吃水标

74-79 bow
船首

74 stem, a bulbous stem (bulbous bow)
船首，球型艏（柱）

75 hawse
锚链

76 hawse pipe
锚链筒

77 anchor cable (chain cable)
锚缆（链索）

78 stockless anchor (patent anchor)
山字锚，无杆锚

79 stocked anchor
普通锚，有杆锚

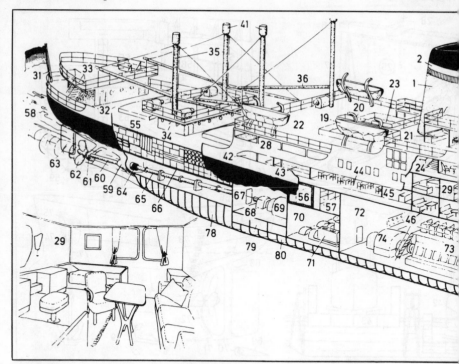

1-71 combined cargo and passenger ship [of the older type]
老式的客货轮
1 funnel
烟窗
2 funnel marking
烟窗标记
3 siren (fog horn)
汽笛（雾笛）
4-11 compass platform (compass bridge, compass flat, monkey bridge)
罗（盘）经台（甲板）
4 antenna lead-in (antenna download)
天线引入线（天线下引线）
5 radio direction finder (RDF) antenna (direction finder antenna, rotatable loop antenna, aural null loop antenna)
无线电测向仪天线（测向仪天线，可旋转的环型天线，消声环型天线）
6 magnetic compass (mariner's compass)
磁罗经（盘）（船用罗经）
7 morse lamp (signalling, *Am.* signaling, lamp)
信号灯
8 radar antenna (radar scanner)
雷达天线
9 code flag signal
信号旗信号
10 code flag halyards
信号旗的升降绳（索）

11 triatic stay (signal stay)
水平撑杆（信号撑杆）
12-18 bridge deck (bridge)
驾驶台甲板
12 radio room
无线电室（报务室）
13 captain's cabin
船长室
14 navigating bridge
驾驶台
15 starboard sidelight [green; port sidelight red]
右舷灯[绿，左舷灯红]
16 wing of bridge
桥翼，船桥的舷翼
17 shelter (weather cloth, dodger)
遮蔽物（挡雨布，防雨布）
18 wheelhouse
舵轮室，驾驶室
19-21 boat deck
小艇甲板
19 ship's lifeboat
救生艇
20 davit
吊柱，吊架
21 officer's cabin
高级船员室
22-27 promenade deck
散步甲板
22 sun deck (lido deck)
阳光甲板（游泳池甲板）
23 swimming pool
游泳池
24 companion ladder (companionway)
升降梯，升降口

25 library (ship's library)
图书馆
26 lounge
休息室
27 promenade
散步甲板
28-30 A-deck
A 甲板
28 semi-enclosed deck space
半封（围）闭式甲板空间
29 double-berth cabin, a cabin
双铺房舱
30 de luxe cabin
豪华舱（头等舱）
31 ensign staff
船尾旗杆
32-42 B-deck (main deck)
B 甲板（主甲板）
32 after deck
后甲板
33 poop
艉楼
34 deckhouse
甲板室
35 samson (sampson) post (king post)
吊杆柱

392

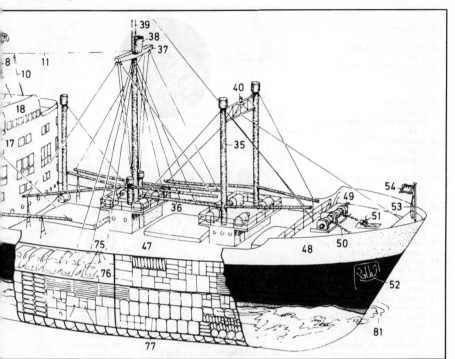

errick boom (cargo boom)
杆（起重杆）
osstrees (spreader)
顶横杆
ow's nest
杆了望台
pmast
桅
rward steaming light
首航行灯
ntilator lead
风器导管
lley (caboose, cookroom,
ip's kitchen)
房
ip's pantry
膳室
ning room
厅
urser's office
务长室
ngle-berth cabin
人舱
redeck
甲板
recastle (fo'c'sle)
首楼
ground tackle
具
indlass
机
chor cable (chain cable)
缆（链索）
mpressor (chain compressor)
缩机（链式压缩机）
chor

53 jackstaff
　船首旗杆
54 jack
　船首旗
55 after holds
　后舱
56 cold storage room (insulated
　hold)
　冷藏室〔隔（绝）热舱〕
57 store room
　储藏室
58 wake
　航系
59 shell bossing (shaft bossing)
　轴包架（轴轴毂）
60 tail shaft (tail end shaft)
　舶轴
61 shaft strut (strut, spectacle
　frame, propeller strut, propeller
　bracket)
　舶轴支架（支架，双环架，推进器架，
　推进器拖架）
62 three-blade ship's propeller
　(ship's screw)
　船用三叶螺旋桨
63 rudder blade (rudder)
　舵面
64 stuffing box
　填料函
65 propeller shaft
　螺旋桨轴
66 shaft alley (shaft tunnel)
　轴道
67 thrust block
　推力轴承
68-74 diesel-electric drive
　柴油机电力推进（驱动）

68 electric engine room
　电动机（引擎）房
69 electric motor
　电动机
70 auxiliary engine room
　辅机房
71 auxiliary engines
　辅机
72 main engine room
　主机房
73 main engine, a diesel engine
　主机，一种柴油发动机
74 generator
　发电机
75 forward holds
　前舱
76 tween deck
　中甲板
77 cargo
　货物
78 ballast tank (deep tank) for
　water ballast
　水压载的压载舱（深舱）
79 fresh water tank
　淡水舱
80 fuel tank
　燃料舱
81 bow wave
　船首波

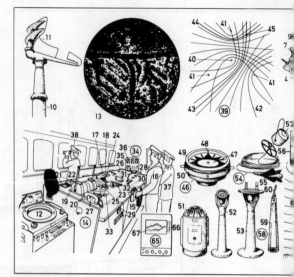

1 **sextant**
六分仪

2 graduated arc
刻度弧

3 index bar (index arm)
指示棒

4 decimal micrometer
十进位测微器

5 vernier
游标

6 index mirror
指示镜

7 horizon glass (horizon mirror)
水平镜

8 telescope
望远镜

9 grip (handgrip)
手柄

10-13 **radar equipment** (radar apparatus)
雷达设备

10 radar pedestal
雷达基座

11 revolving radar reflector
旋转式雷达反射器

12 radar display unit (radar screen)
雷达显示装置（雷达屏幕）

13 radar image (radar picture)
雷达图像

14-38 **wheelhouse**
舵轮室，驾驶室

14 steering and control position
操纵和控制室（位置）

15 ship's wheel for controlling the rudder mechanism
控制舵机的舵轮

16 helmsman (*Am.* wheelsman)
舵手

17 rudder angle indicator
舵角指示器

18 automatic pilot (autopilot)
自航器

19 control lever for the variable-pitch propeller (reversible propeller, feathering propeller, feathering screw)
变距螺旋桨的控制杆（可逆向的螺旋桨，顺流螺旋桨）

20 propeller pitch indicator
螺旋桨螺距指示器

21 main engine revolution indicator
主（发动）机转速指示器

22 ship's speedometer (log)
速率计

23 control switch for bow thruster (bow-manoeuvring, *Am.* maneuvering, propeller)
艏转向推进器控制开关（艏操纵，推进器）

24 echo recorder (depth recorder, echograph)
回音记录器（深度记录器）

25 engine telegraph (engine order telegraph)
车钟（车令钟）

26 controls for the antirolling system (for the stabilizers)
抗摇系统的控制装置

27 local-battery telephone
自给电池电话

28 shipping traffic radio telephone
航运交通无线电话

29 navigation light indicator panel (running light indicator panel)
航海灯指示盘

30 microphone for ship's address system
船行位置呼叫系统用的传声器

31 gyro compass (gyroscopic compass), a compass repeater
迴转罗盘，一种罗盘重发器

32 control button for the ship's siren (ship's fog horn)
（雾）汽笛的控制按钮

33 main engine overload indicator
主机超载指示器

34 detector indicator unit for fixing the ship's position
固定船位置的探测显（指）示装置

35 rough focusing indicator
粗聚胶指示器

36 fine focusing indicator
微聚胶指示器

37 navigating officer
驾驶员

38 captain
船长

39 **Decca navigation system**
迪凯导航系统

40 master station
主台

41 slave station
副台

42 null hyperbola
零值双曲线

43 hyperbolic position line 1
双曲线的位置线 1

44 hyperbolic position line 2
双曲线的位置线 2

45 position (fix, ship fix)
船位（定位）

46-53 **compasses**
罗盘

46 liquid compass (fluid compass, spirit compass, wet compass), a magnetic compass
液体罗盘，一种磁罗盘

47 compass card
罗盘面（卡）

48 lubber's line (lubber's mark, lubber's point)
艏向刻线

49 compass bowl
罗盘碗

50 gimbal ring
平衡环

51-53 gyro compass (gyroscopic compass, gyro compass uni[t])
迴转罗盘

51 master compass (master gy[ro] compass)
主罗盘

52 compass repeater (gyro repe[ater])
罗盘重发器

53 compass repeater with pelo[rus]
带哑罗盘的罗盘重发器

54 **patent log** (screw log, mechanical log, towing log, taffrail log, speedometer)
测程仪（螺旋测程器，机械测程[器]，航[行]测程器，船尾栏杆测程计，速率[计]）

55 rotator
转子，转轮

56 governor
调速器

57 log clock
测程指示表

58-67 **leads**
测锤，测探锤

58 hand lead
手测深锤

59 lead (lead sinker)
测铅

60 leadline
测铅线

61-67 echo sounder (echo sounding machine)
回音测深机

61 sound transmitter
声音发送机

62 sound wave (sound impulse[s])
音波

63 echo (sound echo, echo sig[nal])
回音（回音信号）

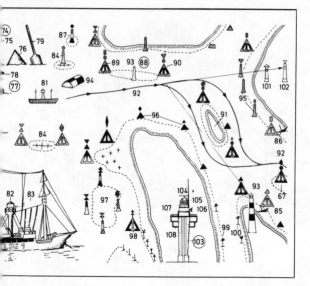

ho receiver (hydrophone)
音接收机（水中听音器）

hograph (echo sounding
achine recorder)
音记录器（回音测深机记录器）

epth scale
度标尺

hogram (depth recording,
epth reading)
度记录图

8 sea marks (floating
avigational marks) **for
10yage and lighting systems**
标（航海浮标），浮标和灯光系统

fairway marks (channel
arks)
道标示

ght and whistle buoy
光和鸣笛浮标

ght (warning light)
光（警灯）

histle

10y
标

10oring chain
船锚（系泊链）

nker (mooring sinker)
锤，系泊水砣

ght and bell buoy
光和钟浮标

ell

nical buoy
形浮标

n buoy
型浮标

pmark
标

ar buoy
标

pmark buoy
标浮标

htship (light vessel)
船

82 lantern mast (lantern tower)
灯塔

83 beam of light
光线，光束

84-102 fairway markings (channel
markings)
航道标志

84 wreck [green buoys]
沉船（绿色浮标）

85 wreck to starboard
右舷沉船标识

86 wreck to port
左舷沉船标识

87 shoals (shallows, shallow
water, *Am*. flats)
浅滩

88 middle ground to port
左舷中洲标识

89 division (bifurcation)
[beginning of the middle
ground; topmark: red cylinder
above red ball]
航道分岔处〔航道中洲的始端，顶标：
红球上红色圆筒〕

90 convergence (confluence) [end
of the middle ground; topmark:
red St. Antony's cross above
red ball]
航道汇合标志〔中洲终端，顶标：红球
上红色圣安东尼十字架〕

91 middle ground
中洲

92 main fairway (main navigable
channel)
主航道

93 secondary fairway (secondary
navigable channel)
副航道

94 can buoy
罐形浮标

95 port hand buoys (port hand
marks) [red]
左舷侧浮标〔红色〕

96 starboard hand buoys
(starboard hand marks)
[black]
右舷侧浮标〔黑色〕

97 shoals (shallows, shallow
water, *Am*. flats) outside the
fairway
在航道外侧的浅滩

98 middle of the fairway (mid-
channel)
航道中央标识

99 starboard markers (inverted
broom)
右舷标识（倒扫帚形）

100 port markers [upward-
pointing broom]
左舷标识（上向扫帚形）

101-102 range lights (leading lights)
导灯

101 lower range light (lower
leading light)
低导灯

102 higher range light (higher
leading light)
高导灯

103 lighthouse
灯塔

104 radar antenna (radar scanner)
雷达天线

105 lantern (characteristic light)
（特别的灯）灯室

106 radio direction finder (RDF)
antenna
无线电探向器天线

107 machinery and observation
platform (machinery and
observation deck)
机械装置和了望台

108 living quarters
住舱

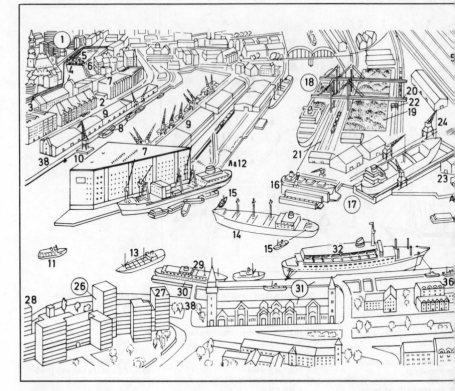

1 dock area 码头区	**15** tug 拖船	**31** passenger terminal 旅客码头
2 free port (foreign trade zone) 自由港（对外贸易区）	**16** floating dock (pontoon dock) 浮船坞（浮码头）	**32** liner (passenger liner, ocean liner) 定期轮（定期客轮，定期远洋轮）
3 free zone frontier (free zone enclosure) 自由区边界	**17** dry dock 乾船坞	**33** meteorological office, a weather station 气象台，气象站
4 customs barrier 海关关卡	**18** coal wharf 煤码头	**34** signal mast (signalling mast) 信号檣
5 customs entrance 海关入口	**19** coal bunker 煤仓	**35** storm signal 暴风雨信号
6 port custom house 港口海关	**20** transporter loading bridge 装卸运货的桥式吊车	**36** port administration offices 港口管理机关
7 entrepôt 仓库	**21** quayside railway 码头边铁路	**37** tide level indicator 潮汐水位指示器
8 barge (dumb barge, lighter) 驳船（无动力驳船，驳船）	**22** weighing bunker 过磅处	**38** quayside road (quayside roadway) 码头边马路
9 break-bulk cargo transit shed (general cargo transit shed, package cargo transit shed) 散装货通栈（一般货物通栈，包捆货物通栈）	**23** warehouse 仓库，货栈	**39** roll-on roll-off (ro-ro) system (roll-on roll-off operation) 水平装卸方式
10 floating crane 水上起重机	**24** quayside crane 码头边起重机	**40** gantry 门式起重机的门架
11 harbour (*Am.* harbor) ferry (ferryboat) 海峡渡轮	**25** launch and lighter 汽艇和驳船	**41** truck-to-truck system (truck-to-truck operation) 车对车装卸方式
12 fender (dolphin) 护舷（系船桩）	**26** port hospital 港口医院	**42** foil-wrapped unit loads 金属箔包装的单位货物
13 bunkering boat 燃料船，油船	**27** quarantine wing 检疫所	**43** pallets 货盘
14 break-bulk carrier (general cargo ship) 散装货船（一般货船）	**28** Institute of Tropical Medicine 热带医学研究所	**44** forklift truck (fork truck, forklift) 堆高机
	29 excursion steamer (pleasure steamer) 游览汽艇	
	30 jetty 突堤码头	

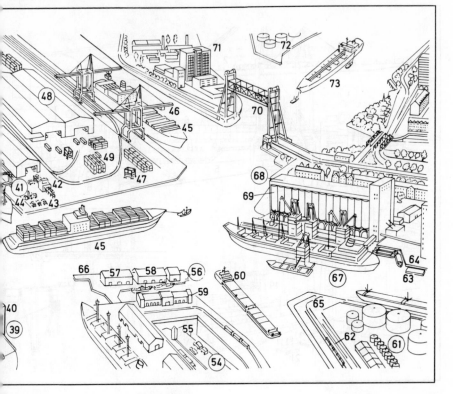

tainer ship
船
asporter container-loading
lge
装卸桥运输机
tainer carrier truck
运输卡车
tainer terminal (container
h)
码头
t load
货物
l store
库
veyor belt (conveyor)
机皮带
t storage shed (fruit
ehouse)
贮藏室
ce building
大楼
an motorway (*Am.* freeway)
高速公路
bour (*Am.* harbor) tunnels
隧道
dock
码头
market

tion room
室
-canning factory
工厂

60 push tow
顶推拖船
61 tank farm
油库
62 railway siding
铁路侧线
63 landing pontoon (landing stage)
栈台，栈桥
64 quay
码头
65 breakwater (mole)
防波堤
66 pier (jetty), a quay extension
突堤码头，延伸码头
67 bulk carrier
散装货船
68 silo
散装仓库
69 silo cylinder
散装仓库圆筒
70 lift bridge
升降桥
71 industrial plant
工业性工厂（场）
72 storage tanks
贮存罐
73 tanker
油轮

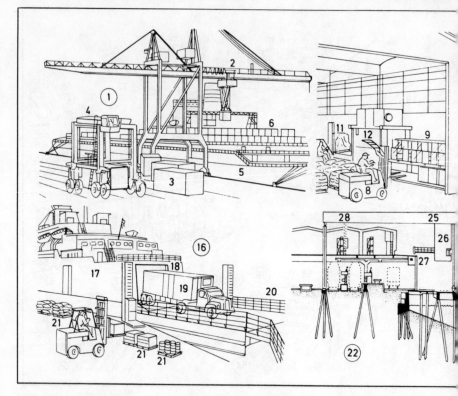

1 container terminal (container berth), a modern cargo-handling berth
货柜码头（新式货物装载码头）
2 transporter container-loading bridge (loading bridge); *sim.*: transtainer crane (transtainer)
货柜装载桥运输机；类似：移动式货柜起重机
3 container
货柜车
4 truck (carrier)
载货车
5 all-container ship
全货柜船
6 containers stowed on deck
堆放甲板上的货柜
7 truck-to-truck handling (horizontal cargo handling with pallets)
车对车搬运（具垫架的水平货物搬运）
8 forklift truck (fork truck, forklift)
堆高机
9 unitized foil-wrapped load (unit load)
单位化金属箔包装的货物
10 flat pallet, a standard pallet
平货盘，标准货盘
11 unitized break-bulk cargo
单位化散装货
12 heat sealing machine
热封口机

13 break-bulk carrier (general cargo ship)
散装货物运输船（一般普通货船）
14 cargo hatchway
货舱口
15 receiving truck on board ship
船上的接货卡车
16 multi-purpose terminal
多用途卸货码头
17 roll-on roll-off ship (ro-ro-ship)
水平装卸船
18 stern port (stern opening)
舳装卸门
19 driven load, a lorry (*Am.* truck)
载货卡车
20 ro-ro depot
水平装卸的货仓
21 unitized load (unitized package)
单位化货物
22 banana-handling terminal [section]
香蕉型装卸码头〔断面图〕
23 seaward tumbler
向海的转筒
24 jib
悬臂
25 elevator bridge
升降桥
26 chain sling
勾环吊链
27 lighting station
照明站

28 shore-side tumbler for loading trains and lorries (*Am.* trucks)
列车和卡车装载用的海岸转筒
29 bulk cargo handling
散装货物的装卸
30 bulk carrier
散装货船
31 floating bulk-cargo elevator
散装货浮升降机
32 suction pipes
吸管
33 receiver
接收器
34 delivery pipe
排出管
35 bulk transporter barge
散装货运驳船
36 floating pile driver
打桩机
37 pile driver frame
打桩机架
38 pile hammer
打桩锤
39 driving guide rail
驱动导轨
40 pile
桩
41 bucket dredger, a dredger
箕斗挖泥船，一种挖泥船
42 bucket chain
箕链
43 bucket ladder
箕梯

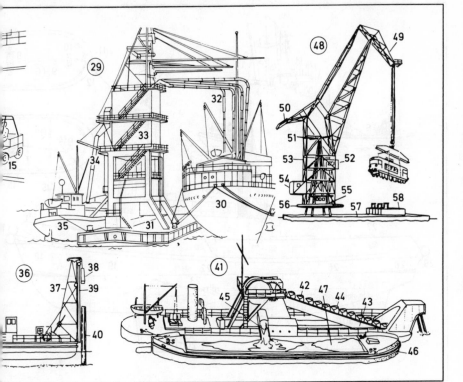

redger bucket
泥箕
ute
槽
opper barge
式驳船
oil
掘出之泥土
oating crane
重机船，水上起重机
o (boom)
臂
ounterweight (counterpoise)
重（对重）
djusting spindle
整轴
rane driver's cabin (crane
river's cage)
重机驾驶室
rane framework
重机架构骨架
inch house
车室
ontrol platform
制，操纵台
rntable
台
ntoon, a pram
底驳船，平底船的一种
gine superstructure (engine
ounting)
动机上的建筑物（船楼）

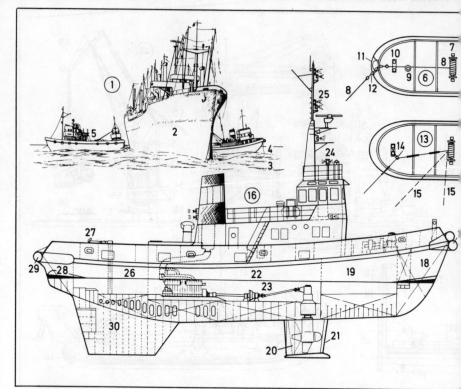

1 salvaging (salving) of a ship
   run aground
   搁浅船的救助
2 ship run aground (damaged
   vessel)
   搁浅船（受损船）
3 sandbank; *also:* quicksand
   沙洲；浮沙，流沙
4 open sea
   公海
5 tug (salvage tug)
   拖船（救难拖船）
6-15 towing gear
   拖曳装置
6 towing gear for towing at sea
   海上的拖曳装置
7 towing winch (towing machine,
   towing engine)
   拖曳绞车（拖曳机）
8 tow rope (tow line, towing
   hawser)
   拖缆，拖索（系船索）
9 tow rope guide
   拖索导柱
10 cross-shaped bollard
   十字形系缆柱
11 hawse hole
   锚链孔
12 anchor cable (chain cable)
   锚缆（链缆）
13 towing gear for work in
   harbours (*Am.* harbors)
   港内作业用的拖船装置

14 guest rope
   系船索
15 position of the tow rope (tow
   line, towing hawser)
   系船索，拖缆的位置
16 tug (salvage tug) [vertical
   elevation]
   拖船（救难拖船）〔立式正面图〕
17 bow fender (pudding fender)
   船首护舷（船首碰垫）
18 forepeak
   船首舱
19 living quarters
   住舱
20 Schottel propeller
   斯科特尔螺桨
21 Kort vent
   科特通气孔
22 engine and propeller room
   发动机和螺桨室
23 clutch coupling
   离合联结器
24 compass platform (compass
   bridge, compass flat, monkey
   bridge)
   罗盘台
25 fire-fighting equipment
   （消防）防火设备
26 stowage
   贮舱
27 tow hook
   拖钩
28 afterpeak
   船尾舱

29 stern fender
   船尾护舷（碰垫）
30 main manoeuvring (*Am.*
   maneuvering) keel
   主操纵龙骨

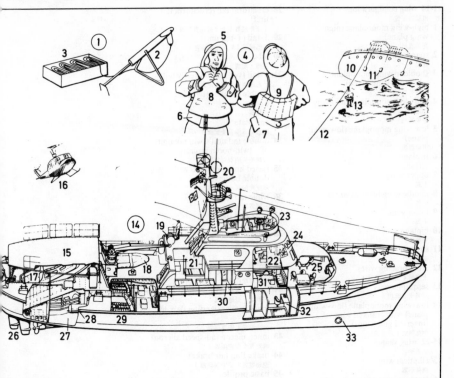

cket apparatus (rocket
n, line-throwing gun)
主索火箭发射器（火箭枪，抛绳枪）
rocket (rocket)
主火箭
cket line (whip line)
索引火箭绳（绕绳）
skins
衣
u' wester (southwester)
水帽
skin jacket
水夹克
skin coat
水外衣
latable life jacket
式救生衣
rk life jacket (cork life
eserver)
木救生衣
anded ship (damaged vessel)
线的船（受损的船）
bag, for trickling oil on the
ter surface
水面上滴油用的油袋
eline
主索
eches buoy
裤形救生衣
cue cruiser
准巡洋舰
licopter landing deck
升机著陆甲板

16 rescue helicopter
救难直升机
17 daughter boat
子船
18 inflatable boat (inflatable
dinghy)
充气艇，橡皮艇（充气小艇）
19 life raft
救生筏
20 fire-fighting equipment for fires
at sea
海难失火用的防火装置
21 hospital unit with operating
cabin and exposure bath
具手术室和御寒室的医院装置
22 navigating bridge
驾驶台
23 upper tier of navigating bridge
驾驶台的上层
24 lower tier of navigating bridge
驾驶台的下层
25 messroom
餐厅
26 rudders and propeller (screw)
舵和螺旋桨
27 stowage
贮藏舱
28 foam can
灭火器（泡沫灭火器）
29 side engines
船侧发动机
30 shower
浴室

31 coxswain's cabin
艇长室
32 crew member's single-berth
cabin
船员单人舱
33 bow propeller
船首（转向）推进器

1-14 wing configurations
机翼的配置

1 high-wing monoplane (high-wing plane)
高单翼机

2 span (wing span)
翼展

3 shoulder-wing monoplane (shoulder-wing plane)
上单翼机

4 midwing monoplane (midwing plane)
中单翼机

5 low-wing monoplane (low-wing plane)
下单翼机

6 triplane
三翼机

7 upper wing
上翼

8 middle wing (central wing)
中翼

9 lower wing
下翼

10 biplane
双翼机

11 strut
支柱

12 cross bracing wires
十字形（交叉）张线

13 sesquiplane
双翼半双翼机

14 low-wing monoplane (low-wing plane) with cranked wings (inverted gull wings)
倒海鸥式下单翼机

15-22 wing shapes
机翼形状

15 elliptical wing
椭圆形翼

16 rectangular wing
长方形翼

17 tapered wing
渐缩翼

18 crescent wing
新月形翼

19 delta wing
三角翼

20 swept-back wing with semi-positive sweepback
半正后掠角的后掠翼

21 swept-back wing with positive sweepback
正后掠角的后掠翼

22 ogival wing (ogee wing)
尖拱翼（S 形机翼）

23-36 tail shapes (tail unit shapes, empennage shapes)
尾翼形状（尾部装置形状，尾翼形状）

23 normal tail (normal tail unit)
（正常）一般的尾翼（一般的机尾装置）

24-25 vertical tail (vertical stabilizer and rudder)
直尾翼（垂直安定面和方向舵）

24 vertical stabilizer (vertical fin, tail fin)
垂直安定面（直尾翅，尾翅）

25 rudder
方向舵

26-27 horizontal tail
水平尾翼

26 tailplane (horizontal stabilizer)
尾面（水平安定面）

27 elevator
升降舵

28 cruciform tail (cruciform tail unit)
十字形尾翼（十字形尾翼装置）

29 T-tail (T-tail unit)
T 形尾翼（T 形尾翼装置）

30 lobe
波瓣，舵囊，整流锥

31 V-tail (vee-tail, butterfly tail)
V 形尾翼（蝴蝶形尾翼）

32 double tail unit (twin tail unit)
双尾翼

33 end plate
端板（双垂直安定面）

34 double tail unit (twin tail unit) of a twin-boom aircraft
双尾桁机的双尾翼装置

35 raised horizontal tail with double booms
双尾桁的高水平尾翼

36 triple tail unit
三尾翼装置

37 system of flaps
襟翼系统

38 extensible slat
外伸式缝翼

39 spoiler
扰流板

40 double-slotted Fowler flap
双缝阜勒氏襟翼

41 outer aileron (low-speed aileron)
外副翼（低速副翼）

42 inner spoiler (landing flap, lift dump)
内扰流板（降落襟翼）

43 inner aileron (all-speed aileron)
内副翼（全速副翼）

44 brake flap (air brake)
制动襟翼（空中制动器）

45 basic profile
基本翼形

46-48 plain flaps (simple flaps)
简单襟翼（单襟翼）

46 normal flap
一般襟翼

47 slotted flap
开缝襟翼

48 double-slotted flap
双缝襟翼

49-50 split flaps
分裂式襟翼

49 plain split flap (simple split flap)
简单分裂式襟翼

50 zap flap
查普襟翼

51 extending flap
伸展式襟翼

52 Fowler flap
阜勒氏襟翼

53 slat
缝翼

54 profiled leading-edge flap (droop flap)
翼形前缘襟翼（下垂襟翼）

55 Krüger flap
克鲁格襟翼

1-31 cockpit of a single-engine (single-engined) racing and passenger aircraft (racing and passenger plane)
单发动机竞赛与载客双用飞机的座舱（驾驶舱）

1 instrument panel
仪表板

2 air-speed (*Am.* airspeed) indicator
空速表

3 artificial horizon (gyro horizon)
人工水平仪

4 altimeter
高度表

5 radio compass (automatic direction finder)
无线电罗盘（自动定位仪）

6 magnetic compass
磁性罗盘

7 boost gauge (*Am.* gage)
增压表

8 tachometer (rev counter, revolution counter)
转速表

9 cylinder temperature gauge (*Am.* gage)
汽缸温度表

10 accelerometer
加速表

11 chronometer
航行表

12 turn indicator with ball
转弯指示器

13 directional gyro
定向陀螺仪

14 vertical speed indicator (rate-of-climb indicator, variometer)
垂直速率表（升降速率指示器）

15 VOR radio direction finder [*VOR*: very high frequency omnidirectional range]
极高频全向导航台无线电定向仪

16 left tank fuel gauge (*Am.* gage)
左油箱油量表

17 right tank fuel gauge (*Am.* gage)
右油箱油量表

18 ammeter
安培计（电流表）

19 fuel pressure gauge (*Am.* gage)
燃油压力表

20 oil pressure gauge (*Am.* gage)
滑油压力表

21 oil temperature gauge (*Am.* gage)
滑油温度表

22 radio and radio navigation equipment
无线电和无线电航行（导航）设备

23 map light
地图灯

24 wheel (control column, control stick) for operating the ailerons and elevators
副翼和升降舵的操纵盘

25 co-pilot's wheel
副驾驶操纵盘

26 switches
开关（电门）

27 rudder pedals
方向舵踏板

28 co-pilot's rudder pedals
副驾驶方向舵踏板

29 microphone for the radio
无线电话筒（扩音器）

30 throttle lever (throttle control)
油门操纵杆

31 mixture control
混合气控制

32-66 single-engine (single-engined) racing and passenger aircraft (racing and passenger plane)
单发动机竞赛与载客两用机

32 propeller (airscrew)
螺旋桨

33 spinner
桨鼻罩

34 flat four engine
平列四缸发动机

35 cockpit
座舱（驾驶舱）

36 pilot's seat
驾驶员座椅

37 co-pilot's seat
副驾驶员座椅

38 passenger seats
旅客座椅

39 hood (canopy, cockpit hood, cockpit canopy)
座舱盖

40 steerable nose wheel
可操纵鼻轮

41 main undercarriage unit (main landing gear unit)
主起落架

42 step
阶座（踏脚）

43 wing
机翼

44 right navigation light (right position light)
右航行灯（右位置灯）

45 spar
翼梁

46 rib
肋

47 stringer (longitudinal reinforcing member)
纵桁（纵向加强桁条）

48 fuel tank
燃油箱

49 landing light
落地灯

50 left navigation light (left position light)
左航行灯（左位置灯）

51 electrostatic conductor
静电放电导体

52 aileron
副翼

53 landing flap
降落襟翼

54 fuselage (body)
机身

55 frame (former)
构架

56 chord
翼弦

57 stringer (longitudinal reinforcing member)
纵桁（纵向加强桁条）

58 vertical tail (vertical stabilizer and rudder)
直尾翼（垂直安定面和方向舵）

59 vertical stabilizer (vertical fin, tail fin)
垂直安定面（直尾翅，尾翼）

60 rudder
方向舵

61 horizontal tail
水平尾翼

62 tailplane (horizontal stabilizer)
尾面（水平安定面）

63 elevator
升降舵

64 warning light (anticollision light)
警告灯（防撞灯）

65 dipole antenna
偶极天线（双极天线）

66 long-wire antenna (long-conductor antenna)
长线天线（长导线天线）

67-72 principal manoeuvres (*Am.* maneuvers) of the aircraft (aeroplane, plane, *Am.* airplane)
飞机的主要动作

67 pitching
俯仰（飞机绕其横轴之角运动）

68 lateral axis
横轴

69 yawing
偏航（飞机绕其垂直轴之运动）

70 vertical axis (normal axis)
垂直轴

71 rolling
侧滚（飞机绕其纵轴之运动）

72 longitudinal axis
纵轴

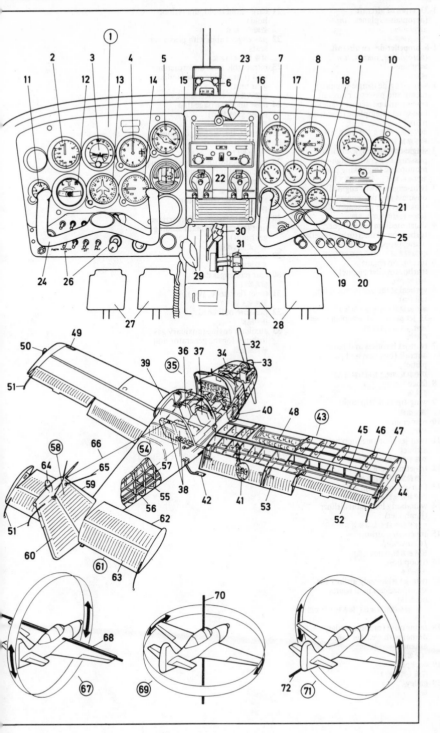

1-33 types of aircraft
(aeroplanes, planes, *Am.*
airplanes)
飞机的种类

1-6 propeller-driven aircraft
(aeroplanes, planes, *Am.*
airplanes)
螺旋桨飞机

1　single-engine (single-engined)
racing and passenger aircraft
(racing and passenger plane), a
low-wing monoplane (low-wing
plane)
单发动机（引擎）竞赛与载客飞机，一
种下单翼飞机

2　single-engine (single-engined)
passenger aircraft, a high-wing
monoplane (high-wing plane)
单发动机客机，一种高单翼飞机

3　twin-engine (twin-engined)
business and passenger aircraft
(business and passenger plane)
双发动机商用与客用飞机

4　short/medium haul airliner, a
turboprop plane (turbopropeller
plane, propeller-turbine plane)
中/短程客机，一种涡轮螺旋桨飞机

5　turboprop engine
(turbopropeller engine)
涡轮发动机

6　vertical stabilizer (vertical fin,
tail fin)
垂直安定面（直尾翅，尾翼）

7-33 jet planes (jet aeroplanes, jets,
Am. jet airplanes)
喷射机

7　twin-jet business and passenger
aircraft (business and passenger
plane)
双喷射发动机之商用与客用飞机

8　fence
折流板

9　wing-tip tank (tip tank)
翼尖油箱

10　rear engine
机尾发动机

11　twin-jet short/medium haul
airliner
双喷射发动机中/短程客机

12　tri-jet medium haul airliner
三喷射发动机中程客机

13　four-jet long haul airliner
四喷射发动机长程客机

14　wide-body long haul airliner
(jumbo jet)
广体长程客机（大型喷射客机）

15　supersonic airliner
[*Concorde*]
超音速客机[协和式飞机]

16　droop nose
下垂机头

17　**twin-jet wide-body airliner** for
short/medium haul routes
(airbus)
中/短程双喷射发动机广体客机（空中巴
士）

18　radar nose (radome, radar
dome) with weather radar
antenna
气象雷达罩

19　cockpit
座舱（驾驶舱）

20　galley
厨房

21　cargo hold (hold, underfloor
hold)
货舱（下货舱）

22　passenger cabin with passenger
seats
具旅客座椅的客舱

23　retractable nose undercarriage
unit (retractable nose landing
gear unit)
收放式鼻轮（收放式前起落架）

24　nose undercarriage flap
(nose gear flap)
鼻轮舱门

25　centre (*Am.* center) passenger
door
中央客舱门

26　engine pod with engine (turbojet
engine, jet turbine engine, jet
engine, jet turbine)
发动机短舱与喷气发动机

27　electrostatic conductors
静电放电导体

28　retractable main undercarriage
unit (retractable main landing
gear unit)
收放式主起落架

29　side window
客舱玻璃窗

30　rear passenger door
后客舱门

31　toilet (lavatory, WC)
盥洗室（厕所）

32　pressure bulkhead
压力隔框

33　auxiliary engine (auxiliary gas
turbine) for the generator unit
辅助发电机

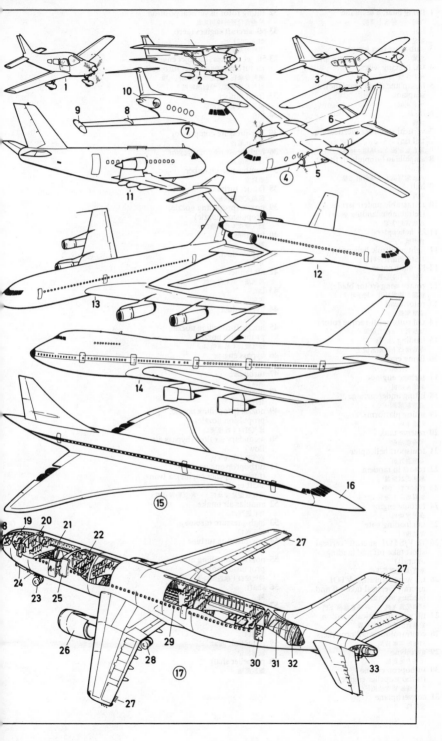

1 **flying boat,** a seaplane
飞船，一种水上飞机

2 hull
船身

3 stub wing (sea wing)
短翼（水翼——水上安定面之俗称）

4 tail bracing wires
尾翼张线

5 floatplane (float seaplane), a
seaplane
水上飞机

6 float
浮筒

7 vertical stabilizer (vertical fin,
tail fin)
垂直安定面（直尾翅，尾翼）

8 **amphibian** (amphibian flying
boat)
水陆两用机（水陆两用飞船）

9 hull
船身

10 retractable undercarriage
(retractable landing gear)
收放式起落架

11-25 **helicopters**
直升机

11 light multirole helicopter
轻型多用途直升机

12-13 main rotor
主转子（主旋翼）

12 rotary wing (rotor blade)
旋翼（旋翼叶片，转子叶）

13 rotor head
旋翼桨毂

14 tail rotor (anti-torque rotor)
尾旋翼（反扭力旋翼片）

15 landing skids
落地滑橇（落地雪橇）

16 flying crane
飞行吊挂机

17 turbine engines
涡轮发动机

18 lifting undercarriage
起重起落架

19 lifting platform
起重平台

20 reserve tank
预备燃油箱

21 transport helicopter
运输直升机

22 rotors in tandem
串连式双旋翼

23 rotor pylon
旋翼塔座（旋翼支柱）

24 turbine engine
涡轮发动机

25 tail loading gate
尾货舱门

26-32 **V/STOL aircraft** (vertical/
short take-off and landing
aircraft)
垂直/短矩起落飞机

26 tilt-wing aircraft, a VTOL
aircraft (vertical take-off and
landing aircraft)
倾斜机翼飞机，一种垂直起落飞机

27 tilt wing in vertical position
於垂直位置的倾斜机翼

28 contrarotating tail propellers
对转尾部螺旋桨

29 gyrodyne
半动力旋翼机

30 turboprop engine
(turbopropeller engine)
涡轮螺旋桨发动机

31 convertiplane
变形机

32 tilting rotor in vertical position
於垂直位置的倾斜旋翼

33-60 **aircraft engines** (aero
engines)
飞机的发动机

33-50 jet engines (turbojet engines,
jet turbine engines, jet turbines)
喷射发动机（涡轮喷射发动机，喷
射涡轮发动机，喷射涡轮机）

33 front fan-jet
前风扇式喷射发动机

34 fan
风扇

35 low-pressure compressor
低压压缩器

36 high-pressure compressor
高压压缩器

37 combustion chamber
燃烧室

38 fan-jet turbine
风扇式喷射涡轮

39 nozzle (propelling nozzle,
propulsion nozzle)
排气喷口（推进喷口）

40 turbines
涡轮

41 bypass duct
分气道

42 aft fan-jet
后风扇式喷射发动机

43 fan
风扇

44 bypass duct
分气道

45 nozzle (propelling nozzle,
propulsion nozzle)
排气喷口（推进喷口）

46 bypass engine
旁通式发动机

47 turbines
涡轮

48 mixer
混合器

49 nozzle (propelling nozzle,
propulsion nozzle)
排气喷口（推进喷口）

50 secondary air flow (bypass air
flow)
副气流（旁通气流）

51 turboprop engine
(turbopropeller engine), a twin-
shaft engine
涡轮螺旋桨发动机，一种双轴发动机

52 annular air intake
环状进气口

53 high-pressure turbine
高压涡轮

54 low-pressure turbine
低压涡轮

55 nozzle (propelling nozzle,
propulsion nozzle)
排气喷口（推进喷口）

56 shaft
轴

57 intermediate shaft
中间轴

58 gear shaft
齿轮轴

59 reduction gear
减速齿轮

60 propeller shaft
螺旋桨轴

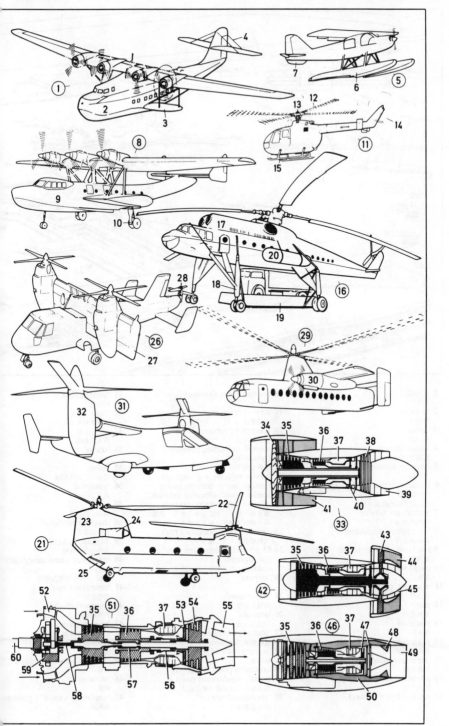

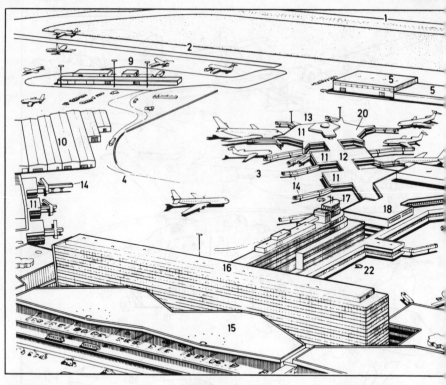

1 runway 跑道	**18** waiting room (lounge) 候机室	**31** 'information' 询问处
2 taxiway 滑行道	**19** airport restaurant 机场餐厅	**32** 'taxis' 计程车搭乘站
3 apron 停机坪	**20** spectators' terrace 接客站台	**33** 'car hire' 汽车出租站
4 apron taxiway 停机坪滑行道	**21** aircraft in loading position (nosed in) 装载中的飞机	**34** 'trains' 火车站
5 baggage terminal 行李站	**22** service vehicles, e.g. baggage loaders, water tankers, galley loaders, toilet-cleaning vehicles, ground power units, tankers 服务车,如:行李装运车,水车,食品 车,厕所清理车,地面电源车,加油车	**35** 'buses' 巴士,公共汽车站
6 tunnel entrance to the baggage terminal 通向行李站的隧道入口		**36** 'entrance' 入口
7 airport fire service 机场消防站		**37** 'exit' 出口
8 fire appliance building 消防设备房	**23** aircraft tractor (aircraft tug) 飞机牵引车(飞机拖车)	**38** 'baggage retrieval' 行李提取处
9 mail and cargo terminal 邮件和货物站	**24-53** airport information symbols (pictographs) 机场标识,指示符号(标识图)	**39** 'luggage lockers' 小件行李存放处
10 cargo warehouse 货仓	**24** 'airport' 机场	**40** 'telephone - emergency calls only' 电话 —— 专供紧急使用
11 assembly point 会合点,集合点	**25** 'departures' 离场(出境)	**41** 'emergency exit' 紧急出口
12 pier 登机走廊	**26** 'arrivals' 到达(入境)	**42** 'passport check' 护照检查处
13 pierhead 登机门	**27** 'transit passengers' 过境旅客	**43** 'press facilities' 新闻记者接待室
14 passenger loading bridge 旅客登机桥	**28** 'waiting room' ('lounge') 候机室	**44** 'doctor' 医疗室
15 departure building (terminal) 出境大楼	**29** 'assembly point' ('meeting point', 'rendezvous point') 集合地点(会合点·集会点)	**45** 'chemist' (*Am.* 'druggist') 药局
16 administration building 管理大楼	**30** 'spectators' terrace' 接送旅客站台	**46** 'showers' 淋浴
17 control tower (tower) 塔台		**47** 'gentlemen's toilet' ('gentlem 男厕所

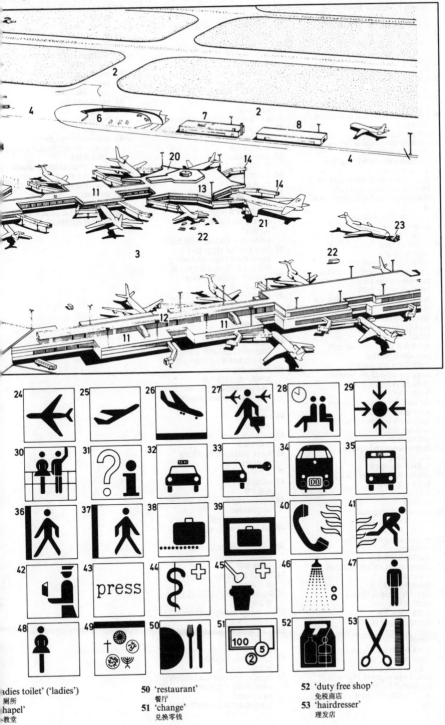

1 Saturn V 'Apollo' booster
(booster rocket) [overall view]
土星五号"阿波罗"增力火箭[全貌]
2 Saturn V 'Apollo' booster
(booster rocket) [overall
sectional view]
土星五号"阿波罗"增力火箭[全体剖面
图]
3 first rocket stage (S-IC)
第一节火箭（S-IC）
4 F-1 engines
F-1 发动机
5 heat shield (thermal protection
shield)
防热板（隔热板）
6 aerodynamic engine fairings
空气动力发动机整流罩
7 aerodynamic stabilizing fins
空气动力安定尾翅
8 stage separation retro-rockets, 8
rockets arranged in 4 pairs
段间分离反向火箭，排成四对的八节火
箭
9 kerosene (RP-1) tank
[capacity: 811, 000 litres]
燃油箱（RP-1）[容量 811,000 公升]
10 liquid oxygen (LOX, LO_2)
supply lines
液态氧（LOX, LO_2)供给管
11 anti-vortex system (device for
preventing the formation of
vortices in the fuel)
反涡流（旋）系统（防止燃料形成涡流
的装置）
12 liquid oxygen (LOX, LO_2)
tank [capacity: 1,315,000
litres]
液态氧容器[容量：1,315,000 公升]
13 anti-slosh baffles
（燃料箱的）防止振动板
14 compressed-helium bottles
(helium pressure bottles)
压缩氦气瓶
15 diffuser for gaseous oxygen
氧气扩散器
16 inter-tank connector (inter-
tank section)
油箱间连接器
17 instruments and system-
monitoring devices
仪器和系统监视装置
18 second rocket stage (S-II)
第二节火箭（S-II）
19 J-2 engines
J-2 发动机
20 heat shield (thermal
protection shield)
防热板（隔热板）
21 engine mounts and thrust
structure
发动机架和推力结构
22 acceleration rockets for fuel
acquisition
获取燃料的加速火箭
23 liquid hygrogen (LH_2)
suction line
液态氢气吸取管路
24 liquid oxygen (LOX, LO_2)
tank [capacity: 1,315,000
litres]
液态氧容器[容量 1,315,000 公升]
25 standpipe
立管
26 liquid hydrogen (LH_2) tank
[capacity: 1,020,000 litres]
液态氢气容器（槽）[容量：1,020,000 公
升]

27 fuel level sensor
燃料液面感测器
28 work platform (working
platform)
工作台
29 cable duct
电缆导管
30 manhole
人孔，进出口
31 S-IC/S-II inter-stage
connector (inter-stage
section)
S-IC/S-II 节间连接器（节间接连部分）
32 compressed-gas container (gas
pressure vessel)
压缩气体容器
33 third rocket stage (S-IVB)
第三节火箭（S-IVB）
34 J-2 engine
J-2 发动机
35 nozzle (thrust nozzle)
喷口（推力喷口）
36 S-II/S-IVB inter-stage
connector (inter-stage
section)
S-II/S-IVB 节间连接器[节间接连部分]
37 four second-stage (S-II)
separation retro-rockets
四具第二节（S-II）分离反向火箭
38 attitude control rockets
姿态控制火箭
39 liquid oxygen (LOX, LO_2)
tank [capacity: 77,200 litres]
液态氧容器[容量：77,200 公升]
40 fuel line duct
燃料管道
41 liquid hydrogen (LH_2) tank
[capacity: 253,000 litres]
液态氢气容器[容量：253,000 公升]
42 measuring probes
探测器，测量探针（器）
43 compressed-helium tanks
(helium pressure vessels)
压缩氦容器
44 tank vent
容器通气口（孔）
45 forward frame section
前框架部分
46 work platform (working
platform)
工作台
47 cable duct
电缆导管
48 acceleration rockets for fuel
acquisition
获取燃料的加速火箭
49 aft frame section
后框架部分
50 compressed-helium tanks
(helium pressure vessels)
压缩氦容器
51 liquid hygrogen (LH_2) line
液态氢气管路
52 liquid oxygen (LOX, LO_2) line
液态氧管路
53 24-panel instrument unit
24 块仪器装置
54 LM hangar (lunar module
hangar)
登月舱棚
55 LM (lunar module)
登月舱
56 Apollo SM (service module),
containing supplies and
equipment
包括供给品和设备的阿波罗配供舱

57 SM (service module) main
engine
配供舱主发动机
58 fuel tank
燃料箱
59 nitrogen tetroxide tank
四氧化氮容器
60 pressurized gas delivery
system
压缩气体输送系统
61 oxygen tanks
氧气箱
62 fuel cells
燃料电池
63 manoeuvring (*Am.*
maneuvering) rocket assemb
火箭操纵装置
64 directional antenna assembly
定向天线装置
65 space capsule (command
section)
太空舱（指挥舱）
66 launch phase escape tower
发射阶段紧急脱离塔

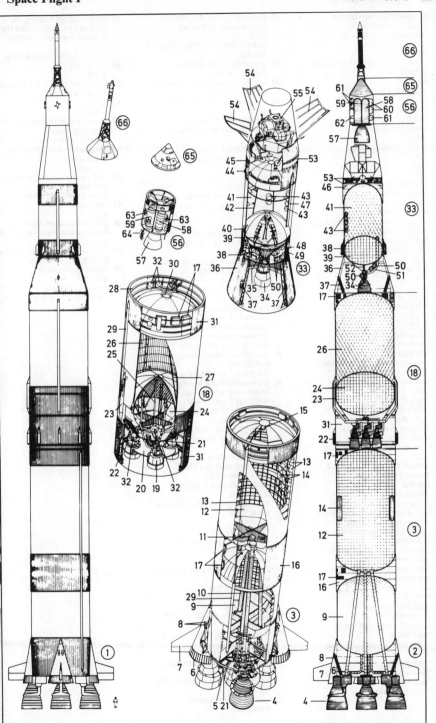

1-45 Space Shuttle-Orbiter
太空梭（太空轨道飞行器）

1 twin-spar (two-spar, double-spar) vertical fin
双梁垂直安定面

2 engine compartment structure
发动机舱结构

3 fin post
垂直安定面支柱，直尾翅支柱

4 fuselage attachment [of payload bay doors]
[酬载舱门的]机身附件

5 upper thrust mount
上推力架

6 lower thrust mount
下推力架

7 keel
龙骨

8 heat shield
隔热板，隔热屏

9 waist longeron
腰（中）部纵梁

10 integrally machined (integrally milled) main rib
整体加工的主肋

11 integrally stiffened light alloy skin
整体加强轻合金蒙皮

12 lattice girder
格子桁

13 payload bay insulation
酬载舱隔热层

14 payload bay door
酬载舱门

15 low-temperature surface insulation
低温表面隔热层

16 flight deck (crew compartment)
驾驶舱（乘员室）

17 captain's seat (commander's seat)
机长座椅

18 pilot's seat (co-pilot's seat)
驾驶员座椅（副驾驶员座椅）

19 forward pressure bulkhead
前部压力舱壁

20 carbon fibre reinforced nose cone
头部碳纤维加强锥体，头部整流罩

21 forward fuel tanks
前燃料箱

22 avionics consoles
航空电子（控制系统）操纵台

23 automatic flight control panel
自动飞行控制板

24 upward observaton windows
向上观测窗

25 forward observation windows
向前观测窗

26 entry hatch to payload bay
酬载舱的舱门入口

27 air lock
气锁（闸）

28 ladder to lower deck
通下舱的梯子

29 payload manipulator arm
酬载机械手臂

30 hydraulically steerable nose wheel
液压转向鼻轮

31 hydraulically operated main landing gear
液压操作主起落架

32 removable (reusable) carbon fibre reinforced leading edge [of wing]
[机翼的可更换（可再度使用）的碳纤维加强前缘

33 movable elevon sections
可动升降副翼部分

34 heat-resistant elevon structure
耐热升降副翼结构

35 main liquid hydrogen (LH$_2$) supply
液态氢气主要供给管路（器）

36 main liquid-fuelled rocket engine
主液态燃料火箭发动机

37 nozzle (thrust nozzle)
喷口（推力喷口）

38 coolant feed line
冷却剂供给管路

39 engine control system
发动机控制系统

40 heat shield
隔热板

41 high-pressure liquid hydrogen (LH$_2$) pump
高压液态氢气泵

42 high-pressure liquid oxygen (LOX) pump
高压液态氧气泵

43 thrust vector control system
推力航向控制系统

44 electromechanically controlled orbital manoeuvring (Am. maneuvering) main engine
机电控制的轨道飞行主发动机

45 nozzle fuel tanks (thrust nozzle fuel tanks)
燃料箱喷咀（燃料箱推力喷咀）

46 **jettisonable liquid hydrogen and liquid oxygen tank** (fuel tank)
可抛弃的液态氢气氧气燃料箱

47 integrally stiffened annular rib (annular frame)
整体加强的环状肋（环状框架）

48 hemispherical end rib (end frame)
半球型端肋（端框架）

49 aft attachment to Orbiter
轨道飞行器的后连接件

50 liquid hydrogen (LH$_2$) line
液态氢气管路

51 liquid oxygen (LOX, LO$_2$) line
液态氧气管路

52 manhole
进入口，人孔，进出口

53 surge baffle system (slosh baffle system)
防止冲激系统

54 pressure line to liquid hydrogen tank
液态氢气箱压力管路

55 electrical system bus
电力系统汇电板

56 liquid oxygen (LOX, LO$_2$) line
液态氧气管路

57 pressure line to liquid oxygen tank
液态氧气箱压力管路

58 **recoverable solid-fuel rocket** (solid rocket booster)
可回收固体燃料火箭（固体燃料火箭增力器）

59 auxiliary parachute bay
辅助降落伞舱

60 compartment housing the recovery parachutes and the forward separation rocket motors
回收降落伞和前分离火箭推进器舱

61 cable duct
电缆导管

62 aft separation rocket motors
后分离火箭推进器

63 aft skirt
后部侧缘

64 swivel nozzle (swivelling, Am. swiveling, nozzle)
旋转喷口（旋转喷气口）

65 **Spacelab** (space laboratory, space station)
太空实验室

66 multi-purpose laboratory (orbital workshop)
多目的实验室（轨道工作室）

67 astronaut
太空人

68 gimbal-mounted telescope
平衡环架望远镜（装於平衡环上的望镜）

69 measuring instrument platfo
测量仪器平台

70 spaceflight module
太空飞行舱

71 crew entry tunnel
（乘员）太空人进舱通道

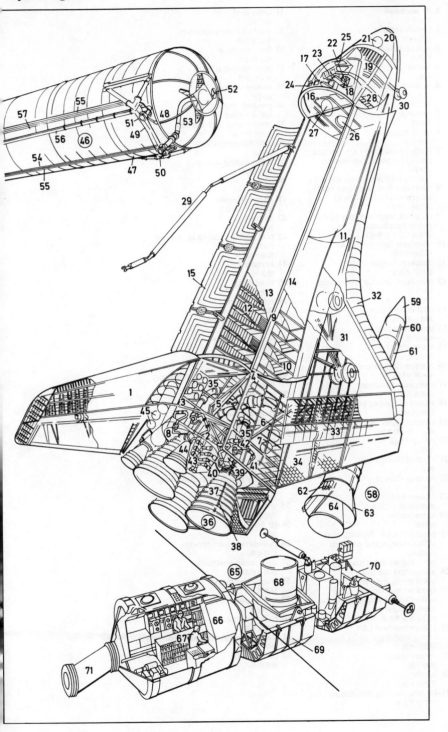

1-30 main hall
营业大厅

1 parcels counter
包裹柜台

2 parcels scales
包裹秤

3 parcel
包裹

4 stick-on address label with
parcel registration slip
贴有包裹挂号条的地址标签

5 glue pot
粘胶筒

6 small parcel
小件包裹

7 franking machine (*Am.* postage
meter) for parcel registration
cards
包裹挂号卡用的邮资打印机（邮资计）

8 telephone box (telephone booth,
telephone kiosk, call box)
电话间（亭）

9 coin-box telephone (pay phone,
public telephone)
投币式电话（收费电话，公用电话）

10 telephone directory rack
电话号码簿架

11 directory holder
住址姓名簿架

12 telephone directory (telephone
book)
电话（号码）簿

13 post office boxes
邮政信箱设备

14 post office box
邮政信箱

15 stamp counter
售邮票柜台

16 counter clerk (counter officer)
邮局柜台职员

17 company messenger
公司收发员

18 record of posting book
邮件记录簿

19 counter stamp machine
柜台（售）邮票机

20 stamp book
邮票夹

21 sheet of stamps
邮票

22 security drawer
保险柜

23 change rack
换币分类架

24 letter scales
邮件秤

25 paying-in (*Am.* deposit), post
office savings, and pensions
counter
存款，邮政储蓄和发放退休金柜台

26 accounting machine
记帐用会计机〔报表（帐目）计算机〕

27 franking machine for money
orders and paying-in slips (*Am.*
deposit slips)
汇票和解款单的盖印机

28 change machine (*Am.*
changemaker)
零钱兑换机

29 receipt stamp
受理日戳

30 hatch
受理口，窗口

31-44 letter-sorting installation
邮件分类装置

31 letter feed
邮件的给送

32 stacked letter containers
装信用容器

33 feed conveyor
给信传送机

34 intermediate stacker
堆置信件盘

35 coding station
标码台

36 pre-distributor channel
邮件预分器通道

37 process control computer
过程控制电脑

38 distributing machine
分信机

39 video coding station
视频标码台

40 screen
屏，幕

41 address display
（收件人）地址显示

42 address
地址

43 post code (postal code, *Am.* zip
code)
邮递区号

44 keyboard
键盘

45 handstamp
手戳

46 roller stamp
滚轮式邮戳

47 franking machine
打印机

48 feed mechanism
给送装置

49 delivery mechanism
排出装置

50-55 postal collection and delivery
邮件的收集与投递

50 postbox (*Am.* mailbox)
邮筒

51 collection bag
邮件袋

52 post office van (mail van)
邮车

53 postman (*Am.* mail carrier, letter
carrier, mailman)
邮差

54 delivery pouch (postman's bag,
mailbag)
投递邮袋

55 letter-rate item
信件投递登记条

56-60 postmarks
邮戳

56 postmark advertisement
广告邮戳

57 date stamp postmark
邮票日期戳

58 charge postmark
邮资戳

59 special postmark
专用邮戳

60 roller postmark
滚轮式邮戳

61 stamp (postage stamp)
邮票

62 perforations
邮票齿孔

1 **telephone box** (telephone booth, telephone kiosk, call box), a public telephone
电话间（亭），公用电话

2 telephone user (*with own telephone:* telephone subscriber, telephone customer)
电话使用人（拥有电话的用户）

3 coin-box telephone (pay phone, public telephone) for local and long-distance calls (trunk calls)
投币式市内与长途电话（收费电话，公用电话）

4 emergency telephone
紧急电话

5 telephone directory (telephone book)
电话（号码）簿

6-26 **telephone instruments** (telephones)
电话

6 standard table telephone
标准台式（桌上型）电话

7 telephone receiver (handset)
电话（听筒）收话器（电话听筒）

8 earpiece
耳机（听筒）

9 mouthpiece (microphone)
送话器（话筒）

10 dial (push-button keyboard)
拨号盘（按钮键盘）

11 finger plate (dial finger plate, dial wind-up plate)
指孔盘（手指拨盘，拨号盘的回转盘）

12 finger stop (dial finger stop)
止拨档

13 cradle (handset cradle, cradle switch)
托架（听筒托架，托架开关）

14 receiver cord (handset cord)
听筒软家（线）

15 telephone casing (telephone cover)
电话机壳

16 subscriber's (customer's) private meter
用户私人用表

17 switchboard (exchange) for a system of extensions
分机系统交换台，内线电话用交换台

18 push button for connecting main exchange lines
连结主交换线用按钮

19 push buttons for calling extensions
分机按钮，内线电话按钮

20 push-button telephone
按钮式电话

21 earthing button for the extensions
分机接地按钮，内线电话接地按钮

22-26 switchboard with extensions
分机（内线）电话和交换台

22 exchange
交换台

23 switchboard operator's set
交换台线生操作机

24 main exchange line
主交换台线

25 switching box (automatic switching system, automatic connecting system, switching centre, *Am.* center)
转换箱（自动转换系统，自动连接系统，转换中心）

26 extension
内线连接线

27-41 **telephone exchange**
电话交换台

27 fault repair service
故障修理服务台

28 maintenance technician
维修技师

29 testing board (testing desk)
实验台

30 telegraphy
电信

31 teleprinter (teletypewriter)
印刷电信机（打字电报机，印刷电信机）

32 paper tape
纸带

33 directory enquiries
查号台

34 information position (operator's position)
询问台

35 operator
接线生

36 microfilm reader
缩影软片放映装置

37 microfilm file
缩影软片档案

38 microfilm card with telephone numbers
带电话号码的缩影软片卡

39 date indicator display
日期指示器显示

40 testing and control station
试验与控制站

41 switching centre (*Am.* center) for telephone, telex, and data transmission services
电话，电报和数据转换中心

42 **selector**, a motor uniselector made of noble metals; *sim.:* electronic selector
选择器，一种由贵金属制造的电动单形选择器；类似：电子选择器

43 contact arc (bank)
接触弧

44 contact arm (wiper)
接触臂（滑臂）

45 contact field
接触区域

46 contact arm tag
接触臂金属头

47 electromagnet
电磁

48 selector motor
选择器电动机

49 restoring spring (resetting spring)
复原簧片

50 **communication links**
通信系统

51-52 satellite radio link
人造卫星无线电通讯

51 earth station with directional antenna
带定向天线的地面站（电台）

52 communications satellite with directional antenna
带定向天线的通讯人造卫星

53 coastal station
海岸站（电台）

54-55 intercontinental radio link
洲际无线电通讯

54 short-wave station
短波站（电台）

55 ionosphere
游离层

56 submarine cable (deep-sea c...
海底电缆（深海电缆）

57 underwater amplifier
水中增幅器

58 **data transmission** (data servi...
数据输送，数据服务台

59 input/output device for data carriers
数据载波的输入输出装置

60 data processor
资料处理器

61 teleprinter
电传印字机

62-64 data carriers
数据载体

62 punched tape (punch tape)
穿孔纸带

63 magnetic tape
磁带

64 punched card (punch card)
穿孔卡片

65 telex link
电报装置

66 teleprinter (page printer)
电传印字机（页印机）

67 dialling (*Am.* dialing) unit
拨号装置

68 telex tape (punched tape, pu... tape) for transmitting the tex... maximum speed
以最快速度发送电文的电报穿孔纸带

69 telex message
电报通信

70 keyboard
键盘

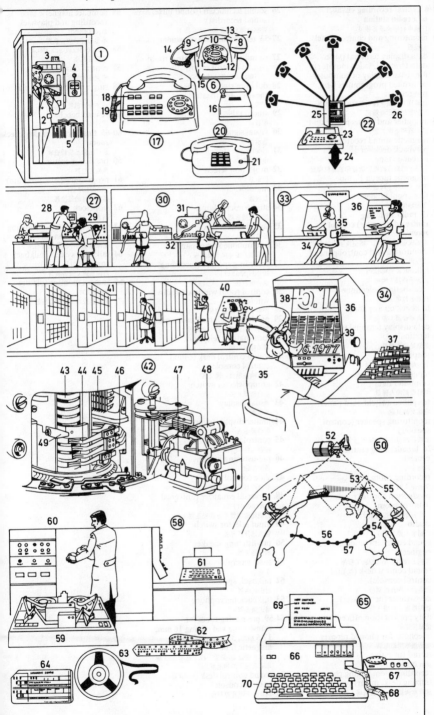

1-6 central recording channel of a radio station
广播电台中央录音频道

1 monitoring and control panel
监控板

2 data display terminal (video data terminal, video monitor) for visual display of computer-controlled programmes (*Am.* programs)
计算机（电脑）控制节目顺序直视显示用的数据显示终端机

3 amplifier and mains power unit
扩大器和电源装置

4 magnetic sound recording and playback deck for $\frac{1}{4}''$ magnetic tape
使用 $\frac{1}{4}$ 吋磁带的磁带录音和放音机座置

5 magnetic tape, a $\frac{1}{4}''$ tape
磁带，一种 $\frac{1}{4}$ 吋磁带

6 film spool holder
磁带轴架

7-15 radio switching centre (*Am.* center) control room
（无线电）收音机广播交换中心控制室

7 monitoring and control panel
监控板

8 talkback speaker
回讲扬声器（喇叭）

9 local-battery telephone
自给电池电话

10 talkback microphone
回讲微音器（麦克风）

11 data display terminal (video data terminal)
数据显示终端机

12 teleprinter
电传印字机

13 input keyboard for computer data
电脑数据输入键盘

14 telephone switchboard panel
电话交换机盘

15 monitoring speaker (control speaker)
监听扬声器（控制扬声器）

16-26 broadcasting centre (*Am.* center)
广播中心

16 recording room
录音室（间）

17 production control room (control room)
制作控制室（控制室）

18 studio
广播室（播音室）

19 sound engineer (sound control engineer)
音响工程师（音响控制工程师）

20 sound control desk (sound control console)
调音台（声音控制台）

21 newsreader (newscaster)
新闻播报（广播）员

22 duty presentation officer
值班传讯员

23 telephone for phoned reports
电话报导用的电话

24 record turntable
录音盘（转盘）

25 recording room mixing console (mixing desk, mixer)
录音室调音台（混音机座，混音器）

26 sound technician (sound mixer, sound recordist)
音响技师（调音员，录音员）

27-53 television post-sync studio
电视后同步配音室

27 sound production control room (sound control room)
音声制作（调整）控制室

28 dubbing studio (dubbing theatre, *Am.* theater)
配音室

29 studio table
配音台

30 visual signal
指示信号

31 electronic stopclock
电子码表

32 projection screen
投影幕

33 monitor
监视器

34 studio microphone
配音室微音器（麦克风）

35 sound effects box
音效箱

36 microphone socket panel
微音器（麦克风）插座板

37 recording speaker (recording loudspeaker)
录音扬声器

38 control room window (studio window)
控制室窗（配音室窗）

39 producer's talkback microphone
制作人回讲微音器（麦克风）

40 local-battery telephone
自给电池电话

41 sound control desk (sound control console)
（音响控制台）调音台

42 group selector switch
组合选择开关

43 visual display
显示盘

44 limiter display (clipper display)
限幅显示表

45 control modules
控制组件

46 pre-listening buttons
预听按钮

47 slide control
滑动控制器（调节器）

48 universal equalizer (universal corrector)
万能均衡装置（万能校正器）

49 input selector switch
输入选择器开关

50 pre-listening speaker
预听扬声器

51 tone generator
发音器

52 talkback speaker
对讲扬声器

53 talkback microphone
回讲微音器

54-59 pre-mixing room for transferring and mixing 16 mm, 17.5 mm, 35 mm perforated magnetic film
转录和混合 16 毫米，17.5 毫米，35 毫米有孔磁带的预混室

54 sound control desk (sound control console)
调音台（声音控制台）

55 compact magnetic tape recording and playback equipment
小型磁带录放音装置

56 single playback deck
单放音机座

57 central drive unit
中央驱动装置

58 single recording and playback deck
单录放音机座

59 rewind bench
倒转柏

60-65 final picture quality check room
最后图像品质检查室

60 preview monitor
预检监控器

61 programme (*Am.* program) monitor
播出节目的监控器

62 stopclock
码表

63 vision mixer (vision-mixing console, vision-mixing desk)
图像混录台（图像混合桌）

64 talkback system (talkback equipment)
回讲系统（回讲装置）

65 camera monitor (picture monitor)
摄影监控器（图像监控器）

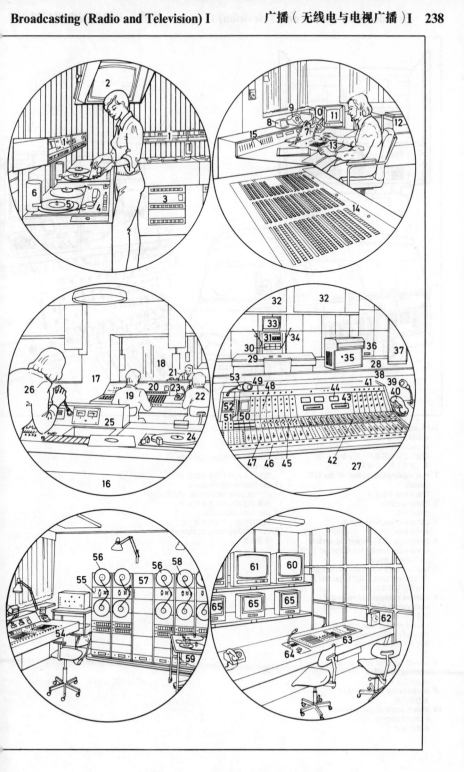

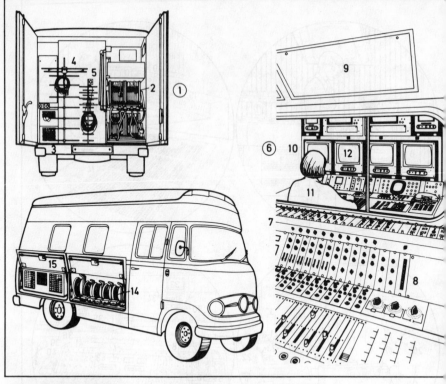

1-15 outside broadcast (OB) vehicle (television OB van; *also:* sound OB van, radio OB van)
转播车（电视转播车，录音转播车，广播，收音（机）广播车）

1 **rear equipment section of the OB vehicle**
转播车后面装备部分

2 camera cable
摄像机电缆

3 cable connection panel
电缆连接板

4 television (TV) reception aerial (receiving aerial) for Channel I
I 频道的电视接收天线

5 television (TV) reception aerial (receiving aerial) for Channel II
II 频道的电视接收天线

6 **interior equipment (on-board equipment) of the OB vehicle**
转播车内部设备

7 sound production control room (sound control room)
调音室（声音制作控制室）（声音控制室）

8 sound control desk (sound control console)
调音枱（声音控制台）

9 monitoring loudspeaker
监控扬声器

10 vision control room (video control room)
影像控制室

11 video controller (vision controller)
影像控制员

12 camera monitor (picture monitor)
摄影机监控器（图象监控器）

13 on-board telephone (intercommunication telephone)
转播车电话（内部连络电话）

14 microphone cable
微音器电缆，麦克风电缆

15 air-conditioning equipment
空调装置

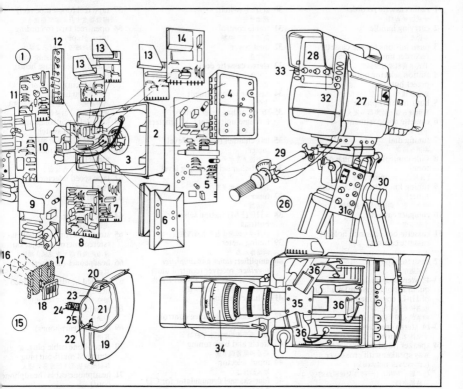

1 **our (*Am.* color) television
(TV) receiver** (colour television
) of modular design
标准组件设计的彩色电视接收机
evision cabinet
视机壳
evision tube (picture tube)
象管（影像管）
(intermediate frequency)
plifier module
增幅组件
our (*Am.* color) decoder
odule
色解码机
IF and UHF tuner
高频和超高频调谐器
rizontal synchronizing
odule
平同步组件
rtical deflection module
直偏转组件
rizontal linearity control
odule
平线性控制组件
rizontal deflection module
平偏转组件
ntrol module
制组件
nvergence module
焦组件
our (*Am.* color) output stage
odule
信号输出级组件

14 **sound module**
音响组件
15 **colour (*Am.* color) picture tube**
彩色映像管
16 **electron beams**
电子束
17 **shadow mask with elongated
holes**
长孔遮板屏
18 **strip of fluorescent (luminescent,
phosphorescent) material**
（发光的，发磷光的）萤光材料片
19 **coating (film) of fluorescent
material**
萤光材料涂层
20 **inner magnetic screen
(screening)**
内磁网屏
21 **vacuum**
真空
22 **temperature-compensated
shadow mask mount**
温度补偿的遮蔽屏架
23 **centring (centering) ring for the
deflection system**
偏转系统的中心环
24 **electron gun assembly**
电子枪组件
25 **rapid heat-up cathode**
急速加热阴极
26 **television (TV) camera**
电视摄影机
27 **camera head**
摄影机头

28 **camera monitor**
摄影机监控器
29 **control arm (control lever)**
控制杆（操纵杆）
30 **focusing adjustment**
聚焦调整装置
31 **control panel**
控制盘
32 **contrast control**
对比度调节装置
33 **brightness control**
亮度调节装置
34 **zoom lens**
可变焦镜头
35 **beam-splitting prism (beam
splitter)**
分光棱镜，分色镜
36 **pickup unit (colour, *Am.* color,
pickup tube)**
拾像装置（彩色摄像管）

1 **radio cassette recorder**
卡式收录音机

2 carrying handle
手提把手

3 push buttons for the cassette
recorder unit
卡式录音机录音按钮

4 station selector buttons (station
preset buttons)
选台按钮

5 built-in microphone
自附微音器，传声器（麦克风）

6 cassette compartment
卡带室

7 tuning dial
调谐标度盘

8 slide control [for volume or
tone]
〔音量或音调〕滑动控制器

9 tuning knob (tuning control,
tuner)
调谐旋钮（调谐控制，调谐器）

10 **compact cassette**
小型卡带

11 cassette box (cassette holder,
cassette cabinet)
卡带盒

12 cassette tape
卡式磁带

13-48 **stero system** (*also:*
quadraphonic system) made up
of Hi-Fi components
由高传真构件组成的（立体）身历声音
响系统（即：四声道系统）

13-14 **stereo speakers**
（立体）身历声扬声器（喇叭）

14 speaker (loudspeaker), a three-
way speaker with crossover
(crossover network)
扬声器（喇叭），一种具交越网路的三
路扬声器

15 tweeter
高音扬声器（喇叭）

16 mid-range speaker
中音（程）扬声器（喇叭）

17 woofer
低音扬声器（喇叭）

18 **record player** (automatic record
changer, auto changer)
唱机（盘），（自动换片唱机）

19 record player housing (record
player base)
唱机（盘）外壳（唱机底座）

20 turntable
转盘

21 tone arm
唱臂

22 counterbalance (counterweight)
配衡，配重

23 gimbal suspension
平衡架方向接头

24 stylus pressure control (stylus
force control)
针压调节（控制）

25 anti-skate control
防滑调节（控制）

26 magnetic cartridge with (conical
or elliptical) stylus, a diamond
带（圆锥形或椭圆形）唱针的一种金钢
石材料做的磁质唱头

27 tone arm lock
唱臂锁

28 tone arm lift
唱臂架

29 speed selector (speed changer)
转速选择器（转速变换器）

30 starter switch
起动器开关

31 treble control
高音（域）控制

32 dust cover
防尘盖

33 **stereo cassette deck**
（立体）身历声卡式带放音（走带）装
置

34 cassette compartment
卡带室

35-36 recording level meters
(volume unit meters, VU meters)
录音水平表（音量计）

35 left-channel recording level
meter
左声道录音水平表

36 right-channel recording level
meter
右声道录音水平表

37 **tuner**
调谐器

38 VHF (FM) station selector
buttons
特高频（调谐）电台选择器按钮

39 tuning meter
调谐指示表

40 **amplifier;** *tuner and amplifier
together:* receiver (control unit)
放大器（扩大器）；调谐器和放大器共
同构成：接收机（控制装置）

41 volume control
音量控制

42 four-channel balance control
(level control)
四声道平衡控制（水平控制）

43 treble and bass tuning
高音和低音调节钮

44 input selector
输入选择器

45 **four-channel demodulator** for CD
4 records
CD4 录音唱带四声道解调器

46 quadra/stereo converter
四声道/立体身历声转换器

47 cassette box (cassette holder,
cassette cabinet)
卡带匣，卡带座

48 record storage slots (record
storage compartments)
唱片储放槽

49 **microphone**
微音器，麦克风

50 microphone screen
微音器（麦克风）筛

51 microphone base (microphone
stand)
微音器（麦克风）座

52 **three-in-one stereo component
system** (automatic record
changer, cassette deck, and
stereo receiver)
三机一体（立体）身历声组合系统：自
动换片装置（唱机，唱盘），卡式录音
座，和（立体）身历声收音机

53 tone arm balance
唱臂平衡器

54 tuning meters
调谐指示表

55 indicator light for automatic
FeO/CrO₂ tape switch-over
氧化铁/二氧化铬带自动转换指示灯

56 **open-reel-type recorder,** a
two of four-track unit
开式卷盘磁带录音机，盘式录音机，一
种二或四轨录音装置

57 tape reel (open tape reel)
磁带卷盘（开式磁带卷盘）

58 open-reel tape (recording
tape, ¼tape)
开式卷盘磁带（¼吋录音带）

59 sound head housing with
erasing head (erase head),
recording head, and
reproducing head (*or:*
combined head)
具消音磁头，录音磁头和放音磁头
（录放音磁头）的录音磁头盒

60 tape deflector roller and end
switch (limit switch)
录音带导向滚轮和终端开关

61 recording level meter (VU
meter)
录音水平表（音量表）

62 tape speed selector
转速选择器

63 on/off switch
开关按钮

64 tape counter
走带计数器

65 stereo microphone sockets
(stereo microphone jacks)
身历声微音器（麦克风）插座

66 **headphones** (headset)
耳机

67 padded headband (padded
headpiece)
加垫头带（加垫式双平式耳机）

68 membrane
振动片（膜）

69 earcups (earphones)
耳机

70 headphone cable plug, a
standard multi-pin plug
耳机电线插头，标准多针插头

71 headphone cable (headphon
cord)
耳机电线（耳机软线）

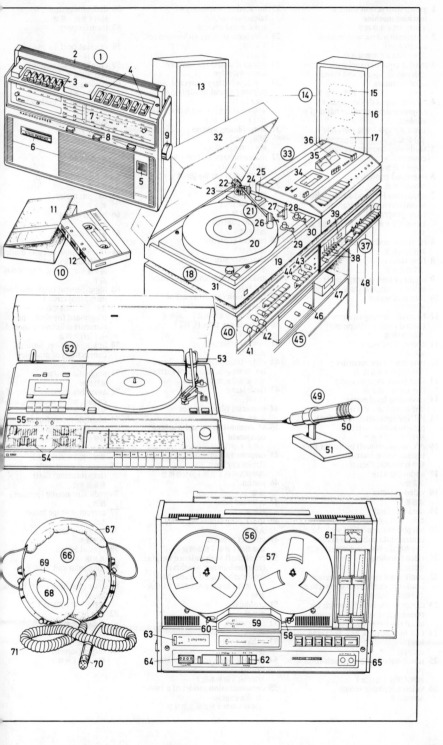

1 group instruction using a
teaching machine
采用教学机的集体教学

2 instructor's desk with central
control unit
其中央控制装置的教师讲台

3 master control panel with
individual diplays and cross
total counters
其个别显示与交叉总计数器的主控板

4 student input device (student
response device) in the hand of a
student
在学生手中的输入装置（学生反应（应答）装置）

5 study step counter (progress
counter)
学习进度计数器

6 overhead projector
架空式投影器

7 apparatus for producing audio
visual learning programmes
(*Am.* programs)
制作视听学习课程（程序）的装置（器具）

8-10 frame coding device
制作编码装置

8 film viewer
纸带检查装置

9 memory unit (storage unit)
储存单元、记忆单元（装置）

10 film perforator
纸带穿孔机

11-14 audio coding equipment
(sound coding equipment)
声音编码装置

11 coding keyboard
编码键盘

12 two-track tape recorder
双轨（磁带）录音机

13 four-track tape recorder
四轨（磁带）录音机

14 recording level meter
录音水平指示表（音量计）

15 PIP (programmed individual
presentation) system
按程序分别显示系统

16 AV (audio-visual) projector for
programmed instruction
程序教学用的视听投影器

17 audio cassette
录音带

18 video cassette
录影带

19 data terminal
数据（资料）终端设备

20 telephone connection with the
central data collection station
与中央数据（资料）收集站连线的电话

21 **video telephone**
电视电话

22 conference circuit (conference
hook-up, conference connection)
会议迴路（会议连线）

23 camera tube switch (switch for
transmitting speaker's picture)
摄像管开关（传播讲话人图像的开关）

24 talk button (talk key, speaking
key)
通话按钮

25 touch-tone buttons (touch-tone
pad)
触摸式按钮（选号盘）

26 video telephone screen
电视电话幕

27 infrared transmission of
television sound
电视声音的红外线传播

28 television receiver (television set,
TV set)
电视机

29 infrared sound transmitter
红外线声音发射机

30 cordless battery-powered
infrared sound headphones
(headset)
不用电线以电池供电的红外线声音接收
耳机（红外线耳机）

31 **microfilming system**
[diagram]
影片微缩系统(简图)

32 magnetic tape station (data
storage unit)
磁带架（资料（数据）储存单元）

33 buffer storage
缓冲储存器

34 adapter unit
适应器装置

35 digital control
数位控置

36 camera control
摄像机控制

37 character storage
字元储存器

38 analogue (*Am.* analog) control
类比控制

39 correction (adjustment) of
picture tube geometry
显（收）像管形状的修正（调整）

40 cathode ray tube (CRT)
阴极射线管

41 optical system
光学装置

42 slide (transparency) of a form
for mixing-in images of forms
混合影像形式的幻灯片

43 flash lamp
闪光灯

44 universal film cassettes
普通影片盒

45-84 **demonstration and teaching
equipment**
示范和教学设备

45 demonstration model of a four-
stroke engine
四冲程发动机（引擎）的示范模型

46 piston
活塞

47 cylinder head
汽缸罩

48 spark plug (sparking plug)
火星塞

49 contact breaker
接触断续（遮断）器断路器

50 crankshaft with balance weights
(counterbalance weights)
(counterbalanced crankshaft)
带（法码）配重的曲轴（配重）（配衡
曲轴）

51 crankcase
曲轴箱

52 inlet valve
进气阀

53 exhaust valve
排气阀

54 coolant bores (cooling water
bores)
冷却剂孔（冷却水孔）

55 demonstration model of a two-
stroke engine
二冲程（引擎）发动机示范模型

56 deflector piston
转向（变流）活塞

57 transfer port
送气口

58 exhaust port
排气口

59 crankcase scavenging
曲轴箱的驱气

60 cooling ribs
冷却肋，散热片

61-67 models of molecules
分子模型

61 ethylene molecule
乙烯分子

62 hydrogen atom
氢原子

63 carbon atom
碳原子

64 formaldehyde atom
甲醛原子

65 oxygen molecule
氧分子

66 benzene ring
苯环

67 water molecule
水（的）分子

68-72 electronic circuits made
modular elements
由基准（本）元件组成的电子线路
路）

68 logic element (logic module)
integrated circuit
逻辑元件，积体电路的一种

69 plugboard for electronic
elements (electronic module
电子元件的插盘

70 linking (link-up, joining,
connection) of modules
组件的连结（接）

71 magnetic contact
磁性接触

72 assembly (construction) of
circuit, using magnetic mod
使用磁性组件的电路构造

73 multiple meter for measuri
current, voltage and resista
测量电流，电压和电阻的多功能表

74 measurement range selecto
量程（测定距离选择器）

75 measurement scale
(measurement dial)
测量刻度盘

76 indicator needle (pointer)
指针

77 current/voltage meter
电流/电压表

78 adjusting screw
调整螺丝

79 optical bench
光具座

80 triangular rail
三角轨

81 laser (teaching laser, instru
laser)
雷射机（教学雷射机）

82 diaphragm
遮光板（光阑）

83 lens system
透镜系统

84 target (screen)
靶，目标（屏幕）

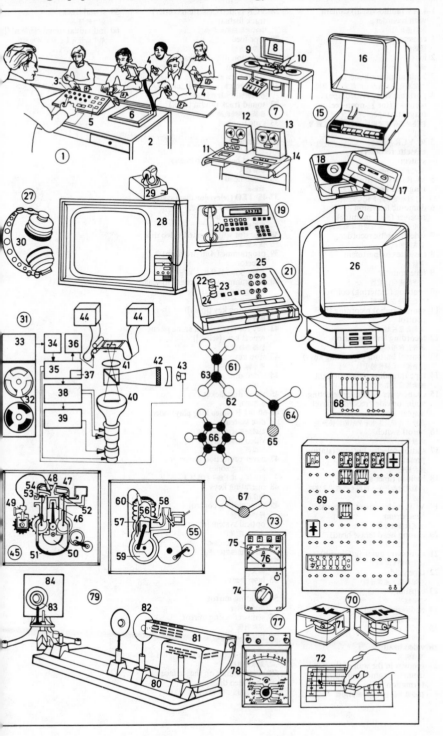

1-4 AV (audio-visual) camera with recorder
录音摄影机

1 camera
摄影机

2 lens
镜头

3 built-in microphone
内装麦克风，机内（内藏式）麦克风

4 portable video (videotape) recorder (for $\frac{1}{4}''$ open-reel magnetic tape
轻便录影带式录影机（$\frac{1}{4}$吋开放盘式磁带适用）

5-36 VCR (video cassette recorder) system
卡式录影机系统

5 VCR cassette (for $\frac{1}{2}''$ magnetic tape)
（$\frac{1}{2}$吋磁带用的）卡式录影带

6 domestic television receiver (*also:* monitor)
家用电视机（亦可用作：监视器）

7 video cassette recorder
卡式录影机

8 cassette compartment
卡带室

9 tape counter
卡带的走带计数器

10 centring (centering) control
中心（调节）控制

11 sound (audio) recording level control
录音音量控制

12 recording level indicator
录音音量指示器

13 control buttons (operating keys)
控制按钮（操作键）

14 tape threading indicator light
插录影带的指示灯

15 changeover switch for selecting audio or video recording level display
选择录音或录影水平显示的转换开关

16 on/off switch
电源开关

17 station selector buttons (station preset buttons)
选台按钮

18 built-in timer switch
内装定时器开关，机内（内藏式）定时器开关

19 VCR (video cassette recorder) head drum
卡式录影机磁鼓

20 erasing head (erase head)
消音（影）磁头

21 stationary guide (guide pin)
固定导梢（导梢）

22 tape guide
卷带导轨，磁带导轨

23 capstan
主导轴

24 audio sync head
同步录音磁头

25 pinch roller
压带轮

26 video head
视频磁头

27 grooves in the wall of the head drum to promote air cushion formation
在磁鼓上促进气垫形成的沟纹

28 VCR (video cassette recorder) track format
卡式录影机的磁轨格式

29 tape feed
供带（方向）

30 direction of video head movement
视频磁头运动的方向

31 video track, a slant track
视频磁轨，一种倾斜磁轨

32 sound track (audio track)
音轨（声频轨迹）

33 sync track
同步磁轨

34 sync head
同步磁头

35 sound head (audio head)
录音磁头

36 video head
录影磁头

37-45 TED (television disc) system
影碟（电视影碟）（系统）

37 video disc player
影碟机

38 disc slot with inserted video disc
插入影碟的碟片槽

39 programme (*Am.* program) selector
节目（次序）选择器

40 programme (*Am.* program) scale (programme dial)
节目刻度盘

41 operating key ([play])
操作键（"播放"）

42 key for repeating a scene (scene-repeat key, [select])
影像重播键

43 stop key
停止键

44 video disc
影碟

45 video disc jacket
影碟护套

46-60 VLP (video long play) video disc system
长时间播放的影碟系统

46 video disc player
影碟机

47 cover projection (*below it:* scanning zone)
投影区（其下是：扫描区）

48 operating keys
操作键

49 slow motion control
慢动作控制

50 optical system [diagram]
光学系统[简图]

51 VLP video disc
长时间播放的影碟

52 lens
镜头

53 laser beam
雷射光束

54 rotating mirror
旋转反射镜

55 semi-reflecting mirror
半反射镜

56 photodiode
光电二极体

57 helium-neon laser
氦氖雷射机

58 video signals on the surface of the video disc
影碟表面上的影像（视频）信号

59 signal track
信号轨迹

60 individual signal element ([
单个信号元（记录的最小单位）

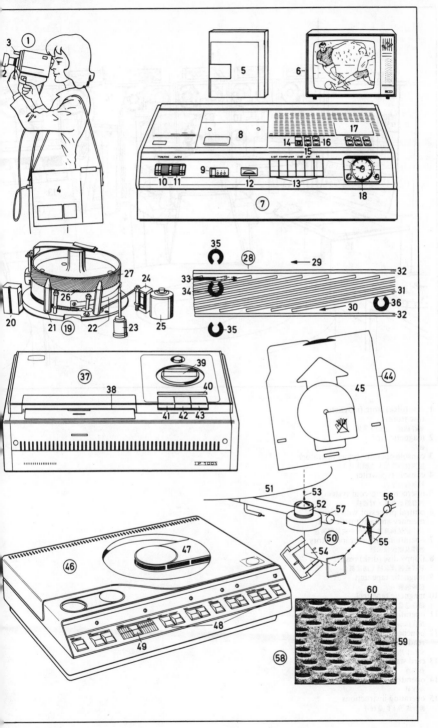

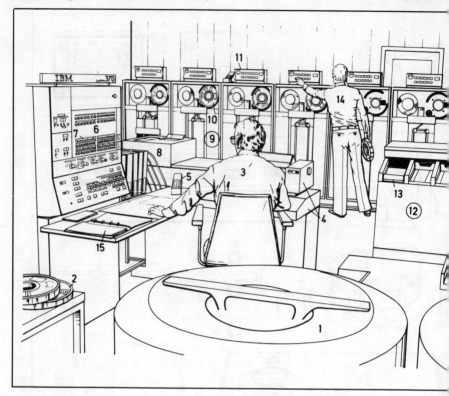

1 **disc (disk) store (magnetic
   disc store)**
   磁碟储存（记忆）装置
2 **magnetic tape**
   磁带
3 **console operator (chief operator)**
   控制台操作员（主操作员）
4 **console typewriter**
   控制台打字机
5 **intercom (intercom system)**
   内部通话系统、对讲机
6 **central processor with main
   memory and arithmetic unit**
   具主记忆和算术单元的中央处理装置
7 **operation and error indicators**
   操作及错误指示器
8 **floppy disc (disk) reader**
   软式磁碟读取机（阅读机）
9 **magnetic tape unit**
   磁带装置
10 **magnetic tape reel**
   磁带卷盘
11 **operating indicators**
   操作指示器
12 **punched card (punch card)
   reader and punch**
   穿孔卡片的读取机和打孔机
13 **card stacker**
   叠卡器
14 **operator**
   操作员
15 **operating instructions**
   操作说明，作业程序

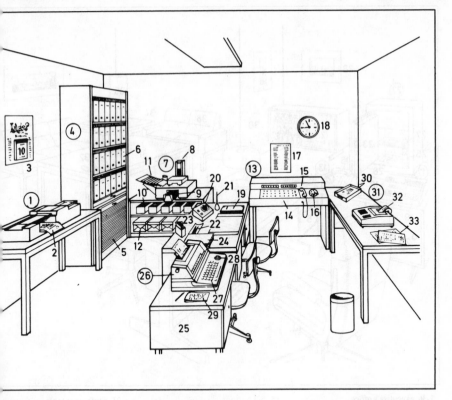

receptionist's office
cretary's office)
处（秘书办公室）
simile telegraph
电讯
nsmitted copy (received
y)
副本（接收副本）
l calendar

g cabinet
（档案）柜
bour door (roll-up door)
门（上卷式门）
(document file)
夹，文件夹
nsfer-type addressing
chine
式复印机
tical stencil magazine
模板箱（仓匣）
ncil ejection
的模板
ncil storage drawer
储存抽屉
er feed
送装置
ck of notepaper
库（储）存
tchboard (internal telephone
ange)
机（内线电话交换）

14 push-button keyboard for
internal connections
内线联系用的按钮键盘
15 handset
手持话机（筒）
16 dial
拨号盘
17 internal telephone list
内线电话（代号）表
18 master clock (main clock)
标准钟
19 folder containing documents,
correspondence, etc. for signing
(to be signed)
待签的卷宗包括文件，信件等
20 intercom (office intercom)
办公室互通电话，内部通话设备
21 pen
钢笔
22 pen and pencil tray
钢笔与铅笔盒
23 card index
卡片索引
24 stack (set) of forms
一叠表格
25 typing desk
打字桌
26 memory typewriter
（记忆式）储存式打字机
27 keyboard
键盘

28 rotary switch for the main
memory and the magnetic tape
loop
主（记忆体）储存器和磁带环的旋转开
关
29 shorthand pad (*Am.* steno pad)
速记簿
30 letter tray
信件盘
31 office calculator
办公室用计算机
32 printer
印表机
33 business letter
商业信件

1-36 executive's office
经理室

1 swivel chair
旋转桌

2 desk
办公桌

3 writing surface (desk top)
桌面

4 desk drawer
办公桌抽屉

5 cupboard (storage area) with door
有门的小柜（储藏柜）

6 desk mat (blotter)
桌垫（吸墨垫）

7 business letter
商业信件

8 appointments diary
约会（定）记事簿

9 desk set
桌上文具（笔墨用具）

10 intercom (office intercom)
办公室互通电话，内部通话设备

11 desk lamp
桌灯

12 pocket calculator (electronic calculator)
袖珍型计算机（电子计算机）

13 telephone, an executive-secretary system
电话，经理秘书的连络装置（内线）

14 dial; *also:* push-button keyboard
拨号盘，即按钮式键盘

15 call buttons
通话按钮

16 receiver (telephone receiver)
听筒（电话听筒）

17 dictating machine
口述录音机

18 position indicator
位置（表）指示器

19 control buttons (operating keys)
控制按钮（操作键）

20 cabinet
柜子

21 visitor's chair
访客座椅

22 safe
保险箱

23 bolts (locking mechanism)
螺栓（闭锁装置）

24 armour (*Am.* armor) plating
防护金属板

25 confidential documents
机密文件

26 patent
专利证明

27 petty cash
小额现金

28 picture
画

29 bar (drinks cabinet)
酒柜

30 bar set
酒柜中成套用具

31-36 conference grouping
会议用设备

31 conference table
会议桌

32 pocket-sized dictating machine (micro cassette recorder)
袖珍型口述录音机（微型卡式录音机）

33 ashtray
烟灰缸

34 corner table
墙角桌子

35 table lamp
枱灯

36 two-seater sofa 'part of the conference grouping'
双座沙发〔会议整组设备的一部分〕

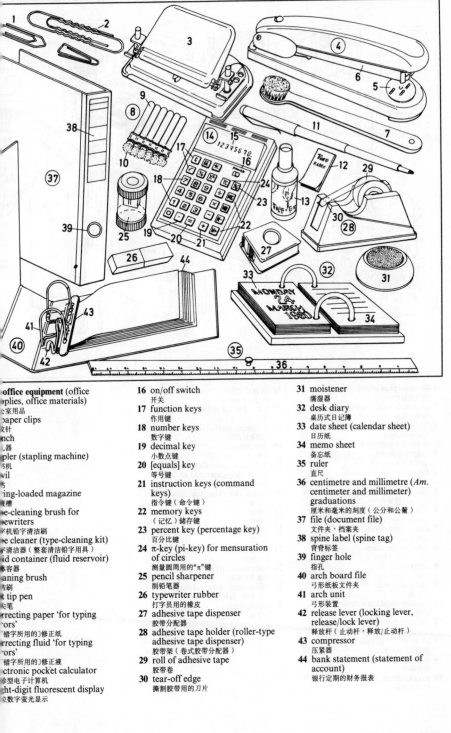

office equipment (office
supplies, office materials)
办公室用品
paper clips
回形针
punch
打孔器
stapler (stapling machine)
订书机
anvil
砧座
spring-loaded magazine
弹簧槽
type-cleaning brush for
typewriters
打字机铅字清洁刷
type cleaner (type-cleaning kit)
铅字清洁器（整套清洁铅字用具）
fluid container (fluid reservoir)
储液容器
cleaning brush
清洁刷
felt tip pen
毡头笔
correcting paper 'for typing
errors'
打字错字所用的修正纸
correcting fluid 'for typing
errors'
打字错字所用的修正液
electronic pocket calculator
袖珍型电子计算机
eight-digit fluorescent display
八位数字荧光显示

16 **on/off switch**
开关
17 **function keys**
作用键
18 **number keys**
数字键
19 **decimal key**
小数点键
20 **[equals] key**
等号键
21 **instruction keys** (command
keys)
指令键（命令键）
22 **memory keys**
（记忆）储存键
23 **percent key** (percentage key)
百分比键
24 **π-key** (pi-key) for mensuration
of circles
测量圆周用的"π"键
25 **pencil sharpener**
削铅笔器
26 **typewriter rubber**
打字员用的橡皮
27 **adhesive tape dispenser**
胶带分配器
28 **adhesive tape holder** (roller-type
adhesive tape dispenser)
胶带架（卷式胶带分配器）
29 **roll of adhesive tape**
胶带卷
30 **tear-off edge**
撕割胶带用的刀片

31 **moistener**
湿润器
32 **desk diary**
桌历式日记簿
33 **date sheet** (calendar sheet)
日历纸
34 **memo sheet**
备忘纸
35 **ruler**
直尺
36 **centimetre and millimetre** (*Am.*
centimeter and millimeter)
graduations
厘米和毫米的刻度（公分和公釐）
37 **file** (document file)
文件夹，档案夹
38 **spine label** (spine tag)
背脊标签
39 **finger hole**
指孔
40 **arch board file**
弓形纸板文件夹
41 **arch unit**
弓形装置
42 **release lever** (locking lever,
release/lock lever)
释放杆（止动杆，释放/止动杆）
43 **compressor**
压紧器
44 **bank statement** (statement of
account)
银行定期的财务报表

1-48　open plan office
　敞开式设计办公室
1　partition wall (partition screen)
　隔墙，隔板
2　filing drawer with suspension
　file system
　具悬挂文件系统的抽屉
3　suspension file
　悬挂文件夹
4　file tab
　文件标签
5　file (document file)
　文件夹（档案夹）
6　filing clerk
　（档案）文件处理员
7　clerical assistant
　助理办事员
8　note for the files
　文件（档案）记录
9　telephone
　电话
10　filing shelves
　文件架
11　clerical assistant's desk
　助理办事员桌
12　office cupboard
　办公室柜子
13　plant stand (planter)
　植物架（播种器）
14　indoor plants (houseplants)
　室内植物
15　programmer
　程式设计师

16　data display terminal (visual
　display unit)
　数据（资料）显示终端机（可见显示装
　置）
17　customer service representative
　顾客服务代表
18　customer
　顾客
19　computer-generated design
　(computer-generated art)
　电脑描绘的设计图样
20　sound-absorbing partition
　隔音板
21　typist
　打字员
22　typewriter
　打字机
23　filing drawer
　文件抽屉
24　customer card index
　顾客卡片索引
25　office chair, a swivel chair
　办公室椅，旋转椅
26　typing desk
　打字桌

d index box
索引盒
ti-purpose shelving
能（用途）架
prietor
者
iness letter
书信
prietor's secretary
者秘书
rthand pad (*Am.* steno pad)
簿
io typist
打字员
ating machine
述）录音机
phone

istics chart
图表
estal containing a cupboard
drawers
小柜子或抽屉的桌架
ing-door cupboard
门小柜子
ce furniture arranged in an
ular configuration
成角型结构的办公家具
l-mounted shelf
於壁上的架子
er tray
盘
l calendar
挂历

43 data centre (*Am.* center)
数据（资料）中心
44 calling up information on the
data display terminal (visual
display unit)
於数据显示终端机（可见显示装置）查
出资料
45 waste paper basket
废纸篓
46 sales statistics
销售统计表
47 EDP print-out, a continuous
fan-fold sheet
电子资料处理，打印输出，一种连续折
扇式纸（数据记录纸）
48 connecting element
连接元件

1 **electric typewriter,** a golf ball typewriter
电动打字机，一种高尔夫球型打字机
2-6 keyboard
字键
2 space bar
间隔棒
3 shift key
换字型键
4 line space and carrier return key
换行和托架返回键
5 shift lock
换字型键锁
6 margin release key
限宽键
7 tabulator key
定位键
8 tabulator clear key
定位的去除键
9 on/off switch
电源开关
10 striking force control (impression control)
打印力控制（印痕控制）
11 ribbon selector
色带选择器
12 margin scale
限宽尺（规）
13 left margin stop
左限停止器
14 right margin stop
右限停止器
15 golf ball (spherical typing element) bearing the types
带字母的球型打字头（球型打字元件）
16 ribbon cassette
色带盒
17 paper bail with rollers
将纸压於筒上的夹紧箍
18 platen
（打字机的）滚筒
19 typing opening (typing window)
打字孔（打字窗）
20 paper release lever
松纸杆
21 carrier return lever
托架返回杆
22 platen knob
滚筒转钮
23 line space adjuster
行距调整器
24 variable platen action lever
可变滚筒操作杆
25 push-in platen action lever
可变进纸卷轴
26 erasing table
擦拭台
27 transparent cover
透明盖
28 exchange golf ball (exchange typing element)
替换的球型字头（替换的打字元件）
29 type
铅字
30 golf ball cap (cap of typing element)
球帽（打字元件帽）
31 teeth
齿
32 **web-fed automatic copier**
卷式自动影印机
33 magazine for paper roll
纸卷（筒）箱
34 paper size selection (format selection)
纸的尺寸选择钮（格式选择）
35 print quantity selection
影印数量选择钮
36 contrast control
浓淡（对比）控制
37 main switch (on/off switch)
（电源开关）总开关
38 start print button
起动影印钮
39 document glass
影印用搁置原件的玻璃
40 transfer blanket
影印纸转动毯带
41 toner roll
影印粉筒
42 exposure system
曝光装置
43 print delivery (copy delivery)
影印纸出口搁板
44 **letter-folding machine**
信件折叠机
45 paper feed
供纸装置
46 folding mechanism
折叠装置
47 receiving tray
接收盘
48 **small offset press**
小型凸版印刷机
49 paper feed
供纸装置
50 lever for inking the plate cylinder
著墨於印版滚筒的手柄
51-52 inking unit (inker unit)
著墨装置
51 distributing roller (distributor)
散墨滚子
52 ink roller (inking roller, fountain roller)
墨滚子
53 pressure adjustment
调压
54 sheet delivery (receiving table)
印刷纸出口搁板
55 printing speed adjustment
印刷速度调整
56 jogger for aligning the piles of sheets
将整叠纸整行的齐纸机
57 pile of paper (pile of sheets)
纸叠
58 folding machine
折叠机
59 gathering machine (collating machine, assembling machine) for short runs
少量纸的集页机（集页机）
60 gathering station (collating station, assembling station)
集页装置
61 adhesive binder (perfect binder) for hot adhesives
热接著剂用的接著胶合机
62 **magnetic tape dictating machine**
磁带录音机
63 headphones (headset, earphones)
耳机
64 on/off switch
电源开关
65 microphone cradle
微音机（麦克风）插孔（台）
66 foot control socket
脚控制插座
67 telephone adapter socket
电话接头插座
68 headphone socket (earpho
socket, headset socket)
耳机插座
69 microphone socket
微音机（麦克风）插座
70 built-in loudspeaker
自附扩音器、内藏式扩音器（喇叭
71 indicator lamp (indicator li
指示灯
72 cassette compartment
卡带室
73 forward wind, rewind, and
buttons
向前快转，倒带（快转），和停止
钮
74 time scale with indexing ma
具刻度的时标
75 time scale stop
时标止动器

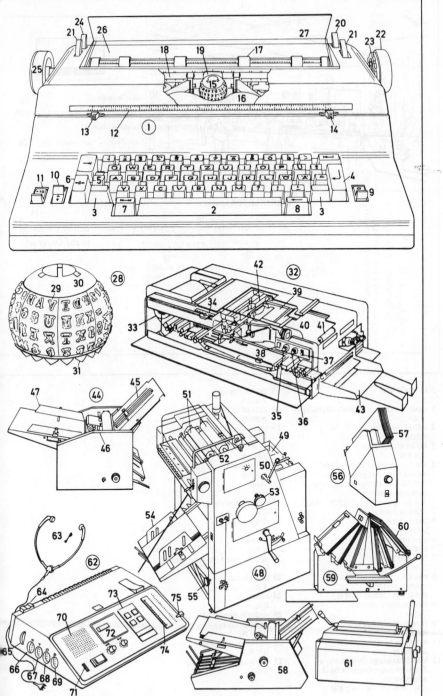

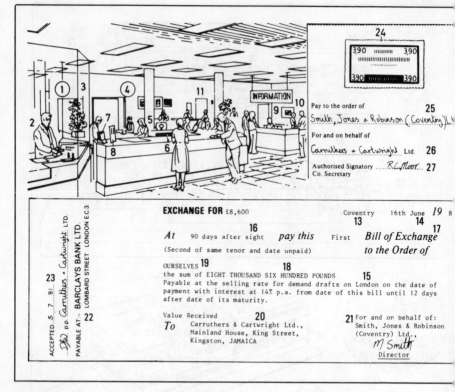

1-11 main hall
主厅

1 cashier's desk (cashier's counter)
出纳柜台

2 teller (cashier)
出纳员

3 bullet-proof glass
防弹玻璃

4 service counters (service and advice for savings accounts, private and company accounts, personal loans)
服务枱（储蓄，私人和公司存款，个人贷款的服务和谘询）

5 bank clerk
银行职员

6 customer
顾客

7 brochures
小册子

8 stock list (price list, list of quotations)
股票行情表（价格表，行情表）

9 information counter
询问枱

10 foreign exchange counter
外汇兑换枱

11 entrance to strong room
保险库入口

12 bill of exchange (bill); here: a draft, an acceptance (a bank acceptance)
汇票；此指支票，银行承兑票据

13 place of issue
开票地点

14 date of issue
开票日期

15 place of payment
付款地点

16 date of maturity (due date)
到期日期

17 bill clause (draft clause)
支票条款

18 value
金额

19 payee (remittee)
受款人（领款人）

20 drawee (payer)
付款人

21 drawer
开票人

22 domicilation (paying agent)
付款地点

23 acceptance
承兑

24 stamp
印花

25 endorsement (indorsement, transfer entry)
背书（转让）

26 endorsee (indorsee)
被背书人

27 endorser (indorser)
背书人

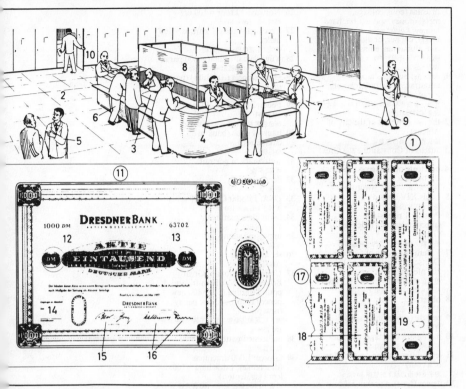

证券交易所 **251**

stock exchange (exchange
or the sale of securities, stocks,
nd bonds)
股票）证券交易所（有价证券交易
，公债，证券）
xchange hall (exchange floor)
易大厅
arket for securities
券市场
oker's post
股票）经纪人位置
vorn stockbroker (exchange
oker, stockbroker, *Am.*
ecialist), an inside broker
式经纪人，场内经纪人
rbstone broker (kerbstoner,
rbstone broker, curbstoner,
tside broker), a commercial
oker dealing in unlisted
curities
外经纪人，经营未挂牌证券的商业经
人
ember of the stock exchange
tockjobber, *Am.* floor trader,
om trader)
股票）证券交易所的成员（股票经纪
，交易所商人）
ock exchange agent
oardman), a bank employee
券交易所代理人，银行雇员
otation board
情板
ock exchange attendat (waiter)
股票）证券交易所服务员

10 telephone box (telephone booth,
telephone kiosk, call box)
电话间（电话亭，公用电话亭）

11-19 securities; *kinds:* share (*Am.*
stock), fixed-income security,
annuity, bond, debenture bond,
municipal bond (corporation
stock), industrial bond,
convertible bond
证券；种类：股票，固定收入证券，年
金，公债，公司债券，市政债券（公司
债券），工业债券，可兑换债券

11 share certificate (*Am.* stock
certificate); *here:* bearer share
(share warrant)
股票（股份）有保证书，此指无记名股
票

12 par (par value, nominal par, face
par) of the share
（股票）证券面值

13 serial number
编号

14 page number of entry in bank's
share register (bank's stock
ledger)
银行股票登记簿的登记页码

15 signature of the chairman of the
board of governors
总裁签名

16 signature of the chairman of the
board of directors
董事长签名

17 sheet of coupons (coupon sheet,
dividend coupon sheet)
息票（股利券）

18 dividend warrnat (dividend
coupon)
股息支付证明（股息单）

19 talon
股息单交换券

1-28 coins (coin, coinage, metal money, specie, *Am.* hard money; *kinds:* gold, silver, nickel, copper, or aluminium, *Am.* aluminum, coins)
硬币（金属货币，种类：金币、银币、镍币、铜币、铝币）

1 Athens: nugget-shaped tetradrachm (tetradrachmon, tetradrachma)
雅典：金块形四德拉克马〔德拉克马为现在希腊货币单位〕

2 the owl (emblem of the city of Athens)
猫头鹰（雅典市的象征）

3 aureus of Constantine the Great
君士坦丁大帝金币

4 bracteate of Emperor Frederick Barbarossa
腓特烈一世（神圣罗马帝国）金币

5 Louis XIV louis-d'or
路易十四法国金币

6 Prussia: 1 reichstaler (speciestaler) of Frederick the Great
普鲁斯：腓特烈大帝的一种银币

7 Federal Republic of Germany: 5 Deutschmarks (DM); 1 DM = 100 pfennigs
德意志联邦共和国：5 德国马克；1 德国马克 = 100 芬尼（辅币）

8 obverse
（货币的）正面

9 reverse (subordinate side)
背面

10 mint mark (mintage, exergue)
（表示造币厂的）刻印

11 legend (inscription on the edge of a coin)
刻字（硬币边缘上的铭刻）

12 device (type), a provincial coat of arms
图案（象征的图案），地方性的徽章

13 Austria: 25 schillings; 1 sch = 100 groschen
奥地利币：25 先令；1 先令 = 100 格罗申（德国的古银币）

14 provincial coats of arms
地方性的徽章

15 Switzerland: 5 franc; 1 franc = 100 centimes
瑞士币：5 法郎；1 法郎 = 100 生丁

16 France: 1 franc = 100 centimes
法国：1 法郎；1 法郎 = 100 生丁

17 Belgium: 100 francs
比利时：100 法郎

18 Luxembourg (Luxemburg): 1 franc
卢森堡：1 法郎

19 Netherlands: 2½ guilders; 1 guilder (florin, gulden) = 100 cents
荷兰：2½ 基尔德；1 基尔德 = 100 分

20 Italy: 10 lire (*sg.* lira)
意大利：10 里拉（单数 lira，复数 lire）

21 Vatican City: 10lire (*sg.* lira)
梵蒂冈市：10 里拉

22 Spain: 1 prseta = 100 centimos
西班牙：1 银币 = 100 生丁

23 Portugal: 1 escudo = 100 centavos
葡萄牙：1 埃斯库多 = 100 分

24 Denmark: 1 krone = 100 òre
丹麦：1 克郎 = 100 欧耳

25 Sweden: 1 krona = 100 òre
瑞典：1 克郎 = 100 欧耳

26 Norway: 1 krone = 100 òre
挪威：1 克郎 = 100 欧耳

27 Czechoslovakea: 1 koruna = 100 heller
捷克：1 克鲁那 = 100 海勒

28 Yugoslavia: 1 kinar = 100 paras
南斯拉夫：1 第那尔 = 100 巴拉

29-39 banknotes (*Am.* bills) (paras money, notes, treasury notes)
钞票（纸币）

29 Federal Republic of Germany: 20 DM
德意志联邦共和国：20 德国马克

30 bank of issue (bank of circulation)
发行银行

31 watermark 'a portrait'
水印〔头像〕

32 denomination
面额

33 USA: 1 dollar ($1) = 100 cents
美国：1 美元 = 100 分

34 facsimile signatures
署名的复印

35 impressed stamp
库印

36 serial number
连续号码

37 United Kingdom of Great Britain and Northern Ireland: 1 pound sterling (£1) = 100 new pence (100p.); *sg.* new penny (new p.)
大不列颠和北爱尔兰联合王国：1 英磅 = 100 新便士

38 guilloched pattern
绳纹饰图案

39 Greece: 1,000 drachmas (drachmae); 1 drachma = 100 lepta (*sg.* lepton)
希腊：1,000 德拉克马 = 100 雷普顿

40-44 striking of coins (coinage, mintage)
造币铸币

40-41 coining dies (minting dies)
铸币印模

40 upper die
上印模

41 lower die
下印模

42 collar
套环

43 coin disc (disk) (flan, planchet, blank)
未加工的钱币

44 coining press (minting press)
铸币冲压机

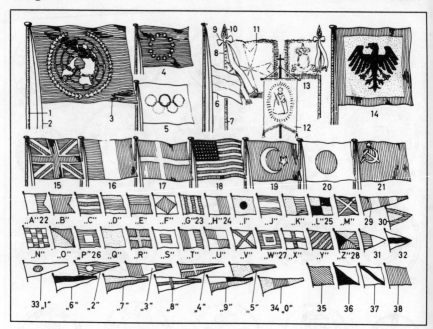

1-3 flag of the United Nations
联合国旗杆
1 flagpole (flagstaff) with truck
顶上具有木冠的旗杆
2 halyard (halliard, haulyard)
升降索
3 bunting
旗布
4 flag of the Council of Europe
欧洲会议旗
5 Olympic flag
奥运会旗
6 flag at half-mast (*Am.* at
half-staff) 'as a token of
mourning'
下半旗（哀悼的表征）

7-11 flag
旗
7 flagpole (flagstaff)
旗杆
8 ornamental stud
饰钉
9 streamer
饰带
10 pointed tip of the flagpole
旗杆尖顶
11 bunting
旗布
12 banner (gonfalon)
旗帜（旌旗）
13 cavalry standard (flag of the
cavalry)
骑兵旗（骑兵的军旗）
14 standard of the German Federal
President 'ensign of head of
state'
德意志联邦总统〔国家元首旗〕
15-21 national flags
国旗

15 the Union Jack (Great Britain)
英国国旗
16 the Tricolour (*Am.* Tricolor)
(France)
三色旗（法国国旗）
17 the Danebrog (Dannebrog)
(Denmark)
丹麦国旗
18 the Stars and Stripes
(Star-Spangled Banner) (USA)
星条旗（美国国旗）
19 the Crescent (Turkey)
新月旗（土耳其国旗）
20 the Rising Sun (Japan)
太阳旗（日本国旗）
21 the Hammer and Sickle (USSR)
锤子与镰刀旗（苏联国旗）
22-34 signal flags, a hoist
信号旗，一串国际信号旗
22-28 letter flags
字母旗
22 letter A, a burgee
(swallow-tailed flag)
字母 A，船的三角旗（燕尾旗）
23 G, pilot flag
G，领港员（领水人）旗
24 H ([pilot on board])
H（领港员在船上）
25 L ([you should stop, I have
something important to
communicate])
L（停船，有要事传送）
26 P, the Blue Peter ([about to set
sail])
P，开航旗（即将出航）
27 W ([I require medical
assistance])
W（要求医药支援）

28 Z, an oblong pennant (oblon
pendant)
Z，长方形（矩形）旗
29 code pennant (code pendant
used in the International Sig
Code
用於国际信号码语的信号三角旗
30-32 substitute flags (repeaters
triangular flags (pennants,
pendants)
代用旗，三角旗
30-34 numeral pennants (numer
pendants)
数字旗（数字三角旗）
33 number 1
数字 1
34 number 0
数字 0
35-38 customs flags
海关旗
35 customs boat pennant (custo
boat pendant)
海关船三角旗
36 [ship cleared through custo
已清关的船上用旗
37 customs signal flag
海关信号旗
38 powder flag '[inflammable
(flammable) cargo]'
易爆危险品旗〔'易燃物'〕

30-36 crests

oat-of-arms (achievement of
s, hatchment, achievement)

（头饰）

ath of the colours (*Am.* colors)

花圈

ntle (mantling)

helmets (helms)

ng helmet (jousting helmet)

马比赛用的头盔

eld

d sinister wavy

右左边的）波纹

t-helmet (pot-helm, heaume)

壶头盔

rred helmet (grilled helmet)

头盔（栅式头盔）

met affronty with visor open

面头盔

marital achievement

arshalled, *Am.* marshaled,

at-of-arms)

姻纹章

ns of the baron (of the husband)

夫的纹章

arms of the family of the

mme (of the wife)

子的纹章

mi-man; *also:* demi-woman

子半身象；女子半身象

st coronet

状饰

13 fleur-de-lis
百合花型的纹章

14 mantling
斗篷

15 bull
公牛

16 unicorn
独角兽

17-23 blazon
纹章解说

17 inescutcheon (heart-shield)
中央饰有纹章的盾

18-23 quarterings one to six
盾面纵横六等分

18, 20, 22, dexter, right
盾章右半边

18-19 chief
盾的上部

19, 21, 23 sinister, left
盾章左半边

22-23 base
盾的底部

24-29 tinctures
色调色彩

24-25 metals
金属

24 or (gold) 'yellow'
金色（黄色）

25 argent (silver) 'white'
银色（白色）

26 sable
黑色

27 gules
红色

28 azure
天蓝色

29 vert
绿色

30 ostrich feathers (treble plume)
鸵鸟羽毛（三重羽饰）

31 truncheon
权杖

32 demi-goat
半身山羊

33 tournament pennons
比赛燕尾旗

34 buffalo horns
水牛角

35 harpy
〔希腊神话〕上半身为女人下半身似鸟
的怪物

36 plume of peacock's feathers
孔雀羽毛饰

37-46 crowns and coronets
王冠与冠饰

37 tiara (papal tiara)
三重冠〔罗马教皇（宗）的三重冠〕

38 Imperial Crown 'German, until 1806'
〔德国至1806年〕王冠

39 ducal coronet (duke's coronet)
公爵冠

40 prince's coronet
王子，（小国）君主的小王冠

41 elector's coronet
〔神圣罗马帝国有权选举皇帝的〕诸侯冠

42 English Royal Crown
英国皇冠王冠

43-45 coronets of rank
显贵的冠饰

43 baronet's coronet
贵族的冠饰

44 baron's coronet (baronial coronet)
男爵的冠冕

45 count's coronet
伯爵的冠冕

46 mauerkrone (mural crown) of a city crest
城市纹章的壁冠

1-98 army weaponry
陆军武器

1-39 hand weapons
手持武器（轻武器）

1 Pl pistol
Pl 型手枪

2 barrel
枪管

3 front sight (foresight)
准星

4 hammer
撞针

5 trigger
板机

6 pistol grip
枪柄

7 magazine holder
弹匣仓

8 MP2 machine
MP2 型机关枪

9 shoulder rest (butt)
肩托（枪托）

10 casing (mechanism casing)
（装填）机匣盖

11 barrel clamp (barrel-clamping nut)
枪管夹（枪管夹紧螺帽）

12 cocking lever (cocking handle)
枪的板机柄

13 palm rest
下护木

14 safety catch
保险（安全掣子）

15 magazine
弹匣

16 G3-A3 self-loading rifle
G3-A3 型自动步枪

17 barrel
枪管

18 flash hider (flash eliminator)
枪口闪光掩盖器

19 palm rest
下护木

20 trigger mechanism
板机

21 magazine
弹匣

22 notch (sighting notch, rearsight)
瞄准具（瞄准槽，表尺座）

23 front sight block (foresight block) with front sight (foresight)
准星座与准星

24 rifle butt (butt)
步枪托

25 44mm anti-tank rocket launcher
44 毫米（反坦克）火箭筒

26 rocket (projectile)
火箭弹（弹）

27 buffer
缓冲器

28 telescopic sight (telescope sight)
望远瞄准器

29 firing mechanism
击发装置

30 cheek rest
颊板托

31 shoulder rest (butt)
肩托（枪托）

32 MG3 machine gun (Spandau)
MG3 型机关枪

33 barrel casing
枪管护盖

34 gas regulator
气体调节器

35 belt-changing flap
弹带变换盖

36 rearsight
瞄准器表尺座（照门）

37 front sight block (foresight block) with front sight (foresight)
准星座与准星

38 pistol grip
手枪枪柄

39 shoulder rest (butt)
肩托（枪托）

40-95 heavy weapons
重型武器

40 120mm AM 50 mortar
120 毫米 AM50 型迫击炮

41 barrel
炮管

42 bipod
双脚架

43 gun carriage
炮托架

44 buffer (buffer ring)
缓冲器（缓冲环）

45 sight (sighting mechanism)
瞄准器（瞄准器装置）

46 base plate
底板（盘）

47 striker pad
缓冲垫

48 traversing handle
横动（转向）把手

49-74 artillery weapons mounted on self-propelled gun carriages
装在自动推进炮车上的火炮

49 175mm SFM 107 cannon
175 毫米 SFM107 大炮

50 drive wheel
驱动轮

51 elevating piston
升降活塞

52 buffer (buffer recuperator)
缓冲器（缓冲复原器）

53 hydraulic system
液压系统

54 breech ring
炮尾环

55 spade
炮车尾部

56 spade piston
炮车尾部活塞

57 155mm M 109 G self-propelled gun
155 毫米 M109G 型自动推进炮

58 muzzle
炮口

59 fume extractor
排烟器

60 barrel cradle
炮管摇架

61 barrel recuperator
炮管复进机

62 barrel clamp
炮管夹

63 light anti-aircraft (AA) machine gun
轻型高射机枪

64 Honest John M 386 rocket launcher
诚实约翰 M386 型火箭炮

65 rocket with warhead
装有弹头的火箭

66 launching ramp
倾斜发射装置

67 elevating gear
俯仰传动机构

68 jack
千斤顶，起重器

69 cable winch
缆索绞车

70 110 SF rocket launcher
110SF 型火箭炮

71 disposable rocket tubes
蜂巢式火箭发射管

72 tube bins
管仓

73 turntable
转台

74 fire control system
射击控制系统

75 2.5 tonne construction vehicle
2.5 吨工程车

76 lifting arms (lifting device)
起重臂（起重装置）

77 shovel
铲斗

78 counterweight (counterpoise)
配重

79-95 armoured (*Am.* armored) vehicles
装甲车辆

79 M 113 armoured (*Am.* armored) ambulance
M113 型装甲救护车

80 Leopard 1 A 3 tank
豹式 1A3 型坦克

81 protection device
防护装置

82 infrared laser rangefinder
红外线雷射测距器

83 smoke canisters (smoke dispensers)
放烟罐（烟雾施放器）

84 armoured (*Am.* armored) turret
装甲炮塔

85 skirt
坦克防护板

86 road wheel
负重轮，稳定轮

87 track
履带

88 anti-tank tank
反战车坦克

89 fume extractor
排烟器

90 protection device
防护装置

91 armoured (*Am.* armored)
装甲输送车

92 cannon
大炮

93 armoured (*Am.* armored) recovery vehicle
装甲修护车

94 levelling (*Am.* leveling) and support shovel
平置和支撑用铲

95 jib
伸重，起重的铁臂

96 25 tonne all-purpose vehicle
25 吨通用车辆

97 drop windscreen (*Am.* drop windshield)
落地式挡风玻璃

98 canvas cover
帆布篷

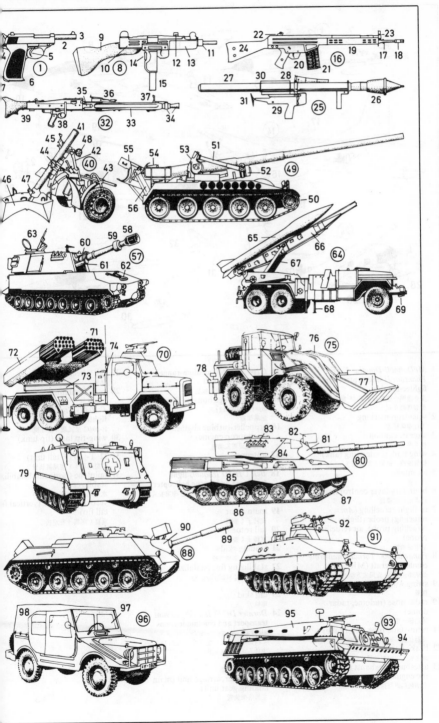

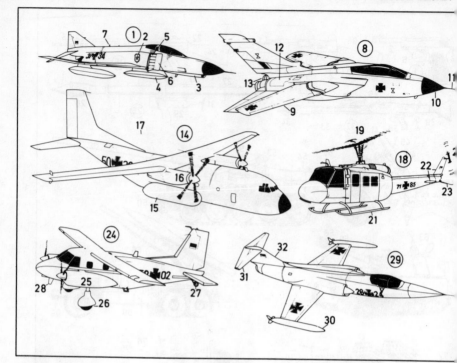

1 *McDonnell-Douglas F-4F Phantom II* **intercepteor and fighter-bomber**
麦克唐纳—道格拉斯 F-4F 幽灵 II 式拦截轰炸战斗机

2 **squadron marking**
飞行中队标志

3 **aircraft cannon**
机关炮

4 **wing tank (underwing tank)**
机翼油箱（机翼下部油箱）

5 **air intake**
进气管

6 **boundary layer control flap**
边界层控制襟翼

7 **in-flight refuelling** (*Am.* refueling) **probe (flight refuelling probe, air refuelling probe)**
空中加油管

8 *Panavia 2000 Tornado* **multirole combat aircraft (MRCA)**
帕纳维亚 2000 旋风式万能战斗机

9 **swing wing**
摇翼

10 **radar nose (radome, radar dome)**
雷达锥，雷达罩

11 **pitot-static tube (pitot tube)**
动静压管

12 **brake flap (air brake)**
减速板（空中制动器）

13 **afterburner exhaust nozzles of the engines**
发动机后燃器排气喷嘴

14 *C160 Transall* **medium-range transport aircraft**
C160 "协同"中程运输机

15 **undercarriage housing (landing gear housing)**
起落架舱

16 **propeller-turbine engine (turboprop engine)**
涡轮螺旋桨发动机

17 **antenna**
天线

18 *Bell UH-ID Iroquois* **light transport and rescue helicopter**
（贝尔公司生产的）UH-ID 印第安式轻型运输和救难直升机

19 **main rotor**
主转子（旋翼）

20 **tail rotor**
尾转子（旋翼）

21 **landing skids**
著陆橇（落地雪橇）

22 **stabilizing fins (stabilizing surfaces, stabilizers)**
安定板

23 **tail skid**
尾橇

24 *Dornier DO28 D-2 Skyservant* **transport and communications aircraft**
（西德多尼尔公司生产的）D028 D-2 空中仆人式运输通讯机

25 **engine pod**
发动机（舱）箱

26 **main undercarriage unit (main landing gear unit)**
主起落架装置

27 **tail wheel**
尾轮

28 **sword antenna**
刀状天线

29 *F-104 G Starfighter* **fighter-bomber**
F-104G 星式战斗轰炸机

30 **wing-tip tank (tip tank)**
翼尖油箱

31-32 **T-tail (T-tail unit)**
T 型尾翼（T 型尾翼装置）

31 **tailplane (horizontal stabilizer, stabilizer)**
水平尾翼（水平安定板）

32 **vertical stabilizer (vertical fin, tail fin)**
垂直（尾翼）安定板

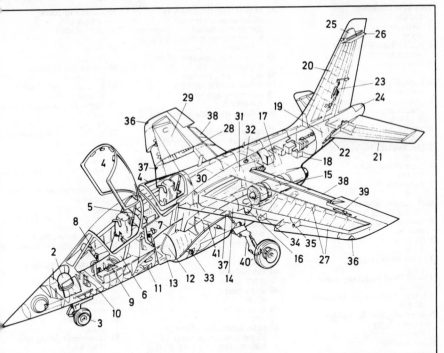

Dornier-Dassault-Breguet
ha Jet Franco-German jet
ner
国达索布雷盖航空公司和西德多尼
同同生产的）阿尔发式喷射教练

t-static tube (pitot tube)
压管
gen tank
瓶，氧气槽
ard-retracting nose wheel
收之鼻轮
kpit canopy (cockpit hood)
罩
opy jack
盖启闭操作啊筒
t's seat (student pilot's seat),
ejector seat (ejection seat)
员弹射座椅（学员弹射座椅）
erver's seat (instructor's
), an ejector seat (ejection
员弹射座椅（教官弹射座椅）
trol column (control stick)
（操纵）杆
ust lever
杆
der pedals with brakes
舵与刹车踏板
t avionics bay
子舱
intake to the engine
机（引擎）进气口
ndary layer control flap
层控制襟翼
intake duct
道

15 turbine engine
涡轮发动机（引擎）
16 reservoir for the hydraulic
system
液压系统油箱
17 battery housing
电瓶舱（电瓶装置舱）
18 rear avionics bay
后电子舱
19 baggage compartment
行李舱
20 triple-spar tail construction
三梁尾翼结构
21 horizontal tail
水平尾翼
22 servo-actuating mechanism for
the elevator
升降舵的辅力致动机构
23 servo-actuating mechanism for
the rudder
方向舵的辅力致动机构
24 brake chute housing (drag chute
housing)
减速伞舱（阻力伞舱）
25 VHF (very high frequency)
antenna (UHF antenna)
特高频天线（超高频天线）
26 VOR (very high frequency
omnidirectional range) antenna
特高频全向天线
27 twin-spar wing construction
双梁机翼结构
28 former with integral spars
整体翼梁框架
29 integral wing tanks
机翼整体油箱

30 centre-section (Am.
center-section) fuel tank
中翼油槽
31 fuselage tanks
机身油箱
32 gravity fuelling (Am. fueling)
point
重力加油口
33 pressure fuelling (Am. fueling)
point
压力加油口
34 inner wing suspension
机翼内侧支承
35 outer wing suspension
机翼外侧支承
36 navigation lights (position
lights)
航行灯（方位灯）
37 landing lights
着陆灯
38 landing flap
降落襟翼
39 aileron actuator
副翼致动器
40 forward-retracting main
undercarriage unit (main
landing gear unit)
向前收之主起落装置
41 undercarriage hydraulic cylinder
(landing gear hydraulic
cylinder)
起落架液压啊筒（著陆架液压啊筒）

1-63 light battleships
轻型战舰

1 destroyer
驱逐舰

2 hull of flush-deck vessel
平甲板船隻的船身

3 bow (stem)
船首

4 flagstaff (jackstaff)
旗杆（船艏旗杆）

5 anchor, a stockless anchor (patent anchor)
锚，无档锚

6 anchor capstan (windlass)
起锚绞盘

7 breakwater (*Am.* manger board)
防波板

8 chine strake
舷缘侧板

9 main deck
主甲板

10-28 superstructures
上层建筑，船楼建筑

10 superstructure deck
船楼甲板

11 life rafts
救生筏

12 cutter (ship's boat)
小艇

13 davit (boat-launching crane)
吊柱吊架

14 bridge (bridge superstructure)
舰桥（船桥）

15 side navigation light (side running light)
侧航行灯

16 antenna
天线

17 radio direction finder (RDF) frame
无线电测向架

18 lattice mast
格子桅

19 forward funnel
前烟窗

20 aft funnel
后烟窗

21 cowl
烟窗帽

22 aft superstructure (poop)
艉部上层建筑（船楼建筑，艉楼）

23 capstan
绞盘

24 companion ladder (companionway, companion hatch)
升降梯（升降口，升降舱口）

25 ensign staff
艉旗杆

26 stern, a transom stern
艉，船尾肋骨

27 waterline
水线

28 searchlight
探照灯

29-37 armament
武器

29 100mm gun turret
100 毫米炮塔

30 four-barrel anti-submarine rocket launcher (missile launcher)
四管反潜艇火箭发射器

31 40mm twin anti-aircraft (AA) gun
40 厘米双高射炮

32 MM 38 anti-aircraft (AA) rocket launcher (missile launcher) in launching container
在发射舱的MM38 型对空火箭发射器（飞弹发射器）

33 anti-submarine torpedo tube
反潜艇鱼雷射管

34 depth-charge thrower
深水炸弹发射装置（投掷器）

35 weapon system radar
武器系统雷达

36 radar antenna (radar scanner)
雷达天线

37 optical rangefinder
光学测距仪

38 destroyer
驱逐舰

39 bower anchor
艏锚

40 propeller guard
螺旋桨护板

41 tripod lattice mast
三角网格桅杆

42 pole mast
杆桅

43 ventilator openings (ventilator grill)
通风机口

44 exhaust pipe
排气管

45 ship's boat
救生艇

46 antenna
天线

47 radar-controlled 127mm all-purpose gun in turret
炮塔上雷达控制 127 毫米多目的（用途）炮

48 127mm all-purpose gun
127 毫米多目的（用途）炮

49 launcher for Tartar missiles
鞑靼飞弹发射器

50 anti-submarine rocket (ASROC) launcher (missile launcher)
反潜艇火箭发射器

51 fire control radar antennas
射击控制雷达天线

52 radome (radar dome)
（雷达）天线罩

53 frigate
（反潜艇）小型驱逐舰

54 hawse pipe
锚链筒

55 steaming light
航海（行）桅灯

56 navigation light (running light)
航海（行）灯

57 air extractor duct
排气管

58 funnel
烟窗

59 cowl
烟窗帽

60 whip antenna (fishpole antenna)
鞭状（钓杆状）天线

61 cutter
小艇

62 stern light
艉灯

63 propeller guard boss
螺旋桨护板毂

64-91 fighting ships
战舰

64 submarine
潜水艇

65 flooded foredeck
浸水前甲板

66 pressure hull
压力船壳

67 turret
塔，炮塔

68 retractable instruments
可伸缩的仪器

69 E-boat (torpedo boat)
E 型快艇（鱼雷快艇）

70 76mm all-purpose gun with turret
76 毫米多目的（用途）炮（塔）

71 missile-launching housing
飞弹发射器外壳

72 deckhouse
甲板室（房舱）

73 40mm anti-aircraft (AA) g
40 毫米高射炮

74 propeller guard moulding (molding)
螺旋桨护板缘饰

75 143 class E-boat (143 class torpedo boat)
143 级 E 型快艇（143 级鱼雷快艇

76 breakwater (*Am.* manger b
防波板

77 radome (radar dome)
（雷达）天线罩

78 torpedo tube
鱼雷射管

79 exhaust escape flue
排气（烟）管道

80 mine hunter
扫雷艇

81 reinforced rubbing strake
加强防擦板

82 inflatable boat (inflatable dinghy)
充气艇（充气小艇）

83 davit
吊柱，吊架

84 minesweeper
扫雷艇，扫雷舰

85 cable winch
钢缆绞车

86 towing winch (towing mach towing engine)
拖缆绞车

87 mine-sweeping gear (parava
扫雷装置（水雷扫除器）

88 crane (davit)
起重装置（吊杆）

89 landing craft
登陆艇

90 bow ramp
船头斜台（登陆舌门）

91 stern ramp
船尾斜台（登陆舌门）

92-97 auxiliaries
辅助舰

92 tender
补给舰（船）

93 servicing craft
驳运船

94 minelayer
布雷艇

95 training ship
教练船

96 deep-sea salvage tug
深海救难艇

97 fuel tanker (replenishing shi
油船（补给船）

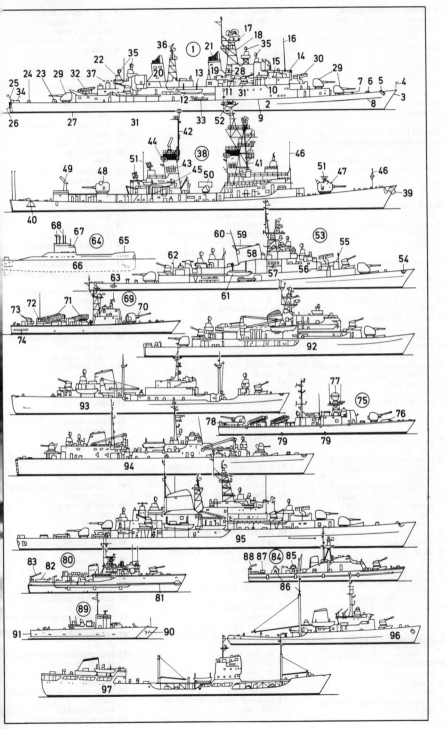

1 **nuclear-powered aircraft carrier** [*Nimitz ICVN 68*] (USA)
"尼米兹 ICVN68"核子动力航空母舰

2-11 body plan
船体正面图

2 flight deck
飞行甲板

3 island (bridge)
司令塔（舰桥）

4 aircraft lift (*Am.* aircraft elevator)
飞行升降机

5 **eight-barrel anti-aircraft (AA) rocket launcher (missile launcher)**
八管高射火箭发射器（导弹发射器）

6 pole mast (antenna mast)
杆樯（天线樯）

7 antenna
天线

8 radar antenna (radar scanner)
雷达天线

8 fully enclosed bow
全闭式船首

10 deck crane
甲板起重机

11 transom stern
方形船尾

12-20 deck plan
甲板平面图

12 angle deck (flight deck)
斜角甲板（飞行甲板）

13 aircraft lift (*Am.* aircraft elevator)
飞机升降机

14 twin launching catapult
双飞机弹射装置

15 hinged (movable) baffle board
铰链阻板（活动阻板）

16 arrester wire
拦阻索

17 emergency crash barrier
紧急栏机网

18 safety net
安全网

19 caisson (cofferdam)
沉箱（堰舱）

20 **eight-barrel anti-aircraft (AA) rocket launcher (missile launcher)**
八管高射火箭发射器（导弹发射器）

21 [*Kara*] *class* **rocket cruiser (missile cruiser)** (USSR)
"卡拉"级火箭巡洋舰（导弹巡洋舰）（苏俄）

22 hull of flush-deck vessel
平甲板船隻的船身

23 sheer
舷弧

24 twelve-barrel underwater salvo rocket launcher (missile launcher)
十二管水中齐发火箭发射器

25 twin anti-aircraft (AA) rocket launcher (missile launcher)
双高射火箭发射器

26 launching housing for 4 short-range rockets (missiles)
四枚短程火箭（导弹）发射装置架

27 baffle board
阻板

28 bridge
舰桥

29 radar antenna (radar scanner)
雷达天线

30 twin 76mm anti-aircraft (AA) gun turret
双 76 毫米高射炮塔

31 turret
塔（炮塔）

32 funnel
烟囱

33 twin anti-aircraft (AA) rocket launcher (missile launcher)
双高射火箭发射器

34 automatic anti-aircraft (AA) gun
自动高射炮

35 ship's boat
救生艇

36 underwater 5-torpedo housing
五管鱼雷发射器

37 underwater 6-salvo rocket launcher (missile launcher)
六管水中齐发火箭发射器

38 helicopter hangar
直升机库

39 helicopter landing platform
直升机著陆平台

40 variable depth sonar (VDS)
可变深度声纳

41 [*California*] class **rocket cruiser (missile cruiser)** (USA)
"加里佛尼亚"级火箭巡洋舰（导弹巡洋舰）（美国）

42 hull
船身

43 forward turret
前炮塔

44 aft turret
后炮塔

45 forward superstructure
船首上层建筑

46 landing craft
登陆艇

47 antenna
天线

48 radar antenna (radar scanner)
雷达天线

49 radome (radar dome)
（雷达）天线罩

50 surface-to-air rocket launcher (missile launcher)
对空火箭发射器

51 underwater rocket launcher (missile launcher)
水中火箭发射器

52 127mm gun with turret
127 毫米炮塔

53 helicopter landing platform
直升机著陆平台

54 **nuclear-powered fleet submarine**
核子动力潜艇

55-74 middle section 'diagram'
中间部分〔简图〕

55 pressure hull
耐压船壳

56 auxiliary engine room
辅机舱

57 rotary turbine pump
旋转涡轮泵

58 steam turbine generator
蒸汽涡轮发电机

59 propeller shaft
螺旋桨轴

60 thrust block
推力轴承

61 reduction gear
减速齿轮（装置）

62 high and low pressure turbine
高低压涡轮

63 high-pressure steam pipe for secondary water circuit (auxiliary water circuit)
二次（辅助）水廻路高压蒸汽管

64 condenser
凝结器

65 primary water circuit
一次水廻路

66 heat exchanger
热交换器

67 nuclear reactor casing (atomic pile casing)
核反应器防护罩（原子堆放护罩）

68 reactor core
反应炉（器）核心

69 control rods
控制杆

70 lead screen
铅屏（遮蔽屏）

71 turret
塔（炮塔）

72 snorkel (schnorkel)
换气装置

73 air inlet
进气口

74 retractable instruments
可伸缩的仪器

75 **patrol submarine** with conventional (diesel-electric) drive
常规驱动（柴油电动）巡逻潜艇

76 pressure hull
耐压船壳

77 flooded foredeck
浸水前甲板

78 outer flap (outer doors) 'for torpedoes'
外闸门〔发射鱼雷用〕

79 torpedo tube
鱼雷发射管

80 bow bilge
艏

81 anchor
锚

82 anchor winch
起锚绞车

83 battery
蓄电池，电瓶

84 living quarters with folding bunks
具折叠床的居住舱

85 commanding officer's cabin
艇长舱（指挥舱）

86 main hatchway
主舱口

87 flagstaff
旗杆

88-91 retractable instruments
可伸缩仪器

88 attack periscope
攻击潜望镜

89 antenna
天线

90 snorkel (schnorkel)
换气装置

91 radar antenna (radar scanner)
雷达天线

92 exhaust outlet
排气口

93 heat space (hot-pipe space)
暖气（管）室

94 diesel generators
柴油发电机

95 aft diving plane and vertical rudder
艉水平舵和垂直舵

96 forward vertical rudder
艏垂直舵

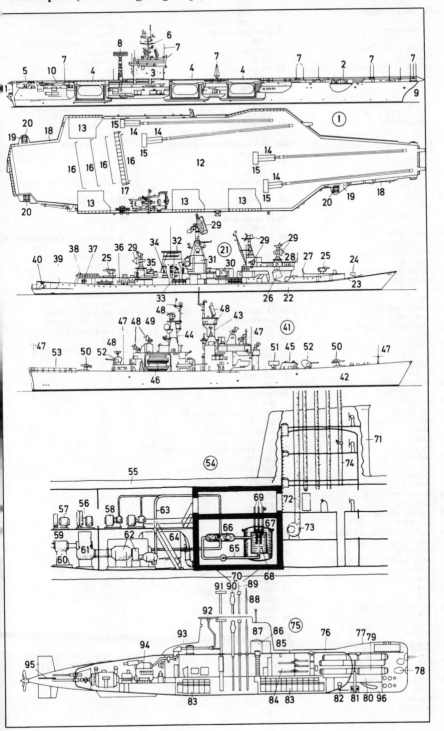

1-85 primary school
小学

1-45 classroom
教室

1 arrangement of desks in a horseshoe
成马蹄形（U型）排列的课桌

2 double desk
双人课桌

3 pupils (children) in a group (sitting in a group)
分组坐的小学生（小孩）

4 exercise book
练习簿

5 pencil
铅笔

6 wax crayon
蜡笔

7 school bag
手提式书包

8 handle
提手

9 school satchel (satchel)
背式书包

10 front pocket
书包正面小口袋

11 strap (shoulder strap)
背带（肩带）

12 pen and pencil case
钢笔和铅笔盒

13 zip
拉链

14 fountain pen (pen)
签字笔（钢笔）

15 loose-leaf file (ring file)
活页纸夹

16 reader
读物，读本

17 spelling book
拼字教科书

18 notebook (exercise book)
笔记簿（练习簿）

19 felt tip pen
毛笔，毡尖笔

20 pupil raising her hand
学生举手

21 teacher
老师

22 teacher's desk
讲台

23 register
点名簿

24 pen and pencil tray
钢笔和铅笔盘

25 desk mat (blotter)
桌垫（吸墨纸）

26 window painting with finger paints (finger painting)
指绘的窗户画

27 pupils' (children's) paintings (watercolours)
儿童画（水彩画）

28 cross
十字架

29 three-part blackboard
三块板组成的黑板

30 bracket for holding charts
挂图表用的托架

31 chalk ledge
粉笔（壁）架

32 chalk
粉笔

33 blackboard drawing
黑板画

34 diagram
图解，示范图

35 reversible side blackboard
正反两面使用的黑板

36 projection screen
放映幕

37 triangle
三角板

38 protractor
分度器

39 divisions
分度

40 blackboard compass
黑板用圆规，两脚规

41 sponge tray
海绵托盘

42 blackboard sponge (sponge)
海绵黑板擦

43 classroom cupboard
教室小柜

44 map (wall map)
地图（挂图）

45 brick wall
砖墙

46-85 craft room
工艺室

46 workbench
工作桌

47 vice (Am. vise)
虎钳

48 vice (Am. vise) bar
虎钳把手

49 scissors
剪刀

50-52 working with glue (sticking paper, cardboard, etc.)
粘胶工作（贴纸，硬纸板等）

50 surface to be glued
表面涂布粘胶，粘贴面

51 tube of glue
一管粘胶

52 tube cap
管帽

53 fretsaw
圆锯，线锯

54 fretsaw blade (saw blade)
锯片（叶）

55 wood rasp (rasp)
木锉

56 piece of wood held in the vice (Am. vise)
虎钳夹住的木块

57 glue pot
粘胶罐

58 stool
凳子

59 brush
刷子

60 pan (dust pan)
盘（灰尘盘）

61 broken china
破碎的瓷器

62 enamelling (Am. enameling)
上瓷釉

63 electric enamelling (Am. enameling) stove
电磁炉

64 unworked copper
未加功的铜器

65 enamel powder
釉粉

66 hair sieve
细筛

67-80 pupils' (children's) work
学生（儿童）作品

67 clay models (models)
粘土（泥塑）模型

68 window decoration of colour (Am. colored) glass
彩色玻璃的窗饰

69 glass mosaic picture (glass mosaic)
玻璃镶嵌画

70 mobile
活动玩具

71 paper kite (kite)
纸风筝

72 wooden construction
木制品

73 polyhedron
多面体

74 hand puppets
玩偶

75 clay masks
粘土（陶）制面具

76 cast candles (wax candles)
蜡烛

77 wood carving
木雕

78 clay jug
陶罐

79 geometrical shapes made of clay
陶制几何模型

80 wooden toys
木制玩具

81 materials
材料，原料

82 stock of wood
木头

83 inks for wood cuts
版画（木刻）用的油墨

84 paintbrushes
画笔

85 bag of plaster of Paris
熟石膏袋

1-45 grammar school; *also:*
upper band of a comprehensive
school (*Am.* alternative school)
初级中学；高级综合中学

1-13 chemistry
化学

1 chemistry lab (chemistry
laboratory) with tiered rows of
seats
一排排阶梯座位的化学实验室

2 chemistry teacher
化学教员（教师）

3 demonstration bench (teacher's
bench)
实验台（教师实验台）

4 water pipe
水管

5 tiled working surface
铺瓷砖的台面

6 sink
水槽（洗涤槽）

7 television monitor, a screen for
educational programmes (*Am.*
programs)
教学用电视机（监控器）

8 overhead projector
投影器

9 projector top for skins
放幻灯片的投影器上部

10 projection lens with right-angle
mirror
带直角反射镜的投影镜头

11 pupils' (*Am.* students') bench
with experimental apparatus
具实验设备的学生实验台

12 electrical point (socket)
电插座

13 projection table
投影台

14-34 biology preparation room
(biology prep room)
生物学准备室

14 skeleton
骨骼；骨架

15 casts of skulls
头颅模型

16 calvarium of Pithecanthropus
Erectus
爪哇直立猿人（头）颅顶化石

17 skull of Steinheim man
斯坦罕姆人的头颅骨

18 calvarium of Peking man (of
Sinanthropus)
北京人（北京猿人）的（头）颅顶化石

19 skull of Neanderthal man,. a
skull of primitive man
尼安德塔人头颅化石（原始人的头
颅）

20 Australopithecine skull (skull of
Australopthecus)
更新世界灵长类动物头颅（已绝种灵长类
头骨）

21 skull of present-day man
现代人头颅

22 dissecting bench
解剖台

23 chemical bottles
化学药瓶

24 gas tap
煤气（瓦斯）栓

25 petri dish
细菌培养皿（碟）

26 measuring cylinder
量筒

27 work folder (teaching material)
工作纸夹（教材）

28 textbook
教科书课本

29 bacteriological cultures
细菌的培养

30 incubator
细菌培养室

31 test tube rack
试管架

32 washing bottle
洗涤瓶

33 water tank
水箱

34 sink
水槽（洗涤槽）

35 language laboratory
语言教室

36 blackboard
黑板

37 console
控制台

38 headphones (headset)
耳机

39 microphone
微音器（麦克风）

40 earcups
耳机套

41 padded headband (padded
headpiece)
加垫头带

42 programme (*Am.* program)
recorder, a cassette recorder
教学用录音机，一种卡式录音机

43 pupil's (*Am.* student's) volume
control
学生用的音量控制

44 master volume control
教师用的音量控制

45 control buttons (operating keys)
控制钮（操作键）

1-25 university (college)
大学（学院）
1 lecture
讲演，讲课
2 lecture room (lecture theatre,
Am. theater)
教室，讲堂
3 university lecturer (lecturer, *Am.*
assistant professor)
大学教师（讲师，[美]助教）
4 lectern
讲台
5 lecture notes
讲义，讲稿
6 demonstrator
示范者
7 assistant
助教，助手
8 diagram
挂图，图表
9 student
学生（男）
10 student
学生（女）
11-25 university library
大学图书馆
11 stack (book stack) with the
stock of books
书库的藏书
12 bookshelf, a steel shelf
书架，钢制书架
13 reading room
阅览室

14 member of the reading room
staff, a librarian
阅览室工作人员，图书馆管理员
15 periodicals rack with periodicals
期刊架
16 newspaper shelf
报纸架
17 reference library with reference
books (handbooks,
encyclopedias, dictionaries)
备有参考书（手册，百科全书，辞典）
的参考书图书馆
18 lending library and catalogue
(*Am.* catalog) room
借书图书馆及目录室
19 librarian
图书馆管理员
20 issue desk
发书台
21 main catalogue (*Am.* catalog)
总目录（索引）
22 card catalogue (*Am.* catalog)
卡片目录（索引）
23 card catalogue (*Am.* catalog)
drawer
卡片目录（索引）抽屉
24 library user
借书人
25 borrower's ticket (library ticket)
借书证

election meeting, a public
eting
（选举）政见发表会，一种公开的集

ommittee
会
irman

mmittee member
会委员
mmittee table
席（桌）

ction speaker (speaker)
发表人（演说者）
trum
台
crophone
扩）音器，麦克风
eting (audience)

n distributing leaflets
传单者
wards
服务人员
nband (armlet)

ner
传用）横幕
card
牌
clamation
，布告

15 heckler
诘问者
16-30 election
选举
16 polling station (polling place)
投票处
17 election officer
选举事务员
18 electoral register
选举人名册
19 polling card with registration
number (polling number)
有登记编号的投票卡片
20 ballot paper with the names of
the parties and candidates
具有党派名称和候选人姓名的选票
21 ballot envelope
选票信封
22 voter
投票人
23 polling booth
投票间（亭）
24 elector (qualified voter)
有选举权者
25 election regulations
选举规则
26 clerk
事务员，办事员
27 clerk with the duplicate list
拿名册副本的办事员
28 election supervisor
选举督察

29 ballot box
（投）票箱
30 slot
投票口

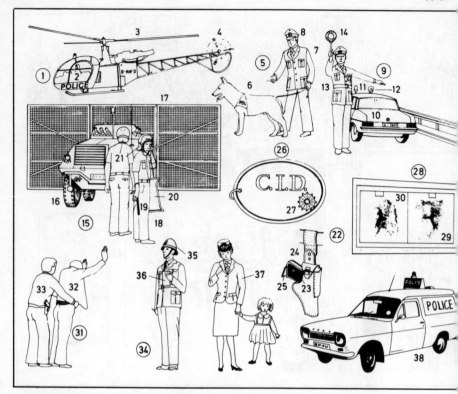

1-33 police duties
警务

1 police helicopter (traffic helicopter) for controlling (*Am.* controling) traffic from the air
从空中指挥交通的警察直升机

2 cockpit
驾驶舱

3 rotor (main rotor)
转子（主转子，主旋翼）

4 tail rotor
尾转子（旋翼）

5 police dog and handler
警犬和训练师

6 police dog
警犬

7 uniform
制服

8 uniform cap, a peaked cap with cockade
制服帽，有帽章的大盘帽

9 traffic control by a mobile traffic patrol
使用交通巡逻车指挥交通

10 patrol car
巡逻车

11 blue light
蓝灯

12 loud hailer (loudspeaker)
扩音器，扬声器

13 patrolman (police patrolman)
巡逻警察

14 police signalling (*Am.* signaling) **disc** (disk)
警察信号牌

15 riot duty
镇暴任务

16 special armoured (*Am.* armored) **car**
特别装甲车

17 barricade
路障

18 policeman (police officer) **in riot gear**
穿镇暴服的警察

19 truncheon (baton)
警棍（警棒）

20 riot shield
镇暴用盾牌

21 protective helmet (helmet)
护盔（头盔）

22 service pistol
警用手枪

23 pistol grip
手枪握把

24 quick-draw holster
快速拔枪枪套

25 magazine
弹匣

26 police identification disc (disk)
警察识别牌

27 police badge
警徽

28 fingerprint identification (dactyloscopy)
指纹证明（指纹）

29 fingerprint
指纹

30 illuminated screen
照明透视屏

31 search
搜查

32 suspect
嫌疑犯

33 detective (plainclothes policeman)
刑事，侦探（便衣警察）

34 English policeman
英国警察

35 helmet
头盔

36 pocket book
袖珍型记事簿

37 policewoman
女警

38 police van
警车

café, *sim.*: espresso bar,
room
店，类似：浓咖啡店，茶馆
nter (cake counter)
（西点柜台）
fee urn
壶
w for the money
eau
，蛋糕
ringue with whipped cream
油的糕饼（蛋白与砂糖制成的）
nee pastry cook
点心学徒
nter assistant
女店员
wspaper shelves (newspaper
k)
架
l lamp

ner seat, an upholstered seat
座位，铺布（皮）面的座位
é table
桌
rble top
里石桌面
tress
务生，女侍者
y
ttle of lemonade
柠檬水

16 lemonade glass
柠檬水玻璃杯
17 chess players playing a game of
chess
下棋者
18 coffee set
整套咖啡器具
19 cup of coffee
一杯咖啡
20 small sugar bowl
小糖罐
21 cream jug (*Am.* creamer)
奶油罐
22-24 café customers
咖啡店顾客
22 gentleman
男士
23 lady
女士
24 man reading a newspaper
看报的男人
25 newspaper
报纸
26 newspaper holder
报纸夹

1-29 restaurant
餐厅

1-11 bar (counter)
柜台

1 beer pump (beerpull)
啤酒泵（生啤酒出酒把手）

2 drip tray
滴盘

3 beer glass
啤酒杯

4 froth (head)
啤酒泡沫

5 spherical ashtray for cigarette and cigar ash
球形烟灰缸

6 beer glass (beer mug)
啤酒玻璃杯（啤酒杯）

7 beer warmer
啤酒加温器

8 bartender (barman, *Am.* barkeeper, barkeep)
酒保

9 shelf for glasses
玻璃杯搁架

10 shelf for bottles
瓶子搁架

11 stack of plates
一叠盘子

12 coat stand
挂衣架

13 hat peg
挂帽钉

14 coat hook
挂衣钩

15 wall ventilator
壁式通风机（换气装置）

16 bottle
瓶

17 complete meal
一盘料理

18 waitress
女侍者，女服务员

19 tray
托盘

20 lottery ticket seller
（奖券）彩票贩卖者

21 menu (menu card)
菜单（菜单卡）

22 cruet stand
调味瓶架

23 toothpick holder
牙签筒

24 matchbox holder
火柴盒立架

25 customer
顾客

26 beer mat
啤酒杯衬垫

27 meal of the day
当日餐点

28 flower seller (flower girl)
卖花人，卖花女

29 flower basket
花篮

30-44 wine restaurant (wine bar)
酒廊（酒吧）

30 wine waiter, a head waiter
酒廊服务员，领班

31 wine list
酒名单

32 wine carafe
玻璃酒瓶

33 wineglass
酒杯

34 tiled stove
瓷砖炉灶

35 stove tile
炉灶瓷砖

36 stove bench
炉灶台

37 wooden panelling (*Am.* paneling)
木制镶板

38 corner seat
角落位置

39 corner table
角落餐桌

40 regular customer
老顾客，常客

41 cutlery chest
刀叉餐具柜

42 wine cooler
酒冷却器

43 bottle of wine
酒瓶

44 ice cubes (ice, lumps of ice)
小冰块

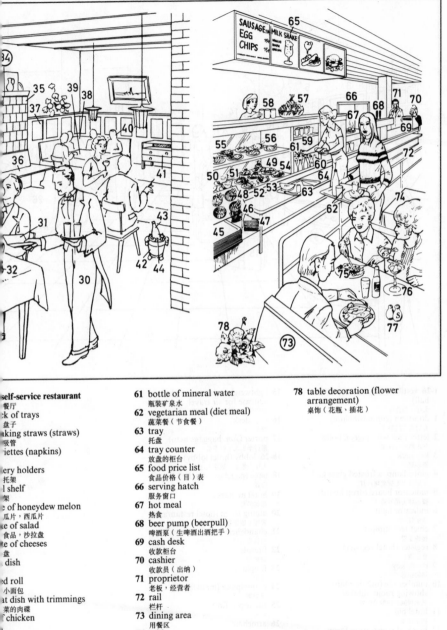

self-service restaurant
自助餐厅
k of trays
盘子
king straws (straws)
吸管
ettes (napkins)

lery holders
托架
l shelf
架
e of honeydew melon
瓜片，西瓜片
e of salad
食品，沙拉盘
te of cheeses
盘
dish

d roll
小面包
at dish with trimmings
菜的肉碟
chicken

ket of fruit
篮
t juice

nks shelf
架
tle of milk
牛奶

61 bottle of mineral water
瓶装矿泉水
62 vegetarian meal (diet meal)
蔬菜餐（节食餐）
63 tray
托盘
64 tray counter
放盘的柜台
65 food price list
食品价格（目）表
66 serving hatch
服务窗口
67 hot meal
热食
68 beer pump (beerpull)
啤酒泵（生啤酒出酒把手）
69 cash desk
收款柜台
70 cashier
收款员（出纳）
71 proprietor
老板，经营者
72 rail
栏杆
73 dining area
用餐区
74 table
餐桌
75 open sandwich
只有一片的三明治（馅等置於面包上）
76 ice-cream sundae
冰淇淋圣代
77 salt cellar and pepper pot
盐罐和胡椒瓶

78 table decoration (flower arrangement)
桌饰（花瓶、插花）

461

旅馆

1-26 **vestibule** (foyer, reception hall)
大厅，招待厅
1 **doorman** (commisionaire)
看门人（门警）
2 **letter rack with pigeon holes**
分小格的信件架
3 **key rack**
钥匙架
4 **globe lamp**, a frosted glass globe
球形灯，毛玻璃球形灯
5 **indicator board** (drop board)
指示牌（吊号牌）
6 **indicator light**
指示灯
7 **chief receptionist**
接待主管
8 **register** (hotel register)
登记簿
9 **room key**
房间钥匙
10 **number tag** (number tab) showing room number
显示房间号码的号码牌
11 **hotel bill**
旅馆账单
12 **block of registration forms**
登记表格本
13 **passport**
护照
14 **hotel guest**
旅客

15 **lightweight suitcase**, a light suitcase for air travel
航空旅行用的轻便手提箱
16 **wall desk**
壁台
17 **porter** (*Am.* baggage man)
搬行李工人，行李员
18-26 **lobby** (hotel lobby)
大厅（旅馆、饭店大厅）
18 **page** (pageboy, *Am.* bell boy)
侍者
19 **hotel manager**
旅馆经理
20 **dining room** (hotel restaurant)
餐厅（旅馆餐厅）
21 **chandelier**
树枝形吊灯
22 **fireside**
壁炉边
23 **fireplace**
壁炉
24 **mantelpiece** (mantelshelf)
壁炉架
25 **fire** (open fire)
炉火
26 **armchair**
扶手椅子

hotel room, a double room
th bath
宿房门，具浴室的双人房
uble door
重门
vice bell panel
务铃按钮板
rdrobe trunk
thes compartment
衣柜
en compartment
麻类衣柜
uble washbasin
洗脸盆
om waiter
司服务员
om telephone
司电话
lour (velours) carpet
绒地毯
wer stand
架
wer arrangement
花
uble bed
人床
nquet room
客室
private party
人宴会
eaker proposing a toast
酒的讲话人

41 **42's neighbour** (*Am.* neighbor)
42 的邻座

42 **43's partner**
43 的同伴

43 **42's partner**
42 的同伴

44–46 **thé dansant** (tea dance) in the foyer
在旅馆大厅的舞会（茶舞）

44 **bar trio**
酒吧三重奏

45 **violinist**
小提琴手

46 **couple dancing** (dancing couple)
双人舞（一对舞伴）

47 **waiter**
服务员，侍者

48 **napkin**
餐巾

49 **cigar and cigarette boy**
卖香烟和雪茄的小孩

50 **cigarette tray**
香烟托盘

51 **hotel bar**
旅馆酒吧

52 **foot rail**
脚踏栏杆

53 **bar stool**
吧台凳

54 **bar**
吧台

55 **bar customer**
酒吧顾客

56 **cocktail glass** (*Am.* highball glass)
鸡尾酒杯

57 **whisky** (whiskey) **glass**
威士忌酒杯

58 **champagne cork**
香槟酒的软木塞

59 **champagne bucket** (champagne cooler)
香槟酒水桶（香槟酒冷却器）

60 **measuring beaker** (measure)
量杯（量度器）

61 **cocktail shaker**
鸡尾酒摇动器

62 **bartender** (barman, *Am.* barkeeper, barkeep)
酒保

63 **barmaid**
酒吧女侍

64 **shelf for bottles**
酒瓶架

65 **shelf for glasses**
酒杯架

66 **mirrored panel**
有镜子的镶板

67 **ice bucket**
冰桶

1 parking meter
停车计时收费表

2 map of the town (street map)
市镇地图（街道图）

3 illuminated board
照明地图板

4 key
按键

5 litter bin (*Am.* litter basket)
垃圾箱

6 street lamp (street light)
路灯

7 street sign showing the name of
the street
街名标示牌

8 drain
排水沟

9 clothes shop (fashion house)
服装（时装）店

10 shop window
橱窗

11 window display (shop window
display)
橱窗陈列品

12 window decoration (shop
window decoration)
橱窗摆饰

13 entrance
入口

14 window
窗

15 window box
窗台

16 neon sign
霓虹灯广告牌

17 tailor's workroom
裁缝师工作室

18 pedestrian
行人

19 shopping bag
购物袋

20 road sweeper (*Am.* street
sweeper)
清道夫

21 broom
扫帚

22 rubbish (litter)
垃圾（废物）

23 tramlines (*Am.* streetcar tracks)
电车路（轨道）

24 pedestrian crossing (zebra
crossing, *Am.* crosswalk)
（斑马线）行人穿越道

25 tram stop (*Am.* streetcar stop,
trolley stop)
电车店

26 tram stop sign (*Am.* streetcar
stop sign, trolley stop sign)
电车站牌

27 tram timetable (*Am.* streetcar
schedule)
电车时刻表

28 ticket machine
售票机

29 [pedestrian crossing] sign
（行人穿越道）路牌

30 traffic policeman on traffic du
(point duty)
执行交通勤务的交通警察

31 traffic control cuff
交通指挥袖套

32 white cap
白色大盘帽

33 hand signal
手势

34 motorcyclist
摩托车骑士

35 motorcycle
摩托车

36 pillion passenger (pillion rider)
坐於摩托车后座者

37 bookshop
书店

38 hat shop (hatter's shop); *for
ladies' hats:* milliner's shop
帽店，女帽制造商

39 shop sign
商店招牌

40 insurance company office
保险公司办公室

artment store

公司

p front

前面

ertisement

s

minated letters

m (*Am.* streetcar, trolley)

niture lorry (*Am.* furniture
ck)

搬运车

ver

天桥

pended street lamp

路灯

p line

线

estrian crossing (*Am.*
sswalk)

穿越道

ffic lights

灯（交通信号灯）

ffic light post

灯柱（交通信号灯柱）

of lights

红绿灯

estrian lights

穿越灯

56 telephone box (telephone booth,
telephone kiosk, call box)
公用电话亭
57 cinema advertisement (film
poster)
电影广告（影片海报）
58 pedestrian precinct (paved zone)
徒步区
59 street café
（街旁）露天咖啡店
60 group seated (sitting) at a table
坐於桌边喝咖啡的人
61 sunshade
遮阳伞
62 steps to the public lavatories
(public conveniences)
通到公共厕所的阶梯
63 taxi rank (taxi stand)
计程车停车处
64 taxi (taxicab, cab)
计程车
65 taxi sign
计程车标帜
66 traffic sign showing [taxi rank]
([taxi stand])
显示计程车停放处的交通标帜
67 taxi telephone
计程车电话
68 post office
邮局
69 cigarette machine
香烟贩卖机
70 advertising pillar
广告柱子，广告张贴处

71 poster (advertisement)
海报（广告）
72 white line
白线
73 lane arrow for turning left
左转的行驶箭头
74 lane arrow for going straight
ahead
直行的行驶箭头
75 news vendor (*Am.* news dealer)
卖报人

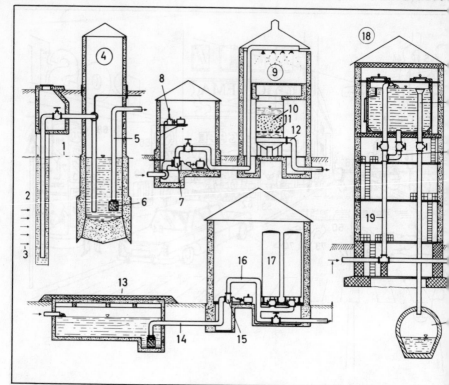

1-66 drinking water supply
饮水供应

1 **water table (groundwater level)**
地下水面（地下水位）

2 **water-bearing stratum (aquifer, aquafer)**
含水层

3 **groundwater stream (underground stream)**
地下水流

4 **collector well for raw water**
生水集水井

5 **suction pipe**
抽水管

6 **pump strainer (with foot valve)**
（装有底阀的）泵滤网

7 **bucket pump with motor**
带马达的斗式泵

8 **vacuum pump with motor**
带马达的真空泵

9 **rapid-filter plant**
快速过滤设备（滤池）

10 **filter gravel (filter bed)**
过滤砂砾

11 **filter bottom, a grid**
滤床，格栅的一种

12 **filtered water outlet**
过滤水出口

13 **purified water tank**
淨水槽

14 **suction pipe with pump strainer and foot valve**
具泵滤网和底阀的抽水管

15 **main pump with motor**
带马达的主泵

16 **delivery pipe**
输水管，供水管

17 **compressed-air vessel (air vessel, air receiver)**
压缩空气容器（贮气器，存气箱）

18 **water tower**
水塔

19 **riser pipe (riser)**
升管（升流管）

20 **overflow pipe**
溢水管

21 **outlet**
出水口

22 **distribution main**
主配水管

23 **excess water conduit**
废水渠

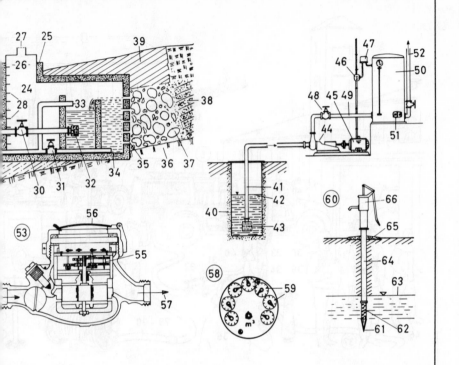

apping a spring
泉水
mber

mber wall
墙壁
hole
孔，检修孔
ilator

irons

g (backing)
物

t control valve
控制阀

t valve
阀

ner

flow pipe (overflow)
管

om outlet
出水口

henware pipes
器）管

ervious stratum
ermeable stratum)
水层

h rubble
石

r-bearing statum (aquifer,
afer)
层

39 loam seal (clay seal)
壌土封层（粘土封层）

40-52 individual water supply
单独供水

40 well
水井

41 suction pipe
抽水管

42 water table (groundwater level)
地下水面（水位）

43 pump strainer with foot valve
具底阀的泵滤网

44 centrifugal pump
离心泵

45 motor
马达

46 motor safety switch
马达安全开关

47 manostat, a switching device
恒定流量装置，一种开关装置

48 stop valve
停止阀

49 delivery pipe
输水管，供水管

50 compressed-air vessel (air vessel, air receiver)
压缩空气容器（贮气器，存气箱）

51 manhole
人孔

52 delivery pipe
输水管，供水管

53 water meter, a rotary meter
水表，旋转式水表

54 water inlet
入水口

55 counter gear assembly
计数装置

56 cover with glass lid
玻璃罩盖

57 water outlet
出水口

58 water-meter dial
水表数字盘

59 counters
计数器

60 driven well (tube well, drive well)
辘轳井（管井，打桩井）

61 pile shoe
桩头

62 filter
过滤器

63 water table (groundwater level)
地下水面（位）

64 well casing
井筒

65 well head
井口

66 hand pump
手摇泵

1-46 fire service drill
(extinguishing, climbing, ladder,
and rescue work)
消防演习（灭火，攀登，爬梯和救护
工作）

1-3 fire station
消防站

1 engine and appliance room
（救火车）消防车和消防装备（器具）
置放室

2 firemen's quarters
消防人员住处（宿舍）

3 drill tower
演习塔

4 fire alarm (fire alarm siren, fire
siren)
火灾警报器

5 fire engine
消防车

6 blue light (warning light), a
flashing light (*Am.* flashlight)
蓝灯（警报灯），闪光信号灯

7 horn (hooter)
警报器，警笛

8 motor pump, a centrifugal pump
马达泵，一种离心泵

9 motor turntable ladder (*Am.*
aerial ladder)
马达旋转云梯

10 ladder, a steel ladder (automatic
extending ladder)
钢梯（自动伸展梯）

11 ladder mechanism
云梯机械装置

12 jack
起重装置

13 ladder operator
云梯操作人员

14 extension ladder
伸展梯

15 ceiling hook (*Am.* preventer)
吊钩（防护钩）

16 hook ladder (*Am.* pompier
ladder)
钩梯

17 holding squad
营救班（拉开救助布的救火人员）

18 jumping sheet (sheet)
救助布（失火时用以接住跳楼者所用的
布）

19 ambulance car (ambulance)
救护车

20 resuscitator (resuscitation
equipment), oxygen apparatus
人工呼吸器，输氧装置

21 ambulance attendant
(ambulance man)
救护人员

22 armband (armlet, brassard)
臂章（臂饰，臂章）

23 stretcher
担架

24 unconscious man
失去知觉者

25 pit hydrant
地下消防栓

26 standpipe (riser, vertical pipe
立管（升管，垂直管）

27 hydrant key
消防栓龙头（开关）

28 hose reel (*Am.* hose cart, hos
wagon, hose truck, hose
carriage)
软管卷轴（软管手推车，软管拖车，软
管手推车，软管托架）

29 hose coupling
软管连接头

30 soft suction hose
吸水软管

31 delivery hose
输水软管

32 dividing breeching
软管分接头

33 branch
水管管口

34 branchmen
水管操作人

35 surface hydrant (fire plug)
地面消防栓

36 officer in charge
消防队长

37 fireman (*Am.* firefighter)
消防队员

38 helmet (fireman's helmet, *A*
fire hat) with neck guard (ne
flap)
具护颈的护盔

39 breathing apparatus
呼吸保护器（装置）

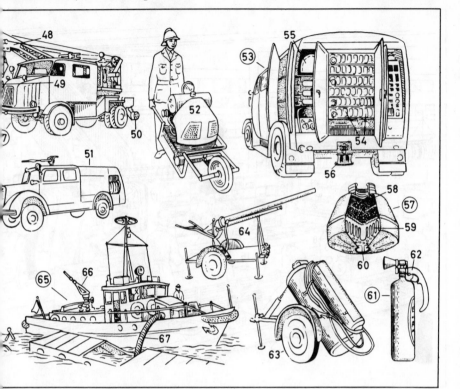

e mask

kie-talkie set
电（通）话机

d lamp
灯

ll axe (*Am.* ax, pompier
chet)
斧

k belt

tline
救生腰带

tective clothing of asbestos
bestos suit) or of metallic
ric
防火衣或金属纤维防火衣

akdown lorry (*Am.* crane
ck, wrecking crane)
车（起重车）

ng crane
机

d hook (draw hook, *Am.* drag
ok)

port roll
卷轴

ter tender
车

table pump
泵

e layer
器具搬运车

54 flaked lengths of hose
   软管卷
55 cable drum
   绳索卷筒
56 winch
   绞车（盘）
57 face mask filter
   防毒面具过滤器
58 active carbon (activated carbon,
   activated charcoal)
   活性碳（活性炭）
59 dust filter
   滤尘器
60 air inlet
   进气口
61 portable fire extinguisher
   轻便灭火器
62 trigger valve
   触发阀
63 large mobile extinguisher
   (wheeled fire extinguisher)
   大型移动式灭火器
64 foam-making branch (*Am.* foam
   gun)
   泡沫喷射器
65 fireboat
   消防艇
66 monitor (water cannon)
   回转喷水管（水炮）
67 suction hose
   吸水软管

1 cashier
收款员，出纳员
2 electric cash register (till)
电动收银机
3 number keys
数目键
4 cancellation button
消除按钮
5 cash drawer (till)
现金抽屉
6 compartments (money compartments) for coins and notes (*Am.* bills)
放纸币和硬币的分格抽屉
7 receipt (sales check)
收据
8 cash total
应付金额
9 adding mechanism
加算器
10 goods
商品货物
11 glass-roofed well
玻璃屋顶天井
12 men's wear department
男装部
13 showcase (display case, indoor display window)
阵列柜
14 wrapping counter
包装柜台
15 tray for purchases
售出物品放置盘

16 customer
顾客
17 hosiery department
袜类部
18 shop assistant (*Am.* salesgirl, saleslady)
店员，女店员
19 price card
价目表
20 glove stand
手套架
21 duffle coat, a three-quarter length coat
连风帽的粗呢大衣，中长(¾)大衣
22 escalator
扶手梯(电梯)
23 fluorescent light (fluorescent lamp)
日光灯
24 office (e.g. customer accounts office, travel agency, manager's office)
办公室(例如：顾客事务室，旅行社，经理办公室)
25 poster (advertisement)
海报(广告)
26 theatre (*Am.* theater) and concert booking office (advance booking office)
剧院和音乐会订位(售票)处(预先售票处)
27 shelves
商品架

28 ladies' wear department
女装部
29 ready-made dress (ready-to-dress, *coll.* off-the-peg dress)
女装成衣
30 dust cover
防尘套
31 clothes rack
衣架
32 changing booth (fitting boo
试衣室
33 shop walker (*Am.* floorwalk floor manager)
商场巡视员(楼层巡视员，楼层经
34 dummy
人像模型
35 seat (chair)
座椅(靠椅)
36 fashion journal (fashion magazine)
时装杂志
37 tailor marking a hemline
正在量裙下摆(底缘)的裁缝(师
38 measuring tape (tape measu
皮尺，量尺
39 tailor's chalk (French chalk
裁缝用粉笔(滑石)
40 hemline marker
下摆(底缘)划线器
41 loose-fitting coat
宽松的外套
42 sales counter
售货(柜)台

m-air curtain
帘

rman (commissionaire)
人

Am. elevator)
（升降电梯）

age (lift car, *Am.* elevator

室（升降室）
perator (*Am.* elevator
rator)
操作人
trols (lift controls, *Am.*
ator controls)
（电梯按钮）
r indicator
指示器
ng door
门，拉门
haft (*Am.* elevator shaft)
升降井
er cable

rol cable
缆
e rail

omer

ery

n goods (table linen and bed

制品（桌布，床单）

58 fabric department
纺织品部
59 roll of fabric (roll of material,
roll of cloth)
布匹
60 head of department (department
manager)
部门经理
61 sales counter
售货（柜）台
62 jewellery (*Am.* jewelry)
department
珠宝部
63 assistant (*Am.* salesgirl,
saleslady), selling new lines (new
products)
卖新产品的（女）店员
64 special counter (extra counter)
特价品柜台
65 placard advertising special offers
特价品广告标语
66 curtain department
窗帘部
67 display on top of the shelves
商品架上的商品陈列

1-40 formal garden (French Baroque garden), palace gardens
正规式公园（法国巴洛克式公园），宫殿式公园

1 grotto (cavern)
洞室（洞窟）

2 stone statue, a river nymph
石像（河中仙女）

3 orangery (orangerie)
栽培橘树的温室

4 boscage (boskage)
密集的灌木

5 maze (labyrinth of paths and hedges)
迷宫〔以小径和（树篱）障碍物所构成的迷宫〕

6 open-air theatre (*Am.* theater)
露天剧场

7 Baroque palace
巴洛克式宫殿

8 fountains
喷泉

9 cascade (broken artificial waterfall, artificial falls)
人造小瀑布

10 statue, a monument
雕像，纪念碑的一种

11 pedestal (base of statue)
雕像底座

12 globe-shaped tree
球形树

13 conical tree
锥形树

14 ornamental shrub
装饰用灌木

15 wall fountain
壁泉

16 park bench
公园长椅

17 pergola (bower, arbour, *Am.* arbor)
藤架（树荫，凉亭）

18 gravel path (gravel walk)
碎石路

19 pyramid tree (pyramidal tree)
尖型树

20 cupid (cherub, amoretto, amorino)
爱神丘彼特

21 fountain
喷水池

22 fountain
喷泉

23 overflow basin
溢流池

24 basin
水池

25 kerb (curb)
镶边石

26 man out for a walk
散步者

27 tourist guide
导游

28 group of tourists
游客群

29 park by-laws (bye-laws)
游园须知

30 park keeper
公园管理人

31 garden gates, wrought iron
公园大门，锻铁门

32 park entrance
公园入口

33 park railings
公园栏杆

34 railing (bar)
栏杆

35 stone vase
石瓶

36 lawn
草坪

37 border, a trimmed (clipped) hedge
道路两旁修整的树篱

38 park path
公园小道

39 parterre
花坛（草坪）

40 birch (birch tree)
白桦（树）

landscaped park (jardin
~~~lais)
式公园（英国式公园）
~~~er bed
~~~ k bench (garden seat)
~~~长椅
~~~er bin (*Am.* litter basket)
~~~箱
~~~y area
~~~区
~~~am
~~~y
~~~dge
~~~k chair
~~~靠背
~~~mal enclosure
~~~围栏
~~~nd
~~~g
~~~waterfowl
~~~，水鸟
~~~d duck with young
~~~鸭的野鸭
~~~ose
~~~mingo
~~~鸟
~~~an
~~~鸟

55 island
　小岛
56 water lily
　睡莲
57 open-air café
　露天咖啡座
58 sunshade
　遮阳伞
59 tree
　树
60 treetop (crown)
　树梢
61 group of trees
　树林
62 fountain
　喷泉
63 weeping willow
　垂柳
64 modern sculpture
　现代雕刻
65 hothouse
　温室，暖房
66 park gardener
　园丁
67 broom
　扫帚
68 minigolf course
　迷你高尔夫球场
69 minigolf player
　打迷你高尔夫球的人
70 minigolf hole
　迷你高尔夫球洞

71 mother with pram (baby
　carriage)
　推婴儿车的母亲
72 courting couple (young couple)
　情侣

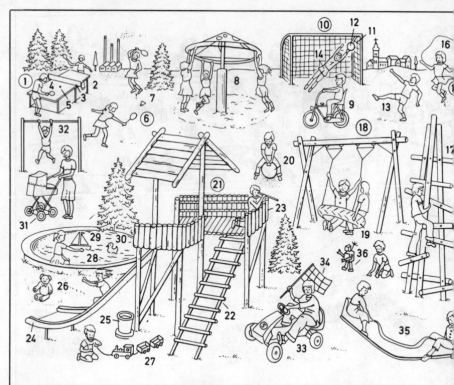

1 table tennis
桌球
2 table
球桌
3 table tennis net
桌球网
4 table tennis racket (raquet)
(table tennis bat)
桌球球拍
5 table tennis ball
桌球（乒乓球）
6 badminton game (shuttlecock
game)
羽毛球
7 shuttlecock
羽毛球
8 maypole swing
五月柱秋千，伞式秋千
9 child's bicycle
儿童自行车
10 football (soccer)
足球
11 goal (goalposts)
球门
12 football
足球
13 goal scorer
射门得分人员
14 goalkeeper
守门员
15 skipping (*Am.* jumping rope)
跳绳

16 skipping rope (*Am.* skip rope,
jump rope, jumping rope)
跳绳用绳
17 climbing tower
攀登塔
18 rubber tyre (*Am.* tire) swing
橡胶轮胎秋千
19 lorry tyre (*Am.* truck tire)
卡车轮胎
20 bouncing ball
大皮球
21 adventure playground
探险游戏场
22 log ladder
木梯
23 lookout platform
了望台
24 slide
滑滑梯
25 litter bin (*Am.* litter basket)
垃圾桶（箱）
26 teddy bear
玩具熊
27 wooden train set
木制火车列车
28 paddling pool
浅戏水池
29 sailing boat (yacht, *Am.*
sailboat)
帆船
30 toy duck
玩具鸭
31 pram (baby carriage)
婴儿车

32 high bar (bar)
单杠
33 go-cart (soap box)
儿童玩具车
34 starter's flag
发号者旗
35 seesaw
跷跷板
36 robot
机器人

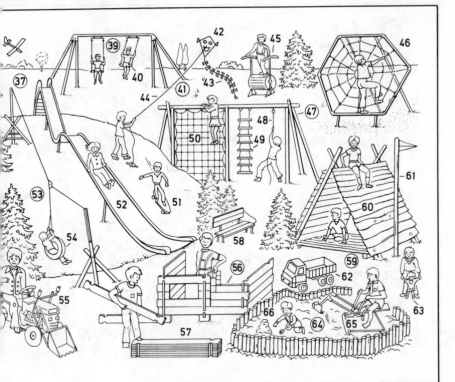

ng model aeroplanes (*Am.*
lanes)
中的模型飞机
del aeroplane (*Am.* airplane)
飞机
ble swing
秋千
ng seat
座位
ng kites
筝

of the kite
尾巴
string
线
olving drum
鼓轮
er's web
网架
nbing frame
架
nbing rope
用绳
ladder
e
nbing net
网
teboard

and-down slide
滑梯

53 rubber tyre (*Am.* tire) cable car
橡胶轮胎缆索车
54 rubber tyre (*Am.* tire)
橡胶轮胎
55 tractor, a pedal car
牵引机，跳板车的一种
56 den
搭栏橱
57 presawn boards
预锯木板
58 seat (bench)
座位（长椅）
59 Indian hut
印第安小屋
60 climbing roof
供攀登的屋顶
61 flagpole (flagstaff)
旗杆
62 toy lorry (*Am.* toy truck)
玩具卡车
63 walking doll
能行走的玩具娃娃
64 sandpit (*Am.* sandbox)
沙坑
65 toy excavator (toy digger)
玩具挖土机
66 sandhill
沙丘

1–21 spa gardens
温泉公园
1–7 salina (salt works)
制盐场
1 thorn house (graduation house)
枝条架（架条制盐装置）
2 thorns (brushwood)
枝条（柴枝）
3 brine channels
盐水槽
4 brine pipe from the pumping station
通泵站的盐水管
5 salt works attendant
制盐场管理人
6–7 inhalational therapy
吸入治疗（疗法）
6 open-air inhalatorium (outdoor inhalatorium)
露天（户外）吸入治疗处
7 patient inhaling (taking an inhalation)
接受吸入疗法的病人
8 hydropathic (pump room) with kursaal (casino)
具娱乐场的水疗院（饮矿泉处）
9 colonnade
柱廊
10 spa promenade
温泉散步场
11 avenue leading to the mineral spring
通往矿泉的道路

12–14 rest cure
休息疗法
12 sunbathing area (lawn)
日光浴区（草坪）
13 deck-chair
躺椅
14 sun canopy
遮阳篷
15 pump room
饮矿泉处
16 rack for glasses
玻璃杯架
17 tap
龙头，栓
18 patient taking the waters
饮矿泉的病人
19 bandstand
音乐台
20 spa orchestra giving a concert
温泉管弦乐队演奏
21 conductor
乐队指挥

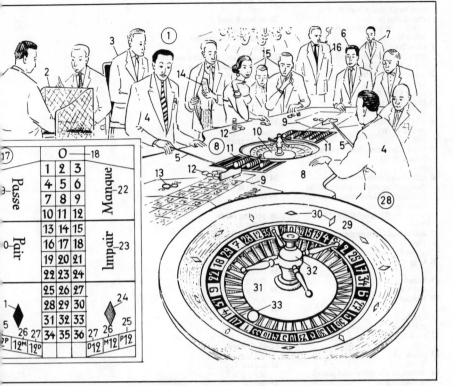

oulette, a game of
nce (gambling game)
赌，一种靠运气的赌博
ing room in a casino
bling casino)
场（赌场）中的赌室
desk
怕，售筹码处
neur (dealer)

pier
收付赌注者
赌金（注）的耙子
d croupier
收付赌注领班
manager
经理
lette table (gaming table,
bling table)
赌桌
lette layout
赌表
lette wheel
赌转轮
k
的赌本
p (check, plaque)

ke
mbership card
员卡

15 roulette player
轮盘赌客
16 private detective (house
detective)
私人保镖
17 roulette layout
轮盘赌表
18 zero (nought, O)
零
19 passe (high) [numbers 19 to
36]
高〔19 至 36 各数〕
20 pair (even numbers)
双（偶数）
21 noir (black)
黑
22 manque (low) [numbers 1 to
18]
低〔1 至 18 各数〕
23 impair [odd numbers]
单〔奇数〕
24 rouge (red)
红
25 douze premier (first dozen)
[numbers 1 to 12]
第一打〔1 至 12 各数〕
26 douze milieu (second dozen)
[numbers 13 to 24]
第二打〔13 至 24 各数〕
27 douze dernier (third dozen)
[numbers 25 to 36]
第三打〔25 至 36 各数〕
28 roulette wheel (roulette)
轮盘赌转轮

29 roulette bowl
轮盘赌托盘
30 fret (separator)
格子
31 revolving disc (disk) showing
numbers 0 to 36
显示 0 至 36 各数的转盘
32 spin
转子
33 roulette ball
轮盘赌球

1-16 chess, a game involving combinations of moves, a positional game
西洋棋，一种靠移动棋子的游戏，一种对阵游戏

1 chessboard (board) with the men (chessmen) in position
棋盘和置於原位的棋子

2 white square (chessboard square)
白方格（白色棋盘方格）

3 black square
黑方格

4 white chessmen (white pieces) [white = W]
白棋（子）

5 black chessmen (black pieces) [black = B]
黑棋（子）

6 letters and numbers for designating chess squares in the notation of chess moves and chess problems
标示记录走棋位置的棋盘格字母和数字

7 individual chessmen (individual pieces)
单一棋子

8 king
王

9 queen
皇后，女王

10 bishop
主教

11 knight
武士，骑士

12 rook (castle)
城堡

13 pawn
卒，兵

14 moves of the individual pieces
单一棋子的移动

15 mate (checkmate), a mate by knight
将军，被骑士将军

16 chess clock, a double clock for chess matches (chess championships)
棋钟，棋赛用的双钟

17-19 draughts (*Am.* checkers)
西洋跳棋

17 draughtboard (*Am.* checkerboard)
西洋跳棋盘

18 white draughtsman (*Am.* checker, checkerman); *also:* piece for backgammon and nine men's morris
白色跳棋子；西洋双六棋和九子棋

19 black draughtsman (*Am.* checker, checkerman)
黑色跳棋子

20 salta
索尔特棋

21 salta piece
索尔特棋棋子

22 backgammon board
西洋双六棋盘

23-25 nine men's morris
九子棋

23 nine men's morris board
九子棋盘

24 mill
连珠

25 double mill
双连珠

26-28 halma
跳棋

26 halma board
跳棋板（盘）

27 yard (camp, corner)
阵地（棋盘四角）

28 halma pieces (halma men) of various colours (*Am.* colors)
不同颜色的棋子

29 dice (dicing)
骰子游戏

30 dice cup
骰子筒

31 dice
骰子

32 spots (pips)
骰子上的点

33 dominoes
骨牌游戏

34 domino (tile)
西洋骨牌

35 double
对子

36 playing cards
纸牌游戏

37 playing card (card)
纸牌、扑克牌

38-45 suits
一组牌

38 clubs
黑梅花

39 spades
黑桃

40 hearts
红心

41 diamonds
红方块

42-45 German suits
德式纸牌

42 acorns
栎子（黑梅花）

43 leaves
叶子（黑桃）

44 hearts
红心

45 bells (hawkbells)
铃（红方块）

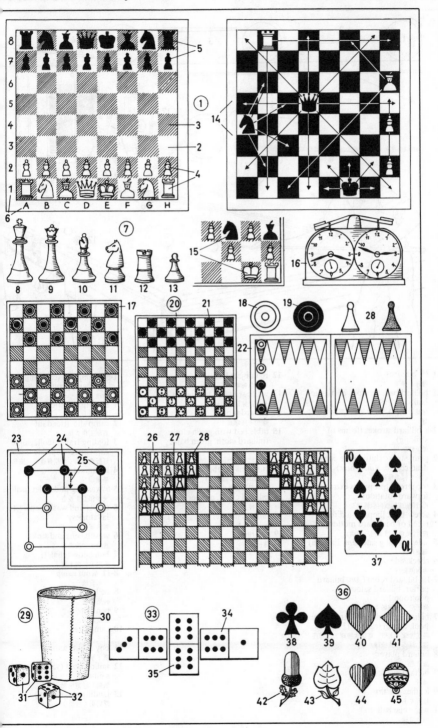

1-19 billiards
撞球，弹子
1 billiard ball, an ivory or plastic ball
撞球（弹子），一种象牙或塑胶制的球
2-6 billiard strokes (forms of striking)
弹子打法
2 plain stroke (hitting the cue ball dead centre, *Am.* center)
定杆（打击母球中心）
3 top stroke [promotes extra forward rotation]
推杆（使球猛烈向前转动）
4 screw-back [imparts a direct recoil or backward motion]
拉杆（使球卷回或向后转动）
5 side (running side, *Am.* English)
侧旋打法
6 check side
返向侧旋打法
7-19 billiard room (*Am.* billiard parlor, billiard saloon, poolroom)
弹子房（撞球场）
7 billiards (English billiards); *sim.:* pool, carom (carrom) billiards
英式撞球；类似：落袋式撞球，母球连撞二球得分式撞球
8 billiard player
撞球者
9 billiard cue (cue)
球杆
10 leather cue tip
球杆皮头
11 white cue ball
白色母球

12 red object ball
红色目标球
13 white spot ball (white dot ball)
有黑点标记的白球
14 billiard table
球枱，撞球桌
15 table bed with green cloth (billiard cloth, green baize covering)
铺绿枱布的枱面
16 cushions (rubber cushions, cushioned ledge)
球桌四边的橡皮衬垫
17 billiard clock, a timer
记时钟
18 billiard marker
记分牌（板）
19 cue rack
球杆架

1-59 camp site (camping site, *Am.* campground)
营地
1 reception (office)
接待处（办公室）
2 camp site attendant
营地工作人员
3 folding trailer (collapsible caravan, collapsible trailer)
可折叠拖车（可摺叠篷车、拖车）
4 hammock
吊床
5-6 washing and toilet facilitie
洗涤和卫生设备
5 toilets and washrooms (*Am.* lavatories)
盥洗室
6 washbasins and sinks
洗脸盆和洗涤槽
7 bungalow (chalet)
平房（斜顶木屋）
8-11 scout camp
童军营地
8 bell tent
钟形帐篷
9 pennon
三角旗
10 camp fire
营火
11 boy scout (scout)
童子军
12 sailing boat (yacht, *Am.* sailboat)
帆船（轻型快艇）
13 landing stage (jetty)
浮码头（栈桥）

atable boat (inflatable ghy)	**32** water carrier (drinking water carrier) 饮用水容器
船（充气橡皮艇）	**33** double-burner gas cooker for propane gas or butane gas 双炉头（丙烷或丁烷）瓦斯炉
broad motor (outboard) 马达	**34** propane or butane gas bottle 丙烷或丁烷瓦斯罐
maran 船体并列的船	**35** pressure cooker 压力锅，快锅
wart (oarsman's bench) 艇座板（划手座板）	**36 frame tent** 框架帐篷
wlock (oarlock) 架	**37** awning 遮篷
r	**38** tent pole 帐篷杆（支柱）
at trailer (boat carriage) 船拖车	**39** wheelarch doorway 圆拱出入口
ge tent 锥形帐篷	**40** mesh ventilator 网状通风口
sheet 篷顶	**41** transparent window 透明玻璃
y line (guy) 素，牵索	**42** pitch number 帐篷号码
t peg (peg) 帐篷桩（钉）	**43** folding camp chair 折叠椅
allet 组	**44** folding camp table 折叠桌
oundsheet ring 面防潮布扣环	**45** camping tableware 露营用桌上餐具
ll end 篷一边的钟状部分（堆放行李）	**46** camper 露营者
ected awning 立遮篷	**47** charcoal grill (barbecue) 炭火烤架
rm lantern, a paraffin lamp 灯，一种蜡（煤）油灯	**48** charcoal 炭，木炭
eping bag 袋	
mattress (inflatable air-bed) 气垫（床）	

49 bellows 送风器
50 roof rack 车顶行李架
51 roof lashing 车顶捆绳
52 caravan (*Am.* trailer) 拖车
53 box for gas bottle 装瓦斯罐的箱子
54 jockey wheel 导轮
55 drawbar coupling 拉杆连结器
56 roof ventilator 车顶通风口
57 caravan awning 拖车遮篷
58 inflatable igloo tent 充气圆顶帐篷
59 camp bed (*Am.* camp cot) 行军床

1-6 surf riding (surfing)
冲浪运动
1 plan view of surfboard
冲浪板平面图
2 section of surfboard
冲浪板剖面图
3 skeg (stabilizing fin)
龙骨之后部（稳定鳍）
4 big wave riding
大浪冲浪运动
5 surfboarder (surfer)
冲浪者
6 breaker
碎浪
7-27 skin diving (underwater swimming)
潜水（水下游泳）
7 skin diver (underwater swimmer)
潜水人
8-22 underwater swimming set
潜水游泳器具
8 knife
小刀
9 neoprene wetsuit
合成橡胶制潜水衣
10 diving mask (face mask, mask), a pressure-equalizing mask
潜水面具（罩），一种均压面罩
11 snorkel (schnorkel)
（换气用）通气管
12 harness of diving apparatus
潜水器具背带
13 compressed-air pressure gauge (*Am.* gage)
压缩空气压力计

14 weight belt
负重腰带
15 depth gauge (*Am.* gage)
深度计
16 waterproof watch for checking duration of dive
潜水计时防水表
17 decometer for measuring stages of ascent
上升时测定用卡计
18 fin (flipper)
蛙鞋
19 diving apparatus (*also*: aqualung, scuba), with two cylinders (bottles)
具两个氧气筒的潜水器具（亦称：水肺）
20 two-tube demand regulator
双筒定（需用）量调节器
21 compressed-air cylinder (compressed-air bottle)
压缩空气筒（压缩空气瓶）
22 on/off valve
开关阀
23 underwater photography
水下摄影
24 underwater camera
水下相机
25 underwater flashlight
水下闪光灯
26 exhaust bubbles
呼出的气泡
27 inflatable boat (inflatable dinghy)
充气船（橡皮艇）

saver (lifeguard)
员
ine
绳
belt (lifebuoy)
圈
m signal
信号
e ball
球
rning sign
告牌
e table, a notice board
owing times of low tide and
h tide
水表，公布高低潮时间的布告板
rd showing water and air
mperature
温和水温布告板
thing platform
浴场跳板
nnon staff
角旗杆
nnon
角旗
ddle boat (peddle boat)
轮船（水上自行车）
rf riding (surfing) behind
otorboat
艇拖拉的冲浪运动
rfboarder (surfer)
浪者
rfboard
浪板
ater ski
水

17 inflatable beach mattress
海滩充气垫
18 beach ball
海滩游戏用皮球
19-23 beachwear
海滩装
19 beach suit
海滩套装
20 beach hat
海滩帽
21 beach jacket
海滩夹克
22 beach trousers
海滩裤
23 beach shoe (bathing shoe)
海滩鞋
24 beach bag
海滩袋
25 bathing gown (bathing wrap)
海滩袍
26 bikini (ladies' two-piece bathing
suit)
比基尼泳装（女士二件式泳装）
27 bikini bottom
比基尼装下部
28 bikini top
比基尼装上部
29 bathing cap (swimming cap)
泳帽
30 bather
游泳者
31 deck tennis (quoits)
掷套环游戏
32 rubber ring (quoit)
套环
33 inflatable rubber animal
充气的浮水（橡皮）动物

34 beach attendant
浴场服务人员
35 sandcastle
沙堡
36 roofed wicker beach chair
有顶篷的沙滩椅
37 underwater swimmmer
潜水泳者
38 diving goggles
潜水镜
39 snorkel (schnorkel)
通气管
40 hand harpoon (fish spear, fish
lance)
鱼叉（鱼矛）
41 fin (flipper) for diving (for
underwater swimming)
潜泳者用的蛙鞋
42 bathing suit (swimsuit)
泳装（泳衣）
43 bathing trunks (swimming
trunks)
泳裤
44 bathing cap (swimming cap)
泳帽
45 beach tent, a ridge tent
沙滩帐篷，脊形帐篷
46 lifeguard station
救生站

1-9 swimming pool with
artificial waves, an indoor pool
人工波浪游泳池，室内游泳池的一种

1 artificial waves
人工波浪

2 beach area
岸区

3 edge of the pool
泳池边

4 swimming pool attendant (pool
attendant, swimming bath
attendant)
泳池服务人员

5 sun bed
日光浴床位

6 lifebelt
救生圈

7 water wings
翼形浮袋

8 bathing cap
泳帽

9 channel to outdoor mineral bath
通向户外矿泉浴池的水道

10 solarium
日光浴室

11 sunbathing area
日光浴场

12 sun bather
日光浴者

13 sun ray lamp
太阳光线灯

14 bathing towel
浴巾

15 nudist sunbathing area
天体日光浴区

16 nudist (naturist)
天体浴者

17 screen (fence)
围墙

18 sauna (mixed sauna)
蒸汽浴（混浴蒸汽浴室）〔三温暖
浴室〕

19 wood panelling (*Am.* paneling)
木嵌板

20 tiered benches
台阶式长凳

21 sauna stove
蒸汽浴炉

22 stones
石块

23 hygrometer
湿度计

24 thermometer
温度计

25 towel
毛巾

26 water tub for moistening the
stone in the stove
沾湿炉中石块用的水桶

27 birch rods (birches) for beating
the skin
拍打皮肤用的桦枝条

28 cooling room for cooling off
(cooling down) after the sauna
蒸汽浴后降温用的降温浴室

29 lukewarm shower
微温淋浴设备

30 cold bath
冷水浴池

31 hot whirlpool (underwater
massage bath)
热水涡流浴室（水中按摩浴室）

32 step into the bath
入浴池的台阶

33 massage bath
按摩浴池

34 jet blower
喷射鼓风机

35 hot whirlpool [diagram]
热水涡流浴池〔简图〕

36 section of the bath
浴池剖面图

37 step
台阶

38 circular seat
环形座位

39 water extractor
抽水机（装置）

40 water jet pipe
喷水管

41 air jet pipe
喷气管

1-32 swimming pool, an
open-air swimming pool
游泳池，露天游泳池
1 changing cubicle
小更衣室
2 shower (shower bath)
淋浴
3 changing room
更衣室
4 sunbathing area
日光浴场
5-10 diving boards (diving
apparatus)
跳板（跳水设备）
5 diver (highboard diver)
跳水者
6 diving platform
跳台
7 ten-metre (*Am.* ten-meter)
platform
十尺高跳台
8 five-metre (*Am.* five-meter)
platform
五公尺高跳台
9 three-metre (*Am.* three-meter)
springboard (diving board)
三公尺高跳台，弹性跳板
10 one-metre (*Am.* one-meter)
springboard
一公尺高跳台，弹性跳板
11 diving pool
跳水池
12 straight header
（直体）头先入水的跳水动作
13 feet-first jump
脚先入水的跳水动作
14 tuck jump (haunch jump)
抱膝跳水
15 swimming pool attendant (pool
attendant, swimming bath
attendant)
游泳池服务人员
16-20 swimming instruction
游泳指导
16 swimming instructor (swimming
teacher)
游泳教练
17 learner-swimmer
学习游泳者
18 float; *sim.:* water wings
浮袋；类似翼形浮袋
19 swimming belt (cork jacket)
救生带（软木救生衣）
20 land drill
陆上游泳练习
21 non-swimmers' pool
浅水池
22 footbath
洗脚池
23 swimmers' pool
深水泳池
24-32 freestyle relay race
自由式接力赛
24 timekeeper (lane timekeeper)
计时员
25 placing judge
终点裁判员
26 turning judge
转身裁判员
27 starting block (starting place)
出发台（点）
28 competitor touching the
finishing line
比赛人员触池壁
29 starting dive (racing dive)
出发跳水

30 starter
发令员
31 swimming lane
泳道
32 rope with cork floats
有软木浮栓的绳索
33-39 swimming strokes
游泳姿式
33 breaststroke
蛙式
34 butterfly stroke
蝶式
35 dolphin butterfly stroke
海豚泳
36 side stroke
侧泳
37 crawl stroke (crawl); *sim.:*
trudgen stroke (trudgen, double
overarm stroke)
自由式；类似：爬泳
38 underwater swimming
潜泳
39 treading water
踩水
40-45 diving (acrobatic diving,
fancy diving, competitive diving,
highboard diving)
跳水（特技跳水，花式跳水，竞技跳
水，高台跳水）
40 standing take-off pike dive
立定起跳梭式跳水
41 one-half twist isander (reverse
dive)
半转体旋式跳水
42 backward somersault (double
backward somersault)
（两次）后空翻跳水
43 running take-off twist dive
跑步起跳转体跳水
44 screw dive
螺旋式跳水
45 armstand dive (handstand dive)
倒立跳水
46-50 water polo
水球
46 goal
球门
47 goalkeeper
守门员
48 water polo ball
水球
49 back
后卫
50 forward
前锋

1-18 taking up positions for
the regatta
就赛舟位置

1 punt, a pleasure boat
平底船，一种游船

2 motorboat
汽艇（快艇）

3 Canadian canoe
加拿大式独木舟

4 kayak (Alaskan canoe, slalom
canoe), a canoe
皮船（阿拉斯加式皮船，回旋划艇），
一种独木舟

5 tandem kayak
双座（前后座）皮船

6 outboard motorboat (outboard
speedboat, outboard)
汽艇（快速汽艇）

7 outboard motor (outboard)
船外（尾）马达

8 cockpit
座舱

9-16 racing boats (sportsboats)
赛船

9-15 shells (rowing boats, *Am.*
rowboats)
轻型划（赛）船（划艇）

9 coxless four, a carvel-built boat
无舵手四人划艇，一种平贴船板的船

10 eight (eight-oared racing shell)
八人赛船

11 cox
舵手

12 stroke, an oarsman
桨手

13 bow ([number one])
船首桨手

14 oar
桨

15 coxless pair
无舵手双人赛船

16 single sculler (single skuller,
racing sculler, racing skuller,
skiff)
单人赛船

17 scull (skull)
桨

18 coxed single, a clinker-built
single
有舵手的小船，船壳板重叠的小船

19 jetty (landing stage, mooring)
码头（浮架码头，停泊处）

20 rowing coach
划船教练

21 megaphone
扩音器

22 quayside steps
码头边台阶

23 clubhouse (club)
会员俱乐部

24 boathouse
船库

25 club's flag
俱乐部旗

26-33 four-oared gig, a touring
boat
四桨小船，一种游艇

26 oar
桨

27 cox's seat
舵手位置

28 thwart (seat)
座板

29 rowlock (oarlock)
桨架

30 gunwale (gunnel)
舷的上缘

31 rising
船侧纵板

32 keel
龙骨

33 skin (shell, outer skin)
[clinker-built]
船的外壳〔重叠搭造的〕

34 single-bladed paddle
(paddle)
单叶桨

35-38 oar (scull, skull)
桨

35 grip
桨柄

36 leather sheath
皮护套

37 shaft (neck)
桨颈

38 blade
桨叶

39 double-bladed paddle (double-
ended paddle)
双叶桨

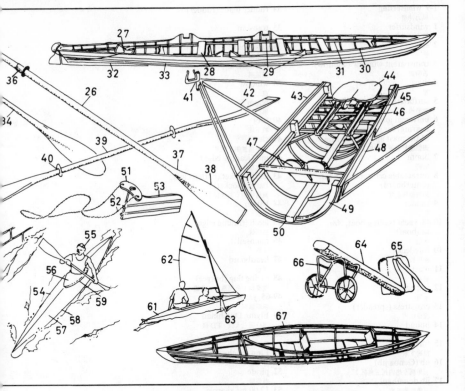

rip ring
消水环
0 sliding seat
滑动座位
owlock (oarlock)
桨架
utrigger
桨外支架
axboard
挡水浪(浪)板
liding seat
滑动座位
unner
滑座轨道
trut
支撑支架
tretcher
脚蹬
kin (shell, outer skin)
船壳
rame (rib)
肋材
elson (keelson)
内龙骨
3 rudder (steering rudder)
舵
oke
舵柄
ines (steering lines)
舵索(操舵绳)
lade (rudder blade, rudder)
舵叶(舵叶)

54-66 folding boats (foldboats, canoes)
摺叠式船(独木舟)
54 one-man kayak
单人皮船
55 canoeist
划独木舟的人
56 spraydeck
防水舱面
57 deck
舱面
58 rubber-covered canvas hull
包橡皮的帆布船壳
59 cockpit coaming (coaming)
座舱栏板
60 channel for rafts alongside weir
筏横靠堰的水道
61 two-seater folding kayak, a touring kayak
双座摺叠式皮船,一种游艇
62 sail of folding kayak
摺叠式皮船的帆
63 leeboard
下风板
64 bag for the rods
杆袋
65 rucksack
背包
66 boat trailer (boat carriage)
运船拖车
67 frame of folding kayak
摺叠式皮船框架
68-70 kayaks
各式皮船

68 Eskimo kayak
爱斯基摩皮船
69 wild-water racing kayak
急流赛艇
70 touring kayak
游玩用皮船

1-9 windsurfing
风力冲浪
1 windsurfer
风力冲浪者
2 sail
帆
3 transparent window (window)
透明窗
4 mast
桅
5 surfboard
冲浪板
6 universal joint (movable
bearing) for adjusting the angle
of the mast and for steering
调整桅杆角度和操纵方向的万向接头
7 boom
帆桁
8 retractable centreboard (*Am.*
centerboard)
伸缩垂板龙骨
9 rudder
舵
10-48 yacht (sailing boat, *Am.*
sailboat)
帆船
10 foredeck
前甲板
11 mast
桅杆
12 trapeze
吊架
13 crosstress (spreader)
桅顶横桁
14 hound
桅肩
15 forestay
前桅支索
16 jib (Genoa jib)
三角帆（热内瓦三角帆）
17 jib downhaul
三角帆降帆索
18 side stay (shroud)
桅杆横支索
19 lanyard (bottlescrew)
小索（短索）
20 foot of the mast
桅杆脚
21 kicking strap (vang)
斜桁支索
22 jam cleat
防松系缆栓
23 foresheet (jib sheet)
前桅帆脚索（三角帆脚索）
24 centreboard (*Am.* centerboard)
case
垂板龙骨框架
25 bitt
系桩
26 centreboard (*Am.* centerboard)
垂板龙骨
27 traveller (*Am.* traveler)
活动铁环
28 mainsheet
主帆脚索
29 fairlead
导索器
30 toestraps (hiking straps)
脚趾带
31 tiller extension (hiking stick)
舵柄分杆
32 tiller
舵柄
33 rudderhead (rudder stock)
舵头

34 rudder blade (rudder)
舵面
35 transom
艉板
36 drain plug
排水塞（栓）
37 gooseneck
鹅颈圈
38 window
窗
39 boom
帆桁
40 foot
帆下缘
41 clew
帆下角铁圈（帆耳）
42 luff (leading edge)
纵帆前缘
43 leech pocket (batten cleat,
batten pocket)
帆后缘袋（条板袋）
44 batten
条板
45 leech (trailing edge)
帆后缘
46 mainsail
主帆
47 headboard
顶板
48 racing flag (burgee)
竞赛旗（燕尾旗，三角旗）
49-65 yacht classes
帆船级别
49 Flying Dutchman
飞行荷兰人级，FD 级
50 O-Joller
O 级小艇
51 Finn dinghy (Finn)
芬兰级
52 pirate
海盗级
53 12.00 m² sharpie
12.00 m² 帆船
54 tempest
暴风雨级
55 star
星级
56 soling
索林级
57 dragon
龙级
58 5.5-metre (*Am.* 5.5-meter) class
5.5 公尺级
59 6-metre (*Am.* 6-meter) R-class
6 公尺 R 级
60 30.00 m² cruising yacht
(coastal cruiser)
30.00 m² 巡航快艇
61 30.00 m² dinghy cruiser
30.00 m² 巡航小帆船
62 25.00 m² one-design keelboat
25.00 m² 统一龙骨船
63 KR-class
KR 级
64 catamaran
双体船
65 twin hull
双体船壳，双体船身

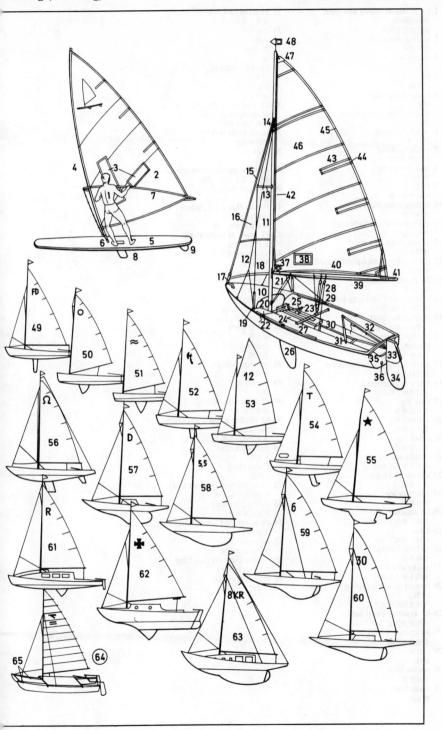

1-13 points of sailing and wind directions
航行方位和风向

1 sailing downwind
顺风航行

2 mainsail
主帆

3 jib
三角帆

4 ballooning sails
满帆

5 centre (*Am.* center) line
中心线

6 wind direction
风向

7 yacht tacking
帆船迎风转向

8 sail, shivering
飘动的帆

9 luffing
转向逆风行驶

10 sailing close-hauled
逆风行驶

11 sailing with wind abeam
侧风行驶

12 sailing with free wind
顺风行驶

13 quartering wind (quarter wind)
船尾风

14-24 regatta course
帆船赛程

14 starting and finishing buoy
起点和终点浮标

15 committee boat
（赛船）委员会船

16 triangular course (regatta course)
三角航线（赛船航程）

17 buoy (mark) to be rounded
船回转浮标（标识）

18 buoy to be passed
通过浮标（标识）

19 first leg
第一段赛程

20 second leg
第二段赛程

21 third leg
第三段赛程

22 windward leg
迎风（逆风）赛程

23 downwind leg
顺风赛程

24 reachng leg
侧风赛程

25-28 tacking
迎风（逆风）转向航行

25 tack
迎风（逆风）转向

26 gybing (jibing)
移帆改向

27 going about
迎风（逆风）转向

28 loss of distance during the gybe (jibe)
移帆改向距离的损失

29-41 types of yacht hull
帆船船身类型

29-34 cruiser keelboat
巡航用龙骨船

29 stern
船尾

30 spoon bow
匙形船首

31 waterline
吃水线

32 keel (ballast keel)
龙骨（压舱龙骨）

33 ballast
压舱物

34 rudder
舵

35 racing keelboat
比赛龙骨船

36 lead keel
铅质龙骨

37-41 keel-centreboard (*Am.* centerboard) yawl
垂板龙骨小帆船

37 retractable rudder
可伸缩的舵

38 cockpit
座舱

39 cabin superstructure (cabin)
舱的上部（建筑）结构

40 straight stem
直船首

41 retractable centreboard (*Am.* centerboard)
可伸缩的垂板龙骨

42-49 types of yacht stern
帆船尾的类型

42 yacht stern
帆船船尾

43 square stern
方形艉

44 canoe stern
独木舟形艉

45 cruiser stern
游艇船尾

46 name plate
船名牌

47 deadwood
船尾鳍

48 transom stern
肋板船尾

49 transom
艉梁

50-57 timber planking
船身（体）外板

50-52 clinker planking (clench planking)
重叠的船身外板

50 outside strake
外列板

51 frame (rib)
船肋骨

52 clenched nail (riveted nail)
钉牢的钉（铆死的钉）

53 carvel planking
平接船身外板

54 close-seamed construction
密缝结构

55 stringer
纵材，承梁纵材

56 diagonal carvel planking
斜平接船身外板

57 inner planking
内层板

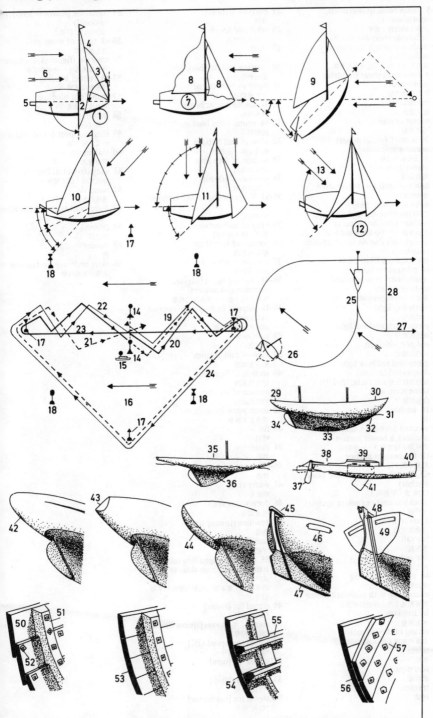

1-5 motorboats (powerboats, sportsboats)
汽艇（动力艇，赛艇）

1 inflatable sportsboats with outboard motor (outboard inflatable)
装有船尾（外）马达的充气赛艇

2 z-drive motorboat (outdrive motorboat)
Z 型驱动汽艇

3 cabin cruiser
舱式游艇

4 motor cruiser
马达游艇

5 30-metre (*Am.* 30-meter) ocean-going cruiser
30 公尺远洋游艇

6 association flag
协会会旗

7 name of craft (*or:* registration number)
船名（或：船舶登记号码）

8 club membership and port of registry (*Am.* home port)
（俱乐部）协会会籍和船籍港标识

9 association flag on the starboard crosstrees
挂在右舷桅顶横杆的协会会旗

10-14 navigation lights of sportsboats in coastal and inshore waters
赛艇在沿海和近海水域的航行灯

10 white top light
白色顶灯

11 green starboard sidelight
绿色右舷灯

12 red port sidelight
红色左舷灯

13 green and red bow light (combined lantern)
绿色和红色船首灯（红绿二色信号灯）

14 white stern light
白色船尾灯

15-18 anchors
锚

15 stocked anchor (Admiralty anchor), a bower anchor
有杆锚（海军锚），一种锚锚

16-18 lightweight anchor
轻量（载）锚

16 CQR anchor (plough, *Am.* plow, anchor)
CQR 锚（犁形锚）

17 stockless anchor (patent anchor)
无杆锚

18 Danforth anchor
丹佛斯式锚

19 life raft
救生筏

20 life jacket
救生衣（夹克）

21-44 powerboat racing
动力艇比赛

21 catamaran with outboard motor
装有船尾（外）马达的双体船

22 hydroplane
水上快艇

23 racing outboard motor
竞赛用船尾（外）马达

24 tiller
舵柄

25 fuel pipe
燃料管

26 transom
艉梁

27 buoyancy tube
浮筒

28 start and finish
出发点和终点

29 start
出发

30 starting and finishing line
起点和终点线

31 buoy to be rounded
供赛艇绕过的浮标

32-37 displacement boats
排水型船

32-34 round-bilge boat
圆底船

32 view of hull buttom
船身（体）底部图

33 section of fore ship
船首剖面图

34 section of aft ship
船尾剖面图

35-37 V-bottom boat (vee-bottom boat)
V 型底船

35 view of hull bottom
船身（体）底部图

36 section of fore ship
船首剖面图

37 section of aft ship
船尾剖面图

38-44 planing boats (surface skimmers, skimmers)
滑航（行）船，（水面滑行快艇）

38-41 stepped hydroplane (stepped skimmer)
加速水面滑行快艇

38 side view
侧视图

39 view of hull bottom
船身底面图

40 section of fore ship
船首剖面图

41 section of aft ship
船尾剖面图

42 three-point hydroplane
三点水上快艇

43 fin
鳍板

44 float
浮筒

45-62 water skiing
滑水

45 water skier
滑水者

46 deep-water start
深水起滑

47 tow line (towing line)
拖缆

48 handle
手把

49-55 water-ski signalling (code of hand signals from skier to boat driver)
滑水信号（滑水者与汽艇驾驶间的手势信号）

49 signal for [faster]
"加速"信号

50 signal for [slower] ([slow down])
"减速"信号

51 signal for [speed OK]
"速度 OK"信号

52 signal for [turn]
"转弯"信号

53 signal for [stop]
"停止"信号

54 signal for [cut motor]
"熄火"信号

55 signal for [return to jetty] ([return to dock])
"返回码头"信号

56-62 types of water ski
滑水板类型

56 trick ski (figure ski), a mono ski
特技滑水板，一种单型滑水板

57-58 rubber binding
橡皮固定装置

57 front foot binding
前足固定装置

58 heel flap
后跟绞链板

59 strap support for second foot
后足套板支座

60 slalom ski
弯道滑水

61 skeg (fixed fin, fin)
导流尾鳍（固定鳍板）

62 jump ski
跳跃滑水板

63 hovercraft (air-cushion vehicle)
气垫船

64 propeller
推进器

65 rudder
舵

66 skirt enclosing air cushion
边缘封闭的气垫

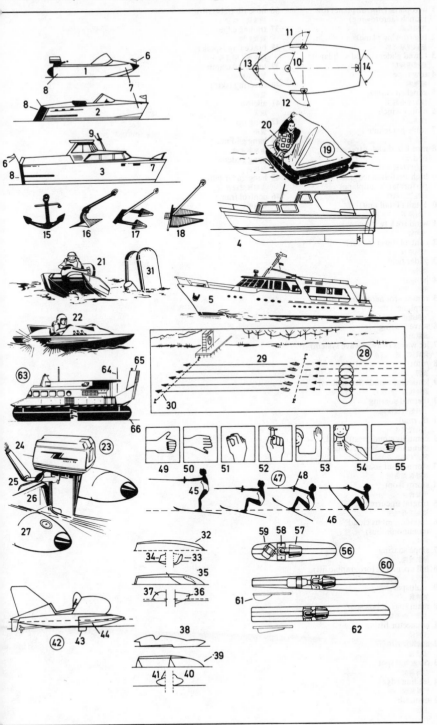

1 aeroplane (*Am.* airplane) tow
launch (aerotowing)
飞机曳航

2 tug (towing plane)
拖机曳航飞机

3 towed glider (towed sailplane)
拖曳滑翔机

4 tow rope
拖曳索

5 winched launch
绞车牵引起飞

6 motor winch
机动绞车

7 cable parachute
引索伞

8 motorized glider (powered
glider)
动力滑翔机

9 high-performance glider (high-
performance sailplane)
高性能滑翔机

10 T-tail (T-tail unit)
T型尾翼

11 wind sock (wind cone)
风向袋

12 control tower (tower)
管制塔台

13 glider field
滑翔机场

14 hangar
机库，棚厂

15 runway for aeroplanes (*Am.*
airplanes)
飞机跑道

16 wave soaring
波状滑翔

17 lee waves (waves, wave system)
背风波（波，波系）

18 rotor
旋转

19 lenticular clouds (lenticulars)
透镜状云，凸状云

20 thermal soaring
上升暖气流滑翔

21 thermal
上升暖气流

22 cumulus cloud (heap cloud,
cumulus, woolpack cloud)
积云（卷毛云）

23 storm-front soaring
风暴锋面滑翔

24 storm front
风暴锋面

25 frontal upcurrent
锋面上升气流

26 cumulonimbus cloud
(cumulonimbus)
积雨云

27 slope soaring
倾斜滑翔

28 hill upcurrent (orographic lift)
小丘上升气流（地形上升）

29 multispar wing
复梁翼

30 main spar, a box spar
主梁，箱形梁

31 connector fitting
连接件

32 anchor rib
锚状肋

33 diagonal spar
对角斜梁

34 leading edge
机翼前缘

35 main rib
主肋

36 nose rib (false rib)
前缘肋（假肋）

37 trailing edge
机翼后缘

38 brake flap (spoiler)
扰流板（阻流板）

39 torsional clamp
扭曲压板

40 covering (skin)
蒙皮

41 aileron
副翼

42 wing tip
翼梢

43 hang gliding
滑翔翼运动

44 hang glider
滑翔翼

45 hang glider pilot
滑翔翼驾驶者

46 control frame
操纵架

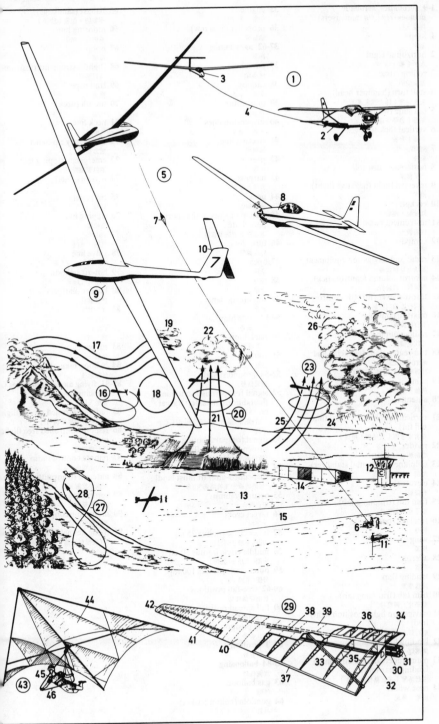

1-9 aerobatics, aerobatic manoeuvres (*Am* maneuvers)
特技飞行
1 loop
筋斗
2 horizontal eight
水平（横）"8"字
3 rolling circle
侧滚圆周
4 stall turn (hammer head)
失速转弯（锤头式失速）
5 tail slide (whip stall)
尾滑（急坠失速）
6 vertical flick spin
直垂上升旋冲
7 spin
旋冲
8 horizontal slow roll
水平慢滚
9 inverted flight (negative flight)
倒飞
10 cockpit
驾驶舱，座舱
11 instrument panel
仪表板
12 compass
罗盘
13 radio and navigation equipment
无线电导航设备
14 control column (control stick)
操纵杆，驾驶杆
15 throttle lever (throttle control)
油门杆（油门控制）
16 mixture control
混合比操纵
17 radio equipment
无线电装置
18 two-seater plane for racing and aerobatics
比赛和特技飞行的双座飞机
19 cabin
机舱，座舱
20 antenna
天线
21 vertical stabilizer (vertical fin, tail fin)
垂直安定面（直尾翅，尾翅）
22 rudder
方向舵
23 tailplane (horizontal stabilizer)
尾面（水平安定面）
24 elevator
升降舵
25 trim tab (trimming tab)
配平片，调整片
26 fuselage (body)
机身
27 wing
机翼
28 aileron
副翼
29 landing flap
降落襟翼
30 trim tab (trimming tab)
配平片，调整片
31 navigation light (position light) [red]
航行灯（方位灯）〔红〕
32 landing light
降落灯
33 main undercarriage unit (main landing gear unit)
主起落架（主起落传动装置）
34 nose wheel
前轮，鼻轮

35 engine
引擎，发动机
36 propeller (airscrew)
螺旋桨
37-62 parachuting
跳伞
37 parachute
降落伞
38 canopy
伞身，伞衣
39 pilot chute
导伞
40 suspension lines
吊索（绳）
41 steering line
操纵绳
42 riser
吊带
43 harness
背带，伞带
44 pack
降落伞包
45 system of slots of the sports parachute
运动降落伞的伞衣缝片方式
46 turn slots
转向翼缝
47 apex
伞顶
48 skirt
伞缘
49 stabilizing panel
安定面
50-51 style jump
跳伞姿势
50 back loop
后筋斗后翻
51 spiral
盘旋
52-54 ground signals
地面信号
52 signal for [permission to jump] ([conditions are safe]) (target cross)
"允许跳伞"信号，（安全信号）（十字标）
53 signal for [parachuting suspended-repeat flight]
"暂停跳伞，重飞"信号
54 signal for [parachuting suspended-aircraft must land]
"暂停跳伞，飞机降落"信号
55 accuracy jump
定点跳伞
56 target cross
十字标
57 inner circle [radius 25 m]
内圈〔半经 25 公尺〕
58 middle circle [radius 50 m]
中圈〔半经 50 公尺〕
59 outer circle [radius 100 m]
外圈〔半经 100 公尺〕
60-62 free-fall positions
自由降落姿势
60 full spread position
四肢伸展姿势
61 frog position
蛙式姿势
62 T position
T 型姿势
63-84 ballooning
驾驶气球
63 gas balloon
气球
64 gondola (ballon basket)
吊篮

65 ballast (sandbags)
压载物，配重（沙袋）
66 mooring line
系留索（绳）
67 hoop
篮圈
68 flight instruments (instrum
飞行装置
69 trail rope
拖绳
70 mouth (neck)
气咀
71 neck line
气咀绳
72 emergency rip panel
紧急裂幅
73 emergency ripping line
紧急裂幅绳
74 network (net)
网
75 rip panel
裂幅
76 ripping line
裂幅绳
77 valve
气阀，气门
78 valve line
气门绳
79 hot-air balloon
热空气气球
80 burner platform
燃烧器台
81 mouth
气球咀
82 vent
排气口
83 rip panel
裂幅
84 balloon take-off
气球起飞
85-91 flying model aeroplanes (*A*
airplanes)
模型飞机
85 radio-controlled model fligh
无线电控制模型机飞行
86 remote-controlled free flight model
飞行模型机
87 remote control radio
遥控无线电
88 antenna (transmitting antenn
天线（发射天线）
89 control line model
线操纵模型机
90 mono-line control system
单线操纵系统
91 flying kennel, a K9-class mo
K9 级模型机棚

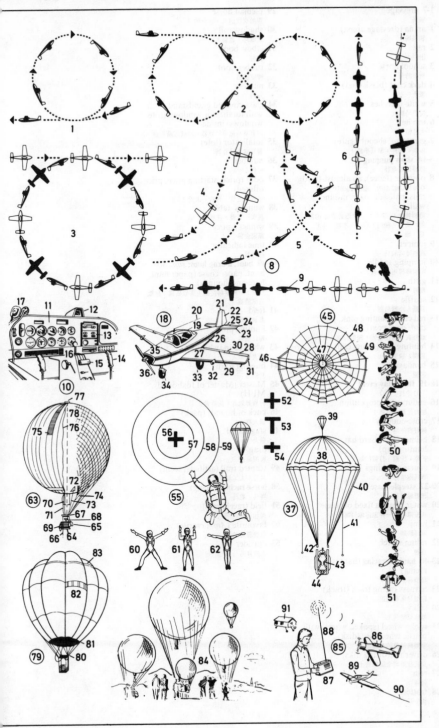

1-7 dressage
驯马

1 arena (dressage arena)
驯马场

2 rail
围栏

3 school horse
所驯的马

4 dark coat (black coat)
黑色外衣

5 white breeches
白色马裤

6 top hat
大礼帽

7 gait (*also:* shcool figure)
步法（亦称：驯马步法）

8-14 show jumping
障碍跳越竞技

8 obstacle (fence), an almost-fixed
obstacle; *sim.:* gate, gate and
rails, palisade, oxer, mound,
wall
障碍物（栏架），一种近於固定的障碍
物；类似：栅门，栏 ，木栅，牛栏，土
堤，墙

9 jumper
跳越障碍的马

10 jumping saddle
跳越障碍用的马鞍

11 girth
鞍带

12 snaffle
轻勒（小型马衔）

13 red coat (hunting pink, pink;
also: dark coat)
红外衣（粉红猎装；深色外衣）

14 hunting cap (riding cap)
猎帽（骑手帽）

15 bandage
护腿

16-19 three-day event
三日竞技（赛）

16 endurance competition
耐力比赛（竞赛）

17 cross-country
越野赛跑道

18 helmet (*also:* hard hat, hard
hunting cap)
护盔（护帽，打猎护帽）

19 course markings
赛马跑道标志

20-22 steeplechase
越野障碍赛

20 water jump, a fixed obstacle
水濠障碍，一种固定障碍物

21 jump
障碍跳越

22 riding switch
马鞭

23-40 harness racing (harness horse
racing)
轻型马车（赛）

23 harness racing track (track)
轻型马车赛跑道

24 sulky
单座双轮马车

25 spoke wheel (spoked wheel) with
plastic wheel disc (disk)
带塑料轮盘的有幅轮子

26 driver in trotting silks
穿竞技用骑士服的骑士

27 rein
缰绳

28 trotter
快步马

29 pieblad horse
黑的斑纹的马，杂色的马

30 shadow roll
遮眼环，遮眼革

31 elbow boot
护肘

32 rubber boot
橡皮护腿

33 number
号码

34 glass-covered grandstand
with totalizator windows (tote
windows) inside
内有赛马赌金计算器的玻璃遮蔽看台

35 totalizator (tote)
赛马赌金计算器

36 number
号码

37 odds (price, starting price, price
offered)
差额（定价，开价，出价）

38 winners' table
赢家一览表，获胜者名单

39 winner's price
赢家金额

40 time indicator
报时器

41-49 hunt, a drag hunt; *sim.:* fox
hunt, paper chase (paper hunt,
hare-and-hounds)
狩猎，一种臭跡狩猎；类似猎狐，撒纸
追纵游戏

41 field
参加比赛者

42 hunting pink
粉红猎装

43 whipper-in (whip)
猎犬管理人

44 hunting horn
狩猎号

45 Master (Master of foxhounds,
MFH)
狩猎筹划者（指辉者）

46 pack of hounds (pack)
猎犬群

47 staghound
猎犬

48 drag
模拟臭跡

49 scented trail (artificial scent)
臭跡（人工臭跡）

50 horse racing (racing)
赛马，跑马

51 field (racehorses)
参加比赛的马

52 favourite (*Am.* favorite)
最被看好的马

53 outsider
无胜算的马

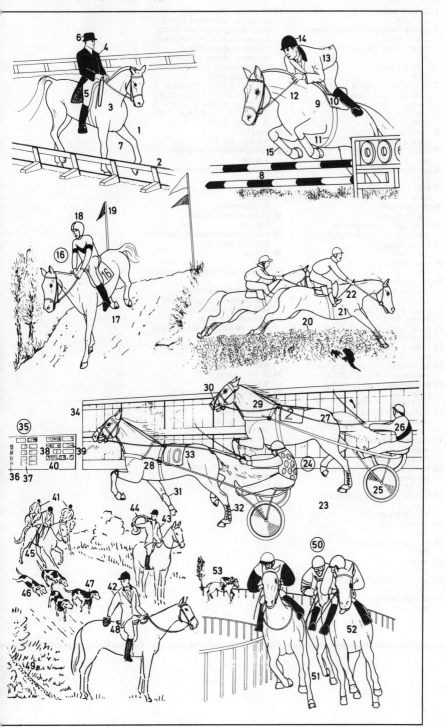

1-23 cycle racing
自行车竞赛

1 cycling track (cycle track); *here:* indoor track
赛车场；（跑道）此指室内车场（跑道）

2-7 six-day race
六日赛

2 six-day racer, a track racer (track rider) on the track
六日赛选手，跑道上的自行车选手

3 crash hat
防护帽

4 stewards
竞赛管理人员；干事

5 judge
裁判

6 lap scorer
计圈员

7 rider's box (racer's box)
选手席

8-10 road race
公路自行车竞赛

8 road racer, a racing cyclist
公路自行车选手，自行车竞赛人员

9 racing jersey
竞赛运动衫

10 water bottle
水壶

11-15 motor-paced racing (long-distance racing)
摩托车领先赛（长距离赛）

11 pacer, a motorcyclist
领先者，摩托车手

12 pacer's motorcycle
领先者骑的摩托车

13 roller, a safety device
滚筒，一种安全装置

14 stayer (motor-paced track rider)
长距离赛选手（摩托车领先赛场选手）

15 motor-paced cycle, a racing cycle
摩托车领先赛车，一种赛车

16 racing cycle (racing bicycle) for road racing (road race bicycle)
公路赛自行车

17 racing saddle, an unsprung saddle
赛车车垫，无弹簧车垫

18 racing handlebars (racing handlebar)
自行车把手（赛车）

19 tubular tyre (*Am.* tire) (racing tyre)
管状车胎（比赛用车胎）

20 chain
链条

21 toe clip (racing toe clip)
踏脚套

22 strap
皮带

23 spare tubula tyre (*Am.* tire)
备用管状车胎

24-38 motorsports
摩托车运动

24-28 motorcycle racing; *disciplines:* grasstrack racing, road racing, sand track racing, cement track racing, speedway [on ash or shale tracks], mountain racing, ice racing (ice speedway), scramble racing, trial, moto cross
摩托车赛；竞赛项目：草地场竞赛，公路赛，沙质跑道竞赛，水泥跑道竞赛，赛车跑道赛（在灰质或页岩跑道），登山赛，冰上赛（冰上赛车跑道），爬行赛，选拔赛，越野赛

24 sand track
沙质跑道（赛车场）

25 racing motorcyc!ist (rider)
竞赛选手

26 leather overalls (leathers)
皮衣

27 racing motorcycle, a solo machine
单人用竞赛摩托车

28 number (number plate)
号码（牌）

29 sidecar combination on the bend
转弯时边车的配合动作

30 sidecar
边车

31 streamlined racing motorcycle [500 cc.]
流线型比赛用摩托车〔500 cc〕

32 gymkhana, a competition of skill; *here:* motorcyclist performing a jump
竞赛，一种竞技比赛；此指赛车手表演障碍跳越

33 cross-country race, a test in performance
越野赛，特技试验

34-38 racing cars
赛车

34 Formula One racing car (a mono posto)
I 型赛车（单人车）

35 rear spoiler (aerofoil, *Am.* airfoil)
后扰流板

36 Formula Two racing car
II 型赛车

37 Super-Vee racing car
超级 V 型赛车

38 prototype, a racing car
标准赛车

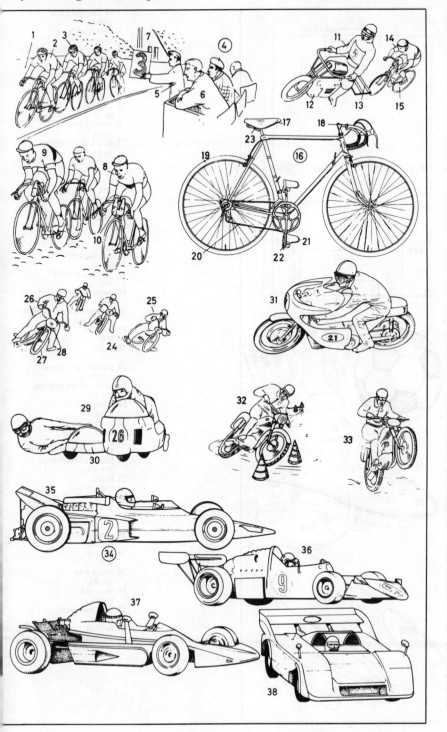

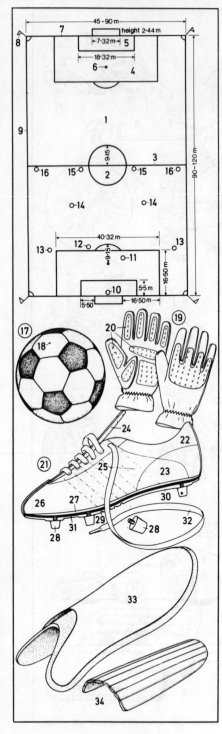

1-16 football pitch
足球场
1 field (park)
球场
2 centre (*Am.* center) circle
中圈
3 half-way line
中线
4 penalty area
罚球区
5 goal area
球门区
6 penalty spot
罚球点
7 goal line (by-line)
球门线，端线
8 corner flag
角旗
9 touch line
边线
10 goalkeeper
守门员
11 spare man
后卫
12 inside defender
内后卫
13 outside defender
边后卫
14 midfield players
中锋
15 inside forward (striker)
前锋
16 outside forward (winger)
侧翼（边锋）
17 football
足球
18 valve
气门
19 goalkeeper's gloves
守门员手套
20 foam rubber padding
泡沫垫料
21 football boot
足球鞋
22 leather lining
皮衬里
23 counter
鞋帮后跟部硬皮
24 foam rubber tongue
泡沫胶鞋舌
25 bands
条纹，条饰
26 shaft
鞋身（帮）
27 insole
鞋内底（软垫）
28 screw-in stud
鞋底针柱
29 groove
槽沟
30 nylon sole
尼龙鞋底
31 inner sole
内衬底
32 lace (bootlace)
鞋带
33 football pad with ankle guard
带护踝的足球垫
34 shin guard
护胫

51 obstruction
阻挡
52 dribble
带球
53 throw-in
掷界外球
54 substitute
替换球员
55 coach
教练
56 shirt (jersey)
球衫（运动衫）
57 shorts
短裤
58 sock (football sock)
袜（足球袜）
59 linesman
边线裁判员
60 linesman's flag
边线裁判员旗
61 sending-off
罚出场
62 referee
裁判员
63 red card; *also:* yellow card
红牌（表示罚出场），黄牌（表示警
告）
64 centre (*Am.* center) flag
中线旗

1 **handball** (indoor handball)
手球（室内手球）

2 handball player, a field player
手球员，场上球员

3 attacker, making a jump throw
进攻球员，跳起掷球

4 defender
防守球员

5 penalty line
罚球线

6 **hockey**
曲棍球

7 goal
球门

8 goalkeeper
守门员

9 pad (shin pad, knee pad)
护垫（护胫，护膝）

10 kicker
球鞋

11 face guard
（守门员）面罩

12 glove
手套

13 hockey stick
曲棍球杆

14 hockey ball
曲棍球

15 hockey player
曲棍球员

16 striking circle
击球圈

17 sideline
边线

18 corner
角

19 **rugby** (rugby football)
橄榄球

20 scrum (scrummage)
并列争球

21 rugby ball
橄榄球

22 **American football** (*Am.*
football)
美式足球

23 football player (player) carrying
the ball
带球的橄榄球员

24 helmet
护盔

25 face guard
面罩

26 padded jersey
衬软垫的运动衫

27 ball (pigskin)
球（橄榄球）

28 **basketball**
篮球

29 basketball
篮球

30 backboard
篮板

31 basket posts
篮架柱

32 basket
篮

33 basket ring
篮圈

34 target rectangle
方形篮标区

35 basketball player shooting
投篮球员

36 end line
端线

37 restricted area
禁区，三秒钟区

38 free-throw line
罚篮线

39 substitute
替补球员

40-69 **baseball**
棒球

40-58 field (park)
棒球场

40 spectator barrier
观众栅栏

41 outfielder
外野手

42 short stop
游击手

43 second base
二垒

44 baseman
守垒员

45 runner
跑垒员

46 first base
一垒

47 third base
三垒

48 foul line (base line)
全线

49 pitcher's mound
投手区，投手板前隆起的土墩

50 pitcher
投手

51 batter's position
打击手位置（击球员）

52 batter
打击手（击球员）

53 home base (home plate)
本垒

54 catcher
捕手

55 umpire
裁判

56 coach's box
跑垒员指导区

57 coach
跑垒指导员

58 batting order
打击顺序

59-60 baseball gloves (baseball
mitts)
棒球手套（棒球合指手套）

59 fielder's glove (fielder's mitt)
垒手及野手手套

60 catcher's glove (catcher's mitt)
捕手手套

61 baseball
棒球

62 bat
球棒

63 batter at bat
打击手击球

64 catcher
捕手

65 umpire
裁判

66 runner
跑垒员

67 base plate
垒包（垫，板）

68 pitcher
投手

69 pitcher's mound
投手板

70-76 **cricket**
板球

70 wicket with bails
具横木的三柱门

71 back crease (bowling crease)
底线（投球限界线）

72 crease (batting crease)
击球限界线

73 wicket keeper of the fielding
防守方三柱门守门员

74 batsman
打击手（击球员）

75 bat (cricket bat)
球棒（板球棒）

76 fielder (bowler)
野手（投手）

77-82 **croquet**
槌球

77 winning peg
起（终）点桩（杆）

78 hoop
柱门

79 corner peg
角桩

80 croquet player
槌球员

81 croquet mallet
槌球的长柄木槌

82 croquet ball
槌球

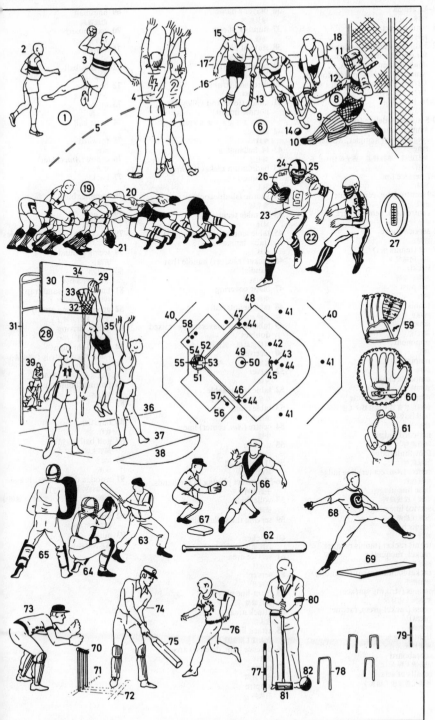

1-42 tennis
网球
1 tennis court
网球场
2-3 doubles sideline (sideline
for doubles matches); *kinds of
doubles:* men's doubles,
women's doubles, mixed doubles
双打边线；双打种类：男子双打、女子
双打，混合双打
3-10 base line
端线的底线
4-5 singles sideline (sideline for
singles matches); *kinds of
singles:* men's singles, women's
singles
单打边线；单打种类：男子单打、女子
单打
6-7 service line
发球线
8-9 centre (*Am.* center) line
中线
11 centre (*Am.* center) mark
中点标识
12 service court
发球区
13 net (tennis net)
网（网球网）
14 net strap
网中心布带
15 net post
网柱
16 tennis player
网球手
17 smash
高压球
18 opponent
对手
19 umpire
裁判
20 umpire's chair
裁判椅
21 umpire's microphone
裁判用扩音器（微音器）（麦克风）
22 ball boy
球童
23 net-cord judge
网绳裁判
24 foot-fault judge
发球裁判
25 centre (*Am.* center) line judge
中线裁判
26 base line judge
端线，底线裁判
27 service line judge
发球线裁判
28 tennis ball
网球
29 tennis racket (tennis racquet,
racket, racquet)
网球拍
30 racket handle (racquet handle)
球拍把手
31 strings (striking surface)
拍面网（击球面）
32 press (racket press, racquet
press)
球拍夹
33 tightening screw
夹紧螺丝
34 scoreboard
记分牌（板）
35 results of sets
各场比赛成绩（结果）

36 player's name
球员姓名
37 number of sets
场数
38 state of play
比赛状况（比数，成绩）
39 backhand stroke
反手击球
40 forehand stroke
正手击球
41 volley (forehand volley at
normal height)
截击（正手截击正常高度的球）
42 service
发球
43-44 badminton
羽毛球
43 badminton racket (badminton
racquet)
羽毛球拍
44 shuttle (shuttlecock)
羽毛球
45-55 table tennis
桌球
45 table tennis racket (racquet)
(table tennis bat)
桌球拍
46 racket (racquet) handle (bat
handle)
球拍柄
47 blade covering
拍身贴面
48 table tennis ball
桌球，乒乓球
49 table tennis players; *here:* mixed
doubles
桌球员此指：混合双打
50 receiver
接球员
51 server
发球员
52 table tennis table
乒乓球桌
53 table tennis net
桌球网
54 centre (*Am.* center) line
中线
55 sideline
边线
56-71 volleyball
排球
56-57 correct placing of the hands
手的正确姿势
58 volleyball
排球
59 serving the volleyball
发球
60 blocker
栏网球员
61 service area
发球区
62 server
发球员
63 front-line player
前排球员
64 attack area
攻击区
65 attack line
攻击线（限制线）
66 defence (*Am.* defense) area
防守区
67 referee
主审裁判
68 umpire
副裁判

69 linesman
边线裁判
70 scoreboard
记分板
71 scorer
记分员
72-78 faustball
拳球
72 base line
底线，端线
73 tape
带，绳
74 faust ball
拳球
75 forward
前锋
76 centre (*Am.* center)
中锋
77 back
后卫
78 hammer blow
鎚击（扣击）
79-93 golf
高尔夫球
79-82 course (golf course, holes
高尔夫球场
79 teeing ground
开球区
80 rough
生杂草的障碍区
81 bunker (*Am.* sand trap)
沙坑（沙地障碍区）
82 green (putting green)
果岭（轻打果岭）
83 golfer, driving
高尔夫球员，挥杆
84 follow-through
打球后手腕伸直的动作（完成动作）
85 golf trolley
打高尔夫球用的手推车
86 putting (holing out)
轻打区
87 hole
球洞
88 flagstick
旗杆
89 golf ball
高尔夫球
90 tee
球座
91 wood, a driver; *sim.:* brassie
(brassy, brassey)
木制球杆，长打杆；类似的：镶铜球
（第二号球杆）
92 iron
铁头高尔夫球杆
93 putter
高尔夫球轻击杆

SCORES	SETS	GAMES
6·3 BORG	2	4
4·6	
2·6 ASHE	2	1

1-33 fencing (modern fencing)
击剑（现代击剑）

1-18 foil
击剑（钝剑）

1 fencing master (fencing instructor)
剑术（击剑）教练

2 piste
击剑场

3 on guard line
预备线

4 centre (*Am.* center) line
中心线

5-6 fencers (foil fencers, foilsmen, foilists) in a bout
比赛中的（钝剑）击剑员

5 attacker (attacking fencer) in lunging position (lunging)
取刺姿的进攻者

6 defender (defending fencer), parrying
取守势的防守者

7 straight thrust, a fencing movement
直刺的击剑动作

8 parry of the tierce
第三姿势防守[格开，挡开来剑]

9 line of fencing
击剑线

10 the three fencing measures [short, medium, and long measure]
三种击剑距离[近，中，长距离]

11 foil, a thrust weapon
钝剑，一种戳刺武器

12 fencing glove
击剑手套

13 fencing mask (foil mask)
护面

14 neck flap (neck guard) on the fencing mask
附于护面上的护颈（盖）

15 metallic jacket
金属夹克

16 fencing jacket
击剑夹克

17 heelless fencing shoes
无跟击剑鞋

18 first position for fencer's salute (initial position, on guard position)
击剑者行礼时所取的第一姿势（开始姿势，预备姿势）

19-24 sabre (*Am.* saber) fencing
军刀对击

19 sabreurs (sabre fencers, *Am.* saber fencers)
军刀赛者

20 (light) sabre (*Am.* saber)
（轻）军刀

21 sabre (*Am.* saber) glove (sabre gauntlet)
军刀手套

22 sabre (*Am.* saber) mask
军刀护面

23 cut at head
劈头部

24 parry of the fifth (quinte)
第五姿势防守

25-33 épée, with electrical scoring equipment
装有电子记分装置的尖头剑术比赛

25 épéeist
尖头剑竞赛者

26 electric épée; *also:* electric foil
电动尖头剑；电动钝剑

27 épée point
剑尖

28 scoring lights
记分灯

29 spring-loaded wire spool
弹簧承载电线卷轴

30 indicator light
指示灯

31 wire
电线

32 electronic scoring equipment
电子记分装置

33 on guard position
预备姿势

34-45 fencing weapons
击剑武器

34 light sabre (*Am.* saber), a cut and thrust weapon
轻型军刀，一种劈刺武器

35 guard
护手

36 épée, a thrust weapon
尖头刀，一种刺的武器

37 French foil, a thrust weapon
法国钝剑，一种刺的武器

38 guard (coquille)
护手

39 Italian foil
意大利钝剑

40 foil pommel
剑的柄端

41 handle
剑柄

42 cross piece (quillons)
交叉柄环

43 guard (coquille)
护手

44 blade
剑身

45 button
钝头

46 engagements
剑之交叉接触

47 quarte (carte) engagement
第四姿势交叉接触

48 tierce engagement (*also:* sixte engagement)
第三姿势交叉接触（即第六姿势交叉接触）

49 circling engagement
迴圈交叉接触

50 seconde engagement (*also:* octave engagement)
第二姿势交叉接触（即第八姿势交叉接触）

51-53 target areas
有效部位

51 the whole body in épée fencing (men)
（男子）击剑的全身

52 head and upper body down to the groin in sabre (*Am.* saber) fencing (men)
（男子）军刀击剑时从头与上身至鼠蹊间的部位

53 trunk from the neck to the groin in foil fencing (ladies and men)
（女子与男子）钝剑击剑是从颈部到鼠蹊间的躯干

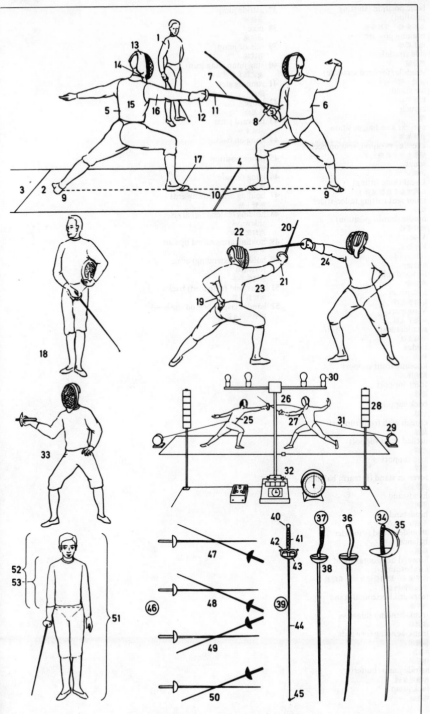

1 basic position (starting position)
基本姿势（开始姿势）
2 running posture
跑步姿势
3 side straddle
侧分腿
4 straddle (forward straddle)
分腿（前分腿）
5 toe stand
以足尖站立
6 crouch
蹲
7 upright kneeling position
直体跪姿
8 kneeling position, seat on heels
跪姿（坐於足跟上）
9 squat
屈腿
10 L seat (long sitting)
L 式坐姿（直腿坐姿）
11 tailor seat (sitting tailor-style)
盘腿
12 hurdle (hurdle position)
跳栏姿势
13 V-seat
V 型姿式
14 side split
纵劈腿
15 forward split
横劈腿
16 L-support
L 型手支撑
17 V-support
V 型手支撑
18 straddle seat
分腿支撑
19 bridge
桥式
20 kneeling front support
跪俯撑
21 front support
俯撑
22 back support
后撑
23 crouch with front support
蹲撑
24 arched front support
弓撑
25 side support
侧撑
26 forearm stand (forearm balance)
前腕倒立
27 handstand
手倒立
28 headstand
头倒立（三点倒立）
29 shoulder stand (shoulder balance)
肩倒立
30 forward horizontal stand (arabesque)
前平衡（一脚向后伸直，一手向前，一手向后伸的姿势）
31 rearward horizontal stand
侧平衡
32 trunk-bending sideways
体侧屈
33 trunk-bending forwards
体前屈
34 arch
体后屈
35 astride jump (butterfly)
伸腿挺身跳
36 tuck jump
缩拢跳

37 astride jump
分腿跳
38 pike
屈体跳
39 scissor jump
剪式跳
40 stag jump (stag leap)
鹿式跳（半劈腿跳）
41 running step
跑步
42 lunge
弓箭步
43 forward pace
向前走步
44 lying on back
仰卧
45 prone position
俯卧
46 lying on side
侧卧
47 holding arms downwards
两臂下垂
48 holding (extending) arms sideways
两臂侧平举
49 holding arms raised upward
两臂上举
50 holding (extending) arms forward
两臂前平举
51 arms held (extended) backward
两臂后平举
52 hands clasped behind the head
两手头后互握

1-11 gymnastics apparatus in men's Olympic gymnastics
男子奥运体操器械

1 long horse (horse, vaulting horse)
纵跳马（跳马）

2 parallel bars
双槓

3 bar
横槓

4 rings (stationary rings)
吊环（静止吊环）

5 pommel horse (side horse)
鞍马

6 pommel
鞍环

7 horizontal bar (high bar)
单槓（高槓）

8 bar
横槓

9 upright
柱，直柱

10 stay wires
支索

11 floor (12 m × 12 m floor area)
地板（12 米 × 12 米徒手操场地）

12-21 auxiliary apparatus and apparatus for school and club gymnastics
辅助器械和学校，俱乐部体操器械

12 springboard (Reuther board)
弹跳板（路德板）

13 landing mat
落地垫

14 bench
长体操凳

15 box
跳箱

16 small box
小跳箱

17 buck
木马

18 mattress
垫子

19 climbing rope (rope)
爬绳

20 wall bars
肋木

21 window ladder
窗形梯

22-39 positions in relation to the apparatus
与器械相关的姿势和位置

22 side, facing
正对跳箱侧面

23 side, facing away
背对跳箱侧面

24 end, facing
正对跳箱端

25 end, facing away
背对跳箱端

26 outside, facing
正对双槓外侧

27 inside, facing
正对双槓内侧

28 front support
前撑，俯撑

29 back support
后撑

30 straddle position
分腿姿势

31 seated position outside
槓上外向正坐

32 riding seat outside
槓外侧坐

33 hang
悬垂

34 reverse hang
后悬垂，吊臂悬垂

35 hang with elbows bent
屈肘悬垂，屈肘向上

36 piked reverse hang
屈体吊臂悬垂

37 straight inverted hang
直臂倒悬垂

38 straight hang
直臂支撑

39 bent hang
屈臂支撑

40-46 grasps (kinds of grasp)
握槓（各种握槓）

40 overgrasp on the horizontal bar
正握单槓

41 undergrasp on the horizontal bar
反握单槓

42 combined grasp on the horizontal bar
正反握单槓

43 cross grasp on the horizontal bar
交叉握单槓

44 rotated grasp on the horizontal bar
扭臂握单槓

45 outside grip on the parallel bars
自外握双槓

46 rotated grasp on the parallel bars
扭臂握双槓

47 leather handstrap
皮护掌

48-60 exercises
各种体操动作

48 long-fly on the horse
跳马的水平腾越

49 rise to straddle on the parallel bars
双槓向上分腿

50 crucifix on the rings
吊环上十字支撑

51 scissors (scissors movement) on the pommel horse
鞍马上的剪式动作

52 legs raising into a handstand on the floor
地板上升腿倒立

53 squat vault on the horse
跳马屈体腾越

54 double leg circle on the pommel horse
鞍马上双腿翻旋

55 hip circle backwards on the rings
吊环上向后复回环

56 lever hang on the rings
吊环上槓杆悬垂

57 rearward swing on the parallel bars
双槓上后向摆越

58 forward kip into upper arm hang on the parallel bars
双槓上挂臂体向前

59 backward underswing on the horizontal bar
单槓上向后弧形腰

60 backward grand circle on the horizontal bar
单槓上向后大翻环

61-63 gymnastics kit
体操服

61 singlet (vest, *Am.* undershirt)
背心

62 gym trousers
体操裤

63 gym shoes
体操鞋

64 wristband
护腕

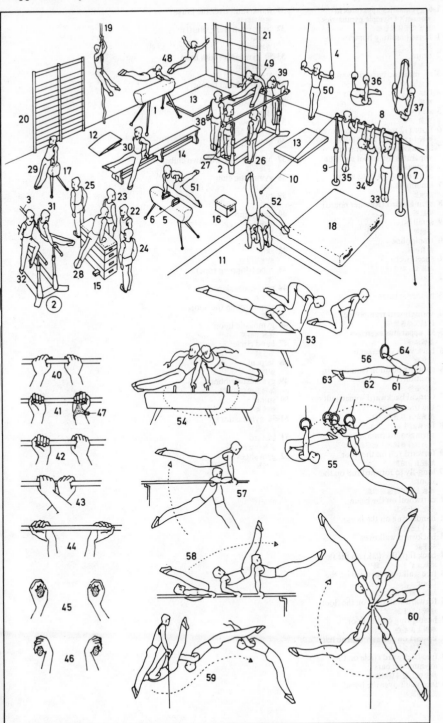

1-6 gymnastics apparatus in women's Olympic gymnastics
奥运女子体操器械

1 horse (vaulting horse)
跳马

2 beam
平衡木

3 asymmetric bars (uneven bars)
高低杠

4 bar
横杠

5 stay wires
支索

6 floor (12 m × 12 m floor area)
地板（12 米 × 12 米徒手操场地）

7-14 auxiliary apparatus and apparatus for school and club gymnastics
辅助器械和学校俱乐部体操器械

7 landing mat
落地垫

8 springboard (Reuther board)
弹跳板

9 small box
小跳箱

10 trampoline
弹簧跳床

11 sheet (web)
跳床面（跳床网）

12 frame
床架

13 rubber springs
橡皮弹簧

14 springboard trampoline
跳板式弹簧跳床

15-32 apparatus exercises
器械体操

15 backward somersault
后空翻

16 spotting position (standing-in position)
保护姿势

17 vertical backward somersault on the trampoline
弹簧跳床垂直后空翻

18 forward somersault on the springboard trampoline
跳板式弹簧跳床上前空翻

19 forward roll on the floor
地板上前滚翻

20 long-fly to forward roll on the floor
地板上水平腾越前滚翻

21 cartwheel on the beam
平衡木上侧翻

22 handspring on the horse
跳马上前手翻

23 backward walkover
后手翻

24 back flip (flik-flak) on the floor
地板上后手（空）翻

25 free walkover forward on the floor
地板上腾身前空翻

26 forward walkover on the floor
地板上前手翻

27 headspring on the floor
地板上头手翻

28 upstart on the asymmetric bars
高低杠腾身向上

29 free backward circle on the asymmetric bars
高低杠上腾身后回旋

30 face vault over the horse
正腾越跳马

31 flank vault over the horse
侧腾越跳马

32 back vault (rear vault) over the horse
背腾越跳马

33-50 gymnastics with hand apparatus
轻器械体操

33 hand-to-hand throw
自抛自接

34 gymnastic ball
体操球

35 high toss
上（高）抛

36 bounce
拍球

37 hand circling with two clubs
手绕双棒

38 gymnastic club
体操棒

39 swing
摆动

40 tuck jump
缩拢跳

41 bar
棒

42 skip
跳绳

43 rope (skipping rope)
绳

44 criss-cross skip
交叉跳

45 skip through the hoop
跳圈

46 gymnastic hoop
体操用藤圈

47 hand circle
单手绕圈

48 serpent
蛇舞

49 gymnastic ribbon
体操用缎（彩）带

50 spiral
螺旋舞

51-52 gymnastics kit
体操服装

51 leotard
紧身运动衣

52 gym shoes
体操鞋

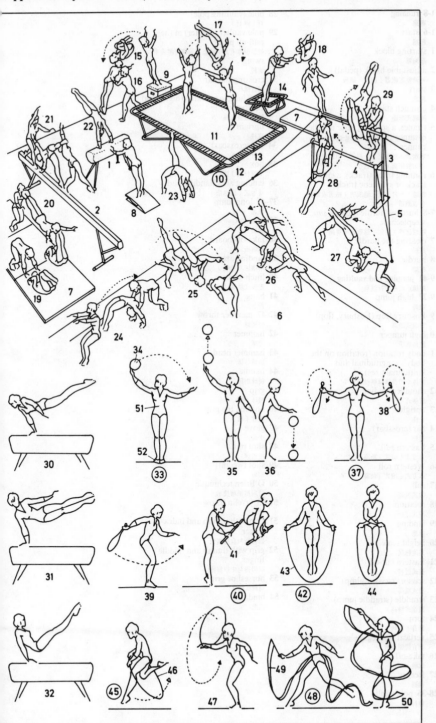

1-8 running
赛跑

1-6 start
起跑

1 starting block
起跑器

2 adjustable block (pedal)
可调整起跑器（脚蹬，踏板）

3 start
起跑

4 crounch start
蹲踞式起跑

5 runner, a sprinter; *also:* **middle-distance runner, long-distance runner**
赛跑者，短跑选手；亦可：中距离选手，长距离（跑）选手

6 running track (track), a cinder track or synthetic track
跑道，一种煤渣（铺成的）跑道或塑胶合成跑道

7-8 hurdles (hurdle racing); *sim.:* **steeplechase**
跳栏比赛；类似：越野障碍赛跑

7 clearing the hurdle
跨栏

8 hurdle
栏架

9-41 jumping and vaulting
跳跃运动和撑杆跳高

9-27 high jump
跳高

9 Fosbury flop (Fosbury, flop)
背浪式跳高

10 high jumper
跳高选手

11 body rotation (rotation on the body's longitudinal and latitudinal axes)
转体（沿身体纵横轴旋转）

12 shoulder landing
肩落式

13 upright
立柱

14 bar (crossbar)
横杆

15 Eastern roll
东方式（剪式）跳高

16 Western roll
西方式（滚式）跳高

17 roll
滚式跳高

18 rotation
滚式过杆

19 landing
落地

20 height scale
高度标尺

21 Eastern cut-off
剪式过杆

22 scissors (scissor jump)
剪式跳高

23 straddle (straddle jump)
腹滚式跳高

24 turn
转身，旋转

25 vertical free leg
垂直摆腿起跳

26 take-off
起跳

27 free leg
摆腿

28-36 pole vault
撑杆跳

28 pole (vaulting pole)
杆（撑杆）

29 pole vaulter (vaulter) in the pull-up phase
处于引体（力）状态下的撑杆跳选手

30 swing
旋转

31 crossing the bar
越过横杆

32 high jump apparatus (high jump equipment)
跳高设备用具

33 upright
立柱

34 bar (crossbar)
横杆

35 box
（撑杆跳）插穴

36 landing area (landing pad)
落地区（落地垫）

37-41 long jump
跳远

37 take-off
起跳

38 take-off board
起跳板

39 landing area
落地区（沙坑）

40 hitch-kick
走步式跳远

41 hang
挺身

42-47 hammer throw
掷链球

42 hammer
链球

43 hammer head
链球球体

44 handle
链球钢链

45 grip
链球手柄

46 holding the grip
握住手柄

47 glove
手套

48 shot put
推铅球

49 shot (weight)
铅球

50 O'Brien technique
背向推铅球技术

51-53 javelin throw
掷标枪

51 grip with thumb and index finger
以拇指与食指握枪

52 grip with thumb and middle finger
以拇指与中指握枪

53 horseshoe grip
马蹄式握法

54 binding
线把

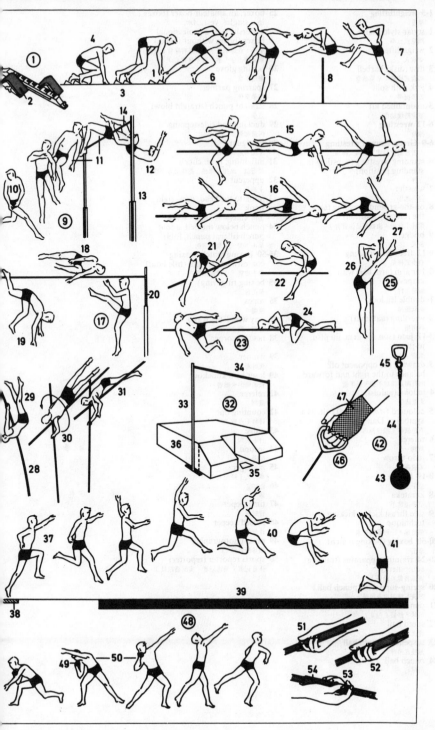

1-5 weightlifting
举重

1 squat-style snatch
蹲踞式抓举

2 weightlifter
举重人

3 disc (disk) barbell
圆盘式杠铃（举重圆盘）

4 jerk with split
箭步挺举

5 maintained lift
举重持续动作

6-12 wrestling
摔角

6-9 Greco-Roman wrestling
（古希腊罗马式）古典式摔角

6 standing wrestling (wrestling in standing position)
立摔

7 wrestler
摔角选手

8 on-the-ground wrestling (here: the referee's position)
撑摔（此指：由裁判员位置看）

9 bridge
桥式

10-12 freestyle wrestling
自由式摔角

10 bar arm (arm bar) with grapevine
缠腿夹臂

11 double leg lock
夹双腿摔

12 wrestling mat (mat)
摔角垫

13-17 judo (sim.: ju-jitsu, jiu jitsu, ju-jutsu)
柔道

13 drawing the opponent off balance to the right and forward
向右前方拉对手使失去平衡

14 judoka (judoist)
柔道选手

15 coloured (Am. colored) belt, as a symbol of Dan grade
有色腰带，段位标志

16 referee
裁判

17 judo throw
柔道摔

18-19 karate
空手道

18 karateka
空手道选手

19 side thrust kick, a kicking technique
侧蹬踢，一种踢腿技术

20-50 boxing (boxing match)
拳击

20-24 training apparatus (training equipment)
训练装置（设备）

20 spring-supported punch ball
弹簧（练习用）吊球

21 punch bag (Am. punching bag)
吊球，沙袋（包）

22 speed ball
速度球

23 suspended punch ball
悬挂式吊球

24 punch ball
吊球

25 boxer, an amateur boxer (boxes in a singlet, vest, Am. undershirt) or a professional boxer (boxes without singlet)
拳手，业馀拳击手（拳击时穿背心）或职业拳击手（拳击时不穿背心）

26 boxing glove
拳击手套

27 sparring partner
练拳拳伴

28 straight punch (straight blow)
直拳

29 ducking and sidestepping
闪避和侧步

30 headguard
（练习用）护盔

31 infighting; here: clinch
接近战，此指：揪扭，抱住对方手臂

32 uppercut
上钩拳

33 hook to the head; here: right hook
击向头部的钩拳，此指：右钩拳

34 punch below the belt, a foul punch (illegal punch, foul)
拳击下身，犯规的击法

35-50 boxing match (boxing contest), a title fight (title bout)
拳击比赛，一种锦标赛

35 boxing ring (ring)
拳击台

36 ropes
围绳

37 stay wire (stay rope)
支索（绳）

38 neutral corner
中立角

39 winner
优胜者

40 loser by a knockout
被击倒的失败者

41 referee
裁判

42 counting out
计秒（点数）

43 judge
台下裁判

44 second
助手

45 manager
举办人（经纪人）

46 gong
锣

47 timekeeper
计时员

48 record keeper
计分员

49 press photographer
报导摄影师

50 sports reporter (reporter)
体育记者（采访记者，实况播报员）

1-57 mountaineering
(mountain climbing, Alpinism)
登山运动

1 hut (Alpine Club hut, mountain
hut, base)
小屋（登山木屋，山地小屋，基地）

2-13 climbing (rock climbing)
'rock climbing technique'
攀登（岩石攀登）〔岩石攀登技术〕

2 rock face (rock wall)
岩壁

3 fissure (vertical, horizontal, or
diagonal fissure)
隙缝（垂直，水平或斜行缝隙）

4 ledge (rock ledge, grass ledge,
scree ledge, snow ledge, ice
ledge)
岩架（岩架，草岩架，碎石岩架，雪岩
架，冰岩架）

5 mountaineer (climber, mountain
climber, Alpinist)
登山者

6 anorak (high-altitude anorak,
snowshirt, padded jacket)
附头巾的御寒外套（高山防风衣，雪
衣，棉夹克）

7 breeches (climbing breeches)
登山裤

8 chimney
直立裂口

9 belay (spike, rock spike)
绳索套（固定）於突起岩石上（岩石
尖）

10 belay
保护绳

11 rope sling (sling)
后方保护绳

12 rope
绳

13 spur
登山用鞋底钉

14-21 snow and ice climbing 'snow
and ice climbing technique'
冰雪攀登〔冰雪攀登技术〕

14 ice slope (firn slope)
冰坡

15 snow and ice climber
冰雪攀登者

16 ice axe (*Am.* ax)
冰斧，冰镐

17 step (ice step)
台阶（冰台阶）

18 snow goggles
护目镜

19 hood (anorak hood)
兜帽（防风外套兜帽）

20 cornice (snow cornice)
雪簷

21 ridge (ice ridge)
山脊（冰脊）

22-27 rope (roped party)
结绳（结绳行进）

22 glacier
冰川

23 crevasse
裂隙，冰隙

24 snow bridge
雪桥

25 leader
响导，领路人

26 second man (belayer)
第二人（保护者）

27 third man (non-belayer)
第三人（非保护者）

28-30 roping down (abseiling,
rapelling)
绕绳下降

28 abseil sling
绕绳下降的后方保护绳

29 sling seat
后方保护绳座

30 Dùlfer seat
杜尔富座

**31-37 mountaineering
equipment** (climbing equipment,
snow and ice climbing
equipment)
登山装备

31 ice axe (*Am.* ax)
冰斧

32 wrist sling
腕带

33 pick
镐尖

34 adze (*Am.* adz)
手斧（铲头）

35 karabiner hole
铁锁孔

36 short-shafted ice axe (*Am.* ax)
短柄冰斧

37 hammer axe (*Am.* ax)
锤斧

38 general-purpose piton
多用途岩钉

39 abseil piton (ringed piton)
绕绳下降岩钉（带环岩钉）

40 ice piton (semi-tubular screw ice
piton, corkscrew piton)
冰岩钉（半管状螺旋岩钉，螺旋形岩
钉）

41 drive-in ice piton
打入式冰岩钉

42 mountaineering boot
登山鞋

43 corrugated sole
波形鞋底

44 climbing boot
攀登鞋

45 roughened stiff rubber upper
粗硬橡皮鞋帮

46 karabiner
铁锁

47 screwgate
螺旋保险栓

48 crampons (lightweight
crampons, twelve-point
crampons, ten-points crampons)
攀登用鞋底钉（轻型鞋底钉，十二齿鞋
底钉，十齿鞋底钉）

49 front points
前齿

50 point guards
鞋底钉护套

51 crampon strap
鞋底钉缚带

52 crampon cable fastener
鞋底钉绳钩扣

53 safety helmet (protective helmet)
安全头盔

54 helmet lamp
头盔灯

55 snow gaiters
雪地鞋罩

56 climbing harness
登山背带

57 sit harness
坐式背带

1-72 skiing
滑雪

1 compact ski
一般雪屐（滑雪板）

2 safety binding (release binding)
安全固定装置

3 strap
带子

4 steel edge
金属刃

5 ski stick (ski pole)
雪杖

6 grip
握柄

7 loop
环

8 basket
雪杖的撑圆

9 ladies' one-piece ski suit
女式连身式滑雪服

10 skiing cap (ski cap)
滑雪帽

11 skiing goggles
滑雪用护目镜

12 cemented sole skiing boot
胶底滑雪鞋

13 crash helmet
护盔

14-30 cross-country equipment
越野赛装备

14 cross-country ski
（距离竞技）越野滑雪

15 cross-country rat trap binding
雪屐鼠夹式固定装置

16 cross-country boot
越野滑雪靴

17 cross-country gear
越野滑雪服

18 peaked cap
遮簷帽，鸭嘴帽

19 sunglasses
太阳眼镜

20 cross-country poles made of bamboo
竹制的越野滑雪雪杖

21-24 ski-waxing equipment
滑雪涂蜡用具（器材）

21 ski wax
雪蜡

22 waxing iron (blowlamp, blowtorch)
涂蜡器（喷灯）

23 waxing cork
涂蜡栓

24 wax scraper
刮蜡器

25 downhill racing pole
下坡赛所用的雪杖

26 herringbone, for climbing a slope
人字形步登坡（分腿滑行）

27 sidestep, for climbing a slope
侧步登坡

28 ski bag
滑雪袋

29 slalom
弯道滑雪比赛

30 gate pole
旗门杆

31 racing suit
比赛服

32 downhill racing
下坡赛

33 [egg] position, the ideal downhill racing position
蛋形姿势，最理想的下坡赛姿

34 downhill ski
下坡用雪屐

35 ski jumping
飞跳姿势

36 lean forward
前倾姿势

37 number
号码

38 ski jumping ski
飞跳用雪屐

39 grooves (3 to 5 grooves)
底槽（3 至 5 条底槽）

40 cable binding
绳索固定装置

41 ski jumping boots
飞跳滑雪鞋

42 cross-country
越野滑雪（速度滑雪）

43 cross-country stretch-suit
越野滑雪弹力服

44 course
滑道

45 course-marking flag
滑道标识旗

46 layers of a modern ski
现代雪屐（滑雪板）的层次

47 special core
特殊心板

48 laminates
积层薄板

49 stabilizing layer (stabilizer)
安定层（安定器）

50 steel edge
钢板边

51 aluminium (*Am.* aluminum) upper edge
铝质上板边

52 synthetic bottom (artificial bottom)
合成底

53 safety jet
安全口

54-56 parts of the binding
固定装置的部件

54 automatic heel unit
足跟部自动装置

55 toe unit
足尖部装置

56 ski stop
雪屐停止（制动）扣

57-63 ski lift
上山吊椅

57 double chair lift
双座上山吊椅

58 safety bar with footrest
带踏脚板的安全杆

59 ski lift
滑行上山

60 track
滑道

61 hook
挂钩

62 automatic cable pulley
自动拉索滑轮

63 haulage cable
拉索

64 slalom
弯道滑雪比赛

65 open gate
开口门

66 closed vertical gate
闭口垂直门

67 open vertical gate
开口垂直门

68 transversal chicane
横断双滑道

69 hairpin
U 型急转滑道

70 elbow
急转

71 corridor
回转滑道

72 Allais chicane
蛇行滑道

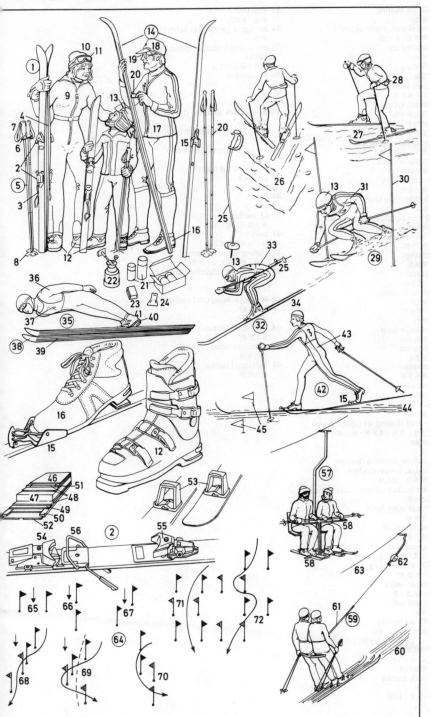

1-26 ice skating
溜冰

1 ice skater, a solo skater
溜冰者，单人溜

2 tracing leg
滑动腿

3 free leg
浮腿

4 pair skaters
双人溜冰者

5 death spiral
固定轴环绕

6 pivot
旋转轴

7 stag jump (stag leap)
鹿式（半劈腿跳）

8 jump-sit-spin
跳跃蹲踞旋转

9 upright spin
直立旋转

10 holding the foot
抱足

11-19 compulsory figures
固定图形

11 curve eight
"8"字形

12 change
变换形

13 three
"3"字形

14 double-three
双"3"字形

15 loop
环形

16 change-loop
变换环形

17 bracket
括弧形

18 counter
外钩手形

19 rocker
内钩手形

20-25 ice skates
溜冰鞋

20 speed skating set (speed skate)
速度（竞速）溜冰鞋，冰刀溜冰鞋

21 edge
刃

22 hollow grinding (hollow ridge, concave ridge)
凹形脊，空心脊

23 ice hockey set (ice hockey skate)
冰球鞋

24 ice skating boot
溜冰靴

25 skate guard
冰刀套

26 speed skater
速度（竞速）溜冰者

27-28 skate sailing
风帆溜冰

27 skate sailor
风帆溜冰者

28 hand sail
手帆

29-37 ice hockey
冰球（冰上曲棍球）

29 ice hockey player
冰球球员

30 ice hockey stick
冰球球杆

31 stick handle
杆柄

32 stick blade
杆刃

33 shin pad
护腿，护具

34 headgear (protective helmet)
护盔

35 puck, a vulcanized rubber disc (disk)
冰球（硬橡胶圆板）

36 goalkeeper
守门员

37 goal
球门

38-40 ice-stick shooting (Bavarian curling)
冰上击柱运动（巴伐利亚冰上溜石运动）

38 ice-stick shooter (Bavarian curler)
冰上击柱者（冰上溜石者）

39 ice stick
冰柱

40 block
石块

41-43 curling
冰上溜石（冰上掷石）

41 curler
冰上溜石者（掷石者）

42 curling stone (granite)
（溜）掷石的石块（花岗岩）

43 curling brush (curling broom, besom)
（掷）溜石笤

44-46 ice yachting (iceboating, ice sailing)
冰帆运动

44 ice yacht (iceboat)
冰上帆船

45 steering runner
方向滑橇

46 outrigged runner
舷外滑橇

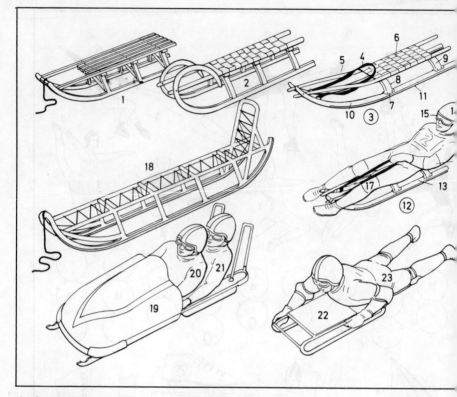

1 toboggan (sledge, *Am.* sled)
平底雪橇（雪橇）
2 toboggan (sledge, *Am.* sled) with
seat of plaid straps
具方格织带座位的平底雪橇
3 junior luge toboggan (junior
luge, junior toboggan)
儿童（小型）雪橇
4 rein
雪橇绳
5 bar (strut)
杆
6 seat
座位
7 bracket
托架
8 front prop
前支柱
9 rear prop
后支柱
10 movable runner
可动滑橇
11 metal face
金属面
12 luge tobogganer
小型滑雪橇者
13 luge toboggan (luge, toboggan)
小型雪橇
14 crash helmet
护盔
15 goggles
护目镜
16 elbow pad
护肘

17 knee pad
护膝
18 Nansen sledge, a polar sledge
南森雪橇，一种极地雪橇
19-21 bobsleigh (bobsledding)
连橇
19 bobsleigh (bobsled), a two-man
bobsleigh (a boblet)
连橇，大雪橇（双人用雪橇）
20 steersman
雪橇驾驶人
21 brakeman
连橇（大雪橇）制动者
22-24 skeleton tobogganing (Cresta
tobogganing)
骨架雪橇滑雪运动
22 skeleton (skeleton toboggan)
骨架雪橇
23 skeleton rider
骨架雪橇滑雪者
24 rake, for braking and steering
用于制动或控制方向的耙齿

anche (snow avalanche,
snowslide); *kinds:* wind
anche, ground avalanche
：种类：风崩，土崩
anche wall, a deflecting wall
erting wall); *sim.:* avalanche
ge
墙，偏向墙（使雪崩改变方向的
；类似：雪崩楔形墙
anche gallery
走廊
wfall

wdrift

w fence
棚栏
anche forest 'planted as
tection against avalanches'
林〔为防止雪崩而种植的〕
et-cleaning lorry (street
ner)
车
w plough (*Am.* snowplow)
chment
附件
w chain (skid chain, tyre
in, *Am.* tire chain)
（防滑链）
ator bonnet (*Am.* radiator
d)
器盖

12 radiator shutter and shutter
opening (louvre shutter)
散热器护板和护板孔
13 snowman
雪人
14 snowball fight
打雪仗
15 snowball
雪球
16 ski bob
骑式雪橇
17 slide
溜冰
18 boy, sliding
溜冰的男孩
19 icy surface (icy ground)
结冰的地面
20 snow-covered roof
雪复盖的屋顶
21 icicle
冰柱
22 man clearing snow
清扫积雪者
23 snow push (snow shovel)
雪铲
24 heap of snow
雪堆
25 horse-drawn sleigh (horse sleigh)
马拉雪橇
26 sleigh bells (bells, set of bells)
雪橇铃
27 foot muff (*Am.* foot bag)
脚套筒

28 earmuff
耳盖（护耳）
29 handsledge (tread sledge); *sim.:*
push sledge
椅式雪橇；类似：手推雪橇
30 slush
雪水，烂泥

1-13 skittles
九柱游戏
1-11 skittle frame
小柱位置
1 front pin (front)
前柱（第一柱）
2 left front second pin (left front second)
左前第二柱
3 running three 'left'
〔左〕前柱间隙
4 right front second pin (right front second)
右前第二柱
5 running three 'right'
〔右〕前柱间隙
6 left corner pin (left corner), a corner (copper)
左角柱（警察，卒）
7 landlord
中央柱（王，主）
8 right corner pin (right corner), a corner (copper)
右角柱（警察，卒）
9 back left second pin (back left second)
左后第二柱
10 back right second pin (back right second)
右后第二柱
11 back pin (back)
后柱
12 pin
小柱
13 landlord
中央柱（王，主）
14-20 tenpin bowling
保龄球（十柱）
14 frame
保龄球各柱位置
15 bowling ball (ball with finger holes)
具指孔的保龄球
16 finger hole
指孔
17-20 deliveries
投球法
17 straight ball
直球
18 hook ball (hook)
弯球
19 curve
曲线球
20 back-up ball (back-up)
歪球
21 boules; sim.: Italian game of boccie, green bowls (bowls)
滚木球：类似意大利滚木球
22 boules player
玩滚木球者
23 jack (target jack)
靶球
24 grooved boule
刻有槽线的木球
25 group of players
一群玩滚木球者
26 rifle shooting
步枪射击
27-29 shooting position
射击姿势
27 standing position
立姿
28 kneeling position
跪姿
29 prone position
卧姿

30-33 targets
靶
30 target for 50 m events (50 m target)
50 公尺赛靶
31 circle
环
32 target for 100 m events (100 m target)
100 公尺赛靶
33 bobbing target (turning target, running-boar target)
活动靶（转动靶，跑猪靶）
34-39 ammunition
弹药
34 air rifle cartridge
空气枪子弹
35 rimfire cartridge for zimmerstutzen (indoor target rifle), a smallbore German single-shot rifle
室内短管步枪（室内靶步枪）用的底弹
发火子弹，一种小口径单发步枪用子弹
36 case head
弹壳
37 caseless round
弹头
38 .22 long rifle cartridge
.22 长步枪弹
39 .222 Remington cartridge
.222 雷明顿子弹
40-49 sporting rifles
运动步枪
40 air rifle
空气枪
41 optical sight
（光学）瞄准器
42 front sight (foresight)
准星
43 smallbore standard rifle
标准小口径步枪
44 international smallbore free rifle
国际小口径自动步枪
45 palm rest for standing position
立姿托盘
46 butt plate with hook
带钩的枪托底板
47 butt with thumb hole
有姆指孔的枪托底板
48 smallbore rifle for bobbing target (turning target)
活动靶射击用的小口径步枪
49 telescopic sight (riflescope, telescope sight)
瞄准器（步枪瞄准器，望远镜瞄准器）
50 optical ring sight
环形瞄准器
51 optical ring and bead sight
环形瞄准器和准星
52-66 archery (target archery)
射箭运动
52 shot
射箭
53 archer
箭手
54 competition bow
比赛用的弓
55 riser
弓臂
56 point-of-aim mark
瞄准记号
57 grip (handle)
弓把
58 stabilizer
安定（防震）器
59 bow string (string)
弓弦

60 arrow
箭
61 pile (point) of the arrow
箭头
62 fletching
箭杆上所粘的羽毛
63 nock
箭扣
64 shaft
箭杆
65 cresting
箭杆上涂染的颜色
66 target
靶
67 Basque game of pelota (jai
巴斯克回力球游戏
68 pelota player
回力球运动者
69 wicker basket (cesta)
柳条球拍
70-78 skeet (skeet shooting), a
of clay pigeon shooting
飞靶射击，一种泥鸽射击运动
70 skeet over-and-under shot
飞靶射击用的双管类枪
71 muzzle with skeet choke
口径收敛的猎枪枪口
72 ready position on call
预备姿势
73 firing position
射击姿势
74 shooting range
靶场
75 high house
高抛靶房
76 low house
低抛靶房
77 target's path
靶的飞行路线
78 shooting station (shooting
射击位置
79 aero wheel
滚轮
80 handle
把手
81 footrest
脚凳
82 go-karting (karting)
小型车赛
83 go-kart (kart)
小型赛车
84 number plate (number)
号码牌
85 pedals
踏板
86 pneumatic tyre (Am. tire)
气胎，车胎
87 petrol tank (Am. gasoline ta
油箱
88 frame
车架
89 steering wheel
方向盘
90 bucket seat
单人圆背摺椅
91 protective bulkhead
防护柜
92 two-stroke engine
二冲程发动机（引擎）
93 silencer (Am. muffler)
消音器，灭音器

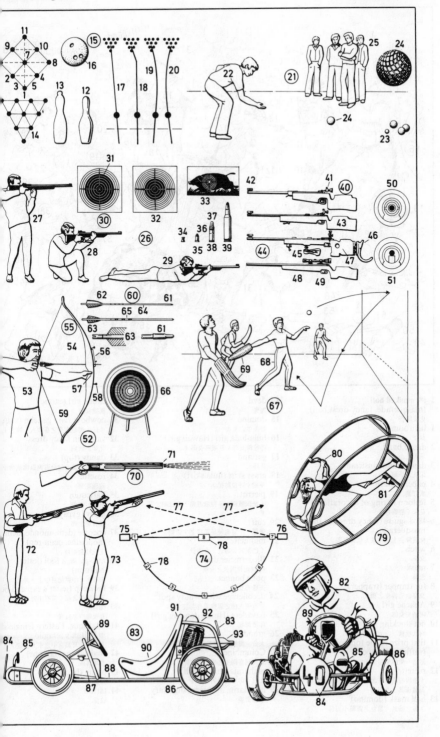

1-48 masked ball
(masquerade, fancy-dress ball)
化装舞会
1 ballroom
舞厅
2 dance band
乐队
3 dance band musician
乐队之乐师
4 paper lantern
纸灯笼
5 festoon (string of decorations)
花采（装饰带）
6-48 disguise (fancy dress) at the masquerade
化装舞会上之化装（化装服装）
6 witch
女巫
7 mask
面具
8 fur trapper (trapper)
身穿软毛兽皮之猎人
9 Apache girl
阿帕契女郎
10 net stocking
网状丝袜
11 first prize in the tombola (raffle), a hamper
置第一奖的奖券篮
12 pierette
（法国哑剧中）著白裤及大扣白色短衣
与戴面具之女丑角
13 half mask (domino)
半截之面具，黑色之露眼小面具

14 devil
魔鬼
15 domino
带头巾之上衣
16 hula-hula girl (Hawaii girl)
呼拉舞女郎（夏威夷女郎）
17 garland
花环
18 grass skirt (hula skirt)
草裙（呼拉裙）
19 pierrot
（法国哑剧中）白衣丑角，走江湖之丑角
20 ruff
襞襟，（宽而硬呈轮状之）皱领
21 midinette
（巴黎时装店之）女店员
22 Biedermeier dress
19世纪德国式之女服
23 poke bonnet
突缘的女帽
24 décolletage with beauty spot
饰有美人痣之露胸紧身女装
25 bayadére (Hindu dancing girl)
印度舞妓
26 grandee
大公、贵族
27 Columbine
意大利喜剧中之半假面女郎
28 maharaja (maharajah)
大君（印度君候的尊称）
29 mandarin, a Chinese dignitary
中国贵族

30 exotic girl (exotic)
异国女郎
31 cowboy; *sim.*: gaucho (vaqu
牛仔，类似南美之畜牧人（牧者）
32 vamp, in fancy dress
化装之妖妇
33 dandy (fop)
好打扮者著（过分讲究服饰或举止
34 rosette
玫瑰花饰
35 harlequin
丑角，谐角
36 gipsy (gypsy) girl
吉普赛女郎
37 cocotte (demi-monde, dem
mondaine, demi-rep)
上流社会娼妓
38 owl-glass, a fool (jester, buffoon)
小丑，（中世纪宫中之）弄臣
39 foolscap (jester's cap and b
丑角所带之帽（带有小铃）
40 rattle
有嘎嘎声之玩具
41 odalisque, Eastern female s
in Sultan's seraglio
女奴（土耳其宫中之东方女奴）
42 chalwar (pantaloons)
土耳其裤
43 pirate (buccaneer)
海盗
44 tattoo
纹身

aper hat
帽

se nose
鼻

apper (rattle)
版，响板（有嘎嘎声之玩具）

apstick
板

fireworks
火类

rcussion cap
管

acker
竹

nger
炮

mping jack
娃娃（玩具）

nnon cracker (maroon,
arroon)
鞭炮

cket
箭炮或冲天炮

aper ball
球

ck-in-the-box
偶匣

carnival procession
欢节（嘉年华会）游行

rnival float (carnival truck)
年华会游行彩车

ing Carnival
年华会国王

59 bauble (fool's sceptre, *Am.*
scepter)
丑角棒

60 fool's badge
丑角所戴之徽章

61 Queen Carnival
嘉年华会皇后

62 confetti
五彩碎纸

63 giant
巨人像（讽刺性人物像）

64 beauty queen
美女皇后

65 fairy-tale figure
神话人物

66 paper streamer
彩色纸带

67 majorette
乐队队长

68 king's guard
国王之护卫

69 buffoon, a clown
小丑

70 lansquenet's drum
16-17 世纪时，德国佣兵所用之军鼓

1-63 travelling (*Am.* traveling) circus
流动马戏团

1 circus tent (big top), a four-pole tent
马戏用帐篷（大顶篷），四柱支撑之大帐篷

2 tent pole
帐柱

3 spotlight
聚光灯

4 lighting technician
灯光技师

5 trapeze platform
（空中飞人用之）秋千台

6 trapeze
秋千吊架

7 trapeze artist
空中飞人

8 rope ladder
绳梯

9 bandstand
乐队台

10 circus band
马戏团乐队

11 ring entrance (arena entrance)
圆型场地入口处（竞技场入口处）

12 wings
舞台两侧

13 tent prop (prop)
帐篷支柱

14 safety net
安全网

15 seats for the spectators
观众席

16 circus box
马戏团包厢

17 circus manager
马戏团经理

18 agent
经纪人

19 entrance and exit
入口与出口

20 steps
台阶

21 ring (arena)
马戏表演场

22 ring fence
表演场之栅栏

23 musical clown (clown)
配乐小丑

24 clown
小丑

25 comic turn (clown act), a circus act
喜戏（滑稽）节目（丑角表演），一种马戏团式之表演

26 circus riders (bareback riders)
马戏团骑手（无鞍骑手）

27 ring attendant, a circus attendant
马戏表演场之工作人员，马戏团服务员

28 pyramid
叠罗汉

29 support
叠罗汉表演之底层支撑者

30-31 performance by liberty ho[rses]
驯马表演

30 circus horse, performing the levade (pesade)
表演后腿直立（前腿上提）的马戏匹

31 ringmaster
驯兽师，表演指挥者

32 vaulter
跳跃上马之演员

33 emergency exit
安全门，太平门

34 caravan (circus caravan, *Am.* trailer)
马戏团使用之大篷车

35 springboard acrobat (springboard artist)
跳板特技表演者

36 springboard
踏板

37 knife thrower
飞刀手

38 circus marksman
射手

39 assistant
助手

40 tightrope dancer
走钢丝（绳索）演员

41 tightrope
绳索，钢丝

42 balancing pole
平衡杆

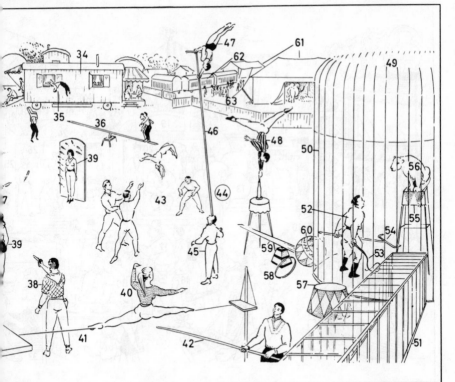

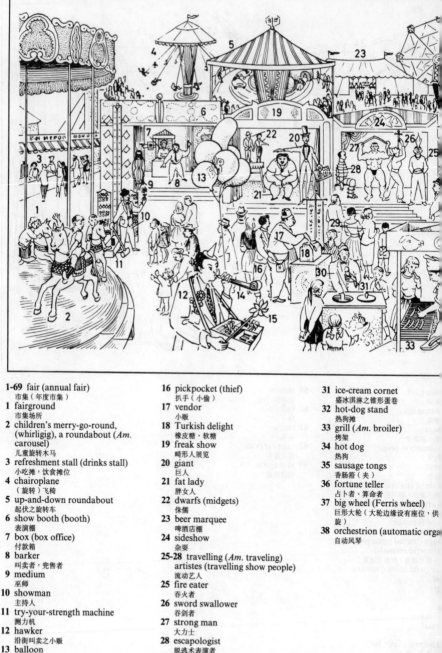

1-69 fair (annual fair)
市集（年度市集）
1 fairground
市集场所
2 children's merry-go-round,
(whirligig), a roundabout (*Am.*
carousel)
儿童旋转木马
3 refreshment stall (drinks stall)
小吃摊，饮食摊位
4 chairoplane
（旋转）飞椅
5 up-and-down roundabout
起伏之旋转车
6 show booth (booth)
表演棚
7 box (box office)
付款箱
8 barker
叫卖者，兜售者
9 medium
巫师
10 showman
主持人
11 try-your-strength machine
测力机
12 hawker
沿街叫卖之小贩
13 balloon
汽球
14 paper serpent
纸蛇
15 windmill
风车

16 pickpocket (thief)
扒手（小偷）
17 vendor
小贩
18 Turkish delight
橡皮糖、软糖
19 freak show
畸形人展览
20 giant
巨人
21 fat lady
胖女人
22 dwarfs (midgets)
侏儒
23 beer marquee
啤酒店棚
24 sideshow
杂耍
25-28 travelling (*Am.* traveling)
artistes (travelling show people)
流动艺人
25 fire eater
吞火者
26 sword swallower
吞剑者
27 strong man
大力士
28 escapologist
脱逃术表演者
29 spectators
观众
30 ice-cream vendor (ice-cream
man)
卖冰淇淋的小贩

31 ice-cream cornet
盛冰淇淋之锥形蛋卷
32 hot-dog stand
热狗摊
33 grill (*Am.* broiler)
烤架
34 hot dog
热狗
35 sausage tongs
香肠箝（夹）
36 fortune teller
占卜者、算命者
37 big wheel (Ferris wheel)
巨形大轮（大轮边缘设有座位，供
旋）
38 orchestrion (automatic organ
自动风琴

nic railway (switchback)
场中，模拟之游览小火车

oggan slide (chute)
雪橇之滑行场（滑行道）

ing boats
彩秋千

ing boat, turning full circle
圆圈之船形秋千

l circle
圆圈

tery booth (tombola booth)
票棚，摇奖棚

eel of fortune
运轮（轮盘赌具）

vil's wheel (typhoon wheel)
风转轮（庵风转轮）

rowing ring (quoit)
环游戏

zes
品

ndwich man on stilts
高跷、身前后挂广告牌的人

ndwich board (placard)
告牌

arette seller, an itinerant
der (a hawker)
香烟者，流动小贩

y
盘

it stall
果摊

ll-of-death rider
车驾驶员

55 hall of mirrors
趣镜室，哈哈镜室

56 concave mirror
凹面镜

57 convex mirror
凸面镜

58 shooting gallery
射击室

59 hippodrome
马戏场，竞技场

60 junk stalls (second-hand stalls)
旧货摊

61 first aid tent (first aid post)
急救站

62 dodgems (bumper cars)
在游乐场中供游客坐的小型电动车，一
面撞别人，一面躲闪别人的游戏（碰碰
车游戏）

63 dodgem car (bumper car)
碰碰车

64-66 pottery stand
陶器摊

64 barker
叫卖者

65 market woman
女商人

66 pottery
陶器

67 visitors to the fair
市集游客

68 waxworks
蜡制品陈列馆

69 wax figure
蜡像

1 treadle sewing machine
脚踏缝纫机
2 flower vase
花瓶
3 wall mirror
壁镜
4 cylindrical stove
圆筒形火炉
5 stovepipe
火炉烟囱
6 stovepipe elbow
烟囱弯肘（头）
7 stove door
炉门
8 stove screen
火炉围屏
9 coal scuttle
煤斗（装煤之容器）
10 firewood basket
柴篮（装柴火的篓子）
11 doll
洋娃娃
12 teddy bear
玩具熊
13 barrel organ
手摇风琴
14 orchestrion
自动风琴
15 metal disc (disk)
金属圆盘
16 radio (radio set, *joc.:* [steam radio]), a superheterodyne (superhet)
收音机，超外差式接收机

17 baffle board
隔音板
18 'magic eye', a tuning indicator valve
电眼，一种调谐指示管
19 loudspeaker aperture
喇叭孔
20 station selector buttons (station preset buttons)
电台选择按钮（电台预置按钮）
21 tuning knob
调谐旋钮
22 frequency bands
波段（刻度盘）
23 crystal detector (crystal set)
晶体检波器（晶体收音机）
24 headphones (headset)
耳机
25 folding camera
折叠式照相机
26 bellows
蛇腹
27 hinged cover
铰盖
28 spring extension
弹簧
29 salesman
店员
30 box camera
盒式照相机
31 gramophone
留声机
32 record (gramophone record)
唱片（留声机唱片）

33 needle head with gramophone needle
装有唱针之唱头
34 horn
留声机之喇叭
35 gramophone box
留声机箱
36 record rack
唱片架
37 portable tape recorder
手提式磁带录音机
38 flashgun
闪光枪
39 flash bulb
闪光灯泡
40-41 electronic flash (electronic flashgun)
电子闪光灯，电子闪光枪
40 flash head
闪光灯头
41 accumulator
蓄电池
42 slide projector
幻灯片放映机
43 slide holder
幻灯片托架
44 lamphouse
灯箱
45 candlestick
烛台
46 scallop shell
扇形贝壳

lery
具（刀、叉、匙等）
dia (cur...
)lis, cup, ...
la tage, ci...
盘
uvenir plate
念盘
ing rack for photographic
ates
化板用之乾燥台
otographic plate
用板
ayed-action release
）（时）放松器（装置）（自拍快门
）
soldiers (*sim.: lead soldiers*)
制士兵（类似於铅制士兵）
er mug (stein)
酒杯（壶）
gle
角（喇叭）
cond-hand books
书
andfather clock
型挂钟（有钟摆的）
ck case
壳
ndulum
摆
ne weight
锤
king weight
计时钟锤
cking chair
椅
lor suit
手服

63 sailor's hat
　　水手帽
64 washing set
　　洗脸用具
65 washing basin
　　洗脸盆
66 water jug
　　水罐
67 washstand
　　脸盆架
68 dolly
　　（洗衣用）搅拌棒，捣衣杵
69 washtub
　　洗衣盆
70 washboard
　　洗衣板（洗衣搓板）
71 humming top
　　起泡陀螺
72 slate
　　石板（瓦）
73 pencil box
　　铅笔盒
74 adding machine
　　计算机（加算机）
75 paper roll
　　纸卷
76 number keys
　　数字键
77 abacus
　　算盘
78 inkwell, with lid
　　带盖的墨水池
79 typewriter
　　打字机

80 [hand-operated] calculating
　　machine (calculator)
　　（手摇）计算机
81 operating handle
　　手摇杆
82 result register (product register)
　　结果记录器
83 rotary counting mechanism
　　(rotary counter)
　　旋转计数器（回转计算装置）
84 kitchen scales
　　厨房用的天平
85 waist slip (underskirt)
　　衬裙
86 wooden handcart
　　木制手车
87 wall clock
　　挂钟，壁钟
88 bed warmer
　　床用取暖器
89 milk churn
　　牛乳桶（牛乳搅拌器）

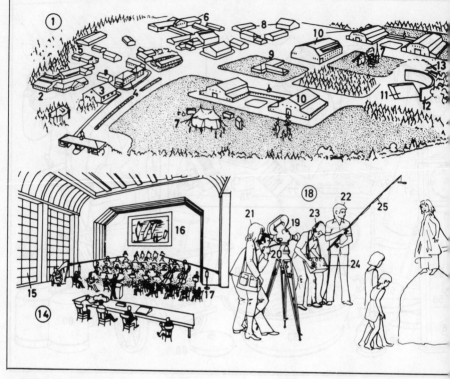

1-13 film studios (studio
complex, *Am.* movie studios)
电影制片厂
1 lot (studio lot)
电影摄影场
2 processing laboratories (film
laboratories, motion picture
laboratories)
显影（冲洗）室
3 cutting rooms
剪辑（接）室
4 administration building (office
building, offices)
行政大楼
5 film (motion picture) storage
vault (film library, motion
picture library)
影片（电影）贮藏库，影片库
6 workshop
片场
7 film set (*Am.* movie set)
布景
8 power house
发电房（厂）
9 technical and research
laboratories
技术研究（实验）室
10 groups of stages
摄影棚群（各种摄影棚）
11 concrete tank for marine
sequences
特殊摄影（水中摄影）用之水泥槽
12 cyclorama
圆形风景画幕

13 hill
小丘
14-60 shooting (filming)
摄影
14 music recording studio (music
recording theatre, *Am.* theater)
（音乐）录音室
15 [acoustic] wall lining
（吸）隔音墙板
16 screen (projection screen)
银幕（放映幕）
17 film orchestra
影片管弦乐团
18 exterior shooting (outdoor
shooting, exterior filming,
outdoor filming)
室外摄影，外景摄影
19 camera with crystal-controlled
drive
晶体控制驱动之摄影机
20 cameraman
摄影师
21 assistant director
助理导演
22 boom operator (boom swinger)
麦克风吊杆操作人员
23 recording engineer (sound
recordist)
录音技师
24 portable sound recorder with
crystal-controlled drive
手提式晶体控制驱动之录音机
25 microphone boom
麦克风吊杆

26-60 shooting (filming) in the
studio (on the sound stage, o
the stage, in the filming hall)
摄影棚内之拍摄（录音棚，拍摄棚，
录影棚）
26 production manager
制片（制作人）
27 leading lady (film actress, filr
star, star)
女主角（女演员，电影明星）
28 leading man (film actor, film
star, star)
男主角（男演员，电影明星）
29 film extra (extra)
临时演员
30 arrangement of microphones
stereo and sound effects
录立体音响与音效用之麦克风配置
31 studio microphone
影棚麦克风
32 microphone cable
麦克风电线
33 side flats and background
背景及侧景屏
34 clapper boy
场记
35 clapper board (clapper) with
slates (boards) for the film tit
shot number (scene number),
and take number
写有片名，镜号（景号），和镜头号
拍板
36 make-up artist (hairstylist)
化妆师（发形设计师）

ghting electrician (studio
ectrician, lighting man, *Am.*
Ter)
光（技）师（摄影棚灯光师工头，组

fusing screen
光屏
ntinuity girl (script girl)
记
n director (director)
演
meraman (first cameraman)
师（第一摄影师）
nera operator, an assistant
meraman (camera assistant)
影助理（摄影助手）
designer (art director)
设计师（艺术指导）
ector of photography
影指导
nscript (script, shooting
ipt, *Am.* movie script)
影剧本（摄影剧本）
istant director
导演
ndproof film camera
undproof motion picture
mera), a wide screen camera
nemascope camera)
隔）音同时录音之摄影机，一种宽
之摄影机（新艺综合体摄影机）
ndproof housing
undproof cover, blimp)
音罩（装置）

49 **camera crane (dolly)**
摄影机之升降移动装置
50 **hydraulic stand**
油压式摄影机架
51 **mask (screen) for protection
from spill light (gobo, nigger)**
遮光板
52 **tripod spotlight (fill-in light,
filler light, fill light, filler)**
三脚架聚光灯
53 **spotlight catwalk**
聚光灯桥
54 **recording room**
录音室
55 **recording engineer (sound
recordist)**
录音（技）师
56 **mixing console (mixing desk)**
配音架，配音台
57 **sound assistant (assistant sound
engineer)**
录音助理
58 **magnetic sound recording
equipment (magnetic sound
recorder)**
磁性带录音设备（磁性带录音机）
59 **amplifier and special effects
equipment, e.g. for echo and
sound effects**
扩大器（机）与特殊效果装置，例如：
用於回声与音效
60 **sound recording camera (optical
sound recorder)**
同步录音摄影机（光学录音机）

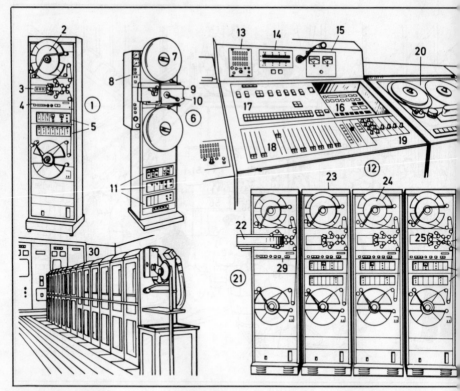

1-46 sound recording and re-recording (dubbing)
录音与混合录音（配音）

1 magnetic sound recording equipment (magnetic sound recorder)
磁性带录音设备（磁性带录音机）

2 magnetic film spool
磁性片盘

3 magnetic head support assembly
磁头组件

4 control panel
控制板（台）

5 magnetic sound recording and playback amplifier
磁性带录音与放音扩大器

6 optical sound recorder (sound recording camera, optical sound recording equipment)
光学录音机（同步录音摄影机，光学录音设备）

7 daylight film magazine
（影）软片盒

8 control and monitoring panel
监控板

9 eyepiece for visual control of optical sound recording
光学录音装置之视觉控制目镜

10 deck
盖板

11 recording amplifier and mains power unit
录音扩大器与电源

12 control desk (control console)
控制（桌）台

13 monitoring loudspeaker (control loudspeaker)
监听喇叭

14 recording level indicators
录音平衡指示器

15 monitoring instruments
监听仪器

16 jack panel
插座板

17 control panel
控制板

18 sliding control
滑动控制

19 equalizer
平衡器

20 magnetic sound deck
磁（性）带音响台

21 mixer for magnetic film
磁性软（影）片用之配音装置

22 film projector
影片放映机

23 recording and playback equipment
录音与放音设备

24 film reel (film spool)
片夹（片盘）

25 head support assembly for the recording head, playback head, and erasing head (erase head)
录音头，放音头及消磁头之支座组件

26 film transport mechanism
放片机器（影片输送装置）

27 synchronizing filter
（声音画面）同步滤波器

28 magnetic sound amplifier
磁性扩大器

29 control panel
控制板

30 film-processing machines (film developing machines) in the processing laboratory (film laboratory, motion picture laboratory)
影片显（冲洗）像（实验）室中之影显（冲洗）像机

o chamber
室

o chamber loudspeaker
喇叭

o chamber microphone
室麦克风

sound mixing (sound
bbing, mixing of several
nd tracks)
配音，数条声带之混录）

xing room (dubbing room)
室

xing console (mixing desk) for
no or stereo sound
立体声之配音混录台

bbing mixers (recording
gineers, sound recordists)
bbing (mixing)
录人员）配音员（录音师）

synchronization (syncing,
bbing, post-synchronization,
st-syncing)
画）同步（后期同步录音）

bbing studio (dubbing
atre, *Am.* theater)
音室

bbing director
音导演

bbing speaker (dubbing
tress)
音员

om microphone
式麦克风

41 microphone cable
麦克风之电线

42-46 cutting (editing)
剪辑（接）

42 cutting table (editing table,
cutting bench)
剪辑台

43 film editor (cutter)
电影剪辑人员

44 film turntable, for picture and
sound tracks
影片画面与声带用之转盘

45 projection of the picture
影片放映

46 loudspeaker
喇叭

1-23 film projection (motion picture projection)
电影放映

1 cinema (picture house, *Am.* movie theater, movie house)
电影院

2 cinema box office (*Am.* movie theater box office)
电影院售票亭

3 cinema ticket (*Am.* movie theater ticket)
电影票

4 usherette
女引座员（女的座位导引员）

5 cinemagoers (filmgoers, cinema audience, *Am.* moviegoers, movie audience)
电影观众

6 safety lighting (emergency lighting)
太平门（出口）灯

7 emergency exit
太平门

8 stage
舞台

9 rows of seats (rows)
座位的排号

10 stage curtain (screen curtain)
舞台的布幕（银幕）

11 screen (projection screen)
银幕

12 projection room (projection booth)
放映室

13 lefthand projector
左侧放映机

14 righthand projector
右侧放映机

15 projection room window with projection window and observation port
其放映窗口与监视口之放映室窗户

16 reel drum (spool box)
片筒，片盒

17 house light dimmers (auditorium lighting control)
戏院调光器（观众席灯光控制）

18 rectifier, a selenium or mercury vapour rectifier for the projection lamps
放映灯用的一种硒或汞汽整流器

19 amplifier
扩大器

20 projectionist
放映师

21 rewind bench for rewinding the film
影片之倒片台

22 film cement (splicing cement)
影片接著剂

23 slide projector for advertisements
放广告之幻灯机

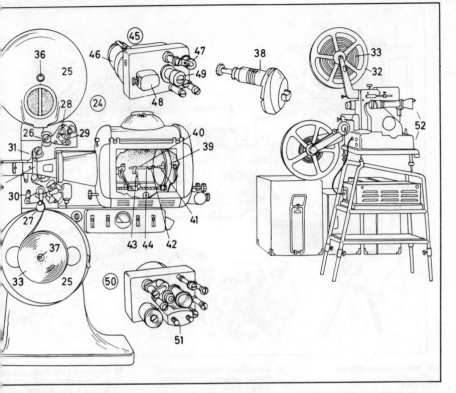

film projectors
影放映机

und projector (film projector,
ema projector, theatre
ojector, *Am.* movie projector)
电影放映机

projector mechanism
映机器

eproof reel drums (spool
xes) with circulating oil
oling system
循环油冷却装置之防火片盒

d sprocket (supply sprocket)
片齿轮

ke-up sprocket
片齿轮

agnetic head cluster
头组件

ide roller (guiding roller) with
aming control
面调整之导轮

op former) for smoothing out
e intermittent movement; *also:*
m break detector
影片间歇转动得以平滑进行之装置
示称：影片中断检测器）

m path
路（道）

m reel (film spool)
片盘

el of film
片卷轮

34 film gate (picture gate, projector
gate) with cooling fan
具冷却（风扇）装置之片门（放映机片
窗）

35 projection lens (projector lens)
放映机镜头

36 feed spindle
供片主轴

37 take-up spindle with friction
drive
磨擦转动之收片（卷片）主轴

38 maltese cross mechanism
(maltese cross movement,
Geneva movement)
十字间歇供（放）片装置

39-44 lamphouse
灯箱

39 mirror arc lamp, with aspherical
(non-spherical) concave mirror
and blowout magnet for
stabilizing the arc (*also:* high-
pressure xenon arc lamp)
反射弧光灯；稳定弧光用之非球面凹镜
和消磁装置（高压氙弧灯）

40 positive carbon (positive carbon
rod)
阳极碳棒

41 negative carbon (negative
carbon rod)
阴级碳棒

42 arc
弧光

43 carbon rod holder
碳棒夹

44 crater (carbon crater)
弧坑（碳棒发火部分），火口

45 optical sound unit [also designed
for multi-channel optical
stereophonic sound and for
push-pull optical sound tracks]
光学录音装置[为多声道光学立体声和推
挽声带用之设计]

46 sound optics
音声用光学装置

47 sound head
声头

48 exciter lamp in housing
带罩框之激磁灯

49 photocell in hollow drum
装纳空心圆筒之光电管

50 attachable four-track magnetic
sound unit (penthouse head,
magnetic sound head)
附加之四轨磁性录音装置（拾音磁头和
还音磁头）

51 four-track magnetic head
四轨磁头

52 narrow-gauge (*Am.* narrow-
gage) cinema projector for
mobile cinema
供流动电影院用之窄规电影放映机

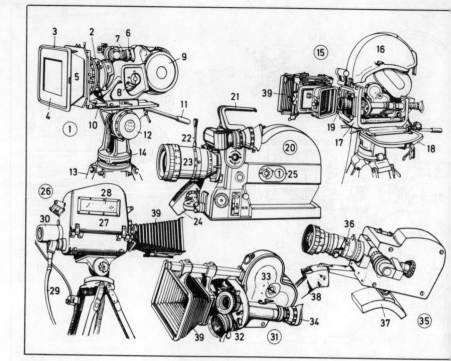

1-39 motion picture cameras
(film cameras)
电影摄影机

1 standard-gauge (*Am.* standard-gage) motion picture camera (standard-gauge, *Am.* standard-gage, 35 mm camera)
标准规格电影摄影机（35毫米）

2 lens (object lens, taking lens)
（透镜）镜头（物镜，摄影镜头）

3 lens hood (sunshade) with matte box
具毛玻璃箱之遮光罩

4 matte (mask)
遮片

5 lens hood barrel
遮光罩筒

6 viewfinder eyepiece
取景器目镜

7 eyepiece control ring
目镜控制圈

8 opening control for the segment disc (disk) shutter
扇形快门开度装置

9 magazine housing
软片盒

10 slide bar for the lens hood
镜头罩滑杆

11 control arm (control lever)
控制杆（操纵杆）

12 pan and tilt head
全景摄影之摇动旋钮

13 wooden tripod
木制三脚架

14 degree scale
刻度盘

15 soundproof (blimped) motion picture camera (film camera)
隔音电影摄影机

16-18 soundproof housing (blimp)
隔音罩

16 upper section of the soundproof housing
隔音罩之上部

17 lower section of the soundproof housing
隔音罩之下部

18 open sidewall of the soundproof housing
隔音罩之敞开侧壁

19 camera lens
摄影机镜头

20 lightweight professional motion picture camera
专业用轻型摄影机

21 grip (handgrip)
柄，把手（手柄）

22 zooming lever
变焦杆

23 zoom lens (variable focus lens, varifocal lens) with infinitely variable focus
具无限可变焦点之变焦镜头（可变焦点镜头）

24 handgrip with shutter release
快门开关手柄

25 camera door
摄影机门

26 sound camera (newsreel camera) for recording sound and picture
声画同步摄影机（新闻摄影机）

27 soundproof housing (blimp)
隔音罩

28 window for the frame counter and indicator scales
画面计算器与指示器刻度窗

29 pilot tone cable (sync pulse cable)
导（频）音电缆（同步脉电缆）

30 pilot tone generator (signal generator, pulse generator)
导（频）音发生器（信号发生器，脉冲发生器）

31 professional narrow-gauge (narrow-gage) motion picture camera, a 16 mm camera
专业窄规（窄影片）电影摄影机（16毫米）

32 lens turret (turret head)
镜头转座

33 housing lock
机箱锁

34 eyecup
目镜罩

35 high-speed camera, a special narrow-gauge (*Am.* narrow-gage) camera
高速摄影机，一种特殊窄规的摄影机

36 zooming lever
变焦杆

37 rifle grip
肩托架

38 handgrip with shutter release
快门开关手柄

39 lens hood bellows
镜头遮光罩蛇腹

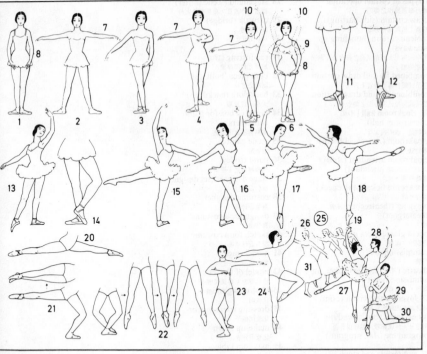

1–5 the five positions (ballet positions)
五种姿势（芭蕾舞姿势）
1 first position
第一种姿势
2 second position
第二种姿势
3 third position
第三种姿势
4 fourth position [open]
第四种姿势（展开式）
fourth position [crossed; extended fifth position]
第四种姿势（交叉式，伸展的第五种姿势）
5 fifth position
第五种姿势
6–12 ports de bras (arm positions)
臂姿势
6 port de bras á coté
侧臂姿势
7 port de bras en bas
臂朝下姿势
8 port de bras en avant
臂朝前姿势
9 port de bras en haut
臂在上姿势
10 dégagé á la quatriéme devant
向前第四种姿势
dégagé á la quatriéme derrière
向后第四种姿势
13 tacé
侧身面向观众之姿势
14 sur le cou-de-pied
动作脚放於支撑脚之舞姿
15 écarté
侧身向旁抬舞之舞姿

16 croisé
侧身面向观众之交叉舞姿
17 attitude
一脚向后举（半弯曲）之姿式
18 arabesque
一脚向后伸直，一脚以脚尖点地，一手向前，一手向后伸之姿势
19 á pointe (on full point)
脚尖点地之舞姿（全脚尖）
20 splits
两腿分开成一直线之舞姿，劈叉
21 cabriole (capriole)
跳跃中以脚碰脚之姿势
22 entrechat (entrechat quatre)
轻跳（两脚在空中交叉或相碰之姿势）
23 préparation [e.g. for a pirouette]
旋转的预备姿势
24 pirouette
旋转
25 corps de ballet
芭蕾舞团
26 ballet dancer (ballerina)
芭蕾舞者（芭蕾女舞者）
27–28 pas de trois
三人舞
27 prima ballerina
芭蕾舞女主角
28 principal male dancer (leading soloist)
芭蕾舞男主角（主要独舞演员）
29 tutu
（芭蕾舞女演员穿的）短裙
30 point shoe, a ballet shoe (ballet slipper)
足尖鞋，芭蕾舞鞋

31 ballet skirt
芭蕾舞裙

1-4 types of curtain operation
舞台布幕操作之类型
1 draw curtain (side parting)
拉幕（由两侧分开型）
2 tableau curtain (bunching up sideways)
由中间向上方两角掀起之舞台幕（向两边反摺型）
3 combined fly and draw curtain
悬吊式舞台幕（垂直上升）
4 combined fly and draw curtain
悬吊式与拉式混合型之舞台幕
5-11 cloakroom hall (_Am._ checkroom hall)
寄物处，衣帽间大厅
5 cloakroom (_Am._ checkroom)
寄物处
6 cloakroom attendant (_Am._ checkroom attendant)
寄物处服务员
7 cloakroom ticket (_Am._ check)
寄存号牌
8 playgoer (theatregoer, _Am._ theatergoer)
戏迷
9 opera glass (opera glasses)
观剧用之眼镜
10 commissionaire
门警
11 theatre (_Am._ theater) ticket, an admission ticket
戏票，入场券
12-13 foyer (lobby, crush room)
休息室（大厅，走廊）
12 usher; _form.:_ box attendant
引座员；传统称呼：包厢服务员
13 programme (_Am._ program)
节目表
14-27 auditorium and stage
观众席与舞台
14 stage
舞台
15 proscenium
前舞台
16-20 auditorium
观众席
16 gallery (balcony)
顶层楼座（包厢）
17 upper circle
第三层楼座
18 dress circle (_Am._ balcony, mezzanine)
二楼特别座，[美]楼座包厢
19 front stalls
一楼正面前排座位（特别座）
20 seat (theatre seat, _Am._ theater seat)
座位（剧场座位）
21-27 rehearsal (stage rehearsal)
排演（舞台彩排）
21 chorus
合唱团
22 singer
歌手
23 singer
歌手（女）
24 orchestra pit
管弦乐队席
25 orchestra
管弦乐队
26 conductor
指挥
27 baton (conductor's baton)
指挥棒
28-42 paint room, a workshop
布景画室（工作房）

28 stagehand (scene shifter)
舞台工作人员，布景更换人员
29 catwalk (bridge)
狭小通道
30 set piece
道具
31 reinforcing struts
加固之斜间撑架
32 built piece (built unit)
制成之道具
33 backcloth (backdrop)
天幕，背景幕
34 portable box for paint containers
颜料容器之手提盒
35 scene painter
绘景师
36 paint trolley
绘画材料之手推车
37 stage designer (set designer)
舞台设计师
38 costume designer
服装设计师
39 design for a costume
服装设计
40 sketch for a costume
服装设计草图
41 model stage
舞台模型
42 model of the set
道具模型（布景模型）
43-52 dressing room
化妆间
43 dressing room mirror
化妆间镜子
44 make-up gown
化妆用外衣
45 make-up table
化妆台
46 greasepaint stick
化妆用涂油彩棒
47 chief make-up artist (chief make-up man)
主化妆师
48 make-up artist (hairstylist)
化妆师（发形设计师）
49 wig
假发
50 props (properties)
小道具（在英国含服装在内）
51 theatrical costume
剧装
52 call light
催场灯（招呼演员准备上台之指示灯）

1-60 stagehouse with machinery (machinery in the flies and below stage)
有机械装置之舞台（舞台上空与台下之机械装置）

1 control room
控制室

2 control console (lighting console, lighting control console) with preset control for presetting lighting effects
（灯光台，灯光控制台）装有灯光效果预设设备之灯光控制台

3 lighting plot (light plot)
灯光标示图

4 grip (gridiron)
格子顶棚（操纵垂幕之舞台天花板里之装置）

5 fly floor (fly gallery)
悬吊长廊

6 sprinkler system for fire prevention (for fire protection)
防火之洒水系统（防火装置）

7 fly man
舞台上方（顶棚）操纵大道具之人

8 fly lines (lines)
吊索

9 cyclorama
弧型背景画幕（大风景画幕）

10 backcloth (backdrop, background)
背景幕

11 arch, a drop cloth
拱门吊幕

12 border
边幕（舞台上方悬挂之布景）

13 compartment (compartment-type, compartmentalized) batten (_Am._ border light)
隔间型边角灯光

14 stage lighting units (stage lights)
舞台灯光设置（舞台照明）

15 horizon lights (backdrop lights)
水平照明灯（背景灯）

16 adjustable acting area lights (acting area spotlights)
可调整的舞台表演区照明灯（表演区聚光灯）

17 scenery projectors (projectors)
布景（背景）之放映机

18 monitor (water cannon) (a piece of safely equipment)
监控器（水枪）（一种安全装置）

19 travelling (_Am._ traveling) lighting bridge (travelling lighting gallery)
移动式照明灯廊（桥）

20 lighting operator (lighting man)
灯光师

21 portal spotlight (tower spotlight)
舞台口聚光灯（塔式聚光灯）

22 adjustable proscenium
可调整之舞台前部装置

23 curtain (theatrical curtain)
舞台幕（剧场台幕）

24 iron curtain (safety curtain, fire curtain)
铁幕（安全幕，防火幕）

25 forestage (apron)
（舞台幕前部分）前舞台

26 footlight (footlights, floats)
脚灯（一舞台前端之照明设备）

27 prompt box
提词人隐藏位置

28 prompter
提词人

29 stage manager's desk
舞台监督工作桌

30 stage director (stage manager)
舞台监督

31 revolving stage
旋转舞台

32 trap opening
舞台活门之开口

33 lift (_Am._ elevator)
升降枪

34 bridge (_Am._ elevator), a rostrum
桥式升降台

35 pieces of scenery
道具

36 scene
舞台全景

37 actor
男演员

38 actress
女演员

39 extras (supers, supernumeraries)
临时演员（临时演员，小配角）

40 director (producer)
导演（制作人）

41 prompt book (prompt script)
提词本

42 director's table (producer's table)
导演工作桌

43 assistant director (assistant producer)
副导演（制作助理）

44 director's script (producer's script)
导演用之剧本

45 stage carpenter
舞台木工

46 stagehand (scene shifter)
管理舞台布景之人员

47 set piece
道具

48 mirror spot (mirror spotlight)
反射聚光灯

49 automatic filter change (with colour filters, colour mediums, gelatines)
滤光镜自动转位装置（带有彩色滤光片、彩色滤光板）

50 hydraulic plant room
水力装置（设备）室

51 water tank
水箱

52 suction pipe
吸水管

53 hydraulic pump
水泵

54 pressure pipe
水压管

55 pressure tank (accumulator)
水压箱（蓄水箱）

56 pressure gauge (_Am._ gage)
水压表

57 level indicator (liquid level indicator)
水平指示器（液面指示器）

58 control lever
控制杆

59 operator
操作人员

60 rams
活塞

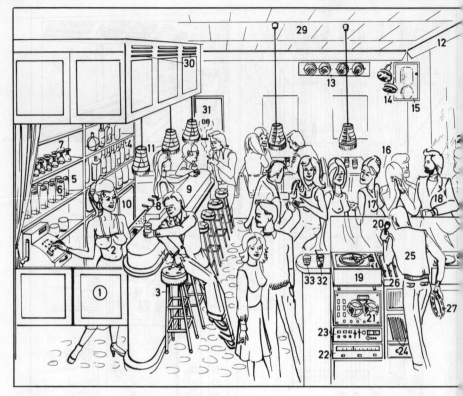

1 bar
　酒吧
2 barmaid
　酒吧女侍（吧柏女侍）
3 bar stool
　酒吧间凳子
4 shelf for bottles
　酒瓶架
5 shelf for glasses
　酒杯架
6 beer glass
　啤酒杯
7 wine and liqueur glasses
　葡萄酒及烈性酒酒杯
8 beer tap (tap)
　生啤酒之龙头（栓）
9 bar
　吧台
10 refrigerator (fridge, *Am.* icebox)
　冰箱（冰柜）
11 bar lamps
　酒吧间照明灯
12 indirect lighting
　间接照明
13 colour (*Am.* color) organ (clavilux)
　（灯光之）色彩机关
14 dancer floor lighting
　舞池照明
15 speaker (loudspeaker)
　喇叭（扬声器）
16 dance floor
　舞池

17-18 dancing couple
　一对舞伴
17 dancer
　跳舞者（女）
18 dancer
　跳舞者（男）
19 record player
　电唱机
20 microphone
　麦克风
21 tape recorder
　（磁带）盘式录音机
22-23 stereo system (stereo equipment)
　立体音响
22 tuner
　调谐器
23 amplifier
　扩大器
24 records (discs)
　唱片
25 disc jockey
　唱片节目主持人
26 mixing console (mixing desk, mixer)
　混频控制台
27 tambourine
　小手鼓（装有小铃之扁鼓）
28 mirrored wall
　镜壁
29 ceiling tiles
　天花板花砖
30 ventilators
　通风口

31 toilets (lavatories, WC)
　盥洗室（化妆室，厕所）
32 long drink
　高杯酒
33 cocktail (*Am.* highball)
　鸡尾酒

nightclub (night spot)
会

akroom (*Am.* checkroom)
处，衣帽间

akroom attendant (*Am.*
ckroom attendant)
处服务员
d

rinet

rinettist (*Am.* clarinetist)
手

mpet
叭

mpeter
叭手

tar

tarist (guitar player)
手

ms
鼓

mmer

aker (loudspeaker)
（扬声器）

rmaid
吧女侍（吧枱女侍）

16 bar stool
吧枱凳子

17 tape recorder
（磁带）盘式录音机

18 receiver
收音机

19 spirits
烈酒

20 cine-projector for porno films
(sex films, blue movies)
色情影片用之放映机

21 box containing screen
装放映幕之箱子

22 stage
舞台

23 stage lighting
舞台灯光

24 spotlight
聚光灯

25 festoon lighting
绵灯照明设备

26 festoon lamp (lamp, light bulb)
绵灯灯泡

27-32 striptease act (striptease
number)
脱衣舞表演

27 striptease artist (stripper)
脱衣舞女

28 suspender (*Am.* garter)
袜吊（袜带）

29 brassiére (bra)
奶罩，（胸罩）

30 fur stole
软毛皮之长围巾

31 gloves
手套

32 stocking
长袜

33 hostess
女侍应生，女服务生

1-33 bullfight (corrida, corrida
de toros)
斗牛

1 mock bullfight
模拟斗牛

2 novillero
见习斗牛士

3 mock bull (dummy bull)
模拟牛

4 novice banderillero (apprentice
banderillero)
初次上场之斗牛士

5 bullring (plaza de toros)
[diagram]
斗牛场（图形）

6 main entrance
主要入口

7 boxes
包厢

8 stands
看台

9 arena (ring)
竞技场

10 bullfighters' entrance
斗牛士入场处

11 torril door
牡牛进场处

12 exit gate for killed bulls
死牛之出口

13 slaughterhouse
屠杀场

14 bull pens (corrals)
牛栏

15 paddock
围场（附有马廐之围场）

16 lancer on horseback (picador)
持矛斗牛士（骑马斗牛士）

17 lance (pike pole, javelin)
矛（标枪）

18 armoured (*Am.* armored) horse
著盔甲之马

19 leg armour (*Am.* armor)
护腿

20 picador's round hat
骑马斗牛士所戴之圆帽

21 banderillero, a torero
徒步斗牛士

22 banderillas (barbed darts)
带钩短矛

23 shirtwaist
短衬衫

24 bullfight
斗牛

25 matador (swordsman), a torero
徒步斗牛士

26 queue, a distinguishing mark of
the matador
发辫，斗牛士之明显标志

27 red cloak (capa)
斗牛士披的红色斗篷

28 fighting bull
被激怒之斗牛

29 montera [hat made of tiny
black silk chenille balls]
斗牛士所戴之黑丝绒球所制之帽

30 killing the bull (kill)
杀牛

31 matador in charity
performances [without
professional uniform]
表演之斗牛士〔未着斗牛士服装〕

32 estoque (sword)
剑

33 muleta
激怒牛用之红布

34 rodeo
牛仔竞技

35 young bull
小公牛

36 cowboy
牛仔

37 stetson (stetson hat)
宽边帽

38 scarf (necktie)
领巾

39 rodeo rider
竞技的骑士

40 lasso
套索

1-2 medieval (mediaeval) notes
中古式音符

1 plainsong notation (neumes, neums, pneumes, square notation)
无伴奏齐唱（单旋律圣歌记谱法，方形记谱法）

2 mensural notation
固定节奏记谱法

3-7 musical note (note)
音符

3 note head
符头

4 note stem (note tail)
符尾

5 hook
行钩

6 stroke
符线

7 dot indicating augmentation of note's value
指示音符值增加的附点记号

8-11 clefs
谱号

8 treble clef (G-clef, violin clef)
高音谱号（G谱号，小提琴谱号）

9 bass clef (F-clef)
低音谱号（F谱号）

10 alto clef (C-clef)
中音谱号（C谱号）

11 tenor clef
次中音谱号

12-19 note values
音值

12 breve (brevis, *Am.* double-whole note)
二全音符记号

13 semibreve (*Am.* whole note)
全音符记号

14 minim (*Am.* half note)
二分音符

15 crotchet (*Am.* quarter note)
四分音符

16 quaver (*Am.* eighth note)
八分音符

17 semiquaver (*Am.* sixteenth note)
十六分音符

18 demisemiquaver (*Am.* thirty-second note)
三十二音符

19 hemidemisemiquaver (*Am.* sixty-fourth note)
六十四分音符

20-27 rests
休止符

20 breve rest
二全休止符

21 semibreve rest (*Am.* whole rest)
全休止符

22 minim rest (*Am.* half rest)
二分休止符

23 crotchet rest (*Am.* quarter rest)
四分休止符

24 quaver rest (*Am.* eighth rest)
八分休止符

25 semiquaver rest (*Am.* sixteenth rest)
十六分休止符

26 demisemiquaver rest (*Am.* thirty-second rest)
三十二分休止符

27 hemidemisemiquaver rest (*Am.* sixty-fourth rest)
六十四分休止符

28-42 time (time signatures, measure, *Am.* meter)
拍子（拍号）

28 two-eight time
八二拍

29 two-four time
四二拍

30 two-two time
二二拍

31 four-eight time
八四拍

32 four-four time (common time)
四四拍（普通拍子）

33 four-two time
二四拍

34 six-eight time
八六拍

35 six-four time
四六拍

36 three-eight time
八三拍

37 three-four time
四三拍

38 three-two time
二三拍

39 nine-eight time
八九拍

40 nine-four time
四九拍

41 five-four time
四五拍

42 bar (bar line, measure line)
小节线

43-44 staff (stave)
谱表（五线谱）

43 line of the staff
谱线

44 space
间（谱线之间）

45-49 scales
音阶

45 C major scale naturals: c, d, e, f, g, a, b, c
C大音阶本位音：c, d, e, f, g, a, b, c

46 A minor scale [natural] naturals: a, b, c, d, e, f, g, a
（自然）小音阶本位音：a, b, c, d, e, f, g, a

47 A minor scale [harmonic]
和声小音阶

48 A minor scale [melodic]
旋律小音阶

49 chromatic scale
半音音阶

50-54 accidentals (inflections, key signatures)
临时记号（变音记号，调号）

50-51 signs indicating the raising of a note
升记号

50 sharp (raising the note a semitone or half-step)
升记号（升高半音记号）

51 double sharp (raising the note a tone or full-step)
重升记号（升高两个半音或一个全音记号）

52-53 signs indicating the lowering of a note
降记号

52 flat (lowering the note a semitone or half-step)
降记号（降低半音记号）

53 double flat (lowering the note tone or full-step)
重降记号（降低两个半音或一个全音记号）

54 natural
还原记号（本位记号）

55-68 keys (major keys and the related minor keys having the same signature)
调子（大调与关系小调，符号相同）

55 C major (A minor)
C大调（A小调）

56 G major (E minor)
G大调（E小调）

57 D major (B minor)
D大调（B小调）

58 A major (F sharp minor)
A大调（升F小调）

59 E major (C minor)
E大调（C小调）

60 B major (G sharp minor)
B大调（升G小调）

61 F sharp major (D sharp minor)
升F大调（升D小调）

62 C major (A minor)
C大调（A小调）

63 F major (D minor)
F大调（D小调）

64 B flat major (G minor)
降B大调（G小调）

65 E flat major (C minor)
降E大调（C小调）

66 A flat major (F minor)
降A大调（F小调）

67 D flat major (B flat minor)
降D大调（降B小调）

68 G flat major (E flat minor)
降G大调（降E小调）

1-5 chord
和弦

1-4 triad
三和弦

1 major triad
大三和弦

2 minor triad
小三和弦

3 diminished triad
减三和弦

4 augmented triad
增三和弦

5 chord of four notes, a chord of
the seventh (seventh chord,
dominant seventh chord)
由四个音叠置而成的七和弦（七和弦，
属七和弦）

6-13 intervals
音程

6 unison (unison interval)
一度（同度）音程

7 major second
大二度

8 major third
大三度

9 perfect fourth
完全四度

10 perfect fifth
完全五度

11 major sixth
大六度

12 major seventh
大七度

13 perfect octave
完全八度

14-22 ornaments (graces, grace
notes)
装饰音（装饰音，装饰音符）

14 long appoggiatura
长倚音

15 acciaccatura (short
appoggiatura)
碎音（短倚音）

16 slide
滑音

17 trill (shake) without turn
无回音之震音

18 trill (shake) with turn
有回音之震音

19 upper mordent (inverted
mordent, pralltriller)
上涟音

20 lower mordent (mordent)
下涟音

21 turn
回音

22 arpeggio
琶音

**23-26 other signs in musical
notation**
乐谱中其他记号

23 triplet; *corresponding groupings:*
duplet (couplet), quadruplet,
quintuplet, sextolet (sextuplet),
septolet (septuplet, septimole)
三连音，相应之连音符：二连音，四连
音，五连音，六连音，七连音

24 tie (bind)
连接线，延音线

25 pause (pause sign)
停留记号，延长记号

26 repeat mark
反复记号

27-41 expression marks (signs of
relative intensity)
表情记号（关系强度记号）

27 marcato (marcando, markiert,
attack, strong accent)
加强记号（强音）

28 presto (quick, fast)
急板（快板）

29 portato (mezzo staccato,
carried)
断奏（连续断奏，带连线的跳音）

30 tenuto (held)
持音

31 crescendo (increasing gradually
in power)
渐强（音量逐渐加强）

32 decrescendo (diminuendo,
decreasing or diminishing
gradually in power)
渐弱（音量逐渐减弱或消失）

33 legato (bound)
圆滑唱（连音）

34 staccato (detached)
断奏，断唱（断音）

35 piano (soft)
弱（柔音）

36 pianissimo (very soft)
很弱

37 pianissimo piano (as soft as
possible)
最弱（尽可能的弱）

38 forte (loud)
强

39 fortissimo (very loud)
很强

40 forte fortissimo (double
fortissimo, as loud as possible)
最强（倍强，尽可能的强）

41 forte piano (loud and
immediately soft again)
强弱（开始强，立刻弱）

42-50 divisions of the compass
音域划分

42 subcontra octave (double contra
octave)
第二列低八度

43 contra octave
中央C起低八度

44 great octave
大八度（五个全音二个半音）

45 small octave
小八度（五个全音一个半音）

46 one-line octave
中央C算起高八度

47 two-line octave
第二列高八度

48 three-line octave
第三列高八度

49 four-line octave
第四列高八度

50 five-line octave
第五列高八度

$A_2 B\flat_2 B_2 C_1$ etc. $B_1 C B c b c' b' c'' b'' c''' b''' c''' b'''' c''''$

1 lur, a bronze trumpet
喇叭，青铜制喇叭

2 panpipes (Pandean pipes, syrinx)
排箫

3 aulos, a double shawm
奥鲁管（双簧吹奏乐器）

4 aulos pipe
奥鲁管的管身

5 phorbeia (peristomion, capistrum, mouth band)
双簧吹奏口缘

6 crumhorn (crummhorn, cromorne, krumbhorn, krummhorn)
克鲁姆双簧管

7 recorder (fipple flute)
英国八孔直笛（直笛同类乐器）

8 bagpipe; *sim.:* musette
风笛（类似法国之小风笛）

9 bag
风袋，风囊

10 chanter (melody pipe)
风笛之笛管

11 drone (drone pipe)
风笛之低音管

12 curved cornett (zink)
弧形短号

13 serpent
蛇形号

14 shawn (schalmeyes); *larger:* bombard (bombarde, pommer)
双簧管（中世纪用之奥博管）；较大型乐器：一种老式双簧管乐器

15 cythara (cithara); *sim. and smaller;* lyre
吉他拉琴（竖琴之一种）；同类较小乐器：里拉琴（古希腊）

16 arm
扶手

17 bridge
琴马

18 sound box (resonating chamber, resonator)
音箱（共鸣室，共鸣器）

19 plectrum, a plucking device
（弹奏弦乐器用的）拨子或弦拨

20 kit (pochette), a miniature violin
袖珍小提琴（小型小提琴）

21 cittern (cithern, cither, cister, citole), a plucked instrument; *sim.:* pandora (bandora, bandore)
西特琴，一种拨弦乐器，类似：潘朵拉琴（类似吉他之古代弦乐器）

22 sound hole
音孔

23 viol (descant viol, treble viol), a viola da gamba; *larger:* tenor viol, bass viol (viola da gamba, gamba), violone (double bass viol)
（六弦提琴，维奥尔）古提琴（高音提琴），一种置於腿上拉的提琴；较大型的：中音提琴，低音提琴，低音大提琴

24 viol bow
琴弓

25 hurdy-gurdy (vielle á roue, symphonia, arominie, organistrum)
摇弦琴

26 friction wheel
磨擦杆（轮）

27 wheel cover (wheel guard)
杆盖（轮盖）

28 keyboard (keys)
琴键

29 resonating body (resonator, sound box)
共鸣体（共鸣器，共鸣箱）

30 melody strings
旋律琴弦

31 drone strings (drones, bourdons)
低音弦

32 dulcimer
扬琴

33 rib (resonator wall)
弦乐器侧边（共鸣壁）

34 beater for the Valasian dulcimer
瓦拉辛扬琴所用之击音器

35 hammer (stick) for the Appenzell dulcimer
阿彭塞耳扬琴之琴槌

36 clavichord; *kinds:* fretted or unfretted clavichord
（击弦）（克拉维卡）古钢琴，种类：有琴格或无琴格之翼琴

37 clavichord mechanism
击弦古钢琴之内部构造（琴键）

38 key (key lever)
琴键

39 balance rail
平衡杆

40 guiding blade
导杆片

41 guiding slot
导沟（导槽）

42 resting rail
支撑杆

43 tangent
切音铜块（板）

44 string
琴弦

45 harpsichord (clavicembalo, cembalo), a wing-shaped stringed keyboard instrument; *sim.:* spinet (virginal)
（拨弦）（哈普西卡）古钢琴，一种翼形拨弦之键盘乐器有：史宾奈古钢琴与维京奈古钢琴

46 upper keyboard (upper manual)
上排键盘（上排手键盘）

47 lower keyboard (lower manual)
下排键盘（下排手键盘）

48 harpsichord mechanism
拨弦古钢琴之内部构造（琴键）

49 key (key lever)
琴键（键杆）

50 jack
钢琴动力杆

51 slide (register)
滑杆（音栓）

52 tongue
琴舌

53 quill plectrum
羽管琴拨

54 damper
制音器

55 string
弦

56 portative organ, a portable organ; *larger:* positive organ (positive)
轻便之风琴；较大型同类的乐器：positive 风琴

57 pipe (flue pipe)
唇管（琴管之气孔）

58 bellows
风箱

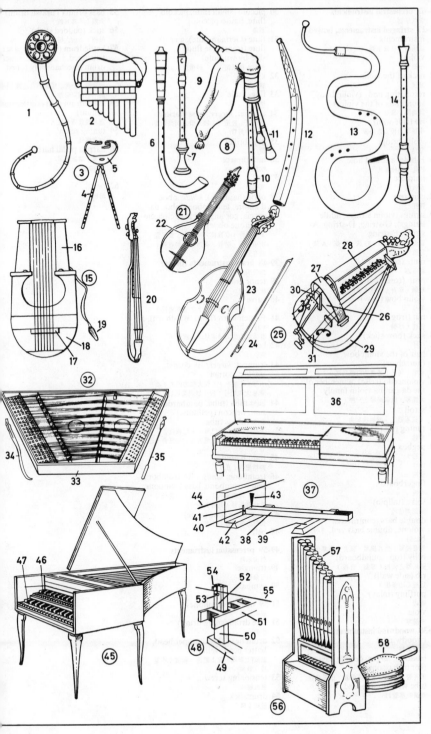

1-62 orchestral instruments
管弦乐器

1-27 stringed instruments, bowed
instruments
弦乐器，弓弦乐器

1 violin
小提琴

2 neck of the violin
琴颈

3 resonating body (violin body,
sound box of the violin)
共鸣体（琴身，音箱）

4 rib (side wall)
小提琴边板（边条板）

5 violin bridge
琴马

6 F-hole, a sound hole
F 孔，一种音孔

7 tailpiece
系弦板

8 chin rest
颚托

9 strings (violin strings, fiddle
strings); G-string, D-string, A-
string, E-string
弦（小提琴弦）：G 弦，D 弦，A 弦，
E 弦

10 mute (sordino)
弱音器

11 resin (rosin, colophony)
松脂，松香（弓弦乐器用）

12 violin bow (bow)
琴弓

13 nut (frog)
弦枕，弓根

14 stick (bow stick)
弓杆

15 hair of the violin bow
(horsehair)
弓毛（马毛，通常为白色马尾）

16 violoncello (cello), a member of
the da gamba violin family
大提琴，低音提琴之一种

17 scroll
（弦乐器之）漩涡状琴头

18 tuning peg (peg)
琴轸

19 pegbox
琴轸头

20 nut
弦枕

21 fingerboard
指板

22 spike (tailpin)
尾部调弦栓

23 double bass (contrabass,
violone, double bass viol, *Am.*
bass)
低音提琴（低音提琴，低音大提琴）

24 belly (top, soundboard)
弦乐器之面板（琴面，音板）

25 rib (side wall)
边板（边条板）

26 purfling (inlay)
镶边

27 viola
中提琴

28-38 woodwind instruments
(woodwinds)
木管乐器

28 bassoon; *larger:* double bassoon
(contrabassoon)
低音管；较大型之同类乐器：倍低音管

29 tube with double reed
双簧吹奏管口

30 piccolo (small flute, piccolo
flute, flauto piccolo)
短笛

31 flute (German flute), a cross
flute (transverse flute,
side-blown flute)
长笛（德国笛），一种横笛

32 key
键

33 fingerhole
指孔

34 clarinet; *larger:* bass clarinet
单簧管（竖笛）；较大型之同类乐器：
低音单簧管

35 key (brille)
键

36 mouthpiece
吹口

37 bell
喇叭口

38 oboe (hautboy); *kinds:* oboe
d'amore; tenor oboes: oboe da
caccia, cor anglais; heckelphone
(baritone oboe)
（奥博管）双簧管；种类有：柔簧管；
次中音管；猎管，英国管；赫克管（上
低音管）

39-48 brass instruments (brass)
铜管乐器

39 tenor horn
次中音号

40 valve
活塞（通指铜管乐器上之变音装置）

41 French horn (horn, waldhorn), a
valve horn
有活塞的法国号（号，无键号）

42 bell
喇叭口

43 trumpet; *larger:* B♭ cornet;
smaller: cornet
小号（小喇叭）；较大型之同类乐器：
降 B 大调短号；较小型同类乐器：短号

44 bass tuba (tuba, bombardon);
sim.: helicon (pellitone),
contrabass tuba
土巴低音号（土巴低音号，本巴敦低音
号）；同类乐器：低音号；倍低音士巴
号

45 thumb hold
拇指把位（孔）

46 trombone; *kinds:* alto trombone,
tenor trombone, bass trombone
长号（伸缩喇叭）；种类：中音长号，
次中音长号，低音长号

47 trombone slide (slide)
长号之伸缩管（U 型）

48 bell
喇叭口

49-59 percussion instruments
打击乐器

49 triangle
三角铁

50 cymbals
钹

51-59 membranophones
膜鸣乐器

51 side drum (snare drum)
小鼓

52 drum head (head, upper head,
batter head, vellum)
鼓皮[上鼓面，敲击鼓面，转皮（小羊
皮）鼓面]

53 tensioning screw
紧鼓螺丝

54 drumstick
鼓槌（棒）

55 bass drum (Turkish drum)
大鼓（土耳其鼓）

56 stick (padded stick)
鼓槌（击鼓大槌）

57 kettledrum (timpano), a scr
tensioned drum; *sim.:* mach
drum (mechanically tuned
drum)
定音鼓，一种以螺丝调音之鼓；同
器：机械定音鼓

58 kettledrum skin (kettledrun
vellum)
定音鼓鼓面（皮）

59 tuning screw
调音螺丝

60 harp, a pedal harp
竖琴，踏板竖琴

61 strings
弦

62 pedal
踏板

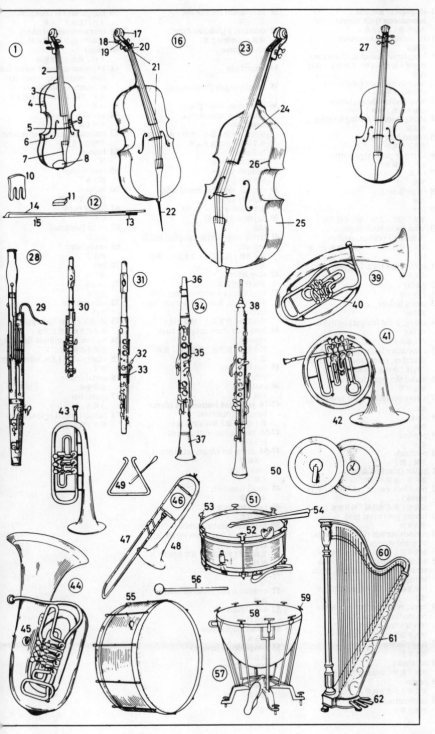

1-46 popular musical instruments (folk instruments)
通俗乐器（民间乐器）

1-31 stringed instruments
弦乐器

1 lute; *large:* theorbo, chitarrone
鲁特琴；较大型的有：泰奥博琴，吉他
隆琴

2 resonating body (resonator)
共鸣体（共鸣器）

3 soundboard (belly, table)
音板（面板，琴板）

4 string fastener (string holder)
系弦板

5 sound hole (rose)
音孔（圆花饰）

6 string, a gut (catgut) string
弦，一种猫肠弦

7 neck
琴颈

8 fingerboard
指板

9 fret
琴格（指板上之格，划分音价之用）

10 head (bent-back pegbox, swanhead pegbox, pegbox)
琴头（弓背琴参斗，天鹅头琴参斗，琴
参斗）

11 tuning peg (peg, lute pin)
调音琴参

12 guitar
吉他（琴）

13 string holder
系弦板

14 string, a gut (catgut) or nylon string
弦，猫肠弦或尼龙弦

15 resonating body (resonating chamber, resonator, sound box)
共鸣体（共鸣室，共鸣器，音箱）

16 mandolin (mandoline)
曼陀林琴

17 sleeve protector (cuff protector)
弦扣

18 neck
琴颈

19 pegdisc
琴参

20 plectrum
琴拨，拨子

21 zither (plucked zither)
齐特琴（拨弦齐特琴）

22 pin block (wrest pin block, wrest plank)
弦栓板（调音弦栓板，调音键板）

23 tuning pin (wrest pin)
调音弦栓

24 melody strings (fretted strings, stopped strings)
旋律琴弦（有音品之琴弦，闭奏弦）

25 accompaniment strings (bass strings, unfretted strings, open strings)
伴奏琴弦（低音弦，无音品琴弦，空
弦）

26 semicircular projection of the resonating sound box (resonating body)
突出半圆形之共鸣箱（共鸣体）

27 ring plectrum
环形琴拨

28 balalaika
俄式三弦琴（类似吉他之俄国弦琴）

29 banjo
班卓琴（亦名五弦琴）

30 tambourine-like body
铃鼓式琴身

31 parchment membrane
羊皮纸膜

32 ocarina, a globular flute
洋埙，一种球状之笛

33 mouthpiece
吹口

34 fingerhole
指孔

35 mouth organ (harmonica)
口琴

36 accordion; *sim.:* piano accordion, concertina, bandoneon
手风琴；同类乐器有：轻便手风琴，六
角手风琴，小六角手风琴

37 bellows
风箱（蛇腹送风器）

38 bellows strap
送风器停止带

39 melody side (keyboard side, melody keys)
旋律键盘部分

40 keyboard (keys)
键盘

41 treble stop (treble coupler, treble register)
高音音栓 [高音音键，高音音栓（整调
器）]

42 stop lever
音栓杆（变音器）

43 bass side (accompaniment side, bass studs, bass press-studs, bass buttons)
低音部分（伴奏部分，低音音键）

44 bass stop (bass coupler, bass register)
低音音栓 [低音音键，低音音栓（整调
器）]

45 tambourine
铃鼓

46 castanets
响板

47-78 jazz band instruments (dance band instruments)
爵士乐队乐器（舞蹈乐队乐器）

47-58 percussion instruments
打击乐器

47-54 drum kit (drum set, drums)
一套鼓器

47 bass drum
大鼓

48 small tom-tom
小印度鼓

49 large tom-tom
大印度鼓

50 high-hat cymbals (choke cymbals, Charleston cymbals, cup cymbals)
礼貌式钹（高领式钹，查尔斯顿钹，杯
形钹）

51 cymbal
钹

52 cymbal stand (cymbal holder)
钹架

53 wire brush
铜丝刷

54 pedal mechanism
踏板装置

55 conga drum (conga)
康茄鼓

56 tension hoop
紧箍环

57 timbales
定音鼓

58 bongo drums (bongos)
（古巴音乐之）小鼓

59 maracas; *sim.:* shakers
响葫芦；同类乐器摇荡器

60 guiro
（拉丁美洲）打击乐器

61 xylophone; *form.:* straw fid *sim.:* marimbaphone (steel marimba), tubaphone
木琴；同类乐器有：马林巴木琴，
木琴

62 wooden slab
木片（板）

63 resonating chamber (sound
共鸣室（音箱）

64 beater
槌

65 jazz trumpet
爵士小号

66 valve
活塞（变音装置）

67 finger hook
指钩

68 mute (sordino)
弱音器

69 saxophone
萨克管

70 bell
喇叭口

71 crook
变音管

72 mouthpiece
吹口

73 struck guitar (jazz guitar)
弹奏式吉他（爵士吉他）

74 hollow to facilitate fingerin
便於手指弹奏之凹瓦

75 vibraphone (*Am.* vibraharp
钟琴

76 metal frame
金属座架

77 metal bar
金属条

78 tubular metal resonator
管状金属共鸣器

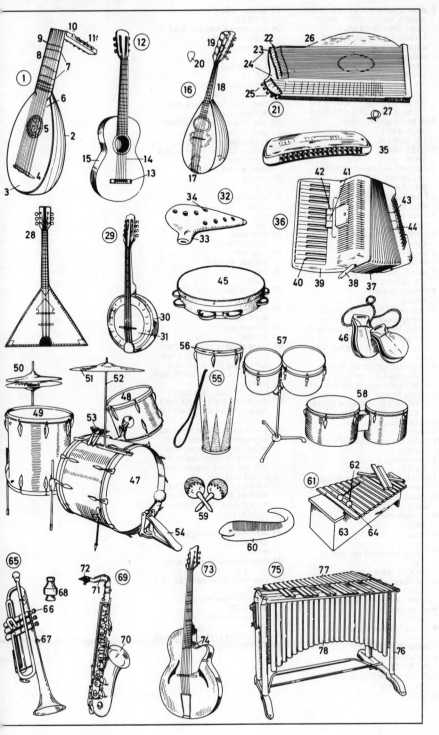

1 piano (pianoforte, upright piano, upright, vertical piano, spinet piano, console piano), a keyboard instrument (keyed instrument); *smaller forms:* cottage piano (pianino); *earlier form:* pantaleon, celesta, with steel bars instead of strings
钢琴（直立式钢琴，小型立式古钢琴，风琴式钢琴），一种键盘乐器；较小型的形式；竖式小钢琴，早期的形式；以钢条替代弦的发音之潘塔龙琴与钢片琴

2-18 piano action (piano mechanism)
钢琴之机械装置

2 iron frame
铁骨架

3 hammer; *collectively:* striking mechanism
琴槌，总称；击槌装置

4-5 keyboard (piano keys)
键盘（钢琴琴键）

4 white key (ivory key)
白键（象牙键）

5 black key (ebony key)
黑键（乌木键）

6 piano case
琴身板（钢琴箱）

7 strings (piano strings)
琴弦（钢琴琴弦）

8-9 piano pedals
钢琴踏板

8 right pedal (sustaining pedal, damper pedal; *loosely:* forte pedal, loud pedal) for raising the dampers
提起制音器之右踏板（支撑踏板，制音踏板；俗称：强音踏板）

9 left pedal (soft pedal; *loosely:* piano pedal) for reducing the striking distance of the hammers on the strings
减少琴槌在琴弦上之打击距离之左踏板（柔音踏板；俗称：弱音踏板）

10 treble strings
高音琴弦

11 treble bridge (treble belly bridge)
高音琴马

12 bass strings
低音琴弦

13 bass bridge (bass belly bridge)
低音琴马

14 hitch pin
系弦钉

15 hammer rail
琴槌杆

16 brace
支架

17 tuning pin (wrest pin, tuning peg)
调音弦栓（调音键，调音琴珍）

18 pin block (wrest pin block, wrest plank)
弦栓板（调音弦栓板，调音键板）

19 metronome
节拍机

20 tuning hammer (tuning key, wrest)
调音槌

21 tuning wedge
调音楔（正音楔）

22-39 key action (key mechanism)
琴键之机械装置

22 beam
梁

23 damper-lifting lever
制音器提杆

24 felt-covered hammer head
以毛毡包裹之琴槌头

25 hammer shank
槌柄

26 hammer rail
槌杆

27 check (back check)
校音器（后校音器）

28 check felt (back check felt)
校音器毡（后校音器毡）

29 wire stem of the check (wire stem of the back check)
校音器之铁丝杆

30 sticker (hopper, hammer jack, hammer lever)
顶杆（提高琴槌之装置）

31 button
音栓

32 action lever
连动杆

33 pilot
导杆

34 pilot wire
导杆线（铁丝）

35 tape wire
拘束带线（铁丝）

36 tape
拘束带

37 damper (damper block)
制音器（制音器块）

38 damper lifter
制音器提杆

39 damper rest rail
制音器架

40 grand piano (horizontal piano, grand, concert grand); *smaller:* baby grand piano, boudoir piano; *sim.:* square piano, table piano
大钢琴（平台钢琴，演奏会用钢琴）；较小型之同类乐器有：小型平台钢琴，闺房钢琴；其他形式：方型钢琴，枱式钢琴

41 grand piano pedals; right pedal for raising the dampers; left pedal for softening the tone (shifting the keyboard so that only one string is struck [una corda] one)
大钢琴踏板；提起制音器用之右踏板；柔音用的左踏板（使用柔音踏板时，只有一弦受击发音，称之"乌那科达"）

42 pedal bracket
踏板木架

43 harmonium (reed organ, melodium)
簧风琴

44 draw stop (stop, stop knob)
拉栓（音栓，音栓旋钮）

45 knee lever (knee swell, swell)
增音器

46 pedal (bellows pedal)
踏板（风箱踏板）

47 harmonium case
簧风琴外箱

48 harmonium keyboard (manual)
簧风琴键板

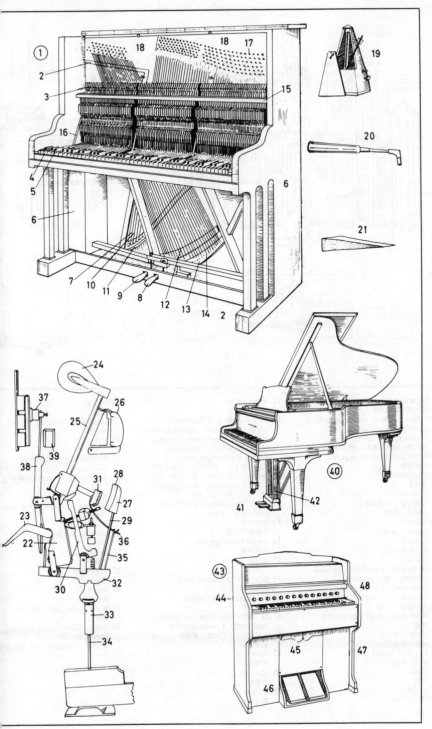

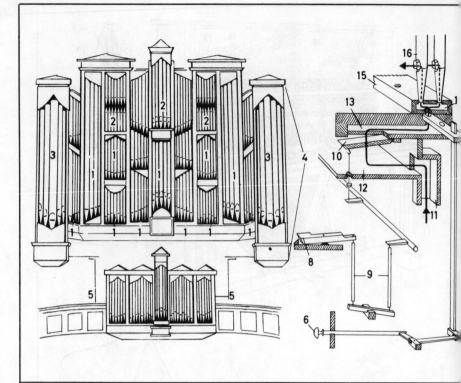

1-52 organ (church organ)
管风琴（教堂风琴）

1-5 front view of organ (organ case) [built according to classical principles]
管风琴正面图（琴身）[依古典原理制造]

1-3 display pipes (face pipes)
正面音管

1 Hauptwerk
主音管

2 Oberwerk
独奏音管（上部音管）

3 pedal pipes
持续音管

4 pedal tower
持续音塔

5 Rückpositiv
合奏音管

6-16 tracker action (mechanical action); *other systems:* pneumatic action, electric ation
连杆机械装置；其他形式：气动装置，电动装置

6 draw stop (stop, stop knob)
拉栓

7 slider (slide)
滑杆（滑动部分）

8 key (key lever)
琴键（琴键杆）

9 sticker
木杆

10 pallet
空气调节阀

11 wind trunk
风道，送风管

12-14 wind chest, a slider wind chest; *other types:* sliderless wind chest (unit wind chest), spring chest, kegellade chest (cone chest), diaphragm chest
风腔（箱），一种滑杆风腔（箱），其他种类：无滑杆风腔（箱）（单一装置风箱），弹簧式风腔（箱），圆锥式风腔（箱），膜片风腔（箱）

12 wind chest (wind chest box)
风腔（风箱）下部

13 groove
（音板）风槽

14 upper board groove
上板风槽

15 upper board
上板

16 pipe of a particular stop
特别音栓之音管

17-35 organ pipes (pipes)
风琴音管

17-22 metal reed pipe (*set of pipes:* reed stop), a posaune stop
金属簧管（音管设备：簧音栓），一种长号音栓

17 boot
音管套

18 shallot
声管簧管

19 tongue
簧片

20 block
塞块

21 tuning wire (tuning crook)
调音管

22 tube
共鸣管

22-30 open metal flue pipe, a salicional
金属开口音管，一种萨尔纳唇管

23 foot
管座

24 flue pipe windway (flue pipe duct)
开口音管，风道

25 mouth (cutup)
吹口

26 lower lip
下簧片

27 upper lip
上簧片

28 languid
簧片

29 body of the pipe (pipe)
管体

30 tuning flap (tuning tongue), tuning device
调音簧片（调音簧舌），一种调音簧

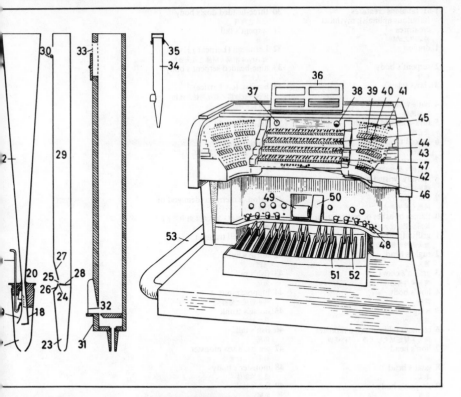

open wooden flue pipe (open
od), principal (diapason)
刂开口音管，管风琴的主要音栓（笛
已松音栓）
p
弯盖
r
耳
ning hole (tuning slot), with
de
板调音孔
pped flue pipe
奏音管
pper
奏器
organ console (console) of an
ectric action organ
子琴之操作部分
usic rest (music stand)
谱架
escendo roller indicator
量渐加强之圆形指示器
ltmeter
压计
op tab (rocker)
伞片
e combination stud (free
mbination knob)
由组合键（旋钮）
ncel buttons for reeds,
uplers etc.
管，联动装置用之止栓钮
anual I, for the Rückpositiv
一键盘，伴奏键盘

43 manual II, for the Hauptwerk
第二键盘，主音管键盘
44 manual III, for the Oberwerk
第三键盘，上部音管键盘
45 manual IV, for the Schwellwerk
第四键盘，增音键盘
46 thumb pistons controlling the
manual stops (free or fixed
combinations) and buttons for
setting the combinations
由扭指活塞控制的键盘音栓（自由或设
定组合），和调节组合的按钮
47 switches for current to blower
and action
电动送风开关
48 toe piston, for the coupler
脚控联动装置活塞
49 crescendo roller (general
crescendo roller)
渐强音量滚轴
50 balanced swell pedal
音乐调节板
51 pedal key [natural]
踏板键（本位者）
52 pedal key [sharp or flat]
踏板键（升高者或降低音）
53 cable (transmission cable)
（输电）电缆

1-61 fabulous creatures
(fabulous animals), mythical
creatures
神话中之动物
1 dragon
龙
2 serpent's body
蛇身
3 claws (claw)
爪
4 bat's wing
蝙蝠翅膀
5 fork-tongued mouth
叉舌嘴
6 forked tongue
叉状舌
7 unicorn [symbol of virginity]
独角兽〔纯洁的象征〕
8 spirally twisted horn
螺旋状独角
9 Phoenix
凤凰（长生鸟）
10 flames or ashes of resurrection
复活（燃）之火焰与灰烬
11 griffin (griffon, gryphon)
鹰身狮身带翅膀怪兽
12 eagle's head
鹰头
13 griffin's claws
鹰头狮身兽之爪
14 lion's body
狮身
15 wing
翅膀
16 chimera (chimaera), a monster
狮头羊身蛇尾之吐火兽，一种怪兽
17 lion's head
狮头
18 goat's head
羊头
19 dragon's body
龙身
20 sphinx, a symbolic figure
人头狮身怪物，一种象征性的形象
21 human head
人头
22 lion's body
狮身
23 mermaid (nix, nixie, water nixie,
sea maid, sea maiden, naiad,
water numph, water elf, ocean
nymph, sea nymph, river
nymph); sim.: Nereids, Oceanids
(sea divinities, sea deities, sea
goddesses); male: nix (merman,
seaman)
人鱼，美人鱼（水妖，女水妖，海上仙
女，保护河，潮泉水之仙女）；类似：
海中仙女，海中女神（海神，女海
神）；雄性：水鬼，水妖（人鱼）
24 woman's trunk
女人身躯
25 fish's tail (dolphin's tail)
鱼尾（海豚尾）
26 Pegasus (favourite, Am. favorite,
steed of the Muses, winged
horse); sim.: hippogryph
飞马（缪司女神最喜爱之马，有翼之
马；类似：马身鹫头，长翅膀之怪物）
27 horse's body
马身
28 wings
翅膀
29 Cerberus (hellhound)
冥府门狗（蛇尾，三狗头之怪物）（地
狱之犬）

30 three-headed dog's body
三头之狗身
31 serpent's tail
蛇尾
32 Lernaean (Lernean) Hydra
近 Argos 市湖，沼泽之九头怪蛇
33 nine-headed serpent's body
九头蛇身
34 basilisk (cockatrice)
传说非洲沙漠之似龙与蛇之怪物
35 cock's head
鸡头
36 dragon's body
龙身
37 giant (titan)
巨人（泰坦神，太阳神）
38 rock
岩石
39 serpent's foot
蛇足
40 triton, a merman (demigod of
the sea)
半人鱼之海神，雄人鱼（海中之半人半
神）
41 conch shell trumpet
响螺（螺号）
42 horse's hoof
马蹄
43 fish's tail
鱼尾
44 hippocampus
马头鱼尾之怪兽
45 horse's trunk
马之躯干
46 fish's tail
鱼尾
47 sea ox, a sea monster
海牛，一种海怪
48 monster's body
海怪的躯体
49 fish's tail
鱼尾
50 seven-headed dragon of St.
John's Revelation (Revelations,
Apocalypse)
圣约翰启示录中之七头龙
51 wing
翅膀
52 centaur (hippocentaur), half
man and half beast
人头马身之怪物，半人半兽
53 man's body with bow and arrow
拿着弓箭之人的躯体
54 horse's body
马身
55 harpy, a winged monster
鸟身人头之女妖，带翅膀之怪物
56 woman's head
女人头
57 bird's body
鸟身
58 siren, a daemon
女海妖，半人半鸟女妖
59 woman's body
女人身
60 wing
翅膀
61 bird's claw
鸟爪

1-40 prehistoric finds
史前时期之发现物

1-9 Old Stone Age (Palaeolithic, Paleolithic period) and **Mesolithic period**
旧石器时代和中石器时代

1 hand axe (*Am.* ax) (fist hatchet), a stone tool
手斧，一种石制工具

2 head of throwing spear, made of bone
由骨头制的投掷矛头

3 bone harpoon
骨制鱼叉

4 head
斧头之头部

5 harpoon thrower, made of reindeer antler
由鹿角所制之鱼叉投掷器

6 painted pebble
彩色之小石块

7 head of a wild horse, a carving
野马头，一种雕刻品

8 Stone Age idol, an ivory statuette
石器时代之崇拜偶像，象牙彫象

9 bison, a cave painting (rock painting) [cave art, cave painting]
野牛，一幅洞穴绘画（岩石绘画）（洞穴艺术，洞穴画）

10-20 New Stone Age (Neolithic period)
新石器时代

10 amphora [corded ware]
双耳瓶（绳纹陶器）

11 bowl [menhir group]
钵（史前时期巨石类）

12 collared flask [Funnel-Beaker culture]
带颈环之长颈瓶（古代杯口文化）

13 vessel with spiral pattern [spiral design pottery]
带有螺旋花纹之器皿（螺旋花饰陶器）

14 bell beaker [beaker pottery]
钟形杯（杯形陶器）

15 pile dwelling (lake dwelling, lacustrine dwelling)
木桩房子（湖边桩屋，湖上桩屋）

16 dolmen (cromlech), a megalithic tomb (*coll.:* giant's tomb); *other kinds:* passage grave, gallery grave (long cist); *when covered with earth:* tumulus (barrow, mound)
都尔门（古代墓址）（环状列石），一种巨石的坟墓；其他种类：长廊墓（长箱形石坟）；用土复盖的称为：塚

17 stone cist, a contracted burail
石棺，一种简陋之葬法

18 menhir (standing stone), a monolith
纪念之巨石柱（立石），一种巨石碑

19 boat axe (*Am.* ax), a stone battle axe
船形斧，一种石制战斧

20 clay figurine (an idol)
陶土之小塑像，一种偶像

21-40 Bronze Age and **Iron Age**; *epochs:* Hallstatt period, La Téne period
青铜器时代和铁器时代；包括初期铁器时期，后期铁器时期

21 bronze spear head
青铜矛头

22 hafted bronze dagger
带柄之青铜短剑

23 socketed axe (*Am.* ax) with haft fastened to rings, a bronze axe
柄栓紧於环上之套筒斧，一种青铜斧

24 girdle clasp
带饰钩

25 necklace (lunula)
颈饰（新月形颈饰）

26 gold neck ring
金颈环

27 violin-bow fibula (safety pin)
乐弓式之扣针（安全别针）

28 serpentine fibula; *other kinds:* boat fibula, arc fibula
蛇形扣针；其他种类：船形扣针，弧形扣针

29 bulb-head pin, a bronze pin
大头别针，一种青铜别针

30 two-piece spiral fibula; *sim.:* disc (disk) fibula
双片之螺旋形扣针；类似：圆盘形扣针

31 hafted bronze knife
带柄之青铜刀

32 iron key
铁钥匙

33 ploughshare (*Am.* plowshare)
犁头

34 sheet-bronze situla, a funerary vessel
青铜水桶，一种随葬器皿

35 pitcher [chip-carved pottery]
有柄水罐（粗刻陶器）

36 miniature ritual cart (miniature ritual chariot)
小型仪式车

37 Celtic silver coin
居尔特银币

38 face urn, a cinerary urn; *other kinds:* domestic urn, embossed urn
人面形骨灰坛，骨灰坛；其他形式：家用坛，布有浮雕之坛

39 urn grave in stone chamber
石室裡的骨灰坛埋葬

40 urn with cylindrical neck
圆筒颈之骨灰坛

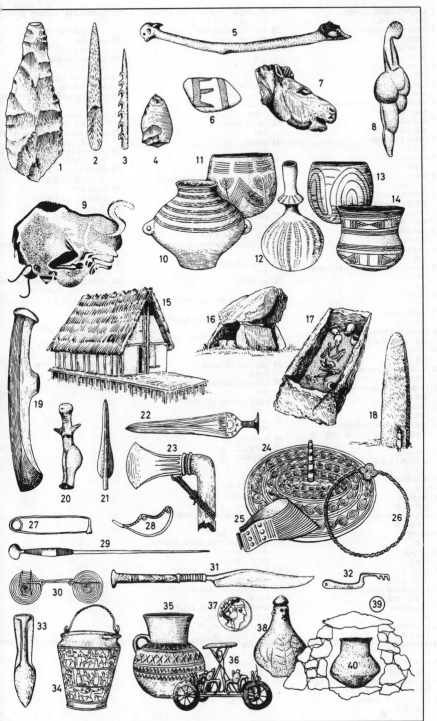

1 **knight's castle** (castle)
  骑士（武士）城堡
2 inner ward (inner bailey)
  内城墙（内壁）
3 draw well
  汲水井
4 keep (donjon)
  城楼（城堡的主楼）
5 dungeon
  地牢
6 battlements (crenellation)
  城垛（枪眼设备）
7 merlon
  枪眼与枪眼间之凸壁
8 tower platform
  塔顶平台
9 watchman
  了望哨
10 ladies' apartments (bowers)
  妇女的房间
11 dormer window (dormer)
  老虎窗（屋顶斜面凸出之天窗）
12 balcony
  阳台，骑楼
13 storehouse (magazine)
  仓库（城堡之弹药库）
14 angle tower
  角塔，角楼
15 curtain wall (curtains, enclosure wall)
  城墙
16 bastion
  稜堡
17 angle tower
  角塔
18 crenel (embrasure)
  枪眼（楔形之枪眼）
19 inner wall
  内墙
20 battlemented parapet
  城垛之胸墙
21 parapet (breastwork)
  胸墙（胸壁）
22 gatehouse
  门楼
23 machicolation (machicoulis)
  （中世纪城堡凸出於入口之）堞眼，枪口
24 portcullis
  格子吊闸（古城堡可升降之铁闸门，吊门）
25 drawbridge
  吊桥
26 buttress
  拱壁，扶壁
27 offices and service rooms
  公务服务间
28 turret
  角楼
29 chapel
  小教堂
30 great hall
  大厅，大会堂
31 outer ward (outer bailery)
  外城墙（外壁）
32 castle gate
  城门
33 moat (ditch)
  城壕（壕沟）
34 approach
  入口
35 watchtower (turret)
  了望台（角楼）
36 palisade (pallisade, palisading)
  栅栏
37 moat (ditch, fosse)
  城壕（壕沟）

38-65 **kinght's armour** (*Am.* armor)
  骑士（武士）之甲胄（盔甲）
38 suit of armour (*Am.* armor)
  整套甲胄（盔甲）
39-42 helmet
  头盔
39 skull
  盔顶
40 visor (vizor)
  （盔之）面颊
41 beaver
  （遮防下巴之）半面甲
42 throat piece
  护喉
43 gorget
  领甲
44 epauliére
  肩甲
45 pallette (pauldron, besageur)
  肩臂甲
46 breastplate (cuirass)
  胸甲
47 brassard (rear brace and vambrace)
  臂铠（后臂甲与前臂甲）
48 cubitiére (cubitiére, couter)
  肘甲
49 tasse (tasset)
  腿甲
50 gauntlet
  护手
51 habergeon (haubergeon)
  无袖铠甲
52 cuisse (cuish, cuissard, cuissart)
  大腿甲
53 knee cap (knee piece, genouilliére, poleyn)
  护膝甲
54 jambeau (greave)
  护胫套
55 solleret (sabaton, sabbaton)
  铁靴
56 pavis (pavise, pavais)
  大盾
57 buckler (round shield)
  圆盾
58 boss (umbo)
  （盾中心之）星标
59 iron hat
  铁帽
60 morion
  无面甲之头盔
61 light casque
  轻便盔
62 types of mail and armour (*Am.* armor)
  铠甲、甲胄之类型
63 mail (chain mail, chain armour, *Am.* armor)
  锁子甲，链甲
64 scale armour (*Am.* armor)
  鳞片甲
65 plate armour (*Am.* armor)
  板片甲
66 **accolade** (dubbing, knighting)
  骑士爵位之授礼仪式
67 liege lord, a knight
  君主，武士之一种
68 esquire
  后补骑士
69 cup bearer
  上酒者，司酒者
70 minstrel (minnesinger, troubadour)
  贵族所养之歌手，吟游诗人

71 **tournament** (tourney, joust, jtilt)
  （中世纪骑士的）马上比武
72 crusader
  十字军战士
73 Knight Templar
  圣堂武士
74 caparison (trappings)
  装饰用马衣马饰
75 herald (marshal at tournament)
  传令官（马上比赛之司令官）
76 tilting armour (*Am.* armor)
  马上比武之武器，盔甲（装备）
77 tilting helmet (jousting helmet)
  马上比武之头盔
78 panache (plume of feathers)
  羽饰（头盔上之装饰羽毛）
79 tilting target (tilting shield)
  马上比武用之小圆盾
80 lance rest
  甲胄胸板上支撑矛柄之处
81 tilting lance (lance)
  马上比武用之长矛
82 vamplate
  矛柄上之护手金属板
83-88 horse armour (*Am.* armor)
  马之护具
83 neck guard (neck piece)
  护颈甲
84 chamfron (chaffron, chafron, chamfrain, chanfron)
  马头甲，马之面甲
85 poitrel
  马前胸甲
86 flanchard (flancard)
  马腹护甲
87 tournament saddle
  马上比武用之马鞍
88 rump piece (quarter piece)
  臀部甲片

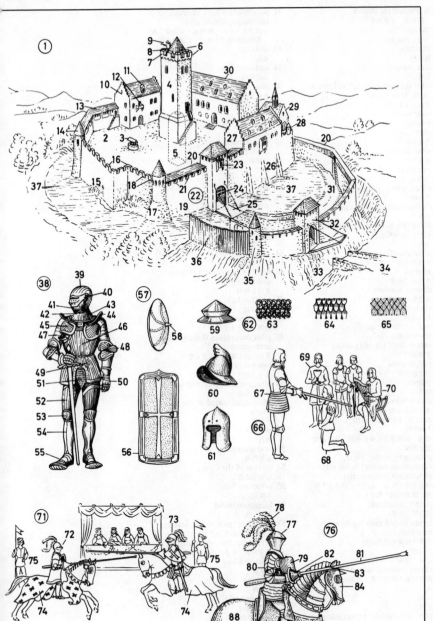

1-30 Protestant church
（基督教）复原教堂

1 chancel
圣坛（高坛）

2 lectern
诵经台

3 altar carpet
坛毯

4 altar (communion table, Lord's table, holy table)
圣坛（圣餐桌）

5 altar steps
圣坛台阶

6 altar cloth
圣坛台布

7 altar candle
蜡烛

8 pyx (pix)
圣饼盒

9 paten (patin, patine)
圣饼碟

10 chalice (communion cup)
圣餐杯

11 Bible (Holy Bible, Scriptures, Holy Scripture)
圣经

12 altar crucifix
耶稣受难像

13 altarpiece
圣坛后之画像

14 church window
教堂窗户

15 stained glass
彩色玻璃

16 wall candelabrum
壁上分枝烛台

17 vestry door (sacristy door)
圣器室门

18 pulpit steps
讲道坛阶梯

19 pulpit
讲道坛

20 antependium
圣坛前之装饰，帷幔

21 canopy (soundboard sounding board)
华盖，坛座罩盖（装於讲坛上使声音响亮之响板）

22 preacher (pastor, vicar, clergyman, rector) in his robes (vestments, canonicals)
身著长袍（礼服、法衣）之讲道人（牧师、助理牧师、教区长）

23 pulpit balustrade
讲道坛之栏杆

24 hymn board showing hymn numbers
有赞美诗编号之告示牌

25 gallery
边座、楼座

26 verger (sexton, sacristan)
教堂司事（教堂司事，圣器收藏室管理人）

27 aisle
通道

28 pew; *collectively:* pews (seating)
教堂之座席（座位）

29 churchgoer (worshippper); *collectively:* congregation
做礼拜者（敬拜者）集体：会众

30 hymn book
赞美诗

31-62 Roman Catholic church
罗马天主教教会

31 altar steps
圣坛台阶

32 presbytery (choir, chancel, sacrarium, sanctuary)
（教堂之）内室，牧师席，司祭席（教士或唱诗班席位，圣所，教堂之内殿）

33 altar
圣坛

34 altar candles
圣坛蜡烛

35 altar cross
圣坛十字架

36 altar cloth
台布

37 lectern
读经台

38 missal (mass book)
弥撒用书（祈祷书）

39 priest
神父

40 server
辅祭

41 sedilia
司祭席（内圣坛之南侧）

42 tabernacle
圣体柜

43 stele (stela)
刻有碑纹之石柱石碑

44 paschal candle (Easter candle)
复活节蜡烛

45 paschal candlestick (Easter candlestick)
复活节烛台

46 sanctus bell
三圣颂铃

47 processional cross
行列圣歌之十字架

48 altar decoration (foliage, flower arrangement)
圣坛装饰（植物，花之布置）

49 sanctuary lamp
教堂内殿灯（圣灯）

50 altarpiece, a picture of Christ
耶稣之画像

51 Madonna, statue of the Virgin Mary
圣母像

52 pricket
烛台

53 votive candles
还愿蜡烛

54 station of the Cross
耶稣受难像

55 offertory box
奉献箱

56 literature stand
书架

57 literature (pamphlets, tracts)
宗教书（宗教小册子）

58 verger (sexton, sacristan)
教堂司事（圣器守司，圣堂杂物员）

59 offertory bag
奉献袋

60 offering
奉献物

61 man praying
祈祷之教徒

62 prayer book
祈祷书

1 **church**
教堂

2 steeple
尖塔

3 weathercock
验风器（通常状如雄鸡，亦称风信鸡）

4 weather vane (wind vane)
风标，风信旗

5 apex
塔尖

6 church spire (spire)
教堂尖塔

7 church clock (tower clock)
教堂时钟

8 belfry window
钟楼窗户

9 electrically operated bell
电动大钟

10 ridge cross
屋脊上之十字架

11 church roof
教堂屋顶

12 memorial chapel
追思礼拜堂

13 vestry (sacristy), an annexe (annex)
圣器收藏室，一种加建之建筑

14 memorial tablet (memorial plate, wall memorial, wall stone)
纪念碑（墙上纪念碑，墙上石碑）

15 side entrance
侧门

16 church door (main door, portal)
教堂大门

17 churchgoer
做礼拜的人

18 graveyard wall (churchyard wall)
墓地围墙（墓地围墙）

19 graveyard gate (churchyard gate, lichgate, lychgate)
墓地大门（墓地大门，有顶盖之墓地门）

20 vicarage (parsonage, rectory)
牧师住宅

21-41 **graveyard** (churchyard, God's acre, *Am.* burying ground)
墓园（墓地）

21 mortuary
停尸间

22 grave digger
挖墓人

23 grave (tomb)
坟墓

24 grave mound
坟堆

25 cross
十字架

26 gravestone (headstone, tombstone)
墓碑（墓石）

27 family grave (family tomb)
家族墓地

28 graveyard chapel
墓园小教堂

29 child's grave
童墓

30 urn grave
骨灰瓮坟墓

31 urn
骨灰瓮

32 soldier's grave
军人墓

33-41 funeral (burial)
葬礼

33 mourners
送葬者

34 grave
墓穴

35 coffin (*Am.* casket)
棺木

36 spade
铲子

37 clergyman
牧师

38 the bereaved
遗族

39 widow's veil, a mourning veil
未亡人面纱，服丧面纱

40 pallbearers
护柩者，棺侧送葬者

41 bier
棺架

42-50 **procession** (religious procession)
宗教之送葬行列仪式

42 processional crucifix
送葬行列的耶稣受难像

43 cross bearer (crucifer)
执十字架者

44 processional banner, a church banner
送葬行列所用教堂之旗帜

45 acolyte
辅祭

46 canopy bearer
持幕盖者

47 priest
神父

48 monstrance with the Blessed Sacrament (consecrated Host)
盛戴圣体之圣体架（神圣的圣体）

49 canopy (baldachin, baldaquin)
幕盖（天盖，织锦）

50 nuns
修女

51 participants in the procession
参加送葬行列者

52-58 **monastery**
修道院

52 cloister
迴廊

53 monastery garden
花园

54 monk, a Benedictine monk
修道士，本笃会修教士

55 habit (monk's habit)
道服（修道士之道服）

56 cowl (hood)
（修道服上之）头巾

57 tonsure
剃发，剃去头发之部分

58 breviary
每日祈祷书（日课经）

59 **catacomb**, an early Christian underground burial place
地下墓窖，早期基督教徒之地下埋葬所

60 niche (tomb recess, arcosolium)
壁龛（坟墓壁龛盦盦）

61 stone slab
石板

1 Christian baptism
(christening)
基督教之洗礼（施洗）

2 baptistery (baptistry)
洗礼所，洗礼堂

3 Protestant clergyman
复原派牧师

4 robes (vestments, canonicals)
礼袍，法衣

5 bands
宽领带

6 collar
衣领

7 child to be baptized (christened)
受洗之小孩

8 christening robe (christening
dress)
洗礼服

9 christening shawl
洗礼围巾

10 font
圣水器

11 font basin
洗礼盆

12 baptismal water
圣水，洗礼水

13 godparents
教父，教母

14 church wedding (wedding
ceremony, marriage ceremony)
教堂婚礼（结婚仪式）

15-16 bridal couple
新婚夫妻

15 bride
新娘

16 bridegroom (groom)
新郎

17 ring (wedding ring)
结婚戒子

18 bride's bouquet (bridal bouquet)
新娘的花束

19 bridal wreath
新娘之花冠

20 veil (bridal veil)
披纱（新娘的披纱）

21 buttonhole
钮孔，插於衣襟钮孔的花束

22 clergyman
牧师

23 witnesses [to the marriage]
婚礼之见证人

24 bridesmaid
女宾相

25 kneeler
跪垫，跪台

26 Holy Communion
圣餐

27 communicants
领受圣餐者

28 Host (wafer)
圣瓶

29 communion cup
圣餐杯

30 rosary
念珠（玫瑰经）

31 paternoster
念珠串里颂主祷文时的大珠子

32 Ave Maria; *set of 10:* decade
福哉玛丽亚，十粒珠子一串（组）

33 crucifix
耶稣受难像

34-54 liturgical vessels
(ecclesiastical vessels)
礼仪用之器皿（教会的器皿）

34 monstrance
圣体显供架

35 Host (consecrated Host, Blessed
Sacrament)
圣体（祝圣之圣体，祝圣圣餐）

36 lunula (lunule)
新月形圣体容器

37 rays
放射状之饰物

38 censer (thurible), for offering
incense (for incensing)
香炉，放置奉献用之香料

39 thurible chain
香炉链

40 thurible cover
香炉盖

41 thurible bowl
香炉钵

42 incense boat
香碗

43 incense spoon
香匙

44 cruet set
一组盛酒或水之壶（圣餐用）

45 water cruet
水瓶

46 wine cruet
酒瓶

47 holy water basin
圣水盒

48 ciborium containing the sacred
wafers
装圣饼之容器

49 chalice
圣餐杯

50 dish for communion wafers
装圣饼之盘子

51 paten (patin, patine)
圣体碟

52 altar bells
圣坛用铃

53 pyx (pix)
圣饼盒

54 aspergillum
洒水器

55-72 forms of Christian crosses
基督教十字架的各种类型

55 Latin cross (cross of the
Passion)
拉丁式十字架（耶稣受难十字架）

56 Greek cross
希腊式十字架

57 Russian cross
俄罗斯式十字架

58 St. Peter's crosss
圣彼得十字架

59 St. Anthony's cross (tau cross)
圣安东尼十字架（T型十字架）

60 St. Andrew's cross (saltire
cross)
圣安德鲁十字架（X型十字架）

61 Y-cross
Y型十字架

62 cross of Lorraine
洛林十字架

63 ansate cross
圆头十字架

64 patriarchal cross
大主教用之十字架

65 cardinal's cross
枢机主教用之十字架

66 Papal cross
教皇用十字架

67 Constantinian cross, a
monogram of Christ (CHR)
康斯坦丁十字架，由基督名字组合而成
之十字架

68 crosslet
小十字架（徽章式）

69 cross moline
锚形十字架

70 cross of Jerusalem
耶路撒冷十字架

71 cross botonnée (cross treflée
三斜式十字架（各端呈叶状之十字架

72 fivefold cross (quintuple cro
五重式十字架

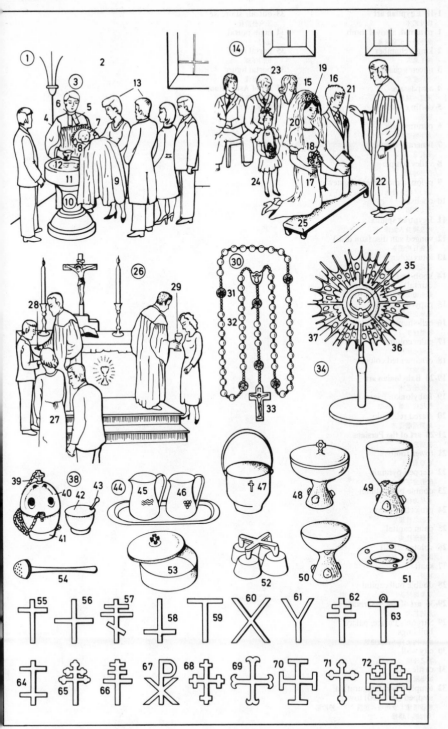

1-18 Egyptian art
埃及艺术
1 pyramid, a royal tomb
金字塔，王室坟墓
2 king's chamber
国王墓穴
3 queen's chamber
王后墓穴
4 air passage
风道，风路
5 coffin chamber
棺室
6 pyramid site
金字塔遗迹
7 funerary temple
葬礼堂
8 valley temple
谷形神殿
9 pylon, a monumental gateway
塔门，纪念碑入口
10 obelisks
方尖石塔
11 Egyptian sphinx
埃及狮身人面像
12 winged sun disc (sun disk)
带翼日轮图案
13 lotus column
莲花饰柱
14 knob-leaf capital (bud-shaped capital)
球形瓣饰柱头（蓓蕾形柱头）
15 papyrus column
纸草花饰图案之圆柱
16 bell-shaped capital
钟型柱头
17 palm column
棕榈形圆柱
18 ornamented column
饰像圆柱
19-20 Babylonian art
巴比伦艺术
19 Babylonian frieze
巴比伦屋簷下饰带
20 glazed relief tile
釉面浮雕瓷砖
21-28 art of the Persians
波斯艺术
21 tower tomb
塔形墓
22 stepped pyramid
阶形金字塔
23 double bull column
双牛饰柱
24 projecting leaves
突出之叶瓣
25 palm capital
棕榈形柱头
26 volute (scroll)
涡形装饰（花纹）
27 shaft
柱身
28 double bull capital
双牛饰柱头
29-36 art of the Assyrians
亚述艺术
29 Sargon's Palace, palace buildings
萨尔冈王宫，宫殿建筑
30 city wall
城之外壁
31 castle wall
城堡围墙
32 temple tower (ziggurat), a stepped (terraced) tower
神庙塔楼（亚述塔式建筑），一种阶形（梯形）塔楼

33 outside staircase
王宫外阶梯
34 main portal
正门
35 portal relief
正门浮雕
36 portal figure
正门雕像
37 art of Asia Minor
小亚细亚艺术
38 rock tomb
石墓

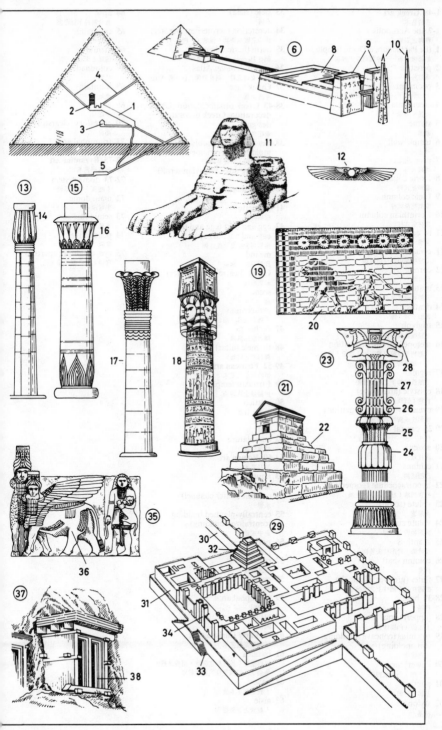

1-48 Greek art
希腊艺术

1-7 the Acropolis
雅典之卫城

1 the Parthenon, a Doric temple
帕德嫩神庙，一种都利亚式神庙

2 peristyle
寺院外柱

3 pediment
（山形墙，三角墙）山形建筑正面

4 crepidoma (stereobate)
柱基（墙基，屋基）

5 statue
雕像

6 temple wall
神庙围墙

7 propylaea
神殿入口

8 Doric column
都利亚式柱

9 Ionic column
爱奥尼亚式柱

10 Corinthian column
哥林多式柱

11-14 cornice
飞檐

11 cyma
（波状花边）反曲线脚

12 corona
台口线

13 mutule
（都利亚式簷饰）外簷头

14 dentils
齿形（装）饰

15 triglyph
三竖线花纹装饰（三槽板纹饰）

16 metope, a frieze decoration
（都利亚建筑屋簷下的）墙面，柱间
壁，横饰带之装饰

17 regula
三槽板纹饰下之短型楞条

18 epistyle (architrave)
台轮（嵌线之最底部）

19 cyma (cymatium, kymation)
波形纹线脚反曲线脚

20-25 capital
柱头

20 abacus
圆柱冠板（顶板）

21 echinus
凸圆线脚

22 hypotrachelium (gorgerin)
柱顶凹槽（柱头房），柱颈

23 volute (scroll)
涡形饰

24 volute cushion
涡形装饰之垫层

25 acanthus
反叶饰（叶形柱头装饰）

26 column shaft
柱身

27 flutes (grooves, channels)
凹圆柱饰（圆柱上之凹槽）

28-31 base
柱基

28 [upper] torus
（上部）凸圆线脚

29 trochilus (concave moulding,
Am. molding)
凹圆线脚

30 [lower] torus
（下部）凸圆线脚

31 plinth
基脚，柱脚

32 stylobate
柱基

33 stele (stela)
石碑

34 acroterion (acroterium, acroter)
碑顶之雕刻饰物（像墩子，吻座）

35 herm (herma, hermes)
刻有 Hermes 神像之石碑

36 caryatid; *male:* Atlas
刻有女像之柱；刻有男像之柱；称 Atlas

37 Greek vase
希腊花瓶

38-43 Greek ornamentation (Greek
decoration, Greek decorative
designs)
希腊装饰图案

38 bead-and-dart moulding (*Am.*
molding), an ornamental band
串珠线脚，一种装饰带

39 running dog (Vitruvian scroll)
涡形条纹

40 leaf ornament
叶形饰

41 palmette
棕榈叶饰

42 egg and dart (egg and tongue,
egg and anchor) cyma
蛋形与尖状之反曲线脚

43 meander
迂迴花纹（蟠螭）

44 Greek theatre (*Am.* theater)
希腊剧场

45 scene
幕

46 proscenium
（舞台前部）前台

47 orchestra
舞台前乐队席

48 thymele (altar)
舞台前之讲坛

49-52 Etruscan art
伊特拉士坎艺术

49 Etruscan temple
伊特拉士坎神庙

50 portico
门廊，柱廊

51 cella
内殿

52 entablature
柱顶线盘

53-60 Roman art
罗马艺术

53 aqueduct
输水道（桥）

54 conduit (water channel)
水道

55 centrally-planned building
(centralized building)
集中式建筑

56 portico
门廊，柱廊

57 reglet
接缝嵌线

58 cupola
圆顶

59 triumphal arch
凯旋门

60 attic
阁楼

61-71 Early Christian art
早期基督教艺术

61 basilica
巴西里佳（长方形之会堂，用于法庭，
集会），巴西里佳风格之教堂

62 nave
（教堂之）本堂

63 aisle
（教堂之）侧廊

64 apse
教堂东首半圆形室

65 campanile
钟楼

66 atrium
前庭（天井）

67 colonnade
柱廊

68 fountain
喷泉

69 altar
祭坛

70 clerestory (clearstory)
高窗

71 triumphal arch
凯旋式拱门

72-75 Byzantine art
拜占庭艺术

72-73 dome system
（圆顶）穹顶系统

72 main dome
主穹顶

73 semidome
半球形顶

74 pendentive
穹隅

75 eye, a lighting aperture
穹顶上之孔眼，采光孔

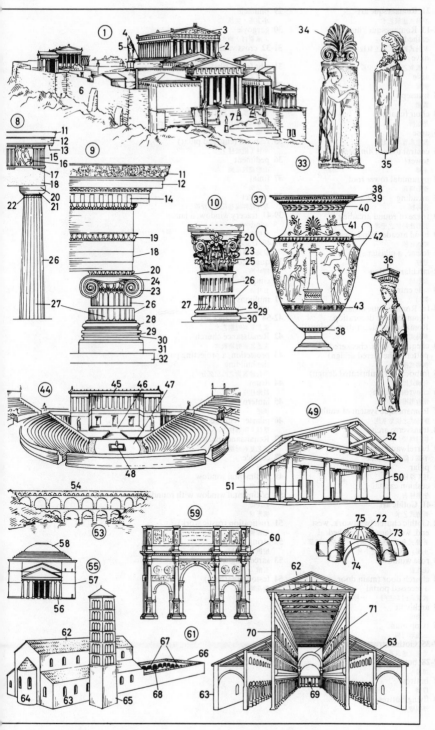

1-21 Romanesque art
罗马式建筑艺术

1-13 Romanesque church, a cathedral
罗马式教堂，天主教教堂之一种

1 nave
（教堂之）本堂，中殿（廊）

2 aisle
侧廊

3 transept
翼廊

4 choir (chancel)
圣坛所

5 apse
教堂东首半圆形室

6 central tower (*Am.* center tower)
主楼

7 pyramidal tower roof
锥形塔顶

8 arcading
连环拱

9 frieze of round arcading
圆形连环拱之壁缘

10 blind arcade (blind arcading)
暗连环拱

11 lesene, a pilaster strip
壁柱

12 circular window
圆形墙

13 side entrance
侧门

14-16 Romanesque ornamentation (Romanesque decoration, Romanesque decorative designs)
罗马式之装饰图案

14 chequered (*Am.* checkered) pattern (chequered design)
棋格式图案

15 imbrication (imbricated design)
鱼鳞式图案

16 chevron design
锯齿形图案

17 Romanesque system of vaulting
罗马式之拱形系统

18 transverse arch
拱门横梁

19 barrel vault (tunnel vault)
半圆（隧道）形拱顶

20 pillar
柱（撑柱）

21 cushion capital
垫形柱头

22-41 Gothic art
哥德式艺术

22 Gothic church [westwork, west end, west facade], a cathedral
哥德式教堂〔西首建筑区；西端，西部正面〕，天主教堂之一种

23 rose window
圆花窗

24 church door (main door, portal), a recessed portal
教堂正门（主门），一种凹形门

25 archivolt
门饰缘

26 tympanum
三角形门楣

27-35 Gothic structural system
哥德式建筑系统

27-28 buttresses
撑墙

27 buttress
撑墙

28 flying buttress
浮拱壁

29 pinnacle
小尖塔，尖顶

30 gargoyle
（承霤口）滴水口

31-32 cross vault (groin vault)
交叉拱顶

31 ribs (cross ribs)
（交叉）拱肋

32 boss (pendant)
悬饰（浮雕）

33 triforium
拱廊（拱门与高窗间部分）

34 clustered pier (compound pier)
柱墩

35 respond (engaged pillar)
半柱（附墙柱）

36 pediment
山形建筑正面

37 finial
尖顶饰

38 crocket
卷叶花样或卷花形之浮雕

39-41 tracery window, a lancet window
窗格花窗户，一种尖形窗

39-40 tracery
窗饰，窗格花

39 quatrefoil
四叶饰

40 cinquefoil
五叶饰

41 mullions
中框

42-54 Renaissance art
文艺复兴时期艺术

42 Renaissance church
文艺复兴时期教堂

43 projection, a projecting part of the building
凸台建筑物之凸出部分

44 drum
鼓形柱座

45 lantern
顶塔

46 pilaster (engaged pillar)
壁柱（附墙柱）

47 Renaissance palace
文艺复兴时期之宫殿

48 cornice
飞檐

49 pedimental window
山形窗

50 pedimental window with round gable
弧形窗

51 rustication (rustic work)
毛面砌石（粗工建筑）

52 string course
层拱，蛇腹层

53 sarcophagus
石棺

54 festoon (garland)
垂花饰

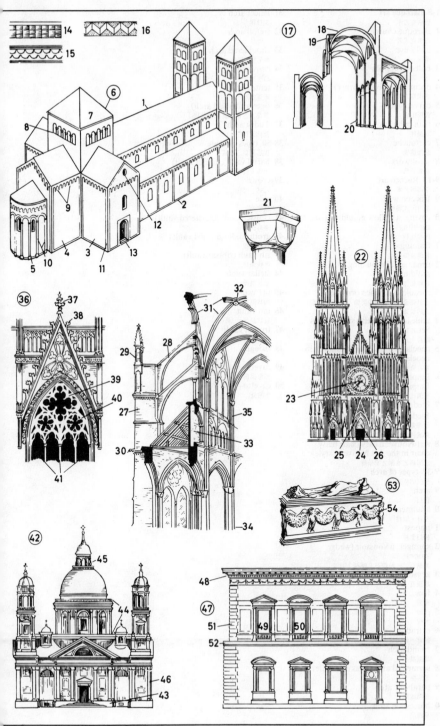

1-8 Baroque art
巴洛克艺术

1 Baroque church
巴洛克式教堂

2 bull's eye
圆窗

3 bulbous cupola
球形圆顶

4 dormer window (dormer)
老虎窗（天窗）

5 curved gable
弧形山墙

6 twin columns
双圆柱

7 cartouche
装饰镜板

8 scrollwork
涡卷装饰

9-13 Rococo art
洛可可艺术

9 Rococo wall
洛可可式墙壁

10 coving, a hollow moulding (*Am.* molding)
凹型线脚，壁带

11 framing
骨架装饰

12 ornamental moulding (*Am.* molding)
花样装饰

13 rocaille, a Rococo ornament
由贝壳或鹅卵石制的装饰，一种洛可可式的装饰

14 table in Louis Seize style (Louis Seize table)
路易十六式的桌子

15 neoclassical building (building in neoclassical style), a gateway
新古典式建筑，市门之一种

16 Empire table (table in the Empire style)
帝国式之桌子

17 Biedermeier sofa (sofa in the Biedermeier style)
彼德麦式样的沙发（19世纪前半德国家具式样之一种）

18 Art Nouveau easy chair (easy chair in the Art Nouveau style)
法国新艺术派之安乐椅

19-37 types of arch
拱门的样式

19 arch
拱门

20 abutment
支柱，墩柱

21 impost
拱门支柱

22 springer, a voussoir (wedge stone)
起拱石，一种拱石（楔石）

23 keystone
拱顶石

24 face
砌面

25 pier
方柱

26 extrados
拱背，外弧线

27 round arch
半圆拱

28 segmental arch (basket handle)
弧形拱

29 parabolic arch
抛物线拱

30 horseshoe arch
马蹄拱

31 lancet arch
尖顶拱

32 trefoil arch
三叶拱

33 shouldered arch
肩形拱

34 convex arch
凸形拱

35 tented arch
帐篷式拱

36 ogee arch (keel arch)
葱花（莲花）拱（龙骨拱）

37 Tudor arch
都铎式拱门

38-50 types of vault
拱形屋顶之样式

38 barrel vault (tunnel vault)
半圆（隧道）形拱顶

39 crown
冠状

40 side
顶侧面

41 cloister vault (cloistered vault)
迴廊拱顶

42 groin vault (groined vault)
穹窿拱顶

43 rib vault (ribbed vault)
穹棱拱顶

44 stellar vault
星状拱顶

45 net vault
网状拱顶

46 fan vault
扇状拱顶

47 trough vault
槽式拱顶

48 trough
槽

49 cavetto vault
凹形拱顶

50 cavetto
中凹处

1-6 Chinese art
中国艺术
1 pagoda (multi-storey,
   multistory, pagoda), a temple
   tower
   宝塔（多层），一种庙塔
2 storey (story) roof (roof of
   storey)
   塔顶
3 pailou (pailoo), a memorial
   archway
   牌楼，一种纪念性的拱道（门）
4 archway
   拱道
5 porcelain vase
   瓷花瓶
6 incised lacquered work
   漆雕艺术

7-11 Japanese art
日本艺术
7 temple
   庙
8 bell tower
   钟塔
9 supporting structure
   支架
10 bodhisattva (boddhisattva), a
   Buddhist saint
   菩萨，佛
11 torii, a gateway
   神社前之牌坊

12-18 Islamic art
伊斯兰（回）教艺术
12 mosque
   清真寺
13 minaret, a prayer tower
   （回教寺院的）尖塔
14 mihrab
   诵经龛
15 minbar (mimbar, pulpit)
   讲经坛
16 mausoleum, a tomb
   陵墓
17 stalactite vault (stalactitic vault)
   钟乳饰圆顶
18 Arabian capital
   阿拉伯式柱头

19-28 Indian art
印度艺术
19 dancing Siva (Shiva), an Indian
   god
   湿婆、婆罗门教中一主神，司破坏，拯
   教之神
20 statue of Buddha
   释迦牟尼像
21 stupa (Indian pagoda), a mound
   (dome), a Buddhist shrine
   佛骨塔，舍利塔（印尼塔），一种圆顶
   土墩，佛龛
22 umbrella
   伞形顶
23 stone wall (*Am.* stone fence)
   石墙
24 gate
   门
25 temple buildings
   寺庙建筑
26 shikara (sikar, sikhara, temple
   tower)
   锡克教庙塔
27 chaitya hall
   神庙大殿厅
28 chaitya, a small stupa
   佛塔，小型之佛骨塔

1-43 studio
画室
1 studio skylight
画室天窗
2 painter, an artist
画家，美术家
3 studio easel
画架
4 chalk sketch, a rough draft
以粉笔所绘素描，草图
5 crayon (piece of chalk)
蜡笔（一支粉笔）
6-19 painting materials
绘画用具
6 flat brush
平头画笔
7 camel hair brush
骆驼毛画笔
8 round brush
圆头画笔
9 priming brush
底色用画笔
10 box of paints (paintbox)
颜料盒
11 tube of oil paint
油画颜料管
12 varnish
油漆
13 thinner
稀释液
14 palette knife
调色刀
15 spatula
抹刀，油漆刀

16 charcoal pencil (charcoal, piece of charcoal)
炭笔
17 tempera (gouache)
不透明颜料（不透明水彩颜料）
18 watercolour (*Am.* watercolor)
水彩颜料
19 pastel crayon
粉腊笔
20 wedged stretcher (canvas stretcher)
张开画布的框（油画框）
21 canvas
油画布
22 piece of hardboard, with painting surface
硬质油画纸板
23 wooden board
木质板
24 fibreboard (*Am.* fiberboard)
纤维板（硬纸板）
25 painting table
颜料桌
26 folding easel
折叠式画架
27 still life group, a motif
静物组合，主题
28 palette
调色板
29 palette dipper
调色杯
30 platform
模特儿台

31 lay figure (mannequin, man⋯
人体模型
32 nude model (model, nude)
裸（人）体模特儿
33 drapery
披衣，衣饰
34 drawing easel
素描架
35 sketch pad
速写本
36 study in oils
油画习作
37 mosaic (tessellation)
镶嵌图
38 mosaic figure
镶嵌画中之人物像
39 tesserae
镶嵌物
40 fresco (mural)
壁画
41 sgraffito
将上层颜料若干处割去以显底色之刻法
42 plaster
石膏
43 cartoon
草图，底图

ulptor
刻家（师）

oportional dividers
例划分器（比例规）

lliper (caliper)
径器

aster model, a plaster cast
膏模特儿，石膏像之一种

ock of stone (stone block)
块

odeller (Am. modeler)
塑家，模型师

ay figure, a torso
像，躯干

ll of clay, a modelling (Am.
odeling) substance
土卷，（造）塑型之材料

odelling (Am. modeling) stand
造）塑型架

ooden modelling (Am.
odeling) tool
制塑形工具（削刀）

ire modelling (Am. modeling)
ol
属丝塑形工具

ating wood
板（敲击用木板）

aw chisel (toothed chisel, tooth
isel)
形齿子（刀），齿形齿子（刀）

at chisel
口凿刀

int (punch)
凿刀

16 iron-headed hammer
铁锤

17 gouge (hollow chisel)
圆口凿刀（凹形凿刀）

18 spoon chisel
匙形凿刀

19 wood chisel, a bevelled-edge chisel
木凿刀，一种斜刃凿刀

20 V-shaped gouge
V形，圆凿刀

21 mallet
木槌

22 framework
骨架

23 baseboard
基座

24 armature support (metal rod)
塑像人体支架（金属杆）

25 armature
塑像头部支架

26 wax model
蜡像模型

27 block of wood
木块

28 wood carver (wood sculptor)
木刻家

29 sack of gypsum powder (gypsum)
石膏粉袋

30 clay box
粘土箱

31 modelling (Am. modeling) clay (clay)
造型粘土

32 statue, a sculpture
塑像，雕塑品

33 low relief (bas-relief)
浅浮雕

34 modelling (Am. modeling) board
浮雕板

35 wire frame, wire netting
金属支架，金属网

36 circular medallion (tondo)
圆形浮雕

37 mask
面具

38 plaque
饰板

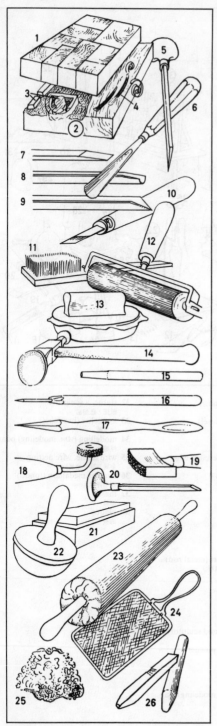

1-13 wood engraving
(xylography), a relief printing
method (a letterpress printing
method)
木刻（木板印刷），一种凸版印刷法
（活版印刷法）

1 end-grain block for wood
engravings, a wooden block
木刻用的木纹板

2 wooden plank for woodcutting,
a relief image carrier
木刻用之厚木板，木刻浮雕像之托板

3 positive cut
正像雕刻（凸刻）

4 plank cut
板刻

5 burin (graver)
雕刻刀

6 U-shaped gouge
U 型圆凿

7 scorper (scauper, scalper)
平刻刀

8 scoop
铲形雕刻工具

9 V-shaped gouge
V 型圆凿

10 contour knife
轮廓刀

11 brush
刷子

12 roller (brayer)
滚筒（用手复印之滚筒）

13 pad (wiper)
打印台（海绵擦）

14-24 copperplate engraving
(chalcography), an intaglio
process; *kinds:* etching,
mezzotint, aquatint, crayon
engraving
铜板雕刻（铜板雕刻术），一种（阴
刻）凹雕，种类有：蚀刻法，网线铜
法，铜板腐蚀法，色笔雕刻法

14 hammer
锤子

15 burin
雕刻刀

16 etching needle (engraver)
蚀刻针

17 scraper and burnisher
刮刀与磨光器

18 roulette
点线机（修版用滚网线刀）

19 rocking tool (rocker)
摇动工具

20 round-headed graver, a graver
(burin)
圆头雕刻刀

21 oilstone
油石（磨石用）

22 dabber (inking ball, ink ball)
涂料棒，散墨器

23 leather roller
皮滚筒

24 sieve
筛子

25-26 lithography (stone
lithography), a planographic
printing method
石版印刷，平版印刷法之一种

25 sponge for moistening the
lithographic stone
润湿石版用的海绵

26 lithographic crayons (greasy
chalk)
石印彩笔（蜡笔）（油性彩笔）

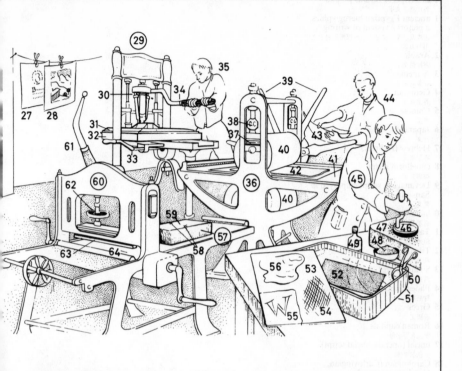

graphic art studio, a printing
~~i~~ce (*Am.* printery)
刷工艺室，印刷室
~~o~~adside (broadsheet, single
~~e~~et)
页印刷
~~ll-colour~~ (*Am.* full-color) print
~~o~~lour print,
~~o~~molithograph)
色印刷
~~t~~en press, a hand press
机（平板平压式印刷机），一种手
印刷机
~~g~~le
~~t~~en
印板
~~e~~ forme (*Am.* form)
~~d~~ mechanism
~~装~~置
~~r~~ (devil's tail)
丙
~~e~~ssman
刷工人
~~o~~pperplate press
版印刷机
~~np~~an
纸格
~~e~~ssure regulator
力调节器
~~r~~ wheel
影轮

40 cylinder
滚筒
41 bed
机台
42 felt cloth
毡布
43 proof (pull)
校样，样张
44 copperplate engraver
铜版雕刻师（工人）
45 lithographer (litho artist),
grinding the stone
磨石之石版印刷师
46 grinding disc (disk)
磨盘
47 grain (granular texture)
颗粒组织
48 pulverized glass
玻璃粉（末）
49 rubber solution
橡胶溶液
50 tongs
夹具
51 etching bath for etching
蚀刻槽
52 zinc plate
锌版
53 polished copperplate
磨光之铜版
54 cross hatch
十字影线（全面直雕）
55 etching ground
铜版上所涂之防蚀剂

56 non-printing area
不印刷的部份
57 lithographic stone
平板印刷用之石头（石板石）
58 register marks
对齐号
59 printing surface (printing image
carrier)
印刷面，版面（印刷图案之承载面）
60 lithographic press
石版印刷机
61 lever
操纵杆
62 scraper adjustment
刮具调节器
63 scraper
刮具
64 bed
版台

1-20 scripts of various peoples
各民族之文字
1 ancient Egyptian hieroglyphics,
a pictorial system of writing
古埃及之象形文字，一种以图形表示之
书写方式
2 Arabic
阿拉伯文字
3 Armenian
亚美尼亚文
4 Georgian
乔治亚文
5 Chinese
中文
6 Japanese
日文
7 Hebrew (Hebraic)
希伯来文
8 cuneiform script
楔形文字
9 Devanagari, script employed in
Sanskrit
梵文
10 Siamese
暹逻文，泰文
11 Tamil
坦米尔文
12 Tibetan
藏文
13 Sinaitic script
西奈文字
14 Phoenician
腓尼基文
15 Greek
希腊文
16 Roman capitals
罗马大写字母
17 uncial (uncials, uncial script)
安色尔字体
18 Carolingian (Carlovingian,
Caroline) minuscule
查里曼王朝用的小写字体
19 runes
古代北欧民族所用之文字
20 Russian
俄文

21-26 ancient writing implements
古代书写工具
21 Indian steel stylus for writing on
palm leaves
印地安人於棕榈叶上书写所用的钢针
22 ancient Egyptian reed pen
古埃及人所用之芦管笔
23 writing cane
竹笔
24 brush
毛笔
25 Roman metal pen (stylus)
罗马人所用之铁笔
26 quill (quill pen)
羽毛笔
27 Korean
韩文

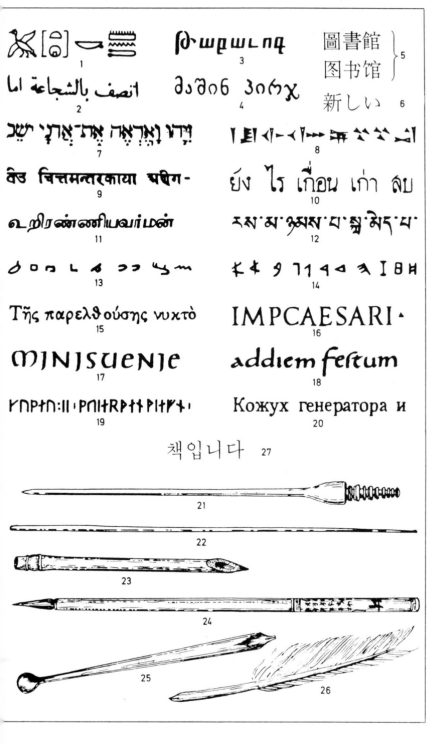

1-15 types (type faces)
字体（铅字字体）

1 Gothic type (German black-letter type)
哥德体字体（德文黑体字型）

2 Schwabacher type (German black-letter type)
萧瓦巴克式字体（德文黑体字型）

3 Fraktur (German black-letter type)
法拉克特式字体（德文黑体字型）

4 Humanist (Mediaeval)
文艺复兴字体（中世纪字体）

5 Transitional
（过渡时期字体）变体字体

6 Didone
古典拉丁字体

7 Sanserif (Sanserif type, Grotesque)
无细线体之铅字（等线黑体字）

8 Egyptian
埃及文字体

9 typescript (typewriting)
打字字体

10 English hand (English handwriting, English writing)
英文手写体

11 German hand (German handwriting, German writing)
德文手写体

12 Latin script
拉丁文字体

13 shorthand (shorthand writing, stenography)
速记体（速记文字）

14 phonetics (phonetic transcription)
音标

15 Braille
点字体（盲人用）

16-29 punctuation marks (stops)
标点符号

16 full stop (period, full point)
句号（点）

17 colon
冒号

18 comma
逗号（点）

19 semicolon
分号

20 question mark (interrogation point, interrogation mark)
问号

21 exclamation mark (*Am.* exclamation point)
惊歎号

22 apostrophe
省字符号（撇号）

23 dash (em rule)
破折号

24 parentheses (round brackets)
括号（圆括弧）（小括号）

25 square brackets
中括号（方括弧）

26 quotation mark (double quotatin marks, paired quotation marks, inverted commas)
引号（双引号，颠倒的逗号）

27 guillemet (French quotation mark)
引号（法文引号）

28 hyphen
连字号

29 marks of omission (ellipsis)
省略号

30-35 accents and diacritical marks (diacritics)
重音符号与读音符号

30 acute accent (acute)
重音符

31 grave accent (grave)
抑音符

32 circumflex accent (circumflex)
抑扬音符（转折音符）

33 cedilla [under C]
变音符（C字下头的尾形符号）

34 diaeresis (*Am.* dieresis)[over e]
分音符号

35 tilde [over n]
n字上头的"~"符号，鼻音符号

36 section mark
章节符号

37-70 newspaper, a national daily newspaper
报纸，全国性之日报

37 newspaper page
报纸（一页的）版面

38 front page
第一版（头版）

39 newspaper heading
报纸标题

40 contents
内容

41 price
价钱

42 date of publication
发行日期

43 place of publication
发行地点

44 headline
大字标题

45 column
专栏

46 column heading
专栏标题

47 column rule
专栏嵌线

48 leading article (leader, editorial)
社论

49 reference to related article
文章所附相关参考资料

50 brief news item
新闻摘要

51 political section
政治栏

52 page heading
版画标题

53 cartoon
漫画

54 report by newspaper's own correspondent
本报记者报导

55 news agency's sign
通讯社标记

56 advertisement (*coll.* ad)
广告，启事

57 sports section
体育栏

58 press photo
新闻照片

59 caption
照片说明

60 sports report
体育报导

61 sports news item
体育新闻

62 home and overseas news section
国内外新闻栏

63 news in brief (miscellaneous news)
简讯（各种新闻消息）

64 television programmes (*Am.* programs)
电视节目栏

65 weather report
气象报告栏

66 weather chart (weather map)
气象图

67 arts section (feuilleton)
文艺栏

68 death notice
死亡通知

69 advertisements (classified advertising)
广告栏（分类广告栏）

70 job advertisement, a vacancy (situation offered)
职业栏（招聘广告栏）

Oxford
1

Oxford
2

Oxford
3

Oxford
4

Oxford
5

Oxford
6

Oxford
7

Oxford
8

Oxford
9

Oxford
10

Oxford
11

Oxford
12

Blue
13

/'ɒksfəd/
14

15

.
16

:
17

,
18

;
19

?
20

!
21

'
22

—
23

( )
24

[ ]
25

" "
26

» «
27

-
28

...
29

é
30

è
31

ê
32

ç
33

ë
34

ñ
35

§
36

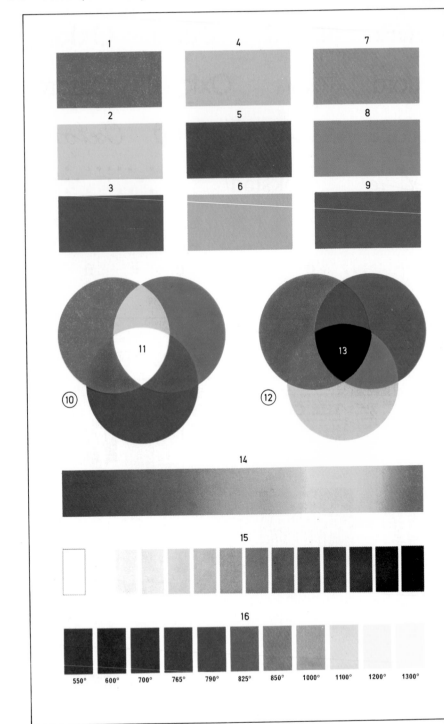

w

色
wn
, 褐色
re (sky blue)
色
nge
, 橙色
n

et

itive mixture of colours (*Am.*
rs)
混合
te

stractive mixture of colours
n. colors)
混合
ck

r spectrum (colours, *Am.*
ors, of the rainbow)
光谱（彩虹的色彩）
y (*Am.* gray) scale
色标）度，灰阶
t colours (*Am.* colors)
, 高温色

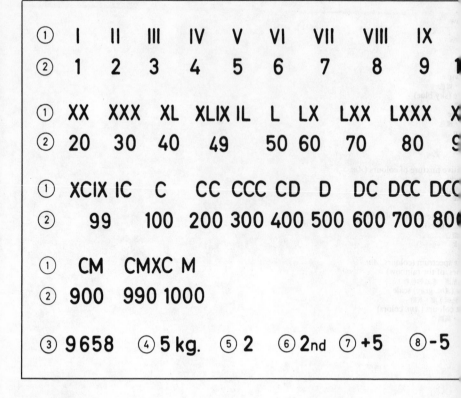

1-26 arithmetic
算术
1-22 numbers
数字
1 Roman numerals
罗马数字
2 Arabic numerals
阿拉伯数字
3 abstract number, a four-figure number [8: units; 5:tens; 6: hundreds; 9: thousands]
不名数，抽象数，四位数〔8:个位；5:十位；6:佰位；9:千位〕
4 concrete number
名数
5 cardinal number (cardinal)
基数
6 ordinal number (ordinal)
序数
7 positive number [with plus sign]
（附加号之）正数
8 negative number [with minus sign]
（附减号之）负数

a,b,c... ⑩ $3\frac{1}{3}$ ⑪ 2,4,6,8 ⑫ 1,3,5,7

3,5,7,11 ⑭ $3+2\sqrt{-1}$ ⑮ $\frac{2}{3}$ ⑯ $\frac{3}{2}$

$\frac{5}{6}$ ⑱ $\frac{12}{4}$ ⑲ $\frac{4}{5}+\frac{2}{7}=\frac{38}{35}$ ⑳ $0\cdot357$

㉑ $0\cdot6666....=0\cdot\overline{6}$ ㉒ ㉓ $3+2=5$

$3-2=1$ ㉕ $3\cdot2=6$ ㉖ $6\div2=3$

$3\times2=6$

---

raic symbols
符号
ed number [3: whole
nber (integer); ⅓:
ction]
数(3：整数；⅓：分数)
n numbers

d numbers

me numbers

nplex number [3: real part;
−1: imaginary part]
(3:实部；2 $\sqrt{-1}$：虚部)
vulgar fractions
分数
per fraction [2: numerator,
rizontal line; 3: denominator]
数(2:分子，水平线；3：分母)
proper fraction, also the
iprocal of item 15
约分数)假分数，也是第 15 项分数
则数
npound fraction (complex
ction)
分数
proper fraction [when
celled down produces a
ole number]
约分数(约分后等於整数)
ctions of different
nominations [35:common
nominator]
同分母之分数(35：公分母)

20 proper decimal fraction with
decimal point and decimal
places [3: tenths; 5: hundredths;
7:thousandths]
（带有小数点和小数位的）真小数（3:十
分位；5:百分位；7:千分位）
21 recurring decimal
循环小数
22 recurring decimal
循环小数
23-26 fundamental arithmetical operations
基本算数运算
23 addition (adding) [3 and 2: the
terms of the sum; +: plus sign;
=: equals sign; 5: the sum]
加法(3 与 2：总和之项；+：加号；=:
等号；5：和)
24 subtraction (subtracting); [3: the
minuend; -: minus sign; 2: the
subtrahend ; 1: the remainder
(difference)]
减法(3:被减数；-：减号；2:减数；
1：余（差）)
25 multiplication (multiplying);
[3:the multiplicand; ×:
multiplication sign; 2: the
multipler; 2 and 3: factors; 6: the
product]
乘法(3:被乘数（式）×:乘号；2:乘
数（式）；2 与 3:乘数；6：积)
26 division (dividing); [6: the
dividend; ÷: division sign; 2:
the divisor; 3: the quotient]
除法；[6：被除数；÷：除号；2：除
数；3：商]

① $3^2 = 9$　　　② $\sqrt[3]{8} = 2$　　　③ $\sqrt{4} =$

④ $3x + 2 = 12$

⑥

⑤ $4a + 6ab - 2ac = 2a(2 + 3b - c)$　　$\log_{10} 3 = 0.477$

⑦ $\dfrac{P[£1000] \times R[5\%] \times T[2\,years]}{100} = I[£100]$

1-24 arithmetic
算术
1-10 advanced arithmetical operations
高等算术运算
1 raising to a power [three squared (3^2): the power; 3: the base ; 2: the exponent (index); 9: value of the power]
乘方〔3 之平方（3^2）:乘方（幂）；3: 底；2:指数；9:乘方值〕
2 evolution (extracting a root); [cube-root of 8: cube root; 8: the radical; 3: the index (degree) of the root; $\sqrt{}$: radical sign; 2; value of the root]
开方〔8 的立方根；8：根数；3：根指数；$\sqrt{}$：根号；2：根值〕
3 square root
平方根
4-5 algebra
代数
4 simple equation [3, 2: the coefficients; x: the unknown quantity]
简单方程式〔3, 2：系数；x：未知数〕
5 identical equation : [a, b, c: algebraic symbols]
恒等式〔a, b, c:代数符号〕

6 logarithmic calculation (taking the logarithm, log); [log: logarithm sign; 3: number whose logarithm is required; 10: the base; 0: the characteristic; 4771: the mantissa; 0,4771: the logarithm]
对数计算〔log:对数符号；3:真数（求对数之数）；10:底；0：（对数之）首数；4771:尾数；0.4771:对数值〕
7 simple interest formula; [P: the principal; R: rate of interest; T: time; I: Interest (profit); %: percentage sign]
简单利息公式〔P：本金；R:利率；T：时间；I：利息；%：百分号〕

⑧ 2 years @ £ 50

4 years @ £ x

⑨ 2 : 50 = 4 : x

⑩ x = £ 100

⑪ 2 + 4 + 6 + 8 ....

⑫ 2 + 4 + 8 + 16 + 32 ....

⑬ $\dfrac{dy}{dx}$

⑭ $\int a x \, dx = a \int x \, dx = \dfrac{a x^2}{2} + C$

⑤ ∞   ⑯ ≡   ⑰ ≈   ⑱ ≠   ⑲ >

⑳ <   ㉑ ∥   ㉒ ∼   ㉓ ◁   ㉔ △

rule of three (rule-of-three
m, simple proportion)
单比例法
tement with the unknown
antity x
x 为未知量的陈述
uation (conditional equation)
程式（条件方程式）
lution

higher mathematics
等数学
ithmetical series with the
ements 2, 4, 6, 8
有 2, 4, 6, 8 等元素之算术（等差）级

ometrical series
何级数（等比级数）
infinitesimal calculus
积分（学）
rivative [dx, dy: the
fferentials; d: differential
gn]
数，微分〔dx, dy: 微分；d: 微分符号〕
egral (integration); [x: the
riable; C: constant of
tegration; S: the integral sign;
: the differential]
分〔x: 变量（数）；C:积分常数；
积分符号；dx: 微分〕
mathematical symbols
学符号
finity
穷（大）

16 identically equal to (the sign of
   identity)
   恒等于（恒等符号）
17 approximately equal to
   约等于，近似于
18 unequal to
   不等于
19 greater than
   大于
20 less than
   小于
21-24 geometrical symbols
   几何符号
21 parallel (sign of parallelism)
   平行（平行符号）
22 similar to (sign of similarity)
   相似於（相似符号）
23 angle symbol
   角之符号
24 triangle symbol
   三角形符号

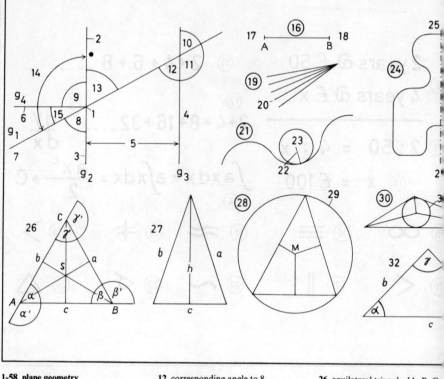

1-58 plane geometry
(elementary geometry, Euclidian geometry)
平面几何学（初等几何学，欧几里德几何学）

1-23 point, line, angle
点，线，角

1 point [point of intersection of g_1 and g_2], the angular point of 8
点〔g_1 与 g_2 之交点〕，角 8 之顶点

2, 3 straight line g_2
直线 g_2

4 the parallel to g_2
平行於 g_2（的直线）

5 distance between the straight lines g_2 and g_3
直线 g_2 与 g_3 间的距离

6 perpendicular (g_4) on g_2
g_2 的垂线（g_4）

7, 3 the arms of 8
角 8 的边

8, 13 vertically opposite angles
角 13 的对顶角

8 angle
角

9 right angle [90°]
直角〔90°〕

10, 11, 12 reflex angle
优角（大於 180°，小於 360°）

10 acute angle, also the alternate angle to 8
锐角，即角 8 的交错角

11 obtuse angle
钝角

12 corresponding angle to 8
角 8 的同位角

13, 9, 15 straight angle [180°]
平角〔180°〕

14 adjacent angle; *here*: supplementary angle to 13
邻角；此指：角 13 之补角

15 complementary angle to 8
角 8 之馀角

16 straight line AB
直线段 AB

17 end A
端点 A

18 end B
端点 B

19 pencil of rays
射线束

20 ray
射线

21 curved line
曲线

22 radius of curvature
曲率半径

23 centre (*Am.* center) of curvature
曲率中心

24-58 plane surfaces
平面

24 symmetrical figure
对称图形

25 axis of symmetry
对称轴

26-32 plane triangles
平面三角形

26 equilateral triangle; [A, B, C: the vertices; a, b, c: the sides; (alpha), β (beta), γ (gamma): interior angles; α′, β′, γ′: the exterior angles the centre (*Am.* center)]
等边三角形；〔A, B, C:顶点；a, b, c: 边；α, β, γ：内角；α′, β′, γ′：外角中心〕

27 isosceles triangle [a, b: the sid (legs); c: the base; h: the perpendicular, an altitude]
等腰三角形〔a, b: 边（腰股）；C:底；h:高，顶垂线〕

28 acute-angled triangle with perpendicular bisectors of the sides
各边带中垂线的锐角三角形

29 circumcircle (circumscribed circle)
外接圆

30 obtuse-angled triangle with bisectors of the angles
带角平分线的钝角三角形

31 inscribed circle
内切圆

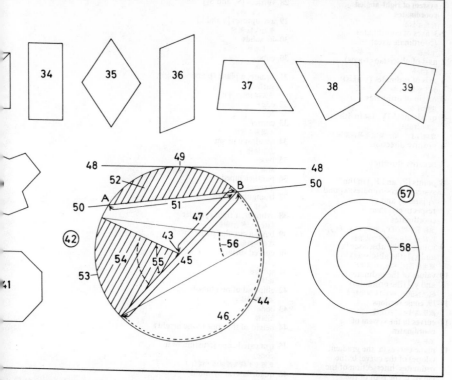

right-angled triangle and the
trigonometrical functions of
angles; [a, b: the catheti; c: the
hypotenuse; γ : the right angle;

$= \sin \alpha$ (sine); $\frac{b}{c} = \cos \alpha$

(cosine); $\frac{a}{b} = \tan \alpha$ (tangent);

$= \cot \alpha$ (cotangent)]

直角三角形及角的三角形函数〔a, b:直角
c: (直角三角形之) 斜边；γ : 直角
$= \sin \alpha$ (正弦) ; $\frac{b}{c} = \cos \alpha$ (馀弦) ;
$= \tan \alpha$ (正切) ; $\frac{b}{a} = \cot \alpha$ (馀切) 〕

quadrilaterals
边形
parallelograms
行四边形
quare [d: a diagonal]
方形 [d:对角线]
ctangle
方形，矩形
ombus (rhomb, lozenge)
形
omboid
菱形，长斜方形
apezium
形
eltoid (kite)
方形（纸鸢形)

39 irregular quadrilateral
不规则四边形
40 polygon
多边形（多角形)
41 regular polygon
正多边形
42 circle
圆
43 centre (*Am.* center)
圆心
44 circumference (periphery)
圆周（周边)
45 diameter
直径
46 semicircle
半圆
47 radius (r)
半径 (r)
48 tangent
切线
49 point of contact (p)
切点 (p)
50 secant
割线
51 the chord AB
弦 AB
52 segment
弓形
53 arc
弧
54 sector
扇形

55 angle subtended by the arc at the centre (*Am.* center) (centre, *Am.* center, angle)
对弧圆心角
56 circumferential angle
圆周角
57 ring (annulus)
环（圆环)
58 concentric circles
同心圆

1 system of right-angled
coordinates
直角坐标系

2-3 axes of coordinates
(coordinate axes)
坐标轴

2 axis of abscissae (x-axis)
横坐标轴（x 轴）

3 axis of ordinates (y-axis)
纵坐标轴（y 轴）

4 origin of ordinates
坐标原点

5 quadrant [I-IV: 1st to 4th
quadrant]
象限〔I-IV：第一象限至第四象限〕

6 positive direction
正向

7 negative direction
负向

8 points [P_1 and P_2] in the
system of coordinates; x_1 and
y_1 [and x_2 and y_2
respectively] their
coordinates
坐标系中的点〔P_1 和 P_2〕；x_1 和 y_1〔
以及 x_2 和 y_2〕分别为其坐标

9 values of the abscissae [x_1
and x_2] (the abscissae)
横坐标值[x_1 和 x_2]（横坐标）

10 values of the ordinates [y_1
and y_2] (the ordinates)
纵坐标值[y_1 和 y_2]（纵坐标）

11-29 conic sections
圆锥曲线，二次曲线

11 curves in the system of
coordinates
坐标系中的曲线

12 plane curves [a: the gradient
(slope) of the curve; b: the
ordinates' intersection of the
curve; c: the root of the
curve]
平面曲线[a：曲线的斜率；b：曲线与纵
轴的交点；c:曲线之根（零点）]

13 inflected curves
拐曲线

14 parabola, a curve of the
second degree
抛物线（二次曲线之一）

15 branches of the parabola
抛物线之分支

16 vertex of the parabola
抛物线的顶点

17 axis of the parabola
抛物线的轴

18 a curve of the third degree
三次曲线

19 maximum of the curve
曲线的最大点（值）

20 minimum of the curve
曲线的最小点（值）

21 point of inflexion (of
inflection)
拐点，反曲点

22 ellipse
椭圆

23 transverse axis (major axis)
横截轴（长轴）

24 conjugate axis (minor axis)
共轭轴（短轴）

25 foci of the ellipse [F_1 and F_2]
椭圆的焦点[F_1 and F_2]

26 hyperbola
双曲线

27 foci [F_1 and F_2]
焦点〔F_1 and F_2〕

28 vertices [S_1 and S_2]
顶点〔S_1 and S_2〕

29 asymptotes [a and b]
渐近线 [a and b]

30-46 solids
立体图形

30 cube
立方体

31 square, a plane (plane
surface)
正方体的一个平面

32 edge
棱

33 corner
（隅角）棱角

34 quadratic prism
方形棱柱

35 base
底面

36 parallelepiped
平行六面体

37 triangular prism
三棱柱

38 cylinder, a right cylinder
圆柱，一种直圆柱

39 base, a circular plane
底面，圆平面

40 curved surface
曲面

41 sphere
球体

42 ellipsoid of revolution
迴转椭球体

43 cone
圆锥体

44 height of the cone (cone height)
圆锥的高

45 truncated cone (frustum of a
cone)
截锥（平截头圆锥体，锥台）

46 quadrilateral pyramid
四边形棱锥

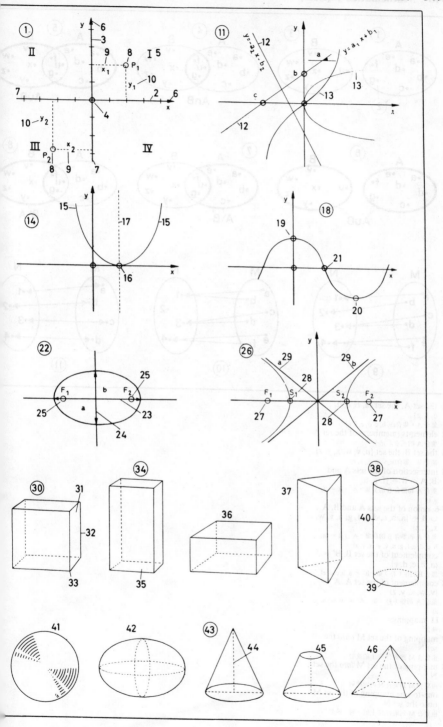

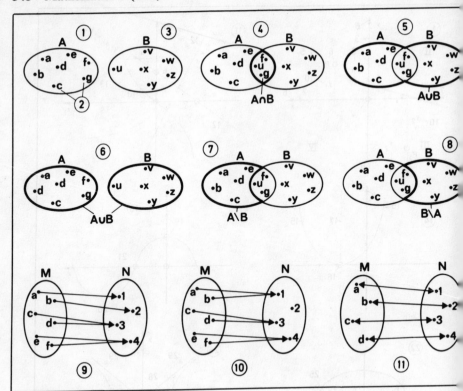

1 the set A, the set {a, b, c, d,
   e, f, g}
   集合 A，集合{a, b, c, d, e, f, g}
2 elememts (members) of the set A
   集合 A 的元素（元）
3 the set B, the set {u, v, w, x, y, z}
   集合 B，集合{u, v, w, x, y, z}
4 intersection of the sets A and
   B, A ∩ B = {f, g, u}
   集合 A 和集合 B 的交集，A ∩ B = {f,
   g, u}
5-6 union of the sets A and B, A
   ∪ B = {a, b, c, d, e, f, g, u, v, w,
   x, y, z}
   集合 A 和集合 B 的联集，A ∪ B = {a,
   b, c, d, e, f, g, u, v, w, x, y, z}
7 complement of the set B, B' =
   {a, b, c, d, e}
   集合 B 的馀（补）集，B' = {a, b, c, d, e}
8 complement of the set A, A' =
   {v, w, x, y, z}
   集合 A 的馀（补）集，A' = {v, w, x, y,
   z}
9-11 mappings
   映射
9 mapping of the set M *onto* the
   set N
   由集合 M 到集合 N 上的映射
10 mapping of the set M *into* the set
   N
   由集合 M 到集合 N 内的映射
11 one-to-one mapping of the set M
   onto the set N
   由集合 M 到集合 N 上的一对一映射

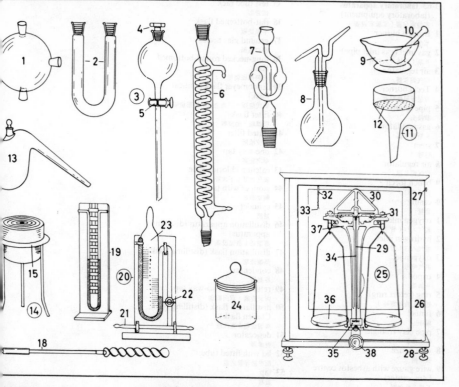

laboratory apparatus
(laboratory equipment)
实验室仪器（实验室设备）

heidt globe
施特球（施特球）

tube
型管

parating funnel
分液漏斗

tagonal ground-glass stopper
角形毛玻璃栓（塞）

o (*Am.* faucet)
塞，旋塞

iled condenser
管冷凝器

lock
全漏斗

ash-bottle
洗瓶

ortar
钵

stle
杵

ter funnel (Büchner funnel)
滤漏斗（布氏漏斗）

ter (filter plate)
板

tort
（曲颈瓶）

ater bath
浴

ipod
脚架

16 water gauge (*Am.* gage)
水位计
17 insertion rings
嵌入环
18 stirrer
搅拌器
19 manometer for measuring
positive and negative pressures
测正负压用之 U 型管
20 mirror manometer for
measuring small pressures
测微压用之反射镜压力计
21 inlet
入口（进）
22 tap (*Am.* faucet)
活塞，旋塞
23 sliding scale
滑尺
24 weighing bottle
称量瓶
25 analytical balance
分析天平
26 case
天平罩
27 sliding front panel
滑动前板
28 three-point support
三点支架
29 column (balance column)
立柱（天平立柱）
30 balance beam (beam)
天平横梁
31 rider bar
游码梁

32 rider holder
游码杆（架）
33 rider
游码
34 pointer
指针
35 scale
刻度尺
36 scale pan
秤盘
37 stop
制动器（吊耳）
38 stop knob
制动旋钮

1-63 laboratory apparatus
(laboratory equipment)
实验室仪器（实验室设备）

1 Bunsen burner
本生灯

2 gas inlet (gas inlet pipe)
瓦斯（气体）入口管

3 air regulator
空气调节器

4 Teclu burner
双层转筒燃烧器

5 pipe union
管接头

6 gas regulator
瓦斯调节器

7 stem
灯管

8 air regulator
空气调节器

9 bench torch
台式喷灯

10 casing
套管

11 oxygen inlet
氧气入口（管）

12 hydrogen inlet
氢气入口（管）

13 oxygen jet
氧气喷咀

14 tripod
三脚架

15 ring (retort ring)
铁圈（曲颈瓶环）

16 funnel
漏斗

17 pipe clay triangle
陶三角管

18 wire gauze
铁丝网

19 wire gauze with asbestos centre
(*Am.* center)
石绵芯铁丝网

20 beaker
烧杯

21 burette (for measuring the
volume of liquids)
量液体体积用的滴管（玻璃量管）

22 burette stand
滴定管架

23 burette clamp
滴定管夹

24 graduated pipette
刻度移液管，吸量管

25 pipette
移液管

26 measuring cylinder (measuring
glass)
量筒

27 measuring flask
量瓶

28 volumetric flask
容量瓶（测定体积的烧瓶）

29 evaporating dish (evaporating
basin), made of porcelain
蒸发皿（磁制品）

30 tube clamp (tube clip,
pinchcock)
螺旋夹

31 clay crucible with lid
带盖陶土坩锅

32 crucible tongs
坩锅钳

33 clamp
烧瓶夹

34 test tube
试管

35 test tube rack
试管架

36 flat-bottomed flask
平底烧瓶

37 ground glas neck
磨口瓶颈

38 long-necked round-bottomed
flask
长颈圆底烧瓶

39 Erlenmeyer flask (conical
flask)
依氏烧瓶，三角烧瓶（锥形烧瓶）

40 filter flask
吸滤瓶，抽滤瓶

41 fluted filter
波纹滤纸

42 one-way tap
单向旋塞

43 calcium chloride tube
氯化钙管（干燥管）

44 stopper with tap
制动旋塞

45 cylinder
量筒

46 distillation apparatus (distilling
apparatus)
蒸馏器（蒸馏设备）

47 distillation flask (distilling flask)
蒸馏烧瓶

48 condenser
冷凝器

49 return tap, a two-way tap
回流旋塞，双向旋塞

50 distillation flask (distilling flask,
Claisen flask)
蒸馏烧瓶（克氏瓶）

51 desiccator
乾燥器

52 lid with fitted tube
配密接导管之盖

53 tap
旋塞

54 desiccator insert made of
porcelain
磁制乾燥器隔板

55 three-necked flask
三口烧瓶

56 connecting piece (Y-tube)
连接管（Y 形管）

57 three-necked bottle
三颈瓶

58 gas-washing bottle
洗气瓶

59 gas generator (Kipp's apparatus,
Am. Kipp generator)
气体发生器（启普发生器）

60 overflow container
溢流容器

61 container for the solid
固体容器

62 acid container
酸容器

63 gas outlet
导气管

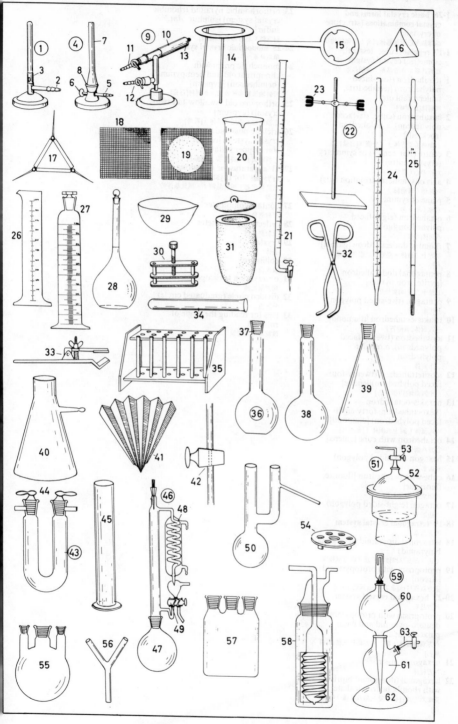

1-26 basic crystal forms and crystal combinations (structure of crystals)
晶体基本形状及晶体组合（晶体结构）
1-17 regular (cubic, tesseral, isometric) crystal system
规则晶系（立方晶系，等轴晶系）
1 tetrahedron (four-faced polyhedron) [tetrahedrite, fahlerz, fahl ore]
四面体[黝铜矿]
2 hexahedron (cube, six-faced polyhedron), a holohedron [rock salt]
六面体（立方体），全面体[岩盐]
3 centre (*Am.* center) of symmetry (crystal centre)
对称中心（晶体中心）
4 axis of symmetry (rotation axis)
对称轴（转动轴）
5 plane of symmetry
对称（平）面
6 octahedron (eight-faced polyhedron)[gold]
八面体[金矿]
7 rhombic dodecahedron [garnet]
斜方十二面体，菱形十二面体[石榴子石]
8 pentagonal dodecahedron [pyrite, iron pyrites]
五角十二面体[黄铁矿]
9 pentagon (five-sided polygon)
五边形
10 triakis-octahedron [diamond]
三八面体[金刚石]
11 icosahedron (twenty-faced polyhedron), a regular polyhedron
二十面体
12 icositetrahedron (twenty-four-faced polyhedron)[leucite]
二十四面体[白榴子石]
13 hexakis-octahedron (hexoctahedron, forty-eight-faced polyhedron) [diamond]
六八面体（四十八面）[金刚石]
14 octahedron with cube [galena]
立方八面体[方铅矿]
15 hexagon (six-sided polygon)
六边形
16 cube with octahedron [fluorite, fluorspar]
八面立方体[氟石]
17 octagon (eight-sided polygon)
八边形
18-19 tetragonal crystal system
四方晶系
18 tetragonal dipyramid (tetragonal bipyramid)
（正）四方双锥体，（正）四方双棱锥
19 protoprism with protopyramid [zircon]
正方双锥柱体[金岩英石(风信子石)]
20-22 hexagonal crystal system
六方晶系
20 protoprism with protopyramid, deutero-pyramid and basal pinacoid [apatite]
六方双锥柱体，第二六方锥和底轴面[磷灰石]
21 hexagonal prism
六方柱体
22 hexagonal (ditrigonal) biprism with rhombohedron [calcite]
菱面六方双柱体（复三角双柱体）[方解石]
23 orthorhombic pyramid (rhombic crystal system) [sulphur, *Am.* sulfur]
斜方锥（斜方晶系）[硫黄]
24-25 monoclinic crystal system
单斜晶系
24 monoclinic prism with clinoprinacoid and hemipyramid (hemihedron) [gypsum]
带斜轴面和半棱锥面之单斜柱[石膏]
25 orthopinacoid (swallow-tail twin crystal) [gypsum]
正轴面（燕尾双晶体）[石膏]
26 triclinic pinacoids (triclinic crystal system) [copper sulphate, *Am.* copper sulfate]
三斜轴面（三斜晶系）[硫酸铜]
27-33 apparatus for measuring crystals (for crystallometry)
结晶测定器（用于晶粒），测量晶体的仪器
27 contact goniometer
接触测角器
28 reflecting goniometer
反射测角器
29 crystal
晶体
30 collimator
视准仪
31 observation telescope
观测望远镜
32 divided circle (graduated circle)
分度盘
33 lens for reading the angle of rotation
读旋角用之透镜

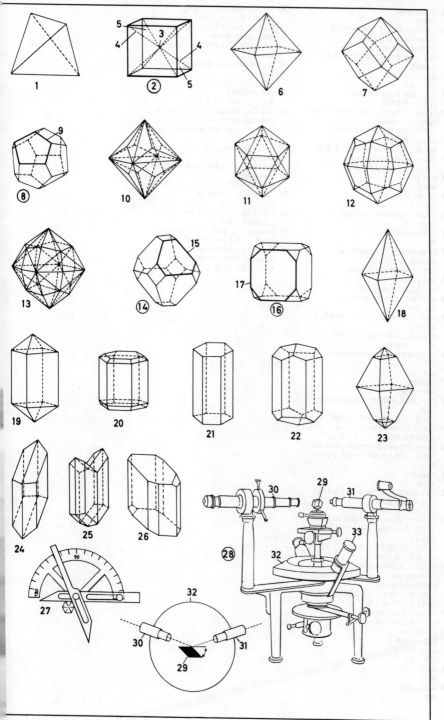

1 totem pole
图腾柱

2 totem, a carved and painted pictorial or symbolic representation
图腾，一种雕刻和绘制的图画，或象征性的图象

3 plains Indian
平原（草原）印第安人

4 mustang, a prairie horse
野马，一种草原马

5 lasso, a long throwing-rope with running noose
套索，一种带有活结的长套索抛绳

6 pipe of peace
印第安人用以表示和平和装饰的长烟管

7 wigwam (tepee, teepee)
（印第安人所居之）锥形帐篷

8 tent pole
帐篷柱

9 smoke flap
排烟口盖

10 squaw, an Indian woman
印第安女人

11 Indian chief
酋长

12 headdress, an ornamental feather headdress
头饰，一种装饰用的羽毛头饰

13 war paint
出征前在脸上所涂的花纹

14 necklace of bear claws
熊爪项链

15 scalp (cut from enemy's head), a trophy
附着头发之头皮（从敌人头上割下的），一种战利品

16 tomahawk, a battle axe (*Am.* ax)
战斧

17 leggings
绑腿，护腿

18 moccasin, a shoe of leather and bast
平底鞋，一种以皮革或韧皮制的鞋子

19 canoe of the forest Indians
森林地带印第安人所用之独木舟

20 Maya temple, a stepped pyramid
（中美）马雅人之神殿，一种阶形金字塔

21 mummy
木乃伊

22 quipa (knotted threads, knotted code of the Incas)
（古秘鲁人之）结绳文字

23 Indio (Indian of Central and South America); here: highland Indian
印第安人（中南美州的印第安人）；此指：高原（地）印第安人

24 poncho, a blanket with a head opening used as an armless cloak-like wrap
斗篷式披巾，南美人当作无袖斗篷外套用的中央开领口的毛毡

25 Indian of the tropical forest
热带森林区的印第安人

26 blowpipe
吹管（吹筒筒）

27 quiver
箭筒（袋）

28 dart
箭

29 dart point
箭头

30 shrunken head, a trophy
收缩的头颅，一种战利品

31 bola (bolas), a throwing and entangling device
系有（铁球）石头的绳索，一种投掷与缠牛的工具

32 leather-covered stone or metal ball
包兽皮的石头或铁球

33 pile dwelling
湖上（边）住居（房屋）

34 duk-duk dancer, a member of a duk-duk (men's secret society)
达克舞者，达克（男人秘密社团）的成员

35 outrigger canoe (canoe with outrigger)
装有舷外（浮）支架的独木舟（小船）

36 outrigger
舷外（浮）支架

37 Australian aborigine
澳洲土著（原住民）

38 loincloth of human hair
人发的腰布，缠腰带

39 boomerang, a wooden missile
回旋镖，一种木制的投掷武器

40 throwing stick (spear thrower) with spears
带矛之投掷杆（标枪）

1 Eskimo
爱斯基摩人

2 sledge dog (sled dog), a husky
拖雪橇之狗（拖小雪橇之狗），一种爱
斯基摩狗

3 dog sledge (dog sled)
狗拉的雪橇

4 igloo, a dome-shaped snow hut
爱斯基摩人所居之雪屋，一种圆顶以雪
块砌成小雪屋

5 block of snow
雪块

6 entrance tunnel
进口通道

7 blubber-oil lamp
鲸油灯

8 wooden missile
木制投掷器

9 lance
长矛

10 harpoon
（捕鲸鱼用系带绳索的）鱼叉

11 skin float
皮制浮标（浮子）

12 kayak, a light one-man canoe
爱斯基摩人用的皮舟，一种单人用的轻
便独木舟

13 skin-covered wooden or bone
frame
包兽皮的木架和骨架

14 paddle
桨

15 reindeer harness
驯鹿装具

16 reindeer
驯鹿

17 Ostyak (Ostiak)
（西伯利亚的）奥斯提亚克人

18 passenger sledge
载人雪橇

19 yurt (yurta), a dwelling tent of
the western and central Asiatic
nomads
（圆顶帐篷）蒙古包，西方和中亚游牧
民族所居住的帐篷

20 felt covering
毛毡盖

21 smoke outlet
排烟口

22 Kirghiz
吉尔吉斯人（中亚西部的住民）

23 sheepskin cap
羊皮帽

24 shaman
黄教僧人（道士）

25 decorative fringe
缘饰，穗状饰物

26 frame drum
木架（框）鼓

27 Tibetan
西藏人

28 flintlock with bayonets
带刺刀之燧发枪

29 prayer wheel
（喇嘛教之）祈祷轮，法轮

30 felt boot
毡靴

31 houseboat (sampan)
船宅（舢板）

32 junk
平底帆船

33 mat sail
蓆帆（粗布帆）

34 rickshaw (ricksha)
人力车（黄包车）

35 rickshaw coolie (cooly)
人力车夫，黄包车夫

36 Chinese lantern
中国灯笼

37 samurai
武士

38 padded armour (*Am.* armor)
带衬垫之盔甲

39 geisha
艺妓

40 kimono
和服

41 obi
（日本和服的）宽腰带

42 fan
扇子

43 coolie (cooly)
苦力，小工

44 kris (creese, crease), a Malayan
dagger
刀身成波状的短剑，马来西亚人用的短
剑

45 snake charmer
耍蛇人

46 turban
（印度男人所包的）头巾

47 flute
笛

48 dancing snake
舞蛇

1 camel caravan
骆驼商队
2 riding animal
骑乘之动物，此指骆驼
3 pack animal
载货之动物（骆驼）
4 oasis
绿州
5 grove of palm trees
棕榈树丛（林）
6 bedouin (beduin)
贝都因人（居住於阿拉伯半岛及北非之
游牧民族）
7 burnous
带有头巾的外衣
8 Masai warrior
马塞族战士（东非）
9 headdress (hairdress)
发式
10 shield
盾
11 painted ox hide
着色（彩色）的牛皮
12 long-bladed spear
长刃的矛
13 negro
黑人
14 dance drum
舞蹈用鼓
15 throwing knife
掷刀，飞刀
16 wooden mask
木制面具
17 figure of an ancestor
祖先雕像
18 slit gong
拍板（中间挖有细缝的长木块，用来敲
击传递信号用）
19 drumstick
鼓槌
20 dugout, a boat hollowed out of a
tree trunk
独木舟，由树干挖空做成的船
21 negro hut
黑人茅舍
22 negress
黑人妇女
23 lip plug (labret)
唇栓（唇饰）
24 grinding stone
磨石
25 Herero woman
赫雷娄族妇女（西南非班图族系之一
族）
26 leather cap
皮帽
27 calabash (gourd)
葫芦或葫芦所制的容器
28 beehive-shaped hut
蜂窝状的茅舍
29 bushman
南非之布希门族人
30 earplug
耳栓
31 loincloth
缠腰布
32 bow
弓
33 knobkerry (knobkerrie), a club
with round, knobbed end
圆头棒，一端为圆球状的棍棒
34 bushman woman making a fire
by twirling a stick
布希门族女人钻木取火
35 windbreak
防风林
36 Zulu in dance costume
着舞蹈服装的祖鲁人

37 dancing stick
舞棒
38 bangle
脚镯
39 ivory war horn
象牙战角
40 string of amulets and bones
一串护身符与骨头
41 pigmy
（居於非洲赤道附近的）小矮人，匹克
米族
42 magic pipe for exorcising evil
spirits
驱邪魔笛
43 fetish
物神

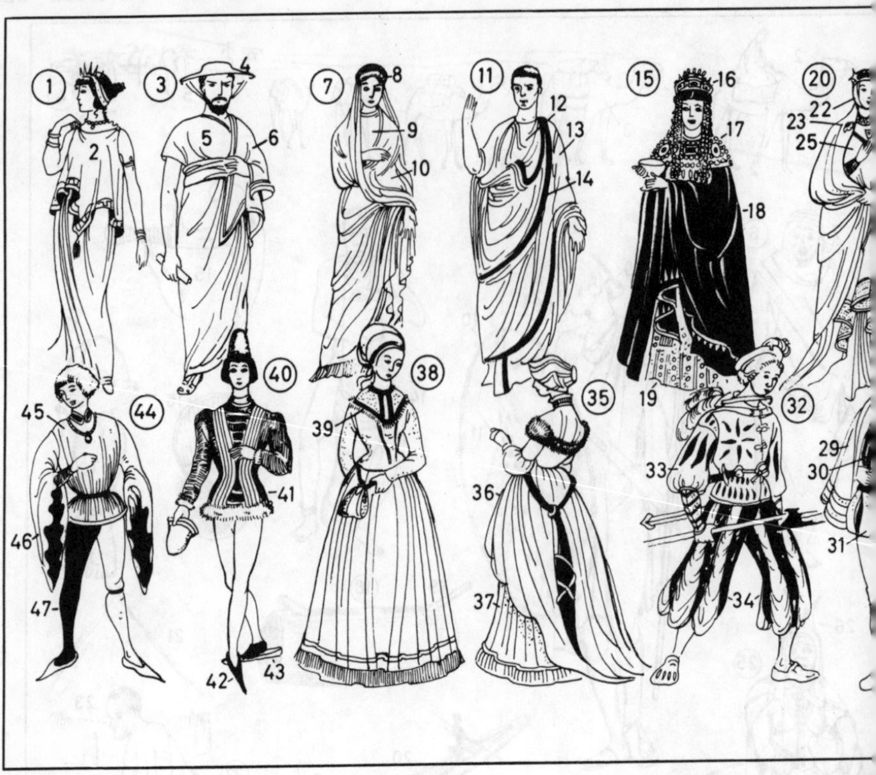

1 Greek woman
希腊妇女
2 peplos
披肩式外衣
3 Greek
希腊男人
4 petasus (Thessalonian hat)
低顶宽边帽
5 chiton, a linen gown worn as a basic garment
衬衣，当为一般衣裳穿著的亚麻长袍
6 himation, woollen (*Am.* woolen) cloak
古希腊人作长袍穿之长方布条，毛料外衣
7 Roman woman
罗马妇女
8 toupee wig (partial wig)
假发
9 stola
（古罗马妇女的）外套
10 palla, a coloured (*Am.* colored) wrap
罩袍，一种彩色披肩
11 Roman
罗马男人
12 tunica (tunic)
短袖上衣
13 toga
宽外袍
14 purple border (purple band)
紫色镶边
15 Byzantine empress
拜占庭帝国女皇
16 pearl diadem
珍珠王冠
17 jewels
珠宝
18 purple cloak
紫色斗篷
19 long tunic
长外衣
20 German princess [13th cent.]
德意志联邦公主（王妃）[13 世纪]
21 crown (diadem)
王冠
22 chinband
颚带
23 tassel
缌，缨
24 cloak cord
斗篷楞条
25 grit-up gown (grit-up surcoat, grit-up tunic)
束发长袍〔束带外衣（上衣）〕
26 cloak
斗篷
27 German dressed in the Spanish style [ca. 1575]
穿西班牙服饰的日尔曼人（约 1575 年）
28 wide-brimmed cap
宽边帽
29 short cloak (Spanish cloak, short cape)
短斗篷（西班牙式斗篷，短披肩）
30 padded doublet (stuffed dou peasecod)
衬垫（填料）紧身上衣（14-18 世纪上衣）（填料紧身上衣）
31 stuffed trunk-hose
填料大脚管短裤
32 lansquenet (German mercen soldier) (ca. 1530)
德国佣兵（约 1530 年）
33 slashed doublet (paned doub
有叉口的紧身上衣
34 Pluderhose (loose breeches, paned trunk-hose, slops)
灯笼裤（宽松的马裤，杂色小布拼做大管裤子）
35 woman of Basle [ca. 1525]
巴塞尔妇女（约 1525 年）
36 overgown (gown)
外长袍
37 undergown (petticoat)
衬裙
38 woman of Nuremberg [ca. 1500]
纽伦堡妇女（约 1500 年）
39 shoulder cape
披肩
40 Burgundian [15th cent.]
勃艮地人（15 世纪）
41 short doublet
短的紧身上衣
42 piked shoes (peaked shoes, copped shoes, crackowes, poulaines)
尖头鞋（14 世纪之靴或鞋）

tens (clogs)
桂，木套鞋（木屐）
ng nobleman [ca. 1400]
经的贵族（约 1400 年）
rt, padded doublet (short,
ilted doublet, jerkin)
科紧身短上衣（男用无袖短皮上衣）
gged sleeves (petal-scalloped
eves)
状袖
se
花袜
gsburg patrician lady [ca.
75]
约 1575 年左右）奥格斯堡的贵族妇女
ffed sleeve
笼袖
ergown (gown, open gown,
eveless gown)
外衣（长外衣，无扣长外衣，无袖长
衣）
ench lady [ca. 1600]
国女（约 1600 年）
llstone ruff (cartwheel ruff,
ff)
盘状襞襟（车轮状襞襟，襞襟）
rseted waist (wasp waist)
腰，束腹
ntleman [ca. 1650]
士（约 1650 年）
de-brimmed felt hat (cavalier
t)
边毡帽（武士帽）

56 falling collar (wide-falling
collar) of linen
亚麻布下翻领（落边宽领）
57 white lining
白色衬里
58 jack boots (bucket-top boots)
长统靴（翻皮长统靴）
59 lady [ca. 1650]
贵妇人（约 1650 年）
60 full puffed sleeves (puffed
sleeves)
灯笼袖
61 gentleman [ca. 1700]
绅士（男士）〔约 1700 年〕
62 three-cornered hat
三角帽
63 dress sword
佩剑
64 lady [ca. 1700]
贵妇人〔约 1700 年〕
65 lace fontange (high headdress of
lace)
（17, 18 世纪时）花边女帽（花边头
饰）
66 lace-trimmed loose-hanging
gown (loose-fitting housecoat,
robe de chambre, negligée,
contouche)
花边宽松长袍（家居穿著的宽松长衣,
卧室内穿的宽松外袍，家常睡袍）
67 band of embroidery
刺绣花条
68 lady [ca. 1880]
贵妇人（约 1880 年）

69 bustle
腰垫
70 lady [ca. 1858]
贵妇人〔约 1858 年〕
71 poke bonnet
帽子撑缘
72 crinoline
用箍扩衬著的裙子
73 gentleman of the Biedermeier
period
彼德麦时期（19 世纪）的德国绅士
74 high collar (choker collar)
高领
75 embroidered waistcoat (vest)
绣花服背心（背心）
76 frock coat
（男人）大礼服
77 pigtail wig
假发辫
78 ribbon (bow)
缎带（蝴蝶结）
79 ladies in court dress [ca. 1780]
穿著朝服（宫庭服）的贵妇人〔约 1780
年〕
80 train
衣裙，拖曳的长裙
81 upswept Rococo coiffure
洛可可式向上梳的发型
82 hair decoration
发饰
83 panniered overskirt
有裙撑的外裙

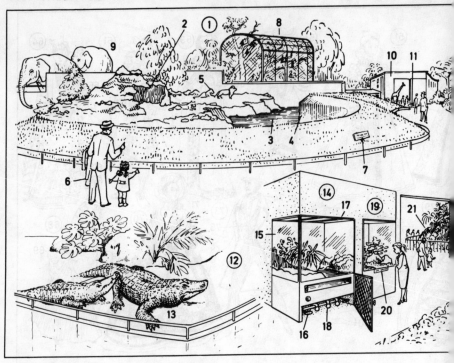

1 outdoor enclosure
 (enclosure)
 户外围场
2 rocks
 岩石
3 moat
 濠沟
4 enclosing wall
 围墙
5 animals on show; *here:* a pride
 of lions
 展示的动物, 此指狮子
6 visitor to the zoo
 动物园游客
7 notice
 布告
8 aviary
 禽舍
9 elephant enclosure
 象的围场
10 animal house (e.g. carnivore
 house, giraffe house, elephant
 house, monkey house)
 动物舍 (如食肉动物舍, 长颈鹿舍, 象
 舍, 猴舍)
11 outside cage, animals' summer
 quarters
 户外笼, 动物夏季放饲场
12 reptile enclosure
 爬虫类围场
13 Nile crocodile
 尼罗河鳄鱼
14 terrarium and aquarium
 陆地动物饲养所和水族馆
15 glass case
 玻璃柜
16 fresh-air inlet
 新鲜空气入口
17 ventilator
 通气口
18 underfloor heating
 地下暖气设备
19 aquarium
 水族馆
20 information plate
 资料 (说明) 牌
21 flora in artificially maintained
 climate
 人工气候培养的植物群

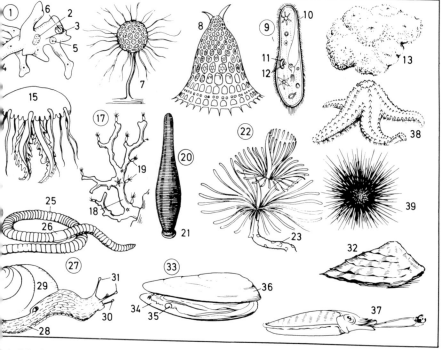

nicellular (one-celled, le-celled) animals
(tozoans)
胞动物（原生动物）
虫，根足类动物
nucleus
核
toplasm
质
udopod
，虚足，假足
retory vacuole (contractile uole, an organelle)
胞（伸缩泡，一细胞器官）
d vacuole

nophrys, a heliozoan
虫
iolarian; *here:* siliceous leton
虫类，此指：含矽质骨骼的放射

per animalcule, a amecium
虫
um

cronucleus (meganucleus)
ronucleus

multicellular animals
ctazoans)
胞动物（后生动物）
h sponge, a porifer (sponge)
，一种多孔动物(海绵动物)

14 medusa, a discomedusa (jellyfish), a coelenterate
水母，腔肠动物的一种
15 umbrella
（水母的）伞罩
16 tentacle
触手
17 red coral (precious coral), a coral animal (anthozoan, reef-building animal)
红珊瑚（珍贵珊瑚），一种珊瑚动物（花虫类动物，构成珊瑚礁的动物）
18 coral colony
珊瑚群体
19 coral polyp
珊瑚虫（水螅型）
20-26 worms (Vermes)
蠕虫（蠕虫形动物）
20 leech, an annelid
水蛭，一种环节动物
21 sucker
吸盘
22 Spirographis, a bristle worm
旋（钢毛）虫，一种多毛类蠕虫
23 tube
（气）管
24 earthworm
蚯蚓
25 segment
环节
26 clitellum [accessory reproductive organ]
环带[副生殖器]
27-36 molluscs (*Am.* mollusks; *also:* testaceans and crustaceans)
软体动物（有壳类和甲壳动物）

27 edible snail, a snail
食用蜗牛，蜗牛的一种
28 creeping foot
爬行足
29 shell (snail shell)
壳（蜗牛壳）
30 stalked eye
柄眼
31 tentacle (horn, feeler)
触手（触角）
32 oyster
牡蛎
33 freshwater pearl mussel
淡水珍珠贻贝
34 mother-of-pearl (nacre)
珍珠母层
35 pearl
珍珠
36 mussel shell
贝壳
37 cuttlefish, a cephalopod
乌贼，一种头足动物
38-39 echinoderms
棘皮动物
38 starfish (sea star)
海星
39 sea urchin (sea hedgehog)
海胆（海刺猬）

1-23 arthropods
节肢动物

1-2 crustaceans
甲壳动物

1 mitten crab, a crab
蟹的一种

2 water slater
水虱（水鼠妇）

3-23 insects
昆虫

3 dragonfly (water nymph), a homopteran (homopterous insect)
蜻蜓，同翅类动物的一种

4 water scorpion (water bug), a rhynchophore
水斧虫（水桩象），一种半翅目昆虫

5 raptorial leg
攫捕足

6 mayfly (dayfly, ephemerid)
蜉蝣

7 compound eye
复眼

8 green grasshopper (green locust, meadow grasshopper), an orthopteron (orthopterous insect)
蚱蜢（绿色蝗虫，草原蚱蜢），一种直翅目昆虫

9 larva (grub)
幼虫

10 adult insect, an imago
成虫，一种成虫

11 leaping hind leg
跳跃的后脚

12 caddis fly (spring fly, water moth), a neuropteran
飞蛾（小蛾），一种脉翅目昆虫

13 aphid (greenfly), a plant louse
蚜虫，一种树虱

14 wingless aphid
无翅蚜虫

15 winged aphid
有翅蚜虫

16-20 dipterous insects (dipterans)
双翅目昆虫

16 gnat (mosquito, midge), a culicid
蚋（蚊），蚊子的一种

17 proboscis (sucking organ)
长嘴（吮食器官）

18 bluebottle (blowfly), a fly
青蝇（绿头蝇），苍蝇的一种

19 maggot (larva)
蛆（幼虫）

20 chrysalis (pupa)
金蛹（蛹）

21-23 Hymenoptera
膜翅目

21-22 ant
蚁

21 winged female
有翅雌蚁

22 worker
工蚁

23 bumblebee (humblebee)
大黄蜂

24-39 beetles (Coleoptera)
甲虫（鞘翅目）

24 stag beetle, a lamellicorn beetle
锹蛾，一种鳃角甲虫

25 mandibles
下颚

26 trophi
口器

27 antenna (feeler)
触角

28 head
头部

29-30 thorax
胸廓

29 thoracis shield (prothorax)
胸盾（前胸）

30 scutellum
小盾片，吸盘

31 tergites
背甲

32 stigma
气孔，气门

33 wing (hind wing)
翅（后翅）

34 nervure
翅脉

35 point at which the wing folds
翅摺点

36 elytron (forewing)
翅鞘（前翅）

37 ladybird (ladybug), a coccinellid
瓢虫，瓢虫科的一种

38 Ergates faber, a longicorn beetle (longicorn)
天牛，长触角的甲虫

39 dung beetle, a lamellicorn beetle
蜣螂，一种鳃角甲虫

40-47 arachnids
蜘蛛类的节肢动物

40 Euscorpius flavicandus, a scorpion
黄蝎，蝎子的一种

41 cheliped with chelicer
带螯角的螯足

42 maxillary antenna (maxillary feeler)
上颚触角

43 tail sting
尾螫针

44-46 spiders
蜘蛛

44 wood tick (dog dick), a tick
原野硬蜱，蜱的一种

45 cross spider (garden spider), an orb spinner
十字虫蜘蛛（花园蜘蛛），一种织网蜘蛛

46 spinneret
（纺织突）吐丝口

47 spider's web (web)
蛛网

48-56 Lepidoptera (butterflies and moths)
鳞翅目（蝴蝶和蛾）

48 mulberry-feeding moth (silk moth), a bombycid moth
家蚕蛾，家蚕蛾科的一种

49 eggs
卵

50 silkworm
蚕

51 cocoon
茧

52 swallowtail, a butterfly
凤蝶，蝴蝶的一种

53 antenna (feeler)
触角

54 eyespot
眼点

55 privet hawkmoth, a hawkmoth (sphinx)
水蜡树蛾（天蛾）

56 proboscis
（昆虫的）吻

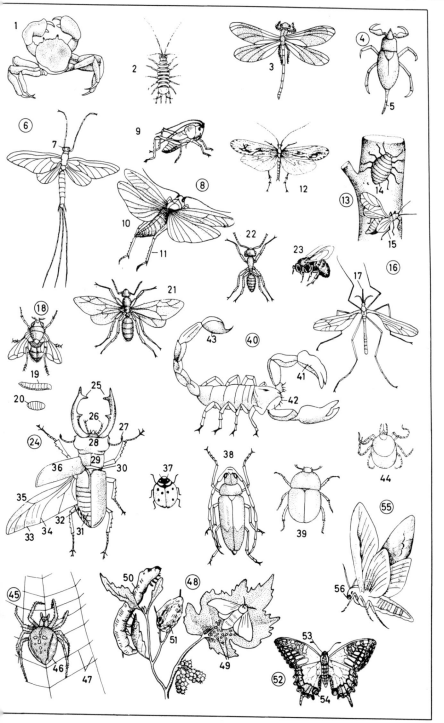

359 Birds I

1-3 flightless birds
不能飞的鸟类

1 cassowary; *sim.:* emu
食火鸡；类似：鹤鹊

2 ostrich
鸵鸟

3 clutch of ostrich eggs [12-14 eggs]
一窝鸵鸟蛋〔12-14 个〕

4 king penguin, a penguin, a flightless bird
企鹅王，企鹅的一种，不能飞的鸟类

5-10 web-footed birds
脚上有蹼的鸟类

5 white pelican, a pelican
白鹈鹕，鹈鹕的一种

6 webfoot (webbed foot)
蹼足

7 web (palmations) of webbed foot (palmate foot)
蹼足的蹼

8 lower mandible with gular pouch
具喉囊的下颌

9 northern gannet (gannet, solan goose), a gannet
北方塘鹅（塘鹅）

10 green cormorant (shag), a cormorant displaying with spread wings
绿鸬鹚（鸬鹚），一种展翅的鸬鹚

11-14 long-winged birds (seabirds)
长翅鸟（海鸟）

11 common sea swallow, a sea swallow (tern); diving for food
普通海燕，潜水觅食的普通海燕

12 fulmar
鼻管

13 guillemot, an auk
海鸠，海雀的一种

14 black-headed gull (mire crow), a gull
黑头鸥

15-17 Anseres
雁类

15 goosander (common merganser), a sawbill
秋沙鸭（一般长咀野鸭），一种有齿突的鸟

16 mute swan, a swan
哑音天鹅，天鹅的一种

17 knob on the bill
咀上的隆突

18 common heron, a heron
一般鹭鸶

19-21 plovers
千鸟类

19 stilt (stilt bird, stilt plover)
高脚沙锥鸟

20 coot, a rail
大鹏，黑鸭

21 lapwing (green plover, peewit, pewit)
田凫

22 quail, a gallinaceous bird
鹌鹑，鹌鸡类的一种

23 turtle dove, a pigeon
斑鸠，鸽子的一种

24 swift
雨燕

25 hoopoe, a roller
戴胜鸟

26 erectile crest
勃起的肉冠

27 spotted woodpecker, a woodpecker; *related:* wryneck
斑点啄木鸟，啄木鸟的一种

28 entrance to the nest
巢的入口

29 nesting cavity
巢

30 cuckoo
杜鹃鸟

1, 3, 4, 5, 7, 9, 10 songbirds
鸣禽类

1 goldfinch, a finch
金翅，金翅属的一种鸟

2 bee eater
蜂虎

3 redstart (star finch), a thrush
红尾鸲，一种鸫类

4 bluetit, a tit (titmouse), a resident bird (non-migratory bird)
蓝山雀，山雀的一种，不迁徙的留鸟

5 bullfinch
红腹灰雀

6 common roller (roller)
颤声金丝雀

7 golden oriole, a migratory bird
金莺，一种迁徙鸟

8 kingfisher
翡翠鸟

9 white wagtail, a wagtail
白鹡鸰，鹡鸰鸟的一种

10 chaffinch
碛鹨（ 欧洲小鸣鸟 ）

1-20 songbirds
鸣禽类

1-3 Corvidae (corvine birds, crows)
乌鸦科（乌鸦）

1 jay (nutcraker)
樫鸟（星鸟）

2 rook, a crow
白咀鸦

3 magpie
喜鹊

4 starling (pastor, shepherd bird)
椋鸟（白头翁的一种）

5 house sparrow
麻雀

6-8 finches
雀科

6-7 buntings
颊白鸟

6 yellowhammer (yellow bunting)
黄雀

7 ortolan (ortolan bunting)
黄雀类之鸟

8 siskin (aberdevine)
金翅雀

9 great titmouse (great tit, ox eye), a titmouse (tit)
大山雀

10 golden-crested wren (goldcrest); *sim.:* firecrest, one of the Regulidae
金冠鹪鹩；类似：红胸戴菊莺

11 nuthatch
五十雀

12 wren
鹪鹩

13-17 thrushes
鸫

13 blackbird
山鸟

14 nightingale (*poet.:* philomel, philomela)
夜莺

15 robin (redbreast, robin redbreast)
知更鸟

16 song thrush (throstle, mavis)
歌鸫，画眉（善鸣的画眉鸟）

17 thrush nightingale
鸫科

18-19 larks
鸫雀，百灵鸟

18 woodlark
土百灵

19 crested lark (tufted lark)
有冠百灵鸟

20 common swallow (barn swallow, chimney swallow), a swallow
一般燕子（谷仓作巢的燕子，烟囱作巢的燕子）

diurnal birds of prey
行类猛禽（食肉禽）
falcons
科
erlin
隼〔鹰隼〕
eregrine falcon
隼
g feathers
部羽毛
rsus
骰骨
eagles
科
hite-tailed sea eagle (white-
iled eagle, grey sea eagle, erne)
尾海鹰
ooked beak
状咀
aw (talon)
（猛禽的爪）
il

mmon buzzard
般秃鹰
accipiters
属
shawk
鹰
mmon European kite (glede,
te)
般欧洲鸢
arrow hawk (spar-hawk)
鹰

13 marsh harrier (moor buzzard,
moor harrier, moor hawk)
白头鹞

14-19 owls (nocturnal birds of
prey)
鸱鸮科（夜行性猛禽）
14 long-eared owl (horned owl)
长耳猫头鹰（枭）
15 eagle-owl (great horned owl)
鹰枭
16 plumicorn (feathered ear, ear
tuft, ear, horn)
耳簇（耳羽，耳簇，耳，角状羽毛）
17 barn owl (white owl, silver owl,
yellow owl, church owl, screech
owl)
草鸮
18 facial disc (disk)
圆形脸盘（面状羽）
19 little owl (sparrow owl)
小猫头鹰（雀枭）

363 Birds V (Exotic Birds)

1 suphur-crested cockatoo, a parrot
有硫黄色冠的鹦鹉，鹦鹉的一种
2 blue-and-yellow macaw
蓝黄色金刚鹦鹉
3 blue bird of paradise
蓝天堂鸟
4 sappho
有羽冠的红雀鸟
5 cardinal (cardinal bird)
红鸟（红锡咀雀）
6 toucan (red-billed toucan), one of the Piciformes
鹦鹉鸟（红咀鹦鹉），鴷形目鸟的一种（巨咀鸟）

1-18 fishes
鱼类

1 man-eater (blue shark, requin),
   a shark
   食人鲨（蓝鲨，鲨鱼）
2 nose (snout)
   鼻
3 gill slit (gill cleft)
   鳃裂
4 mirror carp, a carp
   鲤鱼，镜鲤
5 gill cover (operculum)
   鳃盖
6 dorsal fin
   背鳍
7 pectoral fin
   胸鳍
8 pelvic fin (abdominal fin,
   ventral fin)
   腹鳍
9 anal fin
   臀鳍
10 caudal fin (tail fin)
   尾鳍
11 scale
   鳞
12 catfish (sheatfish, sheathfish,
   wels)
   鲶鱼
13 barbel
   触须
14 herring
   鲱
15 brown trout, a trout
   褐鳟，鳟鱼的一种
16 pike (northern pike)
   梭子鱼（北方梭鱼）
17 freshwater eel (eel)
   淡水鳗鱼
18 sea horse (Hippocampus,
   horsefish)
   海马（海马属）
19 tufted gills
   鳃簇

20-26 Amphibia (amphibians)
两栖类
20-22 salamanders
蝾螈类
20 greater water newt (crested
   newt), a water newt
   鳃螈，一种水蝾螈
21 dorsal crest
   背冠（突）
22 fire salamander, a salamander
   火蝾螈
23-26 salientians (anurans,
   batrachians)
   无尾两栖类
23 European toad, a toad
   欧洲蟾蜍
24 tree frog (tree toad)
   树蛙（树蟾蜍）
25 vocal sac (vocal pouch, croaking
   sac)
   声囊
26 adhesive disc (disk)
   吸盘

27-41 reptiles
爬行类
27, 30-37 lizards
蜥蜴
27 sand lizard
   沙蜥蜴
28 hawksbill turtle (hawksbill)
   玳瑁

29 carapace (shell)
   背甲
30 basilisk
   一种热带美洲蜥蜴
31 desert monitor,. a monitor lizard
   (monitor)
   沙漠大蜥蜴
32 common iguana, an iguana
   一般鬣蜥
33 chameleon, one of the
   Chamaeleontidae
   (Rhiptoglossa)
   变色蜥蜴（变色龙），变色蜥蜴的一
   种
34 prehensile foot
   攀足，卷缠的足
35 prehensile tail
   卷缠尾
36 wall gecko, a gecko
   壁虎，守宫的一种
37 slowworm (blindworm), one of
   the Anguidae
   蛇蜥（盲蛇），蛇蜥科的一种
38-41 snakes
蛇类
38 ringed snake (ring snake, water
   snake, grass snake), a colubrid
   环纹蛇（水蛇，草蛇），无毒蛇的一种
39 collar
   颈
40-41 vipers (adders)
毒蛇，蝮蛇类
40 common viper, a poisonous
   (venomous) snake
   一般蝮蛇，一种毒蛇
41 asp (asp viper)
   （非洲）小毒蛇

1-6 butterflies
蝴蝶

1 red admiral
大西洋红蝴蝶

2 peacock butterfly
孔雀翎蝴蝶

3 orange tip (orange tip butterfly)
黄斑襟粉蝶

4 brimstone (brimstone butterfly)
鼠李粉蝶

5 Camberwell beauty (mourning cloak, mourning cloak butterfly)
黄缘酱蝴蝶，一种紫褐色大蝴蝶（属於欧洲及北美）

6 blue (lycaenid butterfly, lycaenid)
小灰蝶的统称

7-11 moths (Heterocera)
蛾（蛾亚目）

7 garden tiger
灯蛾

8 red underwing
红腹裳夜蛾

9 death's-head moth (death's-head hawkmoth), a hawkmoth (sphinx)
鬼脸天蛾，一种天蛾

10 caterpillar
蠋（一般指鳞翅目的幼虫，毛虫）

11 chrysalis (pupa)
蝶蛹

1 platypus (duck-bill, duck-mole), a monotreme (oviparous mammal)
鸭咀兽，一种单孔类卵生哺乳动物

2-3 marsupial mammals (marsupials)
有袋类哺乳动物

2 New World opossum, a didelphid
（新大陆）美洲负子袋鼠，负子袋鼠类动物

3 red kangaroo (red flyer), a kangaroo
红袋鼠，一种袋鼠类动物

4-7 insectivores (insect-eating mammals)
食虫哺乳类动物

4 mole
鼹鼠

5 hedgehog
刺猬

6 spine
刺毛

7 shrew (shrew mouse), one of the Soricidae
鼩鼱（鼩鼱鼠），鼩鼱首科的一种动物

8 nine-banded armadillo (peba)
犰狳

9 long-eared bat (flitter-mouse), a flying mammal (chiropter, chiropteran)
长耳编蝠，一种飞行的哺乳动物（翼手目）

10 pangolin (scaly ant-eater), a scaly mammal
鲮鲤，又名穿山甲，一种鳞甲的哺乳动物

11 two-toed sloth (unau)
二指树懒

12-19 rodents
啮齿类动物

12 guinea pig (cavy)
天竺鼠

13 porcupine
箭猪，豪猪

14 beaver
海狸

15 jerboa
跳鼠

16 hamster
大颊鼠类

17 water vole
水鼠

18 marmot
土拨鼠

19 squirrel
松鼠

20 African elephant, a proboscidean (proboscidian)
非洲象，长鼻目动物的一种

21 trunk (proboscis)
象鼻

22 tusk
象牙

23 manatee (manati, lamantin), a sirenian
海牛，一种海牛目动物

24 South African dassie (das, coney, hyrax), a procaviid
南非蹄兔，蹄兔科

25-31 ungulates
有蹄类

25-27 odd-toed ungulates
奇蹄类

25 African black rhino, a rhinoceros (nasicorn)
非洲黑犀牛，犀科的一种

26 Brazilian tapir, a tapir
巴西貘

27 zebra
斑马

28-31 even-toed ungulates
偶蹄类

28-30 ruminants
反刍动物

28 llama
骆马

29 Bactrian camel (two-humped camel)
双峰骆驼

30 guanaco
褐色骆马

31 hippopotamus
河马

1-10 ungulates, ruminants
有蹄类，反刍类
1 elk (moose)
红鹿（麋）
2 wapiti (*Am.* elk)
麋鹿
3 chamois
小羚羊
4 giraffe
长颈鹿
5 black buck, an antelope
雄鹿（一种羚羊）
6 mouflon (moufflon)
野羊
7 ibex (rock goat, bouquetin, steinbock)
原羊
8 water buffalo (Indian buffalo, water ox)
水牛（印度水牛）
9 bison
野牛
10 musk ox
麝牛
11-12 carnivores (beasts of prey)
食肉目（肉食兽）
11-13 Canidae
犬科
11 black-backed jackal (jackal)
黑背胡狼（豺类）
12 red fox
红狐
13 wolf
狼
14-17 martens
貂科
14 stone marten (beach marten)
石貂
15 sable
黑貂
16 weasel
鼬，黄鼠狼
17 sea otter, an otter
海獭
18-22 seals (pinnipeds)
海豹科（鳍脚亚目）
18 fur seal (sea bear, ursine seal)
海狗（北极熊）
19 common seal (sea calf, sea dog)
海豹（海狗）
20 walrus (morse)
海象
21 whiskers
须
22 tusk
长牙
23-29 whales
鲸类
23 bottle-nosed dolphin (bottle-nose dolphin)
槌鲸
24 common dolphin
海豚
25 sperm whale (cachalot)
抹香鲸
26 blowhole (spout hole)
鲸鱼喷水孔
27 dorsal fin
背鳍
28 flipper
鳍状肢
29 tail flukes (tail)
鲸尾裂片

1-11 carnivores (beasts of prey)
食肉目（肉食兽）

1 striped hyena, a hyena
条纹土狼，土狼的一种

2-8 felines (cats)
猫科动物

2 lion
狮子

3 mane (lion's mane)
鬃（狮子的鬃毛）

4 paw
脚爪

5 tiger
老虎

6 leopard
豹

7 cheetah (hunting leopard)
印度豹（猎豹）

8 lynx
大山猫属

9-11 bears
熊科

9 raccoon (racoon, *Am.* coon)
浣熊

10 brown bear
大黑熊（马熊）

11 polar bear (white bear)
北极熊（白熊）

12-16 primates
灵长目

12-13 monkeys
猴科动物

12 rhesus monkey (rhesus, rhesus macaque)
恒河猴

13 baboon
狒狒

14-16 anthropoids (anthropoid apes, great apes)
类人猿目（类人猿，大猿）

14 chimpanzee
黑猩猩（非洲人猿）

15 orang-utan (orang-outan)
猩猩

16 gorilla
大猩猩

1 Gigantocypris agassizi
阿氏大介虫

2 Macropharynx longicaudatus
(pelican eel)
长毛巨咽鳗（鹈鹕鳗）

3 Pentacrinus (feather star), a sea
lily, an echinoderm
五角海百合（羽星），一种海百合，棘
皮动物

4 Thaumatolampas diadema, a
cuttlefish [luminescent]
冠乌贼，一种发冷光的墨鱼

5 Atolla, a deep-sea medusa, a
coelenterate
棕色水母，一种属腔肠动物的深海水母

6 Melanocetes, a pediculate
[luminescent]
黑犀鱼属，一种发冷光的柄鳍鱼

7 Lophocalyx philippensis, a glass
sponge
菲律宾丛生海绵，玻璃海绵的一种

8 Mopsea, a sea fan [colony]
柳珊瑚，海扇群的一种

9 Hydrallmania, a hydroid polyp,
a coelenterate [colony]
螅型珊瑚虫，腔肠动物中的水螅珊瑚群

10 Malacosteus indicus, a stomiatid
[luminescent]
印度黑口鱼，发光巨口鱼，属黑口鱼的
一种

11 Brisinga endecacnemos, a sand
star (brittle star), an echinoderm
[luminescent only when
stimulated]
海盘车，棘皮动物的一种，受刺激即发
光的棘皮海星

12 Pasiphaea, a shrimp, a
crustacean
玻璃虾属，褐虾，属於甲壳动物的褐色
小虾

13 Echiostoma, a stomiatid, a fish
[luminescent]
龙口鱼，巨口亚目的发光鱼

14 Umbellula encrinus, a sea pen
(sea feather), a coelenterate
[colony, luminescent]
海伞，属腔肠动物柳珊瑚类群

15 Polycheles, a crustacean
蜘蛛蟹，一种甲壳动物

16 Lithodes, a crustacean, a crab
石蟹，一种甲壳动物

17 Archaster, a starfish (sea star),
an echinoderm
海星，一种棘皮动物

18 Oneirophanta, a sea cucumber,
an echinoderm
长须海参（海黄瓜），一种棘皮动物

19 Palaeopneustes niasicus, a sea
urchin (sea hedgehog), an
echinoderm
盘海胆（海刺蝟），一种棘皮动物

20 Chitonactis, a sea anemone
(actinia), a coelenterate
海葵，一种腔肠动物

1 tree
树
2 bole (tree trunk, trunk, stem)
树干
3 crown of tree (crown)
树冠
4 top of tree (treetop)
树顶
5 bough (limb, branch)
树枝（支干，分支）
6 twig (branch)
小枝
7 bole (tree trunk) [cross section]
树干〔横剖面〕
8 bark (rind)
树皮
9 phloem (bast sieve tissue, inner fibrous bark)
韧皮（韧皮筛管组织，内部有纤维的树皮）
10 cambium (cambium ring)
形成层（形成层圈）
11 medullary rays (vascular rays, pith rays)
髓线（维管线，射出线）
12 sapwood (sap, alburnum)
边材，白木质
13 heartwood (duramen)
心材
14 pith
木髓
15 **plant**
植物
16-18 root
根
16 primary root
主根
17 secondary root
次根
18 root hair
根毛
19-25 shoot (sprout)
芽，苗
19 leaf
叶
20 stalk
主茎，柄
21 side shoot (offshoot)
边枝（蘖枝）
22 terminal bud
顶芽
23 flower
花
24 flower bud
花蕾
25 leaf axil with axillary bud
生有腋芽的叶腋
26 **leaf**
叶
27 leaf stalk (petiole)
叶柄
28 leaf blade (blade, lamina)
叶身（叶缘）叶片
29 venation (veins, nervures, ribs)
叶脉
30 midrib (nerve)
中脉，主脉
31-38 leaf shapes
叶的形状
31 linear
线形叶
32 lanceolate
披针形叶
33 orbicular (orbiculate)
正圆形叶

34 acerose (acerous, acerate, acicular, needle-shaped)
针状形叶
35 cordate
心形叶
36 ovate
卵圆形叶
37 sagittate
箭头形叶
38 reniform
肾形叶
39-42 compound leaves
复叶
39 digitate (digitated, palmate, quinquefoliolate)
掌状叶（有五小叶的复叶）
40 pinnatifid
羽状卡裂复叶
41 abruptly pinnate
分离的羽状复叶
42 odd-pinnate
奇数羽状复叶
43-50 leaf margin shapes
叶缘形状
43 entire
全缘叶
44 serrate (serrulate, saw-toothed)
锯齿叶
45 doubly toothed
双重齿缘叶
46 crenate
圆锯齿缘叶
47 dentate
齿状叶
48 sinuate
波状叶
49 ciliate (ciliated)
有纤毛叶
50 cilium
纤毛
51 **flower**
花
52 flower stalk (flower stem, scape)
花柄（花梗，花茎）
53 receptacle (floral axis, thalamus, torus)
花托
54 ovary
子房
55 style
花柱
56 stigma
柱头
57 stamen
雄蕊
58 sepal
萼片
59 petal
花瓣
60 ovary and stamen [section]
子房和雄蕊〔剖面〕
61 ovary wall
子房壁
62 ovary cavity
子房腔
63 ovule
胚珠
64 embryo sac
胚囊
65 pollen
花粉
66 pollen tube
花粉管
67-77 inflorescences
花序

67 spike (racemose spike)
穗状花序
68 raceme (simple raceme)
总状（单总状）花序
69 panicel
圆锥花序
70 cyme
聚伞花序
71 spadix (fleshy spike)
肉穗花序
72 umbel (simple umbel)
伞形（单伞形）花序
73 capitulum
头状花序
74 composite head (discoid flower head)
复头花序（盘状花头花序）
75 hollow flower head
空心花头花序
76 bostryx (helicoid cyme)
螺旋聚伞花序
77 cincinnus (scorpioid cyme, curled cyme)
蝎尾状聚伞花序
78-82 roots
根
78 adventitious roots
不定根
79 tuber (tuberous root, swollen taproot)
块茎（块茎根，膨胀直根）
80 adventitious roots (aerial roots)
不定根（气生根）
81 root thorns
根刺，根针
82 pneumatophores
呼吸根，排气组织
83-85 blade of grass
草的叶片
83 leaf sheath
叶鞘
84 ligule (ligula)
叶舌
85 leaf blade (lamina)
叶片
86 embryo (seed, germ)
胚（种子，胚芽）
87 cotyledon (seed leaf, seed lobe)
子叶
88 radicle
胚根
89 hypocotyl
胚轴
90 plumule (leaf bud)
幼芽（叶芽）
91-102 fruits
果类
91-96 dehiscent fruits
裂果
91 follicle
荚荛果
92 legume (pod)
豆荚
93 siliqua (pod)
长角（果）
94 schizocarp
乾复裂果，离果
95 pyxidium (circumscissile seed vessel)
盖果（周裂果皮的）
96 poricidal capsule (porose capsule)
孔裂的蒴果（有孔的蒴果）
97-102 indehiscent fruits
（成熟时）不裂开的果实

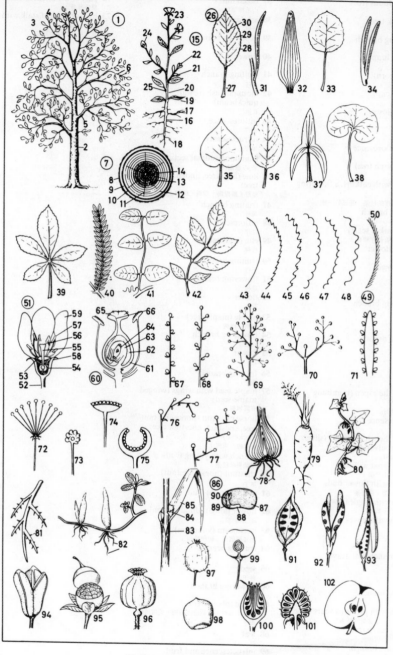

99 drupe (stone fruit) (cherry)
核果（李属）

100 aggregate fruit (compound
fruit) (rose hip)
聚合果（复果）（蔷薇果）

101 aggregate fruit (compound
fruit) (raspberry)
聚合果（复果）（木莓）

102 pome (apple)
梨果（苹果）

1-73 deciduous trees
落叶树

1 oak (oak tree)
橡树

2 flowering branch
花枝

3 fruiting branch
果枝

4 fruit (acorn)
果实（橡实）

5 cupule (cup)
壳斗

6 female flower
雌花

7 bract
苞，苞片

8 male inflorence
雄花序

9 birch (birch tree)
桦树

10 branch with catkins, a flowering branch
带荑荑花序的枝条，花枝的一种

11 fruiting branch
果枝

12 scale (catkin scale)
鳞苞（荑荑花序鳞苞）

13 female flower
雌花

14 male flower
雄花

15 poplar
白杨

16 flowering branch
花枝

17 **flower**
花

18 fruiting branch
果枝

19 fruit
果实

20 seed
种子

21 leaf of the aspen (trembling poplar)
白杨树的叶

22 infructesence
果序列

23 leaf of the white poplar (sliver poplar, silverleaf)
银白杨树叶

24 sallow (goat willow)
阔叶柳（山羊柳）

25 branch with flower buds
带花苞（蕾）枝芽条

26 catkin with single flower
具单花的荑荑花序

27 branch with leaves
叶枝

28 fruit
果实

29 osier branch with leaves
带叶柳枝

30 alder
赤杨木

31 fruiting branch
果枝

32 branch with previous years cone
具有带前一年球果的枝条

33 beech (beech tree)
山毛榉

34 flowering branch
花枝

35 flower
花

36 fruiting branch
果枝

37 beech nut
山毛榉坚果

38 ash (ash tree)
梣树

39 flowering branch
花枝

40 flower
花

41 fruiting branch
果枝

42 mountain ash (rowan, quickbeam)
花楸

43 inflorescence
花序

44 infructescence
果序

45 fruit [longitudinal section]
果实〔纵剖面〕

46 lime (lime tree, linden, linden tree)
酸橙（酸橙树，椴椴，椴树）

47 fruiting branch
果枝

48 inflorescence
花序

49 elm (elm tree)
榆树

50 fruiting branch
果枝

51 flowering branch
花枝

52 flower
花

53 maple (maple tree)
槭树，枫树

54 flowering branch
花枝

55 flower
花

56 fruiting branch
果枝

57 maple seed with wings (winged maple seed)
有翼枫树

58 horse chestnut (horse chestnut tree, chestnut, chestnut tree, buckeye)
七叶树（栗树）

59 branch with young fruits
带幼果的枝条

60 chestnut (horse chestnut)
栗子

61 mature (ripe) fruit
成熟果子

62 flower [longitudinal section]
花〔纵剖面〕

63 hornbeam (yoke elm)
鹅耳枥属树（轭状榆树）

64 fruiting branch
果枝

65 seed
种子

66 flowering branch
花枝

67 plane (plane tree)
悬铃木属树（包括法国梧桐，美国梧桐等）

68 leaf
叶

69 infructescence and fruit
果序和果实

70 false acacia (locust tree)
假刺槐（洋槐）

71 flowering branch
花枝

72 part of the infructescence
果序部分

73 base of the leaf stalk with stipules
具有托叶的叶柄基部

1-71 coniferous trees (conifers)
针叶树

1 silver fir (European sliver fir, common silver fir)
银枞树（欧洲银枞，一般银枞）

2 fir cone, a fruit cone
枞球果，一种球果

3 cone axis
球果轴

4 female flower cone
雌花球果

5 bract scale (bract)
苞鳞（苞片）

6 male flower shoot
雄花枝

7 stamen
雄蕊

8 cone scale
果鳞

9 seed with wing (winged seed)
具翼籽（有翅种子）

10 seed [longitudinal section]
种子〔纵剖面〕

11 fir needle (needle)
籽针（针叶）

12 spruce (spruce fir)
云杉

13 spruce cone
云杉球果

14 cone scale
果鳞

15 seed
种子

16 female flower cone
雌花球果

17 male inflorescence
雄花序

18 stamen
雄蕊

19 spruce needle
云杉叶

20 pine (Scots pine)
松树（苏格兰赤松）

21 dwarf pine
矮松

22 female flower cone
雌花球果

23 short shoot with bundle of two leaves
有两叶维管束的短枝

24 male inflorescences
雄花序列

25 annual growth
一年生果枝

26 pine cone
松果

27 cone scale
果鳞

28 seed
种子

29 fruit cone of the arolla pine (Swiss stone pine)
瑞士五针松果球

30 fruit cone of the Weymouth pine (white pine)
白松果球

31 short shoot [cross section]
短枝〔横剖面〕

32 larch
落叶松

33 flowering branch
花枝

34 scale of the female flower cone
雌花球果的鳞片

35 anther
花药

36 branch with larch cones (fruit cones)
带松果的枝条

37 seed
种子

38 cone scale
果鳞

39 arbor vitae (tree of life, thuja)
侧柏（活树，金钟柏）

40 fruiting branch
果枝

41 fruit cone
果球

42 scale
鳞片

43 branch with male and female flowers
带雌花和雄花的枝条

44 male shoot
雄花枝

45 scale with pollen sacs
带粉囊的鳞片

46 female shoot
雌花枝

47 juniper (juniper tree)
杜松（杜松树）

48 female shoot [longitudinal section]
雌花枝〔纵剖面〕

49 male shoot
雄花枝

50 scale with pollen sacs
带粉囊的鳞片

51 fruiting branch
果枝

52 juniper berry
杜松浆果

53 fruit [cross section]
果实〔横剖面〕

54 seed
种子

55 stone pine
五针松

56 male shoot
雄花枝

57 fruit cone with seeds [longitudinal section]
带籽的果球〔纵剖面〕

58 cypress
柏树

59 fruiting branch
果枝

60 seed
种子

61 yew (yew tree)
紫杉（紫杉树）

62 male flower shoot and female flower cone
雄花枝和雌花球果

63 fruit branch
果枝

64 fruit
果实

65 ceder (cedar tree)
雪松（雪松树）

66 fruiting branch
果枝

67 fruit scale
果鳞

68 male flower shoot and female flower cone
雄花枝和雌花球果

69 mammoth tree (Wellingtonia, sequoia)
红杉（威灵顿树）

70 fruiting branch
果枝

71 seed
种子

1 forsythia
连翘

2 ovary and stamen
子房和雄蕊

3 leaf
叶

4 yellow-flowered jasmine (jasmin, jessamine)
开黄花的茉莉（素馨）

5 flower [longitudinal section] with styles, ovaries and stamens
具花柱，子房和雄蕊的花〔纵剖面〕

6 privet (common privet)
女贞，水蜡树

7 flower
花

8 infructescence
果序列

9 mock orange (sweet syringa)
山梅花

10 snowball (snowball bush, guelder rose)
雪球花

11 flower
花

12 fruits
果实

13 oleander (rosebay, rose laurel)
夹竹桃

14 flower [longitudinal section]
花〔纵剖面〕

15 red magnolia
红木兰

16 leaf
叶

17 japonica (japanese quince)
日本山茶

18 fruit
果实

19 common box (box, box tree)
锦熟黄杨（黄杨，黄杨树）

20 female flower
雌花

21 male flower
雄花

22 fruit [longitudinal section]
果实〔纵剖面〕

23 weigela (weigelia)
锦带花

24 yucca [part of the inflorescence]
丝兰花〔花序部分〕

25 leaf
叶

26 dog rose (briar rose, wild briar)
犬蔷薇（多刺蔷薇，野蔷薇）

27 fruit
果实

28 kerria
棣棠

29 fruit
果实

30 cornelian cherry
西洋山茱萸，樱（桃）树

31 flower
花

32 fruit (cornelian cherry)
果实（樱桃）

33 sweet gale (gale)
香杨梅

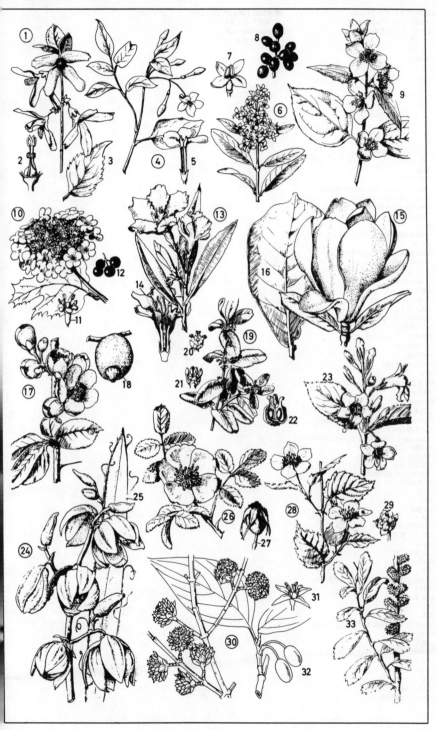

1 tulip tree (tulip poplar,
  saddle tree, whitewood)
  百合木（美国鹅掌楸，白木）
2 carpels
  心皮（雌蕊叶）
3 stamen
  雄蕊
4 fruit
  果实
5 hyssop
  柳薄荷
6 flower [front view]
  花〔前视图〕
7 flower
  花
8 calyx with fruit
  带果的花萼
9 holly
  冬青属植物
10 androgynous (hermaphroditic,
   hermaphrodite) flower
   雌雄同座花（雌雄同体花，两性花）
11 male flower
   雄花
12 fruit with stones exposed
   露核果
13 honeysuckle (woodbine,
   woodbind)
   忍冬（忍冬属植物）
14 flower buds
   花芽（蕾）
15 flower [cut open]
   （剖开的）花
16 Virginia creeper (American ivy,
   woodbine)
   美国地锦（美国常春藤，忍冬）
17 open flower
   开放的花
18 infructescence
   果序
19 fruit [longitudinal section]
   果实〔纵剖面〕
20 broom
   金雀花属植物
21 flower with the petals removed
   除去花瓣后的花
22 immature (unripe) legume (pod)
   未成熟的豆荚
23 spiraea
   绣线菊属植物
24 flower [longitudinal section]
   花〔纵剖面〕
25 fruit
   果实
26 carpel
   心皮
27 blackthorn (sloe)
   黑刺李（黑刺李树）
28 leaves
   （黑刺李）叶
29 fruits
   果实
30 single-pistilled hawthorn (thorn,
   may)
   单雌蕊山楂
31 fruit
   果实
32 laburnum (golden chain, golden
   rain)
   金链花
33 raceme
   总状花序
34 fruits
   果实
35 black elder (elder)
   黑接骨木（接骨木）

36 elder flowers (cymes)
   接骨木花（聚伞花序）
37 elderberries
   接骨木浆果

1 rotundifoliate
(rotundifolious) saxifrage
(rotundifoliate breakstone)
圆叶虎耳草
2 leaf
叶
3 flower
花
4 fruit
果实
5 anemone (windflower)
白头翁属（白头翁）
6 flower [longitudinal section]
花〔纵剖面〕
7 fruit
果实
8 buttercup (meadow buttercup,
butterflower, goldcup, king cup,
crowfoot)
毛茛，金凤花（草地金凤花，毛茛）
9 basal leaf
基生叶
10 fruit
果实
11 lady's smock (ladysmock,
cuckoo flower)
布谷鸟剪秋罗（布谷鸟花）
12 basal leaf
基生叶
13 fruit
果实
14 harebell (hairbell, bluebell)
吊钟柳（山小菜，蓝铃花，圆叶风铃
草）
15 basal leaf
基生叶
16 flower [longitudinal section]
花〔纵剖面〕
17 fruit
果实
18 ground ivy (ale hoof)
连钱草
19 flower [longitudinal section]
花〔纵剖面〕
20 flower [front view]
花〔前视图〕
21 stonecrop
景天
22 speedwell
兔儿尾苗
23 flower
花
24 fruit
果实
25 seed
种子
26 moneywort
金钱草，珍珠菜
27 dehisced fruit
裂果
28 seed
种子
29 small scabious
小山萝蔔属植物
30 basal leaf
基生叶
31 flower of outer series
边花（外丛花）
32 flower of inner series
盘花（裡丛花）
33 involucral calyx with pappus
bristles
带硬冠毛的总苞花萼
34 ovary with pappus
具冠毛的子房
35 fruit
果实

36 lesser celandine
小白屈菜
37 fruit
果实
38 leaf axil with bulbil
带珠芽的叶腋
39 annual meadow grass
一年生草地禾草
40 flower
花
41 spikelet [side view]
小穗状花序〔侧视图〕
42 spikelet [front view]
小穗状花序〔前视图〕
43 caryopsis (indehiscent fruit)
颖果（不裂果）
44 tuft of grass (clump of grass)
一丛草
45 comfrey
紫草科植物
46 flower [longitudinal section]
花〔纵剖面〕
47 fruit
果实

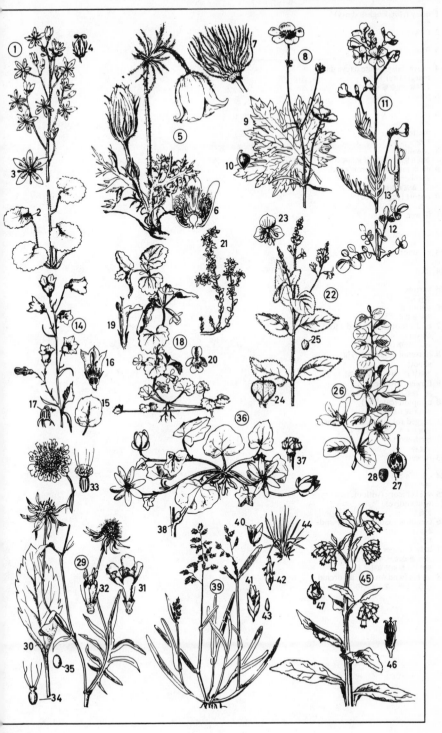

1 daisy (*Am.* English daisy)
雏菊

2 flower
花

3 fruit
果实

4 oxeye daisy (white oxeye daisy, marguerite)
春白菊（牛眼菊，延命菊）

5 flower
花

6 fruit
果实

7 masterwort
星芹

8 cowslip
黄花九轮草，立金花（药用樱草）

9 great mullein (Aaron's rod, shepherd's club)
大毛蕊花（麒麟草，茸菜）

10 bistort (snakeweed)
拳参

11 flower
花

12 knapweed
矢车菊

13 common mallow
一般锦葵

14 fruit
果实

15 yarrow
菊科蓍草

16 self-heal
滁州夏枯草

17 bird's foot trefoil (bird's foot clover)
鸟足三叶草（鸟足苜蓿）

18 horsetail (equisetum) [a shoot]
木贼属的一种（木贼）[一枝]

19 flower (strobile)
花（球穗花序）

20 campion (catchfly)
剪秋罗属（捕虫草）

21 ragged robin (cuckoo flower)
仙翁花（布谷鸟剪秋罗花）

22 birth-wort
马兜铃

23 flower
花

24 crane's bill
牻牛儿苗

25 wild chicory (witloof, succory, wild endive)
野菊苣

26 common toadflax (butter-and-eggs)
柳穿鱼

27 lady's slipper (Venus's slipper, *Am.* moccasin flower)
拖鞋兰（维纳斯拖鞋兰）

28 orchis (wild orchid), an orchid
红门兰（野兰花），兰花

1 wood anemone (anemone, windflower)
白头翁属（毛茛科）

2 lily of the valley
铃兰

3 cat's foot (milkwort); *sim.*: sandflower (everlasting)
猫爪（远志科植物）；类似：不凋花

4 turk's cap (turk's cap lily)
舟形鸟头（舟形鸟头百合）

5 goatsbeard (goat's beard)
假升麻

6 ramson
熊葱

7 lungwort
肺衣

8 corydalis
紫堇属植物

9 orpine (livelong)
紫景天

10 daphne
月桂树，瑞香属植物

11 touch-me-not
小金凤，凤仙花

12 staghorn (stag horn moss, stag's horn, stag's horn moss, coral evergreen)
石松〔石松藓（苔）〕

13 butterwort, an insectivorous plant
捕虫堇，一种食虫植物

14 sundew; *sim.*: Venus's flytrap
茅膏菜；类似：捕蝇草

15 bearberry
熊果

16 polypody (polypod), a fern; *sim.*: male fern, brake (bracken, eagle fern), royal fern (royal osmund, king's fern, ditch fern)
水龙骨属植物，蕨；类似：绵马，欧洲蕨，王紫萁

17 haircap moss (hair moss, golden maidenhair), a moss
毛苔藓，苔藓的一种

18 cotton grass (cotton rush)
画眉菅（莎草科）

19 heather (heath, ling); *sim.*: bell heather (cross-leaved heather)
石南属植物；类似：钟石南（轮生叶欧石南）

20 rock rose (sun rose)
岩玫瑰（半日花）

21 marsh tea
沼生茶树

22 sweet flag (sweet calamus, sweet sedge)
甜旗草（天南星科）

23 bilberry (whortleberry, huckleberry, blueberry); *sim.*: cowberry (red whortleberry), bog bilberry (bog whortleberry), crowberry (crakeberry)
复盆子（越橘）；类似：越橘（红越橘），沼生复盆子（沼生越橘），岩高兰（红莓苔子）

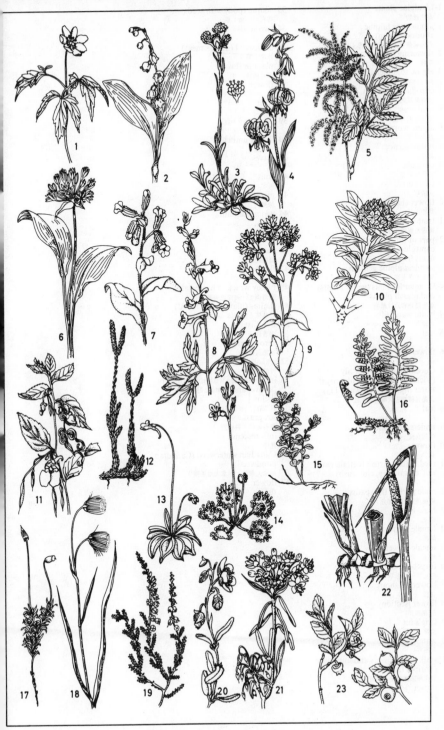

1-13 alpine plants
高山植物

1 alpine rose (alpine rhododendron)
高山蔷薇花（高山杜鹃花）

2 flowering shoot
花枝

3 alpine soldanella (soldanella)
高山钟花

4 corolla opened out
展开的花冠

5 seed vessel with the style
带花柱的种囊

6 alpine wormwood
高山苦艾

7 inflorescence
花序

8 auricula
耳状根春花

9 edelweiss
火绒草

10 flower shapes
花的形状

11 fruit with pappus tuft
带冠毛簇的果实

12 part of flower head (of capitulum)
花头部分（头状花序部分）

13 stemless alpine gentian
高山无茎龙胆

14-57 aquatic plants (water plants) and marsh plants
水生植物和沼泽植物

14 white water lily
白睡莲

15 leaf
叶

16 flower
花

17 Queen Victoria water lily (Victoria regia water lily, royal water lily, Amazon water lily)
王莲属植物（大睡莲，王莲）

18 leaf
叶

19 underside of the leaf
叶的底面

20 flower
花

21 reed mace bulrush (cattail, cat's tail, cattail flag, club rush)
香蒲

22 male part of the spadix
肉穗花序的雄部分

23 male flower
雄花

24 female part
雌部

25 female flower
雌花

26 forget-me-not
忽忘草，相思草

27 flowering shoot
花枝

28 flower [section]
花[剖面图]

29 frog's bit
水鳖（马尿花）

30 watercress
水田芥

31 stalk with flowers and immature (unripe) fruits
带花和未成熟果实的花柄

32 flower
花

33 siliqua (pod) with seeds
带籽的长角（果）

34 two seeds
种子

35 duckweed (duck's meat)
浮萍（紫萍）

36 plant in flower
开花的植物

37 flower
花

38 fruit
果实

39 flowering rush
开花的灯心草

40 flower umbel
伞状花序

41 leaves
叶

42 fruit
果实

43 green alga
绿藻门

44 water plantain
泽泻属

45 leaf
叶

46 panicle
圆锥花序

47 flower
花

48 honey wrack, a brown alga
蜜海藻，一种棕色海藻

49 thallus (plant body, frond)
叶状体（植物体，叶状体）

50 holdfast
固着器

51 arrow head
慈姑属植物

52 leaf shapes
叶的形状

53 inflorescence with male flowers [above] and female flowers [below]
具雄花[上]和雌花[下]的花序

54 sea grass
浒苔属的一种植物

55 inflorescence
花序

56 Canadian waterweed (Canadian pondweed)
加拿大菲藻（加拿大角果藻）

57 flower
花

1 aconite (monkshood,
   wolfsbane, helmet flower)
   附子〔附子属植物，附子草〕
2 foxglove (Digitalis)
   毛地黄
3 meadow saffron (naked lady,
   naked boys)
   草地番红花
4 hemlock (Conium)
   毒芹（毒参）
5 black nightshade (common
   nightshade, petty morel)
   龙葵（一般龙葵，小龙葵）
6 henbane
   黑莨菪〔茄科毒草〕
7 deadly nightshade (belladonna,
   banewort, dwale), a solanaceous
   herb
   毒龙葵，一种茄科毒草
8 thorn apple (stramonium,
   stramony, *Am.* jimson weed,
   jimpson weed, Jamestown weed,
   stinkweed)
   （曼陀草，一种茄科毒草）
9 cuckoo pint (lords-and-ladies,
   wild arum, wake-robin)
   白星海芋（野海芋，延龄草）
10-13 poisonous fungi (poisonous
   mushrooms, toadstools)
   有毒真菌（毒蘑菇，毒伞菌）
10 fly agaric (fly amanita, fly
   fungus), an agaric
   蛤蟆菌，一种伞毒
11 amanita
   鬼笔鹅膏（鳞茎伞菌，有毒伞菌）
12 Satan's mushroom
   魔鬼蘑菇
13 woolly milk cap
   绵毛乳菌盖

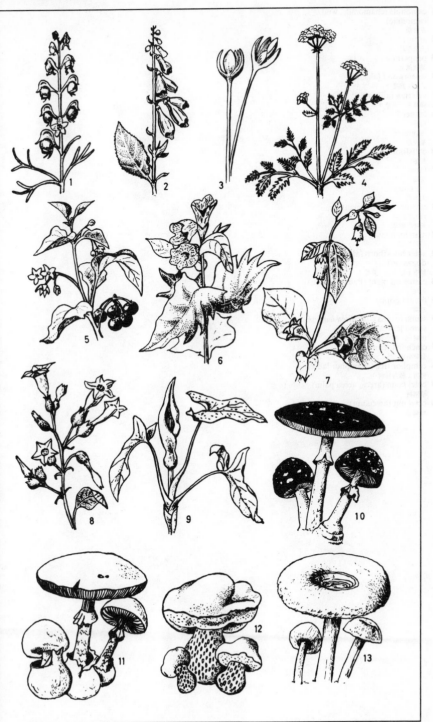

1 camomile (chamomile, wild
   camomile)
   春黄菊
2 arnica
   山金车花
3 peppermint
   胡椒薄荷
4 wormwood (absinth)
   苦艾（洋艾）
5 valerian (allheal)
   缬草（万灵草）
6 fennel
   茴香
7 lavender
   薰衣草
8 coltsfoot
   款冬
9 tansy
   艾菊
10 centaury
   矢车菊
11 ribwort (ribwort plantain,
   ribgrass)
   长叶车前草
12 marshmallow
   药用蜀葵
13 alder buckthorn (alder
   dogwood)
   鼠李（桤木山，茱萸）
14 castor-oil plant (Palma Christi)
   蓖麻
15 opium poppy
   罂粟
16 senna (cassia); *the dried leaflets:*
   senna leaves
   山扁豆，乾小叶，番泻树叶
17 cinchona (chinchona)
   金鸡纳树
18 camphor tree (champhor laurel)
   樟树（樟月桂树）
19 betel palm (areca, areca palm)
   槟榔树
20 betel nut (areca nut)
   槟榔子

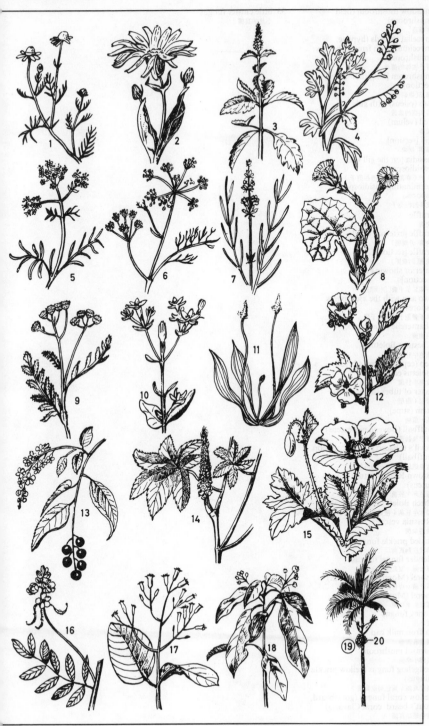

1 meadow mushroom (field mushroom)
洋蘑菇

2 mycelial threads (hyphae, mycelium) with fruiting bodies (mushrooms)
带子实体的菌丝

3 mushroom [longitudinal section]
蘑菇〔纵剖面〕

4 cap (pileus) with gills
带菌摺的菌盖

5 veil (velum)
菌幕

6 gill [section]
菌摺〔剖面〕

7 basidia [on the gill with basidiospores]
担子（在菌摺上具有担孢子）

8 germinating basidiospores (spores)
发芽的担孢子

9 truffle
块菌

10 truffle [external view]
块菌〔外观图〕

11 truffle [section]
块菌〔剖观图〕

12 interior showing asci [section]
内部显示子囊〔剖面图〕

13 two asci with the ascospores (spores)
具子囊孢子的两个子囊

14 chanterelle (chantarelle)
鸡油菌

15 Chestnut Boletus
栗色牛肝菌

16 cep (cepe, squirrel's bread, Boletus edulis)
食用牛肝菌

17 layer of tubes (hymenium)
管层（孢层）

18 stem (stipe)
茎，菌柄

19 puffball (Bovista nigrescens)
卵形马勃菌

20 devil's tobacco pouch (common puffball)
魔鬼烟袋形菌（一般马勃菌）

21 Brown Ring Boletus (Boletus luteus)
棕色环牛肝菌

22 Birch Boletus (Boletus scaber)
桦木牛肝菌（橙黄牛肝菌）

23 Russula vesca
食用伞菌

24 scaled prickle fungus
鳞状皮刺真菌

25 slender funnel fungus
细长漏斗型真菌

26 morel (Morchella esculenta)
羊肚菌（可食用的羊肚菌）

27 morel (Morchella conica)
圆锥形羊肚菌

28 honey fungus
蜜环菌

29 saffron milk cap
橘黄乳菌盖

30 parasol mushroom
高脚小伞菌

31 hedgehog fungus (yellow prickle fungus)
刺皮真菌（黄色刺皮真菌）

32 yellow coral fungus (goatsbeard, goat's beard, coral Clavaria)
黄色珊瑚真菌

33 little cluster fungus
小丛生真菌

1 coffee tree (coffee plant)
咖啡树

2 fruiting branch
果枝

3 flowering branch
花枝

4 flower
花

5 fruit with two beans
[longitudinal section]
有两颗豆的咖啡果[纵剖面]

6 coffee bean; *when processed:*
coffee
咖啡豆，加工后即成：咖啡

7 tea plant (tea tree)
茶树

8 flowering branch
花枝

9 tea leaf; *when processed:* tea
茶树叶，加工后即成：茶叶

10 fruit
茶籽

11 maté shrub (maté yerba maté,
Paraguay tea)
巴拉圭茶树

12 flowering branch with
androgynous (hermaphroditic,
hermaphrodite) flowers
具有雌雄同座花的花枝

13 male flower
雄花

14 androgynous (hermaphroditic,
hermaphrodite) flower
雌雄同座花

15 fruit
果实

16 cacao tree (cacao)
可可树

17 branch with flowers and fruits
带花和果实的可可树枝

18 flower [longitudinal section]
花[纵剖面]

19 cacao beans (cocoa beans); *when
processed:* cocoa, cocoa powder
可可豆，加工后即成：可可，可可粉

20 seed [longitudinal section]
种子[纵剖面]

21 embryo
胚

22 cinnamon tree (cinnamon)
肉桂树

23 flowering branch
花枝

24 fruit
果实

25 cinnamon bark; *when crushed:*
cinnamon
肉桂树皮，弄碎后即成：肉桂

26 clove tree
丁香树

27 flowering branch
花枝

28 flower bud; *when dried:* clove
花苞，干燥后即成：丁香

29 flower
花

30 nutmeg tree
肉豆蔻树

31 flowering branch
花枝

32 female flower [longitudinal
section]
雌花[纵剖面]

33 mature (ripe) fruit
熟果

34 nutmeg with mace, a seed with
laciniate aril
带干皮的肉豆蔻，一种具条裂假种皮的
种子

35 seed [cross section]; *when
dried:* nutmeg
种子[横剖面]，干燥后即成：荳蔻

36 pepper plant
胡椒树

37 fruiting branch
果枝

38 inflorescence
花序

39 fruit [longitudinal section]
with seed (peppercorn); *when
ground:* pepper
具有胡椒子的果实[纵剖面]，磨碎后即
成：胡椒

40 Virginia tobacco plant
维吉尼亚烟草

41 flowering shoot
花枝

42 flower
花

43 tobacco leaf; *when cured:*
tobacco
烟草叶，烤制后即成：烟叶

44 mature (ripe) fruit capsule
成熟的蒴果

45 seed
种子

46 vanilla plant
香兰

47 flowering shoot
花枝

48 vanilla pod; *when cured:* stick of
vanilla
香兰豆荚，焙制后即成：香兰棒

49 pistachio tree
阿月浑子树

50 flowering branch with female
flowers
带雌花的花枝

51 drupe (pistachio, pistachio nut)
核果（阿月浑子树核果）

52 sugar cane
甘蔗

53 plant in bloom
开花期的植物

54 panicle
圆锥花序

55 flower
花

1 rape (cole, coleseed)
油菜（油菜子）

2 basal leaf
基生菜

3 flower [longitudinal section]
花[纵剖面]

4 mature (ripe) siliqua (pod)
熟果荚

5 oleiferous seed
油菜籽

6 flax
亚麻

7 peduncle (pedicel, flower stalk)
花梗，花序柄（花梗，花茎）

8 seed vessel (boll)
种子囊（果荚）

9 hemp
大麻

10 fruiting female (pistillate) plant
结果的雌（雌蕊）性植物

11 female inflorescence
雌花序

12 flower
花

13 male inflorescence
雄花序

14 fruit
果实

15 seed
种子

16 cotton
棉花

17 flower
花

18 fruit
果实

19 lint [cotton wool]
皮棉[原棉]

20 silk-cotton tree (kapok tree, capoc tree, ceiba tree)
木棉树

21 fruit
果实

22 flowering branch
花枝

23 seed
种子

24 seed [longitudinal section]
种子[纵剖面]

25 jute
黄麻

26 flowering branch
花枝

27 flower
花

28 fruit
果实

29 olive tree (olive)
橄榄树

30 flowering branch
花枝

31 flower
花

32 fruit
果实

33 rubber tree (rubber plant)
橡胶树（橡胶植物）

34 fruiting branch
果枝

35 fig
无花果

36 flower
花

37 gutta-percha tree
马来树胶树

38 flowering branch
花枝

39 flower
花

40 fruit
果实

41 peanut (ground nut, monkey nut)
花生（落花生）

42 flowering shoot
花枝

43 root with fruits
带果实的根

44 nut (kernel) [longitudinal section]
坚果（果仁）[纵剖面]

45 sesame plant (simsim, benniseed)
芝麻

46 flowers and fruiting branch
花和果枝

47 flower [longitudinal section]
花[纵剖面]

48 coconut palm (coconut tree, coco palm, cocoa palm)
椰子树

49 inflorescence
花序

50 female flower
雌花

51 male flower [longitudinal section]
雄花[纵剖面]

52 fruit [longitudinal section]
果实[纵剖面]

53 coconut (cokernut)
椰子

54 oil palm
油椰（棕榈树）

55 male spadix
雄肉穗花序

56 infructescence with fruit
带果的果序

57 seed with micropyles (foramina) (foraminate seed)
带珠孔的种子（具小孔的种子）

58 sago palm
西米椰子

59 fruit
果实

60 bamboo stem (bamboo culm)
竹茎（竹竿）

61 branch with leaves
带叶的枝

62 spike
穗状花序

63 part of bamboo stem with joints
具节的一段竹茎

64 papyrus plant (paper reed, paper rush)
纸草植物（莎草科）

65 umbel
伞形花序

66 spike
穗状花序

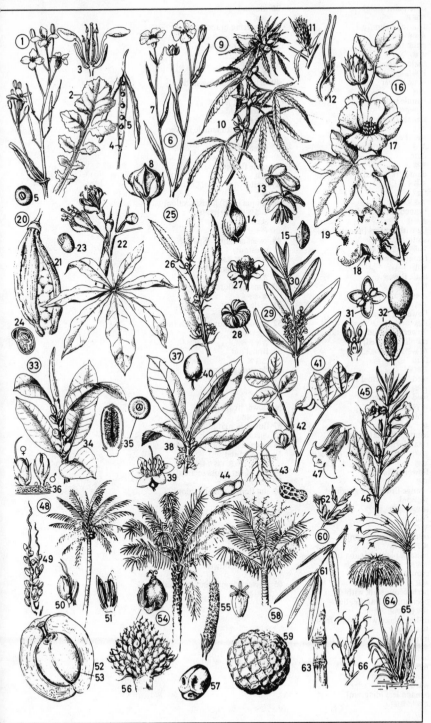

1 date palm (date)
枣椰树

2 fruiting palm
结果的掌叶

3 palm frond
掌状叶

4 male spadix
雄肉穗花序

5 male flower
雄花

6 female spadix
雌肉穗花序

7 female flower
雌花

8 stand of fruit
果串

9 date
枣椰子

10 date kernel (seed)
枣椰子核（种子）

11 fig
无花果树

12 branch with pseudocarps
假果枝

13 fig with flowers [longitudinal section]
具花的无花果[纵剖面]

14 female flower
雌花

15 male flower
雄花

16 pomegranate
石榴树

17 flowering branch
花枝

18 flower [longitudinal section, corolla removed]
花[纵剖面，去掉花冠]

19 fruit
石榴果

20 seed [longitudinal section]
石榴籽[纵剖面]

21 seed [cross section]
种子[横剖面]

22 embryo
胚

23 lemon; *sim.*: tangerine (mandarin), orange, grapefruit
柠檬树；类似：柑橘树，橘子树，葡萄柚树

24 flowering branch
花枝

25 orange flower [longitudinal section]
橘花[纵剖面]

26 fruit
果实

27 orange [cross section]
橘子[横剖面]

28 banana plant (banana tree)
香蕉树

29 crown
树冠

30 herbaceous stalk with overlapping leaf sheaths
具重叠叶梢的草质柄

31 inflorescence with young fruits
具幼果的花序

32 infructescence (bunch of fruit)
果序（果枝）

33 banana
香蕉

34 banana flower
香蕉花

35 banana leaf [diagram]
香蕉叶[简图]

36 almond
杏树

37 flowering branch
花枝

38 fruiting branch
果枝

39 fruit
果实

40 drupe containing seed [almond]
含种子[杏仁]的核果

41 carob
角豆树

42 branch with female flowers
雌花枝

43 female flower
雌花

44 male flower
雄花

45 fruit
果实

46 siliqua (pod) [cross section]
长角果（荚果）[横剖面]

47 seed
种子

48 sweet chestnut (Spanish chestnut)
甜栗树（蜜栗树）

49 flowering branch
花枝

50 female inflorescence
雌花序

51 male flower
雄花序

52 cupule containing seeds (nuts, chestnuts)
含种子的壳斗

53 Brazil nut
巴西栗

54 flowering branch
花枝

55 leaf
叶

56 flower [from above]
花[俯视图]

57 flower [longitudinal section]
花[纵剖面]

58 opened capsule, containing seeds (nuts)
含种子（坚果）的开裂蒴果

59 Brazil nut [cross section]
巴西栗[横剖面]

60 nut [longitudinal section]
坚果[纵剖面]

61 pineapple plant (pineapple)
凤梨

62 pseudocarp with crown of leaves
带叶冠的假果

63 syncarp
聚合果

64 pineapple flower
凤梨花

65 flower [longitudinal section]
花[纵剖面]

Index

Ordering

In this index the entries are ordered as follows:

1. Entries consisting of single words, e.g.: 'hair'.
2. Entries consisting of noun + adjective. Within this category the adjectives are entered alphabetically, e.g. 'hair' is followed by 'hair, closely-cropped'.
   Where adjective and noun are regarded as elements of a single lexical item, they are not inverted, e.g.: 'blue spruce', not 'spruce, blue'.
3. Entries consisting of other phrases, e.g. 'hair curler', 'ham on the bone', are alphabetized as headwords.

Where a whole phrase makes the meaning or use of a headword highly specific, the whole phrase is entered alphabetically. For example 'ham on the bone' follows 'hammock'.

References

The numbers in bold type refer to the sections in which the word may be found, and those in normal type refer to the items named in the pictures. Homonyms, and in some cases uses of the same word in different fields, are distinguished by section headings (in italics), some of which are abbreviated, to help to identify at a glance the field required. In most cases the full form referred to by the abbreviations will be obvious. Those which are not are explained in the following list:

Agr.	Agriculture/Agricultural	*Hydr. Eng.*	Hydraulic Engineering
Alp. Plants	Alpine Plants	*Impl.*	Implements
Art. Studio	Artist's Studio	*Inf. Tech.*	Information Technology
Bldg.	Building	*Intern. Combust. Eng.*	Internal Combustion Engine
Carp.	Carpenter	*Moon L.*	Moon Landing
Cement Wks.	Cement Works	*Music Not.*	Musical Notation
Cost.	Costumes	*Overh. Irrign.*	Overhead Irrigation
Cyc.	Cycle	*Platem.*	Platemaking
Decid.	Deciduous	*Plant Propagn.*	Propagation of Plants
D.I.Y.	Do-it-yourself	*Rm.*	Room
Dom. Anim.	Domestic Animals	*Sp.*	Sports
Equest.	Equestrian Sport	*Text.*	Textile[s]
Gdn.	Garden	*Veg.*	Vegetable[s]

A

Aaron's rod **376** 9
abacus **309** 77
abacus *Art* **334** 20
abattoir **94**
abdomen *Man* **16** 35-37, 36
abdomen *Bees* **77** 10-19
abdomen *Forest Pests* **82** 9
abdomen, lower ~ **16** 37
abdomen, upper ~ **16** 35
abductor hallucis **18** 49
abductor of the hallux **18** 49
aberdevine **361** 8
aborigine, Australian ~ **352** 37
abrasion platform **13** 31
abrasive wheel combination **111** 28, 35
abscissa **347** 9
abseiling **300** 28-30
abseil piton **300** 39
abseil sling **300** 28
absinth **380** 4
absorber attachment **27** 44
absorption dynamometer **143** 97-107
absorption muffler **190** 16
absorption silencer **190** 16
abutment *Bridges* **215** 27, 29, 45
abutment *Art* **336** 20
abutment pier **215** 29
acanthus **334** 25
acceleration lane **15** 16
acceleration rocket **234** 22, 48
accelerator **191** 46
accelerator lock **85** 17
accelerator pedal **191** 46, 94
accelerometer **230** 10
accent, acute ~ **342** 30

accent, circumflex ~ **342** 32
accent, grave ~ **342** 31
accent, strong ~ **321** 27
accents **342** 30-35
acceptance **250** 12, 23
access balcony **37** 72-76
access flap **6** 21, 25
accessories **115** 43-105
accessory shoe **114** 4; **115** 20
accessory shop **196** 24
access ramp **199** 15
acciaccatura **321** 15
accipiters **362** 10-13
accolade **329** 66
accommodation **146** 33
accommodation bureau **204** 28
accommodation ladder **221** 98
accomodation module **146** 33
accompaniment side **324** 43
accompaniment string **324** 25
accordion **324** 36
account, private ~ **250** 4
accounting machine **236** 26
accumulator **309** 41
accumulator *Theatre* **316** 55
accumulator railcar **211** 55
accuracy jump **288** 55
acerate **370** 34
acerose **370** 34
acerous **370** 34
acetylene connection **141** 31
acetylene control **141** 32
acetylene cylinder **141** 2, 22
achene **58** 23
achievement **254** 1-6
achievement, marital ~ **254** 10-13
achievement of arms **254** 1-6
Achilles' tendon **18** 48
acicular **370** 34

acid container **350** 62
Ackermann steering system **85** 31, 37
acolyte **331** 45
aconite **379** 1
acorn **371** 4
acorns **276** 42
acrobat **307** 47
Acropolis **334** 1-7
acroter **334** 34
acroterion **334** 34
acroterium **334** 34
acting area light **316** 16
acting area spotlight **316** 16
actinia **369** 20
Actinophrys **357** 7
action **326** 6-16
action lever **325** 32
activated blade attachment **84** 33
actor **316** 37
actress **316** 38
actuating transistor **195** 19
acuity projector **111** 47
acute **342** 30
ad **342** 56
Adam's apple **19** 13
adapter **112** 55
adapter, four-socket ~ **127** 8
adapter, four-way ~ **127** 8
adapter ring **115** 82
adapter unit **242** 34
adders **364** 40-41
adding **344** 23
adding and subtracting machine **309** 74
adding mechanism **271** 9
addition **344** 23
address **236** 42
address display **236** 41
addressing machine, transfer-type ~ **245** 7

address label **236** 4
address system, ship's ~ **224** 30
A-deck **223** 28-30
adhesion railcar **214** 1
adhesive, hot ~ **249** 61
adhesive binder *Bookbind.* **184** 1
adhesive binder *Office* **249** 61
adhesive tape dispenser **247** 27
adhesive tape dispenser, roller-type ~ **247** 28
adhesive tape holder **247** 28
adjusting cone **187** 58
adjusting equipment **148** 61-65
adjusting knob **116** 54
adjusting nut **143** 35
adjusting screw *Bldg. Site* **119** 79
adjusting screw *Mach. Parts etc.* **143** 107
adjusting screw *Inf. Tech.* **242** 78
adjusting spindle **226** 51
adjusting washer **187** 55
adjustment, circular ~ **14** 62
adjustment, coarse ~ **112** 4
adjustment, fine ~ *Optic. Instr.* **112** 5
adjustment, fine ~ *Photog.* **116** 33
adjustment, fine ~ *Joiner* **133** 36
adjustment, fine ~ *Drawing Off.* **151** 66
adjustment knob **11** 41
administration area **5** 17
administration building *Coal* **144** 18
administration building

Airport 233 16
administration building
  Films 310 4
Admiralty anchor 286 15
admission ticket 315 11
adult insect 358 10
advance booking office 271
  26
adventure playground 273 21
advertisement 98 2; 204 10;
  268 43, 71; 271 25; 312 23;
  342 56, 69
advertising, classified ~ 342
  69
advertising calendar 22 10
advertising pillar 268 70
adze 300 34
aerator 56 15
aerial 213 4
aerial ladder 270 9
aerial sports 288
aerobatic manoeuvres 288
  1-9
aerobatics 288 1-9
aero engines 232 33-60
aerofoil, rear ~ 290 35
aerogenerator 155 42
aeroplane 230 67-72
aeroplane, propeller-driven ~
  231 1-6
aeroplane, types of ~ 231 1-33
aeroplane tow launch 287 1
aerotowing 287 1
aero wheel 305 79
Afghan 70 23
Afghan hound 70 23
A flat major 320 66
Africa 14 14
African hemp 53 9
African marigold 60 20
Afro look 34 26
afterburner exhaust nozzle
  256 13
aftercastle 218 23
after deck 223 32
aftershave lotion 49 38
aft fan-jet 232 42
aft ship 286 34, 37, 41
agaric 379 10
agate 175 22
agent 307 18
aggregate scraper 200 13
agitator *Agr. Mach.* 64 70
agitator *Paperm.* 172 47
agricultural implements 66
agricultural machinery 64; 65
agricultural worker 63 5
agriculture 63
Agulhas Current 14 37
aileron 230 52; 287 41; 288 28
aileron, inner ~ 229 43
aileron, outer ~ 229 41
aileron actuator 257 39
aiming position 86 34
air-bed, inflatable ~ 278 31
air blast 139 56
air-blast circuit breaker 152
  34; 153 51-62
air-bleed duct *Roof &
  Boilerr.* 38 51
air-bleed duct *Intern.
  Combust. Eng.* 190 12
air blower, primary ~ 160 11
air brake 229 44; 256 12
airbridge 233 14
airbus 231 17
air cleaner 191 55
air compressor *Painter* 129 33
air compressor *Offshore
  Drill.* 146 23
air compressor *Railw.* 211 14,
  44; 212 34, 58, 72
air compressor, diesel-

powered ~ 200 39
air compressor, mobile ~ 200
  39
air-conditioning 26 20
air-conditioning equipment
  239 15
air correction jet 192 3
aircraft 229; 230; 231; 232
aircraft, propeller-driven ~
  231 1-6
aircraft, single-engine ~ 230
  1-31, 32-66; 231 1, 2
aircraft, tilt-wing ~ 232 26
aircraft, twin-boom ~ 229 34
aircraft, twin-engine ~ 231 3
aircraft, twin-jet ~ 231 7
aircraft, types of ~ 231 1-33
aircraft cannon 256 3
aircraft carrier, nuclear-
  powered ~ 259 1
aircraft elevator 259 4, 13
aircraft engines 232 33-60
aircraft lift 259 4, 13
aircraft tractor 233 23
aircraft tug 233 23
air currents 9 25-29
air cushion 286 66
air-cushion vehicle 286 63
air duct 155 35
airer 50 32
airer, extending ~ 50 34
air extraction vent 154 21
air extractor duct 258 57
air extractor pipe 133 40
air feed pipe 147 29
air filler neck 196 21
air filter 191 55
air flow 199 45
air flow, secondary ~ 232 50
air force 256; 257
air hose *Garage* 195 54
air hose *Serv. Stat.* 196 18
air inlet *Lorries etc.* 194 16
air inlet *Warships* 259 73
air inlet *Fire Brig.* 270 60
air inlet and outlet 92 14
air intake *Car* 192 60
air intake *Railw.* 209 11
air intake *Air Force* 256 5; 257
  12
air intake, annular ~ 232 52
air intake duct 257 14
air jet pipe 281 41
air line 75 28
airliner, four-jet ~ 231 13
airliner, supersonic ~ 231 15
airliner, tri-jet ~ 231 12
airliner, twin-jet ~ 231 11, 17
airliner, wide-body ~ 231 14,
  17
air lock *Coal* 144 38
air lock *Offshore Drill.* 146 24
air lock *Space* 235 27
air lock *Chem.* 349 7
air masses, homogeneous ~ 8
  1-4
air mattress 278 31
air outlet 168 29
air oxidation passage 165 48
air passage 333 4
airplane *see* aeroplane
airport 233
'airport' 233 24
airport fire service 233 7
airport information symbols
  233 24-53
airport restaurant 233 19
air preheater *Forging* 139 53
air preheater *Power Plant* 152
  11
air pump *Paperm.* 172 40
air pump *Letterpress* 181 6, 35
air receiver 269 17, 50

air refuelling probe 256 7
air regenerator chamber 147
  30
air regulator *Offset Print.* 180
  74
air regulator *Chem.* 350 3, 8
air reservoir, auxiliary ~ 212
  61
air reservoir, main ~ 211 8;
  212 57, 71
air rifle 305 40
air rifle cartridge 305 34
airscrew 230 32; 288 36
air space 74 61
air-speed indicator 230 2
airsports 288
airstream, cold ~ 9 29
airstream, main ~ 192 5
airstream, warm ~ 9 28
air supply 155 24
air survey camera 14 63
air temperature 280 8
air vent cap 38 52
air vessel 269 17, 50
aisle *Map* 15 112
aisle *Forestry* 84 1
aisle *Church* 330 27
aisle *Art* 334 63; 335 2
alarm clock 110 19
alarm clock, electric ~ 43 16
albumen 74 62
alburnum *Carp.* 120 85
alburnum *Bot.* 370 12
Alcor 3 29
Aldebaran 3 25
alder 371 30
alder buckthorn 380 13
alder dogwood 380 13
alder-swamp peat 13 18
ale 93 26
ale hoof 375 18
Alençon lace 102 30
alfalfa grass 136 26
alga, brown ~ 378 48
alga, green ~ 378 43
algebra 345 4-5
alighting board 77 49
alkali-cellulose 169 9
alkali-cellulose crumbs 169 7
Allais chicane 301 72
all-container ship 221 21;
  226 5
Aller rock salt 154 63
allheal 380 5
allonge periwig 34 2
allotment 52 1-32
allotment holder 52 24
all-purpose gun 258 70
all-purpose gun, radar-
  controlled ~ 258 47, 48
all-purpose trailer 62 40
all-purpose vehicle 255 96
all-speed aileron 229 43
alluvial deposit 216 52
all-weather roof 200 38
all-wheel drive 194 1
almond *Tablew. etc.* 45 41
almond *South. Fruits* 384 36
aloe 53 13
alpha particle 1 -31; 227
alpha radiation 1 30-31
Alpine Club hut 300 1
alpine rhododendron 378 1
alpine rose 378 1
alpine soldanella 378 3
alpine strawberry 58 16
alpine wormwood 378 6
Alpinism 300 1-57
Alpinist 300 5
Alsatian 70 25
alsike 69 3

alsike clover 69 3
Altair 3 9
altar 330 4, 33; 334 48, 69
altar bell 332 52
altar candle 330 7, 34
altar carpet 330 3
altar cloth 330 6, 36
altar cross 330 35
altar crucifix 330 12
altar decoration 330 48
altarpiece 330 13, 50
altar steps 330 5, 31
alternative school 261 1-45
alternator 152 23; 153 1
altimeter 230 4
altitude 346 27
altitude scale 7 35
alto clef 320 10
altocumulus 8 15
altocumulus castellanus 8 16
altocumulus floccus 8 16
altostratus 8 8
altostratus praecipitans 8 9
alto trombone 323 46
aluminium foil, asphalted ~
  155 29
aluminum *see* aluminium
A major 320 58
amanita 379 11
amaryllis 53 8
Amazon water lily 378 17
ambulance 270 19
ambulance, armoured ~ 255
  79
ambulance attendant 270 21
ambulance car 270 19
ambulance man 270 21
America 14 12-13
American blight 80 32
American football 292 22
American ivy 51 5; 374 16
A minor 320 55, 62
A minor scale 320 46, 47, 48
ammeter *Car* 191 73
ammeter *Aircraft* 230 18
ammonia 170 24
ammonia scrubber 156 23
ammonia wet collector 156 23
ammonium sulphate 156 36
ammonium sulphate,
  production of ~ 156 35
ammonium sulphate solution
  170 26
ammunition 87 19; 305 34-49
amoeba 357 1
amoretto 272 20
amorino 272 20
amount 271 8
Amphibia 364; 364 20-26
amphibian 232 8
amphibians 364 20-26
amplifier 241 40; 312 19; 317
  23
amplifier, underwater ~ 237 57
amplifier and mains power
  unit 238 3
amplifier equipment 310 59
amplitude adjustment 10 11
amulet 354 40
anaesthesia and breathing
  apparatus 26 1
anaesthesia and respiratory
  apparatus 26 24
anaesthetic, local ~ 24 53
analog *see* analogue
analogue control 242 38
analogue output 112 45
analyser 23 53
analysis, automatic ~ 25 48
analytical balance 349 25
anchor 223 52; 259 81
anchor, lightweight ~ 286
  16-18

anchor, stocked ~ 222 79; 286 15
anchor, stockless ~ 222 78; 258 5; 286 17
anchorage 216 13
anchor cable 218 18; 222 77; 223 50; 227 12
anchor capstan 258 6
anchor hawser 218 18
anchor rib 287 32
anchor rope 218 18
anchors 286 15-18
anchor winch 259 82
ancillary brake valve 211 23
Andromeda 3 24
anemometer 10 28
anemone 375 5; 377 1
aneroid barometer 10 4
aneroid box 10 6
aneroid capsule 10 6
angiographic examination table 27 26
angiography room 27 12
angle Mach. Parts etc. 143 1
angle Maths. 346 1-23; 346 8-13, 8, 55
angle, acute ~ 346 10
angle, adjacent ~ 346 14
angle, alternate ~ 346 10
angle, circumferential ~ 346 56
angle, exterior ~ 346 26
angle, interior ~ 346 26
angle, obtuse ~ 346 11
angle, straight ~ 346 13,9-15
angle brace 118 25; 119 63; 121 57
angle deck 259 12
angle iron 143 1
angle of departure 87 75
angle of descent 87 78
angle of dip 12 3
angle of elevation 87 76
angle of rotation 351 33
angle of the mouth 16 14; 19 19
angle shears 125 2
angle symbol 345 23
angle tie 118 25; 121 57
angle tongs 137 37
angle tower 329 14, 17
angling 89 20-94
angling fence 133 19
Angora cat 73 17
Angoumois grain moth 81 29
Angoumois grain moth caterpillar 81 30
Angoumois moth 81 29
Anguidae 364 37
animal, bovine ~ 73 1
animal, cloven-hoofed ~ 73 9
animal, horned ~ 73 1
animal, inflatable ~ 280 33
animal, rubber ~ 280 33
animal, toy ~ 46 13; 47 6
animal, wild ~ 307 56
animal enclosure 272 49
animal house 356 10
animals, domestic ~ 73 18-36
animals, fabulous ~ 327 1-61
animals, multicellular ~ 357 13-39
animals, one-celled ~ 357 1-12
animals, single-celled ~ 357 1-12
animals, unicellular ~ 357 1-12
ankle guard 291 33
ankle sock, children's ~ 29 30
annealing lehr 162 18
annelid 357 20

annexe 331 13
annuity 251 11-19
annulus 346 57
Annunciation lily 60 12
anode, copper ~ 178 5
anode rod 178 5
anorak Child. Clothes 29 62
anorak Mountain. 300 6
anorak hood 300 19
Anseres 359 15-17
ant 358 21-22
Antarctica 14 18
Antarctic Circumpolar Drift 14 44
Antarctic Continent 14 18
Antarctic Ocean 14 22
antelope 367 5
antenna Meteorol. Instr. 10 59, 68
antenna Forest Pests 82 3
antenna Air Force 256 17
antenna Warships 258 16, 46; 259 7, 47, 89
antenna Airsports 288 20, 88
antenna Articulates 358 27, 53
antenna, maxillary ~ 358 42
antenna, trichotomous ~ 81 5
antenna down-lead 223 4
antenna lead-in 223 4
antenna mast 259 6
antependium 330 20
anthazoan 357 17
anther Soft Fruit 58 45
anther Drupes & Nuts 59 10
anther Conifers 372 35
anthropoid apes 368 14-16
anthropoids 368 14-16
anti-aircraft gun 258 73
anti-aircraft gun, automatic ~ 259 34
anti-aircraft machine gun 255 63
anti-aircraft missile launcher 258 32; 259 5, 20
anti-aircraft rocket launcher 258 32; 259 5, 20
anticline 12 16, 27
anticlinorium 12 20
anticollision light 230 64
anticyclone 9 6
antifriction bearing 143 69
anti-frost layer 198 1; 200 60
antimacassar 207 48
anti-mist windscreen 189 46
anti-mist windshield 189 46
anti-radiation screen 154 74
anti-rolling system 224 26
antirrhinum 51 32
anti set-off apparatus 181 10
anti set-off spray 181 10
anti-skate control 241 25
anti-skid brake switch 211 33
anti-slosh baffle 234 13
anti-submarine missile launcher 258 30, 50
anti-submarine rocket launcher 258 30, 50
anti-submarine torpedo tube 258 33
anti-syphon trap Bathrm. etc. 49 27
anti-syphon trap Plumb. etc. 126 26
anti-tank rocket launcher 255 25
anti-tank tank 255 88
anti-torque rotor 232 14
anti-vortex system 234 11
antler, palmate ~ 88 40
antler, royal ~ 88 8
antler, surroyal ~ 88 9
antlers 88 5-11, 29-31
anurans 364 23-26

anus 20 62
anvil Plumb. 125 22
anvil Blacksm. 137 11, 11-16; 138 33
anvil Forging 139 17, 31, 40
anvil Office 247 5
anvil, clockmaker's ~ 109 7
aorta 18 10; 20 54
aorta, abdominal ~ 18 16
Apache girl 306 9
apartment 37 64-68, 69-71; 46
apartment, ladies' ~ 329 10
apartment building 37 72-76
apartment building, high-rise ~ 37 82
apartment building, multistory ~ 37 77-81
apartment house 37 72-76
apartment house, high-rise ~ 37 82
apartment house, multistory ~ 37 77-81
apatite 351 20
aperture 115 62, 63
aperture control, automatic ~ 117 20
aperture control ring 115 5; 117 4
aperture ring 115 5; 117 4
aperture scale 115 56
aperture setting 117 4
aperture-setting control 114 34
aperture-setting ring 115 5; 117 4
aperture-stop slide 112 16
apex Hunt. 87 77
apex Airsports 288 47
aphid 80 32; 358 13
aphid, winged ~ 82 39; 358 15
aphid, wingless ~ 358 14
apiarist 77 57
apiary 77 56
apiculture 77
à pointe 314 19
Apollo booster 234 1, 2
Apollo service module 234 56
Apollo space capsule 6 9
Apollo spacecraft 6 1
apostrophe 342 22
apparatus, auxiliary ~ 296 12-21; 297 7-14
apparatus exercises 297 15-32
apparatus gymnastics 296; 297
appendix 20 18
appendix, vermiform ~ 20 18
Appenzell dulcimer 322 35
apple 58 56; 99 86; 370 102
apple blossom 58 54
appleblossom weevil 80 10
apple core 58 59
apple pip 58 60
apple skin 58 57
apple stalk 58 61
apple tree 58 51, 52
appliance room 270 1
appliqué 29 20
appoggiatura 321 14, 15
appointments book 22 11
appointments diary 246 8
approach 329 34
approach sign 203 26, 27, 28, 29
approach signs 203 26-29
apricot 59 35
apricot blossom 59 34
apricot branch, flowering ~ 59 33
apricot flower 59 34
apricot leaf 59 36
apricot tree 59 33-36

apron Mach. Tools 149 16
apron Electrotyp. etc. 178 9
apron Airport 233 3
apron Theatre 316 25
apron, butcher's ~ 96 39
apron, composition ~ 164 16
apron, frilled ~ 31 33
apron, leather ~ Arc Weld. 142 11
apron, leather ~ Cotton Spin. 164 16
apron taxiway 233 4
apse 334 64; 335 5
aquafer 12 22; 269 2, 38
aqualung 279 19
aquarium 356 14, 19
Aquarius 4 63
aquatint 340 14-24
aqueduct 334 53
aquifer 12 22; 269 2, 38
Aquila 3 9
arabesque Free Exerc. 295 30
arabesque Ballet 314 18
arachnida 53 16
arbor 272 17
arbor vitae 372 39
arbour 272 17
arc Films 312 42
arc Maths. 346 53, 55
arc, graduated ~ 224 2
arcade, blind ~ 335 10
arcading 335 8
arcading, blind ~ 335 10
arcading, round ~ 335 9
arc fibula 328 28
arch Bldg. Site 119 6
arch Bridges 215 20
arch Free Exerc. 295 34
arch Theatre 316 11
arch Art 336 19
arch, convex ~ 336 34
arch, longitudinal ~ 19 61
arch, parabolic ~ 336 29
arch, reinforced concrete ~ 215 50
arch, round ~ 336 27
arch, segmental ~ 336 28
arch, shouldered ~ 336 33
arch, superciliary ~ 16 5
arch, tented ~ 336 35
arch, transverse ~ 335 18
arch, trellis ~ 52 12
arch, triumphal ~ 334 59, 71
arch, trussed ~ 215 25
arch, Tudor ~ 336 37
arch, types of ~ 336 19-37
Archaster 369 17
arch board file 247 40
arch bridge, spandrel-braced ~ 215 28
arch bridge, stone ~ 215 19
arched front support 295 24
Archer Astron. 3 37; 4 61
archer Sports 305 53
archery 305 52-66
archimedes drill 108 4
architrave 334 18
archivolt 335 25
arch span 215 26
arch unit 247 41
archway 337 4
archway, memorial ~ 337 3
arcing horn 152 47; 153 61
arcosolium 331 60
Arctic Ocean 14 21
arc welder 142 2
arc welding, gas-shielded ~ 142 33
arc welding helmet 142 3, 39
area, epicentral ~ 11 38
area spraying 83 1

areca **380** 19
areca nut **380** 20
areca palm **380** 19
arena *Equest.* **289** 1
arena *Circus* **307** 21
arena *Bullfight. etc.* **319** 9
arena entrance **307** 11
areola **16** 29
argent **254** 25
Argo **3** 45
Aries **4** 53
aril, laciniate ~ **382** 34
arista **68** 12
arithmetic **344** 1-26; **345** 1-24
arithmetic unit **244** 6
arm *Man* **16** 43-48; **17** 12-14
arm *Living Rm.* **42** 22
arm *Flat* **46** 28
arm *Shoem.* **100** 25
arm *Photog.* **115** 93
arm *Joiner* **132** 63
arm *Mach. Parts etc.* **143** 88
arm *Mach. Tools* **150** 24
arm *Music. Instr.* **322** 16
arm *Maths.* **346** 7-3
arm, adjustable ~ **195** 26
arm, hydraulic ~ **85** 21
arm, supplementary ~ **203** 22, 23
arm, upper ~ **16** 43
armadillo **366** 8
armament **258** 29-37
armature **339** 25
armature support **339** 24
armband **263** 11; **270** 22
armband, fluorescent ~ **199** 7
arm bandage **21** 1
arm bar **299** 10
armchair **42** 21; **267** 26
armed forces **255**; **256**; **257**
armlet **263** 11; **270** 22
armonie **322** 25
armor *see* armour
armour **329** 38, 62
armour, knight's ~ **329** 38-65
armour, padded ~ **353** 38
armour, steel tape ~ **153** 50
armour, steel wire ~ **153** 50
armoured car **264** 16
armoured vehicles **255** 79-95
armour plating **246** 24
armpit **16** 26
armpit hair **16** 27
arm positions **314** 7-10
armrest **106** 18; **109** 3; **207** 45, 69; **208** 26
arm sling **21** 2
arms of the baron **254** 10
arms of the family of the femme **254** 11-13
arms of the family of the wife **254** 11-13
arms of the husband **254** 10
armstand dive **282** 45
army **255**
army armament **255** 1-98
army weaponry **255** 1-98
arnica **380** 2
A road **15** 83
arolla pine **372** 29
arpeggio **321** 22
arrangement of desks **260** 1
arrester **152** 35
arrester wire **259** 16
arris **121** 12
arris fillet **121** 31
'arrivals' **233** 26
arrivals and departures board **204** 18
arrival schedule **204** 19
arrival timetable **204** 19
arrow **305** 60

arrow head *Drawing Off.* **151** 26
arrow head *Alp. Plants etc.* **378** 51
art **333**; **334**; **335**; **336**; **337**
art, Babylonian ~ **333** 19-20
art, Baroque ~ **336** 1-8
art, Byzantine ~ **334** 72-75
art, Chinese ~ **337** 1-6
art, computer-generated ~ **248** 19
art, Early Christian ~ **334** 61-71
art, Egyptian ~ **333** 1-18
art, Etruscan ~ **334** 49-52
art, Gothic ~ **335** 22-41
art, Greek ~ **334** 1-48
art, Indian ~ **337** 19-28
art, Islamic ~ **337** 12-18
art, Japanese ~ **337** 7-11
art, Renaissance ~ **335** 42-54
art, Rococo ~ **336** 9-13
art, Roman ~ **334** 53-60
art, Romanesque ~ **335** 1-21
art director **310** 43
artery, carotid ~ **18** 1
artery, femoral ~ **18** 19
artery, frontal ~ **18** 5
artery, iliac ~ **18** 17
artery, pulmonary ~ **18** 11; **20** 55
artery, radial ~ **18** 21
artery, subclavian ~ **18** 7
artery, temporal ~ **18** 3
artery, tibial ~ **18** 20
artery forceps **26** 49
arthropods **358** 1-23
articulates **358**
artillery weapons **255** 49-74
artist **338** 2
artiste agent **307** 18
artistes, travelling ~ **308** 25-28
Art Nouveau easy chair **336** 18
art of Asia Minor **333** 37
art of the Assyrians **333** 29-36
art of the Persians **333** 21-28
arts section **342** 67
ascent, vertical ~ **315** 3
ascent stage **6** 37-47
ascospore **381** 13
ascus **381** 12, 13
ash box door **38** 39
ashpan **210** 6, 7
ash pit **152** 8
ashtray **42** 29; **104** 5; **207** 46, 69; **208** 29; **246** 33
ashtray, spherical ~ **266** 5
ash tree **371** 38
Asia **14** 16
asp **364** 41
asparagus **57** 14
asparagus bed **52** 25
asparagus cutter **56** 10
asparagus knife **56** 10
asparagus patch **52** 5
asparagus server **45** 77
asparagus slice **45** 77
aspen **371** 21
aspergillum **332** 54
asphalt drying and mixing plant **200** 48
asphalt mixer drum **200** 50
asphalt-mixing drum **200** 50
aspiration psychrometer **10** 33
asp viper **364** 41
assay balance **108** 35
assembler **174** 23
assembling machine **249** 59
assembling station **249** 60
assembly of a circuit **242** 72
assembly point **233** 11, 29

assistant *Univ.* **262** 7
assistant *Store* **271** 63
assistant *Circus* **307** 39
assistant, cellarer's ~ **79** 12
assistant, dentist's ~ **24** 18
assistant, doctor's ~ **22** 19
assistant cameraman **310** 42
assistant director *Films* **310** 21, 46
assistant director *Theatre* **316** 43
assistant lecturer **262** 3
assistant producer **316** 43
assistant professor **262** 3
assistant sound engineer **310** 57
association flag **286** 6, 9
association football **291**
asterisk **185** 61
asteroids **4** 47
astride jump **295** 35, 37
astronaut **6** 11; **235** 67
astronomy **3**; **4**; **5**
asymmetric bars **297** 3
asymptote **347** 29
athletics **298**
Atlantic Ocean **14** 20
Atlas **334** 36
atmosphere **7**
atoll **13** 32
Atolla **369** 5
atom **1**; **2**
atomic pile casing **259** 67
atomic power plant **154** 19
atom layer **7** 32
atom models **1** 1-8
atrium *Man* **20** 45
atrium *Art* **334** 66
attachment to Orbiter **235** 49
attack **321** 27
attack area **293** 64
attacker *Ball Games* **292** 3
attacker *Fencing* **294** 5
attacking fencer **294** 5
attack line **293** 65
attack periscope **259** 88
attic **38** 1-29, 18; **334** 60
attitude **314** 17
attitude control rocket **234** 38
aubretia **51** 7
auction room **225** 58
audience **263** 8
audio cassette **242** 17
audio coding equipment **242** 11-14
audio head **243** 35
audio level control **117** 16
audio recording level control **243** 11
audio sync head **243** 24
audio systems **241**
audio track **243** 32
audio typist **248** 33
audiovision **243**
audio-visual camera **243** 1-4
audio-visual projector **242** 16
auditorium **315** 14-27, 16-20
auditorium lighting control **312** 17
auger *Agr. Mach.* **64** 6, 25
auger *Carp.* **120** 65
augmented triad **321** 4
auk **359** 13
aulos **322** 3
aulos pipe **322** 4
aural syringe **22** 74
aureus **252** 3
auricle **17** 56; **20** 24
auricula **378** 8
Auriga **3** 27
auriscope **22** 74
aurora **7** 30
Australia **14** 17

Australopithecus **261** 20
auto **191** 1-56; **195** 34
auto changer **241** 18
autoclave **170** 12, 33
autofocus override switch **117** 11
automatic flight control panel **235** 23
automatic-threading button **117** 83
automobile **191** 1-56; **192**; **193**; **195** 34
automobile models **193** 1-36
automobile tire **191** 15; **196** 27
automotive mechanic **195** 53
autopilot **224** 18
auto-soling machine **100** 2
auxiliaries **258** 92-97
auxiliary brake valve **211** 23
auxiliary-cable tensioning mechanism **214** 48
auxiliary engine room **223** 70; **259** 56
auxiliary parachute bay **235** 59
AV **243**
avalanche **304** 1
avalanche forest **304** 7
avalanche gallery **304** 3
avalanche wall **304** 2
avalanche wedge **304** 2
Ave Maria **332** 32
avenue **274** 11
aviary **356** 8
aviation fuel **145** 57
avionics bay, front ~ **257** 11
avionics bay, rear ~ **257** 18
avionics console **235** 22
awn **68** 12
awner **64** 10
awning *Dwellings* **37** 71
awning *Ship* **218** 15; **221** 116
awning *Camping* **278** 28, 37
awning crutch **218** 14
ax *see* axe
axe **85** 1; **120** 73; **270** 43
axe, bronze ~ **328** 23
axe, socketed ~ **328** 23
axial-flow pump **217** 47-52
axis *Astron.* **4** 22
axis *Maths.* **347** 17
axis, anticlinal ~ **12** 17
axis, celestial ~ **4** 10
axis, conjugate ~ **347** 24
axis, coordinate ~ **347** 2-3
axis, earth's ~ **4** 22-28
axis, floral ~ **370** 53
axis, lateral ~ **230** 68
axis, longitudinal ~ **230** 72
axis, major ~ **347** 23
axis, minor ~ **347** 24
axis, normal ~ **230** 70
axis, polar ~ **113** 15, 18
axis, synclinal ~ **12** 19
axis, transverse ~ **347** 23
axis, vertical ~ **230** 70
axis mount, English-type ~ **113** 22
axis mounting, English-type ~ **113** 22
axis of abscissae **347** 2
axis of ordinates **347** 3
axis of rotation, instantaneous ~ **4** 25
axis of rotation, mean ~ **4** 27
axis of symmetry *Maths.* **346** 25
axis of symmetry *Crystals* **351** 4
axle **187** 61, 76, 81
axle, coupled ~ **210** 36
axle, floating ~ *Agr. Mach.* **65** 33

axle, floating ~ *Motorcycle* 189 34
axle, live ~ 192 65-71
axle, rigid ~ 192 65-71
axle bearing 210 10
axle drive shaft 201 13
azalea 53 12
azimuth 87 74
azure *Heraldry* 254 28
azure *Colour* 343 6

B

baboon 368 13
baby 28 5
baby bath 28 3
baby carriage 28 34; 272 71; 273 31
baby clothes 29 1-12
baby doll 48 25
baby grand piano 325 40
baby pants 28 22
baby pants, rubber ~ 29 10
baby powder 28 14
baby scales 22 42
back *Man* 16 22-25
back *Tablew. etc.* 45 56
back *Horse* 72 29
back *Mills* 91 2
back *Roof* 122 86
back *Bookbind.* 185 41
back *Car* 193 35
back *Swim.* 282 49
back *Ball Games* 293 77
back *Sports* 305 11
backband 71 19
backboard 292 30
backbone *Man* 17 2-5
backbone *Bookbind.* 185 41
back check 325 27
back check felt 325 28
backcloth 315 33; 316 10
back comb 105 6
back crease 292 71
back cushion 42 25
back cut 84 29
backdrop 315 33; 316 10
backdrop light 316 15
back fat 95 40
backfilling 217 7
back flip 297 24
backgammon 276 18
backgammon board 276 22
back gauge 183 17; 185 4, 7
background *Films* 310 33
background *Theatre* 316 10
backhand stroke 293 39
backing 269 29
backing disc, rubber ~ 134 22
backing paper *Photog.* 114 21
backing paper *Paperhanger* 128 5
back left second pin 305 9
back loop 288 50
back of the hand 19 83
backpack unit 6 20
back-pedal brake 187 63
back pin 305 11
back plate 140 36
back-pressure valve, hydraulic ~ 141 8
backrest *Weaving* 166 37
backrest *Railw.* 207 66
backrest, reclining ~ 191 35
back right second pin 305 10
backside 16 40
back sight leaf 87 67
back sight slide 87 69
back standard adjustment 114 55

backstay 219 19
backstitch seam 102 1
back support 295 22; 296 29
back-up ball 305 20
back vault 297 32
backward grand circle 296 60
backward somersault *Swim.* 282 42
backward somersault *Gymn.* 297 15
backward underswing 296 59
backward walkover 297 23
backwater 172 26
bacon 96 2
Bactrian camel 366 29
badge, fool's ~ 306 60
badger 88 48
badging 191 12
badminton 293 43-44
badminton game 273 6
badminton racket 293 43
badminton racquet 293 43
baffle board *Warships* 259 27
baffle board 309 17
baffle board, hinged ~ 259 15
baffle board, movable ~ 259 15
bag *Doc.* 22 33
bag *Hunt.* 86 38
bag *Music. Instr.* 322 9
bag, girl's ~ 29 56
bag, heat-sealed ~ 76 29
bag, paper ~ 98 48
bag, postman's ~ 236 54
bag filter 83 54
bag-full indicator 50 61, 73
baggage compartment 257 19
baggage loader 233 22
baggage man 267 17
'baggage retrieval' 233 38
baggage terminal 233 5, 16
bagging nozzle 83 55
bag net 77 54
bagpipe 322 8
bag sealer 40 47
baguette 97 12
bag wig 34 4
bail 292 70
bailey, inner ~ 329 2
bailey, outer ~ 329 31
bait 86 21
bait, poisoned ~ 83 31
bait, weighted ~ 89 36
bait needle 89 41
baits 89 65-76
bait tin 89 24
bakehouse 97 55-74
baker's shop 97 1-54
bakery 97 55-74
baking ingredient 99 62
baking ingredients 98 8-11
balalaika 324 28
Balance *Astron.* 3 19; 4 59
balance *Paperm.* 173 9
balance beam 349 30
balance cable 214 46
balance cable sleeve 214 74
balance column 349 29
balancer 307 48
balance rail 322 39
balance weight 242 50
balance wheel 110 39
balancing act 307 44
balancing cabins 214 25
balancing knob 116 39
balancing pole 307 42
balcony *Dwellings* 37 18, 69, 73
balcony *Theatre* 315 16; 315 18
balcony *Chivalry* 329 12
balcony, projecting ~ 218 57
baldachin 331 49

baldaquin 331 49
bald patch 34 21
bale 55 31; 63 34; 75 7; 83 13; 169 34; 170 62; 206 10, 11, 23
bale arm 89 62
bale breaker 163 7
bale loader, hydraulic ~ 63 37
bale opener 163 7
baler, high-pressure ~ 63 35
baling press 169 33
balk 63 3
ball *Infant Care etc.* 28 16
ball *Bicycle* 187 31
ball *Aircraft* 230 12
ball *Ball Games* 292 27
ball *Circus* 307 60
ball, ivory ~ 277 1
ball, metal ~ 352 32
ball, paper ~ 306 55
ball, plastic ~ 277 1
ball, steel ~ 143 70
ball, stone ~ 352 32
ball and socket head 114 47
ballast *Station* 205 61
ballast *Railw.* 212 66
ballast *Sailing* 285 33
ballast *Airsports* 288 65
ballast keel 285 32
ballast tank 223 78
ball bearing 143 69; 187 56, 68
ball boy 293 22
ballerina 314 26
ballet 314
ballet dancer 314 26
ballet positions 314 1-6
ballet shoe 314 30
ballet skirt 314 31
ballet slipper 314 30
ball games 291; 292; 293
ballistics 87 73
ball mill 161 1
ball of clay 161 9
ball of the foot 19 58
ball of the thumb 19 75
balloon 308 13
balloon, gas ~ 288 63
balloon, hot-air ~ 288 79
balloon, manned ~ 7 16
balloon basket 288 64
ballooning 288 63-84
ballot box 263 29
ballot envelope 263 21
ballot paper 263 20
ball race 187 68
ballroom 306 1
Balmer series 1 21
baluster 38 29; 123 51
balustrade 38 25; 123 22, 50
bamboo cane 136 31
bamboo culm 383 60
bamboo stem 383 60, 63
banana 99 90; 384 33
banana flower 384 34
banana-handling terminal 226 22
banana leaf 384 35
banana plant 384 28
banana saddle 188 59
banana tree 384 28
band *Ball Games* 291 25
band *Nightclub* 318 3
band *Church* 332 5
band, fluorescent ~ 199 8
band, iron ~ 130 16
band, ornamental ~ 334 38
band, steel ~ 163 5
bandage *First Aid* 21 9
bandage *Equest.* 289 15
bandages, emergency ~ 21 1-13
band brake 143 104

banderilla 319 22
banderillero 319 4, 21
band of barrel 130 8
bandoneon 324 36
bandora 322 21
bandsaw 134 50; 157 48
bandsaw, horizontal ~ 157 48
bandsaw blade 157 53
bandstand 274 19; 307 9
band wheel 104 15
bandwheel cover 133 32
banewort 379 7
banger 306 51
bangle *Jewell.* 36 17
bangle *Ethnol.* 354 38
bangle, asymmetrical ~ 36 26
bangs 34 36
banjo 324 29
bank *Phys. Geog.* 13 4
bank *Post* 237 43
bank *Bank* 250
bank *Roulette* 275 11
bank acceptance 250 12
bank branch 204 31
bank clerk 250 5
bank employee 251 7
banknotes 252 29-39
bank of circulation 252 30
bank of issue 252 30
bank of oars 218 12
bank protection 216 51-55
bank slope 217 28
bank stabilization 216 51-55
bank statement 247 44
banner *Flags* 253 12
banner *Election* 263 12
banner, processional ~ 331 44
banquet room 267 39
bantam 74 56
baptism, Christian ~ 332 1
baptistery 332 2
bar *Horse* 71 41
bar *Office* 246 29
bar *Restaurant* 266 1-11
bar *Hotel* 267 54
bar *Park* 272 34
bar *Playground* 273 32
bar *Gymn.* 296 3, 8; 297 4, 41
bar *Athletics* 298 14, 34
bar *Winter Sp.* 303 5
bar *Circus* 307 50
bar *Disco* 317 1, 9
bar *Nightclub* 318 13, 15
bar *Music. Not.* 320 42
bar *Graphic Art* 340 34
bar, flat ~ 143 10
bar, metal ~ 324 77
bar, round ~ 143 8
bar, sliding ~ 75 21
bar arm 299 10
barb *Bees* 77 10
barb *Fish Farm.* 89 80
barb *Mach. Parts etc.* 143 44
barbecue 278 47
barbel 364 13
bar bender 119 21
barber 106 1
barber's shop 106 1-42
barchan 13 40
barchane 13 40
bar customer 267 55
bareback rider 307 26
barge 216 22, 25; 225 8
barge and push tug assembly 221 92
bargeboard 37 8
bargee 216 26
bargeman 216 26
barge sucker 216 59
bark *Carp.* 120 86
bark *Ship* 219 1-72; 220 21-23
bark *Bot.* 370 8

bark, five-masted ~ **220** 32-34
bark. four-masted ~ **220** 29
bark beetle **82** 22
bark brush **56** 23
barkeep **266** 8; **267** 62
barkeeper **266** 8; **267** 62
barker **308** 8, 64
barkhan **13** 40
barking **85** 23
barking iron **85** 8
bark schooner **220** 20
bark scraper **56** 14
bark spud **85** 8
bark stripping **85** 23
bar lamp **317** 11
barley **68** 1, 26
barley, germinated ~ **92** 23
barley elevator **92** 33
barley hopper **92** 2
barley reception **92** 41
barley silo **92** 31
bar line **320** 42
barmaid **267** 63; **317** 2; **318** 14
barman **266** 8; **267** 62
barn owl **362** 17
barn swallow **361** 20
barograph **10** 4
barouche **186** 35
barque **219** 1-72; **220** 21-23
barque, five-masted ~ **220** 32-34
barque, four-masted ~ **220** 29
barque schooner **220** 20
barrage **217** 57-64, 65-72
barrel *Cooper* **130** 5
barrel *Mach. Tools* **149** 27
barrel *Army* **255** 2, 17, 41
barrel, aluminium ~ **93** 17
barrel, rifled ~ **87** 26
barrel, semi-oval ~ **89** 3
barrel, smooth-bore ~ **87** 27
barrel casing **87** 35; **255** 33
barrel clamp **255** 11, 62
barrel-clamping nut **255** 11
barrel cradle **255** 60
barrelhead **130** 10
barrel organ **309** 13
barrel recuperator **255** 61
barrel-shape **36** 75
barrel-shape, standard ~ **36** 56
barrel stave **130** 9
barrel store **93** 16
barrel vault **335** 19; **336** 38
barricade **264** 17
barrier *Supermkt.* **99** 5
barrier *Railw.* **202** 40
barrier *Hydr. Eng.* **217** 65
barrow *Station* **205** 32
barrow *Prehist.* **328** 16
barrow, road sweeper's ~ **199** 9
barrow, street sweeper's ~ **199** 9
bars **75** 5
bar set **246** 30
bar stool **267** 53; **317** 3; **318** 16
bartender **266** 8; **267** 62
bar trio **267** 44
barysphere **11** 5
basal pinacoid **351** 20
base *Dining Rm.* **44** 23
base *Mills* **91** 33
base *Optic. Instr.* **112** 3; **113** 2
base *Floor etc. Constr.* **123** 21, 63
base *Bookbind.* **183** 25
base *Road Constr.* **200** 59
base *Heraldry* **254** 22-23
base *Mountain.* **300** 1
base *Art* **334** 28-31

base *Maths.* **345** 1, 6; **346** 27; **347** 35, 39
base, horizontal ~ **112** 72
base, round ~ *Hairdresser* **105** 27
base, round ~ *Basketm.* **136** 19
base, round ~ *Electrotyp. etc.* **178** 10
base, woven ~ **136** 20
baseball **292** 40-69, 61
baseball glove **292** 59-60
baseball mitt **292** 59-60
baseboard *Photog.* **116** 27
baseboard *Sculpt. Studio* **339** 23
base course *Dwellings* **37** 17
base course *Carp.* **120** 28
base course *Street Sect.* **198** 3
base course *Road Constr.* **200** 59
base course, concrete ~ **118** 2
base course, natural stone ~ **37** 85
base frame **177** 40
base line **292** 48; **293** 3 - 10, 72
base line judge **293** 26
baseman **292** 44
basement **37** 1; **118** 1
basement stairs **123** 16
basement wall **123** 1
basement window **37** 27; **118** 3
base of goblet **162** 42
base of machine **168** 54
base of statue **272** 11
base of support **214** 81
base plate *Optic. Instr.* **112** 27
base plate *Iron Foundry etc.* **148** 56
base plate *Mach. Tools* **150** 19
base plate *Knitting* **167** 34
base plate *Railw.* **202** 5
base plate *Army* **255** 46
base plate *Ball Games* **292** 67
base unit **39** 9
basic knits **171** 30-48
basic position **295** 1
basidia **381** 7
basidiospore **381** 8
basilica **334** 61
basilisk *Fabul. Creat.* **327** 34
basilisk *Fish etc.* **364** 30
basin *Doc.* **23** 25
basin *Dent.* **24** 12
basin *Park* **272** 24
basis weight **173** 9
basket *Kitch. Utensils* **40** 42
basket *Butch.* **96** 18
basket *Supermkt.* **99** 8
basket *Basketm.* **136** 16
basket *Station* **204** 3
basket *Ball Games* **292** 32
basket *Winter Sp.* **301** 8
basket, rotating ~ **168** 17
basket, wicker ~ **305** 69
basket, wire ~ **55** 50; **66** 25; **188** 23
basketball **292** 28, 29
basketball player **292** 35
basket handle **336** 28
basket maker **136** 33
basket making **136** 1-40
basket post **292** 31
basket ring **292** 33
basketry **136** 1-40
basket weave **171** 11
basketwork **136** 1-40, 16
bas-relief **339** 33
bass **323** 23
bass belly bridge **325** 13
bass bridge **325** 13
bass button **324** 43

bass clarinet **323** 34
bass clef **320** 9
bass coupler **324** 44
bass drum **323** 55; **324** 47
bassinet **28** 30
bassinet covers **28** 31
bassoon **323** 28
bass press-stud **324** 43
bass register **324** 44
bass side **324** 43
bass stop **324** 44
bass string **324** 25; **325** 12
bass stud **324** 43
bass trombone **323** 46
bass tuba **323** 44
bass tuning **241** 43
bass viol **322** 23
bast **136** 29
bastard title **185** 44
bastion **329** 16
bat **292** 62, 75
batch **162** 2
batch feeder **162** 13
batch funnel **162** 13
batching and mixing plant, automatic ~ **201** 19
batch of eggs **80** 2, 30
bath *Bathrm. etc.* **49** 1
bath *Hotel* **267** 27-38
bath *Swim.* **281** 36
bath, cold ~ **281** 30
bath additive **49** 5
bat handle **293** 46
bather **280** 30
bathing beach **280**
bathing cap **280** 29, 44; **281** 8
bathing gown **280** 25
bathing platform **280** 9
bathing shoe **280** 23
bathing suit **280** 42
bathing suit, two-piece ~ **280** 26
bathing towel **281** 14
bathing trunks **280** 43
bathing wrap **280** 25
bath mat **49** 48
batholite **11** 29
bath robe **29** 24
bathroom **49**
bathroom cabinet, mirrored ~ **49** 31
bathroom mule **49** 46
bathroom scales **49** 47
bathroom tissue **49** 11
bathroom tissue holder **49** 10
bath salts **99** 34
bath sponge *Bathrm. etc.* **49** 6
bath sponge *Invertebr.* **357** 13
bat of clay **161** 9
baton **264** 19
baton, conductor's ~ **315** 27
batrachians **364** 23-26
batsman **292** 74
batten *Roof* **122** 17
batten *Sailing* **284** 44
batten, compartmentalized ~ **316** 13
batten, compartment-type ~ **316** 13
batten cleat **284** 43
batten door **37** 34
batten gauge **122** 18
batten pocket **284** 43
batter **292** 52, 63
batterboard **118** 69
batter's position **292** 51
battery *Agr. Mach.* **65** 53
battery *Poultry Farm* **74** 19
battery *Photog.* **114** 66
battery *Car* **191** 50
battery *Warships* **259** 83
battery, rotary ~ **166** 5
battery box **207** 5, 25; **211** 56

battery cage **74** 20
battery cell **110** 7
battery chamber *Photog.* **115** 10
battery chamber *Cine Film* **117** 5
battery compartment **188** 22
battery container **207** 5, 25; **211** 56
battery feeding **74** 23
battery holder **115** 76
battery housing **257** 17
battery railcar **211** 55
battery switch **115** 13
battery system **74** 18
battery tester **25** 52
battery unit **115** 75
batting crease **292** 72
batting order **292** 58
battle axe **352** 16
battle axe, stone ~ **328** 19
battlement **329** 6
battleships, light ~ **258** 1-63
bauble **306** 59
baulk *Agr.* **63** 3
baulk *Carp.* **120** 87
baumkuchen **97** 46
Bavarian curler **302** 38
Bavarian curling **302** 38-40
bay *Phys. Geog.* **13** 7
bay *Game* **88** 7
bay *Carp.* **120** 59
bayadère **306** 25
bay antler **88** 7
bayonet **353** 28
bayonet fitting **127** 65, 69
B-deck **223** 32-42
beach **13** 35-44
beach, raised ~ **11** 54
beach area **281** 2
beach attendant **280** 34
beach bag **280** 24
beach ball **280** 18
beach chair, roofed ~ **280** 36
beach chair, wicker ~ **280** 36
beach grass **15** 7
beach hat **280** 20
beach jacket **280** 21
beach marten **367** 14
beach mattress, inflatable ~ **280** 17
beach shoe **280** 23
beach suit **33** 24; **280** 19
beach tent **280** 45
beach trousers **280** 22
beachwear **280** 19-23
beacon **15** 10, 49
bead **87** 72
bead-and-dart moulding **334** 38
beading **123** 64
beading hammer **125** 15
beading iron **125** 8
beading pin **128** 30
beading swage **125** 15
beak **88** 84
beak, flat ~ **137** 12
beak, hooked ~ **362** 6
beak, round ~ **137** 13
beaker **350** 20
beaker pottery **328** 14
beam *Agr. Mach.* **65** 9, 71
beam *Game* **88** 11, 30
beam *Carp.* **120** 19, 24
beam *Gymn.* **297** 2
beam *Music. Instr.* **325** 22
beam *Chem.* **349** 30
beam, central ~ **27** 3
beam, dipped ~ **191** 20
beam, high ~ **191** 20
beam, low ~ **191** 20
beam, main ~ *Carp.* **120** 38
beam, main ~ *Roof* **121** 66

beam, main ~ *Car* 191 20
beam, tied ~ 215 44
beam bridge 215 7
beam compass 125 11
beam compass, glaziers ~ 124 22
beam entry point 1 64
beam flange 165 30; 166 49; 167 26
beam head 121 33
beaming machine 165 55
beam motion control 166 60
beam of light 224 83
beam setter 195 24
beam splitter 240 35
beam-splitting prism *Optic Instr.* 112 13
beam-splitting prism *Broadcast.* 240 35
beam trammel 125 11
bean 57 8, 11; 382 3, 15
bean, bush ~ 57 8
bean, climbing ~ 57 8
bean flower 57 9
bean plant 52 28; 57 8
bean pole 52 28
beanstalk 57 10
bearberry 377 15
beard *Arable Crops* 68 12
beard *Dom. Anim.* 73 15
beard *Game* 88 73
beard, circular ~ 34 15
beard, full ~ 34 15
beard, round ~ 34 15
bearded couch grass 61 30
beards 34 1-25
bearer cable 119 37; 271 52
bearer share 251 11
bearing, axial-radial ~ 113 3
bearing, centre ~ 177 65
bearing, fixed ~ 215 11
bearing, hydrostatic ~ 5 10
bearing, jewelled ~ 110 33
bearing, lower ~ 192 83
bearing, main ~ 192 23
bearing, movable ~ *Bridges* 215 12
bearing, movable ~ *Sailing* 284 6
bearing, upper ~ 192 73
bearing block 177 61
bearing cup 187 68
bears 368 9-11
beasts of prey 367 11-22; 368 1-11
beater *Hunt.* 86 37
beater *Bakery* 97 70
beater *Music. Instr.* 322 34; 324 64
beater, revolving ~ 64 13
beater, three-blade ~ 163 25
beater drive motor 163 23
beater driving shaft 163 24
beating 86 34-39
beating machine 131 4
beating wood 339 12
beau 306 33
beauty parlor 105 1-39
beauty queen 306 64
beauty salon 105 1-39
beauty shop 105 1-39
beauty spot 306 24
beaver *Chivalry* 329 41
beaver *Mammals* 366 14
beck, flat ~ 137 12
beck, round ~ 137 13
bed *Phys. Geog.* 13 49
bed *Hosp.* 25 10
bed *Joiner* 133 50
bed *Mach. Tools* 150 19, 29
bed *Offset Print.* 180 78
bed *Letterpress* 181 17
bed *Bookbind.* 183 25

bed *Station* 205 61
bed *Graphic Art* 340 41, 64
bed, children's ~ 47 1
bed, double ~ 43 4-13; 267 38
bed, rear ~ 85 49
bed bug 81 39
bedder 91 23
bed frame 43 5
bed linen 271 57
Bedlington terrier 70 18
bed monitor 25 19
bedouin 354 6
bedrock 13 70
bedroom 43
bedroom, twin-berth 207 38
bedroom, two-berth ~ 207 38
bedroom, two-seat ~ 207 38
bedroom lamp 43 19
bedside cabinet 43 17
bedside rug 43 22
bed slide 149 24
bedspread 43 7
bedstead 43 4-6
bed stone 91 23
beduin 354 6
bed unit 46 16
bed unit drawer 46 18
bed unit shelf 46 19
bed warmer 309 88
bee 77 1-25
bee, male ~ 77 5
beech cellulose 169 1
beech gall 82 37
beech nut 371 37
beech tree 371 33
bee eater 360 2
beef 95 14-37
beehive 77 45-50
beehive kiln 161 3
bee house 77 56
beekeeper 77 57
beekeeping 77
beeman 77 57
beer 99 72
beer, bottled ~ 93 26
beer, canned ~ 99 73
beer barrel 93 17
beer bottle 93 26; 205 50
beer can 93 25; 99 73
beer crate 93 24; 99 72
beer filter 93 15
beer glass 45 91; 93 30; 266 3, 6; 317 6
beer marquee 308 23
beer mat 266 26
beer mug 266 6; 309 53
beerpull 266 1, 68
beer pump 266 1, 68
beer tap 317 8
beer warmer 266 7
bees 77
bee shed 77 51
bee smoker 77 59
bee sting ointment 77 68
beeswax 77 67
beet 68 44, 45
beet carrion beetle 80 45
beet cleaner 64 89
beet elevator 64 94
beet elevator belt 64 95
beet harvester 64 85-96
beet hopper 64 96
beetle 82 26, 42
beet leaf 68 47
beetles 358 24-39
beet top 68 46
bee veil 77 58
begonia 53 10
begonia, tuberous ~ 51 19
belay 300 9, 10
belayer 300 26
belfry window 331 8
bell *Plumb. etc.* 126 16

bell *Iron & Steel* 147 6
bell *Railw.* 212 49
bell *Navig.* 224 75
bell *Election* 263 4
bell *Winter Countr.* 304 26
bell *Music. Instr.* 323 37, 42, 48; 324 70
bell, electric ~ 127 15
bell, electrically operated ~ 331 9
belladonna 379 7
Bellatrix 3 13
bell beaker 328 14
bell boy 267 18
bell end 278 27
bellows *Photog.* 114 53; 116 31
bellows *Photomech. Reprod.* 177 10, 26
bellows *Camping* 278 49
bellows *Flea Market* 309 26
bellows *Music. Instr.* 322 58; 324 37
bellows pedal 325 46
bellows strap 324 38
bellows unit 115 85
bell push 127 2
bells 276 45
bell sleeve, pleated ~ 30 54
bell tent 278 8
bell tower 337 8
belly *Sea Fish.* 90 20
belly *Meat* 95 39, 41
belly *Music. Instr.* 323 24; 324 3
belly-band 71 36
belt 30 11; 31 10; 32 39
belt, coloured ~ 299 15
belt, flat ~ 163 49
belt, stretch ~ 31 63
belt buckle 31 12
belt-changing flap 255 35
belt conveying 144 40
belt conveyor 156 2
belt delivery 185 13
belt drive 165 33
belt guard 133 31
beltline 270 45
belt roller 133 18
belt-tensioning lever 133 16
bench *Goldsm. etc.* 108 20
bench *Plumb.* 125 10
bench *Blacksm.* 137 21
bench *Metalwkr.* 140 7
bench *Playground* 273 58
bench *Gymn.* 296 14
bench, collapsible ~ 134 41
bench, oarsman's ~ 278 17
bench, paperhanger's ~ 128 31
bench, pupil's ~ 261 11
bench, student's ~ 261 11
bench, teacher's ~ 261 3
bench, tiered ~ 281 20
bench, woodworker's ~ 132 29-37
bench apron 108 21
bench brush 108 33
bench covering 141 16
bench holdfast 132 36
bench stop 132 36
bench top 132 34
bench torch 350 9
bend 126 46
bending iron *Bldg. Site* 119 77
bending iron *Blacksm.* 137 39
bending machine 125 28, 30
bending table 119 20
bending tool 136 34
bend of hook 89 81
bend sinister wavy 254 6
Benguela Current 14 43
benniseed 383 45

bent hang 296.39
benzene chlorination 170 8
benzene extraction 170 6
benzene ring 242 66
benzene scrubber 156 24
benzol scrubber 156 24
beret 35 27
berlin 186 1
berm 216 38
Bermuda shorts 31 44
berry 58 9, 11; 370 97
berry bush 52 19
berry bushes 58 1-30
berry tree, standard ~ 52 11
besaguer 329 45
besom *Roof & Boilerr.* 38 36
besom *Winter Sp.* 302 43
Bessemer converter 147 55-69
best end of loin 95 7
beta particle 1 32
beta radiation 1 32
Betelgeuse 3 13
betel nut 380 20
betel palm 380 19
bevel *Carp.* 120 81
bevel *Mach. Parts etc.* 143 62
bevel edge 178 44
bevel gear 91 25
bevel gearing 91 25
bevel gear wheel 143 91
bevel wheel 143 91
bez antler 88 7
bez tine 88 7
B flat major 320 64
B flat minor 320 67
bib *Infant Care etc.* 28 43
bib *Ladies' Wear* 30 24
bib and brace *Child. Clothes* 29 40
bib and brace *Ladies' Wear* 30 21
bib and brace overalls 33 44
Bible 330 11
bib skirt 29 41
biceps brachii 18 37
biceps femoris 18 61
bick, flat ~ 137 12
bick, round ~ 137 13
bicycle 187
bicycle, child's ~ 273 9
bicycle, folding ~ 188 1
bicycle, gent's ~ 187 1
bicycle, motor-assisted ~ 188 6
bicycle bell 187 4
bicycle drive 187 35-42
bicycle frame 187 14-20
bicycle kick 291 45
bicycle lamp 187 7
bicycle lock 187 49
bicycle pedal 187 78
bicycle pump 187 48
bicycles 188
bicycle saddle 187 22
bicycle speedometer 187 33
bidet 49 7
Biedermeier dress 306 22
Biedermeier sofa 336 17
bier 331 41
bifurcation 224 89
Big Dipper 3 29
big top 307 1
big wave riding 279 4
big wheel 308 37
bike 187 1
bikini 280 26
bikini bottom 280 27
bikini briefs 32 15
bikini top 280 28
bilberry 377 23
bile duct, common ~ 20 37-38
bilge block 222 40

bilge keel 222 47
bilge shore 222 40
bilge .trake 222 46
bill Game 88 84
bill Bank 250 12
bill Birds 359 17
billboard 118 45
bill clause 250 17
billhook 56 9; 85 11
billiard ball 277 1
billiard clock 277 17
billiard cloth 277 15
billiard cue 277 9
billiard marker 277 18
billiard parlor 277 7-19
billiard player 277 8
billiard room 277 7-19
billiards 277 1-19
billiards, English ~ 277 7
billiards, French ~ 277 7
billiards, German ~ 277 7
billiard saloon 277 7-19
billiard stick 277 9
billiard strokes 277 2-6
billiard table 277 14
bill of exchange 250 12
bills 252 29-39
bin 200 45
bind 321 24
binder 107 6
binder course 198 4
binder injector 200 53
binding Bookbind. 185 40-42
binding Athletics 298 54
binding, parts of ~ 301 54-56
binding, rubber ~ 286 57-58
bindweed 61 26
binoculars 86 6; 111 17; 221
  128
biology preparation room 261
  14-34
biopsy forceps 23 17
biplane 229 10
bipod 255 42
bipod mast 221 24
biprism, ditrigonal ~ 351 22
biprism, hexagonal ~ 351 22
bipyramid, tetragonal ~ 351
  18
birch 51 13; 272 40; 281 27
Birch Boletus 381 22
birch rod 281 27
birch tree 51 13; 272 40; 371 9
bird 86 50
bird, flightless ~ 359 4
bird, gallinaceous ~ 359 22
bird, migratory ~ 360 7
bird, non-migratory ~ 360 4
bird, resident ~ 360 4
bird cherry 59 5
bird-foot 69 11
birds 359; 361; 362; 363
birds, corvine ~ 361 1-3
birds, endemic ~ 360
birds, exotic ~ 363
birds, flightless ~ 359 1-3
birds, indigenous ~ 360
birds, long-winged ~ 359
  11-14
birds, web-footed ~ 359 5-10
bird's foot 69 11
bird's foot clover 376 17
bird's foot trefoil 69 11; 376
  17
birdsmouth 84 28
birds of prey 362
birds of prey, diurnal ~ 362
  1-13
birds of prey, nocturnal ~ 362
  14-19
birth-wort 376 22
biscuit tin, decorative ~ 46 12
bisector 346 28, 30

bishop 276 10
bismarck 97 29
bison 328 9; 367 9
bistort 376 10
bit 140 35
bitch 73 16
biting housefly 81 4
bitt 284 25
bitter 93 26
bitumen 145 64
bituminous distributor 200 46
black 343 13
black arches moth 82 17
black-backed jackal 367 11
black beetle 81 17
blackberry 58 29
blackbird 361 13
blackboard 47 13; 48 16; 261
  36
blackboard, three-part ~ 260
  29
blackboard chalk 48 15
blackboard compass 260 40
blackboard drawing 260 33
blackboard sponge 260 42
black buck 367 5
blackcock 86 11; 88 66
black elder 374 35
Black Forest clock 109 31
Black Forest gateau 97 24
black-headed gull 359 14
black liquor filter 172 28
black liquor storage tank 172
  29
black nightshade 379 5
black rhino 366 25
black salsify 57 35
blacksmith 137; 138
blacksmith's tools 137 22-39
blackthorn 374 27
bladder 20 33, 78
blade Kitch. Utensils 40 40
blade Tablew. etc. 45 54
blade Gdn. Tools 56 36
blade Arable Crops 68 20
blade Paperm. 172 74
blade Bookbind. 185 29
blade Rowing 283 38, 53
blade Fencing 294 44
blade Bot. 370 28
blade, flexible ~ 85 20
blade, front ~ 85 35
blade, lower ~ 23 14
blade, rear ~ 85 40
blade, rotating ~ 39 24
blade bit 145 21
bladebone 95 22, 30, 32, 42
blade coater 173 29-35
blade coating machine 173
  29-35
blade covering 293 47
bladed cone, rotating ~ 172 75
bladed plug, rotating ~ 172 75
bladed shell, stationary ~ 172
  76
blade of grass 370 83-85
blade-slewing gear 200 22
blancmange powder 98 50
blank 252 43
blanket 71 44; 168 56
blanket, rubber ~ 180 54, 79
blanket cylinder 180 24, 37,
  54, 63
blast burner 108 16
blast furnace 147 1
blast furnace plant 147 1-20
blast furnace shaft 147 7
blasting cartridge 158 27
blasting fuse 158 28
blast inlet 148 2
blast lamp 108 16
blast main 147 17, 68; 148 2
blastodisc 74 65

blast pipe Blacksm. 137 6
blast pipe Iron Foundry etc.
  148 2
blast pipe Railw. 210 25
blazer 33 54
blazing star 51 31
blazon 254 17-23
blazonry 254 1-36
bleach 105 1
bleach-hardener 116 10
bleaching 169 21
bleach tube 105 3
bleed 192 27
bleeder 38 65
bleeding heart 60 5
blender 40 46
blending pump 196 1
Blessed Sacrament 331 48;
  332 35
blimp 310 48; 313 16-18, 27
blind Hosp. 25 9
blind Hunt. 86 9
blinder 71 26
blind spot 19 50
blindworm 364 37
blinker 71 26
blob marker 83 9
blob marking 83 6
block Headgear 35 3
block Plumb. 125 21
block Mach. Tools 150 20
block Ship 221 28, 105
block Winter Sp. 302 40
block Music. Instr. 326 20
block, adjustable ~ 298 2
block, charcoal ~ 108 37
block, clay ~ 159 22, 23
block, halftone ~ 178 38
block, hollow ~ 119 24; 159
  21-22, 22, 23
block, pumice concrete ~ 119
  24
block, rubber ~ 187 85
block, tongued and grooved ~
  123 74
block, travelling ~ 145 8
block, wooden ~ 340 1
block and tackle 137 20
block board 132 73
block brake 143 97
blocker 293 60
blocking saw 157 54
block instruments 203 59
block making 178
block mount 178 41
block mountain 12 4-11
block mounting 178 41
block of flats 37 72-76
block of flats, high-rise ~ 37
  82
block of flats, multi-storey ~
  37 77-81
block section panel 203 60
block step 123 17
blood, arterial ~ 18 12
blood, venous ~ 18 11
blood circulation 18 1-21
blood pressure 23 32; 25 1
blood sausage 99 56
blood sedimentation 23 42
blood smear 23 50
bloodstone 108 48
blood vessel 19 33
bloomer 97 8
blooming train 148 50, 70
bloom shears 148 52
blossom 59 9; 69 14; 80 11
blotter 46 23; 246 6; 260 25
blouse, girl's ~ 29 58
blow, straight ~ 299 28
blow-and-blow process 162
  22
blower Furrier 131 10

blower Paperm. 172 4
blower Railw. 211 11
blower, travelling ~ 165 2, 3
blower aperture 165 5
blower fan 191 48; 192 62
blower oil pump 211 45
blower rail 165 6
blowfly 358 18
blowhole 367 26
blowing 162 28, 36
blowing, first ~ 162 24
blowing assembly 165 4
blowing iron 162 39
blowing processes 162 22-37
blowlamp 126 74; 301 22
blow mould 162 26, 34
blowout magnet 312 39
blowpipe Gas Weld. 141 11,
  19; 141 28
blowpipe Ethnol. 352 26
blowpipe lighter 141 27
blow pit 172 13
blow position 147 57
blow tank 172 11
blowtorch 126 74; 301 22
blow valve 172 12
blubber-oil lamp 353 7
blue Colour 343 3
blue Lepidopt. 365 6
blue-and-yellow macaw 363
  2
bluebell 375 14
blueberry 377 23
blue bird of paradise 363 3
bluebottle 61 1; 358 18
blue light 264 11; 270 6
Blue Peter 253 26
blue shark 364 1
blue spruce 51 10
bluetit 360 4
bluff bow 218 25
bluff prow 218 25
blurb 185 39
B minor 320 57, 60
boar Dom. Anim. 73 9
boar Game 88 51
boar, young ~ 88 51
board Bldg. Site 118 22, 87;
  119 16
board Carp. 120 1, 91
board Sawmill 157 35
board Games 276 1
board, illuminated ~ 268 3
board, presawn ~ 273 57
board, squared ~ 120 95
board, unsquared ~ 120 94
board, wooden ~ 338 23
board cutter 183 16
board cutter, rotary ~ 184 20
board-cutting machine,
  rotary ~ 184 20
board feed hopper 184 7
board games 276
boarding 121 75
boarding, horizontal ~ 37 84
boarding platform 194 39
boardman 251 7
board platform 118 28
board-sawing machine 132
  68
board support 132 70
boarhound 86 33
boar hunt 86 31
boaster 158 37
boat, carvel-built ~ 283 9
boat, inflatable ~ 228 18; 258
  82; 278 14; 279 27
boat, ship's ~ 221 107; 258 12,
  45; 259 35
boat, V-bottom ~ 286 35-37
boat, vee-bottom ~ 286 35-37
boat axe 328 19
boat carriage 278 20; 283 66

boat deck 223 19-21
boat elevator 217 29-38
boater 35 35
boat fibula 328 28
boathouse 283 24
boat-launching crane 258 13
boat lift 217 29-38
boat neck 30 34
boats, folding ~ 283 54-66
boatswain 221 114
boat tank 217 33
boat trailer 278 20; 283 66
bobbin Shoem. 100 29
bobbin Dressm. 103 12
bobbin Cotton Spin. 164 52,
  56, 60
bobbin creel 164 28
bobbin lace 102 18
bobbin thread 104 16
bobble 29 4
boblet 303 19
bobsled 303 19
bobsledding 303 19-21
bobsleigh 303 19-21
bobsleigh, two-man ~ 303 19
bobstay 219 15
bob wig 34 2
boccie 305 21
bock beer 93 26
bodhisattva 337 10
bodice 31 30
bodkin Basketm. 136 35
bodkin Composing Rm. 174
  17
bodkin beard 34 13
body Flat 46 3
body Joiner 132 24
body Lorries etc. 194 3, 23
body Aircraft 230 54
body Airsports 288 26
body, bird's ~ 327 57
body, dog's ~ 327 30
body, dragon's ~ 327 19, 36
body, fibre glass ~ 193 14
body, horse's ~ 327 27, 54
body, human ~ 16 1-54
body, interchangeable ~ 213
  40
body, lion's ~ 327 14, 22
body, man's ~ 327 53
body, monocoque ~ 191 1
body, monster's ~ 327 48
body, pituitary ~ 17 43
body, serpent's ~ 327 2, 33
body, tambourine-like ~ 324
  30
body, unitary ~ 191 1
body, woman's ~ 327 59
body brush 71 55
body-fixing plate 192 72
body hammer 195 46
bodyline 175 43
body louse 81 41
body of barrel 130 6
body of wall 217 2
body paper 173 29
body plan 259 2-11
body rotation 298 11
body size 175 46
body temperature 23 3
body tube 113 8, 31-39
bog 13 14-24
bog bilberry 377 23
bogie Bldg. Site 119 32
bogie Power Plant 152 41
bogie Tram 197 9
bogie Railw. 207 4; 208 4; 212
  2; 213 11, 13
bogie open freight car 213 24
bogie open wagon 213 24
bogie wagon 213 26
bog pool 13 23
bog whortleberry 377 23

Bohr-Sommerfeld model 1
  26
boiler Roof & Boilerr. 38 24,
  68
boiler Bakery 97 69
boiler Energy Sources 155 13
boiler Railw. 210 16
boiler, radiant-type ~ 152 5
boiler, vertical ~ 210 62
boiler barrel 210 16
boiler feed pump 152 18
boiler house Market Gdn. 55
  7
boiler house Power Plant 152
  1-21
boiler pressure 210 3
boiler pressure gauge 210 47
boiler room Roof & Boilerr.
  38 38-43
boiler room Market Gdn. 55 7
boiler shop 222 9
boiler suit 30 21
boiling fowl 99 60
boiling water system 154 49
bola 352 31
bolas 352 31
bold 175 2
bold condensed 175 10
boldface 175 2
bole 84 19, 22; 85 23, 41; 370
  2, 7
Boletus edulis 381 16
Boletus luteus 381 21
Boletus scaber 381 22
boll 383 8
bollard 217 12
bollard, cross-shaped ~ 217
  13, 14; 227 10
bollard, double ~ 217 11, 14
bollard, recessed ~ 217 10
bolster Bedrm. 43 11
bolster Tablew. etc. 45 55
bolster plate 85 48
bolster Slaughterho. 94 4
bolt Roof 121 98
bolt Metalwkr. 140 39
bolt Mach. Parts etc. 143 31
bolt Office 246 23
bolt, collar-head ~ 143 32
bolt, countersunk-head ~ 143
  28
bolt, hexagonal-head ~ 143
  13
bolt, square-head ~ 143 39
bolt, T-head ~ 143 41
bolter 91 26
bolt guide pin 140 41
bolt handle 87 22
bolt lever 87 22
bolts 143 13-50
bombard 322 14
bombardon 323 44
bomber jacket 31 42
bombycid moth 358 48
bond Bldg. Site 118 30
bond Stock Exch. 251 1-10,
  11-19
bond, convertible ~ 251 11-19
bond, English ~ 118 62
bond, industrial ~ 251 11-19
bond, municipal ~ 251 11-19
bonding, rubber ~ 192 82
bone 70 33; 354 40
bone, ethmoid ~ 17 39
bone, frontal ~ 17 30
bone, hyoid ~ 20 2
bone, jugal ~ 16 8
bone, lachrimal ~ 17 40
bone, malar ~ 16 8
bone, metacarpal ~ 17 16
bone, nasal ~ 17 41
bone, occipital ~ 17 32
bone, parietal ~ 17 31

bone, sphenoid ~ 17 38
bone, tarsal ~ 17 26
bone, temporal ~ 17 33
bone, zygomatic ~ 16 8; 17 37
bone chisel 24 49
bone-cutting forceps 26 51
bone lace 102 18
bone nippers 26 51
bones 17 1-29
bone saw Slaughterho. 94 19
bone saw Butch. 96 56
bongo drum 324 58
boning knife 96 36
bonnet Car 191 8
bonnet Garage 195 36
bonnet Ship 218 34
bonnet support 195 37
book 42 4; 46 8; 185 36
book, children's ~ 47 17; 48
  23
book, open ~ 185 52
book, second-hand ~ 309 55
book, sewn ~ 185 22
book, unbound ~ 183 32
bookbinder 183 2
bookbinding 183; 184; 185
bookbinding machines 184
  1-23; 185 1-35
bookcase unit 46 7
book cover 185 40
book delivery 184 5
bookjacket 185 37
bookmark, attached ~ 185 70
bookmark, loose ~ 185 71
bookmarker, attached ~ 185
  70
bookmarker, loose ~ 185 71
bookplate 185 51
book-sewing machine 185 16
bookshelf 42 3; 43 14; 262 12
bookshelf unit 46 7
bookshop 268 37
book stack 262 11
boom Bldg. Site 119 36
boom Docks 226 49
boom Sailing 284 7, 39
boom, double ~ 229 35
boomerang 352 39
boom foresail 220 12
boom microphone 311 40
boom operator 310 22
boom swinger 310 22
booster rocket 234 1, 2
boost gauge 230 7
boot Shoem. 100 57
boot Car 191 24; 193 23
boot Music. Instr. 326 17
boot, baby's ~ 101 56
boot, felt ~ 353 30
boot, ladies' ~ 101 12
boot, men's ~ 101 5
boot, pony-skin ~ 101 10
boot, rubber ~ 289 32
boot, Western ~ 101 9
bootee 28 45; 29 5
Boötes 3 30
booth 308 6
bootlace 100 64; 291 32
boot lid 191 7
bootmaker 100
boot space 193 17
borage family 69 13
Boraginaceae 69 13
border Fruit & Veg. Gdn. 52
  18, 22
border Basketm. 136 17
border Park 272 37
border Theatre 316 12
border light 316 13
bore 143 86
bore axis 87 38
bore diameter 87 40
borehole 158 12

borer 80 18
boring machine 175 49
boring mill 138 22
boring mill column 150 31
boring motor 133 7
boring tool 149 51
borrower's ticket 262 25
boscage 272 4
bosh 137 8
bo's'n 221 114
bosom 16 30
boss Chivalry 329 58
boss Art 335 32
bostryx 370 76
bo'sun 221 114
botany 370
bottle Brew. 93 21
bottle Restaurant 266 16
bottle Swim. 279 19
bottle, collapsible ~ 116 9
bottle, non-returnable ~ 93
  29
bottle, three-necked ~ 350 57
bottle, wicker ~ 206 13
bottle, wickered ~ 206 13
bottle basket 79 13
bottle bobbin 167 4
bottle-capping machine 76 46
bottle kiln 161 3
bottle-making machine 162
  21
bottle-nosed dolphin 367 23
bottle-opener 45 47
bottle rack Kitch. 39 6
bottle rack Wine Cell. 79 11
bottlescrew 284 17
bottle warmer 28 21
bottle washer 93 19
bottle-washing machine 93
  19
bottle-washing plant 93 18
bottling 93 22
bottling machine, circular ~
  79 9
bottling machine, semi-
  automatic ~ 79 9
bottom 16 40
bottom, artificial ~ 301 52
bottom, cellular ~ 222 60
bottom, cut-in ~ 119 56
bottom, double ~ 222 60
bottom, synthetic ~ 301 52
bottom bracket bearing 187
  42
bottom fishing 89 20-31
bottom outlet 269 34
bottom plating 222 48
bottom plating, inner ~ 222
  54
bott stick 148 10
boudoir piano 325 40
bough 370 5
bouillon cube 98 27
boule, grooved ~ 305 24
boules 305 21
boules player 305 22
bounce 297 36
bouncing ball 273 20
boundary layer control flap
  256 6; 257 13
boundary ridge 63 3
boundary stone 63 2
bouquet, bridal ~ 332 18
bouquetin 367 7
bourgeois 175 26
bout 294 5-6
Bovista nigrescens 381 19
bow Ladies' Wear 30 46
bow Hairst. etc. 34 7
bow Metalwkr. 140 34
bow Shipbuild. 222 74-79
bow Warships 258 3
bow Rowing 283 13

bow *Music. Instr.* 323 12
bow *Ethnol.* 354 32
bow *Hist. Cost.* 355 78
bow, bulbous ~ 221 45; 222 74
bow, fully enclosed ~ 259 9
bow, rounded ~ 218 25
bow, sliding ~ 205 36
bow and arrow 327 53
bow bilge 259 80
Bowden cable 188 37; 189 12
bow door 221 30
bowed instruments 323 1-27
bowels 20 14-22
bower 272 17
bower, ladies' ~ 329 10
bower anchor 258 39; 286 15
bow fender 227 17
bow gin 87 48
bowl 40 6; 45 63; 105 1; 107 36
bowler 292 76
bow light, green and red ~ 286 13
bowline 218 35
bowling ball 305 15
bowling crease 292 71
bowl lid 107 37
bowls 305 21
bow-manoeuvring propeller 224 23
bow propeller 228 33
bow ramp 258 90
bowsprit 218 20; 219 1
bow stick 323 14
bow string 305 59
bow thruster 224 23
bow-tie 32 47; 33 11, 16
bow trap 87 48
bow wave 223 81
box *Livestock* 75 2
box *Carriages* 186 8
box *Gymn.* 296 15
box *Athletics* 298 35
box *Fair* 308 7
box *Bullfight. etc.* 319 7
box, centrifugal ~ 169 17
box, coach's ~ 292 56
box, crossing keeper's ~ 202 43
box, gateman's ~ 202 43
box, racer's ~ 290 7
box, rider's ~ 290 7
box, small ~ 296 16; 297 9
box attendant 315 12
box camera 309 30
boxcar 213 14, 22
boxer *Dog* 70 10
boxer *Sports* 299 25
box feeder 159 7
box gutter 122 83
boxing 299 20-50
boxing contest 299 35-50
boxing glove 299 26
boxing match 299 20-50, 35-50
boxing ring 299 35
box office 308 7
box pile 217 6
boxroom door 38 20
box spar 287 30
box spur 71 50
box trap 86 20
box tree 373 19
boy scout 278 11
bra 32 1; 318 29
bra, longline ~ 32 4
brace *Bldg. Site* 119 63
brace *Carp.* 120 27, 54
brace *Roof* 121 41, 58, 69, 82
brace *Ship* 219 67
brace *Music. Instr.* 325 16
brace, diagonal ~ *Bldg. Site* 118 88; 119 51

brace, diagonal ~ *Bridges* 215 4
bracelet 36 3
bracelet, cultured pearl ~ 36 9
bracelet, gemstone ~ 36 25
bracelet watch 36 33
braces 29 26, 34; 32 30
braces, adjustable ~ 33 45
braces clip 32 31
brachioradialis 18 39
bracing 215 3
bracing, diagonal ~ 119 14
bracken 15 5; 377 16
bracket *Doc.* 23 10
bracket *Plumb. etc.* 126 6
bracket *Bicycle* 187 77
bracket *School* 260 30
bracket *Winter Sp.* 302 17; 303 7
bracket, chrome ~ 188 60
bracket, round ~ 342 24
bracket, square ~ 342 25
Brackett series 1 23
bract 371 7; 372 5
bracteate 252 4
bract scale 372 5
braid, floral ~ 30 28
braid embroidery 102 31
braid work 102 31
Braille 342 15
brain-stem 17 47; 18 24
brake *Mills* 91 8
brake *Carriages* 186 2, 16
brake *Car* 191 45
brake *Air Force* 257 10
brake *Forest Plants etc.* 377 16
brake, automatic ~ 181 47
brake, auxiliary ~ 212 10
brake, covered ~ 186 33
brake, front ~ 187 5
brake, hydraulic ~ 212 44
brake arm 187 66
brake arm cone 187 67
brake axle 143 99
brake band 143 105
brake block *Mach. Parts etc.* 143 100
brake block *Carriages* 186 16
brake cable 188 37; 189 12
brake casing 187 70
brake chute housing 257 24
brake cone 187 71
brake cylinder pressure gauge 212 7
brake disc 191 17; 192 48
brake drum 138 11, 20
brake flap *Aircraft* 229 44
brake flap *Air Force* 256 12
brake flap *Gliding* 287 38
brake fluid reservoir 191 49
brake line *Motorcycle* 189 12
brake line *Car* 192 53
brake lining *Blacksm.* 138 13
brake lining *Mach. Parts etc.* 143 106
brake lining *Car* 192 52
brake lock 56 38
brake magnet 143 102
brakeman 303 21
brake pedal *Gdn. Tools* 56 40
brake pedal *Offset Platem.* 179 12, 30
brake pedal *Car* 191 45, 95
brake pressure gauge 210 50
brake pulley 143 98
brake shaft 143 99
brake shoe *Blacksm.* 138 12
brake shoe *Mach. Parts etc.* 143 100
brake shoe *Car* 192 51
brake system, dual-circuit ~ 191 72

brake-testing equipment 138 16
brake weight 143 103
brake wheel 91 7
braking disc 191 17; 192 48
braking distance 203 29
braking roller 138 18
branch *Railw.* 203 48
branch *Fire Brig.* 270 33
branch *Maths.* 347 15
branch *Bot.* 370 5, 6
branch *Decid. Trees* 371 10, 25, 27, 32, 59
branch *Conifers* 372 36, 43
branch *Trop. Plants* 382 17
branch *Industr. Plants* 383 61
branch *South. Fruits* 384 12, 42
branch, flowering ~ 58 32, 52; 59 1, 26, 37
branch, fruit-bearing ~ 59 19, 48
branch, fruiting ~ 59 30
branch, left ~ 203 47
branch, right ~ 203 46
branch line 15 23
branchman 270 34
brandy 98 59
brandy glass 45 88
brant 359 5
brant-goose 359 5
brashing 84 12
brass 323 39-48
brassard *Fire Brig.* 270 22
brassard *Chivalry* 329 47
brassica 57 32
brassicas 57 28-34
brassie 293 91
brassière 32 1; 318 29
brassière, longline ~ 32 4
brass instruments 323 39-48
bratwurst 96 11; 308 34
brayer 340 12
Brazil Current 14 35
Brazil nut 384 53, 59
breach 13 34
bread 45 22; 97 2
bread, kinds of ~ 97 6-12; 99 11
bread, wrapped ~ 97 48-50
bread and cheese 266 75
bread basket 45 20
bread-corn 68 1-37
bread counter 99 9
bread crust 97 4
breadth scale 157 58
bread unit 97 56-57
break *Brew.* 93 2
break *Composing Rm.* 175 15
break *Carriages* 186 2
break, covered ~ 186 33
break-bulk cargo, unitized ~ 226 11
break-bulk cargo elevator, floating ~ 226 31
break-bulk cargo transit shed 225 9
break-bulk carrier 225 14; 226 13
breakdown lorry 270 47
breaker *Overh. Irrign.* 67 34
breaker *Swim.* 279 6
breaker spring 67 35
break removal 93 1-5
breakstone; rotundifoliate ~ 375 1
breakwater *Hydr. Eng.* 217 16
breakwater *Docks* 225 65
breakwater *Warships* 258 7, 76
breast *Man* 16 28-29
breast *Horse* 72 19
breast beam 166 46

breast beam board 166 16
breastbone *Man* 17 8
breastbone *Meat* 95 27
breastbox 173 11
breast collar 71 28
breast collar ring 71 27
breast drill 140 58
breast harness 71 26-36
breast of veal 95 4
breastplate 329 46
breast pocket 33 9
breasts 16 28-29
breaststroke 282 33
breastwork 329 21
breather 153 10
breathing apparatus 26 1; 270 39
breathing tube 27 37
breccia 11 27
breeches 300 7
breeches, loose ~ 355 34
breeches, white ~ 289 5
breeches buoy 228 13
breech ring 255 54
breeding comb 77 46
breeds 70
breeze 120 44
brent-goose 359 5
breve 320 12
breve rest 320 20
breviary 331 58
brevier 175 25
brevis 320 12
brewer 92 49
brewery 93 1-31
brewhouse 93 1-31
brewing 92; 93
briar grain 107 41
briar rose 373 26
brick 118 40
brick, cellular ~ 159 28
brick, green ~ 159 16
brick, perforated ~ 159 21-22, 21
brick, radial ~ 159 25
brick, radiating ~ 159 25
brick, solid ~ 159 20
brick, standard ~ 159 18
brick, unfired ~ 159 16
brick cutter 159 15
brickfield 159
brick hammer 118 53
brick kiln 159 19
bricklayer 118 18
bricklayer's tools 118 50-57
brickmason 118 18
brickmason's tools 118 50-57
brick-pressing machine 159 11
brickwork, frost-resistant ~ 122 39
brickwork base 123 15
brickworks *Map* 15 89
brickworks 159
brickyard 159
bride 332 15
bridegroom 332 16
bridesmaid 332 24
bridge *Map* 15 44
bridge *Optician* 111 11
bridge *Station* 205 3
bridge *Ship* 221 6, 12; 223 12-18
bridge *Shipbuild.* 222 26
bridge *Warships* 258 14; 259 3, 28
bridge *Town* 268 48
bridge *Park* 272 47
bridge *Free Exerc.* 295 19
bridge *Sports* 299 9
bridge *Theatre* 315 29; 316 34
bridge *Music. Instr.* 322 17
bridge, cable-stayed ~ 215 46

bridge, covered ~ 215 32
bridge, cross-section of ~ 215
  1
bridge, dental ~ 24 26
bridge, flat ~ 215 52
bridge, iron ~ 15 56
bridge, reinforced concrete ~
  215 49
bridge, rope ~ 215 15
bridge, solid ~ 215 19
bridge, stone ~ 15 50
bridge bearing 215 55
bridge deck 223 12-18
bridge over railway 15 40
bridge ring 89 58
bridges 215
bridge strut 215 30
bridge superstructure 258 14
bridge support 222 12
bridge under railway 15 42
bridle 71 7-13
bridle path 12 46
briefcase 41 17
briefs 32 26
brig 220 17
brigantine 220 14
brightness control 240 33
brille 323 35
brilliant 175 21
brilliant cut 36 44
brimstone butterfly 365 4
brine channel 274 3
brine pipe 274 4
briolette, faceted ~ 36 86
Brisinga endecacnemos 369
  11
brisket, hind ~ 95 25
brisket, middle ~ 95 26
brisket of beef 95 23
bristle 88 52
bristles *Hairst. etc.* 34 23
bristles *Household* 50 47
bristletail 81 14
bristle worm 357 22
broach 109 8
broaching tap 93 14
broach roof 121 22
broach roof, conical ~ 121 24
B road 15 36
broad axe 120 70
broad bean *Veg.* 57 8
broad bean *Fodder Plants* 69
  15
broadcasting 238; 239; 240
broadcasting centre 238
  16-26
broadcasting station 15 33
broadsheet 340 27
broadside 340 27
broadside fire 218 59
broadtail *Ladies' Wear* 30 60
broadtail *Furrier* 131 21
brochure 250 7
broderie anglaise 102 11
broiler 98 6; 308 33
broiler chicken 74 12
broiler rearing 74 11-17
broken thread detector roller
  164 4
broken thread stop motion
  165 19
broker, commercial ~ 251 5
broker, inside ~ 251 4
broker, outside ~ 251 5
bronchus 20 5
Bronze Age 328 21-40
brooch *Ladies' Wear* 30 60
brooch, ivory ~ 36 30
brooch, modern-style ~ 36 19
brooch, pearl ~ 36 7
brood bud bublet 54 27, 29
brood cell 77 31
brood chamber 77 46
brooder 74 3

brook 13 8; 15 80
broom 38 36; 50 46; 62 5; 199
  6; 268 21; 272 67
broom *Shrubs etc.* 374 20
broom, circular ~ 199 40
broom, cylinder ~ 199 42
broom, inverted ~ 224 99
broom, upward-pointing ~
  224 100
broom handle 38 37; 50 49
broom head 50 48
broomstick 38 37; 50 49
brougham 186 3
brow antler 88 6
browband 71 9
brown 343 5
brown ale 93 26
brown bear 368 10
brown leaf-eating weevil 80
  49
Brown Ring Boletus 381 21
brown-tail moth 80 28
brown trout 364 15
brow point 88 6
brow snag 88 6
brow tine 88 6
brush *Roof & Boilerr.* 38 32
brush *Household* 50 42, 53
brush *Bees* 77 7
brush *Forestry* 84 5
brush *Game* 88 47
brush *School* 260 59
brush *Graphic Art* 340 11
brush *Script* 341 24
brush, camel hair ~ 338 7
brush, dry ~ 128 49
brush, flat ~ *Painter* 129 17
brush, flat ~ *Art. Studio* 338 6
brush, rotating ~ 168 46
brush, round ~ 338 8
brush, stiff-bristle ~ 105 16
brush, wire ~ *Gas Weld.* 141
  26
brush, wire ~ *Arc Weld.* 142
  18
brush, wire ~ *Music. Instr.*
  324 53
brush head 50 79
brush head, detachable ~ 49
  30
brushwood *Map* 15 15
brushwood *Forestry* 84 5
brushwood *Spa* 274 2
Brussels lace 102 18
Brussels sprout 57 30
bubble bath 49 3
bubble chamber 1 58
bubble float, oval ~ 89 47
buccaneer 306 43
Büchner funnel 349 11
buck *Dom. Anim.* 73 18
buck *Game* 88 28, 40, 59
buck *Gymn.* 296 17
buck, young ~ 88 39
bucket *Household* 50 54
bucket 91 36
bucket *Bldg. Site* 118 82
bucket chain 226 42
bucket dredger 226 41
bucket elevator 200 49; 201 21
bucket elevator chain 216 57
bucket ladder 226 43
bucket pump 269 7
bucket seat *Car* 193 11
bucket seat *Sports* 305 90
bucket teeth 200 6
bucket-top boot 355 58
buckeye 371 58
buckle 101 52
buckle and knife folder 185 8
buckle and knife folding
  machine 185 8

buckle fold 185 11
buckler 329 57
bucksaw 120 61
bud 54 23, 26; 58 27; 59 22; 60
  16; 61 3
bud, axillary ~ 370 25
bud, terminal ~ 370 22
bud cutting 54 22
Buddha 337 20
budding 54 30
budding knife 54 31
buffalo 367 8
buffalo horn 254 34
buffer *Station* 206 51
buffer *Railw.* 213 7
buffer *Army* 255 27, 44, 52
buffer recuperator 255 52
buffer ring 255 44
buffer storage 242 33
buffet 207 78-79
buffet car, quick-service ~
  207 73
buffet compartment 207
  78-79
buffing machine 108 46
buffing wheel 100 10
buffoon 306 38, 69
bug 81 39
buggy 193 12
buggy, American ~ 186 49
buggy, English ~ 186 48
bugle 309 54
building, centralized ~ 334 55
building, centrally-planned ~
  334 55
building, model ~ 48 28
building, neoclassical ~ 336
  15
building, public ~ 15 54
building berth 222 11-18
building berths 222 11-26
building block 28 41; 48 27
building board, lightweight ~
  123 58
building brick *Infant Care*
  etc. 28 41
building brick *Kindergart.* 48
  27
building brick *Brickwks.* 159
  20
building glazier 124 8
building site 118; 119
building slips 222 11-26
building timber 120 10, 83-96
built piece 315 32
built unit 315 32
bulb, glass ~ 127 57
bulb, old ~ 54 28
bulb-head pin 328 29
bulbil 54 27, 29; 375 38
bulk cargo 221 11
bulk cargo handling 226 29
bulk carrier *Ship* 221 9
bulk carrier *Docks* 225 67;
  226 30
bulk goods 221 11
bulkhead, protective ~ 305 91
bulk material 200 12
bulk transporter barge 226 35
Bull *Astron.* 3 25; 4 54
bull *Dom. Anim.* 73 1
bull *Heraldry* 254 15
bull, mock ~ 319 3
bull, young ~ 319 35
bulldog 70 1
bulldozer 199 16; 200 28
bulldozer blade 200 29
bulldozer for dumping and
  compacting 199 18
bullfight 319 1-33, 24
bullfight, mock ~ 319 1
bullfighting 319
bullfinch 360 5

bull pen 319 14
bullring 319 5
bull's eye 336 2
bull's-eye glass 124 6
bull terrier 70 16
bulrush 136 27
bulwark 221 120; 222 67
bumblebee 358 23
bumper *Tram* 197 12
bumper *Station* 206 51
bumper, front ~ 191 13
bumper, integral ~ 193 33
bumper car 308 62, 63
bumper steel 166 44
bumper steel stop rod 166 45
bump rubber 192 82
bun 34 29
bun, plaited ~ 97 41
bunches 34 30
bunch of fruit 384 32
bunch of grapes 78 5; 99 89
bunch pink 60 6
bungalow 278 7
bunghole 130 7
bunk, folding ~ 259 84
bunk, rear ~ 85 49
bunk-bed 47 1
bunker 293 81
bunkering boat 225 13
Bunsen burner 173 5; 350 1
Bunter downthrow 154 61
bunting 253 3, 11
buntings 361 6-7
bunt line 218 36; 219 71
buoy 90 2; 216 12; 224 71; 285
  17, 18; 286 31
buoy, conical ~ 224 76
buoy, green ~ 224 84
buoy, port hand ~ 224 95
buoy, starboard hand ~ 224 96
buoyancy tube 286 27
buoy rope 90 3
bur 24 37
burden chain 139 44
burette 350 21
burette clamp 350 23
burette stand 350 22
burgee 253 22; 284 48
Burgundian 355 40
burial 331 33-41
burial place, underground ~
  331 59
burin 175 33; 340 5, 15, 20
burner *Power Plant* 152 6
burner *Glass Prod.* 162 6
burner, gas ~ 139 3, 48
burner platform 288 80
burner ventilator 92 17
burning-in oven 179 32
burnisher *Goldsm. etc.* 108 51
burnisher *Watchm.* 109 17
burnishing 109 17
burnous 354 7
burr 88 5, 29
burrow *Soft Fruit* 58 63
burrow *Hunt.* 86 26
burying ground 331 21-41
bus 194 17
bus, double-deck ~ 194 36
bus, double-decker ~ 194 36
bus, electrical system ~ 235 55
busbar 152 29
buses *Lorries etc.* 194
'buses' *Airport* 233 35
bush, rubber ~ 192 67
bushing 162 50
bushing chain, double ~ 190
  49
bushing tip 162 51
bushman 354 29
bushman woman 354 34
business and passenger
  aircraft 231 3, 7

business letter 245 33; 246 7; 248 30
business trip 209 29
bust 42 17
bustle 355 69
bustle pipe 147 53
butane gas 278 33
butane gas container 278 34
butcher 96 38, 58
butcher knife 94 15; 96 37
butcher's shop 96 1-30
butt *Hunt.* 86 47-52, 51; 87 3, 7
butt *Meat* 95 50
butt *Army* 255 9, 24, 31, 39
butt *Sports* 305 47
butt, bound ~ 89 55
butt, cork ~ 89 50
butt end 85 41
butter 98 22; 99 47
butter, branded ~ 76 37
butter-and-eggs 376 26
butter churn 76 33
butter-cream cake 97 24
buttercup 375 8
butter dish 45 36
butterflies 358 48-56; 365 1-6
butterflower 375 8
butterfly *Free Exerc.* 295 35
butterfly *Articulates* 358 52
butterfly nut 143 42; 187 39
butterfly stroke 282 34
butterfly tail 229 31
butterfly valve 192 9
butter knife 45 73
butter-making, continuous ~ 76 33
buttermilk tank 76 18
butter shaping and packing machine 76 32
butter supply pipe 76 34
butterwort 377 13
button *Tram* 197 32
button *Fencing* 294 45
button *Music. Instr.* 325 31
button, staghorn ~ 29 33
button box 103 15
buttonhole 332 21
buttonhole stitch 102 6
button stitch 102 6
butt plate *Hunt.* 87 14
butt plate *Sports* 305 46
buttress *Chivalry* 329 26
buttress *Art* 335 27
buttresses 335 27-28
butt ring 89 58
buzzer, electric ~ 127 15
buzz saw 119 19; 125 24; 134 50
buzz saw blade 132 59
by-line 291 7
bypass air flow 232 50
bypass duct 232 41, 44
bypass engine 232 46
bypass switch 211 25

C

cab *Carriages* 186 26, 28
cab *Lorries etc.* 194 2
cab *Town* 268 64
cab, driver's ~ 64 36; 194 2, 15; 200 11; 208 14; 209 6; 210 39-63, 49; 211 19, 57; 212 5; 213 2
cab, engineer's ~ 208 14; 209 6; 210 39-63, 49; 211 19, 57; 212 5; 213 2
cabbage, green ~ 57 32
cabbage, red ~ 57 32
cabbage, round ~ 57 32

cabbage lettuce 57 36
cabbage white butterfly 80 47, 48
cab frame 65 21
cab heating switch 211 39
cab horse 186 28
cabin *Railw.* 214 20, 28
cabin *Ship* 218 45
cabin *Sailing* 285 39
cabin *Airsports* 288 19
cabin, admiral's ~ 218 27
cabin, captain's ~ 223 13
cabin, commanding officer's ~ 259 85
cabin, coxswain's ~ 228 31
cabin, crane driver's ~ 119 35; 222 16; 226 52
cabin, de luxe ~ 223 30
cabin, double-berth ~ 223 29
cabin, large-capacity ~ 214 52
cabin, officer's ~ 223 21
cabin, single-berth ~ 223 46; 228 32
cabin cruiser 286 3
cabinet 22 40; 246 20
cabinet maker 132 38
cabin pulley cradle 214 66
cabin superstructure 285 39
cable *Sea Fish.* 90 26
cable *Power Plant* 153 41
cable *Music. Instr.* 326 53
cable, auxiliary ~ 214 47
cable, electric ~ 56 32
cable, endless ~ 214 21
cable, high-voltage ~ 153 42
cable, lower ~ 214 46
cable, moisture-proof ~ 127 42
cable, submarine ~ 237 56
cable, thermoplastic ~ 127 42
cable, three-core ~ 127 44
cable binding 301 40
cable boom 195 15
cable box 153 33
cable clip 127 40
cable connection 6 26
cable connection panel 239 3
cable crane berth 222 11-18
cable drum 85 39; 270 55
cable duct 234 29, 47; 235 61
cable ferry 216 1
cable guide 201 7
cable guide rail 214 33
cable manhole 198 17
cable parachute 287 7
cable pattern 30 39
cable pulley, automatic ~ 301 62
cable railway 214 12
cable release 23 9; 114 38; 115 101
cable release, double ~ 115 102
cable release socket 117 6
cable support 214 76
cable suspension lines 214 15-38
cable tunnel 152 20
cable vault 152 21
cableway 214 30
cableway, endless ~ 214 19
cableway gondola 214 52
cableways 214 15-38
cable winch 85 38, 46; 255 69; 258 85
cabochon, high ~ 36 79
cabochon, octagonal ~ 36 81
cabochon, oval ~ 36 80
cabochon, round ~ 36 78
cabochon, simple ~ 36 78
cabochons 36 78-81
caboose 223 42
cabriole 314 21

cabriolet 186 29
cacao bean 382 19
cacao tree 382 16
cachalot 367 25
caddis fly 358 12
caecum 20 17
café 265 1-26
café, open-air ~ 272 57
café customers 265 22-24
café table 265 11
cage *Fish Farm.* 89 1
cage *Coal* 144 23
cage *Circus* 307 50
cage, crane driver's ~ 119 35; 222 16; 226 52
cage, outside ~ 356 11
cage, rotating ~ 168 17
cage, round ~ 307 49
cage, stepped ~ 74 20
cage, tiered ~ 74 20
cage caravan 307 62
cage system 74 18
cage-winding system 144 23
caisson 217 33; 222 32; 259 19
cake 169 19-27, 22
cake counter 99 9; 265 1
cake plate 97 25
cakes 97 17-47
cake tin 40 28, 29
calabash 354 27
calcaneum 17 27
calcite 351 22
calcium chloride tube 350 43
calculating machine 309 80
calculation, logarithmic ~ 345 6
calculator 309 80
calculator, electronic ~ 246 12
calculator dial *Photog.* 114 57
calculator dial *Photograv.* 182 19
calculus, infinitesimal ~ 345 13-14
calendar 22 10
calendar clock 110 19
calendar sheet 247 33
calender 173 36
calendering machine 168 38
calender roll 173 26, 38
calender roller 163 20, 37, 59
calf *Man* 16 53
calf *Farm Bldgs.* 62 33
calf *Dom. Anim.* 73 1
calf *Game* 88 1
calf *Meat* 95 1-13
caliber 87 40
calibre 87 40
California Current 14 39
caliper *see* calliper
call, local ~ 237 3
call, long-distance ~ 237 3
call box 204 46; 236 8; 237 1; 251 10; 268 56
call button 25 6; 127 3; 246 15
calliper *Car* 191 18
calliper *Sculpt. Studio* 339 3
calliper, fixed ~ 192 49
calliper, inside ~ 135 23
calliper, outside ~ 135 18
calliper gauge 149 59
calliper square 85 10
call light 315 52
callosity 72 27
calls for luring game 87 43-47
calm 9 11
calm belts 9 46-47
calms, equatorial ~ 9 46
calor gas container 278 34
calvarium 261 16, 18
calyx 58 8; 374 8
calyx, involucral ~ 375 33
calyx, renal ~ 20 30
cam 190 60

Camberwell beauty 365 5
cambium ring 370 10
came 124 13
camel 366 29
camel caravan 354 1
camera *Atom* 1 60
camera *Optic. Instr.* 112 14, 20
camera *Cine Film* 117 28
camera *Audiovis.* 243 1
camera *Films* 310 19
camera, cartridge-loading ~ 114 11
camera, compact ~ *Cine Film* 117 51
camera, compact ~ *Photomech. Reprod.* 177 32
camera, folding ~ 114 49; 309 25
camera, high-speed ~ 313 35
camera, large-format ~ *Optic. Instr.* 112 25, 36
camera, large-format ~ *Photog.* 114 49, 61
camera, miniature ~ *Doc.* 23 7
camera, miniature ~ *Optic. Instr.* 112 26
camera, miniature ~ *Photog.* 114 1; 115 1
camera, 35 mm ~ *Photog.* 114 1
camera, 16 mm ~ *Cine Film* 117 43
camera, 35 mm ~ *Films* 313 35
camera, 16 mm ~ *Films* 313 31
camera, narrow-gauge ~ 313 35
camera, photogrammetric ~ 112 68
camera, professional press-type ~ 117 66
camera, rapid-sequence ~ 115 77
camera, single-lens reflex ~ 115 1
camera, spectrographic ~ 5 6
camera, stereometric ~ 112 71
camera, subminiature ~ 114 16
camera, Super-8 ~ 117 51
camera, underwater ~ 279 24
camera assistant 117 68; 310 42
camera back 114 54; 115 2
camera body *Photog.* 115 2
camera body *Photomech. Reprod.* 175, 33
camera cable 239 2
camera case 115 103
camera case, underwater ~ 279 24
camera control 242 36
camera crane 310 49
camera door 313 25
camera head 240 27
camera housing, underwater ~ 279 24
camera lens 313 19
cameraman 117 67; 310 20
cameraman, first ~ 310 41
camera monitor 238 65; 239 12; 240 28
camera operator 310 42
camera tube switch 242 23
cam housing 167 13
camomile *Weeds* 61 8
camomile *Med. Plants* 380 1
camp *Games* 276 27
camp *Circus* 307 61
campanile 334 65
camp bed 278 59

camp chair, folding ~ 278 vp
camp cot 278 59
camper 278 46
camp fire 278 10
campground 278 1-59
camphor laurel 380 18
camphor tree 380 18
camping 278
camping eating utensils 278 45
camping site 278 1-59
campion 376 20
camp site 278 1-59
camp site attendant 278 2
camp table, folding ~ 278 44
camshaft 166 56; 190 11, 14
camshaft bearing 192 24
camshaft lubrication 190 13
camshaft wheel 166 55
can Butch. 96 26
can Supermkt. 99 91
can Painter 129 7
can Weaving 166 21
Canadian pondweed 378 56
Canadian waterweed 378 56
canal Map 15 57
canal Hydr. Eng. 217 15-28
canal, auditory ~ 17 34, 58
canal, stomachic-intestinal ~ 77 15-19
canal administration 217 24
canal bed 217 30
canal entrance 217 15-16
Canary Current 14 41
can buoy 224 77, 94
cancel button 326 41
cancellation button 271 4
Cancer 4 56
candelabra 45 16
candidate 263 20
candies 47 31, 32
candies Grocer 98 75-86
candle, cast ~ 260 76
candle, paschal ~ 330 44
candle, wax ~ 77 66; 260 76
candlestick 309 45
candlestick, paschal ~ 330 45
candlewick yarn 35 9
candy 98 75
cane, flowering ~ 58 14
can holder 163 36
Canidae 367 11-13
Canina 3 46
canine 19 17
Canis Major 3 14
Canis Minor 3 15
canister 84 35; 129 16
canned vegetables 98 17
cannon Horse 72 23
cannon Army 255 49, 92
cannon cracker 306 53
canoe 352 19
canoe, Alaskan ~ 283 4
canoe, Canadian ~ 283 3
canoeing 283
canoeist 283 55
canoes 283 54-66
canoe stern 285 44
canoe with outrigger 352 35
canon 13 45
canonicals Church 330 22; 332 4
canopy Infant Care etc. 28 32
canopy Dwellings 37 67
canopy Child. Rm. 47 12
canopy Kindergart. 48 26
canopy Supermkt. 99 24
canopy Aircraft 230 39
canopy Airsports 288 38
canopy Church 330 21; 331 49
canopy bearer 331 46
canopy jack 257 5
cant chisel 132 11

canteen 119 45
canter 72 42
cant hook 85 7
canting table 133 17
cantle 71 39, 46
canvas 338 21
canvas hull, rubber-covered ~ 283 58
canvas stretcher 338 20
canyon 13 45
canyon river 13 51
cap Bees 77 39
cap Drawing Off. 151 40
cap Refuse Coll. 199 8
cap Music. Instr. 326 31
cap Edib. Fungi 381 4
cap, astrakhan ~ 35 34
cap, corduroy ~ 35 25
cap, fox ~ 35 31
cap, leather ~ 35 32; 354 26
cap, linen ~ 35 8
cap, mink ~ 35 17, 20
cap, musquash ~ 35 33
cap, peaked ~ 35 17, 29; 264 8; 301 18
cap, sailor's ~ 35 28
cap, sheepskin ~ 353 23
cap, white ~ 268 32
cap, wide-brimmed ~ 355 28
capa 319 27
capacitor 211 17
cap and bells 306 39
caparison 329 74
cape 30 65; 105 34; 106 4
cape, short ~ 355 29
cape chisel 140 25
capeline 21 3
caper 98 42
capercaillie 88 72
capillary tube stand 23 42
capistrum 322 5
capital Composing Rm. 175 11
capital Art 334 20-25
capital, Arabian ~ 337 18
capital, bell-shaped ~ 333 16
capital, bud-shaped ~ 333 14
capital, Roman ~ 341 16
capital, small ~ 175 14
capitulum 61 14; 370 73; 378 12
capoc tree 383 20
cap of typing element 249 30
capon 73 21
capper 76 46
capping Bees 77 39
capping Coal 144 48
Capricorn 3 36; 4 62
capriole 71 5
caprolactam 170 28
caprolactam oil 170 25
caps, ladies' ~ 35 1-21
caps, men's ~ 35 22-40
capstan Cine Film 117 34
capstan Hydr. Eng. 217 22
capstan Audiovis. 243 23
capstan Warships 258 23
capstan idler 117 35
capsule 384 58
capsule, poricidal ~ 370 96
capsule, porose ~ 370 96
captain 224 38
caption 185 67; 342 59
car Car 191 1-56
car Garage 195 34
car Railw. 213 18
car, four-axled ~ 208 3
car, large-capacity ~ 213 28
car, open ~ 207 59
car accessory 196 28
carapace 364 29
caravan 278 52; 307 34
caravan, collapsible ~ 278 3

caravan, showman's ~ 206 20
caravan awning 278 57
caravanning 278
caravel 218 27-43; 220 37
caraway roll 97 31
caraway stick 97 31
carbide, cemented ~ 149 46
carbine 86 30
carbolic acid 170 14
carbon, active ~ 270 58
carbon, negative ~ 312 41
carbon, positive ~ 312 40
carbon atom 242 63
carbon crater 312 44
carbon disulfide 169 8
carbon disulphide 169 8
carbon disulphide injector 83 33
carbon rod, negative ~ 312 41
carbon rod, positive ~ 312 40
carbon rod holder 312 43
carbon tissue 182 1, 10
carbon tissue, printed ~ 182 8
carbon tissue transfer machine 182 6
carburetor see carburettor
carburettor 189 4; 192 1-15
carburettor, cross-draught ~ 190 79
car carrier, double-deck ~ 213 35
car carrier, two-tier ~ 213 35
carcase 118 1-49
carcass 118 1-49
carcassing 118 1-49
car coat 33 63
card Cotton Spin. 163 34, 51
card Games 276 37
card, patient's ~ 25 5
card, used ~ 195 14
cardan coupling 67 6
cardan joint 67 6, 28
cardan mount 6 36
cardan shaft 64 40, 48; 67 16; 211 51; 212 29, 83
cardan shaft connection 64 63
cardan transmission 189 47
cardboard 260 50-52
card can 163 35
card catalogue 262 22
card catalogue drawer 262 23
card deck 221 79
cardiac rhythm 25 1
cardiac sulcus, longitudinal ~ 20 25
cardigan 31 50; 33 30
cardinal Maths. 344 5
cardinal Birds 363 5
cardinal bird 363 5
card index 245 23
card index box 46 10; 248 27
carding can 163 35
carding engine 163 34, 51
carding machine 163 34
car door 191 4
card sliver 163 38
card stacker 244 13
car ferry 216 10
cargo 223 77
cargo and passenger liner 221 96
cargo and passenger ship 223 1-71
cargo barge 216 25
cargo boom 221 26, 59; 223 36
cargo gear 221 24-29, 59
cargo handling, horizontal ~ 226 7
cargo-handling berth 226 1
cargo-handling gear 221 24-29, 59
cargo hatchway 221 11, 63; 226 14

cargo hold 231 21
cargo ship 221 23
cargo warehouse 233 10
'car hire' 233 33
carload 206 52
car location number 195 48
car models 193 1-36
carnation 60 6
carnival 306
carnival float 306 57
carnival procession 306 57-70
carnival truck 306 57
carnivore house 356 10
carnivores 367 11-22; 368 1-11
carob 384 41
carom billiards 277 7
carousel 308 2
carp 89 26; 364 4
carpel 58 36, 59; 59 13; 374 2, 26
carpenter 120 12
carpenter's tools 120 60-82
carpenter's yard 120 1-59
carpet 44 16
carpet, fitted ~ 41 18; 43 23
carpet, oriental ~ 46 36
carpet, velour ~ 267 35
carpet beater head 50 79
carpet beater nozzle 50 71
carpet brush 50 45
carpet cleaning 50 53-86
carpeting 191 43
carpet sweeper 50 57
carpet sweeper and shampooer, combined ~ 50 76
carp hook 89 86
carp pond 89 6
carpus Man 17 15; 19 76
carpus Horse 72 22
car radio 191 90
carriage Hosp. 26 36
carriage Sawmill 157 12, 52
carriage Knitting 167 39
carriage Tram 197 5, 6, 7
carriage, auxiliary ~ 157 11
carriage, one-horse ~ 186 18, 29
carriage, open ~ 207 61; 208 9
carriage, three-horse ~ 186 45
carriage, two-horse ~ 186 36
carriage apron 149 16
carriage handle 167 41
carriage heating pressure gauge 210 44
carriage horse 186 28
carriage motor 157 15
carriage rail 167 45
carriages 186 1-54, 1-3,26-39,45,51-54
carriages, horse-drawn ~ 186
carriage sprayer 83 38
carriage step 186 13
carrier Bicycle 187 44
carrier Docks 226 4
carrier return lever 249 21
carrion flower 53 15
carrot 57 17
carrot, stump-rooted ~ 57 18
carrycot 28 48
carry-home pack 93 28
carrying axle 210 35
carrying bar 148 16
carrying bogie 197 10
carrying cart 56 26
carrying grip 21 22
carrying handle 241 2
carrying rope 215 16
carrying saddle 73 4
carrying strap 115 9
carrying wheel 214 7
cart 86 39

cart, electric ~ **206** 34
carte engagement **294** 47
cartilage, costal ~ **17** 11
cartilage, thyroid ~ **20** 3
cartoon *Art. Studio* **338** 43
cartoon *Script* **342** 53
cartouche **336** 7
cartridge *Hunt.* **87** 19, 54
cartridge *Slaughterho.* **94** 5
cartridge *Cine Film* **117** 30
cartridge, full-jacketed ~ **87** 55
cartridge, instamatic ~ **114** 15
cartridge, magnetic ~ **241** 26
cartridge, subminiature ~ **114** 17
cartridge chamber **87** 15
cartwheel **297** 21
cartwheel ruff **355** 52
car tyre **191** 15; **196** 27
carvel **218** 27-43; **220** 37
carvel planking **285** 53
carvel planking, diagonal ~ **285** 56
carver **96** 35
carving knife **45** 69; **96** 35
carving set **45** 69-70
car-wash hose **196** 23
car wheel **191** 14
car window, crank-operated ~ **191** 22
caryatid **334** 36
caryopsis **375** 43
cascade **272** 9
case *Meteorol. Instr.* **10** 18
case *Doc.* **22** 33
case *Bookbind.* **185** 40
case *Composing Rm.* **174** 3, 8
case *Lorries etc.* **194** 19
case *Station* **204** 6; **205** 7
case *Chem.* **349** 26
case, cardboard ~ **87** 50
case cabinet **174** 4
case head **305** 36
case maker **184** 6
case-making machine **184** 6
case rack **174** 4
case room **174**; **175**; **176**
cash desk **196** 29; **266** 69; **275** 2
cash drawer **271** 5
cashier **99** 94; **250** 2; **266** 70; **271** 1
cash readout **196** 4
cash register **47** 34; **99** 93; **207** 86
cash register, electric ~ **271** 2
casing *Mach. Parts etc.* **143** 79
casing *Oil, Petr.* **145** 18
casing *Power Plant* **153** 37
casing *Text. Finish.* **168** 16
casing *Army* **255** 10
casing *Chem.* **350** 10
casing, outer ~ **168** 17
casing, protective ~ *Meteorol. Instr.* **10** 39
casing, protective ~ *Railw.* **202** 35
casing cover **143** 80
casing-in machine **185** 27
casino **274** 8; **275** 1
cask **130** 5
casket **331** 35
casque, light ~ **329** 61
Cassegrain cage **5** 4
casserole dish **40** 14
cassette, compact ~ **241** 10
cassette, daylight ~ **177** 50
cassette, 35 mm ~ **114** 7
cassette, single-8 ~ **117** 39
cassette box **241** 11, 47
cassette cabinet **241** 11, 47
cassette compartment **241** 6, 34; **243** 8; **249** 72

cassette deck **241** 52
cassette exit slot **114** 10
cassette holder **241** 11, 47
cassette recorder **117** 73; **261** 42
cassette recorder unit **241** 3
cassette slit **114** 10
cassette tape **241** 12
cassia **380** 16
Cassiopeia **3** 33
cassowary **359** 1
cast **89** 64, 78
cast, long ~ **89** 58
castanets **324** 46
caster **148** 8
castes of bees **77** 1,4,5
cast glass **124** 6
casting **148** 42
casting, continuous ~ **148** 24-29
casting mechanism **174** 25
casting net **89** 31
casting off **167** 66
casting team **148** 13
castle *Map* **15** 74
castle *Games* **276** 12
castle, knight's ~ **329** 1
castle gate **329** 32
castle nut **143** 77
castle wall **333** 31
cast line **174** 27
cast of skull **261** 15
castor *Household* **50** 81
castor *Horse* **72** 27
castor *Pest Contr.* **83** 61
Castor and Pollux **3** 28
castor-oil plant **380** 14
casual **101** 34
casualty **21** 20
cat **62** 3; **73** 17
catacomb **331** 59
catalogue, main ~ **262** 21
catalogue room **262** 18
catalytic cracking plant **145** 70
catamaran **284** 64; **286** 21
cataract **11** 45
catch *Mach. Parts etc.* **143** 29
catch *Railw.* **203** 57
catcher **292** 54, 64
catchfly **376** 20
catchment area **12** 24
catchup **45** 43
cat cracker **145** 48
caterpillar **58** 64; **82** 16, 20, 31, 44, 47; **365** 10; **80** 3, 8, 14, 17, 29, 44, 48
caterpillar hauling scraper **200** 16
caterpillar mounting **200** 3
caterpillar tractor **200** 3
catfish **364** 12
cathedral **335** 1-13, 22
catheter **26** 31
catheter, cardiac ~ **25** 53
catheter gauge unit **27** 30
catheter holder **26** 30
catheterization **27** 30
cathetus **346** 32
cathode **178** 6
cathode ray tube **242** 40
catkin **59** 39; **371** 10, 26
catkin, male ~ **59** 45
catkin scale **371** 12
cat ladder **38** 4; **122** 63
cat litter **99** 38
cats **368** 2-8
cat's foot **377** 3
cat's tail **378** 21
cat's tongue **98** 84
catsuit **29** 19
catsup **45** 43
cattail **378** 21

cattail flag **378** 21
cattle **62** 45; **73** 1-2
cattleship **221** 68
cattle vessel **221** 68
catwalk *Iron & Steel* **147** 38
catwalk *Ship* **221** 3
catwalk *Theatre* **315** 29
cauliflower **57** 31; **99** 84
causticizing agitator **172** 49
causticizing stirrer **172** 49
caustic soda **169** 3, 4, 5, 10; **170** 11
caustic soda solution **170** 10
cautery **24** 43
cavalier hat **355** 55
cavalry saddle **71** 45-49
cavalry standard **253** 13
cave *Phys. Geog.* **13** 76
cave *Map* **15** 85
cave, dripstone ~ **13** 79
cave, limestone ~ **13** 79
cave art **328** 9
cave formations **13** 80-81
cave painting **328** 9
cavern *Phys. Geog.* **13** 76
cavern *Park* **272** 1
cavetto **336** 50
cavetto vault **336** 49
caviare knife **45** 81
cavity **91** 36
cavity, nasal ~ **17** 53
cavity, tympanic ~ **17** 60
cavity of the uterus **20** 80
cavy **366** 12
C-clef **320** 10
cecum **20** 17
cedar tree **372** 65
cedilla **342** 33
ceiba tree **383** 20
ceiling **222** 63
ceiling, concrete ~ **123** 28
ceiling, false ~ **123** 61, 68-69
ceiling beam **120** 38
ceiling construction **123**
ceiling hook **270** 15
ceiling joint **126** 48
ceiling joist **119** 5; **120** 38; **121** 54
ceiling light **24** 20; **75** 8
ceiling paper **128** 53
ceiling paperhanger **128** 50
ceiling plaster **123** 59, 72
ceiling tile **317** 29
celeriac **57** 27
celesta **325** 1
Celestial River **3** 12
Celestial Ship **3** 45
cell **77** 26-30, 27
cell, sealed ~ **77** 32, 33
cella **334** 51
cellarman **79** 18
cellar steps, outside ~ **118** 4
cellar window **37** 27; **118** 3
cell nucleus **357** 2
cello **323** 16
cellulose, refined ~ **172** 78
cellulose, unrefined ~ **172** 77
cellulose sheet **169** 2, 4, 6
cellulose xanthate **169** 9
cembalo **322** 45
cement *Man* **19** 29
cement *Bldg. Site* **118** 43
cement factory **160**
cement-grinding mill **160** 12
cementing pump, high-pressure ~ **146** 34
cement-packing plant **160** 16
cement screed **123** 14
cement silo **119** 30; **160** 15
cement storage tank **146** 15
cement store **201** 22
cement track racing **290** 24-28

cementum, dental ~ **19** 29
cement works **160**
cemetery **15** 106
censer **332** 38
cent **252** 19, 33
Centaur *Astron.* **3** 39
centaur *Fabul. Creat.* **327** 52
Centaurus **3** 39
centaury **61** 1; **380** 10
centavo **252** 23
center *see* centre
centerboard *see* centreboard
centering *see* centring
centime **252** 15, 16
centimeter *see* centimetre
centimetre graduation **247** 36
céntimo **252** 22
central heating, full ~ **38** 38-81
central heating furnace **38** 57
central heating system, coke-fired ~ **38** 38
central heating system, oil-fired ~ **38** 44-60
centre *Turner* **135** 8
centre *Ball Games* **293** 76
centre *Maths.* **346** 26, 43, 55
centre, asbestos ~ **350** 19
centre, live ~ **135** 11
centre angle **346** 55
centreboard **284** 26
centreboard, retractable ~ **284** 8; **285** 41
centreboard case **284** 24
centre circle **291** 2
centre console **191** 38
centre flag **291** 64
centre girder **222** 53
centre lathe **149** 1
centre line *Drawing Off.* **151** 30
centre line *Sailing* **285** 5
centre line *Ball Games* **293** 8-9, 54
centre line *Fencing* **294** 4
centre line judge **293** 25
centre mark **293** 11
centre of curvature **346** 23
centre of symmetry **351** 3
centre plate girder **222** 53
centre punch **134** 31; **140** 64
centre-section fuel tank **257** 30
centre strake **222** 55
centrifuge **23** 59
centrifuge, pendulum-type ~ **168** 14
centrifuge lid **168** 18
centring apparatus, universal ~ **111** 21
centring control **243** 10
centring ring **240** 23
centring suction holder **111** 22
centrosphere **11** 5
cep **381** 16
cepe **381** 16
cephalopod **357** 37
Cerberus **327** 29
cereal **68** 1
cereal product **99** 62
cereal products **98** 35-39
cereals **68** 1-37
cerebellum **17** 45; **18** 23
cerebrum **17** 42; **18** 22
cesta **305** 69
Cetus **3** 11
chaffinch **360** 10
chaffron **329** 84
chafron **329** 84
chain **74** 14; **75** 15; **99** 95; **118** 30

chain *Bicycle* 187 36
chain *Cyc. Racing* 290 20
chain armour 329 63
chain cable 222 77; 223 50; 227 12
chain compressor 223 51
chain curtain 139 50
chain cutter 120 17
chain delivery 180 43
chain drive 187 35-42
chain feeder 74 25
chain ferry 216 1
chain grinder, continuous ~ 172 53, 66
chain gripper 180 56
chain guard 187 37; 188 46
chain guide 120 15
chain mail 329 63
chain mortiser 132 49
chain mortising machine 132 49
chain reaction 1 41, 48
chain saw 120 14
chain sling *Forging* 139 44
chain sling *Docks* 226 26
chain stay 187 20
chain stitch 102 2
chain-tensioning device 157 41
chain transmission 187 35-39
chain wheel 187 35
chair 42 34; 271 35
chair, adjustable ~ 105 17; 106 16
chair, barber's ~ 106 16
chair, cane ~ 43 3
chair, dentist's ~ 24 3
chair, double ~ 214 18
chair, folding ~ 28 33
chair, gaffer's ~ 162 45
chair, glassmaker's ~ 162 45
chair, hairdresser's ~ 105 17; 106 16
chair, single ~ 214 16
chair, steel ~ 67 2
chair, tubular steel ~ 41 21
chair, two-seater ~ 214 17, 18
chair, umpire's ~ 293 20
chair, visitor's ~ 246 21
chair grip 21 21
chair lift 214 16-18
chair lift, double ~ 301 57
chairman 263 1
chairman of board of directors 251 16
chairman of board of governors 251 15
chairoplane 308 4
chaise 186 34
chaise, closed ~ 186 54
chaise, covered ~ 186 54
chaise, one-horse ~ 186 29
chaitya 337 28
chaitya hall 337 27
chalaza 74 63
chalcography 340 14-24
chalet 278 7
chalice 330 10; 332 49
chalk 48 15; 260 32; 338 5
chalk, French ~ 104 24
chalk, tailor's ~ 104 24
chalk ledge 260 31
chalk sketch 338 4
chalwar 306 42
Chamaeleontidae 364 33
chamber *Atom* 1 66
chamber *Forest Pests* 82 36
chamber *Hunt.* 87 20
chamber *Water* 269 24
chamber, king's ~ 333 2
chamber, photographic ~ 113 40
chamber, queen's ~ 333 3

chamber, stone ~ 328 39
chamber wall 269 25
chameleon 364 33
chamfer 143 62
chamfering hammer 125 14
chamfrain 329 84
chamfron 329 84
chamois 367 3
chamomile 61 8; 380 1
chamotte slab 141 16
champagne bottle 99 78
champagne bucket 267 59
champagne cooler 267 59
champagne cork 267 58
champagne glass 45 86
champagne glasses 45 85-86
chancel 330 1, 32; 335 4
chandelier 267 21
chanfron 329 84
'change' *Airport* 233 51
change *Winter Sp.* 302 12
change-gear box 149 7
change-gear handle 132 56
change gears 10 14
change-loop 302 16
change machine 197 33; 204 22; 236 28
changemaker 236 28
changeover switch 50 59; 243 15
change points, electric ~ 197 37
change rack 236 23
change-speed gear 163 29; 211 50
change wheel 164 40
changing booth 271 32
changing cubicle 282 1
changing room 282 3
changing top 28 4
changing unit 28 11
channel *Overh. Irrign.* 67 13
channel *Railw.* 202 32
channel *Swim.* 281 9
channel *Rowing* 283 60
channel *Art* 334 27
channel, distributary ~ 13 2
channel, navigable ~ 224 92, 93
channel iron 143 7
channel markings 224 84-102
channel marks 224 68-83
chantarelle 381 14
chanter 322 10
chanterelle 381 14
chapel *Map* 15 61, 107
'chapel' *Airport* 233 49
chapel *Chivalry* 329 29
chaplet 34 32
chaplet hairstyle 34 31
chaps 70 26
chapter heading 185 60
char-a-banc, covered ~ 186 33
character 174 7, 44; 175 38
characteristic 345 6
characteristic light 221 48; 224 105
character storage 242 37
charcoal 278 48
charcoal, activated ~ 270 58
charcoal grill 278 47
charcoal pencil 338 16
chard 57 28
charge postmark 236 58
charger 25 51
charging car 144 8; 156 6
charging chamber 154 79
charging conveyor 144 42
charging door 38 61; 139 4
charging machine 147 25
charging opening 139 49
charging platform 147 4

charging position 147 55, 56
Charioteer 3 27
charity performance 319 31
Charles's Wain 3 29
Charleston cymbals 324 50
charlock 61 18
charm 36 35
chart 22 32; 76 8; 260 30
chart, illustrated ~ 22 16
chase 181 38
chasing 87 28
chasing hammer 108 41
chassis *Overh. Irrign.* 67 14
chassis *Blacksm.* 138 28
chassis *Car* 191 2
check *Roulette* 275 12
check *Theatre* 315 7
check *Music. Instr.* 325 27
check brake 143 97
checker 276 18, 19
checkerboard 276 17
checkerman 276 18, 19
checkers 276 17-19
check felt 325 28
check light 195 21, 22
checkmate 276 15
checkout 99 92
check rail 202 23
checkroom 315 5; 318 1
checkroom attendant 315 6; 318 2
checkroom hall 315 5-11
check side 277 6
cheek *Man* 16 9
cheek *Hunt.* 87 4
cheekbone 16 8; 17 37
cheek piece 71 8
cheek rest 255 30
cheek strap 71 8
cheese 98 5; 266 52
cheese, cross-wound ~ 164 58
cheese, round ~ 99 42
cheese, whole ~ 99 40
cheeseboard 45 35
cheesecake 97 23
cheese counter 99 39
cheese dish 40 7
cheesefly 81 15
cheese knife 45 72
cheese machine 76 47
cheetah 368 7
chef 207 34
chelicer 358 41
cheliped 358 41
chemical bottle 116 10; 261 23
'chemist' 233 45
chemistry 261 1-13
chemistry laboratory 261 1; 349; 350
chemistry teacher 261 2
chequer-board cut 36 66
cheroot 107 4
cherry *Drupes & Nuts* 59 5, 6-8
cherry *Goldsm. etc.* 108 7
cherry *Bot.* 370 99
cherry blossom 59 3
cherry flan 97 22
cherry flower 59 3
cherry fruit 59 6-8
cherry fruit fly 80 18
cherry leaf 59 2
cherry stone 59 7
cherry tree 59 1, 11-18
cherub 272 20
chess 265 17; 276 1-16
chessboard 47 20; 276 1
chessboard square 276 2
chess championship 276 16
chess clock 276 16
chessman 276 1, 4, 5, 7

chess match 276 16
chess move 276 6
chess player 265 17
chess problem 276 6
chess square 276 6
chest *Man* 16 28-30; 17 8-11
chest *Paperm.* 172 25
chest grip 21 37
chestnut *Horse* 72 27
chestnut *Decid. Trees* 371 60
chestnut *South. Fruits* 384 52
Chestnut Boletus 381 15
chestnut tree 371 58
chest of drawers 41 8
chevron design 335 16
chew 107 19
chewing tobacco 107 19
chianti 98 61
chianti bottle 99 77
chibonk 107 32
chibonque 107 32
chick 74 2
chicken 62 36; 73 19-26; 96 24
chicken run 74 11
chick-pea 69 19
chick unit 74 1
chicory 57 40
chief 254 18-19
chignon 34 29
child 260 3
child, small ~ 28 42
child carrier seat 187 21
children's room 47
chilling roll 180 28
chill roller 180 28
chimera 327 16
chimney *Map* 15 38
chimney *Dwellings* 37 10
chimney *Roof & Boilerr.* 38 5
chimney *Bldg. Site* 118 21
chimney *Carp.* 120 47
chimney *Roof* 122 13
chimney *Blacksm.* 137 7
chimney *Power Plant* 152 15
chimney *Energy Sources* 155. 12
chimney *Railw.* 210 22
chimney *Mountain.* 300 8
chimney bond 118 66
chimney brick 159 28
chimney flashing 122 14
chimney swallow 361 20
chimney sweep 38 31
chimney sweeper 38 31
chimpanzee 368 14
chin 16 15
china, broken ~ 260 61
china cabinet 44 26
china manufacture 161
china painter 161 17
China reed 136 28
China rose 60 15
chinband 355 22
chinch 81 39
chinchona 380 17
Chinese lantern 52 15
chine strake 258 8
chin rest 323 8
chintuft 34 10
chip *Basketm.* 136 12
chip *Roulette* 275 12
chip basket 136 11
chip container 170 40
chip crusher 172 5
chip distributor 172 3
chip extractor 157 51
chip-extractor opening 132 48
chip packer 172 3
chip pan 40 41
chipper 172 1
chipping hammer *Blacksm.* 137 38

chipping hammer *Gas Weld.* 141 25
chipping hammer *Arc Weld.* 142 17
chip remover 157 50
chiropter 366 9
chiropteran 366 9
chisel 120 71
chisel, bevelled-edge ~ 132 7; 339 19
chisel, blacksmith's ~ 137 38
chisel, broad ~ 158 37
chisel, flat ~ 140 26; 339 14
chisel, hollow ~ 339 17
chisel, pneumatic ~ 148 45
chisel, toothed ~ 339 13
chisels 132 7-11
chitarrone 324 1
chiton 355 5
Chitonactis 369 20
chivalry 329
chive 57 22
chlorine 170 7
chlorine ion 1 10
chlorobenzene 170 9, 11
chock *Bldg. Site* 119 40
chock *Iron Foundry etc.* 148 61
chocolate 98 80
chocolate, bar of ~ 98 78
chocolate box 98 79
chocolate liqueur 98 83
choir 330 32; 335 4
choir organ 326 5, 42
choke cymbals 324 50
choke flap 192 6
choker 36 16
choker collar 355 74
cholecystography 27 4
chopper 188 56
chopper drum 64 34
chopping board 96 57
chord *Aircraft* 230 56
chord *Music. Not.* 321 1-5, 5
chord *Maths.* 346 51
chord, lower ~ 121 73, 79
chord, upper ~ 121 74, 80
chorus 315 21
chow 70 21
christening 332 1
christening dress 332 8
christening robe 332 8
christening shawl 332 9
Christian 330 61
chromatic scale 320 49
chromolithography 340 28
chronometer 230 11
chrysalis 77 30, 32; 80 4, 25, 43; 81 3, 21, 24; 82 13, 21, 32; 358 20; 365 11
chrysanthemum 51 29; 61 7
chuck *Meat* 95 19
chuck *D.I.Y.* 134 48
chuck *Turner* 135 6
chuck, four-jaw ~ 149 35
chuck, independent ~ 149 35
chuck, quick-action ~ 132 54
chuck, self-centring ~ 149 37
chuck, three-jaw ~ 149 37
chuck, two-jaw ~ 135 10
church 51 53, 61, 107; 330; 331 1; 332
church, Baroque ~ 336 1
church, Gothic ~ 335 22
church, Protestant ~ 330 1-30
church, Renaissance ~ 335 42
church, Roman Catholic ~ 330 31-62
church, Romanesque ~ 335 1-13
church banner 331 44
church clock 331 7
church door *Church* 331 16

church door *Art* 335 24
churchgoer 330 29; 331 17
church landmark 15 64
church organ 326 1-52
church owl 362 17
church roof 331 11
church spire 331 6
church wedding 332 14
church window 330 14
churchyard 331 21-41
churchyard gate 331 19
churchyard wall 331 18
chute *Docks* 226 45
chute *Fair* 308 40
chute, spiral ~ 144 28
chute, three-way ~ 92 34
ciborium 332 48
cigar, Brazilian ~ 107 2
cigar and cigarette boy 267 49
cigar box 107 1
cigar case 107 8
cigar cutter 107 9
cigarette, filter-tipped ~ 107 12
cigarette, Russian ~ 107 14
cigarette beetle 81 25
cigarette case 107 10
cigarette holder 107 16
cigarette lighter 107 27, 30
cigarette machine 268 69
cigarette packet 107 11
cigarette paper 107 17
cigarette roller 107 15
cigarettes and tobacco kiosk 204 47
cigarette seller 308 51
cigarette tip 107 13
cigarette tray 267 50
cigarillo 107 3
cigar lighter 191 88
ciliate 370 49
ciliate infusorian 357 9
cilium *Man* 19 41
cilium *Invertebr.* 357 10
cilium *Bot.* 370 50
cinchona 380 17
cincinnus 370 77
cine camera 117 1
cine film 117
cinema 312 1
cinema, mobile ~ 312 52
cinema advertisement 268 57
cinema audience 312 5
cinema box office 312 2
cinemagoer 312 5
cinema projector 312 24
cinema projector, narrow-gauge ~ 312 52
cinemascope camera 310 47
cinema ticket 312 3
cine projector 117 78; 318 20
cinnamon 382 25
cinnamon bark 382 25
cinnamon tree 382 22
cinquefoil 335 40
circle *Sports* 305 31
circle *Maths.* 346 42
circle, circumscribed ~ 346 29
circle, divided ~ *Optic. Instr.* 113 27
circle, divided ~ *Crystals* 351 32
circle, graduated ~ *Optic. Instr.* 113 27
circle, graduated ~ *Crystals* 351 32
circle, inner ~ 288 57
circle, inscribed ~ 346 31
circle, middle ~ 288 58
circle, outer ~ 288 59
circle, upper ~ 315 17
circles, concentric ~ 346 58
circles, polar ~ 14 11

circle template 151 70
circling engagement 294 49
circuit, integrated ~ *Clocks* 110 16
circuit, integrated ~ *Inf. Tech.* 242 68
circuit, primary ~ 154 2, 42
circuit, secondary ~ 154 7, 45
circuit breaker 127 19, 33, 36; 152 34; 153 51-62
circuit breaker, miniature ~ 41 20
circuit breaker consumer unit 127 33
circular broom 199 40
circular saw attachment 84 33; 134 52
circular saw blade 132 59
circulation, atmospheric ~ 9 46-52
circulation pump 154 43, 54
circulatory system 18 1-21
circumcircle 346 29
circumference *Cooper* 130 23
circumference *Maths.* 346 44
circumference, staved ~ 130 2
circumflex 342 32
circus 307
circus, travelling ~ 307 1-63
circus act 307 25
circus attendant 307 27
circus band 307 10
circus box 307 16
circus caravan 206 20; 307 34
circus horse 307 30
circus manager 307 17
circus marksman 307 38
circus rider 307 26
circus tent 307 1
circus trailer 307 34
cirrocumulus 8 14
cirrostratus 8 7
cirrus 8 6
cist, long ~ 328 16
cist, stone ~ 328 17
cistern 49 16
cithara 322 15
cittern 322 21
city 15 51
city banner 218 22
city wall 333 30
Claisen flask 350 50
clamp *Atom* 2 43
clamp *Overh. Irrign.* 67 30
clamp *Goldsm. etc.* 108 34
clamp *Joiner* 132 51; 133 9
clamp *Bookbind.* 183 18; 185 3
clamp *Chem.* 350 33
clamp, horizontal ~ 14 57
clamp, vertical ~ 14 55
clamp handle 133 8
clamping device *Atom* 2 43
clamping device *Mach. Tools* 150 15
clamping plate, hinged ~ 117 90
clamping screw 133 23
clamping shoe 133 10
clamp lever 132 67
clamp tip 149 46
clamp tip tool 149 45
clapper *Carnival* 306 47
clapper *Films* 310 35
clapper board 310 35
clapper boy 310 34
clappers 162 42
clarinet 318 4; 323 34
clarinettist 318 5
clasp, white gold ~ 36 10
clasp nut 149 19
classes, social ~of bees 77 1,4,5

classification siding 206 47
classification track 206 47
classification yard 206 42
classification yard switch tower 206 44
classifier 172 50
classroom 260 1-45
classroom cupboard 260 43
clavicembalo 322 45
clavichord 322 36
clavichord mechanism 322 37
clavicle 17 6
clavilux 317 13
claw 327 3; 362 7
claw, bird's ~ 327 61
claw, double ~ 77 8
claw chisel 339 13
claw head 120 75
claws, griffin's ~ 327 13
clay 160 1; 260 79; 339 8, 31
clay, impure ~ 159 2
clay, raw ~ 159 2
clay box 339 30
clay column *Brickwks.* 159 14
clay column *Porcelain Manuf.* 161 8
clay pigeon shooting 305 70-78
clay pit *Map* 15 88
clay pit *Brickwks.* 159 1
cleaner, centrifugal ~ 173 11
cleaner, ultrasonic ~ 109 23
cleaning brush *Hunt.* 87 62
cleaning brush *Office* 247 10
cleaning fluid 111 32
cleaning machine *Brew.* 92 36
cleaning machine *Watchm.* 109 30
cleaning plant 144 20
cleaning rag 50 55
cleaning rod 87 61
cleaning shop 148 38-45
cleaning tank 178 1
cleaning tow 87 63
cleanout door 38 39
cleansing pond 89 6
clear-felling system 84 4-14
clearing *Map* 15 2
clearing *Forestry* 84 13
clearstory 334 70
cleat *Carp.* 120 45
cleat *Floor etc. Constr.* 123 67
cleaver, butcher's ~ 94 18
cleaving hammer 85 5
clefs 320 8-11
cleft, anal ~ 16 41
clench planking 285 50-52
clerestory 334 70
clergyman 330 22; 331 37; 332 22
clergyman, Protestant ~ 332 3
clerical assistant 248 7
clerk 263 26, 27
clew 284 41
click 110 34
click beetle 80 37, 38
click wheel 110 35
cliff 13 28
cliff face 13 28
cliffline 13 25-31
cliffs 13 25-31
climate, artificially maintained ~ 356 21
climate, boreal ~ 9 56
climate, equatorial ~ 9 53
climates 9 53-58
climates, polar ~ 9 57-58
climatic map 9 40-58
climatology 9
climber *Flower Gdn.* 51 5
climber *Fruit & Veg. Gdn.* 52 5

climber *Indoor Plants* 53 2
climber *Veg.* 57 8
climber *Mountain.* 300 5
climbing 300 2-13
climbing boot 300 44
climbing breeches 300 7
climbing equipment 300
31-57
climbing frame 273 47
climbing harness 300 56
climbing net 273 50
climbing plant 53 2
climbing roof 273 60
climbing rope 273 48; 296 19
climbing tower 273 17
clinch 299 31
clinker cooler 160 9
clinker pit 152 8
clinker planking 285 50-52
clinker store 160 10
clinoprinacoid 351 24
clip *Atom* 2 18
clip *Bicycle* 187 62
clip *Railw.* 202 9
clipper display 238 44
clippers, electric ~ 105 21; 106
32
clipper ship, English ~ 220 36
clitellum 357 26
clitoris 20 88
Clivia minata 53 8
cloak 355 18, 26
cloak, red ~ 319 27
cloak, short ~ 355 29
cloak, Spanish ~ 355 29
cloak, woollen ~ 355 6
cloak cord 355 24
cloakroom 48 34; 207 70; 315
5; 318 1
cloakroom attendant 315 6;
318 2
cloakroom hall 315 5-11
cloakroom ticket 315 7
cloche 35 12
clock 191 38; 211 37; 212 16
clock, double ~ 276 16
clock, electric ~ 191 79
clock, main ~ 245 18
clock case 110 26; 309 57
clockmaker 109 1
clocks 110
clockwork 110 36
clockwork drive 10 14
clockwork mechanism 110 36
clod 63 7
clog 101 44; 355 43
cloister 331 52
cloister vault 336 41
closed vertical gate 301 66
close-up bellows attachment
115 85
close-up equipment 115
81-98
close-up lens 117 55
closing gear 90 27
closing head 143 59
closure rail 202 26
cloth 166 12; 271 59
cloth, damask ~ 45 2
cloth, felt ~ 340 42
cloth, flannel ~ 128 48
cloth, linen ~ 206 11
cloth, sterile ~ 26 38
cloth, unraised ~ 168 33
clothes, children's ~ 29
clothes, teenagers' ~ 29 48-68
clothes brush 50 44; 104 31
clothes closet 43 1
clothes closet door 46 2
clothes compartment 212 63;
267 30
clothes line 38 23; 50 33
clothes louse 81 41

clothes moth 81 13
clothes rack 271 31
clothes rack, movable ~ 103
17
clothes shop 268 9
clothing, protective ~ 84 26;
270 46
cloth roller 166 20
cloth-shearing machine,
rotary ~ 168 42
cloth take-up motion 166 19
cloth take-up roller 166 47
cloth temple 166 13
cloud, lenticular ~ 287 19
cloud chamber photograph 2
26
cloud chamber track 2 27
cloud cover 9 20-24
clouds 8 1-19, 1-4, 5-12,
13-17
clouds, luminous ~ 7 22
clouds, noctilucent ~ 7 22
clout 121 94
clout nail 121 94; 122 96
clove 382 28
clove carnation 60 7
clove pink 60 7
clover, four-leaf ~ 69 5
clover broadcaster 66 26
clove tree 382 26
clown 306 69; 307 24
clown, musical ~ 307 23
clown act 307 25
club 283 23
club hammer 126 77
clubhouse 283 23
club membership 286 8
club rush 378 21
clubs 276 38
clump of grass 375 44
cluster of eggs 80 2, 30
cluster of grapes 78 5
cluster of stars 3 26
clutch 191 44
clutch, dry ~ 190 78
clutch, fluid ~ 65 37
clutch, main ~ 65 39
clutch, multi-plate ~ 190 78
clutch, single-plate ~ 190 71
clutch coupling 227 23
clutch flange 177 55
clutch lever 188 32
clutch pedal 191 44, 96; 192
28
C major 320 55, 62
C major scale 320 45
C minor 320 59, 65
coach *Lorries etc.* 194 17
coach *Ball Games* 291 55; 292
57
coach, four-axled ~ 208 3
coach, second ~ 209 7
coach body 186 5; 207 2; 208
6
coach bolt 202 7
coach box 186 8
coach door 186 11
coaches 186
1-3,26-39,45,51-54
coach horse 186 28
coachman 186 32
coach screw 202 7
coach step 186 13
coach wagons 186
1-3,26-39,45,51-54
coagulating bath 169 15
coal 170 1
coal bunker 152 2; 225 19
coal conveyor 152 1
coal distillation, dry ~ 170 2
coal feed conveyor 199 37
coal mill 152 4
coal mine 144 1-51

coal scuttle 309 9
coal seam 144 50
coal shovel 38 43
coal tar 170 3
coal tar extraction 156 18
coal tower 156 5
coal tower conveyor 156 4
coal wharf 225 18
coaming 283 59
coarse dirt hose 50 84
coarse fishing 89 20-31
coastal cruiser 284 60
coastal lake 13 44
coaster 221 99
coaster brake 187 63
coasting vessel 221 99
coat 29 54; 30 60; 33 2
coat, black ~ 289 4
coat, braided ~ 186 23
coat, cloth ~ 30 61; 33 66
coat, dark ~ 289 4, 13
coat, fur ~ 30 60
coat, gallooned ~ 186 23
coat, loden ~ 29 31; 30 64
coat, loose-fitting ~ 271 41
coat, mink ~ 131 24
coat, ocelot ~ 131 25
coat, oilskin ~ 228 7
coat, poncho-style ~ 30 68
coat, poplin ~ 33 60
coat, red ~ 289 13
coat, three-quarter length ~
271 21
coat belt 33 59
coat button 33 64
coat collar 33 58
coater 173 31, 34
coat hanger 41 3
coat hook 41 2; 207 50; 266
14
coating, bituminous ~ 200 58
coating of fluorescent
material 240 19
coat-of-arms 254 1-6
coat-of-arms, marshalled ~
254 10-13
coat-of-arms, provincial ~
252 12, 14
coat pocket 33 61
coat rack 41 1
coat stand 266 12
coat-tail 33 14
cob 59 49
cobalt bomb 2 28
cobnut 59 49
coccyx 17 5; 20 60
coccinellid 358 37
cochlea 17 63
cock *Farm Bldgs.* 62 37
cock *Dom. Anim.* 73 21
cockade 264 8
cockatrice 327 34
cockchafer 82 1
cockchafer grub 82 12
cocker spaniel 70 38
cocking handle 255 12
cocking lever 255 12
cocking piece 121 30
cock pheasant 88 77
cock pigeon 73 33
cockpit *Aircraft* 230 1-31, 35;
231 19
cockpit *Police* 264 2
cockpit *Rowing* 283 8
cockpit *Sailing* 285 38
cockpit *Airsports* 288 10
cockpit canopy 230 39; 257 4
cockpit coaming 283 59
cockpit hood 230 39; 257 4
cockroach 81 17
cockscomb 73 22
cock's foot 69 25
cock's head 69 10

cock's tread 74 65
cocktail 317 33
cocktail fork 45 76
cocktail glass 267 56
cocktail shaker 267 61
cocoa *Grocer* 98 66
cocoa *Trop. Plants* 382 19
cocoa bean 382 19
cocoa palm 383 48
cocoa powder 382 19
coconut 383 53
coconut oil 98 23
coconut palm 383 48
coconut tree 383 48
cocoon *Forest Pests* 82 21
cocoon *Articulates* 358 51
coco palm 383 48
cocotte 306 37
cod 90 22
code flag halyard 223 10
code flag signal 223 9
cod end 90 22
code pendant 253 29
code pennant 253 29
coding keyboard 242 11
coding station 236 35
cod line 90 23
codling moth 58 62
codlin moth 58 62
coefficient 345 4
coelenterate 357 14; 369 5, 9,
14, 20
coffee 98 65-68, 67; 99 68-70,
68; 265 19
coffee *Trop. Plants* 382 6
coffee, instant ~ 99 70
coffee, pure ~ 98 65
coffee bean 382 6
coffee cup 44 29
coffee grinder, electric ~ 39
24; 98 69
coffee maker 39 38
coffee plant 382 1
coffee pot 44 28
coffee roaster 98 70
coffee service 44 27
coffee set 44 27; 265 18
coffee table 42 28
coffee tree 382 1
coffee urn 265 2
cofferdam 259 19
coffin 331 35
coffin chamber 333 5
cog *Mach. Parts etc.* 143 83
cog *Ship* 218 18-26
cog, wooden ~ 91 9
cognac 98 59
cog railroad 214 4-5
cog railway 214 4-5
cog wheels 143 82-96
coiffure, upswept ~ 355 81
coiffures 34 27-38
coil 89 21
coiled-coil filament 127 58
coiler 148 72
coiler top 163 62
coil spring 191 28; 192 68
coin 252 1-28
coin, Celtic ~ 328 37
coin, gold ~ 36 37
coin, silver ~ 328 37
coinage 252 1-28, 40-44
coin-box telephone 236 9;
237 3
coin bracelet 36 36
coin disc 252 43
coining dies 252 40-41
coining press 252 44
coins 252 1-28
coins, aluminium ~ 252 1-28
coins, copper ~ 252 1-28
coins, gold ~ 252 1-28
coins, nickel ~ 252 1-28

coins, silver ~ **252** 1-28
coin setting **36** 38
coke **147** 2
coke guide **156** 9
coke loading **156** 15
coke loading bay **156** 12
coke oven **144** 7; **156** 8, 16
coke-oven gas processing **156**
  16-45
coke-quenching car **144** 11
coke-quenching tower **144** 10
cokernut **383** 53
coke side bench **156** 13
coke wharf **156** 12
coking coal **156** 33
coking coal tower **144** 9
coking plant *Coal* **144** 7-11
coking plant *Coking* **156** 1-15
coking plant *Synth. Fibres*
  170 2
col **12** 47
cold-drawing **170** 46
cold house **55** 33
cold light source **23** 8
cold room **94** 21-24
cold shelf **96** 12; **98** 3
cold storage room **223** 56
cold store **94** 21-24; **225** 50
cold tap **126** 29
cold water tank **92** 9
cole **383** 1
Coleoptera **358** 24-39
coleseed **383** 1
collar *Jewell.* **36** 16
collar *Dog* **70** 13
collar *Game* **88** 27
collar *Roof* **121** 35, 70
collar *Money* **252** 42
collar *Church* **332** 6
collar *Fish etc.* **364** 39
collar, braided ~ **186** 22
collar, cowl ~ **30** 3
collar, Dutch ~ **71** 28
collar, fur ~ **30** 63
collar, fur-trimmed ~ **30** 63
collar, galerooned ~ **186** 22
collar, ground glass ~ **115** 53,
  64
collar, high ~ **355** 74
collar, integral ~ **143** 33
collar, knitted ~ **33** 31
collar, matt ~ **115** 53, 64
collar, padded ~ **101** 20
collar, pointed ~ **71** 15
collar, stand-up ~ **30** 43
collar, turndown ~ **30** 5; **31** 69
collar, wide-falling ~ **355** 56
collar beam **121** 35, 38, 70
collar beam roof **121** 34
collar beam roof structure
  121 37
collar bearing **148** 73
collarbone **17** 6
collating machine **249** 59
collating station **249** 60
collecting bin **201** 20
collecting hopper **92** 20
collecting tank **172** 26
collecting vessel **10** 40, 45
collection **74** 36
collection bag **236** 51
collector **155** 19
collector bow **205** 36
collector well **269** 4
college **262** 1-25
college lecturer **262** 3
colliery **144** 1-51
collimator **111** 46; **351** 30
colon **342** 17
colon, ascending ~ **20** 19
colon, descending ~ **20** 21
colon, transverse ~ **20** 20
colonnade **274** 9; **334** 67

colophony **323** 11
color *see* colour
Colorado beetle **80** 52
colour **343**
colour analyser **116** 36
colour analyser lamp **116** 37
colour chemicals **116** 52
colour computer **177** 51
colour conversion filter step
  117 38
colour correction, selective ~
  177 51
colour correction unit **177** 39
colour decoder module **240** 5
colour developer **116** 10
colour enlarger **116** 40
colour filter **316** 49
colour indicator **127** 37
colour light distant signal **203**
  9, 14
colour light signal **203** 3
colour medium **316** 49
colour-mixing knob **116**
  43-45
colour organ **317** 13
colour output stage module
  240 13
colour pickup tube **240** 36
colour picture tube **240** 15
colour print **340** 28
colour printing paper **116** 51
colour processing chemicals
  116 52
colours of the rainbow **343** 14
colour television receiver **240**
  1
colour television set **240** 1
colposcope **23** 5
coltsfoot **380** 8
colubrid **364** 38
Columbian **175** 30
columbine *Gdn. Flowers* **60**
  10
Columbine *Carnival* **306** 27
column *Photog.* **116** 42
column *Forging* **139** 10
column *Mach. Tools* **150** 10
column *Bookbind.* **185** 65
column *Script* **342** 45
column *Chem.* **349** 29
column, angled ~ **116** 28
column, bent ~ **113** 21
column, central ~ **114** 46
column, Corinthian ~ **334** 10
column, Doric ~ **334** 8
column, Ionic ~ **334** 9
column, ornamented ~ **333** 18
column, spinal ~ **17** 2-5
column, vertebral ~ **17** 2-5
column box **119** 11, 73
column heading **342** 46
column rule **342** 47
column shaft **334** 26
coma position **21** 24
comb *Infant Care etc.* **28** 8
comb *Dom. Anim.* **73** 22
comb *Hairdresser* **105** 6
comb, adjustable ~ **165** 26
comb, top ~ **163** 67
combat sports **299**
comber **163** 56, 63
comber draw box **163** 60
comb foundation **77** 43
combination, two-piece ~ **30**
  45
combination cutting pliers
  126 60; **127** 53
combination lever **210** 30
combination rib weave **171** 25
combination toolholder **149**
  41
combine **64** 1-33
combined grasp **296** 42

combine harvester **63** 31; **64**
  1-33
combing cylinder **163** 68
combing machine **163** 56
comb setting **165** 36
combustion chamber **232** 37
combustion chamber,
  external ~ **147** 16
comfrey **375** 45
comic turn **307** 25
comma **342** 18
command key **247** 21
command module **6** 9
command section **234** 65
commencement of speed
  restriction **203** 39, 42
commissionaire **267** 1; **271**
  44; **315** 10
commissure, labial ~ **16** 14;
  19 19
committee **263** 1-2
committee boat **285** 15
committee member **263** 2
committee table **263** 3
common box **373** 19
common buzzard **362** 9
common comfrey **69** 13
common denominator **344** 19
common dolphin **367** 24
common European kite **362**
  11
common flea **81** 42
common groundsel **61** 12
common heron **359** 18
common housefly **81** 2
common iguana **364** 32
common mallow **376** 13
common merganser **359** 15
common myrtle **53** 11
common nightshade **379** 5
common orache **61** 24
common pheasant **88** 77
common privet **373** 6
common puffball **381** 20
common roller **360** 6
common salt **170** 13
common sea-swallow **359** 11
common silver fir **372** 1
common swallow **361** 20
common time **320** 32
common toadflax **376** 26
common vetch **69** 18
common viper **364** 40
communicant **332** 27
communication line **127** 23
communication link **237** 50
communications satellite **237**
  52
communion cup **330** 10; **332**
  29
communion table **330** 4
communion wafer **332** 50
commutator cover **211** 18
companion hatch **258** 24
companion ladder **221** 123;
  223 24; **258** 24
companionway **221** 123; **222**
  23; **223** 24; **258** 24
company account **250** 4
company messenger **236** 17
compartment *Forestry* **84** 2
compartment *Railw.* **207** 13;
  208 24
compartment *Store* **271** 6
compartment, secretarial ~
  205 37; **209** 25
compartment, special ~ **205**
  26
compartment, twin-berth ~
  207 38
compartment, two-berth ~
  207 38

compartment, two-seat ~ **207**
  38
compartment batten **316** 13
compartment door **207** 14
compartment window **207** 52;
  208 8
compass *Drawing Off.* **151** 52
compass *Airsports* **288** 12
compass, divisions of ~ **321**
  42-50
compass, fluid ~ **224** 46
compass, gyroscopic ~ **224** 31,
  51-53
compass, liquid ~ **224** 46
compass, magnetic ~ **223** 6;
  224 46; **230** 6
compass, mariner's ~ **223** 6
compass, ratchet-type ~ **151**
  64
compass, spirit ~ **224** 46
compass, wet ~ **224** 46
compass bowl **224** 49
compass brick **159** 25
compass bridge **223** 4-11; **227**
  24
compass card **224** 47
compasses **224** 46-53
compass flat **223** 4-11; **227** 24
compass head **151** 53
compass plane **132** 28
compass platform **223** 4-11;
  227 24
compass repeater **224** 31, 52,
  53
compass saw **120** 63; **126** 70;
  132 3
compendium of games **47** 18
compensating airstream **192** 4
compensating roller **181** 45
compensation pendulum **109**
  33
compensator **181** 45
compensator level **112** 69
competition bow **305** 54
competitor **282** 28
complementary angle **346** 15
complement of set **348** 7, 8
composing frame **174** 2
composing room **174**; **175**;
  176
composing rule **174** 14
composing stick **174** 13
composition *Composing Rm.*
  175 1-17
composition *Art. Studio* **338** 4
composition, computer-
  controlled ~ **176** 14
compositor **174** 5
compost heap **52** 6
comprehensive school **261**
  1-45
compress **27** 4
compressed-air bottle **279** 21
compressed-air braking
  system **208** 21
compressed-air cylinder **279**
  21
compressed-air hose **174** 38
compressed-air inlet **153** 53
compressed-air line *Joiner*
  133 45
compressed-air line *Blacksm.*
  138 5
compressed-air pipe *Forging*
  139 22
compressed-air pipe
  Metalwkr. **140** 17
compressed-air pressure
  gauge **279** 13
compressed-air reservoir
  Agr. Mach. **64** 92
compressed-air reservoir
  Offshore Drill. **146** 21

compressed-air supply 213 20
compressed-air system 138 1
compressed-air tank
   Blacksm. 138 4
compressed-air tank Power
   Plant 153 51
compressed-air vessel 269 17,
   50
compressed-gas container
   234 32
compressed-helium bottle
   234 14
compressed-helium tank 234
   43, 50
compression bandage 21 17
compression plate 2 25
compressor Painter 129 33
compressor Blacksm. 138 3
compressor Oil, Petr. 145 45
compressor Energy Sources
   155 4
compressor Ship 223 51
compressor Office 247 43
compressor, high-pressure ~
   232 36
compressor, low-pressure ~
   232 35
computer 23 53; 177 70; 195 1
computer cable 195 3, 38
computer centre 244
computer data 238 13
computer harness 195 3, 38
computer plug, main ~ 195 2,
   39
computer test, automatic ~
   195 53
computing scale 98 12
concave 64 11
concave ridge 302 22
concentrator 172 24, 42, 44,
   48, 62
concert grand 325 40
concertina 324 36
conch shell trumpet 327 41
concrete, heavy ~ 119 72
concrete, rammed ~ 118 1
concrete, tamped ~ 118 1
concrete aggregate 118 36;
   119 26
concrete bucket 119 38
concrete mixer 47 40; 118 33;
   119 29; 201 23
concrete-mixing plant 201 19
concrete pump hopper 201 24
concreter 119 9
concrete road construction
   201 1-24
concrete scraper 200 13
concrete spreader 201 5
concrete spreader box 201 6
concrete tamper 119 83
concrete test cube 119 84
concrete-vibrating
   compactor 201 10
concrete vibrator 119 88
condensate 172 17
condenser Brew. 92 6
condenser Optic. Instr. 112 8;
   113 32
condenser Oil, Petr. 145 44
condenser Nucl. Energy 154
   17, 35
condenser Energy Sources
   155 8
condenser Synth. Fibres 170 5
condenser Paperm. 172 30
condenser Warships 259 64
condenser Chem. 350 48
condenser, coiled ~ 349 6
condenser, universal ~ 112 66
condensing locomotive 210
   69
condensing tender 210 69

condition report 195 7
conductor Power Plant 153 34,
   43
conductor Spa 274 21
conductor Theatre 315 26
conductor, copper ~ 127 43
conductor, electrostatic ~ 230
   51; 231 27
conductor, high-voltage ~
   152 33
conduit 334 54
cone Phys. Geog. 11 24
cone Mach. Parts etc. 143 67
cone Synth. Fibres 169 27
cone Bicycle 187 58
cone Maths. 347 43
cone Decid. Trees 371 32
cone, cross-wound ~ 165 8, 24
cone, pyrometric ~ 161 6
cone, truncated ~ 347 45
cone axis 372 3
cone breaker 172 82
cone chest 326 12-14
cone creel 165 9
cone drum box 163 30
cone height 347 44
cone nozzle 83 23
cone refiner 172 27, 60, 73, 83
cone scale 372 8, 14, 27, 38
cone-winding frame 165 1
cone-winding machine 169
   26
coney 366 24
confectionery 97 17-47; 98
   75-86
confectionery unit 97 67-70
conference circuit 242 22
conference connection 242 22
conference grouping 246
   31-36
conference hook-up 242 22
conference table 246 31
confetti 306 62
configuration, angular ~ 248
   39
confluence 224 90
conga drum 324 55
congregation 330 29
conifers 372 1-71
Conium 379 4
connecting corridor 208 11
connecting door, sliding ~
   207 19
connecting element 248 48
connecting hose 208 16, 21
connecting lead 25 20, 56
connecting piece 350 56
connecting rod Agr. 63 20
connecting rod Intern.
   Combust. Eng. 190 21
connecting rod Railw. 210 11
connecting-rod bearing 192
   25
connecting seal, rubber ~ 207
   8; 208 12
connecting shaft 63 20
connecting system, automatic
   ~ 237 25
connection, internal ~ 245 14
connection, pneumatically
   sprung ~ 194 45
connection, rubber ~ 194 45
connection of modules 242 70
connection rebar 119 10, 71
connector Moon L. 6 28
connector Weaving 166 52
connector, thermoplastic ~
   127 29
connector fitting 287 31
consignment, general ~ 206 4
consignment, mixed ~ 206 4
consignment note 206 30
console Joiner 133 24

console Serv. Stat. 196 29
console School 261 37
console Music. Instr. 326
   36-52
console operator 244 3
console piano 325 1
console typewriter 244 4
consolidating beam 201 2
constant of integration 345 14
constellations 3 9-48
construction, close-seamed ~
   285 54
construction, wooden ~ 260
   72
construction of circuit 242 72
construction set 48 22
construction site 118; 119
construction unit, precast ~
   215 58
construction vehicle 255 75
consulting room 23 1
contact, auxiliary ~ 153 57
contact, magnetic ~ 242 71
contact arc 237 43
contact arm 237 44
contact arm tag 237 46
contact breaker 242 49
contact field 237 45
contact goniometer 351 27
contact maker 127 38-39
contact sleeve, metal ~ 166 31
contact spring 127 28
contact wire maintenance
   vehicle 211 41, 44-54
contact wire voltage indicator
   211 28
container 206 57; 221 22; 226
   3, 6
container Chem. 350 61
container, plastic ~ 83 25
container, railroad-owned ~
   206 19
container, railway-owned ~
   206 19
container, shielded ~ 154 82
container berth 225 48; 226 1
container car 206 58
container carrier truck 225 47
container for vegetables 96 51
container platform 194 27
container ship 221 89; 225 45
container station 206 54
container terminal 225 48;
   226 1
container wagon 206 58
containment, steel ~ 154 21
continents 14 12-18
continuity girl 310 39
continuity tester 127 55
continuous feed grate 199 34
continuous filament process
   162 48
continuous reheating furnace
   148 69
continuous rolling mill train
   148 66-75
contouche 355 66
contour 15 62
contour, submarine ~ 15 11
contour knife 340 10
contrabass 323 23
contrabassoon 323 28
contrabass tuba 323 44
contracted burial 328 17
contractile vacuole 357 5
contra octave 321 43
contrast control 240 32; 249
   36
contrast medium injector 27
   15
control, digital ~ 242 35
control, manual ~ 115 52
control, sliding ~ 311 18

control and monitoring panel
   311 8
control arm 240 29; 313 11
control board 153 1
control box Moon L. 6 23
control box Mach. Tools 150
   36
control box Offset Platem.
   179 33
control button Hosp. 25 30
control button Cine Film 117
   98
control button Text. Finish.
   168 40
control button Navig. 224 32
control button Audiovis. 243
   13
control button Office 246 19
control button School 261 45
control cable 271 53
control column 230 24; 257
   8; 288 14
control console Power Plant
   153 1-6
control console Photomech.
   Reprod. 177 5
control console Films 311 12
control console Theatre 316 2
control desk Hosp. 27 10
control desk Brew. 93 1
control desk Iron & Steel 147
   66
control desk Power Plant 153
   1-6
control desk Nucl. Energy 154
   80
control desk Offset Print. 180
   16
control desk Photograv. 182
   28
control desk Films 311 12
control desk, driver's ~ 212 32
control desk, engineer's ~ 212
   32
control device 26 7
control frame 287 46
control gear 164 38
control grip Pest Contr. 83 19
control grip Photog. 115 76
control handle, cranked ~ 168
   52
control knob Hosp. 25 49; 27
   41
control knob Electrotyp. etc.
   178 15
controller 197 27
controller, rear ~ 197 8
controller handwheel 211 20;
   212 12
control lever Agr. Mach. 64
   59
control lever Pest Contr. 83 21
control lever Cine Film 117 63
control lever Cotton Spin. 163
   28
control lever Road Constr.
   201 8, 12
control lever Navig. 224 19
control lever Broadcast. 240
   29
control lever Films 313 11
control lever Theatre 316 58
control line model 288 89
control linkage 190 30
control loudspeaker 311 13
control mechanism 181 26
control module 238 45; 240 1
control panel Hosp. 26 20; 27
   10
control panel Roof & Boilerr.
   38 67
control panel Dairy. 76 11
control panel Brew. 93 1, 20

control panel *Offshore Drill.* 146 28
control panel *Power Plant* 153 1
control panel *Nucl. Energy* 154 80
control panel *Paperm.* 173 43
control panel *Photomech. Reprod.* 177 36, 60
control panel *Offset Platem.* 179 10, 17
control panel *Offset Print.* 180 74
control panel *Bookbind.* 185 2
control panel *Broadcast.* 240 31
control panel, bracket-mounted ~ 177 6
control panel, electric ~ 168 25, 58
control panel, hinged ~ 177 6
control platform 226 55
control point 203 25
control rod *Nucl. Energy* 154 24
control rod *Warships* 259 69
control rod drive 154 23
control room *Hosp.* 25 1-9
control room *Offshore Drill.* 146 32
control room *Power Plant* 152 19, 28; 153 1-8
control room *Railw.* 214 65
control room *Broadcast.* 238 17
control room *Theatre* 316 1
control room, central ~ *Dairy.* 76 7
control room, central ~ *Brew.* 92 25
control room window 238 38
controls 25 29; 153 6; 271 48
control speaker 238 15
control station 217 45
control stick 230 24; 257 8; 288 14
control switch *Hosp.* 25 29
control switch *Offset Print.* 180 74
control switch *Navig.* 224 23
control tap 172 9
control tower 233 17; 287 12
control unit *Hosp.* 26 7
control unit *Opticn.* 111 29
control unit *Blacksm.* 138 31
control unit *Mach. Tools* 150 36
control unit *Photomech. Reprod.* 177 51
control unit *Electrotyp. etc.* 178 29, 36
control unit *Offset Platem.* 179 33
control unit *Audio* 241 40
control unit, central ~ *Hosp.* 25 1, 20
control unit, central ~ *Inf. Tech.* 242 2
control unit, electric ~ 168 58
control valve 153 52
control weight 166 63
control well 117 98
control wheel *Text. Finish.* 168 40
control wheel *Railw.* 212 81
convenience outlet 127 5
convenience outlet, double ~ 127 6
convent 15 63
convergence 224 90
convergence module 240 12

conversion filter step 117 38
converter 92 42
converter bottom, solid ~ 147 47
converter chimney 147 67
converter top, conical ~ 147 45
converter tube 27 19
convertible 193 9
convertiplane 232 31
conveyances 186 1-54
conveyor *Poultry Farm* 74 22
conveyor *Dairy.* 76 23
conveyor *Bldg. Site* 118 77
conveyor *Synth. Fibres* 169 32
conveyor *Paperm.* 172 79
conveyor *Photograv.* 182 30
conveyor *Refuse Coll.* 199 36
conveyor *Docks* 225 51
conveyor belt *Dairy.* 76 23
conveyor belt *Bldg. Site* 118 77
conveyor belt *Synth. Fibres* 169 32
conveyor belt *Paperm.* 172 79
conveyor belt *Photograv.* 182 30
conveyor belt *Docks* 225 51
conveyor brattice 163 13
conveyor trolley 74 39
conveyor unit 83 59
cook, head ~ 207 34
cooker 96 47
cooker, calor gas ~ 278 33
cooker, double-burner ~ 278 33
cooker, electric ~ 39 12; 46 32
cooker, gas ~ 39 12; 278 33
cooker hood 39 17; 46 31
cooker unit 39 12-17
cooking liquor 172 46
cooking pot 39 29; 40 12
cookroom 223 42
coolant 149 44
coolant bore 242 54
coolant-collecting plant 92 7
coolant feed line 235 38
coolant flow passage 154 29
coolant pump 190 61
coolant pump, primary ~ 154 25
coolant supply pipe 138 26; 149 25
coolant system 154 55
coolant tray 149 44
cooler *Oil, Petr.* 145 44
cooler *Coking* 156 27
coolie 353 43
cooling 170 34
cooling aggregate 39 5
cooling compressor 92 22
cooling cylinder 170 27
cooling fan 312 34
cooling rib 189 20; 190 80; 242 60
cooling roll 173 25
cooling roller 180 28
cooling room 281 28
cooling system 154 48
cooling table 97 67
cooling tank 162 15
cooling tower *Coal* 144 15
cooling tower *Nucl. Energy* 154 39
cooling tower *Synth. Fibres* 170 43
cooling unit 209 21; 212 26, 77
cooling water *Nucl. Energy* 154 18
cooling water *Railw.* 212 65, 78
cooling water bore 242 54
cooling water flow circuit 154 10

cooling water heat exchanger 155 3
cooling water pipe *Opticn.* 111 31
cooling water pipe *Power Plant* 152 27
cooling water pipe *Car* 191 10
cooling water temperature gauge 212 21
cooling water thermostat 190 62
cool shelf 266 49
coon 368 9
cooper 130 11
coordinate 347 2-3, 8
coordinate, right-angled ~ 347 1
coot 359 20
cop, full ~ 163 2
cope 148 19
copier, automatic ~ 249 32
copier, web-fed ~ 249 32
coping stone 37 37
copper 305 6, 18
copper, unworked ~ 260 64
copper cylinder, polished ~ 182 7
copper plate 179 9
copperplate, polished ~ 340 53
copperplate engraver 340 44
copperplate engraving 340 14-24
copperplate press 340 36
copper sulphate 351 26
copy 176 3; 177 18
copy, received ~ 245 2
copy, transmitted ~ 245 2
copyboard 177 14, 22, 30
copy cylinder 177 64
copy delivery 249 43
copyholder 177 15
copying camera, overhead ~ 177 1
copying stand 115 90, 92, 93
copypod 115 90
copy stand 115 90, 92, 93
coquille 294 38, 43
coral, precious ~ 357 17
coral, red ~ 357 17
coral animal 357 17
coral Clavaria 381 32
coral colony 357 18
coral evergreen 377 12
coral polyp 357 19
coral reef 13 32
cor anglais 323 38
cord 206 12
cord, warp-faced ~ 171 26, 27
cordate 370 35
corded ware 328 10
cordon, horizontal ~ 52 17, 29
cordon, quadruple ~ 52 1
cordon, vertical ~ 52 2
core *Phys. Geog.* 11 5
core *Soft Fruit* 58 36, 59
core *Iron Foundry etc.* 148 36
core *Power Plant* 153 17, 36
core *Electrotyp. etc.* 178 18
core, soft-lead ~ 87 56
core, special ~ 301 47
core bit 145 21
core print 148 37
corking machine, semi-automatic ~ 79 10
corkscrew 40 18; 45 46
corkscrew piton 300 40
cormorant 359 10
corn 68 1, 31
corn camomile 61 8
corn campion 61 6
corn cob 68 36

corn cockle 61 6
cornea 19 47
cornelian cherry 373 30, 32
corner *Games* 276 27
corner *Ball Games* 291 41; 292 18
corner *Sports* 305 6; 305 8
corner *Maths.* 347 33
corner bottom slate 122 77
corner brace 120 26
corner flag 291 8
corner kick 291 41
corner peg 292 79
corner seat 207 58; 265 10; 266 38
corner section 42 26
corner stile 120 52
corner strut 120 52
corner stud 120 52
corner table 246 34
corner unit 39 27
corner work 149 51
cornet 323 43
cornett, curved ~ 322 12
cornfield 63 32
corn flower 61 1
corn head 64 35
cornice *Carp.* 120 34
cornice *Mountain.* 300 20
cornice *Art* 334 11-14; 335 48
corn marigold 61 7
corn poppy 61 2
corn removal 92 38
corn salad 57 38
corn spurrey 69 12
corn stem 68 5
corn weevil 81 16
corolla 59 11; 378 4
corolla, papilionaceous ~ 57 1
corona 334 12
corona, solar ~ 4 39
Corona Borealis 3 31
coronet, baronet's ~ 254 43
coronet, baronial ~ 254 44
coronet, count's ~ 254 45
coronet, ducal ~ 254 42
coronet, elector's ~ 254 41
coronet, prince's ~ 254 40
coronets 254; 254 37,38,42-46
coronets of rank 254 43-45
corporation stock 251 11-19
corps de ballet 314 25
corpus callosum 17 44
corpus cavernosum and spongiosum 20 67
corral 319 14
correcting fluid 247 13
correcting lens 115 22
correcting paper 247 12
correction lens 115 72
corrector, universal ~ 238 48
corrector plate 113 11
correspondence 245 19
correspondence file 22 12
correspondent 342 54
corresponding angle 346 12
corrida 319 1-33
corridor *Railw.* 207 11
corridor *Winter Sp.* 301 71
corridor compartment coach 207 1-21
Corvidae 361 1-3
corydalis 377 8
cosine 346 32
cosmetics 99 27-35
cosmetics gondola 99 23
cossack trousers 30 44
costume, theatrical ~ 315 51
costume designer 315 38
costumes, historical ~ 355
cot, collapsible ~ 28 1
cotangent 346 32

cottage, dikereeve's ~ 216 45
cottage, ferryman's ~ 216 45
cottage cheese 76 45
cottage piano 325 1
cotter punch 137 31
cotton *Cotton Spin.* 163 1-13
cotton *Industr. Plants* 383 16
cotton bale, compressed ~ 163 3
cotton bobbin 100 29
cotton boll, ripe ~ 163 1
cotton feed 163 9
cotton-feeding brattice 163 8
cotton grass 377 18
cotton reel 104 9
cotton rush 377 18
cotton spinning 163; 164
cotton wool ball 99 30
cotton wool packet 99 28
cotyledon 370 87
couch *Doc.* 22 43
couch *Weeds* 61 30
coucher 173 49
couch grass 61 30
couchman 173 49
coudé ray path 5 3
coudière 329 48
coulee 13 45
coulter 65 10
coulter, disc ~ 64 66; 65 69
coulter, drill ~ 65 76
coulter, rolling ~ 64 66; 65 69
coulter, skim ~ 65 68
counter *Child. Rm.* 47 28
counter *Shoem.* 100 59
counter *Shoes* 101 37
counter *Cotton Spin.* 163 61
counter *Composing Rm.* 175 41
counter *Offset Print.* 180 74
counter *Railw.* 207 31
counter *Café* 265 1
counter *Restaurant* 266 1-11
counter *Water* 269 59
counter *Ball Games* 291 23
counter *Winter Sp.* 302 18
counter *Flea Market* 309 83
counter, cashier's ~ 250 1
counter, extra ~ 271 64
counter, special ~ 271 64
counterbalance 241 22
counterbalance weight 242 50
counterblow hammer 139 5
counterbrace 215 35
counter clerk 236 16
counter gear assembly 269 55
counter officer 236 16
counterpoise *Optic. Instr.* 113 19
counterpoise *Hydr. Eng.* 217 76
counterpoise *Docks* 226 50
counterpoise *Army* 255 78
counter stamp machine 236 19
counter tube 2 21
counter tube casing 2 20
counterweight *Overh. Irrign.* 67 37
counterweight *Optic. Instr.* 113 19
counterweight *Bldg. Site* 119 33
counterweight *Forging* 139 34
counterweight *Hydr. Eng.* 217 76
counterweight *Docks* 226 50
counterweight *Audio* 241 22
counterweight *Army* 255 78
counting, automatic ~ 74 52
counting beads 47 14
counting blocks 48 17
counting mechanism 309 83

counting out 299 42
country estate 15 94
countryside in winter 304
coupé *Carriages* 186 3
coupé *Car* 193 28
couple 267 46; 272 72; 317 17-18
couple, bridal ~ 332 15-16
coupler *Bldg. Site* 119 53
coupler *Plumb. etc.* 126 43
coupler *Music. Instr.* 326 41
couplet 321 23
coupling *Agr. Mach.* 65 61
coupling *Bldg. Site* 119 53
coupling *Railw.* 208 16; 210 2; 212 82; 214 18
coupling, front ~ 65 50
coupling, unlinked ~ 208 19
coupling bolt 202 15
coupling hook 122 64
coupling hose 208 21
coupling link 208 17
coupling screw 208 18
coupling spindle 148 58
coupon 251 17
coupon sheet 251 17
courbette 71 6
course *Weaves* 171 42
course *Rivers* 216 9
course *Ball Games* 293 79-82
course *Winter Sp.* 301 44
course, damp-proof ~ 123 4
course, first ~ 118 67
course, second ~ 118 68
course, triangular ~ 285 16
course counter 167 43
course-marking flag 301 45
course markings 289 19
courser 70 24
court dress 355 79
courtesy light 191 77
court shoe 101 29
court shoe, fabric ~ 101 54
court shoe, sling-back ~ 101 53
couter 329 48
cove 13 7
cover *Dining Rm.* 44 5
cover *Tablew. etc.* 45 3-12
cover *Optic. Instr.* 113 13
cover *Photog.* 115 11
cover *Bldg. Site* 118 22
cover *Bookbind.* 185 40
cover *Bicycle* 187 30
cover *Water* 269 56
cover, canvas ~ 255 98
cover, glass ~ *Kitch. Utensils* 40 7
cover, glass ~ *Energy Sources* 155 33
cover, hinged ~ 309 27
cover, nylon ~ 207 68
cover, porous ~ 199 21
cover, screw-in ~ 115 11
cover, screw-on ~ 83 40
cover, soundproof ~ 310 48
cover, terry ~ 49 14
cover, transparent ~ 249 27
coverall 29 23
covering 287 40
covering, felt ~ 353 20
covering, green baize ~ 277 15
covering material 184 12
cover projection 243 47
cover with filter 2 14
coving 336 10
cow 73 1
cowberry 377 23
cowboy 306 31; 319 36
cowboy boot 101 9
cowcatcher 210 34
cow corn 68 31
cowl *Blacksm.* 137 7

cowl *Warships* 258 21, 59
cowl *Church* 331 56
cowl collar 30 3
cowl neck jumper 30 2
Cowper's gland 20 75
cowshed *Farm Bldgs.* 62 7
cowshed *Livestock* 75 14
cowslip 376 8
cox 283 11
coxed single 283 18
coxless four 283 9
coxless pair 283 15
CQR anchor 286 16
Crab *Astron.* 4 56
crab *Shipbuild.* 222 14, 28
crab *Articulates* 358 1
crab *Deep Sea Fauna* 369 16
crab apple tree 58 51
crab louse 81 40
cracker 306 50
cracker, catalytic ~ 145 48
crackowe 355 42
cradle 237 13
cradle, bouncing ~ 28 2
cradle, double ~ 214 68
cradle, two-wheel ~ 214 69
cradle frame, lightweight ~ 189 17
cradle switch 237 13
craft room 260 46-85
crakeberry 377 23
cramp 119 58; 120 66
cramp iron 119 58; 121 97
crampon 300 48
crampon cable fastener 300 52
crampon strap 300 51
Crane *Astron.* 3 42
crane *Warships* 258 88
crane, floating ~ 225 10; 226 48
crane, flying ~ 232 16
crane, hammer-headed ~ 222 7
crane, overhead ~ 222 20
crane, polar ~ 154 38
crane, revolving ~ 146 3
crane, travelling ~ 147 41; 222 20
crane cable 222 13
crane framework 226 53
crane hoist, auxiliary ~ 147 61
crane hook 139 45
crane motor 157 28
crane's bill 53 1; 376 24
crane track 119 27
crane truck 270 47
crank *Agr. Mach.* 64 43
crank *Bicycle* 187 41
crank *Road Constr.* 201 18
crankcase 190 40; 242 51
crankcase scavenging 242 59
crank drive 217 53
crankshaft 166 50; 190 23; 192 29
crankshaft, counterbalanced ~ 242 50
crankshaft bearing 190 22; 192 23
crankshaft bleed 192 22
crankshaft drilling 192 22
crankshaft tributary 192 22
crankshaft wheel 166 51
crash bar 188 18
crash barrier 259 17
crash hat 290 3
crash helmet 301 13; 303 14
crate 76 30; 206 5
crater 312 44
crater, volcanic ~ 11 16
cravat 32 40
craw 73 20
crawl 282 37

crawl stroke 282 37
crayon 47 26; 338 5
crayon, wax ~ 48 11; 260 6
crayon engraving 340 14-24
cream 99 27, 46
cream, whipped ~ 97 28; 265 5
cream cake 97 21, 24
creamer 265 21
creamery butter machine 76 33
cream heater 76 13
cream jar 28 13; 99 27
cream jug 265 21
cream maturing vat 76 31
cream pie 97 24
cream puff 97 27
cream roll 97 17
cream separator 76 14
cream supply pump 76 40
cream tank 76 19
cream tube 99 33
crease *Men's Wear* 33 6
crease *Ball Games* 292 72
crease *Ethnol.* 353 44
creatures, fabulous ~ 327 1-61
creatures, mythical ~ 327 1-61
creek *Phys. Geog.* 13 8
creek *Map* 15 80
creel *Fish Farm.* 89 25
creel *Cotton Spin.* 164 28, 58
creel *Weaving* 165 25
creel, full ~ 164 41
creeper 51 5; 52 5; 53 2; 57 8
creeping foot 357 28
creese 353 44
crenate 370 46
crenel 329 18
crenellation 329 6
crepe paper 49 11
crepidoma 334 4
crescendo 321 31
crescendo roller 326 49
crescendo roller indicator 326 37
crescent *Astron.* 4 3, 7
crescent *Bakery* 97 32
crescent *Supermkt.* 99 13
Crescent *Flags* 253 19
crescent-forming machine 97 64
crescent moon 4 3, 7
crescent roll 97 32; 99 13
crescent wing 229 18
crest *Horse* 72 12, 14
crest *Dom. Anim.* 73 22
crest *Heraldry* 254 1
crest, dorsal ~ 364 21
crest, erectile ~ 359 26
Cresta tobogganing 303 22-24
crest coronet 254 12
crested lark 361 19
crested newt 364 20
cresting 305 65
crest of dam 217 59
crests 254 1, 11, 30-36
crevasse 12 50; 300 23
crew compartment 6 41; 235 16
crew cut 34 11
cricket 292 70-76
cricket bat 292 75
crimping 170 59
crimping iron 106 26
crimson clover 69 4
crinoline 355 72
crispbread 97 50
criss-cross skip 297 44
cristobalite 1 12
croaking sac 364 25

crocket 335 38
croisé 314 16
croissant 97 32; 99 13
crojack 220 26
crojack yard 220 25
cromlech 328 16
crook 324 71
crook of the arm 16 44
crop 73 20
crops, arable ~ 68
croquant 98 85
croquet 292 77-82
croquet ball 292 82
croquet mallet 292 81
croquet player 292 80
Cross Astron. 3 44
cross Plumb. etc. 126 50
cross School 260 28
cross Church 331 25
cross, ansate ~ 332 63
cross, cardinal's ~ 332 65
cross, Constantinian ~ 332 67
cross, fivefold ~ 332 72
cross, Greek ~ 332 56
cross, Latin ~ 332 55
cross, Papal ~ 332 66
cross, patriarchal ~ 332 64
cross, processional ~ 330 47
cross, quintuple ~ 332 72
cross, Russian ~ 332 57
cross, saltire ~ 332 60
cross, St. Andrew's ~ 332 60
cross, St. Anthony's ~ 332 59
cross, St. Peter's ~ 332 58
cross arm 152 37
cross arms 10 30
crossbar Goldsm. etc. 108 5
crossbar Bicycle 187 16
crossbar Ball Games 291 36
crossbar Athletics 298 14, 34
cross beam 119 57
cross bearer 331 43
cross bond, English ~ 118 65
cross botonnée 332 71
crossbrace 215 35
cross bracing wire 229 12
crossbuck 202 41
cross chain conveyor 157 22
cross conveyor 157 20
cross-country Equest. 289 17
cross-country Winter Sp. 301
  42
cross-country binding 301 15
cross-country boot 301 16
cross-country equipment 301
  14-20
cross-country gear 301 17
cross-country lorry 194 1
cross-country motorcycle 189
  16
cross-country pole 301 20
cross-country race 290 33
cross-country ski 301 14
cross-country stretch-suit
  301 43
cross-country tyre 194 4
cross-cut 134 31
cross-cut, octagonal ~ 36 53
cross-cut, oval hexagonal ~
  36 63
cross-cut, round hexagonal ~
  36 65
cross-cut, trapezium ~ 36 58
cross-cut chain saw 157 38
cross-cut chisel 140 25
cross-cut saw 120 14
crosses, Christian ~ 332 55-72
crossfall 200 57
cross fold knife 185 12
cross fold unit, third ~ 185 14
cross grasp 296 43
cross hairs 87 32
cross hairs, double ~ 115 66

cross hatch 340 54
cross head Forging 139 37
cross head Railw. 210 27
crossing 205 15
crossing, intercom-
  controlled ~ 202 47
crossing, telephone-
  controlled ~ 202 47
crossing keeper 202 42
crossing the bar 298 31
crossjack 220 26
crossjack yard 220 25
cross joint 151 50
cross lacing 29 37
crosslet 332 68
cross moline 332 69
cross of Jerusalem 332 70
cross of Lorraine 332 62
cross of the Passion 332 55
crossover 241 14
crossover, double ~ 203 49-52
crossover network 241 14
cross piece Bldg. Site 119 61
cross piece Shipbuild. 222 15
cross piece Fencing 294 42
cross rib 335 31
cross slide 149 23, 39; 150 12
cross-slide guide 174 48
cross spider 358 45
cross stitch 102 5
cross stitch, Russian ~ 102 9
cross strut 119 67
cross tie Roof 121 30
crosstie Station 205 60
crosstie, concrete ~ 202 37
crosstie, coupled ~ 202 14, 38
crosstie, steel ~ 202 36
cross total counter 242 3
crosstrees 223 37; 284 13
crosstrees, starboard ~ 286 9
cross treflée 332 71
cross vault 335 31-32
crosswalk 198 11; 268 24, 51
cross-winding the threads
  165 11
cross wire, overhead ~ 197 42
cross wires 87 32
crotchet 320 15
crotchet rest 320 23
crouch 295 6, 23
crouch start 298 4
croup 72 31
croupier 275 4
croupier, head ~ 275 6
crow 86 50, 51; 361 2
crowbar 158 32
crowberry 377 23
crowfoot 375 8
crown Man 16 1; 19 37
crown Dent. 24 28
crown Forging 139 36
crown Bridges 215 31
crown Park 272 60
crown Art 336 39
crown Hist. Cost. 355 21
crown South. Fruits 384 29
crown, gold ~ 24 28
crown, mural ~ 254 46
crown block 145 4
crown cork 93 27
crown cork bottle-opener 45
  47
crown cork closure 93 27
crown cork opener 45 47
crown of hooks 81 38
crown-of-the-field 61 6
crown of tree 370 3
crownpiece 71 10
crowns 254 37,38,42-46
crown safety platform 145 3
crown wheel Clocks 110 41
crown wheel Mach. Parts etc.
  143 93

crows 361 1-3
crow's nest 223 38
crucible, clay ~ 350 31
crucible, graphite ~ 108 10
crucible tongs 108 11; 350 32
crucifer 331 43
crucifix Gymn. 296 50
crucifix Church 332 33
crucifix, processional ~ 331
  42
crude benzene, production of
  ~ 156 41
crude benzene tank 156 42
crude benzol, production of ~
  156 41
crude benzol tank 156 42
crude oil production 145
  22-27
crude phenol tank 156 40
crude tar tank 156 32
cruet set 332 44
cruet stand 266 22
cruiser 286 5
cruiser keelboat 285 29-34
cruiser stern 285 45
cruising yacht 284 60
cruising yawl 284 61
crumb 97 3
crumhorn 322 6
crupper 71 34; 72 31
crupper-strap 71 34
crusader 329 72
crushed grape transporter 78
  16
crusher 172 5
crusher, coarse ~ 158 19
crusher, fine ~ 158 19
crusher, gyratory ~ 158 19
crusher, primary ~ 158 17
crusher, rotary ~ 158 19
crush hat 35 36
crush room 315 12-13
crust 97 4, 5
crust, earth's ~ 11 1
crust, outer ~ 11 1
crustacean 369 12, 15, 16
crustaceans 357 27-36; 358
  1-2
crusta petrosa 19 29
crutch 148 15
Crux 3 44
cryosurgery 22 63
Cryptolestes 81 27
crystal 351 29
crystal centre 351 3
crystal combinations 351
  1-26
crystal cone 77 21
crystal detector 309 23
crystal forms 351 1-26
crystallography 351
crystallometry 351 27-33
crystal plate glass 124 5
crystals 351 1-26
crystal set 309 23
crystal system 351 1-17
cub 88 42
cube Kindergart. 48 21
cube Maths. 347 30
cube Crystals 351 2, 14, 16
cube root 345 2
cube sugar 98 53
cubic crystal system 351 1-17
cubitière 329 48
cuckoo 359 30
cuckoo clock 109 31
cuckoo flower 375 11; 376 21
cuckoo pint 379 9
cucumber 57 13; 99 83
cue 277 9
cue ball, white ~ 277 11
cue rack 277 19
cue tip, leather ~ 277 10

cuff 25 16; 30 14; 32 45
cuff, fur ~ 30 62
cuff, fur-trimmed ~ 30 62
cuff, inflatable ~ 23 34
cuff, ribbed ~ 30 30
cuff link 32 46; 36 21
cuff protector 324 17
cuff slit 30 48
cuirass 329 46
cuish 329 52
cuissard 329 52
cuisse 329 52
culicid 358 16
culm Arable Crops 68 6
culm Coking 156 14
culotte 31 48; 29 59
cultivator Market Gdn. 55 21
cultivator Agr. Mach. 65 55
cultivator, three-pronged ~
  56 13
cultivator attachment 56 21
culture, bacteriological ~ 261
  29
cumulonimbus 8 17; 287 26
cumulonimbus cloud 287 26
cumulus 8 1; 287 22
cumulus cloud 287 22
cumulus congestus 8 2
cumulus humilis 8 1
cup Bicycle 187 79
cup Decid. Trees 371 5
cup, baby's ~ 28 27
cup, hemispherical ~ 10 30
cup, rust-proof ~ 122 102
cup, zinc ~ 122 102
cup bearer 329 69
cupboard 246 5
cupboard, children's ~ 47 21
cupboard, sliding-door ~ 248
  38
cupboard base unit 42 6
cupboard unit 42 7
cupboard unit, two-door ~ 46
  6
cup cymbals 324 50
cupid 272 20
cupola Iron Foundry etc. 148
  1
cupola Art 334 58
cupola, bulbous ~ 336 3
cupola furnace 148 1
cupule 59 42; 371 5; 384 52
curb 198 6; 272 25
curb bit 71 13, 52
curb chain 71 12
curbstone 198 7
curbstone broker 251 5
curbstoner 251 5
curd cheese 76 38, 45
curd cheese machine 76 38
curd cheese packet 76 45
curd cheese packing machine
  76 44
curd cheese pump 76 39
curds separator 76 41
curettage 26 52
curette 22 50; 26 52
curing floor 92 18
curing kiln 92 30
curl 34 3
curl brush 105 13
curl clip 105 14
curler Hairdresser 105 4
curler Winter Sp. 302 41
curling 302 41-43
curling broom 302 43
curling brush 302 43
curling iron 105 5; 106 31
curling stone 302 42
curling tongs 105 5; 106 31
curly kale 57 34
currant 58 12, 14; 98 9
currant bush 52 19; 58 10

current 216 9
current, cold ~ 9 29
current, three-phase ~ 153 42
current, warm ~ 9 28
current collector *Lorries etc.*
  194 41
current collector *Tram* 197 2,
  23
current collector *Railw.* 207
  24, 75; 211 2, 30
current control pedal 142 31
current meter *Railw.* 212 18
current meter *Rivers* 216 43
current rating 127 37
currents, oceanic ~ 14 30-45
current transformer 153 58
current/voltage meter 242 77
currycomb 71 54
curtail step 123 18, 42
curtain *Dining Rm.* 44 13
curtain *Railw.* 207 56
curtain *Chivalry* 329 15
curtain, iron ~ 316 24
curtain, theatrical 316 23
curtain department 271 66
curtain lace 167 29
curtain operation, types of ~
  315 1-4
curtain rail 44 15
curtain wall 329 15
curvature 346 22
curve *Sports* 305 19
curve *Maths.* 347 11, 18
curve, ballistic ~ 87 79
curve, hypsographic ~ 11
  6-12
curve, inflected ~ 347 13
curve, plane ~ 347 12
curved electrotype casting
  machine 178 13
curved plate casting machine
  178 13
curve eight 302 11
curvet 71 6
cushion 42 23; 47 8; 202 6
cushion, gilder's ~ 129 50
cushion, rubber ~ 277 16
cushion capital 335 21
cusp 20 48
customer 98 43; 99 2, 18; 111
  2; 248 18; 250 6; 266 25;
  271 16, 55
customer accounts office 271
  24
customer area 207 78
customer card index 248 24
customer service
  representative 248 17
customs 217 24
customs barrier 225 4
customs boat pendant 253 35
customs boat pennant 253 35
customs entrance 225 5
customs flags 253 35-38
customs launch 221 100
customs signal flag 253 37
cut *Metalwkr.* 140 28
cut *Fencing* 294 23
cut, antique ~ 36 49
cut, cold ~ 96 14
cut, positive ~ 340 3
cut, round ~ 36 42-43
cut, standard ~ 36 48
cut and thrust weapon 294 34
cutlery 45; 309 47
cutlery chest 266 41
cutlery drawer 39 10; 44 21
cutlery holder 266 48
cutlet 95 12
cut nippers, detachable-jaw ~
  140 67
cutoff knife and roughing
  station 184 3

cuts 36 42-86
cuts, fancy ~ 36 68-71
cutter *Paperhanger* 128 42
cutter *Joiner* 132 20
cutter *Drawing Off.* 151 15
cutter *Brickwks.* 159 15
cutter *Paperm.* 173 44
cutter *Composing Rm.* 175 33,
  51
cutter *Ship* 220 8
cutter *Warships* 258 12, 61
cutter *Films* 311 43
cutter, automatic ~ 162 19
cutter, fine ~ 133 37
cutter, rotary ~ *Forestry* 85 26
cutter, rotary ~ *Bookbind.* 184
  22
cutter, spherical ~ 108 7
cutter, universal ~ 134 28
cutter bar 64 3
cutter for metal watch straps
  109 19
cutter spindle 175 60
cutting *Map* 15 84
cutting *Synth. Fibres* 170 60
cutting *Films* 311 42-46
cutting, shooting ~ 54 24
cutting, sprouting ~ 54 24
cutting attachment 141 19
cutting bench 117 96; 311 42
cutting blade 183 19
cutting cylinder *Gdn. Tools*
  56 35
cutting cylinder *Text. Finish.*
  168 44
cutting drum 64 34
cutting edge 45 57; 66 14; 85
  2
cutting edge, cemented
  carbide ~ 149 48, 50
cutting edge, razor's ~ 106 40
cutting head 175 51
cutting-in brush 129 20
cutting machine *Furrier* 131 5
cutting machine *Gas Weld.*
  141 34
cutting machine *Synth. Fibres*
  169 30
cutting machine, universal ~
  141 36
cutting nozzle 141 38
cutting-off machine 125 16
cutting pliers 127 51
cutting point 136 35
cutting room 310 3
cutting scale, illuminated ~
  185 6
cutting shears 103 3
cutting table *Dressm.* 103 4
cutting table *Cine Film* 117 96
cutting table *Composing Rm.*
  175 52
cutting table *Films* 311 42
cutting template 103 13
cutting tip, adjustable ~ 149
  45, 46
cutting tip, cemented carbide
  ~ 149 50
cutting unit *Gdn. Tools* 56 33,
  41
cutting unit *Agr. Mach.* 64 8
cuttlefish 357 37; 369 4
cuttling device 168 35
cutup 326 25
cutwater 215 56
cutworm 80 44
cyan filter adjustment 116 45
cyclamen 53 5
cycle 187 1
cycle, motor-paced ~ 290 15
cycle racing 290 1-23

cycle serial number 187 51
cycle track 290 1
cycling track 290 1
cyclohexanol, pure ~ 170 18
cyclohexanol, raw ~ 170 16
cyclohexanone 170 20
cyclohexanoxime 170 22
cyclone 4 38; 9 5
cyclone heat exchanger 160 6
cyclorama 310 12; 316 9
cyclotron 2 49
Cygnus 3 23
cylinder *Cooper* 130 27
cylinder *Metalwkr.* 140 45
cylinder *Cotton Spin.* 163 43
cylinder *Offset Print.* 180 79
cylinder *Railw.* 210 32
cylinder *Swim.* 279 19
cylinder *Graphic Art* 340 40
cylinder *Chem.* 350 45
cylinder, developed ~ 182 13
cylinder, grooved ~ 165 10
cylinder, high-pressure ~ 153
  23
cylinder, hydraulic ~ 64 8;
  194 26
cylinder, low-pressure ~ 153
  25
cylinder, medium-pressure ~
  153 24
cylinder, perforated ~ 163 21
cylinder, right ~ 347 38
cylinder, steel ~ 180 54
cylinder arm 177 68
cylinder crankcase 190 19
cylinder diameter 167 16
cylinder head 190 45; 242 47
cylinder head gasket 190 48
cylinder lock 140 44
cylinder oil 145 63
cylinder-processing machine
  182 9
cylinder temperature gauge
  230 9
cylinder trimmer 85 25
cylinder trolley 141 23
cylinder undercasing 163 55
cyma 334 11, 19
cymatium 334 19
cymbal 324 51
cymbal holder 324 52
cymbals 323 50
cymbal stand 324 52
cyme 370 70; 374 36
cyme, curled ~ 370 77
cyme, helicoid ~ 370 76
cyme, scorpioid ~ 370 77
cypress 372 58
cythara 322 15

D

dabber 340 22
dachshund 70 39
dactyloscopy 264 28
dado, oil-painted ~ 129 15
daemon 327 58
da gamba violin 323 16
dagger, bronze ~ 328 22
dagger, hafted ~ 328 22
dagger, Malayan ~ 353 44
dahlia 51 20; 60 23
dairy 76 1-48
dairy cow 62 34; 75 17
dairy cow shed 75 14
dairy plant 76 1-48
dairy product 99 43
daisy 376 1
dam *Map* 15 69
dam *Game* 88 1
dam *Energy Sources* 155 38
dam *Hydr. Eng.* 217 57-64

damp course 123 4
dampener 180 23, 52, 61
dampening roller 180 23, 52,
  61
dampening unit 180 39, 61
damper *Offset Print.* 180 23,
  52, 61
damper *Car* 191 26; 192 69
damper *Music. Instr.* 322 54;
  325 37
damper, electromagnetic ~ 11
  40
damper block 325 37
damper door 210 6
damper lifter 325 38
damper-lifting lever 325 23
damper pedal 325 8
damper rest rail 325 39
damping roller 180 23, 52, 61
damping unit 180 39, 61
dam sill 217 79
dance band 306 2
dance band instruments 324
  47-78
dance costume 354 36
dance drum 354 14
dance floor 317 16
dance floor lighting 317 14
dancer 317 17, 18
dancer, principal ~ 314 28
dancing girl, Hindu ~ 306 25
dancing snake 353 48
dancing stick 354 37
dandelion 51 34; 61 13
dandy 306 33
dandy brush 71 55
Danebrog 253 17
Danforth anchor 286 18
danger zone 2 50
Dan grade 299 15
Danish pastry 97 30
Dannebrog 253 17
daphne 377 10
dark beer 93 26
darkroom equipment 116
  1-60
darkroom lamp 116 21
dark slide 114 64
darning stitch 102 17
dart 352 28
dart, barbed ~ 319 22
dart point 352 29
das 366 24
dash 342 23
dashboard *Carriages* 186 6
dashboard *Car* 191 57-90
dashboard *Tram* 197 29
dashboard lighting 197 30
dassie 366 24
data, technical ~ 151 32
data carrier 237 59, 62-64
data centre 248 43
data collection station,
  central ~ 242 20
data display terminal 238 2,
  11; 248 16, 44
data output 112 44
data print-out 195 7
data processor 237 60
data recording back 115 67
data service 237 58
data storage unit 242 32
data terminal 242 19
data transmission 237 58
data transmission service 237
  41
date 384 9
date and second button 110 4
date indicator display 237 39
date kernel 384 10
date of issue 250 14
date of maturity 250 16
date of publication 342 42

date palm 384 1
date sheet 247 33
date stamp postmark 236 57
daughter boat 228 17
davit 221 78, 101; 223 20; 258 13, 83, 88
day cream 99 27
dayfly 358 6
daylight film magazine 311 7
daylight-loading tank 116 5
day nursery 48
dead axle 210 35
deadly nightshade 379 7
dead man's handle 211 21; 212 13
deadwood 285 47
de-aerator 152 16
de-airing pug mill 161 7
de-airing pug press 161 7
dealer 275 3
death notice 342 68
death's-head hawkmoth 365 9
death's-head moth 365 9
death spiral 302 5
debarking 85 23
debenture bond 251 11-19
debenzoling 156 27
decade 332 32
decatizing cylinder, perforated ~ 168 50
decay, spontaneous ~ 1 28
Decca navigation system 224 39
decimal, recurring ~ 344 21, 22
decimal fraction, proper ~ 344 20
decimal key 247 19
decimal place 344 20
decimal point 344 20
deck Rowing 283 57
deck Films 311 10
deck, lower ~ Offshore Drill. 146 35
deck, lower ~ Lorries etc. 194 37
deck, lower ~ Space 235 28
deck, main ~ Offshore Drill. 146 37
deck, main ~ Ship 221 80; 223 32-42
deck, main ~ Warships 258 9
deck, middle ~ 146 36
deck, orthotropic ~ 215 2
deck, top ~ 146 37
deck, upper ~ Lorries etc. 194 38
deck, upper ~ Railw. 213 36
deck, woven ~ 215 18
deck beam 222 57
deck bucket 221 113
deck-chair 37 47; 51 2; 221 111; 274 13
deck crane 221 5, 61
deck crane Warships 259 10
decker 172 24, 42, 44, 48, 62
deck hand 221 112
deckhouse 221 6, 39; 223 34; 258 72
decking, woven ~ 215 18
deck plan 259 12-20
deck plating 222 56
deck slab 215 6
deck space 223 28
deck tennis 280 31
declination axis 113 5, 17
declination bearing 113 6
declination gear 113 4
decoder 110 18
décolletage 306 24
decometer 279 17
decoration, Greek ~ 334 38-43

decoration, Romanesque ~ 335 14-16
decorative glass worker 124 8
decorative pieces 35 4
decoy bird 86 48
decrescendo 321 32
dedication, handwritten ~ 185 50
dedusting fan 83 53
dedusting screen 83 56
deep freeze 96 21; 98 74; 99 57
deep-sea cable 237 56
deep-sea fauna 369
deep-sea fishing 90 1-23
deep-sea floor 11 10
deep-sea medusa 369 5
deep-sea salvage tug 258 96
deep-sea trench 11 12
deep tank 223 78
deep-water start 286 46
deer, antlerless ~ 88 1
deer fence 84 7
deer stalking 86 1-8
defence area 293 66
defender Ball Games 292 4
defender Fencing 294 6
defending fencer 294 6
deflection system 240 23
deflector piston 242 56
defroster vent 191 42; 192 64
dégagé 314 11, 12
degree 345 2
degree scale 313 14
dehydrogenation 170 19
delayed-action release 115 15
delay indicator 205 24
delicatessen shop 98 1-87
deliveries 305 17-20
delivery 184 5; 185 23, 35
delivery blower 181 33
delivery cylinder 180 42, 65
delivery hose 270 31
delivery mechanism Offset Print. 180 45
delivery mechanism Post 236 49
delivery pile 180 44; 181 9
delivery pipe Docks 226 34
delivery pipe Water 269 16, 49, 52
delivery pouch 236 54
delivery reel 173 28
delivery roller 164 59
delivery table 181 31; 184 14, 19
delivery tray 185 15
delivery tube 65 77
delivery unit 180 45
delivery valve 67 9
delphinium 60 13
delta 13 1
delta connection 153 21
delta wing 229 19
deltoid 346 38
demand regulator, two-tube ~ 279 20
demesne 15 94
demi-goat 254 32
demigod 327 40
demijohn 206 13
demi-man 254 11
demi-mondaine 306 37
demi-monde 306 37
demi-rep 306 37
demisemiquaver 320 18
demisemiquaver rest 320 26
demi-woman 254 11
demonstration bench 261 3
demonstration equipment 242 45-84
demonstration model 242 45, 55

demonstrator 262 6
den 273 56
Deneb 3 23
denims 31 60; 33 22
denomination Money 252 32
denomination Maths. 344 19
denominator 344 15
dental surgeon 24 1
dentate 370 47
dent corn 68 31
dentil 334 14
dentine 19 31
denting draft 171 6
dentist 24 1
denture 24 25
department manager 271 60
department store 268 41; 271
departure building 233 15
'departures' 233 25
departure schedule 204 20
departure time indicator 205 23
departure timetable 204 20
deposit counter 236 25
deposit slip 236 27
depot 144 17
depression 9 5
depth adjustment 64 88; 65 60; 157 45
depth-charge thrower 258 34
depth gauge D.I.Y. 134 47
depth gauge Swim. 279 15
depth gauge attachment rule 149 68
depth of focus 11 34
depth reading 224 67
depth recorder 224 24
depth recording 224 67
depth scale 224 66
depth wheel 65 59, 63
derailment guard 214 75
derivative 345 13
derrick Phys. Geog. 12 33
derrick Offshore Drill. 146 12
derrick Ship 221 67
derrick boom 221 26, 59; 223 36
derrick boom, heavy-lift ~ 221 25, 62
derrick mast 221 60
descant viol 322 23
descent stage 6 28-36
desert monitor 364 31
desert zone 9 54
desiccator 350 51
desiccator insert 350 54
design 151 16
design, chequered ~ 335 14
design, computer-generated ~ 248 19
design, imbricated ~ 335 15
design, knitted ~ 30 37
design, modular ~ 240 1
design, quilted ~ 30 31
design for costume 315 39
designs, decorative ~ 334 38-43; 335 14-16
desk 46 22; 246 2
desk, cashier's ~ 250 1
desk, clerical assistant's ~ 248 11
desk, double ~ 260 2
desk, instructor's ~ 242 2
desk, stage manager's ~ 316 29
desk, teacher's ~ 260 22
desk chair 46 27
desk diary 247 32
desk drawer 46 26; 246 4
desk lamp 246 11
desk mat 46 23; 246 6; 260 25
desk set 246 9

desk top 246 3
desk unit 46 21
dessert bowl 45 6
dessert plate 45 6
dessert spoon 45 61, 66
destination board 205 21, 38
destination indicator 205 22
destination sign 197 20
destroyer 258 1, 38
desulfurization see desulphurization
desulfurizing see desulphurizing
desulphurization 156 28
desulphurizing 169 20
desulphurizing plant 145 46, 68
detaching roller 163 71
detangling brush 105 2
detective 264 33
detector indicator unit 224 34
detonator cap 87 58
detritus 12 45
deutero-pyramid 351 20
Deutschmark 252 7
Devanagari 341 9
developer 27 33
developer, first ~ 116 10
developing dish 116 25
developing dish, semi-automatic ~ 116 56
developing dish, thermostatically controlled ~ 116 56
developing solution 116 9
developing spiral 116 2
developing tank Photog. 116 1, 20
developing tank Photograv. 182 11
developing tank, multi-unit ~ 116 3
developing tank thermometer 116 8
developing tray 116 25
deviation mirror 113 11
device 252 12
devil 306 14
devil's tail 340 34
devil's tobacco pouch 381 20
devil's wheel 308 46
de-waxing 145 50
dew claw 88 23, 57
dewlap 73 24
dexter 254 18,20,22
D flat major 320 67
diabetics file 22 26
diacritics 342 30-35
diadem 355 21
diadem, pearl ~ 355 16
diaeresis 342 34
diagnostic test bay 195 1-23
diagonal 346 33
diagram Drawing Off. 151 11
diagram School 260 34
diagram Univ. 262 8
dial 204 5; 237 10; 245 16
dial finger plate 237 11
dial finger stop 237 12
dialling unit 237 67
dial wind-up plate 237 11
diameter 346 45
diamond Composing Rm. 175 21
diamond Audio 241 26
diamond Crystals 351 10, 13
diamonds 276 41
diaper, disposable ~ 28 22
diaphragm Meteorol. Instr. 10 27
diaphragm Man 20 9, 26
diaphragm Dent. 24 33
diaphragm Inf. Tech. 242 82

diaphragm, bladed ~ 2 33
diaphragm chest 326 12-14
diaphragm spring 190 29
diathermy unit 23 22
diazo plate 179 32, 34
dibber 54 7; 56 1
dibble 54 7; 56 1
dice 276 29, 31
dice cup 47 42; 276 30
dicing 276 29
dictating machine 22 27; 209 30; 246 17; 248 34
dictating machine, pocket-sized ~ 246 32
dictionary 262 17
dictionary, medical ~ 22 22
didelphid 366 2
Didone 342 6
die Metalwkr. 140 32
die Brickwks. 159 13
die, lower ~ 252 41
die, steel ~ 175 36
die, upper ~ 252 40
die and stock 140 32
die blank 175 35
die block, lower ~ 139 14, 39
die block, upper ~ 139 13, 38
die case 174 42, 46
die head 143 57
diesel-electric drive 223 68-74; 259 75
diesel engine Energy Sources 155 5
diesel engine Intern. Combust. Eng. 190 4
diesel engine Railw. 211 47; 212 25, 51
diesel engine Ship 223 73
diesel engine, auxiliary ~ 209 19
diesel engine, eight-cylinder ~ 212 73
diesel engine, five-cylinder in-line ~ 190 3
diesel engine, four-cylinder ~ 65 44
diesel engine, six-cylinder ~ Agr. Mach. 64 28
diesel engine, six-cylinder ~ Railw. 209 23
diesel engine, underfloor ~ 209 23
diesel fuel 146 26
diesel generator 259 94
diesel generator unit 209 5
diesel-hydraulic locomotive 212 1, 24, 47; 213 1
diesel locomotive 212 1, 68
diesel locomotive, single-engine ~ 208 1
diesel locomotives 212 1-84
diesel oil 145 56
diesel railcar 208 13; 211 41
diesel tank 146 13
diesel trainset 209 1
die stock 125 27
diet meal 266 62
difference 344 24
differential Agr. Mach. 65 32
differential Intern. Combust. Eng. 190 75
differential Maths. 345 13, 14
differential gear 65 32; 190 75
differential sign 345 13
diffuser Photog. 114 60
diffuser Paperm. 172 11, 13
diffuser Space 234 15
diffusing screen 310 38
digester 172 7
digger 64 59
digger, toy ~ 273 65
digging bucket 200 5

digging bucket arm 200 4
digging bucket teeth 200 6
digging fork 66 22
Digitalis 379 2
digital readout Clocks 110 2
digital readout Optic. Instr. 112 47
digitate 370 39
digitated 370 39
digitus I 19 52, 64
digitus II 19 53, 65
digitus III 19 54, 66
digitus IV 19 55, 67
digitus V 19 56, 68
digitus anularis 19 67
digitus medius 19 66
digitus minimus 19 56, 68
dike 216 34, 39
dike, main ~ 216 32
dike batter 216 40
dike ramp 216 47
dikereeve 216 46
dike slope 216 40
diligence 186 39
dimension line 151 25
diminished triad 321 3
diminuendo 321 32
dimmer switch 127 17
dimple 16 16
dinar 252 28
diner 207 22-32
dinghy, inflatable ~ 228 18; 258 82; 278 14; 279 27
dining area 266 73
dining car 207 22-32
dining car kitchen 207 33
dining chair 44 10
dining compartment 207 32, 77
dining room 44; 223 44; 267 20
dining set 42 33-34; 44 1-11
dining table 42 33; 44 1; 45 1; 46 34
dinner dress 33 7
dinner plate 39 42; 44 7; 45 4
dinner service 44 33
dinner set 44 33
diopter control ring 117 15
dioptric adjustment ring 117 15
dip, true ~ 12 3
diploma 106 42
dipole antenna 230 65
dipper stick 200 4
dipstick 190 47
dipterans 358 16-20
dipyramid, tetragonal ~ 351 18
direct current motor 150 9
direction, negative ~ 347 7
direction, positive ~ 347 6
directional antenna Moon L. 6 4, 44
directional antenna Post 237 51, 52
directional antenna assembly 234 64
directional gyro 230 13
direction finder, automatic ~ 230 5
direction finder antenna 223 5
director 310 40; 316 40
director of photography 310 44
directory enquiries 237 33
directory holder 236 11
direct-vision frame finder 117 57
dirndl 31 26
dirndl, girl's ~ 29 36
dirndl apron 31 31

dirndl blouse 31 29
dirndl dress 31 26
dirndl necklace 31 28
disc Flat 46 15
disc Agr. Mach. 65 83
disc Disco 317 24
disc, adhesive ~ 364 26
disc, carborundum ~ 24 35
disc, facial ~ 362 18
disc, germinal ~ 74 65
disc, insertable ~ 115 96
disc, metal ~ 309 15
disc, plain ~ 65 84
disc, revolving ~ 275 31
disc, serrated-edge ~ 65 85
disc, silver ~ 10 24
disc, solar ~ 4 36
disc barbell 299 3
disc brake Intern. Combust. Eng. 190 74
disc brake Car 191 17-18; 192 48-55
disc brake Railw. 208 4
disc brake, front ~ 189 32
disc brake calliper 189 33
disc clutch 139 21
disc coulter drive 64 68
disc fibula 328 30
disc floret 375 32
discharge, pneumatic ~ 213 18
discharge connection valve 213 21
discharge conveyor 64 83
discharge door 139 2; 213 25
discharge flap 213 25
discharge flume 91 41
discharge opening Forging 139 2
discharge opening Sawmill 157 56
discharge opening Hydr. Eng. 217 56
discharge pipe 64 37
discharge structure 217 44
discharging chute 147 39
discharging position 147 58
disc jockey 317 25
discomedusa 357 14
discotheque 317
disc pack 176 34
disc slot 243 38
disc stack 176 34
disc store 244 1
discussion tube arrangement 112 22
disc wheel 191 14
disgorger 89 40
disguise 306 6-48, 33
dish 332 50
dish, three-compartment ~ 40 8
dish drainer 39 33
dish rack 39 41
dish thermometer 116 13
dishwasher 39 40
dishwashing machine 39 40
disinfectant powder 83 60
disintegrator 172 5
disk see disc
dislocation 11 50
dispenser 22 64
displacement 11 50
displacement boats 286 32-37
display 47 30; 271 67
display, digital ~ Clocks 110 20
display, digital ~ Optic. Instr. 112 47
display, individual ~ 242 3
display, visual ~ Railw. 211 34
display, visual ~ Broadcast. 238 2, 43

display cabinet 44 26; 46 9
display cabinet unit 42 5
display case 271 13
display counter 99 10
display pipes 326 1-3
display window, indoor ~ 271 13
dissecting bench 261 22
dissolver 172 37
dissolving tank 172 37
distance 346 5
distance-measuring instrument 112 70
distance piece Bees 77 41
distance piece Bldg. Site 119 81
distance scale 115 4
distance setting 114 28; 117 3
distance-setting ring 114 39; 115 8
distant signal identification plate 203 24
distillation 170 17
distillation, gradual ~ 170 4
distillation apparatus 350 46
distillation column 145 37, 49
distillation flask 350 47, 50
distillation plant 145 66
distillation product, heavy ~ 145 40
distillation product, light ~ 145 39
distilling apparatus 350 46
distilling flask 350 47, 50
distributary 13 2
distributing machine 236 38
distributing mechanism 174 20
distributing pipe 126 8
distributing roller 181 7, 62; 249 51
distribution board 157 67
distribution main 269 22
distribution pipe, main ~ 38 71
distribution steel 119 69
distributor Composing Rm. 174 20
distributor Letterpress 181 7, 62
distributor Intern. Combust. Eng. 190 9, 27
distributor Office 249 51
distributor cylinder 62 23
distributor roller 181 7, 62
distributor shaft 190 27
distributor unit 62 22
district boundary 15 103
district heating main 198 28
ditch 329 33, 37
ditch fern 377 16
divan, double ~ 43 4-13
diver 282 5
dividend 344 26
dividend coupon 251 18
dividend coupon sheet 251 17
dividend warrant 251 18
divider Bakery 97 56
divider and rounder 97 63
dividing 344 26
dividing breeching 270 32
diving 282 38
diving, acrobatic ~ 282 40-45
diving, competitive ~ 282 40-45
diving, fancy ~ 282 40-45
diving apparatus 279 12, 19; 282 5-10
diving board 282 9
diving boards 282 5-10
diving goggles 280 38

diving mask 279 10
diving plane, aft ~ 259 95
diving platform 282 6
diving pool 282 11
division Navig. 224 89
division School 260 39
division sign 344 26
division sign 344 26
divisor 344 26
D major 320 57
D minor 320 63
Dobermann terrier 70 27
dock Horse 72 34
dock Shipbuild. 222 36-43
dock, emptied (pumped-out) ~ 222 43
dock, floating ~ Shipbuild. 222 34-43, 41
dock, floating ~ Docks 225 16
dock area 225 1
dock basin 222 36
dock bottom 222 31
dock crane 222 34
dock floor 222 31
dock gate 222 32
docking a ship 222 41-43
docking hatch 6 45
docking target recess 6 47
docks 225; 226
dockside crane 222 34
dock structure 222 37-38
dockyard 222 1-43
doctor 22; 23
'doctor' 233 44
doctor blade 168 44
document 245 19
document, confidential ~ 246 25
document file 245 6; 247 37; 248 5
document glass 249 09
dodecahedron, pentagonal ~ 351 8
dodecahedron, rhombic ~ 351 7
dodgem 308 62
dodgem car 308 63
dodger 223 17
doe Dom. Anim. 73 18
doe Game 88 40, 59
doe, barren ~ 88 34
doe, young ~ 88 39
doffer 163 42
doffer comb, vibrating ~ 163 39
dog Dom. Anim. 73 16
dog Game 88 42
dog Bldg. Site 119 58
dog Roof 121 97
dog Intern. Combust. Eng. 190 39
dog, three-headed ~ 327 30
dog, toy ~ 47 7, 41
dog biscuit 99 37
dog bowl 70 32
dog brush 70 28
dogcart 186 18
dog comb 70 29
dog flange 190 39
dog food 99 36
dog lead 70 30
dog rose 373 26
dogs Dog 70
dogs Forging 139 33
dog sled 353 3
dog sledge 353 3
dog's outfit 70 28-31
Dog Star 3 14
dog tick 358 44
do-it-yourself 134
do-it-yourself enthusiast 134 61
do-it-yourself work 134 1-34

doldrums 9 46
dolina 13 71
doll 309 11
doll, sleeping ~ 47 11
doll, walking ~ 273 63
dollar 252 33
doll's pram 47 10; 48 24
dolly Flea Market 309 68
dolly Films 310 49
dolmen 328 16
dolphin 225 12
dolphin butterfly stroke 282 35
dome Brew. 92 45
dome Art 337 21
dome, high ~ 36 79
dome, imperial ~ 121 25
dome, main ~ 334 72
dome, revolving ~ 5 12
dome cover 38 48
dome shutter 5 14
dome system 334 72-73
domiciliation 250 22
dominant seventh chord 321 5
domino Games 276 34
domino Carnival 306 13, 15
dominoes 276 33
domino panel 203 66
donjon 329 4
donkey 73 3
door Farm Bldgs. 62 17
door Carriages 186 11
door Tram 197 32
door Railw. 207 20, 22
door, bottom ~ 210 7
door, double ~ Tram 197 14
door, double ~ Railw. 208 7
door, double ~ Hotel 267 27
door, driver's ~ 193 2
door, folding ~ Tram 197 14
door, folding ~ Railw. 207 39; 208 7
door, front ~ Dwellings 37 65
door, front ~ Hall 41 25
door, front ~ Household 50 30
door, front ~ Floor etc. Constr. 123 24
door, front ~ Car 193 5
door, glass ~ 44 18
door, hinged ~ 194 12
door, ledged ~ 37 34
door, main ~ Church 331 16
door, main ~ Art 335 24
door, outer ~ 259 78
door, outward-opening ~ 194 35
door, rear ~ Car 193 3, 6, 20
door, rear ~ Lorries etc. 194 11
door, revolving ~ 213 9
door, side ~ Lorries etc. 194 8, 12
door, side ~ Railw. 213 9
door, sliding ~ Farm Bldgs. 62 16
door, sliding ~ Brew. 92 47
door, sliding ~ Lorries etc. 194 8
door, sliding ~ Railw. 213 15
door, vertical-lift ~ 139 51
doorbell 127 2
door frame 41 26
door handle Hall 41 28
door handle Carriages 186 12
door handle Car 191 5
door-lifting mechanism 139 55
door lock Hall 41 27
door lock Metalwkr. 140 36-43
door lock Car 191 6
doorman 267 1; 271 44

dormer 37 56; 38 7; 121 6; 329 11; 336 4
dormer window 37 56; 38 7; 121 6; 329 11; 336 4
dormer window, hipped ~ 121 13
dorsum manus 19 83
dorsum of the foot 19 61
dorsum of the hand 19 83
dorsum pedis 19 61
dosimeter 2 8-23
dosing mechanism 83 60
dosser 78 15
dosser carrier 78 14
dot 178 39
dot, French ~ 102 13
dot ball, white ~ 277 13
double 276 35
double backward somersault 282 42
double bass 323 23
double bassoon 323 28
double bass viol 322 23; 323 23
double bull capital 333 28
double bull column 333 23
double edger 157 57
double flat 320 53
double-lap roofing 122 2
double leg circle 296 54
double leg lock 299 11
double mill 276 25
double overarm stroke 282 37
doubles 293 2-3
doubles, mixed ~ 293 49
double sharp 320 51
doubles match 293 2-3
doubles sideline 293 2-3
doublet, padded ~ 355 30, 45
doublet, paned ~ 355 33
doublet, quilted ~ 355 45
doublet, short ~ 355 41, 45
doublet, slashed ~ 355 33
doublet, stuffed ~ 355 30
double-three 302 14
double unit for black 180 12-13
double unit for cyan 180 8-9
double unit for magenta 180 10-11
double unit for yellow 180 6-7
double-whole note 320 12
doubling frame 164 57
doubling of slivers 164 5
dough mixer 97 55, 59
doughnut 97 29
douze dernier 275 27
douze milieu 275 26
douze premier 275 25
dovetail halving 121 89
dowel hole 120 22, 23
dowel hole borer 133 6
dowel hole boring machine 133 6
down-draught carburettor 192 1-15
down-gate 148 21
downhill racing 301 32
downhill racing pole 301 25
downhill racing position 301 33
downhill ski 301 34
downpipe 37 13; 38 10; 122 29; 147 63
downspout 37 13; 38 10
downtake 147 13
down-town 268
down tube 187 17
downy mildew 80 20, 21
drachma 252 39
Draco 3 32
draff 92 50

draft Weaves 171 4, 11, 13, 19, 21, 27
draft Bank 250 12
draft see draught
draft, rough ~ 338 4
draft board 168 7
draft clause 250 17
drafting 164 12, 13
drafting machine 151 2
drafting roller 164 21, 22, 29
draft mark 222 73
drag Iron Foundry etc. 148 20
drag Equest. 289 48
drag chute housing 257 24
drag hook Horse 71 14
drag hook Fire Brig. 270 49
drag hunt 289 41-49
drag lift 214 15
Dragon Astron. 3 32
dragon Sailing 284 57
dragon Fabul. Creat. 327 1, 50
dragon, seven-headed ~ 327 50
dragon beam 120 42
dragon figurehead 218 16
dragonfly 358 3
dragon piece 120 42
dragon ship 218 13-17
drain Street Sect. 198 23
drain Rivers 216 37
drain Town 268 8
drainage 144 46
drainage basin 12 24
drainage ditch Road Constr. 200 63
drainage ditch Rivers 216 33
drainage layer 199 25
drainage sluice 216 34
drainage tube 26 47
drain cock 178 34
drain cover 198 24
drain pipe 198 25; 199 26
drain plug 284 36
drake 73 35
drapery 338 33
draught beam 65 18
draughtboard 276 17
draught mark 222 73
draughts 276 17-19
draughtsman 276 18, 19
drawbar 64 47, 61; 65 18
drawbar coupling Agr. Mach. 65 30
drawbar coupling Camping 278 55
drawbar frame 65 26
drawbar support 64 62
drawbar trailer 194 22
drawbench 108 2
drawbridge 329 25
draw cord 29 67
draw curtain 315 1
drawee 250 20
drawer Dent. 24 17
drawer Hall 41 9
drawer Flat 46 11
drawer Bedrm. 43 18
drawer Bathrm. etc. 49 34
drawer Bank 250 21
draw frame 164 1
draw frame, four-roller ~ 164 9
draw frame, simple ~ 164 9
draw frame cover 164 7
draw hoe 66 1
draw hook 270 49
drawing Drawing Off. 151 16
drawing Synth. Fibres 170 55
drawing, final ~ 170 47
drawing, preliminary ~ 170 45
drawing, rolled ~ 151 10
drawing bench 108 2

drawing board 151 1
drawing board adjustment 151 5
drawing easel 338 34
drawing floor 120 11
drawing head 151 4
drawing ink cartridge 151 36
drawing ink container 151 63
drawing-in roller 168 12
drawing knife 120 79
drawing machine 162 7
drawing office 151
drawing pen, tubular ~ 151 37, 38
drawing roll 162 11
drawing table 151 6
draw-in wire 127 30
drawknife 120 79
draw-off tap 126 34
drawshave 120 79
draw stop 325 44; 326 6
drawstring 29 64, 67
drawstring waist 31 66
draw well 329 3
draw wire 127 30
draw works 145 11
dredger 216 56; 226 41
dredger, hydraulic ~ 216 59
dredger bucket 226 44
dredging bucket 216 58
dredging machine, floating 216 56
dress 31 9
dress, button-through ~ 30 10
dress, jersey ~ 29 28
dress, knitted ~ 29 28; 30 33
dress, off-the-peg ~ 271 29
dress, peasant-style ~ 30 27
dress, ready-made ~ 271 29
dress, ready-to-wear ~ 271 29
dress, shirt-waister ~ 30 10
dress, two-piece ~ 30 33; 31 11
dress, wrap-around ~ 30 25
dress, wrapover ~ 30 25
dressage 289 1-7
dressage arena 289 1
dress and jacket combination 31 6
dress circle 315 18
dress form 103 6
dress guard 104 14
dressing, sterile gauze ~ 21 6
dressing axe 158 38
dressing comb 105 15; 106 28
dressing floor 92 8
dressing gown 29 24; 32 35
dressing machine 83 52
dressing material 26 34
dressing room 315 43-52
dressing room mirror 315 43
dressing stool 43 24
dressing table 43 25; 105 19
dressing-table mirror 43 29
dressmaker 103 1
dress shirt 32 43
dress sword 355 63
dribble 291 52
drier Synth. Fibres 170 38
drier Paperm. 173 22
drier Offset Print. 180 14, 27
drier, swivel-mounted ~ 105 25
drier felt 173 23
driers 50 23-34
drift net fishing 90 1-10
drill Dent. 24 6, 17
drill Agr. Mach. 65 74
drill Goldsm. etc. 108 4
drill Turner 135 22
drill, electric ~ 56 19; 120 21; 134 16, 50-55
driller 158 9

drilling bit 145 21
drilling cable 145 7
drilling line 145 7
drilling machine, electric ~ 108 6
drilling machine, radial-arm ~ 150 18
drilling machine, suspended ~ 108 6
drilling pipe 145 19
drilling platform 146 1-37; 221 66
drilling rig 145 1; 146 1-39
drilling vessel, semisubmersible ~ 221 64
drill pipe 145 6
drill spindle 150 23
drill stand 134 54
drill tower 270 3
drink, soft ~ 96 30
drinker, mechanical ~ 74 16
drinking bowl, mechanical ~ 74 16
drinking fountain 205 33
drinking straw 266 46
drinking trough 74 6
drinking water carrier 278 32
drinking water supply 269 1-66
drinking water tank 146 16
drinks cabinet 246 29
drinks cupboard 42 20
drinks gondola 99 71
drinks shelf 266 59
drinks stall 308 3
drip, intravenous ~ 25 13; 26 9
drip fuel line 190 53
drip ring 283 40
dripstone 13 80
drip tray 266 2
drive Composing Rm. 175 37
drive Railw. 214 2
drive, clockwork ~ 10 14
drive, conventional ~ 259 75
drive, crystal-controlled ~ 310 19, 24
drive, fluid ~ 65 37
drive, hydraulic ~ 139 9, 15
drive, main ~ 214 63
drive belt 103 10
drive-belt gear 109 21
drive chain 188 17
drive clutch 177 54
drive connection 67 19
drive gearbox 163 57; 168 10, 32
drive mechanism 110 43
drive motor Poultry Farm 74 37
drive motor Dressm. 103 9
drive motor Forging 139 25
drive motor Mach. Tools 150 9
drive motor Cotton Spin. 163 12, 23, 49
drive motor Text. Finish. 168 55
drive motor Composing Rm. 175 61
drive motor Electrotyp. etc. 178 12, 28
drive motor Offset Platem. 179 11
drive motor Hydr. Eng. 217 47
drive pulley, fast-and-loose ~ 163 50
drive pulley, main ~ 163 50
driver Carriages 186 32
driver Bicycle 187 72
driver Serv. Stat. 196 8
driver Ship 219 30

driver Equest. 289 26
driver Ball Games 293 91
driver plate 149 55
driver's brake valve 210 53; 211 22; 212 11
driver's position Agr. Mach. 64 33
driver's position Tram 197 25
drive shaft Car 192 30
drive shaft Hydr. Eng. 217 49
drive unit Shoem. 100 8
drive unit Photomech. Reprod. 177 56
drive unit, central ~ 238 57
drive well 269 60
drive wheel Agr. Mach. 65 80
drive wheel Shoem. 100 8
drive wheel Text. Finish. 168 4
drive wheel Offset Print. 180 66
drive wheel Army 255 50
drive wheel unit 209 3
driving 86 34-39
driving axle 210 37
driving axle gearing 64 30
driving barrel 187 73
driving cylinder 165 32
driving drum 165 32, 35
driving gear Cotton Spin. 163 57
driving gear Railw. 210 2-37
driving guide rail 226 39
driving pinion 214 8
driving plate Turner 135 9
driving plate Mach. Tools 149 55
driving shaft 163 24
driving trailer car 211 62
driving unit 209 2
driving wheel tyre 64 31
drizzle 9 33
drone Bees 77 5
drone Music. Instr. 322 11
drone cell 77 36
drone pipe 322 11
drone string 322 31
droop flap 229 54
droop nose 231 16
drop 98 76
drop, plain ~ 36 85
drop board 267 5
drop cloth 316 11
drop compass 151 59
drop forging 139
drop grate 210 5
drop grate lever 210 40
drop hammer, air-lift ~ 139 24
drop hammer, short-stroke ~ 139 11
drop net 89 29
drop pin 165 37
droppings removal 74 23-27
dropping worm 149 18
drop pin roller 165 39
drop windscreen 255 97
drop windshield 255 97
drop wire 166 34
drop worm 149 18
drove 158 37
drove chisel 158 37
'druggist' 233 45
drum Meteorol. Instr. 10 5, 16, 20
drum Household 50 29
drum Agr. Mach. 64 12
drum Painter 129 9
drum Cooper 130 13
drum Nucl. Energy 154 77
drum Nightclub 318 10
drum Music. Instr. 323 57
drum Art 335 44

drum, hollow ~ 312 49
drum, lansquenet's ~ 306 70
drum, revolving ~ 273 45
drum brake 188 36
drum brake, front ~ 189 11
drum brake, rear ~ 189 13
drum head 323 52
drum kit 324 47-54
drummer 318 11
drum of paint 129 9
drums 324 47-54
drum set 324 47-54
drumstick Supermkt. 99 59
drumstick Music. Instr. 323 54
drumstick Ethnol. 354 19
drupe 59 41, 43, 49; 370 99; 382 51; 384 40
drupes 59 59, 1-36
dryas 51 7
dry bulb thermometer 10 34
dry cell battery 127 27
dry cooling tower 154 39
dry dock 222 31-33; 225 17
drying 169 24; 170 58
drying cabinet 116 23
drying chamber 170 49
drying cylinder 165 50, 53; 173 22
drying cylinder, heated ~ 173 33
drying floor 92 16
drying kiln 92 29
drying machine 169 31
drying rack Agr. 63 28, 29
drying rack Flea Market 309 49
drying section 168 28
drying shed 159 17
dry-seed dressing 83 52
dry zone, equatorial ~ 9 54
D sharp minor 320 61
dual film-tape recording 117 70
dual film-tape reproduction 117 75
dual film-tape system 117 7
dubbing Films 311 1-46, 37-41
dubbing Chivalry 329 66
dubbing actor 311 39
dubbing director 311 38
dubbing mixer 311 36
dubbing room 311 34
dubbing speaker 311 39
dubbing studio Broadcast. 238 28
dubbing studio Films 311 37
dubbing theatre Broadcast. 238 28
dubbing theatre Films 311 37
duck 73 35
duck, toy ~ 49 4; 273 30
duck, wild ~ 86 41; 272 51
duck-bill 366 1
duck hunting 86 40
ducking 299 29
duckling 73 35
duck-mole 366 1
duck shooting 86 40
duck's meat 378 35
duckweed 378 35
duct 163 11
duct, cystic ~ 20 38
duct, hepatic ~ 20 37
duct, spermatic ~ 20 74
ductor 181 63
ductor roller 181 63
duct roller 181 64
due date 250 16
duffle coat 271 21
dugout 218 7; 354 20
duk-duk dancer 352 34

dulcimer 322 32
Dülfer seat 300 30
dumb barge 225 8
dumb barge, tug-pushed ~ 221 94
dummy *Infant Care etc.* 28 15
dummy *Store* 271 34
dummy, dressmaker's ~ 103 6
dummy bull 319 3
dummy funnel 221 16
dump body 194 25; 200 8
dump car 213 37
dump chest 172 81
dumping bucket 214 34
dumping device 147 44, 59
dump truck 47 38; 147 64; 200 7
dump truck, three-way ~ 194 24
dune, crescentic ~ 13 40
dune, migratory ~ 13 39
dune, travelling ~ 13 39
dune, wandering ~ 13 39
dune buggy 193 12
dung 63 15
dungarees 29 40; 30 21
dung beetle 358 39
dungeon 329 5
dunging, mechanical ~ 74 23-27
dunging chain 74 27
dunging conveyor 74 27
dung tank 221 72
dunnage 222 62u.63
duodenum 20 14, 43
duplet 321 23
duplicate list 263 27
duramen 120 84; 370 13
dust, fine ~ 158 22
dust, lunar ~ 6 14
dust bag container 50 62
dustbin 199 3
dustbin-tipping device 199 2
dust brush 109 18
dust cap 187 57, 82
dust catcher *Goldsm. etc.* 108 45
dust catcher *Iron & Steel* 147 14
dust-collecting chamber 163 11
dust-collecting machine 147 14
dust collector *Goldsm. etc.* 108 45
dust collector *Cement Wks.* 160 7
dust collector *Refuse Coll.* 199 47
dust container 50 86
dust counter 112 42
dust cover *Bookbind.* 185 37
dust cover *Audio* 241 32
dust cover *Store* 271 30
dust discharge flue 163 22
dust escape flue 163 22
dust exhauster 108 43
dust extraction fan 163 10
dust extractor 92 40; 172 1
dust filter 270 59
dust hood 133 20
dust jacket 185 37
dust pan 50 52; 260 60
dust removal fan 83 53
dust removal screen 83 56
dust-settling chamber 172 6
dust shield 10 7
Dutch clover 69 2
'duty free shop' 233 52
duty presentation officer 238 22
duvet, quilted ~ 43 8
dwale 379 7

dwarf 308 22
dwarf French bean 57 8
dwarf pine 372 21
dwelling 37
dwelling, lacustrine ~ 328 15
dye liquor padding trough 165 47
dye spray 100 35
dyke *see* dike
dynamo 187 8
dynastarter 209,13

E

Eagle 3 9
eagle fern 377 16
eagle owl *Hunt.* 86 48, 51
eagle owl *Birds* 362 15
eagles 362 5-9
ear *Man* 16 18
ear *Arable Crops* 68 2
ear *Dog* 70 2
ear *Horse* 72 1
ear *Dom. Anim.* 73 11
ear *Game* 88 16, 32, 44, 61
ear *Music. Instr.* 326 32
ear *Birds* 362 16
ear, external ~ 17 56-58
ear, feathered ~ *Game* 88 78
ear, feathered ~ *Birds* 362 16
ear, internal ~ 17 62-64
ear, middle ~ 17 59-61
earcup 241 69; 261 40
earflap 35 31
ear lobe 17 57
earmuff 304 28
earphone *Hairst. etc.* 34 38
earphone *Audio* 241 69
earphone *Office* 248 35; 249 63
earphones 34 37
earphone socket *Cine Film* 117 10
earphone socket *Office* 249 68
ear piece *Forestry* 84 23
earpiece *Post* 237 8
earplug 354 30
earrings 36 13
earrings, drop ~ 36 11
earrings, pendant ~ 36 11
earth 4 8, 30
Earth 4 45
earth 6 17
earth, composted ~ 55 15
earth, excavated ~ 118 78
earth, prepared ~ 55 15
earth core 11 5
earthing button 237 21
earthing clamp 142 35
earth moth 80 42
earthquake 11 32-38
earthquake, submarine ~ 11 53
earthquake focus 11 32
earth station 237 51
earthworm 357 24
earthworm, artificial ~ 89 67
ear tuft 362 16
earwig 81 11
easel 116 35
easel, folding ~ 338 26
East Australian Current 14 38
Easter candle 330 44
Easter candlestick 330 45
easterlies 9 48, 49
Eastern cut-off 298 21
Eastern roll 298 15
east point 4 14
easy chair 336 18
eaves 38 11; 121 4; 122 36
eaves, rafter-supported ~ 37 9

eaves course 122 49, 76
eaves fascia 122 42
eaves joint 122 76
E-boat 258 69, 75
écarté 314 15
ECG 23 28
ECG amplitude 25 49
ECG analyser 25 45
ECG analysis 25 50
ECG impulse 25 46
ECG lead 25 43
ECG machine, portable ~ 23 46
ECG monitor 25 2, 21, 28, 47
ECG recorder 25 41
ECG recording unit 25 27
ECG rhythm 25 48
E-channel 143 7
echinoderm 369 3, 11, 17, 18, 19
echinoderms 357 38-39
Echinops 53 14
echinus 334 21
Echiostoma 369 13
echo 224 63
echo chamber 311 31
echo chamber loudspeaker 311 32
echo chamber microphone 311 33
echogram 224 67
echograph 224 24, 65
echo receiver 224 64
echo recorder 224 24
echo signal 224 63
echo sounder 224 61-67
echo sounding machine 224 61-67
echo sounding machine recorder 224 65
eclipse 4 33
eclipse, lunar ~ 4 29-35, 34-35
eclipse, solar ~ 4 29-35, 32, 39, 41
ecliptic 3 2; 4 22
economizer *Power Plant* 152 26
economizer *Railw.* 210 23
Edam cheese 99 42
edelweiss 378 9
edge *Tablew. etc.* 45 57
edge *Forestry* 85 2
edge *Winter Sp.* 302 21
edge *Maths.* 347 32
edge, aluminium ~ 301 51
edge, front ~ 122 88
edge, hidden ~ 151 24
edge, matching ~ 128 21
edge, non-matching ~ 128 22
edge, razor's ~ 106 40
edge, steel ~ 301 4, 50
edge, upper ~ 301 51
edge, visible ~ 151 23
edge board, lower ~ 118 74
edge board, upper ~ 118 73
edge mill 159 8
edge of platform 205 19
edge of pool 281 3
edge runner mill 159 8
edge sander 133 12
edge-sanding machine 133 12
edge-veneering machine 133 26
edging *Flower Gdn.* 51 15
edging *Optician* 111 35
edging, concrete ~ 52 20
edging, hoop ~ 55 38
edging machine 111 24
editing 311 42-46
editing table 117 96; 311 42
editorial 342 48
EDP print-out 248 47

eaves course 122 49, 76
education, nursery ~ 48 1-20
education, pre-school ~ 48 1-20
eel 364 17
eel hook 89 87
efface 314 13
efflux viscometer 129 38
E flat major 320 65
E flat minor 320 68
egg *Man* 20 84
egg *Poultry Farm* 74 58
egg *Bees* 77 26, 27
egg *Gdn. Pests* 80 15, 55
egg *Forest Pests* 82 19
egg *Articulates* 358 49
egg and anchor cyma 334 42
egg and dart cyma 334 42
egg and tongue cyma 334 42
egg box 74 42, 45; 99 50
egg collection 74 22, 34
egg collection system 74 34
egg-counting board 89 19
egg gallery 82 23
egg integument 74 59
egg-packing machine, fully automatic ~ 74 46
egg position 301 33
egg production 74 34-53
eggshell 74 59
egg timer 110 31
egg weigher 74 43
Egyptian 342 8
eight 283 10
eighth note 320 16
eighth rest 320 24
ejection seat 257 6, 7
ejector seat 257 6, 7
E-layer 7 27
elbow *Man* 16 43
elbow *Overh. Irrign.* 67 6
elbow *Horse* 72 20
elbow *Winter Sp.* 301 70
elbow boot 289 31
elbow coupling 126 40
elbow joint 126 51, 52
elbow pad 303 16
elbow screw joint 126 40, 45
elbow snips 125 2
elder 374 35
elderberry 374 37
elder flower 374 36
election 263 16-30
election meeting 263 1-15
election officer 263 17
election regulations 263 25
election speaker 263 5
election supervisor 263 28
elector 263 24
electoral register 263 18
electric action organ 326 36-52
electrical fitter 127 1
electrical point 261 12
electrical socket 261 12
electrical system bus 235 55
electric engine room 223 68
electrician 127 1
electricity cable 198 14, 19
electricity meter 127 32
electricity meter cupboard 127 31
electricity transmission line 15 113
electric light bulb 127 56
electric power plant 152 1-28
electrocardiogram monitor 25 2, 21, 28
electrocardiograph 23 28; 25 41
electrode *Hosp.* 25 26, 35, 38
electrode *Slaughterho.* 94 8
electrode *Arc Weld.* 142 10
electrode *Iron & Steel* 147 52

electrode, central ~ 2 3
electrode, platinum-iridium
  ~ 24 44
electrode, strap-on ~ 23 30
electrode arm 142 24
electrode case 142 7
electrode exit point 25 34
electrode holder 142 9, 20
electrode lead 25 25
electromagnet 237 47
electron 1 3, 17, 27, 32
electron, free ~ 1 25
electron beam 240 16
electron gun 113 31
electron gun assembly 240 24
electronic circuits 242 68-72
electronics, remote ~ 112 53
electronics cabinet 177 69
electron microscope 113 30
electron shell 1 6, 8
electron spin 1 4
electroplating bath 178 4
electroplating tank 178 4
electroplating vat 178 4
electrotome 22 38
electrotype, curved ~ 178 21
electrotyping 178
electrotyping plant 178 1-6
element, electronic ~ 242 69
element, fissionable ~ 1 49
element, front ~ 115 7
element, fusible ~ 127 36
element, oscillating ~ 110 9
element of set 348 2
elephant 366 20
elephant, toy ~ 47 6
elephant enclosure 356 9
elephant house 356 10
elevating conveyor 200 49
elevating drum, rotary ~ 64
  74
elevating gear 255 67
elevating piston 255 51
elevation, front ~ 151 17
elevation, side ~ 151 18
elevator *Offshore Drill.* 146 8
elevator *Synth. Fibres* 170 36
elevator *Aircraft* 229 27; 230
  63
elevator *Air Force* 257 22
elevator *Store* 271 45
elevator *Airsports* 288 24
elevator *Theatre* 316 33, 34
elevator, chain and slat ~ 64
  7
elevator, open-web ~ 64 69
elevator bridge 226 25
elevator car 271 46
elevator carrier 174 22
elevator controls 271 48
elevator operator 271 47
elevator shaft *Offshore Drill.*
  146 20
elevator shaft *Store* 271 51
elevon section, movable ~ 235
  33
elevon structure, heat-
  resistant ~ 235 34
elk 367 1, 2
ellipse 347 22
ellipse template 151 71
ellipsis 342 29
ellipsoid of revolution 347 42
elm tree 371 49
elytron 82 10; 358 36
E major 320 59
embankment *Map* 15 104
embankment *Refuse Coll.*
  199 14
embankment *Rivers* 216 49
embossing platen 183 29
embrace 205 53
embrasure 329 18

embroidery 29 29; 30 42; 355
  67
embryo *Arable Crops* 68 16
embryo *Bot.* 370 86
embryo *Trop. Plants* 382 21
embryo *South. Fruits* 384 22
embryo plant 68 14
embryo sac 370 64
emergency brake 214 3, 71
emergency brake valve 210 57
emergency cable 214 47
emergency-cable tensioning
  mechanism 214 48
emergency crash barrier 259 17
'emergency exit' 233 41
emergency exit 307 33; 312 7
emergency flare stack 146 11
emergency lighting 312 6
emergency telephone 237 4
emery paper 135 25
eminence, frontal ~ 16 4
eminence, thenar ~ 19 75
E minor 320 56
emission control 190 73
Emmental cheese 99 41
empennage shapes 229 23-36
Empire table 336 16
empress, Byzantine ~ 355 15
emptying system, dust-free ~
  199 2
em rule 342 23
emu 359 1
emulsion 129 4
emulsion paint 129 4
emulsion paste 128 28
emulsion tube 192 10
enamel 19 30
enamelling 260 62
enamelling stove, electric ~
  260 63
enamel powder 260 65
enchasing hammer 108 41
enclosing wall 356 4
enclosure, outdoor ~ 356 1
enclosure wall 329 15
encyclopaedia 42 18; 262 17
end *Basketm.* 136 23
end *Mach. Parts etc.* 143 23
end, hipped ~ 122 10
end, partial-hipped ~ 121 17
end, round ~ 143 50
end, rounded ~ 143 20
end, west ~ 335 22
end frame, hemispherical ~
  235 48
end-grain block 340 1
endive 57 39
endive leaf 57 39
endleaf 185 49
end line 292 36
end mill 150 43
end moraine 12 55
endorsee 250 26
endorsement 250 25
endorser 250 27
endpaper 185 49
end pier 215 27
end plate 229 33
end rib, hemispherical ~ 235
  48
end ring 89 52
end support 150 40
end switch 241 60
endurance competition 289
  16
energy 1 55
energy, solar ~ 155 17-36
energy level 1 15, 27
energy system 6 6, 8
engagement 294 46
engine *Moon L.* 6 30
engine *Oil, Petr.* 145 12
engine *Aircraft* 231 26

engine *Airsports* 288 35
engine, air-cooled ~ 188 7;
  189 3, 50
engine, auxiliary ~ *Ship* 223
  71
engine, auxiliary ~ *Aircraft*
  231 33
engine, eight-cylinder ~ 190 1
engine, four-cylinder ~ 189
  50
engine, four-stroke ~ 189 3,
  50
engine, main ~ *Railw.* 209 4
engine, main ~ *Ship* 221 81;
  223 73
engine, rear ~ *Garage* 195 49
engine, rear ~ *Aircraft* 231 10
engine, side ~ 228 29
engine, single-cylinder ~ 188
  26; 189 3
engine, twin-shaft ~ 232 51
engine, two-stroke ~ 188 7,
  26; 242 55; 305 92
engine, water-cooled ~ 189
  31, 39
engine and propeller room
  227 22
engine and transmission
  control wheel 212 67
engine compartment 195 35
engine compartment
  structure 235 2
engine control system 235 39
engine driver 208 2
engineer 208 2
engineering workshop 222 8
engineer's brake valve 210 53;
  211 22; 212 11
engine fairing, aerodynamic
  ~ 234 6
engine mount 234 21
engine mounting 190 38; 191
  53; 226 58
engine oil 196 15
engine oil temperature gauge
  212 19
engine order telegraph 224 25
engine pod 231 26; 256 25
engine room *Ship* 221 10
engine room *Fire Brig.* 270 1
engine room ventilator 212 37
engine superstructure 226 58
engine telegraph 224 25
English *Composing Rm.* 175
  29
English *Billiards* 277 5
English daisy 376 1
English hand 342 10
English ryegrass 69 26
English setter 70 41
engraver 340 16
engraving 36 41
engraving ball 108 34
engraving machine 177 52
engraving system 177 66
enlarger 116 26
enlarger head 116 41
enlarging meter 116 53
enlarging photometer 116 53
ensign of head of state 253 14
ensign staff 223 31; 258 25
entablature 334 52
entire 370 43
entrance 77 48; 99 4; 208 10
'entrance' 233 36
entrance 307 19
entrance, bullfighters' ~ 319
  10
entrance, main ~ 319 6
entrance, side ~ 331 15; 335
  13
entrance and exit door 197 14
entrance hall 41 1-29

entrance tunnel 353 6
entrechat 314 22
entrepôt 225 7
entry/exit hatch 6 38
entry hatch 6 10; 235 26
epaulière 329 44
épée 294 25-33, 36
épée, electric ~ 294 26
épéeist 294 25
épée point 294 27
ephemerid 358 6
epicalyx 58 22
epicenter 11 33
epicentre 11 33
epididymis 20 73
epiglottis 17 51
epistyle 334 18
equalizer 311 19
equalizer, universal ~ 238 48
'equals' key 247 20
equals sign 344 23
equation, conditional ~ 345 9
equation, identical ~ 345 5
equation, simple ~ 345 4
equator 14 1
equator, celestial ~ 3 3
Equatorial Countercurrent 14
  33
equestrian sport 289
equilibrist 307 48
equinoxes 3 6-7
equipment carrier 177 58
equipment locker 212 35
equipment section 239 1
equisetum 376 18
equitation 71 1-6
erase head 241 59; 243 20;
  311 25
eraser 151 42
eraser, glass ~ 151 47
eraser, pencil-type ~ 151 41
erasing head 241 59; 243 20;
  311 25
erasing knife 151 43
erasing knife blade 151 44
erasing shield 151 35
erasing table 249 26
erasion 26 52
erection shop 222 4
Ergates faber 358 38
ergometer, bicycle ~ 23 26
ergometry 23 26-31
ergot 68 4
Eridamus 3 12
Erlenmeyer flask 173 2; 350
  39
ermine moth 80 5
erne 362 5
error indicator 244 7
eruption 7 21
escalator 271 22
escape wheel 110 40
escapologist 308 28
escarpment 13 57
escudo 252 23
Eskimo 353 1
Eskimo kayak 283 68
esophagus 17 49
espalier 37 33; 52 1,2,16,17,29
espalier, free-standing ~ 52
  16
espalier fruit tree 52
  1,2,16,17,29
esparto grass 136 26
espresso bar 265 1-26
esquire 329 68
estate 193 15
estate car 193 15
estoque 319 32
etchant 178 24; 182 16
etching 340 14-24
etching bath 178 31; 340 51
etching ground 340 55

etching machine *Electrotyp. etc.* 178 23
etching machine *Photograv.* 182 15
etching needle 340 16
etching solution 178 24; 182 16
etching tank 178 24, 31; 182 16
ethmoid 17 39
ethnology 352; 353; 354
ethylene molecule 242 61
Eurobottle 93 26
Europe 14 15
European silver fir 372 1
European Southern Observatory 5 1-16
European toad 364 23
Euscorpius flavicaudus 358 40
evacuating pump, centrifugal ~ 67 11, 23
evaporating basin 350 29
evaporating dish 350 29
evaporator 155 6
evening dress 33 13
evening gown 30 53
evening sandal 101 27
evening suit 33 7
everlasting 377 3
ever-ready case 115 103
evolution 345 2
ewe 73 13; 75 10
examination couch 22 43; 23 4
examination table 27 1, 26
excavation *Bldg. Site* 118 69-82
excavation *Garage* 195 28
excavation side 118 72
excavator 118 76, 81; 200 1
excavator, large-scale ~ 159 3
excavator, toy ~ 273 65
excavator, universal ~ 158 13
excess water conduit 269 23
exchange *Post* 237 17, 22
exchange *Stock Exch.* 251 1-10
exchange broker 251 4
exchange floor 251 1
exchange golf ball 249 28
exchange hall 251 1
exchange rate 204 32
exchange typing element 249 28
excited state 1 19
exciter lamp 312 48
exclamation mark 342 21
exclamation point 342 21
exclusion principle 1 7
excretory vacuole 357 5
excursion steamer 221 101-128; 225 29
executive-secretary system 246 13
exercise book 47 24; 260 4, 18
exercises 296 48-60
exergue 252 10
exhaust *Agr. Mach.* 64 38
exhaust *Railw.* 209 12, 22
exhaust, upsweept ~ 188 15; 189 15
exhaust bubbles 279 26
exhaust casing 212 69
exhaust escape flue 258 79
exhaust fan *Brew.* 92 15
exhaust fan *Joiner* 133 33
exhaust gas 160 4
exhaust gas stack 154 37
exhaust manifold 190 36, 73
exhaust mast 221 17
exhaust muffler 212 42, 48
exhaust outlet 259 92

exhaust pipe *Photograv.* 182 25
exhaust pipe *Car* 191 51
exhaust pipe *Ship* 221 76
exhaust pipe *Warships* 258 44
exhaust pipe, four-pipe ~ 189 51
exhaust port 242 58
exhaust repair 195 52
exhaust silencer 212 42, 48
exhaust system 195 51
exhaust valve 190 46; 242 53
'exit' 233 37
exit 307 19
exit, emergency ~ 99 79
exit gate 319 12
ex libris 185 51
exosphere 7 31
exotic 306 30
expansion line 1 61
expansion tank 38 24
experimental apparatus 261 11
explosion, atomic ~ 7 11
exponent 345 1
exposing lamp 182 3
exposure bath 228 21
exposure control device 176 9
exposure control switch 117 17
exposure counter 115 17
exposure meter 114 29
exposure meter, hand-held ~ 114 56
exposure meter control step 117 37
exposure meter needle 115 57
exposure system 249 42
exposure time balancing knob 116 39
exposure timer 116 24; 179 18
expression marks 321 27-41
express locomotive 205 35
express train car 207 1-21
express train carriage 207 1-21
express train coach 207 1-21
express train compartment 207 43
extension *Joiner* 133 13
extension *Post* 237 17, 19, 21, 22-26, 26
extension arm 132 63
extension bar 151 57
extension bellows 115 85
extension cord 127 10
extension ladder 270 14
extension lead 127 10
extension plug 127 11
extension socket 127 12
extension tube *Household* 50 70
extension tube *Photog.* 115 81
extensor, common ~ 18 57, 63
extensor, radial ~ 18 56
extensor carpi radialis longus 18 56
extensor communis digitorum 18 57, 63
extinguisher, mobile ~ 270 63
extra 310 29; 316 39
extra bold 175 9
extracting a root 345 2
extraction fan 199 32
extraction forceps 24 47
extraction of phenol 170 3
extraction vent 49 20
extractor 170 37
extractor duct, movable ~ 142 15
extractor fan 133 33
extractor grid 100 13

extractor support 142 16
extrados 336 26
extremity, fimbriated ~ 20 82
extrusion press 159 11; 161 7
eye *Man* 16 7; 19 38-51
eye *Horse* 72 4
eye *Dom. Anim.* 73 32
eye *Game* 88 15, 33, 43. 60
eye *Fish Farm.* 89 82
eye *Mills* 91 19
eye *Blacksm.* 137 29
eye *Weaving* 166 28, 29
eye *Art* 334 75
eye, compound ~ *Bees* 77 20-24
eye, compound ~ *Articulates* 358 7
eye, simple ~ 77 2
eye, stalked ~ 357 30
eyeball 19 45
eye-bright 61 27
eyebrow *Man* 19 38
eyebrow *Roof* 121 23
eyecup 115 73; 117 14; 313 34
eyeground 22 32
eyelash 19 41
eyelet *Shoem.* 100 63
eyelet *Glaz.* 124 23
eyelet *Weaving* 166 28
eyelet, hook, and press-stud setter 100 53
eyelet embroidery 102 11
eyelid, lower ~ 19 40
eyelid, upper ~ 19 39
eye muscles 19 44
eyepiece 113 20; 115 42; 117 14; 311 9
eyepiece, binocular ~ 23 6
eyepiece control ring 313 7
eyepiece focusing knob 112 56
eyespot 358 54

F

fabled beings 327
fabric *Bldg. Site* 118 1-49
fabric *Knitting* 167 29, 48
fabric *Text. Finish.* 168 39, 51, 64
fabric *Weaves* 171 29
fabric *Store* 271 59
fabric, air-dry ~ 168 22
fabric, metallic ~ 270 46
fabric, non-woven ~ 103 27
fabric, printed ~ 168 57
fabric, raised ~ 168 36
fabric, shrink-resistant ~ 168 26
fabric, tubular ~ 167 1, 9
fabric, woollen ~ *Dressm.* 103 27
fabric, woollen ~ *Text. Finish.* 168 1
fabric, woven ~ 166 12
fabric box 167 10
fabric container 167 10
fabric department 271 58
fabric drum 167 10
fabric-finishing machine, decatizing ~ 168 49
fabric for upholstery 134 60
fabric guide roller 168 5
fabric-plaiting device 168 30
fabric-raising machine 168 31
fabric roll 167 29
fabric roller 166 20
fabric shaft 171 21, 23
fabric wallhanging 128 18
fabulous creatures 327
facade, west ~ 335 22

extractor support 142 16

face *Man* 16 4-17
face *Horse* 72 5
face *Clocks* 110 25
face *Blacksm.* 137 28
face *Composing Rm.* 174 31; 175 42
face *Art* 336 24
face, metal ~ 303 11
face compress 106 25
face guard 292 11, 25
face mask *Fire Brig.* 270 40
face mask *Swim.* 279 10
face mask filter 270 57
face par 251 12
face pipes 326 1-3
facet 77 20
face urn 328 38
face vault 297 30
facing 24 32
facing, decorative ~ 30 47
facsimile signature 252 34
facsimile telegraph 245 1
factor 344 25
factory number 187 51
factory ship *Sea Fish.* 90 11
factory ship *Ship* 221 86
fahlerz 351 1
fahl ore 351 1
fair 308
fair, annual ~ 308 1-69
fairground 308 1
fairing 189 43
fairing, integrated ~ 189 44
fairing, metal ~ 188 50
fairlead 284 29
fairway 216 21
fairway, main ~ 224 92
fairway, secondary ~ 224 93
fairway markings 224 84-102
fairway marks 224 68-83
fair-weather cumulus 8 1
fairy-tale figure 306 65
falcon 86 46
falconer 86 42
falconry 86 42-46
falcons 362 1-4
fall 221 106
falling wedge 85 4
fallow 63 1
fallow buck 88 40
fallow deer 88 40-41
falls 11 45
falls, artificial ~ 272 9
false acacia 371 70
false oat 69 22
family grave 331 27
family tomb 331 27
fan *Roof & Boilerr.* 38 58
fan *Agr. Mach.* 64 15; 65 52
fan *Pest Contr.* 83 49
fan *Game* 88 75
fan *Energy Sources* 155 14
fan *Weaving* 165 23
fan *Intern. Combust. Eng.* 190 7
fan *Refuse Coll.* 199 35, 46
fan *Aircraft* 232 34, 43
fan *Ethnol.* 353 42
fan, low-pressure ~ 199 33
fan blower 179 22
fan clutch 190 8
fancy appliqué 35 7
fancy dress 306 6-48, 32
fancy-dress ball 306 1-48
fan drift 144 22
fan drive, hydrostatic ~ 212 62
fan fold sheet, continuous ~ 248 47
fang 19 36
fan-jet turbine 232 38
fanlight 37 35
fan nozzle 83 4

fan tail **73** 29
fan vault **336** 46
faradization unit **23** 37
farm **15** 101
farm buildings **62**
farmer **62** 6
farmhand **63** 5
farming **63**
farm labourer **63** 5
farmland **63** 17
farm produce **68** 1-47
farm road **63** 18
farmstead **62**
farm track **63** 18
farm vehicle engineering **138**
farmworker **63** 5
farmyard **62** 17
farmyard hedge **62** 35
farmyard manure **63** 15
farrowing and store pen **75** 40
farrowing rails **75** 43
fascia panel **191** 57-90
fascine **216** 53
fashion catalogue **104** 6
fashion doll **47** 9; **48** 32
fashion house **268** 9
fashion journal **104** 4; **271**·36
fashion magazine **104** 4; **271** 36
fast and slow motion switch **117** 87
fastback **193** 29
fast breeder **154** 1
fast-breeder reactor **154** 1
fastening *Plant Propagn.* **54** 13
fastening *Station* **206** 12
fat **end 95** 53
fat lady **308** 21
fattening pond **89** 6
faucet *Kitch.* **39** 36
faucet *Plumb. etc.* **126** 34
faucet *Electrotyp. etc.* **178** 34
faucet *Chem.* **349** 5, 22
faucet, outlet ~ **37** 41
fault *Phys. Geog.* **12** 4
fault *Coal* **144** 51
fault, distributive ~ **12** 8
fault, multiple ~ **12** 8
fault, normal ~ **12** 7
fault-block mountain **12** 4-11
faulting **12** 4-20
fault line **12** 5
faults, complex ~ **12** 8-11
fault throw **12** 6
fault trace **12** 5
faustball **293** 72-78, 74
favorite **289** 52
favourite **289** 52
fawn **88** 39
fawn, female ~ **88** 34
F-clef **320** 9
F-contact **115** 14
feather *Headgear* **35** 6, 12
feather *Dom. Anim.* **73** 31
feather *Mach. Parts etc.* **143** 73
feed *Iron & Steel* **147** 51
feed *Mach. Tools* **149** 9
feed adjustment **100** 28
feed board **180** 32, 49, 67; **181** 4, 21, 30; **185** 9
feed chain **172** 67
feed chain drive **172** 69
feed channel **157** 55
feed conveyor **236** 33
feed conveyor, endless-chain ~ **74** 25
feed dispenser **74** 13

feed drum **180** 33, 34
feeder *Agr. Mach.* **64** 72
feeder *Poultry Farm* **74** 49-51
feeder *Brtckwks.* **159** 7
feeder *Offset Print.* **180** 31, 48, 68, 74
feeder *Letterpress* **181** 22, 24
feeder *Bookbind.* **185** 25
feeder, automatic ~ **181** 5
feeder, mechanical ~ **74** 13, 23
feeder broom **199** 44
feeder mechanism **181** 22
feeder panel **153** 4
feeder-selecting device **167** 40
feeder skip **118** 35
feed gearbox **149** 8
feed gear lever **149** 10
feed guide **184** 23
feed hopper *Poultry Farm* **74** 24
feed hopper *Bookbind.* **185** 26
feed-in **173** 13
feed indicator **157** 9
feeding, mechanical ~ **74** 23-27
feeding apparatus **181** 22
feeding bottle **28** 19
feeding bowl **70** 32
feeding-in **164** 15
feeding passage **75** 3
feeding place **86** 28
feeding site **80** 50
feeding trough *Poultry Farm* **74** 21
feeding trough *Livestock* **75** 37
feeding trough, adjustable ~ **74** 4
feed mechanism *Agr. Mach.* **65** 78
feed mechanism *Mach. Tools* **149** 18
feed mechanism *Post* **236** 48
feed mechanism *Graphic Art* **340** 33
feed motor **177** 43
feed pawl **157** 44
feed pipe **96** 50
feed pump *Nucl. Energy* **154** 13
feed pump *Railw.* **210** 9
feed roll **85** 19
feed roller **85** 24; **157** 4, 40
feed roller, fluted ~ **163** 52
feed runner **147** 22
feed screw **149** 15
feed setting **100** 28
feed shaft **149** 33
feed spindle **312** 36
feed spool **117** 31
feed sprocket **312** 26
feed supply pipe **74** 15
feed table *Sawmill* **157** 63
feed table *Offset Print.* **180** 32, 49, 67
feed table *Letterpress* **181** 4, 21, 30
feed table *Bookbind.* **184** 12, 21; **185** 9, 34
feed-through insulator **153** 12, 35
feed-through terminal **153** 12, 35
feed trip **149** 18
feed tripping device **149** 18
feed valve **210** 20
feedwater heater **210** 23
feedwater line **154** 12, 30
feedwater preheater **210** 23
feedwater steam circuit **154** 45
feedwater tank **152** 17

feedwater tray, top ~ **210** 29
feeler *Agr. Mach.* **64** 86
feeler *Forest Pests* **82** 3
feeler *Weaving* **166** 32
feeler *Invertebr.* **357** 31
feeler *Articulates* **358** 27, 53
feeler, maxillary ~ **358** 42
feeler gauge **140** 53
feeler support wheel **64** 88
feet-first jump **282** 13
felines **368** 2-8
feller **84** 20
felling **84** 27
felling wedge **84** 4, 30
felling wedge, hydraulic ~ **84** 25
felt **173** 51
felt, dry ~ **173** 23
felt nail **122** 96
felt pen **48** 18
felt tip pen **247** 11; **260** 19
female, winged ~ **358** 21
femur **17** 22
fence *Joiner* **132** 65
fence *Refuse Coll.* **199** 13
fence *Aircraft* **231** 8
fence *Swim.* **281** 17
fence *Equest.* **289** 8
fence, electrified ~ **62** 46
fence, paling ~ **52** 10
fence, protective ~ **84** 7
fence, stone ~ **337** 23
fence, timber ~ **118** 44
fence, wicker ~ **216** 54
fence, wire ~ **15** 39
fence, wire netting ~ **84** 7
fence, wooden ~ **37** 53
fence adjustment handle **132** 66
fence rack **63** 28
fencers **294** 5-6
fencer's salute **294** 18
fencing **294**
fencing, modern ~ **294** 1-33
fencing glove **294** 12
fencing instructor **294** 1
fencing jacket **294** 16
fencing mask **294** 13, 14
fencing master **294** 1
fencing measure **294** 10
fencing movement **294** 7
fencing shoe, heelless ~ **294** 17
fencing weapons **294** 34-45
fender *Horse* **71** 40
fender *Tram* **197** 12
fender *Hydr. Eng.* **217** 9
fender *Docks* **225** 12
fender, front ~ *Bicycle* **187** 13
fender, front ~ *Car* **191** 3; **191** 3, 13
fender, integral ~ **193** 33
fender, wooden ~ **218** 26
fender pile *Hydr. Eng.* **217** 9
fender pile *Shipbuild.* **222** 35
F-1 engine **234** 4
fennel **380** 6
fen peat **13** 17
fermentation room **97** 72
fermentation thermometer **93** 9
fermentation trolley **97** 73
fermentation vessel **93** 8
fermenter **93** 8
fermenting cellar **93** 7
fern **377** 16
ferret **86** 24
ferreter **86** 25
ferreting **86** 23
ferries **221**
Ferris wheel **308** 37
ferroconcrete construction **119** 1-89

ferrule **45** 53
ferry, flying ~ **216** 10
ferryboat **216** 11, 15; **225** 11
ferry cable **216** 2
ferry landing stage **216** 7
ferryman **216** 17
ferry rope **216** 2
fertilizer, artificial ~ **63** 14
fertilizer, chemical ~ **63** 14
fertilizer, lime ~ **63** 14
fertilizer, nitrogen ~ **63** 14
fertilizer, phosphoric acid ~ **63** 14
fertilizer, potash ~ **63** 14
fertilizer spreader **62** 21
fescue **69** 24
festoon *Carnival* **306** 5
festoon *Art* **335** 54
festoon lamp **318** 26
festoon lighting **318** 25
fetish **354** 43
fetlock **72** 24
fettler **148** 43
fettling shop **148** 38-45
feuilleton **342** 67
F-hole **323** 6
fiber *see* fibre
fibre **77** 23
fibre, glass ~ **151** 48
fibre, loose ~ **168** 43
fibreboard **338** 24
fibula **17** 24
fibula, serpentine ~ **328** 28
fibula, spiral ~ **328** 30
fibula, two-piece ~ **328** 30
fiddle string **323** 9
field *Agr.* **63** 4, 17
field *Equest.* **289** 41, 51
field *Ball Games* **291** 1; **292** 40-58
field, fallow ~ **63** 1
field bean **69** 15
field bindweed **61** 26
field camomile **61** 8
field chopper, self-propelled ~ **64** 34-39
fielder **292** 76
field eryngo **61** 32
field glasses **86** 6
field guard **63** 13
field illumination **112** 33
fielding side **292** 73
field lens **115** 40
field mangel **69** 21
field marigold **61** 7
field mushroom **381** 1
field pests **80** 37-55
field player **292** 2
field poppy **61** 2
field sprinkler **67** 32
fig **383** 35; **384** 11, 13
fighter-bomber **256** 1, 29
fighting bull **319** 28
fighting ships **258** 64-91
fighting ships, modern ~ **259**
figure, clay ~ **48** 13; **339** 7
figure, plasticine ~ **48** 13
figure, satirical ~ **306** 63
figure, symbolic ~ **327** 20
figure, symmetrical ~ **346** 24
figure, wax ~ **308** 69
figurehead **218** 16
figures, compulsory ~ **302** 11-19
figure ski **286** 56
figurine, clay ~ **328** 20
filament **169** 17, 22; **170** 44
filament, continuous ~ **169** 1-34
filament, solid ~ **169** 15
filament lamp **127** 56
filament tow **169** 28, 30
file *Doc.* **22** 12, 26

file *Metalwkr.* **140** 16
file *Office* **245** 6; **247** 37; **248** 5
file, flat ~ **108** 49; **140** 27
file, half-round ~ **140** 29
file, rough ~ **140** 8
file, round ~ **108** 47; **140** 29
file, smooth ~ **140** 8
file handle **108** 50
filet **102** 22
file tab **248** 4
filigree work **102** 30
filing cabinet **245** 4
filing clerk **248** 6
filing drawer **248** 2, 23
filing machine **140** 15
filing shelf **248** 10
fill, sanitary ~ **199** 10
filler *Tobacc. etc.* **107** 7
filler *Paperhanger* **128** 3
filler *Power Plant* **153** 38
filler *Films* **310** 52
filler hoist **200** 51
filler hole **213** 19
filler light **310** 52
filler opening **200** 52
filler rod **141** 12
fillet *Meat* **95** 13
fillet *Carp.* **120** 45
fillet *Floor etc. Constr.* **123** 57, 67
fillet *Bookbind.* **183** 3
fillet, tilting ~ **121** 31
fillet gauge **142** 36
filleting knife **89** 38
fillet of beef **95** 24
fillet of pork **95** 44
filling *Dent.* **24** 30
filling *Tablew. etc.* **45** 38
filling *Hydr. Eng.* **217** 7
filling *Water* **269** 29
filling compound **153** 38
filling end **162** 2
filling inlet **50** 12
filling knife **128** 35
filling machine **76** 21, 26
filling material **24** 51
filling station **196** 1-29
fill-in light **310** 52
fill light **310** 52
film *Atom* **2** 10, 13
film *Photog.* **114** 9
film *Composing Rm.* **176** 25
film, cine ~ **117**
film, exposed ~ **117** 42
film, unexposed ~ **117** 41
film actor **310** 28
film actress **310** 27
film advance **114** 32
film advance lever, single-stroke ~ **115** 16
film agitator, automatic ~ **116** 19
film and sound cutting table **117** 96
film and tape synchronizing head **117** 102
film back **115** 80
film break detector **312** 30
film camera **27** 20
film camera, soundproof ~ **310** 47; **313** 15
film cameras **313** 1-39
film cassette **112** 65
film cassette, miniature ~ **114** 7
film cassette, universal ~ **242** 44
film cement **312** 22
film clip **116** 14
film copier, automatic ~ **176** 28
film-developing machine **311** 30

film director **310** 40
film dosimeter **2** 8
film drier **116** 23
film editor **311** 43
film extra **310** 29
film feed spool **117** 79
film former **178** 24
film gate **117** 30; **312** 34
film gate opening **117** 40
filmgoer **312** 5
filming **310** 14-60, 26-60
filming, exterior ~ **310** 18
filming, outdoor ~ **310** 18
filming agent **178** 24
filming speed selector **117** 12
film laboratory **310** 2, 30
film library **310** 5
film magazine **113** 40
film marker **117** 95
film matrix case **176** 17
film of fluorescent material **240** 19
film orchestra **310** 17
film path **312** 31
film perforator **117** 95; **242** 10
film poster **268** 57
film-processing machine **311** 30
film processor, automatic ~ **177** 72
film projection **312** 1-23
film projector **311** 22; **312** 24
film projectors **312** 24-52
film reel **311** 24; **312** 32
film-ring dosimeter **2** 11
films **310**; **311**; **312**; **313**
filmscript **310** 45
film set **310** 7
filmsetter **176** 7
filmsetting **176**
film speed setting **117** 18
film spool **114** 8; **311** 24; **312** 32
film spool holder **238** 6
film star **310** 27, 28
film storage vault **310** 5
film studios **310** 1-13
film title **310** 35
film transport **114** 32
film transport handle **116** 7
film transport mechanism **311** 26
film turntable **117** 99; **311** 44
film viewer **117** 91; **242** 8
film wind **114** 32
film window **114** 18; **115** 28, 34
filter *Atom* **2** 9, 12, 14
filter *Weaving* **165** 14
filter *Synth. Fibres* **170** 32
filter *Paperm.* **172** 20
filter *Water* **269** 62
filter *Chem.* **349** 12
filter, fluted ~ **350** 41
filter adjustment **116** 43, 44, 45
filter bed **269** 10
filter bottom **269** 11
filter cake **161** 13
filter change, automatic ~ **316** 49
filtered water outlet **269** 12
filter flask **350** 40
filter funnel **349** 11
filter gravel **269** 10
filter lens **142** 40
filter mount **115** 6
filter pick-up **112** 57
filter plate **349** 12
filter press *Porcelain Manuf.* **161** 12

filter press *Synth. Fibres* **169** 12
filter screen **116** 22
fimbria **20** 82
fin *Swim.* **279** 18
fin *Bathing* **280** 41
fin *Motorboats etc.* **286** 43
fin, abdominal ~ **364** 8
fin, anal ~ **364** 9
fin, caudal ~ **364** 10
fin, dorsal ~ *Fish etc.* **364** 6
fin, dorsal ~ *Mammals* **367** 27
fin, fixed ~ **286** 61
fin, pectoral ~ **364** 7
fin, pelvic ~ **364** 8
fin, ventral ~ **364** 8
fin, vertical ~ *Aircraft* **229** 24; **230** 59; **231** 6; **232** 7
fin, vertical ~ *Space* **235** 1
fin, vertical ~ *Air Force* **256** 32
fin, vertical ~ *Airsports* **288** 21
final image tube **113** 39
final picture quality checking room **238** 60-65
finch **360** 1
finches **361** 6-8
finds, prehistoric ~ **328** 1-40
fine cut **107** 25
fine focusing indicator **224** 36
finger, fifth ~ **19** 68
finger, fourth ~ **19** 67
finger, little ~ **19** 68
finger, middle ~ **19** 66
finger, pivoted ~ **74** 36
finger, second ~ **19** 65
finger, third ~ **19** 66
fingerboard **323** 21; **324** 8
finger guard **83** 20; **85** 15
finger hole *Office* **247** 39
finger hole *Sports* **305** 16
fingerhole *Music. Instr.* **323** 33; **324** 34
finger hook **324** 67
fingernail **19** 80
finger pad **19** 78
finger paint **260** 26
finger painting **260** 26
finger plate **237** 11
fingerprint **264** 29
fingerprint identification **264** 28
finger stop **237** 12
fingertip **19** 79
finial **335** 37
fining bath **162** 4
fining lap **111** 37, 38
finish **286** 28
finish, gloss ~ **128** 32
finished malt collecting hopper **92** 20
finishing **168** 1-65; **170** 57
finishing bur **24** 38
finishing layer **123** 40
finishing line **282** 28; **286** 30
finishing machine **100** 3
finishing of textile fabrics **168**
finishing press **183** 4
finishing train **148** 71
Finn **284** 51
Finn dinghy **284** 51
fin post **235** 3
fipple flute **322** 7
fir cone **372** 2
fire, blacksmith's ~ **137** 1-8; **138** 34
fire, open ~ **267** 25
fire alarm **270** 4
fire alarm siren **270** 4
fire appliance building **233** 8
fire-arm **87** 2
fireboat **270** 65
firebox **210** 4
fire control radar antenna **258** 51

fire control system **255** 74
fire crest **361** 10
fire curtain **316** 24
fire department **270**
firedoor handle handgrip **210** 63
fire eater **308** 25
fire engine **270** 5
fire extinguisher **196** 9
fire extinguisher, portable ~ **270** 61
fire extinguisher, wheeled ~ **270** 63
firefighter **270** 37
fire-fighting equipment **227** 25; **228** 20
fire gable **121** 9
fire gun **221** 4
fire hat **270** 38
firehole door **210** 61
firehole shield **210** 60
fireman **270** 37
fire nozzle **221** 4
fireplace **267** 23
fire plug **270** 35
fire prevention **316** 6
fire protection **316** 6
fire salamander **364** 22
fire service **270**
fire service drill **270** 1-46
fireside **267** 22
fire siren **270** 4
fire station **270** 1-3
fire tube **210** 17
firewood basket **309** 10
fireworks **306** 49-54
firing mechanism **255** 29
firing mould **161** 4
firing pin **87** 21
firing position **305** 73
firing process **161** 2
firing sequence insert **195** 13
firing trigger **87** 11
firmer chisel **134** 30
firn basin **12** 48
fir needle **372** 11
firn field **12** 48
firn slope **300** 14
first aid **21**
first aid dressing **21** 5
first aid kit **21** 4
first aid post **308** 61
first aid station **204** 44
first aid tent **308** 61
first base **292** 46
first-class section **207** 17
first floor **37** 2; **118** 7
first-floor landing **123** 23
first position **294** 18
Fish *Astron.* **4** 64
fish *Grocer* **98** 19
fish *Fish etc.* **364**
fish, canned ~ **96** 28
fish, female ~ **89** 13
fish basket **89** 25
fishbolt **202** 13
fishbone stitch **102** 7
fish-canning factory **225** 59
fish culture **89** 1-19
fish dish **266** 53
fish dock **225** 56
fish egg **89** 12
fishes **364** 1-18
fish farming **89** 1-19
fish fork **45** 8, 65
fish hook **89** 79
fishing **89** 26
fishing boat **89** 27; **90** 24
fishing line **89** 63
fishing lugger **90** 1
fishing pliers **89** 37

fishing tackle **89** 37-94
fishing tackle, suspended ~ **90** 29
fish knife *Tablew. etc.* **45** 8, 64
fish knife *Fish Farm.* **89** 39
fish ladder **89** 93
fish lance **280** 40
fish market **225** 57
fish pass **89** 93
fishplate **202** 12
fishpole antenna **258** 60
fish spawn **89** 12
fish spear **280** 40
fishtail bit **145** 21
fish way **89** 93
fission 1 43, 46
fission, nuclear ~ 1 34
fission fragment 1 44, 47, 51
fission fragments 1 37-38
fissure 11 52
fissure, diagonal ~ **300** 3
fissure, horizontal ~ **300** 3
fissure, vertical ~ **300** 3
fissure bur 24 39
fist 16 48
fist hatchet **328** 1
fitch **129** 19
fitter **140** 1
fitting booth **271** 32
fitting of the frame 111 10
fitting-out quay **222** 5-9
fittings **126** 38-52
five-four time **320** 41
fix **224** 45
flag *Flags* **253** 7-11
flag *Town* **268** 44
flag, club's ~ **283** 25
flag, linesman's ~ **291** 60
flag, Olympic ~ **253** 5
flag, swallow-tailed ~ **253** 22
flag at half-mast **253** 6
flag at half-staff **253** 6
flag dressing **221** 85
flag of the Council of Europe **253** 4
flag of the United Nations **253** 1-3
flagpole **253** 1, 7; **273** 61
flags **253**
flags, national ~ **253** 15-21
flags, triangular ~ **253** 30-32
flagstaff **253** 1, 7; **258** 4; **259** 87; **273** 61
flagstick **293** 88
flagstone **51** 17
flail rotor **64** 73
flame regulator **107** 31
flamingo **272** 53
flan **252** 43
flancard **329** 86
flan case **97** 47
flanchard **329** 86
flange *Cooper.* **130** 28
flange *Mach. Parts etc.* **143** 2, 5
flange *Electrotyp. etc.* **178** 44
flange *Hydr. Eng.* **217** 67
flange, bottom ~ **215** 10
flange, top ~ **215** 9
flange mount **130** 20
flanging, swaging, and wiring machine **125** 25
flank *Man* **16** 32
flank *Game* **88** 26
flank *Meat* **95** 2, 15-16
flank *Bldg. Site* **119** 6
flank, thick ~ **95** 15, 36
flank, thin ~ **95** 16
flank vault **297** 31
flans **97** 22-24
flap *Child. Clothes* **29** 35
flap *Horse* **71** 40, 47
flap *Aircraft* **229** 37

flap, double-slotted ~ **229** 48
flap, extending ~ **229** 51
flap, fur ~ **35** 32
flap, normal ~ **229** 46
flap, outer ~ **259** 78
flap, slotted ~ **229** 47
flap, split ~ **229** 49
flap extension **78** 19
flaps, plain ~ **229** 46-48
flaps, simple ~ **229** 46-48
flaps, split ~ **229** 49-50
flap valve **192** 63
flare, pork ~ **95** 45
flash, battery-portable ~ **114** 65
flash, electronic ~ **114** 65, 68; **309** 40-41
flash, single-unit ~ **114** 68
flash bar **114** 75
flash bulb **309** 39
flash contact **114** 30
flash cube **114** 74
flash cube contact **114** 13
flash cube unit **114** 73
flash eliminator **255** 18
flashgun **114** 68; **309** 38
flashgun, electronic ~ **309** 40-41
flash head **114** 67; **309** 40
flash hider **255** 18
flash lamp *Photomech. Reprod.* **177** 37
flash lamp *Inf. Tech.* **242** 43
flashlight *Electr.* **127** 26
flashlight *Fire Brig.* **270** 6
flashlight, underwater ~ **279** 25
flash socket **115** 14
flash switch **114** 33
flash tube **176** 26
flask, collared ~ **328** 12
flask, conical ~ **350** 39
flask, flat-bottomed ~ **350** 36
flask, long-necked ~ **350** 38
flask, round-bottomed ~ **350** 38
flask, three-necked ~ **350** 55
flask, volumetric ~ **173** 3
flat *Dwellings* **37** 64-68, 69-71
flat *Flat* **46**
flat *Music. Not.* **320** 52
flat-bed cylinder press, two-revolution ~ **181** 1
flat-bed knitting machine **167** 35
flat-bed offset machine **180** 75
flat-bed offset press **180** 75
flatcar **206** 24; **213** 5, 11, 40
flat clearer **163** 44
flat four engine **230** 34
flat glass production **162** 1-20
flat plate keel **222** 49
flats *Cotton Spin.* **163** 45, 46
flats *Navig.* **224** 87, 97
flatter **137** 35
flatworm **81** 35
flauto piccolo **323** 30
flavourings **382**
flax **383** 6
flay brush **129** 21
flaying knife **94** 13
flea **81** 42
flea beetle **80** 39
flea market **309**
fleet of lorries **206** 25
fleet submarine, nuclear-powered ~ **259** 54
flesh *Soft Fruit* **58** 24, 35, 58
flesh *Drupes & Nuts* **59** 6
fletching **305** 62
fleur-de-lis **254** 13
flews **70** 26

flex **50** 66, 77
flex hook **50** 65
flexor, radial ~ **18** 40
flexor, ulnar ~ **18** 58
flexor carpi radialis **18** 40
flexor carpi ulnaris **18** 58
flies **316** 1-60
flight, negative ~ **288** 9
flight board **77** 49
flight deck *Space* **235** 16
flight deck *Warships* **259** 2, 12
flight instrument **288** 68
flight of wild ducks **86** 41
flight refuelling probe **256** 7
flik-flak **297** 24
flint **107** 28
flint corn **68** 31
flintlock **353** 28
flint maize **68** 31
flip-over numeral **110** 20
flipper *Swim.* **279** 18
flipper *Bathing* **280** 41
flipper *Mammals* **367** 28
flip-up window **142** 4
flitch of bacon **96** 2
flitter-mouse **366** 9
float *Bldg. Site* **118** 57
float *Plumb. etc.* **126** 15
float *Weaves* **171** 40
float *Car* **192** 15
float *Rivers* **216** 12
float *Hydr. Eng.* **217** 34
float *Aircraft* **232** 6
float *Swim.* **282** 18
float *Motorboats etc.* **286** 44
float *Theatre* **316** 26
float, cork ~ *Fish Farm.* **89** 43
float, cork ~ *Swim.* **282** 32
float, lead-weighted ~ **89** 48
float, plastic ~ **89** 44
float, polystyrene ~ **89** 46
float, quill ~ **89** 45
float, skin ~ **353** 11
float, sliding ~ **89** 43, 48
float, spherical ~ **90** 19
float, wooden ~ **90** 6
float bath **162** 16
float chamber **192** 14
float glass process **162** 12
floating thread, diagonal ~ **171** 38
floating thread, loose ~ **171** 41
floating vessel **221** 65
floating yarn, diagonal ~ **171** 38
floating yarn, loose ~ **171** 41
float lever **65** 43
float line **90** 4
floatplane **232** 5
floats **89** 43-46
float seaplane **232** 5
float shaft **217** 35
flood bed **216** 41
flood containment area **216** 42
flood damage **216** 5
floodgate **217** 77
flood plain **13** 62
flood wall **216** 32
floor **296** 11; **297** 6
floor, blind ~ **123** 38, 73
floor, concrete ~ **118** 16
floor, false ~ **120** 43; **123** 68
floor, ferroconcrete ~ **119** 8
floor, first ~ **37** 2, 3; **118** 7, 14
floor, inserted ~ **120** 43; **123** 68
floor, reinforced concrete ~ **119** 8; **123** 35
floor, ribbed ~ **123** 35
floor, second ~ **37** 3; **118** 14
floor, upper ~ **37** 3; **118** 14
floor and carpet cleaning **50** 53-86

floorboard **120** 36
floor brick **159** 24
floor brush **129** 27
floor ceiling **222** 63
floor cleaning **50** 53-86
floor cloth **50** 55
floor construction **123**
floor filling **120** 44; **123** 69
floor grinding machine **138** 7
floor indicator **271** 49
flooring block, hollow ~ **159** 26
floor manager **271** 33
floor nozzle **50** 71
floor plate **222** 59
floor socket **127** 23
floor socket, sunken ~ **127** 24
floor trader **251** 6
floorwalker **271** 33
flop **298** 9
floppy disc reader **244** 8
flora **356** 21
florin **252** 19
flour **91** 28; **97** 52
flour beetle **81** 18
flour corn **68** 31
flour silo **97** 74
flow **216** 9
flow chart **76** 9
flow coating machine **129** 34
flow diagram **76** 9; **92** 25
flower *Soft Fruit* **58** 4
flower *Drupes & Nuts* **59** 9
flower *Weeds* **61** 10, 19, 22
flower *Arable Crops* **68** 42
flower *Fodder Plants* **69** 7, 14
flower *Gdn. Pests* **80** 11
flower *Bot.* **370** 23, 51
flower *Decid. Trees* **371** 17, 26, 35, 40, 52, 55, 62
flower *Shrubs etc.* **373** 5, 7, 11, 14, 31; **374** 6, 7, 15, 21, 24
flower *Flowers etc.* **375** 3, 6, 16, 19, 20, 23, 40, 46; **376** 2, 5, 11, 19, 23
flower *Alp. Plants etc.* **378** 16, 20, 28, 31, 32, 37, 47, 57
flower *Trop. Plants* **382** 4, 17, 18, 29, 42, 55
flower *Industr. Plants* **383** 12, 17, 27, 31, 36, 39, 46, 47
flower *South. Fruits* **384** 13, 18, 56, 57, 65
flower, amaranthine ~ **60** 21
flower, androgynous ~ *Shrubs etc.* **374** 10
flower, androgynous ~ *Trop. Plants* **382** 12, 14
flower, female ~ *Drupes & Nuts* **59** 38
flower, female ~ *Decid. Trees* **371** 6, 13
flower, female ~ *Conifers* **372** 43
flower, female ~ *Shrubs etc.* **373** 20
flower, female ~ *Alp. Plants etc.* **378** 25; **378** 53
flower, female ~ *Trop. Plants* **382** 32, 50
flower, female ~ *Industr. Plants* **383** 50
flower, female ~ *South. Fruits* **384** 7, 14, 42, 43
flower, forced ~ **55** 24
flower, fumariaceous ~ **60** 5
flower, hermaphroditic ~ *Shrubs etc.* **374** 10
flower, hermaphroditic ~ *Trop. Plants* **382** 12, 14
flower, male ~ *Drupes & Nuts* **59** 39

flower, male ~ *Decid. Trees* 371 14
flower, male ~ *Conifers* 372 43
flower, male ~ *Shrubs etc.* 373 21; 374 11
flower, male ~ *Alp. Plants etc.* 378 23, 53
flower, male ~ *Trop. Plants* 382 13
flower, male ~ *Industr. Plants* 383 51
flower, male ~ *South. Fruits* 384 5, 15, 44, 51
flower, open ~ 374 17
flower, withered ~ 58 55
flower arrangement 266 78; 267 37; 330 48
flower basket 266 29
flower bed *Fruit & Veg. Gdn.* 52 18
flower bed *Market Gdn.* 55 37
flower bed *Park* 272 41
flower box 37 20
flower bud *Soft Fruit* 58 27
flower bud *Bot.* 370 24
flower bud *Decid. Trees* 371 25
flower bud *Shrubs etc.* 374 14
flower bud *Trop. Plants* 382 28
flower cone, female ~ 372 4, 16, 22, 34, 62, 68
flower garden 51 1-35
flower girl 266 28
flower head *Weeds* 61 14
flower head *Alp. Plants etc.* 378 12
flower head, discoid ~ 370 74
flower head, hollow ~ 370 75
flowering branch *Decid. Trees* 371 2, 10, 16, 34, 39, 51, 54, 66, 71
flowering branch *Conifers* 372 33
flowering branch *Trop. Plants* 382 8, 12, 23, 27, 31, 50
flowering branch *Industr. Plants* 383 22, 26, 30, 38
flowering branch *South. Fruits* 384 17, 24, 37, 49, 54
flowering rush 378 39
flowering shoot *Alp. Plants etc.* 378 2, 27
flowering shoot *Trop. Plants* 382 41, 47
flowering shoot *Industr. Plants* 383 42
flower pot 54 8
flowers, wild ~ 375; 376
flower seller 266 28
flower shoot 59 28
flower shoot, male ~ 372 6, 62, 68
flower stalk *Drupes & Nuts* 59 4
flower stalk *Bot.* 370 52
flower stalk *Industr. Plants* 383 7
flower stand 204 48; 267 36
flower stem 370 52
flower umbel 378 40
flower vase 309 2
flower window 37 68
flowmeter *Hosp.* 26 3
flowmeter *Dairy.* 76 4
flow path 154 51
flow pipe *Roof & Boilerr.* 38 74
flow pipe *Plumb. etc.* 126 23
flow pipe *Energy Sources* 155 10
fluate 128 7

flue 155 25
flueblock 38 40
flue brush 38 35
flue pipe 322 57
flue pipe, metal ~ 326 23-30
flue pipe, open ~ 326 23-30, 31-33
flue pipe, stopped ~ 326 34
flue pipe, wooden ~ 326 31-33
flue pipe duct 326 24
flue pipe windway 326 24
flue tube 210 8
fluid container 247 9
fluid reservoir 247 9
fluid transmission 212 27, 52
fluorescent display, eight-digit ~ 247 15
fluorescent material 240 18
fluorescent tube 127 61, 62
fluorite 351 16
fluoroscope, mobile ~ 26 14
fluorspar 351 16
fluothane container 26 26
flush-deck vessel 258 2; 259 22
flushing lever *Bathrm. etc.* 49 17
flushing lever *Plumb. etc.* 126 19
flushing valve 126 37
flush pipe 126 17
flute *Mills* 91 17
flute *Music. Instr.* 323 31
flute *Art* 334 27
flute *Ethnol.* 353 47
flute, globular ~ 324 32
flute, small ~ 323 30
fluting 157 6
flux *Goldsm. etc.* 108 36
flux *Plumb.* 125 7
flux *Gas Weld.* 141 18
flux *Iron & Steel* 147 2
fly *Men's Wear* 33 48
fly *Fish Farm.* 89 65
fly *Articulates* 358 18
fly agaric 379 10
fly amanita 379 10
fly and draw curtain 315 4
fly curtain 315 3
flyer 164 25
fly floor 316 5
fly frame 164 19
fly frame operative 164 24
fly frame operator 164 24
fly front 33 62
fly fungus 379 10
fly gallery 316 5
flying boat 232 1
flying boat, amphibian ~ 232 8
flying buttress 335 28
Flying Dutchman 284 49
fly leaf 185 49
fly line 316 8
fly man 316 7
fly nut *Mach. Parts etc.* 143 42
fly nut *Bicycle* 187 39
flysheet 278 22
fly swat 83 32
fly title 185 44
flywheel *Weaving* 166 15
flywheel *Intern. Combust. Eng.* 190 20
F major 320 63
F minor 320 66
foal 73 2
foam bath 49 3
foam can 228 28
foam canister 83 6
foam feed pipe 83 10
foam gun 270 64
foam-making branch 270 64
focal length setting 117 3

focimeter 111 33
fo'c'sle 218 10, 19; 221 13; 223 48
focus 347 25, 27
focus, seismic ~ 11 32
focusing adjustment 240 30
focusing aid 115 60
focusing device 5 11
focusing hood 114 23; 115 68
focusing ring 114 39; 115 8
focusing screen *Optic. Instr.* 112 21
focusing screen *Photog.* 115 39
focusing screen *Photomech. Reprod.* 177 2, 34
focusing screens, interchangeable ~ 115 58-66
focusing stage 115 86
focusing telescope 115 74
focusing wedge 115 55
focus setting 114 28; 117 3
fodder plants 69 1-28
fodder silo 62 11, 43
fodder tank 221 73
fog 9 31
fog, high ~ 8 4
fog headlamp and rear lamp switch 191 64
fog horn 223 3
fog horn, ship's ~ 224 32
fog lamp, rear ~ 191 67
fog lamp warning light 191 63
foil 294 1-18, 11
foil, electric ~ 294 26
foil, French ~ 294 37
foil, Italian ~ 294 39
foil fencers 294 5-6
foilists 294 5-6
foil mask 294 13
foil pommel 294 40
foilsmen 294 5-6
fold 185 54
fold, asymmetrical ~ 12 13
fold, gluteal ~ 16 42
fold, nasolabial ~ 16 11
fold, normal ~ 12 12
fold, reclined ~ 12 15
fold, recumbent ~ 12 15
fold, symmetrical ~ 12 12
fold-away table 207 53
foldboats 283 54-66
folder *Offset Print.* 180 15, 29
folder *Letterpress* 181 55
folder *Photograv.* 182 27
folder *Office* 245 19
folder-feeding station 184 17
folder unit *Offset Print.* 180 15, 29
folder unit *Letterpress* 181 55
folder unit *Photograv.* 182 27
folding 12 4-20
folding machine 249 58
folding mechanism 249 46
fold mountains 12 12-20
fold plate 185 10
fold unit 74 1
foliage 330 48
foliage plant 39 37
folk instruments 324 1-46
follicle *Man* 20 84
follicle *Bot.* 370 91
follower *Metalwk.* 140 43
follower *Composing.Rm.* 175 57
follow-through 293 84
font 332 10
fontage, lace ~ 355 65
font basin 332 11
food, canned ~ 96 25; 98 15-20
food, frozen ~ 99 58-61

food compartment 207 83
food pests 81 15-30
food price list 266 65
food slicer 40 38
food store, self-service ~ 99 1-96
food vacuole 357 6
fool 306 38
foolscap 306 39
foot *Man* 16 54; 17 26-29; 19 52-63
foot *Shoem.* 100 23
foot *Photog.* 114 71
foot *Joiner* 132 29
foot *Blacksm.* 137 15
foot *Bookbind.* 185 58
foot *Sailing* 284 40
foot *Music. Instr.* 326 23
foot, palmate ~ 73 36; 359 7
foot, prehensile ~ 364 34
foot, rubber ~ 114 45
foot, second ~ 286 59
foot, serpent's ~ 327 39
foot, webbed ~ 73 36; 359 6, 7
footage counter 117 52
foot bag *Infant Care etc.* 28 38
foot bag *Winter Countr.* 304 27
football 273 12; 291 17; 292 22
football boot 291 21
football game 273 10
football pad 291 33
football pitch 291 1-16
football player 292 23
football sock 291 58
footband 185 42
foot bar lever 100 27
footbath 282 22
footbed, surgical ~ 101 50
foot binding, front ~ 286 57
footboard 186 7, 13
foot brake 188 52
footbridge 15 78
foot control 139 27
foot control socket 249 66
foot-fault judge 293 24
footferry 15 60
foot gear-change control 188 55; 190 77
foot gearshift control 188 55; 190 77
footing 123 2
foot lever 83 34
footlight 316 26
footman 186 20
foot margin 185 58
foot muff *Infant Care etc.* 28 38
foot muff *Winter Countr.* 304 27
foot muscle 18 49
footnote 185 62
foot of bed 43 4
foot of goblet 162 42
foot of machine 133 25
foot of mast 284 20
foot passenger ferry 15 60
footpath 15 43
footpath under railway 15 44
foot pedal *Pest Contr.* 83 34
foot pedal *Forging* 139 27
foot pedal *Arc Weld.* 142 31
foot pedal *Letterpress* 181 12
foot pedal *Bookbind.* 183 18
footpiece *Mach. Tools* 149 12
footpiece *Carriages* 186 13
footprints 126 59
foot rail 267 52
footrest *Hairdresser* 105 18; 106 19
footrest *Bicycle* 187 47
footrest *Motorcycles etc.* 188 44

footrest *Railw.* 207 57
footrest *Winter Sp.* 301 58
footrest *Sports* 305 81
footrope *Sea Fish.* 90 9, 18
footrope *Ship* 219 46
foot scraper 123 25
foot switch *Hosp.* 27 21
foot switch *Dressm.* 103 26
foot switch *Sawmill* 157 66
foot switch, electric ~ 50 2
foot treadle 83 34
foot valve 269 6, 14, 43
footwear 101
fop 306 33
forage harvester, self-
    propelled ~ 64 34-39
forage plants 69 1-28
foramen 383 57
forceps, obstetrical ~ 26 53
forcing 55 24
forcing bed 55 16
forcing house 55 4
forearm *Man* 16 46
forearm *Horse* 72 21
forearm balance 295 26
forearm stand 295 26
forebay 217 39
forecarriage 65 14-19
forecastle 218 10, 19; 221 13;
    223 48
fore course 218 41; 219 55
foredeck 223 47; 284 10
foredeck, flooded ~ 258 65;
    259 77
fore edge 185 57
fore edge margin 185 57
fore end 95 51
forefinger 19 65
forefoot 72 22-26
foregrip 87 13
forehand 72 18-27
forehand stroke 293 40
forehand volley 293 41
forehead *Man* 16 4-5
forehead *Horse* 72 3
foreign counter 204 31
foreign exchange counter
    204 31; 250 10
foreign trade zone 225 2
foreleg 70 5; 88 25, 64
forelock 72 2
foremast 218 42; 219 2-4; 220
    21; 221 2
foremast, lower ~ 219 2
forepart 218 49
forepaw 70 6
forepeak 227 18, 28
fore royal 219 60
fore royal stay 219 13
fore royal yard 219 37
foresail 219 41; 219 55
foresail, square ~ 220 13
foresheet 284 23
fore ship 286 33, 36, 40
foresight 255 3, 23, 37; 305
    42
foresight block 255 23, 37
foreskin 20 70
forest 84 1-34
forestage 316 25
forestay 219 10; 284 15
forest Indian 352 19
forest labourer 84 18
forest pests 82
forestry 84; 85
forestry office 15 3
forest track 84 3
foretop 219 50
fore topgallant mast 219 4
fore topgallant rigging 219 18
fore topgallant sail 218 52
fore topgallant stay 219 12
fore topmast 219 3

fore topmast crosstrees 219 51
fore topmast rigging 219 17
fore topmast stay 219 11
fore topmast staysail 219 20
forewing 358 36
foreyard 219 32
forge 137 1-8, 1, 34
forget-me-not 378 26
forging and sizing press 139
    18
forging press, hydraulic ~ 139
    35
fork *Tablew. etc.* 45 7, 58
fork *Agr. Impl.* 66 3, 7, 22
fork *Horse* 71 29
fork *Optic. Instr.* 113 12
fork *Quarry* 158 33
fork, protective ~ 307 54
fork, rear ~ 188 14; 189 7
fork, swinging-arm ~ 188 14;
    189 7
fork blade 187 12
fork column 187 14
fork end 187 12
forklift 93 23; 206 16; 225 44;
    226 8
forklift truck 93 23; 206 16;
    225 44; 226 8
fork mount 113 24
fork mounting 113 12, 24
forks, front ~ 187 10-12
forks, telescopic ~ 188 8
fork spanner 134 2
fork truck 93 23; 206 16; 225
    44; 226 8
fork wrench 134 2
form *Office* 245 24
form *see* forme
formaldehyde atom 242 64
format selection 249 34
forme 174 10
forme, locked up ~ 181 36
forme bed 180 78; 181 17
forme-inking roller 181 18,
    27, 61
forms 36 42-86
Formula One racing car 290
    34
Formula Two racing car 290
    36
formwork 119 54-76
forsythia 373 1
forte 321 38
forte fortissimo 321 40
forte pedal 325 8
forte piano 321 41
fortissimo 321 39
fortress 15 74
fortune teller 308 36
forward *Swim.* 282 50
forward *Ball Games* 293 75
forward, reverse and still
    projection switch 117 88
forward horizontal stand 295
    30
forwarding agent 206 28
forwarding office 206 26
forwarding roll 180 4
forward kip 296 58
forward pace 295 43
forward roll 297 19, 20
forward somersault 297 18
forward split 295 14
forward straddle 295 4
forward walkover 297 26
forward wind button 249 73
Fosbury flop 298 9

fosse 329 37
fossette 16 16
foul 291 50; 299 34
foul line 292 48
foundation *Bees* 77 43
foundation *Floor etc. Constr.*
    123 2
foundation base 123 3
foundation pile 5 28
foundation trench 118 75
founder 148 8
fountain 272 8, 21, 22, 62; 334
    68
fountain pen 260 14
fountain roller 181 64; 249 52
Fourcault glass-drawing
    machine 162 8
Fourcault process 162 1
four-channel balance control
    241 42
four-channel demodulator
    241 45
four-channel level control
    241 42
four-eight time 320 31
four-four time 320 32
four-masters 220 28-31
four-to-pica 175 20
four-two time 320 33
four-wheel drive 194 1
fowl, domestic ~ 73 19-36
fowl run 74 11
foxglove 379 2
fox hunt 289 41-49
fox terrier, wire-haired ~ 70
    15
foyer 5 25; 267 1-26, 44-46;
    315 12-13
fraction 344 10, 19
fraction, complex ~ 344 17
fraction, compound ~ 344 17
fraction, improper ~ 344 16,
    18
fraction, proper ~ 344 15
fractionating column 145 37
fractions, vulgar 344 15-16
fractocumulus 8 12
fractostratus 8 11
Fraktur 342 3
frame *Agr. Mach.* 65 8, 90
frame *Bees* 77 40
frame *Optic.* 111 5
frame *Forging* 139 16
frame *Basketm.* 136 22
frame *Iron Foundry etc.* 148
    57
frame *Mach. Tools* 149 65
frame *Knitting* 167 33
frame *Railw.* 207 3; 208 5
frame *Shipbuild.* 222 58
frame *Aircraft* 230 55
frame *Rowing* 283 49, 67
frame *Sailing* 285 51
frame *Gymn.* 297 12
frame *Sports* 305 14, 88
frame, aluminium ~ 50 19
frame, annular ~ 235 47
frame, bone ~ 353 13
frame, C-shaped ~ 26 19; 27 17
frame, ferroconcrete ~ 119 2
frame, heated ~ 55 16
frame, iron ~ 325 2
frame, lower ~ 148 20
frame, metal ~ *Opticn.* 111 7
frame, metal ~ *Music. Instr.*
    324 76
frame, plate glass ~ 179 15
frame, reinforced concrete ~
    119 2

frame, sectional ~ 65 56
frame, shell ~ 111 8
frame, tortoiseshell ~ 111 8
frame, tubular ~ 188 9, 49
frame, upper ~ 148 19
frame, wire ~ 339 35
frame, wooden ~ 353 13
frame bar 64 51
frame-clamping machine 133
    42
frame-coding device 242
    8-10
frame counter 115 17; 313 28
frame-cramping machine
    133 42
frame drum 353 26
frame end plate 164 26
frame hive 77 45-50
frame-mounting device 133
    48
frame number 187 51
frame sample 124 2
frame-sanding pad 133 34
frame saw, vertical ~ 157 2
frame section, aft ~ 234 49
frame section, forward ~ 234
    45
frame slipway 222 19-21
frame stand 133 43
frame tent 278 36
frame timber 119 64
frame timber, bolted ~ 119
    74
frame vent 55 17
frame wood 124 3
frame wood sample 124 2
framework 339 22
framework support 214 77
framing 336 11
framing chisel 132 11
framing control 312 29
framing table 132 62
franc 252 15, 16, 17, 18
Frankfurter 96 8
Frankfurter garland cake 97
    42
Frankfurter sausage 96 8
franking machine 22 24; 236
    7, 27, 47
freak show 308 19
free backward circle 297 29
free combination knob 326 40
free combination stud 326 40
free exercise 295
free-fall positions 288 60-62
free flight model, remote-
    controlled ~ 288 86
free kick 291 43
free leg *Athletics* 298 27
free leg *Winter Sp.* 302 3
free leg, vertical ~ 298 25
free port 225 2
freestyle relay race 282 24-32
freestyle wrestling 299 10-12
free-throw line 292 38
free walkover forward 297 25
freeway *Map* 15 16
freeway *Docks* 225 54
free-wheel hub 187 63
freezer 22 63; 96 21; 97 65; 98
    74
freezer, upright ~ 39 7
free zone enclosure 225 3
free zone frontier 225 3
freight agent 206 28
freight barge 216 25
freight car 206 6
freight car, flat ~ 206 21
freight car, open ~ 213 8, 33
freight car, special ~ 213 33
freight depot *Map* 15 91
freight depot *Station* 206
freighter 221 57

freight house 206 7, 26-39
freight house door 206 37
freight office 206 26
freight truck 206 15
French chalk 271 39
French horn 323 41
French lady 355 51
French toast 97 54
French window 37 21
frequency band 309 22
fresco 338 40
fresh-air inlet 356 16
fresh-air inlet and control 191 85
fresh-air regulator 191 86
fresh meat counter 99 51
fresh milk filling and packing plant 76 20
fresh milk tank 76 15
fresh oil tank 65 46
freshwater eel 364 17
freshwater pearl mussel 357 33
fresh water tank 221 70; 223 79
Fresnel lens 115 64
fret Roulette 275 30
fret Music. Instr. 324 9
fretsaw 135 12; 260 53
fretsaw blade 135 13; 260 54
friction drive 116 33; 312 37
friction pad 192 49
friction tape 127 34
friction wheel 322 26
fridge Kitch. 39 2
fridge Flat 46 33
fridge Disco 317 10
frieze 335 9
frieze, Babylonian ~ 333 19
frieze decoration 334 16
frigate 258 53
frill 31 34; 32 44
frill collar 31 46
frill front 32 44
fringe 34 36
fringe, decorative ~ 353 25
fringe region 7 34
frit 162 2
frit feeder 162 13
frit funnel 162 13
frock coat 355 76
frog Agr. Mach. 65 8
frog Road Constr. 200 26
frog Railw. 202 24
frog Music. Instr. 323 13
frog position 288 61
frog's bit 378 29
frond 378 49
front 305 1
front, cold ~ 8 13; 9 27
front, extended ~ 200 10
front, hinged ~ 213 10
front, occluded ~ 9 25
front, warm ~ 8 5; 9 26
frontalis 19 4
front axle pivot pin 65 48
front axle suspension 65 49
front band 71 9
front element mount 115 6
front fan-jet 232 33
front-line player 293 63
front panel, sliding ~ 349 27
front roller underclearer 164 44
fronts 9 25-29
fronts, cold ~ 8 13-17
fronts, warm ~ 8 5-12
front seat headrest 193 7
front seat head restraint 193 7
front sight block 255 23, 37
front support Free Exerc. 295 21, 23
front support Gymn. 296 28

front wheel drive 191 52
front wheel drum brake 188 36
froth 266 4
fruit Weeds 61 11, 20, 23
fruit Restaurant 266 57
fruit Decid. Trees 371 4, 19, 28, 45, 69
fruit Conifers 372 53, 64
fruit Shrubs etc. 373 12, 18, 22, 27, 29, 32; 374 4, 8, 12, 19, 25, 29, 31, 34
fruit Flowers etc. 375 4, 7, 10, 13, 17, 24, 35, 37, 47; 376 3, 6, 14
fruit Alp. Plants etc. 378 11, 38, 42
fruit Trop. Plants 382 3, 5, 10, 15, 17, 24, 39
fruit Industr. Plants 383 14, 18, 21, 28, 32, 40, 43, 52, 56, 59
fruit South. Fruits 384 19, 26, 39, 45
fruit, aggregate ~ Soft Fruit 58 28
fruit, aggregate ~ Bot. 370 100, 101
fruit, canned ~ 98 16
fruit, compound ~ Soft Fruit 58 28
fruit, compound ~ Bot. 370 100, 101
fruit, dehisced ~ 375 27
fruit, immature ~ 378 31
fruit, indehiscent ~ 375 43
fruit, mature ~ Decid. Trees 371 61
fruit, mature ~ Trop. Plants 382 33
fruit, ripe ~ Decid. Trees 371 61
fruit, ripe ~ Trop. Plants 382 33
fruit, soft ~ 58 1-30
fruit, stewed ~ 45 30
fruit, unripe ~ 378 31
fruit, young ~ Decid. Trees 371 59
fruit, young ~ South. Fruits 384 31
fruit and vegetable counter 99 80
fruit and vegetable garden 52 1-32
fruit bowl 45 29, 40
fruit capsule, mature ~ 382 44
fruit capsule, ripe ~ 382 44
fruit cone 372 2, 29, 30, 36, 41, 57
fruit dish 45 28
fruit flan 97 22; 99 20
fruit garden 52
fruiting body 381 2
fruiting branch Decid. Trees 371 3, 11, 18, 31, 36, 41, 47, 50, 56, 64
fruiting branch Conifers 372 40, 51, 59, 63, 66, 70
fruiting branch Trop. Plants 382 2, 37
fruiting branch Industr. Plants 383 34, 46
fruiting branch South. Fruits 384 38
fruiting palm 384 2
fruit juice 98 18; 266 58
fruit juice bottle 99 74
fruit juice can 99 75
fruit knife 45 71
fruit pests 80 1-19
fruit picker 56 22
fruit pip 58 37, 60

fruit preserver 40 23
fruits 370 91-102
fruits, dehiscent ~ 370 91-96
fruits, indehiscent ~ 370 97-102
fruits, Mediterranean ~ 384
fruits, southern ~ 384
fruits, subtropical ~ 384
fruits, tropical ~ 384
fruit scale 372 67
fruit spoon 45 66
fruit stall 308 53
fruit storage shed 225 52
fruit tree, standard ~ 52 30
fruit trees, dwarf ~ 52 1,2,16,17,29
fruit warehouse 225 52
frustum of a cone 347 45
frying pan 40 4
fry pond 89 6
F sharp major 320 61
F sharp minor 320 58
fuchsia 53 3
fuel cell 234 62
fuel gas 145 52
fuel gauge 191 38, 65
fuel-handling hoist 154 27
fuel hand pump 190 64
fuel-injection engine 190 1
fuel injector 190 32
fuel inlet 192 13
fuel leak line 190 53
fuel level sensor 234 27
fuel line 190 31
fuel line duct 234 40
fuel oil 38 50
fuel oil, heavy ~ 145 59
fuel oil, light ~ 145 58
fuel oil tank 212 75
fuel pin 154 4
fuel pipe 286 25
fuel pressure gauge 230 19
fuel pressure line 190 52
fuel pressure pipe 190 52
fuel pressure regulator 190 17
fuel rod 154 4
fuel storage 154 28
fuel supply pipe 190 31
fuel tank Moon L. 6 7, 29, 37
fuel tank Agr. Mach. 65 42
fuel tank Motorcycles etc. 188 10, 28
fuel tank Motorcycle 189 2
fuel tank Railw. 209 20; 212 56
fuel tank Ship 223 80
fuel tank Aircraft 230 48
fuel tank Space 234 58
fuel tank, forward ~ 235 21
fuel tank, jettisonable ~ 235 46
fuel tank, main ~ 212 4
fuel tanker 258 97
fuel tender 210 67
fuel warning light 191 71
full circle 308 43
full-colour print 340 28
full-cone indicator 165 7
fuller's earth 199 38
fulling machine, rotary ~ 168 1
fulling roller, bottom ~ 168 6
fulling roller, top ~ 168 3
full point 342 16
full spread position 288 60
full-step 320 51, 53
full stop 342 16
full title 185 46
fulmar 359 12
fume extraction equipment 142 13
fume extractor 255 59, 89
fumigation chamber, mobile ~ 83 15

fumigation plant, vacuum ~ 83 11
fumigator, vacuum ~ 83 11
function, trigonometrical ~ 346 32
function key 247 17
funeral 331 33-41
fungi, edible ~ 381
fungi, esculent ~ 381
fungi, poisonous ~ 379 10-13
funicular 214 12
funicular railway car 214 13
funnel Photog. 116 12
funnel Ship 221 8, 40, 75, 84; 223 1
funnel Warships 258 58; 259 32
funnel Chem. 350 16
funnel, aft ~ 258 20
funnel, forward ~ 258 19
Funnel-Beaker culture 328 12
funnel marking 223 2
fur marker 131 22
furnace 199 29
furnace, continuous ~ 139 1
furnace, electric ~ 147 51-54
furnace, gas ~ 139 47
furnace, gas-fired ~ 139 47; 140 11
furnace, low-shaft ~ 147 51-54
furnace, stationary ~ 147 23
furnace bed 38 66
furnace incline 147 2
furnace lift 147 2
furnace thermometer 38 64
furniture 174 8; 181 40
furniture lorry 268 47
furniture truck 268 47
furrier 131 1
furrow Agr. 63 8
furrow Mills 91 17
furrow, gluteal ~ 16 42
furrow wheel 65 16
fur seal 367 18
fur-sewing machine 131 9
fur side 131 12, 17
furskin 131 5
furskin, cut ~ 131 14
furskin, uncut ~ 131 6
furskins 131 11-21
fur trapper 306 8
fur worker 131 8, 23
fuse Electr. 127 19, 36
fuse Quarry 158 28
fuse box Hall 41 19
fuse box Weaving 166 23
fuse carrier 127 68
fuse cartridge 127 36
fuse holder 127 35
fuselage 230 54; 288 26
fuselage attachment 235 4
fuselage tank 257 31
fuse wire 127 68

G

gable 37 15; 121 5; 122 25
gable, curved ~ 336 5
gable, round ~ 335 50
gable end 37 15; 122 25
gable roof 37 5; 121 1
gable slate 122 80
gaffer 310 37
gaffsail 220 1
gaff topsail 219 31
gag Horse 71 53
gag Fish Farm. 89 42
gag bit 71 53
gage see gauge

gaillardia 60 19
gait 289 7
gaiter, leather ~ 191 92
gaits of the horse 72 39-44
Galaxy 3 35
gale 373 33
galena 351 14
galingale 53 17
gall *Gdn. Pests* 80 33
gall *Forest Pests* 82 34
gallant soldier 61 31
gall bladder 20 11, 36
galleries under bark 82 23-24
gallery *Forest Pests* 82 24
gallery *Coal* 144 29
gallery *Theatre* 315 16
gallery *Church* 330 25
gallery, drilled ~ 192 21
gallery grave 328 16
galley *Composing Rm.* 174 12, 44
galley *Ship* 218 44-50; 223 42
galley *Aircraft* 231 22
galley loader 233 22
galley slave 218 48
gall gnat 80 40
gall midge 80 40
gallop, full ~ 72 43-44, 43, 44
gallows 221 87
gall wasp 82 33
galvanometer 11 44
gamba 322 23
gambling casino 275 1
gambling game 275 1-33
gambling table 275 8
gambrel 94 21
gambrel roof 121 18
gambrel stick 94 21
game 86 28; 88
game, furred ~ 86 35
game, positional ~ 276 1-16
game, winged ~ 86 41
game of chance 275 1-33
game path 86 16
game preserve 86 1-8
gaming room 275 1
gaming table 275 8
gamma radiation 1 33, 40
gammon steak 95 54
gander 73 34
gang mill 157 2
gang stitcher 184 15
gangway 38 3
gangway, central ~ *Railw.* 208 23
gangway, central ~ *Ship* 218 46
gannet 359 9
gantry *Photomech. Reprod.* 177 13
gantry *Shipbuild.* 222 26
gantry *Docks* 225 40
gantry crane 157 27; 206 55; 222 20, 25
gantry support 214 24
garage *Dwellings* 37 32, 79
garage *Garage* 195
garage, agent's ~ 195 1-55
garage, distributor's ~ 195 1-55
garage driveway 37 52
garbage 199 17
garbage can 199 3
garbage can dumping device 199 2
garbage container 199 4
garbage disposition 199
garbage incineration unit 199 28
garbage truck 199 1
garden 37 57
garden, Baroque ~ 272
garden, formal ~ 272 1-

garden, front ~ 37 58
garden chair 37 49
gardener 55 20
garden fence 52 10
garden flowers 60
garden gate 272 31
garden hedge 51 9
garden hoe 66 1
garden hose 37 42; 56 27
garden house 52 14
garden ladder 52 8
garden light 37 38
garden mould 55 15
garden pansy 60 2
garden parasol 37 48
garden path 51 14; 52 23
garden pests 80
garden pond 51 16
garden rake 51 4
garden rose 60 15
garden seat 272 42
garden shed 52 3
garden shovel 55 14
garden sieve 55 13
garden spider 358 45
garden strawberry 58 16
garden table 37 50
garden tiger 365 7
garden tools 56
garden wall 37 37
gargoyle 335 30
garland 306 17; 335 54
garnet 351 7
Garratt locomotive 210 64
garter 318 28
gas, liquid ~ 145 53
gas, natural ~ 12 30
gas appliances 126 12-25
gas bottle 278 53
gas cap 12 30
gas circulation unit 83 16
gas-collecting main 156 17
gas compressor 156 26
gas connection 141 31
gas control 141 32
gas cooler *Offshore Drill.* 146 27
gas cooler *Coking* 156 19
gas cooling 156 29
gas cutting installation 148 67
gas cylinder 138 35
gas cylinder manifold 141 1
gas drying 156 30
gas extractor 156 21
gas fitter 126 1
gas fitter's tools 126 58-86
gas flue 152 12
gas generator 350 59
gas holder 156 25
gas hose 141 9
gas inlet 350 2
gas inlet pipe 350 2
gaskin 72 36
gas lighter 107 30
gas main 198 21
gas main, high-pressure ~ 156 45
gas main, low-pressure ~ 156 44
gas meter *Plumb. etc.* 126 5
gas meter *Coking* 156 31
gas oil component 145 42
gasoline can 196 25
gasoline canister 84 36
gasoline inlet 192 13
gasoline pump 196 1
gasoline pump, self-service ~ 196 8
gasoline pump hose 196 2
gasoline station 196 1-29
gasoline tank 188 10, 28; 189 2; 305 87
gasometer 144 12

gas outlet *Oil, Petr.* 145 29
gas outlet *Chem.* 350 63
gas pipe *Pest Contr.* 83 14
gas pipe *Forging* 139 54
gas pipe *Metalwkr.* 140 12
gas pipe *Oil, Petr.* 145 29
gas pipe *Iron & Steel* 147 18, 27
gas pliers *Plumb. etc.* 126 58
gas pliers *Metalwkr.* 140 68
gas pressure vessel 234 32
gas regenerator chamber 147 28
gas regulator 255 34; 350 6
gas-separating plant 145 69
gas separator 145 28
gas station 196 1-29
gas supply 27 41
gas tap 261 24
gastrocnemius 18 62
gas tube 83 35
gas turbine 209 9
gas turbine, auxiliary ~ 231 33
gas turbine, twin-shaft ~ 209 23
gas turbine controller 209 16
gas turbine driving unit 209 8
gas turbine fuel tank 209 17
gas turbine trainset 209 1
gas-washing bottle 350 58
gas water 156 39
gas welder 141
gas welding torch 130 14
gate 202 40; 289 8; 337 24
gate, removable ~ 118 46
gate, sliding ~ 217 18, 55
gate, vertical ~ 217 31, 38
gate, wrought iron ~ 272 31
gate and rails 289 8
gateau 99 15; 265 4
gateaux 97 22-24
gatehouse 329 22
gateman 202 42
gate pole 301 30
gateway 336 15; 337 11
gateway, monumental ~ 333 9
gatherer and wire stitcher 184 15
gathering and wire-stitching machine 184 15
gathering machine 249 59
gathering station 249 60
gaucho 306 31
gauge 76 6
gauntlet 329 50
gauze 183 33; 185 20
gauze, sterile ~ 22 58
gauze, wire ~ 350 18, 19
gauze roll holder 185 19
G-clef 320 8
gear *Gdn. Tools* 56 20
gear *Iron Foundry etc.* 148 63
gear *Road Constr.* 201 11
gear *Hydr. Eng.* 217 48
gear, epicyclic ~ 143 94
gear, planetary ~ 143 94
gearbox *Agr. Mach.* 65 79
gearbox *Turner* 135 4
gearbox *Cotton Spin.* 164 2, 33, 39
gearbox, five-speed ~ 189 6
gear-change *Agr. Mach.* 65 35
gear-change *Motorcycles etc.* 188 31
gear-change, floor-type ~ 191 91
gear-change, two-speed ~ 188 12
gear-change lever 189 28
gear-change pattern 192 47
gear control 149 2
gearing *Agr. Mach.* 64 50, 65

gearing *Overh. Irrign.* 67 21
gearing *Road Constr.* 201 11
gearing, helical ~ 143 89
gearing, multi-speed ~ 190 72
gearing, multi-step ~ 190 72
gear lever 191 91; 192 46
gear meter 76 4
gears *Agr. Mach.* 64 50, 65
gears *Overh. Irrign.* 67 21
gear shaft 232 58
gear shaft, intermediate ~ 190 57
gearshift 65 23, 35; 188 31
gearshift, two-speed ~ 188 12
gearshift lever *Motorcycle* 189 28
gearshift lever *Car* 191 91; 192 46
gearshift pattern 192 47
gearshift rod 192 41
gearshift switch 134 46
gear wheel, helical ~ 192 34, 36, 39, 43
gear wheel, herringbone ~ 143 87
gear wheel, stepped ~ 143 82
gear wheels 143 82-96
gecko 364 36
Geiger counter 2 19
Geiger-Müller counter 2 19
geisha 353 39
gelatine 316 49
gelding 73 2
Gemini 3 28; 4 55
general cargo ship 225 14; 226 13
general cargo transit shed 225 9
general practice 22 1-74
general practitioner 23 2
general service lamp 127 56
generator *Nucl. Energy* 154 15, 47, 53
generator *Energy Sources* 155 46
generator *Intern. Combust. Eng.* 190 76
generator *Railw.* 211 46
generator *Ship* 223 74
generator exhaust 146 2
generator unit 231 33
Geneva movement 312 38
Genoa jib 284 16
genouillère 329 53
gentleman *Café* 265 22
gentleman *Hist. Cost.* 355 54, 61, 73
'gentlemen' 233 47
'gentlemen's toilet' 233 47
geodesy 14 46-62
geography, physical ~ 11; 12; 13
geology 12 1-33
geometrical shape 260 79
geometrid 80 16; 82 28
geometry 346; 347
geometry, elementary ~ 346 1-58
geometry, Euclidian ~ 346 1-58
geranium 53 1
gerbera 51 26
germ 370 86
German brown trout 364 15
German hand 342 11
German pointer 70 40
German sheepdog 70 25
German shepherd 70 25
geyser *Phys. Geog.* 11 21
geyser *Plumb. etc.* 126 12-13
G flat major 320 68
gherkin, pickled ~ 98 29
ghost train 308 5

giant 308 20; 327 37
giant figure 306 63
gib *Plumb.* 125 3
gib *Mach. Parts etc.* 143 74
gig 186 34
gig, four-oared ~ 283 26-33
Gigantocypris agassizi 369 1
gilder 183 2
gilding *Painter* 129 40
gilding *Bookbind.* 183 1
gilding and embossing press
  183 26
gill *Dom. Anim.* 73 24
gill *Edib. Fungi* 381 4, 6
gill, tufted ~ 364 19
gill cleft 364 3
gill cover 364 5
gill slit 364 3
gillyflower 60 7
gimbal ring 224 50
gimbal suspension 241 23
gimlet 120 65
gimping 102 28
gimping needle 102 29
gingerbread 97 51
gipsy girl 306 36
gipsy moth 80 1
giraffe 367 4
giraffe house 356 10
girder, steel ~ 143 3-7
girdle 32 5
girdle clasp 328 24
girl, exotic ~ 306 30
girt 120 50
girth 71 18, 36; 289 11
girth, emergency ~ 71 23
girth, second ~ 71 23
glacier *Phys. Geog.* 12 49
glacier *Mountain.* 300 22
glacier snout 12 51
glacier table 12 56
gladiolus 51 28; 60 11
gland, bulbourethral ~ 20 75
gland, parotid ~ 19 9
gland, pituitary ~ 17 43
gland, prostate ~ 20 76
gland, submandibular ~ 19 11
gland, submaxillary ~ 19 11
gland, suprarenal ~ 20 29
gland, thyroid ~ 20 1
glans penis 20 69
glass 54 9
glass, armoured ~ 109 29
glass, bullet-proof ~ 250 3
glass, coloured ~ 260 68
glass, crystal ~ 45 86
glass, frosted ~ 124 5
glass, laminated ~ 124 5
glass, lined ~ 124 6
glass, molten ~ 162 23, 31, 50
glass, ornamental ~ 124 6
glass, patterned ~ 124 5
glass, pulverized ~ 340 48
glass, raw ~ 124 6
glass, shatterproof ~ 124 5
glass, stained ~ 124 6; 330 15
glass, tapered ~ 45 85
glass, thick ~ 124 5
glass, wired ~ 124 6
glassblower 162 38
glassblowing 162 38-47
glass case 356 15
glass cloth 130 29
glass cutter, diamond ~ 124 25
glass cutter, steel ~ 124 26
glass cutters 124 25-26
glass-drawing machine 162 8
glasses 111 9
glass fibre, production of ~
  162 48-55
glass fibre products 162 56-58
glass filament 162 52
glass forming 162 38-47

glass furnace 162 1, 49
glass holder 124 9
glasshouse pot, covered ~ 162
  46
glassmaker 162 38
glassmaking 162 38-47
glass mosaic picture 260 69
glass paper 135 25
glass pliers 124 19
glass ribbon 162 10
glass sponge 369 7
glass wool 162 58
glassworker 124 8
glazier 124; 124 8
glazing sheet 116 58
glazing sprig 124 24
glede 362 11
glider 287 3
glider, high-performance ~
  287 9
glider, motorized ~ 287 8
glider, powered ~ 287 8
glider field 287 13
gliding 287
globe 42 13
globe, frosted glass ~ 267 4
globe, solar ~ 4 36
globe, terrestrial ~ 4 8
globe artichoke 57 41
globe lamp 267 4
globe thistle 53 14
glove 33 67; 292 12; 298 47;
  318 31
glove, catcher's ~ 292 60
glove, fielder's ~ 292 59
glove, goalkeeper's ~ 291 19
glove box lock 191 89
glove compartment lock 191
  89
glove stand 271 20
glow plug 190 66
gloxinia 53 7
glue 48 4; 260 50-52, 51
glue, joiner's ~ 132 13
glue cylinder 184 10
glue-enamel plate 179 32
glue pot 132 12, 13; 183 15;
  236 5; 260 57
glue roller 184 10; 185 33
glue size 128 4
glue tank 184 9; 185 32
glue well 132 13
gluing 183 14
gluing cylinder 184 10
gluing machine 185 31
gluing mechanism 184 4
glume 68 11
gluteus maximus 18 60
G major 320 56
G minor 320 64
gnat 358 16
goaf 144 37
goal *Playground* 273 11
goal *Swim.* 282 46
goal *Ball Games* 291 35; 292 7
goal *Winter Sp.* 302 37
goal area 291 5
goalkeeper *Playground* 273 14
goalkeeper *Swim.* 282 47
goalkeeper *Ball Games* 291
  10; 292 8
goalkeeper *Winter Sp.* 302 36
goal kick 291 38
goal line 291 7
goalpost 273 11; 291 37
goal scorer 273 13
Goat *Astron.* 3 36; 4 62
goat *Dom. Anim.* 73 14
goatee beard 34 10
goat's beard *Forest Plants etc.*
  377 5
goatsbeard *Forest Plants etc.*
  377 5

goat's beard *Edib. Fungi* 381
  32
goatsbeard *Edib. Fungi* 381 32
goat willow 371 24
gob *Coal* 144 37
gob *Glass Prod.* 162 40
gobbler 73 28
goblet, hand-blown ~ 162 41
gobo 310 51
gob of molten glass 162 23, 31
go-cart 273 33
god, Indian ~ 337 19
godet 30 52
Godet wheel 169 16
godparent 332 13
God's acre 331 21-41
'GO' gauging member 149 57
goggles 140 21; 303 15
going about 285 27
go-kart 305 83
go-karting 305 82
gold *Heraldry* 254 24
gold *Crystals* 351 6
gold and silver balance 108 35
goldcrest 361 10
goldcup 375 8
gold cushion 183 6
golden chain 374 32
golden crested wren 361 10
golden maidenhair 377 17
golden oriole 360 7
golden rain 374 32
goldfinch 360 1
gold finisher 183 2
gold knife 183 7
gold leaf 129 45, 52; 183 5
gold size 129 44
goldsmith 108 17
golf 293 79-93
golf ball *Office* 249 15
golf ball *Ball Games* 293 89
golf ball cap 249 30
golf ball typewriter 249 1
golf course 293 79-82
golfer 293 83
golf trolley 293 85
gondola *Supermkt.* 99 23, 43,
  62
gondola *Railw.* 214 20
gondola *Airsports* 288 64
gondola cableway 214 19
gonfalon 253 12
gong 299 46
goods 271 10
goods, bulky ~ 206 18
goods, general ~ 206 4
goods depot 15 91
goods lorry 206 15
goods office 206 26
goods shed 206 7, 26-39
goods shed door 206 37
goods shelf 47 36; 98 14
goods station 206
goods van 206 6; 213 22
goods van, covered ~ 213 14
goods wagon, covered ~ 213
  14
goods wagon, open ~ 213 8
goosander 359 15
goose 73 34; 272 52
gooseberry 58 9
gooseberry bush 52 19; 58 1
gooseberry cane, flowering ~
  58 2
gooseberry flan 97 22
gooseberry flower 58 6
goosefoot 61 25
gooseneck 284 37
gorge 13 52
gorgerin 334 22
gorget 329 43
gorilla 368 16
goshawk 362 10

'GO' side 149 60
gosling 73 34
gouache 338 17
gouge 132 9; 135 15; 339 17
gouge, U-shaped ~ 340 6
gouge, V-shaped ~ 339 20;
  340 9
gourd 354 27
governor 224 56
gown 105 34; 106 4; 355 25,
  36, 66
gown, linen ~ 355 5
gown, open ~ 355 50
gown, sleeveless ~ 355 50
graben 12 11
grace notes 321 14-22
graces 321 14-22
grade crossing, protected ~
  202 39
grade crossing, unprotected ~
  202 49
grade crossings 202 39-50
grader 200 19
grader levelling blade 200 21
grader ploughshare 200 21
gradient 347 12
grading 74 44
grading, automatic ~ 74 52
graduated measuring rod 14
  47
graduation house *Map* 15 32
graduation house *Spa* 274 1
graftage 54 30-39
grafting 54 30-39
grain *Arable Crops* 68 1-37, 4,
  37
grain *Brew.* 92 50
grain *Graphic Art* 340 47
grain, farinaceous ~ 68 13
grain auger 64 20
grain harvest 63 31-41
grain leaf 68 8, 19
grain lifter 64 2
grain pest 81 27
grain tank 64 23
grain tank auger 64 24
grain tank unloader 64 25
grain unloader spout 64 26
grain weevil 81 16
grammar school 261 1-45
gramophone 309 31
gramophone box 309 35
gramophone needle 309 33
gramophone record 309 32
granary weevil 81 16
grand 325 40
grandee 306 26
grandfather clock 110 24; 309
  56
grand piano 325 40
grand piano pedal 325 41
grandstand, glass-covered ~
  289 34
granite 302 42
gran turismo car 193 32
granular texture 340 47
grape 80 21; 99 89
grape-berry moth 80 22, 23,
  24
grape crusher 78 17
grapefruit 384 23
grape gatherer 78 11
grape phylloxera 80 26
grapevine *Wine Grow.* 78 2-9
grapevine *Sports* 299 10
grape worm 80 23, 24
graphic art 340
graphic art studio 340 27-64
graphite 1 54
grapnel 218 11
grapple 218 11
grappling iron 218 11
grasp, kinds of ~ 296 40-46

grasping arm 2 47
grass 136 26
grass, paniculate ~ 69 27
grassbox 56 29
grasshopper, artificial ~ 89 68
grassland 15 18
grassland, marshy ~ 15 19
grassland, rough ~ 15 5
grass ledge 300 4
grass shears 56 48
grass snake 364 38
grasstrack racing 290 24-28
grass verge 200 56
grate 199 33
graticule *Map* 14 1-7
graticule *Hunt.* 87 31-32
graticule *Photomech. Reprod.*
177 4
graticule adjuster screw 87 30
graticule system 87 31
grating 141 14
grating spectrograph 5 5
graupel 9 35
grave *Church* 331 23, 34
grave *Script* 342 31
grave, child's ~ 331 29
grave, soldier's ~ 331 32
grave digger 331 22
gravel 118 36; 119 26
gravel filter layer 199 23
grave mound 331 24
graver 175 33; 340 5
graver, round-headed ~ 340
20
gravestone 331 26
graveyard 331 21-41
graveyard chapel 331 28
graveyard gate 331 19
graveyard wall 331 18
gravity fault 12 7
gravity fuelling point 257 32
gravity hammer, air-lift ~
139 24
gravity mixer 118 33
gravure cylinder 182 10
gravure cylinder, etched ~
182 22
gravure cylinder, printed ~
182 17
gravure etcher 182 18
gravure printing 182
gravy boat 45 17
gravy ladle 45 18
gray *see* grey
grayhound 70 24
grease gun 195 30
grease nipple 143 81
greasepaint stick 315 46
greasy chalk 340 26
great apes 368 14-16
Great Bear 3 29
great brain 17 42; 18 22
Great Dane 70 14
Great Dog 3 14
Greater Bear 3 29
greater burnet saxifrage 69 28
Greater Dog 3 14
greater water newt 364 20
great hall 329 30
great horned owl 362 15
great mullein 376 9
great organ 326 1, 43
great primer 175 30
great tit 361 9
great titmouse 361 9
greave 329 54
Greek 355 3
Greek woman 355 1
green *Ball Games* 293 82
green *Colour* 343 4
green bowls 305 21
green cloth 277 15
green cormorant 359 10

greenfly 358 13
greengage 59 24
green grasshopper 358 8
greenhouse, heated ~ 55 32
greenhouse, polythene ~ 55
40
greenhouse, unheated ~ 55 33
green liquor, uncleared ~ 172
41
green liquor preheater 172 43
green locust 358 8
green oak roller moth 82 43
green oak tortrix 82 43
green plover 359 21
Greenwich meridian 14 5
grenzanhydrite 154 67
Gretchen style 34 31
greyhound 70 24
grey scale 343 15
grey sea eagle 362 5
grid *Cotton Spin.* 163 26
grid *Water* 269 11
grid *Theatre* 316 4
grid hearth 139 1
gridiron 316 4
griffin 327 11
grill *Painter* 129 12
grill *Station* 204 38
grill *Fair* 308 33
grinder *Painter* 129 29
grinder *Metalwkr.* 140 18
grinder, continuous ~ 172 53,
66
grinder, pneumatic ~ 148 44
grinder chuck 157 46
grinding, hollow ~ 302 22
grinding cylinder 161 1
grinding disc 340 46
grinding machine 140 18
grinding machine, universal
~ 150 1
grinding machine bed 150 6
grinding machine table 150 7
grinding-roller bearing 163
41
grinding stone *Paperm.* 172
71
grinding stone *Ethnol.* 354 24
grinding wheel *Dent.* 24 36
grinding wheel *D.I.Y.* 134 23
grinding wheel *Blacksm.* 137
19; 138 8
grinding wheel *Metalwkr.* 140
19
grinding wheel *Mach. Tools*
150 4
grinding wheel *Sawmill* 157
43
grindstone 172 71
grip *Photog.* 114 37
grip *Cine Film* 117 61
grip *Bicycle* 187 3
grip *Navig.* 224 9
grip *Rowing* 283 35
grip *Athletics* 298 45
grip *Winter Sp.* 301 6
grip *Sports* 305 57
grip *Films* 313 21
gripper 180 65
gripper bar 180 56
gripping jaw 149 36
grip sole 101 19
grist 92 42
grit guard 148 40
gritter, self-propelled ~ 200
41
grocer 98 41
grocer's shop 98 1-87
groceryman 98 41
grocery store 98 1-87
groin 16 38
groin *see* groyne
groin vault 335 31-32; 336 42

groom *Carriages* 186 27
groom *Church* 332 16
groove *Iron Foundry etc.* 148
59
groove *Sawmill* 157 6
groove *Ball Games* 291 29
groove *Winter Sp.* 301 39
groove *Music. Instr.* 326 13
groove *Art* 334 27
groove, anal ~ 16 41
grooving 157 6
groschen 252 13
Grotesque 342 7
grotto 272 1
ground 123 9
ground, fallow ~ 63 1
ground, icy ~ 304 19
ground avalanche 304 1
ground control 6 44
ground floor 37 2; 118 7
ground-floor landing 123 23
ground game 86 35
ground ivy 375 18
ground layer 7 7
ground nut 383 41
ground-nut oil 98 24
ground power unit 233 22
groundsheet ring 278 26
ground signals 288 52-54
ground state level 1 18
ground tackle 223 49-51
groundwater 12 21
groundwater level 269 1, 42,
63
groundwater stream 269 3
groundwood 172 68
groundwood mill 172 53-65
groundwood pulp 172 77, 78
group 260 3; 268 60
group instruction 242 1
group selector switch 238 42
grove 354 5
grower 55 20
grower, commercial ~ 55 20
growing stock 74 1
growler 186 26
growth, annual ~ 372 25
groyne *Phys. Geog.* 13 37
groyne *Rivers* 216 19
groyne head *Phys. Geog.* 13
38
groyne head *Rivers* 216 20
grub 58 64; 77 29; 81 20; 358
9; 80 6, 19, 36, 41, 46, 53,
54; 82 25, 36
grubber 55 21; 65 55
grub screw 143 48
Grus 3 42
G sharp minor 320 60
GT car 193 32
guanaco 366 30
guard *Blacksm.* 138 9
guard *Metalwkr.* 140 20
guard *Fencing* 294 35, 38, 43
guard, king's ~ 306 68
guard, protective ~ 168 45
guard board 118 29
guard cam 167 57
guard for V-belt 180 58
guard iron 210 34
guard netting 118 90
guard rail *Roof & Boilerr.* 38
28
guard rail *Agr. Mach.* 64 55
guard rail *Forestry* 84 8
guard rail *Floor etc. Constr.*
123 53
guard rail *Weaving* 165 31
guard rail *Railw.* 202 23
guard rail *Ship* 221 121
guard rail *Shipbuild.* 222 66
gudgeon pin 192 26
guelder rose 373 10

guest rope 227 14
gugelhupf 97 33
guide 23 21
guide, stationary ~ 243 21
guide bar *Cotton Spin.* 164 17
guide bar *Weaving* 165 38
guide bearing 113 14
guide block 174 48; 176 18
guide chain 65 13
guide-chain crossbar 65 12
guide dog 70 25
guide groove 217 75
guide notch 117 36
guide pin 243 21
guide post 15 110
guide rail *Weaving* 165 3
guide rail *Railw.* 214 56
guide rail *Store* 271 54
guide rod 200 27
guide roller *Sawmill* 157 5
guide roller *Cotton Spin.* 164
18
guide roller *Films* 312 29
guide step 117 36
guide tractor 141 19
guiding blade 322 40
guiding roller 312 29
guiding slot *Weaving* 165 11
guiding slot *Music. Instr.* 322
41
guilder 252 19
guillemet 342 27
guillemot 359 13
guilloline *Plumb.* 125 26
guilloline *Bookbind.* 183 16;
185 1
guilloline cutter, automatic ~
185 1
guinea fowl 73 27
guinea pig 366 12
guiro 324 60
guitar 318 8; 324 12, 73
guitarist 318 9
guitar player 318 9
gulden 252 19
gules 254 27
Gulf Stream 14 30
gull 359 14
gullet *Man* 17 49; 20 23, 40
gullet *Bees* 77 19
gullet *Forestry* 84 28
gull wing, inverted ~ 229 14
gully 12 44
gum 19 15
gun 218 50
gun, pneumatic ~ 94 3
gun, self-cocking ~ 87 23
gun, self-propelled ~ 255 57
gun barrel, rifled ~ 87 34
gun carriage 255 43
gun carriage, self-propelled ~
255 49-74
gun dog 86 7
gunnel 283 30
gunport 218 59
gunport shutter 218 60
gun slit 86 52
gun turret 258 29
gunwale 283 30
gutta-percha tree 383 37
gutter *Dwellings* 37 6, 11
gutter *Roof & Boilerr.* 38 9
gutter *Roof* 122 28, 92
gutter *Bookbind.* 185 55
gutter *Street Sect.* 198 10
gutter, parallel ~ 122 83
gutter bracket 122 32
guy *Wine Grow.* 78 8
guy *Camping* 278 23
guy line 278 23
guy pole 152 31
guy wire *Wine Grow.* 78 8
guy wire *Energy Sources* 155 44

gybe 285 28
gybing 285 26
gymkhana 290 32
gymnastic ball 297 34
gymnastic club 297 38
gymnastic hoop 297 46
gymnastic ribbon 297 49
gymnastics 297 33-50
gymnastics, men's ~ 296 1-11
gymnastics, Olympic ~ 296 1-11; 297 1-6
gymnastics, women's ~ 297
gymnastics apparatus 296 1-11; 297 1-6
gymnastics kit 296 61-63; 297 51-52
gym shoe 296 63; 297 52
gym trousers 296 62
gypsum Sculpt. Studio 339 29
gypsum Crystals 351 24, 25
gypsum crusher 160 14
gypsum powder 339 29
gypsum store 160 13
gyro compass 224 31, 51-53
gyro compass unit 224 51-53
gyrodyne 232 29
gyro horizon 230 3
gyro repeater 224 52

H

habergeon 329 51
habit 382 53
habit, monk's ~ 331 55
hack 186 26
hacking knife 128 37
hackney carriage 186 26
hackney coach 186 26
hacksaw 134 3, 17; 136 40; 138 23; 140 9; 150 14
hacksaw frame 126 71
haematite 108 48
haft 137 30
hail 9 36
hail, soft ~ 9 35
hair 16 3
hair, bobbed ~ 34 34
hair, closely-cropped ~ 34 11
hair, curled ~ 34 33
hair, curly ~ 34 18
hair, long ~ 34 1
hair, pinned-up ~ 34 28
hair, shingled ~ 34 34
hair, swept-back ~ 34 28
hair, swept-up ~ 34 28
hairbell 375 14
hairbrush 28 7; 105 10
haircap moss 377 17
hair clip 105 11
hair curler 106 31
haircut 106 3
haircuts 34 1-25
haircutting scissors 105 7; 106 34
hair decoration 355 82
hairdress 354 9
hairdresser 105 35; 106 1
'hairdresser' Airport 233 53
hairdresser, ladies' ~ 105
hairdresser, men's ~ 106
hairdresser's tools 105 1-16
hairdressing salon, ladies' ~ 105 1-39
hairdressing salon, men's ~ 106 1-42
hair drier, hand-held ~ 105 33; 106 22
hair element 10 9
hair-fixing spray 105 24
hair moss 377 17
hairpin Needlewk. 102 29

hairpin Winter Sp. 301 69
hairpin work 102 28
hair sieve 260 66
hair spray 105 24
hairstyle 106 3
hairstyles 34 1-25
hairstyles, girls' ~ 34 27-38
hairstyles, ladies' ~ 34 27-38
hairstylist 310 36; 315 48
hair tonic 106 10
hair trigger 87 12
hairworm 80 51
hake 65 19
hake chain 65 17
half-barrier crossing 202 45
half chicken 266 56
half mask 306 13
half-moon 4 4, 6
half nonpareil 175 20
half note 320 14
half nut 149 19
half rest 320 22
half-step 320 50, 52
half-title 185 43, 44
halftone dot 178 39
half-way line 291 3
hall 41 1-29
hall, main ~ 236 1-30; 250 1-11
halliard 253 2
hall manager 275 7
hall mirror 41 6
hall of mirrors 308 55
Hallstatt period 328 21-40
hallux 19 52
halma 276 26-28
halma board 276 26
halma man 276 28
halma piece 276 28
halogen lamp 177 31
halothane container 26 26
halt 15 27
halter 71 7-11
halter top 31 64
halved joint 121 86
halving joint 121 86
halyard 253 2
ham 95 51
hame 71 14
hammer 85 5; 126 78; 134 7; 137 26; 139 26
hammer Army 255 4
hammer Athletics 298 42
hammer Music. Instr. 322 35; 325 3
hammer Graphic Art 340 14
hammer, anvil and stirrup 17 61
hammer, bricklayer's ~ 118 53
hammer, brickmason's ~ 118 53
hammer, carpenter's ~ 120 74
hammer, flat-face ~ 137 35
hammer, glazier's ~ 124 18
hammer, iron-headed ~ 339 16
hammer, machinist's ~ D.I.Y. 134 40
hammer, machinist's ~ Metalwkr. 140 23
hammer, shoemaker's ~ 100 37
hammer, stonemason's ~ 158 35
Hammer and Sickle 253 21
hammer axe 300 37
hammer blow 293 78
hammer crusher Quarry 158 20
hammer crusher Cement Wks. 160 2
hammer cylinder 139 30

hammer drill 158 11
hammer drill, electric ~ 134 43
hammer forging 139
hammer guide 139 29
hammer head Airsports 288 4
hammer head Athletics 298 43
hammer head, felt-covered ~ 325 24
hammer jack 325 30
hammer lever 325 30
hammer mill 160 2
hammer rail 325 15, 26
hammer shank 325 25
hammer throw 298 42-47
hammock 278 4
ham on the bone 96 1; 99 52
hamper 306 11
hamster 366 16
hand 16 47, 48; 17 15-17; 19 64-83
hand apparatus 297 33-50
hand axe 328 1
handball 292 1
handball player 292 2
hand bindery 183 1-38
hand book 262 17
hand bookbindery 183 1-38
hand brace 140 13
hand brake 187 5; 191 72; 212 33
hand brake lever 188 33; 191 93
hand brake wheel 212 64, 80
hand camera, large-format ~ 114 36
handcart 120 6
handcart, wooden ~ 309 86
hand circle 297 47
hand circling 297 37
handclap 117 69
hand-composing room 174 1
hand compositor 174 5
hand control 195 8
hand cream 99 27
hand cultivator 55 21
hand die 126 85
hand die, electric ~ 125 12
hand drill 140 13
hand flat knitting machine 167 35
hand gallop 72 42
hand glass Hairdresser 105 23; 106 7
hand glass Optician 111 16
handgrip Photog. 114 37
handgrip Cine Film 117 5, 61
handgrip Bicycle 187 3
handgrip Navig. 224 9
handgrip Films 313 21, 24, 38
hand guard 94 10
hand hair drier 105 33; 106 22
hand hammer, blacksmith's 137 23
hand harpoon 280 40
handicraft 48 3
hand-ironing pad 104 30
hand-iron press 103 18
handkerchief 33 10
hand ladle 148 23
hand lamp 270 42
hand lance 83 46
handle Atom 2 39
handle Hosp. 26 12
handle Tablew. etc. 45 51, 59, 62
handle Household 50 9, 63
handle Market Gdn. 55 27
handle Agr. Mach. 65 2
handle Agr. Impl. 66 17
handle Pest Contr. 83 19

handle Forestry 85 3
handle Hairdresser 106 37
handle Joiner 132 10, 18
handle D.I.Y. 134 47
handle Metalwkr. 140 5
handle Carriages 186 12
handle School 260 8
handle Motorboats etc. 286 48
handle Fencing 294 41
handle Athletics 298 44
handle Sports 305 57, 80
handle, bound ~ 89 55
handle, cork ~ 89 50
handle, double ~ 148 15
handle, fixed ~ 129 7
handle, insulated ~ 127 54
handle, tubular ~ 50 64
hand lead 224 58
handlebar 187 2; 188 45
handlebar, adjustable ~ 188 3
handlebar, semi-rise ~ 188 11
handlebar fittings 188 30-35
handlebar grip 187 3
handlebar moustache 34 8
handlebars 34 8
handlebar stem 187 10
hand lever Joiner 132 55
hand lever Bookbind. 183 31
hand-lever press 183 26
hand luggage 194 19
hand mirror Hairdresser 105 23; 106 7
hand mirror Optician. 111 16
hand net 89 2
handpiece 24 6
hand press 340 29
hand pump 83 26; 269 66
hand puppet 260 74
handrail Roof & Boilerr. 38 28
handrail Hall 41 23
handrail Floor etc. Constr. 123 53, 79
handrail Ship 221 122
handrailing 215 70
hand rammer 148 32
hand-removing tool 109 10
handrest 112 58
hand saw 120 60; 126 72; 134 27
handscrew 132 14
handset 237 7; 245 15
handset cord 237 14
handset cradle 237 13
hand-setting room 174 1
hand shank 148 14
hand shears Tailor 104 11
hand shears Bldg. Site 119 87
hand signal 268 53
handsledge 304 29
hand spray Pest Contr. 83 24
hand spray Hairdresser 105 30; 106 13
hand spray Painter 129 35
hand spray Offset Platem. 179 7
handspring 297 22
handstamp 236 45
handstand 295 27; 296 52
handstand dive 282 45
hand steel shears 119 22
handstrap, leather ~ 296 47
hand-to-hand throw 297 33
hand towel 28 9; 49 23; 106 24
hand vice 140 24
hand weapons 255 1-39
handwheel Shoem. 100 24
handwheel Cooper 130 19
handwheel Cotton Spin. 163 18
handwheel Knitting 167 7, 30

handwheel *Paperm.* **172** 74
handwheel *Bookbind.* **183** 23
handwheel *Road Constr.* **201** 9
handwriting, English ~ **342** 10
handwriting, German ~ **342** 11
hang **296** 33, 35; **298** 41
hangar **287** 14
hanger **215** 41
hang glider **287** 44
hang glider pilot **287** 45
hang gliding **287** 43
Hansa cog **218** 18-26
Hansa ship **218** 18-26
hansom **186** 29
hansom cab **186** 29
harbour **216** 14; **225; 226**
harbour ferry **225** 11
harbour tunnel **225** 55
hardboard **338** 22
hardcore **123** 12
hardener **130** 33
hardie **137** 32
hard-rock drill **158** 11
hard-top **193** 26
hardwood cutting **54** 25
hardy **137** 32
hare **86** 35; **88** 59
hare-and-hounds **289** 41-49
harebell **375** 14
hare calf **87** 44
hare hunting **86** 34-39
harlequin **306** 35
harmonica **324** 35
harmonium **325** 43
harmonium case **325** 47
harmonium keyboard **325** 48
harness *Horse* **71** 7-25
harness *Airsports* **288** 43
harness horse racing **289** 23-40
harness of diving apparatus **279** 12
harness racing **289** 23-40
harness racing track **289** 23
harp **323** 60
harpoon **353** 10
harpoon, bone ~ **328** 3
harpoon thrower **328** 5
harpsichord **322** 45
harpsichord mechanism **322** 48
harpy **254** 35; **327** 55
harrow, disc ~ **65** 82
harrow, rotary ~ **65** 89
harrow, spike-tooth ~ **65** 88
harrow, three-section ~ **65** 88, 89
hasp **71** 14
hat **35** 9
hat, Alpine ~ **35** 23
hat, carpenter's ~ **120** 13
hat, felt ~ **35** 15, 24; **355** 55
hat, fox ~ **35** 19
hat, hard ~ **289** 18
hat, huntsman's ~ **86** 5
hat, iron ~ **329** 59
hat, knitted ~ **35** 10
hat, ladies' ~ **41** 11
hat, lightweight ~ **35** 37
hat, loden ~ **35** 23
hat, men's ~ **35** 13
hat, mink ~ **35** 18
hat, mohair ~ **35** 6, 11
hat, paper ~ **306** 45
hat, picador's ~ **319** 20
hat, sailor's ~ **309** 63
hat, Thessalonian ~ **355** 4
hat, three-cornered ~ **355** 62
hat, trilby-style ~ **35** 14
hat, Tyrolean ~ **35** 24

hat, wide-brimmed ~ **35** 38; **355** 55
hat, woollen ~ **29** 57; **35** 10, 26
hat and light luggage rack **208** 28
hat box **205** 11
hatch *Roof & Boilerr.* **38** 14
hatch *Roof* **122** 24
hatch *Post* **236** 30
hatchback **193** 18
hatchboard **222** 65
hatch coaming **222** 64
hatch cover **222** 65
hatcher **74** 30
hatchery **89** 11-19
hatchet **270** 43
hatchet iron **125** 5
hatching compartment **74** 30
hatching jar **89** 17
hatching tray **74** 31, 32
hatchment **254** 1-6
hatch platform **6** 34
hatchway **222** 64-65
hatchway, main ~ **259** 86
H atom **1** 26
hat peg **266** 13
hats, ladies' ~ **35** 1-21
hats, men's ~ **35** 22-40
hat shop **268** 38
hatter's shop **268** 38
haubergeon **329** 51
haulage *Forestry* **85** 42
haulage *Rivers* **216** 27
haulage cable *Railw.* **214** 14, 26, 37, 42, 45
haulage cable *Winter Sp.* **301** 63
haulage cable driving pulley **214** 62
haulage cable guide wheel **214** 61
haulage cable roller **214** 32, 49, 60
haulage cable sleeve **214** 73
hauling **216** 27
hauling capstan **217** 22
haulm conveyor **64** 76
haulm conveyor agitator **64** 77
haulm conveyor drive **64** 78
haulm elevator **64** 90
haulm stripper **64** 73
haulm stripper, flexible ~ **64** 76
haulyard **253** 2
haunch *Horse* **72** 35
haunch *Game* **88** 21, 37
haunch jump **282** 14
Hauptwerk **326** 1
hautboy **323** 38
haute école **71** 1-6
Havana cigar **107** 2
Hawaii girl **306** 16
hawk, male ~ **86** 46
hawkbells **276** 45
hawker **308** 12, 51
hawking **86** 42-46
hawkmoth **82** 27; **358** 55; **365** 9
hawksbill turtle **364** 28
hawse **222** 75
hawse hole **227** 11
hawse pipe **222** 76; **258** 54
hawthorn **374** 30
hay **75** 13
hay, tedded ~ **63** 25
hay fork, three-pronged ~ **66** 3
hay harvest **63** 19-30
haymaking **63** 19-30
hay rack, double ~ **75** 12
hayrake **66** 23
hay tripod **63** 30

hazard flasher **191** 76
hazard flasher switch **191** 68
hazel **59** 49
hazel branch, flowering ~ **59** 44
hazel bush **59** 44-51
hazel grouse **88** 69
hazel hen **88** 69
hazel leaf **59** 51
hazelnut **59** 49
hazel tree **59** 44-51
H-beam **143** 6
head *Man* **16** 1-18; **17** 42-55
head *Arable Crops* **68** 2
head *Horse* **72** 1-11
head *House Insects etc.* **81** 33, 36
head *Forest Pests* **82** 2
head *Game* **88** 12
head *Brew.* **93** 31
head *Tobacc. etc.* **107** 23
head *Carp.* **120** 58
head *Roof* **122** 87
head *Mach. Parts etc.* **143** 14, 52
head *Weaves* **171** 31
head *Composing Rm.* **175** 39
head *Hydr. Eng.* **217** 25
head *Restaurant* **266** 4
head *Music. Instr.* **323** 52; **324** 10
head *Prehist.* **328** 4
head *Articulates* **358** 28
head, bald ~ **34** 22
head, binocular ~ **112** 12
head, cock's ~ **327** 35
head, combined ~ **241** 59
head, composite ~ **370** 74
head, countersunk ~ **143** 46
head, eagle's ~ **327** 12
head, goat's ~ **327** 18
head, human ~ **327** 21
head, lion's ~ **327** 17
head, partly bald ~ **34** 20
head, pig's ~ **95** 43
head, rotating ~ **64** 52
head, shrunken ~ **352** 30
head, woman's ~ **327** 56
head and neck **19** 1-13
head badge **187** 15
headband **183** 35
headband, padded ~ **241** 67; **261** 41
head bandage **21** 3
head beam **183** 21
headboard *Bedrm.* **43** 6
headboard *Sailing* **284** 47
headbox **173** 11
head cellarman **79** 17
headcheese **96** 9
headdress **354** 9; **355** 65
headdress, feather ~ **352** 12
headdress, ornamental ~ **352** 12
head drum **243** 19, 27
header *Carp.* **120** 41
header *Roof* **121** 71
header *Ball Games* **291** 46
header joist **120** 41
header tank **212** 78
head frame **144** 3
headgear **35; 144** 1; **302** 34
headguard **299** 30
heading **130** 10
heading bond **118** 60
heading course **118** 64
head interlocking point **171** 34
headlamp **187** 7; **189** 10; **191** 20
headlight **189** 10; **191** 20
head line *Man* **19** 73
headline *Sea Fish.* **90** 7

headline *Script* **342** 44
head margin **185** 56
head of department **271** 60
head of railcar **197** 3
headphone cable **241** 71
headphone cable plug **241** 70
headphone cord **241** 71
headphones **241** 66; **249** 63; **261** 38; **309** 24
headphone socket **117** 10; **249** 68
headpiece **71** 7-11
head piece **183** 21
headpiece, padded ~ **241** 67; **261** 41
head post **123** 54
headrace **91** 41
head rail **120** 58
headrest *First Aid* **21** 13
headrest *Railw.* **207** 67
headrest, adjustable ~ **191** 33; **207** 47
headrest, integral ~ **193** 31
headrest cushion, down-filled ~ **207** 68
head restraint, adjustable ~ **191** 33
head restraint, integral ~ **193** 31
head rule **342** 40
headset **241** 66; **249** 63; **261** 38; **309** 24
headset socket **249** 68
headspring **297** 27
headstall **71** 7-11
headstand **295** 28
headstock **150** 2
headstock, geared ~ **149** 2
headstock, movable ~ **150** 26
headstone **331** 26
head support assembly **311** 25
heald, wire ~ **166** 27
heald eyelet **166** 28
heald frame **166** 4
heald frame guide **166** 3
heald shaft **166** 4
heald shaft guide **166** 3
heald shaft guiding wheel **166** 36
health insurance certificate **22** 9
heap cloud **8** 1, 2, 17; **287** 22
heart **18** 14; **20** 8, 24-25, 45-57
heart cherry **59** 5
hearth *Blacksm.* **137** 1-8, 1; **138** 34
hearth *Iron & Steel* **147** 24
heart line **19** 74
heart plank **120** 93
heart rhythm **25** 1
hearts **276** 40, 44
heartsease pansy **60** 2
heart-shield **254** 17
heartwood *Carp.* **120** 84
heartwood *Bot.* **370** 13
heartwood plank **120** 93
heat **1** 55
heat colour **343** 16
heater **172** 32
heater, electric ~ **174** 45; **179** 3
heater, gas ~ **126** 25
heater, water-controlled ~ **192** 60-64
heater box **192** 61
heater plug **190** 55
heat exchanger *Nucl. Energy* **154** 6, 44
heat exchanger *Coking* **156** 27
heat exchanger *Cement Wks.* **160** 4, 6
heat exchanger *Paperm.* **172** 19

heat exchanger *Car* 192 61
heat exchanger *Railw.* 207 6;
  209 15; 212 36, 55
heat exchanger *Warships* 259
  66
heat exchanger, auxiliary ~
  212 43
heat exchanger exhaust 160 7
heat extractor 182 5
heath 15 5
heath and moor 15 5
heather 377 19
heating, underfloor ~ 356 18
heating box 183 27
heating coupling hose 208 20
heating element 172 32
heating engineer 126
heating oil 38 50
heating oil tank 212 75
heating pipe 55 8
heating regulator 207 54
heating system 207 6
heating system, hot-water ~
  38 38-81
heating unit, electric ~ 174 45
heat pump 155 22
heat pump system 155 1
heat reservoir 155 20
heat-sealing machine 76 27;
  226 12
heat shield *Motorcycles etc.*
  188 16
heat shield *Space* 234 5, 20;
  235 8, 40
heat space 259 93
heat transfer fluid 155 31
heaume 254 7
Heaviside-Kennelly Layer 7
  27
heavy-duty boot 101 39
heavy liquor pump 172 34
heavy vehicle elevator 221 56
heavy vehicle lift 221 56
heckelphone 323 38
heckler 263 15
heddle, wire ~ 166 27
heddle eyelet 166 28
hedge *Map* 15 98
hedge *Dwellings* 37 59
hedge *Fruit & Veg. Gdn.* 52 32
hedge, trimmed ~ 272 37
hedgehog 366 5
hedgehog fungus 381 31
hedge mustard 61 16
hedge shears 56 49
hedge trimmer 134 55
hedge trimmer, battery-
  operated ~ 56 17
hedge-trimming attachment
  134 55
heel *Man* 19 63
heel *Agr. Impl.* 66 15
heel *Bakery* 97 5
heel *Shoem.* 100 67
heel, high ~ 101 28
heel, raised ~ 101 33
heelbone 17 27
heel flap 286 58
heel trimmer 100 4
heel unit, automatic ~ 301 54
height adjuster 106 17
height-adjuster bar 106 17
height adjustment *Hosp.* 27 3
height adjustment *Photog.*
  116 34
height adjustment *Sawmill*
  157 49
height adjustment crank 64
  57
height adjustment wheel 132
  60
height and angle adjustment
  177 21

height gauge 22 69
height of shank 175 45
height of shoulder 175 45
height scale *Sawmill* 157 60
height scale *Athletics* 298 20
height to paper 175 44
helicon 323 44
helicopter deck 146 7
helicopter hangar 221 52; 259
  38
helicopter landing deck 228
  15
helicopter landing platform
  259 39, 53
helicopter platform 221 19
helicopters 232 11-25
heliostat 5 29
heliozoan 357 7
heliport 146 7
heliport deck 146 7
helium atom (model) 1 5
helium-neon laser 243 57
helium nucleus 1 30-31
helium pressure bottle 234
  14
helium pressure vessel 234
  43, 50
heller 252 27
hellhound 327 29
helm 218 13
helmet *Police* 264 35
helmet *Equest.* 289 18
helmet *Ball Games* 292 24
helmet *Chivalry* 329 39-42
helmet, barred ~ 254 8
helmet, fireman's ~ 270 38
helmet, grilled ~ 254 8
helmet, protective ~ *Police*
  264 21
helmet, protective ~
  Mountain. 300 53
helmet, protective ~ *Winter
  Sp.* 302 34
helmet affronty 254 9
helmet flower 379 1
helmet lamp 300 54
helmets 254 4,7-9
helms 254 4,7-9
helmsman 224 16
helper 21 19
helve 85 3
hemidemisemiquaver 320 19
hemidemisemiquaver rest
  320 27
hemihedron 351 24
hemipyramid 351 24
hemisphere, northern ~ 3
  1-35
hemline marker 271 40
hemlock 379 4
hemp 383 9
hem stitch work 102 14
hen 62 36; 73 19
hen, fattened ~ 98 7
henbane 379 6
hen pheasant 88 77
herald 329 75
heraldic beasts 254 15-16
heraldic tent 254 14
heraldry 254 1-36
herb, primulaceous ~ 53 5
herb, solanaceous ~ 53 6; 379
  7
Hercules 3 21
herd 86 15
Herdsman 3 30
Herero woman 354 25
herm 334 35
herma 334 35
hermes 334 35
heron 86 46; 359 18
herring 364 14
herringbone 301 26

herringbone stitch 102 9
herring drift net 90 2-10
herring lugger 90 1
Hessian fly 80 40
Heterocera 365 7-11
hexagon 351 15
hexagonal crystal system 351
  20-22
hexahedron 351 2
hexakis-octahedron 351 13
hexoctahedron 351 13
H-girder 143 6
hibernation cocoon 80 31
hide 88 56
hide, raised ~ 86 14-17, 14
hide beetle 81 22
hieroglyphics, ancient
  Egyptian ~ 341 1
Hi-Fi component 241 13-48
high 9 6
high-altitude anorak 300 6
highball 317 33
highball glass 267 56
high bar *Playground* 273 32
high bar *Gymn.* 296 7
highboard diver 282 5
highboard diving 282 40-45
high chair, baby's ~ 28 33
high-draft draw frame 164 14
high-draft speed frame 164
  19
high-draft system 164 14
high frequency 7 26
high-hat cymbals 324 50
high house 305 75
high jump 298 9-27
high jump apparatus 298 32
high jump equipment 298 32
high jumper 298 10 J
highland Indian 352 23
high-moor bog 13 19
high-mountain region 12
  39-47
high performance sailplane
  287 9
high-pile lining 101 3
high-pressure area 9 6
high-pressure belt 9 47
high-pressure manometer
  141 4
high-pressure xenon arc
  lamp 312 39
high-rise handlebar 188 57
high-riser 188 56
high school 261
high school riding 71 1-6
high seat 86 14
high-speed plate, automatic ~
  39 15
high-tension voltage
  indicator 211 29
high tide 280 7
high toss 297 35
high-water line 13 35
high-water mark 13 35
highway construction 201
  1-24
hiking boot 101 18
hiking stick 284 31
hiking strap 284 30
hill *Phys. Geog.* 13 66
hill *Films* 310 13
hillside spring 12 38
hill upcurrent 287 28
himation 355 6
hind 86 13
hind, young ~ 88 1
hinge 188 2
hip *Man* 16 33
hip *Horse* 72 32
hip *Roof* 121 12
hip bone 17 18
hip circle backwards 296 55

hip dormer window 121 13
hip end 121 11
hip grip 21 38
hipped-gable roof 121 16
hippocampus *Fabul. Creat.*
  327 44
Hippocampus *Fish etc.* 364 18
hippocentaur 327 52
hippodrome 308 59
hippogryph 327 26
hippopotamus 366 31
hip rafter 121 62
hip roof 37 64; 121 10, 60
hip tile 122 9
historical ship, types of ~ 218
hitch 65 61
hitch, adjustable ~ 64 60
hitch, front ~ 65 50
hitch-kick 298 40
hitch pin 325 14
hive 77 45-50, 52
hive-bee 77 1-25
hock 72 37
hockey 292 6
hockey ball 292 14
hockey player 292 15
hockey stick 292 13
hod 122 22
hod hook 122 23
hoe 66 24
hoe and fork, combined ~ 56
  7
hoe handle 66 2
hog 94 11
hogpen 62 8; 75 35
hoist *Oil, Petr.* 145 11
hoist *Flags* 253 22-34
hoist, builder's ~ 118 31
hoist, inclined ~ 158 16; 159
  5
hoisting gear 206 56; 217 74
hoisting gear bridge 217 73
hoisting gear cabin 217 71
hoisting rope 120 37
hold 223 55, 75
hold, insulated ~ 223 56
hold, underfloor ~ 231 21
hold-down, automatic ~ 157
  65
holdfast *Carp.* 120 66
holdfast *Alp. Plants etc.* 378
  50
holding device 157 47
holding forceps 23 12
holding press 183 4
holding squad 270 17
hold pillar 222 61
hole *Phys. Geog.* 13 34
hole *Ball Games* 293 87
hole, elongated ~ 240 17
hole, square ~ 140 43
holes 293 79-82
holing out 293 86
hollowing tool 135 17
hollow of the throat 16 20
hollow-shaft boring bit 133 7
holly 374 9
holohedron 351 2
holster 264 24
Holy Bible 330 11
Holy Communion 332 26
Holy Scripture 330 11
holy table 330 4
holy water basin 332 47
home and overseas news
  section 342 62
home base 292 53
home plate 292 53
home port 286 8
homogenizer 76 12
honey 77 33
honey, strained ~ 77 62-63
honey bag 77 18

honey-bee 77 1-25
honey cell 77 33
honeycomb 77 31-43, 45
honeycomb, artificial ~ 77 42
honeycomb, natural ~ 77 60
honeycomb weave 171 29
honeydew melon 266 50
honey extractor 77 61
honey fungus 381 28
honey gland 59 18
honey in the comb 77 64
honey jar 77 63
honey pail 77 62
honey sac 77 18
honey separator 77 61
honeysuckle 374 13
honey super 77 45
honey wrack 378 48
hood Infant Care etc. 28 26
hood Child. Clothes 29 2
hood Ladies' Wear 30 69
hood Headgear 35 2
hood Blacksm. 137 7
hood Carriages 186 42
hood Car 191 8
hood Garage 195 36
hood Aircraft 230 39
hood Mountain. 300 19
hood Church 331 56
hood, collapsible ~ 186 52;
 193 10
hood, convertible ~ 193 10
hood, detachable ~ 31 21
hood, falcon's ~ 86 44
hood, folding ~ 28 35
hood, protective ~ 157 65
hood drawstring 29 64
hood support 195 37
hoof Horse 72 26
hoof Game 88 24
hoof, horse's ~ 327 42
hoofprints 86 8
hook Roof & Boilerr. 38 22
hook Horse 71 14
hook Shoem. 100 62
hook Oil, Petr. 145 9
hook Sports 299 33
hook Winter Sp. 301 61
hook Sports 305 18, 46
hook Music. Not. 320 5
hook, blunt ~ 26 50
hook, butcher's ~ 96 55
hook, closed ~ 89 85
hook, concealed ~ 89 75
hook, double ~ 89 83
hook, open ~ 89 83
hook, treble ~ 89 85
hookah 107 42
hook-and-ride band 140 50
hook ball 305 18
hook belt 270 44
hook disgorger 89 40
hook ladder 270 16
hooks 89 79-87
hoop Airsports 288 67
hoop Ball Games 292 78
hoop Circus 307 58
hoopoe 359 25
hoop of barrel 130 8
hooter Motorcycles etc. 188 53
hooter Fire Brig. 270 7
hop boiler 92 52
hop garden 15 114
hop growing 83 27
hopper Agr. Mach. 64 59
hopper Wine Grow. 78 18
hopper Mills 91 13
hopper Cotton Spin. 163 31
hopper Music. Instr. 325 30
hopper, endless-floor ~ 64 84
hopper barge 226 46
hopper delivery roller,
 wooden ~ 163 32

hopper feeder 163 33
hopsack weave 171 11
horizon 13 21
horizon, artificial ~ 230 3
horizon glass 224 7
horizon light 316 15
horizon mirror 224 7
horizontal bar 296 7
horizontal boring and milling
 machine 150 25
horizontal deflection module
 240 10
horizontal eight 288 2
horizontal linearity control
 module 240 9
horizontally-opposed twin
 engine 189 47
horizontal milling spindle
 150 39
horizontal slow roll 288 8
horizontal synchronizing
 module 240 7
horn Horse 71 38
horn Motorcycles etc. 188 53
horn Car 191 60
horn Railw. 212 70
horn Fire Brig. 270 7
horn Flea Market 309 34
horn Music. Instr. 323 41
horn Invertebr. 357 31
horn Birds 362 16
horn, spirally twisted ~ 327 8
hornbeam 371 63
horned owl 362 14
horns 88 29-31
horse Horse 71; 72
horse Dom. Anim. 73 2
horse Carp. 120 18
horse Gymn. 296 1; 297 1
horse, armoured ~ 319 18
horse, piebald ~ 289 29
horse, toy ~ 47 15
horse, wild ~ 328 7
horse, winged ~ 327 26
horse armour 329 83-88
horse bean 69 15
horse box 75 2
horse brush 71 55
horse chestnut 371 60
horse chestnut tree 371 58
horsefish 364 18
horsehair 323 15
horsehair brush 100 12
horse latitudes 9 47
horsemanship 289
horse racing 289 50
horse-radish 57 20
horse's head 72 1-11
horse sleigh 304 25
horse stall 75 2
horsetail 376 18
horst 12 10
hose Household 50 75
hose Bldg. Site 118 38
hose Serv. Stat. 196 2; 196 23
hose Fire Brig. 270 54
hose Hist. Cost. 355 47
hose, rotary ~ 145 13
hose carriage 270 28
hose cart 270 28
hose connection 83 30
hose connector 56 45
hose coupling 270 29

hose layer 270 53
hosepipe 118 38; 196 23
hose reel 56 26; 270 28
hose truck 270 28
hose wagon 270 28
hosiery 271 56
hosiery department 271 17
hosiery mill 167 1-66
hosiery shelf 99 25
hospital 25; 26; 27
hospital bed 25 10
hospital unit 228 21
Host 331 48; 332 28, 35
hostess 318 33
hot-air duct 139 52
hot-air gun 130 25
hot-air sterilizer 22 71
hotbed 55 16
hotbed vent 55 17
hot-blast pipe 147 19
hot-blast stove 147 15
hotel 267
hotel bar 267 51
hotel bill 267 11
hotel guest 267 14
hotel lobby 267 18-26
hotel manager 267 19
hotel porter 204 17
hotel register 267 8
hotel restaurant 267 20
hotel room 267 27-38
hotel sticker 205 9
hothouse 55 4; 272 65
hot-pipe space 259 93
hotplate 39 15; 207 30
hotplate, electric ~ 45 45
hot reservoir 155 20
hot-shoe contact 114 72
hot-shoe flash contact 115 21
hot tap 126 28
hot water supply 155 26
hot water tank 38 68
hot water tank Brew. 92 10
hot water tank Paperm. 172
 18
hound Hunt. 86 33
hound Sailing 284 14
hour and minute button 110 3
hour axis 5 8
hour axis drive 5 7
hourglass 110 31
hour hand 110 13
house Dwellings 37 54
house Farm Bldgs. 62 1
house Bldg. Site 118 1-49
house, detached ~ 37 1-53
house, dikereeve's ~ 216 45
house, duplex ~ 37 64-68
house, ferryman's ~ 216 45
house, semi-detached ~ 37
 69-71
house, solar ~ 155 17
house, solar-heated ~ 155 17
house, terraced ~ 37 58-63
house, timber ~ 37 84-86
houseboat 353 31
house cat 62 3
housecoat Underwear etc. 32
 20
housecoat Hist. Cost. 355 66
house cricket 81 7
house detective 275 16
house dress 31 36
housefly 81 1, 2
house frock 31 36
household appliances 50
household utensils 50
house insects 81 1-14
houseleek 51 7
house light dimmer 312 17
houseplant 42 36; 248 14
houseplants 53
house sparrow 361 5

house spider 81 9
house telephone 127 3
house wall 120 29
housewife 39 1
housing Meteorol. Instr. 10 18
housing Iron Foundry etc. 148
 57
housing Films 312 48
housing, protective ~ 10 39
housing, soundproof ~ 310
 48; 313 16-18, 27
housing development 37
 54-57
housing estate 37 54-57
housing lock 313 33
hover 74 3
hovercraft 286 63
hub 187 26
hub, centre ~ 187 59
hub, front ~ 187 52
hub assembly, front ~ 187 52
hub barrel 187 69
hub body 187 69
hub shell 187 69
huckleberry 377 23
hula-hula girl 306 16
hula skirt 306 18
hull Aircraft 232 2, 9
hull Warships 258 2; 259 22,
 42
hull bottom 286 32, 35, 39
hull frame 222 29
human flea 81 42
Humanist 342 4
human louse 81 40, 41
humblebee 358 23
humerus 17 12
humidifier 79 22
hummock 13 42
hump 206 46
hundreds 344 3
hunt 289 41-49
Hunter Astron. 3 13
hunter 86 1
hunting 86 1-52, 9-12, 14-17
hunting cap 289 14
hunting cap, hard ~ 289 18
hunting clothes 86 2
hunting dog 86 33
hunting equipment 87 41-48
hunting horn 87 60; 289 44
hunting knife 87 42
hunting knife, double-edged
 ~ 87 41
hunting leopard 368 7
hunting pink 289 13, 42
hunting rifle 86 4
hunting rifles 87 1-40
hunting screen 86 9
hunting weapons 87
huntsman 86 1
hurdle Free Exerc. 295 12
hurdle Athletics 298 8
hurdle position 295 12
hurdle racing 298 7-8
hurdles 298 7-8
hurdy-gurdy 322 25
hurst 91 20
husk 59 50; 68 33
husk corn 68 31
husky 70 22; 353 2
hut 300 1
hut, beehive-shaped ~ 354 28
hut, Indian ~ 273 59
Hydra 3 16
Hydra, Lernaean ~ 327 32
Hydrallmania 369 9
hydrangea 51 11
hydrant key 270 27
hydraulic engineering 217
hydraulic lift pad 195 27
hydraulic plant 92 13
hydraulic plant room 316 50

hydraulic system *Agr. Mach.* 64 65
hydraulic system *Paperm.* 173 37
hydraulic system *Army* 255 53
hydraulic system *Air Force* 257 16
hydrocyanic acid 83 15
hydro-extraction 169 23
hydro-extractor, pendulum-type ~ 168 14
hydro-extractor lid 168 18
hydroformer 145 47
hydrogenation 170 16
hydrogen atom 1 15; 242 62
hydrogen atom (model) 1 1
hydrogen balloon 10 56
hydrogen bomb explosion 7 12
hydrogen cooler 153 27
hydrogen inlet *Synth. Fibres* 170 15
hydrogen inlet *Chem.* 350 12
hydrogen sulphide scrubber 156 22
hydrogen sulphide wet collector 156 22
hydrogen tank 6 6
hydropathic 274 8
hydrophone 224 64
hydroplane 286 22
hydroplane, stepped ~ 286 38-41
hydroplane, three-point ~ 286 42
hydrosphere 11 2
hydroxylamine inlet 170 21
hyena 368 1
hygrograph 10 8, 50
hygrometer *Drawing Off.* 151 39
hygrometer *Offset Platem.* 179 28
hygrometer *Swim.* 281 23
hygrometer element 10 9
hymenium 381 17
Hymenoptera 358 21-23
hymn board 330 24
hymn book 330 30
hymn number 330 24
hyoid 20 2
hyperbola 347 26
hyperbolic position line 224 43, 44
hyphae 381 2
hyphen 342 28
hypocentre 11 32
hypocotyl 370 89
hypophysis cerebri 17 43
hypotenuse 346 32
hypotrachelium 334 22
hyrax 366 24
hyssop 374 5

I

ibex 367 7
ibis 359 5
ice 266 44
ice, glacial ~ 12 48-56
ice accident 21 28-33
ice axe 300 16, 31
ice axe, short-shafted ~ 300 36
iceboat 302 44
iceboating 302 44-46
icebox 39 2; 46 33; 317 10
ice breaker 221 50
ice bucket 267 67
ice cream 308 31
ice-cream cornet 308 31
ice-cream man 308 30

ice-cream sundae 266 76
ice-cream vendor 308 30
ice-crystal cloud 8 6
ice-crystal cloud veil 8 7
ice cube 266 44
ice hockey 302 29-37
ice hockey player 302 29
ice hockey set 302 23
ice hockey skate 302 23
ice hockey stick 302 30
ice ledge 300 4
ice pellets 9 35
ice piton 300 40, 41
ice racing 290 24-28
ice ridge 300 21
ice sailing 302 44-46
ice skater 302 1
ice skates 302 20-25
ice skating 302 1-26
ice skating boot 302 24
ice slope 300 14
ice speedway 290 24-28
ice step 300 17
ice stick 302 39
ice-stick shooter 302 38
ice-stick shooting 302 38-40
ice yacht 302 44
ice yachting 302 44-46
icicle 304 21
icing, chocolate ~ 97 34
icing sugar 98 54
icosahedron 351 11
icositetrahedron 351 12
identification mark 163 6
identification number 85 33
identification tally 74 55
idle air bleed 192 2
idle mixture adjustment screw 192 11
idling adjustment 190 51
idling air jet 192 2
idling jet 192 1
idol 328 20
igloo 353 4
igloo tent, inflatable ~ 278 58
ignition distributor 190 9, 27
iguana 364 32
ileum 20 16
ilium 17 18
illegal punch 299 34
illumination, incident ~ 112 59, 63
illumination, vertical ~ 112 59, 63
illumination beam path 112 6
illumination optics 112 7
illumination path 112 6
image beam 115 35
image converter 26 15, 18; 27 19
imago 358 10
imbrication 335 15
imitation motorcycle fork 188 58
immersion heater 40 17
immersion roller 165 45
immersion vibrator 119 88
impact crusher 158 20
impact wrench 195 44
impair 275 23
impeller wheel 217 52
Imperial Crown 254 38
impost 336 21
impounding reservoir 217 57
impregnating spray 50 40
impression-adjusting wheel 180 81
impression control 249 10
impression cylinder 180 35, 64; 181 2, 44, 59
impression-setting wheel 180 81
impression tray 24 56

imprint 342 40
imprint, publisher's ~ 185 48
impulse generator, programmed ~ 25 33
impulse meter, automatic ~ 25 42
incense boat 332 42
incense spoon 332 43
inchworm 80 17
incident light measurement 114 60
incident neutron 1 42
incisor 19 16, 34
inclined cable anchorage 215 48
inclined cable system 215 51
incubation tank, long ~ 89 18
incubator 261 30
incubator, Californian ~ 89 15
incus and stapes 17 61
indention 175 16
index 345 1, 2
index arm 224 3
index bar 224 3
index cards 22 7
index finger 19 65
indexing mark 249 74
indexing table, rotary ~ 150 42
index mirror 224 6
index plate 151 51
Indian 352 25
Indian chief 352 11
Indian corn 68 31
Indian cress 53 4
Indian meal moth 81 28
Indian Ocean 14 23
indicator *Hosp.* 26 28
indicator *Motorcycle* 189 37, 45
indicator *Tram* 197 22
indicator, rear ~ 189 42
indicator and dimming switch 191 59
indicator board *Station* 204 32
indicator board *Hotel* 267 5
indicator for rough and fine adjustment 148 65
indicator lamp *Sawmill* 157 62
indicator lamp *Cotton Spin.* 164 8
indicator lamp *Office* 249 71
indicator light *Hosp.* 25 6
indicator light *Motorcycle* 189 37, 45
indicator light *Serv. Stat.* 196 7
indicator light *Tram* 197 22
indicator light *Railw.* 203 14
indicator light *Audio* 241 55
indicator light *Office* 249 71
indicator light *Hotel* 267 6
indicator light *Fencing* 294 30
indicator light, front ~ 191 19
indicator light, rear ~ 189 42
indicator needle *Photog.* 114 58
indicator needle *Inf. Tech.* 242 76
indicator plate 203 12
indicator scale 114 58; 313 28
indigo dyeing and sizing machine 165 40
Indio 352 23
individual-section machine 162 21
indoor target rifle 305 35
indorsee 250 26
indorsement 250 25
indorser 250 27

induced-draught fan 152 14
induction coil 11 44
industrial plant 225 71
inert-gas atmosphere 162 16
inert-gas supply 142 34
inert-gas torch 142 33
inert-gas welding 142 33
inert-gas welding equipment 138 29
inertial measurement unit 6 43
inescutcheon 254 17
infant care 28
infants' wear 29 13-30
in-feed scale 157 61
infighting 299 31
infiltration drain 216 37
infinity 345 15
inflating bulb 25 17
inflator 22 37
inflections 320 50-54
inflight antenna 6 46
inflight refuelling probe 256 7
inflorescence 371 43, 48; 378 7, 53, 55; 382 38; 383 49; 384 31
inflorescence, female ~ 59 46; 68 32; 383 11; 384 50
inflorescence, male ~ 59 39; 68 35; 371 8; 372 17, 24; 383 13
inflorescences 370 67-77
'information' 233 31
information bureau 204 29
information clerk 204 49
information counter 250 9
information office 204 29
information plate 356 20
information position 237 34
information technology 242
infrared drier 173 32
infrared laser rangefinder 255 82
infrared sound headphones 242 30
infrared sound transmitter 242 29
infrared transmission 242 27
infraspinatus 18 53
infringement 291 50
infructescence 61 15; 371 22, 44, 69, 72; 373 8; 374 18; 383 56; 384 32
infusion apparatus 25 11
infusion bottle 25 12
infusion device 25 14
ingot 148 48
ingot mould 147 32
ingot tipper 148 49
ingress/egress hatch 6 38
ingress/egress platform 6 34
inhalation 274 7
inhalational therapy 274 6-7
inhalator 23 24
inhalatorium 274 6
inhaler 26 2, 29
inhaling apparatus 23 24
inhaling tube 26 2, 29
initial 175 1
initial position *Fish Farm.* 89 33
initial position *Fencing* 294 18
injection condenser 172 16
injection nozzle 190 32, 54
injection pump *Intern. Combust. Eng.* 190 65
injection pump *Railw.* 211 48
injection pump drive 190 57
injection timer unit 190 58
ink 260 83
ink ball 340 22
ink duct 180 22; 181 65

inker **180** 21, 50, 60, 77
inker unit **180** 6-13, 40, 51, 60, 71, 76; **181** 7, 8, 19, 28, 50, 57; **249** 51-52
ink fountain **180** 22; **181** 65
ink fountain roller **181** 64
inking ball **340** 22
inking roller **180** 21, 50, 60, 77; **249** 52
inking unit **180** 6-13, 40, 51, 60, 71, 76; **181** 7, 8, 19, 28, 50, 57; **249** 51-52
ink pad **22** 30
ink plate **181** 8
ink roller **180** 21, 50, 60, 77; **249** 52
ink slab **181** 8
ink unit, tubular ~ **151** 68
inkwell **309** 78
inlay **323** 26
inlet *Paperm.* **172** 77
inlet *Chem.* **349** 21
inlet filter **146** 26
inlet manifold **190** 18; **192** 13
inlet valve **242** 52
inlet vent **191** 47
inner tube **187** 30
input **117** 27
input keyboard **238** 13
input/output device **237** 59
input selector **241** 44
input selector switch **238** 49
input unit **176** 30
inscription **252** 11
insect, odonate ~ **358** 3
insect, orthopterous ~ **358** 8
insectivores **366** 4-7
insects **358** 3-23
insects, dipterous ~ **358** 16-20
insert, wood ~ **85** 4
insertion ring **349** 17
inshore fishing **90** 24-29
inside defender **291** 12
inside forward **291** 15
insolation **155** 18
insole **291** 27
inspection apparatus **79** 20
inspection window **38** 62
inspector **205** 44
instep **19** 61
instruction, programmed ~ **242** 16
instruction key **247** 21
instruction laser **242** 81
instrument, keyed ~ **325** 1
instrument, plucked ~ **322** 1-19
instrument basin **27** 5
instrument cabinet **24** 16
instrument housing *Atom* **2** 5, 22
instrument housing *Meteorol. Instr.* **10** 59
instrument panel *Offset Print.* **180** 74
instrument panel *Railw.* **212** 31
instrument panel *Aircraft* **230** 1
instrument panel *Airsports* **288** 11
instruments, dental ~ **24** 4
instruments, orchestral ~ **323** 1-62
instruments, retractable ~ **258** 68; **259** 74, 88-91
instruments for gynecological and proctological examinations **23** 3-21
instruments for minor surgery **22** 48-50
instrument table **22** 45
instrument table, mobile ~ **26** 37

instrument tray **24** 5; **26** 39
instrument unit **234** 53
insufflator **23** 18
insulating board **122** 44
insulating casing **10** 26
insulating tape **127** 34
insulation *Slaughterho.* **94** 10
insulation *Energy Sources* **155** 36
insurance company office **268** 40
intaglio printing **182**
intaglio process **340** 14-24
intake muffler **191** 54
intake pipe **189** 5
intake silencer **190** 16; **191** 54
integer **344** 10
integral **345** 14
integral sign **345** 14
integration **345** 14
intensive care unit **25** 1-30
interceptor **256** 1
Intercity train **205** 34; **209** 1-22
intercom *Doc.* **22** 34
intercom *Garage* **195** 55
intercom *Computer* **244** 5
intercom *Office* **245** 20; **246** 10
intercommunication telephone **239** 13
intercom system *Railw.* **202** 48; **203** 69
intercom system *Computer* **244** 5
interest **345** 7
interference technician **237** 28
interior equipment **239** 6
interlacing point **171** 28
interleaving device **181** 11
intermediate frequency amplifier module **240** 4
intermediate image screen **113** 37
internal combustion engine, single-cylinder ~ **190** 6
internal combustion engine, two-stroke ~ **190** 6
internal combustion engines **190**
internal facing tool **149** 51
International Signals Code **253** 29
interrogation mark **342** 20
interrogation point **342** 20
interrupter **153** 55
intersection **347** 12
intersection of sets **348** 4
interspacing **175** 13
inter-stage connector **234** 31, 36
inter-stage section **234** 31, 36
inter-tank connector **234** 16
inter-tank section **234** 16
intervals **321** 6-13
intestine **77** 15
intestine, large ~ **20** 17-22
intestine, small ~ **20** 14-16
intestines **20** 14-22
intestinum crassum **20** 17-22
intestinum tenue **20** 14-16
intrusion **11** 30
inundation area **216** 41
inverness **186** 32
invertebrates **357**
inverted comma **342** 26
inverted flight **288** 9
involucre **59** 50
ion chamber **2** 2, 17
ionization chamber **2** 2, 17
ionizing particle **1** 58
ionosphere *Atmos.* **7** 23

ionosphere *Post* **237** 55
iris *Man* **19** 42
iris *Flower Gdn.* **51** 27
iris *Gdn. Flowers* **60** 8
iron *Shoem.* **100** 9
iron *Tailor* **104** 29
iron *Ball Games* **293** 92
iron, electric ~ **50** 6
iron, light-weight ~ **50** 6
iron, molten ~ **148** 11
iron, slater's ~ **122** 84
iron, square ~ **143** 9
Iron Age **328** 21-40
iron and steel works **147**
ironer **103** 19
iron foundry **148** 1-45
iron handle **50** 9
ironing board **50** 16
ironing-board cover **50** 17
ironing head **50** 4
ironing machine, electric ~ **50** 1
ironing surface *Household* **50** 16
ironing surface *Dressm.* **103** 23
ironing table **50** 15
iron ladle **147** 12, 21, 42
iron pyrites **351** 8
iron runout **147** 11
irons **50** 1-20
iron well **50** 18
irradiation table **2** 36
irrigation, overhead ~ **67**
irrigation system, portable ~ **67** 3
irrigation unit, long range ~ **67** 18
ischium **17** 19
island *Phys. Geog.* **13** 6
island *Warships* **259** 3
island *Park* **272** 55
isobar **9** 1
isocheim **9** 42
isohel **9** 44
isohyet **9** 45
isometric crystal system **351** 1-17
isosceles triangle **346** 27
isoseismal **11** 37
isothere **9** 43
isotherm **9** 40
issue desk **262** 20
Italian ryegrass **69** 26
italics **175** 7
ITOS satellite **10** 64
ivory carver **135**

J

jack *Ship* **223** 54
jack *Army* **255** 68
jack *Fire Brig.* **270** 12
jack *Sports* **305** 23
jack *Music. Instr.* **322** 50
jack, hydraulic ~ **85** 45
jackal **367** 11
jack boot **355** 58
jack chain, endless ~ **157** 17
jacket **29** 51; **31** 2; **33** 2
jacket, baby's ~ **28** 25; **29** 9
jacket, casual ~ **33** 39
jacket, cork ~ **282** 19
jacket, denim ~ **33** 21
jacket, leather ~ **33** 43
jacket, metallic ~ **294** 15
jacket, mink ~ **30** 1
jacket, oilskin ~ **228** 6
jacket, padded ~ **300** 6
jacket, pile ~ **29** 44
jacket, poplin ~ **31** 37
jacket, short-sleeved ~ **33** 26

jacket, suede ~ **30** 58
jacket button **33** 55
jacket crown **24** 28
jacket flap **185** 38
jack-in-the-box **306** 56
jack panel **311** 16
jack plane **132** 16
jack rafter **121** 61, 63
jack spur, screwed ~ **71** 50
jack spur, strapped ~ **71** 51
jackstaff **223** 53; **258** 4
jackstay **221** 118
jacob's ladder **221** 91
jai alai **305** 67
jam **98** 52
jam, whole-fruit ~ **98** 51
jamb **118** 11; **120** 32, 51
jambeau **329** 54
jam cleat **284** 22
Jamestown weed **379** 8
Japan Current **14** 31
Japanese quince **373** 17
japonica **373** 17
jardin anglais **272** 41-72
javelin **319** 17
javelin throw **298** 51-53
jaw *Man* **16** 17
jaw *Hosp.* **26** 46
jaw *Joiner* **132** 33
jaw *Metalwkr.* **140** 3
jaw, lower ~ *Man* **17** 35
jaw, lower ~ *Horse* **72** 11
jaw, upper ~ **17** 36; **19** 27
jawbone, lower ~ **17** 35
jawbone, upper ~ **17** 36
jaws, inside ~ **149** 71
jaws, outside ~ **149** 70
jaw trap **87** 48
jay **361** 1
jazz band instruments **324** 47-78
jazz guitar **324** 73
jazz trumpet **324** 65
jeans **31** 60; **33** 22
jejunum **20** 15
jellyfish **357** 14
jelly roll **97** 19
J-2 engine **234** 19, 34
jenny **222** 14, 28
jerboa **366** 15
jerkin **355** 45
jerkin head roof **121** 16
jerk with split **299** 4
jersey **291** 56
jersey, padded ~ **292** 26
jess **86** 45
jester **306** 38
jet **83** 19
jet, main ~ **192** 12
jet aeroplanes **231** 7-33
jet airplanes **231** 7-33
jet blower **281** 34
jet condenser **172** 16
jet engine **231** 26
jet engines **232** 33-50
jet fuel tank **146** 18
jet nozzle **153** 29
jet of water **272** 22
jet planes **231** 7-33
jet pump **216** 62
jets **231** 7-33
jet stream level **7** 5
jet trainer **257** 1-41
jet turbine **231** 26
jet turbine engine **231** 26
jet turbine engines **232** 33-50
jet turbines **232** 33-50
jetty *Map* **15** 59
jetty *Docks* **225** 30, 66
jetty *Park* **272** 46
jetty *Camping* **278** 13
jetty *Rowing* **283** 19
jewel **110** 33; **355** 17

jewel box **36** 31
jewel case **36** 31
jewellery **36**; **36** 1
jewellery department **271** 62
jewelry **36** 1
jib *Bldg. Site* **119** 36
jib *Ship* **220** 2
jib *Docks* **226** 24, 49
jib *Army* **255** 95
jib *Sailing* **284** 16; **285** 3
jib, flying ~ **219** 23
jib, inner ~ **219** 21
jib, outer ~ **219** 22
jib boom **218** 51; **219** 1
jib crane **222** 34
jib downhaul **284** 17
jibe **285** 28
jibing **285** 26
jib sheet **284** 23
jib stay **219** 14
jig **134** 42
jiggering **161** 14
jig saw **108** 12
jigsaw puzzle **48** 9
jigsaw puzzle piece **48** 10
jimpson weed **379** 8
jimson weed **379** 8
job advertisement **342** 70
jockey **22** 68
jockey cap **35** 8
jockey roller **181** 45
jockey wheel **278** 54
jogger **249** 56
join **122** 94
joiner **132** 38; **133**
joiner's tools **132** 1-28
joining of modules **242** 70
joint *Phys. Geog.* **13** 50
joint *Plumb. etc.* **126** 38
joint *Railw.* **202** 11
joint *Industr. Plants* **383** 63
joint, pre-packed ~ **96** 22
joint, universal ~ **284** 6
joint and side pasting
  attachment **185** 28
joint cutter **201** 16
joint-cutting blade **201** 17
jointed charlock **61** 21
jointer **133** 37
joint vice **108** 34
joist **121** 54
joist shuttering **119** 12
joke **306** 56
jollying **161** 14
Jordan **172** 27, 60, 73, 83
Jordan refiner **172** 27, 60, 73, 83
journal **143** 63
joust **329** 71
jousting helmet *Heraldry* **254** 4
jousting helmet *Chivalry* **329** 77
judge *Cyc. Racing* **290** 5
judge *Sports* **299** 43
judo **299** 13-17
judoist **299** 14
judoka **299** 14
judo throw **299** 17
jug **39** 30
jug, clay ~ **260** 78
juice extractor **40** 19
ju-jitsu **299** 13-17
jumbo derrick boom **221** 25, 62
jumbo jet **231** 14
jump **289** 21
jumper *Child. Clothes* **29** 43
jumper *Equest.* **289** 9
jumper, child's ~ **29** 47
jumper, cowl neck ~ **30** 2
jumper, polo neck ~ **30** 7
jumper, short-sleeved ~ **31** 61

jumping **298** 9-41
jumping hoop **307** 58
jumping jack **306** 52
jumping rope **273** 15, 16
jumping saddle **289** 10
jumping sheet **270** 18
jump rope **273** 16
jump-sit-spin **302** 8
jump ski **286** 62
jumpsuit **31** 53
jump throw **292** 3
junior hacksaw **127** 52
juniper berry **372** 52
juniper tree **372** 47
junk **353** 32
junk stall **308** 60
Jupiter **4** 48
just **329** 71
justifying scale **174** 35
jute **383** 25

K

kail **57** 34
kale **57** 34
kangaroo **366** 3
kapok tree **383** 20
karabiner **300** 46
karabiner hole **300** 35
karate **299** 18-19
karateka **299** 18
karst formation **13** 71-83
karst spring **13** 74
kart **305** 83
karting **305** 82
kayak **283** 4; **353** 12
kayak, folding ~ **283** 61, 62, 67
kayak, one-man ~ **283** 54
kayak, two-seater ~ **283** 61
kayaks **283** 68-70
Keel *Astron.* **3** 46
keel *Shipbuild.* **222** 22
keel *Space* **235** 7
keel *Rowing* **283** 32
keel *Sailing* **285** 32
keel, lead ~ **285** 36
keel, vertical ~ **222** 53
keel arch **336** 36
keel block **222** 39
keel-centreboard yawl **285** 37-41
keel plate **222** 49
keelson **222** 53; **283** 50
keep **329** 4
keep net **89** 28
kegellade chest **326** 12-14
kelly **145** 14
kelson **222** 53; **283** 50
kerb **198** 6; **272** 25
kerbstone **198** 7
kerbstone broker **251** 5
kerbstoner **251** 5
kerf **84** 28
kernel **68** 13; **383** 44
kerosene **145** 60
kerosene tank **234** 9
kerria **373** 28
ketchup **45** 43
kettle, brass ~ **42** 14
kettle, whistling ~ **39** 16; **40** 10
kettledrum **323** 57
Keuper **154** 57
key *Map* **14** 27-29
key *Metalwkr.* **140** 33-35
key *Town* **268** 4
key *Music. Instr.* **322** 28, 38, 49; **323** 32, 35; **324** 40; **326** 8
key, black ~ **325** 5
key, ebony ~ **325** 5
key, flat ~ **140** 48

key, gib-headed ~ **143** 74
key, iron ~ **328** 32
key, ivory ~ **325** 4
key, sunk ~ **143** 73
key, white ~ **325** 4
key action **325** 22-39
keyboard *Composing Rm.* **174** 32, 37; **176** 2
keyboard *Post* **236** 44; **237** 70
keyboard *Office* **245** 27; **249** 2-6
keyboard *Music. Instr.* **322** 28; **324** 40; **325** 4-5
keyboard, lower ~ **322** 47
keyboard, upper ~ **322** 46
keyboard console **176** 1
keyboard instrument **325** 1
keyboard operator **176** 4
keyboard send-receive
  teleprinter **176** 31
keyboard side **324** 39
keyboard unit **176** 1
keyhole **140** 40
keyhole saw **120** 63; **126** 70; **132** 3
key lever **322** 38, 49; **326** 8
key mechanism **325** 22-39
key rack **267** 3
keys *Mach. Parts etc.* **143** 73-74
keys *Music. Not.* **320** 55-68
key seat **143** 85
key signatures **320** 50-54
key slot **143** 85
keystone **336** 23
keyway **143** 66, 85
kick-back guard **132** 47; **157** 59
kicker **292** 10
kicking strap **284** 21
kick stand **187** 34
kickstarter **188** 39, 43; **189** 38
kidney, left ~ **20** 30-31
kidney, right ~ **20** 28
kidney dish **23** 45
kidney vetch **69** 6
kieselguhr **93** 3
kieselguhr filter **93** 4
kill *Hunt.* **86** 38
kill *Bullfight. etc.* **319** 30
killer **94** 1
kiln **92** 19
kiln, circular ~ **159** 19
kiln, rotary ~ **160** 8
kilning floors **92** 16-18
kilns **161**
kilometer *see* kilometre
kilometre sign **216** 44
kimono **353** 40
kindergarten **48**
king **276** 8
King Carnival **306** 58
king cup **375** 8
kingfisher **360** 8
king penguin **359** 4
king pin roof structure **121** 42
king post **223** 35
king post, ventilator-type ~ **221** 58
king's fern **377** 16
Kipp generator **350** 59
Kipp's apparatus **350** 59
Kirghiz **353** 22
Kirschner beater **163** 25
kit **322** 20
kitchen **39**
kitchen *Butch.* **96** 31-59
kitchen *Railw.* **207** 29, 80
kitchen, ship's ~ **223** 42
kitchen appliances **40**
kitchen cabinet **207** 35
kitchen chair **39** 43
kitchen clock **39** 20; **109** 34

kitchen cupboard **39** 8
kitchen lamp **39** 39
kitchen roll **40** 1
kitchen scales **309** 84
kitchen table **39** 44
kitchen unit **46** 29
kitchen utensils **40**
kite *Playground* **273** 41, 42
kite *Maths.* **346** 38
kite *Birds* **362** 11
kite, paper ~ **260** 71
kite string **273** 44
knapsack **86** 3
knapsack sprayer, plunger-
  type ~ **83** 43
knapweed **376** 12
kneading machine **97** 55
knee *Man* **16** 50
knee *Horse* **72** 22
knee-breeches **33** 40
kneecap *Man* **17** 23
knee cap *Chivalry* **329** 53
kneeler **332** 25
knee lever **325** 45
kneeling front support **295** 20
kneeling position *Free Exerc.* **295** 8
kneeling position *Sports* **305** 28
knee mounting **113** 21
knee pad *Ball Games* **292** 9
knee pad *Winter Sp.* **303** 17
knee piece **329** 53
knee roll **71** 48
knee stand **33** 41
knee swell **325** 45
knife *Tablew. etc.* **45** 7, 50
knife *Forestry* **85** 11
knife *Paperhanger* **128** 38
knife *Paperm.* **172** 74
knife *Swim.* **279** 8
knife, bookbinder's ~ **183** 13
knife, bronze ~ **328** 31
knife, butcher's ~
  Slaughterho. **94** 15
knife, butcher's ~ *Butch.* **96** 37
knife, cobbler's ~ **100** 50
knife, electrician's ~ **127** 63
knife, gardener's ~ **56** 9
knife, gilder's ~ **129** 51
knife, hafted ~ **328** 31
knife, shoemaker's ~ **100** 50
knife, surgical ~ **26** 43
knife blade **96** 32
knife case **94** 12
knife coulter **65** 10
knife handle **96** 34
knife rest **45** 11
knife thrower **307** 37
knight *Games* **276** 11
knight *Chivalry* **329** 67
knighting **329** 66
Knight Templar **329** 73
knit **101** 43
knits **171**
knits, basic ~ **171** 30-48
knit stitch **101** 43
knitting **167**
knitting head **167** 21
knitting machine, circular ~ **167** 1
knitting machine, flat ~ **167** 18
knives, butcher's ~ **96** 31-37
knob **359** 17
knob, adjustable ~ **151** 3
knobkerrie **354** 33
knobkerry **354** 33
knob-leaf capital **333** 14
knockout **299** 40
knock-over bit **167** 52
knot *Meteorol. etc.* **9** 12

knot *Ladies' Wear* 31 47
knot *Underwear etc.* 32 42
knot *Roof* 122 68
knot, French ~ 102 13
knot hole cutter 132 53
knot hole moulding machine 132 52
knot stitch, twisted ~ 102 13
knotted work 102 21
knotter 172 54; 173 13
knotting machine 85 18
knuckle *Man* 19 82
knuckle *Meat* 95 38, 42, 49
knuckle, fore ~ 95 5, 8
knuckle, hind ~ 95 1, 10
knuckle of pork 96 17
Kocher's forceps 22 49
kohlrabi 57 26
Korean 341 27
Kort vent 227 21
koruna 252 27
kraft pulp mill 172 1-52
KR-class 284 63
kris 353 44
krona 252 25
krone 252 24, 26
Krüger flap 229 55
krummhorn 322 6
Kuroshio 14 31
Kuro Siwo 14 31
kursaal 274 8
kymation 334 19

L

label 54 4
laboratory 23 41-59
laboratory, multi-purpose ~ 235 66
laboratory and research microscope 112 1·
laboratory apparatus *Doc.* 23 57
laboratory apparatus *Paperm.* 173 2-10
laboratory apparatus *Chem.* 349 1-38; 350 1-63
laboratory equipment *Doc.* 23 57
laboratory equipment *Paperm.* 173 2-10
laboratory equipment *Chem.* 349 1-38; 350 1-63
laboratory microscope 112 1
laboratory technician 23 41
laboratory timer 116 18
laborer *see* labourer
labourer, bricklayer's ~ 118 19
labourer, builder's ~ 118 19
Labrador Current 14 40
labret 354 23
laburnum 374 32
labyrinth 17 62
lace 100 64; 291 32
lace, cotton ~ 31 32
lace, Venetian ~ 102 30
lace fastening 101 21
lackey 186 20
lackey moth 80 13
lacolith 11 30
lacquered work, incised ~ 337 6
lacquey 186 20
lactam oil 170 37
ladder *Moon L.* 6 35
ladder *Roof & Boilerr.* 38 15
ladder *Child. Rm.* 47 5
ladder *Fruit & Veg. Gdn.* 52 8
ladder *Bldg. Site* 118 42
ladder *Railw.* 211 43
ladder *Hydr. Eng.* 217 8
ladder *Space* 235 28

ladder, aluminium ~ 50 35
ladder, arched ~ 5 20
ladder, extending ~ 270 10
ladder, standard ~ 118 86
ladder, steel ~ 270 10
ladder dredge, multi-bucket ~ 216 56
ladder hook 122 15, 69
ladder mechanism 270 11
ladder operator 270 13
ladder scaffold 118 86-89
'ladies' 233 48
'ladies' toilet' 233 48
ladies' wear 30; 31
ladies' wear department 271 28
ladle 130 32
ladle, crane-operated ~ 147 60
ladle, drum-type ~ 148 6
ladle, mobile ~ 148 6
lady *Café* 265 23
lady *Hist. Cost.* 355 59, 64, 68, 70, 79
ladybird 358 37
ladybug 358 37
lady-finger 69 6
lady's finger 69 6
ladysmock 375 11
lady's slipper 376 27
lady's smock 375 11
lager 93 26
lager cellar 93 12
lagging 38 72
lagoon 13 33
lake 13 3
lake, coastal ~ 13 44
lake, ox-bow ~ 15 75
lake dwelling 328 15
lamantin 366 23
lamb 73 13; 75 11
lamb's lettuce 57 38
lamellicorn 82 1
lamellicorn beetle 358 24, 39
lamina 68 20; 370 28, 85
laminate 301 48
lamp *Dent.* 24 19
lamp *Dining Rm.* 44 12
lamp *Watchm.* 109 12
lamp *Carriages* 186 9
lamp *Street Sect.* 198 14
lamp *Nightclub* 318 26
lamp, directional ~ 22 44
lamp, fluorescent ~ 49 32; 271 23
lamp, front ~ 188 29
lamp, individual ~ 26 11
lamp, pendant ~ 44 12
lamp, rear ~ 187 46
lamp, side ~ 191 20
lamp bracket *Photomech. Reprod.* 177 16
lamp bracket *Bicycle* 187 6
lamp compartment 177 41
lampholder 127 60
lamphouse 112 28, 59; 116 29; 309 44; 312 39-44
lamphouse connector 112 60
lamp housing 116 29
lamp post 198 18
lam rod 166 54
lance *Gdn. Tools* 56 25
lance *Bullfight. etc.* 319 17
lance *Chivalry* 329 81
lance *Ethnol.* 353 9
lanceolate 370 32
lancer 319 16
lance rest 329 80
lancet arch 336 31
lancet window 335 39-41
land 87 39
landau 186 36
landaulette 186 36

land drill 282 20
landfill, sanitary ~ 199 10
landing *Floor etc. Constr.* 123 34-41
landing *Athletics* 298 19
landing, intermediate ~ 123 52-62
landing area 298 36, 39
landing beam 123 34, 55
landing beam, main ~ 123 66
landing craft 258 89; 259 46
landing flap 229 42; 230 53; 257 38; 288 29
landing gear, hydraulically operated ~ 235 31
landing gear, main ~ 235 31
landing gear, retractable ~ 232 10
landing gear housing 256 15
landing gear hydraulic cylinder 257 41
landing gear unit, forward-retracting ~ 257 40
landing gear unit, main ~ 230 41; 231 28; 257 40; 288 33
landing gear unit, retractable ~ 231 28
landing light 230 49; 257 37; 288 32
landing mat 296 13; 297 7
landing net 89 2
landing pad *Moon L.* 6 33
landing pad *Athletics* 298 36
landing pontoon 225 63
landing skid 232 15; 256 21
landing stage 225 63; 278 13; 283 19
landing unit, main ~ 256 26
landlord 305 7, 13
landside 65 5, 67
landslide 11 46
landslip 11 46
land surveying 14 46-62
land wheel 65 15
lane *Map* 15 112
lane *Forestry* 84 1
lane arrow 268 73, 74
lane timekeeper 282 24
language laboratory 261 35
languid 326 28
lansquenet 355 32
lantern *Carriages* 186 9
lantern *Ship* 218 44; 221 48
lantern *Navig.* 224 105
lantern *Art* 335 45
lantern, Chinese ~ 353 36
lantern, combined ~ 286 13
lantern, paper ~ 52 15; 306 4
lantern mast 224 82
lantern tower 224 82
lanyard 284 19
lap *Dom. Anim.* 73 23
lap *Roof* 122 100
lap *Cotton Spin.* 163 58, 64
lap, carded ~ 163 47
lapboard 136 7
lap cradle 163 15
lapel 31 23; 33 5
lapel, silk ~ 33 8
lapping plate 125 4
lap riveting 143 56
lap scorer 290 6
lap-turner, movable ~ 163 19
lapwing 359 21
larch 372 32
larch cone 372 36
lard 96 5
large cabbage white butterfly 80 47
larks 361 18-19
larkspur 60 13
larmier 88 14
larry 144 8; 156 6

larry car 144 8; 156 6
larva 58 64; 77 29; 80 6, 19, 36, 38, 41, 46; 81 20; 358 9, 19; 82 12, 25, 36
larva, first-generation ~ 80 23
larva, mature ~ 80 53
larva, second-generation ~ 80 24
larva, young ~ 77 28; 80 54
larynx 20 2-3
laser 242 81
laser beam 243 53
lashing *Bldg. Site* 118 30
lashing *Ship* 218 32; 221 119
lasso 319 40; 352 5
last 100 34
last, iron ~ 100 54
last, wooden ~ 100 32
latch bolt 140 37
latch needle 167 12, 56, 61
lateen sail 218 29; 220 3
lateen spanker 218 29
lateen yard 218 30
lateral 144 30
lath 123 70
lath, double ~ 122 43
lath, tilting ~ 122 43
lath, toothed ~ 122 26
lath axe 122 21
lathe 135 1
lathe, watchmaker's ~ 109 20
lathe bed 135 2; 149 31
lathe carrier 149 54
lathe foot 149 12
lathe spindle 149 20
lathe tool 149 48, 52
lathe tools 149 45-53
lathing 123 71
latissimus dorsi 18 59
latitude 14 6
latrine 118 49
lattice casing 221 84
lattice girder 235 12
lattice mast 258 18
lattice structures 1 9-14
lattice swing bridge 215 63
launch 225 25
launcher 258 49
launching container 258 32
launching housing 259 26
launching ramp 255 66
launch phase escape tower 234 66
lauter battery 92 51
lauter tun 92 50
lava plateau 11 14
lava stream 11 18
lavatories 317 31
lavatory 49 12; 146 29; 207 16, 42, 72; 211 59; 231 31; 278 5
lavatory, public ~ 268 62
lavender 380 7
lawn 37 46; 51 33; 272 36; 274 12
lawn aerator 56 15
lawn mower, electric ~ 56 31
lawn mower, motor ~ 56 28
lawn rake 51 3; 56 3
lawn sprinkler 37 43; 56 43
lay-by 217 27
layer 54 11, 12
layer, bast ~ 54 35
layer, bituminous ~ 200 58
layer, level ~ 123 39
layer, raffia ~ 54 35
layer, top ~ 123 41
layer cloud 8 3, 4. 8. 9. 10
layering 54 10
layette 28
layette box 28 18
lay figure 338 31

laying battery 74 19
laying hen 74 57
laying-on trowel 118 56
laying up 216 14
lay shaft 192 37
L-D converter 147 45-50
lead Kitch. 39 25
lead Dog 70 30
lead Slaughterho. 94 9
lead Arc Weld. 142 25
lead Navig. 224 59
lead, electric ~ Household 50 77
lead, electric ~ Gdn. Tools 56 32
lead, oval ~ 89 88
lead, pear-shaped ~ 89 90
lead, spare ~ 151 46
lead came 124 13
leader Dwellings 37 13
leader Roof & Boilerr. 38 10
leader Fish Farm. 89 78
leader Photog. 114 9
leader Carriages 186 46
leader Mountain. 300 25
leader Script 342 48
lead hammer 124 11
leading article 342 48
leading edge Sailing 284 42
leading edge Gliding 287 34
leading edge, carbon fibre reinforced ~ 235 32
leading-edge flap, profiled ~ 229 54
leading lady 310 27
leading light, higher ~ 224 102
leading light, lower ~ 224 101
leading lights 224 101-102
leading man 310 28
leading soloist 314 28
lead-in tube 153 40
lead knife 124 12
leadline 224 60
leads 89 88-92; 224 58-67
leadscrew 149 19, 32
leadscrew handwheel 149 13
leadscrew reverse-gear lever 149 6
lead shot 89 89
lead sinker 224 59
leaf 58 3, 53; 59 17; 68 8; 333 24; 370 19, 26; 371 21, 23, 27, 29, 68; 372 23; 373 3, 16, 25; 374 28; 375 2; 378 15, 18, 19, 41, 45; 384 55, 62
leaf, alternate pinnate ~ 59 40
leaf, basal ~ 375 9, 12, 15, 30; 383 2
leaf, pinnate ~ 57 3
leaf, sprouting ~ 59 29
leaf, ternate ~ 58 19
leaf, trifoliate ~ 58 19
leaf, young ~ 59 29
leaf axil 370 25; 375 38
leaf blade 68 20; 370 28, 85
leaf bud 59 47; 370 90
leaf cluster, rooted ~ 54 17
leaf drop 80 20
leaf fat 95 45
leaflet 263 9
leaf margin shapes 370 43-50
leaf ornament 334 40
leaf roller 82 43
leaf shapes 370 31-38
leaf sheath 68 9, 21; 370 83; 384 30
leaf stalk 370 27; 371 73
leaf tendril 57 4
leaf vegetables 57 28-34
leakage steam path 153 28
lean forward 301 36
lean-to roof 37 78; 121 7

leaping hind leg 358 11
learner-swimmer 282 17
learning programme, audio-visual ~ 242 7
lease rod 166 38
leash 70 30
leather beetle 81 22
leathers 290 26
leather side 131 13, 18
leaves 276 43
leaves, compound ~ 370 39-42
lebkuchen 97 51
lectern 262 4; 330 2, 37
lecture 262 1
lecture notes 262 5
lecturer 262 3
lecture room 262 2
lecture theatre 262 2
lederhosen 29 32
ledge Photograv. 182 23
ledge Mountain. 300 4
ledge, cushioned ~ 277 16
ledger 118 26
ledger tube 119 48
leeboard 220 7; 283 63
leech Sailing 284 45
leech Invertebr. 357 20
leech pocket 284 43
leek 57 21
lee waves 287 17
left 254 19,21,23
left corner pin 305 6
left front second pin 305 2
left hook 299 33
left luggage locker 204 21
left luggage office 204 27
left tank fuel gauge 230 16
leg Man 16 49-54; 17 22-25
leg Game 88 21, 37, 81
leg Meat 95 1, 38
leg Mach. Parts etc. 143 2
leg Maths. 346 27
leg, back ~ 82 8
leg, broken ~ 21 11
leg, downwind ~ 285 23
leg, first ~ 285 19
leg, fractured ~ 21 11
leg, front ~ 82 6
leg, hind ~ Dog 70 7
leg, hind ~ Horse 72 33-37
leg, hind ~ Bees 77 3, 6-9
leg, hind ~ Game 88 22, 63
leg, middle ~ 82 7
leg, second ~ 285 20
leg, third ~ 285 21
leg, tubular ~ 114 44
leg, vertical ~ 143 4
leg, windward ~ 285 22
leg armour 319 19
legato 321 33
leg boot, high ~ 101 7, 13
leg boot, men's ~ 101 7, 13
legend 252 11
leg feather 362 3
leggings 28 24; 29 45; 352 17
leg holder 23 11
leg of mutton piece 95 22, 29
leg ring 74 54
legs 82 6-8
leg space ventilation 191 81
leg support 23 10, 11
legume 57 6; 370 92
legume, immature ~ 374 22
legume, unripe ~ 374 22
Leguminosae 57 1-11
leg vice 140 10
Leine rock salt 154 64
leisure centre 281
lemon 384 23
lemonade 265 15
lemonade glass 265 16
lemon peel, candied ~ 98 10

lemon squeezer 40 9
lending library 262 18
length adjustment 100 20
lengthening arm 151 57
lengths of material 104 2
length stop 157 68
lens Man 19 48
lens Photog. 115 32, 84; 116 32
lens Composing Rm. 176 23
lens Audiovis. 243 2, 52
lens Films 313 2
lens Crystals 351 33
lens, bifocal ~ 111 15
lens, concave and convex ~ 111 41
lens, convex and concave ~ 111 42
lens, fisheye ~ 115 44
lens, flat ~ 111 38
lens, flush ~ 114 5
lens, interchangeable ~ 112 62; 115 43
lens, long focal length ~ 115 48
lens, long-focus ~ 115 49
lens, medium focal length ~ 115 47
lens, negative ~ 111 37
lens, normal ~ 115 3-8, 46; 117 49
lens, plano-concave ~ 111 39, 40
lens, positive ~ 111 37
lens, short focal length ~ 115 45
lens, special ~ 111 38
lens, standard ~ 115 3-8, 46; 117 49
lens, telephoto ~ 115 48
lens, variable focus ~ 117 2
lens, varifocal ~ 117 2
lens, wide-angle ~ 115 45; 117 48
lens barrel 115 3
lens carrier 177 27
lens case 115 104
lens head 117 46-49
lens hood 313 3, 10
lens hood barrel 313 5
lens hood bellows 313 39
lens panel 112 18
lens pouch, soft-leather ~ 115 105
lens standard 114 52
lens surface 111 37
lens system 242 83
lens turret 117 46; 313 32
lenticular 287 19
Lent lily 60 3, 12
Leo 3 17; 4 57
Leonberger 73 16
leopard 368 6
leotard 297 51
Lepidoptera 358 48-56; 365
lepton 252 39
lesene 335 11
Lesser Bear 3 34
lesser celandine 375 36
Lesser Dog 3 15
lesser housefly 81 1
less-than-carload freight 206 4
let-off motion 166 59
let-off weight lever 166 62
let-out section 131 7
let-out strip 131 7
letter 174 44
letter, capital ~ 175 11
letter, double ~ 175 6
letter, initial ~ 175 1
letter, lower case ~ 175 12
letter, small ~ 175 12

letter, upper case ~ 175 11
letter carrier 236 53
letter container 236 32
letter feed 236 31
letter flags 253 22-28
letter-folding machine 249 44
lettering 129 40
lettering brush 129 41
lettering stencil 151 69
letter matrix 174 47; 176 16
letterpress machine, rotary ~ 181 41
letterpress machine, web-fed ~ 181 41
letterpress press, rotary ~ 181 41
letterpress printing 181
letterpress printing machines 181 1-65
letterpress printing method 340 1-13
letter rack 267 2
letter-rate item 236 55
letters, illuminated ~ 268 45
letter scales 236 24
letter-sorting installation 236 31-44
letter spacing 175 13
letter tray 245 30; 248 41
lettuce 57 36
lettuce leaf 57 37
leucite 351 12
levade Horse 71 4
levade Circus 307 30
levee 13 9; 216 49
level 14 48
level, lower ~ 217 17
level, motor-driven ~ 112 69
level, upper ~ 217 25
level crossing 15 26
level crossing, protected ~ 202 39
level crossing, unprotected ~ 202 49
level crossings 202 39-50
level indicator 316 57
leveling see levelling
levelling 14 46
levelling and support shovel 255 94
levelling beam 201 3, 4
levelling blade 200 18
levelling staff 14 47
lever Plumb. etc. 126 19
lever Sawmill 157 46
lever Cotton Spin. 164 42
lever Office 249 50
lever Graphic Art 340 61
lever for normal and coarse threads 149 4
lever hang 296 56
lever mechanism 203 54
liberty horses 307 30-31
Libra 3 19; 4 59
librarian 262 14, 19
library, municipal ~ 262 11-25
library, national ~ 262 11-25
library, regional ~ 262 11-25
library, scientific ~ 262 11-25
library, ship's ~ 223 25
library ticket 262 25
library user 262 24
license plate 189 8
lichgate 331 19
licker-in 163 53
licker-in roller 163 53
licker-in undercasing 163 54
lid Kitch. Utensils 40 13
lid Electrotyp. etc. 178 37
lid Chem. 350 52
lid, glass ~ 269 56
lid, hinged ~ 127 24

lid, sliding ~ **179** 2
lid clip **50** 83
lido deck **223** 22
Lieberkühn reflector **115** 97
liege lord **329** 67
lifebelt **221** 124; **222** 24; **280** 3; **281** 6
lifebelt light **221** 125
lifebelt *Offshore Drill.* **146** 19
lifeboat **221** 78, 107; **223** 19
lifeboat launching gear **221** 101-106
lifebuoy *Ship* **221** 124
lifebuoy *Shipbuild.* **222** 24
lifebuoy *Bathing* **280** 3
lifebuoy light **221** 125
lifeguard **280** 1
lifeguard station **280** 46
life jacket **286** 20
life jacket, cork ~ **228** 9
life jacket, inflatable ~ **228** 8
life line **19** 72
lifeline **221** 103; **228** 12; **280** 2
life preserver, cork ~ **228** 9
life raft **228** 19; **258** 11; **286** 19
life rocket **228** 2
lifesaver **21** 36; **280** 1
life saving **228**
life support pack **6** 20
life support system **6** 20
lift *Ship* **219** 47
lift *Store* **271** 45
lift *Theatre* **316** 33
lift, hydraulic ~ **195** 25, 26
lift, vertical ~ **170** 36
liftback **193** 29
lift bridge **225** 70
lift cage **271** 46
lift car **271** 46
lift chair **214** 16
lift chair, double ~ **214** 17
lift controls **271** 48
lift device **103** 24
lift dump **229** 42
lifter *Agr. Mach.* **64** 59
lifter *Sawmill* **157** 46
lifter rail **164** 30
lifter roller **181** 63
lifting arm **255** 76
lifting bolt **164** 37
lifting crane **270** 48
lifting device **255** 76
lifting gear **206** 56
lifting hook **85** 6
lifting motor **150** 22
lifting platform **232** 19
lifting rod **65** 29
lifting rod adjustment **65** 25
lifting spindle **217** 36
lifting undercarriage **232** 18
lift-off hinge **140** 49
lift operator **271** 47
lift platform **173** 40
lift shaft **271** 51
ligament, falciform ~ **20** 34
ligature *First Aid* **21** 14-17
ligature *Composing Rm.* **175** 6
ligature-holding forceps **26** 44
light **106** 8; **210** 46; **224** 69
light, flashing ~ **270** 6
light, fluorescent ~ **271** 23
light, leaded ~ **124** 14
light, polar ~ **7** 30
light, rear ~ **187** 46; **189** 9
light, supplementary ~ **203** 17
light ale **93** 26
light and bell buoy **224** 74
light and whistle buoy **224** 68
light beer **93** 26
light box **179** 25

light bulb **127** 69; **318** 26
light-emitting diode readout **110** 2
lighter **216** 25; **225** 8, 25
lighter, disposable ~ **107** 30
lighter, tug-pushed ~ **221** 94
lighterman **216** 26
light face **175** 8
lighthouse *Map* **15** 8
lighthouse *Navig.* **224** 103
lighting, external ~ **197** 32
lighting, indirect ~ **317** 12
lighting, internal ~ **197** 32
lighting aperture **334** 75
lighting bridge, travelling ~ **316** 19
lighting console **316** 2
lighting control console **316** 2
lighting effects **316** 2
lighting electrician **310** 37
lighting gallery, travelling ~ **316** 19
lighting man **310** 37; **316** 20
lighting operator **316** 20
lighting plot **316** 3
lighting station **226** 27
lighting technician **307** 4
lightning **9** 39
lightning arrester **152** 35
lightning conductor **38** 30
lightning rod **38** 30
light plot **316** 3
light railway diesel locomotive **200** 24
light rays **1** 62
light readout **195** 9
lights, set of ~ **268** 54
light section tube **112** 38
light-sensitive section **77** 22
lightship *Map* **15** 13
lightship *Ship* **221** 47
lightship *Navig.* **224** 81
light source *Atom* **1** 59
light source *Optic. Instr.* **112** 52
light source, photometric ~ **112** 50
light stop **5** 22
light vessel **221** 47; **224** 81
ligula **68** 22; **370** 84
ligule **68** 22; **370** 84
lily **60** 12
lily of the valley **377** 2
limb **370** 5
limb, fractured ~ **21** 10
limb, moon's ~ **4** 41
limbing machine **85** 18
limbs **16** 43-54
lime **147** 56
lime, reconverted ~ **172** 52
lime bunker **147** 62
lime kiln **15** 86
limerick **89** 84
lime slaker **172** 51
limestone **160** 1
lime tree **371** 46
limiter display **238** 44
limit switch **241** 60
limousine **193** 1
linden plant **53** 9
linden tree **371** 46
line *Horse* **71** 33
line *Composing Rm.* **175** 4
line *Carriages* **186** 31
line *Railw.* **202** 1-38
line *Theatre* **316** 8
line *Maths.* **346** 1-23
line, curved ~ **346** 21
line, equinoctial ~ **3** 3
line, horizontal ~ **344** 15
line, local ~ **15** 25
line, straight ~ **346** 2-3, 5, 16
linear **370** 31

line block **178** 42
line-casting machine **174** 19
line cut **178** 42
line engraving **178** 42
line etching **178** 42
line glass **124** 6
line guide **89** 60
linen **206** 11
linen, dirty ~ **50** 22
linen bin **50** 21
linen compartment **267** 31
linen drawer **44** 22; **47** 22
linen goods **271** 57
linen shelf **43** 2
linen tester **177** 23
line-of-battle ship **218** 51-60
line of fencing **294** 9
line of latitude **14** 2
line of life **19** 72
line of longitude **14** 4
line of the head **19** 73
line of the heart **19** 74
line of the staff **320** 43
line plate **178** 42
liner **221** 82; **225** 32
lines *Horse* **71** 25
lines *Rowing* **283** 52
line shooting **89** 20
linesman *Railw.* **202** 44
linesman *Ball Games* **291** 59; **293** 69
lines of the hand **19** 72-74
line space adjuster **249** 23
line space and carrier return key **249** 4
line steam injector **210** 41
line-throwing gun **228** 1
lingerie **32** 1-15
lining *Bldg. Site* **119** 54
lining *Hist. Cost.* **355** 57
lining, fireproof ~ **147** 48
lining, knitwear ~ **101** 17
lining, leather ~ **291** 22
lining, refractory ~ **147** 48
lining, tricot ~ **101** 17
lining board *Bldg. Site* **118** 41; **119** 18
lining board *Floor etc. Constr.* **123** 54
lining paper **128** 5
lining paper, shredded ~ **128** 8
link **36** 39
link, lower ~ **65** 28
link, top ~ **65** 27
linkage, three-point ~ **64** 45; **65** 72
linking of modules **242** 70
link-up of modules **242** 70
linotype line-composing machine **174** 19
linotype matrix **174** 29
lint **383** 19
lintel **37** 25; **118** 9
lintel, reinforced concrete ~ **118** 13
Linz-Donawitz converter **147** 45-50
Lion *Astron.* **3** 17; **4** 57
lion **307** 56; **356** 5; **368** 2
lip, lower ~ *Man* **19** 26
lip, lower ~ *Horse* **72** 10
lip, lower ~ *Music. Instr.* **326** 26
lip, upper ~ *Man* **19** 14
lip, upper ~ *Horse* **72** 8
lip, upper ~ *Music. Instr.* **326** 27
lip of the pudendum **20** 87
lip of the vulva **20** 87
lip plug **354** 23
liquefied-gas tanker **221** 35
liqueur **98** 58

liqueur decanter **45** 48
liqueur glass **45** 89; **317** 7
liquid-column barometer **10** 1
liquid crystal readout **110** 2
liquid feed pipe **74** 26
liquid hydrogen and liquid oxygen tank, jettisonable ~ **235** 46
liquid hydrogen line **234** 51; **235** 50
liquid hydrogen pump, high-pressure ~ **235** 41
liquid hydrogen suction line **234** 23
liquid hydrogen supply, main ~ **235** 35
liquid hydrogen tank **234** 26, 41
liquid level indicator **316** 57
liquid manure channel **75** 44
liquid manure silo **62** 13
liquid oxygen line **234** 52; **235** 51, 56
liquid oxygen pump, high-pressure ~ **235** 42
liquid oxygen supply line **234** 10
liquid oxygen tank **234** 12, 24, 39
liquid stage **148** 27
liquor **168** 14
liquor, weak ~ **172** 45
liquor preheater **172** 8
liquor pump **172** 33
liquor supply pipe **92** 48
lira **252** 20, 21
literature **330** 57
literature stand **330** 56
litho artist **340** 45
Lithodes **369** 16
lithographer **340** 45
lithographic crayon **340** 26
lithographic press **340** 60
lithographic stone **340** 25, 57
lithography **340** 25-26
lithosphere **11** 1
litter *Poultry Farm* **74** 8
litter *Livestock* **75** 6
litter *Town* **268** 22
litter basket **37** 63; **205** 55; **272** 43; **273** 25
litter bin **37** 63; **205** 55; **268** 5; **272** 43; **273** 25
litter receptacle **196** 12; **207** 55
Little Bear **3** 34
little brain **17** 45; **18** 23
little cluster fungus **381** 33
Little Dipper **3** 34
Little Dog **3** 15
little owl **362** 19
livelong **377** 9
live power take-off **65** 31
live power take-off shaft **65** 31
liver **20** 10, 34-35
livery **186** 21
live sound **117** 100
livestock, small **213** 28
livestock ramp **206** 1
living quarters **224** 108; **227** 19; **259** 84
living room **42**
lizards **364** 27, 30-37
llama **366** 28
load **73** 5
load, driven ~ **226** 19
load, foil-wrapped ~ **226** 9
load, unitized ~ **226** 9, 21
load hook **270** 49
loading bridge **221** 90; **226** 2
loading chamber **116** 6

loading crane 85 28, 44
loading deck 221 34
loading dock 206 9
loading door 207 23
loading foreman 205 30; 206 29
loading gauge 206 22
loading platform *Lorries etc.* 194 3
loading platform *Ship* 221 90
loading siding 206 17
loading strip 206 8
loading supervisor 206 36
loaf, French ~ 97 12
loaf, long ~ 97 8
loaf, round ~ 97 6, 7; 99 14
loaf, small ~ 97 7
loaf, white ~ 97 9
loaf of bread 97 2
loam 120 44; 159 2
loan, personal ~ 250 4
lobby 267 18-26; 315 12-13
lobe 229 30
lobe, pulmonary ~ 20 7
lobe, upper ~ 20 7
lobe of the liver 20 35
lobster fork 45 79
local-battery telephone 224 27; 238 9, 40
lock *Map* 15 58
lock *Hunt.* 87 9
lock *Hydr. Eng.* 217 20
lock approach 217 26
lock chamber 217 20
lock gate 217 18, 32
lock indicator panel 203 63
locking bolt 117 62
locking lever *Atom* 2 40
locking lever *Motorcycles etc.* 188 2
locking lever *Office* 247 42
locking mechanism 246 23
locking nut 143 30; 187 54
lock lever 203 55
locknut 143 30; 187 54
locksmith 140 1
lock washer 202 8
locomotive, articulated ~ 210 64
locomotive, electric ~ 205 35; 211 1
locomotive, elevation of ~ 212 51-67
locomotive, fireless ~ 210 68
locomotive, mainline ~ 212 1
locomotive boiler 210 2-37
locust tree 371 70
loft 37 4; 38 18
log *Forestry* 84 20, 31
log *Maths.* 345 6
log, mechanical ~ 224 54
log, sawn ~ 157 33
log, ship's ~ 224 22
logarithm 345 6
logarithm sign 345 6
log capacity scale 157 10
log chain, endless ~ 157 17
log clock 224 57
log dump 85 32; 157 31
log grips 85 29; 157 13, 39
log grips, pivoted ~ 157 29
logic element 242 68
logic module 242 68
log-kicker arm 157 19
log ladder 273 22
loin *Game* 88 18, 35
loin *Meat* 95 3
loin *Butch.* 96 4
loin, pork ~ 95 46
loincloth 352 38; 354 31
loins *Man* 16 24
loins *Horse* 72 30
loin strap 71 32

long-conductor antenna 230 66
long-distance racing 290 11-15
long-distance runner 298 5
long drink 317 32
long-eared bat 366 9
long-eared owl 362 14
long-fly 296 48; 297 20
long haul airliner 231 13, 14
long horse 296 1
longicorn 358 38
longicorn beetle 358 38
longitude 14 7
long johns 32 29
long jump 298 37-41
long line 90 28
long-line fishing 90 28-29
long-lining 90 28-29
long measure 294 10
long primer 175 27
long rifle cartridge 305 38
longship 218 13-17
long sitting 295 10
longwall face, cut ~ 144 34
longwall face, ploughed ~ 144 33
longwall faces 144 33-37
long-wire antenna 230 66
lookout platform 273 23
loom, automatic ~ 166 1, 35
loom framing 166 24
loop *Knitting* 167 62, 66
loop *Weaves* 171 39
loop *Airsports* 288 1
loop *Winter Sp.* 301 7; 302 15
loop, closed ~ 171 36
loop, open ~ 171 30
loop, platinum ~ 23 15
loop, primary ~ 154 2, 42
loop, secondary ~ 154 7, 45
loop antenna 223 5
loo paper 49 11
looper 80 17
loop fastening 30 41
loop formation 167 65
loop former 312 30
loose-leaf file 260 15
Lophocalyx philippensis 369 7
lopping 85 11
lords-and-ladies 379 9
Lord's table 330 4
lorries 194
lorry 226 19
lorry, heavy ~ 194 20; 200 7
lorry, light ~ 194 1, 5
lorry, toy ~ 47 38; 273 62
lorry tyre 273 19
lorry wheel 138 21
lorry with trailer 213 34
loser 299 40
lot 310 1
lottery booth 308 44
lottery ticket seller 266 20
lotus column 333 13
loud hailer 264 12
loud pedal 325 8
loudspeaker 42 10; 241 14; 264 12; 311 46; 317 15; 318 12
loudspeaker, built-in ~ 249 70
loudspeaker aperture 309 19
louis-d'or 252 5
Louis Seize table 336 14
lounge *Living Rm.* 42
lounge *Ship* 223 26
lounge *Airport* 233 18
'lounge' *Airport* 233 28
lourer 321 29
louvre shutter 304 12
love-lies-bleeding 60 21

low 9 5
low box 172 26
lower cable sleeve 214 74
lower fore topgallant sail 219 58
lower fore topgallant yard 219 35
lower fore topsail 219 56
lower fore topsail yard 219 33
Lower Keuper 154 57
lower main topgallant sail 219 64
lower main topgallant yard 219 41
lower main topsail 219 62
lower main topsail yard 219 39
Lower Muschelkalk 154 60
lower station platform 214 51
low house 305 76
low-moor bog 13 14
low-pressure area 9 5
low-pressure manometer 141 6
low-pressure regulator 190 59
low relief 339 33
low-speed aileron 229 41
low-temperature surface insulation 235 15
low tide 280 7
low-voltage bushing 152 44
low-voltage terminal 152 44
lozenge 346 35
L-seat 295 10
L-support 295 16
lubber's line 224 48
lubber's mark 224 48
lubber's point 224 48
lubricant pump, automatic ~ 210 42
lubricating nipple 143 81
lubricating oil 145 62
lubricating oil refinery 145 67
lubricating system, pressure-feed ~ 192 16-27
lubrication hole 187 62
lubrication system 65 45
lubricator 187 62, 65
lubricator, automatic ~ 210 42
lucerne 69 9
ludo 47 19
luff 284 42
luffing 285 9
luffing jib crane 222 23
luge 303 13
luge, junior ~ 303 3
luge toboggan 303 13
luge toboggan, junior ~ 303 3
luge tobogganer 303 12
luggage 205 7-12
luggage carrier 187 44
luggage clerk 204 9
luggage compartment *Car* 193 17, 23
luggage compartment *Lorries etc.* 194 13
luggage compartment *Railw.* 207 71; 208 15
luggage counter 204 4
luggage label 205 8
luggage locker 194 18
'luggage lockers' 233 39
luggage rack 207 51; 208 27
luggage receipt 204 8
luggage rest 204 43
luggage sticker 204 7
lugger 90 1
lugsail 220 4
lug strap 166 22
lumbar region 72 30
lumber 120 2
lumber, rough ~ 120 83
lumberer 84 18

lumbering 84 15-37
lumberjack 84 18
lumber-jacket 30 38
lumberman 84 18
lumber room door 38 20
luminescent 369 14
luminescent material 240 18
lump coal 156 14
lunar module 234 55
lunar module hangar 234 54
lunation 4 2-7
lung 18 13; 20 6-7
lung, right ~ 20 6
lunge 295 42
lunging 294 5
lunging position 294 5
lungwort 377 7
lunula *Man* 19 81
lunula *Prehist.* 328 25
lunula *Church* 332 36
lunule 19 81
lupin 51 23
lur 322 1
lute 324 1
lute pin 324 11
lycaenid butterfly 365 6
lychgate 331 19
Lyman series 1 20
lymph gland, submandibular ~ 19 10
lynx 368 8
lynx fur 131 20
lynx skin 131 15
lynx skin, let-out ~ 131 16
Lyoner sausage 96 10
Lyra 3 22
Lyre *Astron.* 3 22
lyre *Music. Instr.* 322 15
lyre flower 60 5

M

maar 11 25
macadam spreader 200 31
macaroni 98 33
macaroon, coconut ~ 97 37
mace 382 34
machicolation 329 23
machicoulis 329 23
machine, four-cylinder ~ 189 49
machine, heavy ~ 189 43
machine, heavy-weight ~ 189 43
machine, high-performance ~ 189 43
machine, multi-magazine ~ 174 19
machine base 168 15
machine bed 177 57
machine chest 172 86; 173 1, 13
machine control lever 167 44
machine drum 323 57
machine gun 255 8, 32
machine hood 173 27
machine housing 200 2
machine part 111 30
machine parts 143
machine processor 116 60
machinery and observation deck 224 107
machinery and observation platform 224 107
machinery shed 62 15
machine tap 150 44
machine tools 149; 150
machine wire 173 14
machining centre 150 41
mackerel sky 8 14
MacPherson strut unit 192 72-84

macramé **102** 21
macro equipment **115** 81-98
macro frame **117** 56
macro lens attachment **117** 55
macronucleus **357** 11
Macropharynx longicaudatus **369** 2
macrophoto stand **115** 94
macro zoom lens **117** 53
madeira glass **45** 84
Madonna **330** 51
Madonna lily **60** 12
magazine *Doc.* **22** 4
magazine *Flat* **46** 20
magazine *Hunt.* **87** 17
magazine *Cine Film* **117** 45
magazine *Office* **249** 33
magazine *Army* **255** 15, 21
magazine *Police* **264** 25
magazine *Chivalry* **329** 13
magazine, rotary ~ **114** 77
magazine, spring-loaded ~ **247** 6
magazine back **115** 80
magazine holder **255** 7
magazine housing **313** 9
magazine repeater **87** 2
magazine rifle **87** 2
magazine spring **87** 18
magenta filter adjustment **116** 43
maggot *Gdn. Pests* **80** 19
maggot *Articulates* **358** 19
'magic eye' **309** 18
magmatism, plutonic ~ **11** 29-31
magnesium plate **179** 9
magnet 1 **63**; 2 **51**; **108** 32; **212** 38
magnetic disc store **244** 1
magnetic film **311** 21
magnetic film spool **311** 2
magnetic head, four-track ~ **312** 51
magnetic head cluster **312** 28
magnetic head support assembly **311** 3
magnetic sound amplifier **311** 28
magnetic sound deck **311** 20
magnetic sound head **312** 50
magnetic sound recorder **310** 58; **311** 1
magnetic sound recording and playback deck **238** 4
magnetic sound recording and playback amplifier **311** 5
magnetic sound recording equipment **310** 58; **311** 1
magnetic sound unit, attachable ~ **312** 50
magnetic sound unit, four-track ~ **312** 50
magnetic tape **237** 63; **238** 4, 5; **244** 2
magnetic tape dictating machine **249** 62
magnetic tape loop **245** 28
magnetic tape recording and playback equipment **238** 55
magnetic tape reel **244** 10
magnetic tape station **242** 32
magnetic tape unit **244** 9
magnifier **175** 34
magnifying glass **175** 34; **177** 23
magnitude 3 **14**
magpie **361** 3
magpie moth larva **58** 5
maharaja **306** 28
mahlstick **129** 47

mail **329** 62, 63
mail and cargo terminal **233** 9
mailbag **236** 54
mailbox **236** 50
mail carrier **236** 53
mailcoach **186** 39, 53
mailcoach driver **186** 40
mailman **236** 53
mail van **236** 52
main air pressure gauge **212** 6
main air reservoir pressure gauge **212** 8
main beam warning light **191** 69
main course **218** 33; **219** 61
main drive unit **113** 15
main engine revolution indicator **224** 21
main engine room **223** 72
main exchange line **237** 18, 24
main line **203** 45
mainmast **218** 40; **219** 5-7; **220** 22
mainmast, lower ~ **219** 5
main royal sail **219** 66
main royal stay **219** 13
main royal staysail **219** 26
main royal yard **219** 43
mainsail **218** 33; **219** 61; **220** 11; **284** 46; **285** 2
mains button **195** 11
mainsheet **284** 28
mains power unit **311** 11
mainstay **219** 10
maintained lift **299** 5
maintenance technician **237** 28
main title **185** 46
maintop **219** 52
main topgallant mast **219** 7
main topgallant rigging **219** 18
main topgallant sail **218** 53
main topgallant stay **219** 12
main topgallant staysail **219** 25
main topmast **219** 6
main topmast crosstrees **219** 53
main topmast rigging **219** 17
main topmast stay **219** 11
main topmast staysail **219** 24
main topsail **218** 38
main topsail yard **218** 39
main yard **218** 37; **219** 38
maize **68** 1, 31
maize billbug **81** 26
maize cob **68** 36
maize kernel **68** 37
majorette **306** 67
major keys **320** 55-68
major second **321** 7
major seventh **321** 12
major sixth **321** 11
major third **321** 8
major triad **321** 1
majuscule **175** 11
maker-up **174** 5
make-up artist **310** 36; **315** 48
make-up artist, chief ~ **315** 47
make-up gown **315** 44
make-up man, chief ~ **315** 47
make-up table *Offset Platem.* **179** 23
make-up table *Theatre* **315** 45
Malacosteus indicus **369** 10
malaria mosquito **81** 44
malleolus, external ~ **19** 59
malleolus, inner ~ **19** 60
malleolus, internal ~ **19** 60
malleolus, lateral ~ **19** 59
malleolus, medial ~ **19** 60

malleolus, outer ~ **19** 59
malleolus fibulae **19** 59
malleolus medialis **19** 60
malleolus tibulae **19** 60
mallet **118** 54; **120** 67; **125** 18; **132** 5; **158** 36; **278** 25; **339** 21
malleus **17** 61
malt, green ~ **92** 23
malt beer **93** 26
malt elevator **92** 35
maltese cross mechanism **312** 38
maltese cross movement **312** 38
malting **92** 1-41
maltings **92** 1
malting tower **92** 1
malt silo **92** 37
mamma **16** 28-29
mammal, flying ~ **366** 9
mammal, oviparous ~ **366** 1
mammal, scaly ~ **366** 10
mammals **366**; **367**; **368**
mammals, insect-eating ~ **366** 4-7
mammals, marsupial ~ **366** 2-3
mammoth tree **372** 69
Man **16**; **17**; **18**; **19**; **20**
manager **299** 45
manatee **366** 23
manati **366** 23
mandarin *Carnival* **306** 29
mandarin *South. Fruits* **384** 23
mandible *Man* **17** 35
mandible *Articulates* **358** 25
mandible, lower ~ **359** 8
mandolin **324** 16
mandrel **125** 19
mane **72** 13
mane, lion's ~ **368** 3
man-eater **364** 1
maneuver *see* manoeuvre
maneuvering *see* manoeuvring
mangelwurzel **69** 21
manger board **258** 7, 76
mangle **165** 46
mangold **69** 21
mangoldwurzel **69** 21
manhole *Roof & Boilerr.* **38** 45
manhole *Brew.* **93** 13
manhole *Cooper* **130** 18
manhole *Space* **234** 30; **235** 52
manhole *Water* **269** 26, 51
manhole cover *Roof & Boilerr.* **38** 46
manhole cover *Cooper* **130** 19
manhole cover *Street Sect.* **198** 17
manikin **338** 31
manipulator 2 **38**
manipulator, mechanical ~ **139** 32
manipulators 2 **47**
man-made fibres **169**; **170**
mannequin **338** 31
manoeuvres, principal, of aircraft **230** 67-72
manoeuvring keel **227** 30
manoeuvring rocket assembly **234** 63
manoeuvring rockets 6 **5**, 39
manometer **25** 22; **67** 10; **83** 42; **178** 8; **196** 20; **349** 19
manostat **269** 47
manque **275** 22
mansard dormer window **121** 19

mansard roof **121** 18
mantelpiece **267** 24
mantelshelf **267** 24
mantissa **345** 6
mantle *Phys. Geog.* **11** 3
mantle *Iron & Steel* **147** 46
mantle *Heraldry* **254** 3
mantle clock **42** 16
mantling **254** 3, 14
manual **325** 48; **326** 42, 43, 44, 45
manual, lower ~ **322** 47
manual, upper ~ **322** 46
manual feed station **184** 2
manure **63** 15
manure distributor **62** 21
manure fork, four-pronged ~ **66** 7
manure gutter **75** 20
manure hoe **66** 8
manure removal **74** 23-27; **75** 21
manure spreader **62** 21; **63** 39
manuscript **174** 6; **176** 3
manway **154** 32
map *Map* **14**; **15**
map **204** 15; **260** 44; **268** 2
maple seed **371** 57
maple tree **371** 53
map light **230** 23
map of the world **14** 10-45
mapping **348** 9, 10
mapping, one-to-one ~ **348** 11
mappings **348** 9-11
map projections **14** 8-9
map signs **15** 1-114
map symbols **14** 27-29; **15** 1-114
maraca **324** 59
marcando **321** 27
marcato **321** 27
mare **73** 2
margarine **98** 21; **99** 48
margin **185** 55-58
margin, back ~ **185** 55
margin, inside ~ **185** 55
margin, outside ~ **185** 57
margin, upper ~ **185** 56
margin control **180** 5, 20
margin release key **249** 6
margin scale **249** 12
margin stop, left ~ **249** 13
margin stop, right ~ **249** 14
marguerite **51** 24; **376** 4
marimba, steel ~ **324** 61
marimbaphone **324** 61
marine sequence **310** 11
mark **285** 17
mark, port hand ~ **224** 95
mark, starboard hand ~ **224** 96
marker **85** 12
marker, port ~ **224** 100
marker, starboard ~ **224** 99
market for securities **251** 2
market garden **55** 1-51, 3
market place **15** 52
market square **15** 52
market woman **308** 65
markiert **321** 27
marking, axillary ~ **88** 74
marking hammer **85** 12
marking iron **85** 12
marking out **104** 21
markings, graduated ~ **115** 65
mark of omission **342** 29
marks, diacritical ~ **342** 30-35
marl **160** 1
marmot **366** 18
maroon **306** 53
marquise **36** 55
marriage ceremony **332** 14

Mars 4 46
marsh *Phys. Geog.* 13 14-24
marsh *Map* 15 20
marshal 329 75
marshaling *see* marshalling
marshalling yard 206 42
marshalling yard signal box
206 44
marsh harrier 362 13
marshmallow *Bakery* 97 36
marshmallow *Med. Plants*
380 12
marsh plants 378 14-57
marsh tea 377 21
marsupials 366 2-3
marten 86 22
martens 367 14-17
martinet 218 36
marzipan 98 82
Masai warrior 354 8
mash 93 10
mash copper 92 44
masher 92 49
mashhouse 92 42-53
mashing process 92 42-53
mash kettle 92 44
mash thermometer 93 9
mash tub 92 43
mash tun 92 43, 44
mask *Hosp.* 27 48
mask *Swim.* 279 10
mask *Carnival* 306 7
mask *Films* 310 51; 313 4
mask *Sculpt. Studio* 339 37
mask, clay ~ 260 75
mask, pressure-equalizing ~
279 10
mask, wooden ~ 354 16
mask drum 177 48
masked ball 306 1-48
masking frame 116 35
masking tape 128 16
mask-scanning head 177 47
masonry bonds 118 58-68
masonry dam 217 58
masquerade 306 1-48, 6-48
mass 11 43
mass, continental ~ 11 7
massage bath 281 33
mass book 330 38
masseter 19 7
massif 12 39
mast 219 1-9; 221 77; 284 4,
11
mast, full-rigged ~ 220 16
mast, half-rigged ~ 220 15
Master 289 45
master arm 2 42
master brewer 92 49
master butcher 96 38
master clock 245 18
master compass 224 51
master control panel 242 3
master furrow 91 18
master gyro compass 224 51
Master of foxhounds 289 45
master selector 195 8
master/slave manipulator 2
47
master station 224 40
master switch 153 2
master turner 135 20
master volume control 261 44
masterwort 376 7
mat 299 12
matador 319 2, 25, 31
match 107 22
matchbox 107 21
matchbox holder 266 24
match head 107 23
mate 276 15
maté 382 11
material *School* 260 81

material *Store* 271 59
material, basic ~ 169 1
material, radioactive ~ 1 28
materials store 146 6
maté shrub 382 11
mathematics 344; 345; 346;
347; 348
mathematics, higher ~ 345
11-14
matinée coat 29 3
matrix *Man* 20 79
matrix *Composing Rm.* 174
21, 31
matrix, punched ~ 175 37
matrix, stamped ~ 175 37
matrix-boring machine 175
49
matrix case 174 42, 46; 176 17
matrix clamp 175 59
matrix disc 176 20
matrix drum 176 27
matrix-engraving machine
175 49
matrix for hand-setting 174
28
matrix holder 24 55
matrix mimic board 153 8
mat sail 353 33
matte 313 4
matte box 313 3
matter 174 15; 181 37
matter, front ~ 185 43-47
matter, machine-set ~ 174 27
matter, preliminary ~ 185
43-47
matting, reed ~ 55 6
matting, straw ~ 55 6
mattress 47 3; 296 18
mattress, foam ~ 43 10
matt weave 171 11
maturing 169 7
mauerkrone 254 46
mausoleum 337 16
mavis 361 16
maw worm 81 31
maxilla 17 36; 19 27
maximum 347 19
maximum thermometer 10
53
may 374 30
Maya temple 352 20
May bug 82 1
mayfly 358 6
maypole swing 273 8
maze 272 5
M-cardan 67 29
meadow 13 13; 62 44; 63 22
meadow buttercup 375 8
meadow fescue grass 69 24
meadow flowers 375; 376
meadow foxtail 69 27
meadow grass 375 39
meadow grasshopper 358 8
meadow mushroom 381 1
meadow saffron 379 3
meal, complete ~ 266 17
meal, deepfreeze ~ 96 23
meal, deep-frozen ~ 96 23
meal, hot ~ 266 67
meal, ready-to-eat ~ 96 23
meal beetle 81 18
meal of the day 266 27
meal worm beetle 81 18
meander *Phys. Geog.* 13 11
meander *Art* 334 43
meander core 13 12
mean low water 15 9
mean sea level 146 39
measure *Hotel* 267 60
measure *Music. Not.* 320
28-42
measure line 320 42
measurement chamber 112 43

measurement dial 242 75
measurement range selector
Atom 2 4, 23
measurement range selector
Optic. Instr. 112 46
measurement range selector
Inf. Tech. 242 74
measurement scale 242 75
measuring and control unit
178 3
measuring arm 142 38
measuring beaker 267 60
measuring cylinder *Doc.* 23
43
measuring cylinder *Photog.*
116 11
measuring cylinder *Paperm.*
173 4
measuring cylinder *School*
261 26
measuring cylinder *Chem.*
350 26
measuring device 112 51
measuring flask 350 27
measuring glass 10 47; 350 26
measuring instrument 153 30
measuring instrument
platform 235 69
measuring instruments 149
56-72
measuring machine,
universal-type ~ 112 67
measuring probe 234 42
measuring rod *Map* 14 47
measuring rod *Cine Film* 117
59
measuring rod *Quarry* 158 26
measuring scale 149 63
measuring tank 130 22
measuring tape 103 2; 271 38
measuring vessel 93 3;
130 33
measuring worm 80 17
meat 96 1-4, 59; 99 53
meat, canned ~ 98 20
meat, cold ~ 96 14
meat, minced ~ 96 16
meat, roast ~ 45 27
meat, smoked ~ 96 3
meat axe 94 18
meat chopper 40 39
meat counter 99 51
meat dish 266 55
meat grinder 96 53
meathook 96 55
meat inspector 94 24
meat joints 95
meat mincer 96 53
meat-mixing trough 96 40
meat plate 45 26
meat platter 45 26
meat product 99 53
meat salad 96 13
meat saw 94 20
mechanic 140 1
mechanical finger car 159 18
mechanical pulp mill 172
53-65
mechanism casing 255 10
medallion 339 36
Mediaeval 342 4
medical card 22 8
medical laboratory
technician 23 41
medical record 22 8
medicament, water-soluble ~
25 14
medicine 22 23
medicine cabinet 49 49
medicine case 24 7
medicine cupboard 22 35
medicine sample 22 41
Mediterranean 14 25

medium 308 9
medium haul airliner 231 12
medium measure 294 10
medulla oblongata 17 47; 18
24
medusa 357 14
meeting 263 8
meeting, public ~ 263 1-15
meeting point 233 29
meganucleus 357 11
megaphone 283 21
megaphone exhaust pipe 189
51
meiobia 9 3
Melanocetes 369 6
melodium 325 43
melody key 324 39
melody pipe 322 10
melody side 324 39
melody string 322 30; 324 24
melon 57 23
melter 148 7
melting bath 162 3, 14
melting furnace *Iron Foundry
etc.* 148 1
melting furnace *Electrotyp.
etc.* 178 19
melting plant 148 1-12
melting pot *Goldsm. etc.* 108
8
melting pot *Synth. Fibres* 170
30
member, diagonal ~ 215 35
member, upright ~ 119 59
member, vertical ~ 215 36
member of set 348 2
membership card 275 14
membrane 241 68
membrane, parchment ~ 324
31
membrane, periodontal ~ 19
28
membrane, tympanic ~ 17 59
membrane, vitelline ~ 74 64
membranophones 323 51-59
memorial chapel 331 12
memorial plate 331 14
memorial tablet 331 14
memory, main ~ 244 6; 245
28
memory key 247 22
memory typewriter 245 26
memory unit 176 11; 242 9
memo sheet 247 34
menagerie 307 63
menhir 328 18
menhir group 328 11
men's wear 33
men's wear department 271
12
menu 266 21
menu card 266 21
Mercator projection 14 9
Mercury 4 43
mercury barometer 10 1
mercury battery 25 32
mercury column 10 2
mercury manometer 25 18
meridian 14 4
meridian circle 113 26
meridian of Greenwich 14 5
meridian of longitude 14 4
meridians 14 1-7
meridian telescope 113 29
meringue 97 26; 265 5
merlin 362 1
merlon 329 7
mermaid 327 23
merman 327 23, 40
merry-go-round 308 2
mesa 13 59
mesh 171 37
mesh connection 153 21

mesh gauge **102** 25
mesh pin **102** 25
mesh ventilator **278** 40
Mesolithic period **328** 1-9
messroom **228** 25
metacarpal **17** 16
metal, noble ~ **237** 42
metal-blocking device **111** 34
metal feeder **174** 26
metal feeder, automatic ~ **174** 40
metal runner **147** 35
metals **254** 24-25
metal shears **108** 23; **125** 1
metalworker **140** 1
metalwork shop **140** 1-22
metatarsus **17** 28
metazoans **357** 13-39
meteor **7** 18
meteorite crater **6** 16
meteorological instruments **10**
meteorological office **225** 33
meteorological watch office **9** 7
meteorology **8; 9**
meter *Atom* **2** 6
meter *Photog.* **114** 62
meter *Blacksm.* **138** 19
meter *Serv. Stat.* **196** 14
meter *Music. Not.* **320** 28-42
meter, customer's ~ **237** 16
meter, multiple ~ **242** 73
meter, private ~ **237** 16
meter, rotary ~ **269** 53
meter, subscriber's ~ **237** 16
meter cell **114** 3, 24; **115** 37
metering pump **169** 13
metope **334** 16
metre tape measure **103** 2
metronome **325** 19
mezzanine **315** 18
mezzo staccato **321** 29
mezzotint **340** 14-24
micro attachment **115** 89
micro cassette recorder **246** 32
microfilm card **237** 38
microfilm file **237** 37
microfilming system **242** 31
microfilm reader **237** 36
micrometer **142** 37; **149** 62; **173** 10; **224** 4
micrometer eyepiece **14** 53
micrometer head **14** 52
micronucleus **357** 12
microphone **22** 15; **117** 8, 24, 74; **197** 26; **209** 31; **224** 30; **230** 29; **237** 9; **241** 49; **261** 39; **263** 7; **310** 30; **317** 20
microphone, built-in ~ **241** 5; **243** 3
microphone, umpire's ~ **293** 21
microphone base **241** 51
microphone boom **310** 25
microphone boom, telescopic ~ **117** 23
microphone cable **239** 14; **310** 32; **311** 41
microphone connecting cord **117** 25
microphone connecting lead **117** 25
microphone cradle **249** 65
microphone screen **241** 50
microphone socket **249** 69
microphone socket panel **238** 36
microphone stand **241** 51
microprism collar **115** 54
microprism spot **115** 58, 59, 62, 63

micropyle **383** 57
microscope **111** 19; **112** 1
microscope, metallurgical ~ **112** 23
microscope, surgical ~ **112** 31
microscope, universal ~ **112** 54
microscope, wide-field ~ **112** 23, 54
microscope body **113** 31-39
microscope camera, fully automatic ~ **112** 64
microscope for reflected light **112** 23
microscope stage **112** 9
microscope tube **113** 31-39
microwave treatment unit **23** 36; **24** 23
mid-channel **224** 98
middle-distance runner **298** 5
middle ground **224** 91
middle ground to port **224** 88
middle mast **220** 33
Middle Muschelkalk **154** 59
middle of the fairway **224** 98
middle section **259** 55-74
middling **91** 2
midfield player **291** 14
midge **358** 16
midget **308** 22
midi bus **194** 34
midinette **306** 21
midrib **370** 30
mihrab **337** 14
milch-cow **62** 34; **75** 17
mild **93** 26
mildew **80** 20
milestone **15** 109
milk **266** 60
milk, canned ~ **98** 15
milk, homogenized ~ **99** 44
milk, long-life ~ **99** 44
milk, pasteurized ~ **99** 44
milk, sterilized ~ **76** 16
milk bag **99** 45
milk carton **76** 22
milk churn **309** 89
milker **62** 34; **75** 17, 25
milk glass **124** 5
milk heater **76** 13
milking parlour **75** 23
milk jug **44** 31
milkman **75** 25
milk pipe **75** 27
milk pot **40** 15
milk processing area **76** 12-48
milk reception **76** 1
milk tanker **76** 2
milk tub filler **76** 21
milkwort **377** 3
Milky Way **3** 35
mill **276** 24
miller **91** 15
millet **68** 28
millibar scale **10** 3
millimeter graduation **247** 36
millimetre scale **10** 3
milliner **35** 1
milliner's shop **268** 38
milling machine **142** 41
milling machine, rotary ~ **168** 1
milling machine, universal ~ **150** 32
milling machine table **150** 33
milling roller, bottom ~ **168** 4, 6
milling roller, top ~ **168** 3
millrace **91** 44
mills **91**
mill spindle **91** 12
millstone **91** 16, 19, 21

millstone, upper ~ **91** 22
millstone casing **91** 20
millstone ruff **355** 52
millstream **91** 44
mill weir **91** 42
mill wheel, breast ~ **91** 37
mill wheel, middleshot ~ **91** 37
mill wheel, overshot ~ **91** 35
mill wheel, undershot ~ **91** 39
milometer **187** 33
mimbar **337** 15
minaret **337** 13
minbar **337** 15
mince **96** 16
mincemeat **96** 16
mincer **40** 39; **96** 53
mincing machine **96** 52, 53
mine **15** 34
mine, disused ~ **15** 35
mine car **144** 45
mine fan **144** 16
minehead buildings **154** 70
mine hunter **258** 80
minelayer **258** 94
mineral bath, outdoor ~ **281** 9
mineral spring **274** 11
mineral water **266** 61
minesweeper **258** 84
mine-sweeping gear **258** 87
mini **193** 19
miniature film cassette **112** 35
minibus **194** 9; **195** 47
minigolf course **272** 68
minigolf hole **272** 70
minigolf player **272** 69
minim **320** 14
minim rest **320** 22
minimum **347** 20
minimum thermometer **10** 54
mining, underground ~ **144** 21-51
minion **175** 24
minionette **175** 23
mink **30** 60
mink skin **131** 11
mink skin, let-out ~ **131** 19
minnesinger **329** 70
minor keys **320** 55-68
minor planets **4** 47
minor triad **321** 2
minstrel **329** 70
mintage **252** 10, 40-44
minting dies **252** 40-44
minting press **252** 44
mint mark **252** 10
minuend **344** 24
minus blue filter adjustment **116** 44
minuscule **175** 12
minuscule, Carolingian ~ **341** 18
minus green filter adjustment **116** 43
minus red filter adjustment **116** 45
minus sign **344** 8, 24
minute hand **110** 12
Mira **3** 11
mirabelle **59** 25
mire crow **359** 14
mirror **43** 29; **49** 33; **105** 20; **106** 6; **111** 4; **177** 38; **188** 35; **189** 30; **207** 49
mirror, angled ~ **177** 28
mirror, auxiliary ~ **115** 38
mirror, concave ~ **5** 32; **308** 56; **312** 39
mirror, convex ~ **308** 57
mirror, flat ~ **5** 3
mirror, illuminating ~ **14** 59
mirror, main ~ **5** 1; **113** 10
mirror, primary ~ **5** 1; **113** 10

mirror, right-angle ~ **261** 10
mirror, rotating ~ **243** 54
mirror, secondary ~ **5** 2; **113** 11
mirror, semi-reflecting ~ **243** 55
mirror, triple ~ **104** 1
mirror arc lamp **312** 39
mirror assembly **176** 21
mirror carp **364** 4
mirror lens **115** 50
mirror manometer **349** 20
mirror reflex system **115** 31
mirror spot **316** 48
mirror spotlight **316** 48
mirror system **176** 24
missal **330** 38
missile **258** 49
missile, short-range ~ **259** 26
missile, wooden ~ **352** 39; **353** 8
missile cruiser **259** 21, 41
missile launcher, underwater ~ **259** 37, 51
missile-launching housing **258** 71
miter *see* mitre
miter angle **120** 82
mitre **124** 4
mitre block **124** 30
mitre board **124** 31
mitre box *Glaz.* **124** 30
mitre box *Joiner* **132** 43
mitre gate **217** 19
mitre joint **124** 4
mitre shoot **124** 31
mitre square **120** 82
mitring machine **124** 7
mitt, catcher's ~ **292** 60
mitt, fielder's ~ **292** 59
mitten crab **358** 1
mixed asphalt outlet **200** 54
mixer *Dent.* **24** 51
mixer *Kitch. Utensils* **40** 45
mixer *Cine Film* **117** 26
mixer *Synth. Fibres* **170** 53
mixer *Aircraft* **232** 48
mixer *Broadcast.* **238** 25
mixer *Films* **311** 21
mixer *Disco* **317** 26
mixer, double shaft ~ **159** 10
mixer, hand ~ **39** 22
mixer, high-speed ~ **79** 5
mixer, propeller-type ~ **79** 5
mixer drum **200** 15
mixer operator **118** 32
mixer tap **39** 36; **49** 2; **106** 14; **126** 27
mixing **169** 2
mixing chamber **83** 62
mixing chest **173** 1
mixing console *Cine Film* **117** 26
mixing console *Broadcast.* **238** 25
mixing console *Films* **310** 56; **311** 35
mixing console *Disco* **317** 26
mixing desk *Cine Film* **117** 26
mixing desk *Broadcast.* **238** 25
mixing desk *Films* **310** 56; **311** 35
mixing desk *Disco* **317** 26
mixing drum **118** 34; **200** 15
mixing faucet **39** 36; **49** 2; **106** 14; **126** 27
mixing machine **200** 15
mixing plant, central ~ **201** 19
mixing plant, stationary ~ **201** 19
mixing room **311** 34
mixing screw **83** 59

mixing spoon **40** 3
mixing tank **172** 35
mixture, additive ~ **343** 10
mixture, subtractive ~ **343** 12
mixture control **230** 31; **288** 16
Mizar **3** 29
mizen *see* mizzen
mizzen **218** 29; **219** 30
mizzen, lower ~ **219** 8
mizzen mast **218** 31; **219** 8-9; **220** 23, 24, 30, 34
mizzen stay **219** 10
mizzen staysail **219** 27
mizzen top **219** 54
mizzen topgallant sail **218** 54
mizzen topgallant stay **219** 12
mizzen topgallant staysail **219** 29
mizzen topmast **219** 9
mizzen topmast rigging **219** 17
mizzen topmast stay **219** 11
mizzen topmast staysail **219** 28
moat **329** 33, 37; **356** 3
mobile **260** 70
moccasin **101** 30; **352** 18
moccasin flower **376** 27
mock orange **373** 9
model, clay ~ **260** 67
model, dressmaker's ~ **103** 6
model, nude ~ **338** 32
model, plaster ~ **339** 4
model, wax ~ **339** 26
model aeroplane **273** 37, 38
model aeroplanes **288** 85-91
model coat **103** 7
model dress **103** 5
model flight, radio-controlled ~ **288** 85
model hat **35** 7
modeling *see* modelling
modeller **339** 6
modelling board **48** 14; **339** 34
modelling clay **48** 12; **339** 31
modelling stand **339** 9
modelling substance **339** 8
modelling tool **161** 20
modelling tool, wire ~ **339** 11
modelling tool, wooden ~ **339** 10
model of set **315** 42
model of skull **261** 15
models of molecules **242** 61-67
model stage **315** 41
moderator 1 **54**
modular elements **242** 68-72
module, electronic ~ **242** 69
module, lunar ~ **6** 12
module, magnetic ~ **242** 72
moistener **247** 31
moisturising cream **99** 27
molar **19** 18, 35
mold *see* mould
molder **97** 57
mole *Map* **15** 48
mole *Hydr. Eng.* **217** 15
mole *Docks* **225** 65
mole *Mammals* **366** 4
molecular rearrangement **170** 23
molluscs **357** 27-36
monastery *Map* **15** 63
monastery *Church* **331** 52-58
monastery garden **331** 53
money **252**; **265** 3
money, hard ~ **252** 1-28
money, metal ~ **252** 1-28
money, paper ~ **252** 29-39
money compartment **271** 6

money order **236** 27
moneywort **375** 26
monitor **23** 27; **26** 15, 16, 33; **27** 23
monitor *Cine Film* **117** 97
monitor *Broadcast.* **238** 33
monitor *Audiovis.* **243** 6
monitor *Fire Brig.* **270** 66
monitor *Theatre* **316** 18
monitor *Fish etc.* **364** 31
monitor, six-channel ~ **27** 31
monitoring and control panel **238** 1, 7
monitoring controls **153** 5
monitoring instrument **311** 15
monitoring loudspeaker **239** 9; **311** 13
monitoring speaker **238** 15
monitoring unit, mobile ~ **25** 24
monitor lizard **364** 31
monitor support, swivel-mounted ~ **27** 24
monitor unit **25** 44
monk **89** 9
monk, Benedictine ~ **331** 54
monkey bridge **223** 4-11; **227** 24
monkey house **356** 10
monkey nut **383** 41
monkeys **368** 12-13
monkshood **379** 1
monochlorobenzene **170** 9
monoclinic crystal system **351** 24-25
monogram **36** 41
mono-line control system **288** 90
monolith **328** 18
monoplane, high-wing ~ **229** 1; **231** 2
monoplane, low-wing ~ **229** 5, 14; **231** 1
monoplane, midwing ~ **229** 4
monoplane, shoulder-wing ~ **229** 3
mono posto **290** 34
monorail car **144** 43, 44
monoski **286** 56
mono sound **311** 35
monotreme **366** 1
monotype caster **174** 39
monotype casting machine **174** 39
monotype composing and casting machine **174** 32-45
monotype composing machine **174** 32
monsoon **9** 52
monster **327** 16
monster, winged ~ **327** 55
monstrance **331** 48; **332** 34
montera **319** 29
monument *Map* **15** 92
monument *Park* **272** 10
moon **4** 1-9, 31, 45
moon, full ~ **4** 5
moon, new ~ **4** 2
moon, waning ~ **4** 7
moon, waxing ~ **4** 3
moon landing **6**
moor buzzard **362** 13
moor harrier **362** 13
moor hawk **362** 13
mooring **283** 19
mooring bitt, cross-shaped ~ **217** 13, 14
mooring bitt, double ~ **217** 14
mooring chain **224** 72
mooring line **288** 66
mooring sinker **224** 73
moose **367** 1

mop, gilder's ~ **129** 54
mopboard **123** 21, 63
moped **188** 24
moped, battery-powered ~ **188** 20
moped headlamp **188** 29
mopeds **188**
Mopsea **369** 8
moraine, lateral ~ **12** 53
moraine, medial ~ **12** 54
morainic filter layer **199** 24
Morchella conica **381** 27
Morchella esculenta **381** 26
mordant **178** 24; **182** 16
mordent, inverted ~ **321** 19
mordent, lower ~ **321** 20
mordent, upper ~ **321** 19
morel **381** 26, 27
morello **59** 5
morello cherry **59** 5
morion **329** 60
morse **367** 20
morse lamp **223** 7
mortadella **96** 7
mortar *Army* **255** 40
mortar *Chem.* **349** 9
mortar bed **123** 27
mortar pan **118** 39
mortar trough **118** 20, 39, 84
mortar tub **118** 39
mortice *see* mortise
mortise **120** 17
mortise, forked ~ **121** 85
mortise and tenon joint **121** 84, 85
mortise axe **120** 72
mortise chisel **132** 8
mortise lock **140** 36-43
mortiser **120** 17
mortising chain, endless ~ **132** 50
mortuary **331** 21
mosaic **338** 37
mosaic figure **338** 38
mosque **337** 12
mosquito **358** 16
moss **377** 17
moss phlox **60** 14
moss pink **60** 14
moth **58** 64; **81** 13; **82** 15, 18, 45, 48
moth, female ~ **82** 30
moth, male ~ **82** 29
moth, night-flying ~ **82** 14
moth, nocturnal ~ **82** 14
mother **28** 6; **272** 71
mother-of-pearl **357** 34
mother sheep **75** 10
moths **358** 48-56; **365** 7-11
motif *Child. Clothes* **29** 20
motif *Art. Studio* **338** 27
motion, longitudinal ~ **149** 17
motion picture camera, lightweight ~ **313** 20
motion picture camera, narrow-gauge ~ **313** 31
motion picture camera, professional ~ **313** 20, 31
motion picture camera, soundproof ~ **310** 47; **313** 15
motion picture camera, standard-gauge ~ **313** 1
motion picture cameras **313** 1-39
motion picture laboratory **310** 2; **311** 30
motion picture library **310** 5
motion picture projection **312** 1-23
motion pictures **310**; **311**; **312**; **313**
motion picture storage vault **310** 5

motions, rotary ~ **4** 22-28
moto cross **290** 24-28
motor *Forestry* **84** 34
motor *Watchm.* **109** 13
motor *Iron Foundry etc.* **148** 64
motor *Weaving* **165** 12, 34
motor *Electrotyp. etc.* **178** 14
motor *Tram* **197** 5, 7
motor *Water* **269** 45
motor, auxiliary ~ **211** 17
motor, built-in ~ **164** 33
motor, built-on ~ **164** 2
motor, electric ~ *Roof & Boiler.* **38** 59
motor, electric ~ *Pest Contr.* **83** 53
motor, electric ~ *Blacksm.* **138** 2
motor, electric ~ *Weaving* **166** 18
motor, electric ~ *Railw.* **212** 34
motor, electric ~ *Ship* **223** 69
motor, synchronous ~ **176** 19
motor, three-phase ~ **164** 35
motor, two-stroke ~ **56** 30
motor base plate **164** 36
motor bedplate **164** 36
motorboat **283** 2
motorboat landing stage **216** 7
motorboats **286** 1-5
motor car **191** 1-56; **192**; **193**; **195** 34
motor car mechanic **195** 53
motor coach **194** 17
motor cruiser **286** 4
motor cultivator **56** 18
motorcycle **189**; **268** 35
motorcycle, heavyweight ~ **189** 31
motorcycle, light ~ **188** 39; **189** 1, 16
motorcycle, lightweight ~ **189** 1
motorcycle, pacer's ~ **290** 12
motorcycle chain **189** 22
motorcycle racing **290** 24-28
motorcycles **188**
motorcycles, heavy ~ **189** 31-58
motorcycles, heavyweight ~ **189** 31-58
motorcycles, large-capacity ~ **189** 31-58
motorcycle stand **189** 21
motorcycle tyre **189** 26
motorcyclist **268** 34; **290** 11
motor drive **115** 76
motor drive, attachable ~ **115** 78
motor drive gear **167** 31
motor ferry **216** 6
motor grader **200** 19
motor pump **270** 8
motor safety switch **269** 46
motor saw **84** 22, 27; **85** 13
motor scooter **188** 47
motor ship **223**
motorsports **290** 24-38
motor truck, heavy ~ **194** 20
motor turntable ladder **270** 9
motor uniselector **237** 42
motor unit **50** 82
motor vehicle mechanic **195** 53
motorway *Map* **15** 16
motorway *Docks* **225** 54
motor winch **287** 6
moufflon **367** 6
mouflon **367** 6
mould *Bldg. Site* **119** 84
mould *Iron & Steel* **147** 37

mould *Glass Prod.* 162 47
mould *Paperm.* 173 48
mould, fixed ~ 178 22
mouldboard 65 4, 64
moulder *Bakery* 97 57
moulder *Iron Foundry etc.* 148 30
moulding, concave ~ 334 29
moulding, hollow ~ 336 10
moulding, ornamental ~ 336 12
moulding box, closed ~ 148 18
moulding box, open ~ 148 33
moulding department 148 30-37
moulding press, hydraulic ~ 178 7
moulding sand 148 35
moulding shop 148 30-37
mould loft 222 3
mould wall 148 29
mound *Equest.* 289 8
mound *Prehist.* 328 16
mound *Art* 337 21
mountain ash 371 42
mountain climber 300 5
mountain climbing 300 1-57
mountaineer 300 5
mountaineering 300 1-57
mountaineering boot 300 42
mountaineering equipment 300 31-57
mountain hut 300 1
mountain racing 290 24-28
mountain railroads 214 1-14
mountain railways 214 1-14
mountain range 12 39
mountain ridge 12 36
mountains, folded ~ 12 12-20
mountain slope 12 37
mountain top 12 35
mounting, German type ~ 113 16
mounting, mobile ~ 27 22
mounting, underfloor ~ 127 22
mount of the frame 111 10
mourner 331 33
mourning cloak butterfly 365 5
mourning veil 331 39
mousetrap 83 36
moustache, English-style ~ 34 19
moustache, military ~ 34 19
moustache, waxed ~ 34 13
mouth *Man* 16 13; 19 14-37
mouth *Horse* 72 9
mouth *Forestry* 84 28
mouth *Game* 88 13, 45
mouth *Joiner* 132 21
mouth *Airsports* 288 70, 81
mouth *Music. Instr.* 326 25
mouth, fork-tongued ~ 327 5
mouth band 322 5
mouth gag 22 48
mouth lamp 24 42
mouth mirror 24 41
mouth organ 324 35
mouthpiece *Hosp.* 27 38
mouthpiece *Tobacc. etc.* 107 40
mouth piece *Electrotyp. etc.* 178 17
mouthpiece *Post* 237 9
mouthpiece *Music. Instr.* 323 36; 324 33, 72
mouthwash 49 36
movable-comb hive 77 45-50
movable-frame hive 77 45-50
movable half 215 66

move 276 14
movie audience 312 5
moviegoer 312 5
movie house 312 1
movie projector 312 24
movie script 310 45
movie set 310 7
movie studios 310 1-13
movie theater 312 1
movie theater box office 312 2
movie theater ticket 312 3
moving iron 137 39
mower, electric ~ 56 31
mower, hand ~ 56 34
mower, motor ~ 56 28
mower, riding ~ 56 37
mower, rotary ~ 63 19
mud drum 210 28
mudguard, front ~ 187 13
mudguard, rear ~ 187 43
mud pump 145 16
muffle furnace 140 11
muffler *Car* 191 29
muffler *Railw.* 209 12, 22, 24; 211 49
muffler *Sports* 305 93
mulberry-feeding moth 358 48
mule *Dom. Anim.* 73 8
mule *Shoes* 101 25
mule, open-toe ~ 101 22
mule cop 165 15
muleta 319 33
mull 183 33; 185 20
mullion *Dwellings* 37 35
mullion *Art* 335 41
mull roll holder 185 19
multiple cable system 215 51
multiple drying machine 169 31
multiple-frame viewfinder 114 41
multiple meter 127 41
multiple-unit train 211 60
multiplicand 344 25
multiplication 344 25
multiplication sign 344 25
multiplier 344 25
multiplier phototube 112 51
multiplier reel 89 59
multiplying 344 25
multirole combat aircraft 256 8
multirole helicopter, light ~ 232 11
multi-tier transport 74 35
mummy 352 21
Munich beer 93 26
mural 338 40
Muschelkalk 154 58, 59, 60
muscle, contractile ~ 77 17
muscle, deltoid ~ 18 35
muscle, pectoralis ~ 18 36
muscle, sternocleidomastoid ~ 18 34; 19 1
muscle, sternomastoid ~ 18 34; 19 1
muscle, temporal ~ 19 3
muscle, thenar ~ 18 41
muscles, ocular ~ 19 44
muscles of facial expression 19 6
muscles of the neck 19 12
muscular system 18 34-64
musculature 18 34-64
musette 322 8
mushroom 381 2, 3
mushrooms, poisonous ~ 379 10-13
musical instrument, automatic ~ 308 38
musical instruments 322;

323; 324; 325; 326
musical instruments, popular ~ 324 1-46
musical notation 320; 321
music recording studio 310 14
music recording theatre 310 14
music rest 326 36
music stand 326 36
music systems 241
musk ox 367 10
mussel shell 357 36
mustang 352 4
mustard *Weeds* 61 16
mustard *Grocer* 98 28
mute 323 10; 324 68
mute swan 359 16
mutton spanker 218 29
mutule 334 13
muzzle *Dog* 70 3, 31
muzzle *Game* 88 45
muzzle *Army* 255 58
muzzle *Sports* 305 71
mycelium 68 4; 381 2
myrtle 53 11
Myrtus 53 11

N

Na atom 1 8
nacre 357 34
nadir 4 13
naiad 327 23
nail 19 80
nail, clenched ~ 285 52
nail, galvanized ~ 122 74
nail, riveted ~ 285 52
nail, wire ~ 121 95; 122 74; 143 51
nail, wooden ~ 121 92
nail bag 122 72
nail claw 120 75
nail grip 100 56
nail polish 99 32
nail puller 100 47
nail punch 134 32
nail varnish 99 32
naked boys 379 3
naked lady 379 3
name plate 118 47; 285 46
Nansen sledge 303 18
nape of the neck 16 21
napkin 45 9; 266 47; 267 48
napkin ring 45 10
nappy, disposable ~ 28 22
narcissus 53 8; 60 3
narghile 107 42
narghileh 107 42
narrow-gauge diesel locomotive 200 24
narrow-gauge track system 159 4
nasicorn 366 25
nasturtium 53 4
natural 320 45, 46, 54
natural-gas engine 155 5
naturist 281 16
naum keag 100 7
nave 334 62; 335 1
navel 16 34
navette 36 55
navigating bridge 223 14; 228 22, 23, 24
navigating officer 224 37
navigation 224
navigational marks, floating ~ 224 68-108
navigational television receiver mast 221 37
navigation equipment 288 13
navigation light *Air Force* 257 36

navigation light *Warships* 258 56
navigation light *Airsports* 288 31
navigation light, left ~ 230 50
navigation light, right ~ 230 44
navigation light, side ~ 258 15
navigation light indicator panel 224 29
navigation lights 286 10-14
navvy 118 76
navy 258
navy plug 107 25
navy yard 222 1-43
Neanderthal man 261 19
neck *Man* 16 19-21
neck *Horse* 72 12, 15
neck *Game* 88 3
neck *Meat* 95 6, 20
neck *Mach. Parts etc.* 143 64
neck *Weaves* 171 33
neck *Rowing* 283 37
neck *Airsports* 288 70
neck *Music. Instr.* 324 7, 18
neck, cylindrical ~ 328 40
neck, ground glass ~ 350 37
neckband 36 16
neck brush 106 27
neckerchief 31 57
neck flap *Fire Brig.* 270 38
neck flap *Fencing* 294 14
neck guard *Fire Brig.* 270 38
neck guard *Fencing* 294 14
neck guard *Chivalry* 329 83
neck interlocking point 171 35
necklace 36 2; 328 25; 352 14
necklace, coral ~ 36 34
necklace, cultured pearl ~ 36 12
necklace, ivory ~ 36 28
necklace, pearl ~ 36 32
neckline *Ladies' Wear* 30 34
neck line *Airsports* 288 71
neck of violin 323 2
neck piece 329 83
neck ring, gold ~ 328 26
neck strap 71 30
necktie 319 38
nectary 59 18
needle *Mach. Parts etc.* 143 76
needle *Drawing Off.* 151 56
needle *Conifers* 372 11
needle, hypodermic ~ 22 65; 24 54
needle, right-angle ~ 151 67
needle, surgical ~ 22 57
needle, tapered ~ 190 51
needle bar 167 28
needle bed 167 51, 55
needle butt 167 60
needle cage 143 75
needle cam 167 14
needle cylinder *Knitting* 167 8, 11
needle cylinder *Bookbind.* 185 21
needled part of the cylinder 163 70
needle file 108 22
needle head 309 33
needle holder 22 59
needle holder, cylindrical ~ 167 8, 11
needle hook 167 64
needle-matching system 114 29
needlepoint 102 30
needle point attachment 151 54
needlepoint lace 102 30
needle-raising cam 167 59

needle roller bearing 143 75-76
needles in parallel rows 167 53
needle trick 167 15
needlework 102
negative carrier 116 30
negative flight 288 9
negligée 355 66
negress 354 22
negro 354 13
negro hut 354 21
nematode 80 51
Neolithic period 328 10-20
neon sign 268 16
Neptune 4 51
Nereid 327 23
nerve 370 30
nerve, auditory ~ 17 64
nerve, femoral ~ 18 31
nerve, optic ~ Man 19 51
nerve, optic ~ Bees 77 23, 24
nerve, peroneal ~ 18 33
nerve, radial ~ 18 28
nerve, sciatic ~ 18 30
nerve, thoracic ~ 18 26
nerve, tibial ~ 18 32
nerve, ulnar ~ 18 29
nerves 19 33
nervous system 18 22-33
nervure Articulates 358 34
nervure Bot. 370 29
nest 359 28
nesting cavity 359 29
Net Astron. 3 48
net Hunt. 86 27
net Sea Fish. 90 8
net Airsports 288 74
net Ball Games 293 13
net background 102 16
net-cord judge 293 23
net curtain 42 35; 44 14
net fabric 167 29
net post 293 15
net sonar cable 90 14
net sonar device 90 17
net stocking 306 10
net strap 293 14
netting 102 22
netting, wire ~ 339 35
netting loop 102 23
netting needle 102 26
netting thread 102 24
nettle 61 33
net vault 336 45
network 288 74
neume 320 1
neutral conductor 127 13
neutral corner 299 38
neutral point 153 22
neutron 1 30, 39, 45, 52, 53
neutron bombardment 1 36, 50
nevé 12 48
new-born baby 28 5
newel 123 43
newel, open ~ 123 76
newel, solid ~ 123 77, 78
newel post 123 43
Newfoundland dog 70 34
news, miscellaneous ~ 342 63
newscaster 238 21
news dealer 205 17; 268 75
news in brief 342 63
news item 342 50
newspaper 182 31; 205 51; 265 25; 342 37-70
newspaper, folded ~ 181 56
newspaper delivery unit 182 29
newspaper heading 342 39
newspaper holder 265 26

newspaper page 342 37
newspaper rack 265 8
newspaper shelf 262 16; 265 8
newspaper typesetting 176 29
newsreader 238 21
newsreel camera 313 26
New Stone Age 328 10-20
news trolley 205 16
news vendor 205 17; 268 75
New World opossum 366 2
nib 122 51
nib size 151 40
niche 331 60
nick 175 47
nigger 310 51
night-care cream 99 27
nightclub 318 1-33
nightdress 32 16
nightgown 32 16
nightie 32 16
nightingale 361 14
nightshirt 32 37
night spot 318 1-33
nightwear 32
nightwear, ladies' ~ 32 16-21
nightwear, men's ~ 32 35-37
Nile crocodile 356 13
nimbostratus 8 10
nine-eight time 320 39
nine-four time 320 40
nine men's morris 276 18, 23-25
nine men's morris board 276 23
nipper, bottom ~ 163 65
nipper, top ~ 163 66
nippers 100 40, 41
nipping press 183 20
nipple 16 28
nipple key 126 63
nitrogen tetroxide tank 234 59
nitrous oxide 26 3
nix 327 23
nixie 327 23
nobleman 355 44
nock 305 63
node 68 7
node, lymph ~ 19 10
nodosity 80 27
nogging piece 120 55
noir 275 21
nominal par 251 12
non-belayer 300 27
nonpareil 175 23
non-printing area 340 56
noodle 98 34; 99 65
Norfolk Island pine 53 16
North America 14 12
North Atlantic Drift 14 30
North Equatorial Current 14 32
Northern Cross 3 23
Northern Crown 3 31
northern gannet 359 9
northern pike 364 16
north light 121 21
north point 4 16
North Pole 14 3
North Sea 14 26
North Star 3 1, 34
Norton tumbler gear 149 8
nose Man 16 10
nose Dog 70 4
nose Horse 72 6
nose Fish etc. 364 2
nose, false ~ 306 46
noseband 71 7
nose cone, carbon fibre reinforced ~ 235 20
nose gear flap 231 24
nose landing gear unit, retractable ~ 231 23

nosepiece, revolving ~ 112 11, 30
nose rib 287 36
nose-section fairing 235 20
nose undercarriage flap 231 24
nose undercarriage unit, retractable ~ 231 23
nose wheel 288 34
nose wheel, forward-retracting ~ 257 3
nose wheel, hydraulically steerable ~ 235 30
nose wheel, steerable ~ 230 40
nosing 123 20
nostril 72 7
notation, mensural ~ 320 2
notation, square ~ 320 1
notch Phys. Geog. 13 30
notch Forestry 84 28
notch Hunt. 87 66, 70
notch Army 255 22
notch, wedge-shaped ~ 54 38
note 185 62
note, marginal ~ 185 68
note, musical ~ 320 1-2
notebook 47 24; 260 18
note head 320 3
notepaper 245 12
notes 252 29-39
notes, medieval ~ 320 1-2
note stem 320 4
note tail 320 4
note values 320 12-19
'NOT GO' gauging member 149 58
'NOT GO' side 149 61
notice 356 7
notice board 204 12
nougat 98 81
novice 319 2
novillero 319 2
nozzle Household 50 67
nozzle Overh. Irrign. 67 33
nozzle Pest Contr. 83 46
nozzle Serv. Stat. 196 3
nozzle Aircraft 232 39, 45, 49, 55
nozzle Space 234 35; 235 37
nozzle, pistol-type ~ 83 28
nozzle, revolving ~ 56 44
nozzle, swivelling ~ 235 64
nozzle fuel tank 235 45
nuclear energy 154
nuclear power plant 154 19
nuclear reactor casing 259 67
nuclear research ship 221 9
nucleus 1 43
nucleus, atomic ~ 1 2, 16, 29, 35, 49, 51
nude 338 32
nudist 281 16
nudist sunbathing area 281 15
null hyperbola 224 42
number Equest. 289 33, 36
number Cyc. Racing 290 28
number Winter Sp. 301 37
number Sports 305 84
number, abstract ~ 344 3
number, cardinal ~ 344 5
number, complex ~ 344 14
number, concrete ~ 344 4
number, even ~ 344 11
number, four-figure ~ 344 3
number, mixed ~ 344 10
number, negative ~ 344 8
number, odd ~ 344 12
number, ordinal ~ 344 6
number, positive ~ 344 7
number, prime ~ 344 13
number, whole ~ 344 10, 18
number disc 189 18

nosepiece, revolving
number key Office 247 18
number key Store 271 3
number key Flea Market 309 76
'number one' 283 13
number plate 189 8; 290 28; 305 84
numbers 344 1-22
number sign 197 21
number tab 267 10
number tag 267 10
numeral, Arabic ~ 344 2
numeral, Roman ~ 344 1
numeral pendants 253 33-34
numeral pennants 253 33-34
numerator 344 15
nun 331 50
nun moth 82 17
nursery 47
nursery child 48 2
nursery education 48 1-20
nursery gardener 55 20
nursery hand 55 45, 46
nursery sapling 83 15
nursery teacher 48 1
nut Bldg. Site 119 75
nut Music. Instr. 323 13, 20
nut Bot. 370 98
nut Industr. Plants 383 44
nut South. Fruits 384 52, 58, 60
nut, castellated ~ 143 24, 77
nut, castle ~ 143 24
nut, hexagonal ~ 143 18
nut, round ~ 143 35
nutation 4 24
nutcracker 361 1
nutcrackers 45 49
nuthatch 361 11
nutmeg 382 34, 35
nutmeg tree 382 30
nuts 59 59, 37-51
Nydam boat 218 1-6
nylon 101 4
nylon 6 fibres 170 1-62
nylons pack 99 26
nylon-thread cop 133 4
nymph, artificial ~ 89 66

O

oak 51 12
oak apple 82 34
oak gall 82 34
oak-gall wasp 82 33
oak tree 51 12; 371 1
oar 218 5; 278 19; 283 14, 26, 35-38
oarlock 278 18; 283 29, 41
oarsman 218 3; 283 12
oasis 354 4
oat-grass 69 22
oat panicle 68 27
oats 68 1
oats, rolled ~ 98 37
obelisk 333 10
Oberwerk 326 2
obi 353 41
object ball, red ~ 277 12
objective, interchangeable ~ 112 62
objective aperture 113 35
objective lens 113 36
objective turret 112 11, 30
object lens 114 26; 313 2
object stage 112 9
oblique, external ~ 18 43
obliquus externus abdominis 18 43
oboe 323 38
O'Brien technique 298 50
observation opening 5 13

observation port *Agr. Mach.* 64 27
observation port *Films* 312 15
observation room 5 33
observation shaft 5 30
observation telescope 351 31
observation window 25 8
observation window, forward ~ 235 25
observation window, upward ~ 235 24
observatory 5 1-16; 9 7
observatory, solar ~ 5 29-33
observatory dome 5 12
obstacle, almost-fixed ~ 289 8
obstacle, fixed ~ 289 20
obstruction 291 51
obverse 252 8
ocarina 324 32
occipitalis 18 50; 19 2
occipitofrontalis 19 4
occiput 16 2
occlusion 9 25
ocean *Phys. Geog.* 13 26
ocean *Map* 14 19-26
ocean current, cold ~ 14 27
ocean current, warm ~ 14 28
ocean currents 14 30-45
ocean drifts 14 30-45
Oceanid 327 23
ocean liner 221 82; 225 32
ocean nymph 327 23
ocean station vessel 9 7
ocellus *Dom. Anim.* 73 32
ocellus *Bees* 77 2
octagon 351 17
octahedron 351 6, 14, 16
Octans 3 43
Octant 3 43
octave, five-line ~ 321 50
octave, four-line ~ 321 49
octave, great ~ 321 44
octave, one-line ~ 321 46
octave, small ~ 321 45
octave, three-line ~ 321 48
octave, two-line ~ 321 47
octave engagement 294 50
odalisque 306 41
odd-pinnate 370 42
odds 289 37
odds-and-ends box 195 31
odonatan 358 3
Oertz rudder 222 69-70
oesophagus *Man* 17 49; 20 23, 40
oesophagus *Bees* 77 19
offcut 120 96
off-end framing 165 14
offering 330 60
offertory bag 330 59
offertory box 330 55
office *Coal* 144 18
office *Station* 205 13
office *Railw.* 207 41
office *Office* 245; 246; 247; 248; 249
office *Camping* 278 1
office *Chivalry* 329 27
office, executive's ~ 246 1-36
office, manager's ~ 271 24
office, open plan ~ 248 1-48
office, physician's ~ 22 1-74
office, purser's ~ 223 45
office, receptionist's ~ 245 1-33
office, secretary's ~ 245 1-33
office building *Coal* 144 18
office building *Offshore Drill.* 146 14
office building *Docks* 225 53
office building *Films* 310 4
office calculator 245 31
office chair 248 25

office cupboard 248 12
office equipment 247 1-44
office furniture 248 39
office intercom 245 20; 246 10
office machinery 249
office materials 247 1-44
officer in charge 270 36
officer of the watch 221 126
offices 217 24; 310 4
offices, administrative ~ 222 1
office supplies 247 1-44
offset machine, four-colour ~ 180 30
offset machine, rotary ~ 180 1, 18
offset machine, sheet-fed ~ 180 30
offset machine, single-colour ~ 180 46, 59
offset plate 179 1
offset plate, coated ~ 179 16
offset platemaking 179
offset press *Paperm.* 173 21
offset press *Office* 249 48
offset press, four-colour ~ 180 1, 18, 30
offset press, rotary ~ 180 1, 18
offset press, sheet-fed ~ 180 30, 70
offset press, single-colour ~ 180 46, 59
offset printing 180
offshoot 370 21
offshore drilling 146
offshore drilling rig supply vessel 221 32
offside 291 42
off switch 10 15
ogee arch 336 36
ogee wing 229 22
oil 98 24
oil, crude ~ *Phys. Geog.* 12 31
oil, crude ~ *Oil, Petr.* 145 28-35, 36-64
oil, mineral ~ 145
oil, viscous ~ 84 35
oil and vinegar bottle 45 42
oil bag 228 11
oil bath air cleaner *Agr. Mach.* 65 54
oil bath air cleaner *Railw.* 212 79
oil bath air filter *Agr. Mach.* 65 54
oil bath air filter *Railw.* 212 79
oil bleeder screw 190 24
oil burner 38 58-60
oil can 196 16
oil-circulating pump *Power Plant* 152 45
oil-circulating pump *Railw.* 211 12
oil conservator 152 42; 153 9
oil cooler *Power Plant* 152 46
oil cooler *Car* 192 19
oil cooler *Railw.* 211 11
oil drain plug 190 24
oil drilling 145 1-21
oiler 109 4
oil filler neck 190 28
oil filter 190 43; 192 20
oil-firing system 199 30, 35
oil furnace 145 36
oil gallery, main ~ 192 21
oil gauge *Roof & Boilerr.* 38 54
oil gauge *Power Plant* 153 11
oil heating furnace 38 57
oil level pipe 38 53
oil paint 338 11
oil palm 383 54
oil pipe 190 13

oil pipeline 145 65
oil pressure gauge *Sawmill* 157 7
oil pressure gauge *Aircraft* 230 20
oil pressure limiting valve 190 67
oil pressure warning light 191 73
oil production 145 22-27
oil products 145 52-64
oil pump 190 42; 192 16
oil pump drive 190 25
oil reservoir 64 29, 93
oil rig 146 1-39
oil scraper ring 190 37
oil stand 109 5
oilskins 228 4
oilstone 340 21
oil sump *Agr. Mach.* 65 45
oil sump *Intern. Combust. Eng.* 190 41
oil sump *Car* 192 17
oil tank *Roof & Boilerr.* 38 44
oil tank *Agr. Mach.* 64 93
oil tank *Oil, Petr.* 145 34
oil tank *Motorcycle* 189 36
oil temperature gauge *Car* 191 38
oil temperature gauge *Aircraft* 230 21
oil temperature sensor 195 16, 40
oil-to-air cooling unit 209 18
ointment, tube of ~ 22 47
O-Joller 284 50
Old Stone Age 328 1-9
old woman's tooth 132 26
oleander 373 13
olive oil 98 24
olive tree 383 29
omnibus, horse-drawn ~ 186 37
on-board equipment 239 6
on-board telephone 239 13
one-design keelboat 284 62
one-half twist isander 282 41
Oneirophanta 369 18
one-second theodolite 112 73
one-two 291 49
one-way tap 350 42
on full point 314 19
on guard line 294 3
on guard position 294 18, 33
onion 57 24
onion skin 57 25
on-line disc storage unit 176 32
on-load tap changer 153 13
on/off switch *Railw.* 211 30
on/off switch *Audio* 241 63
on/off switch *Audiovis.* 243 16
on/off switch *Office* 247 16; 249 9, 37, 64
on/off valve 279 22
on-ramp 15 16
on-the-ground wrestling 299 8
open gate 301 65
open-hearth furnace 147 21-30
opening 122 24
opening, pharyngeal ~ 19 24
opening control 313 8
open-newel staircase 123 76
open-reel tape 241 58
open vertical gate 301 67
open work 102 27
opera glass 315 9
opera hat 35 36
operating cabin 228 21

operating handle 309 81
operating indicator 244 11
operating instructions 244 15
operating key 243 13, 41, 48; 246 19; 261 45
operating lamp 27 25
operating lamp, shadow-free ~ 26 10
operating lamp, swivel-mounted ~ 26 11
operating lever *Pest Contr.* 83 21
operating lever *Cine Film* 117 63
operating lever *Road Constr.* 201 12
operating mechanism housing 153 60
operating table 26 8, 36
operating table, pedestal ~ 26 5
operating theatre 26 1-33
operating valve 153 52
operation indicator 244 7
operations, arithmetical ~ 344 23-26; 345 1-10
operator *Post* 237 35
operator *Computer* 244 14
operator *Theatre* 316 59
operator, chief ~ 244 3
operator's position 237 34
operator's set 237 23
operculum 364 5
ophthalmic test stand 111 43
ophthalmometer 111 44
ophthalmoscope 22 62
opium poppy 380 15
opponent 293 18
optical bench 114 50; 242 79
optical instruments 112; 113
optical sound recorder 310 60; 311 6
optical sound recording 311 9
optical sound recording equipment 311 6
optical sound unit 312 45
optical system 242 41; 243 50
optician 111 1
optic plate, right-hand ~ 195 18
optometer 111 44
or 254 24
orange *Colour* 343 7
orange *South. Fruits* 384 23, 27
orange flower 384 25
orange peel, candied ~ 98 11
orangery 272 3
orange tip butterfly 365 3
orange tree 55 49
orang-outan 368 15
orang-utan 368 15
orbicular 370 33
orbicularis oculi 19 5
orbicularis oris 19 8
orbiculate 370 33
orbit, moon's ~ 4 1
orbital manoeuvring main engine 235 44
orb spinner 358 45
orchard 15 108
orchard sprayer, mobile ~ 83 38
orchestra *Theatre* 315 25
orchestra *Art* 334 47
orchestra pit 315 24
orchestrion 308 38; 309 14
orchid 376 28
orchis 376 28
order 250 19
ordinal 344 6
ordinate 347 10
ore 147 2

öre 252 24, 25, 26
ore deposit 11 31
organ 326 1-5, 1-52
organ, automatic ~ 308 38
organ, portable ~ 322 56
organ, portative ~ 322 56
organ, positive ~ 322 56
organ, suctorial ~ 81 36
organ case 326 1-5
organ console 326 36-52
organelle 357 5
organistrum 322 25
organ of equilibrium and
  hearing 17 56-65
organ pipes 326 17-35
organs, internal ~ 20 1-57
orifice, cardiac ~ 20 41
original 177 18
origin of ordinates 347 4
Orion 3 13
ornament, Rococo ~ 336 13
ornamental 53 16
ornamentation, Greek ~ 334
  38-43
ornamentation, Romanesque
  ~ 335 14-16
ornaments 321 14-22
orogenis 12 4-20
orogeny 12 4-20
orographic lift 287 28
orpine 377 9
orthopinacoid 351 25
orthopteron 358 8
ortolan 361 7
ortolan bunting 361 7
Orton cone 161 6
oscillation counter 110 17
osier branch 371 29
osier rod 136 15
osier stake 136 14
ossicles, auditory ~ 17 61
Ostiak 353 17
ostrich 359 2
ostrich egg 359 3
ostrich feather 254 30
Ostyak 353 17
os uteri externum 20 85
otter 367 17
otter boards 90 13
Otto-cycle engine 190 1
Otto-cycle internal
  combustion engine 190 2
outboard 278 15; 283 6, 7
outboard inflatable 286 1
outboard motor 278 15; 283
  7; 286 1, 21
outboard motorboat 283 6
outboard speedboat 283 6
outdrive motorboat 286 2
outer case 187 30
outfall 216 36
outfielder 292 41
outflow condenser 92 4
outhouse 62 14
outlet Electr. 127 5
outlet Paperm. 172 78
outlet Water 269 21
outlet, double ~ 127 6
outlet cock 178 34
outlet control valve 269
  30
outlet duct 92 19
outlet structure 217 44
outlet to brake line 192 53
outlet tunnel 217 62
outlet valve 269 31
outline drawing 129 46
output 117 28
output gear box 212 53
outrigger Rowing 283 42
outrigger Ethnol. 352 36
outrigger canoe 352 35
outriggers 283 9-16

outside broadcast vehicle 239
  1-15
outside defender 291 13
outside forward 291 16
outside grip 296 45
outsider 289 53
ovary Man 20 83
ovary Soft Fruit 58 40
ovary Bot. 370 54, 60
ovary Shrubs etc. 373 2, 5
ovary Flowers etc. 375 34
ovary, epigynous ~ 58 7
ovary, perigynous ~ 59 14
ovary cavity 370 62
ovary wall 370 61
ovate 370 36
oven 39 13; 97 66, 71
oven, electric ~ 207 30
oven window 39 14
overall 33 56
overalls, hairdresser's ~ 106 2
overalls, leather ~ 290 26
over-and-under shotgun 305 70
overblouse 31 61
overblouse, girl's ~ 29 48
overburden 158 2
overburden excavator 159 3
overdress 31 17
overfall 91 43
overfeed, initial ~ 168 26
overflow Roof & Boilerr. 38
  69
overflow Bathrm. etc. 49 25,
  45
overflow Fish Farm. 89 5
overflow Water 269 33
overflow basin 272 23
overflow container 350 60
overflow pipe 38 69; 269 20,
  33
overflow spillway 217 60
overfold 12 14
overgown 355 36, 50
overgrasp 296 40
overhead bicycle kick 291 45
overhead camshaft 189 3;
  190 14
overhead contact wire. 197
  41; 205 58
overhead line support 152 31
overhead projector 261 8
overhead spray washing plant
  169 29
overhead wire maintenance
  vehicle 211 41
overhead wire voltage
  indicator 211 28
overlap angle 128 51
overlay flooring 123 62
overload indicator 224 33
oversite concrete 123 13
overskirt, panniered ~ 355 83
over tile 122 58
overtop 29 48
overtop, knitted ~ 30 4; 31 65
oviduct 20 81
ovule 58 39; 59 14; 370 63
ovum 20 84
owl 252 2
owl-glass 306 38
owls 362 14-19
ox Dom. Anim. 73 1
ox Slaughterho. 94 2
ox Meat 95 14-37
oxer 289 8
ox eye 361 9
oxeye daisy 376 4
oxeye daisy, white ~ 51 24
Oxford 101 31
Oxford shoe 101 31
ox hide, painted ~ 354 11
oxidation 170 19
oxidation, controlled ~ 169 7

oxide ceramic 149 46
oxteam 63 16
oxygen apparatus Moon L. 6
  18
oxygen apparatus Fire Brig.
  270 20
oxygen atom 1 13
oxygen-blowing converter
  147 45-50
oxygen connection 141 30
oxygen control 141 29
oxygen cylinder Hosp. 27 45
oxygen cylinder Gas Weld.
  141 3, 21
oxygen cylinder Road Constr.
  200 40
oxygen flow meter 26 4
oxygen hose 141 10
oxygen inlet 350 11
oxygen jet 350 13
oxygen lance 147 49
oxygen molecule 242 65
oxygen supply 25 22
oxygen tank Moon L. 6 6
oxygen tank Space 234 61
oxygen tank Air Force 257 2
oxygen treatment 25 23
oxymeter 27 13
oxysphere 11 1
oyster 357 32
oyster fork 45 80
oyster round 95 11
ozone layer 7 13, 19

P

pace 72 40
pacemaker 25 36
pacemaker, cardiac ~ 25 31,
  37
pacemaker, internal ~ 25 37
pacemaker, short-term ~ 25
  25
pacemaker battery 25 51
pacemaker control unit 25 40
pacemaker impulse 25 44
pacemaker unit 25 30
pacer 290 11
Pacific Ocean 14 19
pack Dom. Anim. 73 5
pack Hunt. 86 33
pack Airsports 288 44
pack, disposable ~ 93 28
package, unitized ~ 226 21
package cargo transit shed
  225 9
package freight 206 4, 27
pack animal 354 3
packing, sterile ~ 26 31
packing box 210 33
packing box dispenser 74 53
packing machine 76 36
pack of hounds 86 33; 289 46
pack saddle 73 4
pad Horse 71 49
pad Game 88 46
pad Shoem. 100 16
pad Ball Games 292 9
pad Graphic Art 340 13
pad, bakelite ~ 166 64
pad, leather ~ Goldsm. etc.
  108 27
pad, leather ~ Weaving 166 64
pad, suctorial ~ 77 9
pad, unsterile ~ 26 23
pad bridge 111 12
padding, foam rubber ~ 291
  20
paddle Brew. 92 46
paddle Electrotyp. etc. 178 25,
  33
paddle Ship 218 8

paddle Ethnol. 353 14
paddle, double-bladed ~ 283
  39
paddle, double-ended ~ 283
  39
paddle, single-bladed ~ 283
  34
paddle boat 280 12
paddling pool 37 44; 273 28
paddock 319 15
padlock 38 21
page Bookbind. 185 53
page Hotel 267 18
page, double-column ~ 185
  64
page, front ~ 342 38
pageboy 267 18
pageboy style 34 35
page cord 174 16
page heading 342 52
page number 185 63; 251 14
page printer 237 66
pagoda, Indian ~ 337 21
pagoda, multi-storey ~ 337 1
pail 50 54
pailoo 337 3
pailou 337 3
paint 129 6, 7-8, 9; 338 10
paintbox 48 6; 338 10
paintbrush 48 7; 129 3; 260
  84
paint bucket 129 10
paint container 315 34
Painter Astron. 3 47
painter Painter 129 2
painter Art. Studio 338 2
painting 129 1; 260 27
painting, watercolour ~ 48 5
painting materials 338 6-19
painting surface 338 22
painting table 338 25
paint kettle 129 8
paint roller 129 11
paint room 315 28-42
paint scraper 129 22
paint trolley 315 36
pair 275 20
pairing season 86 9-12
pair skater 302 4
pajamas 32 17, 36
palace, Baroque ~ 272 7
palace, Renaissance ~ 335 47
palace buildings 333 29
palace gardens 272 1-40
Palaeolithic period 328 1-9
Palaeopneustes niasicus 369
  19
palate, hard ~ 19 20
palate, soft ~ 19 21
pale ale 93 26
palette 338 28
palette dipper 338 29
palette knife 338 14
paling 52 10
palisade Equest. 289 8
palisade Chivalry 329 36
palisading 329 36
palla 355 10
pallbearer 331 40
pallet Porcelain Manuf. 161
  20
pallet Station 206 32
pallet Docks 225 43; 226 7
pallet Music. Instr. 326 10
pallet, flat ~ 226 10
pallet, standard ~ 226 10
pallette 329 45
palm 88 41
Palma Christi 380 14
palma manus 19 71
palmate 370 39
palmation 73 36; 359 7
palm capital 333 25

palm column 333 17
palmette 334 41
palm frond 384 3
palm of the hand 19 71
palm rest 255 13, 19; 305 45
palm tree 354 5
palpebra, lower ~ 19 40
palpebra, upper ~ 19 39
pampas grass 51 8
pamphlet 330 57
pan Household 50 52
pan Carp. 120 59
pan School 260 60
panache 329 78
Panama hat 35 16
pan and tilt head 114 48; 313 12
pancreas 20 44
Pandean pipes 322 2
pandora 322 21
pane 66 10; 137 27
panel 120 59
panel, front ~ 32 24
panel, mirrored ~ 267 66
panelboard 157 67
panelling, metal ~ 208 6
panelling, wood ~ 281 19
panelling, wooden ~ 266 37
panel pin 124 29
pane of glass 124 16
pangolin 366 10
pan grinding mill 159 8
Panhard rod 192 70
panicle 68 27; 370 69; 378 46; 382 54
pan loaf 97 10
pannier 78 15
panpipes 322 2
pan set 40 12-16
pansy 60 2
pantaleon 325 1
pantaloons 306 42
pantie briefs 32 8
pantie-corselette 32 3
pantie-girdle 32 2
pantie-hose 29 42; 32 12
panties, long-legged ~ 32 10
pantile 122 54
pantograph Map 14 65
pantograph Composing Rm. 175 58
pantograph Tram 197 23
pantograph carriage 175 53
pantry, ship's ~ 223 43
pants, long ~ 32 11
paper Photog. 116 50
paper Drawing Off. 151 14
paper Paperm. 173 2-10
paper Offset Print. 180 47
paper Letterpress 181 46
paper Office 249 57
paper, asphalted ~ 153 48
paper, blank ~ 180 2, 69; 181 23, 30
paper, coated ~ 173 35
paper, cork ~ 128 18
paper, metallic ~ Paperhanger 128 18
paper, metallic ~ Power Plant 153 44
paper, metallized ~ 153 44
paper, natural ~ 128 18
paper, printed ~ 180 57; 181 9, 25
paper, raw ~ 173 29
paper, unprinted ~ 180 2, 69; 181 23, 30
paper, wood ~ 128 18
paper bag, cone-shaped ~ 98 49
paper bail 249 17
paper chase 289 41-49
paper clip 247 1, 2

paper edge, butted ~ 128 20
paper feed 245 11; 249 45, 49
paper feed and delivery 181 14
paper feeding and delivery unit 181 14
paperhanger 128
paper hanging 128 18-53
paperhanging brush 128 40
paperhanging kit 128 33
paper hunt 289 41-49
paper machine 173 11, 13-28
papermaking 172; 173
papermaking by hand 173 46-51
paper punch 22 28
paper recorder 25 56, 57
paper recorder unit 27 33
paper reed 383 64
paper release lever 249 20
paper ribbon 174 34
paper roll 249 33; 309 75
paper roller 128 47
paper rush 383 64
paper size selection 249 34
paper speed scale 116 54
paper stand 151 13
paper tape 237 32
paper towel 196 11
paper-towel dispenser 196 10
paper tower 174 33, 43
pappus 375 34
pappus bristle 375 33
pappus tuft 378 11
paprika 57 42
papyrus column 333 15
papyrus plant 383 64
par 251 12
para 252 28
parabola 347 14
parachute Meteorol. Instr. 10 57
parachute Airsports 288 37
parachuting 288 37-62
paraffin 145 60
paraffin lamp 278 29
paraffin oil 145 60
paragon 175 31
Paraguay tea 382 11
parallel 346 4
parallel bars 296 2
parallelepiped 347 36
parallel of latitude 14 2
parallelograms 346 33-36
parallels 14 1-7
Paramecium 357 9
parapet Dwellings 37 19
parapet Bridges 215 70
parapet Chivalry 329 21
parapet, battlemented ~ 329 20
parasites 81
parasites of man 81 31-42
parasol mushroom 381 30
paravane 258 87
parcel Station 204 2
parcel Post 236 3, 6
parcel registration card 236 7
parcel registration slip 236 4
parcels counter 236 1
parcels office 204 1
parcels scales 236 2
parent 54 15
parentheses 342 24
parent plant 54 15
paring knife 100 51
parison 162 47
parison mould 162 26
park Map 15 97
park Park 272
park Ball Games 291 1; 292 40-58
park, landscaped ~ 272 41-72

parka 29 66
parka coat 29 66
park bench 272 16, 42
park by-law 272 29
park chair 272 48
park entrance 272 32
park gardener 272 66
parking meter 268 1
park keeper 272 30
park path 272 38
park railing 272 33
park tree 272 59
parlour, herringbone ~ 75 23
parquet floor 123 74
parquet strip 123 62
parrot 363 1
parrying 294 6
parry of the fifth 294 24
parry of the quinte 294 24
parry of the tierce 294 8
parsley 57 19
parsonage 331 20
part, imaginary ~ 344 14
part, real ~ 344 14
parterre 272 39
Parthenon 334 1
partial-hip end 121 17
parting, centre ~ 34 9
parting, side ~ 34 14
parting kiss 205 52
parting-off tool 149 53
parting tool Turner 135 24
parting tool Mach. Tools 149 53
partition 75 38
partition, framed ~ 120 48
partition, glass ~ 25 8
partition, sound-absorbing ~ 248 20
partition, wooden ~ 38 19
partition screen 248 1
partition wall Bldg. Site 119 25
partition wall Office 248 1
part load 206 4
part-load goods 206 27
partridge 88 70
partridge call 87 47
party 263 20
party, private ~ 267 40-43
party blouse 30 55
party skirt 30 56
par value 251 12
Paschen series 1 22
pas de trois 314 27-28
Pasiphaea 369 12
pass Phys. Geog. 12 47
pass Ball Games 291 47
pass, short ~ 291 49
passage 71 3
passage, barred ~ 307 51
passage grave 328 16
passe 275 19
passenger 204 24; 205 6; 208 30; 221 97, 109
passenger aircraft 231 2
passenger cabin 231 22
passenger car 208 3
passenger coach 207 1-21; 208 3
passenger compartment 207 13
passenger door, centre ~ 231 25
passenger door, rear ~ 231 30
passenger ferry 216 1
passenger liner 221 82; 225 32
passenger seat Car 191 36
passenger seat Lorries etc. 194 14
passenger seat Aircraft 230 38; 231 22

passenger sledge 353 18
passenger terminal 225 31
passenger vehicle 191 1-56; 195 34
passerines 361
Passiflora 53 2
passion flower 53 2
passport 267 13
'passport check' 233 42
pastas 98 32-34
paste 128 26
paste, heavy-duty ~ 128 24
pasteboard 128 31
paste brush 128 27
pastel crayon 338 19
pastern 72 25
pasting machine 128 25
pastor Church 330 22
pastor Birds 361 4
pasture, rough ~ 15 5
patch pocket 29 68; 30 22; 31 56; 33 38; 35 37
pâté 96 15
patella 17 23
paten 330 9; 332 51
patent 246 26
patent anchor 222 78; 258 5; 286 17
patent key 187 50
patent log 224 54
patent valve 187 31
paternoster 332 31
path, central ~ 55 42
path, gravel ~ 272 18
path, unfenced ~ 15 102
patient 22 2, 3; 24 2; 274 7, 18
patients file 22 6
patin 330 9; 332 51
patine 330 9; 332 51
patrician lady 355 48
patrol car 264 10
patrolman 264 13
patrol submarine 259 75
patten 355 43
pattern Iron Foundry etc. 148 34
pattern Composing Rm. 175 55
pattern, chequered ~ 335 14
pattern control chain 167 19
pattern repeat 171 12
pattern stencil 168 62
pattern table 175 56
pauldron 329 45
Pauli exclusion principle 1 7
Pauli principle 1 7
pause 321 25
pause sign 321 25
pavais 329 56
pavement 37 60; 198 8, 9
paving 198 8
paving, brick ~ 123 7
paving, flagstone ~ 123 26
paving brick 159 27
pavis 329 56
Pavo 3 41
paw 88 46, 50; 368 4
paw, hind ~ 70 8
pawn 276 13
payee 250 19
payer 250 20
paying agent 250 22
paying-in counter 236 25
paying-in slip 236 27
payload bay 235 26
payload bay door 235 14
payload bay insulation 235 13
payload manipulator arm 235 29
pay phone 236 9; 237 3
pea 57 1, 7
peach 59 31

peach blossom 59 27
peach flan 97 22
peach flower 59 27
peach leaf 59 32
peach tree 59 26-32
Peacock Astron. 3 41
peacock Dom. Anim. 73 30
peacock butterfly 365 2
pea flower 57 2
pea jacket 221 127
peak 11 6; 12 40
peanut 45 41; 383 41
pear 58 33
pear blossom 58 38
pearl Jewell. 36 8
pearl Game 88 30
pearl Composing Rm. 175 22
pearl Invertebr. 357 35
pearl barley 98 35
pear pip 58 37
pears 99 87
pear-shape, faceted ~ 36 84
pear-shape, plain ~ 36 83
pear-shape, standard ~ 36 54
pear-shapes 36 82-86
pear stalk 58 34
pear tree 58 31, 32
peasecod 355 30
peat 55 31; 206 10
pea tendril 57 4
peavy 85 9
peba 366 8
pebble, painted ~ 328 6
pectoralis, greater ~ 18 36
pectoralis major 18 36
pedal Joiner 132 72
pedal Bicycle 187 40, 78
pedal Sports 305 85
pedal Music. Instr. 323 62;
    325 41, 46
pedal, adjustable ~ 298 2
pedal, left ~ 325 9
pedal, right ~ 325 8
pedal bracket 325 42
pedal car 273 55
pedal crank 188 25
pedal cylinder 163 27
pedal drive 188 25
pedal frame 187 83
pedal harp 323 60
pedal key 326 51, 52
pedal lever 163 28
pedal mechanism 324 54
pedal pipe 326 3
pedal roller 163 27, 28
pedal tower 326 4
peddle boat 280 12
pedestal Optic. Instr. 113 2
pedestal Office 248 37
pedestal Park 272 11
pedestal Circus 307 55
pedestal crane 146 3
pedestal grinding machine
    138 7
pedestal mat 49 18
pedestrian 268 18
pedestrian crossing 198 11;
    268 24, 51
'pedestrian crossing' sign 268
    29
pedestrian lights 268 55
pedestrian precinct 268 58
pedicel 59 4; 383 7
pediculate 369 6
pediment Phys. Geog. 13 65
pediment Art 334 3; 335 36
peduncle 59 4; 383 7
peeler 133 1
peeling machine 133 1
peen 66 10; 137 27
peewit 359 21
peg Floor etc. Constr. 123 11
peg Camping 278 24

peg Music. Instr. 323 18; 324
    11
Pegasus Astron. 3 10
Pegasus Fabul. Creat. 327 26
pegbox 323 19
pegbox, bent-back ~ 324 10
pegbox, swan-head ~ 324 10
pegdisc 324 19
pein 137 27
Pekinese dog 70 19
Peking man 261 18
pelargonium 53 1
pelican 359 5
pelican eel 369 2
pellitone 323 44
pelorus 224 53
pelota 305 67
pelota player 305 68
pelvis 17 18-21
pelvis, renal ~ 20 31
penalty 291 40
penalty area 291 4
penalty kick 291 40
penalty line 292 5
penalty spot 291 6
pen and pencil case 260 12
pen and pencil tray 245 22;
    260 24
pencil 47 26; 129 41; 260 5
pencil, carpenter's ~ 120 77
pencil, clutch-type ~ 151 45
pencil, coloured ~ 48 11
pencil, lead ~ 118 51
pencil attachment 151 62
pencil box 309 73
pencil holder 22 31
pencil lead 151 46
pencil of rays 346 19
pencil point attachment 151
    55
pencil sharpener 247 25
pencil silhouette 31 14
pen clip 2 18
pendant 335 32
pendant, gemstone ~ 36 14
pendant, oblong ~ 253 28
pendants 253 30-32
pendeloque 36 54
pendentive 334 74
pendulum Atom 2 35
pendulum 110 27; 309 58
pendulum device 2 35
pendulum spray 83 27
penguin 359 4
peninsula 13 5
penis 20 66
penlight pocket 6 24
pen meter 2 15
pennant, oblong ~ 253 28
pennants 253 30-32
pennon 278 9; 280 11
pennon staff 280 10
penny, new ~ 252 37
pensions counter 236 25
Pentacrinus 369 3
pentagon 351 9
pentaprism 115 41, 70
pentaprism viewfinder,
    interchangeable ~ 115 69
penthouse 37 83
penthouse head 312 50
penthouse roof 37 55
pent roof 37 55, 78; 121 7
penumbra 4 34
peplos 355 2
pepper 382 39
peppercorn 382 39

peppermint 380 3
pepper plant 382 36
pepper pot 266 77
percentage focusing chart 177
    7
percentage key 247 23
percentage sign 345 7
percent key 247 23
perch 86 49
percolation of a river 13 73
percussion cap Hunt. 87 59
percussion cap Carnival 306
    49
percussion drill, electric ~ 134
    43
percussion instruments 323
    49-59; 324 47-58
percussion screwdriver 138 6
percussor 22 73
peregrine falcon 362 2
perennial 52 22
perennial, flowering ~ 52 9
perfect binder 184 1; 249 61
perfect fifth 321 10
perfect fourth 321 9
perfecting unit 181 49
perfecting unit for black 180
    12-13
perfecting unit for cyan 180
    8-9
perfecting unit for magenta
    180 10-11
perfecting unit for yellow 180
    6-7
perfect octave 321 13
perforated brick 159 21
perforation 236 62
perforator Paperhanger 128
    12
perforator Composing Rm.
    176 5
perfume bottle 43 27; 105 36
perfume spray 43 26; 106 21
pergola 37 80; 51 1; 272 17
pericarp 57 6
pericementum 19 28
perineum 20 64
period 342 16
periodical 262 15
periodicals rack 262 15
periodontium 19 28
periphery 346 44
peristomion 322 5
peristyle 334 2
peritoneum 20 58
perlon fibres 170 1-62
Permian 154 62
peroneus longus 18 64
perpendicular 346 6, 27, 28
perpetual frost climate 9 58
Persian cat 73 17
Persian lamb 30 60
personnel carrier, armoured
    ~ 255 91
Peru Current 14 42
pesade 71 4; 307 30
peseta 252 22
pest control 83
pestle 349 10
petal 58 43; 59 11; 370 59
petasus 355 4
pet foods 99 36-37
petiole 370 27
petri dish 173 7; 261 25
petrol can 196 25
petrol canister 84 36
petroleum Phys. Geog. 12 31
petroleum Oil, Petr. 145 41
petroleum gas, liquefied ~
    145 53
petroleum reservoir 12 27
petrol lighter 107 27
petrol motor 83 41

petrol pump 196 1
petrol pump, self-service ~
    196 8
petrol pump hose 196 2
petrol station 196 1-29
petrol tank 188 10, 28; 189 2;
    305 87
petticoat 355 37
petty cash 246 27
petty morel 379 5
petunia 53 6
pew 330 28
pewit 359 21
Pfund series 1 24
phaeton 86 18; 186 38
phalange 17 17, 29; 19 77
phalanx 17 17; 19 77
pharmacopoeia 22 23
pharynx 19 24
phases, lunar ~ 4 2-7
pheasant 88 77
pheasant cock 88 77
pheasant hen 88 77
pheasant's eye 60 4
phenol 170 3, 14, 16
phenol extraction 156 39
philomel 361 14
philomela 361 14
philtrum 16 12
phloem 370 9
phlox 60 14
Phoenix 327 9
phonetics 342 14
phonetic transcription 342 14
phorbeia 322 5
phoropter 111 44
phosphorescent material 240
    18
photocell 312 49
photocomposition 176
photocomposition system 176
    29
photodiode 114 70; 243 56
photoengraving, halftone ~
    178 38
photogrammetry 14 63-66;
    112 67
photographic plate 309 49, 50
photographic unit 176 14
photography 114; 115; 116
photography, underwater ~
    279 23
photogravure 182
photomechanical
    reproduction 177
photometer 23 54
photometer, microscopic ~
    112 49
photometry 23 52, 53
photomicrographic camera
    attachment 112 36
photomicro mount adapter
    112 64
photomicroscope 112 34
photomicroscope adapter 115
    89
photomultiplier 112 51
photosetting 176
photosetting system 176 29
phototheodolite 112 67
phototopography 14 63-66
phototypesetting 176 1
photo-unit 176 14
piaffe 71 1
pianino 325 1
pianissimo 321 36
pianissimo piano 321 37
piano Music. Not. 321 35
piano Music. Instr. 325 1, 40
piano accordion 324 36
piano action 325 2-18
piano case 325 6
pianoforte 325 1

piano keys 325 4-5
piano mechanism 325 2-18
piano pedal 325 9
piano pedals 325 8-9
piano string 325 7
pica 175 28
picador 319 16
piccolo 323 30
Piciformes 363 6
pick 158 31; 300 33
pick counter 166 2
picker 166 64
picker head 184 11
picking bowl 166 67
picking cam 166 66
picking knife 136 38
picking stick 166 17, 22
picking stick buffer 166 65
picking stick return spring 166 68
pickpocket 308 16
pick stick 166 17
pickup attachment 62 41; 63 27
pickup reel 64 4
pickup sucker 184 8
pickup truck 194 1, 5
pickup unit 240 36
picture 43 20; 246 28
picture, panoramic ~ 24 21
picture frame 43 21
picture gate 312 34
picture house 312 1
picture monitor 238 65; 239 12
picture rail 128 29
picture tube 240 3
picture tube geometry 242 39
pier Bridges 215 21, 54
pier Docks 225 66
pier Airport 233 12
pier Art 336 25
pier, clustered ~ 335 34
pier, compound ~ 335 34
pier, reinforced concrete ~ 215 61
piercing saw 108 12
piercing saw blade 108 13
pierette 306 12
pierhead 233 13
pierrot 306 19
pies 97 22-24
pig Farm Bldgs. 62 10
pig Dom. Anim. 73 9
pig Livestock 75 39
pig Slaughterho. 94 11
pig Meat 95 38-54
pig Iron & Steel 147 40
pig, solidifying ~ 148 25
pig-casting machine 147 34-44
pigeon 73 33; 359 23
pigeon hole 267 2
pig iron, molten ~ 147 55
pig iron ladle 147 12, 21, 42
pig iron runout 147 11
piglet 73 9; 75 42
pigment paper 182 1, 8, 10
pigmy 354 41
pigpen 62 8; 75 35
pigskin 292 27
pigsty 62 8; 75 35
pigtail Hairst. etc. 34 6
pigtail Tobacc. etc. 107 18
pigtail wig 34 5; 355 77
pig trap 146 31
pike Fish Farm. 89 17
pike Free Exerc. 295 38
pike Fish etc. 364 16
pike, spawning ~ 89 11
piked reverse hang 296 36

pike pole 319 17
pi-key 247 24
pilaster 335 46
pilaster strip 335 11
pile 226 40
pile, steel ~ 217 4
pile delivery unit 180 55
pile driver, floating ~ 226 36
pile driver frame 226 37
pile dwelling 328 15; 352 33
pile feeder 180 73
pile feeder, automatic ~ 180 48
pile foundation 216 8
pile hammer 226 38
pile of arrow 305 61
pile shoe 269 61
pileus 381 4
piling 157 25
pillar Mach. Tools 150 21
pillar Shipbuild. 222 61
pillar Art 335 20
pillar, engaged ~ 335 35, 46
pillar guide 139 42
pillar stand Atom 2 29
pillar stand Optic. Instr. 112 32
pillar tap 126 31
pillion footrest 188 44
pillion passenger 268 36
pillion rider 268 36
pillow 27 27; 43 12-13; 47 4
pillowcase 43 12
pillow lace 102 18
pillowslip 43 12
pilot Railw. 210 34
pilot Music. Instr. 325 33
pilot, automatic ~ 224 18
pilot boat 221 95
pilot chute 288 39
pilot flag 253 23
pilot light 50 10
pilot light, covered ~ 38 60
'pilot on board' 253 24
pilot tone cable 313 29
pilot tone generator 313 30
pilot tone socket 117 7
pilot wire 325 34
Pilsener beer 93 26
pimehinketone 170 20
pin Roof 121 93
pin Turner 135 9
pin Metalwkr. 140 47
pin Mach. Parts etc. 143 31
pin Sports 305 12
pin, bronze ~ 328 29
pin, cylindrical ~ 143 40
pin, diamond ~ 36 18
pin, front ~ 305 1
pin, grooved ~ 143 40
pin, split ~ 143 19, 25, 78
pin, tapered ~ 143 37
pinacoid, triclinic ~ 351 26
pinafore, bib top ~ 29 41
pinafore dress 29 13; 30 8; 31 8
pin block 324 22; 325 18
pincers Shoem. 100 40, 41
pincers Plumb. etc. 126 65
pincers D.I.Y. 134 13
pincers Basketm. 136 37
pincers Metalwkr. 140 69
pincers, caudal ~ 81 12
pinch bar 158 32
pinchcock 350 30
pinch roller 243 25
pinch roller, rubber ~ 117 35
pincushion 104 20
pine 372 20
pineapple 99 85
pineapple flower 384 64
pineapple gall 82 40
pineapple plant 384 61

pine beauty 82 46
pine cone 372 26
pine hawkmoth 82 27
pine moth 82 28
pine weevil 82 41
pin groove 143 49
pin holder 109 16
pinion Game 88 76
pinion Mach. Parts etc. 143 92
pink Equest. 289 13
pink Colour 343 4
pinnacle 335 29
pinnate 370 41
pinnatifid 370 40
pinnipeds 367 18-22
pin slit 143 49
pin slot 143 49
pin vice 109 16
pin wire 124 28
pip 276 32
pipe Living Rm. 42 12
pipe Ship 221 3
pipe Music. Instr. 322 57; 326 16, 29
pipe, briar ~ 107 39
pipe, cast-iron ~ 37 14
pipe, cement ~ 200 62
pipe, clay ~ 107 34
pipe, Dutch ~ 107 34
pipe, earthenware ~ 269 35
pipe, long ~ 107 35
pipe, magic ~ 354 42
pipe, perforated ~ 200 62
pipe, polyester ~ 67 26
pipe, short ~ 107 33
pipe, vertical ~ Dwellings 37 14
pipe, vertical ~ Fire Brig. 270 26
pipe bender 125 28
pipe-bending machine Plumb. 125 28
pipe-bending machine Plumb. etc. 126 82
pipe bowl 107 36
pipe cleaner 107 46, 48
pipe clip Roof 122 31
pipe clip Plumb. etc. 126 56
pipe connection, quick-fitting ~ 67 28
pipe cutter 126 84
pipe-cutting machine 126 10
pipeline 145 65
pipe of peace 352 6
pipe rack Living Rm. 42 11
piperack Offshore Drill. 146 4
pipe repair stand 126 11
pipes 326 17-35
pipe scraper 107 45
pipe stem 107 38
pipe still 145 36
pipe support 67 7, 25
pipe supports 126 53-57
pipe union 350 5
pipe vice 126 81
pipe wrench 126 61; 127 47; 134 11
piping 30 13; 31 7
pirate Sailing 284 52
pirate Carnival 306 43
pirn 166 30
pirn, empty ~ 166 21
pirn holder, spring-clip ~ 166 33
pirouette 314 24
Pisces 4 64
pisciculture 89 1-19

pistachio 382 51
pistachio nut 382 51
pistachio tree 382 49
piste 294 2
pistil 59 13
pistol 255 1
pistol, captive-bolt ~ 94 3
pistol grip Hunt. 87 6
pistol grip D.I.Y. 134 44
pistol grip Army 255 6, 38
pistol grip Police 264 23
piston Drawing Off. 151 60
piston Intern. Combust. Eng. 190 37
piston Inf. Tech. 242 46
piston, hydraulic ~ 139 41
piston pin 192 26
piston pump lever 83 45
piston ring 190 37
piston rod Intern. Combust. Eng. 190 21
piston rod Car 192 75
piston rod Railw. 210 33
pit Blacksm. 138 17
pit Coal 144 1-51
pitcher Ball Games 292 50, 68
pitcher Prehist. 328 35
pitcher's mound 292 49, 69
pitching 230 67
pitching, stone ~ 216 55
pitch number 278 42
pitch of rivets 143 60
pith 370 14
pithead building 144 4
pithead frame 144 3
pithead gear 144 1
Pithecanthropus erectus 261 16
pith ray 370 11
pit hydrant 270 25
piton 300 38
piton, ringed ~ 300 39
pitot-static tube 256 11; 257 1
pitot tube 256 11; 257 1
pivot Hairdresser 106 36
pivot Bridges 215 69
pivot Winter Sp. 302 6
pivot bearing 91 10
pivoting half 215 66
pivoting section 215 66
pivoting span 215 66
pivot pier 215 65
pix 330 8; 332 53
placard 263 13; 271 65; 308 50
place 44 5; 45 3-12
place card 45 13
place mat 44 4
place of issue 250 13
place of payment 250 15
place setting 44 5; 45 3-12
placing judge 282 25
plaid strap 303 2
plain, alluvial ~ 13 10
plainclothes policeman 264 33
plain part of the cylinder 163 69
plains Indian 352 3
plainsong notation 320 1
plain-tile roofing 122 2
plait 97 41
plait, coiled ~ 34 38
plaiter 168 30, 33
plaiting-down platform 168 37
plaits 34 30
plaits, coiled ~ 34 32
plan Drawing Off. 151 19
plan Railw. 207 10-21, 26-32, 38-42, 61-72, 76
planchet 252 43
plane Carp. 120 64

plane *Aircraft* 230 67-72
plane *Maths.* 347 31
plane, abyssal ~ 11 10
plane, circular ~ 347 39
plane, high-wing ~ 229 1; 231 2
plane, horizontal ~ 4 12
plane, low-wing ~ 229 5, 14; 231 1
plane, midwing ~ 229 4
plane, propeller-driven ~ 231 1-6
plane, shoulder-wing ~ 229 3
plane, two-seater ~ 288 18
plane, types of ~ 231 1-33
plane geometry 346 1-58
plane iron 132 20
plane of symmetry 351 5
planer, two-column ~ 150 8
planer table 150 11
planes 132 15-28
planetarium 5 17-28
plane tree 371 67
plane triangles 346 26-32
planets 4 42-52
planing boats 286 38-44
planing machine, two-column ~ 150 8
plank 55 22; 118 87; 120 1, '91; 157 34, 35
plank, unsquared ~ 120 94
plank, wooden ~ 340 2
plank cut 340 4
planking 119 52
planking, inner ~ 285 57
plank platform 118 28
plank roadway 118 79
plan of locomotive 211 10-18
planographic printing method 340 25-26
plant 370 15; 382 53
plant, anagraceous ~ 53 3
plant, asclepiadaceous ~ 53 3
plant, climbing ~ 51 5; 52 5; 57 8
plant, cyperaceous ~ 53 17
plant, ericaceous ~ 53 12
plant, female ~ 383 10
plant, flowering ~ 58 17
plant, fruit-bearing ~ 58 17
plant, gesneriaceous ~ 53 7
plant, indoor ~ 42 36; 248 14
plant, insectivorous ~ 377 13
plant, liliaceous ~ 53 13
plant, pistillate ~ 383 10
plant, pneumatic ~ 92 12
plant, potted ~ 55 25
plant, ranunculaceous ~ 60 13
plant, tiliaceous ~ 53 9
plant, tuberous ~ 68 38
plantation, young ~ 84 11, 12
plant body 378 49
planter 248 13
plant in flower 378 36
plant louse 358 13
plants, alpine ~ 378 1-13
plants, aquatic ~ 378 14-57
plants, drupaceous ~ 59 1-36
plants, farinaceous ~ 68 1-37
plants, indoor ~ 53
plants, leguminous ~ 57 1-11
plants, medicinal ~ 380
plants, poisonous ~ 379
plants, pomiferous ~ 58 31-61
plants, propagation of ~ 54
plants, tropical ~ 382
plants of forest, marsh and heathland 377
plant stand 248 13
plants used in industry 383
plaque *Roulette* 275 12
plaque *Sculpt. Studio* 339 38
plaster *Hosp.* 26 54

plaster *Paperhanger* 128 2
plaster *Art. Studio* 338 42
plaster, adhesive ~ 21 7; 22 55
plaster cast 339 4
plaster cup 134 18
plasterer 118 83
plastering 118 83-91
plaster mould 161 15
plaster of Paris 128 2; 260 85
plasticine 48 12
plate 266 11
plate, baby's ~ 28 28
plate, bottom ~ 45 3
plate, curved ~ 178 21
plate, deep ~ 44 6; 45 5
plate, front ~ 85 35
plate, halftone ~ 178 38
plate, presensitized ~ 179 31
plate, rear ~ 85 40
plate, sliding ~ 183 28
plate, steel ~ 96 54
plate armour 329 65
plateau 13 46
plate clamp *Electrotyp. etc.* 178 27
plate clamp *Offset Platem.* 179 8
plate-coating machine 179 1
plate cylinder *Offset Print.* 180 25, 38, 53, 62
plate cylinder *Letterpress* 181 51, 60
plate cylinder *Office* 249 50
plate-drying cabinet, vertical ~ 179 27
plate girder bridge 215 52
plate magazine 113 40
plate mount 178 41
plate mounting 178 41
platen *Letterpress* 181 13, 15, 29
platen *Bookbind.* 183 24
platen *Office* 249 18
platen *Graphic Art* 340 31
platen knob 249 22
platen machine 181 13, 29
platen press 181 13, 29; 340 29
platen variable 249 25
plate rack 178 35
plate rod 178 6
plate whirler 179 1
platform *Wine Grow.* 78 20
platform *Shoes* 101 8
platform *Bldg. Site* 118 87; 119 52
platform *Station* 205 1, 14
platform *Swim.* 282 7, 8
platform *Circus* 307 5
platform *Art. Studio* 338 30
platform, continental ~ 11 8
platform, covered ~ 218 49
platform, intermediate ~ 145 5
platform, operator's ~ 168 23
platform, wave-cut ~ 13 31
platform clock 205 46
platformer 145 47
platform lighting 205 48
platform loudspeaker 205 27
platform mailbox 205 56
platform number 205 4
platform post box 205 56
platform railing 118 24
platform roofing 205 5
platform scale 204 5
platform seat 205 14
platform sole 101 8
platform telephone 205 57
platform truck 194 6
platypus 366 1
play area 272 44
playback deck 238 4
playback deck, single ~ 238 56

playback head 311 25
player 48 20
player's name 293 36
playgoer 315 8
playground, children's ~ 273
playing card 276 36
playing card, French ~ 276 37
play pen 28 39
playsuit 29 11, 19, 22
plaza de toros 319 5
pleasure boat 283 1
pleasure steamer 221 101-128; 225 29
pleasure vehicle 186 33
pleat, front ~ 31 25
plectrum 322 19; 324 20
Pleiades 3 26
Pleiads 3 26
pleiobar 9 2
plexus, brachial ~ 18 27
pliers, flat-nose ~ 126 62; 140 66
pliers, multiple ~ 134 12
pliers, round-nose ~ 126 64; 127 50
pliers, shoemaker's ~ 100 38
plinth *Dwellings* 37 17
plinth *Carp.* 120 28
plinth *Art* 334 31
plinth, natural stone ~ 37 85
Plough *Astron.* 3 29
plough *Agr.* 63 6
plough *Brew.* 92 24
plough, four-furrow ~ 63 40
plough, mounted ~ 65 62
plough, reversible ~ 65 62
plough, single-bottom ~ 65 1
plough anchor 286 16
plough beam 65 9, 71
plough bottom 65 4-8, 64-67
plough frame 65 70
plough handle 65 3
ploughshare 65 7, 65; 328 33
plough stilt 65 3
plovers 359 19-21
plow 63 6
plow *see* plough
plowshare 328 33
plucking device 322 19
Pluderhose 355 34
plug *Tobacc. etc.* 107 19
plug *Plumb. etc.* 126 55
plug *Metalwkr.* 140 45
plug, double-jointed ~ 89 70
plug, earthed ~ 127 9
plug, multi-pin ~ 241 70
plug, single-jointed ~ 89 69
plug, three-pin ~ 127 67
plugboard 242 69
plug gauge 149 56
plugging 123 69
plugging sand bucket 158 29
plug point 127 5
plug point, double ~ 127 6
plug socket 50 78
plum 59 25
plum, black-skinned ~ 59 20
plum, oval ~ 59 20
plumb bob 118 50, 71
plumber 125; 125 17; 126; 126 1
plumber's tools 126 58-86
plumbing fixtures 126 26-37
plume *Heraldry* 254 36
plume *Chivalry* 329 78
plumicorn 88 78; 362 16
plum leaf 59 21
plummet *Fish Farm.* 89 91
plummet *Bldg. Site* 118 50, 71
plum slice 97 43
plum stone 59 23
plum tree 59 19-23
plumule 370 90

plunger *Oil, Petr.* 145 23
plunger *Glass Prod.* 162 32
plunger *Car* 192 7
plus sign 344 7, 23
Pluto 4 52
pneumatic pick longwall face 144 35
pneumatophore 370 82
pneume 320 1
poacher 86 29
pochette 322 20
pocket, front ~ 30 23; 33 46; 260 10
pocket, inset ~ 29 63; 31 4
pocket billiards 277 7
pocket book 264 36
pocket calculator 246 12
pocket calculator, electronic ~ 247 14
pocket camera 114 16
pocket chamber 2 15
pocket flap 33 18
pocket meter 2 15
pocket timetable 204 42; 205 45
pocket torch 127 26
pocket train schedule 204 42; 205 45
pod 57 6; 61 20, 23; 69 8, 16; 370 92, 93; 378 33; 384 46
pod, immature ~ 374 22
pod, mature ~ 383 4
pod, pouch-shaped ~ 61 11
pod, ripe ~ 383 4
pod, unripe ~ 374 22
pod corn 68 31
poet's daffodil 60 4
poet's narcissus 60 4
point *Game* 88 10, 31
point *Mach. Parts etc.* 143 23, 54
point *Sculpt. Studio* 339 15
point *Maths.* 346 1-23
point, angular ~ 346 1
point, diamond ~ 24 40
point, equinoctial ~ 3 6, 7
point, front ~ 300 49
point, typographic ~ 175 18
pointer *Hosp.* 26 28
pointer *Dog* 70 40, 43
pointer *Photog.* 114 58
pointer *Inf. Tech.* 242 76
pointer *Chem.* 349 34
point guard 300 50
pointing 122 55
pointing sill 121 47
point lace 102 30
point light exposure lamp 179 21
point lock 202 28
point-of-aim mark 305 56
point of Aries 3 6
point of arrow 305 61
point of contact 346 49
point of hook 89 80
point of inflexion 347 21
point of intersection 346 1
point of release 89 34
point paper design 171 4, 27
points, equinoctial ~ 3 6-7
points, manually-operated ~ 202 16
points, remote-controlled ~ 202 27
points, single ~ 203 45-48
points change indicator 197 39
point shoe 314 30
point size 175 46
points knob 203 62
points lever 203 55
points mechanism, electric ~ 197 43

points mechanism, electrohydraulic ~ 197 43
points mechanism, electromechanical ~ 197 43
points motor 202 35
points of sailing 285 1-13
points of the horse 72 1-38
point source lamp 182 4
points signal 197 38; 202 19
points signal, electrically illuminated ~ 202 33
points signal lamp 202 19
points signals 203 45-52
point wire 202 30
poison gland 77 14
poison sac 77 13
poitrel 329 85
poke bonnet 306 23; 355 71
poker 38 41; 137 5
polar bear 368 11
Polaris 3 1, 34
polarizer 112 14
polarizing filter 112 19
polar sledge 303 18
polar wind zone 9 51
pole Fruit & Veg. Gdn. 52 28
pole Horse 71 21
pole Fish Farm. 89 30
pole Mills 91 32
pole Carriages 186 19, 30
pole Rivers 216 16
pole Athletics 298 28
pole, bamboo ~ 307 46
pole, celestial ~ 3 1; 4 24, 26
pole, geographical ~ 14 3
pole, hooked ~ 77 55
pole, terrestrial ~ 14 3
pole chain 71 20
pole horse 186 47
pole mast 258 42; 259 6
Pole Star 3 1, 34
pole vault 298 28-36
pole vaulter 298 29
poleyn 329 53
polhode 4 28
police 264
police badge 264 27
police dog 70 25; 264 5, 6
police duties 264 1-33
police helicopter 264 1
police identification disc 264 26
police launch 221 100
policeman 264 18, 34
police officer 264 18
police patrolman 264 13
police signalling disc 264 14
police van 264 38
policewoman 264 37
polishing 109 17
polishing and burnishing machine 108 42
polishing bonnet, lamb's wool ~ 134 21
polishing brush 100 11
polishing iron 108 51
polishing machine attachment 109 15
polishing wheel 108 44
polish rod 145 27
political section 342 51
Politzer bag 22 37
polje 13 72
pollen 77 3, 35; 370 65
pollen basket 77 6
pollen comb 77 7
pollen sac 372 45, 50
pollen tube 370 66
pollex 19 64
polling booth 263 23
polling card 263 19
polling number 263 19

polling place 263 16
polling station 263 16
polo jumper, striped ~ 30 20
polo neck jumper 30 7
polo outsole 101 24
polo saddle, high-back ~ 188 13
polyamide 170 34, 35, 37, 41
polyamide chip, dry ~ 170 39
polyamide cone 170 51, 52
polyamide fibres 170 1-62
polyamide filament 170 43
polyamide staple 170 61, 62
polyamide thread 170 46
polyanthus narcissus 60 4
Polycheles 369 15
polyester resin 130 17
polygon 346 40
polygon, eight-sided ~ 351 17
polygon, five-sided ~ 351 9
polygon, regular ~ 346 41
polygon, six-sided ~ 351 15
polyhedron 260 73
polyhedron, eight-faced ~ 351 6
polyhedron, forty-eight-faced ~ 351 13
polyhedron, four-faced ~ 351 1
polyhedron, regular ~ 351 11
polyhedron, six-faced ~ 351 2
polyhedron, twenty-faced ~ 351 11
polyhedron, twenty-four-faced ~ 351 12
polymerization 170 33, 54
polyp, hydroid ~ 369 9
polypod 377 16
polypody 377 16
pome 370 102
pomegranate 384 16
Pomeranian 70 20
pomes 58
pommel 296 6
pommel horn 71 38
pommel horse 296 5
pommer 322 14
pompier 270 43
pompier ladder 270 16
pompon 29 4
pompon dahlia 60 23
poncho 352 24
pond Map 15 79
pond Park 272 50
pons 17 46
pons cerebelli 17 46
pons cerebri 17 46
pontic, porcelain ~ 24 29
pontoon 226 57
pontoon, bottom ~ 222 38
pontoon bridge 15 46
pontoon dock 222 34-43; 225 16
pony 75 4
ponytail 34 27
poodle 70 36
pool, indoor ~ 281 1-9
pool, non-swimmers' ~ 282 21
pool, swimmers' ~ 282 23
pool attendant 281 4; 282 15
pool billiards 277 7
poolroom 277 7-19
poop 223 33; 258 22
poor man's weatherglass 61 27
popcorn 68 31
pop group 306 2
poplar 371 15
pop musician 306 3
poppy 51 30; 61 2
poppy flower 61 4
poppy seed 61 5

porcelain manufacture 161
porcelain painter 161 17
porcupine 366 13
porifer 357 13
pork 95 38-54
pork, collared ~ 96 9
porridge oats 98 37
port Ship 220 27
port Docks 225; 226
port administration offices 225 36
portal 331 16
portal, main ~ 333 34
portal, recessed ~ 335 24
portal figure 333 36
portal frame 215 38
portal relief 333 35
portal spotlight 316 21
portato 321 29
portcullis 329 24
port custom house 225 6
port de bras à coté 314 7
port de bras en avant 314 9
port de bras en bas 314 8
port de bras en haut 314 10
porter Brew. 93 26
porter Station 205 31; 206 33
porter Hotel 267 17
porthole 117 64
porthole, ornamental ~ 218 57
port hospital 225 26
portico 334 50, 56
port liner 190 73
port of registry 286 8
ports de bras 314 7-10
posaune stop 326 17-22
position 224 45
position indicator 246 18
position light 257 36; 288 31
position light, left ~ 230 50
position light, right ~ 230 44
positions 314 1-6
positions, arm ~ 314 7-10
positive 322 56
post Dent. 24 34
post Wine Grow. 78 7
post Forestry 84 17; 85 30, 47
post Mills 91 34
post Carp. 120 25
post Roof 121 40, 81
post Paperm. 173 50
post Ball Games 291 37
post, broker's ~ 251 3
post, principal ~ 120 53
postage meter 22 24; 236 7
postage stamp 236 61
postal code 236 43
postal collection 236 50-55
postal delivery 236 50-55
postbox 236 50
post code 236 43
post crown 24 31
poster 98 2; 204 10; 268 71; 271 25
posthorn 186 41
post horse 186 43
postman 236 53
postmark, special ~ 236 59
postmark advertisement 236 56
postmarks 236 56-60
post office 236; 237; 268 68
post office box 236 13, 14
post office savings counter 236 25
post office van 236 52
post-synchronization 311 37-41
post-syncing 311 37-41
post-sync sound 117 101
post windmill 91 31
pot Kitch. 39 29

pot Kitch. Utensils 40 12
pot Plant Propagn. 54 8
pot, baby's ~ 28 47
pot, centrifugal ~ 169 17
potash salt bed 154 65
potash salt seam 154 65
potato 68 38, 40
potato, flat-oval ~ 68 38
potato, Irish ~ 68 38
potato, kidney-shaped ~ 68 38
potato, long ~ 68 38
potato, pear-shaped ~ 68 38
potato, purple ~ 68 38
potato, red ~ 68 38
potato, round ~ 68 38
potato, round-oval ~ 68 38
potato, white ~ 68 38
potato, yellow ~ 68 38
potato apple 68 43
potato basket 66 25
potato beetle 80 52
potato berry 68 43
potato chipper 40 43
potato crisp 45 41
potato dish 45 31
potato fork 66 5
potato harvester 64 59-84
potato haulm 68 41
potato hoe 66 24
potato hook 66 6
potato plant 68 38
potato planter 66 21
potato rake 66 20
potato server 45 75
potato top 68 41
potato tuber 68 40
potential transformer 153 59
pot-helm 254 7
pot-helmet 254 7
pot holder 39 18
pot holder rack 39 19
pot plant 39 37; 44 25; 55 25
potsherd 161 21
potter's wheel 161 11
pottery 308 66
pottery, chip-carved ~ 328 35
pottery stand 308 64-66
potting bench 55 12
potting table 55 12
potty 28 47
pouch, gular ~ 359 8
poulaine 355 42
poulard 98 7; 99 58
poultry 73 19-36
poultry farming 74 1-27
poultry keeping 74
poultry management, intensive ~ 74 1-27
pounce bag 129 49
pouncing 129 48
pound, lower ~ 217 29
pound, upper ~ 217 37
pound lock gate 217 31
pound sterling 252 37
pouring end 147 34
pouring floor, sinking ~ 148 24
pouring ladle lip 147 43
powder, black ~ 87 53
powder, smokeless ~ 87 53
powder box 43 28; 49 35
powder charge 87 57
powder flag 253 38
powder tin 99 29
power 345 1
powerboat racing 286 21-44
powerboats 286 1-5
power control 100 22
power hacksaw 138 23
power hammer 137 9
power house Hydr. Eng. 217 21

power house *Shipbuild.* 222 33
power house *Films* 310 8
power lift 65 24-29
power line 127 23
powerpack unit 114 66
power plant *Coal* 144 13
power plant *Power Plant* 152; 153
power plant *Glass Prod.* 162
power regulator 100 22
power saw *Forestry* 84 22, 27; 85 13
power saw *Blacksm.* 138 23
power screwdriver 195 23
power shovel 200 1
power source 110 7
power station *Coal* 144 13
power station *Offshore Drill.* 146 1
power station *Power Plant* 152; 153
power station *Glass Prod.* 162
power station *Hydr. Eng.* 217 64
power supply *Arc Weld.* 142 25
power supply *Energy Sources* 155 21
power supply, external 115 79
power take-off 63 21; 64 49
power take-off clutch 65 40
power take-off gear 65 38
power take-off gear-change 65 23, 40
power take-off shaft 63 21; 64 49
power transformer 152 30, 39
power unit 84 34
power zooming arrangement 117 19
prairie horse 352 4
pralltriller 321 19
pram *Infant Care etc.* 28 34
pram *Docks* 226 57
pram *Park* 272 71
pram *Playground* 273 31
pram, wicker ~ 28 30; 48 24
pram jacket 29 3
pram suit 29 1
prayer book 330 62
prayer tower 337 13
prayer wheel 353 29
preacher 330 22
precession 4 24
precipitation 8 18
precipitation, scattered ~ 8 19
precipitation, types of ~ 8 18-19
precipitation area 9 30
precipitation gauge 10 44
precipitator, electrostatic ~ *Power Plant* 152 13
precipitator, electrostatic ~ *Coking* 156 20
precipitator, electrostatic ~ *Cement Wks.* 160 7
precipitator, electrostatic ~ *Paperm.* 172 39
precision balance 108 35
precision bench lathe 109 20
precision file 140 8
precision lathe 138 20
predator, small ~ 86 19, 20, 22
pre-distributor channel 236 36
pre-drying 165 50
preheater 212 41
preheater, high-pressure ~ 152 26
preheater, low-pressure ~ 152 25
preheater pressure gauge 210 43

preheater unit 185 30
prehistory 328
prelims 185 43-47
pre-listening button 238 46
pre-listening speaker 238 50
premasher 92 42
premixer 97 58
pre-mixing room 238 54-59
premolar 19 18
préparation 314 23
preparation and sterilization room 26 34-54
preparation level 64 16
preparation of surfaces 128 1-17
preparation room 26 34-54
prepuce 20 70
presbytery 330 32
prescription 22 3, 20
present-day man 261 21
preserve 98 51
preserving jar 40 25
preset control 316 2
presorter 172 21
presorting 64 82
press *Joiner* 133 51
press *Ball Games* 293 32
press, first ~ 173 19
press, rotary ~ *Text. Finish.* 168 38
press, rotary ~ *Letterpress* 181 57
press, second ~ 173 20
press, web-fed ~ 181 57
press-and-blow process 162 30
press attachment 100 15
press bar 100 17
press bed 180 78; 181 17
press bowl, heated ~ 168 41
press camera 114 36
presser 103 19
'press facilities' 233 43
press finishing 168 38
pressing *Glass Prod.* 162 33
pressing *Paperm.* 173 50
pressing cloth 104 32
pressing cushion 104 28
pressing mechanism 184 13
pressing pad 104 28
pressman 340 35
press mould 162 34
press photo 342 58
press photographer 299 49
press roll 173 37
press roller 64 64
pressure, atmospheric ~ 9 4
pressure, barometric ~ 9 4
pressure adjustment 249 53
pressure adjustment, calibrated ~ 185 5
pressure bulkhead 231 32
pressure bulkhead, forward ~ 235 19
pressure chamber 83 44
pressure cloth 116 59
pressure cooker *Kitch. Utensils* 40 21
pressure cooker *Camping* 278 35
pressure cylinder 133 46
pressure foot 133 47
pressure fuelling point 257 33
pressure gas 156 28
pressure gauge *Hosp.* 25 53; 26 29
pressure gauge *Overh. Irrign.* 67 10
pressure gauge *Pest Contr.* 83 42
pressure gauge *Blacksm.* 138 15

pressure gauge *Electrotyp. etc.* 178 8
pressure gauge *Offset Print.* 180 74
pressure gauge *Garage* 195 29
pressure gauge *Serv. Stat.* 196 20
pressure gauge *Railw.* 211 24
pressure gauge *Theatre* 316 56
pressure graph 27 31
pressure hull 258 66; 259 55, 76
pressure indicator 25 55
pressure line 235 54, 57
pressure pipe *Market Gdn.* 55 8
pressure pipe *Hydr. Eng.* 217 50
pressure pipe *Theatre* 316 54
pressure pipeline 217 41
pressure piston 133 52
pressure plate 115 24
pressure point 21 14
pressure pot 129 31
pressure pump, hydraulic ~ 178 11
pressure-reducing valve 141 5
pressure regulator *Gas Weld.* 141 5
pressure regulator *Graphic Art* 340 38
pressure release valve 155 7
pressure tank 316 55
pressure trace 25 57
pressure transducer 27 32
pressure valve 40 22
pressure weight 168 2
pressurized gas delivery system 234 60
pressurized-water reactor 154 19
pressurized-water system 154 40
presto 321 28
pretzel *Bakery* 97 44
pretzel *Supermkt.* 99 16
preventer 270 15
preview monitor 238 60
price 289 37
price card 271 19
price display 196 6
price label 96 6
price list *Butch.* 96 19
price list *Grocer* 98 73
price list *Bank* 250 8
price offered 289 37
pricket 330 52
pricking off 54 5
pricking out 54 5
priest 330 39; 331 47
prima ballerina 314 27
primary 153 15
primary school 260 1-85
primary voltage bushing 152 43
primary voltage terminal 152 43
primates 368 12-16
prime focus cage 5 2
Prime meridian 14 5
primer 128 6
prime steam line 154 31
priming brush 338 9
primitive man 261 19
princess, German ~ 355 20
principal 345 7
principal diapason 326 31-33
print delivery 249 43
print drier, heated ~ 116 57
print drier, rapid ~ 116 57
printer *Garage* 195 6
printer *Office* 245 32

printer, rotating ~ 111 27
printery 340 27-64
printing, rotary ~ 178 21
printing cylinder 177 67
printing-down frame 179 13
printing element 178 39
printing image carrier 340 59
printing office 340 27-64
printing paper 180 47
printing paper, photographic ~ 116 51
printing plate 178 38
printing speed adjustment 249 55
printing surface 340 59
printing unit 180 41, 80
printing unit, first ~ 181 48
printing unit, lower ~ 180 7, 9, 11, 13
printing unit, reversible ~ 182 26
printing unit, second ~ 181 52
printing unit, upper ~ 180 6, 8, 10, 12
print-out machine 195 6
print quantity selection 249 35
print tongs 116 47
'Prinz Heinrich' cap 35 28
prism, hexagonal ~ 351 21
prism, monoclinic ~ 351 24
prism, quadratic ~ 347 34
prism, triangular ~ 347 37
private detective 275 16
privet 373 6
privet hawkmoth 358 55
prize 306 11; 308 48
probe *Dent.* 24 46
probe *Photog.* 114 63; 116 55
probe, bulb-headed ~ 22 53; 26 40
probe, hollow ~ 26 41
probe, olive-pointed ~ 22 53; 26 40
probe exposure meter 114 61
probe lead 116 38
proboscidean 366 20
proboscidian 366 20
proboscis *Articulates* 358 17, 56
proboscis *Mammals* 366 21
procaviid 366 24
process and reproduction camera, universal ~ 177 24
process camera, overhead ~ 177 1
process camera, vertical ~ 177 32
process control computer 236 37
processing drum 116 48
processing laboratory 310 2; 311 30
processing machine 179 31
processing plant 144 5
processing unit, central ~ 176 29
procession, religious ~ 331 42-50
processionary moth 82 14
processor, automatic ~ 116 60
processor, central ~ 244 6
proclamation 263 14
proctoscope 23 17, 19, 21
proctoscopy 23 18
Procyon 3 15
produce, agricultural ~ 68 1-47
producer 316 40
product 344 25
production control room 238 17
production line 173 13-28

production manager 310 26
production oil and gas
  separator 146 9
product register 309 82
profile 118 69
profile, basic ~ 229 45
profiling tool 161 14
profit 345 7
program *see* programme
program card 195 5, 10
program input 177 71
programme 315 13
programme, computer-
  controlled ~ 238 2
programme, educational ~
  261 7
programme dial 243 40
programmed individual
  presentation system 242 15
programme monitor 238 61
programmer 248 15
programme recorder 261 42
programme scale 243 40
programme selector 243 39
program selector control 50
  26
program selector switch 25 50
progress counter 242 5
projectile 255 26
projection *Films* 311 45
projection *Art* 335 43
projection, conical ~ 14 8
projection, cylindrical ~ 14 9
projection booth 5 27; 312 12
projection dome 5 21
projectionist 312 20
projection lamp 312 18
projection lens 261 10; 312 35
projection room 312 12
projection room window 312
  15
projection screen *Optic. Instr.*
  112 24
projection screen *Broadcast.*
  238 32
projection screen *School* 260
  36
projection screen *Films* 310
  16; 312 11
projection table 261 13
projection window 312 15
projector 5 23; 316 17
projector, lefthand ~ 312 13
projector, overhead ~ 242 6
projector, righthand ~ 312 14
projector attachment 112 55
projector gate 312 34
projector lens 312 35
projector mechanism 312
  25-38
projector switch 195 20
projector top 261 9
promenade 223 27
promenade deck 223 22-27
prominence, laryngeal ~ 19
  13
prominence, solar ~ 4 40
prompt book 316 41
prompt box 316 27
prompter 316 28
prompt script 316 41
prone position *Free Exerc.*
  295 45
prone position *Sports* 305 29
prong *Tablew. etc.* 45 60
prong *Agr. Impl.* 66 4
proof 340 43
proofing press 180 75
proof press 180 75
prop *Household* 50 37
prop *Circus* 307 13
prop *Theatre* 315 50
prop, front ~ 303 8

prop, rear ~ 303 9
propagation 54 10, 14, 27
propagation of plants 54
propane gas 278 33
propane gas container 278 34
propeller *Brew.* 92 46
propeller *Energy Sources* 155
  45
propeller *Life-Sav.* 228 26
propeller *Aircraft* 230 32
propeller *Motorboats etc.* 286
  64
propeller *Airsports* 288 36
propeller, feathering ~ 224 19
propeller, reversible ~ 224 19
propeller, ship's ~ 221 44; 222
  72; 223 62
propeller, three-blade ~ 223
  62
propeller, variable-pitch ~
  224 19
propeller bracket 223 61
propeller guard 258 40
propeller guard boss 258 63
propeller guard moulding 258
  74
propeller mixer 79 6
propeller pitch indicator 224
  20
propeller post 222 71
propeller pump 217 47-52
propeller shaft *Car* 192 30, 65
propeller shaft *Ship* 223 65
propeller shaft *Aircraft* 232
  60
propeller shaft *Warships* 259
  59
propeller strut 223 61
propeller-turbine engine 256
  16
propeller-turbine plane 231 4
propelling nozzle 232 39, 45,
  49, 55
property 315 50
proportion, simple ~ 345 8-10
proportional dividers 339 2
proprietor 248 29; 266 71
prop stand 187 34; 188 51
propulsion nozzle 232 39, 45,
  49, 55
propylaea 334 7
propylaeum 334 7
propylon 334 7
proscenium 315 15; 334 46
proscenium, adjustable ~ 316
  22
prostate 20 76
protection device 255 81, 90
prothorax 82 4; 358 29
proton 1 2, 16, 31
protoplasm 357 3
protoprism 351 19, 20
protopyramid 351 19, 20
prototype 290 38
protozoans 357 1-12
protractor 260 38
protrusion, massive ~ 11 29
protuberance, frontal ~ 16 4
prow, rounded ~ 218 25
pruner 56 11
pruning knife 56 9
pruning saw 56 16
pruning shears 56 50
prussic acid 83 15
pseudocarp 58 21; 384 12, 62
pseudopod 357 4
psychrometer 10 52
pubis 17 20
public conveniences 268 62
publicity calendar 22 10
puck 302 35
pudding fender 227 17
pudenda 16 39

puffball 381 19
puff paste 97 18
puff pastry 97 18
pug 70 9; 123 69
pug dog 70 9
pull 340 43
pull-down table 207 53
pullet 74 9
pullet fold unit 74 5
pulley *Cotton Spin.* 164 48
pulley *Bicycle* 187 9
pulley, glass ~ 169 16
pulley cradle 214 36, 53
pulley cradle, main ~ 214 67
pullover, heavy ~ 33 52
pullover, men's ~ 33 51
pullover, short-sleeved ~ 33
  32
pull rod *Mach. Parts etc.* 143
  101
pull rod *Railw.* 202 20
pull-switch 127 16
pull-through 87 64
pull-up phase 298 29
pulmonary function test 27 36
pulp 58 24, 35, 58; 59 6
pulp, chemical ~ 172 77, 78
pulp, dental ~ 19 32
pulp, mechanical ~ 172 77, 78
pulp-drying machine 172 61
pulper 172 80
pulpit 330 19; 337 15
pulpit balustrade 330 23
pulpit steps 330 18
pulp machine 172 61
pulpstone 172 71
pulp water pump 172 55, 63
pulsator 75 32
pulse cable 117 72
pulse-generating camera 117
  71
pulse generator 313 30
pulse generator socket 117 7
pulse rate 23 27
pulse shape 23 37
pump *Agr. Mach.* 65 45
pump *Shoes* 101 29
pump *Oil, Petr.* 145 22
pump *Synth. Fibres* 170 31
pump, centrifugal ~ *Wine
  Cell.* 79 7
pump, centrifugal ~ *Rivers*
  216 60
pump, centrifugal ~ *Water*
  269 44
pump, centrifugal ~ *Fire Brig.*
  270 8
pump, direct-connected ~ 83
  41
pump, hydraulic ~ *Agr.
  Mach.* 64 29, 91
pump, hydraulic ~ *Theatre*
  316 53
pump, main ~ 269 15
pump, motor-driven ~ 83 41
pump, portable ~ 270 52
pump, power take-off-driven
  ~ 67 14, 15
pump compass 151 59
pump compression spring 174
  41
pump connection 67 8
pumpernickel 97 49
pumping plant 217 39-46
pumping rod 145 25
pumping station *Offshore
  Drill.* 146 22
pumping station *Hydr. Eng.*
  217 43
pumping station *Shipbuild.*
  222 33
pumping station *Spa* 274 4
pumping unit 145 22

pumpkin 57 23
pump pressure spring 174 41
pump room *Brew.* 92 11
pump room *Spa* 274 8, 15
pumps 2 52
pump shaft 199 19
pump strainer 269 6, 14, 43
punch *Shoem.* 100 45, 46
punch *Goldsm. etc.* 108 19,
  30, 31
punch *Office* 247 3
punch *Sculpt. Studio* 339 15
punch, foul ~ 299 34
punch, hollow ~ 125 13
punch, illegal ~ 299 34
punch, revolving ~ 100 44
punch, rotary ~ 100 44
punch, round ~ 137 36; 140
  65
punch, steel ~ 175 36
punch, straight ~ 299 28
punch bag 299 21
punch ball 299 24
punch ball, spring-supported
  ~ 299 20
punch ball, suspended ~ 299
  23
punch blank 175 35
punch card 237 64
punch card reader 244 12
punch cutter 175 32
punched card 237 64
punched card reader 244 12
punched tape 176 6, 8, 12;
  237 62, 68
punched tape input 176 30
punched tape reader 176 13,
  15
punching bag 299 21
punch tape 176 6, 8, 12; 237
  62, 68
punch tape input 176 30
punch tape reader 176 13, 15
punctuation marks 342 16-29
punt 216 15; 283 1
punt pole 89 30; 216 16
pup 73 16
pupa 77 30, 32; 80 4, 25, 43;
  81 21, 24; 82 13, 21, 32; 358
  20; 365 11
pupa, coarctate ~ 81 3
pupil *Man* 19 43
pupil *School* 260 3
puppy 73 16
pure culture plant 93 6
purfling 323 26
purge valve 6 25
purified water tank 269 13
purlin 119 55; 121 39, 51, 76
purlin, concrete ~ 119 4
purlin, inferior ~ 119 3; 121
  44; 122 40
purlin roof 121 46
purlin roof structure 121 52,
  60
purple clover 69 1
purple medick 69 9
purse wig 34 4
push button 203 67; 237 18,
  19; 241 3
push-button keyboard 237
  10; 245 14; 246 14
push-button telephone 237
  20
pushchair 28 37
pushchair, doll's ~ 48 31
pusher ram 156 7
pushing frame 200 30
push sledge 304 29
push tow 225 60
push tug 221 93
putlock 118 27
putlog 118 27

putter 293 93
putting 293 86
putting green 293 82
putty 124 17
putty knife 124 27; 129 24
puzzle 48 9
pyelogram 27 6
pyelogram cassettes 27 14
pyelography 27 4
pygmy poodle 70 36
pyjamas 32 17, 36
pyjama top 32 18
pyjama trousers 32 19
pylon Railw. 214 31, 77
pylon Art 333 9
pylon, tubular steel ~ 214 78
pylorus 20 42
pyramid Fruit & Veg. Gdn. 52
16
pyramid Circus 307 28
pyramid Art 333 1
pyramid, glass ~ 5 19
pyramid, orthorhombic ~ 351
23
pyramid, quadrilateral ~ 347
46
pyramid, stepped ~ 333 22;
352 20
pyramid site 333 6
pyramid tree 52 16; 272 19
pyrheliometer 10 23
pyrite 351 8
pyrometer 178 16
pyx 330 8; 332 53
pyxidium 370 95

Q

quack grass 61 30
quadrant 347 5
quadraphonic system 241
13-48
quadra/stereo converter 241
46
quadrilateral, irregular ~ 346
39
quadrilaterals 346 33-39
quadruplet 321 23
quail 359 22
quail call 87 45
quake, tectonic ~ 11 32-38
quake, volcanic ~ 11 32-38
quantity, unknown ~ 345 4, 8
quant pole 89 30; 216 16
quantum jump 1 15
quantum jumps 1 20-25
quantum transitions 1 20-25
quarantine wing 225 27
quarrier 158 5
quarry Map 15 87
quarry Quarry 158 1
quarryman 158 5
quarry worker 158 5
quarte engagement 294 47
quarter Shoem. 100 61
quarter Carp. 120 25
quarter, first ~ 4 4
quarter, last ~ 4 6
quarter, third ~ 4 6
quarter baulk 120 90
quarter gallery 218 57
quarterings 254 18-23
quartering wind 285 13
quarter light 191 23
quarter note 320 15
quarter of beef 94 22
quarter piece 329 88
quarter rest 320 23
quarters, firemen's ~ 270 2
quarter vent 191 23
quarter wind 285 13
quartz 110 15

quartz-halogen lamp 179 21;
182 3
quartz watch, electronic ~ 110
14
quatrefoil 335 39
quaver 320 16
quaver rest 320 24
quay 222 5; 225 64
quayside crane 225 24
quayside railway 225 21
quayside road 225 38
quayside roadway 225 38
quayside steps 283 22
quay wall 217 1-14
queen Bees 77 4, 38
queen Games 276 9
queen bee 77 4
Queen Carnival 306 61
queen cell 77 37
queen-excluder 77 47
queen post 121 46, 52, 68
queen truss 121 65
Queen Victoria water lily 378
17
quenching car 156 10
quenching tower 156 11
quenching trough 137 8
question mark 342 20
queue 34 6; 319 26
quickbeam 371 42
quick grass 61 30
quick hitch 65 86
quicksand 227 3
quid 107 19
quill 341 26
quillons 294 42
quill pen 341 26
quill plectrum 322 53
quilting 29 39; 30 17
quilt stitching 29 39; 30 17
quince, apple-shaped ~ 58 49
quince, pear-shaped ~ 58 50
quince leaf 58 47
quince tree 58 46
quinquefoliolate 370 39
quintuplet 321 23
quipa 352 22
quitch grass 61 30
quiver 352 27
quoin 181 39
quoit 280 32; 308 47
quoits 280 31
quotation 250 8
quotation board 251 8
quotation mark, double ~ 342
26
quotation mark, French ~ 342
27
quotient 344 26

R

rabbet plane 132 25
rabbit 73 18; 86 23; 88 65
rabbit burrow 86 26
rabbit fence 84 7
rabbit hole 86 26
rabbit net 86 27
raccoon 368 9
race, inner ~ 143 72
race, outer ~ 143 71
race board 166 42
racehorse 289 51
raceme 58 15; 374 33
raceme, simple ~ 370 68
raceway 91 44
racical sign 345 2
racing 289 50
racing, motor-paced ~ 290
11-15
racing and passenger aircraft
230 1-31, 32-66; 231 1

racing bicycle 290 16
racing boats 283 9-16
racing car 290 36, 38
racing cars 290 34-38
racing cycle 290 15, 16
racing cyclist 290 8
racing dive 282 29
racing flag 284 48
racing handlebar 290 18
racing jersey 290 9
racing keelboat 285 35
racing motorcycle 290 27
racing motorcycle,
streamlined ~ 290 31
racing motorcyclist 290 25
racing outboard motor 286 23
racing saddle 290 17
racing sculler 283 16
racing shell, eight-oared ~
283 10
racing suit 301 31
racing toe clip 290 21
racing tyre 290 19
rack Kitch. Utensils 40 31
rack Composing Rm. 174 8
rack Garage 195 10
rack Railw. 214 9, 10
rack, removable ~ 40 24
rack and pinion 112 39
rack-and-pinion railway 214
4-5
rack-and-pinion railways
214 7-11
racket 293 29
racket handle 293 30, 46
racket press 293 32
rack for glasses 274 16
rack head 163 16, 18
racking disc 118 61
rack mountain railway 214
4-5
rack railroad 214 4-5
rack railroad car 214 5
rack railroad locomotive,
electric ~ 214 4
rack railway coach 214 5
rack railway locomotive,
electric ~ 214 4
rack railways 214 7-11
rack railway trailer 214 5
rack track 217 69
racoon 368 9
racquet see racket
radar antenna 223 8; 224 104;
258 36; 259 8, 29, 48, 91
radar apparatus 224 10-13
radar display unit 224 12
radar dome Aircraft 231 18
radar dome Air Force 256 10
radar dome Warships 258 52,
77; 259 49
radar equipment 224 10-13
radar image 224 13
radar nose 231 18; 256 10
radar pedestal 224 10
radar picture 224 13
radar reflector 10 58
radar reflector, revolving ~
224 11
radar scanner 223 8; 224 104;
258 36; 259 8, 29, 48, 91
radar screen 224 12
radial side of the hand 19 69
radiant energy 10 23
radiation, solar ~ 155 18
radiation detectors 2 1-23
radiation meters 2 1-23
radiation monitor 2 1
radiation shield 2 31, 46
radiation shielding 2 31
radiation unit 24 23
radiator Doc. 23 23
radiator Roof & Boilerr. 38 76

radiator Agr. Mach. 65 51
radiator Plumb. etc. 126 20
radiator Energy Sources 155
15
radiator Car 191 9
radiator Railw. 212 54
radiator bonnet 304 11
radiator brush 129 21
radiator grill 191 11
radiator heating 155 27
radiator hood 304 11
radiator rib 38 77; 126 21
radiators 6 8
radiator shutter 304 12
radical 345 2
radicle 370 88
radio 238; 239
radioactive waste storage 154
56
radio antenna 197 34
radio cassette recorder 241 1
radio communication set 197
28
radio compass 230 5
radio direction finder
antenna 223 5; 224 106
radio direction finder frame
258 17
radio equipment 197 28; 230
22; 288 13, 17
radiographer 27 11
radio interference service 237
27
radiolarian 357 8
radio link, intercontinental ~
237 54-55
radiometer 10 71
radio navigation equipment
230 22
radio OB van 239 1-15
radiophone 22 14
radio room 223 12
radioscope box 74 47
radioscope table 74 43
radiosonde 10 59
radiosonde assembly 10 55
radio station 238 1-6
radio switching centre
control room 238 7-15
radio system 6 26
radio telephone 212 23
radish 57 15
radish, white ~ 57 16
radius Man 17 13
radius Mills 91 2
radius Maths. 346 47
radius of curvature 346 22
radome Aircraft 231 18
radome Air Force 256 10
radome Warships 258 52, 77;
259 49
raffia 136 29
raffle 306 11
raft 283 60
rafter 121 28, 36; 122 19
rafter, common ~ 121 56
rafter, principal ~ 121 55
rafter end 121 45; 122 41
rafter head 121 45; 122 41
rafter roof 121 27
rag bolt 143 43
rag felt 122 62
ragged robin 376 21
rail Atom 2 37
rail Livestock 75 16
rail Joiner 133 41
rail Mach. Tools 150 12
rail Railw. 202 1
rail Station 205 59; 206 38
rail Railw. 214 10
rail Restaurant 266 72
rail Equest. 289 2
rail Birds 359 20

rail, triangular ~ 242 80
rail bottom 202 4
rail brake 206 48
railcar 205 25
railcar, articulated ~ 197 1, 13
railcar, front ~ 211 61
railcar, light ~ 208 13
railcar, short-distance ~ 208 13
railcar, six-axle ~ 197 13
railcar, twelve-axle ~ 197 1
rail clip 202 9
rail foot 202 4
rail guard 210 34
rail head 202 2
railing Bldg. Site 118 89
railing Park 272 34
rail joint 202 11
railroad see railway
railroad map 204 33
railroad policeman 205 20
railroad station 15 41
railroad ticket 204 36
railroad track 202; 203
rail service, interurban ~ 197 1
rail service, urban ~ 197 13
railway, funicular ~ 214 12
railway, light ~ 200 23
railway, main line ~ 15 21
railway, narrow-gauge ~ Map 15 90
railway, narrow-gauge ~ Road Constr. 200 23
railway guide, official ~ 204 50
railway information clerk 204 49
railway line 202; 203
railway map 204 33
railway policeman 205 20
railway siding 225 62
railway station 15 41
railway ticket 204 36
railway vehicles 207; 208; 209; 210; 211; 212; 213
rail web 202 3
rain 8 18; 9 32
rainbow 7 4
rainbow, colours of the ~ 343 14
rainbow dressing 221 85
rain cape 41 4; 196 26
rain cloud 8 10
raincoat 29 31
rain cover 10 41
rain gauge 10 38, 44
rainwater pipe 37 13; 38 10; 122 29
rain zone, temperate ~ 9 55
rain zone, tropical ~ 9 53
raisin 98 8
raising of livestock 75
raising to a power 345 1
rake Roof & Boilerr. 38 42
rake Gdn. Tools 56 4
rake Blacksm. 137 4
rake Roulette 275 5
rake Winter Sp. 303 24
rake, wire-tooth ~ 51 3; 56 3
rake, wooden ~ 66 23
raking back 118 61
Ram Astron. 4 53
ram Dom. Anim. 73 13
ram Blacksm. 137 10
ram Forging 139 12
ram Ship 218 9
ram Theatre 316 60
ram, lower ~ 139 7
ram, upper ~ 139 6
rambler 52 5
ram guide 139 8
ram longwall face 144 36

rammer 200 26
rammer, pneumatic ~ 148 31
ramp Bldg. Site 119 41
ramp Floor etc. Constr. 123 30
ramp Station 206 1
ramp Ship 221 55
ram piston 65 24
ramson 377 6
randing 136 1, 4
randing, oblique ~ 136 3
rangefinder 255 82
rangefinder, optical ~ 258 37
rangefinder window 114 40
range light, higher ~ 224 102
range light, lower ~ 224 101
range lights 224 101-102
range selector 114 59
range switch 114 59
rape 383 1
rapelling 300 28-30
rapid adjustment compass 151 64
rapid feeding system 74 23
rapid-filter plant 269 9
rapid heat-up cathode 240 25
rapid-loading system 115 25
rapid scale 98 12
rapid-veneer press 133 49
rapping iron 136 36
raptorial leg 358 5
Raschel fabric 167 29
rasp 260 55
rasp, shoemaker's ~ 100 49
raspberry 58 28; 370 101
raspberry bush 58 25
raspberry flower 58 26
ratan chair cane 136 32
rate-of-climb indicator 230 14
rate of interest 345 7
rattan chair cane 136 32
rattle Infant Care etc. 28 44
rattle Carnival 306 40, 47
rattle, baby's ~ 28 44
rat trap binding 301 15
Rautek grip 21 18
ravine 13 52
raw coal bunker 144 41
raw material Cement Wks. 160 1, 4
raw material Synth. Fibres 169 1-12
raw material store 160 3
raw meal silo 160 5
raw milk pump 76 3
raw milk storage tank 76 5
raw mill 160 4, 7
ray Church 332 37
ray Maths. 346 20
ray, medullary ~ 370 11
ray, vascular ~ 370 11
ray floret 375 31
rays, sun's ~ 4 9
razor, open ~ 106 38
razor, straight ~ 106 38
razor handle 106 39
R-class 284 59
reach, lower ~ 217 29
reach, upper ~ 217 37
reaching leg 285 24
reactor 154 3, 41, 50
reactor, nuclear ~ 1 48; 154 19
reactor building 154 20
reactor core 259 68
reactor pressure vessel 154 22
reader 260 16
reading adjustment 10 10
reading lamp 43 15
reading microscope 113 28
reading room 262 13
reading room staff 262 14
readout, digital ~ 110 2; 112 47

readout, fast ~ 195 12
ready position 305 72
reamer 109 8; 140 31
reamer, angled ~ 125 9
rear brace 329 47
rearing of livestock 75
rear of the railcar 197 4
rear seat headrest 193 8
rear seat head restraint 193 8
rearsight 255 22, 36
rear vault 297 32
rear-view mirror 188 35; 189 30
rear-view mirror, inside ~ 191 39
rearward horizontal stand 295 31
rearward swing 296 57
rear window heating switch 191 82
rebate plane 132 25
receipt 98 44; 271 7
receipt stamp 236 29
receiver Meteorol. Instr. 10 63
receiver Hunt. 87 16
receiver Docks 226 33
receiver Audio 241 40
receiver Office 246 16
receiver Ball Games 293 50
receiver Nightclub 318 18
receiver, tilting-type ~ 148 5
receiver cord 237 14
receiver surface, blackened ~ 155 29
receiving hopper 147 5
receiving table 249 54
receiving tray 249 47
receiving truck 226 15
receptacle 370 53
reception Doc. 22 5
reception Camping 278 1
reception hall 267 1-26
receptionist, chief ~ 267 7
recess 217 70
reciprocal 344 16
recirculation pump 154 43, 54
record 46 15; 309 32; 317 24
record chamber, automatic ~ 241 18
record changer, automatic ~ 241 52
recorder Meteorol. Instr. 10 61
recorder Hosp. 25 3
recorder Music. Instr. 322 7
recorder, eight-channel ~ 27 28
recorder, open-reel-type ~ 241 56
recorder, potentiometric ~ 23 55
recording, photographic ~ 27 33
recording amplifier 311 11
recording and playback deck, single ~ 238 58
recording and playback equipment 311 23
recording arm 10 7, 12, 15, 21
recording channel, central ~ 238 1-6
recording drum 10 5, 16, 20
recording engineer 310 23, 55; 311 36
recording head Cine Film 117 33
recording head Audio 241 59
recording head Films 311 25
recording instrument 10 61
recording level control 117 16
recording level display 243 15
recording level indicator 243 12; 311 14

recording level meter 241 35, 36, 61; 242 14
recording level meters 241 35-36
recording loudspeaker 238 37
recording mechanism 10 42
recording meter 138 19
recording paper 25 4; 27 29, 34, 40
recording pen 10 13
recording rain gauge 10 38
recording room 238 16; 310 54
recording room mixing console 238 25
recording sensitivity selector 117 16
recording space 177 49
recording speaker 238 37
recording tape 241 58
record keeper 299 48
record of posting book 236 18
record player 241 18; 317 19
record player base 241 19
record player housing 241 19
record rack 309 36
record storage compartment 241 48
record storage slot 241 48
record turntable 238 24
recovery parachute 235 60
recovery vehicle, armoured ~ 255 93
rectangle 346 34
rectifier Blacksm. 138 30
rectifier Electrotyp. etc. 178 2
rectifier Films 312 18
rector 330 22
rectory 331 20
rectoscope 23 16, 17
rectoscopy 23 18
rectum 20 22, 61
rectus abdominis 18 44
red 343 1
red admiral 365 1
red-billed toucan 363 6
redbreast 361 15
redcap 205 31
red card 291 63
red clover 69 1
red deer 88 1, 1-27
red flyer 366 3
red fox 88 42; 367 12
red kangaroo 366 3
red magnolia 373 15
redstart 360 3
red swing filter 116 46
reducing coupler 126 39, 41
reducing elbow 126 49
reducing socket 126 39, 41
reducing valve 141 5
reduction drive lever 149 3
reduction gear Paperm. 172 69
reduction gear Aircraft 232 59
reduction gear Warships 259 61
reduction gearing, multi-step ~ 64 71
red underwing 365 8
red whortleberry 377 23
red wine glass 45 83
reed Basketm. 136 28
reed Weaving 166 10
reed Music. Instr. 326 41
reed, double ~ 323 29
reed mace 136 27
reed mace bulrush 378 21
reed organ 325 43
reed pen 341 22
reed pipe, metal ~ 326 17-22
reed stop 326 17-22

reed-threading draft 171 6
reef 219 72
reefer 221 127
reel, fixed-spool ~ 89 32, 61
reel, multiplying ~ 89 59
reel, spring-tine ~ 64 4
reel, stationary-drum ~ 89 61
reel arm, foldaway ~ 117 92
reel drum 312 16
reel drum, fireproof ~ 312 25
reel gearing 64 5
reeling machine 173 41
reel of film 312 33
reel oven 97 71
reels 89 59-64
reel stand 180 3, 19
referee 291 62; 293 67; 299
  16, 41
referee's position 299 8
reference book 262 17
reference library 262 17
refill 151 46
refill lead 151 46
refiner 172 84
refiner, conical ~ 172 27, 60,
  73, 83
refining bath 162 4
reflected-light microscope
  112 23
reflecting goniometer 351 28
reflector Atom 1 65
reflector Optic. Instr. 113 1
reflector Bicycle 187 45
reflector, glass ~ 187 86
reflector, swivel-mounted ~
  114 69
reflector pedal 187 78
reflex angle 346 10,11-12
reflex camera, twin-lens ~
  114 22
reflex finder 117 44
reflex mirror 115 33
reflex system 115 31
reformer 145 47
reformer, catalytic ~ 145 71
refractometer 111 44
refractometer, dipping ~ 112
  48
refractor 113 16
refreshment kiosk 205 49
refreshment stall 308 3
refrigeration system 93 11
refrigerator 39 2; 46 33; 317
  10
refrigerator car 213 39
refrigerator shelf 39 3
refrigerator van 213 39
refrigerator wagon 213 39
refuse 199 17
refuse, compacted and
  decomposed ~ 199 22
refuse collection vehicle 199 1
refuse container 199 4
refuse disposal 199
refuse incineration unit 199
  28
regatta 283 1-18
regatta course 285 14-24, 16
register School 260 23
register Hotel 267 8
register Music. Instr. 322 51
register device 177 12
register mark 340 58
registration form 267 12
registration number Election
  263 19
registration number
  Motorboats etc. 286 7
registration number Script
  342 43
reglet 334 57
regula 334 17
regular crystal system 351 1-17

regular customer 266 39, 40
regular grade gasoline 145 54
regular grade petrol 145 54
regulating handle 133 14
regulating valve 38 75
regulator 109 32
regulator main valve 210 13
regulator valve 210 13
Regulidae 361 10
rehearsal 315 21-27
reheating 162 27, 35
reichstaler 252 6
rein 71 33; 186 31; 289 27;
  303 4
reindeer 353 16
reindeer harness 353 15
reinforced concrete
  construction 119 1-89
reinforcement 119 54-76, 68
reinforcement, projecting ~
  119 10, 71
reinforcement, steel-bar ~
  123 37
reinforcement beading 125 8
reinforcement binding 119
  66
reinforcement rod 119 23
reinforcing member,
  longitudinal ~ 230 47, 57
reinforcing rib Road Constr.
  200 9
reinforcing rib Hydr. Eng.
  217 78
reinforcing steel 119 23
reinforcing strut 315 31
reins 71 25, 33
rejects chest 172 59
relay 186 43
relay horse 186 43
release First Aid 21 34
release Weaving 165 35
release, delayed-action ~ 309
  51
release binding 301 2
release grip 21 34
release lever Slaughterho. 94
  6
release lever Office 247 42
release/lock lever 247 42
release phase 75 33
release valve 210 58
relief image carrier 340 2
relief printing method 340
  1-13
relief tile, glazed ~ 333 20
remainder 344 24
remains 15 72
Remington cartridge 305 39
remitter 250 19
remnant 103 16
remote control jack 117 9
remote control panel 157 14
remote control radio 288 87
remote control socket 117 9
rendering, exterior ~ 122 38
rendering coat 123 6
rendezvous point 233 29
rendezvous radar antenna 6
  42
reniform 370 38
rennet vat 76 48
repair bay 196 22
repairer 161 19
repair quay 222 10
repair shop 196 22
repeater 87 2
repeaters 253 30-32
repeating rifle 87 2
repeat mark 321 26
replenishing ship 258 97
report 342 54
reproducing head 241 59
reptile enclosure 356 12

reptiles 364 27-41
requin 364 1
re-recording 311 1-46
re-reeler 173 41
re-reeling machine 173 41
rescue 21 18-23, 28-33, 34-38
rescue cruiser 221 18; 228 14
rescue helicopter 221 20; 228
  16
rescuer 21 29, 34
research laboratory 310 9
research microscope 112 1, 66
research microscope,
  binocular ~ 23 51
research rocket 7 24
reserve fuel tank 212 60
reserve tank 232 20
reservoir Hydr. Eng. 217
  39-46
reservoir Air Force 257 16
reservoir, impounded ~ 217
  57
reservoir rock 12 29
reset button Cine Film 117 86
reset button Car 191 77
resetting button 127 20
resetting spring 237 49
residential area 15 28
residue 145 43
resin 323 11
resin, synthetic ~ 130 26
resistor 153 56
resonating body 322 29; 323
  3; 324 2, 15, 26
resonating chamber 322 18;
  324 15, 63
resonating sound box 324 26
resonator 322 18, 29; 324 2, 15
resonator, tubular metal ~
  324 78
resonator wall 322 33
respiration, artificial ~ 21
  24-27
respirator 21 27; 26 25
respiratory apparatus 21 27;
  26 24
respiratory functions 23 31
respiratory machine 26 1
respiratory rate 23 27
respond 335 55
'restaurant' 233 50
restaurant 266 1-29
restaurant car 207 22-32
restaurant car, self-service ~
  207 73
rest cure 274 12-14
resting rail 322 42
restoring spring 237 49
restricted area 292 37
rests 320 20-27
result register 309 82
results of sets 293 35
resuscitation 21 24-27
resuscitation, mouth-to-
  mouth ~ 21 26
resuscitation, mouth-to-nose
  ~ 21 26
resuscitation apparatus 21 27
resuscitation equipment 270
  20
resuscitator 21 27; 270 20
retailer 98 41
retail shop 98 1-87
retail store 98 1-87
retaining plate 167 56
retarder 206 48
reticella lace 102 30
reticule 115 61
Reticulum 3 48
retina 19 49
retort 349 13
retort ring 350 15
retoucher 182 14

retouching and stripping desk
  177 19
retrieving 86 36
retrofocus position 115 84
return 38 79
return pipe 38 56, 79, 80; 126
  24
return spring Knitting 167 37
return spring Car 192 55
return tap 350 49
Reuther board 296 12; 297 8
rev counter 189 41; 191 38;
  212 22; 230 8
rev counter, electric ~ 191 70
rev counter, electronic ~ 188
  40
reveal 37 26; 118 10; 120 31
revenue stamp 107 26
revers collar 30 9
reverse 252 9
reverse dive 282 41
reverse gear 192 44
reverse hang 296 34
reverse shaft 149 34
reversing catch 87 24
reversing clutch 115 27
reversing gear 210 18; 211 53;
  212 74
reversing gears 65 41
reversing ring 115 83
reversing wheel 210 56
revertive signal panel 153 7
revetment 216 51-55
revolution counter 189 41;
  191 38; 212 22; 230 8
revolution counter, electric ~
  191 70
revolution counter, electronic
  ~ 188 40
revolving die hammer 85 12
reward 86 43
rewind 114 6; 115 12
rewind bench 238 59; 312 21
rewind button 249 73
rewind cam 115 29
rewind crank 114 6; 115 12
rewinder Cine Film 117 93
rewinder Paperm. 173 41
rewind handle Photog. 114 6;
  115 12
rewind handle Cine Film 117
  93
rewinding 170 50
rewind release button 115 27
rewind station 173 41
rhesus macaque 368 12
rhesus monkey 368 12
rhinoceros 366 25
Rhiptoglossa 364 33
rhizome 58 18
rhizopod 357 1
rhomb 346 35
rhombic crystal system 351 23
rhombohedron 351 22
rhomboid 346 36
rhombus 346 35
rhubarb flan 97 22
rhynchophore 358 4
rib Meat 95 3
rib Floor etc. Constr. 123 36
rib Basketm. 136 24
rib Shipbuild. 222 58
rib Aircraft 230 46
rib Rowing 283 49
rib Sailing 285 51
rib Music. Instr. 322 33; 323 4,
  25
rib Art 335 31
rib Bot. 370 29
rib, annular ~ 235 47
rib, false ~ 287 36
rib, flat ~ 95 21
rib, fore ~ 95 18

rib, main ~ *Space* **235** 10
rib, main ~ *Gliding* **287** 35
rib, middle ~ **95** 19
rib, prime ~ **95** 18
rib, top ~ **95** 31
ribbon **34** 7; **355** 78
ribbon, corded ~ **35** 13
ribbon, fancy ~ **35** 14
ribbon cassette **249** 16
ribbon of glass **162** 10
ribbon selector **249** 11
ribbon window **37** 86
Ribes **58** 1-15
ribgrass **380** 11
rib randing **136** 2
ribs, false ~ **17** 10
ribs, true ~ **17** 9
rib vault **336** 43
rib weave, combined ~ **171** 19
ribwort **380** 11
ribwort plantain **380** 11
rice *Arable Crops* **68** 1; **68** 29
rice *Grocer* **98** 38
rice grain **68** 30
rickshaw **353** 34
rickshaw coolie **353** 35
rickstand **63** 28, 29
riddle **55** 13
ride *Map* **15** 112
ride *Forestry* **84** 1
rider *Cyc. Racing* **290** 25
rider *Chem.* **349** 33
rider bar **349** 31
rider holder **349** 32
ridge *Phys. Geog.* **12** 36; **13** 60
ridge *Dwellings* **37** 7
ridge *Roof* **121** 2; **122** 93
ridge *Mountain.* **300** 21
ridge, concave ~ **302** 22
ridge, hollow ~ **302** 22
ridge beam **121** 48
ridge board **121** 48
ridge capping piece **122** 99
ridge course **122** 47, 79
ridge course tile **122** 4
ridge cross **331** 10
ridge hook **122** 65
ridge joint **122** 79
ridge purlin **121** 43
ridge rope **221** 118
ridge tent **278** 21; **280** 45
ridge tile **122** 3, 8, 52
ridge turret **121** 14
ridge vent **55** 11
ridging hoe **56** 5
riding animal **354** 2
riding cap **289** 14
riding seat **296** 32
riding switch **289** 22
riffler **172** 2; **173** 13
rifle, self-loading ~ **255** 16
rifle, short ~ **86** 30
rifle, single-loading ~ **87** 1
rifle, triple-barrelled ~ **87** 23
rifle barrel **87** 26
rifle butt **255** 24
rifle cleaning kit **87** 61-64
rifle grip *Photog.* **115** 100
rifle grip *Films* **313** 37
riflescope **87** 29; **305** 49
rifle shooting **305** 26
rifling **87** 36
rifling calibre **87** 37
rig **219** 1-72
Rigel 3 13
rigging **219** 1-72
rigging, running ~ **219** 67-71
rigging, standing ~ **219** 10-19
right **254** 18, 20, 22
right angle **346** 9, 32
right corner pin **305** 8
right front second pin **305** 4
right hook **299** 33

right tank fuel gauge **230** 17
rim *Bicycle* **187** 28
rim *Motorcycle* **189** 25
rim *Car* **191** 16; **192** 77
rim brake **187** 5
rimfire cartridge **305** 35
rind **120** 86; **370** 8
ring *Jewell.* **36** 4
ring *Forestry* **85** 4
ring *Fish Farm.* **89** 56
ring *Cotton Spin.* **164** 51, 54
ring *Sports* **299** 35
ring *Circus* **307** 21
ring *Bullfight. etc.* **319** 9
ring *Church* **332** 17
ring *Maths.* **346** 57
ring *Chem.* **350** 15
ring, all-round ~ **89** 58
ring, annual ~ **84** 24
ring, asymmetrical ~ **36** 27
ring, diamond ~ **36** 23, 24
ring, front ~ **113** 7
ring, gemstone ~ **36** 15
ring, man's ~ **36** 20
ring, rubber ~ *Kitch. Utensils* **40** 26
ring, rubber ~ *Bathing* **280** 32
ring, spring-steel ~ **89** 51
ring and bead sight, optical ~ **305** 51
ring attendant **307** 27
ring cake **97** 33; **99** 22
ringed snake **364** 38
ring entrance **307** 11
ring fence **307** 22
ring file **260** 15
ring finger **19** 67
ring for the carrying strap **115** 9
ring frame **164** 34
ring gauge **108** 25, 27
ring gemstones **36** 72-77
ringmaster **307** 31
ring net **90** 25
ring plectrum **324** 27
ring rail **164** 42, 54
ring-rounding tool **108** 26
rings **296** 4
ring sight, optical ~ **305** 50
ring snake **364** 38
ring spindle, standard ~ **164** 45
ring spinning frame **164** 34
ring tube *Cotton Spin.* **164** 52
ring tube *Weaving* **165** 11
riot duty **264** 15
riot gear **264** 18
riot shield **264** 20
rip panel **288** 75, 83
rip panel, emergency ~ **288** 72
ripper **200** 20
ripping line **288** 76
ripping line, emergency ~ **288** 73
ripple marks **13** 41
riprap **216** 51
rise adjustment **133** 21
rise adjustment wheel **133** 22
rise and fall adjustment wheel **132** 60
riser *Floor etc. Constr.* **123** 33, 48
riser *Iron Foundry etc.* **148** 22
riser *Water* **269** 19
riser *Fire Brig.* **270** 26
riser *Airsports* **288** 42
riser *Sports* **305** 55
riser gate **148** 22
riser pipe **269** 19
rise to straddle **296** 49
rising **283** 31
Rising Sun **253** 20
ritual cart, miniature ~ **328** 36

ritual chariot, miniature ~ **328** 36
river *Phys. Geog.* **13** 61
river *Map* **15** 76
river *Rivers* **216** 31
river, navigable ~ **15** 45
river, subterranean ~ **13** 83
river arm **13** 2; **216** 3
river arm, blind ~ **216** 18
riverbank **216** 5
riverbed **13** 68
river bend **13** 11
river branch **13** 2; **216** 3
river branch, blind ~ **216** 18
river engineering **216**
river ferry **216** 10
river island **216** 4
river islet **216** 4
river mouth **13** 1
river nymph **272** 2; **327** 23
river police **217** 24
rivers **216**
river terrace **13** 49, 63
rivet **143** 57-60
rivet head **143** 57
riveting **143** 56
riveting machine **138** 27
rivet shank **143** 58
riving hammer **85** 5
rivulet *Phys. Geog.* **13** 8
rivulet *Map* **15** 80
road **37** 61
road, bituminous ~ **200** 55
road, good ~ **15** 30
road, main ~ **15** 83
road, metalled ~ **15** 30
road, poor ~ **15** 99
road, secondary ~ **15** 36
road, unmetalled ~ **15** 99
road bridge **15** 55
road building **200**; **201**
road-building machinery **200** 1-54
road coach **186** 39
road construction **200**; **201**
road form **201** 15
road layers **198** 1-5
road making **200**; **201**
road-metal spreading machine **200** 31
road over railway **15** 22
road race **290** 8-10
road race bicycle **290** 16
road racer **290** 8
road racing **290** 16, 24-28
road ripper **200** 20
road roller **200** 36
roadster *Bicycle* **187** 1
roadster *Car* **193** 26
road surface **215** 8; **217** 1
road sweeper **199** 5; **268** 20
road-sweeping lorry **199** 41
roadway, orthotropic ~ **215** 2
road wheel **255** 86
roast **45** 27
roasting chicken **98** 6
roasting drum **98** 71
roasting round **95** 11
robe de chambre **355** 66
robes **330** 22; **332** 4
robin **361** 15
robin redbreast **361** 15
robot **273** 36
rocaille **336** 13
rock **13** 25; **327** 38; **356** 2
rock, blasted ~ **158** 4
rock, coal-bearing ~ **144** 49
rock, impermeable ~ **12** 23; **13** 78
rock, impervious ~ **12** 23; **13** 78

rock, loose ~ **158** 4
rock, piece of ~ **6** 15
rock, sedimentary ~ **12** 1; **13** 48
rock, stratified ~ **13** 48
rock bit **145** 21
rock climbing **300** 2-13
rocker *Child. Rm.* **47** 16
rocker *Winter Sp.* **302** 19
rocker *Music. Instr.* **326** 39
rocker *Graphic Art* **340** 19
rocker arm **190** 33
rocker arm mounting **190** 34
rocker switch **127** 4
rockery **37** 40; **51** 6
rocket *Life-Sav.* **228** 2
rocket *Army* **255** 26, 65
rocket *Carnival* **306** 54
rocket, short-range ~ **259** 26
rocket apparatus **228** 1
rocket cruiser **259** 21, 41
rocket engine **6** 3
rocket engine, liquid-fuelled ~ **235** 36
rocket engine, main ~ **235** 36
rocket gun **228** 1
rocket launcher **255** 64, 70
rocket launcher, underwater ~ **259** 37, 51
rocket line **228** 3
rocket stage, first ~ **234** 3
rocket stage, second ~ **234** 18
rocket stage, third ~ **234** 33
rocket tube **255** 71
rock face *Phys. Geog.* **12** 43; **13** 28
rock face *Quarry* **158** 15
rock face *Mountain.* **300** 2
rock garden **37** 40; **51** 6
rock goat **367** 7
rocking chair **309** 61
rocking tool **340** 19
rock island **13** 12
rock ledge **300** 4
rock painting **328** 9
rock plant **51** 7
rock rose **377** 20
rock salt **351** 2
rockslide **11** 46
rock slip **11** 46
rock spike **300** 9
rock terrace **13** 47
rock tomb **333** 38
rock wall **300** 2
rod, carbon-fibre ~ **89** 57
rod, glass ~ **89** 49, 57
rod, iron ~ **130** 3
rod, metal ~ **339** 24
rod, polished ~ **145** 27
rod, telescopic ~ **89** 53
rodents **366** 12-19
rodeo **319** 34
rodeo rider **319** 39
rod rest **89** 23
rods **89** 49-58
rod section **89** 54
rod tip **89** 35
roe *Game* **88** 28-39
roe *Fish Farm.* **89** 12
roe, female ~ **88** 34
roebuck **86** 17; **88** 28
roe call **87** 43
roe deer **88** 28-39
roll *Kitch. Utensils* **40** 31
roll *Tablew. etc.* **45** 21
roll *Horse* **71** 48
roll *Bakery* **97** 13
roll *Supermkt.* **99** 12
roll *Restaurant* **266** 54
roll *Athletics* **298** 17
roll, double ~ **97** 15
roll, lower ~ **148** 55
roll, upper ~ **148** 54

roll, white ~ **97** 14
roll bar *Agr. Mach.* **65** 21
roll bar *Motorcycles etc.* **188** 18
roll bar *Car* **193** 13
roll bearing **148** 60
roll cutter **173** 42
roller *Hairdresser* **105** 12
roller *Cooper* **130** 26
roller *Glass Prod.* **162** 11
roller *Weaving* **165** 57
roller *Road Constr.* **200** 37
roller *Station* **206** 39
roller *Hydr. Eng.* **217** 65
roller *Office* **249** 17
roller *Cyc. Racing* **290** 13
roller *Graphic Art* **340** 12
roller *Birds* **359** 25; **360** 6
roller, bottom ~ **164** 10
roller, fluted ~ **164** 10
roller, grooved ~ **130** 30
roller, lambskin ~ **130** 31
roller, leather ~ **340** 23
roller, lower ~ *Iron Foundry etc.* **148** 55
roller, lower ~ *Cotton Spin.* **164** 10
roller, rubber ~ **182** 8
roller, rubber-disc ~ **64** 82
roller, steel ~ **164** 10
roller, submersible ~ **217** 68
roller, three-wheeled ~ **200** 36
roller, top ~ **164** 11
roller, upper ~ *Iron Foundry etc.* **148** 54
roller, upper ~ *Cotton Spin.* **164** 11
roller, wire-covered ~ **168** 34
roller bearing **164** 47
roller bit **145** 21
roller chain *Bicycle* **187** 36
roller chain *Intern. Combust. Eng.* **190** 25
roller chain, double ~ **190** 10
roller covering **50** 3
roller guide **201** 4
roller path **148** 50
roller postmark **236** 60
roller printing machine, ten-colour ~ **168** 53
rollers **148** 54-55
roller stamp **236** 46
roller table **157** 23
roller top **217** 66
roller trestle **157** 26
rollfilm **114** 19
rollfilm spool **114** 20
roll holder **40** 1
rolling **230** 71
rolling circle **288** 3
rolling dam **217** 65-72
rolling mill **148** 46-75
rolling plant **159** 9
rolling road **138** 16
rolling shutter frame **37** 29
rolling stock **207**; **208**; **209**; **210**; **211**; **212**; **213**
roll-on roll-off operation **225** 39
roll-on roll-off ship **226** 17
roll-on roll-off system **225** 39
roll-on roll-off trailer ferry **221** 54
rollover device **139** 43
rolls *Bakery* **97** 13-16
rolls *Iron Foundry etc.* **148** 54-55
roll stand **148** 56-60
roll unit **97** 61
roll-up door **245** 5
Roman **355** 11
Roman woman **355** 7

romper **29** 21
romper suit **29** 22
roof **37** 5; **38**; **121**; **122**; **337** 2
roof, cement ~ **122** 97
roof, flat ~ **37** 77
roof, glass ~ **55** 5
roof, hipped ~ **37** 64; **121** 10, 60
roof, imperial ~ **121** 25
roof, mission-tiled ~ **122** 56
roof, pantiled ~ **122** 53
roof, paper ~ **122** 90
roof, pitched ~ **38** 12
roof, plain-tiled ~ **122** 50
roof, sliding ~ **193** 24; **194** 10; **213** 22
roof, Spanish-tiled ~ **122** 56
roof, split-tiled ~ **122** 45
roof, swivelling ~ **213** 26, 27
roof, tiled ~ **122** 1
roof beam **121** 29
roof board **122** 61
roof boarding **122** 61
roof cable **211** 5
roof cladding **38** 1
roof course **122** 78
roof covering **38** 1
roofer **122**
roof guard **38** 8
roof hook **38** 6
roofing, cement ~ **122** 90-103
roofing, paper ~ **122** 90-103
roofing felt **122** 62
roofing nail **143** 55
roofing paper **122** 62
roof ladder **38** 4; **122** 63
roof lashing **278** 51
roof opening **213** 23
roof rack **278** 50
roofs, styles and parts of ~ **121** 1-26
roof sheathing **122** 61
roof structures of timber **121** 27-83
roof trestle **122** 66
roof truss **120** 7; **121** 78
roof valley **121** 15; **122** 11, 82
roof ventilator **278** 56
rook *Games* **276** 12
rook *Birds* **361** 2
room, double ~ **267** 27-38
room, heated ~ **169** 24
room divider **42** 19
room key **267** 9
room number **267** 10
room telephone **267** 34
room thermostat **38** 78
room trader **251** 6
room waiter **267** 33
rooster **62** 37; **73** 21
root *Man* **19** 36
root *Plant Propagn.* **54** 21
root *Arable Crops* **68** 17, 45
root *Horse* **72** 34
root *Maths.* **347** 12
root *Bot.* **370** 16-18
root *Industr. Plants* **383** 43
root, adventitious ~ **370** 78, 80
root, aerial ~ **370** 80
root, primary ~ **370** 16
root, secondary ~ **370** 17
root, tuberous ~ **370** 79
root crops **68** 38-45
rooter **200** 20
root gall **80** 27
root hair **68** 18; **370** 18
root louse **80** 26
roots **54** 12; **370** 78-82
rootstock **54** 33
root thorn **370** 81
rope *First Aid* **21** 30
rope *Weaving* **166** 61
rope *Swim.* **282** 32

rope *Gymn.* **296** 19; **297** 43
rope *Mountain.* **300** 12, 22-27
roped party **300** 22-27
rope ladder **221** 91; **273** 49; **307** 8
rope-pulley hoist **118** 91
ropes **299** 36
rope sling **300** 11
ropeway, aerial ~ **15** 67
ropeway, double-cable ~ **214** 25, 30
ropeway gondola **214** 52
ropeways **214** 15-38
ropeways, endless ~ **214** 15-24
ropeways, single-cable ~ **214** 15-24
ropeway support **214** 76
roping down **300** 28-30
ro-ro depot **226** 20
ro-ro-ship **226** 17
ro-ro system **225** 39
ro-ro trailer ferry **221** 54
rosary **332** 30
rose *Market Gdn.* **55** 28
rose *Game* **88** 5, 29
rose *Music. Instr.* **324** 5
rose, bush ~ **52** 13
rose, climbing ~ **52** 12
rose, double ~ **60** 17
rose, ivory ~ **36** 29
rose, rambling ~ **52** 12
rose, standard ~ **51** 25; **52** 21
rosebay **373** 11
rosebud **60** 16
rose cut **36** 45
rose-ear **70** 2
rose hip **370** 100
rose laurel **373** 13
rose thorn **60** 18
rose tree, standard ~ **52** 13, 21
rosette **306** 34
rose window **335** 23
rosin **323** 11
rostrum **263** 6; **316** 34
rotary engine, two-rotor ~ **190** 5
rotary-table machine **150** 41
rotary-table shot-blasting machine **148** 39
rotary turbine pump **259** 57
rotated grasp **296** 44, 46
rotation **298** 18
rotation axis **351** 4
rotator **224** 55
rotisserie **40** 32
rotor *Clocks* **110** 32
rotor *Intern. Combust. Eng.* **190** 68
rotor *Aircraft* **232** 22
rotor *Gliding* **287** 18
rotor, main ~ **232** 12-13; **256** 19; **264** 3
rotor, tail ~ **256** 20
rotor, tilting ~ **232** 32
rotor blade *Energy Sources* **155** 45
rotor blade *Aircraft* **232** 12
rotor head **232** 13
rotor pylon **232** 23
rouge **275** 24
rough **293** 80
rough focusing indicator **224** 35
roughing file **134** 9
roughing-out hammer **195** 46
roughing wheel **111** 36
roulette *Roulette* **275** 1-33, 28
roulette *Graphic Art* **340** 18
roulette ball **275** 33

roulette bowl **275** 29
roulette layout **275** 9, 17
roulette player **275** 15
roulette table **275** 8
roulette wheel **275** 10, 28
round **95** 14
round, caseless ~ **305** 37
roundabout **308** 2
round bar reinforcement **119** 80
round-bilge boat **286** 32-34
round end **95** 52
rounding machine *Bakery* **97** 63
rounding machine *Plumb.* **125** 30
roundwood **120** 35; **157** 30
round worm **81** 31
route **203** 68
route indicator **203** 20, 21
route lever **203** 58
route of the paper **180** 26
route of the sheets **180** 33
route of the web **180** 26
router plane **132** 26
route sign **197** 21
route straight ahead **203** 45, 49, 50
roving **164** 29
roving bobbin **164** 23
row **312** 9
rowan **371** 42
rowboats **283** 9-15
rowing **283**
rowing boat **89** 27
rowing boat, Germanic ~ **218** 1-6
rowing boats **283** 9-15
rowing coach **283** 20
rowlock **278** 18; **283** 29, 41
row of needles **167** 27
row of needles, back ~ **167** 46
row of needles, front ~ **167** 47
row of seats, tiered ~ **261** 1
royal **88** 8
Royal Crown, English ~ **254** 42
royal fern **377** 16
royal osmund **377** 16
royal water lily **378** 17
rubber, synthetic ~ **164** 11
rubber belt, studded ~ **64** 79
rubber plant **383** 33
rubber solution **340** 49
rubber tree **383** 33
rubber tyre cable car **273** 53
rubber tyre swing **273** 18
rubbing strake, reinforced ~ **258** 81
rubbish **268** 22
rubble **11** 47
rubble, rough ~ **269** 37
ruby **175** 22
ruby, synthetic ~ **110** 33
Rückpositiv **326** 5
rucksack **283** 65
rudder *Ship* **218** 6, 24; **221** 43
rudder *Shipbuild.* **222** 69
rudder *Ship* **223** 63
rudder *Life-Sav.* **228** 26
rudder *Aircraft* **229** 25; **230** 60
rudder *Air Force* **257** 23
rudder *Rowing* **283** 51-53, 53
rudder *Sailing* **284** 9, 34; **285** 34
rudder *Motorboats etc.* **286** 65
rudder *Airsports* **288** 22
rudder, retractable ~ **285** 37
rudder, vertical ~ **259** 95, 96
rudder angle indicator **224** 17
rudder blade **221** 43; **222** 69; **223** 63; **283** 53; **284** 34
rudderhead **284** 33

rudder pedal **230** 27; **257** 10
rudder pedal, co-pilot's ~ **230** 28
rudder post **222** 70
rudder stock **222** 68; **284** 33
ruff *Carnival* **306** 20
ruff *Hist. Cost.* **355** 52
rugby **292** 19
rugby ball **292** 21
rugby football **292** 19
rule **151** 33
rule, folding ~ **120** 76; **134** 33
rule, glazier's ~ **124** 21
rule of three sum **345** 8-10
rule pocket **33** 49
ruler **151** 33; **247** 35
ruling pen **151** 49
ruling pen attachment **151** 58, 61
rum **98** 57
ruminant **73** 1
ruminants **366** 28-30; **367** 1-10
rummer **45** 87
rump *Horse* **72** 31
rump *Game* **88** 20, 36
rump *Meat* **95** 14, 35
rump piece **329** 88
runch **61** 18
rune **341** 19
rung **38** 17; **50** 38
runner *Plant Propagn.* **54** 14, 16
runner *Soft Fruit* **58** 20
runner *Mills* **91** 22
runner *Iron Foundry etc.* **148** 21
runner *Rowing* **283** 45
runner *Ball Games* **292** 45, 66
runner *Athletics* **298** 5
runner, movable ~ **303** 10
runner, outrigged ~ **302** 46
runner bean **52** 28; **57** 8
runner gate **148** 21
running **298** 1-8
running axle **210** 35
running-boar target **305** 33
running dog **334** 39
running gear, front ~ **191** 52
running head **185** 66
running light **258** 56
running light, side ~ **258** 15
running light indicator panel **224** 29
running posture **295** 2
running side **277** 5
running step **295** 41
running step indicator **211** 36
running take-off twist dive **282** 43
running three **305** 3, 5
running title **185** 66
running track **298** 6
running wheel **64** 41, 56; **214** 7, 70
runout **147** 54
runway *Hunt.* **86** 16
runway *Airport* **233** 1
runway *Gliding* **287** 15
rush *Phys. Geog.* **13** 17
rush *Basketm.* **136** 27
rusk **97** 54
Russula vesca **381** 23
rustication **335** 51
rustic work **335** 51
rutting mane **88** 27
rutting season **86** 9-12
rye **68** 1, 2
rye bread **97** 10, 49; **99** 14
rye-bread roll **97** 16
rye flour **97** 52
ryegrass, perennial ~ **69** 26

S

sabaton **329** 55
saber *see* sabre
sable *Ladies' Wear* **30** 60
sable *Heraldry* **254** 26
sable *Mammals* **367** 15
sabot **101** 47
sabre, light ~ **294** 20, 34
sabre fencer **294** 19
sabre fencing **294** 19-24
sabre gauntlet **294** 21
sabre glove **294** 21
sabre mask **294** 22
sabreur **294** 19
sack **38** 34
sacker **92** 39
Sacrament **331** 48
sacrarium **330** 32
sacristan **330** 26, 58
sacristy **331** 13
sacristy door **330** 17
sacrum **17** 21; **20** 59
saddle *Phys. Geog.* **12** 16, 42
saddle *Mach. Tools* **149** 13
saddle, adjustable ~ **188** 4
saddle, English ~ **71** 45-49
saddle, reciprocating ~ **185** 24
saddle, unsprung ~ **290** 17
saddle, western ~ **71** 37-44
saddle apron **188** 6
saddleback roof **37** 5; **121** 1
saddle bag **187** 25
saddle clip **126** 53
saddle-pad **71** 17, 31
saddle roof **37** 5; **121** 1
saddles **71** 37-49
saddle seat **71** 37
saddle spring **187** 23
saddle stitching **31** 45
saddle tree **374** 1
safe **246** 22
safelight **116** 21
safety bar **301** 58
safety binding **301** 2
safety bonnet **85** 36
safety brake **85** 15
safety catch *Atom* **2** 40
safety catch *Household* **50** 25
safety catch *Hunt.* **87** 8, 24
safety catch *Army* **255** 14
safety catch, sliding ~ **87** 25
safety chain **126** 3
safety current **127** 2
safety curtain **316** 24
safety device **290** 13
safety equipment **316** 18
safety glass **124** 5
safety glasses **140** 21
safety helmet **84** 23; **140** 22; **158** 10; **300** 53
safety helmet, shock-resisting ~ **127** 48
safety hood **85** 36
safety jet **301** 53
safety key **140** 48
safety latch **50** 25
safety lighting **312** 6
safety lock **140** 44
safety net *Warships* **259** 18
safety net *Circus* **307** 14
safety nut **187** 64
safety pin **328** 27
safety rail **119** 43
safety valve *Roof & Boiler* **38** 70
safety valve *Railw.* **210** 3
safety wall **122** 35
saffron milk cap **381** 29
saggar **161** 2
sagger **161** 2
Sagittarius **3** 37; **4** 61
sagittate **370** 37
sago **98** 39
sago palm **383** 58
sail **219** 1-72; **283** 62; **284** 2; **285** 8
sail, ballooning ~ **285** 4
sail, brailed-up ~ **218** 21
sail, fore-and-aft ~ **220** 15
sail, furled ~ **218** 21
sail, square ~ **218** 21, 33; **219** 55-66; **220** 16
sail axle **91** 5
sailboat *Playground* **273** 29
sailboat *Camping* **278** 12
sailboat *Sailing* **284** 10-48
sailboat, single-masted ~ **220** 6-8
sailboats, mizzen-masted ~ **220** 9-10
sailboats, two-masted ~ **220** 11-17
sailing **284**; **285**
sailing barge, ketch-rigged ~ **220** 9
sailing boat *Playground* **273** 29
sailing boat *Camping* **278** 12
sailing boat *Sailing* **284** 10-48
sailing boat, single-masted ~ **220** 6-8
sailing boats, mizzen-masted ~ **220** 9-10
sailing boats, two-masted ~ **220** 11-17
sailing close-hauled **285** 10
sailing downwind **285** 1
sailing ship **219**; **220**
sailing ships, development of ~ **220** 35-37
sailing ships, four-masted ~ **220** 28-31
sailing vessels, three-masted ~ **220** 18-27
sailing with free wind **285** 12
sailing with wind abeam **285** 11
sailor suit **309** 62
sailplane **287** 3
sailplane, high-performance ~ **287** 9
sails, fore-and-aft ~ **219** 20-31
sail shapes **220** 1-5
sail top **91** 6
sainfoin **69** 10
saint, Buddhist ~ **337** 10
Saint Andrew's cross bond **118** 65
salad **266** 51
salad bowl **45** 23
salad chicory **57** 40
salad cream **96** 29
salad drawer **39** 4
salad fork **45** 68
salad oil **98** 24; **99** 66
salad plants **57** 36-40
salad servers **45** 24
salad spoon **45** 67
salamander **364** 22
salamanders **364** 20-22
sal-ammoniac block **125** 6
sales area **99** 4
sales check **98** 44; **271** 7
salesclerk **98** 13
sales counter **271** 42, 61
salesgirl **97** 1; **98** 31; **99** 17; **271** 18, 63
saleslady **97** 1; **98** 31; **99** 17; **271** 18, 63
salesman **309** 29
sales premises **111** 1-19
sales shelf **99** 23
sales statistics **248** 46
salicional **326** 23-30
salientians **364** 23-26
salina *Map* **15** 32
salina *Spa* **274** 1-7
sallow **371** 24
salon, men's ~ **106** 1-42
salon mirror **105** 20; **106** 6
saloon, lower ~ **194** 37
saloon, upper ~ **194** 38
saloon car **193** 4, 25
salt **98** 40
salt, common ~ **1** 9
salta **276** 20
salta piece **276** 21
salt cake storage tank **172** 36
salt cellar **266** 77
salt mine **154** 57-68, 72
salt water outlet **145** 33
salt water pipe **145** 33
salt water tank **146** 17
salt works *Map* **15** 32
salt works *Spa* **274** 1-7
salt works attendant **274** 5
saltzstange **97** 31
salvage **227**
salvage tug **227** 5, 16
salvaging **227** 1
Salvator beer **93** 26
salving **227** 1
sampan **353** 31
sample beam **115** 36
sample sagger **161** 2
sample scoop **98** 72
samson post **223** 35
samson post, ventilator-type ~ **221** 58
samurai **353** 37
sanctuary **330** 32
sanctuary lamp **330** 49
sanctus bell **330** 46
sand *Map* **15** 6
sand *Bldg. Site* **118** 36; **119** 26
sandal **101** 51
sandal, ladies' ~ **101** 49
sandal court shoe **101** 27
sandbag **216** 50; **288** 65
sandbank **227** 3
sand bed **123** 8
sand belt, endless ~ **133** 15
sand box *Railw.* **212** 59, 76
sandbox *Playground* **273** 64
sand delivery pipe **148** 38
sand deposit **216** 52
sand dome **210** 14
sander **129** 30
sander, orbital ~ **134** 53
sander, single-belt ~ **133** 30
sander control **211** 32
sander switch **211** 32
sandhill **273** 66
sand hills **15** 6
sanding **129** 28
sanding attachment, orbital ~ **134** 53
sanding belt, endless ~ **133** 15
sanding belt regulator **133** 14
sanding disc **134** 25
sanding dust extractor **133** 28
sanding machine, single-belt ~ **133** 30
sanding table **133** 35
sanding valve **210** 55
sanding wheel **133** 27
sand lizard **364** 27
sandpaper **128** 14; **129** 25; **135** 25
sandpaper block **128** 13; **129** 26
sand pipe **210** 15, 19
sandpit **273** 64
sand star **369** 11
sand table **173** 13
sand track racing **290** 24-28

sand trap *Paperm.* **173** 13
sand trap *Ball Games* **293** 81
sand tube **210** 15
sandwich **45** 39
sandwich, open ~ **45** 37
sandwich board **308** 50
sandwich man **308** 49
sanitary articles **99** 35
San-José scale **80** 35
Sanserif **342** 7
Sanserif type **342** 7
Sanskrit **341** 9
sap **120** 85; **370** 12
sappho **363** 4
sapwood **120** 85; **370** 12
sarcophagus **335** 53
sardine server **45** 78
sardines in oil **98** 19
Sargon's Palace **333** 29
sartorius **18** 45
Satan's mushroom **379** 12
satchel **260** 9
sate **137** 34
satellite **4** 45
satellite radio link **237** 51-52
satellite sounding **7** 33
satin stitch **102** 10
Saturn **4** 49
Saturn V **234** 1, 2
sauceboat **45** 17
sauce ladle **45** 18
saucepan **40** 16
saucer **44** 30
sauna, mixed ~ **281** 18
sauna stove **281** 21
sausage **98** 4; **99** 54
sausage, broiled ~ **308** 34
sausage, grilled ~ **308** 34
sausage, pork ~ **99** 55
sausage, scalded ~ **96** 8
sausage filler **96** 49
sausage fork **96** 44
sausage meat **96** 41, 52
sausages **96** 6-11
sausage stand **308** 32
sausage stuffer **96** 49
sausage tongs **308** 35
savings account **250** 4
savoy **57** 33
savoy cabbage **57** 33
saw, butcher's ~ **94** 19
saw, circular ~ **119** 19; **125** 24; **134** 50
saw, free-cutting ~ **84** 32
saw, two-handed ~ **120** 68
saw, vertical frame ~ **157** 2
sawbill **359** 15
saw blade **120** 62; **150** 16; **157** 3, 47; **260** 54
saw carriage **132** 71; **133** 38
saw chain **84** 35; **85** 14; **85** 15; **120** 14
saw frame **138** 25; **150** 17; **157** 8
saw guide **85** 16
saw handle **132** 4
sawing shed **120** 3
sawmill **144** 6; **157** 1
saw rasp **134** 6
saw set **132** 42
saw-sharpening machine **157** 42
saw tooth **96** 33
sawtooth roof **121** 20
saxboard **283** 43
saxifrage, rotundifoliate ~ **375** 1
saxophone **324** 69
scaffold **118** 25; **122** 34; **222** 18
scaffold, steel ~ **5** 18
scaffold, supporting ~ **14** 50
scaffold, tubular steel ~ **119** 46

scaffold board **122** 70
scaffolding **215** 62
scaffolding, tubular steel ~ **119** 46
scaffolding joint **118** 30
scaffold pole **118** 23
scaffold standard **118** 23
scalding colander **96** 45
scale *Map* **14** 29
scale *Chem.* **349** 35
scale *Fish etc.* **364** 11
scale *Decid. Trees* **371** 12
scale *Conifers* **372** 34, 42, 45, 50
scale, triangular ~ **151** 34
scale, wax ~ **77** 25
scale adjustment **116** 34
scale armour **329** 64
scaled prickle fungus **381** 24
scale insect **80** 35
scale louse **80** 35
scale pan *Kitch. Utensils* **40** 37
scale pan *Chem.* **349** 36
Scales *Astron.* **3** 19; **4** 59
scales *Doc.* **22** 66
scales *Kitch. Utensils* **40** 35
scales *Child. Rm.* **47** 33
scales *Supermkt.* **99** 88
scales *Photog.* **114** 58
scales *Music. Not.* **320** 45-49
scaling hammer **137** 38
scallop shell **309** 46
scalp **352** 15
scalpel **26** 43
scalper **340** 7
scaly ant-eater **366** 10
scanner **177** 39
scanner film **177** 72
scanning drum **177** 45
scanning head **177** 46, 63
scanning zone **243** 47
scantling **120** 10
scape **370** 52
scapula **16** 23; **17** 7
scar **11** 48
scarecrow **52** 27
scarf *Ladies' Wear* **31** 57
scarf *Men's Wear* **33** 65
scarf *Headgear* **35** 16
scarf *Bullfight. etc.* **319** 38
scarf joint, oblique ~ **121** 88
scarf joint, simple ~ **121** 87
scarifier **200** 20
scarlet pimpernel **61** 27
scarlet runner **52** 28; **57** 8
scarlet runner bean **57** 8
scarp **13** 57
scatter cushion **42** 27; **46** 17
scauper **340** 7
scaur **11** 48
scaw **11** 48
scene *Theatre* **316** 36
scene *Art* **334** 45
scene number **310** 35
scene painter **315** 35
scene-repeat key **243** 42
scenery **316** 35
scenery projector **316** 17
scene shifter **315** 28; **316** 46
scenic artist **315** 35
scenic railway **308** 39
scent, artificial ~ **289** 49
sceptre, fool's ~ **306** 59
schalmeyes **322** 14
schedule **204** 16
schedule, engineer's ~ **210** 52
Scheidt globe **349** 1
schilling **252** 13
schizocarp **370** 94
schnapps **98** 56
schnauzer **70** 35
schnecke **97** 38

schnorkel *Warships* **259** 72, 90
schnorkel *Swim.* **279** 11
schnorkel *Bathing* **280** 39
school **260**; **261**
school bag **260** 7
school book **47** 25
school children's wear **29** 31-47
school figure **289** 7
school horse **289** 3
school satchel **260** 9
schooner, four-masted ~ **220** 28
schooner, three-masted ~ **220** 18
schooner, topsail ~ **220** 11-13
Schottel propeller **227** 20
Schwellwerk **326** 45
scion **54** 37
scion bud **54** 23, 34
scissor-blade **106** 35
scissor jump **295** 39; **298** 22
scissors *Shoem.* **100** 43
scissors *School* **260** 49
scissors *Gymn.* **296** 51
scissors *Athletics* **298** 22
scissors, angled ~ **22** 51
scissors, bull-nosed ~ **128** 34
scissors, curved ~ **26** 42
scissors movement **296** 51
scoop *Doc.* **22** 50
scoop *Hosp.* **26** 52
scoop *Graphic Art* **340** 8
scoop thermometer **92** 53
scooter **188** 47
scooters **188**
scoreboard **293** 34, 70
scorer **293** 71
scoring equipment, electrical ~ **294** 25-33
scoring equipment, electronic ~ **294** 32
scoring light **294** 28
scorper **340** 7
Scorpio **3** 38; **4** 60
Scorpion *Astron.* **3** 38; **4** 60
scorpion *Articulates* **358** 40
scorzonera **57** 35
Scots pine **372** 20
Scottish terrier **70** 17
scouring machine, open-width ~ **168** 8
scouring nozzle **216** 62
scouring tunnel **217** 62
scouring wheel **100** 6
scout **278** 11
scout camp **278** 8-11
scrag **95** 6
scrag end **95** 6
scramble racing **290** 24-28
scrambling motorcycle **189** 16
scrap box **141** 15
scraper *Butch.* **96** 42
scraper *Paperhanger* **128** 10
scraper *Painter* **129** 23
scraper *Graphic Art* **340** 63
scraper, pointed ~ **140** 63
scraper, triangle ~ **140** 63
scraper adjustment **340** 62
scraper and burnisher **340** 17
scraper blade **200** 17
scraper floor, movable ~ **62** 24
scrap iron charging box **147** 26
scrap iron feed **147** 65
scray entry, curved ~ **168** 47
scree **11** 47; **12** 45; **13** 29
screech owl **362** 17
screed **123** 41
screeding beam **201** 14
screeding board **201** 14

scree ledge **300** 4
screen *Hunt.* **86** 9
screen *Fish Farm.* **89** 10
screen *Bldg. Site* **118** 85
screen *Paperm.* **172** 57
screen *Refuse Coll.* **199** 11
screen *Post* **236** 40
screen *Inf. Tech.* **242** 84
screen *Swim.* **281** 17
screen *Films* **310** 16, 51; **312** 11
screen, all-matt ~ **115** 58, 59, 60, 65
screen, centrifugal ~ **172** 22, 56
screen, crystal glass ~ **179** 24
screen, fluorescent ~ **74** 40
screen, ground glass ~ **112** 24; **115** 58, 59, 60, 61, 65, 66; **177** 2, 34
screen, illuminated ~ **177** 20; **264** 30
screen, inner ~ **240** 20
screen, lead ~ **259** 70
screen, magnetic ~ **240** 20
screen, matt ~ *Optic. Instr.* **112** 24
screen, matt ~ *Photog.* **115** 61, 66
screen, protective ~ **154** 74
screen, rotary ~ **172** 2
screen, secondary ~ **172** 58
screen, vibrating ~ **158** 21
screen curtain **312** 10
screen frame, mobile ~ **168** 60
screen holder, hinged ~ **177** 3
screening **156** 14
screening, inner ~ **240** 20
screening, magnetic ~ **240** 20
screenings **158** 22
screen magazine **177** 9
screen printing **168** 59
screen printing operator **168** 65
screen table **168** 63
screen work **136** 4
screw *First Aid* **21** 16
screw *Metalwkr.* **140** 4
screw *Weaving* **165** 36
screw *Life-Sav.* **228** 26
screw, cheese-head ~ **143** 36
screw, cross-head ~ **143** 26
screw, feathering ~ **224** 19
screw, hexagonal socket head ~ **143** 27
screw, main ~ **148** 62
screw, self-tapping ~ **143** 26
screw, ship's ~ **221** 44; **222** 72; **223** 62
screw, slotted ~ **143** 36
screw, three-blade ~ **223** 62
screw-back **277** 4
screw base **127** 59
screw block **136** 8
screw clamp **120** 66
screw conveyor **92** 26
screw-cutting machine **125** 27; **126** 86
screw die **140** 61
screw dive **282** 44
screwdriver **109** 6; **126** 69; **127** 46; **134** 4; **140** 62
screwdriver, cross-point ~ **134** 5
screwgate **300** 47
screw groove **143** 38
screw joint **126** 42
screw log **224** 54
screw post **222** 71
screws **143** 13-50
screw slit **143** 38
screw slot **143** 38
screw tap **140** 60

screw thread 50 50
screw wrench 126 67
scrim 183 33; 185 20
scrim roll holder 185 19
script *Films* 310 45
script *Script* 341; 342
script, cuneiform ~ 341 8
script, director's ~ 316 44
script, Latin ~ 342 12
script, producer's ~ 316 44
script, Sinaitic ~ 341 13
script, uncial ~ 341 17
script girl 310 39
scripts 341 1-20
Scriptures 330 11
scroll *Music. Instr.* 323 17
scroll *Art* 333 26; 334 23
scroll, Vitruvian ~ 334 39
scroll-opening roller 168 13
scrollwork 336 8
scrotum 20 71
scrubber 156 22, 23, 24
scrubbing agent 156 37
scrubbing brush 50 56
scrubbing oil tank 156 43
scrub board 123 21, 63
scrum 292 20
scrummage 292 20
scuba 279 19
scull 283 17, 35-38
sculptor 339 1
sculpture 339 32
sculpture, modern ~ 272 64
scut 88 19, 62
scutcher, double ~ 163 14
scutcher lap 163 47
scutcher lap holder 163 48
scutch grass 61 30
scutellum 82 5; 358 30
scythe 66 12
scythe blade 66 13
scythe sheath 66 18
scythestone 66 19
sea 13 26; 14 19-26
sea, epeiric ~ 14 26
sea, epicontinental ~ 14 26
sea, marginal ~ 14 26
sea, open ~ 227 4
sea anemone 369 20
sea bear 367 18
seabirds 359 11-14
sea calf 367 19
sea couch grass 61 30
sea cucumber 369 18
sea deity 327 23
sea divinity 327 23
sea dog 367 19
sea fan 369 8
sea feather 369 14
sea fishing 90
Sea Goat 3 36; 4 62
sea goddess 327 23
sea grass 378 54
sea hedgehog 357 39; 369 19
sea horse 364 18
seakale beet 57 28
seal 190 69
seal, clay ~ 269 39
seal, loam ~ 269 39
sea ladder 221 91
sea lead 89 92
sea level 11 11
sea lily 369 3
sealing tape 126 75
seals 367 18-22
seam 144 29
sea maid 327 23
sea maiden 327 23
seaman 327 23
sea marks 224 68-108
seam binding 103 14; 104 19
seamless engraving
  adjustment 177 53

sea monster 327 47
seam roller 128 36
sea nymph 327 23
sea otter 367 17
sea ox 327 47
sea pen 369 14
seaplane 232 1, 5
seaquake 11 53
search 264 31
searchlight 258 28
Sea Serpent 3 16
seaside pleasure boat 221 15
sea star 357 38; 369 17
sea strait 14 24
seat *Man* 16 40
seat 24 24; 41 10; 44 11; 65
  22; 71 45; 212 63; 271 35;
  273 58; 283 28; 303 6; 307
  15; 312 9; 315 20
seat *Mach. Parts etc.* 143 65
seat, back ~ 193 22
seat, captain's ~ 235 17
seat, child's ~ 187 21
seat, circular ~ 281 38
seat, coachman's ~ 186 8
seat, commander's ~ 235 17
seat, conical ~ 143 67
seat, co-pilot's ~ 230 37; 235
  18
seat, cox's ~ 283 27
seat, double ~ 197 19; 207 63
seat, driver's ~ 186 8; 191 34;
  210 59
seat, engineer's ~ 210 59
seat, fireman's ~ 210 59
seat, folding ~ 193 22; 207 12
seat, instructor's ~ 257 7
seat, observer's ~ 257 7
seat, pilot's ~ 230 36; 235 18;
  257 6
seat, rear ~ 191 31
seat, reclining ~ 191 34; 207
  44, 64
seat, single ~ 197 17; 207 62
seat, sliding ~ 283 41-50, 44
seat, student pilot's ~ 257 6
seat, upholstered ~ 207 44;
  208 25; 265 10
seat cushion 42 23
seated position 296 31
seating 330 28
seating group 42 21-26
seat pillar 187 24
seat stay 187 19
seat stick 86 10
seat tube 187 18
seat upholstery 207 65
sea urchin 357 39; 369 19
seawater desalination plant
  146 25
sea wave, seismic ~ 11 53
sea wing 232 3
secant 346 50
secateurs 56 50; 78 12
second 299 44
secondary 153 16
secondary school 261
second base 292 44
second-class seating
  arrangement 211 58
second-class section 207 10;
  208 22
seconde engagement 294 50
second-hand stall 308 60
second indicator 110 21
second man 300 26
second-stage separation
  retro-rocket 234 37
seconds timer 129 39
secretary 209 27
secretary, proprietor's ~ 248
  31
section *Forestry* 84 2

section *Drawing Off.* 151 28
section *Bookbind.* 183 12
section *Railw.* 203 29
section, hollow ~ 215 5
section, middle ~ 215 68
section, tubular ~ 215 5
section line *Map* 15 112
section line *Forestry* 84 1
section line *Drawing Off.* 151
  27
section mark 342 36
section of warp rib fabric 171
  14
sections 143
sections, conic ~ 347 11-29
sector 346 54
securities 251 11-19
security 251 1-10
security, fixed-income ~ 251
  11-19
security, unlisted ~ 251 5
security drawer 236 22
sedan 193 4, 25
sedge *Phys. Geog.* 13 17
sedge *Indoor Plants* 53 17
sedilia 330 41
sediment *Phys. Geog.* 13 69
sediment *Doc.* 23 50
sediment filter, stainless steel
  ~ 79 8
sediment filter, stainless steel
  ~ 79 8
sedimentary filter
seed *Plant Propagn.* 54 3
seed *Soft Fruit* 58 23
seed *Drupes & Nuts* 59 8
seed *Agr.* 63 12
seed *Arable Crops* 68 13, 15,
  25
seed *Bot.* 370 86
seed *Decid. Trees* 371 20, 65
seed *Conifers* 372 9, 10, 15, 28,
  37, 54, 57, 60, 71
seed *Flowers etc.* 375 25, 28
seed *Alp. Plants etc.* 378 33, 34
seed *Trop. Plants* 382 20, 34,
  35, 39, 45
seed *Industr. Plants* 383 15,
  23, 24, 57
seed *South. Fruits* 384 10, 20,
  21, 47, 52, 58
seed, foraminate ~ 383 57
seed, oleiferous ~ 383 3, 5
seedbed preparation 63 31-41
seed capsule 61 5
seed corn 63 12
seed-dressing machine 83 52
seed dusting 83 52
seed fish 89 13
seed-harrow, combination ~
  Agr. 63 41
seed-harrow, combination ~
  Agr. Mach. 65 87
seed hopper 65 75
seed leaf 370 87
seedling *Plant Propagn.* 54 6
seedling *Market Gdn.* 55 23
seedling *Forestry* 84 7, 9
seedling box 55 51
seedling nursery 84 6
seedling plant 54 6
seedlip 63 11
seed lobe 370 87
seed pan 54 2
seed pike 89 11
seed potato 68 39
seed sowing 54 1
seed tuber 68 39
seed vessel 57 6; 378 5; 383 8
seed vessel, circumscissile ~
  370 95
seesaw 273 35; 307 59
Seger cone 161 6
seggar 161 2
segment *Maths.* 346 52
segment *Invertebr.* 357 25

segment disc shutter 313 8
seismograph, horizontal ~ 11
  39
seismology 11 32-38
seismometer 11 39
seizing 90 5
selector 237 42
selector, electronic ~ 237 42
selector fork 192 42, 45
selector head 192 44
selector motor 237 48
self-discharge freight car 213
  24
self-discharge wagon 213 24
self-feeder 74 13
self-heal 376 16
self-rescue 21 33
self-service restaurant 266
  45-78
self-service station 196 1-29
self-threading guide 165 18
self-time lever 115 15
self-timer 115 15
selvedge 166 11; 171 20, 24
selvedge shaft 171 22
selvedge thread draft 171 20
semaphore arm 203 2
semaphore arm,
  supplementary ~ 203 8
semaphore signal 203 1, 7, 12
semibold 175 3
semibreve 320 13
semibreve rest 320 21
semicircle 346 46
semicolon 342 19
semidome 334 73
semiquaver 320 17
semiquaver rest 320 25
semitone 320 50, 52
semi-trailer *Lorries etc.* 194
  30-33
semi-trailer *Station* 206 59
semolina 98 36
sending-off 291 61
senna 380 16
senna leaf 380 16
sensing element 10 22
sepal 58 8, 44; 59 12; 370 58
separating funnel 349 3
separating layer 7 10
separating rail 164 30
separation plant 199 31
separation rocket motor, aft ~
  235 62
separation rocket motor,
  forward ~ 235 60
separator *Bldg. Site* 119 81
separator *Offshore Drill.* 146
  28
separator *Cotton Spin.* 164 43
separator *Paperm.* 172 31
separator *Roulette* 275 30
separator, centralized ~ 172
  15
septimole 321 23
septolet 321 23
septum 77 43
septum, interventricular ~ 20
  52
septum, ventricular ~ 20 52
septuplet 321 23
sequestrum forceps 26 45
sequoia 372 69
seraglio, Sultan's ~ 306 41
serial number *Stock Exch.*
  251 13
serial number *Money* 252 36
series, arithmetical ~ 345 11
series, geometrical ~ 345 12
series, inner ~ 375 32
series, outer ~ 375 31
series of moulds 147 36
Serpens 3 20

Serpent *Astron.* 3 20
serpent *Gymn.* 297 48
serpent *Music. Instr.* 322 13
serpent, nine-headed ~ 327 33
serpent, paper ~ 308 14
serrate 370 44
serratus anterior 18 42
serrulate 370 44
server *Ball Games* 293 51, 62
server *Church* 330 40
service 293 42
service area 293 61
service bell panel 267 28
service bridge 217 72
service building 154 36
service bunker 156 3
service counter 250 4
service court 293 12
service girder, adjustable ~ 119 78
service line 293 6-7
service line judge 293 27
service module 6 2
service module main engine 234 57
service pistol 264 22
service riser 126 7
service room 329 27
service station 196 1-29
service tray 105 31
service vehicle 233 22
servicing craft 258 93
serviette 45 9; 266 47
serviette ring 45 10
serving, jute ~ 153 49
serving area 207 79
serving cutlery 45 69-70
serving fork 45 70
serving hatch 266 66
serving spoon 45 74, 75
serving trolley 45 32
servo-actuating mechanism 257 22, 23
servo cylinder 192 50
servo unit 192 50
sesame plant 383 45
sesquiplane 229 13
set *Plant Propagn.* 54 20
set *Blacksm.* 137 34
set *Composing Rm.* 175 48
set *Ball Games* 293 37
set *Maths.* 348 1, 3
set collar 143 33
set designer 310 43; 315 37
set hammer 137 33
set head 143 57
set of rolls 148 54-55
set piece 315 30; 316 47
sets 348
set screw 127 21
set square 151 7
set square, adjustable ~ 151 4
set square, steel ~ 108 28
sett 137 34
settee 42 24
setting 54 18
setting and hatching machine 74 28
setting lever 115 15
setting lotion 106 23
setting rule 174 14
setting stick 174 13
set trigger 87 12
set trigger, second ~ 87 11
Seven Sisters 3 26
seventh chord 321 5
sewer, combined ~ 198 27
sewing 183 8, 34
sewing cord 183 10
sewing frame 183 9
sewing machine *Dressm.* 103 8

sewing machine *Tailor* 104 12
sewing machine *Bookbind.* 185 16
sewing machine cotton 103 12
sewing machine drawer 104 18
sewing machine table 104 17
sewing machine thread 103 12
sewing mechanism 133 5
sewing needle 185 21
sewing silk 104 10
sewing thread 183 11
sex organs, female ~ 20 79-88
sex organs, male ~ 20 66-77
sextant 224 1
sextolet 321 23
sexton 330 26, 58
sextuplet 321 23
sgraffito 338 41
shading 55 6
shading panel 55 9
shadow 34 17
shadow mask 240 17
shadow mask mount, temperature-compensated ~ 240 22
shadow roll 289 30
shaft *Farm Bldgs.* 62 20
shaft *Agr. Mach.* 64 59
shaft *Mach. Parts etc.* 143 61
shaft *Nucl. Energy* 154 69
shaft *Cotton Spin.* 164 42
shaft *Weaving* 166 4
shaft *Carriages* 186 19, 30
shaft *Aircraft* 232 56
shaft *Rowing* 283 37
shaft *Ball Games* 291 26
shaft *Sports* 305 64
shaft *Art* 333 27
shaft, intermediate ~ 232 57
shaft, main ~ *Coal* 144 24
shaft, main ~ *Car* 192 40
shaft alley 223 66
shaft bossing 223 59
shaft chain 71 20
shaft furnace 147 1
shaft guide 166 3
shaft strut 223 61
shaft tunnel 223 66
shag *Tobacc. etc.* 107 25
shag *Birds* 359 10
shake 321 17, 18
shaker 324 59
shallot 328 18
shallows 224 87, 97
shaman 353 24
shampoo 106 20
shampoo basin 105 29; 106 12
shampoo bottle 105 32
shampooing head 50 79
shampoo spray 105 30; 106 13
shampoo unit 105 28; 106 11
shank *Man* 16 52
shank *Meat* 95 14, 33
shank *Shoem.* 100 68
shank *Metalwkr.* 140 33
shank *Mach. Parts etc.* 143 15, 53
shaper 150 45
shapes game 48 19
shaping, final ~ 162 28, 36
shaping hammer 108 40
shaping machine *Dairy.* 76 35
shaping machine *Mach. Tools* 150 45
shaping pad 104 23
shard 161 21
share *Agr. Mach.* 65 7, 58, 65
share *Stock Exch.* 251 11-19
share, pointed ~ 65 65
share, three-bladed ~ 64 67
share certificate 251 11

share register 251 14
share warrant 251 11
shark 364 1
sharp 320 50
sharpie 284 53
shave 136 39
shave, clean ~ 34 25
shaver, electric ~ 49 37
shaving 120 80
shavings 132 40; 135 26
shawl 31 71
shawm 322 14
shawm, double ~ 322 3
shearing train 148 74, 75
shears 128 34
shears, tinner's ~ 125 1
sheatfish 364 12
sheath *Arable Crops* 68 9
sheath *Forestry* 84 30
sheath, lead ~ 153 39, 47
sheath, leather ~ 283 41
sheathfish 364 12
sheathing paper 122 62
shed 166 40
shedding tappet 166 57
shed roof 37 78; 121 7
sheep 73 13
sheepdog 70 25
sheep pen 75 9
sheer 259 23
sheer strake 222 44
sheet *Household* 50 5
sheet *Offset Print.* 180 17, 47
sheet *Ship* 219 68
sheet *Office* 249 57
sheet *Fire Brig.* 270 18
sheet *Gymn.* 297 11
sheet, blank ~ 180 69; 181 23, 30
sheet, corrugated ~ 122 98
sheet, linen ~ 43 9
sheet, plastic ~ 76 28
sheet, printed ~ 180 55, 57; 181 25
sheet, single ~ 340 27
sheet, unprinted ~ 180 69; 181 23, 30
sheet cloud 8 3, 4, 8, 9, 10
sheet counter 181 54
sheet delivery 249 54
sheet feeder 180 31, 48, 68, 74; 181 24; 184 16; 185 25
sheet feeder, automatic ~ 181 5
sheet-feeding station 184 16
sheet glass 124 5
sheet glass production 162 1-20
sheeting support 119 86
sheet metal 128 17
sheet-metal screw 143 26
sheet of glass 162 10
sheet of stamps 236 21
sheet pile 119 17
sheet pile bulkhead 217 5
sheet pile wall 119 17; 217 5
sheet piling 119 17; 217 5
sheet shears 125 26
sheet zinc 122 14
shelf 44 19; 98 14; 100 36; 195 14; 271 27
shelf, continental ~ 11 8
shelf, revolving ~ 39 28
shelf, steel ~ 262 12
shelf, wall-mounted ~ 248 40
shelf for bottles 266 10; 267 64; 317 4
shelf for glasses 266 9; 267 65; 317 5
shelf unit 46 1
shell *Cooper* 130 23
shell *Shipbuild.* 222 44-49
shell *Rowing* 283 33, 48

shell *Ball Games* 293 33
shell *Invertebr.* 357 29
shell *Fish etc.* 364 29
shell, soft ~ 59 42
shell, steel ~ 154 21
shell bit 135 16
shell bossing 223 59
shell membrane 74 60
shell plating 222 44-49
shells 283 9-15
shell shelter 223 17
shelving 248 28
shepherd bird 361 4
shepherd's purse 61 9; 376 9
shepherd's weatherglass 61 27
sherd 161 21
sherry glass 45 84
shield *Game* 88 55
shield *Plumb. etc.* 126 33
shield *Ship* 218 17
shield *Heraldry* 254 5
shield *Ethnol.* 354 10
shield, concrete ~ 154 20
shield, concrete and lead ~ 1 57
shield, protective ~ 2 46
shield, round ~ 329 57
shield, sliding ~ 2 32
shield budding 54 30
shielding, protective ~ 2 46
shielding-gas supply 142 34
shielding wall, lead ~ 2 46
shield volcano 11 13
shifting spanner 126 68
shift key 249 3
shift lock 249 5
shift pattern 192 47
shikara 337 26
shin 95 22, 28
shinbone 17 25
shingle 34 34
shin guard 142 12; 291 34
shin pad 292 9; 302 33
ship, five-masted ~ 220 35
ship, four-masted ~ 220 31
ship, full-rigged ~ 220 24-27, 31, 35
ship, stranded ~ 228 10
shipbuilding 222
shipbuilding sheds 222 3-4
shipbuilding yard 222 1-43
'ship cleared through customs' 253 36
ship-drawing office 222 2
ship fix 224 45
ship of the line 218 51-60
shipper 206 28
shipping traffic radio telephone 224 28
ship run aground 227 2
ship under construction 222 30
shipyard 222 1-43
shirt 30 26; 291 56
shirt, boy's ~ 29 61
shirt, casual ~ 32 38; 33 37
shirt, check ~ 33 50
shirt, knitted ~ 33 36
shirt, short-sleeved ~ 33 33
shirt-blouse 30 40
shirt button 33 34
shirts, men's ~ 32 38-47
shirt top 30 45
shirtwaist 319 23
shirt-waister dress 30 10
Shiva 337 19
shoals 224 87, 97
shoat 75 42
shock absorber *Moon L.* 6 32
shock absorber *Car* 191 26; 192 69
shock absorber *Railw.* 207 4
shock absorber, telescopic ~

188 41; 189 23
shock treatment 25 26
shock wave 11 35
shoe Mills 91 14
shoe Bldg. Site 119 50
shoe, bast ~ 122 75
shoe, chisel-shaped ~ 65 58
shoe, copped ~ 355 42
shoe, diamond-shaped ~ 65 58
shoe, finished ~ 100 1
shoe, hemp ~ 122 75
shoe, high-heeled ~ 101 33
shoe, laced ~ 101 31
shoe, peaked ~ 355 42
shoe, piked ~ 355 42
shoe, repaired ~ 100 1
shoe, slater's ~ 122 75
shoe brake 143 97
shoe brush 50 41
shoe buckle 101 52
shoe care utensils 50 39-43
shoelace 100 64
shoemaker 100
shoe polish 50 39, 43
shoes 41 16; 101
shoe sieve 64 19
shoe spray 50 40
shoot 54 37; 370 19-25
shoot, female ~ 372 46, 48
shoot, long ~ 78 3
shoot, male ~ 372 44, 49, 56
shoot, short ~ 372 23, 31
shooting Hunt. 86 47-52
shooting Films 310 14-60, 26-60
shooting, exterior ~ 310 18
shooting, outdoor ~ 310 18
shooting box 305 78
shooting brake 193 15
shooting gallery 308 58
shooting positions 305 27-29
shooting range 305 74
shooting script 310 45
shooting seat 86 10
shooting star 7 25
shooting station 305 78
shooting stick 86 10
shop 195
shop, goldsmith's ~ 215 53
shop assistant 97 1; 98 13, 31; 99 17; 271 18
shop front 268 42
shopkeeper 98 41
shopper 50 87
shopping bag 98 45; 99 3; 268 19
shopping trolley 50 87; 99 1
shop shelf 47 36
shop sign 268 39
shop walker 271 33
shop window 268 10
shop window decoration 268 12
shop window display 268 11
shorthand 342 13
shorthand pad 245 29; 248 32
shorthand writing 342 13
short measure 294 10
short/medium haul airliner 231 4; 231 11
short run 184 1; 249 59
shorts 33 25; 291 57
shorts, children's ~ 29 25
shorts, ladies' ~ 31 39
shorts, leather ~ 29 32
short standing 75 22
short stop 292 42
short wave 7 26
short-wave station 237 54
short-wave therapy apparatus 23 22, 39
shot Athletics 298 49

shot Sports 305 52
shote 75 42
shot firer 158 25
shotgun, over-and-under ~ 87 33
shot number 310 35
shot put 298 48
shoulder Phys. Geog. 12 41
shoulder Man 16 22
shoulder Horse 72 18
shoulder Game 88 17, 38
shoulder Meat 95 5, 9
shoulder Composing Rm. 175 40
shoulder balance 295 29
shoulderblade 16 23; 17 7
shoulder button 31 15
shoulder cape 355 39
shoulder girdle 17 6-7
shoulder guard 142 5
shoulder iron 38 33
shoulder landing 298 12
shoulder rest 255 9, 31, 39
shoulder stand 295 29
shoulder strap 260 11
shoulder strap, frilled ~ 29 14
shovel 55 14; 137 2; 200 1; 255 77
shovel, mechanical ~ 118 81
shovel, wooden ~ 91 24
shovel bucket 118 82
show booth 308 6
showcase 271 13
shower Meteorol. 8 19
shower Meteorol. etc. 9 37
shower Life-Sav. 228 30
shower Swim. 282 2
shower, lukewarm ~ 281 29
shower adjustment rail 49 43
shower attachment, extendible ~ 126 30
shower base 49 44
shower bath 282 2
shower cubicle 49 39
shower curtain 49 40
shower head, adjustable ~ 49 41
shower nozzle 49 42
'showers' 233 46
show jumping 289 8-14
showman 308 10
show people, travelling ~ 308 25-28
shredding 169 6
shrew 366 7
shrew mouse 366 7
shrimp 369 12
shrine 337 21
shrine, Buddhist ~ 337 21
shrink foil 76 25
shrink ring 130 24
shrink-sealing machine 76 24
shroud 219 16; 284 18
shrub, anemophilous ~ 59 44-51
shrub, ornamental ~ 272 14
shrub, wind-pollinating ~ 59 44-51
shrub bed 55 37
shrubs, ornamental ~ 373; 374
shuck 68 33
shunter 206 43
shunting engine 206 43
shunting locomotive 206 43
shutter Market Gdn. 55 9
shutter Mills 91 4
shutter, folding ~ 37 30
shutter, louvred ~ 212 84
shutter, rolling ~ 37 28
shutter, side ~ 119 55
shutter board 118 41; 119 18, 76

shutter catch 37 31
shuttering 119 54-76; 123 10
shuttering, bottom ~ 119 54
shuttering board 119 76
shuttering strut 119 13
shutter opening 304 12
shutter release 114 12, 31; 115 18; 117 6; 313 24, 38
shutter release button 114 12; 115 18
shutter speed control 114 35; 115 19
shutter speed setting knob 115 19
shutter weir 217 65-72
shuttle Needlewk. 102 20
shuttle Weaving 166 9, 26
shuttle Ball Games 293 44
shuttle box 166 9
shuttlecock 273 7; 293 44
shuttlecock game 273 6
shuttle eye 166 29
shuttle tip, metal ~ 166 25
sickle 56 8
side Man 16 32
side Optician. 111 13
side Joiner 132 23
side Weaves 171 32
side Billiards 277 5
side Art 336 40
side Maths. 346 26, 27
side, subordinate ~ 252 9
side, woven ~ 136 18
side batten 222 62
side blackboard 260 35
sideboard Dining Rm. 44 20
sideboard Tablew. etc. 45 44
side board Farm Bldgs. 62 25
sideboards 34 24
sideburns 34 24
sidecar 290 30
sidecar body 189 54
sidecar combination 290 29
sidecar crash bar 189 55
sidecar machine 189 53
sidecar wheel 189 57
sidecar windscreen 189 58
sidecar windshield 189 58
side cast, two-handed ~ 89 32
side ceiling 222 62
side comb 105 6
side control 180 5, 20
side drum 323 51
side elevation 207 1, 22-25, 37, 60, 74
side flat 310 33
side frame 165 12; 167 20
side girder, longitudinal ~ 222 52
side grafting 54 36
side grip 134 45
side horse 296 5
side joint 111 14
side lay control 180 5, 20
sidelight 189 56; 191 20; 223 15
sidelight, green ~ 286 11
sidelight, headlight, and parking light switch 191 62
sidelight, port ~ 286 12
sidelight, red ~ 286 12
sidelight, starboard ~ 286 11
sideline 292 17; 293 2 - 3, 4 - 5; 293 55
side margin control 180 5, 20
sidemarker lamp 189 56; 191 20
side note 185 68
side of pork 94 23
side panel, removable ~ 188 48
side parting 315 1
side planking 62 25

side pocket 33 12
siderostat 5 16
side rudder 218 6
side shoot 370 21
sideshow 308 24
side slit 30 49
side split 295 15
side stake 206 24
side stay 284 18
sidestep 301 27
sidestepping 299 29
side stop 200 34, 44
side straddle 295 3
side strake 222 45
side stringer 222 50
side stroke 282 36
side support Shipbuild. 222 40
side support Free Exerc. 295 25
side thrust kick 299 19
side trappings 71 16
side view 207 1, 22-25, 37, 60, 74
sidewalk 37 60; 198 9
sidewall Electrotyp. etc. 178 45
sidewall Railw. 213 29
side wall Music. Instr. 323 4, 25
side-whiskers 34 24
side window blower 191 61
siding 206 50
Siemens-Martin open-hearth furnace 147 21-30
sieve Market Gdn. 55 13
sieve Graphic Art 340 24
sieve, louvred-type ~ 64 17
sieve, reciprocating ~ 64 19
sieve, upright ~ 55 13
sieve extension 64 18
sifter 91 26
sight 87 65; 255 45
sight, front ~ 87 71; 255 3, 23, 37; 305 42
sight, optical ~ 305 41
sight, telescopic ~ 87 29; 255 28; 305 49
sight graticule 87 31-32
sighting mechanism 255 45
sighting notch Hunt. 87 66
sighting notch Army 255 22
sight scale division 87 68
sign, chequered ~ 203 30
sign, illuminated ~ 203 38
signal 205 42
signal, distant ~ 203 7-24
signal, main ~ 203 1, 1-6
signal, visual ~ 238 30
signal and radar mast 221 7
signal arm 203 2
signal box 203 53
signal box, electrically-operated ~ 203 61
signal box, manually-operated ~ 203 53
signal element 243 60
signal flags 253 22-34
signal generator 313 30
signaling see signalling
signal knob 203 62
signal lever 203 56
signal light Power Plant 153 3
signal light Cotton Spin. 164 8
signal light Railw. 212 15
signal light Ship 221 125
signalling equipment 203
signalling lamp 223 7
signalling mast 225 34
signal mast Map 14 51
signal mast Docks 225 34
signal position 203 4, 5, 10, 11
signals, supplementary ~ 203 25-44

signal stay **223** 11
signal tower **14** 51
signal tower, electrically-operated ~ **203** 61
signal tower, manually-operated ~ **203** 53
signal track **243** 59
signature *Bookbind.* **183** 12; **185** 69
signature *Stock Exch.* **251** 15, 16
signature, cross-folded ~ **185** 15
signature, parallel-folded ~ **185** 13
signature code **185** 69
signboard **118** 45
signet ring **36** 40
sign for day running **203** 36
sign for night running **203** 38
sign of parallelism **345** 21
sign of similarity **345** 22
signs, conventional ~ **15** 1-114
signs, zodiacal ~ **4** 53-64
signs of the zodiac **4** 53-64
signwriting brush **129** 41
sikar **337** 26
sikhara **337** 26
silencer **191** 29; **209** 12, 22, 24; **211** 49; **305** 93
silhouette **25** 39
silicon atom **1** 14
siliqua *Weeds* **61** 20, 23
siliqua *Bot.* **370** 93
siliqua *Alp. Plants etc.* **378** 33
siliqua *South. Fruits* **384** 46
siliqua, mature ~ **383** 4
siliqua, ripe ~ **383** 4
silk-cotton tree **383** 20
silk moth **358** 48
silk taffeta **35** 36
silkworm **358** 50
sill *Phys. Geog.* **11** 31
sill *Car* **193** 21
sill rail **120** 56
silo **225** 68
silo, above-ground ~ **62** 11
silo, polythene ~ **62** 43
silo cylinder **225** 69
silo pipe **62** 12
silver **254** 25
silver-disc pyrheliometer **10** 23
silver fir **372** 1
silverfish **81** 14
silverleaf **371** 23
silver owl **362** 17
silver poplar **371** 23
silverside **95** 34
silversmith **108**
sima **11** 4
simple interest formula **345** 7
simsim **383** 49
Sinanthropus **261** 18
sine **346** 32
singer **315** 22, 23
single, clinker-built ~ **283** 18
single-hand control **185** 7
single-loader **87** 1
singles **293** 4-5
single sculler **283** 16
single-shot rifle **305** 35
singles match **293** 4-5
singles sideline **293** 4-5
single-system recording **117** 8
singlet **296** 61
single-trip bottle **93** 29
sinister **254** 19,21,23
sink *Phys. Geog.* **11** 49; **13** 71
sink *Kitch.* **39** 35
sink *Forestry* **84** 28
sink *Bakery* **97** 68

sink *Coal* **144** 47
sink *Energy Sources* **155** 16
sink *School* **261** 6, 34
sink *Camping* **278** 6
sinker *Sea Fish.* **90** 10
sinker *Knitting* **167** 58
sinker *Navig.* **224** 73
sinker, oval ~ **89** 88
sinkhole **11** 49; **13** 71
sink unit **39** 33-36
Sinningia **53** 7
sinter terraces **11** 23
sinuate **370** 48
sinus, frontal ~ **17** 55
sinus, sphenoidal ~ **17** 54
siphon barometer **10** 1
siphon tube **10** 43
siren *Ship* **223** 3
siren *Fabul. Creat.* **327** 58
siren, ship's ~ **224** 32
sirenian **366** 23
Sirius **3** 14
sirloin **95** 17; **96** 4
sisal **35** 13
siskin **361** 8
site fence **118** 44
site hut **118** 48; **119** 44
site of battle **15** 93
site office **118** 48
sit harness **300** 57
situla, sheet-bronze ~ **328** 34
Siva **337** 19
six-day race **290** 2-7
six-day racer **290** 2
six-eight time **320** 34
six-four time **320** 35
sixte engagement **294** 48
sixteenth note **320** 17
sixteenth rest **320** 25
six-to-pica **175** 19
sixty-fourth note **320** 19
sixty-fourth rest **320** 27
size **128** 4
size press **173** 24
sizing **162** 53
sizing and edging machine **132** 57
sizing machine **165** 52
skateboard **273** 51
skate guard **302** 25
skate sailing **302** 27-28
skate sailor **302** 27
skeet **305** 70-78
skeet choke **305** 71
skeet shooting **305** 70-78
skeg **279** 3; **286** 61
skeletal **194** 30-33
skeleton *Man* **17** 1-29
skeleton *School* **261** 14
skeleton *Winter Sp.* **303** 22
skeleton, siliceous ~ **357** 8
skeleton construction **119** 1
skeleton rider **303** 23
skeleton toboggan **303** 22
skeleton tobogganing **303** 22-24
skep **77** 52
sketch for costume **315** 40
sketch pad **338** 35
skew notch **120** 54
skew notch, double ~ **121** 91
skew notch, single ~ **121** 90
ski, compact ~ **301** 1
ski, modern ~ **301** 46
ski bag **301** 28
ski bob **304** 16
ski cap **35** 39; **301** 10
skid chain **304** 10
skidder **85** 34
skidder, short-haul ~ **85** 27
skife knife **100** 51
skiff **283** 16
skiing **301** 1-72

skiing boot, cemented sole ~ **301** 12
skiing cap **35** 39; **301** 10
skiing goggles **301** 11
ski jumping **301** 35
ski jumping boot **301** 41
ski jumping ski **301** 38
ski lift **301** 57-63, 59
skim coulter **65** 11
skimmer **96** 43
skimmer, stepped ~ **286** 38-41
skimmer rod **148** 17
skimmers **286** 38-44
skim milk tank **76** 17
skin *Shipbuild.* **222** 44-49
skin *School* **261** 9
skin *Gliding* **287** 40
skin, light alloy ~ **235** 11
skin, outer ~ *Rowing* **283** 33, 48
skin, outer ~ *Ball Games* **293** 33
skin diver **279** 7
skin diving **279** 7-27
skip *Road Constr.* **200** 25
skip *Railw.* **213** 38; **214** 34
skip *Gymn.* **297** 42, 45
skip hoist *Iron & Steel* **147** 3
skip hoist *Road Constr.* **200** 14
ski pole **301** 5
skipping **273** 15
skipping rope **273** 16; **297** 43
skip rope **273** 16
skip-winding system **144** 25
skirt *Child. Clothes* **29** 52
skirt *Ladies' Wear* **30** 9; **31** 3, 24
skirt *Army* **255** 85
skirt *Motorboats etc.* **286** 66
skirt *Airsports* **288** 48
skirt, aft ~ **235** 63
skirt, girl's ~ **29** 46
skirt, grass ~ **306** 18
skirt, inverted pleat ~ **30** 51
skirt, loden ~ **30** 67
skirt, long ~ **30** 45
skirt, pleated ~ **30** 32
skirt, wrap-around ~ **31** 13
skirt, wrapover ~ **31** 13
skirting **123** 21
skirting board **123** 21, 63
skirt suit **31** 1
skirt suit, girl's ~ **29** 50
ski stick **301** 5
ski stop **301** 56
ski suit, ladies' ~ **301** 9
ski suit, one-piece ~ **301** 9
skittle frame **305** 1-11
skittles **305** 1-13
skiving knife **100** 51
ski wax **301** 21
ski-waxing equipment **301** 21-24
skull *Man* **17** 1, 30-41
skull *School* **261** 15, 17, 19, 21
skull *Rowing* **283** 35-38
skull *Chivalry* **329** 39
skull, australopithecine ~ **261** 20
sky **3** 1-8
sky, northern ~ **3** 1-35
sky, southern ~ **3** 36-48
sky blue **343** 6
skydiving **288** 37-62
skylight **38** 2; **121** 8; **122** 12
skysail **220** 32
slab **120** 96
slab, reinforced concrete ~ **123** 28
slab, stone ~ **51** 17; **331** 61
slab, wooden ~ **324** 62
slab cake **97** 34; **99** 21

slacks **29** 49
slacks, lightweight ~ **31** 52
slack suit **30** 57
slade **65** 6, 66
slag escape **147** 9
slag ladle **147** 10
slag spout **148** 12
slalom **301** 29, 64
slalom canoe **283** 4
slalom ski **286** 60
slant track **243** 31
slapstick **306** 48
slat **229** 53
slat, extensible ~ **229** 38
slate *Roof* **122** 85
slate **309** 72
slate hammer **122** 73
slater *House Insects etc.* **81** 6
slater *Roof* **122** 71
slate roof **122** 61-89
slath **136** 21
slating batten **122** 17
slaughterer **94** 1
slaughterhouse *Slaughterho.* **94**
slaughterhouse *Bullfight. etc.* **319** 13
slaughterman **94** 1
slave, female ~ **306** 41
slave driver **218** 47
slave galley **218** 44-50
slave station **224** 41
sled **303** 1, 2
sled dog **353** 2
sledge **303** 1, 2
sledge dog **353** 2
sledge hammer **137** 22; **158** 6
sleeper *Bldg. Site* **119** 39
sleeper *Station* **205** 60
sleeper *Railw.* **207** 36
sleeper, concrete ~ **202** 37
sleeper, coupled ~ **202** 14, 38
sleeper, steel ~ *Railw.* **202** 36
sleeper, steel ~ *Hydr. Eng.* **217** 3
sleeper and strampler **29** 23
sleeping bag *Infant Care etc.* **28** 17
sleeping bag *Camping* **278** 30
sleeping car **207** 36
sleeping doll **47** 11
sleeve **30** 15
sleeve, batwing ~ **31** 16
sleeve, braided ~ **186** 24
sleeve, dagged ~ **355** 46
sleeve, full ~ **355** 60
sleeve, gallooned ~ **186** 24
sleeve, kimono ~ **30** 36
sleeve, petal-scalloped ~ **355** 46
sleeve, protective ~ **142** 6
sleeve, puffed ~ **31** 27; **355** 49, 60
sleeve, sliding ~ **192** 32, 35
sleeve, turned-up ~ **31** 62
sleeve, turnover ~ **30** 6
sleeve, turn-up ~ **30** 6
sleeve board **50** 20
sleeve protector **324** 17
sleigh, horse-drawn ~ **304** 25
sleigh bell **304** 26
slender funnel fungus **381** 25
slewing crab **222** 21
slew turntable **200** 22
sley **166** 41, 53
sley cap **166** 6
slice *Bakery* **97** 43
slice *Blacksm.* **137** 2
slice, sugared ~ **97** 43
slicer **96** 31
slicker **81** 14
slide *Inf. Tech.* **242** 42
slide *Playground* **273** 24

slide *Winter Countr.* 304 17
slide *Music. Not.* 321 16
slide *Music. Instr.* 322 51; 323 47; 326 7, 33
slide, bed ~ 177 59
slide bar 313 10
slide calliper 85 10
slide chair 202 22
slide control 238 47; 241 8
slide-copying adapter 115 88
slide-copying attachment 115 87
slide holder 309 43
slide projector 114 76; 309 42; 312 23
slider 326 7
slide rail 206 38
sliding door 271 50
sliding scale 349 23
sliding weight 22 68; 40 36
sliding-weight scales *Doc.* 22 66
sliding-weight scales 40 35
sling *First Aid* 21 2
sling *Mountain.* 300 11
sling pump 101 53
sling ring 87 5
sling seat 300 29
slip *Underwear etc.* 32 13
slip *Plant Propagn.* 54 20
slip *Roof* 122 48
slip casting 161 15
slip fault 12 7
slip-off slope 13 58
slipper *Shoes* 101 41
slipper *Station* 206 49
slipper animalcule 357 9
slipper brake 206 49
slip road 15 16
slips 222 11-26
slip sock, woollen ~ 101 42
slipway 222 11-18
slipway crane 222 23
slipway floor 222 17
slipway frame 222 19
slipway portal 222 11
slipways 222 11-26
slit, side ~ 30 49
slit gong 354 18
slitter 181 42
sliver 164 15, 21
sliver, carded ~ 163 38
sliver, carded and combed ~ 163 72
sliver, coiled ~ 163 35
sliver, doubled ~s 164 12
sliver, thin ~ 164 13
sliver can 164 3, 20
sloe 374 27
slope 347 12
slope, continental ~ 11 9
slope soaring 287 27
slops 355 34
slosh baffle system 235 53
slot *Glass Prod.* 162 9
slot *Weaving* 166 32
slot *Garage* 195 5
slot *Election* 263 30
slot *Airsports* 288 45
slotted board 2 45
slouch hat 35 21
slow motion control 243 49
slow-running jet 192 1
slowworm 364 10
slubbing frame 164 19
slug 174 27
slug-casting machine 174 19
slug-composing machine 174 19
slug of clay 161 10
sluice dam 217 73-80
sluice gate 217 53-56, 77
sluice valve 217 53-56

slump fault 12 7
slush 304 30
slush pump 145 16
smack 221 49
small-arm 87 2
small beer 93 26
smallbore free rifle 305 44
smallbore rifle 305 48
smallbore standard rifle 305 43
small cabbage white butterfly 80 48
small ermine moth 80 5
small of the back 16 25
small of the butt 87 7
small scabious 375 29
small-shot cartridge 87 49
small-shot charge 87 51
smash 293 17
smear 23 15, 50
smelting section 147 8
smith 137; 138
smith forging 139
smock overall 31 35
smock windmill 91 29
smokebox door 210 26
smoke canister 255 83
smoke dispenser 255 83
smoke extract 38 81
smoke flap 352 9
smoke house 96 48
smoke outlet 38 81; 210 22; 353 21
smoker's companion 107 44
smokestack *Power Plant* 152 15
smokestack *Railw.* 210 22
smoke tube 210 8
smoking requisites 107
smoother 128 11
smoothing blade 200 18
smoothing plane 132 15; 134 1
snaffle 289 12
snail 357 27
snail, edible ~ 357 27
snail shell 357 29
snake, poisonous ~ 364 40
snake, venomous ~ 364 40
snake charmer 353 45
snakes 364 38-41
snakeweed 376 10
snapdragon 51 32
snap gauge 149 59
snap lid 127 24
snapping beetle 80 37
snapping bug 80 37
snare drum 323 51
snath 66 16
snathe 66 16
snead 66 16
sneath 66 16
snedding machine 85 18
snipe 88 83
snorkel *Warships* 259 72, 90
snorkel *Swim.* 279 11
snorkel *Bathing* 280 39
snout 73 10; 88 53; 364 2
snow 8 18; 9 34; 304 24; 353 5
snow and ice climber 300 15
snow and ice climbing 300 14-21
snow and ice climbing equipment 300 31-57
snow avalanche 304 1
snowball *Winter Countr.* 304 15
snowball *Shrubs etc.* 373 10
snowball bush 373 10
snowball fight 304 14
snow blower 213 17
snow bridge 300 24
snow chain 304 10

snow cornice 300 20
snowdrift 304 5
snowdrop 60 1
snowfall 10 48; 304 4
snow fence 304 6
snow forest climate 9 56
snow gaiter 300 55
snow goggles 300 18
snow guard 38 8
snow guard bracket 122 16
snow hut 353 4
snow ledge 300 4
snowman 304 13
snow plough, rotary ~ 213 17
snow plough attachment 304 9
snow plough signs 203 34-35
snow push 304 23
snowshirt 300 9
snow shovel 304 23
snowslide 304 1
snow suit 29 38
snuff 107 20
snuff box 107 20
soaking pit 148 46
soaking pit crane 148 47
soaking tub 136 13
soap 49 22
soap box 273 33
soap dish 49 21
soap dispenser 50 27
soaring 287
soccer 291
soccer game 273 10
sock 291 58
sock, knee-length ~ 29 53; 32 32; 33 42
sock, long ~ 32 34
sock, surgical ~ 101 50
socket *Hairdresser* 106 15
socket *Plumb.* 125 20
socket *Plumb. etc.* 126 43
socket *Electr.* 127 7
socket, double ~ 127 6
socket, earthed ~ 127 5, 6, 13
socket, four-way ~ 127 8
socket, surface-mounted ~ 127 13
socket, switched ~ 127 7
socket, three-pin ~ 127 66
socket, three-pole ~ 127 13
socket, tinner's ~ 125 20
socket, underfloor ~ 127 22
socket outlet box 127 25
socks, men's ~ 32 32-34
soda bottle 42 32
soda-lime absorber 27 39
soda water 98 87
soda water bottle 42 32
sodium atom 1 8
sodium chloride 1 9; 170 13
sodium ion 1 11
sodium pump, primary ~ 154 5
sodium pump, secondary ~ 154 8
sodium sulphate storage tank 172 36
sodium system, primary ~ 154 2
sodium system, secondary ~ 154 7
sofa 336 17
sofa, two-seater ~ 246 36
soffit 122 27
soft corn 68 31
soft pedal 325 9
soil covering 200 64
soil injector 83 33
solan goose 359 9
solar cell 155 34
solar collector 155 28, 32
solarium 281 10

solar panel 10 66
solar radiation shielding 10 36
solar sensor 10 69
solar spectrum 343 14
solar system 4 42-52
soldanella 378 3
solder 108 38
solder, tin-lead ~ 126 76
soldering apparatus 125 5-7
soldering borax 108 39
soldering fluid 125 7
soldering flux 108 36
soldering gun *Goldsm. etc.* 108 14
soldering gun *D.I.Y.* 134 56
soldering iron *Plumb.* 125 5
soldering iron *Plumb. etc.* 126 73
soldering iron *D.I.Y.* 134 19, 57
soldering iron, electric ~ 127 45
soldering iron, high-speed ~ 134 58
soldering stone 125 6
solder wire, tin-lead ~ 134 20
soldier, lead ~ 309 52
soldier, tin ~ 309 52
sole *Agr. Mach.* 65 6, 66
sole *Shoem.* 100 66
sole *Joiner* 132 22
sole, cemented ~ 101 11
sole, corrugated ~ 300 43
sole, inner ~ 291 31
sole, natural-colour ~ 101 15, 38
sole, nylon ~ 291 30
sole, plastic ~ 101 2
sole, PVC ~ 101 2
sole, rubber ~ 101 38
sole, wooden ~ 101 45
sole bar reinforcement 213 12
sole leather 100 31
sole-leather shears 100 39
solenoid valve 139 23
sole of the foot 19 62
sole-plate *Household* 50 7
sole-plate *Road Constr.* 200 33
sole-plate *Railw.* 202 5
sole press, automatic ~ 100 14
sole stitcher 100 26
sole-stitching machine 100 26
sole trimmer 100 5
solid-fuel rocket, recoverable ~ 235 58
solidification 170 35, 43
solid-newel staircase 123 77
solid rocket booster 235 58
solids 347 30-46
solid stage 148 26
solid-web girder 121 72
solid-web girder bridge 215 7
solifluction lobe 11 51
solifluction tongue 11 51
soling 284 56
solleret 329 55
solo machine 290 27
solo organ 326 45
solo seat 189 19
solo skater 302 1
solstice 3 8
solution 345 10
solution, viscous ~ 169 15
solvent fumes 182 25
Somali Current 14 36
sombrero 35 5
songbirds 360 1,3,4,5,7,9,10; 361 1-20
song thrush 361 16
soot 38 34
sordino 323 10; 324 68

Soricidae 366 7
sort 174 7, 28
sorter 172 57
sorter, rotary ~ 172 23
sorter, secondary ~ 172 58
sorting machine 74 38
sorting siding 206 47
sorting table 64 81
sound assistant 117 68; 310 57
soundboard Music. Instr. 323 24; 324 3
soundboard Church 330 21
sound box 322 18, 29; 323 3; 324 15, 63
sound camera 117 22; 313 26
sound camera, Super-8 ~ 117 1
sound coding equipment 242 11-14
sound connecting cord 117 8
sound control console 238 20, 41, 54; 239 8
sound control desk 238 20, 41, 54; 239 8
sound control engineer 238 19
sound control room 238 27; 239 7
sound dubbing 311 34-36
sound echo 224 63
sound editor 117 96
sound effect 310 30
sound effects box 238 35
sound engineer 238 19
sound film 117 82
sound film cartridge, Super-8 ~ 117 29
sound head Cine Film 117 33
sound head Audiovis. 243 35
sound head Films 312 47
sound head housing 241 59
sound hole 322 22; 323 6; 324 5
sound impulse 224 62
sounding balloon 7 17
sounding board 330 21
sound mixer 238 26
sound mixing 311 34-36
sound module 240 14
sound OB van 239 1-15
sound optics 312 46
sound production control room 238 27; 239 7
sound projector 117 81; 312 24
sound recorder, portable ~ 310 24
sound recording 311 1-46
sound recording camera 310 60; 311 6
sound recording equipment 117 7
sound recording level control 243 11
sound recording selector switch 117 13
sound recordist Broadcast. 238 26
sound recordist Films 310 23, 55; 311 36
sound source 117 27
sound source, external ~ 117 8
sound technician 238 26
sound track Cine Film 117 82
sound track Audiovis. 243 32
sound track system 117 21
sound transmitter 224 61
sound turntable, first ~ 117 100
sound turntable, second ~ 117 101

sound wave 224 62
sound wave propagation 7 14
soup ladle 45 14
soup plate 44 6; 45 5
soup seasoning 98 30
soup spoon 45 61
soup tureen 44 8; 45 15
soup vegetable 68 25
sources of energy, modern ~ 155
source water inlet 155 2
sour cherry 59 5
souring chamber 159 6
sour milk vat 76 42
South America 14 13
South Equatorial Current 14 34
Southern Cross 3 44
Southern Ocean 14 22
Southern Triangle 3 40
south point 4 17
South Pole 14 3
southwester 35 30; 228 5
sou'wester 35 30; 228 5
souvenir plate 309 48
sow Dom. Anim. 73 9
sow Livestock 75 41
sow Hunt. 86 32
sow Game 88 48, 51
sow bug 81 6
sower 63 10
sowing 54 1; 63 10-12
sow pig 75 42
spa 274
space Composing Rm. 175 5, 17
space Music. Not. 320 44
space, popliteal ~ 16 51
spaceband 174 24
space bar 249 2
space capsule 6 9, 10; 234 65
spacecraft 6 1
space flight 234; 235
spaceflight module 235 70
Spacelab 235 65
space laboratory 235 65
spacer 119 81
Space Shuttle-Orbiter 235 1-45
space station 235 65
space suit 6 18-27
space suit helmet 6 22
spacing bracket 126 54
spacing clip 126 57
spacing lines 10 58
spacing material 174 8
spade 56 2; 331 36
spade Fish Farm. 89 82
spade Army 255 55
spade, semi-automatic ~ 56 12
spade piston 255 56
spades 276 39
spadix 370 71; 378 22
spadix, female ~ 384 6
spadix, male ~ 383 55; 384 4
spa gardens 274 1-21
spaghetti 98 32
spale 136 12
spale basket 136 11
span Bridges 215 14
span Aircraft 229 2
span, clear ~ 215 13
span, wire rope ~ 221 102
Spandau 255 32
Spanish chestnut 384 48
Spanish paprika 57 42
spanker 219 30
spanker boom 218 28; 219 44
spanker boom topping lift 219 48
spanker gaff 219 45
spanker peak halyard 219 49

spanker sheet 219 69
spanker vang 219 70
span of oxen 63 16
spa orchestra 274 20
spa promenade 274 10
spar 230 45
spar, diagonal ~ 287 33
spar, integral ~ 257 28
spar, main ~ 287 30
spar buoy 224 79
spar ceiling 222 62
spare man 291 11
spare part Watchm. 109 22
spare part Garage 195 32
spare rib 95 41
spare tyre Lorries etc. 194 4
spare tyre Cyc. Racing 290 23
spare wheel 191 25; 194 33
spar-hawk 362 12
spark arrester 210 24
spark gap 153 62
spark-ignition engine 190 1, 2
sparking plug 190 35; 242 48
spark plug 190 35; 242 48
spark-plug cap 188 27
Sparmannia 53 9
sparring partner 299 27
sparrow hawk 362 12
sparrow owl 362 19
spars 219 32-45
spatula Dent. 24 50
spatula Hosp. 25 7
spatula Art. Studio 338 15
spatula, plastic ~ 128 44
spawn 89 12
spawner 89 13
speaker Living Rm. 42 10
speaker Election 263 5
speaker Hotel 267 40
speaker Disco 317 15
speaker Nightclub 318 12
speaker, three-way ~ 241 14
speaking key 242 24
spear, long-bladed ~ 354 12
spear head, bronze ~ 328 21
spear thrower 352 40
special effects equipment 310 59
special offer 96 20; 271 65
specialty shop 195 1-55
specie 252 1-28
speciestaler 252 6
specimen insertion air lock 113 33
specimen stage adjustment 113 34
spectacle fitting 111 1-4
spectacle frame Opticn. 111 5, 10-14
spectacle frame Ship 223 61
spectacle lens 111 15
spectacles 111 5, 9
spectator 308 29
spectator barrier 292 40
spectators' terrace 233 20
'spectators' terrace' 233 30
spectrograph 5 33
speculum, aural ~ 22 74
speculum, rectal ~ 23 19
speculum, vaginal ~ 23 13
speed ball 299 22
speedboat 283 2
speed change lever 149 5
speed changer 241 29
speed code number 203 37
speed control 179 29
speed indicator 203 18
speed indicator, distant ~ 203 19
speedo 188 19, 34; 191 38, 74
speedometer Motorcycles etc. 188 19, 34, 40
speedometer Motorcycle 189 40

speedometer Car 191 38, 74
speedometer Tram 197 31
speedometer Railw. 211 35; 212 9
speedometer Navig. 224 54
speedometer, ship's ~ 224 22
speedometer drive 192 38, 39
speed recorder 210 54
speed restriction, permanent ~ 203 41, 42
speed restriction, temporary ~ 203 39, 40
speed restriction sign 203 36-38, 41, 44
speed restriction signs 203 36-44
speed restriction warning sign 203 43
speed selector 241 29
speed skate 302 20
speed skater 302 26
speed skating set 302 20
speedway 290 24-28
speedwell 375 22
speleothems 13 80-81
spelling book 260 17
spelt 68 24
spelt, green ~ 68 25
spencer 220 1
sperm whale 367 25
sphagnum mosses 13 20, 22
sphenoid 17 38
sphere 347 41
sphere, celestial ~ 4 23
sphere, plain ~ 36 82
sphere, solar ~ 4 36
sphere unit 2 38
spherical typing element 249 15
sphincter, anal ~ 20 63
sphinx Fabul. Creat. 327 20
sphinx Articulates 358 55
sphinx Lepidopt. 365 9
sphinx, Egyptian ~ 333 11
sphygmograph 26 32
sphygmomanometer 25 15
Spica 3 18
spice jar 39 32
spice packet 99 67
spice rack 39 31; 47 29
spices 382
spider legs 115 91
spiders 358 44-46
spider's web Playground 273 46
spider's web Articulates 358 47
spike Arable Crops 68 2
spike Mountain. 300 9
spike Music. Instr. 323 22
spike Industr. Plants 383 62, 66
spike, fleshy ~ 370 71
spike, racemose ~ 370 67
spikelet 68 3, 10; 69 23; 375 41, 42
spill light 310 51
spillway 217 60
spin Roulette 275 32
spin Airsports 288 7
spinach 57 29
spinal cord 17 48; 18 25
spindle Watchm. 109 17
spindle Mach. Tools 149 66; 150 27
spindle Cotton Spin. 164 43
spindle Bookbind. 183 22
spindle Bicycle 187 60, 80
spindle, horizontal ~ 150 40
spindle, main ~ 149 11
spindle, screwed ~ 149 66

spindle catch **164** 49
spindle drive **164** 31
spindle oil **145** 61
spindle rail **164** 50
spindle rotation speed **150** 35
spindle shaft **164** 46
spindle speed **164** 38, 40
spindle top **126** 32
spine *Man* **17** 2-5
spine *Bookbind.* **183** 14; **185** 41
spine *Mammals* **366** 6
spine label **247** 38
spine of the book **183** 1
spinet **322** 45
spine tag **247** 38
spinet piano **325** 1
spinner *Fish Farm.* **89** 74, 75
spinner *Aircraft* **230** 33
spinner, long ~ **89** 76
spinneret *Synth. Fibres* **169** 14; **170** 41
spinneret *Articulates* **358** 46
spinneret hole **170** 41, 42
spinning **170** 57
spinning bath **169** 15
spinning jet **169** 14; **170** 41, 42
spiraea **374** 23
spiral *Photog.* **116** 2
spiral *Airsports* **288** 51
spiral *Gymn.* **297** 50
spiral design pottery **328** 13
spire **331** 6
spire ball **331** 5
spirit glass **45** 90
spirit lamp **24** 57
spirit level *Map* **14** 61
spirit level *Bldg. Site* **118** 55
spirit level *Plumb. etc.* **126** 79
spirit level *D.I.Y.* **134** 29
spirits **98** 56-59; **318** 19
spirograph **27** 36
Spirographis **357** 22
spirometer **23** 31
spirometry **27** 36-50
spit *Phys. Geog.* **13** 5
spit *Kitch. Utensils* **40** 33
spitz **70** 20
splashboard **186** 6
spleen **20** 12, 27
splenius of the neck **18** 51
splice, wet ~ **117** 89
splice graft **54** 39
splice grafting **54** 39
splicer **117** 89
splicing cement **312** 22
splicing head **133** 29
splint *First Aid* **21** 12
splint *Sawmill* **157** 16
splint, emergency ~ **21** 10
splint bone **17** 24
splinter **157** 16
split-image rangefinder **115** 55, 59, 64
splits **314** 20
splitter **94** 17
splitting hammer **85** 5
spoil **226** 47
spoiler **229** 39; **287** 38
spoiler, front ~ **193** 36
spoiler, inner ~ **229** 42
spoiler, rear ~ **193** 34; **290** 35
spoiler rim **193** 30
spoil heap **144** 19
spoke *Mach. Parts etc.* **143** 88
spoke *Bicycle* **187** 27
spoke *Motorcycle* **189** 24
spoke end **187** 29
spoke flange **187** 29
spoke nipple **187** 29
spokeshave **132** 27
spoke wheel **289** 25
sponge *Bathrm. etc.* **49** 6

sponge *School* **260** 42
sponge *Graphic Art* **340** 25
sponge *Invertebr.* **357** 13
sponge holder **23** 12
sponge tray **260** 41
spool **162** 55
spool box **312** 16
spool box, fireproof ~ **312** 25
spool holder **185** 17
spool knob **114** 27
spoon *Tablew. etc.* **45** 61
spoon *Fish Farm.* **89** 73
spoon, wooden ~ **40** 2
spoon bait **89** 73
spoonbill **359** 5
spoon bit **135** 16
spoon bow **285** 30
spoon chisel **339** 18
spore **381** 8, 13
sporting coupé **193** 28
sporting gun **86** 4
sporting guns **87** 1-40
sporting rifle **86** 4
sporting rifles **87** 1-40; **305** 40-49
sport parachute **288** 45
sport parachuting **288** 37-62
sports, various ~ **305**
sportsboat, inflatable ~ **286** 1
sportsboats *Rowing* **283** 9-16
sportsboats *Motorboats etc.* **286** 1-5, 10-14
sports news item **342** 61
sports report **342** 60
sports reporter **299** 50
sports section **342** 57
spot **276** 32
spot, central ~ **115** 65
spot, clear ~ **115** 66
spot ball, white ~ **277** 13
spotlight **307** 3; **318** 24
spotlight catwalk **310** 53
spotted bruchus **81** 19
spotted woodpecker **359** 27
spotting position **297** 16
spot welder, foot-operated ~ **142** 29
spot welding **142** 22
spot welding electrode holder **142** 23
spout **91** 14
spout, swivel-mounted ~ **64** 37
spout hole **367** 26
spray *Doc.* **22** 60
spray *Pest Contr.* **83** 8
spray boom **83** 3
spray can **106** 23
spray canister **83** 44
spraydeck **283** 56
sprayer *Gdn. Tools* **56** 24
sprayer *Letterpress* **181** 10, 34
sprayer, semi-mounted ~ **83** 47
sprayer, tractor-mounted ~ **83** 2
spray fluid tank **83** 5, 50
spray gun *Pest Contr.* **83** 18
spray gun *Painter* **129** 32
spray gun *Letterpress* **181** 34
spray gun, airless ~ **129** 37
spraying **129** 28
spraying tube **83** 29
spray line, oscillating ~ **67** 1
spray nozzle *Household* **50** 13
spray nozzle *Intern. Combust. Eng.* **190** 54
spray pipe **172** 72
spray tank **83** 39
spray tube **83** 22
spray unit *Pest Contr.* **83** 58
spray unit *Offset Platem.* **179** 5, 6

spray unit, airless ~ **129** 36
spreader *Paperhanger* **128** 46
spreader *Ship* **223** 37
spreader *Sailing* **284** 13
spreader cylinder **62** 23
spreader unit **62** 22
spreading flap **200** 42
spring *Map* **15** 82
spring *Metalwkr.* **140** 46
spring *Knitting* **167** 38
spring *Carriages* **186** 15
spring, artesian ~ **12** 26
spring, rubber ~ **297** 13
spring attachment **11** 42
spring barrel **110** 38
springboard *Swim.* **282** 9, 10
springboard *Gymn.* **296** 12; **297** 8
springboard *Circus* **307** 36
springboard acrobat **307** 36
springboard artist **307** 35
springboard trampoline **297** 14
spring bolt **140** 37
spring bow compass **151** 64
spring buffer **214** 50
spring bumper **214** 50
spring chest **326** 12-14
springer **336** 22
spring extension **309** 28
spring fly **358** 12
spring form **40** 27
spring pin tool **109** 9
spring ring hinge **151** 65
spring snowflake **60** 1
spring suspension **83** 7
spring tine **65** 57
spring tine, double ~ **64** 42, 54
spring vice **140** 10
spring washer **143** 34; **202** 8
sprinkler **55** 19
sprinkler, oscillating ~ **56** 46
sprinkler, revolving ~ **56** 43; **62** 29; **67** 4, 32
sprinkler cart **62** 27
sprinkler hose **62** 30
sprinkler nozzle **67** 27
sprinkler stand **62** 28
sprinkler system **316** 6
sprinkling can **51** 21; **55** 26
sprinkling device **55** 19
sprinter **298** 5
spritsail **218** 43; **220** 5
sprocket **143** 90; **187** 38, 74
sprocket piece **121** 30
sprocket wheel **187** 38
sprout *Veg.* **57** 30
sprout *Bot.* **370** 19-25
spruce **372** 12
spruce cellulose **169** 1
spruce cone **372** 13
spruce fir **372** 12
spruce-gall aphid **82** 38
spruce needle **372** 19
spur *Dom. Anim.* **73** 26
spur *Game* **88** 82
spur *Mountain.* **300** 13
spurrey **69** 12
spurs **71** 50-51
spur vein **72** 28
spur wheel, helical ~ **143** 89
sputum **23** 25
spyhole *Hall* **41** 29
spyhole *Iron Foundry etc.* **148** 4
squadron marking **256** 2
square *Metalwkr.* **140** 57
square *Maths.* **346** 33; **347** 31
square, black ~ **276** 3
square, glazier's ~ **124** 20
square, iron ~ **120** 78
square, white ~ **276** 2
squared timber store **157** 32

square root **345** 3
squash **57** 23
squat **295** 9
squat-style snatch **299** 1
squat vault **296** 53
squaw **352** 10
squaw corn **68** 31
squeegee *Photog.* **116** 49
squeegee *Text. Finish.* **168** 61
squeeze phase **75** 34
squeeze roller **165** 46
squirrel **366** 19
squirrel's bread **381** 16
stabilizer *Photog.* **116** 10
stabilizer *Motorcycles etc.* **188** 5
stabilizer *Railw.* **214** 55
stabilizer *Navig.* **224** 26
stabilizer *Air Force* **256** 22
stabilizer *Winter Sp.* **301** 49
stabilizer *Sports* **305** 58
stabilizer, horizontal ~ **229** 26; **230** 62; **256** 31; **288** 23
stabilizer, vertical ~ **229** 24; **230** 59; **231** 6; **232** 7; **256** 32; **288** 21
stabilizer and rudder, vertical ~ **229** 24-25; **230** 58
stabilizer bar **192** 71
stabilizing fin *Air Force* **256** 22
stabilizing fin *Swim.* **279** 3
stabilizing fin, aerodynamic ~ **234** 7
stabilizing layer **301** 49
stabilizing panel **288** 49
stabilizing surface **256** 22
stabilizing wing **117** 60
stable **62** 2; **75** 1
stable fly **81** 4
stableman **186** 27
staccato **321** 34
stack *Forestry* **84** 15
stack *Univ.* **262** 11
stack bearer **157** 37
stacker, intermediate ~ **236** 34
stacker truck **159** 18
stacking machine **162** 20
stack of logs **84** 16
staff **320** 43-44
staff compartment **207** 81
staff lavatory **207** 82
staff toilet **207** 82
staff washroom **207** 26
staff WC **207** 82
stag, rutting ~ **86** 12; **88** 4
stag beetle **358** 24
stag call **87** 46
stage *Films* **312** 8
stage *Theatre* **315** 14-27, 14
stage *Nightclub* **318** 22
stage, mechanical ~ **112** 10, 29; **115** 98
stage, microscopic ~ **112** 9
stage, revolving ~ **316** 31
stage, universal ~ **112** 17
stage base **112** 15
stage carpenter **316** 45,
stagecoach **186** 39
stagecoach, English ~ **186** 53
stage curtain **312** 10
stage designer **315** 37
stage director **316** 30
stagehand **315** 28; **316** 46
stagehouse **316** 1-60
stage light **316** 14
stage lighting **318** 23
stage lighting unit **316** 14
stage manager **316** 30
stage plate **115** 95
stage rehearsal **315** 21-27
stage separation retro-rocket **234** 8

staghorn 377 12
stag horn moss 377 12
staghound 289 47
staging *Photograv.* 182 12
staging *Shipbuild.* 222 18
stag jump 295 40; 302 7
stag leap 295 40; 302 7
stag's horn 377 12
stag's horn moss 377 12
staining dish 23 50
staining vat 130 15
staircase 37 72; 118 22
staircase, dog-legged ~ 123 42-44
staircase, outside ~ 333 33
staircase, quarter-newelled ~ 123 75
staircase, spiral ~ 123 76, 77
staircase, winding ~ 123 76, 77
staircase bolt 123 46
staircase construction 123
staircase of locks 217 17-25
staircase window 37 81; 123 65
stair light 41 22
stairs, concrete ~ 123 16
stair well 120 46
stake *Wine Grow.* 78 7
stake *Forestry* 84 17
stake *Plumb.* 125 23
stake *Basketm.* 136 6
stake *Roulette* 275 13
stake net 89 94
stalactite 13 80, 82
stalactite vault 337 17
stalagmite 13 81, 82
stalk 58 13, 34, 61; 68 6; 370 20; 378 31
stalk, herbaceous ~ 384 30
stalking 86 1-8
stall 75 2
stallion 73 2
stalls, front ~ 315 19
stall turn 288 4
stamen 58 45; 59 10, 39; 370 57, 60; 372 7, 18; 373 2, 5; 374 3
stamp *Doc.* 22 29
stamp *Slaughterho.* 94 24
stamp *Post* 236 21, 61
stamp *Bank* 250 24
stamp, impressed ~ 252 35
stamp book 236 20
stamp counter 236 15
stanchion 221 117
stanchion, hinged ~ 213 6
stanchion, steel ~ 213 6
stand *Hosp.* 25 11; 26 9, 29
stand *Overh. Irrign.* 67 2
stand *Shoem.* 100 54
stand *Optic.* 111 5
stand *Optic. Instr.* 112 2
stand *Basketm.* 136 10
stand *Composing Rm.* 175 50
stand *Photomech. Reprod.* 177 29
stand *Motorcycles etc.* 188 51
stand *Circus* 307 57
stand *Bullfight. etc.* 319 8
stand, hydraulic ~ 310 50
stand, raised ~ 86 14, 14-17
standard *Bldg. Site* 119 47, 59
standard *Forging* 139 19
standard *Photomech. Reprod.* 177 11
standard adjustment 114 51
standard lamp 46 37
Standard meridian 14 5
standard of the German Federal President 253 14
standby drive 214 64
standing-in position 297 16

standing matter 174 11
standing matter rack 174 9
standing position 305 27
standing press 183 20
standing room portion 197 18
standing stone 328 18
standing take-off pike dive 282 40
standing type 174 11
standing type rack 174 9
standing wrestling 299 6
standpipe *Farm Bldgs.* 62 12
standpipe *Oil, Petr.* 145 13
standpipe *Paperm.* 173 12
standpipe *Space* 234 25
standpipe *Fire Brig.* 270 26
standpipe coupler 67 5
stapelia 53 15
staple fiber lap 169 31
staple fibre 169 1-34
staple fibre, viscose rayon ~ 169 28-34
staple fibre layer 169 31
staple length 170 60
stapler 22 25; 247 4
staple shaft 144 27
stapling machine 247 4
star *Sailing* 284 55
star *Films* 310 27, 28
star, binary ~ 3 29
star, circumpolar ~ 3 5
star, double ~ 3 29
star, principal ~ 3 9
star, variable ~ 3 11
star connection 153 20
star finch 360 3
starfish 357 38; 369 17
starling 361 4
star map 3 1-35
star network 153 20
stars, fixed ~ 3 9-48
Stars and Stripes 253 18
Star-Spangled Banner 253 18
start *Motorboats etc.* 286 28, 29
start *Athletics* 298 1-6, 3
starter 282 30
starter, electric ~ 56 39
starter and steering lock 191 75
starter battery 212 46
starter button, electric ~ 189 52
starter motor *Intern. Combust. Eng.* 190 44
starter motor *Railw.* 212 30
starter pedal 188 25
starter's flag 273 34
starter switch 241 30
starting and braking device, automatic ~ 168 20
starting and finishing buoy 285 14
starting and stopping handle 166 8
starting and stopping lever 165 17; 180 80; 181 32
starting block *Swim.* 282 27
starting block *Athletics* 298 1
starting dive 282 29
starting gear ring 192 31
starting handle 163 17
starting lever 178 20
starting motor 190 44
starting place 282 27
starting position 295 1
starting price 289 37
starting resistance 135 3
starting resistor 135 3
starting rod 167 22
starting signal 205 47
start print button 249 38

start-stop lever 163 40
star wheel *Mach. Tools* 149 43
star wheel *Graphic Art* 340 39
Stassfurt salt 154 66
Stassfurt seam 154 65
stately home 15 96
statement of account 247 44
state of play 293 38
static air tank 196 19
station, coastal ~ 237 53
station, lower ~ 214 39
station, top ~ 214 57
station, upper ~ 214 57
stationary rings 296 4
station bookstall 204 26
station bookstand 204 26
station clock 204 30
station foreman 205 41
station hall 204
station mailbox 204 11
station of the Cross 330 54
station platform 205
station post box 204 11
station preset button 241 4; 243 17; 309 20
station restaurant 204 13
station selector button 241 4; 243 17; 309 20
station sign 205 28
station wagon 193 15
statistics chart 248 36
statue 272 10; 334 5; 339 32
statue, stone ~ 272 2
statuette, ivory ~ 328 8
stave *Cooper* 130 2
stave *Music. Not.* 320 43-44
stay, triatic ~ 223 11
stayer 290 14
stay pole 152 31
stay rope 299 37
stay-warm plate 28 28
stay wire 296 10; 297 5; 299 37
St. Bernard dog 70 37
steady, fixed ~ 150 30
steam 50 11
steam and recirculation water flow path 154 51
steam boiler 152 5
steam chest 210 31
steam collector 210 21
steam coupling hose 208 20
steam dome 210 12
steam extraction 103 26
steam extractor 103 25
steam-generating station 152 1-28
steam generator 154 9, 26, 44
steam heater 172 38
steam hole 50 14
steaming light 223 40; 258 55
steaming light mast 221 51
steam iron 103 20; 131 3
steam line 154 11
steam locomotives 210 1-69
steam pipe 172 64
steam pipe, high-pressure ~ 153 33
steam press 104 26
steam pressing unit 104 26
'steam radio' 309 16
steam reversing gear 210 18
steam slit 50 14
steam spray gun 131 2
steam sterilizer 22 39
steam storage locomotive 210 68
steam trawler 221 46
steam tube 210 17
steam turbine 152 23; 153 23-30; 154 14, 46, 52
steam turbine generator 259 58

steel 94 100
steel, finished ~ 148 68
steel bender 119 21
steel-casting ladle 147 31
steel grit delivery pipe 148 38
steel ingot 147 33
steel lattice bridge 215 34
steel-leg vice 126 80
steel-wheel glass cutter 124 26
steelworks 147 21-69
steep face 12 43
steeping 169 4
steeping floor 92 8, 28
steeping tank 92 8
steeple 331 2
steeplechase *Equest.* 289 20-22
steeplechase *Athletics* 298 7-8
steep liquor 92 6
steering, hydraulic power ~ 65 41
steering alignment 195 17, 22
steering alignment, visual ~ 195 41
steering and control position 224 14
steering arm 192 79
steering axle 64 32
steering column 192 56
steering column, controlled-collapse ~ 191 57
steering drop arm 192 58
steering gear 192 56-59
steering head 187 11
steering line *Rowing* 283 52
steering line *Airsports* 288 41
steering oar 218 6
steering rudder 283 51-53
steering runner 302 45
steering system, rear-wheel ~ 64 39
steering tube 187 14
steering wheel 191 37; 305 89
steering wheel spoke 191 58
steersman *Ship* 218 2
steersman *Winter Sp.* 303 20
stein 309 53
steinbock 367 7
Steinheim man 261 17
stela 330 43; 334 33
stele 330 43; 334 33
stem *Forestry* 84 19
stem *Tobacc. etc.* 107 38
stem *Metalwkr.* 140 33
stem *Ship* 218 4; 221 83, 108
stem *Chem.* 350 7
stem *Bot.* 370 2
stem *Edib. Fungi* 381 18
stem, bulbous ~ 222 74
stem, prostrate ~ 58 20
stem, straight ~ 285 40
stem, wire ~ 325 29
stem cutting 54 25
stemless alpine gentian 378 13
stemming sand bucket 158 29
stem post 218 4
stem rudder 218 24
stem stitch 102 4
stencil ejection 245 9
stencil knife 129 43
stencil lettering guide 151 69
stencil magazine, vertical ~ 245 8
stencil storage drawer 245 10
stenography 342 13
steno pad 245 29; 248 32
stenter 165 54; 168 21
stenter clip 168 24
stenter pin 168 24
step *Roof & Boilerr.* 38 27
step *Hall* 41 24

step *Carriages* **186** 13
step *Tram* **197** 15
step *Aircraft* **230** 42
step *Swim.* **281** 32, 37
step *Mountain.* **300** 17
step, bottom ~ **123** 18, 42
step, top ~ **123** 19
step, wedge-shaped ~ **123** 31
step bearing **91** 10
step-cut, hexagonal ~ **36** 62
step-cut, octagonal ~ **36** 52
step-cut, rectangular ~ **36** 50
step-cut, rhombus ~ **36** 59
step-cut, round hexagonal ~ **36** 64
step-cut, square ~ **36** 51
step-cut, trapezium ~ **36** 57
step-cut, triangular ~ **36** 60-61
step fault **12** 8
step irons **269** 28
stepladder **50** 35; **126** 2; **129** 5
steppe zone **9** 54
stepping stones **37** 45
steps *Dwellings* **37** 39
steps *Household* **50** 35
steps *Station* **204** 25; **205** 2
steps *Circus* **307** 20
steps, front ~ **37** 66
steps, wooden ~ **38** 25
stereobate **334** 4
stereo cassette deck **241** 33
stereo component system, three-in-one ~ **241** 52
stereo effect **310** 30
stereo equipment **42** 9; **317** 22-23
stereo microphone jack **241** 65
stereo microphone socket **241** 65
stereomicroscope, wide-field ~ **112** 61
stereoplanigraph **14** 66
stereo receiver **241** 52
stereoscope **14** 64
stereo sound **311** 35
stereo speakers **241** 13-14
stereo system **42** 9; **241** 13-48; **317** 22-23
sterilization room **26** 34-54
sterilizer **76** 12
sterilizer, small ~ **26** 35
stern **221** 14; **222** 66-72; **258** 3, 26; **285** 29
stern, gilded ~ **218** 55-57
stern, lower ~ **218** 58
stern, square ~ **285** 43
stern, upper ~ **218** 55
sterncastle **218** 23
stern fender **227** 29
stern frame **222** 70-71
stern gallery **218** 56
stern light **258** 62
stern light, white ~ **286** 14
stern loading door **221** 31
stern opening **221** 55; **226** 18
stern port **221** 55; **226** 18
stern post **218** 1
stern ramp **221** 88; **258** 91
stern towing point **221** 53
sternum **17** 8
stethoscope **23** 35
stetson hat **319** 37
steward *Ship* **221** 110
steward *Election* **263** 10
steward *Cyc. Racing* **290** 4
stick **322** 35; **323** 14, 56
stick, forked ~ **54** 13
stick, French ~ **97** 12
stick blade **302** 32
sticker *Slaughterho.* **94** 14

sticker *Music. Instr.* **325** 30; **326** 9
stick handle **302** 31
sticking knife **94** 14
sticking paper **260** 50-52
sticking plaster **21** 7; **22** 55
stiffener **215** 53
stiffening **101** 37
stifle **72** 33
stifle joint **72** 33
stigma *Soft Fruit* **58** 41
stigma *Drupes & Nuts* **59** 16
stigma *Articulates* **358** 32
stigma *Bot.* **370** 56
stile *Roof & Boilerr.* **38** 16
stile *Household* **50** 36
stile *Carp.* **120** 25
stile *Roof* **121** 40
stiletto **102** 12
stiletto beard **34** 13
stiletto heel **101** 28
stillhunting **86** 1-8
stilling basin **217** 61
stilling box **217** 61
stilling pool **217** 61
still life group **338** 27
stilt **359** 19
stilt bird **359** 19
stilt plover **359** 19
stilts **308** 49
stimulants **382**
sting **77** 11
stinging nettle **61** 33
stinging organs **77** 10-14
sting sheath **77** 12
stinkweed **379** 8
stipe **381** 18
stipple paint **129** 53
stippler **129** 18
stippling roller **129** 13
stipule **57** 5; **58** 48; **371** 73
stirrer *Dairy.* **76** 43
stirrer *Paperm.* **172** 47
stirrer *Chem.* **349** 18
stirrup *Horse* **71** 43
stirrup *Bldg. Site* **119** 70
stirrup iron **71** 43
stirrup leather **71** 42
stitch, flat ~ **102** 10
stitch, knotted ~ **102** 13
stitch, ornamental ~ **102** 3
stitch, overcast ~ **102** 8
stitch, Russian ~ **102** 9
stitching **183** 8, 34
stitching, decorative ~ **31** 5
stitching machine **100** 21
stitching wire feed mechanism **184** 18
stock *Plant Propagn.* **54** 33
stock *Hunt.* **87** 3,4,6,13
stock *Joiner* **132** 24
stock *Paperm.* **173** 1, 2-10
stock *Stock Exch.* **251** 1-10
stock *Stock Exch.* **251** 11-19
stock, round ~ **139** 1
stock, square ~ **143** 9
stockbroker, sworn ~ **251** 4
stock certificate **251** 11
stock chest **172** 85; **173** 1
stock cube **98** 26
stock exchange **251** 1-10
stock exchange agent **251** 7
stock exchange attendant **251** 9
stocking **318** 32
stocking, knee-high ~ **32** 9
stockings pack **99** 26
stockjobber **251** 6
stock ledger **251** 14
stock list **250** 8
stock preparation plant **172** 79-86
stocks **222** 11-26

stock saddle **71** 37-44
stogy **101** 39
stoker, travelling-grate ~ **152** 3
stola **355** 9
stole, fur ~ **318** 30
stollen **97** 11
stomach *Man* **16** 35-37; **20** 13, 41-42
stomach *Bees* **77** 16
stomatid **369** 10, 13
stone *Agr.* **63** 9
stone *Mills* **91** 21
stone *Clocks* **110** 33
stone *Quarry* **158** 8
stone *Swim.* **281** 22
stone *Sculpt. Studio* **339** 5
stone *Shrubs etc.* **374** 12
stone, crushed ~ **158** 24
stone, dressed ~ **158** 30
stone, lower ~ **91** 23
Stone Age idol **328** 8
stone block **339** 5
stone catcher **64** 9
stone chippings **158** 23
stonecrop **51** 7; **61** 17; **375** 21
stone-crushing plant **158** 18
stone-dressing device **172** 70
stone fruit **59** 41, 43, 49; **370** 99
stone lithography **340** 25-26
stone marten **367** 14
stonemason **158** 34
stonemason's tools **158** 35-38
stone pine **372** 55
stones, faceted ~ **36** 42-71
stone spreader **200** 31
stone trap **64** 9
stool **24** 14; **27** 50; **260** 58
stop *Bookbind.* **185** 11
stop *Railw.* **214** 35
stop *Music. Instr.* **325** 44; **326** 6
stop *Chem.* **349** 37
stop and start lever **163** 31
stop and tail light **189** 9
stop and tail light unit **188** 38
stop bar **133** 11
stop bath **116** 10
stop board **203** 25, 33
stop boards **203** 31-32
stop button *Clocks* **110** 22
stop button *Office* **249** 73
stopclock **238** 62
stopclock, electronic ~ **238** 31
stopcock, flange-type ~ **130** 21
stop-cylinder machine **181** 20
stop-cylinder press **181** 20
stop fillet **119** 62
stop key **243** 43
stop knob *Music. Instr.* **325** 44; **326** 6
stop knob *Chem.* **349** 38
stop lever **324** 42
stop line **268** 50
stop motion **166** 43
stop-motion device **168** 19
stopper *Overh. Irrign.* **67** 36
stopper *Iron & Steel* **147** 31
stopper *Music. Instr.* **326** 35
stopper *Chem.* **350** 44
stopper, ground glass ~ **349** 4
stopper, octagonal ~ **349** 4
stopping device **168** 19
stopping handle **164** 6, 32
stopping point **203** 25, 31-32
stop plate **157** 18
stop rod blade **166** 43
stops **342** 16-29
stop signal **203** 1
stop signal, electric ~ **203** 3
stop signals **203** 1-6

stop tab **326** 39
stop valve *Plumb. etc.* **126** 4
stop valve *Gas Weld.* **141** 7
stop valve *Water* **269** 48
storage area **246** 5
storage bin **200** 35
storage box *Child. Rm.* **47** 2
storage box *D.I.Y.* **134** 34, 39
storage cell **77** 35
storage chamber **154** 71, 76
storage container **130** 17
storage cupboard **207** 27
storage door **39** 6
storage reservoir **217** 57
storage shelf **174** 10
storage siding **206** 50
storage tank *Brew.* **93** 13
storage tank *Oil, Petr.* **145** 72
storage tank *Paperm.* **172** 17, 41, 45, 46
storage tank *Docks* **225** 72
storage tank gauge **76** 10
storage unit *Dent.* **24** 8
storage unit *Composing Rm.* **176** 11
storage unit *Inf. Tech.* **242** 9
storage vessel **10** 46
store area **5** 17
storehouse **329** 13
storekeeper **98** 41
store room **223** 57
storey roof **337** 2
storm front **287** 24
storm-front soaring **287** 23
storm lantern **278** 29
storm signal **225** 35; **280** 4
stout **93** 26
stove, cylindrical ~ **309** 4
stove, tiled ~ **266** 34
stove bench **266** 36
stove door **309** 7
stovepipe **309** 5
stovepipe elbow **309** 6
stove screen **309** 8
stove tile **266** 35
stowage **227** 26; **228** 27
straddle **298** 23
straddle jump **298** 23
straddle position **296** 30
straddle seat **295** 18
straight ball **305** 17
straightedge *Paperhanger* **128** 39
straightedge *Metalwkr.* **140** 56
straightedge rule **179** 26
straight hang **296** 38
straight header **282** 12
straight inverted hang **296** 37
straight thrust **294** 7
strainer *Paperm.* **172** 54
strainer *Water* **269** 32
strainer, basket ~ **67** 12
strainer, rotary ~ **172** 23
strain insulator **152** 38
strait **14** 24
Strait of Gibraltar **14** 24
straits bridge **215** 57
strake, outside ~ **285** 50
stramonium **379** 8
stramony **379** 8
strampler **29** 23
strand **162** 54
strand of fruit **384** 8
strand of moulds **147** 36
strap *Clocks* **110** 5
strap *Bldg. Site* **119** 60, 65
strap *School* **260** 11
strap *Cyc. Racing* **290** 22
strap *Winter Sp.* **301** 3
strap hinge **140** 51
strap support **286** 59
stratification **12** 1
stratocumulus **8** 3

stratosphere 7 8
stratosphere aircraft 7 15
stratovolcano 11 15
stratum, impermeable ~ *Phys. Geog.* 12 28
stratum, impermeable ~ *Water* 269 36
stratum, impervious ~ *Phys. Geog.* 12 28
stratum, impervious ~ *Water* 269 36
stratum, porous ~ 12 29
stratum, water-bearing ~ *Phys. Geog.* 12 22
stratum, water-bearing ~ *Water* 269 2, 38
stratus 8 4
straw *Agr.* 63 34, 36
straw *Livestock* 75 7
straw *Basketm.* 136 30
straw *Station* 206 23
straw *Restaurant* 266 46
straw baler 63 35
strawberry 58 21
strawberry flan 97 22
strawberry plant 58 16
straw field 324 61
straw hive 77 52
straw press 63 35
straw shaker 64 14
strawwalker 64 14
straw yard system 74 1-17
stream *Phys. Geog.* 13 8
stream *Map* 15 80
stream *Park* 272 45
stream, subglacial ~ 12 52
stream, underground ~ 269 3
streamer 253 9
streamer, paper ~ 306 66
streamlining, integrated ~ 189 44
street 37 61; 198 13
street, cross-section of a ~ 198
street café 268 59
streetcar 197; 268 46
streetcar schedule 268 27
streetcar service 197 13
streetcar stop 268 25
streetcar stop sign 197 36; 268 26
streetcar track 268 23
street cleaner 199 41; 304 8
street cleaning 199
street-cleaning lorry 199 41; 304 8
street corner 198 12
street lamp 37 62; 268 6
street lamp, suspended ~ 268 49
street light 37 62; 268 6
street map 204 15; 268 2
street sign 268 7
street sweeper 199 5; 268 20
stretcher *Fire Brig.* 270 23
stretcher *Rowing* 283 47
stretcher, emergency ~ 21 23
stretcher, wedged ~ 338 20
stretcher bar 202 29
stretch girdle 32 5
stretching 170 46, 55
stretching, final ~ 170 47
stretching, preliminary ~ 170 45
stretching bond 118 59
stretching course 118 63
stretching machine 100 18
streusel cake 97 35
streusel slice 97 43
stridulating apparatus 81 8
stridulating mechanism 81 8
strike *Phys. Geog.* 12 2
strike *Composing Rm.* 175 37
striker *Hunt.* 87 21

striker *Ball Games* 291 15
striker pad 255 47
striking circle 292 16
striking force control 249 10
striking mechanism 325 3
striking of coins 252 40-44
striking surface *Tobacc. etc.* 107 24
striking surface *Ball Games* 293 31
striking weight 110 28; 309 60
string *Roof & Boilerr.* 38 26
string *Basketm.* 136 28
string *Sports* 305 59
string *Music. Instr.* 322 44, 55; 323 9, 61; 325 7
string, catgut ~ 324 6, 14
string, chalked ~ 128 45
string, fretted ~ 324 24
string, gut ~ 324 6, 14
string, nylon ~ 324 14
string, open ~ 324 25
string, outer ~ 123 44
string, stopped ~ 324 24
string, unfretted ~ 324 25
string, wreathed ~ 123 49
string briefs 32 23
string course 335 52
stringed instruments 323 1-27; 324 1-31
stringer *Roof & Boilerr.* 38 26
stringer *Shipbuild.* 222 50
stringer *Aircraft* 230 47, 57
stringer *Sailing* 285 55
stringer, outer ~ 123 44
string fastener 324 4
string holder 324 4, 13
strings 293 31
string vest 32 22
strip 148 66-75
stripe, magnetic ~ 117 82
striped hyena 368 1
strip flooring 123 62
stripper *Paperhanger* 128 1, 9
stripper *Nightclub* 318 27
stripping 89 11
stripping knife 128 15; 134 37
stripping table 179 23
strip steel 143 11
striptease act 318 27-32
striptease artist 318 27
striptease number 318 27-32
strip window 37 86
strobile 376 19
stroke *Rowing* 283 12
stroke *Music. Not.* 320 6
stroke, plain ~ 277 2
strokes 136 1-4
stroller 28 37
strong beer 93 26
strong man 308 27
strong room 250 11
structural parts of ship 222 44-61
structural system, Gothic ~ 335 27-35
structure, geological ~ 154 57-68
structure, longitudinal ~ 222 44-56
structures, molecular ~ 1 9-14
strut *Bldg. Site* 119 63, 67
strut *Carp.* 120 27, 54
strut *Roof* 121 58, 69, 82
strut *Ship* 223 61
strut *Aircraft* 229 11
strut *Rowing* 283 46
strut *Winter Sp.* 303 5
strut, diagonal ~ *Bldg. Site* 118 88
strut, diagonal ~ *Bridges* 215 4
stub 84 14

stub axle 192 78
stubble beard 34 23
stubble field 63 33
stub wing 232 3
stud *Carp.* 120 25
stud *Roof* 121 40
stud *Mach. Parts etc.* 143 22
stud, ornamental ~ 253 8
stud, rubber ~ 187 84
stud, screw-in ~ 291 28
student 262 9, 10
student input device 242 4
student response device 242 4
studio *Broadcast.* 238 18
studio *Art. Studio* 338 1-43
studio, artist's ~ 338
studio, sculptor's ~ 339
studio apartment 37 74
studio complex 310 1-13
studio easel 338 3
studio electrician 310 37
studio flat 37 74
studio lot 310 1
studio microphone *Broadcast.* 238 34
studio microphone *Films* 310 31
studio skylight 338 1
studio table 238 29
studio window 238 38
study in oils 338 36
study step counter 242 5
stuff 173 1, 2-10
stuff box 173 11
stuff chest 172 85, 86; 173 1, 13
stuffing box *Oil, Petr.* 145 26
stuffing box *Railw.* 210 33
stuffing box *Ship* 223 64
stuff preparation plant 172 79-86
stump 84 14
stump of tooth 24 27
stunner, electric ~ 94 7
stunning device 94 3
stupa 337 21, 28
Stuttgart Planetarium 5 17-28
sty 62 8
style 58 42; 59 15; 68 34; 370 55; 373 5; 378 5
style jump 288 50-51
styling scissors 106 34
stylobate 334 32
stylus 341 25
stylus, conical ~ 241 26
stylus, elliptical ~ 241 26
stylus, steel ~ 341 21
stylus force control 241 24
stylus pressure control 241 24
sub-base course, bituminous ~ 198 2
sub-base course, gravel ~ 200 60
sub-base course, hardcore ~ 200 60
subcontra octave 321 42
sub-drainage 200 61
subfloor 123 38, 73
subgrade grader 201 1
subheading 342 41
submarine 258 64
substation, outdoor ~ 152 29-35
substitute 291 54; 292 39
substitute flags 253 30-32
substitute signal 203 6
substructure *Oil, Petr.* 145 2
substructure *Offshore Drill.* 146 38
subtitle 185 47
subtracting 344 24
subtraction 344 24
subtrahend 344 24

succory 57 40; 376 25
sucker *House Insects etc.* 81 37
sucker *Optician.* 111 23
sucker *Invertebr.* 357 21
sucker rod 145 25
sucking organ 358 17
suction 162 25, 28, 36
suction apparatus *Dent.* 24 11
suction apparatus *Poultry Farm* 74 41
suction box *Poultry Farm* 74 41
suction box *Cotton Spin.* 164 44
suction box *Paperm.* 173 15
suction control 50 72
suction control, fingertip ~ 50 74
suction control, sliding ~ 50 74
suction dredger 216 59
suction electrode 23 29
suction feeder 180 72
suction head 217 51
suction hose *Household* 50 75
suction hose *Fire Brig.* 270 67
suction hose, soft ~ 270 30
suction pipe *Roof & Boilerr.* 38 55
suction pipe *Docks* 226 32
suction pipe *Water* 269 5, 14, 41
suction pipe *Theatre* 316 52
suction pipe, trailing ~ 216 59
suction port 199 43
suction pump 216 62
suction roll 173 16
suction slot 168 43
suction tube 10 37
sugar 98 53-55
sugar, confectioner's ~ 98 54
sugar, refined ~ 98 55
sugar beet 68 44
sugar beet eelworm 80 51
sugar bowl 44 32; 265 20
sugar cane 382 52
sugar loaf 99 64
suit, asbestos ~ 270 46
suit, casual ~ 33 17
suit, denim ~ 31 58; 33 20
suit, extra-vehicular ~ 6 18-27
suit, jersey ~ 29 17
suit, men's ~ 33 1
suit, one-piece ~ 29 17
suit, quilted ~ 29 38
suit, single-breasted ~ 33 1
suit, two-piece ~ 29 12
suitcase 194 19; 204 6; 205 7
suitcase, light ~ 267 15
suitcase, lightweight ~ 267 15
suite, upholstered ~ 42 21-26
suiting 104 3
suits 276 38-45
suits, German ~ 276 42-45
suit trousers 33 3
sulfate *see* sulphate
sulfide *see* sulphide
sulfur *see* sulphur
sulfuric *see* sulphuric
sulky 289 24
sulphate pulp mill 172 1-52
sulphur 351 23
sulphur-crested cockatoo 363 1
sulphuric acid 170 23, 24
sulphuric acid, production of ~ 156 34
sulphuric acid supply 156 33
sultana 98 8
sum 344 23
Sumatra cigar 107 2

summer **121** 67
summer beam **121** 67
summer blouse **31** 22
summer coat **31** 20
summer dike **216** 48
summer dress **31** 9
summerhouse **52** 14
summer quarters **356** 11
summer slacks **31** 52
summer solstice **3** 8
summer wear **31**
summit **12** 40
sump *Coal* **144** 47
sump *Intern. Combust. Eng.* **190** 41
sump filter **192** 18
sun **4** 10-21, 29, 36-41, 42
sun bather **281** 12
sunbathing area *Dwellings* **37** 46
sunbathing area *Spa* **274** 12
sunbathing area *Swim.* **281** 11; **282** 4
sun bed **281** 5
sun blind **37** 71
sun canopy **274** 14
sun deck **223** 22
sundew **377** 14
sundial **110** 30
sun disc, winged ~ **333** 12
sundress, child's ~ **29** 13
sun filter **6** 22
sunflower **51** 35; **52** 7; **69** 20
sunflower oil **98** 24
sunglasses **6** 19; **111** 6; **301** 19
sunglass pocket **6** 19
sun hat **29** 16; **35** 37
sunlight **155** 18
sun lounge **37** 70
sun parlor **37** 70
sun ray lamp **281** 13
sun roof **37** 75
sunroof, steel ~ **193** 24
sun rose **377** 20
sun sensor **10** 69
sunshade *Dwellings* **37** 48, 71
sunshade *Town* **268** 61
sunshade *Park* **272** 58
sunshade *Films* **313** 9
sun spectacles **111** 6
sunspot **4** 37, 38
sun terrace **37** 75
supatap **126** 35
super *Bees* **77** 45
super *Theatre* **316** 39
Super-calender **173** 36
supercilium **19** 38
super grade gasoline **145** 55
super grade petrol **145** 55
superheater **152** 9
supermarket **99** 1-96
supernumerary **316** 39
superstructure *Weaving* **165** 6
superstructure *Ship* **221** 10, 69
superstructure, aft ~ **258** 22
superstructure, compact ~ **221** 33
superstructure, forward ~ **259** 45
superstructure deck **258** 10
superstructures **258** 10-28
Super-Vee racing car **290** 37
supplementary angle **346** 14
supply pipe *Butch.* **96** 50
supply pipe *Plumb. etc.* **126** 9
supply sprocket **312** 26
supply table **74** 51
supply vessel **221** 32
support *Plant Propag.* **54** 33
support *Roof* **121** 83
support *Knitting* **167** 38
support *Offset Platem.* **179** 20
support *Shipbuild.* **222** 27

support *Circus* **307** 29, 45
support, adjustable ~ **67** 22
support, intermediate ~ **214** 29, 76
support, single-pylon ~ **214** 23
support, three-point ~ **349** 28
support, tubular steel ~ **214** 78
support cable **2** 30
supporters **254** 15-16
support guide rail **214** 79
supporting cable **214** 27, 38, 41, 44
supporting cable anchorage **214** 59
supporting cable brake **214** 71
supporting cable guide **214** 58
supporting cable guide rail **214** 79
supporting insulator **153** 54
supporting pulley **163** 46
supporting structure **337** 9
supporting wall **121** 77
support insulator **153** 54
support roll **270** 50
support truss **214** 80
suppressor **190** 35
surcoat **355** 25
surf **13** 27
surface, asphalt ~ **200** 58
surface, bituminous ~ **198** 5
surface, curved ~ **347** 40
surface, flat ~ **111** 39
surface, hatched ~ **151** 29
surface, icy ~ **304** 19
surface, lunar ~ **6** 13
surface, nap ~ **168** 31
surface, plane ~ **347** 31
surface, raised ~ **168** 31
surface, special ~ **111** 40, 41, 42
surface boundary layer **7** 7
surface chart **9** 1-39
surface condenser **152** 24
surface finisher **200** 43
surface-finish microscope **112** 37
surface hydrant **270** 35
surface not to be machined **151** 20
surfaces, plane ~ **346** 24-58
surface skimmers **286** 38-44
surface synoptic chart **9** 1-39
surface-to-air missile launcher **259** 50
surface-to-air rocket launcher **259** 50
surface to be machined **151** 21
surface to be superfinished **151** 22
surface wave **11** 36
surfacing **111** 36
surfboard **279** 1, 2; **280** 15; **284** 5
surfboarder **279** 5; **280** 14
surfer **279** 5; **280** 14
surfing **279** 1-6; **280** 13
surf riding **279** 1-6; **280** 13
surge baffle system **235** 53
surge diverter **152** 35
surgery **22** 32-74
surge tank **217** 40
surgical instruments **26** 40-53
surgical unit **26** 1-54
sur le cou-de-pied **314** 14
surroyal **88** 9
survey illumination **112** 52
surveying **14** 46-62
surveying, geodetic ~ **14** 46-62
surveying level **14** 48
surveyor's level **14** 48
suspect **264** 32

suspender *Underwear etc.* **32** 6
suspender *Bridges* **215** 41
suspender *Nightclub* **318** 28
suspenders **29** 26, 34; **32** 30; **33** 45
suspension **168** 16
suspension, steel and rubber ~ **207** 4
suspension and haulage cable **214** 21
suspension arm, lower ~ **192** 84
suspension bridge **215** 39
suspension bridge, primitive ~ **215** 15
suspension cable *Railw.* **214** 27, 38, 41, 44
suspension cable *Bridges* **215** 40
suspension cable anchorage *Railw.* **214** 59
suspension cable anchorage *Bridges* **215** 43
suspension cable bearing **214** 33
suspension cable brake **214** 71
suspension cable guide **214** 58
suspension cable guide rail **214** 79
suspension damper **192** 76
suspension file **248** 3
suspension file system **248** 2
suspension gear **214** 54
suspension gear bolt **214** 72
suspension line **288** 40
suspension line, double-cable ~ **214** 25, 30
suspension line gondola **214** 52
suspension lines, single-cable ~ **214** 15-24
suspension line support **214** 76
suspension rope **215** 17
suspension spring **192** 74
sustaining pedal **325** 8
suture material **22** 56; **26** 21
swab **137** 3
swab dispenser **22** 36
swage block *Goldsm. etc.* **108** 18
swage block *Blacksm.* **137** 17
swage block *Metalwkr.* **140** 14
swage head **143** 57
swallow **361** 20
swallowhole **11** 49; **13** 71
swallowtail **358** 52
swallow-tail twin crystal **351** 25
swamp **13** 24
Swan *Astron.* **3** 23
swan **272** 54; **359** 16
swan-neck **37** 12; **122** 30
swan's neck **37** 12; **122** 30
swarf **149** 44
swarm cluster of bees **77** 53
swarming net **77** 54
swarm of bees **77** 53
swath **63** 23, 36
swathe **63** 23, 36
swather **63** 19
swather, rotary ~ **63** 26; **64** 40-45
swath rake **64** 44
swath reaper **63** 19
sweater **29** 43; **31** 51
sweater, short-sleeved ~ **33** 32
sweepback, positive ~ **229** 21
sweepback, semi-positive ~ **229** 20
sweeper, mechanical ~ **199** 39
sweet **98** 75, 80

sweet bread **97** 40
sweet calamus **377** 22
sweet cherry **59** 5
sweet chestnut **384** 48
sweet corn **68** 31
sweet flag **377** 22
sweet gale **373** 33
sweet pepper **57** 42
sweets **47** 31, 32
sweet sedge **377** 22
sweet syringa **373** 9
sweet william **60** 6
swell **325** 45
swell organ **326** 2, 44
swell pedal, balanced ~ **326** 50
swift **359** 24
swimming **282**
swimming bath **281**
swimming bath attendant **281** 4; **282** 15
swimming belt **282** 19
swimming cap **280** 29, 44
swimming instruction **282** 16-20
swimming instructor **282** 16
swimming lane **282** 31
swimming pool **223** 23; **281** 1-9
swimming pool, open-air ~ **282** 1-32
swimming pool attendant **281** 4; **282** 15
swimming strokes **282** 33-39
swimming teacher **282** 16
swimming trunks **280** 43
swimsuit **280** 42
swing *Gymn.* **297** 39
swing *Athletics* **298** 30
swing, double ~ **273** 39
swing boat **308** 41, 42
swing bridge, flat ~ **215** 67
swing door **207** 18
swing-grippers **180** 33
swing pipe **172** 10
swing seat **273** 40
swing wing **256** 9
Swiss chard **57** 28
Swiss cheese **99** 41
Swiss roll **97** 19
Swiss stone pine **372** 29
switch *Electr.* **127** 7
switch *Garage* **195** 4, 12
switch *Aircraft* **230** 26
switch, main ~ *Joiner* **132** 58
switch, main ~ *Railw.* **211** 3, 31
switch, main ~ *Office* **249** 37
switch, manually-operated ~ **202** 16
switch, remote-controlled ~ **202** 27
switch, rotary ~ *Electr.* **127** 18
switch, rotary ~ *Office* **245** 28
switchback **308** 39
switch blade **202** 21
switchboard *Post* **237** 17, 22-26
switchboard *Office* **245** 13
switch engine **206** 43
switcher **206** 43
switches, single ~ **203** 45-48
switching box **237** 25
switching centre **237** 25, 41
switching device **269** 47
switching system **153** 5
switching system, automatic ~ **237** 25
switch knob **203** 62
switch lever *Mach. Tools* **149** 11; **150** 35
switch lever *Railw.* **203** 55
switch lock **202** 28
switch signal **197** 38; **202** 19

switch signal, electrically
  illuminated ~ **202** 33
switch signal lamp **202** 19
switch signals **203** 45-52
switch stand **202** 17
switch tongue **202** 21
switch tower **15** 24
switch tower, electrically-
  operated ~ **203** 61
switch tower, manually-
  operated ~ **203** 53
switch yard **206** 42
swivel *Fish Farm.* **89** 77
swivel *Oil, Petr.* **145** 10
swivel arm **26** 13; **104** 27; **105**
  26
swivel chair **246** 1; **248** 25
swivel coupling **50** 69
swivel head **50** 60
swivel mechanism **65** 73
swivel motor **132** 69
swivel nozzle **235** 64
swivel saddle **188** 21
swivel tap **126** 36
swop platform **194** 23
sword **319** 32
sword antenna **256** 28
sword lily **60** 11
swordsman **319** 25
sword swallower **308** 26
S-wrench, adjustable ~ **126**
  66
symbol, algebraic ~ **344** 9; **345**
  5
symbols, geometrical ~ **345**
  21-24
symbols, mathematical ~ **345**
  15-24
symphisis, pubic ~ **20** 65
symphonia **322** 25
syncarp **384** 63
sync head **243** 34
synchro **153** 32
synchromesh gearbox, four-
  speed ~ **192** 28-47
synchronization **311** 37-41
synchronization start **117** 65
synchronization unit **117** 77
synchronizing cone **192** 33
synchronizing filter **311** 27
syncing **311** 37-41
syncline **12** 18
sync pulse cable **313** 29
sync start **117** 65, 69
sync track **243** 33
synthetic fibres **169**; **170**
syringe **22** 54, 65
syringe, hypodermic ~ **24** 53
syringe, multi-purpose ~ **24**
  10
syrinx **322** 2
system, ancillary ~ **211** 34
system, planetary ~ **4** 42-52
system camera **115** 1-105
system-monitoring device
  234 17
system of accessories **115**
  43-105
system of coordinates **347** 8,
  11
system of flaps **229** 37

T

tabard **30** 50
tabby weave **171** 1
tabernacle **330** 42
table *Forging* **139** 20
table *Restaurant* **266** 74
table *Playground* **273** 2
table *Music. Instr.* **324** 3
table *Art* **336** 14, 16

table, auxiliary ~ *Blacksm.*
  137 14
table, auxiliary ~ *Mach. Tools*
  150 28
table, director's ~ **316** 42
table, flat ~ **36** 46, 72, 73, 74
table, producer's ~ **316** 42
table, revolving ~ **148** 41
table, rotary ~ **145** 15
tableau curtain **315** 2
table bed **277** 15
tablecloth **45** 2
table decoration **45** 19; **266**
  78
table en cabochon **36** 47
table en cabochon, antique ~
  36 76
table en cabochon,
  rectangular ~ **36** 77
table feed drive **150** 34
table lamp **46** 24; **246** 35
tableland **13** 46
table leg **44** 2
table linen **271** 57
table napkin **45** 9
table pedestal **26** 6
table piano **325** 40
table rise adjustment **133** 23
table runner **46** 35
table telephone, standard ~
  237 6
table tennis **293** 45-55
table tennis ball **273** 5; **293** 48
table tennis bat **273** 4; **293** 45
table tennis game **273** 1
table tennis net **273** 3; **293** 53
table tennis player **293** 49
table tennis racket **273** 4; **293**
  45
table tennis table **293** 52
table top *Dining Rm.* **44** 3
table top *Arc Weld.* **142** 14
table-top tripod **115** 99
table tripod **115** 99
tableware **45**
tabulator clear key **249** 8
tabulator key **249** 7
tachograph **210** 54
tachometer *Weaving* **166** 2
tachometer *Knitting* **167** 43
tachometer *Letterpress* **181** 54
tachometer *Car* **191** 38
tachometer *Railw.* **212** 22
tachometer *Aircraft* **230** 8
tack **285** 25
tacking **285** 25-28
tackle **219** 1-72; **221** 27, 104
taffrail log **224** 54
tagetes **60** 20
tail *Horse* **72** 38
tail *Roof* **122** 89
tail *Bookbind.* **185** 58
tail *Birds* **362** 8
tail *Mammals* **367** 29
tail, cruciform ~ **229** 28
tail, curly ~ **73** 12
tail, docked ~ **70** 12
tail, dolphin's ~ **327** 25
tail, falcate ~ **73** 25
tail, fish's ~ **327** 25, 43, 46, 49
tail, horizontal ~ **229** 26-27,
  35; **230** 61; **257** 21
tail, normal ~ **229** 23
tail, prehensile ~ **364** 35
tail, raised ~ **229** 35
tail, serpent's ~ **327** 31
tail, tufted ~ **73** 6
tail, vertical ~ **229** 24-25; **230**
  58
tailband **185** 42
tail bracing wire **232** 4

tailcoat **33** 13
tail end shaft **223** 60
tail fin *Aircraft* **229** 24; **230**
  59; **231** 6; **232** 7
tail fin *Air Force* **256** 32
tail fin *Airsports* **288** 21
tail fin *Fish etc.* **364** 10
tail fluke **367** 29
tailgate **193** 16, 20; **195** 50
tailings auger **64** 21
tailings outlet **64** 22
tail line **122** 81
tail loading gate **232** 25
tail margin **185** 58
tail of kite **273** 43
tailor **104** 22; **271** 37
tailor's chalk **271** 39
tailor seat **295** 11
tailpiece **323** 7
tailpin **323** 22
tailplane **229** 26; **230** 62; **256**
  31; **288** 23
tailpole **91** 32
tail propeller **232** 28
tail rotor **232** 14; **264** 4
tails **33** 13
tail shaft **223** 60
tail shapes **229** 23-36
tail skid **256** 23
tail slide **288** 5
tail sting **358** 43
tailstock *Turner* **135** 7
tailstock *Mach. Tools* **149** 29;
  150 5
tailstock *Photomech. Reprod.*
  177 62
tailstock barrel **149** 27
tailstock barrel adjusting
  handwheel **149** 30
tailstock barrel clamp lever
  149 28
tailstock centre **149** 26
tail unit, cruciform ~ **229** 28
tail unit, double ~ **229** 32, 34
tail unit, normal ~ **229** 23
tail unit, triple ~ **229** 36
tail unit shapes **229** 23-36
tail vice **132** 37
tail wheel **256** 27
take-down weight **167** 32
take number **310** 35
take-off **298** 26, 37
take-off, balloon ~ **288** 84
take-off board **298** 38
take-off stand **165** 41
taker-in **163** 53
take-up roll **117** 80
take-up spindle **312** 37
take-up spool *Photog.* **115** 25
take-up spool *Cine Film* **117**
  32, 80
take-up sprocket **312** 27
taking lens **313** 2
talkback equipment **238** 64
talkback microphone **238** 10,
  53
talkback microphone,
  producer's ~ **238** 39
talkback speaker **238** 8, 52
talkback system **238** 64
talk button **242** 24
talk key **242** 24
talon *Stock Exch.* **251** 19
talon *Birds* **362** 7
talus **11** 47; **12** 45
tambour door **245** 5
tambourine *Disco* **317** 27
tambourine *Music. Instr.* **324**
  45
tamer **307** 52
tamper **200** 26; **201** 13
tamping beam **200** 32; **201** 2
tandem **186** 50

tandem kayak **283** 5
tang **45** 52, 60
tangent *Music. Instr.* **322** 43
tangent *Maths.* **346** 32, 48
tangent screw **14** 56
tangerine **384** 23
tank *Cooper* **130** 1
tank *Lorries etc.* **194** 30
tank *Army* **255** 80
tank, bottom ~ **222** 38
tank, concrete ~ **310** 11
tank, side ~ **222** 37
tank, spherical ~ **145** 73; **221**
  36
tank bottom valve **38** 49
tank car **213** 31
tank construction engineer
  130
tanker *Docks* **225** 73
tanker *Airport* **233** 22
tanker terminal **145** 74
tank farm **225** 61
tank for sterilized milk **76** 16
tank furnace **162** 1
tank inlet **38** 47
tank locomotive **210** 65
tank margin plate **222** 51
tank reel **116** 2
tank spiral, multi-unit ~ **116**
  4
tank top **222** 54
tank top plating **222** 54
tank vent **234** 44
tank wagon **213** 31
tansy **380** 9
tap *Doc.* **23** 49
tap *Metalwkr.* **140** 60
tap *Power Plant* **153** 18
tap *Spa* **274** 17
tap *Disco* **317** 8
tap *Chem.* **349** 5, 22; **350** 44,
  53
tap, outside ~ **37** 41
tap bar **148** 9
tap changer **211** 10
tapchanger driving
  mechanism **211** 13
tape *Ball Games* **293** 73
tape *Music. Instr.* **325** 36
tape, adhesive ~ **98** 47; **134**
  38; **247** 29
tape, magnetic ~ **25** 46
tape, varnished-cambric ~
  153 46
tape cassette **117** 76
tape counter **241** 64; **243** 9
tape deflector roller **241** 60
tape feed **243** 29
tape guide **243** 22
tape measure **103** 2; **271** 38
tape punch **176** 5
taper, wax ~ **77** 65
tape recorder **117** 70; **317** 21;
  318 17
tape recorder, four-track ~
  242 13
tape recorder, portable ~ **309**
  37
tape recorder, two-track ~
  242 12
tape reel, open ~ **241** 57
taper thread, female ~ **126** 47
tape speed selector **241** 62
tapestry wallpaper **128** 18
tape threading indicator light
  243 14
tape wire **325** 35
tapeworm **81** 35
tap hole **147** 50
tapir **366** 26
tappet **166** 57
tappet shaft **166** 56
tapping **153** 18

tapping a spring 269 24-39
tapping bar 148 9
tapping hole 147 50
tapping spout 148 3
taproot, swollen ~ 370 79
tap wrench 140 30
tar 170 4
tar and bitumen heater 200 46
target Inf. Tech. 242 84
target Sports 305 30, 32, 66, 77
target, bobbing ~ 305 33, 48
target, turning ~ 305 33, 48
target archery 305 52-66
target areas 294 51-53
target cross 288 56
target jack 305 23
target rectangle 292 34
targets 305 30-33
tar-spraying machine 200 46
tar storage tank 200 47
tarsus Man 17 26
tarsus Birds 362 4
tartlet 97 20
tasse 329 49
tassel Headgear 35 24
tassel Arable Crops 68 35
tassel Hist. Cost. 355 23
tasset 329 49
tatting 102 19
tatting shuttle 102 20
tattoo 306 44
tau cross 332 59
Taurus 3 25; 4 54
taxi 268 64
taxicab 268 64
taxi rank 268 63, 66
'taxis' 233 32
taxi sign 268 65
taxi stand 268 63, 66
taxi telephone 268 67
taxiway 233 2
T-cut 54 32
tea Grocer 98 65-68
tea Supermkt. 99 68-70
tea Trop. Plants 382 9
tea bag 98 68
teacher 260 21
teaching equipment 242; 242
  45-84
teaching laser 242 81
teaching machine 242 1
teaching material 261 27
tea dance 267 44-46
tea leaf 382 9
team of oxen 63 16
tea packet 99 69
tea plant 382 7
tea plate 39 34
tear bag 88 14
tear-off edge 247 30
tea room 265 1-26
teat Infant Care etc. 28 20
teat Livestock 75 19
teat cup 75 30
teat cup cluster 75 26
tea tree 382 7
technical drawing 151 16
technical laboratory 310 9
Teclu burner 350 4
tectogenis 12 4-20
tedder, rotary ~ 63 24; 64
  46-58
teddy bear 28 46; 273 26; 309
  12
teddy bear, rocking ~ 48 30
tee 126 44, 47
tee Ball Games 293 90
teeing ground 293 79
tee-iron 143 3
teepee 352 7
tee-square 151 9
teeth 19 16-18
teeth, false ~ 24 25

teeth grinder 157 43, 45
teething ring 28 12
teeth of knock-over bit 167
  52
telecobalt unit 2 28
telegraphy 237 30
telemetry antenna 10 70
telephone 22 18; 41 7; 202 48;
  238 23; 246 13; 248 9
telephone, public ~ 236 9; 237
  1, 3
telephone, toy ~ 47 35
telephone adapter socket 249
  67
telephone answering and
  recording set 22 13
telephone answering device
  22 13
telephone book 236 12; 237 5
telephone booth 204 46; 236
  8; 237 1; 251 10; 268 56
telephone box 204 46; 236 8;
  237 1; 251 10; 268 56
telephone cable 198 15
telephone cable pipeline 198
  16
telephone casing 237 15
telephone connection 242 20
telephone cover 237 15
telephone customer 237 2
telephone directory 236 12;
  237 5
telephone directory rack 236
  10
'telephone - emergency calls
  only' 233 40
telephone exchange 237
  27-41
telephone exchange, internal
  ~ 245 3
telephone index 22 21
telephone instruments 237
  6-26
telephone kiosk 204 46; 236
  8; 237 1; 251 10; 268 56
telephone line, customers' ~
  198 20
telephone line, subscribers' ~
  198 20
telephone list, internal ~ 245 17
telephone number 237 38
telephone receiver 237 7; 246
  16
telephones 237 6-26
telephone service 237 41
telephone subscriber 237 2
telephone switchboard panel
  238 14
telephone user 237 2
telephoto lens 117 47
teleprinter 176 31; 237 31, 61,
  66; 238 12
telescope 14 60; 42 15; 224 8
telescope, gimbal-mounted ~
  235 68
telescope, monocular ~ 111 18
telescope, reflecting ~ 113 1
telescope, refracting ~ 113 16
telescope, surveyor's ~ 14 48
telescope magnifier 113 38
telescope mountings 113
  16-25
telescope mounts 113 16-25
telescope sight 87 29; 255 28;
  305 49
teletype 176 31
teletypewriter 237 31
television 238; 239
television cabinet 240 2
television camera 10 67; 112
  36; 154 78; 240 26
television disc system 243
  37-45

television engineering 240
television mast 15 33
television OB van 239 1-15
television post-sync studio
  238 27-53
television programmes 342 64
television receiver 242 28
television receiver, domestic
  ~ 243 6
television receiving aerial 239
  4, 5
television reception aerial
  239 4, 5
television set 42 8; 46 14; 242
  28
television sound 242 27
television tube 240 3
telex link 237 65
telex message 237 69
telex service 237 41
telex tape 237 68
teller 250 2
tempera 338 17
temperature 9 8
temperature gauge 179 4
temperature gauge, distant-
  reading ~ 210 48
temperature graph 7 37
temperature regulation flap
  10 65
temperature regulator 191 84
temperature scale 7 36
temperature selector 50 8
tempest 284 54
template 126 83
template, circular ~ 141 35
temple Man 16 6
temple Weaving 166 13
temple Art 337 7
temple, Doric ~ 334 1
temple, Etruscan ~ 334 49
temple, funerary ~ 333 7
temple buildings 337 25
temple tower 333 32; 337 1,
  26
temple wall 334 6
temporalis 19 3
tender Railw. 210 38
tender Warships 258 92
tender platform 210 2
tendo calcaneus 18 48
tendril 57 4
tendril, thorny ~ 58 30
tennis 293 1-42
tennis ball 293 28
tennis court 293 1
tennis net 293 13
tennis player 293 16
tennis racket 41 13; 293 29
tennis shoe 101 36
tenon saw 132 44
tenor clef 320 11
tenor horn 323 39
tenor trombone 323 46
tenor viol 322 23
tenpin bowling 305 14-20
tens 344 3
tension and slub-catching
  device 165 13
tension bar 167 49
tension cable, inclined ~ 215
  47
tension cable pulley 214 43
tension compensator 165 51
tension equalizer 165 51
tension hoop 324 56
tensioning device Agr. Mach.
  64 94
tensioning device Railw. 208
  18
tensioning lever 208 18
tensioning screw 323 53

tension roller Joiner 133 13
tension roller Letterpress 181
  45
tension weight Knitting 167
  50
tension weight Railw. 214 41,
  42
tension weight shaft 214 40
tent 80 7
tent, four-pole ~ 307 1
tentacle 357 16, 31
tenter 165 54; 168 21
tenter clip 168 24
tenter pin 168 24
tent peg 278 24
tent pole 278 38; 307 2; 352 8
tent prop 307 13
tenuto 321 30
tepee 352 7
teres major 18 55
teres minor 18 54
tergites 358 31
term 344 23
terminal Docks 226 16
terminal Airport 233 15
terminal box 211 16
termination of speed
  restriction 203 40
tern 359 11
terrace 37 36
terracette 13 64
terrarium 356 14
terrestrial meridian 14 4
terrier 70 15, 16, 17, 18, 27, 39
terry towel 49 9
tessellation 338 37
tessera 338 39
tesseral crystal system 351
  1-17
testaceans 357 27-36
test equipment 195 17
testicle, right ~ 20 72
testing and control station
  237 40
testing board 237 29
testing desk 237 29
testing device for waterproof
  watches 109 26
testing kit 138 14
testis 20 72
test meter, universal ~ 127 41
test oil and gas separator 146
  10
test separator 146 10
test tube 350 34
test tube rack 173 8; 261 31;
  350 35
tether 75 15-16
tetradrachm 252 1
tetragonal crystal system 351
  18-19
tetrahedrite 351 1
tetrahedron 351 1
text 237 68
textbook 261 28
thalamus 370 53
thallus 378 49
Thaumatolampas diadema
  369 4
T-head bolt 202 10
theater see theatre
theatergoer 315 8
theatre Astron. 5 26
theatre Theatre 315; 316
theatre, Greek ~ 334 44
theatre, open-air ~ 272 6
theatregoer 315 8
theatre projector 312 24
theatre seat 315 20
theatre ticket 315 11
thé dansant 267 44-46
theodolite 14 52-62
theorbo 324 1

thermal 287 21
thermal protection shield 234 5, 20
thermal soaring 287 20
thermograph 10 19, 51
thermometer *Meteorol. Instr.* 10 25
thermometer *Infant Care etc.* 28 29
thermometer *Text. Finish.* 168 27
thermometer *Swim.* 281 24
thermometer, ladle-type ~ 92 53
thermometers 10 53-54
thermometer screen 10 49
thermometer shelter 10 49
thermometric scale 7 36
thermoplastic 130 15
thermos jug 40 5
thermo time switch 190 63
thickener 172 24, 42, 44, 48, 62
thicknesser 132 45
thicknessing machine 132 45
thicknessing table 132 46
thief 308 16
thigh 16 49; 17 22
thigh bone 17 22
thill 186 19, 30
thiller 186 28
thill horse 186 28
thimble, graduated ~ 149 64
thinner *Painter* 129 16
thinner *Art. Studio* 338 13
thinning 84 37
thinning razor 105 9; 106 41
thinnings, small-sized ~ 84 37
thinning scissors 105 8; 106 33
thinning shears 105 8; 106 33
third base 292 47
third man 300 27
thirty-second note 320 18
thirty-second rest 320 26
thistle 61 32
Thomas converter 147 55-69
thoracic shield 82 4; 358 29
thorax *Man* 16 28-30; 17 8-11
thorax *Articulates* 358 29-30
thorn *Gdn. Flowers* 60 18
thorn *Spa* 274 2
thorn apple 379 8
thorn house *Map* 15 32
thorn house *Spa* 274 1
thousands 344 3
thread *Overh. Irrign.* 67 38
thread *Mach. Parts etc.* 143 16, 68
thread *Glass Prod.* 162 54
thread *Cotton Spin.* 164 53
thread *Weaving* 165 21
thread *Knitting* 167 17, 36
thread *Bookbind.* 183 11
thread, coarse ~ 149 4
thread, female ~ 126 41, 45
thread, male ~ 126 38, 51
thread, metal ~ 102 30
thread, mycelial ~ 381 2
thread, normal ~ 149 4
thread, sleeved ~ 162 57
thread chaser 135 14
thread clearer 165 20
thread container 22 61
thread cop 185 18
thread-cutting machine 125 27; 126 86
thread guide *Shoem.* 100 30
thread guide *Knitting* 167 3, 54, 64

thread head 187 75
threading draft 171 5
threading key 127 30
thread interlacing 171 26
thread pitch 149 9
thread spool 185 18
thread tapper 108 15
threadworm 80 51
three 302 13
three-day event 289 16-19
three-decker 218 51-60
three-eight time 320 36
three-four time 320 37
three-masters 220 18-27
three-phase generator 153 26
three-phase plug 127 14
three-two time 320 38
threshing drum 64 12
throat *Man* 16 19; 19 14-37, 24
throat *Horse* 72 16
throat *Forestry* 84 28
throatlash 71 11; 72 16
throatlatch 71 11; 72 16
throat piece 329 42
throstle 361 16
throttle control 230 30; 288 15
throttle lever 230 30; 288 15
throttle twist grip 188 30; 189 29
throttle valve *Hosp.* 27 43
throttle valve *Car* 192 9
through-the-lens reflex finder 117 44
thrower 161 9
throw-in 291 53
throwing act 307 43
throwing knife 354 15
throwing ring 308 47
throwing spear 328 2
throwing stick 352 40
thrush 360 3
thrushes 361 13-17
thrush nightingale 361 17
thrust bearing 221 29
thrust block 223 67; 259 60
thrust lever 257 9
thrust mount, lower ~ 235 6
thrust mount, upper ~ 235 5
thrust nozzle 234 35; 235 37
thrust nozzle fuel tank 235 45
thrust structure 234 21
thrust vector control system 235 43
thrust washer 190 56
thrust weapon 294 11, 36, 37
thuja 372 39
thumb 19 64
thumb hold 323 45
thumb hole 305 47
thumb nut 119 75
thumb piston 326 46
thundercloud 7 2
thunderstorm 9 38
thurible 332 38
thurible bowl 332 41
thurible chain 332 39
thurible cover 332 40
thwart 278 17; 283 28
thymele 334 48
tiara, papal ~ 254 37
Tibetan 353 27
tibia 17 25
tibialis anterior 18 47
tick *Bedrm.* 43 13
tick *Articulates* 358 44
tick, drill ~ 43 10
tick bean 69 15
ticket 204 36
ticket agent 204 39
ticket-cancelling machine 197 16

ticket clerk 204 39
ticket counter 197 33; 204 35
ticket machine 268 28
ticket office 204 34
ticket printer, hand-operated ~ 204 41
ticket-printing machine 204 40
ticket-stamping machine 204 40
tidal power plant 155 37
tide level indicator 225 37
tidemark 13 35
tide table 280 7
tie *Ladies' Wear* 30 46
tie *Underwear etc.* 32 41
tie *Bldg. Site* 119 39
tie *Roof* 121 59
tie *Station* 205 60
tie *Music. Not.* 321 24
tie, concrete ~ 202 37
tie, coupled ~ 202 14, 38
tie, diagonal ~ 121 30
tie, double ~ 121 50
tie, simple ~ 121 49
tie, steel ~ 202 36
tie beam 121 53
tie belt 29 55; 31 19
tie fastening 101 21
tiepin 36 22
tier, lower ~ 228 24
tier, upper ~ 228 23
tierce engagement 294 48
tiercel 86 46
tie rod 65 47
tier of oars 218 12
tie shoe 101 31
tie tube 119 49
tie-up 171 22, 23
tie-up of shafts 171 9
tiger 307 56; 368 5
tightening screw 293 33
tightrope 307 41
tightrope dancer 307 40
tights 29 42; 32 12
tilbury 186 44
tilde 342 35
tile *Bathrm. etc.* 49 19
tile *Games* 276 34
tile, flat interlocking ~ 122 60
tile, interlocking ~ 122 59
tile, plain ~ 122 6, 46
tile beard 34 16
tile cutter 122 33
tile hammer 122 20
tile roofings 122 45-60
tiles 122 45-60
tiling batten 122 17
till 207 86; 271 5
till, electric ~ 271 2
tillage 69 1-28
tiller 218 13; 284 32; 286 24
tiller extension 284 31
tillering 68 5
tilt 329 71
tilt block 12 9
tilting armour 329 76
tilting device 147 44, 59
tilting helmet 254 4; 329 77
tilting lance 329 81
tilting shield 329 79
tilting table 133 17
tilting target 329 79
tilt wing 232 27
timbale 324 57
timber 85 42
timber, end-grained ~ 120 92
timber, halved ~ 120 88
timber, long ~ 120 2
timber, round ~ 120 35; 157 30
timber, sawn ~ 157 22
timber, small ~ 84 37

timber, squared ~ 120 10; 157 36
timber, stacked ~ 84 15
timber, standing ~ 84 4
timber, undressed ~ 120 83
timber, yarded ~ 84 15
timber cutting 84 15-37
timber dog 121 97
timberjack 84 18
timber joints 121 84-98
timber planking 285 50-57
time *Music. Not.* 320 28-42
time *Maths.* 345 7
time ball 280 5
time indicator 289 40
timekeeper 282 24; 299 47
timer *Doc.* 23 40
timer *Hosp.* 27 35
timer *Kitch.* 39 21
timer *Watchm.* 109 35
timer *Photog.* 116 18
timer *Photograv.* 182 20
timer *Billiards* 277 17
timer, synchronous ~ 24 52
timer switch, built-in ~ 243 18
time scale *Meteorol. Instr.* 10 17
time scale *Office* 249 74
time scale stop 249 75
time schedule 151 12
time signatures 320 28-42
timetable 204 16, 18
timetable, driver's ~ 210 52
timetable, official ~ 204 50
time weight 110 29; 309 59
timing machine, electronic ~ 109 27
timpano 323 57
tin 129 7
tin, molten ~ 162 17
tinctures 254 24-29
tine *Tablew. etc.* 45 60
tine *Agr. Impl.* 66 4
tine *Game* 88 10, 31
tine bar 64 53
tinner's snips 125 1
tip, adjustable ~ 149 47
tip, controlled ~ 199 10
tip, cork ~ 107 13
tip, gold ~ 107 13
tip, oxide ceramic ~ 149 47
tip, pointed ~ 253 10
tip-cart, three-way ~ 62 18
tip heap 144 19
tipper 200 7
tipper, three-way ~ 194 24
tipper wagon 213 37
tipping body *Lorries etc.* 194 25
tipping body *Road Constr.* 200 8
tipping bucket 214 34
tipping car 147 64
tipping cylinder 62 19
tipping device 147 44, 59
tipping truck 119 28
tipping wagon 119 28
tippler, three-way ~ 92 34
tip tank 231 9; 256 30
tip-up seat 207 12
tire *see* tyre
tired swimmer grip 21 38
T-iron 143 3
tissue, erectile ~ 20 67
tit 360 4; 361 9
titan 327 37
title block 151 31
title bout 299 35-50
title fight 299 35-50
title page 185 45
title panel 151 31
titmouse 360 4; 361 9

tjalk **220** 6
T-joint **126** 44, 47
T-junction joint **126** 44, 47
toad **364** 23
toadstools **379** 10-13
toast **45** 34
toaster **40** 30
toat **132** 18
tobacco *Tobacc. etc.* **107** 25
tobacco *Trop. Plants* **382** 43
tobacco, raw ~ **83** 13
tobacco beetle **81** 25
tobacco factory **83** 11
tobacco leaf **382** 43
tobacco plant **382** 40
tobacco pouch **107** 43
tobacco presser **107** 47
toboggan **303** 1, 2, 13
toboggan, junior ~ **303** 3
toboggan cap **35** 39
toboggan slide **308** 40
toe, big ~ **19** 52
toe, first ~ **19** 52
toe, fourth ~ **19** 55
toe, great ~ **19** 52
toe, little ~ **19** 56
toe, second ~ **19** 53
toe, third ~ **19** 54
toecap **100** 58; **101** 16, 40
toecap remover **100** 52
toe clip **290** 21
toenail **19** 57
toe piston **326** 48
toe post sandal **101** 48
toe stand **295** 5
toestrap **284** 30
toe unit **301** 55
toffee **98** 77
toga **355** 13
toggle **340** 30
toggle action *Letterpress* **181** 16
toggle action *Bookbind.* **183** 30
toggle fastening **30** 66
toggle-joint action **181** 16; **183** 30
toggle-joint press **183** 26
toggle-lever press **183** 26
toilet **49** 12; **146** 29; **207** 16, 42, 72; **211** 59; **231** 31; **278** 5
toilet bowl **49** 13
toilet cistern **126** 14
toilet-cleaning vehicle **233** 22
toilet lid **49** 14
toilet pan **49** 13
toilet paper **49** 11
toiletries **99** 27-35
toilet roll holder **49** 10
toilets **317** 31
toilet seat **49** 15
toilet water **105** 37; **106** 9
tomahawk **352** 16
tomato **57** 12; **99** 82
tomato plant **55** 44
tomb **331** 23; **337** 16
tomb, giant's ~ **328** 16
tomb, megalithic ~ **328** 16
tomb, royal ~ **333** 1
tombola **306** 11
tombola booth **308** 44
tomb recess **331** 60
tombstone **331** 26
tom cat **73** 17
tondo **339** 36
tone **320** 51, 53
tone arm **241** 21
tone arm balance **241** 53
tone arm lift **241** 28
tone arm lock **241** 27
tone generator **238** 51

toner roll **249** 41
tongs *Atom* **2** 44
tongs *Glass Prod.* **162** 44
tongs *Graphic Art* **340** 50
tongs, concreter's ~ **119** 85
tongs, flat ~ **137** 24
tongs, round ~ **137** 25
tongue *Man* **17** 52; **19** 25
tongue *Tablew. etc.* **45** 52
tongue *Game* **88** 2
tongue *Shoem.* **100** 65
tongue *Shoes* **101** 32
tongue *Music. Instr.* **322** 52; **326** 19
tongue, foam rubber ~ **291** 24
tongue, forked ~ **327** 6
tonsil **19** 23
tonsil, palatine ~ **19** 23
tonsure **331** 57
tool **195** 43
tool, stone ~ **328** 1
tool bag **187** 25
tool bit holder **149** 45
tool box *D.I.Y.* **134** 35
tool box *Mach. Tools* **150** 13
tool box *Railw.* **212** 45
tool cabinet **134** 1-34
tool case **127** 49
tool cupboard **134** 1-34
tool grinder **137** 18
tool-grinding machine **137** 18
tool post **149** 21
tool rest **135** 5; **149** 22
tools **119** 77-89
tool shank **149** 49
tool shed **37** 32; **52** 3; **55** 1
tool slide **149** 22
tool trolley **195** 42
tooth *Man* **19** 28-37
tooth *Mach. Parts etc.* **143** 83
tooth *Composing Rm.* **174** 30
tooth *Office* **249** 12
tooth, bicuspid ~ **19** 18
tooth, canine ~ **19** 17
tooth, molar ~ **19** 18, 35
tooth, porcelain ~ **24** 29
tooth, premolar ~ **19** 18
toothbrush, electric ~ **49** 29
toothed **370** 45
toothing, external ~ **143** 96
toothing, internal ~ **143** 95
toothing, spiral ~ **143** 92-93
toothing plane **132** 17
tooth mug **49** 28
toothpaste box **99** 31
toothpick holder **266** 23
tooth pulp **19** 32
tooth-root elevator **24** 48
tooth scaler **24** 45
top **12** 40; **193** 10; **323** 24
top, collapsible ~ *Carriages* **186** 52
top, collapsible ~ *Car* **193** 10
top, convertible ~ **193** 10
top, elasticated ~ **32** 33
top, fireclay ~ **108** 9
top, fixed ~ **186** 14
top, folding ~ **194** 10
top, hard ~ **193** 27
top, humming ~ **309** 71
top, leather ~ **35** 19
top, marble ~ **265** 12
top, shirred ~ **29** 15
top clearer **164** 22
top gases **145** 38
top hat **35** 36; **186** 25; **289** 6
top light, white ~ **286** 10
top lighting, incident ~ **112** 63
topmark **224** 78, 90
topmark buoy **224** 80
topmast **223** 39

topography, fluvial ~ **13** 1-13
topper **64** 85
topping **266** 54
topping knife **64** 87
top rail **221** 122
top ring **89** 52
top roller, light ~ **164** 18
tops **145** 38
topsail schooner, three-masted ~ **220** 19
top side *Meat* **95** 37
top side *Paperm.* **173** 31
top slide **149** 22, 42
top stroke **277** 3
top tube **187** 16
torch **127** 26
torch lighter **141** 27
torcular **26** 48
torero **319** 21, 25
torii **337** 11
torpedo boat **258** 69, 75
torpedo housing, underwater ~ **259** 36
torpedo tube **258** 78; **259** 79
torque converter **190** 70
torque converter bearing **211** 54
torque converter lever **65** 34
torque wrench **195** 45
torril door **319** 11
torsional clamp **287** 39
torso **339** 7
Torsteel **119** 82
torten **97** 22-24
tortrix moth **80** 9
torus *Art* **334** 28, 30
torus *Bot.* **370** 53
totalizator **289** 35
totalizator window **289** 34
tote **289** 35
totem **352** 2
totem pole **352** 1
tote window **289** 34
toucan **363** 6
touch line **291** 9
touch-me-not **377** 11
touch-tone button **242** 25
touch-tone pad **242** 25
toupee wig **355** 8
toupet **34** 2
touring bicycle **187** 1
touring boat **283** 26-33
touring cycle **187** 1
touring cycle handlebar **187** 2
touring kayak **283** 61, 70
touring moped **188** 24
tourist **272** 28
tourist guide **272** 27
tournament **329** 71
tournament pennon **254** 33
tournament saddle **329** 87
tourneur **275** 3
tourney **329** 71
tourniquet, emergency ~ **21** 15
tourniquet, surgeon's ~ **26** 48
tow **170** 57, 58, 59, 60
towage **227**
towel **106** 25; **281** 25
towel, paper ~ **40** 1; **106** 5
towel rail **49** 8
tower *Map* **15** 53
tower *Bldg. Site* **119** 34
tower *Bridges* **215** 42
tower *Airport* **233** 17
tower *Gliding* **287** 12
tower, central ~ **335** 6
tower, lattice steel ~ **152** 36
tower, stepped ~ **333** 32
tower, terraced ~ **333** 32
tower clock **331** 7
tower crane **47** 39; **119** 31
tower platform **329** 8

tower roof, pyramidal ~ **335** 7
tower slewing crane **119** 31
tower spotlight **316** 21
tower tomb **333** 21
tow hook **227** 27
towing **216** 27
towing engine *Rivers* **216** 29
towing engine *Salvage* **227** 7
towing engine *Warships* **258** 86
towing gear **227** 6, 6-15, 13
towing hawser **216** 24; **227** 8, 15
towing line **286** 47
towing log **224** 54
towing machine **227** 7; **258** 86
towing mast **216** 28
towing path **216** 30
towing plane **287** 2
towing track **216** 30
towing vehicle **194** 21, 29
towing winch **227** 7; **258** 86
tow line **216** 24; **227** 8, 15; **286** 47
town **15** 51; **268**
town banner **218** 22
town centre **268**
tow path **216** 30
tow rope *Rivers* **216** 24
tow rope *Salvage* **227** 8, 15
tow rope *Gliding* **287** 4
tow rope guide **227** 9
toy, soft ~ **46** 13; **47** 6, 7, 41
toy, wooden ~ **260** 80
toy duck **28** 10
toys **48** 21-32
toy shop **47** 27
T position **288** 62
trace **71** 22, 24, 35
trace monitor **25** 54
tracer **153** 45
tracer element **153** 45
tracery **335** 39-40
tracery window **335** 39-41
trachea **17** 50; **20** 4
tracing head **141** 37
tracing leg **302** 2
tracing wheel **129** 42
track *Atom* **2** 37
track *Hunt.* **86** 8
track *Cine Film* **117** 82
track *Station* **205** 59-61
track *Railw.* **202** 1-38
track *Army* **255** 87
track *Equest.* **289** 23
track *Cyc. Racing* **290** 2
track *Winter Sp.* **301** 60
track, cinder ~ **298** 6
track, indoor ~ **290** 1
track, sand ~ **290** 24
track, synthetic ~ **298** 6
track, unfenced ~ **15** 102
track and field events **298**
track and signal indicator **203** 64
track-clearing vehicle **213** 17
track diagram control layout **203** 65
track diagram control panel **203** 66
tracker action **326** 6-16
track format **243** 28
trackhound **70** 42, 43
track indicator **65** 81
track inspection railcar **213** 32
track racer **290** 2
track rider **290** 2
track rider, motor-paced ~ **290** 14
track rod **65** 47
track-rod ball-joint **192** 80
tracksuit **33** 27

tracksuit bottoms 33 29
tracksuit top 33 28
trackwalker 202 44
tract 330 57
traction motor 211 6
traction motor blower 211 15
tractive effort indicator 211 26
tractive unit 194 21, 29
tractor 62 38; 64 46; 65 20; 67 17; 85 43; 194 21, 29; 273 55
tractor, narrow-track ~ 78 21
tractor driver 62 39
tractor unit 85 43
trader, itinerant ~ 308 51
trades 9 48, 49
tradesman 98 41
trade winds 9 48, 49
traffic control 264 9
traffic control cuff 268 31
traffic helicopter 264 1
traffic light post 268 53
traffic lights 268 52
traffic patrol 264 9
traffic policeman 268 30
traffic sign 268 66
trail 86 8
trail, scented ~ 289 49
trailer Farm Bldgs. 62 40
trailer Agr. 63 27, 38
trailer Blacksm. 138 10
trailer Lorries etc. 194 22
trailer Station 206 3, 35
trailer Camping 278 52
trailer, collapsible ~ 278 3
trailer, folding ~ 278 3
trailer, tip-up ~ 56 42
trailer frame 138 28
trailering 278
trailer wagon 200 25
trailing arm 191 27; 192 66
trailing cable hanger 133 39
trailing cable support 133 39
trailing edge Sailing 284 45
trailing edge Gliding 287 37
trailing link arm 192 81
trail rope 288 69
train 355 80
train, electric ~ 197
train, interurban ~ 197
train, local ~ 208 1-12
train, short-distance ~ 208 1-12
train, suburban ~ 205 25
train control system, inductive ~ 211 7, 38; 212 14, 38
train deck 221 80
trainee pastry cook 265 6
trainer Shoes 101 35
trainer Circus 307 31
train ferry Map 15 12
train ferry Ship 221 74
train heating generator 212 39
train heating system 212 17, 18
train heating system transformer 212 40
train heating voltage indicator 211 27
training apparatus 299 20-24
training equipment 299 20-24
training ship 258 95
training shoe 101 35
train plate, bottom ~ 110 37
'trains' 233 34
train schedule 204 50
train service, local ~ 208 1-30
trainset 209 1
trainset, experimental ~ 209 23

train set, wooden ~ 47 37; 48 29; 273 27
trajectory 89 36
tram 197; 268 46
tramline 268 23
trammel 125 11
trampoline 282 10; 297 10
tram service 197 13
tram stop 197 35; 268 25
tram stop sign 197 36; 268 26
tram timetable 268 27
transept 335 3
Trans-Europe Express 209 1-22
Trans-Europe Express, electric ~ 205 34
transfer blanket 249 40
transfer cylinder 180 36
transfer drum 180 36
transfer entry 250 25
transfer port 242 57
transformer Clocks 110 8
transformer Power Plant 153 9-18
transformer Railw. 211 10
transformer, high-tension ~ 211 4
transformer, mobile ~ 152 30, 39
transformer, transportable ~ 152 30, 39
transformer connection 153 19
transformer station Brew. 92 21
transformer station Hydr. Eng. 217 46
transformer tank 152 40
transforming section 23 56
transillumination 112 60
transistor, actuating ~ 195 19
Transitional 342 5
'transit passengers' 233 27
transit shed 225 9
transmission 209 18
transmission cable 326 53
transmission line 154 16
transmission line, high-voltage ~ 152 32
transmission oil 209 15; 212 36, 43
transmission oil temperature gauge 212 20
transmissometer 10 60
transmitted-light microscope 112 14
transmitter 10 59, 62
transmitting antenna 288 88
transom Dwellings 37 35
transom Ship 221 42
transom Sailing 284 35; 285 49
transom Motorboats etc. 286 26
transom stern 221 42; 258 26; 259 11; 285 48
transparency 242 42
transparency arm 177 44
transparent gage 59 25
transplanting Plant Propagn. 54 5
transplanting Forestry 84 10
transport aircraft, medium-range ~ 256 14
transport and communications aircraft 256 24
transport and rescue helicopter 256 18
transporter, suction ~ 74 49
transporter container-

loading bridge 225 46; 226 2
transporter loading bridge 225 20
transport helicopter 232 21
transport lug 152 48
transport roller Cine Film 117 34
transport roller Joiner 132 72
transport sprocket 115 26
transport vehicle 62 18
transtainer 226 2
transtainer crane 226 2
transversal chicane 301 68
transverse motion 149 17
trap Bathrm. etc. 49 27
trap Hunt. 86 20
trap Plumb. etc. 126 26
trapdoor 38 13
trapercius 18 52
trapeze Sailing 284 12
trapeze Circus 307 6
trapeze artist 307 7
trapezium 346 37
trap opening 316 32
trapper 306 8
trapping 86 19-27, 19
trappings Horse 71 16
trappings Chivalry 329 74
trash bin Doc. 22 70
trash bin Butch. 96 46
trash can 199 3
trash conveyor 64 80
travel agency 271 24
travel centre 204 28
traveler see traveller
traveling see travelling
traveller Cotton Spin. 164 51, 55
traveller Sailing 284 27
Travellers' Aid 204 45
travelling bag 205 10
travelling box 77 44
traverse 152 37
traversing handle 255 48
trawler 90 11; 221 86
trawl fishing 90 11-23
trawling 90 11-23
trawl warp 90 12
tray Living Rm. 42 30
tray Pest Contr. 83 17
tray Game 88 8
tray Café 265 3, 14
tray Restaurant 266 19, 45, 63
tray Fair 308 52
tray, revolving ~ 204 37
tray, round ~ 44 24
tray counter 266 64
tray for purchases 271 15
tray thermometer 116 13
tread 50 38; 123 32, 47
tread, rubber ~ 187 85
treading water 282 39
treadle Poultry Farm 74 63
treadle Dressm. 103 11
treadle Tailor 104 13
treadle control 168 48
treadle lever 166 58
treadle sewing machine 309 1
treadling diagram 171 10
tread sledge 304 29
treasury notes 252 29-39
treble belly bridge 325 11
treble bridge 325 11
treble clef 320 8
treble control 241 31
treble coupler 324 41
treble plume 254 30
treble register 324 41
treble stop 324 41
treble string 325 10
treble tuning 241 43
treble viol 322 23

tree 272 59, 61; 370 1
tree, conical ~ 272 13
tree, globe-shaped ~ 272 12
tree, pyramidal ~ 52 16; 272 19
tree brush 56 23
tree cake 97 46
tree calliper, steel ~ 84 21
tree felling 84 15-37
tree frog 364 24
tree guard 118 80
tree nursery Map 15 111
tree nursery Market Gdn. 55 3
tree nursery Forestry 84 6, 10
tree of life 372 39
tree pruner 56 11
trees, coniferous ~ Map 15 1
trees, coniferous ~ Conifers 372 1-71
trees, deciduous ~ 371 1-73
trees, mixed ~ 15 14
trees, non-coniferous ~ 15 4
trees, ornamental ~ 373; 374
trees, young ~ 84 10-11
tree scraper 56 14
tree stake 52 31
tree stump 84 14
tree toad 364 24
treetop 272 60; 370 4
tree trunk 84 19; 370 2, 7
tree trunk, hollowed-out ~ 218 7
trefoil arch 336 32
trek, roped ~ 300 22-27
trellis 89 5
trellis, wire ~ 78 9
trembling poplar 371 21
trenchcoat 33 57
trestle Overh. Irrign. 67 7
trestle Carp. 120 18, 19
trestle Shipbuild. 222 27
trestle, paperhanger's ~ 128 52
trestle rope 122 67
triad 321 1-4
triakis-octahedron 351 10
trial 290 24-28
trial frame 111 3
trial lens case 111 45
triangle Fish Farm. 89 85
triangle Drawing Off. 151 7, 8
triangle Railw. 203 13
triangle School 260 37
triangle Music. Instr. 323 49
triangle, acute-angled ~ 346 28
triangle, equilateral ~ 346 26
triangle, obtuse-angled ~ 346 30
triangle, pipe clay ~ 350 17
triangle, right-angled ~ 346 32
triangle cut 36 67
triangles, plane ~ 346 26-32
triangle sign 203 13
triangle symbol 345 24
triangulation point 14 49; 15 71
triangulation station 14 49; 15 71
Triangulum Australe 3 40
triceps brachii 18 38
trichopteran 358 12
trick button 117 84
trick ski 286 56
triclinic crystal system 351 26
Tricolour 253 16
triforium 335 33
trigger Slaughterho. 94 6
trigger Army 255 5
trigger guard 87 10
trigger mechanism 255 20
trigger valve 270 62
triglyph 334 15

trilby hat **35** 22
trill **321** 17, 18
trim **46** 5
trimaran **278** 16
trimmer *Carp.* **120** 41
trimmer *Roof* **121** 71
trimmer *Paperhanger* **128** 43
trimmer joist **120** 41
trimming, fur ~ **30** 59
trimming, lace ~ **31** 32
trimming, leather ~ **30** 18
trimming blade **85** 22
trimming knife **128** 38
trimming machine **85** 18
trimmings **266** 55
trimming tab **288** 25, 30
trimming table **132** 64
trimming tool **162** 43
trim tab **288** 25, 30
triplane **229** 6
triple-spar tail construction **257** 20
triplet **321** 23
trip mileage recorder **191** 74, 77
tripod *Photog.* **114** 42; **115** 99
tripod *Paperm.* **173** 6
tripod *Chem.* **349** 15; **350** 14
tripod, wooden ~ **313** 13
tripod bush **115** 30
tripod crane **222** 6
tripod lattice mast **258** 41
tripod leg **114** 43
tripod socket **115** 30
tripod spotlight **310** 52
trireme **218** 9-12
triton **327** 40
trochilus **334** 29
troika **186** 45
trolley *Blacksm.* **138** 35
trolley *Lorries etc.* **194** 42
trolley *Tram* **197**
trolley *Station* **206** 14
trolley *Town* **268** 46
trolley, electric ~ **205** 29
trolley, metal ~ **74** 31
trolley bus **194** 40
trolley bus trailer **194** 44
trolley shoe **194** 42
trolley shoe, aluminium alloy ~ **197** 24
trolley shoe, carbon ~ **197** 24
trolley stop **197** 35; **268** 25
trolley stop sign **197** 36; **268** 26
trolley wire **197** 41; **205** 58
trolley wire contact point **197** 40
trombone **323** 46
trombone slide **323** 47
tropaeolum **53** 4
trophus **358** 26
trophy **352** 15, 30
tropic of Cancer **3** 4
tropics **14** 10
tropopause **7** 9
troposphere **7** 1
trot **72** 41
trotter *Meat* **95** 38, 42, 48
trotter *Equest.* **289** 28
trotting silks **289** 26
troubadour **329** 70
trough *Phys. Geog.* **12** 18
trough *Mills* **91** 14
trough *Railw.* **202** 34
trough *Art* **336** 48
trough, equatorial ~ **9** 46
trough, outdoor ~ **62** 9
trough gutter **122** 83
trough mixer, double shaft ~ **159** 10
trough plane **12** 19
trough surface **12** 19

trough valley **13** 55
trough vault **336** 47
trouser leg **33** 6
trouser pocket **33** 47
trousers, boy's ~ **29** 60
trouser suit **30** 57
trouser turn-up **31** 40
trout **364** 15
trout breeding **89** 14
trout fry **89** 16
trout pond **89** 6
trout rearing **89** 14
trowel *Gdn. Tools* **56** 6
trowel *Bldg. Site* **118** 52
trub **93** 2
trub removal **93** 1-5
truck *Bldg. Site* **119** 32
truck *Power Plant* **152** 41
truck *Sawmill* **157** 16
truck *Refuse Coll.* **199** 38
truck *Railw.* **207** 4; **208** 4; **212** 2; **213** 13
truck *Docks* **226** 4, 19
truck *Flags* **253** 1
truck, electric ~ **205** 29; **206** 2, 34
truck, heavy ~ **194** 20; **200** 7
truck, large-capacity ~ **158** 14
truck, light ~ **194** 1, 5
truck, toy ~ **47** 38; **273** 62
truck farm **55** 1-51, 3
trucks **194**
truck tire **273** 19
truck-to-truck handling **226** 7
truck-to-truck operation **225** 41
truck-to-truck system **225** 41
truck with trailer **213** 34
trudgen **282** 37
trudgen stroke **282** 37
truffle *Grocer* **98** 86
truffle *Edib. Fungi* **381** 9, 10, 11
trumpet **318** 6; **323** 43
trumpet, bronze ~ **322** 1
trumpet daffodil **60** 3
trumpeter **318** 7
trumpet narcissus **60** 3
truncheon *Heraldry* **254** 31
truncheon *Police* **264** 19
trunk *Man* **16** 22-41
trunk *Forestry* **84** 19
trunk *Car* **191** 24; **193** 23
trunk *Mammals* **366** 21
trunk *Bot.* **370** 2
trunk, horse's ~ **327** 45
trunk, main ~ **88** 11
trunk, round ~ **120** 83
trunk, woman's ~ **327** 24
trunk-bending forwards **295** 33
trunk-bending sideways **295** 32
trunk call **237** 3
trunk-hose, paned ~ **355** 34
trunk-hose, stuffed ~ **355** 31
trunk lid **191** 7
trunk line **15** 21
trunk pipeline **145** 35
trunk road **15** 17
trunks **32** 27
truss **215** 3
trussed arch bridge **215** 23
trussed-rafter roof **121** 34
truss element **215** 24
trusser **130** 12
truss joint **215** 37
truss post **121** 68
truss tower **155** 43
trying plane **132** 39
trysail **220** 1

try square **120** 69; **132** 6; **134** 26
try-your-strength machine **308** 11
tsetse fly **81** 43
T-shirt **31** 38
T-shirt, children's ~ **29** 27
T-square **151** 9
tsunami **11** 53
T-tail **229** 29; **256** 31-32; **287** 10
T-tail unit **229** 29; **256** 31-32; **287** 10
tub *Market Gdn.* **55** 48
tub *Wine Grow.* **78** 10
tub, wooden ~ **91** 27
tuba **323** 44
tubaphone **324** 61
tube *Hosp.* **25** 13; **26** 17
tube *Optician* **111** 18
tube *Optic. Instr.* **113** 8
tube *Bicycle* **187** 30
tube *Music. Instr.* **323** 29; **326** 22
tube *Invertebr.* **357** 23
tube *Edib. Fungi* **381** 17
tube, diaphragmed ~ **10** 27
tube, eustachian ~ **17** 65
tube, fallopian ~ **20** 81
tube, steel ~ **155** 30
tube, telescopic ~ **65** 77
tube, uterine ~ **20** 81
tube bin **255** 72
tube cap **260** 52
tube centre section **113** 9
tube clamp **40** 20; **350** 30
tube clip **40** 20; **350** 30
tube connection **6** 26
tube holder **22** 46
tuber *Arable Crops* **68** 40
tuber *Bot.* **370** 79
tuberose **60** 9
tuberosity **80** 27
tube support **27** 47
tube valve **187** 31
tube well **269** 60
tubing **145** 20, 24
tub plant **55** 47
tuck and miss stitch **171** 44, 47
tuck jump **282** 14; **295** 36; **297** 40
tuck stitch, pulled-up ~ **171** 45, 48
tuck stitch, staggered ~ **171** 46
tue iron **137** 6
tuff **73** 7
tuff deposit **11** 26
tuft **73** 7
tufted lark **361** 19
tuft of grass **375** 44
tug *Shipbuild.* **222** 42
tug *Docks* **225** 15
tug *Salvage* **227** 5, 16
tug *Gliding* **287** 2
tulip poplar **374** 1
tulip tree **374** 1
tulle background **102** 16
tulle lace **102** 15
tulle work **102** 15
tumble drier **50** 28
tumbler *Metalwkr.* **140** 38
tumbler *Restaurant* **266** 3
tumbler, seaward ~ **226** 23
tumbler, shore-side ~ **226** 28
tumbler lever **149** 10
tumbler reverse lever **149** 14
tumbler spring **140** 42
tumbling separator, mechanical ~ **64** 75
tumulus **328** 16
tun **92** 45

tun, wooden ~ **91** 27
tundra climate **9** 57
tuner **241** 9, 37; **317** 22
tuner, automatic ~ **23** 38
tunic *Ladies' Wear* **30** 29
tunic *Ship* **221** 115
tunic *Hist. Cost.* **355** 12, 25
tunic, long ~ **355** 19
tunica **355** 12
tunic dress **30** 29
tunic top **30** 29
tuning control **241** 9
tuning crook **326** 21
tuning device **326** 30
tuning dial **241** 7
tuning flap **326** 30
tuning fork element **110** 9
tuning fork principle **110** 6
tuning fork watch **110** 6
tuning hammer **325** 20
tuning hole **326** 33
tuning key **325** 20
tuning knob **241** 9; **309** 21
tuning meter **241** 39, 54
tuning peg **323** 18; **324** 11; **325** 17
tuning pin **324** 23; **325** 17
tuning screw **323** 59
tuning slot **326** 33
tuning tongue **326** 30
tuning wedge **325** 21
tuning wire **326** 21
tunnel *Map* **15** 70
tunnel *Soft Fruit* **58** 63
tunnel *Station* **204** 23
tunnel *Railw.* **214** 6
tunnel, plastic ~ **55** 40
tunnel, underground ~ **198** 29
tunnel entrance **233** 6
tunnel kiln **161** 5
tunnelling machine **144** 32
tunnel vault **335** 19; **336** 38
tup *Blacksm.* **137** 10
tup *Forging* **139** 12, 26
turban **353** 46
turbine **67** 20; **209** 18; **232** 40, 47
turbine, high and low pressure ~ **259** 62
turbine, high-pressure ~ **232** 53
turbine, low-pressure ~ **232** 54
turbine, reversible ~ **155** 39
turbine, supercharged ~ **212** 51
turbine engine **232** 17, 24; **257** 15
turbine exhaust **146** 5
turbine house **152** 22; **217** 43
turbine inlet **155** 40, 41
turbine monitoring panel **153** 30
turbine transmission **209** 10
turbine unit **209** 24
turbogenerator **154** 34
turbogenerator set **154** 33
turbogenerator unit **153** 23-30
turbojet engine **231** 26
turbojet engines **232** 33-50
turbopropeller engine **231** 5; **232** 30, 51
turbopropeller plane **231** 4
turboprop engine **231** 5; **232** 30, 51; **256** 16
turboprop plane **231** 4
tureen **45** 15
turkey **73** 28
turkey cock **73** 28
turkey hen **73** 28
turkey leg **99** 59
Turkish delight **308** 18

turk's cap 377 4
turk's cap lily 377 4
turn *Athletics* 298 24
turn *Music. Not.* 321 21
turnbuckle 130 4; 202 31
turner *Brew.* 92 24
turner *Turner* 135 20
turnery 135 1-26
turn indicator *Car* 191 76
turn indicator *Aircraft* 230 12
turn indicator light 189 37, 45
turn indicator light, front ~ 191 19
turning head, multiple ~ 149 41
turning judge 282 26
turning tools 135 14,15,24
turnip moth 80 42
turnout 203 51, 52
turn slot 288 46
turntable *Porcelain Manuf.* 161 11
turntable *Electrotyp. etc.* 178 26
turntable *Lorries etc.* 194 31
turntable *Bridges* 215 64
turntable *Docks* 226 56
turntable *Audio* 241 20
turntable *Army* 255 73
turntable glazing machine 161 16
turn-up 30 35; 31 54; 33 35
turpentine separator 172 14
turret *Mach. Tools* 149 40
turret *Warships* 258 47, 67. 70; 259 31, 52, 71
turret *Chivalry* 329 28, 35
turret, aft ~ 259 44
turret, armoured ~ 255 84
turret, forward ~ 259 43
turret head 117 46; 313 32
turret lathe 149 38
turtle dove 359 23
tusk 88 54; 366 22; 367 22
tutu 314 29
tuyère 147 20
TV set 42 8; 46 14
tween deck 223 76
tweeter 241 15
tweezers 22 52; 109 14; 174 18
twig 370 6
twilight area 4 21
twin anti-aircraft gun 258 31
twin anti-aircraft gun turret 259 30
twin anti-aircraft missile launcher 259 25, 33
twin anti-aircraft rocket launcher 259 25, 33
twin columns 336 6
twin edger 157 57
twin engine, horizontally-opposed ~ 189 47
twin etching machine 178 30
twin hull 284 65
twin launching catapult 259 14
Twins 3 28; 4 55
twin seat 188 42
twin seat, racing-style ~ 189 14
twin set 31 49
twin-spar wing construction 257 27
twin tail unit 229 32, 34
twist bit 134 49; 140 59
twist drill 134 49; 140 59
twist grip *Pest Contr.* 83 19
twist grip *Motorcycles etc.* 188 31
twist grip throttle control 188 30; 189 29

twist of tobacco 107 18
twitch grass 61 30
two-eight time 320 28
two-four time 320 29
two-high mill 148 53
two-line brevier 175 30
two-line primer 175 31
two-pipe system 126 22
two-seater 193 28
two-stroke blending pump 196 13
two-toed sloth 366 11
two-two time 320 30
two-way tap 350 49
tympan 340 37
tympanum 335 26
type *Letterpress* 181 37
type *Office* 249 15, 29
type *Money* 252 12
type, black-letter ~ 342 1, 2, 3
type, bold ~ 175 2
type, bold condensed ~ 175 10
type, boldfaced ~ 175 2
type, extra bold ~ 175 9
type, Gothic ~ 342 1
type, heavy ~ 175 2
type, italic ~ 175 7
type, light face ~ 175 8
type, Schwabacher ~ 342 2
type, semibold ~ 175 3
type area 185 59
type bed 180 78; 181 17
typecase 174 3
type casting 175 32-37
type character 174 7; 175 38
type cleaner 247 8
type-cleaning brush 247 7
type-cleaning kit 247 8
type disc 176 20
type face 174 31; 175 42
type faces 342 1-15
type forme 340 32
typefounding 175 32-37
type height 175 44
type line 175 43
type magazine 174 21
type matrix 174 47; 176 16
type matter 174 15; 175 1-17; 181 37
types 342 1-15
typescript *Composing Rm.* 174 6
typescript *Script* 342 9
typesetter 174 5
typesetting, computer-controlled ~ 176 14
typesetting computer 176 10
type size 175 18, 46
types of ship 221
typewriter 209 28; 248 22; 309 79
typewriter, electric ~ 249 1
typewriter rubber 247 26
typewriting 342 9
typing compartment 209 26
typing desk 245 25; 248 26
typing opening 249 19
typing window 249 19
typist 248 21
typographer beetle 82 22
tyre 191 15
tyre, high-pressure ~ 187 30
tyre, pneumatic ~ 187 30; 305 86
tyre, rubber ~ 273 54
tyre, tubular ~ 290 19, 23
tyre chain 304 10
tyre pressure gauge 196 17
tyre tread 189 27

U

udder 75 18
ulna 17 14
ulnar side of the hand 19 70
ultra large crude carrier 221 1
umbel 383 65
umbel, simple ~ 370 72
Umbellula encrinus 369 14
umbo 329 58
umbra 4 35
umbrella *Hall* 41 15
umbrella *Station* 205 12
umbrella *Art* 337 22
umbrella *Invertebr.* 357 15
umbrella, telescopic ~ 41 12
umbrella stand 41 14
umpire 292 55, 65; 293 19, 68
unau 366 11
uncial 341 17
underbrush 84 5
undercarriage 194 32
undercarriage, retractable ~ 232 10
undercarriage housing 256 15
undercarriage hydraulic cylinder 257 41
undercarriage unit, forward-retracting ~ 257 40
undercarriage unit, main ~ 230 41; 231 28; 256 26; 257 40; 288 33
undercarriage unit, retractable ~ 231 28
underclothes, ladies' ~ 32 1-15
underclothes, men's ~ 32 22-29
undercut *Forestry* 84 28
undercut *Meat* 95 13
undercut swing saw 157 24, 64
underframe 207 3; 208 5
undergown 355 37
undergrasp 296 41
undergrowth 84 5
underlip 72 10
under-ridge tile 122 5
undershirt 296 61
underside 173 34
underskirt 309 85
understructure 191 2
under tile 122 57
underwater case 117 57
underwater housing 117 57
underwater massage bath 281 31
underwater salvo missile launcher 259 24
underwater salvo rocket launcher 259 24
underwater swimmer 279 7; 280 37
underwater swimming 279 7-27; 282 38
underwater swimming set 279 8-22
underwear 32
underwear, ladies' ~ 32 1-15
underwear, men's ~ 32 22-29
underwing tank 256 4
underwood 84 5, 32
uneven bars 297 3
ungulates 366 25-31; 367 1-10
ungulates, even-toed ~ 366 28-31
ungulates, odd-toed ~ 366 25-27
unicorn 254 16; 327 7
uniform 264 7
uniform cap 264 8
Union Jack 253 15
union of sets 348 5-6

unison 321 6
unison interval 321 6
unit, assistant's ~ 24 9
unit, slide-in ~ 27 32
unit indicator 174 36
unit load 225 49; 226 9
unit load, foil-wrapped ~ 225 42
units 344 3
university 262 1-25
university lecturer 262 3
university library 262 11-25
university professor 262 3
unloading unit 62 42
unrefined oil tank 221 71
unwind station 173 39
up-and-down roundabout 308 5
up-and-down slide 273 52
upcurrent, frontal ~ 287 vp
upholstery 134 59
upper, corduroy ~ 101 26
upper, rubber ~ 300 45
upper, soft-leather ~ 101 46
upper, terry ~ 101 23
upper arm hang 296 58
upper board 326 15
upper board groove 326 14
uppercut 299 32
upper fore topgallant sail 219 59
upper fore topgallant yard 219 36
upper fore topsail 219 57
upper fore topsail yard 219 34
upper hatch 6 45
upper-leather shears 100 42
upper main topgallant sail 219 65
upper main topgallant yard 219 42
upper main topsail 219 63
upper main topsail yard 219 40
Upper Muschelkalk 154 58
Upper Permian 154 62
upright *Gymn.* 296 9
upright *Athletics* 298 13, 33
upright *Music. Instr.* 325 1
upright kneeling position 295 7
upright spin 302 9
upsett 136 25
upsetting block 137 16
upstart 297 28
upward ventilator 154 81
U-rail 214 22
Uranus 4 50
ureter 20 32
urethra 20 68
urethroscope 23 20
urine sediment chart 23 58
urn 328 40; 331 31
urn, cinerary ~ 328 38
urn, domestic ~ 328 38
urn, embossed ~ 328 38
urn grave 328 39; 331 30
Ursa Major 3 29
Ursa Minor 3 34
ursine seal 367 18
usher 315 12
usherette 312 4
uterus 20 79
utility room door 118 6
utility room window 118 5
U-tube 349 2
U-valley 13 55
uvula 19 22

V

vacancy **342** 70
vacuum **240** 21
vacuum back **177** 35
vacuum box **173** 15
vacuum chamber 2 52; **83** 12; **159** 12
vacuum cleaner *Household* **50** 80
vacuum cleaner *Goldsm. etc.* **108** 43
vacuum cleaner, cylinder ~ **50** 68
vacuum cleaner, upright ~ **50** 58
vacuum equipment **145** 51
vacuum film holder **177** 8
vacuum frame **179** 13; **182** 2
vacuum line **74** 50; **75** 29
vacuum printing frame **179** 13
vacuum pump *Intern. Combust. Eng.* **190** 59, 60
vacuum pump *Water* **269** 8
vacuum pump switch **179** 19
vacuum ripening tank **169** 11
vacuum timing control **190** 9
vagina **20** 86
Valaisian dulcimer **322** 34
Valenciennes **102** 18
valerian **380** 5
valley *Phys. Geog.* **13** 52-56
valley *Roof* **121** 15; **122** 11, 82
valley, dry ~ **13** 75
valley, synclinal ~ **13** 56
valley, U-shaped ~ **13** 55
valley, V-shaped ~ **13** 53, 54
valley bottom **13** 67; **215** 60
valley floor **13** 67
valley glacier **12** 49
valley rafter **121** 64
valleyside **13** 57-70
valley station **214** 39
valley station platform **214** 51
valley temple **333** 8
value **250** 18
value, note's ~ **320** 7
valve *Roof & Boilerr.* **38** 73
valve *Bicycle* **187** 31
valve *Airsports* **288** 77
valve *Ball Games* **291** 18
valve *Music. Instr.* **323** 40; **324** 66
valve, aortic ~ **20** 49
valve, atrioventricular ~ **20** 46, 47
valve, bicuspid ~ **20** 47
valve, mitral ~ **20** 47
valve, pulmonary ~ **20** 50
valve, sliding ~ **217** 55
valve, tricuspid ~ **20** 46
valve control house **217** 42, 63
valve horn **323** 41
valve house **217** 42, 63
valve housing **217** 54
valve line **288** 78
valve sealing cap **187** 32
valves of the heart **20** 46-47
valve tube **187** 31
vambrace **329** 47
vamp *Shoem.* **100** 60
vamp *Carnival* **306** 32
vamplate **329** 82
van, medium ~ **194** 7
Vandyke beard **34** 13
vane, curved ~ **91** 38
vane, flat ~ **91** 40
vang **284** 21
vanilla **382** 48
vanilla plant **382** 46
vanilla pod **382** 48
vans **194**

vaquero **306** 31
variable **345** 14
variable depth sonar **259** 40
variable focus lens **313** 23
variable platen action lever **249** 24
varifocal lens **313** 23
variometer **230** 14
varnish **338** 12
varnishing **129** 14
vas deferens **20** 74
vase, Greek ~ **334** 37
vase, hand-painted ~ **161** 18
vase, porcelain ~ **337** 5
vase, stone ~ **272** 35
vastus lateralis **18** 46
vastus medialis **18** 46
vat *Fish Farm.* **89** 4
vat *Paperm.* **172** 25; **173** 47
vat, concrete ~ **79** 3
vat, stainless steel ~ **79** 4
vatman **173** 46
vault **79** 1
vault, cloistered ~ **336** 41
vault, groined ~ **336** 42
vault, ribbed ~ **336** 43
vault, stalactitic ~ **337** 17
vault, stellar ~ **336** 44
vault, types of ~ **336** 38-50
vaulter *Athletics* **298** 29
vaulter *Circus* **307** 32
vaulting **298** 9-41
vaulting, Romanesque ~ **335** 17
vaulting horse **296** 1; **297** 1
vaulting pole **298** 28
V-belt **64** 78
V-belt drive **180** 58
V-cardan **67** 31
VCR cassette **243** 5
veal **95** 1-13
vee-belt drive **180** 58
vee-neck **31** 68
vee-tail **229** 31
Vega **3** 22
vegetable, frozen ~ **99** 61
vegetable basket **99** 81
vegetable crate **55** 43
vegetable dish **45** 25
vegetable garden **52**
vegetable oil **98** 23
vegetable patch **52** 26
vegetable plants **57**
vegetable plate **45** 33
vegetable platter **45** 33
vegetable plot **52** 26; **55** 39
vegetables **57**
vegetables, canned ~ **96** 27
vegetable spoon **45** 74
vegetarian meal **266** 62
vehicle **195** 47
vehicle, articulated ~ **194** 28
vehicle, electrically-powered ~ **188** 20
vehicle ferry **15** 47
vehicle ramp **206** 1
vehicles **186** 1-54
vehicles, horse-drawn ~ **186** 1-54
vehicle tanker **194** 28
veil **381** 5
veil, bridal ~ **332** 20
veil, widow's ~ **331** 39
vein **370** 29
vein, frontal ~ **18** 6
vein, iliac ~ **18** 18
vein, jugular ~ **18** 2
vein, portal ~ **20** 39
vein, pulmonary ~ **18** 12; **20** 56
vein, subclavian ~ **18** 8
vein, temporal ~ **18** 4
velum **381** 5

velum palati **19** 21
vena cava, inferior ~ **18** 15; **20** 57
vena cava, superior ~ **18** 9; **20** 53
venation **370** 29
vendor **308** 17
veneer **133** 2
veneer-peeling machine **133** 1
veneer-splicing machine **133** 3
V-engine **190** 1
vent *Phys. Geog.* **11** 28
vent *Airsports* **288** 82
vent, volcanic ~ **11** 17
ventilating tile **122** 7
ventilation control knob **26** 27
ventilation drum **74** 29
ventilation drum motor **74** 33
ventilation flap *Market Gdn.* **55** 41
ventilation flap *Railw.* **213** 16, 29, 30
ventilation shaft *Brew.* **92** 14
ventilation shaft *Coal* **144** 21
ventilation slit **50** 30
ventilation switch **191** 83
ventilation system **6** 26
ventilation system, automatic ~ **191** 30
ventilation window **55** 10
ventilator *Bathrm. etc.* **49** 20
ventilator *Poultry Farm* **74** 10, 17
ventilator *Railw.* **207** 9
ventilator *Ship* **221** 41
ventilator *Water* **269** 27
ventilator *Disco* **317** 30
ventilator *Zoo* **356** 17
ventilator, hinged ~ **55** 10
ventilator grill **258** 43
ventilator lead **223** 41
ventilator opening **258** 43
ventilators **55** 10-11
vent mast **221** 38
vent pipe **155** 11
vent prop **55** 18
ventral part **95** 39
ventricle **20** 51
vents **55** 10-11
venturi **192** 8
venturi throat **190** 15
Venus *Astron.* **4** 44
Venus *Prehist.* **328** 8
Venus's flytrap **377** 14
Venus's slipper **376** 27
verge **37** 8; **121** 3
verger **330** 26, 58
vermouth **98** 62
Vermes **357** 20-26
vermuth **98** 62
vernier *Metalwkr.* **140** 55
vernier *Navig.* **224** 5
vernier calliper gauge **140** 52; **149** 67
vernier depth gauge **140** 54; **149** 72
vernier scale **149** 69
vert **254** 29
vertebra, cervical ~ **17** 2
vertebra, coccygeal ~ **17** 5; **20** 60
vertebra, dorsal ~ **17** 3
vertebra, lumbar ~ **17** 4
vertebra, thoracic ~ **17** 3
vertex *Man* **16** 1
vertex *Maths.* **346** 26; **347** 16, 28
vertex refractionometer **111** 33
vertical backward somersault **297** 17

vertical deflection module **240** 8
vertical drive head **150** 38
vertical flick spin **288** 6
vertical milling spindle **150** 37
vertical/short take-off and landing aircraft **232** 26-32
vertical speed indicator **230** 14
vertical tangent screw **14** 54
vesicle, germinal ~ **74** 66
vesicle, seminal ~ **20** 77
vessel, completed ~ **162** 29, 37
vessel, damaged ~ **227** 2; **228** 10
vessel, funerary ~ **328** 34
vessels, ecclesiastical ~ **332** 34-54
vessels, liturgical ~ **332** 34-54
vessel with spiral pattern **328** 13
vest *Infant Care etc.* **28** 23
vest *Underwear etc.* **32** 7
vest *Men's Wear* **33** 4, 15
vest *Gymn.* **296** 61
vest *Hist. Cost.* **355** 75
vest, envelope-neck ~ **29** 7
vest, knitted ~ **33** 53
vest, short-sleeved ~ **32** 28
vest, sleeveless ~ **29** 6; **32** 25
vest, wrapover ~ **29** 8
vest and shorts set **32** 21
vestibule *Railw.* **207** 21
vestibule *Hotel* **267** 1-26
vestments **330** 22; **332** 4
vestry **331** 13
vestry door **330** 17
VHF and UHF tuner **240** 6
VHF antenna **257** 25
VHF station selector button **241** 38
viaduct **215** 59; **268** 48
vibrating beam **201** 13
vibrating cylinder **119** 89
vibrating head **119** 89
vibrating poker **119** 89
vibration, macroseismic ~ **11** 38
vibration damper **190** 26
vibrator **201** 13
vicar **330** 22
vicarage **331** 20
vice **109** 28; **134** 10; **138** 24; **260** 47, 56
vice, front ~ **132** 30
vice, parallel-jaw ~ **140** 2
vice bar **260** 48
vice handle **132** 31
vice screw **132** 32
Victoria regia water lily **378** 17
video cassette **242** 18
video cassette recorder **243** 7
video cassette recorder system **243** 5-36
video coding station **236** 39
video controller **239** 11
video control room **239** 10
video data terminal **238** 2, 11
video disc **243** 38, 44, 58
video disc jacket **243** 45
video disc player **243** 37, 46
video head **243** 26, 36
video head movement, direction of ~ **243** 30
video long play video disc system **243** 46-60
video monitor **238** 2
video recorder, portable ~ **243** 4
video signal **243** 58
videotape recorder, portable

769

~ 243 4
video telephone 242 21
video telephone screen 242 26
video track 243 31
vielle à roue 322 25
Vienna sausage 96 8
view, front ~ 151 17
view, lateral ~ 27 3
view, side ~ 151 18
viewer editor 117 91
viewfinder, rectangular ~ 114
  14
viewfinder, right-angle ~ 115
  71
viewfinder, universal ~ 114
  41
viewfinder eyepiece *Photog.*
  114 2; 115 22
viewfinder eyepiece *Films* 313
  6
viewfinder hood 114 23; 115
  68
viewfinder image 115 51
viewing lens 114 25
viewing screen 117 94
view point 15 68
Viking ship 218 13-17
village 15 105
vine *Wine Grow.* 78 2-9
vine *Pest Contr.* 83 51
vinegar 98 25
vine layer 83 15
vine leaf 78 4
vine pests 80 20-27
vine root louse 83 33
vine shoot 78 2
vine stem 78 6
vine tendril 54 22
vineyard *Map* 15 65
vineyard *Wine Grow.* 78 1, 21
vineyard area 78 1-21
vineyard tractor 83 48
viniculture 78
viniculturist 78 13
viol 322 23
viola 323 27
viola da gamba 322 23
viol bow 322 24
violet 343 9
violin 323 1
violin, miniature ~ 322 20
violin body 323 3
violin bow 323 12
violin-bow fibula 328 27
violin bridge 323 5
violin clef 320 8
violinist 267 45
violin string 323 9
violoncello 323 16
violone 322 23; 323 23
vipers 364 40-41
Virgin 3 18; 4 58
virginal 322 45
Virginia creeper 51 5; 374 16
Virgin Mary 330 51
Virgo 3 18; 4 58
vis-à-vis 186 51
viscose 169 13-27, 15
viscose process 169 1-34
viscose rayon 169 1-12, 34
viscose rayon cake 169 18
viscose rayon thread 169
  13-27
viscose spinning solution 169
  10, 28-34
viscous drive 190 8
vise *see* vice
vision controller 239 11
vision control room 239 10
vision mixer 238 63
vision-mixing console 238 63
vision-mixing desk 238 63
visitor 356 6

visor *Forestry* 84 23
visor *Heraldry* 254 9
visor *Chivalry* 329 40
visual display 23 27
visual display unit 248 16, 44
viticulture 78
viticulturist 78 13
vitreous body 19 46
vixen 88 42
VLP video disc 243 51
V-neck 31 68
vocal pouch 364 25
vocal sac 364 25
Voith transmission 209 14;
  212 74
vol-au-vent 97 18
volcanism 11 13-28
volcano, active ~ 11 15
volcano, composite ~ 11 15
volcano, extinct ~ 11 25, 28
volcano, subterranean ~ 11 20
vole and mole trap 83 37
volley 293 41
volley, forehand ~ 293 41
volleyball 293 56-71, 58, 59
voltage meter 212 17
voltage regulator, automatic
  ~ 153 31
voltage transformer 153 59
voltmeter 326 38
volume, respiratory ~ 26 28
volume control 117 85; 241
  41
volume control, pupil's ~ 261
  43
volume control, student's ~
  261 43
volume readout 196 5
volumetric flask 350 28
volume unit meters 241 35-36
volute 333 26; 334 23
volute cushion 334 24
VOR antenna 257 26
VOR radio direction finder
  230 15
voter 263 22
voter, qualified ~ 263 24
votive candle 330 53
voussoir 336 22
V-seat 295 13
V-support 295 17
V-tail 229 31
vulcanicity 11 13-28
vulva 16 39
V-valley 13 53
V-way *Joiner* 132 61
V-way *Composing Rm.* 175
  54

W

wad, felt ~ 87 52
wafer *Bakery* 97 45
wafer *Church* 332 28
wafer, sacred ~ 332 48
waffle 97 45
waffle iron, electric ~ 40 34
waggonette 186 2
wagon 213 18
wagon, flat ~ 206 21, 24; 213
  5, 11, 40
wagon, large-capacity ~ 213
  28
wagon, open ~ 213 33
wagon, special ~ 213 33
Wagoner 3 27
wagon load 206 52
wagon truck 200 25
wagtail 360 9
waist *Man* 16 31
waist *Shoem.* 100 68
waist, corseted ~ 355 53

waistband *Ladies' Wear* 31 41
waistband *Men's Wear* 33 23
waistcoat 33 4, 15
waistcoat, denim ~ 31 59
waistcoat, embroidered ~ 355
  75
waistcoat, knitted ~ 33 53
waistcoat, quilted ~ 30 16
waist longeron 235 9
waist slip 32 14; 309 85
waiter 267 47
waiter, head ~ 266 30
waiting room *Doc.* 22 1
waiting room *Station* 204 14
waiting room *Airport* 233 18
'waiting room' *Airport* 233 28
waitress 265 13; 266 18
wake 223 58
wake-robin 379 9
waldhorn 323 41
walk 71 2; 72 39
walkie-talkie set 270 41
walking stick 41 5
walking-stick umbrella 205
  12
walkway *Dwellings* 37 60
walkway *Street Sect.* 198 9
walkway *Hydr. Eng.* 217 72
wall *Map* 15 95
wall *Carp.* 120 29
wall *Equest.* 289 8
wall *Ball Games* 291 44
wall, brick ~ 118 8; 123 29;
  260 45
wall, concrete ~ 123 1
wall, framed ~ 120 48
wall, glass ~ 37 16
wall, hollow-block ~ 118 15
wall, inner ~ 329 19
wall, mirrored ~ 317 28
wall, outer ~ 121 32, 77; 122
  37
wall, Rococo ~ 336 9
wall, rubble concrete ~ 119 7
wall, side ~ 42 2; 46 4; 222 37
wall, slatted ~ 213 29
wall, stone ~ 337 23
wall, timber ~ 119 25; 120 9
wall barley 61 28
wall bars 296 20
wall brush, flat ~ 129 17
wall calendar 22 17; 245 3;
  248 42
wall candelabrum 330 16
wall chart 195 32
wall clock 109 32; 309 87
wall connection 25 23
wall cupboard 39 8; 46 30
wall desk 267 16
wall espalier 52 1
wall fountain 272 15
wall gecko 364 36
wall joist 120 39
wall lamp 265 9
wall lining, 'acoustic' ~ 310 15
wall map 260 44
wall memorial 331 14
wall mirror 309 3
wall-of-death rider 308 54
wall outlet 127 5
wall outlet, double ~ 127 6
wallower 91 11
wallpaper 128 18, 19
wallpaper, synthetic ~ 128 18
wallpaper-cutting board 128
  41
wallpapering 128 18-53
wallpaper paste 128 23
wallpaper-stripping liquid
  128 1
wallpaper-stripping machine
  128 9

wall pepper 51 7
wall plaster 123 60
wall plate 120 40, 49
wall shelf 104 8
wall shelf unit 104 8
wall socket 39 26; 127 5
wall socket, double ~ 127 6
wall stone 331 14
wall string 123 45
wall stringer 123 45
wall switch 127 16
wall unit 42 1; 44 17; 46 1
wall ventilator 266 15
walnut 59 41, 43
walnut tree 59 37-43, 37
walrus 367 20
wane 120 89
waney edge 120 89
Wankel engine, two-rotor ~
  190 5
wapiti 367 2
ward, inner ~ 329 2
ward, outer ~ 329 31
wardrobe 43 1
wardrobe door 46 2
wardrobe trunk 267 29
warehouse *Station* 206 53
warehouse *Docks* 225 23
warhead 255 65
war horn, ivory ~ 354 39
warm-air brush 106 30
warm-air comb 105 22; 106
  29
warm-air curtain 271 43
warm-air regulator 191 87
warm house 55 4, 32
warm-up regulator 190 50
warning cross 202 41
warning light 191 67, 72, 76,
  80; 202 46, 50; 224 69; 230
  64; 270 6
warning sign 280 6
warp *Sea Fish.* 90 12
warp *Weaving* 165 43; 166 39
warp *Knitting* 167 24
warp *Weaves* 171 14
warp *Hydr. Eng.* 217 23
warp, wire ~ 90 15
warp paint 352 13
warp beam 165 29, 42; 166
  48; 167 24
warp beam, sized ~ 165 56
warping capstan 217 22
warping machine 165 22
warping machine frame 165
  27
warp-knitting machine 167
  23
warp let-off motion 166 61
warp rib fabric 171 14
warp rib weave 171 13
warp thread 166 39; 171 1-29,
  2, 17, 18
warp thread, lowered ~ 171 8
warp thread, raised ~ 171 7
warren 86 23
warship, Roman ~ 218 9-12
warships 258; 259
washbasin 24 15; 49 24; 126
  27, 31; 278 6
washbasin, double ~ 267 32
washbasin pedestal 49 27
washboard *Floor etc. Constr.*
  123 21, 63
washboard *Flea Market* 309
  70
wash-bottle 349 8
washer *Photog.* 116 15
washer *Mach. Parts etc.* 143
  17, 34
washer *Sawmill* 157 21
washer *Bicycle* 187 55
washer, lead ~ 122 103

washing 169 19; 170 48, 56
washing and toilet facilities 278 5-6
washing basin 309 65
washing bottle 261 32
washing drum 50 24
washing floor 92 3, 27
washing line 38 23; 50 33
washing machine 157 21
washing machine, automatic ~ 50 23
washing machines 50 23-34
washing set 309 64
washing trough 165 49
washing unit, compressed-air ~ 92 3
washing-up area 207 28
washing-up brush 50 51
wash liquor, weak ~ 172 44
washroom 207 15; 278 5
washstand Railw. 207 40
washstand Flea Market 309 67
wash tank Photog. 116 15
wash tank Oil, Petr. 145 30
washtub 309 69
wash water, weak ~ 172 44
wasp 82 35
wasp waist 355 53
waste 144 37
waste, medium-activity ~ 154 72
waste, nuclear ~ 154 57-68
waste, radioactive ~ 154 57-68, 77
waste bin 22 70; 96 46
waste-gas heat exchanger 155 9
wastepaper basket 46 25; 248 45
waste pipe Bathrm. etc. 49 45
waste pipe Street Sect. 198 26
waste steam exhaust 210 22
waste tray, mobile ~ 26 22
waste water discharge 156 38
waste water outlet 217 62
waste water pump Paperm. 172 63
waste water pump Refuse Coll. 199 20
watch, automatic ~ 110 32-43
watch, waterproof ~ 109 26; 279 11
watchdog 62 32; 70 25
watches 110
watchglass-fitting tool 109 11, 29
watchkeeper 221 126
watchmaker 109 1
watchman 329 9
watch strap 110 5
watch strap, metal ~ 109 19
watch-testing machine 109 24
watch-timing machine 109 25
watchtower 329 35
water 48 8
water, artesian ~ 12 21
water, baptismal ~ 332 12
water, entrapped ~ 13 16
water, raw ~ 269 4
water, rising ~ 12 26
water, running ~ 89 1
water, shallow ~ 224 87, 97
water, underlying ~ 12 32
water and brine separator 145 32
water appliances 126 12-25
water ballast 223 78
water barrel 52 4
water bath 132 12; 349 14
water bath, constant

temperature ~ 23 48
Water Bearer 4 63
water bottle 290 10
water buffalo 367 8
water bug 358 4
water butt 52 4
water canister 83 57
water cannon 270 66; 316 18
Water Carrier Astron. 4 63
water carrier Camping 278 32
water channel 334 54
water circuit, auxiliary ~ 259 63
water circuit, primary ~ 259 65
water circuit, secondary ~ 259 63
water-collecting tank 92 5
watercolour 260 27; 338 18
water connection 179 5
water container 103 22
water cooler 189 35
water-cooling system Moon L. 6 26
water-cooling system Iron Foundry etc. 148 28
watercress 378 30
water cruet 332 45
water elf 327 23
water extractor 281 39
waterfall 11 45
waterfall, artificial ~ 272 9
water feed pipe 103 21
waterfowl 272 51-54
waterfowling 86 40
water gauge Map 15 29
water gauge Roof & Boilerr. 38 63
water gauge Railw. 210 45
water gauge Chem. 349 16
water glass 24 13
water heater 145 31
water heater, electric ~ 126 13
water heater, gas ~ 126 12
water heater, instantaneous ~ 126 12-13
watering can 51 21; 55 26
water inlet Fish Farm. 89 7
water inlet Plumb. etc. 126 18
water inlet Water 269 54
water inlet pipe 168 11
water jet pipe 281 40
water jet pump 23 49
water jug 309 66
water jump 289 20
water level 13 77
water lily 51 18; 272 56
waterline 258 27; 285 31
water main 198 22
watermark 252 31
water meter 269 53
water-meter dial 269 58
watermill Map 15 77
watermill Mills 91 35-44
water molecule 242 67
water moth 358 12
water newt 364 20
water nixie 327 23
water nymph Fabul. Creat. 327 23
water nymph Articulates 358 3
water outlet Fish Farm. 89 8
water outlet Energy Sources 155 23
water outlet Water 269 57
water outlet pipe 116 17
water overfall 91 43
water ox 367 8
water pipe Market Gdn. 55 30
water pipe Poultry Farm 74 7, 26
water pipe Tobacc. etc. 107 42

water pipe Power Plant 152 7
water pipe Paperm. 172 65
water pipe School 261 4
water plantain 378 44
water plants 378 14-57
water polo 282 46-50
water polo ball 282 48
water preheater 152 10
waterproofing 123 5
water pump 190 61
waters, coastal ~ 286 10-14
waters, inshore ~ 286 10-14
water scorpion 358 4
water ski 280 16
water ski, types of ~ 286 56-62
water skier 286 45
water skiing 286 45-62
water slater 358 2
Water Snake Astron. 3 16
water snake Fish etc. 364 38
water supply 27 46; 269
water supply, individual ~ 269 40-52
water supply pipe Brew. 92 48
water supply pipe Photog. 116 16
water table 13 77; 269 1, 42, 63
water tank Market Gdn. 55 2, 29
water tank Gas Weld. 141 17
water tank Refuse Coll. 199 27
water tank Railw. 210 66
water tank School 261 33
water tank Theatre 316 51
water tanker 233 22
water tap 39 36; 49 26; 126 31
water temperature 280 8
water temperature gauge 191 38, 66
water tender 270 51
water tower Map 15 81
water tower Market Gdn. 55 2
water tower Coal 144 14
water tower Water 269 18
water trough 137 8
water tub 281 26
water-tube boiler 152 5
water vole 366 17
waterway engineering 217
water wings 281 7; 282 18
Watling Street thistle 61 32
wattle 73 24
wave 13 36; 287 17
wave, seismic ~ 11 36
waves, artificial ~ 281 1-9
wave soaring 287 16
wave system 287 17
waxing cork 301 23
waxing iron 301 22
wax scraper 301 24
wax separation 145 50
waxworks 308 68
waybill 206 30
wayside flowers 375; 376
WC 49 12; 207 16, 42, 72; 211 59; 231 31; 317 31
weaponry 255 1-98
weapons, heavy ~ 255 40-95
weapon system radar 258 35
weasel 367 16
weather 8 1-19
weather chart 9 1-39; 342 66
weather cloth 223 17
weathercock 331 3
weather map 9 1-39; 342 66
weather radar antenna 231 18
weather report 342 65
weather satellite 10 64
weather ship 9 7
weather station 9 7; 225 33

weather vane 121 26; 331 4
weave, plain ~ 171 1, 4, 24
weaver 136 5
weaves Basketm. 136 1-4
weaves Weaves 171 1-29
weaving 165; 166
weaving draft 171 29
weaving machine 166 1, 35
web Dom. Anim. 73 36
web House Insects etc. 81 10
web Paperm. 173 30, 45
web Letterpress 181 43, 58
web Railw. 202 3
web Gymn. 297 11
web Articulates 358 47
web Birds 359 7
webfoot 359 6
web-offset press 180 1, 18
wedding ceremony 332 14
wedding ring 36 5; 332 17
wedding ring box 36 6
wedding ring sizing machine 108 24
wedge 119 15; 132 19; 158 7
wedge, hardwood ~ 121 96
wedge, optical ~ 176 22
wedge heel 101 55
wedge stone 336 22
weed 379 8
weeding hoe 51 22
weeds 61
weekend house 37 84-86
weeping willow 272 63
weevil 80 10, 49; 82 42
weft feeler 166 31
weft feeler, electric ~ 166 14
weft pirn 166 7
weft replenishment 166 5
weft thread 171 1-29, 3
weft thread, lowered ~ 171 15
weft thread, raised ~ 171 16
weft yarn 163 2
weigela 373 23
weigela 373 23
weighbridge 206 41
weighbridge office 206 40
weighing apparatus 92 32; 170 29
weighing bottle 349 24
weighing bunker 225 22
weighing machine 206 31
weighing platform 22 67
weigh office 199 12
weight Roof & Boilerr. 38 32
weight Sea Fish. 90 10
weight Clocks 110 32
weight Railw. 202 18
weight Athletics 298 49
weight, iron ~ 90 21
weight belt 279 14
weighting disc 165 21
weightlifter 299 2
weightlifting 299 1-5
weights, lead ~ 89 88-92
weir Map 15 66
weir Hydr. Eng. 217 65-72
weir Rowing 283 60
weir sill 217 79
welder electrode arm 142 30
weld gauge 142 36
welding bench 141 13; 142 21
welding current adjustment 142 31
welding generator 142 26
welding glove, five-fingered ~ 142 32
welding glove, three-fingered ~ 142 8
welding goggles 141 24
welding lead 142 19
welding nozzle 141 33
welding paste 141 18
welding rod 141 12

welding table 142 13
welding torch 141 11, 19, 28
welding transformer 125 29;
  142 1, 27
well *Astron.* 5 24
well *Map* 15 100
well *Carp.* 120 46
well *Joiner* 132 35
well *Oil, Petr.* 145 17
well *Water* 269 40
well, artesian ~ 12 25
well, driven ~ 269 60
well, glass-roofed ~ 271 11
well casing 269 64
well head 269 65
wellington boot 101 14
Wellingtonia 372 69
wels 364 12
welt, knitted ~ 29 65; 31 70
welt, stretch ~ 31 43
welt cutter 100 48
welt pincers 100 38
West Australian Current 14
  45
westerlies 9 50
Western roll 298 16
west point 4 15
West Wind Drift 14 44
westwork 335 22
wet and dry bulb
  thermometer 10 52
wet bulb thermometer 10 35
wet felt, first ~ 173 17
wet felt, second ~ 173 18
wether 73 13
wet oil tank 145 30
wetsuit, neoprene ~ 279 9
wetting trough 165 44
Weymouth pine 372 30
Whale 3 11
whales 367 23-29
wharve 164 48
wheat 68 1, 23
wheat and rye bread 97 6, 8
wheat beer 93 26
wheat flour 97 52; 99 63
wheatgerm bread 97 48
wheatgerm oil 98 24
wheel *Overh. Irrign.* 67 24
wheel *Clocks* 110 11
wheel *Bicycle* 187 1
wheel *Aircraft* 230 24
wheel, back ~ 186 17
wheel, co-pilot's ~ 230 25
wheel, front ~ 186 4; 187
  26-32
wheel, light alloy ~ 189 48
wheel, rear ~ 186 17
wheel, rubber-tyred ~ 64 32
wheel, ship's ~ 224 15
wheel, spoked ~ 289 25
wheel adjustment 64 58
wheel alignment 195 17, 21
wheel alignment, visual ~ 195
  41
wheel and axle drive 212 28
wheel and axle set 212 3; 213
  3
wheelarch doorway 278 39
wheelbarrow 56 47; 118 37;
  119 42
wheelbarrow sprayer 83 38
wheel brush, wire ~ 134 24
wheel cover 322 27
wheel cylinder 192 54
wheel disc, plastic ~ 289 25
wheeler 186 47
wheel flange lubricator 211
  52
wheel guard *Tram* 197 11
wheel guard *Music. Instr.* 322
  27
wheelhead slide 150 3

wheelhorse 186 47
wheelhouse 223 18; 224
  14-38
wheel lock 187 49
wheel mirror 195 41
wheel nut 187 53
wheel of fortune 308 45
wheel plough 65 1
wheel ratchet 110 10
wheel rim 187 28; 189 25; 191
  16; 192 77
wheelsman 224 16
wheel tapper 205 39
wheel-tapping hammer 205
  40
whelp 73 16
whetstone 66 19
whetting anvil 66 11
whetting hammer 66 9
whip *Bldg. Site* 118 30
whip *Equest.* 289 43
whip *Circus* 307 53
whip antenna 258 60
whip line 228 3
whipper-in 289 43
whipping unit 97 70
whip stall 288 5
whirler 179 1
whirligig 308 2
whirlpool, hot ~ 281 31, 35
whirlpool separator 93 2
whisk 39 23
whiskers *Hairst. etc.* 34 12
whiskers *Mammals* 367 21
whisky 42 31
whisky glass 267 57
whistle *Kitch. Utensils* 40 11
whistle *Railw.* 211 9; 212 49
whistle *Navig.* 224 70
whistle lever 211 40
whistle valve handle 210 51
white 107 29
white *Poultry Farm* 74 62, 67
white *Heraldry* 254 25
white *Colour* 343 11
white bear 368 11
white clover 69 2
white light, supplementary ~
  203 15
white line 268 72
white owl 362 17
white oxeye daisy 376 4
white pelican 359 5
white pine 372 30
white poplar 371 23
white-tailed eagle 362 5
white-tailed sea eagle 362 5
white wagtail 360 9
white water lily 378 14
white water pump 172 63
whitewood 374 1
wholemeal bread 97 48
whole note 320 13
whole rest 320 21
whortleberry 377 23
wick 107 29
wickerwork 136 4, 16
wicket 292 70
wicket keeper 292 73
wide screen camera 310 47
width *Roof* 122 91, 95
width *Composing Rm.* 175 48
width adjustment 100 19
width scale 157 58
width-setting tree 100 55
Wiener 96 8
wig 105 38; 315 49
wig, full-bottomed ~ 34 2
wig, partial ~ 355 8
wig block 105 39
wiggler 89 72
wigwam 352 7
wild animal cage 307 49

wild animal tamer 307 52
wild arum 379 9
wild barley 61 28
wild boar 86 32; 88 51
wild briar 373 26
wild camomile 380 1
wild cherry 59 5
wild chicory 376 25
wild endive 376 25
wildfowling 86 40
wild morning glory 61 26
wild mustard 61 18
wild oat 61 29
wild orchid 376 28
wild pear tree 58 31
wild radish 61 21
wild sow 86 32; 88 51
wild strawberry 58 16
wild-water racing kayak 283
  69
willow rod 136 15
willow stake 136 14
Wilson chamber 2 24
Wilson cloud chamber 2 24
winch 270 56
winched launch 287 5
winch house 226 54
wind arrow 9 9
wind avalanche 304 1
wind box 147 69
windbreak 354 35
wind chest 326 12, 12-14
wind chest box 326 12
wind cone 287 11
wind cripple 13 43
wind direction 9 9-19; 285 6
wind-direction indicator 10
  31
wind directions 285 1-13
wind-direction shaft 9 9
wind-direction symbols 9
  9-19
windflower 375 5; 377 1
wind gauge 10 28
wind generator 55 34; 155 42
winding, low-voltage ~ 153
  16
winding, primary ~ 153 15
winding, secondary ~ 153 16
winding crown 110 42
winding engine house 144 2
winding gear 217 74
winding handle 117 50
winding inset 144 26
wind knob 110 23
windlass 223 49; 258 6
windmill *Map* 15 31
windmill *Mills* 91 1-34
windmill *Fair* 308 15
windmill, Dutch ~ 91 29
windmill, German ~ 91 31
windmill arm 91 1
windmill cap, rotating ~ 91 30
windmill sail 91 1
windmill vane 91 1
window 2 16; 6 40; 25 8; 28
  36, 49; 75 31; 77 50; 186 10;
  268 14; 284 38
window, circular ~ 335 12
window, double casement ~
  37 22
window, heated ~ 191 80
window, lead glass ~ 154 75
window, pedimental ~ 355 49,
  50
window, rear ~ 191 32, 80
window, side ~ 231 29
window, single casement ~ 37
  23
window, sliding ~ 207 7
window, transparent ~ 278
  41; 284 3
window box 268 15

window breast 37 24
window decoration 260 68;
  268 12
window display 98 1; 268 11
window frame 133 44
window glass 124 5
window head 37 25; 118 9;
  120 57
window jamb 120 51
window ladder 296 21
window ledge 118 12; 120 33
window lintel 120 57
window opening 120 30
window painting 260 26
window shutter 37 30
window sill 37 24; 118 12;
  120 33
window vent 55 10
windpipe 17 50; 20 4
wind power plant 155 42
wind pump 15 73
windrow 63 36
wind screen 5 15
windscreen, panoramic ~ 191
  21
windscreen wiper 191 41; 197
  32
wind shaft 91 5
windshield 5 31
windshield, panoramic ~ 191
  21
windshield wiper 191 41
wind sock 287 11
wind speed 9 10
wind-speed barb 9 10
wind-speed feather 9 10
wind-speed indicator 10 29
wind-speed meter 10 29
windsurfer 284 1
windsurfing 284 1-9
wind systems 9 46-52
wind trunk 326 11
wind vane 10 32; 55 36; 331 4
wind wheel 55 35
wine 99 76; 266 43
wine, bottled ~ 98 60-64
wine, red ~ 98 64
wine, sparkling ~ 98 63
wine, white ~ 98 60
wine bar 266 30-44
wine bottle 79 14
wine carafe 266 32
wine cask 79 2
wine cellar 79 1-22
wine cooler 266 42
wine cruet 332 46
wineglass 44 9; 45 12, 82, 83;
  79 19; 266 33; 317 7
wine grower 78 13
wine growing 78
wine in bottles 98 60-64
wine jug 79 15
wine list 266 31
wine press, horizontal ~ 79 21
wine restaurant 266 30-44
wine tasting 79 16
wine vat 79 3
wine vault 79 1-22
wine waiter 266 30
wing *House Insects etc.* 81 8
wing *Game* 88 76, 79
wing *Sea Fish.* 90 16
wing *Aircraft* 230 43
wing *Airsports* 288 27
wing *Fabul. Creat.* 327 15, 28,
  51, 60
wing *Decid. Trees* 371 57
wing *Conifers* 372 9
wing, bat's ~ 327 4
wing, central ~ 229 8
wing, cranked ~ 229 14
wing, elliptical ~ 229 15
wing, front ~ 191 3

wing, hind ~ **358** 33
wing, lower ~ **229** 9
wing, membranous ~ **82** 11
wing, middle ~ **229** 8
wing, multispar ~ **287** 29
wing, ogival ~ **229** 22
wing, rectangular ~ **229** 16
wing, rotary ~ **232** 12
wing, swept-back ~ **229** 20, 21
wing, tapered ~ **229** 17
wing, upper ~ **229** 7
wing case **82** 10
wing configurations **229** 1-14
Winged Horse **3** 10
winger **291** 16
wing mirror, left-hand ~ **191** 40
wing mirror, right-hand ~ **191** 56
wing nut **143** 42; **187** 39
wing of bridge **223** 16
wing rail **202** 25
wings **307** 12
wing shapes **229** 15-22
wing span **229** 2
wing suspension, inner ~ **257** 34
wing suspension, outer ~ **257** 35
wing tally **74** 55
wing tank **256** 4
wing tank, integral ~ **257** 29
wing tip **287** 42
wing-tip tank **231** 9; **256** 30
wing wall *Rivers* **216** 35
wing wall *Hydr. Eng.* **217** 80
winker **71** 26
winner **299** 39
winner's price **289** 39
winners' table **289** 38
winning peg **292** 77
winnowing **64** 15
winter boot **101** 1
winter coat **30** 61
winter dike **216** 32
winter dress **30** 12
winter green **57** 34
winter moth **80** 16
winter slacks **30** 19
winter sports **301**; **302**; **303**
winter wear **30**
wiper *Post* **237** 44
wiper *Graphic Art* **340** 13
wiper/washer switch and horn **191** 60
wire *Paperm.* **173** 14
wire *Fencing* **294** 31
wire, gold ~ **108** 3
wire, iron ~ **143** 12
wire, overhead ~ **194** 43
wire, silver~ **108** 3
wire and sheet roller **108** 1
wireless mast **15** 33
wireman **127** 1
wire side **173** 34
wire spool, spring-loaded ~ **294** 29
wire stripper and cutter **134** 15
wire strippers **127** 64
wireworm **80** 38
witch **306** 6
witchgrass **61** 30
withers *Dog* **70** 11
withers *Horse* **72** 17
witloof **376** 25
witness **332** 23
wobbler, double-jointed ~ **89** 70
wobbler, round ~ **89** 71
wobbler, single-jointed ~ **89** 69
wolf **367** 13

wolfsbane **379** 1
womb **20** 79
wood *Forestry* **84** 1-34
wood *School* **260** 82
wood *Ball Games* **293** 91
wood *Sculpt. Studio* **339** 27
wood, coniferous ~ **15** 1
wood, deciduous ~ **15** 4
wood, mixed ~ **15** 14
wood, open ~ **326** 31-33
wood, rough ~ **135** 21
wood anemone **377** 1
woodbind **374** 13
woodbine **51** 5; **374** 13, 16
wood carver **339** 28
wood carving **260** 77
wood chip paper **128** 18
wood chisel **339** 19
wood cut **260** 83
wood cutting *Forestry* **84** 15-37
woodcutting *Graphic Art* **340** 2
wood engraving **340** 1, 1-13
wood file **132** 2
wood grouse **88** 72
wood haulage way **84** 3
wood ibis **359** 5
woodland strawberry **58** 16
woodlark **361** 18
wood louse **81** 6
woodpecker **359** 27
wood pulp, chemical ~ **172** 77, 78
wood pulp paper **128** 18
wood rasp **132** 1; **134** 8; **260** 55
wood screw **122** 101; **132** 41; **143** 45
wood screw thread **143** 47
wood sculptor **339** 28
woodsman **84** 18
wood stork **359** 5
wood tick **358** 44
wood-turning lathe **134** 51; **135** 1
woodwind instruments **323** 28-38
woodwinds **323** 28-38
woodworking adhesive **134** 36
woofer **241** 17
woolly apple aphid **80** 32, 33
woolly apple aphid colony **80** 34
woolly milk cap **379** 13
woolpack cloud **8** 1; **287** 22
work **118** 17
workbench **97** 60, 62; **100** 33; **104** 7; **108** 20; **109** 2; **111** 20; **124** 15; **125** 10; **137** 21; **140** 7; **260** 46
workbench, collapsible ~ **134** 41
workbench lamp **109** 12
workboard **136** 7
work clamp *Joiner* **132** 51
work clamp *Arc Weld.* **142** 35
worker *Bees* **77** 1, 6-9, 10-19
worker *Articulates* **358** 22
worker bee **77** 1
worker cell **77** 34
work folder **261** 27
working, open-cast ~ **158** 1
working area **162** 5
working bath **162** 5
working deck **221** 19, 34
working face **158** 3
working passage **75** 24
working platform **118** 17; **145** 5; **211** 42; **234** 28, 46
workings, underground ~ **144** 21-51

working surface, tiled ~ **261** 5
working top **39** 11
workman's cap **35** 40
workpiece **104** 25; **133** 44; **139** 46; **140** 6; **141** 20; **142** 28; **148** 51; **150** 20
workpiece, blocked ~ **139** 28
workpiece, preshaped ~ **139** 28
work platform **118** 17; **211** 42; **234** 28, 46
workroom, dressmaker's ~ **103** 1-27
workroom, furrier's ~ **131** 1-25
workroom, tailor's ~ **104** 1-32; **268** 17
works **15** 37
workshop **62** 17; **146** 30; **310** 6; **315** 28-42
workshop, bootmaker's ~ **100** 1-68
workshop, carpenter's ~ **120** 4
workshop, cooper's ~ **130** 1-33
workshop, fitter's ~ **140** 1-22
workshop, glazier's ~ **124** 1
workshop, joiner's ~ **132** 1-73
workshop, locksmith's ~ **140** 1-22
workshop, mechanic's ~ **140** 1-22
workshop, optician's ~ **111** 20-47
workshop, orbital ~ **235** 66
workshop, shoemaker's ~ **100** 1-68
workshop, tank construction engineer's ~ **130** 1-33
workshop, turner's ~ **135** 1-26
workshop area **5** 17
workshop door **120** 5
workshop trolley **109** 22
work top **50** 31
worm **192** 59
worm-and-nut steering gear **192** 56-59
worm gear sector **192** 57
wormhole **58** 65
worms **357** 20-26
wormwood **380** 4
worshipper **330** 29
wort **92** 50, 51, 52
wort boiler **92** 52
wort cooler **93** 5
wort cooling **93** 1-5
wound **21** 8
wrap, coloured ~ **355** 10
wrapper *Tobacc. etc.* **107** 5
wrapper *Bookbind.* **185** 37
wrapping, jute ~ **163** 4
wrapping counter **271** 14
wrapping material **98** 46-49
wrapping paper **98** 46
wreath **123** 52
wreath, bridal ~ **332** 19
wreath of the colours **254** 2
wreath piece **123** 49
wreck **224** 84
wrecking crane **270** 47
wreck to port **224** 86
wreck to starboard **224** 85
wren **361** 12
wrench **134** 14
wrench, open-end ~ **134** 2
wrest **325** 20
wrestler **299** 7
wrestling **299** 6-12
wrestling, Greco-Roman ~ **299** 6-9
wrestling mat **299** 12
wrest pin **324** 23; **325** 17
wrest pin block **324** 22; **325** 18

wrest plank **324** 22; **325** 18
wrist *Man* **19** 76
wrist *Horse* **72** 22
wristband **296** 64
wrist joint **2** 41
wrist sling **300** 32
wristwatch, automatic ~ **110** 32-43
wristwatch, electronic ~ **110** 1
writing, English ~ **342** 10
writing, German ~ **342** 11
writing cane **341** 23
writing surface **47** 23; **246** 3
writing system, pictorial ~ **341** 1
writing unit **46** 21
wrought-iron craftsman **140** 1
wryneck **359** 27

X

xanthate **169** 10
X-contact **115** 14
xenon lamp **177** 17
xenon lamp housing **177** 42
X-radiation **1** 33, 56
X-ray **25** 39
X-ray apparatus **24** 21; **27** 6
X-ray cassette **27** 2
X-ray control unit, central ~ **27** 9
X-ray examination table **27** 1
X-ray generator **24** 22
X-ray head **27** 18
X-ray image intensifier **27** 16
X-ray support, telescopic ~ **27** 8
X-ray technician **27** 11
X-ray tube **27** 17, 18
X-ray unit **27** 1-35
xylography **340** 1-13
xylophone **324** 61

Y

yacht **273** 29; **278** 12; **284** 10-48
yacht classes **284** 49-65
yacht hull, types of ~ **285** 29-41
yachting **284**; **285**
yachting cap **35** 29
yacht stern **285** 42
yacht stern, types of ~ **285** 42-49
yacht tacking **285** 7
yankee corn **68** 31
yard **276** 27
yardmaster **206** 45
yard radio **212** 50; **213** 4
yarn **164** 53, 56; **167** 17, 36; **169** 17, 25
yarn, doubled ~ **164** 60
yarn, glass ~ **162** 56, 57
yarn, inlaid ~ **171** 43
yarn, sleeved ~ **162** 57
yarn, viscose rayon ~ **169** 1-34, 27
yarn count **164** 40
yarn-distributing beam **167** 25
yarn-dividing beam **167** 25
yarn feeder **167** 6
yarn-forming frame, intermediate ~ **164** 27
yarn guide *Shoem.* **100** 30
yarn guide *Knitting* **167** 3, 54, 64
yarn guide support post **167** 2
yarn length recorder **165** 28

yarn package **165** 15; **170** 48
yarn package container **165**
    16
yarn-tensioning device **167** 5
yarrow **376** 15
yawing **230** 69
yawl **220** 10
y-axis **347** 3
Y-connection **153** 20
Y-cross **332** 61
yeast **93** 6
yeast, baker's ~ **97** 53
yeast bread **97** 11
yeast propagation **93** 6
yellow *Heraldry* **254** 24
yellow *Colour* **343** 2
yellow bunting **361** 6
yellow card **291** 63
yellow coral fungus **381** 32
yellow filter adjustment **116**
    44
yellow flag **60** 8
yellow-flowered jasmine **373**
    4
yellowhammer **361** 6
yellow iris **60** 8
yellow light **203** 16
yellow lupin **69** 17
yellow meal beetle **81** 23
yellow owl **362** 17
yellow prickle fungus **381** 31
yellow water flag **60** 8
yerba maté **382** 11
yew tree **372** 61
yoghurt maker **40** 44
yoke *Bldg. Site* **119** 64
yoke *Power Plant* **153** 14
yoke *Rowing* **283** 51
yoke, adjustable ~ **65** 14
yoke, bolted ~ **119** 74
yoke, front ~ **33** 19
yoke, kimono ~ **31** 18
yoke elm **371** 63
yoke mount, English-type ~
    113 23
yoke mounting, English-type
    ~ **113** 23
yolk **74** 68
yolk sac **74** 64
Y-tube **350** 56
yucca **373** 24
yurt **353** 19
yurta **353** 19

zircon **351** 19
zither **324** 21
zone, arid ~ **9** 54
zone, paved ~ **268** 58
zone, tropical ~ **9** 53
zoo **356**
zoological gardens **356**
zooming lever **117** 54; **313** 22,
    36
zoom lens **112** 41; **240** 34; **313**
    23
zoom lens, interchangeable ~
    117 2
zoom stereomicroscope **112**
    40
Zulu **354** 36

Z

zap flap **229** 50
Z-drive motorboat **286** 2
zebra **366** 27
zebra crossing **198** 11; **268** 24
Zechstein, leached ~ **154** 62
Zechstein, lixiviated ~ **154** 62
Zechstein shale **154** 68
zenith *Astron.* **4** 11
zenith *Hunt.* **87** 77
zero **275** 18
zero adjustment **2** 7
zero isotherm **9** 41
zero level **7** 6, 20
ziggurat **333** 32
zimmerstutzen **305** 35
zinc plate **179** 9; **180** 53; **340**
    52
zinc plate, etched ~ **178** 40
zinc plate, photoprinted ~ **178**
    32
zink **322** 12
zinnia **60** 22
zip **31** 55; **33** 28; **260** 13
zip, front ~ **29** 18
zip, inside ~ **101** 6
zip code **236** 43

索 引
汉语索引检字说明

1. 本索引是根据最通用的字典部首目录编排而成。

2. 检索方法：

　(1)《部首目录》共有 174 个基本部首。部首次序是按部首笔画数目排列。检索时，根据汉语词条第一个字的部首，从《部首目录》内查出该字部首的页码，然后查《检字表》。

　(2)《检字表》内，同一部首的字按笔画画数排列（部首画数不计算在内）。《中文索引》词条再按第二字或第三字分类即可找到。

3. 汉语词条后的第一个黑体数字，表示正文中的图号，紧跟的幼体阿拉伯数字，表示该图内英文词条的排序号。只需从汉语词条后的数字，便可找到相应的图和英文词条。

4. 汉语词条之前若由英文字母或阿拉伯数字起头，则均按英文字母顺序或阿拉伯数字大小排列，列入其他项内。

（一）部首目录

一 画

部首	号
丶	1
一	2
丨	3
丿	4
乙(一乛乚)	5

二 画

部首	号
亠	6
冫	7
冖	8
讠(言)	9
二	10
十	11
厂	12
匚	13
卜(⺊)	14
刂	15
冂	16
八(丷)	17
人(入)	18
亻	19
勹	20
匕	21
几	22
儿	23
厶	24
又	25
廴	26
卩(巳)	27
阝(在左)	28
阝(在右)	29
凵	30
刀(勹)	31
力	32

三 画

部首	号
氵	33
忄	34
宀	35
广	36
门	37
辶	38
寸	39
扌	40
工	41
土	42
士	43
艹	44
大	45
弋	46
小(⺌)	47
口	48
囗	49
巾	50
王	51
韦	52
木	53
犬	54
歹	55
车	56
戈	57
比	58
瓦	59
止	60
支	61
日	62
水	63
贝	64
见	65
父	66

四 画

部首	号
牛(牜)	67
手	68
毛	69
气	70
片	71
斤	72
爪(爫)	73
月	74
欠	75
风	76
殳	77
爿	78
母	79
毋	80
氺	81

五 画

部首	号
穴	82
立	83
疒	84
衤	85
示	86
石	87
龙	88
业	89
目	90
田	91
罒	92
钅(金)	93
矛	94
矢	95
禾	96
白	97
瓜	98
鸟	99
用	100
疋	101
皮	102

(二)　检字表

起	850
超	850
越	850

赤 部 (152)
| 赫 | 850 |

豆 部 (153)
豆	850
豉	850
登	850
豌	850

酉 部 (154)
配	850
酬	850
酪	850
酸	850
酵	850
酿	850
醋	850

里 部 (155)
| 里 | 850 |
| 野 | 850 |

足(⻊)部 (156)
| 足 | 850 |

四至六画
距	851
趾	851
跗	851
跑	851
路	851
跨	851
跟	851
跪	851
跷	851
跳	851

七至九画
踩	851
踢	851
踪	851
踏	851
蹄	851

十画以上
蹰	851
蹲	851
蹼	851

豸 部 (157)
豹	851
貂	851
貘	851

采 部 (158)
| 釉 | 851 |
| 释 | 851 |

身 部 (159)
身	851
躯	851
躺	851

角 部 (160)
角	851
解	851
触	851

青 部 (161)
青	851
静	851
靛	851

其 部 (162)
| 基 | 851 |
| 期 | 851 |

雨 部 (163)
雨	851
雪	851
雷	851
零	851
雾	852
震	852
霓	852
霉	852
露	852

隹 部 (164)
隼	852
难	852
集	852
雅	852
雄	852
雏	852
雌	852
雕	852

鱼(鱼)部 (165)
鱼	852
鲁	852
鲜	852
鲤	852
鲶	852
鲸	852
鲮	852
鲱	852
鳃	852

鳍	852
鳗	852
鳟	852
鳞	852

革 部 (166)
靶	852
靴	852
鞋	852
鞍	852
鞑	852
鞘	852
鞭	852
鞫	852

骨 部 (167)
骨	852
骰	852
髁	852
髓	852
髋	852

鬼 部 (168)
| 鬼 | 852 |

髟 部 (169)
髻	852
鬃	852
鬓	852
髭	852
鬈	852

麻 部 (170)
麻	852
摩	853
磨	853
魔	853

鹿 部 (171)
鹿	853
麾	853
麋	853
麝	853

鼠 部 (172)
鼠	853
鼩	853
鼹	853

其 他 (173)
A	853
B	853
C	853
D	853

E	853
F	853
G	853
H	853
I	853
J	853
K	853
L	853
M	853
O	853
P	853
R	853
S	853
T	853
U	853
V	853
W	853
X	853
Y	853
Z	853
α	853
β	853
γ	853
π	853

阿拉伯数字
| 罗马数字 | 853 |

(三) 中文索引

准备的工作 173 50
18，17 42-55，88 12
56，353 46
3
梳成醒的发型 34 28
的跳水动作 282 12
370 73
部分 378 12
面 38
12
49 1-13
1
295 28
28
21 3
锥加强锥体 235 20
4，7-9，264 21，35，42
300 54
46
261 15
面 207 17
华舱) 223 30
之海神 327 40
座 3 39
4，6
243 55
帆的枪 220 15
的后掠翼 229 20
148 66
加工 148 66-68
裹机 79 10
温控制显影盆 116 56
形制瓶机 79 9
56 12
翼机 232 29
5
254 32
42 17
6 56
194 30-33，206 59
式跳水 282 41
346 47
5 35
320 49
185 43，44
甲板空间 223 28
交道口 202 45
6 46
336 27
335 19，336 38
121 86
334 73
杯的横什 10 30
肋 235 48
喷雾器 83 47
295 40
具 306 13
34
探船 221 64
13
脉弓 18 10
219 7
，218 53
帆 219 65
帆 219 42
帆 219 64
帆桁 219 41
索帆 219 25
315 19

主开关 211 31
主反射镜 113 10
主厅 250 1-11
主气流 192 5
主气压计 212 6
主中桅上帆 219 63
主中桅上帆桁 219 40
主中桅下帆 219 62
主中桅下帆桁 219 39
主中桅支索帆 219 24
主中桅帆顶横杆 219 53
主台 224 40
主甲板 221 80，258 9
主平台梁 123 66
主(发动)机 209 4，221 81，223 73
主(发动)机转速指示器 224 21
主夹板 110 37
主肋 243 22
主肋骨 95 18
主导轴 243 22
主动臂 2 42
主机房 223 72
主机插头 195 2
主机插座 195 39
主机超载指示器 224 33
主帆 218 33，220 11，284 46，285 2
主帆桁 218 37，219 38
主桨 284 28
主坑道 144 24
主驱动装置 214 63
主油道 192 21
主油箱 212 4
主送风管 147 17
主选择开关 195 8
主罗盘 224 51
主穹顶 334 72
主审裁判 293 67
主贮气器 211 8，212 57，71
主贮气器压力计 212 8
主顶帆 219 61
主顶桅支索帆 219 26
主顶桅帆桁 219 43
主泵 218 12
主茎 370 20
主音管 326 1
主配(水)管 38 71，269 22
主柱 120 53
主持人 308 10
主要道路 15 83
主要驱动滑轮 163 50
主轴 183 22，192 40
主轴台 149 2，150 2
主轴左右手动作用转换杆 149 11
主轴转速变换杆 150 35
主席 263 1
主根 370 16
主航道 224 92
主教 276 10
主起落架 230 41，256 26，257 40，288 33
主舱口 259 86
主索 215 40
主锚座 215 43
主桅 218 40，219 5-7，220 22
主桅帆 219 61
主桅楼 219 52
主液态燃料火箭发动机 235 36
主减震器 6 32

主副聚焦装置 5 11
主旋翼 232 12-13，256 19
主蒸汽管道 154 31
主喷嘴 192 12
主楼 335 6
主橡 335 6
主滑轮托架 214 67
主聚焦笔和副镜架 5 2
主槽 91 18
主操纵龙骨 227 30
主螺杆 149 32
主螺丝 148 62
永冻气候 9 58
亲本 54 15
举办人 299 45
举重 91 1-5
举重人 299 2
举重持续动作 299 5
举起手的学生 260 20

一部

一二挡的换挡叉 192 42
一二挡滑动套筒 192 36
一人分的一套餐具 44 5
一人座位 197 17
一马二轮双座有盖小马车 186 29
一小组游戏者 48 20
一个接一个成排的窗户 37 86
一公尺高跳台 282 10
一车肥料 63 15
一双机械手(主动/被动机械手)的爪臂 2 47
一丛草 375 44
一包烟草 107 25
一包香烟 107 27
一对舞伴 317 17-18
一次水回路 259 65
一次电压端子 152 43，44
一次电路 154 2，42
一次纳泵 154 5
一次冷却剂泵 154 2
一次绕阻 153 15
一次鼓风机 160 11
一年生植物 53 14
一块肉 96 59
一块腰肉 96 4
一串护身符与骨头 354 40
一串桨果 58 11
一串葡萄 78 5
一组盛酒或水之壶 332 44
一组牌 276 38-45
一杯咖啡 265 19
一垒 292 46
一览表 195 32
一秒纬线仪 14 61
一种小蝶的幼虫 58 64
一种具交越网之三音路扬声器 241 14
一种宽松非正式外衣 33 54
一种堆积的云 8 1
一挡的螺旋齿轮 192 36
一套木工工具 120 20
一套珠宝物物 36 1
一套服器 324 47-54
一般用途的车床刀具 149 52
一般壳鹰 362 9
一般诊疗 22 1-74
一般尾翼 22

一般欧洲鸢 362 11
一般清洗钟表用的清洗机 109 30
一般翅蛇 364 40
一般响蛇 376 13
一般燕子 361 20
一般襟翼 229 46
一般蠕蜥 364 32
一副餐具(餐具摆设) 45 3-12
一盘料理 266 17
一盒香烟纸 107 17
一脚向后伸直 314 18
一脚向后举(半弯曲)之姿式 314
一排排阶梯座位的化学实验室 261 1
一窝鸵鸟蛋 359 3
一氯苯 170 9
一楼正面前排座位 315 19
一群玩滚木球者 305 25
一叠表格 245 24
一叠盘子 266 11
一管粘胶 260 51
七叶树 371 58
七头龙 327 50
七和弦 321 5
丁字尺 151 9
丁字铁 143 3
丁坝 216 19
丁坝头 216 20
丁型头螺栓 143 41
丁型接头 126 44
丁型螺栓 202 10
丁砌层 118 64
丁砌法 118 60
丁香树 382 26
丈夫的纹章 254 10
三、四挡的换挡叉 192 45
三、四挡的滑动套筒 192 32
三十二分休止符 320 26
三十二分音符 320 18
三八面体 351 10
三人舞 314 27-28
三口烧瓶 350 55
三公尺高跳台 282 9
三爪夹头 149 37
三日竞技 289 16-19
三出叶 58 19
三头之狗身 327 30
三头马车 186 45
三头钩 89 85
三叶拱 336 32
三叶草种子撒播机 66 26
三叶型头 66 17
三叶搅拌机 163 25
三只单眼睛 77 2
三圣颂铃 332 46
三机一体自历声组合系统自动换片装置 241 52
三列三座八汽缸的大轿车 193 1
三次曲线 347 18
三色旗 253 16
三尖瓣 20 46
三向倾卸卡车 194 24
三连音 321 23
三芯电缆 127 44
三块板组成的黑板 260 29
三尾翼装置 229 36
三角号志 203 13
三角肌 18 35
三角轨 242 80
三角网络枪杆 258 41
三角帆 219 23，284 16，285 3
三角帆降帆索 284 17

布头 103 16
布兰德斯特计印板 89 19
布告 263 14，356 7
布希门族女人钻木取火 354 34
布谷鸟鸣钟 109 31
布谷鸟剪秋罗 375 11
布谷鸟孵秋罗花 376 21
布纹检验器 177 23
布套用的布料 134 60
布拉克系 1 23
布的织边 166 11
布毒饵管 83 31
布面大衣 33 66
布袋木偶 260 74
布景 310 7
布景之放映机 316 17
布景设计师 310 43
布景画室 315 28-42
布景模型 315 42
布雷艇 258 94
丙烷炉焊棒 125 5
丙烷炉焊接装置 125 5-7
丙烷或丁烷瓦斯罐 278 34
东方式跳高 298 15
东地毯 46 36
东北信风 9 48
东点 4 14
东南信风 9 49
东澳大利亚洋流 14 38
再加热 162 27，35
再转换石灰 172 52
亚述艺术 333 29-36
亚洲 14 16
亚美尼亚文 341 3
亚麻 383 6
亚麻布下翻领 355 56
亚麻布帽 35 8
亚麻制品 271 57
亚麻类衣柜 267 31
百分比键 247 23
百日草 60 22
百叶窗 25 9
百叶箱 10 49
百合木 374 1
百合花形的纹章 254 13
百合科植物 53 13
百灵鸟 361 18-19
百货公司 268 41
百科全书 42 18
百慕达短裤 31 44
百褶裙 30 32
死亡通知 342 68
死火山道 11 28
死生之出口 319 12
死骨锯 26 45
求偶炫耀的黑色公鸭 86 11
来伯吉恩反射器 115 97
来福线式夹 115 100
来福枪管 87 26，34
更衣室 282 3
更换用品柜 28 11
更换篷 28 4
更新世界灵长类动物头颅 261 20
束带长袍 355 25
束紧带 29 67
束腰 355 53
束腰带 30 46
束腰圈 31 66
两个下燃带：沙漠和草原带 9 54
两个温带多雨带 9 55
两马前后纵驾两轮马车 186 50
两手头去后互撑 295 52
两头尖的卵形宝石 36 55
两件式套装 29 12，30 45
两栖类 364 20-26
两臂上举 295 49
两臂下垂 295 47

两臂后平举 295 51
两臂侧平举 295 48
两臂前平举 295 50
巫师 308 9
武士 353 37
武仙星座 3 21
武器 353 21
武器系统雷达 258 35
表土 144 48，158 2
表尺 87 8
表尺沟 87 70
表尺刻度 87 68
表尺游标 87 67
表示方向的方法 9 9-19
(表示造形厂的)�印 252 17
表拆卸工具 109 10
表带 110 5
(表面安装式)接地墙插座 127 6
表面波 11 36
表面修整的显微镜 112 37
表面凝结器 152 24
表演之斗牛士 319 31
表演后腿直立的马戏团马匹 307 30
表演场之栅栏 307 22
表演 308 6
表情记号 321 27-41
奉献物 330 59
奉献袋 330 50
奉献箱 330 55
事务长室 223 45
事务 263 26
事故刹车手柄的旁通开关 211 25
事故刹车手柄(装置) 211 21，212 13
事故或危险闪光灯开关 191 68
枣刺虫 80 28
枣椰子 384 9
枣椰子核 384 10
枣椰树 384 1
画 43 20，246 28
画面计算器与指示器刻度窗 313 28
画室 338 1-43
画室天窗 338 1
画眉草(莎草科) 377 18
画笔 48 7,129 19，260 84
画家 338 2
画框 338 1
画架 338 3
面包心 97 3
面包片 45 22
面包设备 97 56-57
面包房 97 55-74
面包店 97 1-54
面包的种类 97 6-12
面包和糕饼柜抬 99 1
面包点心学徒 265 6
面包篮 45 20
面包卷架 40 31
面包架 97 74
面条 98 34
面具 306 7，13，339 37
面板 323 6
面食 98 32-34
面粉 91 28，97 52
面粉饲槽 97 74
面部表情肌 19 6
面颊 329 40
面罩 27 48，292 25
面膜 252 32
面霜盒 28 13
歪球 305 21
夏至 3 8
夏季外衣 31 20

夏季轻便裤 31 52
夏季季风 9 52
夏季堤 216 48
夏季短衫 31 22
哥林多式柱 334 10
哥萨克裤子 30 44
哥登氏专利的女袜平针织机 167 18
哥德式艺术 335 22-41
哥德式建筑系统 335 27-35
哥德式教堂 335 1
哥德体字体 342 1
爽身粉 99 29
棘下肌 18 53
棘皮动物 357 38-39
棘轮 110 10
棘螺栓 143 43
整平刮板 200 18
整平梁 201 3，14
整平梁的滚轮导槽 201 4
整行排铸字模 174 29
整体头枕 173 59
整体加工的主肋 235 10
整体加强的环形肋 235 47
整体加强轻合金蒙皮 235 11
整体式保险杆 193 33
整体翼梁框架 257 28
整块胶合板 132 73
整组Z形扳手 134 2
整组红缘灯 268 54
整枝后的人工幼林 84 12
整经机 165 22
整经机架 165 27
整卷印刷用纸 173 30，45
整面辊 200 43
整流维 229 30
整流器 138 30，178 2
整流器盖(罩) 211 18
整套甲胄 329 38
整套沙拉用具 45 24
整套管式制图笔 151 38
整盒相纸 116 51
整锯齿工具 132 42
整叠盘子 266 45
赛式假发 34 4

I部

中子 1 30
中子撞击 1 36，50
中小型柴油液压机车 212 47
中文 341 5
中分 34 9
中心X射线控制装置 27 9
中心电极 2 3
中心仪表台 191 38
中心冲 134 31 140 64
中心壳 187 59
中心板列 222 55
中心柱 114 46
中心控制 243 10
中凹处 336 50
中央X算起高八度 321 46
中央起低八度 321 43
中央处理单位 244 6
中央驱动装置 238 57
中央饰有纹章的盾 254 17
中央柱 305 7
中央客舱门 231 25
中央通道(路) 55 42，208 23
中央通路式客车 208 9
中央控制室 76 7，92 25
中央暖气炉 38 57

中古式音符 320 1-2
中世纪的有盖桥 215 32
(中世纪骑士的)马上比武
中立角 299 38
中甲板 146 36，223 76
中耳 17 59-61
中压汽缸 153 24
中肋骨和颈与肩部的肉 95 26
中间支架 214 29
中间平台 145 5
中间过道 207 26
中间齿轮轴 190 57
中间轴 232 57
中间轴承 177 65
中间显像屏 113 37
中间部分 215 68
中间部分(简图) 259 55-71
中壳灰岩层 154 59
中级饱 132 39
中块辊轧机组 148 70
中线 291 3，293 8-9，54 4
中线裁判 293 25
中线旗 291 64
中国艺术 337 1-6
中国式灯笼 52 15
中国灯笼 353 36
中国狗的一种 70 21
中国贵族 306 29
中性点 153 22
中单翼机 229 4
中洲 224 91
中脉 370 30
中指 19 66
(中美马雅人之神殿 352
中卷叶 107 6
中括号 342 25
中型公车 194 34
中型有盖卡车 194 7
中型沙发 42 24
中音扬声器 241 16
中音谱号 320 10
中点标识 293 11
中统禅 32 32，33 42
中框 335 41
中椀 220 33，223 39
中椀支索 219 11
中椀主帆桁 218 39
中射式水车 91 37
中胸肉 95 26
中锋 291 14，293 76
中圈 288 58，291 2
中程运输机 256 14
中黑体铅字 175 3
中焦距镜头 115 47
中/短程客机 231 4
中/短程双喷射发动机广体客
231 17
中提琴 323 27
中腿 82 7
中殿 335 1
中碛 12 54
中频放大组件 240 4
中翼 229 8
中翼油槽 257 30
书 46 8，185 36
书皮 185 37
书包正面小口袋 260 10
书写导板 151 69
书写和格插物 129 40
书写刷 129 41
书名页 185 45
书芯 185 44
书库的藏书 262 11
书壳滚筒 184 10
书店 268 37
书帖 183 12

后挂车底架 85 49
后挡泥板 187 43
后客舱门 231 30
后勬觥 288 50
后舱 223 55
后座 191 31
后座头枕 193 8
后座搁脚板 188 44
后桅下桁横板 220 25
后桅支索帆 219 27
后桅帆船 220 9-10
后桅塔 259 44
后桅楼 219 54
后桅横帆 220 26
后桅冲刷阀 216 61
后部侧缘 235 63
后部操纵器 197 8
后脑肉 95 25
后烟窗 258 20
后框架部份 234 49
后胸爪 7
后排针 167 46
后链轮 187 38
后悬垂 296 34
后颈 16 21
后腿 70 7, 72 33-37, 82 8,
   88 22·63
后腿肉 95 14
后窗 191 32
后窗加温开关 191 82
后窗加温警示灯 191 80
后量规 183 17, 185 4
后量规之单手控制器 185 7
后跟铰链板 286 58
后鼓轮刹车 189 13
后雾灯警示灯号 191 67
后膝关节 72 33
后撑 295 22, 296 29
各边带中垂线的锐角三角形 346
   28
各民族的文字 341 1-20
各式汽船 283 68-70
各式面包 99 11
各季节开始时的太阳视轨道 4
   10-21
各场比赛成绩 293 35
各种衣料 104 2
各种冻肉 96 14
各种形状的琢磨 36 42-86
各种体操动作 296 48-60
各种贮气瓶 127
各种油漆罐 129 7-8
各种点心 97 17-47
各种狩猎方式 86 1-52
各种屠宰 96 31-37
(各种)跳水 282 40-45
各种握杠 296 40-46
各种壁橱柜 42 1
希伯来文 341 7
希腊:1000德拉克马;
   1德拉克马=100雷普顿 252 39
希腊文 341 15
希腊艺术 334 1-48
希腊式十字架 332 56
希腊妇女 355 1
希腊男人 355 3
希腊花瓶 334 37
希腊剧场 334 44
希腊装饰图案 334 38-43
卵 358 49
卵块 80 2·30
卵形马勃菌 381 19
卵圆形叶 370 36
卵坑道 82 23
卵带 74 63
卵巢 20 83
垂式耳坠 36 11

垂花饰 335 54
垂钓 89 20-31
垂板龙骨 284 26
垂板龙骨小帆船 285 37-41
垂板龙骨框架 284 24
(垂直)入射照明(顶入射照明) 112
   63
垂直上升旋冲 288 6
垂直边 143 4
垂直气压掘起长壁工作面 144 35
垂直支柱 119 59
垂直安定面 229 24, 230 59,
   231 6, 232 7, 256 32, 288 21
垂直安定面支柱 235 3
垂直驱动头 150 38
垂直偏转组件 240 8
垂直摆腿起跳 298 25
垂直管 37 14
垂柳 272 63
垂球 118 50
重力加油口 257 32
重升记号 320 51
重质混凝土 119 72
重型车辆升降机 221 56
重型车床 194 20
重型吊杆 221 25·62
重型武器 255 40-95
重型摩托车 189 31-58
重子核 1 35
重复花样 171 12
重复分裂 1 46
重音符号 342 30
重音符号与读音符号 342 30-35
重降记号 320 53
重接按钮 127 20
重量平衡器 67 37
重氮基生产 179 34
重叠式双管猎枪 87 33
重叠的船身外板 285 50-52
重置按钮 187 86
重蒸馏物 145 40
重锤 11 43, 167 32
重整製置 145 59
重燃料油 145 59
重瓣玫瑰 60 17
复叶 370 39-42
复头皮序 370 74
复合字 175 6
复合标线片系统 87 31
复位弹簧 192 55
复制台 115 90·92
复制台的悬臂 115 93
复活之火焰与灰烬 327 10
复活节蜡烛 330 44
复活节蜡烛台 330 45
复砂活板 200 42
复背斜 12 17
复卷器 170 50, 173 41
复梁裳 287 29
复原派牧师 332 3
复原簧片 237 49
复叠 77 20-24, 358 7
复断层 12 8-11
复盖屋顶 121 18
复盖尘埃的月球表面 6 13
复盖防水布罩的船载救生艇 221
   107
复造物 355 6
复经合成橡皮的上滚轮 164 11
复数 344 14
乘方 345 1

乘车型刈草机 56 37
(乘员)太空人进 通道 235 71
乘法 344 25
乘客座位 191 36, 194 14
舞厅 306 1
舞台 315 14, 318 22
舞台上方(顶棚)操纵大道具之人
   316 7
舞台工作人员 315 28
舞台口乘电灯 316 21
舞台木工 316 45
舞台布幕操作之类型 315 1-4
舞台设计系统 315 37
舞台全景 316 36
舞台灯光 318 23
舞台灯光设置 316 14
舞台两侧 307 12
舞台的布幕(银幕) 312 10
舞台表演区照明灯 316 16
舞台活门之开口 316 32
舞台前之讲坛 334 48
舞台前部 315 15, 334 46
舞台前部装置 316 22
舞台监督 316 30
舞台监督之工作桌 316 29
舞台幕 315 2, 316 23
舞台模型 315 41
舞池 317 16
舞池照明 317 14
舞蛇 353 48
舞棒 354 37
舞娘 82 16
舞蹈用鞋 354 14
孵化机 74 28
孵化室 74 30
孵化盘 74 3
孵化盘金属手推车 74 31
孵卵巢室 77 31
孵卵器 74 3
靠头之物 21 13
靠背 207 66
靠垫 42 25
靠椅 207 64
靠椅扶手 106 18

乙部(→ 丁乚)

乙炔气瓶 141 2, 22
乙炔控制钮 141 32
乙炔接头 141 31
乙烯分子 242 61
丁望台 273 23, 329 35
了望哨 329 9
飞刀手 307 37
飞马 27 3
飞马星座 3 10
飞车驾驶员 308 54
飞机引航 287 1
飞机的发动机 232 33-60
飞机的主要动作 230 67-72
飞机的种类 231 1-33
飞机牵引车 233 23
飞机跑道 287 15
飞行中队标志 256 2
飞行天线 6 46
飞行升降机 259 4, 13
飞行吊扯机 232 16
'飞行荷兰人'级 284 49
飞行装置 259 2
飞行模型机 288 86
飞轮 166 15, 190 20
飞弹发射器 258 32
飞弹发射器外壳 258 71
飞船 232 1

飞兜 29 35
飞翔的野鸭 86 41
飞跳用雪展 301 38
飞跳姿势 301 35
飞跳滑雪鞋 301 41
飞蛾 82 15
飞靶射击 305 70-78
飞靶射击用的双管类枪 3
飞燕草 60 13
飞蝶,一种脉翅目昆虫 3
飞笛 120 34, 334 11-14
   335 48
乡间宅地 15 94
尺 247 35
尺寸线 151 25
尺侧屈腕肌 18 58
尺度矫正 162 53
尺骨 17 14
尺骨神经 18 29
尺蠖蛾 82 28·31
巴比伦艺术 333 19-20
巴比伦屋簷下饰带 333 1
巴尔麦系 1 21
巴西里佳风格之教堂 334
巴洛克艺术 336 1-8
巴洛克式教堂 336 1
巴洛克式宫殿 272 7
巴斯克回力球游戏 305 62
巴塞尔妇女 355 35
司令塔 259 3
司机 208 2
司机门 193 2
司机位置 210 59
司机驾驶台 212 32
司机室 211 19
炉的位置 210 39
司祭席 330 41
司酒者 329 69
矛 319 17
民间乐器 324 1-46
乳牛 62 34, 75 17
乳牛棚 75 14
乳化管 192 10
乳头 16 28, 75 19
乳头皲 16 29
乳白玻璃 124 5
乳状胶 128 28
乳冻点心粉 98 50
乳制品陈列架 99 43
乳房 16 28-29
乳油槽 76 7
乳品厂 76 1-48
乳品厂图表 76 13
乳品接收设备 76 1
乳品搬运车 76 2
乳胶漆 129 4
乳酪装箱机 76 21
乳酪 98 5
乳酪刀 45 72
乳酪秤 45 35
乳酪柜台 99 39
乳酪蛋糕 97 23
乳酪盘 266 52
乳罩 32 1

一部

六十四分休止符 320 27
六十四分音符 320 19
六八面体 351 13
六月二十一日(夏至)太阳的视
   4 20

冷热水龙头 49 26
冷热水混合龙头 49 2，106 14
冷锋 8 13，9 27
冷锋上的云 8 13-17
冷凝器 145 44，154 17，35，155 8
冷藏车 213 39
冷藏库 225 50
冷藏室 94 21-24，99 57，223 54
冷藏架 266 49
冷藏柜（室）96 21，97 65
冷藏箱 98 3
冷藏蔬菜 99 61
冶炼区 147 8
净水槽 269 13
净化池 89 9
净盆盆 94 7
净跨径 215 13
凉拌肉食 96 13
凉亭 52 14，272 17
凉焦台 156 12
凉鞋 101 51
准直仪 111 46
准备於下一个信号灯处停车 203 7，9，16
准备运送的人造纤维 169 34
准备运送的聚醚胺酯 170 52
准备和消毒室 26 34-54
准备姿势 314 23
准星 87 72，255 3，305 42
准星座与准星 255 23，37
谢谢的花 58 55
减三和弦 321 3
减色混合 343 12
减压阀 141 5，155 7
减红过滤调整装置 116 45
减法 344 24
减速伞轮 257 24
减速驱动杆 149 3
减速板 256 12
减速齿轮 232 59
减速信号 286 50
减蓝过滤调整装置 116 43
减蓝过滤调整装置 116 44
减震器 190 26，191 26，192 69
减磨齿样头 163 16
凝灰岩 11 19
凝灰岩沉积 11 26
凝固生铁 148 25
凝态发酵乳制造器 40 44
凝乳酪包 76 41
凝乳酪包装机 76 44
凝乳酪包 76 39
凝结式火车头 210 69
凝结液贮存槽 172 17
凝结器 154 17，259 64

一部

写字台 46 21
写有片名，镜号和镜头号之拍板 310 35
军人胡 34 19
军人慕 331 32
军刀 294 20
军刀手套 294 21
军刀对击 294 19-24
军刀击剑时从头与上身至鼠蹊间的部位 294 52
军刀护甲 294 22
军刀赛者 294 19
军鼓 306 70
农夫 62 6

农田 63 17
农民式服装 30 27
农妇 62 4
农场 15 101
农场工人 63 5
农场小路 63 18
农家的中庭 62 31
冠乌鴞 369 4
冠状 337 4
冠状头饰 254 12
冠状轮 110 41，143 93
冥王星 4 52
冥府门狗 327 29

讠(言)部

计分员 299 48
计时动锤 110 29
计时员 282 24，299 47
计时器 23 40，27 35，182 20
计程车 268 64
计程车电话 268 67
计程车标志 268 65
计程车停车处 268 63
'计程车停车处'的交通标志 268 66
计程车搭乘站 233 32
计量表 76 6
计量泵 169 13
计量器 2 6，114 62，196 14
计数装置 269 55
计数管 2 21
计数器套 2 20
计数器 163 61，269 59
计数器标度盘 182 19
计算器 309 80
计算块 48 17
计算和控制装置 178 3
计算刻度盘 114 57
计算器标度盘 182 19
计算器电池 115 37
订口 185 55
订书之线球 183 11
订书机 22 25，247 4
订书线 183 10
订书铁丝之供应装置 184 18
训练装置 299 20-24
记分穿 183 9
记分员 293 71
记分牌(板) 277 18，293 34，70
记忆式打字机 245 26
记忆单元 176 11
记忆键 247 22
记时钟 277 17
记录仪 10 61
记录电表电压的感应线圈 11 44
记录机械装置 10 42
记录各镜头曝光数据的装置 115 67
记录杆 10 7，12，21
记录杆的停止开关 10 15
记录喇叭 177 49
记录纸 27 29，34，40
记录纸带 25 4
记录表 18 19
记录笔 10 13
记录筒 10 20
记录器 25 3，10 6
记帐用会计机 236 26
记圈员 290 6
讲台 260 22，262 4
讲课(演) 262 1
讲道坛之栏杆 330 23
讲道(经)坛 330 19，337 15

讲道坛阶梯 330 18
讲稿 262 5
访客座椅 246 21
设备用电缆 198 19
设通风细缝的前门 50 30
设陷阱诱捕野兽的方式 86 19-27
证券 251 11-19
证券市场 251 2
证券交易所 251 1-10
证券交易所代理人 251 5
证券交易所成员 251 6
证券交易所服务员 251 9
诊断试车台 195 1-23
诊疗室(床) 22 43，23 4
诊察室 23 1
试衣室 271 32
试配眼镜 111 1-4
试配镜架 111 3
试验与控制站 237 40
试验用油，汽分离器 146 10
试验仪器 138 14
试验台 237 29
试探具 116 55
试管 350 34
试管架 173 8，261 31，350 35
诚实约翰M386型火箭炮 255 64
诋诃者 263 15
询问处 204 29
询问台 237 34，250 9
语言教室 261 35
误点指示牌 205 24
诱饵 86 21
诱饵重联的轨迹 89 36
诵经台 330 2
诵经龛 330 16
诸侯冠 254 41
读卡机和打孔机 244 12
读本 260 16
读音台 330 37
读旋角用之透镜 351 33
读数显微镜 113 28
读数调整 10 10
调子 320 55-68
调车用小型柴油机车 212 68
调车机车 206 43
调车场 206 42，46
调车场用无线电 212 50
调车场长 206 45
调车场信号箱 206 44
调节切削刃的液压缸 64 8
调节间隔法 175 13
调节纱线张力的张量盘 165 21
调节织针尺寸标尺 167 42
调节阀 38 75
调节喷射的控制手把 83 19
调节器阀 210 13
调压 249 53
调色刀 338 14
调色盘 338 29
调色板 338 28
调味包 99 67
调味汁容器 45 17
调料勺 45 18
调味品 39 31，47 29
调味品盒 39 32
调味瓶架 266 22
调前或调后的旋钮 110 23
调速器 224 56
调音台 238 20，239 8
调音弦栓 324 23，325 17
调音弦栓板 324 22
调音室 239 7
调音槌 325 20
调音琴轸 324 11
调音榫 325 21
调音管 326 21

调音簧舌 326 30
调音榫丝 323 59
调焦光楔 115 55
调焦环 226 42
调焦率图表 177 7
调诸电视选择器按钮 241
调谐标度盘 241 7
调谐指示器 241 39，54
调谐旋钮 241 9，309 21
调谐器 241 37，317 22
调谐选择器 50 8
调整(板) 181 8
调整之导轮 312 29
调整刀片间隙用的手轮 17
调整片 288 30
调整铲斗、漏斗提升器、和的控制杆 64 59
调整轴 37
调整炮枪角度和操纵方向的头 284 6
调整监视器用的控制开关和 25 29
调整梳机装置的螺钉 165
调整装置 148 61-65
调整截割喷嘴用的刀尖块架环
调整螺钉 119 79
调整螺丝 242 78
谱号 320 8-11
诸线 320 43-44

二部

二二拍 320 30
二十四面体 351 12
二十面体 351 11
三拍 320 38
二门轿车 193 25
二分体止阀 320 22
二分点 3 6-7
二分音符 320 14
二牛拉车 63 16
二四拍 320 12
二次水翻落高压蒸汽管 2
二次电路 154 7，45
二次曲线 347 11-29
二次纳泵 154 8
二次绝组 153 16
二全音符记号 320 12
二冲程发动机 56 30，305
二冲程发动机示范模型 24
二冲程混合泵 196 13
二尖瓣 20 47
二件式套装 31 11
二转子汪克尔引擎(旋转发动机 190 5
二翅转页版平台印刷机 18
二全 292 43
二指树獭 366 11
二段轧机 148 53
二等车剖面图 207 10
二等车厢 209 7
二等客车的区划 208 22
二等座位配置 211 58
二挡的螺旋齿轮 192 43
二速换挡 188 12
二氧化碳气瓶 138 32
二氧化碳贮量计 27 49
二道筛 172 58
二硫化碳 169 8
二楼 315 18
二楼特别座 315 18
干电池 127 27

压印机 340 29
压印板 181 15，340 31
压印滚筒 180 35，64，181 2，44，59
压布 116 59
压出过量的苛性钠 169 5
压舌板 24 50，25 7
压光机 109 17
压在切口过碳素纸上之橡皮滚轮 182 8
压花板 183 29
压花玻璃 124 5
压杆 100 17
压迫绷带 21 17
压条 54 11
压刨床 132 45
压床 133 50
压吹制法 162 30
压纸格 340 37
压纸装置 185 3
压板 115 24
压板紧饰 54 10
压实的棉花包 163 3
压带轮 243 25
压挤滚轮 165 46
压砖机 159 11
压砖设备 159 9
压型机附件 100 15
压紧器 247 63
压载物 212 66
压舱物 285 33
压铸玻璃 124 6
压辊滚轮 128 36
压滤机 161 12，169 12
压榨机 173 24
压榨辊子 64 64
压榨辊轮的液压系统 173 37
(压)模 159 13
压机 97 57
压缩输送系统 234 60
压缩机 138 3，145 45，155 4，223 51
压(缩)板 2 25
压缩空气入口 153 53
压缩空气压力计 279 13
压缩(空)气(体)容器 234 32，269 17，50
压缩空气系统 138 1
压缩空气制动系统连接软管 208 21
压缩空气供给装置 213 20
压缩空气软管 174 38
压缩空气管 279 21
压缩空气管 133 45
压缩空气管路 138 5
压缩空气罐(筒) 64 92，153 51
压缩氮气瓶 234 14
压缩空气瓶 234 43，50
压缩储气筒 146 21
压槽与书脊侧上胶配件 185 28
压缩缸 120 55
厕所(盥洗室) 49 12，146 29，207 16，42，72，82，211 59，231 31，317 31
厘米和毫米的刻度 247 36
厚木板 55 22，119 76，157 34
厚载肋角 95 15，36
厚绒布鞋帮 101 23
厚玻璃 124 5
厚套泳衫 33 52
原子层 7 32
原子核 1 2，16，29
原子弹爆炸高度 7 11
原子模型 1 1-8
原木 120 2，83

原木体积标尺 157 10
原木运输量 157 17
原生质 357 3
原羊 367 7
原油 13 1，145 41
原油加工流程简图 145 36-64
原油的处理(简图) 145 28-35
原料 160 1，260 81
原料库 160 3
原料和水混合的磨料筒 161 1
原料贮藏 173 1
原料准备设备(简图) 172 79-86
原野硬蜱 358 44
原煤仓 144 41
原稿 174 6，176 3，177 18
原稿板架 177 14，22，30
原稿圆筒 177 17
原稿夹框 177 15
厢式四轮轻便马车 186 54
厩舍 81 4
厨师领班 207 34
厨房 207 29，80，223 42，231 20
厨房用的天平 309 84
厨房灯 39 39
厨房设备 46 29
厨房钟 39 20，109 34
厨房柜子 207 35
厨房桌 39 44
厨房椅子 39 43
雁类 359 15-17

广部

(左边的)波纹 254 6
(左)支线 203 47
左心房腔 20 47
左右手动作和离合转换轴 149 34
左右控制装置 180 20
左后第二柱 305 9
左角柱 305 6
左声道录音水平表 241 35
左肾 20 30-31
左侧放映机 312 14
左侧露后视镜 191 40
左油箱油量表 230 16
左转的行驶箭头 268 73
左限停止器 249 13
左前第二柱 305 2
左航行灯 230 50
左(倾)顶骨 17 31
左舷中洲标志 224 88
左舷灯 223 15
左舷沉船标志 224 86
左舷标志 224 100
左舷侧浮标(红色) 224 95
左踏板 325 9
右边镜片 195 18
(右)支线 203 46
右心导管压力计(血压计) 25 53
右心房腔 20 46
右后第二柱 305 10
右角柱 305 8
右声道录音水平表 241 36
右肾 20 28
右肺 20 6
右侧放映机 312 14
右侧后视镜 191 56
右油箱油量表 230 17
右限停止器 249 14
右前第二柱 305 3
右航行灯 230 44
右舷灯 223 15
右舷标志 224 99
右舷侧浮标 224 96

右踏板 325 8
右擎丸 20 72
灰尘沉淀室 172 6
灰尘刷 109 18
灰尘抽出器 92 40
灰尘(袋)容器 50 62，86
灰岩洞 13 79
灰渣盆地 13 72
灰泥桶 122 22，134 18
灰度 343 15
灰盘底门 210 7
在谷粒中的稻螟幼虫 81 30
在扶手上的烟灰盒 207 46
在航道外侧的浅滩 224 97
在热压器内聚合 170 33
在旅馆大厅的舞台 267 44-46
在猎物的发情期和交配期狩猎 86 9-12
在禁猎地潜随猎物 86 1-8
在蜂窝中的蜂蜜 77 64
在数据显示终端机上查出资料 248 44
在磁盘上促进气垫形成的沟纹 243 27
在腊转木材的林业工人 84 18
有门的小柜 246 5
有叉紧身上衣 355 33
有小贴袋的布质遮阳帽 35 37
有三层桨座的战船 218 9-12
有片头的底片 114 9
有办外汇业务的银行分行 204 31
有牛脂的腿肉 95 22
有车篷的长形游览马车 186 33
有孔砖和空心砖块 159 21-22
有孔滚筒的盖子 163 21
有边台 214 20
有车缆道 214 19
有包扎的手把 89 55
有凹槽的滚筒 165 10
有耳盖的狐皮帽 35 31
有羽冠的红雀鸟 363 4
有轨电车 268 46
有轨电车车头 197 2
有轨电车车尾 197 4
有轨电车停靠标志 197 36
有轨电车停靠站 197 35
有尖顶的教堂 15 107
有纤毛叶 370 49
有压缩空气洗涤装置的洗涤层 92 3
有机械装置之舞台 316 1-60
有色瀑带 299 15
有花饰的垂边软帽 35 21
有两叶维管束的短枝 372 23
有杆瓣 222 79，286 15
有把手(柄)的打孔器 100 46
有卵的果室 77 27
有声电影放映机 312 24
有声放映机 117 81
有肘和蹄的肩胛骨肉 95 42
有护栏的平交道口 202 39
有伸缩性短内裤 32 5
有折痕(裤线)的裤管 33 6
有角剪 22 51
有围兜尽带的连身工作服 33 44
有毒马铃薯浆果 68 43
有毒真菌 379 10-13
有固定节奏记谱法 320 2
有线道玻璃 124 6
有软毛耳盖的帽子 35 32
有软毛猎物 86 35
有软木牙栓的绳索 282 32
有肩胛骨的前腿肉 95 42
有选举权者 263 24
有套钩和骑带的铰链 140 50
有饰边背带 29 14

有拇指孔的枪托底板 305
有顶篷的沙滩椅 280 36
有拉链的运动衫 33 28
有柄水罐 328 35
有轴指把收集器 74 36
有活字的铅字盘 174 44
有活塞的法国圆号 323 41
有配药装置的消毒刑罐 83
有配重的曲轴 242 50
有面对面座位的马车 186
有透明窗的婴儿车 28 34
有给取附件的拖车 63 27
有冠百灵鸟 361 19
有带的风衣 33 57
有翼音之盘 321 18
有翅衬虫 82 39，358 15
有翅雌蚁 358 21
有效动力输出轴 65 31
有效部份 294 51-53
有烟灰盒的扶手 207 69
有载接插部 153 13
有剖面线的面 151 29
有袋目哺乳动物 366 2-3
有弹性的茎杆摘除器的输送带 76
有盖汤盆 44 8
(有盖和柄的)糖罐 44 32
有盖的熔化玻璃罐 162 46
有舵手的小船 283 18
有领螺栓 143 32
(有帽尖的)貂皮帽 35 17
有硫黄色冠的鹦鹉 363 1
有黑点标记的白球 277 13
有辐轮子 289 25
有棱纹的袖口 30 30
有罩的钟 42 16
有蜻的密封果案 77 32
有池塘的香烟 147 23
有嘎嘎声之玩具 306 40
有槛窗台 37 24
有管的窄道 221 3
有管理的垃圾场 199 10
有蜜的密封果案 77 33
有槽板 2 45
有槽铅条 124 13
有槽销 143 40
有槽涡轮 130 30
有槽螺丝 143 36
有篷的四轮马车 186 1
有篷快艇 213 14
有篷摇篮 28 30
有蹄类 366 25-31，367 1-10
有赞美诗编号之告示牌 330
有镜子的镶板 267 66
有翼鞭柄 371 57
存车线 206 50
存版 174 11
存取物品盖 6 21
存款、邮政储金及发放退休金柜 236 25

匚部

匹克米族 354 41
区间长时限速的限速号志 203
区间列车 208 1-12
区间列车 208 1-30
区间距离少于5%制动距离时的 近标志 203 29
区域供热总管 198 28
区域喷淋 83 1
巨人 308 20，327 37
巨人像 306 63

308 37
木 3 20
363 6
4 56
照相机 114 11
提箱(包) 22 33
章 22 29
技师 23 41
233 44
22 22

架 5 4
127 65
262 22
抽屉 262 23
245 23
盒 248 27
273 19
音机 241 1
相机 117 73
机录音按钮 241 3
机 243 7
机系统 243 5-36
机的磁轨格式 243 28
机磁鼓 243 9
带 243 5
夕 241 12
59
火箭巡洋舰 259 21
卡带座 241 47
带计数器 243 9
241 6,34,243 8,249
241 11
86 30
35 18
35 6
体状态下的撑杆跳选手
9
2 20
1法郎 252 18
177 31

一行草 63 23
干 63 36
车装载用的海岸转筒
8
站与开车时间表 204 18
发生器 212 39
电压指示器 211 27
系统变压器罩 212 40
点通知栏 204 12
机 195 6,245 32
04 21
非台 120 11
条板 128 29
128 45
船的人 283 55
218 3
奴隶 218 48
218 5
东 283 20
船 89 27
98 58
36 39
2 8-23
网模 175 36
252 11
rmes神像之石碑 334 35
盘柱 334 36

刻有碑纹之石柱石碑 330 43
刻有槽线的木球 305 24
刻度尺 349 35
刻度弧 224 2
刻度套管 149 64
刻度(圆)盘 113 27,242 75,
313 14
刻度移液管 350 24
剌毛 366 6
剌毛蓐麻 61 33
剌皮寄菌 381 31
刺状卷须 58 30
刺穿和凋谢了的花 80 11
刺绣 29,39 42
刺绣花边 355 67
刺蝟 366 5
剌浪子编底 163 54
到达(入境) 233 26
到舱门与台架的梯子 6 35
到站时间差 204 19
到期日期 250 16
刹车片 192 51
刹车分泵 192 54
刹车夹 191 18,192 49
刹车灯和尾灯装置 188 38
刹车衬 117 52
刹车衬 138 13,143 106
刹车块 138 12,186 16
刹车线 189 12
刹车油储存器 191 49
刹车鼓 192 54
刹车鼓 138 11
刹车锥体 187 71
刹车锥体 179 12,191 45,95
刹车鞘 187 70
刹车臂 187 66
刹车臂锥型螺帽 187 67
制女帽的人 35 1
制片 310 26
制动气缸压力计 212 7
制动压力计 210 50
制动杆 56 38
制动轮 91 7
制动盘 191 17-18
制动旋钮 349 38
制动塞 350 44
(制动)辊子 138 18
制动磁铁 143 102
制动器 91 8,206 49
制动器(吊耳) 349 37
制动踏板 56 40
制动襟翼 229 38
制作人回讲微音器 238 39
制作视听学习课程的装置 242 7
制作控制室 238 17
制作编码的装置 242 8-10
制图台(桌) 151 6
制图规 151 4
制图板 151 1
制图板调整装置 151 5
制图墨水器 151 63
制图墨水盒 151 36
制果糕的设备 97 67-70
制服 186 21,264 7
制服帽 264 8
制音器 322 54,325 37
制音器罩 325 39
制音器提杆 325 23,38
制瓶机 162 21
制盐场 15 32,274 1-7
制盐场管理人 274 5
制栓弹簧 140 42
制模板 48 14
制模粘土 48 12
制凝乳 76 48
制凝乳酪机 76 38

刮刀 96 42,120 79,129 23,
136 38,151 43,185 29
刮刀与磨光器 340 17
刮刀转动齿轮 200 22
刮刀涂布机 173 29-35
刮线小刀片 151 44
刮具 340 63
刮具调节器 340 62
刮除约 26 52
刮除器 128 10
刮胡膏 99 33
刮匙 22 50,26 52
刮管器 146 31
刮蜡器 301 24
刷子 260 59,340 11
刷毛 50 47
刷头 50 48
刷胶用刷子 128 27,40
刷胶机 128 25
剃刀柄 106 39
剃发 331 52
剃光的面颊 34 25
削发剃刀 105 9,106 41
削发剃刀 105 8,106 33
削铅笔器 247 25
剖面A-B 151 28
剖面线 151 27
剧本 316 44
剧角 5 26,334 44
剧院和音乐会订位处 271 26
剧装 315 51
剥皮刀 94 13
剥皮机 133 1
剥线和剪线钳 127 64,134 15
剥树皮用的铲 85 8
剥气流 232 50
副台 224 41
副导演 310 46,316 43
副驾驶员舵踏板 230 28
副驾驶员座椅 230 25
副驾驶操纵盘 230 25
副标题 185 47
副轴 192 37
副航带最高压带 9 47
副航道 224 93
副裁判 293 68
副萼 58 22
副萼 20 73
副翼 230 52,287 41,288 28
副翼和升降舵的操纵盘 230 24
副翼致动器 257 39
割刀 128 37
割刀杆 64 3
割道 346 50
割草部件 56 33
割断工具 135 24,149 53
剑 319 32
剑兰 51 28
剑尖 294 27
剑身 294 44
剑的柄端 294 40
剑柄 294 41

门部
丹麦:1克朗=100欧耳 252 24
丹麦枭 70 14
丹麦国旗 253 17
丹麦糕饼 97 30
丹佛斯式铺 286 18
内爪 327 11
内卡锌 135 23
内切齿 346 31
内龙骨 283 50
内外照明的控制按钮 197 32

内耳 17 62-64
内衣 28 23,271 56
内后卫 291 12
内帆 219 21
内有赛马赌金计算器的玻璃遮蔽看台 289 34
内忧流板 229 42
内层板 285 57
内齿轮 143 95
内侧和外侧头 18 62
内侧拉链 101 6
内线电话一览表 245 17
内接连接线 237 26
内衬底 291 31
内拉滚轮 168 12
内径 143 86
内钩手形 302 19
内城墙 329 2
内部温计赛 381 12
内部通讯(联络)系统 202 48,
203 69
内部通信设备 246 10
内部通话装置 195 55
内部控制平交道口 202 47
内部器官,内脏 20 1-57
内容 342 40
内舱底板 222 54
内圆角规 142 36
内副翼 229 43
内圈 143 72,288 57
内装麦克风 241 5
内装定时器开关 243 18
内装扬声器 249 70
内殿 330 32,334 51
内磁网屏 240 20
内墙 329 19
内踝 19 60
同心圆 346 58
同步 311 37-41
同步马达 176 19
同步计时器 24 52
同步录音磁头 243 24
同步录音摄影机 117 22
同步驱动链轮 192 33
同步起动拍手信号 117 69
同步起动摄影机 117 65
同步装置(器) 117 77,153 32
同步磁头 243 34
同步磁轨 243 33
同度音程 321 6
网 288 74,293 13
网心布带 293 14
网目屏箱 177 9
网约 96 43
网状丝袜 306 10
网状纱底 102 16
网状组织 171 37
网状帘子 42 35
网状通气窗 278 40
网状拱顶 336 45
网状窗帘 44 14
网线三角裤 32 23
网线汗衫 32 22
网址 293 15
网点 178 39
网苦星座 3 48
网球 293 1-42
网球手 293 16
网球场 293 1
网球拍 41 13,293 29
网球鞋 101 34
网绳裁判 293 23
网眼饰针 102 25
网腹 90 20
肉豆蔻树 382 30
肉鸡 74 12
肉鸡的饲育 74 11-17

肉店 96 1-30
肉贩 96 38
肉桂树 382 22
肉桂树皮 382 25
肉趾 88 46
肉距 88 82
肉垂 45 26
肉穗花序的雄部分 378 22
肉罐头 98 20

八(ン)部

八二拍 320 28
八人赛艇 283 10
八九拍 320 39
八三拍 320 33
八六拍 320 34
八分休止符 320 24
八分音符 320 16
八凸凹圆形 36 81
八边平台形 36 74
八边形 351 17
八边形交叉状切割 36 53
八边阶状切割 36 52
八四拍 320 31
八字钩 34 8
八角形毛玻璃塞 349 4
八位数字荧光显示 247 15
八线记录器 27 28
八面立方体 351 16
八面体 351 16
八缸V型燃料喷射火花点火引擎 190 1
八缸柴油引擎 212 73
八管高射火箭发射器 259 5, 20
公牛 254 15
公司收发员 236 17
公用电话 237 1
(公用)电话间(亭) 204 46, 236 8, 268 56
公用设备室门 118 6
公用设备室门 118 5
公务服务间 329 27
公共马车 186 37
公共汽车站 233 35
公共建筑物 15 54
公共露天场地 37 76
公鸡 62 37, 73 21
公告 204 10
公事包 41 17
公园 15 97, 272 1-40
公园入口 272 32
公园大门 272 31
公园小道 272 38
公园长椅 272 16, 42
公园栅栏 272 33
公园管理人 272 30
公园靠椅 272 48
公兔 88 59
公海 227 4
公寓屋顶 37 77
公路自行车选手 290 8
公路自行车竞赛 290 8-10
公路赛自行车 290 16
分子结构 1 9-14
分子模型 242 61-67
分小格的信件架 267 2
分开式瓦屋顶 122 45
分气道 147 41, 44
分水角 215 56
分浪滚轮 163 71
分切刀 45 69
分号 342 19
分布钢筋 119 69
分节机架 65 56
分禾器 64 1

分机电话和交换台 237 22-26
分机系统交换台 237 17
分机按钮 237 19
分机接地按钮 237 21
分光式反射观景器 117 44
分光棱镜 112 13
分色镜 240 35
分针 110 12
分级(产品) 74 44
分纱棒 166 38
分块剪切机 148 52
分块滚子机组 148 50
分拣台 64 81
分拣橡皮带 64 73
分析天平 349 25
分析心电图用的程式选择开关 25 50
分析原料和浆张用的实验室仪器 173 2-10
分组用的小学生 260 3
分批进料 162 2
分垫器 128
分类机 74 38
分音符号 342 34
分信机 236 38
分段腐蚀 182 12
分度 260 39
分度板 151 51
分度圆盘 113 27
分度盘 351 32
分度器 260 38
分厘卡 142 37, 149 62
分配管 126 8
分离用的设备 199 31
分离的羽状复叶 370 41
分离器 172 31
分离器控制盘 146 28
分烧护架 75 43
分烧护栅 75 40
分液漏斗 349 3
分接头 113 58
分接头交换器的驱动机构 211 13
分裂式襟翼 229 49-50
分裂前之原子襟翼 1 43
分裂碎片 1 37-38, 44, 47, 51
分割机 97 56
分割器和划圆机 97 63
分割影像的测距器 115 55
分腿 295 4
分腿支撑 295 18
分腿姿势 296 30
分腿跳 295 37
分馏塔 145 37
分蘖后的谷物茎 68 5
半面甲 329 41
并列争球 292 20
并条机 164 1
并紧螺帽 143 30
并紧帽 143 30
共轭轴 347 24
共鸣室(器) 322 18, 29, 324 2, 15, 63
共鸣管 326 22
共鸣箱(体) 322 29, 323 3, 324 2, 15, 63
共鸣壁 322 33
兑换零钱 233 51
兵(卒) 276 13
谷叶 68 19
谷冰沟 12 49
谷地类型 13 52-56
谷形神殿 333 8
谷底 13 67, 215 60
谷坡 13 1-37
谷物收割和苗床整地 63 31-41

谷物制品 98 35-39
谷类 68 1-37
谷类害虫的一种 81 27
谷种 63 12
谷粒木螺钻 64 20
谷象 81 26
谷象鼻虫 81 16
卷云 8 6
卷片曲柄 117 50
卷片齿轮 312 27
卷布滚轮 166 20, 47
卷布滚轮上的织品 167 29
卷叶形花样或卷花形之浮雕 335 38
卷叶蛾 82 45
卷发 34 3, 33
卷发(器) 105 4, 12, 14
卷发头 105 4
卷发刷 105 13
卷曲的尾巴 73 12
卷层云 8 7
卷纸托架 40 1
卷扬电动机 150 22
卷扬动力机房 144 2
卷取纸机 181 5
卷线固定轴 89 61
卷线轴 162 55
(卷线的)线轴 89 59-64
卷袖 31 62
卷袖或袖口翻边 30 35
卷积云 8 14
卷烟器 107 15
卷盘 116 2
卷筒纸 173 64
卷筒纸支架 180 3, 19
卷筒纸宽度分切机 181 42
具一个平面的平凹透镜 111 39
具八地板的电炉 207 30
具八蘖孢子的两个子囊 381 13
具个别显示与交叉总计数器的主控板 242 3
具手术室和御寒室的医院装置 228 21
具毛玻璃面的遮光罩 313 3
具水冷式引擎的重型摩托车 189 1
具印纸器的转速器 181 54
具中央控制单位的教师讲台 242 2
具中央控制单元的教师讲台 242 2
具方格织带座位的平底雪 303 1
具无限可变焦点之变焦镜头 313 23
具无泽环和分割影像测距器的夫瑞奈棱镜马达 115 54
具半带的驱动马达 163 49
具未印刷纸堆的给纸台 181 30
具电动机的空气压缩机 212 34
具节的小佛兰 383 63
具幼果的花序 384 31
具企口缝块的镶木地板 123 74
具交流发电机的蒸气涡轮 152 23
具有托�的叶柄基部 371 73
具有固定轴的两手操作的侧撤网 89 32
具有空心轴撤刀叉块的搪孔马达 133 7
具有带前一年球果的枝条 371 32
具有胡椒子的果实 382 39
具有桥梁调节装置的测隙片支承轮 64 88
具有雌雄同座花的花枝 382 12

具有圆锥形或椭圆形金钢石针之磁晶唱头 241 26
具冷却装置的片门 312 3
具花柱、子房和雄蕊的花 59 7
具回动机构的付特液体传动 212 74
具两个氧气筒的潜水器具 279 19
具护颏的护盔 329 61
具折叠床的居住舱 259 84
具羽毛的子房 375 34
具单色花的美冕花序 371 26
具刻度的时标 249 74
具刻度盘的磅秤 204 5
具放钉子、螺丝和插头的小箱 134 39
具抽气孔的钢安全外壳 154 21
具底阀的泵浦吸网 269 43
具指孔的保龄球 305 15
具通风舌门的侧壁 213 29
具吃纸夹之递纸滚筒 180 33
具纸感光速度标尺的调整 116 54
具垂直孔的空心粘土砖块 159 23
具垂直孔的有孔砖 159 21
具测量仪表的涡轮监控盘 152 3
具泵浦同和底阀的抽水管 270 31
具重叠叶柄的萃质柄 384 33
具显微镜线和分割影像测距器的无泽屏 115 59
具显微棱镜光点的全无泽屏 115 58
具栓的钢铸浇螺 147 31
具润版滚之润版装置 180 61
具桁条结构的四披屋顶 121 36
具部因人 327 8
具特殊表面的凹凸透镜 111 42
具斜接头的支撑 120 54
具宽大把的铲子 199 8
具烧结碳化物刀头的车床刀 149 48
具膜膜曲率计和验光计的光室 111 44
具雄花和雌花的花序 378 53
具屬片的裙裤 164 43
具瘕囊的下颚 359 8
具零钱兑换机的售票计算器 33 1
具磁性条纹的有声影片 117 4
具精密无泽中心光点和刻度线屏 115 65
具棟木的三柱子 292 70
具翼棘子 372 9
单一冲程底片调节杆 115 16
单一光源电子闪光灯 114 68
单一棋子 276 7
单一棋子的移动 276 14
单人皮船 283 54
单人用竞赛摩托车 290 27
单人圆背摺椅 305 90
单人座 189 19
单人轮 223 46
单人赛船 283 16
单个灯 26 11
单个信号元 243 60
单马二轮马车 186 34
单手绕圈 297 47
单片机 31 13
单片离合器 190 71
单叶桨 283 34
单打边线 293 4-5
单发动机客机 231 2
单发动机柴油火车头 208 1
单发动机竞赛和载客两用机 231 2 32-66, 231 1
单发猎枪 87 1

机和单字铸版机 174
员的运输 144 44
应的运输 144 43
印刷机 180 46，59
相凸板 178 38
片 370 72
350 42
属箔包装的货物 226 9
225 49，226 21
装货物 226 11
器 174 36
73 32，296 7
后大週环 296 60
后弧形摆 296 59
65 1
121 49
式 345 7
体声之配音混录台 311
米卡式带 117 39
看机台 238 58
238 56
面)屋顶 37 55，78，121
顶 180 17
力物 357 1-12
从系统 288 90
275 2
盘 203 45-48
340 27
架 214 23
花行 370 68
告机 133 30
水 269 40-52
中程内燃机 190 6
中程发动机 188 26
料袋头 121 90
轮马车 289 24
式玻璃窗 37 23
船 220 6-8
系 351 24-25
西装 33 1
束腰洋装 30 10
207 62
合 121 87
道 214 15-24
远镜 111 18
山楂 374 30
竖笛 318 4，323 34
轮 65 32，190 75
187 10-12
37 65，41 25，123 24
阶 37 66
219 4
上帆 219 59
上帆桁 219 36
下帆 219 35
下帆桁 219 35
帆 218 52
上帆具 219 18
193 5
65 14-19
303 8
式喷射发动机 232 33
297 26
213 3
上帆 219 57
上帆桁 219 34
下帆 219 33
支索帆 219 20
索片 219 18
桅顶横杆 219 51
楼 219 50

前电子枪 257 11
前甲板 223 47，284 10
前平衡 295 30
前灯 187 7，189 10，191 20
前池 217 39
前列腺 20 76
前帆 219 1
前护板 85 35
前足下落时的飞奔步法 72 43
前足固定装置 286 57
前纵心沟 20 25
前肘 95 8
前扰流板 193 36
前齿 300 49
前环 113 7
前虎钳 132 30
前抵肩 33 19
前轮 186 4，187 26-32，288 34
前轮驱动的前行齿轮 191 52
前轮架 65 14-19
前轮圆盘制动器 189 32
前轮鼓式刹车 188 36
前顶帆 219 60
前顶帆桁 219 37
前拉链 29 18
前视图 151 17
前庭 334 66
前柱 305 1
前柱间隙 305 3，5
前轴支轴鞘 65 48
前轴架 65 49
前指示灯 191 19
前挡泥板 187 13
前舱 223 75
前座头枕 193 7
前座 218 42，219 2-4，220 21，221 2
前枪支架 284 15
前(枪)218 41，219 55
前枪帆 220 1
前枪帆脚索 284 23
前枪剑帆 220 1
前枪塔 259 43
前枪横梁 220 13
前舷 187 2
前部压力舱壁 235 19
前烟囱 258 19
前倾姿势 301 36
前框架部分 234 45
前犁 65 11，68
前脚爪 70 6
前脚(足) 72 22-26
前排针 167 47
前排障具 293 63
前腿 70 5，82 6，88 25，64
前腿肉 95 5
前腕侧 72 19
前锋 282 50，291 15，293 75
前联结装置 65 50
前摆把 87 41
前缘肋 287 36
前锯肌 18 42
前毂 187 52
前鼓轮列车 189 11
前瞄准器 87 71
前雾灯和前雾灯开关 191 64
前置定位斜臂 192 81
前置定位臂 192 66
前端轨道装置 211 61
前舞台 316 25
前滚翻 297 19
前撑 296 28
前额 16 4-5
前额隆凸部 16 4
前镜片 115 7
前镜片座 115 6
前燃料箱 235 21

前褶 31 25
前臂 16 46，72 21
前臂弯曲处 16 44
前翼(前挡板) 191 3
首级枪支架 219 51
酋长 352 11
着于礼服下的衬衫 32 43
着长披肩的车夫 186 32
着色的牛皮 354 11
着陆板(降落板)，前板 77 49
着陆镜 256 21
着鲜于连版滚筒的手柄 249 50
着舞蹈服装的祖鲁人 354 36
着墨于印版滚筒的手柄 249 50
着墨装置 249 51-52
兽皮 88 56
兽笼篷车 307 62
兽瓜 343 2
黄包车 353 34
黄包车夫 353 35
黄色 343 2
黄色双面印刷装置 180 6-7
黄色过滤调整装置 116 44
黄色羽扇豆 69 17
黄色珊瑚真菌 381 32
黄花九轮草 376 8
黄花素馨 373 4
黄李子 59 25
黄金菊 61 8
黄莺 360 7
黄教徒人 353 24
黄道 3 2
黄道十二宫的符号 4 53-64
黄道轴 4 22
黄麻 383 25
黄麻包装布 163 4
黄麻护线 153 49
黄菖蒲 60 8
黄缘酱螂蝶 365 5
黄棕色松鸡 88 69
黄斑蜂粉螺 365 3
黄蜂 82 35
黄鼠狼 367 16
黄酸酯溶解于苛性钠中以制备粘胶纺丝溶液 169 10
黄蝎 358 40

人(入)部

人力车 353 34
人力车夫 353 35
人力喷雾(漆)器 129 35
人马星座 3 37
人马座 4 61
人工水平仪 230 3
人工气候培养的植物群 356 21
人工幼林 84 11
人工吹制和(高)脚玻璃杯 162 41
人工呼吸器 21 27，26 25，270 20
人工波浪 281 1
人工养殖的珍珠手镯 36 9
人工养殖的珍珠项链 36 12
人工起泡游泳池 281 1-9
人工蜜蜂巢 77 42
人工操作 202 16
人孔 130 18，234 30，235 52，269 26，51
人中 16 12
人头 327 21
人头马身之怪物 327 52
人头狮身怪物 327 20
人字传动轮 143 87
人字形交叉缝 102 9
人字形步登坡 301 26

人字闸门 217 19
人行桥 15 78
人行道 15 43，37 60，154 32，198 9，11
人员专用道 154 32
人员车辆运输 144 39
人体 16 1-54
人体支架 339 24
人体内的寄生虫 81 31-42
人体模型 338 31
人体摆波 15 60
人鱼 327 23
人面形骨灰坛 328 38
人造小瀑布 272 9
人造牛油 98 21，99 48
人造卫星无线电通讯 237 51-52
人型楼梯 123 42-44
人像模型 271 34
人墙 291 44
人口 77 48，208 10，233 36，268 13，329 34，349 21
人口与出口 307 19
人口坡道 199 15
人口通道 353 6
人水口 269 54
人场券 315 11
人浴池的台阶 281 32
人射中子 1 42
人射照明 112 63
人射照明灯箱 112 59
从不同的声源的输入 117 27
从内酸胶油中分离聚醯胺用的抽出器 170 37
从自动到手动开关 195 4
从纤维纺丝液至纤维胶人造丝 169 28-34
从纤维胶液至粘胶人造丝 169 13-27
从动臂 175 57
从动臂 191 7
从空中指挥交通的警察直升机 264 1
从轮轴 210 35
从挤压辊转换到吹制模 162 34
从牵伸滚轮出来的纺条 164 29
从带砂滤器和结筛器的原料贮槽进料 173 13
从玻璃瓶模转换到吹制模 162 26
从高台隐藏处狩猎 86 14-17
从原料到纤维胶人造丝 169 1-12
从粗磨机热交换器排出灰尘的收尘器 160 7
从喷丝孔压挤出来的喷丝头 170 41
从煤气水中抽取 156 39
(从滚筒去除过量油漆用的)铁格子 129 12
以X为未知量陈述 345 8
以毛毡包裹之琴槌头 325 24
以印花粉印花样 129 48
以沥青涂黑铝铂的接受器表面 155 29
以拇指与中指捏枪 298 52
以拇指与食指捏枪 298 51
以经纱为棱枝花的图案 171 13
以拳救球 291 39
以粉笔所绘素描 338 4
以巴巴表示的气压值 9 4
以链或细绳或缚绳于鹰架上的接合点 118 30
以输送器集蛋 74 22
以螺栓固定的架材 119 74
仓库 144 17，206 53，225 7，23，329 13
从生性蔷薇 52 13
丛毛 73 7
丛毛尾巴 73 6

部

双手柄

双手柄 148 15
双户公寓(住宅) 37 64-68
双飞机弹射装置 259 14
双节损饵 89 70
双叶桨 283 39
双打边线 293 2-3
双目检查显微镜 23 51
双目镜 23 8
双目镜头 112 12
双发动机商客用飞机 231 3
双连珠 276 25
双向犁 65 62
双向旋塞 350 49
双曲线1 347 26
双曲线位置线1 224 43
双曲线位置线2 224 44
双托架 214 68
双轨磁带录音机 242 12
双耳瓶 328 10
双杠 296 2
双杠上挂臂体向前 296 58
双杠上向后摆荡 296 57
双杠向上分腿 296 49
双层公共汽车 194 36
双层运输车 213 35
双层定位夹 177 26
双层板条(斜板条) 122 43
双层转筒燃烧器 350 4
双系条 121 50
双系船柱 217 11
双快门栓 115 102
双体船 284 64
双体船壳 284 65
双体船身 284 65
双尾桁机的双尾翼装置 229 34
双尾桁的高水平尾翼 229 35
双尾翼 229 33
双件四户公寓 37 69-71
双鱼座 4 64
双轮小马车 186 18
双轮托架 214 69
双轮轻便马车 186 44
双炉头 278 33
双股纱线的缠结 164 60
双钩 89 83
双栏页 185 64
双阀水龙头 126 35
双面印刷装置 181 49
双面经线绞向交织图 171 26
双面经线纹面图 171 27
双面腐蚀机 178 30
双轴套链 159 10
双轴槽形搅拌机 159 10
双重门 267 27
双重录音的声体装置 117 75
双重齿轮叶 370 45
双柱及活门门槛式屋顶 121 46
双柱龙门绝床 150 8
双柱屋架结构 121 52
双洗脸盆 267 32
双套穿集團组扣 171 48
双翅目昆虫 358 16-20
双峰骆驼 366 29
双扇门式玻璃窗 37 22
双圆柱 336 6
双缺口社接头 121 91
双桅帆船舵 220 9
双桅帆船 220 11-17,14,17
双座上山吊椅 301 57
双座车辅室 207 38
双座皮艇 283 5
双座打稻机 163 14
双座沙发 246 36
双座秋千 273 39
双座轿式四轮马车 186 3
双座跑车 193 26
双座摺叠式皮船 283 61

双高射火箭发射器 259 25,33
双(偶数) 275 20
双插座 127 6
双梁机翼结构 257 27
双梁垂直安定面 235 1
双弹齿 64 42,54
双脚榄 221 24
双脚架 207 1
双搭扣厚呢上衣 221 127
双排座 207 63
双辅房舱 223 29
双楣条式干草架 75 12
双接插平瓦屋顶 122 2
双筒定(需用)量调节器 279 20
双筒望远镜 86 6,111 17,221 128
双喷射发动机商用与客用飞机 231 7
双喷射发动机短/中程客机 231 8
双缆索道 214 25
双缝卓勒氏襟翼 229 40
双缝襟翼 229 48
双焦镜片 111 15
双管(供热)系统 126 22
双管类枪 305 70
双撑门 208 7
双滚链链 190 10
双颚夹头 135 10
双镜头反射照相机 114 22
双簧吹奏门缘 322 5
双簧吹奏管口 323 29
双簧管 322 14,323 38
双翼机 229 10,13
双卡台 207 18
发令员 282 30
发号者旗 273 34
发电厂 144 13,217 21
发电机 154 15,47,53,155 46,190 76,211 46,223 74
发电站(所) 146 1,217 64,310 8
发行时间 342 42
发行地点 342 43
发行银行 252 30
发夹 105 11
发式 354 9
发动机 6 30,145 12,288 35
发动机上的建筑物 226 58
发动机进气口 257 12
发动机后燃器排气喷口 256 13
发动机的十字(万向)接头装置 6 36
发动机油温计 212 19
发动机和螺旋桨室 227 22
发动机架和推力结构 234 21
发动机结构 235 2
发动机(舱)箱 195 35,256 25
发动机控制系统 235 39
发动机短舱与喷气发动机 231 26
发动机罩 195 36
发动机罩支柱 195 37
发动机罩 195 35
发芽的担孢子 381 8
发针 105 11
发条匣 110 38
发条盒 110 38
发泡炒油饼 97 28
发饰 355 82
发刷 28 7,105 10
发型 106 3
发音器 238 51
发射段内紧急脱离塔 234 66

发射角 87 75
发射斜轨 255 66
发射控制系统 255 74
发烟罐 255 83
发钯 107 26
发球 293 42,59
发球区 293 12,61
发球员 293 51,62
发球棒 293 6-7
发球线裁判 293 27
发情的牡鹿 86 12
发情期的牡鹿鹿 88 4
发喷雾器 83 29
发酵面包 97 11
发酵室 93 7,97 72
发酵温度计 93 9
发酵槽 93 8
发鲜 319 26
叠卡机 244 13
叠合边 128 21
叠罗汉 307 28
叠罗汉表演之底层支撑者 307 29

廴部

延长记号 321 25
延长线 127 10
延长线插头 127 11
延长线插座 127 12
延长管 50 70
延长端 200 10
延长臂 132 63
延长臂(杆) 151 57
延迟放松器 309 51
延伸喷头 225 66
延伸管 115 81
延音线 321 24
延膝 17 47,18 24
延绳钓的 90 28-29
迪凯导航系统 224 39
建造工场 222 4
建造中的船 222 30
建造和填塞用的立体方块 48 21
建筑工地顺列 118 49
建筑用木材 120 83-96
建筑物的遗迹 15 72
翻片凸杆 115 29
翻片杆(装置) 114 6,115 12
翻片钮 115 27
翻转罗盘 224 51-53
翻转炉 97 71
翻转弧形榫子 5 20
翻转滑道 301 71
翻转缩绒机 168 1
翻卷柄(翻卷机) 117 93
翻旋门 207 18
翻翘交叉接触 294 49
翘窗 331 52

卩(㔾)部

卫生门 99 35
卫生设备 126 26-37
卫生纸 49 11
卫生纸推架 49 10
卫星探测范围 7 33
印於书套耳页广告 185 39
印花 107 26,250 24
印花后的织物 168 57
印花粉袋 129 49
印版台 180 78,181 17
印版着墨装置 180 6-13

印版滚筒 180 25,38,5
181 51,60
印刷工人 340 35
印刷工艺室 340 27-64
印刷之纸堆 180 57
印刷甲虫 82 22
印刷电信机 237 31
印刷机之起动与停止踏板
印刷机上部之着墨装置 6,8,10,12
印刷机下部之着墨装置 7,9,11,13
印刷纸出口捆板 249 54
印刷纸张喷粉器 181 10
印刷面 340 59
印刷速度调节 249 55
印刷装置 180 41
印刷装置的起动杆和停止杆 80
印刷滚筒 177 67
印第安人 352 3,23,25
印第安人於棕榈叶上书写的针 341 21
印第安女人 352 10
印第安小屋 273 59
印第安式轻型运输机教生机型 256 18
印度艺术 337 19-28
印度洋 14 23
印度黑口鱼 369 10
印度舞妓 306 25
印溶咖啡 99 70
卸货活板 213 25
卸料槽 147 39
卸料槽 172 81
卸螺组件 62 42
卸粮槽 64 21
卸粮输送器 64 83

阝部(在左)

防风林 354 35
防火山墙 121 9
防火片盒 312 25
防水幕 316 24
防水大衣 30 64
防水胶布 228 7
防水夹克 228 6
防水层 123 5
防水衫 49 16
防水表的测试装置 109 25
防水舱面 283 56
防火罩 30 67
防止火花器 210 24
防止冲激系统 235 53
防止脱轨装置 214 34
防止脱轨装置 214 75
防止倾炉过压的安全阀 292
防守方三柱门守门员 292
防守队员 292 4
防守区 293 66
防守者 294 6
防尘衣(皮套) 2 48,191
防尘套 271 30
防尘衣 187 57,82,24
防压阀安全盖帽 85 36
防护外罩(壳) 10 39
防护网 118 90
防护衣 84 26
防护金属板 246 24
防护屏栅层 2 46
防护袖 142 6
防护厚皮 88 55
防护帽 228 5,290 3

168 45，255 8i，90
138 9，140 20
305 91
258 7，76
板 283 43
13 37，15 48，217 15，
5 65
13 38
栓 284 22
过滤器 270 57
10 41
340 55
84 7
录音之摄影机 310 47
310 48
234 20
250 3
38 8
304 6
29 38
122 102
玻璃 189 46
124 5
开关 211 33
(控制) 241 25
304 10
101 19
127 42
123 4
305 58
76 27
37
18，69，73，329 12
48
223 22
175 5
312 40
87 39
39
24
178 6
铅管 242 40
312 41
66
20 69
体 20 67
87
88
86
23 13
的下叶板 23 14
23 5
88
71
塔 333 22
12 8
42
24，268 62
网 217 17-25
练习 282 20
255 1-98
饲养所和水族馆 356 14
1
虫 369 1
树 382 49
洋流 14 37
喷射教练机 257 1-41
村女服装 31 26
10-31
字 341 2
柱头 337 18
字 344 2
太空船 6 1
供船 234 56
郎 8
154 63

阿斯特拉罕羔羊皮帽 35 34
阿基米德钻 108 4
阿富汗猎狗 70 23
阿彭塞耳场琴之琴槌 322 35
陈列柜 271 13
陈列柜台、糕饼陈列柜台 99 10
陈列架 47 30
陈列假发的木头架 105 39
陈列橱 46 9
阻气板 192 6
阻板 259 27
阻挡 291 51
附於护п上的护须 294 14
附工具棚的车库 37 32
附头巾的御寒外衣 300 6
附有风帽的御寒马克 29 62
附有领的巴拿马帽 35 16
附件系统 115 43-105
附件插座板 114 4，115 20
附重 202 18
附点记号 320 7
附玻璃盖的乳酪盘 40 7
附着头发的头皮 352 15
附属的建筑物 62 14
附属修理间 196 24
降A大调 320 66
降B大调 320 64
降B小调 320 67
降D大调 320 67
降E大调 320 66
降E小调 320 68
降G大调 320 68
降水计 10 44
降水区 9 30
降水性高层云 8 9
降水型 8 18-19
降记号 320 52-53
降结肠 20 21
降落灯 288 32
降落伞 10 57，288 37
(降)落角 87 78
降落级 6 28-36
降落垫 6 33
降落襟翼 230 53，257 38，288 29
限速号志 203 36-38，44
限速警示标志 203 43
限宽尺 249 12
限宽键 249 6
限深轮 65 59，63
限幅显示表 238 44
陨石 7 18
陨石坑 6 16
除气流水器 152 16
除去腐败后的花 374 21
除去高温沉淀物所用的旋涡分离器 93 2
除尘网 83 56
除尘粗糠屑 87 63
除芒器 64 10
除法 344 26
除草锄 51 22，66 1
除霜(器)通气孔 192 64
除霜通气孔 191 42
酸幕 337 16
陶三角管 350 17
陶土之小塑像 328 20
陶制烟斗 107 34
陶瓷器的碎片 161 21
陶器 308 66
陶(器)管 269 35
陶器堆 308 64-66
陶罐 260 78
陶坑 11 49
隐蔽棱边 151 24

隘口 12 47
隔间 208 24
隔间型边角灯光 316 13
隔板(墙) 75 38，248 1
隔音电影摄影机 313 15
隔音板 248 20，309 17
隔音罩 313 16-18，27
隔音罩之上部 313 16
隔音罩之下部 313 17
隔音罩敞开侧壁 313 18
隔音墙 310 15
隔热层 38 72，235 15
隔热板(屏) 122 44，234 5，235 8，40
隔墙 119 25，248 1
隔膜 20 26，24 33
障碍物 289 8
障碍跳越 289 21
障碍跳越竞技 289 8-14
隧道 15 70，214 6
隧道开掘机 144 32

阝部(在右)

邮车 236 52
邮件分类装置 236 31-44
邮件记录簿 236 18
邮件和货物站 233 9
邮件给送 236 31
邮件预分器通道 236 36
邮局 268 68
邮局柜台职员 236 16
邮政马车 186 39，53
邮政马车夫 186 40
邮政信箱 236 14
邮政信箱设备 236 13
邮差 236 53
邮资戳 236 58
邮递区号 236 43
邮票 236 21，61
邮票日期戳 236 57
邮票夹 236 20
邮票齿孔 236 62
邮筒 236 47
邮戳 236 56-60
邻角 346 14
邻座 267 41
郊区列车 205 25
部分断面经过经纱 171 14
部件移动装置 177 58
耶稣之画像 330 50
耶稣受难像 330 54
都市高速公路 225 54
都利亚式柱 334 8
都德式拱门 336 37

凵部

击发装置 255 29
(击弦)古钢琴 322 36
击弦古钢琴的内部结构 322 37
击弦板 323 7
击剑 294 1-33
击剑手套 294 12
击剑夹克 294 16
击剑员 294 5-6
击剑袖 294 6
击剑的全身 294 51
击剑� 294 7
击剑武器 294 34-45
击剑者行礼时所取的第一姿势 294 18
击剑教练 294 1
击球员 292 51，52，74

击球限界线 292 72
击球圈 292 16
凸凹透镜 111 42
凸台建筑物之凸出部分 335 43
凸形拱 336 34
凸状云 287 19
凸版印刷机 181 1-65
凸版轮转印刷机 181 41
凸轮轴 190 14
凸轮轴承 190 11，192 24
凸轮轴润滑油管 190 13
凸轮箱 167 13
凸缘 308 57
凸圆线脚 334 21
凸缘 130 28，143 5
凸缘型停止旋塞 130 21
凸缘座 130 20
凸缘，踏步挑头 123 20
凹印滚筒 182 70
凹形线脚 334 29，336 10
凹形拱顶 336 49
凹狄系船柱 217 10
凹板(面) 64 11
凹版腐蚀工 182 18
凹版滚筒 182 17，22
凹面镜 5 32，308 56
凹圆柱饰 334 27
凹槽 12 18
幽门 20 42

刀(ク)部

刀口 45 57，56 36
刀刃 45 54，56 36，106 40，302 21
刀刃根部 66 15
刀叉台 45 11
刀叉托架 266 48
刀叉抽屉 44 21
刀叉餐具柜 266 41
刀片(身) 40 40，96 32
刀状天线 256 28
刀身成波状的短剑 353 44
刀和刃 45 7
刀具 175 51
刀具主轴 175 60
刀背 45 56
刀柄 45 51，96 34，149 49
刀架 135 5，150 13
刀架滑座(板) 177 59
刀根 45 52
刀箱 94 12
危险地带(区) 2 50
负向 347 7
负重腰带 279 14
负数 344 8
龟甲虫 81 22
龟头 20 69
免税商店 233 54
兔儿尾苗 375 22
兔子 73 18，88 65
兔子 87 44
兔的短尾巴 88 62
剪刀 100 43，128 34，260 49
剪刀片 106 35
剪式过杆 298 21
剪式踊 295 39
剪式跳高 298 22
剪枝刀 56 50
剪秋罗属 376 20
剪草剪刀 56 48
剪钳 127 51，140 67
剪辑台 311 42
剪辑台 311 43
剪辑室 310 3

象牙

象牙 366 22
象牙玫瑰花 36 29
象牙战角 354 39
象牙项链 36 28
象牙胸针 36 30
象的围场 356 9
象限 347 5
象鼻 366 21
象鼻虫 80 49
赖曼系 1 20
劈刀 94 17
劈叉 314 20
劈头部 294 23
劈锤 85 5

力部

办公大楼 225 53
办公室 205 13，271 24
办公室计算机 245 31
办公室(处) 146 14，217 24
办公室电话，内部通话设备 246 10
办公室用品 247 1-44
办公室设备 248 39
办公室柜子 248 2
办公桌 246 12
办公桌抽屉 246 4
办公椅 46 27，248 25
加工厂 144 5
加工处理层 92 18
加工处理器 92 30
加工角内面刀 149 51
加工表面 151 21
加工船 90 11
加奶油的糕饼 265 5
加压盘 183 24
加压脚 133 47
加压装置 184 13
加压煤气的去硫 156 28
加色混合 343 10
加那利洋流 14 41
'加利福利亚'级火箭巡视舰 259 41
加利福尼亚洋流 14 39
加利福尼亚卵孵化器 89 15
加护病房设备 25 1-30
加法 344 23
加固之斜闸撑架 315 31
加劲杆 215 53
加油筒咀 143 81
加油管咀 109 28
加垫头带 241 67，261 41
加速水面滑行快艇 286 38-41
加速火箭 234 48
加速表 230 10
'加速'信号 286 49
加料台 147 4
加料机 147 25
加拿大式独木舟 283 3
加拿大菲藻 378 56
加热干燥滚筒 173 33
加热器 172 32
加热箱塞 190 55
加热箱 183 27
加氢中和硫酸 170 24
加硫酸使分子式新排列 170 23
加强记号 321 27
加强肋 200 9，217 78
加强防擦板 258 81
加强铁箍 130 16
加煤机 152 3
加算机 309 74
加算器 271 9

动力分导装置从动泵 67 15
动力分导装置(输出轴) 63 21
动力升降装置 65 24-29
动力杆 322 50
动力油缸活塞 65 24
动力起动器 209 13
动力调整器 100 22
动力驱动 286 1-5
动力臂比赛 286 21-44
动力装置 84 34
动力滑翔机 138 23
动力滑翔机 287 8
动叶轮 217 52
动物园游客 356 6
动物围栏 272 49
动物展览 307 63
动物：猪：肉，猪肉 95 38-54
动轴 192 65-71
动脉钳 22 49，26 49
动脉压脉管 256 11，257 1
助手 22 19，299 44
助手的器具柜 24 9
助教 262 7
助理办事员 248 7
助理办事员员 248 11
助理导演 310 21
助演者 307 45
男士 265 7
男士无边或及有边帽 35 22-40
男士内(睡)衣裤 32 22-29
男士戒指 36 20
男士时装 33 1-67
男士衬衫 33 38-47
男士套头衫 33 51
男士的胡须和发型 34 1-25
男士理发厅 106 1-42
男士帽 35 13
男士短裤 32 32-34
男子半身像 339 5
(男仆所穿的)制服 186 21
男仆服班 186 20
男主角 310 28
男长统靴 101 5
男式高统靴 101 7，13
'男厕所' 233 47
男性生殖器 20 66-77
男孩长裤 29 60
男孩衬衫 29 61
男爱好 271 12
男睡衣 32 37
男演员 316 37
男爵的冠冕 254 44
勃起状态 254 46
勃起的肉冠 359 26

氵部

汇流排 152 29
汇票 250 12
汇票和缴款单的盖印机 236 27
池塘 281 3
汤杓 45 14
汤的调味料 98 30
汤盆 44 6，45 5，15
汤料块 98 26
汽水 98 87
汽水瓶 42 32
汽车小客车 193 12
汽车甲板 221 79
'汽车出租站' 233 33
汽车收音机 191 90
汽车附件 196 28

汽车轮胎 196 27
汽车修理工人 195 53
汽车渡船 216 10
包 210 12
汽油 211 9
汽油打火机 107 27
汽油成分 145 42
汽油的油泵 196 1
汽油瓶箱 278 53
汽油桶 84 36，196 25
汽缸 210 32
汽缸 145 63
汽缸罩 242 47
汽笛 211 9，212 70，223 3
汽笛杆 211 40
汽笛固定手柄 210 51
汽笛控制按钮 224 32
汽锅给水系 152 18
汽艇 283 2，6，286，1-5
汽艇和驳船 225 25
汽艇拖拉的冲浪运动 280 13
没有尖顶的小教堂 15 61
沟纹钢滚 164 10
沟桥 15 46
沟轮 65 16
沟橡 121 64
沟槽 91 17，162 9
沟槽给棉滑轮 163 52
沙丁鱼叉 45 78
沙丘 13 5
沙地(丘) 15 6
沙坑 273 64，293 81，298 39
沙拉叉 45 68
沙拉油 98 24，99 66
沙拉盘 266 51
沙拉匙 45 67
沙拉酱 96 29
沙拉碗 45 23
沙质跑道 290 24
沙网 227 3
沙滩帐篷 280 45
沙袋 288 65，299 21
沙堡 280 35
沙漠大蜥蜴 364 31
沙蜥 110 31
沙箱 212 59，76
沙咀 13 5
沉子 90 10
沉积物 13 69
沉积岩 13 48
沉积岩的层理 12 1
沉箱 224 84
沉淀残渣和过滤麦芽汁用的过滤槽 92 50
沉箱 259 19
沥青 145 64
沥青纸 153 48
沥青底基层 198 2
沥青路面 198 5
沿矿层的坑道 144 29
沿海船 221 99
泳池边 281 3
泳池服务人员 281 4
泳道 282 31
泳裙 281 8，280 29，44
泳裤 280 43
泳装(泳衣) 280 42
沾湿炉中石块用的水桶 281 26
泪骨 17 40
法兰绒布 128 48
法兰结 102 13
法栀 353 29
法国：1法郎=100生丁 252 16
法国号 323 41
法国式的面包 97 12

法国妇女 355 51
法国国营铁路公司 209
法国钝剑 294 37
法国新艺术派安乐椅
浅戏水池 37 44，273 2 21
浅浮雕 339 33
浅滩 224 87
浅水平衡锤 217 76
浅水坝 217 73-80
浅水闸门 217 77
浅水阀 217 53-56
浅放口 192 27
沼生菜芽 377 21
沼泽 15 20，14-24
沼泽地 13 24
沼泽草地 15 19
沼泥浆 13
波江星座 3 12
波纹 254 6
波纹钢板 350 41
波形瓦 122 54
波形瓦屋顶 122 53
波斯叶 370 48
波形石棉水泥瓦屋顶 12
波纹线脚反曲线脚 3
波形鞋底 300 43
波形薄板 122 98
波状的短剑 353 44
波状滑翔 287 16
波斯艺术 333 21-28
波段 309 22
泽西属 378 44
泥水匠 118 83
泥块 63 7
泥炭层 55 31，206 10
泥浆泵 145 16
泥塑家 339 7
泥塑模型 260 67
泛滥平原 13 62
注水口 50 12
注水式浮坞 222 41
注油孔 187 62
注油池 195 30
注浆用的石膏模 161 15
沸水系统 154 49
川流 13 61，261 31
河口 13 1
河马 366 31
河中岛 216 4
河中拖船 216 23
河谷 13 57-70
河岸塌陷部分 216 5
河流 15 76
河流阶地 13 49，63
河流地形学 13 1-13
河流的三角洲 13 1
河道中停泊驳船处 217 2
河道闸门 217 31
河堤草地 15 7
油闸撑杆 230 30，288
油门销 85 17
油门踏板 191 46，94
油分离机 76 14
油气分离器 146 9
(油井的)铁架塔 12 33
油毛毡 122 62
油石 340 21
油台 109 5
油过滤器 192 20
油池 190 41，192 19
油池过滤器 192 18
油池式空气清洁器 212 1
油灰 124 17

24 27，129 24
彩机器 310 50
157 7
灯 190 67
灯 191 73
38 53
冷却装置 209 18
152 46，192 19，211
5 61
145 74
225 73，258 97
338 36
338 21
管 338 11
36
153 11
42，192 16
的滚轮键 190 25
16
气滤清器 65 54，212
鱼 98 19
瓶 45 42
5 13，258 97
8 11
383 1
191 38
器 195 16，40
38 54
191 38，65
灯 191 71
闸 8 12
338 15
129 2
129 22
129 3
129 8，10
129 11
129 6，7
20，24
145 35
22 47
接器 234 16
344，145 34，192 17
38 47
38 49
30，196 25
3 31
228 28
器 83 10
291 20
活 291 24
器 270 64
49 3
13 80-81
13 76
72 1
电通讯 237 54-55
管 196 23
350 58
小镜橱 49 31
105 28，106 11
106 10
105 29，106 12
105 32，106 20
332 12
332 9
332 8
332 11
所) 332 2
1 384
干衣器 50 23-24
309 70
309 69

洗衣槽 50 24
洗净液 111 32
洗涤 169 19，170 56
洗涤机 157 21
洗涤层 92 27
洗涤刷 50 51
洗涤油槽 156 43
洗涤和卫生设备 278 5-6
洗涤剂分配器 50 27
洗涤(物)槽 39 35，97 68，165 49，261 6，34
洗涤瓶 261 32
洗涤机 111 32
洗涤器 116 15
洗瓶 349 8
洗瓶机 93 19
洗瓶设备 93 18
洗脚用具 309 64
洗脸盆 24 15，49 24，309 65
洗脸盆之水龙头 126 31
洗脸盆和洗涤槽 278 6
洗罐机 39 40
洗濯槽 49 6
洗餐具间 207 34
洋 14 19-26
洋娃娃 47 9，309 11
洋槐 371 70
洋流 14 30-45
洋葱 57 24
洋葱头 57 25
洋蕈 324 32
洋蘑菇 381 1
洛可可式艺术 336 9-13
洛可可式向上梳发型 355 81
洛可可式墙壁 336 9
洛林十字架 332 62
派和糕饼 97 22-24
酒水机 62 27
酒水机 62 29
酒水机(立)架 62 28
酒水系统 316 6
酒水软管 62 30
酒水壶 51 21，55 26
酒水器喷嘴 67 27
洒水管 55 19，332 54
浇水管 56 27
浇注嘴 147 34
浇桶注口 147 43
浇铸班(组) 148 13
活火山 11 15
活书签 185 71
活式火车头 210 64
活字 174 7，15
活字库 174 21
活字字模 174 47
活字(铅字)制造(铸造) 175 32-37
活字盘 174 3，12
活动支承 215 12
活动吊车 222 14，28
活动扳手 126 68
活动顶尖 135 11
活动挡板 62 24
活动废物盘 26 22
活动的筛网框 168 60
活动架 40 24
活动卷绳器 163 19
活动家具 219 67-71
活动铁环 284 27
活动靶 305 33
活动鞍座 188 21
活页夹成 260 15
活版 340 32
活板门 38 13
活版填料之长度 181 40

活版填料架 174 8
活闸门槛 121 47
活鱼笼 89 28
活塞 151 60，190 37，242 46，316 60，323 40，324 66，349 5，22
活塞式泵杆 83 45
活塞杆 192 75，210 33
活塞销 192 26
洪水河床 216 41
浓积云 8 2
浓淡(对比)控制 249 36
浓液 172 34
浓缩的肉汤块 98 27
浓缩的汤料块 98 26
浓缩器 172 24，42，48，62
测力机 308 11
测定仪器 149 56-72
测定域选择器 112 46
测径尺 84 21
测径器 339 3
测标(信号塔，信号柱) 14 51
测铅 224 58-67，59
测铅设备 224 59
测深锤 224 58-67
测距仪的观测窗 114 40
测量 14 46-62
测量入射光用的漫射体 114 60
测量电流 242 73
测量电流、电压和电阻的多功能电表 242 73
测量仪器平台 235 69
漫杆 117 59
测量纸张定量的秤 173 9
测量角度用的仪器 14 52-62
测量范围选择器 242 74
测量刻度 149 63
测量刻度盘 242 75
测量架 14 43
测量高温 161 6
测量臂 130 22
测量探针 234 42
测量温度极值的温度表 10 53-54
测量装置 112 51
测量照明用的光源 112 52
测量照相机 112 68
测量臂 142 38
测程仪 224 57
测程指示表 224 57
测厚片 64 86
测微规 140 53
测微尺 149 62
测微计 173 10
测微计钮 14 52
测微用之反射镜压力计 349 20
测微目镜 14 53
浒苔属的一种植物 378 54
浣熊 368 9
涟波 13 41
消去的索引卡片 22 7
消防人员住处 270 2
消防车 270 5
消防车及消防设备放置室 270 1
消防队长 270 36
消防员 270 5
消防设备 227 25
消防设备房 233 8
消防斧 270 43
消防站 270 1-3
消防栓龙头 270 27
消防起重车 270 47
消防艇 270 65
消防演习 270 1-46
消防器具搬运车 270 53
消毒布 26 58
消毒纱布 22 58
消毒纱布敷料 21 6

消毒剂罐 83 60
消毒药品分量分配器 22 36
消弧角 152 47，153 61
消音排气器(管) 212 42，48
消音磁头 243 20
消音器 191 29，211 49，305 93
消除按钮 271 4
消除矮林和杂草的易削锯 84 32
流入管 38 74
流水中的网箱 89 1
流出位置 147 58
流出粘度计 129 38
流出槽 147 54
流动马戏团 307 1-63
流动艺人 308 25-28
流动涂层机 129 34
流行玩具其娃娃 48 32
流线型车罩 189 44
流线型比赛用摩托车 290 31
流线型舵 222 69-70
流送管线 155 10
流星 7 25
流理设备 39 33-36
流速计 216 43
流域 12 24
流量 76 4
流程图 76 9
浴巾 281 14
浴池剖面图 281 36
浴场服务人员 280 34
浴缸 49 1
浴室 228 30
浴室防滑垫子 49 48
浴室拖鞋 49 46
浴室磨砂 49 47
浴盐 49 5，99 34
涂布的卷筒纸 173 35
涂布感光液之平板 179 16
涂布感光液用之平板烘版机 179 1
涂抹刀 128 46
涂抹灰泥 118 83-91
涂抹镘刀 118 56
涂金用的刷把 129 54
涂底层 123 6
涂染料滚轮 168 61
涂胶于金箔 129 52
涂料棒 340 22
涂漆 129 14
涂漆的护壁 129 15
涂蜡栓 301 23
涂蜡器(喷灯) 301 22
浸入式加热器 40 17
浸入式振动器 119 88
浸水前甲板 258 65，269 77
浸液用之凝结器 92 6
浸渍叉 89，28
浸渍盆 136 13
润饰梳 105 15，106 28
润版装置 180 39
润版滚 180 23，52
润肤膏 99 27
润湿石版用海绵 340 25
润湿槽 165 44
润湿器 247 31
润滑油 145 62
润滑油循环泵 152 45
润滑油精炼厂 145 67
润滑器 187 65
海马 364 18
海上用梯 221 91
海上拖曳缆管 227 6
海上铅探补给船 221 32
海上铅锤 89 92
海牛 327 47，366 23

海水入口 155 40，41
海水去盐设备 146 25
海水浴场跳板 280 9
海平面 11 11，146 39
海伞 369 14
海关入口 225 5
海关关卡 225 4
海关或水警汽艇 221 100
海关船三角旗 253 35
海关信号旗 253 37
海关旗 253 35-38
海鸠 359 13
海报(广告) 268 71，271 25
海狗 367 18
海底电缆 237 56
海底等高线 15 11
海怪的躯体 327 48
海岸站(电台) 237 53
海神 327 40
海星 357 38，369 17
海(浮)标 13 26
海胆 369 41
海蚀台地 13 31
海蜇 366 14
海豹 367 19
海豹科 367 18-22
海浴场服务员 280 34
海象 367 20
海绿 61 27
海湾 13 7
海葵 369 20
海滨游艇 221 15
海港渡轮 225 11
海港隧道 225 55
海滩 13 35-44
海滩失火用的防火装置 228 20
海滩充气垫 280 17
海滩式夹克 280 21
海滩套装 280 19
海滩袋 33 24，280 19-23
海滩游戏用皮球 280 18
海滩裤 280 22
海滩帽 280 20
海滩鞋 280 20
海德堡圆盘机 181 29
海獭 367 17
酒名单 266 31
酒吧 30-44，317 1，318 13
酒吧女侍 267 63，317 2，318 14
酒吧三重奏 267 44
酒吧间照明灯 317 11
(酒)吧间凳子 267 53，317 3，318 16
酒吧顾客 267 55
酒冷却器 266 42
酒杯 45 12，89 79 19，266 33
酒杯架 317 5，267 65
酒柜 246 29
酒柜中成套器具 246 30
酒类 98 56-59
酒保 266 8，267 62
酒瓶 266 43，332 46
酒瓶(子)搁架 266 10，267 64

酒瓶架 79 11，267 64，317 4
酒壶 79 15
酒廊 266 9
酒廊服务员 266 30
酒桶仓库 93 16
酒窝 16 16
酒窖 79 1-22
酒窖店员 79 18
酒窖经理 79 17
(酒精)水平仪 134 29
酒精灯 24 57
涡形系纹 334 39
涡形装饰 333 26，334 23
涡形装饰之垫座 334 24
涡轮 67 20，232 40，47
涡轮发电机 154 34
涡轮发电机组 154 33
涡轮发动机 232 17，24，257 15
涡轮机室 217 43
涡轮机海水入口 155 40
涡轮机排气装置 146 5
涡轮机海水入口 155 41
涡轮螺旋桨发动机 232 30，51，256 16
涡卷装饰 336 8
浮石研磨机 100 7
浮石混凝土空心砖 119 24
浮动车轴 189 34
浮动杆 65 43
浮动轴 65 33
浮式玻璃制造法 162 12
浮线组织 171 40
浮标 216 12，224 71
浮标索(绳) 90 3，4，7
浮标(筒) 89 43-48，90 2，126 256 16
浮拱壁 335 28
浮船 221 65
浮船坞(浮具头) 222 34-43，225
浮袋 281 7，282 18
浮球 126 15
浮萍 378 35
浮筒 192 15，217 34，232 6，286 27，44
浮筒升降井 217 35
浮筒室 192 14
浮腿 302 3
浮雕板 339 34
淬火塔 156 11
液化气运输船 221 35
液化石油气(液化气) 145 53
液汁抽出器 79 9
液压千斤顶 85 45
液压止回阀 141 8
液压动力转向及回动 65 41
液压伐木车 84 25
液压式制版压型机 178 9
液压机顶梁 139 36
液压驱动装置 139 9，15，212 27，52
液压汽缸 194 26
液压系统 255 53
液压系统的齿轮装置 64 65
液压系统油箱 257 16
液压转向鼻轮 235 30
液压制动器 212 44
液压泵 64 29，91，178 11
液压扇罩装配机 63 37
液压活塞 139 41
液压扇提升装置 212 62
液压提升装置 195 25
液压提升装置台 195 27
液压提升装置之调整臂 195 26
液压锻制机 139 35
液压操作主起落架 235 31

液压臂 85 21
液体石炭酸 170 24
液体状态 148 27
液体罗盘 224 46
液体离合器 65 37
液体容器 247 9
液态粪便沟 75 44
液态氢气主要供给管路 235 35
液态氢气吸取用管路 234 23
液态氢气容器(槽) 234 26，41
液态氢气箱压力管路 235 54
液态氧气管路 234 51，235 50
液态氧气管路 235 56
液态氧气供给管 234 10
液态氧气容器 234 12，24，39
液态氧气管路 234 52，235 51，56
液氧 172 33
液底肥池(槽) 62 13
液罐车 213 31
淡水珍珠蛤贝 357 33
淡水舱 223 79
淡水槽 221 70
淡水鳗鱼 364 17
淡积云 8 1
淡黄带白斑的雄鹿 88 40
渐近线(a和b) 347 29
渐弱 321 32
渐强 321 27
渐强音量滚轴 326 49
渐缩翼 229 17
淋巴结 19 10
淋浴 233 46，282 2
淋浴间的地板 49 44
淋浴室(间) 49 43
淋浴调节杆 49 43
淋浴喷嘴 49 42
清溶镁灰残留物 154 62
深水池 282 23
深水炸弹发射装置 258 34
深水起滑 286 46
深红三叶草 69 4
深成岩浆活动 11 29-31
深色啤酒 93 26
深度计 279 15
深度伦证器 224 67
深度规辅助尺 149 68
深度标尺 224 66
深度调节带 65 60
深海底 11 10
深海教难船 258 96
深海海 11 12
清扫机 199 39
清扫积雪者 304 22
清齿牙器 24 45
清选机 92 36
清泥器 210 28
清洁剂 247 7，10
清洁刷子 50 56
清洁油油器 65 46
清洗设备 14 20
清洗阀用的存取口盖 6 25
清洗槽 178 1
清除矮林和杂草用的高速锯 84 32
清真寺 337 12
(清真寺)尖塔 337 13
清理工 148 41
清理场 148 38-45
清道夫 199 5，268 20
清道夫手推车 199 9
清路车 304 8
渔帆船 217 19
渔船码头 225 56
渔罐工厂 225 59

混合气控制 230 31
混合槽 172 35
混合比操纵 288 16
混合麦芽和水的转化器 92
混合纤维素板 169 2
混合成像的幻灯片 242 42
混合沥青出口 200 54
混合室 83 62
混合筒 200 15
混合棱形容器 171 19，48
混合操作台 117 26
混淤人员 311 36
和树林 15 14
混凝土 119 72
混凝土夹钳 119 85
混凝土天花板 123 28
混凝土边饰 119 11
混凝土立方体模子 119 84
混凝土轨枕 202 37
混凝土吊桶(输送斗) 119
混凝土和铝屏蔽 1 57
混凝土地面 123 13
混凝土屏蔽 154 20
混凝土泵漏斗 201 24
混凝土梁 119 4
混凝土骨材 118 36，119
混凝土捣棒 119 83
混凝土振动压实机 201 10
混凝土铲运机 200 13
混凝土基层 118 2
混凝土搅拌机(玩具) 47 40 33，119 29
混凝土铺设装置 201 19
混凝土铺设机 201 20
混凝土路的铺筑 201 1-24
混凝土倾倒手轮 201 9
混凝土撒播机 201 6
混凝土撒播机 201 6
混频控制台 317 26
游乐场中模拟之游览小火车 39
游戏蛇 29 11
游动滑车 145 8
游园须知 272 29
游码 349 33
游码杆 349 32
游码梁 349 31
游玩区 272 44
游玩用龙船 283 70
游泳池 223 23，282 1-35
游泳池服务人员 282 15
游泳者 280 30
游泳指导 282 16-20
游泳姿式 282 33-39
游泳教练 282 16
游标 140 55，224 5
游标卡尺 140 52，149 67
游标刻度 149 69
游标深度尺(规) 140 54，14
游览汽艇 225 29
游客群 272 28
游隼 362 2
游离层 7 23，237 55
游离室 2 2，17
游离窗 2 16
游艇船尾 285 45
游艇桅 35 29
温床(框) 55 16
温床通风口 55 17
温室 55 4，32，272 3，65
温度 9 8
温度计 10 25，51，28 29，27，179 4，281 24
温度运转调整器 190 50

安全壁 122 35
安全螺帽 187 64
安定层 301 49
安定面 256 22，288 49
安定器 305 58
安哥拉山羊毛帽 35 11
安培计 230 18
安装木板 121 75
安装摄像仪的观测室 5 33
守门员 273 14，282 47 291 10，292 8，302 36
守门员手套 291 19
（守门员）面罩 292 11
守垒员 292 44
完工机（完成最后一道手续的机器）100 3
完工机组 148 71
完全八度 321 13
完全五度 321 10
完全四度 321 9
完成，加工 168 1-65
完成动作 293 84
完整枪弹 87 55
宠物食品 99 36-37
宝石 110 33
宝石手镯 36 25
宝石坠子 36 14
宝石戒指 36 15
宝瓶座 4 63
宝塔 337 1
宗教之送葬行列仪式 331 42-50
宗教书 330 57
定心吸力托盘 111 22
定日镜 5 29
定向天线 6 4
定向天线桅 234 64
定向灯 22 44
定向陀螺仪 230 13
定杆 277 2
定位 224 45
定位孔插床 133 6
定位托架 126 54
定位式旋转开关 127 18
定位环 143 33
定位的去除键 249 8
定位垫块 119 81
定位装置 177 12
定位键 249 7
定时器 39 21，109 35
定点跳伞 288 55
定星镜 5 16
定音鼓 323 57，324 57
定音鼓的鼓面 323 58
定调器之电池充电器 25 51
定调器控制钮 25 40
定调器装置的控制按钮 25 30
定距片 77 41
定期客轮（定期越洋轮）221 82，225 32
定期客货轮 221 96
实心中柱式螺旋楼梯 123 77
实心玻璃柱杆 89 49
实况录音用的初次录音装置 117 100
实况播报员 299 50
实验台 261 3
实验室仪器组（设备）349 1-38，350 1-63
实验室和研究用显微镜 112 1
（实验室）暗房计时器 116 18
实腹版梁 121 72
实腹梁桥 215 7
宫殿建筑 333 29
客舱 231 22
客舱玻璃窗 231 29

室女星座和角宿大星 3 18
室女座 4 58
室内分隔设计 42 19
室内植物 42 36，248 14
室内温度调节器 38 78
室内短管步枪用的底部发火子弹 305 35
室内照明灯 24 20
宴会礼衫 30 55
宴会裙 30 56
宴客室 267 39
家用电视机 243 6
家虫 81 1-14
家具组 42 21-26
家具搬运车 268 47
家居服，长便袍 32 20
家居简便洋装 31 36
家兔 88 65
家庭主妇 39 1
家庭里菜园园主 52 24
家蚕蛾体 81 2
家蚕蛾 358 48
家畜船 221 68
家猫 62 3
家族墓地 331 27
家禽 73 19-36
宽V形谷 13 54
宽大的罩衫 33 56
宽边草帽 355 55
宽边炮 35 38，319 37，355 28
宽外炮 355 13
宽尾毛皮 131 21
宽松的外套 271 41
宽松的阔领 30 3
宽松的裤子 29 49
宽松睡衣裤 32 17，36
宽度 122 91，95
宽度调整 100 19
宽度调整靴楦 100 55
宽领带 332 5
宽罩型洋服 30 8
宽腰带 353 41
容量显示(器) 196 5
容量瓶 350 28
容器通气孔 234 44
寄存号牌 315 7
寄物处，衣帽间大厅 315 5-11，5
寄物处服务员 315 6，318 2
密封门 77 33
密封实验室 77 33
密缝的灌木 272 4
密结构 285 54
富可法制玻璃熔炉 162 1
富可法玻璃拉制机 162 8
寒洋流 14 27
塞子，阻塞器 67 36，148 61
塞块 326 20
塞规 149 56
塞栓 126 55
寝室灯 43 19
蜜环圈 381 28
蜜海藻 378 48
蜜服 77 3
蜜蜂 77 1-25
蜜蜂蛹� 77 25
蜜蜂薰烟器 77 59
蜜蜡 77 67
蜜蜡芯 77 65
蜜蜡烛 77 66
蜜囊 77 18
赛马（跑马）289 50
赛马跑道标志 289 19
赛马赌金计算器 289 35
赛车 193 28，290 34-38

赛车车垫 290 17
赛车车场 290 1
赛车把手 290 18
赛车型双人座 189 14
赛船 283 9-16
（赛船）委员会船 285 15
赛跑 298 1-8
赛跑者 298 5

广部

广体长程客机 231 14
广告月历 22 10
广告邮戳 236 56
广告(栏) 98 2，268 43，271 25，342 56，69
广告柱子 268 70
广告牌 308 50
广角镜头 115 45，117 48
广域冶金显微镜 112 23
广域体视显微镜 112 61
广播中心 238 16-26
广播台 15 33
广播电台中央录音频道 238 1-6
庄园 15 94
庄家 275 3
庄家的赌本 275 11
应付金额 271 8
应急担架 21 23
应急供氧装置 6 18
应急缆索 214 47
床 46 16
床边小地毯 43 22
床头凳 43 6
床头柜 43 17
床头监测器 25 19
床用取暖器 309 88
床身 150 29
床身滑台 149 24
床垫 43 10，47 3
床单 43 4-6，297 12
床框 43 5
床脚板 43 4
床铺抽屉 46 18
床铺架 46 19
床罩 43 7
库印 252 35
库德式光路的平面镜 5 3
序数 346 6
匏立不相容原理 1 7
匏立定律 1 7
店主 98 41
店员 97 1，98 13，31，99 17，271 18，309 29
庙 337 7
庙塔 337 1
废水泵 172 63，199 20
废水泵 269 23
废水排出 156 38
废气泵 49 45，198 26
废气热交换器 155 9
废弃的矿山 15 35
废玻璃 26 25，248 45
废物 268 22
废物箱 47 46，196 12，207 55
废铁进料箱(斗) 147 26
废铁槽 147 65
废料坑 172 59
废料箱 141 15
废盐矿的地质结构 154 57-68
底部干燥器 116 23
底片计数器 114 18，115 28，34
底片头 116 14，30
底片自动搅拌器 116 10
底片壳夹缝 114 10

底片振动手柄 116 7
底片板送装置 114 32
底片卷筒轴 114 20
底片盒 114 64
底色用画笔 338 9
底托架轴承 187 42
底条加强材 213 12
底层楼板 123 38，73
底层设备 39 9
底图 338 43
底板 116 27，150 19，202 5
底线 292 71，293，3-10
底线裁判 293 26
底面 347 35，39
底架 207 3，208 5
底盘 222 38
底部 254 22-23
底部出水口 269 34
底座 112 3，113 2，11
底座板 112 27
底盘 45 3，148 56，19 194 32，255 46
底绳 90 9，18
底铣滚轮的驱动轮 168 4
底楼(层) 37 2，118 7
底座 128 6
底模板 119 54
底槽 301 39
座位（部）24 24，44 22，212 63，303 6，3
座位栓号 312 9
座板 283 28
座垫 207 65
座舱框 214 16-18
座舱 214 28，230 35，8，285 38，288 19
座舱 65 21
座舱栏杆 283 59
座舱盖启闭操作唧筒 25
座舱(罩)230 39，257 4
座椅(靠椅)271 35
座管 187 18
座菖蒲 51 28，60 11
康茄舞 324 55
康斯坦丁十字架 332 67
腐饰(制石)机 178 23，1
腐蚀植物层 13 15
腐蚀植物层 178 24，31，182
鹰 327 12
鹰身狮身带翅膀怪兽 327
鹰头狮身兽之爪 327 13
鹰隼 362 5-9
鹰的头罩 86 44
鹰的足带 86 45
鹰眼 118 23
鹰架顶板横木 118 26
鹰科 362 5-9
鹰隼 362 1
鹰猎 86 42-46
鹰猎者 86 42
鹰属 362 10-13
鹰咀豆 69 19

门部

门 337 24
门厅 41 1-29
门厅镜子 41 6
门式起重机机架 222 26
门式起重机的门架 225 4
门把手 41 28
门齿 19 16，34
门顶气窗 37 35

通风口

通风口 191 47，317 30
通风口支柱 55 18
通风孔，换气窗 49 20
通风井 144 21
通风瓦 122 7
通风开关 191 83
通风(气)孔(口) 49 20，55 10-11
通风机 221 41
通风机口 258 43
通风式干湿球温度表 10 33
通风舌门 213 16，30
通风设备 74 10，17
通风坑 172 13
通风树 120 88
通风活性 55 41
通风控制旋钮 26 27
通风窗 55 40
通风管式吊杆柱 221 58
通风橹 221 38
通风管道 92 14
通风滚筒 74 29
通风滚筒马达 74 33
通风槽 172 11
通风导管 223 41
通讯人造卫星 237 52
通讯社标记 342 55
通用车辆 255 96
通用观景镜 114 41
'通过'规件(端) 149 57
通过浮标 285 18
'通过'端 149 58
通过静脉插入电极 25 38
通至集尘室的管道 163 11
通向月台的台阶 205 2
通向矿泉浴池的水道 281 9
通向行李站台的隧道入口 233 6
通向刹车站的出口 192 53
通向站台的地下道 204 23
通向站台的阶梯 204 25
通条 87 61
通到公共厕所的阶梯 268 62
通往矿泉的道路 274 11
通话按钮 242 24，246 15
通信系统 237 50
通信档案夹 22 12
通航河道 15 45
通道 307 51，330 27
通路板 38 3
逻辑元件 242 68
道床 205 61
道服 331 35
道具 315 30，316 35，47
道具模型 315 42
道路两旁修整的树篱 272 37
遗体 331 38
遥测天线 10 70
遥测温度计 210 48
遥控无线电 288 87
遥控电子设备 112 53
遥控板 157 14
遥控转辙器 202 27
遥控插座 117 9
杆 313 4
遮光板 55 9，310 51
遮光单 37 29
遮光罩筒 313 5
遮阳伞 268 61，272 58
遮阳板 121 23
遮阳帽 29 16
遮阳篷 37 71，274 14
遮热板 188 16
遮盖 113 13
遮蔽环 289 30
遮眼革 289 30
遮蔽屏幕 240 22
遮蔽容器 154 82

遮蔽框 116 35
遮篷 221 116
遮篷索 221 118
暹逻文 341 10
避雷针 38 30
避雷器 152 35

寸部

对子 276 35
对分材 120 88
对分鸠尾榫 121 89
对齿锻锤 139 5
对齐号 340 58
对讲机 22 34，244 5，245 20
对讲机扬声器 238 52
对折裙 30 10
对角长壁工作面 144 36
对角罗纱 171 38
对角斜梁 287 33
对转尾部螺旋桨 232 28
对弧圆心角 346 55
对空火箭发射器 259 50
对流层 7 1
对称层顶 7 9
对称中心 351 3
对称平面 351 5
对称图形 346 24
对称轴 345，351 4
对称褶曲 12 12
寺庙建筑 337 25
寺院外柱 334 2
导气管 155 35，350 63
导丝轮 89 54
导轨 2 37，202 26，214 56，221 121，271 54
导灯 224 101-102
导伞 288 29
导向杆 200 27
导向轴承 113 14
导向滚子 157 5
导体 153 34，43
导块 19 24
导杆 164 17，325 33
导杆片 322 40
导杆线 322 34
导纱(线) 167 3，54
导纱支柱 167 2
导纱滚轮 165 57
导纱器 167 6
导纱器放纱于针钩上 167 64
导轮 278 54
导线杆 100 30
导纱滚轮 168 5
导流尾鳍 286 61
导流活塞 242 56
导索器 284 29
导链 65 13
导链装置 120 15
导链轮杆 65 12
导液管 26 47
导棒 165 38
导豹 272 27
导管架 26 30
导频音发生器 313 30
导频音电缆 313 29
导数 345 13
导演 316 40
导演工作桌 316 42
导槽 117 36，217 75，322 41
导纱逆转齿轮杆 149 6
封闭的气垫 286 66
封面 185 40

封面材料 184 12
封垫 190 69
封域绝缘音 153 38
封装底板 122 42
耐力比赛 289 16
耐火炉衬 147 48
耐火板复盖的工作台 141 16
耐火泥顶 108 9
耐压船壳 259 55，76
耐热升降副翼结构 235 34
射门得分人员 273 13
射手 307 38
射击乌鸦或大鸥鹊的靶垛 86 51
射击位置 305 78
射击室 308 58
射击姿势 305 27-29，73
射击控制雷达天线 258 51
射束进入点 1 64
射线 346 20
射线束 346 19
射程内的兽群 86 15
射箭 305 52
射箭运动 305 52-66

扌部

扑克牌 276 37
扒手(小偷) 308 16
扒钉 121 97
打入式冰岩钉 300 41
打孔器 22 28，100 45，102 12，108 19，31，247 3
打孔锥 102 12
打孔器盒 108 30
打火石 107 28
打水板 67 34
打水快弹簧 67 35
打印内控制 249 10
打印台(盒) 22 30，340 13
打印机 230 28
打击手击球 292 63
打击手位置 292 51
打击乐器 323 49-59，324 47-58，60
打击顺序 292 58
打包铁皮 163 5
打字孔(窗) 249 19
打字用橡皮擦 247 26
打字字体 342 9
打字机 209 28，248 22，309 79
(打字机的)滚筒 249 18
打字间 248 21
打字室 209 26
打字桌 245，248 26
打结花边 102 21
打点重锤 110 28
打甘 269 60
打桩机 226 37
打桩机架 226 37
打桩锤 226 38
打捆卷棉机 163 47
打雪仗 304 14
扣 166 10
扣子 36 10
扣击 293 78
扣座 166 41，53
扣锁 38 21
扣盖 166 6
扣揩绳 206 12
执十字架者 331 43
执照 106 42
扫 38 36，62 5，199 6，268 21，272 67
扫帚柄(把手) 38 37
扫描头 177 46，63

扫描滚筒 177 45
扫描器 177 39
扫雪机 213 17
扫雪艇 258 80，84
扩大器 312 19，317 23
扩大器和电源装置 238 3
扩大器和特殊效果设备
扩音器 264 12，283 21
托叶 57 5，58 48，111
托板(制造模型的工具) 161
托架 100 25，133 24，1
托架 131，303 7
托架开关 237 13
托架返回杆 249 21
托座弹珠 39 19
托座 126 6
托梁模板 119 12
托盘 42 30，83 17，265 266 19，63，308 52
托盘温度计 116 13
托腿架 13 10
扶手 38 28，41 23，42 28，123 50，53，79，45，228 26，322 16
扶手栏杆 221 122
扶手梯(电梯) 271 22
扶手椅(子) 42 21，267 24
扶垫器 54 2
扶壁 329 26
扶摇器 64 2
投手 292 50，68
投手区，投手板前隆起的土 292 49
投手板 292 69
投币式市内与长途电话 23
投币式电话 236 9
投环游戏 308 47
投递邮袋 236 54
投算人 263 22
投票 263 30
投票卡片 263 23
投票处 263 16
投票间 263 23
投票箱 263 29
投球法 305 17-20
投球界限球 292 71
投梭转子 166 67
投梭盘 166 16
投梭棒回动弹簧 166 68
投梭棒缓冲冲皮 166 65
投影台 261 13
投影区 243 47
投影屏 112 24，238 32
投影圆凸 5 21
投影镜头 261 10
投影器 261 8
投影器上部 261 9
投篮球员 292 35
投掷杆 352 40
报刊摄影师 299 49
报务室 223 12
报时钟 309 60
报时器 280 5
报刊 289 40
报纸 205 51，265 25，342 37-70
报纸夹 265 26
报纸收纳装置 182 29
报纸标题 342 39
报纸类 262 16，265 8
报纸照相排版系统资料处理机 176 29
报刊 86 43
折尺 120 76，134 33
折伞 41 12

...85 54
...网范围 12 12-20
...181 53
...纸装置 184 17
...置 180 15，29，185
...85 10
...185 69
...机) 181 55，182 27
...51
...121 18
...121 19
...31 8
...207 39
...28 35
...68 30，35，249 58
...194 10
...臂 117 92
...框架 283 67
...的帆 283 62
...338 26
...窗遮光罩 114 23
...283 54-66
...207 12
...78 44
...78 43
...座椅 193 22
...93 9
...287 39
...195 45
...轴承 211 54
...190 70
...器 65 34
...296 46
...296 44
...122 39
...的控制装置 224 26
...盔 127 48
...9，26 12；50 63，55
17，305 80，313 21
...刷了叶脉的毛虫 80 8
...素转化成纤维素黄酸
酯
...229 39，287 38
...193 30
...叭）42 10，311 46，
318 12
...32
...实验)室 310 9
...5，20
...87 10
...255 12
...70 47
...342 32
...342 31
...44
...71 26-36
...4 35，38，43，329 50
...329 82
...140 21，300 18，303 15
...4 28
...404 14
...9 31，303 16
...55，202 23
...5
...29，255 85
...497 11
...216 51-55
...216 38

护栏 84 8，133 41，165 31，
　222 16
护面 294 13
护枢者 331 40
护胫 142 12，291 34
护胫板 329 54
护胫套裤 29 45
护舷木 217 9
护舷栏 222 35
护链装置 188 46
护出塞 289 18，292 24，299 30，
　301 13，302 34，303 14
护腿 289 15，302 33，319 19，
　352 17
护腿套裤 28 24
护腕 296 64
护喉 296 13
护颈 294 14
护颈甲 329 83
护颈装置 329 54
护照 126 33，267 13
'护照检查'处 233 42
护膝 292 9，303 17
护膝甲 329 53
拆包机 163 7
拆挡写字格 47 23
抛石 216 51
抛光杆 145 27
抛光的铜滚筒 182 7
抛光圆盘 134 21
抛物线 347 14
抛物线的分支 347 15
抛物线的顶点 347 16
抛物线拱 336 29
抛掷表演 307 43
招人广告栏 342 70
招呼站 15 27
拉刀 109 8
拉丁文字体 342 12
拉丁式十字架 332 55
拉力装置 208 18
拉力滚筒 133 13
拉马车的马 186 28
拉(开)幅机 168 21
拉布拉多羊洋流 14 40
拉杆 64 47，143 101，152
　31，220 20，277 4
拉杆支座 64 62
拉杆架 65 26
拉杆联结器 65 30，278 55
拉伸 170 55
拉伸至达到高抗拉强度 170 46
拉线用于 127 16
拉制台 108 2
拉制机 162 7
拉制粘土坯的拉坯工人 161 9
拉索 301 63
拉栓 325 44，326 6
拉紧重锤升降井 214 40
拉紧绳索滑轮 214 43
拉链 31 55，260 13
拉链或钮扣洞遮盖 33 48
拉综针 166 54
拉菲亚树的纤维 136 29
拉歌尔式经纬针织机 167 23
栏网球员 293 60
栏阻索 259 16
栏截袭炸战斗机 256 1
拖车 63 38，138 10，194 22，
　206 3，278 52
拖车车厢 211 62
拖车架 138 28
拖车渡轮 221 54
拖车遮篷 278 57

拖(斗)车 200 25
拖网板 90 13
拖网索 90 12
拖网渔业 90 11-23，221 86
拖网机 90 11
拖曳绞车 227 7
拖曳船 222 42
拖机，曳航飞机 287 2
拖板 206 32
拖拉出来的细丝 169 28
拖线切割成一般纤维长度 170 60
拖线的干燥 170 58
拖线的卷累 170 59
拖钩 227 27
拖索 214 14
拖索导柱 227 9
拖船 225 15，227 5，16
拖船索 217 23
拖船推进的无动力驳船 221 94
拖绳(缆) 216 24，286 47，288
　69
拖雪橇的狗 353 2
拖缆 216 24，227 8，286 47
拖缆导柱 227 9
拖缆位置 227 15
拖缆绞车 258 86
拖缆滑翔机 287 3
拖裙 355 80
拖鞋兰 376 27
担子 381 7
担架 270 23
拍子 320 28-42
拍打皮肤用的桦枝条 281 27
拍地毯用的架子 37 51
拍身贴面 293 47
拍卖 354 18
拍卖室 225 58
拍岸浪 13 47
拍岸海浪 13 36
拍面网 293 31
拍球 297 36
拍摄速度选择器 117 12
拍摄速度调整 117 18
拍摄镜头 26 17
拇指 19 64
拇指肌 18 41
拇指把位 323 45
拇指和食指握枪 298 51
拇指球 19 75
拇趾 19 52
抽风机 152 14
抽水马桶 49 13
抽水机 281 39
抽水泵 216 62
抽水站和水库 217 39-46
抽水管 269 5，41
抽丝后做成花边装饰的刺绣 102
　14
抽出器支架 142 16
抽尘器格栅 100 13
抽吸 162 25，28，36
抽屉 41 9，43 18，46 11，49
　34，248 2
抽油烟机 46 31
抽油杆 145 22
抽取泉水 269 24-39
抽除麦粒 92 38
抽样杓 98 72
抽热器 182 5
抽滤瓶 350 40
抽曲线 347 13
拐点 347 21
拌和数 118 34
抹刀 338 15

抹子 118 52，57
抹平混凝土工 119 9
抹鱼子酱用的刀 45 81
抹香鲸 367 25
披衣 338 33
披纱 332 20
披针形叶 370 32
披肩 30 65，31 71，105 34，
　106 4，355 39
披肩式外衣 355 2
拔牙钳 24 57
拔钉钳 120 75
披藻钻 40 18，45 46
拘束带 325 36
拘束带伐 325 35
抱子甘蓝 57 30
抱足 302 10
抱腰法 21 38
抱膝跳水 282 14
拨子 322 19，324 20
拨土板 65 4，64
拨无头针用的金属丝 124 28
拨火棒 38 41
拨号盘 237 10，245 16，246
　14
拨号装置 237 67
拨灰耙子 38 42
拨弦古钢琴之内部构造 322 46
拥抱 205 53
拾取轮 64 4
拾取轮驱动装置 64 5
拾取附件 62 41
拾像装置 240 36
持音 326 4
持续音塔 326 4
持续音管 326 3
持幕盖音 326 5
持鞭子的奴隶监管 218 47
挂于右舷枪顶横杆的协会会旗
　286 9
挂历 245 3，248 42
挂瓦木条 122 17
挂式电动钻孔机 108 6
挂衣台 41 2，266 14
挂衣架 41 3，266 12
挂肉钩 96 21，97，96 55
挂图 262 8
挂图表用的托架 260 30
挂钟 309 87
挂钩 38 22，301 61
挂锁 38 21
挂帽钉 266 13
挡水库 283 40
挡风玻璃 191 21
挡风玻璃雨刷 191 41
挡光板 9
挡位 192 47
挡板 65 18，178 9
挡板调整手柄 132 66
挡泥板 186 6
挡雨布 223 17
挡雪板托架 122 16
括号 342 24
括弧形 302 17
挑签瓶底 122 27
指孔 247 39，305 16，323 33，
　324 34
指孔盘 237 11
指甲 19 80
指甲油 99 32
指甲弧影 19 81
指示风速的风速翼 9 10
指示灯 25 6，50 10，157 62，
　164 8，196 7，249 71，267
　6，294 30
指示列车前方停车点的停车牌
　203 31-32

指示信号 238 30
指示停止于指定点的停止板 203 25
指示棒 224 3
指示器 189 37，45，197 22
指示牌 267 5
指示镜 224 6
指令键 247 21
指尖 19 79
指纹 264 29
指纹证明 264 28
指针 242 76，349 34
指拨 323 21，324 8
指挥 315 26
指挥舱 6 9，259 85
指挥棒 315 27
指垫 19 78
指钩 324 67
指绘的窗户画 260 26
指南针(罗盘) 288 12
指骨 17 17，19 77
指推式吸尘开关 50 74
(拴牲畜用的)系链 75 15-16
按钮 203 67
按钮式电话 237 20
按钮键盘 245 14
按摩浴池 281 33
按身 298 41
挺杆 166 57
拱 119 6，215 20
拱门 336 19
拱门支柱 336 21
拱门帘幕 316 11
拱门饰缘 335 25
拱门的样式 336 19-37
拱门横梁 335 18
拱形屋顶之样式 336 38-50
拱极星的界圈 3 5
拱背 336 26
拱顶 215 31
拱顶石 336 23
拱道 337 4
拱廊(拱门与高窗间的部分) 335 33
拱跨 215 26
拱壁 329 26
挪威：1克郎=100欧耳 252 26
挖土工人 118 76
挖土机 118 81，200 1
挖斗 200 5
挖斗升降机链 216 57
挖泥 200 6
挖掘臂 200 4
挖泥斗(爪) 216 58，226 44
挖泥船 216 56
挖掘出之泥土 226 47
挖掘用叉 66 22
挖掘机 159 3
挖掘的泥土 118 78
挖墓人 331 22
拼字教科书 260 17
拼图玩具 48 9
拼图玩具块(片) 48 10
挤压 162 33
挤压节拍 75 34
挤压机 159 11
挤乳人 75 25
挤乳台(间) 75 23
挤乳(导)管 75 27
挤乳杯 75 30
挤梭子鱼卵 89 11
振动片 241 68
振动式集棉滚筒梳 163 39
振动筛 158 21
振荡计数器 110 17
振荡洒水器 56 46

振荡要素 110 9
振幅调整 10 11
捕手 292 54，64
捕手手套 292 60
捕虫者 377 13
捕鱼小船 90 24
捕鱼钳 89 37
捕(流)鲑漂网 90 2-10
捕猎者 86 25
捕鼠机 83 36
捕蜂群网 77 54
捕鲸帆船 90 1
换币分类架 236 23
换气装置 259 72，90
换向环 115 83
换向逆转杆 149 14
换向离合器 115 27
换行和托架返回键 249 4
换字型键 249 3
换字型键盘 249 5
换齿轮手柄 132 56
换挡杆 190 77
换挡控制踏板 190 77
换挡提把 188 31
换镜旋座 112 11，30
捣衣杆 309 68
捣实梁 201 2
捣实混凝土的地下室 118 1
捣紧机 200 32
捣紧梁 200 32
捆孔用的绳缆 90 5
捆好之报纸堆 182 31
捆版器 174 16
捆索系索 218 32
捞工 173 14
挽缰(绳) 71 24，35
探针 24 46，114 63
探针孔 166 32
探针导线 116 38
探空气球到达高度 7 17
探视孔 41 29
探险游戏场 273 21
探测器 234 42
探照灯 258 28
接口环(圈) 115 82
接目镜 113 20，115 42
接收机 10 63
接收盘 249 47
接收器 87 16，226 33
接近战 299 31
接近标志 203 26-29
接地插头 127
接合主螺杆螺帽用的手杆 149 19
接合进给机械用的下降螺杆 149 18
接合点凹槽 6 47
接芽 54 23
接住跳楼者所用的布 270 18
接线生 237 35
接线总长 245 13
接受吸入疗法的病人 274 7
接送客站台 233 20
接送旅客站台 233 30
接待主管 267 7
接待处 278 1
接待室 22 5
接钩绳 89 78
接串木花 374 37
接骨木果实 374 36
接球 291 48
接球员 293 50
接触区域 237 45
接触式断路器 242 49
接触线电压指示器 211 28
接触线维修车 211 41

接触线维修车的机械设备 211 44-54
接触弧 237 43
接触测角器 351 27
接触弹簧 127 28
接触触簧 127 38-39
接触臂 237 44
接触臂金属头 237 46
接触嵌线 334 57
接楼向附件导座的导块 174 48
接橙 54 37
推力杆 257 9
推力轴承 221 29，223 67，259 64
推土航向控制系统 235 43
推土机 199 16，200 28
推土机刮板 200 29
推木臂 157 19
推进机器的曲柄 201 18
推进、回转和静止的放映开关 117 88
推进架 200 30
推进溜板 156 7
推进器拖架 223 61
推进器柱 222 71
推进器(螺旋桨) 222 72，286 64
推杆 277 3
推拨销 143 37
推铅球 298 48
推婴儿车的母亲 272 71
控制开关 178 36
控制龙头 172 9
控制台 93 1，147 66，153 1-6，179 10，180 16，182 28，261 37，311 16
控制台打字机 244 4
控制台操作员 244 3
控制曲柄 168 52
控制杆 83 21，117 63，201 8，12，259 69，316 58
控制机 38 67，76 11，153 1，185 2，311 4，17，29
控制组件 238 45，240 11
控制阀 153 52
控制柄 89 62
控制(按)钮 117 98，243 13，246 19
控制按钮和控制轮 168 40
控制钮(操作键) 178 15，261 45
控制室 25 1-9，146 32，152 19，28，153 1-8，214 65，316 1
控制室窗 238 38
控制站 217 45
控制杆 166 63
控制盘 27 10，93 20，154 80，173 43，177 36，60，179 17，240 31，316 1
控制排气量的排气歧管口衬垫 190 73
控制舵机的舵轮 224 15
控制棒 154 24
控制棒驱动装置 154 23
控制装置 26 7，111 29，138 31，153 6，168 58，178 29，179 33，181 26
控制器 150 36，179 33
控制踏板 168 48
描述血压曲线的纸带记录器 25 44-54
描绘锤 129 42
描跟头 141 37
描跟器 153 45
掩蔽纸带 128 16
捻线机 164 57
掷刀 354 15

掷套环游戏 280 31
掷界外球 291 53
掷标枪 298 51-53
掷链球 298 42-47
卷于锥形筒上可使用的纤维丝纱 169 27
卷尺 103 2
卷式自动影印机 249 32
卷形小面包 266 54
卷纸轴架 164 28
卷轴机 165 55
卷轴顶部 163 62
卷轴筒 217 22
卷纹盘 217 22
卷袖 31 62
卷棉箱 163 48
卷筒纸 181 43，46，58
卷筒纸之宽度分切器 181
卷筒纸左右控制装置 180
卷筒玻璃丝 162 57
卷缠尾 364 35
掏空用的刀具 135 17
排水孔 38 65
排水口 89 8，216 36，2
排水管 199 25
排水沟 198 10，200 63，33，37，268 8
排水设备 144 46
排水栓 178 34
排水型船 286 32-37
排水渠(明沟) 216 33
排水罐 284 36
排水隧道 217 62
排水管 116 17，199 26
排水机 155 16
排风机 92 15，133 33
排气口 242 58，259 92，
排气孔盖 38 52
排气风扇 199 32
排气系统 195 51
排气系统维修 195 52
排气组织 370 82
排气歧管 190 36
排气阀 190 46，242 53
排气烟囱 154 37
排气枪 221 17
排气喷口 232 39，45，49
排气阀 212 69
排气管 64 38，133 40，1
51，209 12，210 25，22
258 44，57
排气管道 258 79
排出的模组 245 9
排出装置 236 49
排出管 226 34
排он原理 1 7
排尘风道 163 22
排字工人 174 5
排字架 174 2
排字量规 174 14
排油烟机 39 17
排泄腔 357 5
排版框 181 38
排除松纤维的抽吸口 168 4
排屑口 132 48
排料口 139 42
排骨肉 95 47
排烟口 38 81，353 21
排烟口盖 352 9
排烟通风口 352 21
排烟器 255 59，89
排球 293 56-71，58
排粪链 74 27
排障器 210 34
排演 315 21-27
排箫 322 2
搭栏槛 273 56

切入刷 129 20
切片刀 96 31
切开的三明治 45 37
切瓦器 122 33
切皮革的刀 100 51
切肉刀 94 18，96 35
切肉用的刀叉 45 69-70
切肉的屠夫 96 58
切纸机 173 44
切线 346 48
切鱼(片)刀 89 38
切顶器 64 85
切点(P) 346 49
切削刀 100 48
切削刃 66 14
切削压铁 100 9
切削机 150 41
切削圆筒 64 34
切砖机 159 15
切音铜块(板) 322 43
切甜菜顶刀 64 87
切割台 175 52
切割机 141 34
切割树干的动力锯 84 22
切割部件 56 41
切割喷嘴 141 38
切割滚刀 63 15
切缝刀片 201 17
切缝机 201 16
切管工 126 10
切管器 126 84
至工地场的门 62 17
至摄影机的输出 117 28
地下火山 11 20
地下水位(面) 269 1，63
地下水流 269 3
地下作业(采矿) 144 21-51
地下河 11 83
地下室窗子 37 27
地下室(窖) 37 1，79 1
地下室楼梯 123 16
地下室墙壁 123 17
地下排水道 200 61
地下暖气设备 356 18
地下墓窖 331 59
地下隧道 198 29
地中海 14 25
地方铁路线 15 25
地方性徽章 252 12，14
地区喷雾 83 1
地平面 4 12
地壳 11 1
地牢 329 5
地址 236 42
地址显示 236 41
地址标签 236 4
地极 14 3
地极移动轨迹 4 28
地轮 65 15
地函 11 3
地图 260 44
地图灯 230 23
地图投影(法) 14 8-9
地图符号 15 1-114
地板 296 11，297 6
地板上水平腾越前滚翻 297 20
地板上后手(空) 297 24
地板上头手翻 297 26
地板上前手翻 297 27
地板上前滚翻 297 19
地板上腾身前空翻 297 25
地板吸尘嘴 50 71
地板和地毯的清扫 50 53-86
地板刷 50 46，129 27
地板刷柄 50 49
地板插座 127 23
地质学 12 1-33

地板砖 159 24
地垒 12 10
地面 123 9
地面天气图 9 1-39
地面防潮布扣环 278 26
地面层 7 7，123 23
地面层砖墙 123 29
地面信号 288 52-54
地面消防栓 270 35
地面站 237 51
地面控制定向性天线 6 44
地轴的运动 4 22-88
地核 11 5
地壂 12 11
地球 11 8，30，6 17
地球上的全蚀带 4 33
地球上的气候 9 53-58
地球上的层状构造 11 1-5
地球上的经纬线 14 1-7
地球仪 42 13
地球和卫星月球 4 45
地球表面陆高海深 11 6-12
地毯 41 18，43 23，44 16
地毯衬 50 54
地毯拍打器头 50 79
地毯清扫和洗涤两用机器 50 76
地毯清扫器 50 57
地震(学) 11 32-38
地震波 11 36
地震的效应 11 45-54
地震屋 11 32
地磅房 206 40
地磅/桥秤 206 41
地窖 81 6
坐于桌边喝咖啡的人 268 60
坐于摩托车后座者 268 36
坐台 41 10
坐式背带 300 57
坐位 273 58
坐垫 42 23
坐标系中的曲线 347 11
坐标系中的点 347 8
坐标轴 347 2-3
坐标原点 347 4
坐骨 17 19
坐椅握法 21 21
均力板 140 36
均匀气团所见到的云 8 1-4
均热坑炉 148 46
均热坑炉起重机 148 47
坟堆 331 24
坟墓 331 23
坝顶 217 59
坝槛 217 79
块状钗 143 97
块茎 370 79
块茎根 370 79
块菌 381 9，10，11
块煤和屑煤筛分 156 14
场内经纪人 251 4
场外经纪人 251 5
场记 310 34
场院树篱 62 35
场数 293 37
赤(红)孤 88 42，367 12
赤杨木 371 30
赤杨沼泽泥炭 13 18
赤道 14 1
赤道气候:热带 9 53
赤道逆流 14 33
赤道槽 9 46
赤鹿 88 1-27
坛毯 330 3
坩锅钳 108 11，350 32
坑 138 17
坑口井架 144 1，3
坑口建筑物 144 4，154 70

坑内小坑 144 27
坑底车场装卸处 144 26
坑道 195 28
坑道窨 161 5
(坑)隧道开掘机 144 32
坚果 370 98，384 60
坚果(果仁) 383 44
坚果筲 59 37-51
坞门 222 32
垃圾 199 17，268 22
垃圾车 199 1
垃圾容器 199 4
垃圾桶 199 3，205 55，273 25
垃圾桶倾倒装置 199 2
垃圾筒 22 70
垃圾焚烧装置 199 28
垃圾箱 37 63，96 46，196 12，268 5，273 25，273 25
幸运轮 308 45
坦米尔文 341 11
型铁钻 137 17，140 14
型坯 108 11
城门 329 32
城市纹章的壁冠 254 46
城堞(之胸墙) 329 6，20
城垛 15 74，276 12
城堡之弹药库 329 13
城堡围墙 333 31
城堡的主楼 329 4
城墙 15 95
城墙(之外墙) 329 15，333 30
城楼 329 4
城镇 15 51
城堞 329 33，37
垫子 47 8，296 18
垫材 222 62，63
垫形柱头 335 21
垫板 120 45
垫草 74 8，75 6
垫圈 143 17，187 55
埋头 143 46
埋头键 143 73
埋头螺栓 143 28
埃及艺术 333 1-18
埃及文字体 342 8
埃及狮身人面像 333 11
埃佛勒斯峰 7 3
堆于甲板上的货柜 226 6
堆肥 52 6
堆肥撒布机 62 21
堆高机 93 23，225 44，226 8
堆积机 162 20
堆积的木材 84 15
堆积的衬板 118 41
堆置信件盘 236 34
堵头布 183 35
堵塞杆 148 10
堤 216 32
堤防(河堤) 15 104，199 14，216 49
堤防坡道 216 47
堤防斜坡 216 40
堤防管理人 216 46
堤防管理人住屋 216 45
堤顶 216 39
堤排水闸 216 34
塔 258 67，259 71
塔门 333 9
塔台 233 17
塔尖 331 5
塔式回转起重机 119 31
塔式起重机玩具 47 39
塔传动轮 143 82
塔形屋顶 121 22
塔形墓 333 21
塔顶 337 2

塔顶气 145 38
塔顶平台 329 8
塔架 119 34
堰 15 66，69，217 57-
堡状高积云和絮状高积云
堡形螺帽 143 24
堞眼 329 23
填(补)料 24 30
填料 128 3
填料 200 52，213 19
填料大脚管短榫 355 31
填料函 223 64，145 26
填料紧身短上衣 24 51
填料搅拌器 355 45
填料端，分批进料 162
填料器 200 51
填弹塞 87 52
填装机 76 26
填煤管、土等的楼板 12
填塞砂桶 158 29
墙上插座 39 26
墙角桌子 246 34
墙面 334 16
墙面的准备 128 1-17
墙梁 120 39
墙钟，挂钟 109 32
墙脚 37 17
墙(壁) 120 29
墙壁月历 22 17
墙壁抹灰面 123 60
墙壁挂钩 44 17
增三和弦 321 4
增加跳动斜度的摆式喷雾
27
增压表 230 7
增音器 325 45
增湿器 79 22
墨斗(槽) 180 22，181 6
墨西哥湾流 14 30
墨滚子 249 52，340 12
墨槽与滚 181 64
墨沟 329 33，37
壁上分枝烛台 330 16
壁上挂历 248 42
壁灯 265 9
壁式通风机 266 15
壁式碗柜 39 8
壁式碗碟相柜 46 30
壁纸 128 18
壁纸的长度 128 19
壁纸封接边 128 20
壁纸剥离液 128 1
壁纸剥除器 128 9
壁纸粘剂 128 23
壁虎 364 36
壁画 338 40
壁龛 267 24
壁炉 267 22
壁炉台 267 24
壁带 336 10
壁柱 335 11，46
壁泉 272 15
壁凳 331 60
壁脚板 123 21，63
壁镜 309 3
壁橱架本体 46 3
壁橱架支架 46 1
塑像 339 32
塑像人体支架 339 24
塑像头部支架 339 25
塑胶片 76 28
塑胶刮板 128 44
塑胶浮标 89 44
塑胶容器 83 25

牛乳 **99** 45
55 40
口器 **40** 47
器 11
第 2
器 **269** 39

人 **353** 22
器 **324** 12
318 9
器 **322** 15
郎 **306** 36
23，**357** 29
71 5
60
器2 47
步 **311** 37-41
摄影机 **313** 26
番值围 7 14
器 **224** 61
面同步滤波器 **311** 27
装置 **242** 11-14
器 **117** 21
器 **326** 18
64 25
国王 **306** 58
皇后 **306** 61
游行 **306** 57-70
会游行彩车 **306** 57
9 15

53 39
马 **132** 53
132 52
315 13
盘 **243** 40
器 **243** 39
器 **234** 31，36
物 **358** 1-23
325 19
192 9，**27** 43
3 50
器3 45
23，26，**59** 22，**61** 3，
9-25
54 30
刀 **54** 31
4，**69** 7，14，**370** 23，
371 17，35，40，52，55，
373 7，11，14，31，**374**
，15，24，**375** 3，6，16，
20，23，40，46，**376** 2，
，19，23，**378** 16，20，
32，37，47，57，**382** 4，
21，42，**383** 3，12，17，
31，36，39，47，**384** 18，
57，65
糊 **355** 65
袍 **355** 66
饰 **31** 32
204 48
370 53
器 **382** 28
52 18，**272** 41
52 18，**55** 37，**272** 39
370 67-77，**371** 43，48，
7，55，**382** 38，**383** 49

花园 **37** 57，**51** 1-35，**331** 53
花园小路 **51** 14
花园池塘 **51** 16
花园耙子 **51** 4
花园桌 **37** 50
花园靠椅 **37** 49
花环 **306** 17
花环腊肠饼 **97** 42
花枝 **59** 28，**371** 2，16，34，
39，**51**，54，66，71，**372** 33，
27，**382** 3，7，**382** 3，8，
27，31，41，47，**383** 22，26，
30，38，42，**384** 17，24，37，
49，54
花和果枝 **383** 46
花的形状 **378** 10
花饰铅条窗 **124** 14
花柄 **370** 52
花架 **54** 8，**248** 13
花冠 **34** 32，**59** 11
花冠状发冠 **34** 31
花茎 **370** 52
花柱 **58** 42，**59** 15，68 **34**，**370**
55
花药 **372** 35
花瓶 **309** 2
花粉 **370** 65
花粉贮存室 **77** 35
花粉梳 **77** 7
花粉管 **370** 66
花粉篮 **77** 6
花样冰鞋 **36** 68-71
花菜 **99** 84
花采 **306** 5
花梗(柄) **59** 4，**370** 52，**383** 7
花托 **37** 68
花椰菜 **57** 31，**99** 84
花萼 **58** 8
花楸 **371** 42
花篮 **266** 29
花蕾(芽) **58** 27，**370** 24，**374**
14
花瓣 **58** 43，**370** 59，**59** 11
芦苇 **136** 28
芦荟 **53** 13
芦笋 **57** 14
芦笋地(床) **52** 25
芦笋铲 **45** 77
芦笋割刀 **56** 10
苏格兰猎 **70** 17
芬兰级 **284** 51
芫青蛾 **80** 42
苋属花 **60** 21
荠菜 **99** 28
苍蝇拍 **83** 32
苍鹰 **362** 10
芭蕾舞女主角 **314** 27
(芭蕾舞女演员穿的)短裙 **314** 29
芭蕾舞团 **314** 25
芭蕾舞男主角 **314** 28
芭蕾舞者 **314** 26
芭蕾舞裙 **314** 31
芭蕾舞鞋 **314** 30
苹果 **58** 56，**99** 86
苹果毛虫 **80** 32
苹果毛虫群体 **80** 34
苹果皮 **58** 57
苹果花 **58** 54
苹果花象鼻虫 **80** 10
苹果形的榴梓 **58** 49
苹果的小种子 **58** 60
苹果树 **58** 51
苹果卷叶蛾 **58** 62
苹果核 **58** 61
苹果蠹蛾 **80** 13
苔原气候 **9** 57

茅草 **61** 30，**136** 26
茅膏菜 **377** 14
英文2点铅字 **175** 19
英文3点铅字 **175** 20
英文4点铅字 **175** 21
英文5点铅字 **175** 22
英文6点铅字 **175** 23
英文7点铅字 **175** 24
英文8点铅字 **175** 25
英文9点铅字 **175** 26
英文10点铅字 **175** 27
英文12点铅字 **175** 28
英文14点铅字 **175** 29
英文16点铅字 **175** 30
英文20点铅字 **175** 31
英文手写体 **342** 10
英式二轮单座马车 **186** 48
英式轭铁型座架 **113** 23
英式砌法 **118** 62
英式轴型座架 **113** 22
英式髭 **34** 19
英式髭f **34** 19
英国八孔直笛 **322** 7
英国式十字砌法 **118** 65
英式马鞍 **71** 45-49
英国快速帆船'浪花'号(1867)年
220 36
英国国旗 **253** 15
英国塞特种猎狗 **70** 41
英国警察 **264** 34
苗圃 **15** 110
苗圃工人 **55** 45，46
茎 **381** 18
茎干缝 **102** 4
茎叶升降器 **64** 90
茎叶摘除器 **64** 73
茎叶输送带的三角皮带驱动装置
64 78
茎叶输送带搅动器 **64** 77
(茎)秆 **68** 6
(茎)秆节 **68** 7
(茎)秆打包机 **63** 35
茎细 **34** 25
茚化搅拌器 **172** 49
茚化钠 **169** 3
茚化钠溶液 **170** 10
苦力 **353** 43
苦艾 **380** 4
苦艾酒 **98** 62
苦苣苔科植物 **53** 7
苯环 **242** 66
苯的提取和输送 **170** 6
苯的氯化 **170** 8
苯酚 **170** 14
苯清洁器 **156** 24
苞 **371** 7
苞片 **371** 7，**372** 5
苞鳞 **372** 5
茄科草本植物 **53** 6
药用大蒜芥 **61** 16
药用鼠尾 **380** 12
药局 **233** 45
药典 **22** 23
药物样品 **22** 41
药剂喷雾器 **56** 24
药瓶 **27** 2
药液喷雾箱 **83** 39
药箱 **24** 7
药橱(柜) **22** 35，**49** 49
荚果(荚) **69** 8，16
荧光灯管座 **127** 62
荧光材料 **240** 18
荧光材料涂层 **240** 19
荧光屏(幕) **74** 40
荧光灯管(日光灯管) **127** 61
荧光臂章 **199** 7
荐骨 **17** 21，**20** 59

茶 **98** 65-68
茶、咖啡等 **99** 68-70
茶树 **382** 7
茶树叶 **382** 9
茶盘 **39** 34
茶袋 **98** 68
茼蒿菊 **51** 24
荠菜 **61** 9
荠菜花 **61** 10
荠菜果 **61** 11
茴香 **380** 6
茧 **358** 51
茧内的蛾蛹
草地 **13** 13，**15** 18，**51** 33，**63**
22
草地禾草 **375** 39
草地通气器 **56** 15
草地番红花 **379** 3
草坪 **272** 36
草图 **338** 43
草的叶片 **370** 83-85
草耙 **75** 7
草鸦 **362** 17
草莓 **58** 21
草莓派 **97** 22
草莓植物 **58** 16
草耙子 **51** 3，**56** 3
草盖鸡场系统 **74** 1-17
草裙 **306** 18
草裙舞女郎 **306** 16
草箱 **56** 29
草履虫 **357** 9
获取燃料的加速火箭 **234** 22
获胜者名单 **289** 38
荷兰、21基尔德 **252** 19
荷兰单桅帆船 **220** 6
荷包牡丹 **60** 5
荷花 **272** 56
(莫尔斯)信号灯 **223** 7
莲花饰柱 **333** 13
莱茵岩盐 **154** 64
莱菲麻层 **54** 35
莴苣 **57** 36
莴苣叶 **57** 37
莎草科植物 **53** 17
菲律宾丛生海绵 **369** 7
董宝莲 **53** 11
营火 **278** 10
营业大厅 **236** 1-30
营地 **278** 1-59
营地工作人员 **278** 2
营养完全的狗食物 **99** 36
营救者 **21** 29
营救班 **270** 17
营巢 **359** 29
萨尔冈王宫 **333** 29
萨克管 **324** 69
菌幕 **381** 5
菌褶 **381** 6
菩萨 **337** 10
萝卜 **57** 15
萝藦属 **53** 15
萝藦属科植物 **53** 15
菊苣苇 **57** 35
菊花 **51** 29
菊苣 **57** 40
菊科苦草 **376** 15
菊苣苣 **57** 39
著墨装置 **180** 6-13，40，
51，60，71，76，**181**
28，50
著墨滚轮 **180** 21，**50**，77
菱形 **346** 35
菱形十二面体 **351** 7
菱形阶状切割 **36** 59
菱形锄齿 **65** 58
菱面六方双柱体 **351** 22

菜虫 80 48
菜豆 57 11
菜单 266 21
菜粉蝶 80 47
菜篮 99 81
葬礼 331 33-41
葬礼堂 333 7
菠菜 57 29
菠菜 361 6
蒿类之鸟 361 7
葵花籽油 98 24
董事长签名 251 16
葫芦 354 27
萼片 58 44，59 12，370 58
蒸头形圆屋顶 121 25
蒸花拱 336 36
韭菜 57 21
葡萄 99 89
葡萄干 97 43
葡萄干饼 97 43
葡萄牙：1 埃斯库多＝100 分 252 23
葡萄叶 78 4
葡萄压汁器 78 17
葡萄园 15 65，78 1-21
葡萄园牵引机 78 21，83 48
葡萄采集桶 78 10
葡萄采集(者)人 78 11
葡萄茎 78 6
葡萄树行 83 51
葡萄害虫 80 20-27
葡萄根瘤虫 80 26
葡萄酒及烈性酒酒杯 317 7
葡萄酒瓶 79 14
葡萄酒盏 79 2
葡萄栽培者 78 13
葡萄植物 52 5
葡萄锈壁虱 80 22
葡萄锈壁虱第一代幼虫 80 23
葡萄锈壁虱第二代幼虫 80 24
葡萄蔓 78 2
葡萄藤 78 2-9
蓄水层 12 22
蓄电池 259 83，309 41
蓄电池轨道车 211 55
蓄电瓶 191 50
蓄电池箱 188 22，207 5，15
蓄洪区 216 42
蓄着披头长发 34 1
落下网 89 29
落水管 122 29
落叶松 372 32
落叶树 371 1-73
落叶树林 15 4
落叶病 80 20
落石堆 11 47，12 45
落地 298 19
落地大时钟 110 24
落地灯 38 16
落地灯 46 37，230 49，257 37
落地式挡风玻璃 255 97
落地式摆钟 157 24，64
落地垫 296 13，297 2
落地雪橇 256 21
落地滑橇 232 15
落针滚轮 165 39
落锤气缸 139 30
落锤滑槽 139 29
苦荬果 370 91
蒙皮 287 40

蒸发皿 350 29
蒸发器 155 6
蒸汽 50 11
蒸汽口(孔) 50 14
蒸汽加热器 172 38
蒸汽机车 210 1-69
蒸汽产生器 154 9，26
蒸汽灯炮 221 51
蒸汽和电热交换器 207 6
蒸汽和再循环水流通道 154 51
蒸汽拖网渔船 221 46
蒸汽室 210 31
蒸汽浴 281 18
蒸汽浴后降温用的降温浴室 281 28
蒸汽浴炉 281 21
蒸汽涡轮发电机 259 58
蒸汽涡轮机 154 14，46，52，153 23-30
蒸汽排出器 103 25
蒸汽涡炉 152 5
蒸汽喷枪 131 2
蒸汽喷射器 210 41
蒸汽储压火车头 210 68
蒸汽管 172 64
蒸汽管线 154 11
蒸汽熨斗 131 3
蒸汽熨烫装置 104 26
蒸纱机 168 49
蒸笼 96 47
蒸煮贮槽 172 46
蒸馏 170 17
蒸馏烧瓶 350 47，50
蒸馏塔 145 49
蒸馏装置 145 66
蒸馏器 350 46
蓝山雀 360 4
蓝天鸟 363 3
蓝色 343 3
蓝灯 264 11，270 6
蓝黄色金刚鹦鹉 363 2
蒲公英 51 34，61 13
蒲公英花序 61 14
蒲草 51 8
蓬子 331 9
蓬顶电缆 211 5
幕 334 45
幕盖 334 45
墓穴 331 34
墓地大门 331 19
墓园小教堂 331 28
墓碑 331 26
蓖麻 380 14
荷蕾 60 16
蔓生植物 52 5
蔓藤花棚 51 1
慕尼克啤酒 93 26
蔷薇果 370 100
蔬菜上桌用的匙 45 74
蔬菜板 52 26，55 39
蔬菜板条箱 55 43
蔬菜盆 45 25
蔬菜容器 96 51
蔬菜盘 45 33
蔬菜篓 266 62
蔬菜罐头 96 27，98 17
薄木板 157 35
薄板 133 2，157 35
薄板剥离机 133 1
薄荷油 125 26
薄板编结机 133 3
薄金属肋肉 95 16
薄金属片 128 17
薄金属板螺丝 143 26
薄饼 97 45

(薄锌板做成的)烟囱泛水 122 14
藏文 341 12
藏书之印记 185 51
藤本上的芽插 54 22
藤条科 136 32
藤架 37 80
藤椅 43 3
藜 61 25
蘑菇 381 3

大部

大力士 308 27
大二度 321 7
大七度 321 12
大八度 321 44
大丁菊 51 26
大于 345 19
大三角帆 220 3
大三和弦 321 1
大三度 321 8
大山雀 361 9
大山猫 268 8
大公 306 26
大厅 267 1-26，329 30
大六度 321 10
大爪草 69 12
(大气)边缘区 7 34
大气层温度递升的上限 7 20
大气环流 9 46-52
大火星座和天狼星 3 14
大毛蕊花 376 9
大区域的稳定降雨或降雪 8 18
大头钉 143 55
大头别针 328 29
大写字体 175 11
大印度鼓 324 49
大皮球 273 12
大礼服 355 76
大礼帽 186 25，289 6
大主教用之十字架 332 64
大衣口袋 33 61
大衣钩 207 50
大衣钮扣 33 64
大会堂 329 30
大字标题 342 44
大动脉 20 54
大动脉瘤 20 49
大西洋 14 20
大西洋红娥蝶 365 1
大光圈镜头用的显微稜镜光点 115 62
大麦 68 26
大麦升降机 92 33
大麦贮窖 92 2
大麦接收 92 4
大麦储仓 92 31
大君 306 28
大丽花 51 20
大丽菊属 60 23
大块牛肉 94 22
大坐骨神经 18 30
大围领套头衫 30 2
大陆 14 12-18
大陆台地 11 9
大陆块 11 7
大陆坡 11 9
大陆棚 11 8
大学 262 1-25
大学讲师 262 3
大学图书馆 262 11-25
大岩桐 53 7
大拇指 19 64
大批货物 206 18

大油漆桶 129 9
大鸥 86 48
大钩 145 9
大炮 255 92
大肠 20 17-22
大盾 329 56
大洲 14 12-18
大胡子 34 15
大型手提照相机 114 36
大型折叠照相机 114 49
大型柔软玩具狗 47 41
大型移动式灭火器 270
大型照相机 112 25
大型照相机用的试探曝光... 61
大钢琴 325 40
大钢琴踏板 325 41
大脑 17 42，18 22
大栈 357 11
大浪冲浪运动 279 4
大酒杯 45 87
大胸椎 18 36
大铁钳 100 41
大圆肌 18 55
大容量的卡车 158 14
大量货车 158 14
大桶 52 4，89 4，130 1
大理石桌面 265 12
大猎犬 86 33
大麻 383 9
大脚趾 19 52
大黄派 97 22
大黄蜂 358 23
大教堂 15 53
大盘帽 35 29
大雪橇 303 19
大琹菜 69 18
大槌 125 18，137 22
大腿 16 49
大腿甲 329 52
大腿肉 95 54
大腿前端肉 95 51
大腿动脉止血带 21 15
大提琴 323 16
大帽钉(头) 121 94，122
大颊腺类 366 16
大猩猩 368 16
大鼓 323 55，324 47
大熊星座和其目视双星开... 3 29
大锤 158 36
大篷车 206 20，307 34
大鹅 359 20
大臀肌 18 60
大翻领 31 23
大糖炮 306 53
太平门 307 33，312 7
太平门(出口)灯 312 6
太平洋 14 19
太阳 4 29，36-41，42
太阳穴 16 3
太阳电池版 10 66
太阳虫 357 7
太阳光线灯 281 13
太阳光线的方向 4 9
太阳光谱 343 14
太阳面(球) 4 38
太阳能电池 155 34
太阳能收集器 155 19
太阳能住宅 155 17
太阳能的利用 155 17-36
太阳眼镜 301 19，111 6
太阳眼镜盒 6 19
太阳黑子 4 37
太阳黑子附近的气旋 4 38
太阳感应器 10 69

光学录音装置之视觉控制目镜
311 95
光学测距器 258 37
(光学)瞄准仪 305 41
光具座 114 50
光度计 23 54
光度计光源 112 50
光度测法用的电脑和分析器 23
53
光度测法用的吸光架 23 52
光栅摄谱仪 5 5
光射线路径 1 62
光圈环 115 5
光圈刻度 115 56
光圈调整环 115 5
光圈调整装置 114 34
光圈控制环 115 5
光楔 176 22
光源 1 59
光谱摄影机 5 5
雀科 361 6-8
衖膺 362 12
常规驱动巡逻潜艇 259 75
常客 266 40

口部

口对口人工呼吸法 21 26
口述录音机 22 27
口套 70 31
口轮匝肌 19 8
口腔灯 24 42
口腔和咽喉 19 14-37
口腔(镜) 24 41
口琴 324 35
口袋盖 33 18
口器 358 26
台口宽 334 12
台上裁判 299 43
台布 330 36
台灯 46 24，246 35
台式喷灯 350 9
台式精密车床 109 20
台阶 37 39，123 17，281 37
台阶式长椅 281 20
台阶形的排式住宅 37 58-63
台刷 108 33
台板(面) 116 27，142 14，182
23
台虎(钳) 109 28，138 24
台轮 334 18
台架 120 18，139 19，222 18
台架压床 133 15
台面升降调整台 133 22
台面升降调整装置 133 21
台面板 132 34
台座 307 55
台脚 132 32
古代书写工具 341 21-26
古代北欧民族所用之文字 341 11
古代墓穴 328 16
(古罗马妇女的)外套 355 9
古典式摔角 299 6-9
古希藓泥沼层 13 22
古埃及人所用之芦管笔 341 22
古埃及之象形文字 341 1
叶子 58 3，53，59 17，68 8，
276 43，370 26，371 68
叶片 68 20，370 28，85
叶舌 68 22，370 84
叶状体 378 49
叶状膜片 2 33
叶形饰 334 40
叶芽 59 47
叶或花像鸟足的植物 69 11

叶枝 371 27
叶的形状 370 31-38，378 52
叶的底面 378 19
叶卷须 57 4
叶柄 370 27
叶脉 370 29
叶菜类 57 28-34
叶缘形状 370 43-50
叶鞘 68 9，21，370 83
叫卖者 308 8，64
号印 85 33
号角 309 54
号志灯光 153 3
号志回转盘 153 7
号码 289 33，36，290 28，301
37
号码盘 189 18
号码牌 305 84
只有一片的三文治 266 75
舌 17 52，19 25
舌针 167 12，61
舌针的扣板 167 56
舌阀 192 63
舌骨 20 2
吐司 45 34
吐丝口 358 46
名数 344 4
吃水线 285 31
吃水标 222 73
吃去的部分，被食部分 80 50
(吃鱼用的)叉 45 65
(吃鱼用的)刀 45 8
吃鱼用的刀和鱼叉 45 8
吃草的红色雌鹿 86 13
吃甜点用的匙 45 66
吊于吊架上的救生艇 221 78
吊斗升降系统 144 25
吊斗升降车 147 4，200 14，213
38，214 34
吊车轨道 222 24
吊灯 46 4
吊式门架 177 13
吊式钢板照相机 177 1
吊式麦克风 311 40
吊衣柜 267 30
吊杆 221 59，223 58
吊杆柱 223 35
吊杆轮 221 60
吊床 278 4
吊环 87 5，296 4
吊环上十字支撑 296 50
吊环上向后复回环 296 55
吊环上杠杆悬垂 296 56
吊柱 258 13，83
吊钩 85 6，270 15，49
吊钟柳 367 14
吊带 29 26，34，32 30，288 42
吊带夹子 32 31
吊重齿轮 217 74
吊架 221 101，223 20
吊索(架) 119 37，120 37，215
17，41，219 47，221 106，271
52，284 12，288 40，316 8
吊桥 215 39，329 25
吊袜带 32 6
吊舱 214 52
吊舱滑轮托架 214 66
吊球 299 24
吊锤 224 73
吸入运输装置 74 49
吸入疗法(治疗) 274 6-7
吸入装置 23 12
吸入棉箱 164 44
吸入器管 26 2，226 32
吸水井 329 3
吸水头 217 51

吸水软管 270 30，67
吸水装置 24 11
吸水滚轮 173 16
吸水管 316 52
吸引电极 23 29
吸气消音器 190 16
吸气管 26 2
吸尘口 199 43
吸尘扇 163 10
吸尘控制 50 72
吸尘器 108 43，147 14
吸式给纸机 180 72
吸收的中子 1 53
吸收式测功器 143 97-107
吸收装置的配件 27 44
吸吮器官 81 36
吸纸头 184 11
吸纸器 184 8
吸泥机 216 59
吸油管 38 55
吸取筒 153 73
吸烟者的用具 107 44
吸盘 77 9，81 37，111 23，357
21，364 26
吸量管 350 24
吸滤瓶 350 40
吸管 10 37，22 72
吸隔音墙板 310 15
吸墨纸 46 23
吹口 27 38，323 36，324 33，
72，326 25
吹气风扇 191 48，192 62
吹风机 105 33，106 22，179 22
吹张器 22 37
吹制 162 28，36
吹制过程 162 22
吹制法 162 22-37
吹炼过程 147 57
吹气转炉 147 45-50
吹管 162 39，352 26
吹管点火器 141 27
鸣禽类 360 1，3，4，5，7，
9，10，361 1-20
吟游诗人 329 70
听诊 263 8
听诊器 22 73，23 53
听打字员 248 33
听觉神经 17 64
听骨 17 61
听筒 237 8，245 15，246 16
听筒软索 237 14
吧台 267 54，317 9，318 15
吧台凳 267 53
吞火者 308 25
吞剑者 308 26
君子兰 53 8
君士坦丁大帝金币 252 3
吻别 205 52
咀嚼烟草 107 19
呼出的气泡 279 26
呼吸计 23 31
呼吸保护器 270 39
呼吸量指针式指示器 26 28
呼吸管 21 27，153 10
呼吸器 21 27，153 10
咖啡 98 65，67，99 68
咖啡豆 382 6
咖啡豆烘烤炉 98 70
咖啡杯 44 29
咖啡壶 44 28
咖啡店 265 1-26
咖啡店顾客 265 22-24
咖啡果 382 5
咖啡树 282 1
咖啡壶 44 28，265 2
咖啡桌 42 28，265 11

咖啡器具 265 18
哑音天鹅 359 16
咽喉 19 24
品脱葡萄酒 79 16
咖啡杆 180 56
哈巴狗 70 9
哈哈镜车 308 55
(哈普西卡)古钢琴 322 45
哈蜜瓜片 266 50
响板 306 47，324 46
响葫芦 324 59
响螺(号) 327 41
屏栓(饰) 354 23
唾液盆 24 12
喷齿类动物 366 12-19
唱片 46 15，309 32，31
唱片节目主持人 317 25
唱片架 309 36
唱片储放槽 241 19
唱头 309 33
唱机 241 18
唱机外壳 241 19
唱臂 241 21
唱臂平衡器 241 53
唱臂导架 241 28
唱臂锁 241 27
告出物品放置盘 271 15
告报小贩 205 17
告报手推车 205 16
告解亭机 236 19
告解票柜台 236 15
告�烟者，流动小贩 308
告示类 204 34
告示机 268 28
告示员 204 37
告(票)货柜柜 204 35，27
42，61
告唤亭 204 47
告筹知处 275 2
啤酒厂 93 1-31
啤酒过滤器 93 15
啤酒加温器 266 7
啤酒花和植园 15 114
啤酒泡沫 266 4
啤酒杯 93 30，266 3，6
309 53，317 6
啤酒杯衬垫 266 26
啤酒店棚 308 23
啤酒泵 266 1，68
啤酒玻璃杯 266 6
啤酒桶 93 17
啤酒酿造者 92 49
啤酒箱堆 93 24
喀斯特层的水位(地下水面)
77
喀斯特泉 13 74
咳(吸管) 88 84
喇叭 188 53，322 1
喇叭孔 309 19
喇叭口 323 37，42，48，
喇叭水仙 60 3
喷水池 272 21
喷水管 281 40
喷气管 281 41
喷丝孔 170 42
喷灯 126 74
喷杆 83 3
喷沙精制或磨光的石南纹烟
107 41
喷气燃料槽 146 18
喷气轮 56 25，83 18 181 3
喷油定时装置 190 58
喷油泵 190 65
喷(油)嘴 55 28，67 33，
72，190 54，196 3，2
喷泉 272 8，22，62，33,4
喷洒液箱 83 5，50
喷洒装置 83 58

帆船船身类型 285 29-41
帆船赛艇 285 14-24
帐篷 307 61
帐篷边的钟状部份 278 27
帐篷支柱 307 13
帐篷(支柱)杆 278 38，307 2
帐篷号角 278 42
帐篷式拱 336 35
帐篷顶 278 22
帐篷柱 352 8
帐篷桩(钉) 278 24
帕申系 1 22
帕纳维亚2000旋风式万能战斗机 256 8
帕德嫩神庙 334 1
带X射线头的X射线头 27 18
带十字接头的肘管 67 6
带十字接头的速套管连接器 67 28
带子 301 3
带子实体的菌丝 381 2
带牛皮的肉豆蔻 382 34
带小鸭的野鸭 272 51
带风门的灰盘 210 6
带方形的从动轮 140 43
带方向转动装置的水平对置式双缸引擎 189 47
带日光滤器的太空头套 6 22
带开关的三脚插座 127 66
带水柜的火车头 210 65
带计转器自行车速率计 187 33
带手轮的人孔盖 130 19
带手指防护装置锯链的安全制动器 85 15
带分接头变换器的变压器 211 10
带分数 344 10
带切割附件和导向器的熔接气焊 141 19
带内螺纹的异径管节 126 41
带内螺纹的异径管头 126 45
带头巾之上衣 306 15
带卡口的灯泡 127 69
带乔之投掷杆伇(标枪) 352 40
带尼龙套下凹枕头 207 68
带电池槽的手柄 117 5
带电煤栏 61
带四声道解调器 241 45
带幼虫的枝条 371 59
带叶的枝 383 61
带叶柳枝 371 29
带皮革或电木衬垫的弹棉机 166 64
带外螺纹的肘管接头 126 51
带吊斗的装料车 213 37
带字母的球型打字头 249 15
带有电动机的除尘风扇 83 53
带有水管的外衣 347 2
带有花和果实的可可树枝 382 17
带有鸣叫声的羽翼 88 3
带有呼换按钮的室内电话 127 3
带有面甲和耳罩的安全盔 84 23
带有棚条盖的坛子 206 13
带有钢质和橡胶悬挂装置和减震器的转向架 207 4
带有珍珠的钻石戒指 36 23
带有兜帽的皮毛外套 29 66
带有混合螺旋的输送装置 83 59
带有喷嘴的手动喷枪 83 46
带有螺旋花纹之器皿 328 13
带式运送机 156 2
带羽毛的钟形帽 35 12
带羽饰的毛帽 35 6
带行驶里程记录的速率表 191 74
带哑罗盘的受夏重发器 224 53
带衣柜的座位 212 63
带后舱口的三门轿车 193 18

带托盘的分馏塔 145 37
带连接器的双人座 214 18
带连接器的煤水平台 210 2
带进路指示器的远方信号灯 203 20
带卵子的滤泡 20 84
带状运送机 144 40
带花和未成熟果实的花柄 378 31
带花苞的枝芽条 371 25
带花环的树 120 8
带花饰的模特儿帽 35 7
带条绞链 140 51
带岔道的高速公路 15 16
带护罩的转辙电动机 202 35
带护藤的足球盔 291 33
带拖刀之熔丝枪 353 28
带拖架车 213 34
带变换管的景像变换器 27 19
带侧边车的摩托车 189 53
带侧柱的平板货车 206 24
带线路图的控制台 203 65
带线路图的控制盘 203 66
带定向天线的通讯人造卫星 237 52
带钐 143 104
带轮罩 133 32
带转向架的自卸敞篷车 213 24
带转向架的标准平板车 213 11
带松果的枝条 371 12
带细根的叶簇 54 17
带钩饰 328 24
带果的花萼 374 8
带果的果序 383 56
带果实的根 383 43
带金属镶板的车厢 208 6
带冠毛簇的果实 378 11
带柄之青铜刀 328 31
带柄之青铜短剑 328 22
带显示不大于5%刹车距离显示板的臂形志志 203 12
带钢 143 11
带钢卷 148 73
带指针的刻度盘 114 58
带保险丝的开关座架 127 68
带钩枪托底板 305 46
带钩短矛 319 22
带籽的长角(果) 378 33
带籽的果实 372 57
带重锤的刷子 38 32
带配菜的西餐 266 55
带格子套的烟管 221 84
带珠孔的种子 383 57
带珠球的叶液 355 8
带倒车齿轮的换档器头 192 44
带倒刺的鱼钩尖 89 80
带校正透镜的观景窗目镜 115 22
带版压条 54 12
带消音器的轮机装置 209 24
带消音器的排气管(装置) 209 12，22
带粉豫的鳞片 372 45，50
带(绳) 293 73
带球 291 52
带球形装置的操作器 2 38
带插入键和环的钢拉线 127 30
带盖的墨水池 309 78
带盖陶瓷坩埚 350 31
带斜轴面和半梭椎面之单斜柱 351 24
带深度规的手柄 134 47
带眼罩的接目镜 117 14
带速度指示器的远方信号灯 203 18
带速率器和电子转速计的仪表盘 188 40

带菌摺的菌盖 381 4
带裁刀之给纸台 184 21
带硬刮毛的总苞花蕊 375 33
带缝纫针之针滚筒 185 21
带循环油冷却装置之防火片盒 312 25
带销的驱动盘 135 9
带茉满花序的枝条 371 10
带隐钩旋转弧形诱饵 89 75
带距离线的雷达指示器 10 58
带鼓风机的油冷却器 211 11
带煤水车的高速列车 210 38
带滤色器的软片套 2 14
带锯条 157 53
带照相机和超偏振镜的透射光显微镜 112 14
带塑料轮盘的有辐轮子 289 25
带蜂窝的蜂房上层活动架 77 45
带罩框之激磁灯 312 48
带增压轮机的柴油引擎 212 51
带雌花的花枝 382 50
带雌花和雄花的枝条 372 43
带滚筒的花篮 206 10
带踏脚板的安全杆 301 58
带腊帆的斜桅 219 1
带鞋植的立架 100 4
带雕刻马头的船艉支架 218 14
带褶喇叭袖 30 54
带翼旦形图案 333 12
带繁殖蜂窝的育蜂室 77 46
带鳌角的盘架 358 41
帝国式之桌子 336 16
帽子撑绦 355 71
帽形头盔 254 7
帽形盒 205 11
帽饰 35 4
帽和轻型行李架 208 28
帽店 268 38
帽兜 35 2
帽模 35 3
幅铇刀 132 27

山部

山毛榉 371 33
山毛榉虫瘿 82 37
山毛榉坚果 371 37
山鸟 361 13
山羊 73 14，296 17
山羊胡 34 10
山羊胡须 73 15
山谷台 214 51
山谷站 214 39
山岳地区 12 43
山形建筑正面 334 3，335 36
山形屋顶 121 1
山形窗 334 4
山(形)墙(头) 37 15，121 5，122 25
山岭 13 60
山肩 12 41
山坡 12 37
山顶 11 6，12 40
山顶站 214 57
山金车花 380 2
山脉 12 39
山扁豆 380 16
山前侵蚀平原(足面) 13 65
山脊 12 36，13 60，300 21
山崩 11 46
山梅花 373 9
山腰梁 12 39
山鞍 12 16，42
山墙石板瓦 122 80
山墙簷口 121 3
岛 13 6

岔尖 202 21
岩石 13 25，327 38，35 3
岩石阶地 13 47
岩石块 6 15
岩石岛 13 12
岩石园 51 6
岩石采掘面 158 15
岩生植物 51 7
岩床 11 31
岩玫瑰 377 20
岩梁 300 4
岩洞 15 85
岩基 11 30
岩峯山 11 29
岩壁 12 43，300 2
岸 13 4
岸区 217 28
岸坡 217 28
岸壁 217 1-4
炭(木炭) 278 48
炭火烤架 278 47
炭灰箱门 38 39
炭块 108 37
炭笔 338 16
炭盘 157 53
峡谷 13 45，52
峡谷河川 13 51
峯 11 6
嵌入式镜头 114 5
嵌入环 349 17
嵌心绣法 102 22
嵌有金丝网的玻璃 124 6
嵌装 123 57，67，143 7，51
(嵌装式)接地插座 127 5
崖 11 48

彳部

行人 268 18
行人穿越口 268 55
行人穿越道 268 24，51
'行人穿越道'路牌 268 29
行车路线和终点站标志 一
行列圣歌之十字架 330 4
行车虫(幼虫) 82 14，16
行军床 278 59
行李 205 7-12
行李台 204 43
行李员 204 9，267 17
行李间 207 71
行李收据 204 8
行李架 207 51，208 27
行李标签 204 7，205 8
行李站 233 5
行李舱 257 19
行李寄存处 204 27
行李寄存柜 204 21
行李寄存处 207 70
行李锁柜(过解处) 194 18
行李提取处 233 38
行李箱 191 24，193 17 一194 13
行李箱盖 191 7
行纸路线 268 29
行驶轮 64 41，56
行政区域分界线 15 103
行星齿轮 143 94
行星和行星符号 4 42-52
行情板 251 8
行距(间) 175 5
行距调整器 249 23
往复移动之骑马钉鞍座 一
很弱 321 36
很强 321 39
待洗衣物箱 50 21
待触发按扣机 87 11

食用牛肝菌 381 16
食用肉 96 1-4，99 53
食用伞菌 381 23
食用蜗牛 357 27
食虫哺乳类动物 366 4-7
食肉目 367 11-12，368 1-11
食肉检查员的戳记 94 24
食胞 357 6
食物保管室 207 83
食物道 77 19
食指 19 66
食品切片机 40 38
食品价目表 266 65
食品杂货商 98 41
食品冷冻室 204 1
食品售货亭 205 49
食盐 1 9，98 40
食粉甲虫 81 18
食管(道) 17 49，20 23，40
食腐烂蔬菜的甲虫 80 45
食糖 98 53-55
饮水供应 269 1-66
饮水槽 74 6，146 16
饮水器 278 32
饮用水容器 278 32
饮矿泉处 274 15
饮矿泉的病人 274 18
饮食摊位 308 3
饮料陈列架 99 71
饮料吸管 266 46
饮料架 266 59
饮料柜 42 20
饲养通道 75 3
饲养槽 75 37
饲料分送器 74 13
饲料供给管 74 15
饲料甜菜 69 21
饲料植物 69 1-28
饲料袋 62 43
饲料221 73
饲槽 74 21
饰边 31 34
饰孔刺绣，穿孔刺绣 102 11
饰有美人虑之露胸紧身女装 306 24
饰钉 253 8
饰板 339 38
饰线用之工具 183 3
饰物(护身符) 36 35
饰带 253 9
饰缘 102 3
饰像圆柱 333 18
饼模 40 28，29
饵针 89 27
饵罐 89 24
蚀刻针 340 16
蚀刻钢刀 340 51
馅饼 97 18
馈电屏 153 4
馈电维体 153 12，35
馈钱器 74 49-51
餐刀 45 50
餐巾 45 9，266 47，267 48
餐巾/餐巾抽屉 44 22
餐厅 223 44，228 25，233 50，266 1
餐车 207 22-32
餐车厨房 207 33
餐饮部 207 78-79
餐具 207 85，309 47
餐具抽屉 44 20，45 44
餐具柜(架) 44 20，45 44
餐具垫 44 4
餐室 207 32，77
餐桌 42 33，44 1，45 1，46 34，266 74
餐桌餐巾类 45 19
餐盘 39 42，45 4
餐椅 44 10

ヨ（ヨ）部

灵长目 368 12-16
灵猩 70 24
录立体音响与音效用之麦克风配置 310 30
录放音磁头的录音头盒 241 59
录音水平控制 117 16
录音水平表(音量指示表) 241 35-36，61，242 14
录音及放音设备 311 23
录音卡带 242 17
录音头，放音头及消磁头之支座组件 311 25
录音头盒 241 59
录音机 209 30，261 42
录音扩音器与电源 311 11
录音设备 310 58
录音助手 117 68
录音助理 310 57
录音技师 310 23，55
录音扬声器 238，37
录音和混合录音 311 1-46
录音室 238 16，310 14，54
录音室调音台 238 25
录音带 242 17
录音带转向滚轮和终端开关 241 60
录音平衡指示器 243 12，311 14
录音音量表示表 242 14
录音音量控制 117 16，243 11
录音盘 238 24
录音装置 117 7
录音装置用的导频音或脉动发生器插座 117 7
录音感度选择器 117 16
录音摄影机 310 60
录音摄像头 243 35
录影摄像头 243 36

尸部

尼龙 101 4
尼龙长袜 99 26
尼龙绒巾 133 4
尼龙鞋底 291 30
'尼米兹 ICVN 68' 核子动力航空母舰 259 1
尼安德塔人的头颅化石 261 19
尼罗河鳄鱼 356 13
尿沉淀图表 23 58
尿道 20 68
尿道球腺 20 75
尿道镜 23 17
尾股 16 40
层云 8 4
层云 8 4
层玻璃 124 5
层的分界 13 21
层琉 335 52
层架式鸡笼 74 20
层架式鸡笼快速饲养 74 23
层架式鸡笼系统 74 18
层积云 8 3
尾 362 8
尾巴 70 12，72 38，88 47，49，58
尾羽 88 67，80
尾轮 256 27
尾面 229 26，230 62
尾骨 17 5，20 60
尾钳 81 12
尾座 149 29，177 62
尾座圆筒 149 27
尾座筒夹杆 149 28

尾座筒调整手轮 149 30
尾部调弦栓 323 22
尾旋翼(转子) 232 14，256 20，264 4
尾椎 17 5
尾滑 288 5
尾鳍 256 23
尾鳌 81 12
尾鳌针 358 43
尾翼形状 229 23-36
尾翼张绘 232 4
尾鳍 364 10
尾秃头 34 20
局部阵雨式的降水 8 17，19
局部排水沟 122 11，82
局部麻醉用的皮下注射器 24 53
居尔特银币 328 37
居住单位 146 33
昼行性鸟兽 23 58
屋外变电所 152 29-35
屋角底石板瓦 122 77
屋顶 37 7
屋顶边沟 37 11，38 9
屋顶用梯 122 63
屋顶层 122 57
屋顶板 122 61
屋顶钩 38 6
屋顶型式及其各部分 121 1-26
屋(顶桁)架 120 7，121 78
屋顶排水沟 122 11，82
屋顶窗 37 56
屋架梁 121 29
屋面油纸 122 62
屋面复盖层 38 1
屋脊 37 7，121 2，12，122 93
屋脊上之十字架 331 10
屋脊小塔 121 14
屋脊瓦 122 4
屋脊瓦 122 4
屋脊形帐篷 278 21
屋脊通风口 55 11
屋脊挂钩 122 65
屋脊盖顶片 122 99
屋脊接缝 122 79
屋簷板 37 8
屋簷 37 9，38 11，121 4，122 36
屋簷雨 122 5
屈光度控制环 117 15
屈体吊臂悬垂 296 36
屈肘悬垂 296 35
屈臂悬垂 296 39
屏，幕 236 40
展开的花冠 378 4
展示的动物 356 5
展翅飞行的猎物 86 41
屠刀 96 37
屠夫 94 1
屠夫的围裙 96 39
屠牛枪 94 3
屠宰厂 94 15
屠杀场 319 13
犀牛 366 25
履带牵引机 200 3
履带牵引式铲运机 200 16

己(巳)部

己醛环胶 170 28
己醛环胺的形成 170 25
已印好之纸堆 181 25
已印刷好的收纸堆 181 9

已印刷过之单张纸的收纸装 180 55
已成形长颈瓶的吹模 162
已折叠好之报纸 181 56
已修整板材 120 95
已清洗过的瓶子 93 21
已展开的圆木 157 33
已曝光影片 117 42
包扎材料 26 34
包在子房中心内的胚珠 59
已成形长颈瓶的吹模 352
包骨皮的木架或骨架 353
包掮 319 7
包装机 76 8
包装好的面包 97 48-50
包装材料 98 46-49
包装纸 98 46
包装相台 271 14
包装箱分配器 74 53
包裹处理室 204 1
包裹柜台 236 2
包裹秤 236 2
包橡的帆布皮艇船壳 283 68
异形钢筋 119 82，
异国女郎 306 30
异径肘头 126 49
异径管节 126 39
色选择器 249 11
色带盒 249 16
色调配彩 254 24-29
色彩机关 317 13
色彩调整旋钮 116 43-45
色情影片用之放映机 318

弓部

弓 354 32
弓毛 323 15
弓杆 323 14
弓把 305 57
弓形 346 52
弓形纸板文件夹 247 40
弓形集电器 205 36
弓形装置 247 41
弓弦 305 59
弓弦乐器 323 1-25
弓框捕捉器 87 48
弓锯 134 3，17，136 40 9，150 14
弓锯架 126 71
弓箭步 295 42
弓撑 295 24
引入线 166 34
引入管 153 40
引水船 221 95
引水泵 91 41
引号(双引号、颠倒的逗号) 26
引号(法文引号) 342 27
引导织品进给开报机 168
引纱导杆 165 18
引诱鸟的树 86 47
引诱猎物的杆 87 43-47
引座员 315 12
引索伞 287 7
引擎 145 12，288 35
引擎方向接头装置 6 36
引擎支架 190 38
引擎和传动控制制 212 67
引擎架 191 53

通风口 212 37
油热交换器 212 55
91 8
158 25
5, 323 9, 61, 324
46 51
17
23 1-27
面板 323 24
面 322 33
13, 20
25 18
330 38
器 165 51
少装置 165 13
167 50
67 49
181 45
2 48, 89 42
的框 338 20
18 35
94
的网 86 27
53
2 42
44
口 168 47
91 38
机 178 13
336 28
159 25
画幕 316 9
335 50
322 12
136 34
缝针 22 57
123 52
工作台 119 20
用的扳手 119 77
(斜梁) 123 49
座) 113 21
具 137 39
5 2
26 42
5 18
286 60
比赛 301 29, 64
6 26
125 28, 126 82
46 26
7 1-19, 1
277 2-6
7 7-19
5 37
17, 255 15, 21, 264
255 7
87 18
57
89 51
28 2
65 57
40 27
19, 305 34-39
158 27
他 324 73
盖 255 35
257 6, 7
87 79
87 73
296 12, 297 8
15, 20
46, 186 15, 309 28
167 38
299 20

弹簧环铰接装置 151 65
弹簧承载电线卷轴 294 29
弹簧垫圈 143 34, 202 8
弹簧圆规 151 64
弹簧悬架 83 7
弹簧缓冲器 214 50
弹簧销钉 109 9
弹簧跳床 297 10
弹簧跳床垂直后空翻 297 17
弹簧帽 247 6
弹簧螺栓 140 37
弱 321 35
弱音器 323 10, 324 68
强 321 38
强力粘合剂 128 24
强度均匀的降水 8 18
强弱 321 41

子(孑)部
子午仪 113 26
子午环 113 26
子午线望远镜 113 29
子叶 370 87
子房 58 40, 370 54
子房和雄蕊 370 60, 373 2
子房腔 370 55
子房壁 370 61
子宫 20 79
子宫外口 20 85
子宫腔 20 80
子船 228 17
子弹 87 55
孑孓鱼饵 89 72
孔径 f=1:3.5或更大的镜头显微棱镜光点 115 63
孔径光阑滑动片 112 16
孔雀 73 30
孔雀毛饰 254 36
孔雀的羽毛 73 31
孔雀星座 3 41
孔雀肉 61 7
孔雀翎斑 73 32
孔雀翎眼 73 32
孔裂的蒴果 370 96
学习进度计数器 242 5
学习游泳者 282 17
学生(儿童)作品 260 67-80
学生(女) 262 10
学生用的音量控制 261 43
学生(男) 262 9
学生应答装置 242 4
学生实验台 261 11
学生举手 260 20
学服 29 31-47
学前小童教育 48 1-20

女部
女人头 327 56
女人身 327 59
女人身躯 327 24
女士 265 23
女士发型 34 27-38
女士连身式滑雪服 301 9
女士有边帽和无边帽 35 1-21
女士凉鞋 101 49
女士滑裤 31 39
女子理发厅和美容院 105 1-39
女丑角 306 24
女司膳员 312 4
女奴 306 41
女主角 306 33
女用中统袜 32 9
女用衬衫 29 58

女式靴子 101 12
女贞 373 6
女巫 306 6
女场记 310 39
女芭蕾舞演员 314 26
女服务生 265 13
女运动裤 98 31, 306 21
女性生殖器 20 79-88
女侍者(女侍应生) 266 18, 318 33
'女厕所' 233 48
女孩外套 29 54
女孩紧身连衫裙 29 36
女孩夏服 29 13
女孩裙子 29 46
女海妖 327 58
女轻便高跟鞋 101 29
女帽 306 23
女商人 308 65
女候相 332 24
女裙开叉处所附的三角布片 30 52
女装成衣 271 29
女服部 271 28
女演员 316 38
奶油 99 46
奶油刀 45 73
奶油成形包装机 76 32
奶油卷 99 17
奶油供应泵 76 40
奶油松饼 97 27
奶油蛋糕 97 24
奶油碟 45 36
奶油熟化桶 76 31
奶油罐 265 21
奶瓶 28 19
奶瓶保温器 28 21
奶罩 318 29
奶嘴 28 15
妇女内衣 32 1-15
妇女的发型和少女发型 34 27-38
妇女的房间 329 10
妇女宽边帽 41 11
妇女睡衣衬裤 32 16-21
妇科和直肠检查器具 23 3-21
好打扮者 306 33
妻子的纹章 254 11-23
委员会 263 1-2
委员会委员 263 2
委员席(桌) 263 3
妥蛇人 353 45
姜味面包 97 51
娃娃车 48 24
娃娃车篷 48 26
娃娃头 34 35
要屠宰的动物，牛 94 2
要屠宰的猪 94 11
婆塞 15 74
姿态控制火箭 234 38
婚礼之见证人 332 23
婴儿 28 5
婴儿上衣 28 25, 29 9
婴儿车 28 30, 37, 273 31
婴儿车上短上衣 29 3
婴儿套装 28 3
婴儿用的高脚椅 28 33
婴儿全套用品箱 28 18
婴儿用 28 16
婴儿学步鞋 101 56
婴儿服装 29 1-12
婴儿短上衣 48 25
婴儿粉盒 28 14
婴儿浴盆 28 3
婴儿橡皮质尿兜裤 29 10
嫁接 54 30-39

嫁接于树干上的玫瑰(花) 51 25
嫁接于树干上的浆果树 52 11
嫁接于树干上的蔷薇(树) 52 21
嫌疑犯 264 32
嫩叶 59 29
嫩芽(新梢)插枝 54 24

幺部
幻灯片托架 309 43
幻灯片放映机 309 42
幻灯片复制附件 115 87
幻灯片复制接合器 115 88
幻灯机 114 76
幼儿 28 42
幼儿之轻便短靴 28 45
幼儿用围栏 28 39
幻儿摇摇响玩具 28 44
幼虫 77 29; 80 3, 6, 14, 17, 19, 29, 36, 41, 46, 54, 81 20, 82 20, 25, 44, 47, 358 9, 19
幼虫挖的坑道 82 24
幼芽 370 90
幼体 77 28
幼狐 88 42
幼苗 54 6, 84 9
幼苗箱 55 51
幼树 84 10-11
幼稚园儿童 48 2
幼稚园教师 48 1

纟(糹)部
约会记事薄 246 8
纤毛 357 10, 370 50
纤匍枝 54 16
纤维板 338 24
纤维胶人造丝饼 169 18
纤维素板浸于苛性钠中 169 4
纪念之巨石柱 328 18
纪念性的拱道(门) 337 3
纪念盘 309 48
纪念碑 15 92, 331 10
纪念碑入口 333 9
毛毛狗 70 20
丝兰花 373 24
丝件的洗涤 170 48
丝饼的处理过程 169 19-27
丝带 34 7
丝绒地毯 267 35
丝绸翻领 33 8
红 275 24
红门兰 376 28
红三叶草 69 1
红木兰 373 15
红方块 276 41
红外镜 276 40, 44
红鸟 363 5
红外衣 289 13
红外线干燥器 173 32
红外线灯机 242 30
红外线声发射机 242 29
红外线雷射测距器 255 82
红色 254 27, 343 1
红色左舷灯 286 12
红色目标球 277 12
红杉 372 69
红豆草 69 10
红胫鹬 361 63
红珊瑚 357 17
红胸翠菊鸳 361 10
红袋鼠 366 3
红脾 291 63
红鹿 367 1

红(葡萄)酒 98 64
红(葡萄)酒杯 45 83
红腹灰雀 360 5
红腹裳夜鹰 365 8
红鹤 272 53
红醋栗 58 12
红醋栗树 58 10
红咀鸥鸶 363 6
纯环己醇 170 18
纯果酱 98 51
纽芬兰狗 70 34
纽伦堡妇女 355 38
纺纱用品的整理 170 57
纺织筒管 164 23
纺织品部 271 58
纺锭 166 30
纺锭固定用的弹簧夹 166 33
纬纱 171 3
纬纱纺锭 166 7，30
纬纱补充旋转转台 166 5
纬线 14 2
纬线触杆的金属接触套 166 31
纬度 14 6
纹身 306 44
纹章 254 1-6
纹章盾的支撑兽 254 15-16
纹章解说 254 17-23
纵向纺织物 222 44-56
纵向横向移动的搬操杆 149 17
纵帆前缘 284 42
纵帆斜桁顶帆 219 31
纵材 222 50，285 55
纵坐标轴 347 3
纵坐标值 347 10
纵轴 230 72
纵桁 230 47，57
纵肋马 296 1
纵劈腿 295 14
纸尺寸选择钮 249 34
纸毛巾 106 5
纸风筝 260 71
纸灯笼 52 15，306 4
纸卷 173 30
纸卷箱 249 33
纸质打字机色带 174 34，237 32
纸架 151 13
纸草植物 383 64
纸板裁切机 183 16
纸带穿孔器(机) 176 5，242 10
纸带器 174 33，43
纸带检查装置 242 8
纸料槽 172 86
纸浆干燥机 172 61
纸浆水泵 172 55，63
纸浆槽 173 47
纸堆 180 47
纸袋 98 48
纸筷 306 55
纸蛇 308 14
纸帽 306 45
纸牌游戏 276 36
纸叠 249 57
纹刀 140 31
纹车 145 11
纹车牵引起飞 287 5
纹车室 226 54
纹肉机 40 39，96 53
纹肉槽 96 40
纹帆索 219 71
纹架 221 87
纹盘(车) 258 23，270 56
纹接夹板 117 90
纹链阻板 259 15
纱分配轴 167 25
纱布 189 5
纱布卷架 185 19
纱(线) 164 53，167 17

纱线计长器 165 28
纱线张力装置 167 5
纱线清理装置 165 20
纱管顶部 164 52
绕点站指示牌 205 22
绕点站牌 205 21，38
绕点裁判员 282 25
绕点触地壁运动员 282 28
绅士 355 54，61
练习簿 47 24，260 4
练拳拳伴 299 27
绊创膏 21 7，22 55
绊创青膏 26 54
组合刀具夹架 149 41
组合选择开关 238 42
组合播种耙 63 41，65 87
组件的连接 242 70
组版 175 1-17
经由小船上岸的旅客 221 97
经由混合硬平织制造的连续细丝、
　纤维人造丝和纤维胶人造丝纱
　169 1-34
经纪人 307 18
经纪人交易柜台 251 3
经纱 165 43，166 39，171 2
经纱下沉 171 8
经纱升起 171 7
经纱轴 166 59
经纱放出器 166 59
经纱放出器索 166 61
经纱梁 166 48
经纬仪 14 52-62
经线 14 4
经度 14 4
经轴 165 42，167 24
经轴凸缘 165 30，166 49，167 26
经纱运动控制装置 166 60
经纱架 165 41
经理室 246 1-36
经者室 248 29
经者秘书 248 31
织布机 166 1
织布机框架 166 24
织布的准备过程 165 1-57
织边轴的穿孔 171 5
织边穿轴筒 171 20
织(成)品 166 12，168 39，51
织网桥面 215 18
织网蜘蛛 358 45
织针凸轮 167 14
织补针迹 102 17
织物卷紧装置 166 19
织物卷滚轮 166 47
织品穿轴 171 21
织品穿轴筒 171 21
织品窗 167 10
织梭箱和梭子 166 9
细木匠工具 132 1-28
细木匠工作室 132 1-73
细切断器和锯木机 133 37
细长的面包卷 97 15
细长漏斗型真菌 381 25
细条地板 123 62
细体铅字 175 8
细通心面 98 32
细柳条 136 15
细胞核 357 2
细菌的培养 261 29
细菌培养皿 261 25
细菌培养室 261 30
细筛 260 66
细缝 57 22

线 167 36，346 1-23
线上磁碟贮存装置 176 32
线讯部分 183 34
线把 298 54
线形叶 370 31
线条 31 14
线条凸板 178 42
线(轴) 89 21，185 18
线轴团 100 29
线轴架 103 13
线圈 171 30，167 62
线圈在圈头交织 171 39
线路 202 1-38
线纵操纵模型机 288 89
绉褶模式 31 46
络头 71 7-11
绑索 221 119
统计图表 248 36
给水泵 154 13，210 23
给水预热器(给水加热器) 210 23
给水竿 89 7
给水管线 154 12
给水槽 152 17
给书装置 185 14
给电源用的集电器 207 75
给纱选择装置 167 40
给纸与收纸装置 181 14
给纸台(桌) 180 32，49，67，
　181 4，21，185 9
给纸机 180 48，68
给纸机护板 181 24
给纸机械 181 22
给纸和收纸用的气泵 181 6
给纸板装置 184 7
给纸导规 184 23
给纸装置 180 31，184 7，185
　26
给纸滚筒 180 34
给纸器 185 25
给纸器控制开关之仪表盘 180 74
给送装置 236 48
给信传送机 236 33
给料口 178 17
给料槽 172 67
给棉口 163 8
绝缘把毛 127 54
绝缘带 127 34
绝缘材料 155 36
绝壁 12 43
绝顶夹克 29 44
绒球 29 4
绒球大丽花 60 23
绒球支持钳 26 44
结合层 198 4
结网针 102 26
结网绳 102 24
结网圈(环) 102 23
结冰的地面 304 19
结果记录牌 309 82
结果的树枝 59 19
结果的雌性植物 383 10
结果的掌叶 384 2
结果枝 59 30，48
结绳 300 22-27
结绳文字 352 22
结婚仪式 332 14
结婚登录 254 10-13
结婚戒指 36 5，332 17
结婚戒指打造机 108 24
结婚戒指盒 36 6
结晶测定器 351 27-33
结晶玻璃 124 5
绘画用具 338 6-19
绘画材料之手推车 315 36
绘架星座 3 47

绘景师 315 35
绕线式灯丝 127 58
绕线模 126 83
绕绳下降 300 28-30
绕绳下降岩钉 300 39
绣花西服背心 355 75
绣成菊福植物 374 23
绣球花 51 11
绦虫 81 35
绦虫头部 81 36
绳 297 43，300 12
绳纹饰图案 252 38
绳股 162 54
绳线订书 183 8
绳线装订机 185 16
绳结 122 68
绳索 307 41，352 31
绳索套(固定)于突起岩
　300 9
绳索固定装置 301 40
绳索滑轮吊车 118 91
绳绑 221 91，273 49，320 12
维吉尼亚烟草 382 40
维京海盗船 218 13-17
维修技师 237 28
维管变 370 11
绿色 254 29，343 8
绿色右舷灯 286 11
绿色和红色船首灯 286
绿蛰虫 358 8
绿麦芽 92 23
绿巨象 81 19
绿洲 354 4
绿液预热器 172 43
绿箭 51 9
绿藻门 378 43
缆车双座 214 17
缆车座 214 16
缆车箱 30 39
缆索支承架 214 76
缆索导轨 214 33
缆索铁道 214 12
缆索绞车 85 38，46，25
缆索起重机 222 11-18
缆索铁道 214 12
缆索圆筒 85 39
缆索渡船 216 1
缆道 152 20，214 15-38
缆绳导轮 201 7
绵毛乳菌盖 379 13
绶带花圈 254 2
综丝(线) 166 27
综梁(轴) 166 3，4
综眼 166 28
棚带 21 9
缓冲座 100 16，255 47
缓冲钢板 166 44
缓冲钢板防止杆 166 45
缓冲储存器 242 33
缓冲器 206 51，213 7，
　27，44，52
缓冲橡胶块 192 82
缓和剂 152 10
缎纹刺绣针迹 102 10
编印用横的突出板 136 8
编织底 136 20
编织法式样 136 1-4
编织面 136 18
编织缝线 101 43
编织组成 101 47
编枝棚栏 216 54
编码键盘 242 11
编结头 133 29
编结彩饰 102 31

黑白斑纹的马

黑白斑纹的马 289 29
黑头鸥 359 14
黑丝绒球所制之帽 319 29
黑色 254 26，343 13
黑色双面印刷装置 180 12-13
黑色外衣 289 4
黑色雄松鸡 88 66
黑色跳棋子 276 19
黑(块) 275 21
黑麦 68 1
黑体铅字 175 2
黑体凝缩活字 175 10
黑板 47 13，48 16，261 36
黑板用圆规 260 40
黑板画 260 33
黑刺李 374 27
黑刺李(叶) 374 28
黑背胡狼 367 11
黑莓 58 29
黑苞脊 379 9
黑梅花 276 38
黑犀鱼鳔 369 6
黑接骨木 374 35
黑液贮槽 172 29
黑液滤器 172 28
黑啤酒 93 26
黑棋(子) 276 5
黑貂 367 15
黑猩猩 368 14
黑键 325 5
黑潮 14 31
(煮)咖啡壶 39 38
煮沸麦芽汁用的锅炉 92 52
煮熟的烟熏香肠 96 7
煮熟的禽肉 99 60
焦化设备 170 2
焦油的分离 156 18
焦油的分馏 170 4
焦油和酚的提取 170 3
焦点 347 27
焦炭装载 156 15
焦距测定器 111 33
焦煤导路 156 9
焦煤的倾卸 156 1
焦煤塔 144 9
照片说明 342 59
照片架 116 35
照明反光镜的调整装置 14 58
照明毛玻璃屏 177 20
照明光束路径 112 6
照明光学部件 112 7
照明地图板 268 3
照明站 226 27
照明路线 112 6
照明透视屏 264 30
照相打字之键盘操作台 176 1
照相打字组版之电脑 176 10
照相机系 115 103
(照相机)机身 115 2
照相机系统 115 1-105
照相机或投影机附件的接合器 112 55
照相机背 115 23
照相机械 115 5
照相测量用的全能测量机器 112 67
照相锌板 178 32
照相台 2 36
黑肉 96 3
黑衣草 380 7
熟石膏 128 2
熟石膏袋 260 85
熟果 382 33
熟果荚 383 4
熟的香肠 96 7
熊爪项链 352 14

熊果 377 15
熊科 368 9-11
熊蔥 377 6
燕麦(片) 98 37
燕麦圆锥花序 68 27
燕尾 33 14
燕尾双晶体 351 25
燕尾服 33 13
燕尾旗 253 22

斗部

斗牛 319 1-33，24
斗牛士 319 4
斗牛士入场处 319 10
斗牛士披的红色斗篷 319 27
斗牛士所戴的黑丝绒球所制之帽 319 29
斗牛场 319 5
斗式驳船 226 46
斗篷 254 3，14，355 26
斗篷式大衣 30 68
斗篷式披肩 352 24
斗篷楼条 355 24
斜口锯箱 132 43
斜边盖子 132 7
斜方肌 18 52
斜方晶系 351 23
斜方锥 351 23
斜行 71 3
斜行平接船身外板 285 56
斜角甲板 259 12
斜角规 120 81
斜角铰刀 125 9
斜体铅字 175 7
斜纹毛织品衬里 101 17
斜纹粗布夹克 33 21
斜纹粗布服 31 58，33 20
斜纹粗布裤(牛仔裤) 33 22
斜纹粗布背心 31 59
斜纹编织 136 3
斜拉杆 121 30
斜拉索 215 47
斜坡 206 1
斜坡道 119 41
斜坡滑用 287 27
斜齿轮 91 25
斜杠机 218 43，220 5
斜屋顶 38 12
斜面移动轮 143 91
斜面凿 132 11
斜脊瓦 122 9
斜索桥 215 46
斜桁文索 284 21
斜桁顶横帆 220 4
斜桁帆 220 1
斜桁机 219 31
斜索系统 215，51
斜索锚座 215 48
斜接 124 4
斜接用的角板 133 19
斜接机 124 7
斜面滑槽 124 31
斜嵌接合 121 88
斜锯架 124 30
斜榫尺 120 82
斜撑 118 88，119 14，121 41
斜撑支架 283 46

文部

文艺复兴字体 342 4
文艺复兴时期艺术 335 42-54
文艺复兴时期之宫殿 335 47
文艺复兴时期教堂 335 42

文艺栏 342 67
文氏管 192 8
文氏喉管 190 15
文件记录 248 8
文件处理员 248 6
文件夹 245 6，247 37，248 5
文件抽屉 248 23
文件架 248 10
文件柜 245 4
文件标签 248 4
齐行标尺 174 35
齐行楔 174 24
齐特琴 324 21

方部

方山 13 59
方术 120 74
方石英晶体 1 12
方头雪茄烟 107 4
方头螺栓 143 39
方尖石搭 333 10
方向轴 212 29
方向装置 241 23
方向盘 191 37，305 89
方向盘轮辐 191 58
方向舵 229 25，230 60，288 22
方向舵与刹车踏板 257 10
方向舵的辅力致动机构 257 23
方向舵踏板 257 10
方向槽 322 45
方形木材 157 36
方形木材堆积场场 157 32
方形闪光灯 114 74
方形闪光灯接点 114 13
方形闪光装置 114 73
方形阶状切割 36 51
方形船尾 259 11
方形艇 285 43
方形楼柱 347 34
方位角 87 74
方柱 336 25
方铁杆 143 9
方铁杆 145 14
方格号志 203 30
方眼花边网 102 22
方程式 345 9
方糖 98 53
放于定位上的龙骨 222 22
放大机 116 26
放大机头 116 41
放大机光度计 116 53
放大机测光计 116 53
放大机的光源 116 29
放大照明机台的台板 115 95
放大镜 175 34
放大器 241 40
放广告之幻灯机 312 23
放片机器 311 26
放气阀 213 21
放风筝 273 41
放出的中子 1 39，45，52
放长山猫毛皮 131 16
放长皮条 131 7
放长前的山猫皮 131 15，17
放长貂皮 131 9
放(扩)大器 241 40，312 19
放压阀 155 7
放纸币和硬币的分格抽屉 271 6
放乳节拍 75 33
放牧马鞍 71 37-44
放映的牛 241 40
放空水的船坞 222 43
放钓线 89 20

放饵处 86 28
放油栓 190 24
放映师 312 20
放映机 312 25-38
放映机镜头 312 35
放映灯用硒或汞汽整流器
放映室 5 27，312 12
放映室窗户 312 15
放映幕 260 36
放钻子的抽屉 24 17
放样间 222 3
放射虫类 357 8
放射状之饰物 332 37
放射性物质的自发衰变 1
放射性废料储放于盐矿中
放储能解压 74 48
放射线照射台 74 47
放射线照射装置 74 47
放热器肋 126 21
放热器(热)辐射器 126 20
放盘的柜台 266 64
放焦台 156 13
放置毛巾 47 22
於木头上切螺纹用的单用螺 135 14
於加热间烘乾 169 24
於定位上的船体构架 222
於垂直位置的倾斜机翼 23
於斜位置的倾斜旋翼 23
施工用吊车 118 31
施工用品吊车 118 31
施肥曲柄 66 8
施特球 349 1
旁注 185 68
旁通式发动机 232 46
旅行车 193 15
旅行袋 205 10
旅行读物 205 18
旅行推销员 209 28
旅行摩托车 188 24
旅客 204 24，205 6，221 109，267 14
旅客包房车厢 207 13
旅客码头 225 31
旅客座椅 230 38
旅客救护床 204 45
旅客登记桥 233 14
旅客登记簿 267 8
旅馆 267 18-26
旅馆房间 267 27-38
旅馆帐单 267 11
旅馆经理 267 19
旅馆标签 205 9
旅馆酒吧 267 51
旅馆搬运工 204 17
旅馆餐厅 267 20
连旗 253 12
旋切加刀 85 26
旋风转轮 308 46
旋冲 288 7
旋花 61 26
旋坯 161 14
旋转 287 18，298 30，3
旋转刀片的锥座 172 75
旋转马达 132 69
旋转飞椅 308 4
旋转切口 184 22
旋转开关 245 28
旋转车顶 213 27
旋转车顶的转向架车 213
旋转分度工作台 150 42
旋转毛刷 168 46
旋转反射镜 243 54
旋转刈辐割草机 63 19
旋转龙头 126 36
旋转扣孔针 100 44
旋转珠击机 148 39
旋转计数器 309 83

盒 114 77
刊幅机 63 26，64
门 213 9
视器支架 27 24
磷石机 158 19
达反射器 224 11
草机 64 46-58
打机 64 13
器 50 69
机 172 23
器 67 4，32，56 43
39 28
302 6
射镜 114 69
铁 85 12
机 146 3
车 64 52
教 215 65
外罩 168 17
诱饵 89 74
式卸载管 64 37
头 50 60，145 10
轮 64 74
246 1
口 235 64
咀 56 44
置 65 73
轮 273 45
轮泵 259 57
台 316 31
板 111 27
26 13，104 27
音阶 320 48
弦 322 30，324 24
盘部分 324 39
虫 357 22
215 69
350 53
床 150 18
232 12，264 3
数 232 13
座 232 23
268 44
口 301 30
253 3，11
253 1，7，259 87，273
293 88
顶 253 10
253 7-11

电站 152 1-28
1 116
象 11 13-28
11 17
维 11 24
板 221 80
车时刻表 204 50
刻简表 204 42
站 15 41，233 34
票 204 36
警报器 270 4
间隙 153 62
点头引擎的剖面图 190 2
73 28
99 59
屏 309 8
烟囱 309 5
218 50
137 5
4 46

火星塞 190 35，242 48
火星塞盖 188 27
火绒草 378 9
火药 87 57
火柴 107 22
火柴头 107 23
火柴盒 107 21
火柴盒架 266 24
火腿 96 1，99 52
火焰形钻子 24 38
火焰调节器 107 31
火煤瓶 364 22
火箱 210 4
火箱主发动机的喷嘴 6 3
火箭炮 306 54
火箭弹 255 26，65，306 54
火箭救生绳 228 3
火箭操纵装置 234 63
灭火枪 221 4
灭火器 196 9
灭菌乳槽 76 16
灭菌器 76 7
灯，(电)灯 106 8
灯光 224 69
灯光师 310 37，316 20
灯光技师 307 4
灯光和鸣笛浮标 224 68
灯光和钟浮标 224 74
灯光标示图 316 3
灯光显示 195 9
灯光装饰字母 268 45
灯光箱 179 25
灯芯 107 29
灯芯绒帽 35 25
灯芯绒鞋帮 101 26
灯芯草 378 26
灯形轮 91 11
灯的托架 177 16
灯架 187 6
灯室 177 41，224 105
灯座 127 60
灯船 15 13，224 81
灯笼袖 31 27，355 49，60
灯笼裤 355 34
灯塔船 221 47
灯蛾 365 7
灯管 350 7
灯(箱)室 112 28，116 29，309
44，312 39-44
钎枪 108 14，141 11
钎接用的鼓风燃烧器 108 16
钎接用的熔接剂 108 36，141 18
钎接导管 142 19
钎接剂 125 7
钎接块(石) 125 6
钎接锤 125 15
钎接喷灯 108 16
钎接棒 108 38
钎接硼砂 108 39
(炊)具 39 12-17
炉门 61，309 7
炉门握把 210 63
炉门盖(罩) 210 60
炉火 267 25
炉内温度计 38 64
炉床 38 66，147 24
炉耙 137 4
炉灶台 266 36
炉灶砖 266 33
炉篦低压风扇 199 33
炮口 255 58
炮车尾活塞 255 55
炮车尾部活塞 255 56
炮托架 255 43
炮尾环 255 54
炮门挡板 218 60

炮塔上雷达控制127毫米多目的炮
258 47
炮管 255 41
炮管夹 255 62
炮管复进机 255 61
炮管摇架 255 60
炼油厂 145 65-74
炼焦厂 144 7-11
炼焦炉电池组 156 8
炼焦炉组 144 7
炼焦炉煤气的处理 156 16-45
炸马铃薯锅 40 41
焙室炉 144 11
烙铁 126 73，134 19
烤肉 45 27
烤肉叉 40 32
烤肉箱 40 32
烤鸡 98 6
烤架 98 33
烤面包机 40 30
烤箱 39 13，97 66
烤面粉 39 14
烘烤配料 98 8-11
烘烤配料和谷类品的陈列架 99 62
烘烤鼓轮 98 71
烘乾机层 92 16-18
烟斗 42 12
烟斗的燃斗 107 36
烟斗刮刀 107 45
烟斗架 42 11
烟斗柄 107 38
烟斗嘴 107 37
烟灰类 306 49-54
烟灰缸 42 29，104 5，208 29，246 33
烟囱 15 38，37 10，38 5，118
21，120 47，122 13，137 7，
152 15，155 12，210 22，221
8，40，75，223 1，258 58，
259 32
烟囱砖 159 28
(烟囱)的通烟道清洁刷 38 35
烟囱标记 223 2
烟囱弯帽 309 6
烟囱砌法 118 66
烟囱清理者 38 31
烟囱道清洁刷 38 35
烟囱帽 258 21，59
烟草厂的真空熏蒸消毒器(机)
83 11
烟草叶 382 43
烟草甲虫 81 25
烟草加压器 107 47
烟草卷 107 18
烟草袋 107 43
烟道 152 12，155 25
烟熏室 96 48
烟管 210 8
烟管除垢针 107 48
烟管除锈器 107 46
烟酒门 107 40
烟咀 107 40
烟灯 45 16，309 45，330
52
烛式悬架 192 72-84
烛灯器 24 43
烧杯 173 8
烧结中央暖气系统 38 44-60
烧结碳化物或氧化陶磁的调整截
割喷咀 141 46
烧焊夹 350 33
烧焦炭的中央暖气系统 38 38
烧碰 169 3
烫平垫 104 28
烫发钳 105 5，106 26
烫金工 183 2
烫金机 183 4

资金压花机 183 26
资袖板 50 20
资滤器 90 45
焰割装置 148 67
焚烧炉 199 29
煤 170 1
煤斗 309 9
煤仓 152 2，156 3
煤水平台 210 2
煤气集中运输 144 45
煤气主管 156 17
煤气压缩机 156 26
煤气冷却 156 29
煤气冷却器 156 19
煤气抽出器 156 21
煤气表 156 31
煤气栓 261 24
煤气干燥 156 30
煤气蓄热室 147 28
煤气罐 144 12
煤尘集收袋 38 34
煤层 144 1-51，225 19
煤矿 144 1-51
煤码头 225 18
煤铲 38 43，137 2
煤干燥蒸馏用的焦化设备 170 2
煤塔 156 5
煤塔运送机 156 4
煤渣坑 152 8
"熄火"信号 286 54
熄焦车 144 11
熄焦塔 144 10
熔工 148 7
熔化设备 148 1-12
熔化的锡 162 17
熔化罐 162 3，14
熔化罐 108 8，170 30
熔炉 178 19
熔岩高原 11 18
熔岩高原 11 14
熔接工作台 142 21
熔接气炬 141 28
熔接台 141 13
熔接电压调节用的脚踏板 142 31
熔接护目镜 141 24
熔接条 141 12
熔接氧炬 141 11
熔接喷咀 141 33
熔断器 127 19，36
熔炉 148 8
熔铁炉 148 1
熔铁流入位置 147 55
熔渣出口 147 9
熔渣流槽 148 12
熔渣槽 147 10
熔解的玻璃原料 162 40
熨斗 104 29
熨斗手把 50 9
熨斗升降装置 103 24
熨斗底板 50 7
熨斗托架 50 18
熨衣工 103 19
熨烫斗 50 4
熨烫用具 50 1-20
熨烫板 104 32
熨烫板 50 16
熨烫板罩布 50 17
熨烫的无纺毛织物 103 27
燃气轮机 209 9
燃气轮机驱动装置 209 8
燃气轮机控制器 209 16
燃气轮机燃料槽 209 17
燃气器 139 3，48
燃油压力表 230 19
燃油压力调节器 190 17
燃油表 191 65

燃油舱

燃油舱 223 80
燃油装置 199 30
燃油装置所用的风扇 199 35
燃油箱 230 48，234 9
燃油器 38 58-60
燃烧送风机 92 17
燃烧室(器) 152 6，232 37
燃烧模 161 4
燃烧器台 162 6，288 80
燃料气 145 52
燃料仓 154 28
燃料电池 234 62
燃料压力调节器 190 17
燃料压力管 190 52
燃料补给车 210 67
燃料单格 190 31
燃料供给管 190 31
燃料船 225 13
燃料液面感测器 234 27
燃料喷射器 190 32
燃料棒 154 4
燃料贮箱 286 25
燃料管道 234 40
燃料输送吊车 154 27
燃料箱 6 7，29，37，65 42，
188，28，189 2，209 20，230
48，234 58
燃料箱吸气管 235 45
燃料槽 212 56，221 71
燃料槽油箱 188 10
爆竹 306 50

心部

心 153 17
心电图分析用的程序选择开关 25 50
心电图仪 23 28
心电图记录装置 25 27
心电图记录器 25 41
心电图节律纸带上的自动分析 25 48
心电图监视器 25 2，21，28，47
心电图振幅控制旋钮 25 49
心皮 59 13，374 2，26
心导管液压计 27 30
心材 120 84，370 13
心形叶 370 35
心形端果 148 37
心房 20 24，45
心室 20 51
心室隔膜 20 52
心轴 125 19，187 60，80
心轴调节 126 32
心脏 18 14，20 8，24-25，45-57
心脏定调器 25 31
心瓣 20 46-47
忍冬属植物 374 13
念珠(玫瑰经) 332 30
念珠串里领主祷文时的大珠子 332 31
急转 301 70
急板 321 28
急速加热阴极 240 25
急流赛艇 283 69
急救包 21 4
急救(包札用的)药品 21 5
急救用的手提心电图仪 23 46
急救药品 21 5
急救站 204 44，308 61
急救绷带法 21 1-13
急下水道 198 27
总开关 153 2，211 3，31，249 37

总水管 198 22
总目录 262 21
总状花序 58 15，370 68，374 33
总肝管 20 37
总苞 59 50
总胆管 20 37-38
总裁签名 251 15
息票 251 17
悬吊长廊 316 5
悬吊式与拉式混合型之舞台幕 315 4
悬吊式舞台幕 315 4
悬吊齿轮 214 72
悬吊物的外壳 168 16
悬吊弹簧 192 74
悬吊装置 214 54
悬吊减震器 192 76
悬吊路灯 268 49
悬饰(浮雕) 335 32
悬垂 296 33
悬挂干燥上的架子 248 40
悬挂式吊球 299 23
悬挂的文件夹 248 3
悬铃木属树 371 67
悬浮钓具 90 29
悬崖 13 28，57
悬崖线 13 25-31
悬蹄，伪蹄 88 23，57
悬臂 226 24，49
悬臂式起重机 222 23
慈菇属植物 378 51
意大利 252 20
意大利产红葡萄酒 98 61
意大利钝剑 294 39
意大利黑麦草 69 26
意大利歌剧中之半假面美女郎 306 27
感光区 77 22
感光板用之干燥台 309 49
感应元件 10 22
感应电疗设备 23 37
感应列车系统 211 7，212 14
感应列车系统用的控制器 211 38
感应式列车控制系统的磁石 212 38
感染霉病的葡萄 80 21
感情线 19 74

户部

户外地下室阶梯 118 4
户外围场 356 1
户外饲槽 62 9
户外笼 356 11
启动程序输入 195 13
启事 342 56
房子 62 1
房间电话 267 34
房间号码的号码牌 267 10
房间服务员 267 33
房间钥匙 267 9
房架 118 1-49
肩 16 22
肩甲 329 44
肩肉 95 50
肩扣 31 15
肩托 255 9，31，39
肩托架 313 37
肩形拱 336 33
肩胛骨 16 7-6
肩胛骨 16 23，17 7，95 30，32
肩部 88 17，38

肩部中弹受伤而后被击毙的雄鹿 86 17
肩铁 38 33
肩倒立 295 29
肩端 122 10
肩袋 29 56
肩隆 70 17
肩落地 298 12
肩胛肉 95 9
肩臂甲 329 45
扁方形 346 38
扁平肋骨 95 21
扁平钳 137 27
扁凹头 137 31
扁条 143 10
扁豆，马豆 69 15
扁桃体 19 23
扁凿 140 26
扁钮锯 140，140 27
扁圆钳 126 62
扇子 353 42
凤风机风道 144 22
扇形 346 54
扇形贝壳 309 46
扇形尾 73 29
扇形尾羽 88 75
扇形快门开度控制 313 8
扇形喷雾嘴 83 4
扇状拱顶 336 46

礻部

礼仪用之器皿 332 34-54
礼服手绸 33 10
礼服和上衣的组合装 31 6
礼袍，法衣 332 4
礼帽 35 12
礼貌式钱 324 50
社论 342 48
祈祷之教徒 330 61
祈祷书 330 62
视网膜 19 49
视场透镜 115 40
视场照明 112 47
视神经 19 51，77 24
视神经纤维 77 23
视准管 351 30
视频标码站 236 39
视频磁头 243 26
视频磁头运动方向 243 30
视频磁轨 243 31
神父 330 39，331 47
神社前之牌坊 337 11
神话人物 306 65
神话中之动物 327 1-61
神庙入口 337 27
神庙围墙 334 6
神庙塔楼 333 32
神经系统 18 22-23
神经和血管 19 33
神殿入口 334 7
神龛雕像 354 17
福哉玛利亚 332 32

王部

王 276 8，305 13
王子冠 254 40
王后墓穴 333 3
王冠 254 37，42，355 21
王冠与冠饰 254 37-46
王室坟墓 333 1
王宫外阶梯 333 33

王莲属植物 378 17
玉米 68 31
玉米收割台 64 35
玉米粒 68 37
玉米螟 81 28
玉米穗轴 68 36
环 301 7，305 31，346 5
环己酮的形成 170 20，22
环节 357 25
环扣 30 41
环形 302 15
环形软片剂量计 2 11
环形胡须 34 15
环形众磨带 133 15
环形座位 281 38
环形蛋糕 97 33，99 22
环形琴弦 324 27
环形格局 71 50
环形雏箱 305 50
环形瞄准器及准星 305 51
环形瞄准眼链 132 50
环状阀 302 15
环状发生腰带 270 45
环纹蛇 364 38
环带 357 26
环梁 121 38，70
环管 357 19
环管纱 165 15
环礁 13 32
玫瑰耳 70 2
玫瑰花式切割 36 45
玫瑰花饰 306 34
玫瑰花布 60 16
玫瑰花刺 60 18
现代人的头颅 261 21
现代苔藓泥沼层 13 20
现代雪屐的层次 301 46
现代雕刻 272 64
现金出纳机 47 34
现金抽屉 271 5
现金数目显示器 196 4
玩具 48 21-32
玩具卡车 47 38，273 62
玩具电话 47 35
玩具动物 47 6
玩具店 47 27
玩具挖土机 273 65
玩具鸭 28 10，49 4，273 3
玩具娃娃车 47 10
玩具娃娃 48 31
玩具熊 28 46，273 26，309
玩偶匣 306 56
玩滚木球者 305 22
珍珠 36 8，357 35
珍珠王冠 355 16
珍珠母层 357 34
珍珠矿华阶地 11 23
珍珠项链 36 32
珊瑚虫 357 19
珊瑚项链 36 34
珊瑚群体 357 18
珊瑚礁 13 32
珐琅质 19 30
玳瑠 364 28
玳瑁耳 111 8
玻璃刀 124 25-26
玻璃门 44 18
玻璃工人 124 8，162 38
玻璃工人坐椅 162 45
玻璃片 54 9
玻璃反射镜 187 86
玻璃水杯 48 8
玻璃布 130 29
玻璃丝 130 42
玻璃灯泡 127 57
玻璃匠工作房 124 1

[124 21
尺圆规 124 22
角尺 124 20
124 18
124 9
151 48
身 193 14
丝 162 52
品 162 56-58
的生产 162 48-55
曾强合成树脂制造的滚筒
130 17
聚酯树脂造成的贮储
130 17
燎 151 47
9 46
162 38-47
179 15
274 16
架 266 9
356 15
162 58
135 25
55 5
天井 271 11
369 12
340 48
124 19
进给装置 162 13
155 33
269 56
124 10
37 16
162 49
画 260 69
55 17
271 62
36 31
3 27
128 30
直 54 27
324 29
具 165 1-16
镜子 105 20,106 6
105 35,106 1
233 53
105 7,106 34
14 60,42 15,224 8,
头 115 48
各种座架 113 16-25
放大镜 113 38
瞄准器 87 29,255 28
273 11,282 46,291 35,
7,302 37
291 5
291 7
291 37
291 38
木 291 36
277 9
头 277 10
277 19
277 14
291 1
盒 293 36
347 41
标 90 19
221 45
267 4
圆围 336 3
梨形 36 82-86
272 12
头 114 47
灰缸 266 5
盒 222 74

球形瓣饰柱头 333 14
球形罐 221 36
球果轴 372 3
球衫 291 56
球拍夹 293 32
球拍把手 293 30
球拍柄 293 46
球洞 293 87
球盖甘蓝 57 26
球轴承 187 56
球面槽 108 7
球面槽 145 73
球桌 273 2
球桌四边的橡皮衬垫 277 16
球座 293 90
球根秋海棠 51 19
球蓟 51 19
球棒 292 62,75
球童 293 22
球帽 292 10
球鞋 292 10
斑马 366 27
斑鸠 359 23
斑砂岩降侧 154 61
斑点啄木鸟 359 27
琶音 321 22
琴弓 322 24,323 12
琴马 322 17,323 5
琴头 322 10
琴舌 322 52
琴身 323 3
琴身板 325 6
琴弦 225 7,322 44
琴拨 324 20
琴轸 323 18,324 19
琴轸头 323 19
琴弦 324 5
琴颈 323 2,324 7,18
琴槌杆 325 3
琴槌 325 15
琴键 322 28,38,49,326 8
琴键之机械装置 325 22-39
瑞士币(法郎 252 15
瑞士五针松果球 372 29
瑞士乳酪 99 41
瑞典卷 97 19
瑞典:1克郎=100欧耳 252 25
瑞香属植物 377 10

韦部

韧皮 370 9
韩文 341 27

木部

木乃伊 352 21
木马 296 17
木工工作场 120 4
木工工具 120 60-82
木工车床 51,135 1
木工台 132 29-37
木工用铅笔 120 77
木工用锤 120 74
木工场 120 1-59
木工(匠) 120 12,132 38
木工粘着剂 134 36
木片 324 62
木片包装机 172 3
木片条 136 11
木片条篮子 136 11
木心板 120 93
木头 260 82
木块 339 27
木杆 326 9

木钉 121 92
木条 71 41
木条量尺(规) 122 18
木材的屋顶结构 121 27-83
木材的道路运输 85 42
木材接合 121 84-98
木材堆支座 157 37
木齿 91 9
木板 118 87,119 16
木板门 37 34
木板支架 117 30
木板平台 118 28
木板堆 120 1,157 25
木板输运车 157 16
木板墙 120 9
木板壁 38 19
木质板 338 23
木质浮标 90 6
木制三脚架 313 13
木制手车 309 86
木制开口音管 326 31-33
木制火车列车 273 27
木制火车轨 47 37,48 29
木制投掷器 353 8
木制玩具 260 80
木制品 260 72
木制面具 354 16
木制绝缘套 10 26
木制草耙 66 23
木制铲 91 24
木制球杆 293 91
木制帽箱传送滚轮 163 32
木制塑型工具 339 10
木制模型建筑物 48 28
(木制)鞋型 100 32
木制镶瓜 266 37
木刻(木版印刷) 340 1-13
木刻用的木纹板 340 1
木刻用的油墨 260 83
木刻用之厚木板 340 2
木刻家 339 28
木刻浮雕像之托板 340 2
木底鞋 101 44
木套箱 355 43
木星 4 48
木栅栏 37 53
木炭 278 48
木莓 370 101
木钻 120 65
木屑,刨花 120 80,135 26
木屑去除器 157 50
木屑抽除装置 157 51
木贼属的一种 376 18
木梯 273 22
木梯及扶手栏杆 38 25
木桶 55 48,91 27
木桶板条 130 9
木桶的撞条 130 8
(木桶的)塞子 130 7
木匙组 40 2
木槌 118 54,120 67,125 18,
132 5,278 25,339 21
木锥 134 8,260 55
木凿刀 339 19
木嵌板 281 19
木琴 324 61
木棉树 383 20
木楔 132 19
木碰垫 218 26
木管乐器 323 28-38
木鞋底 101 45
木雕 260 77
木螺纹 143 47
木螺丝 122 101,132 41,143
45
木螺钻 64 6

木髓 370 14
杀牛 319 30
权杖 254 31
杂志 22 4,46 20
杂货铺 98 1-87
杂耍 308 24
杂种三叶草 69 3
机力锯 85 13
机力锤 137 9
机力螺丝攻 150 44
机工(榫头)锯 140 23
机车正视图 212 51-67
机车平面图 211 10-18
机车锅炉和驱动装置 210
2-37
机内麦克风 243 3
机内定时器开关 243 18
机台 340 41
机长座椅 235 17
机电控制的轨道飞行主发动机
235 44
机关炮 256 3
机动刈草机 56 28
机动性火箭 6 5
机动绞车 85 7
机身 230 54,288 26
机身附件 235 4
机身油箱 257 31
机尾发动机 231 10
机尾板 164 26
机库 287 14
机场 233 24
机场消防站 233 7
机场餐厅 233 19
机匣盖 255 10
机油 196 15
机背 114 54
机背标准调整装置 114 55
机型超大型油轮 221 1
机架(台) 65 90,112 2,115
98,139 19,148 57,167 33,
175 50,177 11
机舱 230 56
机座 177 57
机脚 100 23,133 25
机密文件 246 25
机械台 112 10,29
机器部分 111 30
机械铲 118 81
机械排字条 174 27
机械装置和了望台 224 107
机械滚转分离器 64 75
机械操作手车 159 18
机械操纵杆 167 44
机窗 117 64
机摇臂 150 24
机器锁 313 33
机器人 273 36
机器外壳 200 2
机器房 62 15
机器送出的织品 168 9
机器底座 168 15,54
机器罩 173 27
机翼 230 43,288 27
机翼下油箱 256 4
机翼内侧支承 257 34
机翼外侧支承 257 35
机翼后缘 287 37
机翼形状 229 15-22
机翼前缘 287 34
机翼的配置 229 1-14
机翼整体油箱 257 29
杜尔富座 300 30
杜松(树) 372 47
杜松果 372 52
杜鹃鸟 359 30

829

杜鹃花　53 12
极　14 3
极北气候　9 56
极光　7 37
极地气候　9 57-58
极地风带　9 51
极地雪橇　303 18
极地起重机　154 38
极轴　113 18
极轴主驱动装置　113 18
极高频全向导航台无线电定向仪
　230 15
极圈　14 11
李树　59 19-23
李树叶　59 21
李核　59 23
杆　303 5，307 46
杆刃　302 32
杆顶安全台　145 3
杆顶滑车　145 4
杆柄　302 31
杆枪　258 42，259 6
杆盖　322 27
杆袋　283 64
杏仁　59 35
杏仁　45 41
杏花　59 34
杏树　59 33-36
杏树叶　59 36
条件报告　195 7
条纹　291 25
条纹土狼　368 1
条纹套头羊领衫　30 20
条板　284 44
条板箱　76 30，206 5
条播机　65 74
条播犁刀(头)　65 76
材料　260 81
材料仓库　146 6
材料架　100 36
杠上外向正坐　296 31
杠外侧坐　296 32
村庄　15 105
构架　230 55，139 16
构架台　132 62
构架式船台　222 19-21
构轴(框架)　120 48
枪口闪光遮盖器　255 18
枪机　87 9
枪托　87 3，4，6，13
枪托的腰部　87 7
枪托底板　87 14
枪身活板架　87 28
枪刷，擦膛刷　87 62
枪柄　255 6
枪栓　94 4
枪栓柄　87 22
枪眼　329 18
枪眼与枪眼间之凸壁　329 7
枪膛　87 54
枪管　255 2，17，33
枪管夹　255 11
枪管壳　87 35
枪膛轴　87 38
枪膛清扫绳　87 64
枕头　27 27，43 12-13，47 4
枕机　18 50，19 2
枕套　43 12
枕骨　17 32
枕骨部　16 2
枢机主教用之十字架　332 65
枢机　106 36
枢轴原木卡钩　157 29
板　120 96
板片状甲　329 65

板石铺砌　123 26
板材　120 91
板条　123 70，71
板条用的连续轧钢机　148 66-75
板条斧　122 21
板状矽藻土计量器　93 3
板刻　340 4
板架　44 19，178 35
板桩墙　119 17，217 5
板球　292 70-76
松土机　200 20
松木象鼻虫　82 41
松节油分离器　172 14
松纸杆　249 20
松果　372 26
松树　372 20
松树乔　122 21
松树天蛾　82 27
松树蛾　82 28
松香(脂)　323 11
松紧带镶边　31 43
松紧腰带　31 63
松紧螺旋扣　202 31
松散岩石床　158 4
松散浮沙　171 41
松鼠　366 19
林中小道　84 3
林务局　15 3
林地　84 1-34
林间小路　15 102
林间车道　84 1
林班　84 2
林诺铸版机　174 19
柜子　246 20
柜台　47 28，207 31，265 1，
　266 1-11
柜台的收银抽屉　207 86
柜台店员　265 7
枝条　274 2
枝条架　274 1
枞球果　372 2
果心　58 36，59
果仁　58 60
果仁糖　98 85
果汁　98 18，266 58
果肉　58 24，58
果树篮子　52 8
果串　58 11
果序(列)　371 22，44，72，
　373 8，374 18，384，32
果序和果实　371 69
果枝　371 3，11，18，31，36，
　41，47，50，56，64，372 40，
　51，59，63，66，70，382 2，
　37，383 34，384 38
果岭　293 82
果实　58 28，371 4，19，28，
　45，372 53，64，373 12，18，
　22，27，29，32，374 4，19，
　25，29，31，34，375 4，7，
　10，13，17，24，378 3，42，
　376 3，6，14，378 38，42，
　382 15，24，383 14，18，
　21，28，32，40，52，59，
　384，26，39，45
果实采集器　56 22
果实序　61 15
果类　370 91-102
果球　372 41
果菜园　52 1-32
果菜园小路　52 23
果酱　98 52
果鳞　372 8，14，27，38，67
枫树　371 53
析色器　116 36

析色器灯　116 37
相机　112 20
相机之暗匣　177 10
相机机身　177 25，33
相似于　345 22
相纸类　116 50
栅栏　37 53，75 5，99 5，199
　13，202 40，329 36
栏　185 65
栏外标题　185 66
栏杆　37 19，75 5，118 89，
　123 22，50，215 70，221
　122，266 72，272 34，
栏杆柱　38 29，123 43，51
栏栅　121 54
栏栅梁　121 67
栏架　298 8
栎子　276 42
柿毛虫　80 1
柿量尺蠖　80 16
架子　307 57
架空电线　194 43
架空线　197 42
架空式投影器　242 6
架空线　197 41
架空线支架　152 36
架空线接触点　197 40
架空喷洒设备　169 29
架柱　222 27
架锯　120 61
柏油纸板屋顶　122 90
柏油贮槽　200 47
柏油混合筒　200 50
柏油喷洒车　200 46
柏油路的典型横断面　200 55
柏油路面　200 58
柏树　372 58
柳叶菜科　53 3
柳条　136 6，14
柳条织品图案　171 11
柳条球拍　305 69
柳穿鱼　376 26
柳珊瑚　369 8
柳薄荷　374 5
柔性刀片　85 20
柔道　299 13-17
柔道选手　299 14
柔道摔　299 17
柠檬水玻璃杯　265 16
柠檬果皮蜜饯　98 10
柠檬树　384 23
染色大水桶　130 15
染色皿　23 50
染色喷雾器　100 35
染液浸槽　165 47
柱门　292 78
柱子(形)模架　119 11，73
柱头　58 41，59 16，334 20-
　25，370 56
柱导槽　139 42
柱身　333 27，334 26
柱顶凹槽　334 30
柱顶线盘　334 52
柱座　112 32
柱基　334 28-31，32
柱脚　334 31
柱廊　274 9，334 50，56，67
柱塞　145 23，162 32，192 7
柱塞背负负喷雾机　83 43
柱梢　162 32
柱(撑柱)　78 7，120 25，121
　40，81，335 20，34
栈台　225 63
栈桥　278 13

栈桥绳　122 67
标尺调整器　116 34
标记　191 12
标示记录走棋位置的棋盘□
　数字　276 6
标码台　236 35
标线片　87 31-32
标线片调整具螺丝　87 30
标志符号　342 16-29
标语牌　263 13
标准小口径步枪　305 43
标准子午线　14 5
标准时　36 48
标准台式电话　237 6
标准平板车　213 5
标准传统式切割　36 49
标准环形锭子　164 45
标准规格电影摄影片　313
标准单字排字机　174 32
标准螺纹和粗牙螺纹手柄
标准钟　245 18
标准砖　118 58
标准圆形切割　36 42-43
标准装置　114 51
标准梨形　36 54
标准桃形　36 56
标准敞篷货车　213 8
标准赛车　290 38
标准镜头　115 3-8，46，□
标签　54 4
标题　185 62
标题栏　151 31
柄　66 17，114 37，370 □
柄眼　357 30
查号台　237 33
查里曼王朝的小写字体　34
查普襟翼　229 50
树　272 59，370 1
树干　84 19，370 2，7
树干剥皮　85 23
树木支柱　52 31
树皮　120 86，370 8
树皮下的坑道　82 23-24
树皮刮刀　56 14
树皮刮削　56 23
树身　84 19
树形蛋糕　97 46
树林　272 61
树顶　370 4
树枝　370 5
树枝形吊灯　267 21
树的保护栏　118 80
树苗圃　55 3，84 6
树冠　370 3，384 29
树架　37 33
树桩　84 14
树莓花　58 26
树莓矮灌木　58 25
树梢　272 60
树辐　364 24
树篱修剪机　134 55
桌子　27 31
桌之高度和角度之调整器　17
桌上三角架　115 99
桌上文具　246 9
桌历式日记簿　247 32
桌布　45 2
桌面　246 11
桌饰　266 78
桌面　44 3，246 3
桌垫　246 6，260 25
桌球　273 1，5，293 45-55
桌球员　293 49
桌球网　273 3，293 53
桌球球拍　273 4，293 46

3 26，275 30
重底 222 60
329 24
477 4
33 50
316 4
258 18
215 63
235 12
254 8
159 28
55 49
7，123 11，226 40
61
座 119 50
216 8
79
潜艇 259 54
34
154 19
内受控制的链式反应 1
防护罩 259 67
99，382 51
59 1-36
43
59 37-43
97 35
，68 17，370
78-82
18，370 18
57 27
81
18
80 27
68 38-45
9 46
垫板 133 34
51
6 22，149 65
124 3
119 64
124 2
机 133 34
窝 77 45-50
披 136 22-24
装置 133 48
278 36
133 43
3 26
光程 115 36
40 43
4 23
柄 161 2
整用的控制器 113 34
气闸 113 33
8，278 19，283 14，
353 14
3 12
83 38
83 35
78 18，283 29，41
83 37
230 33
1-9，221 77，284 4
84 11
台 223 38
284 20
索 284 18
84 14
223 37
行 284 13
219 16
24，193 21，325 22
20 87
21 33
119 56

桁条 121 39，51，76
桁架 215 3
桁架节点 215 37
桁架式橡屋顶 121 34
桁架构件 215 24
桁架拱 215 25
桁架拱析 215 25
桁架塔 155 43
桦木牛肝菌 381 22
桦树 59 31
桃子 59 31
桃派 97 22
桃色 59 27
桃金娘料 53 11
桃树 59 26-32
桃树叶 59 32
档位 192 47
档位调整手柄 132 66
校正板 113 11
校正钮头 115 72
校音器 325 27
校音器之铁丝杆 325 29
校音器毡 325 28
校样 340 43
校准压力调节器 185 5
栗子 371 60
栗色牛肝菌 381 15
桡动脉 18 21
桡侧伸腕长肌 18 56
桡侧屈肌 18 40
桡神经 18 28
桥门架 215 38
桥支架 222 12
桥拱 215 27，29，45
桥式 295 19，299 9
桥式升降台 316 34
桥式通道 147 38
桥的半翘旋部分 215 66
桥面板 215 6
桥脑 17 46
桥梁支承 215 55
桥梁横断面 215 1
桥塔 215 42
桥墩 215 21，54
桥撑 215 30
桥翼 215 16
栽植橘树的温室 272 3
栖木 86 49
柴油 145 56
柴油火车头 212 1-84
柴油火车头驾驶室 212 5
柴油发电机 259 94
柴油发电机装置 209 5
柴油发动机 211 47，212 25
柴油发动机的剖面图 190 4
柴油机电力推进(驱动) 223
68-74
柴油轨道列车 208 13
柴油液压火车头 212 1，24
柴油输入过滤器 146 26
柴油槽 146 13
柴篮 309 10
梨(子) 58 33，99 87
梨花 58 38
梨形的榅桲 58 50
梨形铅锤 89 90
梨果 370 102
梨果肉 58 35
梨果类植物 58 31-61
梨果梗 58 34
梨的小种子 58 37
梨树 58 31
梨树枝 58 32
梢 121 93
梢捆 216 53
梯子 21 32，47 5，38 15，118
42，211 43，217 8

梯子两侧的直条框 50 36
梯子竖框 38 16
梯子脚蹬横木 38 17
梯头钩 122 15，69
梯形 346 37
梯形交叉状切割 36 58
梯形阶状切割 36 57
梯形塔楼 333 32
梯架 118 86-89
梯架立柱 118 86
梯架踏板 50 38
梵文 341 9
梵蒂冈市：10里拉 252 21
检车锤 205 40
检讨(分析)管装置 112 22
检字手盘 174 13
检查员 205 44
检查室 38 62
检查箱容量观察口 64 27
检疫所 225 27
检修出入孔 38 45
检修出入孔盖 38 46
检修员 205 39
检验食品用的浸渍折射计 112 48
检验器 37 20
检眼镜 22 62
检管装置 112 22
梗 102 4
梗形线迹 102 4
梳子 28 8
梳妆台 43 25，105 19
梳妆台镜 43 29
梳妆凳子 43 24
梳理缠结的发刷 105 2
梳梯机 163 34
梳梯机的拉箱 163 60
梳梯机的拉条 163 51
梳梯机梳条 163 38
梳棉滚筒 163 68
梳棉罐之柱杆 163 36
梭子 166 26
梭子鱼 364 17
梭子鱼孵化瓶 89 17
梭口 166 40
梭织的绕线轮(梭) 102 20
梭结花边 102 18，19
梭道 166 40
梭眼 166 29
桶 130 5
桶身 130 6
桶形 36 75
桶钩 122 23
桶栽植物 55 47
桶盖 130 10
斜桁 383 16
棣棠 373 28
棉花 383 16
棉花供给 163 1-13，9
棉花捆包商标 163 6
棉纱花边 31 32
棉绒进给 164 15
棉条并合 164 5
棉条筒 164 3，20
棉绒卷筒 104 9
棉卷支架 163 15
棉被 43 8
棉箱的开关杆 163 31
桶绒给棉机 163 33
森林 84 1-34
森林砍伐 84 15-37
椅子 42 34，46 27
(椅子)的座部 44 11
椅式雪橇 304 29
椅套 207 48
椰子 383 53
椰子油 98 23
椰子树 383 48

植物 370 15
植物架 248 13
棕色 343 5
棕色水母 369 5
棕色环牛肝菌 381 21
棕榈叶饰 334 41
棕榈形柱头 333 25
棕榈形圆柱 333 17
棕榈树丛 354 5
棕熊 368 10
棋钟 276 16
棋格式图案 335 14
棋盘 47 20
棋盘状切割 36 66
棋盘和原位的棋子 276 1
棺木 331 35
棺架 331 41
棺室 333 5
棕鸟 361 4
槌头 126 78，134 7，40
棒 297 41
棒状闪光灯 114 75
棒球 292 40-69，61
棒球运动员 292 59-60
棒球场 292 40-58
椭圆 347 22
椭圆六边交叉状切割 36 63
椭圆平台型 36 72
椭圆凸圆形 36 80
椭圆形气泡浮标 89 47
椭圆形铅锤 89 88
椭圆形黑皮李子 59 20
椭圆形模板 151 71
椭圆形翼 229 15
椭圆的焦点 347 25
椭圆柱图模板 151 71
椭圆舳 218 25
楔 158 7
楔块 119 15，158 7
楔形切口 54 38
楔形文字 341 8
楔形后脚 101 55
楔形阶 123 31
楔形垫枕 43 11
楔形薄块 119 40
椴树 58 46
椴树叶 58 47
槌 324 64
槌杆 325 26
槌柄 325 25
槌球 292 77-82，82
槌球员 292 80
槌球的长柄木槌 292 81
槌鲸 367 23
楼 121 28，36，122 19
楼支撑屋簷 37 9
楼头 121 45，122 41
楼屋顶 121 27
棚(框顶) 120 58
榆树 371 49
椴科植物 53 9
楼层指示器 271 49
楼板 120 36
楼板填料 123 69
楼座 330 25
楼梯井 120 46
楼梯灯 41 22
楼梯间 37 72
楼梯间盖(板) 118 72
楼梯(间)窗(户) 37 81，123
65
楼梯栏杆柱 123 78
楼梯斜梁 38 26
楼梯最低梯级 123 42
楼梯最高梯级 123 19
楼梯端柱 123 54
楼梯踏板 123 32，47

楼梯踢脚板 123 33，48
楼梯螺栓 123 46
模 173 48
模仿摩托车前叉 188 58
模拟牛 319 3
模拟斗牛 319 1
模拟臭迹 289 48
模拟输出 112 45
模板 119 18，123 10
模板支撑 119 13
模板和钢筋 119 54-76
模板储藏抽屉 245 10
模板矮花门 129 43
模砂 148 35
模型 148 1
模型飞机 273 37，38，288 85-91
模型师 339 6
模特儿台 338 30
榫眼 137 29
榫眼斧 120 72
榫眼和榫接 121 84
榫眼凿 132 8
榫帽 132 44
榫实 59 49
榛树 59 44-51
榛树叶 59 7
柠檬酸 40 9
榨葡萄的运输机 78 16
槟榔子 380 20
槟榔树 380 19
横木 119 61
横栏 218 21，219 55-66
横列计数器 167 43
横向运送机 157 20
横向坡度 200 57
横向铣轴 150 12
横向滑台 150 12
横杆 108 5，192 70，297 4，298 14，34
横杆球关节 192 80
横杠 296 3，8
横坑 144 30
横担 152 37
横钉的木板壁 37 84
横折叠刀 185 12
横坐标轴 347 2
横坐标值 347 9
横轴 230 68
横结肠 20 20
横梁 119 57，61，222 15
横流道 148 21
横舵柄 283 51
横断双滑道 301 68
横断锯 120 14
横幕 263 12
横滑台 149 23，39
横管 119 48
横截轴 347 23
横膈膜 20 9
横撑 119 12
横脚腿 295 15
樱树 373 30
樱桃 59 5，6-8
樱桃叶 59 2
樱桃肉 59 6
樱桃花 59 3，9
樱桃苍蝇 80 18
樱桃派 97 22
樱桃树 59 1-18
樱桃核 59 7
威树 371 53
橄榄头探针 22 53
橄榄形探针 26 40
橄榄油 98 24
橄榄树 383 29

橄榄球 292 19，21，27
橄榄球员 292 23
槽 336 48
槽口刨 132 25
槽式拱顶 336 47
槽沟 291 29
槽形卷轴 116 2
槽顶 92 45
槽钢 202 32
槽铁 143 7
樑树 380 18
橡皮奶嘴 28 20
橡皮洗片滑杆 117 35
橡皮动物 280 33
橡皮固定螺丝 187 84
橡皮护腿 289 32
橡皮固定装置 286 57-58
橡皮块 187 85
橡皮衬套 192 67
橡皮衬垫圆盘 134 22
橡皮垫圈 122 103
橡皮弹簧 297 13
橡皮圈 40 26
橡皮滚轮 182 8
橡皮滚筒 180 24，37，54，63，79
橡皮糖 98 84，308 18
橡树 371 1
橡树卷叶蛾 82 43
橡胶连接密封圈 207 8，208 12
橡胶轮胎 273 19
橡胶轮胎秋千 273 18
橡胶轮胎缆索车 273 53
橡胶网 383 33
橡胶护板 114 45
橡胶溶液 340 49
橡胶滚筒 116 49
橘子 384 27
橘皮蜜饯 98 11
橘花 384 25
橘乳菌盖 381 29
橱柜 267 15
橱柜底座部分 42 6
橱窗 268 10
橱窗陈列品 268 11
橱窗摆饰 268 12
橙 343 7
秦吾属之杂草 61 12

犬部
犬齿 19 17
犬蔷薇 373 26

歹部
残月 4 7
残油 145 43
残株田地 63 33
残屑输送器 64 80

车部
车门 186 11，191 4，207 20，22
车门把手 186 12，191 5
车门锁 191 6
车内后视镜 191 39
车夫座位 186 8
车对车装卸方式 225 41
车对车搬运 226 7
车立方柱 85 30，47
车头标记 187 15
车灯 186 9

车后部 193 35
车杠 186 19，30
车把 187 2，188 45
车把主干 187 10
车把配件 188 30-35
车把握套 187 3
车身 186 5，207 2
车身用锤 195 46
车库 37 79
车库车道 37 52
车床工 135 20
车床工厂 135 1-26
车床工具 149 45-53
车床床身 149 31
车床尾座 135 7
车床尾座顶尖 149 26
车床轴 149 20
车床牵引具 149 54
车床脚架 149 12
车场无线电天线 213 4
车间过道 207 19
车尾机架 165 14
车尾闸板 193 16，195 50
车体固定板 192 72
车位号码 195 48
车顶开口 213 23
车顶行李架 278 50
车顶通风口 278 57
车顶捆捆 278 51
车轮 191 14
车轮定位检查灯 195 21
车轮和转向调整试验设备 195 17
车轮轴 62 20
车轮螺帽 187 53
车垫 191 43
车架 187 14-20，305 88
车架横杆 187 16
车胎 191 15
车钟 224 25
车钟和汽笛 212 49
车削刀具 135 14，15，24
车轴轴承 210 10
车铃 187 4
车站书报摊 204 26
车站内邮筒 204 11
车站时钟 204 18
车站领班 205 41
车站餐厅 204 13
车梯 197 15
车厢加热压力计 210 44
车票日期印刷机 204 40
车辆码头 15 47
车窗 186 10，207 52，208 8
车锁 187 49
车缝线 30 17
车缝饰纹 30 31
车辕 186 19，30
车箱灯开关和里程记录器归按零钮 191 77
车篷 47 12
轧光机 173 36
轧光滚轮 173 26，38
轧钢厂 148 46-75
轧票机 197 16
轨条扣件 202 9
轨条接头 202 11
轨底 202 4
轨辙监视器 25 54
轨枕 119 39，205 60
轨道 205 59-61
轨道工作室 235 66
轨道飞行器之后连接件 235 49
轨道巡视员 204 44
轨道式砂磨机 134 53
轨道和信号指示器 203 64

轨道检查车 213 32
轨腹 202 3
轨槽 217 70
轫块 138 12，143 100
轫柄 143 99
轫带 143 105
轫鼓 138 11
轫滑轮 143 98
转子 190 68，275 32
转子叶 155 45
转写式复印机 245 7
转台 161 1，226 56，2
转台上轴场 161 16
转台手动控制的信号 115
转向(车)架 152 41
转向头 187 11
转向机柱 192 56
转向把手 255 48
转向齿轮 192 56-59
转向架 119 32，197 9，212 2，213 13
转(向)轴 192 78
转向轮上的橡胶轮胎 64
转向逆风行驶 285 9
转向指示灯 189 37，45
转向指示灯和危险闪光灯的灯号 191 76
转向指示灯和前灯减光开关 59
转向垂臂 192 59
转向调整检查灯 195 22
转向翼缝 187 14
转向翼缝 288 29
转向臂 192 79
转动起重机 222 21
转动筒 187 73
转动滚筒的自动释压踏板
转身 298 24
转身裁判员 282 26
转轮 186 11
转轮，转子 224 55
转炉 89 77
转炉整体炉底 147 47
转速计数指示器 166 2
转速选择器 241 29，62
转速表 189 41，212 22
转接器 242 34
转弯时边车的配合动作 29
'转弯'信号 286 52
转弯指示器 230 12
转换开关 50 59
转换器 202 17
转换箱 237 25
转盘 145 15，178 26，19 31，204 37，215 64，2 20，275 31
转塔 149 40
转塔式车床 149 38
转帽式风车 91 29
转速表 212 22，230 8
转满圈之船形秋千 308 42
转播之船形秋千 308 42
转播 239 1-15
转播车内部设备 239 6
转播车电话 239 13
转播车后面装组部分 239
转辙号志 202 19
转辙杆 203 55
转辙指示器 197 39
转辙器 202 29
转辙器上可移动的短轨条(尖) 202 21
转辙器闸 202 28
转辙器拉线 202 30
转辙器和信号按钮 203 62

号 197 38，203 45-52
明 志 202 33
14
式的夹皮 31 42
4，110 11
间 222 8
152 22
65 1
83
用的一弧型版铸造 178 21
机之着墨装置 181 57
切割机 184 20
器 65 81
189 25，191 16，
87 30
计 196 17
面 189 27
87 61，76
力机构 212 28
212 3，213 3
几构 64 58
03 57
会 200 23
275 1-33
托盘 275 29
转轮 275 10，28
表 275 9，17
客 275 15
桌 275 8
球 275 33
189 25
187 26
143 88，187 27，
24
纹接管 187 29
340 10
159 8
2 10，176 25
动复制机 176 28
描用的软片自动显影机 72
量计 2 8
眼光板用的照相室 113 40
112 65，313 9
之长闸中 318 30
巴 89 50
生衣 228 9
帮 101 46
头袋 115 105
飞 59 42
17 11
为 95 2，15-16
磁碟读取机 244 8
动物 357 27-36
具动物 46 13
元具狗 47 7
291 27
座位 208 25
靠背座椅 207 44
呢帽 35 15，22
芯 87 56
221 91
50 75，118 38，196 2，
0 54
分接头 270 32
连接头 270 29
接头 56 45，83 30
卷 287 27
卷轴 270 28
联结 83 30
143 61，150 27，187 81，
2 56
成对的穿吊 171 9

轴包架 223 59
轴向—径向轴承 113 3
轴承杯 187 68
轴承座 143 65，177 61
轴承颈 143 64
轴流式抽水机 217 47-52
轴道 223 66
轴颈 143 63
轴打区 293 86
轻合金车轮 189 48
轻快帆船 218 27-43
轻快的四轮敞篷马车 186 38
轻质上滚子 164 18
轻纤维板 123 58
轻武器 87 2，255 1-39
轻便之风琴 322 56
轻便手提箱 267 15
轻便火水壶 270 61
轻便式录影机 243 4
轻便轨道列车 208 13
轻便的平底半高跟布鞋 101 54
轻便套鞋 101 41
轻便泵 270 52
轻便铁路 200 23
轻便铁路柴油机车 200 24
轻便盔 329 61
轻型马车(舆) 289 23-40
轻型马赛跑道 289 23
轻型弓锯 127 52
轻型军刀 294 34
轻型多用途直升机 232 11
轻型划船 283 9-15
轻型货车 194 5
轻型炮架型车架 189 17
轻型战舰 258 1-63
轻型高射机枪 255 63
轻型摩托车 188 39，189 1
轻勒 289 12
轻量锚 286 16-18
轻跳 314 22
轻熏腌物 145 39
轻燃料油 145 58
轻机械体操 297 33-50
载人气球到达高度 7 16
载人雪橇 353 18
载货之动物 354 3
载货车 226 4
载货车台 18 21
载货台 194 3
载货卡车 226 19
(载)带物架 187 44
较大的地狱虎耳草 69 28
辅机 223 71
辅机房 223 70
辅机舱 259 56
辅助马达用的电容器 211 17
辅助工作台 137 14，150 28
辅助反射镜 115 38
辅助火电机 211 33
辅助白灯 203 15
辅助托车 157 11
辅助制动阀 211 23
辅助制动器 212 10
辅助系统用的可见显示 211 34
辅助肚管 71 23
辅助贮气器 212 61
辅助信号 203 25-44
辅助降落伞舱 235 59
辅助舱 6 2，259 56
辅助舰 258 92-97
辅助柴油发动机 209 19
辅助起重吊车 147 61
辅助接触 153 57
辅助机械和学校 296 12-21

辅助器械和学校俱乐部体操器械 297 7-14
辅助缆索 214 47
辅助缆索拉紧装置 214 48
辅助臂形号志臂 203 8
辅絮 330 40，331 45
辊子架 148 56-60
输入/输出装置 237 59
输入选择开关 238 49
输入选择器 241 44
输水软管 237 59
输水道(桥) 334 53
输水管 269 49，52
输片齿轮 115 26
输片滑轮 117 34
输出齿轮箱 212 53
输电线 154 16
输电线路 154 16
输纸轮 180 4
输尿管 20 32
输送小车 74 39
输送机 118 77
输送阀 67 9
输送带 169 32
输送带(器、机) 118 77，182 30，225 51
输送滚轮 164 59
输送管 65 77
输卵管 20 81，82
输料管 96 50
输液瓶 25 12
输液装置的立架 25 11
输棉口 163 13
输精管 20 74
辐条 187 27
辐射仪 10 71
辐射屏蔽层 2 31，46
辐射监测器 2 1
辐射探测器 2 1-23
辐射器 23 23
辕马 186 47
辕杆 71 21
辕杆链 71 20
辙叉 202 24
辙轮 166 55
辙轴(挺杆轴) 166 56

戈部

成马蹄形(U形)排列的课桌 260 1
成虫 358 10
成层火山 11 15
成形机 76 35，97 64
成形槌 108 40
成角度的支柱 116 28
成束的盛器 165 16
成束的纱 164 55
成套辊子 148 54-55
成套餐具 44 33
成品麦芽收集漏斗 92 20
成品瓶(容器)的输送 162 29，37
成卷的绘图 151 10
成排的书 42 4
成圈 167 65
成熟的幼虫 80 53
成熟棉花 163 1
成熟的蒴果 382 44
成熟果子 371 61
戏水犬 70 1
戏水池 37 44
戏迷 315 11
戏院调光器 312 17
戏票 315 11

戏剧和音乐会订位(售票)处 271 26
戒指 36 4
戒指成圆环工具 108 26
戒指宝石 36 72-77
戒指量具 108 25，27
战斗轰炸机 256 29
战场遗骸 15 93
战斧 352 16
战舰 218 51-60
咸脆饼 97 44
威耳生雾室 2 24
威士忌酒 98 56
威士忌酒库 267 57
威士忌酒瓶架 42 31
裁刀 128 42，151 15
裁刀与铣背机 184 22
裁切标尺 185 6
裁纸机 185 1
裁判用扩音器 293 21
裁判(员)(椅) 291 62，292 55，65，293 19，20，299 16，41
裁剪刀 103 3，151 15
裁剪下的毛皮 131 14
裁前布 103 7
裁剪样板 103 13
裁缝工作室 103 1-27
裁缝用粉笔 271 39
裁缝划笔 104 24
裁缝(师) 103 1，104 22，271 37
裁缝师工作室 104 1-32，268 17
割制修边机 132 57
裁壁纸板 128 41
截击 293 41
截流水力 3 16
截锥 347 45
戴胜鸟 359 25
戴菊莺 361 10

比部

比压器 153 59
比利时：100法朗 252 17
比快步稍慢的步伐 71 1
比例尺 14 29
比例尺的滑座 175 53
比例划分器 339 2
比流器 153 58
比基尼三角裤 32 15
比基尼泳装 280 26
比基尼装上部 280 27
比基尼装下部 280 27
比赛人员触地壁 282 28
比赛用的弓 305 54
比赛龙骨船 285 35
比赛成绩 293 38
比赛衫 290 9
比赛状况 293 38
比赛服 301 31
比赛和特技飞行的双座飞机 288 18
比赛燕尾旗 254 33

瓦部

瓦尖 122 51
瓦形胡须 34 16
瓦的下边线 122 81
瓦和瓦屋顶 122 45-60
瓦拉辛扬赛所用之制音器 322 34
瓦屋顶 122 1
瓦斯入口管 350 2

瓦斯加热器(炉) 126 25
瓦斯匠和铅管工 126 1
瓦斯炉 139 47
瓦斯和供水设备 126 12-25
瓦斯香烟打火机 107 30
瓦斯总管 198 21
瓦斯热水器 126 12
瓦斯钳 126 58
瓦斯调节器 350 6
瓦斯控制钮 141 32
瓦斯筒用的手推车 138 35
瓦斯蓄热室 147 28
瓦斯熔接气炬 130 14
瓦斯管 139 54，140 12，141 9，147 18，27
瓦斯管螺旋钳 126 59
瓦锤 122 20
瓷牙 24 29
瓷花瓶 337 5
瓷制干燥器隔板 350 54
瓷砖 49 19
瓷砖炉灶 266 34
瓷器画工 161 17
瓷器橱 44 26
瓶子 266 16
瓶子搁架 266 10
瓶形筒管 167 4
瓶状窑 161 3
瓶架 39 6
瓶盖机 76 46
瓶装牛奶 266 60
瓶装红葡萄酒 99 77
瓶装花露水 105 37
瓶装果汁 99 74
瓶装矿泉水 266 61
瓶装洗发精 105 32
瓶装香槟酒 99 78
瓶装面霜 99 27
瓶装柠檬水 265 15
瓶装啤酒 93 26，205 50
瓶装葡萄酒 98 60-64，99 76

止部

止血法 21 14-17
止板 157 18
止挡 214 35
止推垫圈 190 56
步法 289 7
步枪托 255 24
步枪的擦拭用具 87 61-64
步 249 31
齿轨铁路电动机车 214 4
齿轨铁路系统 214 7-11
齿条登山铁路 214 4-5
齿状叶 370 47
齿刨 132 17
齿形轨 277 69
齿形轨条 214 9，11
齿形板条 122 26
齿形凿子(刀) 339 13
齿条(装)饰 334 14
齿条和齿轮 112 39
齿条登山铁路 214 4-5
齿间距 143 84
齿轮 56 20，143 82-96
齿轮传动装置 67 21
齿轮轴 232 58
齿轮变速器 65 35
齿轮变换杆 189 28
齿轮装置 201 11
齿轮装置 65 79，135 4，164 39
齿质 19 31
齿冠 19 37，24 28
齿根 19 36

齿根膜 19 28
齿髓 19 15
齿髓 19 32

夊部

敲板 306 48，339 12
敲铁 136 36
(敲)搅打机 131 4

日部

日文 341 6
日历纸 247 33
日历钟 110 19
日本山茶 373 17
日本艺术 337 7-11
(日本和服的)宽腰带 353 41
日尔曼人 355 27
日光下装片显影罐 116 5
日光灯 49 32，271 23
日光灯管 127 61
日光休息室 37 70
日光屋顶 37 75
日光浴区(场) 37 46，274 12，281 11，282 4
日光浴床位 281 5
日光浴者 281 12
日光浴室 281 10
日全蚀时的月球边缘 4 41
日蚀 4 32
日蚀和月蚀 4 29-35
日耳 4 40
日课经 331 58
日晷 110 30
日期和秒的按钮 110 4
日期指示器显示 237 39
早期基督教艺术 334 61-71
早金莲 53 4
时针 110 13
时间进度表 151 12
时间表 204 16
时间标尺 10 17
时和分的按钮 110 3
时钟 211 37，212 16
时轴 5 8
时轴驱动装置 5 7
时轴止动器 249 75
时装目录 104 6
时装杂志 104 4，271 36
时髦物件 36 19
时髦钻石戒指 36 24
昆虫 358 3-23
易燃危险品旗 253 38
明轮船 280 12
明宦暗箱 177 50
明暗开关 127 17
昏迷(厥)的姿态 21 24
弭宿星团 5 24
星号 185 61
星鸟 52 1
星芹 376 7
星级 284 55
星形凸饰 149 43
星系拱顶 336 44
星条旗 253 18
星座重和星名 3 9-48
星接 153 20
星象仪竖井 5 24
春分点 3 6
春白菊 376 4
春黄菊 380 1

映射 348 9-11
映像管 240 3
显示汇率的指示板 204 32
显示房间号码的号码牌 267 10
显示器 238 43
显示停止信号的电动色灯停止信号 203 3
显贵的冠饰 254 43-45
显微光度计 112 49
显微附件 115 89
显微照相机 112 34
显微棱镜系统 115 54
显微镜 111 19
显微镜台 112 9
显微镜照相机附件 112 36
显微镜镜身 113 31-39
显微镜镜筒 113 31-39
显微管形状的修正 242 39
显影室 310 2
显影盆 116 25
显影箱 116 48
显影滚筒 182 13
显影槽 116 20，182 11
显影槽温度计 116 8
显影罐 116 1
晒印夹 116 47
晒衣绳 50 33
智慧线 19 73
晨衣 29 24
曼陀林琴 324 16
曼陀草 379 8
晚礼服 30 53，33 7
晚香玉 60 9
匙 45 61
匙弓 73
匙头钻 135 16
匙的凹槽 45 63
匙形诱饵 89 73
匙形船首 285 30
匙形凿刀 339 18
匙齿 140 35
匙柄 45 62，140 33
晶体 351 29
晶体结构 351 1-26
晶体基本形状及晶系组合 351 1-26
晶体检波器 309 23
晶状体 19 48
晶格结构 1 9-14
晾干织品 168 22
晾衣架 50 32
晾衣夹 38 23
晴天 61 17，375 21
晴天积云 8 1
晴芬德系 1 24
普通分数 344 15-16
普通汽油 145 54
普通圆盘耙片 65 84
普通家蝇 81 2
普通海燕 359 11
普通橡 121 56
普通影片箱 242 44
普鲁斯·腓特烈大帝银币 252 6
暂时限速的终点 203 40
暂时限速的起点 203 39
'暂停跳伞——飞机降落'信号 288 54
'暂停跳伞——重飞'信号 288 53
暗连环拱 335 10
暗房灯 116 21
暗房装备 116 1-60
暗气炉刷 129 21
暖气室 259 93
暖气通气道 38 40
暖气调节器 191 87，207 54

暖气管 55 8
暖房 55 4，272 65
暖房植株 14 28
暖脚袋 28 38
暖锋 8 5，9 26
暖锋上见到的云 8 5-12
暴风雨信号 284 54
暴风雨后信号 225 35
暴风信号 280 4
曙暮光区域的界厚 4 21
曝光计 114 56
曝光计电池 114 3，24
曝光计指针 179 18
曝光计指针 115 57
曝光计控制臂 117 37
曝光计调整 115 17
曝光灯 182 5
曝光时间调整旋钮 116 39
曝光定时器 116 15
曝光控制装置 176 9
曝光装置 249 42

日部

曲线 346 21
曲线的最大点(值) 347 19
曲线的最小点(值) 347 20
曲线球 305 19
曲轴 190 23，192 29
曲轴轮 166 51
曲轴轴承 190 22
曲轴轴承盖 190 22
曲轴箱 192 22
曲轴箱 190 40，242 51
曲轴箱的驱气 242 59
曲面 347 40
曲柄 64 43
曲柄传动装置 217 53
曲流 13 11
曲率中心 346 23
曲率半径 346 22
曲棍球 349 13
曲棍球杆 292 14
曲棍球杆 292 13
曲棍球员 292 15
冒口 148 22
冒号 342 17
替补球员 292 39
替换的球型字头 249 28
替换球型 291 54
最上端牛腿肉 95 34
最后伸拉 170 47
最后图像品质检查室 238 60
最低温度表 10 54
最终(末级)显像管 113 39
最高峰 12 40
最高温度表 10 53
最被看好的马 289 52
最弱 321 37
最强 321 40
量子跃迁 1 20-25
血压 23 32
量血压用可膨胀的臂带 23 34
量杆 158 26
量水 10 47，267 60
量油尺 190 47
量瓶 173 3，350 27
量氧计 27 13
量雪尺 10 48
量筒 23 43，116 11，173 4，261 26，350 26，45
量程选择器 2 4，23
量器 196 14

牛入场处　319 11
牡蛎　357 32
牡蛎叉　45 80
物神　354 43
物镜　113 36
物镜孔径控制器　113 35
物镜旋转塔　112 30
物镜旋转盘　112 11
牧夫星座　3 30
牧师　331 37，332 22
牧师住宅　331 20
牧场　15 18
(牧)草地　62 44
牧草的收获作业　63 19-30
牲口　73 1-2
牧牛儿童　376 24
牵引　216 27
牵引力指示器　211 26
牵引马达　211 3
牵引马达鼓风机　211 15
牵引发动机　216 29
牵引机　64 46，46，65 20，
　67 17，85 43，273 55
牵引机上的喷雾器　83 2
牵引司机台　62 39
牵引式驳船　216 22
牵引杆　64 61，65 18
牵引板　168 7
牵引炮　216 28
牵引调节板　65 19
牵引调节板链　65 17
牵引装置　194 21，29
牵引缆车　214 15
牵引缆索　214 26，37，45
牵引缆索导轮　214 61
牵引缆索驱动滑轮　214 62
牵引缆索拉紧重锤　214 42
牵引缆索套管　214 73
牵引缆索滚轮　214 32，49，60
牵伸后的棉条轮　164 13
牵伸前的并合棉卷　164 12
牵伸滚轮　164 22
牵转具　139 33
牵转具凸轮　190 39
牵狗的绳或皮带　70 30
牵索支架　133 39
特写和放大用的设备　115 81-98
特写蛇腹附件　115 85
特写镜头　117 55
特价品　96 20
特价品广告标语　271 65
特价品价格表　96 19
特价品柜台　271 64
特价品盘　96 18
特别音栓之音管　326 16
特别装甲车　264 16
特技飞行　288 1-9
特技试验　290 33
特技潜水板　286 56
特技演员　307 47
特种心形　301 47
特殊无盖货车　213 33
特殊和平面镜精研磨轮　111 38
特殊画面按钮　117 84
特殊摄影用之水泥槽　310 11
特高频天线　257 25
特高频全向天线　257 26
特高频和超高频调谐器　240 6
特黑体铅字　175 9
犁　63 6
犁刀　65 10
犁头　65 7，65，328 33
犁托　65 4
犁把　65 3
犁沟　63 8
犁体　65 4-8，64-47

犁形镗　286 16
犁侧板　65 5，67
犁底　65 6，66
犁架　65 70
犁柄　65 4
犁柱　65 9
犁梁　65 9
犁辕　65 71

手部

手　16 47，17 15-17，19 64-83
手巾，毛巾　49 23
手工艺品　48 3
手工书籍装订所　183 1-35
手工造纸　173 46-51
手工给料台　184 2
手工排字用之字模　174 28
手工排字房　174 1
手工绳线装钉架　183 9
手工裁剪刀　104 11
手工熨斗　103 18
手工熨烫垫　104 30
手风琴　324 36
手术刀　22 43
手术台托架　26 30
手术台基座　26 6
手术灯　27 25
手术的显微镜　112 31
手术室　1 1-33
手民　174 5
手写题辞　185 50
手网　89 2
手关节　19 82
手动平针织机　167 35
手动光圈调整用的光圈环　117 4
手动杆　183 31
手动版牙　150 20
手动或自动曝光控制开关　117 17
手动泵　83 26
手动钢剪　119 22
手动喷雾器　83 24
手动操作印票机　204 41
手动燃(油)料泵　190 64
手动螺旋(丝)　132 14
手把　286 48
手纹　19 72-74
手杆　132 55
手杖　41 5
手护栏　19 33
手套　33 67，292 12，298 47，
　318 31
手套架　271 20
手电车　187 5，212 33
手电车杆　191 93
手电车和双迴路刹车系统的警示灯
　191 72
手电车轮　212 64，80
手刹车摇柄　188 33
手斧　300 34，328 1
手柜钳　140 24
手或脚钢　36 17
手轮　100 24，167 30
手枪式喷咀　83 28
手枪式握柄　134 44
手枪握把　264 23
手势　268 33
手的尺骨侧　19 70
手的正确姿势　293 56-57
手的桡骨侧　19 69
手背　19 83
手柄　2 39，65 2，106 37，117
　61，132 18，140 5，148 14，
　224 9，255 38，340 34
手按喷雾器　179 7
手持电动打孔模　125 12

手持武器　255 1-39
手持喷雾器　105 30，106 13
手测深锤　224 58
手绕双棒　297 37
手绘花瓶　161 18
手指护板　83 20
手倒立　295 27
手捣杆　148 32
手部侯养器　99 27
手球　292 1
手球员　292 2
手推车　56 47，97 73，119 42，
　120 6，205 32，206 14
手推刈草机　56 34
手剪(钢筋手剪)　119 87
手搅拌器　39 22
手提灯　270 42
手提行李(皮箱)　194 19
手提式书包　260 7
手提式晶体控制驱动之录音机
　310 24
手提带子　28 50
手提箱　206 4，205 7
手提曝光计　114 56
手锯　120 60，126 72，134 27
手掌　19 71
手摇风琴　309 13
手摇杆　309 81
手摇柄　64 43
手摇泵　269 66
手摇钻　140 13
手锤　126 77
手镜　105 23，106 7，111 16
手操作车票印刷机　204 41
手操作号志箱　203 53
手臂姿势　314 7-10
手臂朝上姿势　314 10
手臂下垂姿势　314 8
手臂朝前姿势　314 9
手臂绷带　21 1
手戳　236 45
手镯　36 3，17
手镯表　36 33
承兑　250 23
承包商家牌　118 47
承梁　45 55
承梁板　85 48，120 40，49
承雷口　335 30
拜占庭艺术　334 72-75
拜占庭帝国女王　355 15
拳　16 48
拳手　299 25
拳击　299 20-50
拳击手台　299 19
拳击手套　299 26
拳击比赛　299 35-50
拳击台　299 35
拳师犬　70 10
拳参　376 10
拳球　299 24
掌状叶　370 39，384 3
掌状物　88 41
掌趾　19 72-74
掌骨　17 16
犁子　110 34，143 29
掌车轮　110 21
驱动重量　143 103
攀足　364 34
攀登　300 2-13
攀登网　273 50
攀登的屋顶　273 60
攀登架　273 47
攀登塔　273 17
攀缘在拱架上的蔷薇　52 12
攀缘豆类　52 28
攀缘植物　51 5，52 5，53 2

毛部

毛　81 40
毛巾　28 9，49 9，281 2
毛巾架　49 8
毛皮　131 11-21
毛皮工人　131 8，23
毛皮大衣　30 60
毛皮放长切割机　131 5
毛皮放长用的吹风机　131
毛皮饰边　30 59
毛皮袖口　131 22
毛皮袖口　30 62
毛皮领　30 63
毛布　173 51
毛虫　80 3，14，29
毛地黄　379 2
毛雨　9 33
毛刷　50 53，105 10，26
毛织软鞋　101 42
毛线帽　35 10，26
毛线鞋　29 5
毛毡盖　353 20
毛苢薢　377 17
毛面砌石　335 51
毛玻璃　124 5
毛玻璃片　115 58
毛玻璃屏　112 24，115 58，
　60，61，65，66
毛毡化(大头钉)　122 96
毛笔　18 8，260 19，341
毛发　375 8
毛料外衣　355 6
毛葛大衣　33 60
毛葛短外衣　31 37
毛帽(安哥拉山羊毛帽)　35
毡布　340 42
毡尖笔　247 11
毡靴　353 30

气部

气力捣锤　148 31
气力磨轮　148 44
气力鋬　148 45
气门　187 31，288 77，29
　358 32
气门封帽　187 32
气门绳　288 32
气升式落锭　139 24
气生根　370 80
气压计　10 4
气压感应盒　10 6
气动货货车　213 18
气动弹力橡胶连接部分　19
气冷式二冲程发动机　188
气冷式四缸四冲程引擎　19
气冷式单缸四冲程引擎(带
　轮轴)　189 3
气体分离装置　145 69
气体分离器　145 28
气体发生器　350 59
气体冷却器　146 27
气体调节器　255 34
气体循环系管　83 16
气闸　146 24，235 27
气泡水平器　118 55
气泡水准仪　14 61
气泡室　1 66
气炬点火器　141 27
气堡　172 40
气胎，车胎　305 86

4 61
救生衣 228 8
286 63
油箱 190 19
便裘 230 9
准车 141 23
144 38
9 40-58
288 63，308 13
飞 288 84
288 81
207 9
42 30
星 10 64
225 33
或海洋气象观测船 9 7
告栏 342 65
342 66
象 9 30-39
达罩 231 18
17 50，20 4，83 14，35，29
288 70
马 288 71
丁 177 41
夏 177 42
原子模型 1 1
入口 170 15，350 12
枪 10 56
扣器 153 27
子 242 62
子的波耳 — 索末菲模型 1
子的能阶 1 15
爆炸高度 7 12
物 128 7
容器 26 26
气 156 23
e)原子模型 1 5
雷射机 243 57
子 242 65
170 19
亚氮流量计 26 3
铁/二氧化铬带自动转换指示 241 55
入口 234 15
扩器 234 15
治疗用的接头部分 25 23
供给用的测压计 25 22
瓶 27 45，141 3，21，257
流量计 26 4
接头 141 30
控制钮 141 29
筒 200 40
喷咀 350 13
管 141 10
导管 147 49
京子 1 13
定器 27 42
170 7
化钠 170 13
化钙盐 1 9
化钙管 350 43
和苛性钠的蒸发 170 11
离子 1 10

部
书口 184 5
书之装置 185 23
书台 184 14，19，185 35
片主轴 312 37
片(盘)轴 117 32，80

收付赊注者 275 4
收纸台 181 31
收纸吹风器 181 33
收纸单位 181 33
收放式落雪器 180 45
收放式主起落架 231 28
收放式前起落架 231 23
收放式起落架 232 10
收音机 309 16，318 18
收费站 236 9
收银 98 44，271 7
收银机 99 93
收款箱 266 70
收款柜台 266 69
收集冷却液和切屑的冷却液盘 149 44
收集站连线的电话 242 20
收集器 10 45
收缩肌肉 77 17
政见发表人 263 5
政治栏 342 51
故障修理服务台 237 27
致动晶体设备 195 19
教父，教母 332 13
教师用的音量控制 261 44
教学用电视机 261 7
教练 291 55
教练船 258 95
教练鞋 101 35
教皇用十字架 332 66
教科书(本) 47 25，261 28
教室 260 1-45，262 2
教堂 331 1
(教堂)本堂 334 62
教堂之座席(位) 330 28
教堂大门 331 16
教堂小柜 260 43
教堂内殿灯 330 49
教堂正门 335 24
教堂司事 330 26，58
教堂东南半圆形室 334 64，335 5
教堂尖塔 331 8
教堂时钟 331 7
教堂屋顶 331 11
教堂标志 15 64
教堂婚礼 332 14
教堂窗户 330 14
救生火箭 228 2
救生甲板 223 19-21
救生衣 286 20
救生员 21 36，280 1
救生带(圈) 221 124，281 6，282 19
救生站 280 46
救生索 221 103，228 12，280 2
救生索火箭发射器 228 1
救生筏 228 19，258 11，286 19
救生圈灯 221 125
救生艇 19，223 19，258 45，259 35
救生艇下水装置 221 101-106
救护人员 270 21
救护车 270 19
救助者 21 19
救助者被溺水者紧抱时的解困法 21 34
救难巡洋舰 228 14
救难直升机 221 20
敏锐度投影器 111 47
数字 344 1-22
数字0 253 34
数字1 253 33
数字(目)键 247 18，271 3，309 76
数字显示 112 47
数字显示器 110 2
数字旗 253 33-34

数位控制 242 35
数学符号 345 15-24
数据中心 248 43
数据记录纸 248 47
数据终端设置 242 19
数据显示终端机 238 2，11
数据载体 237 62-64
数据载波的输入输出装置 237 59
数据输出 112 44
数据输入 237 58
散发传单者 263 9
散光屏 310 38
散步甲板 223 22-27，27
散步者 272 26
散热片 38 77，189 20，190 80
散热百叶窗 212 84
散热器 38 76，65 51，126 20，155 15，191 9，212 54
散热器护板和护板孔 304 12
散热器护罩 191 11
散热器盖 304 11
散浆机 172 80
散装仓库 225 68
散装仓库圆筒 225 69
散装材料 200 12
散装货运驳船 226 35
散装货(物) 206 4，27
散装货物运输船 226 13
散装货物的装卸 226 29
散装货物舱口 221 11
散装货浮升降机 226 31
散装货栈 225 9
散装货柜 225 14，67，226 30
散弹 87 51
散弹药筒 87 49
散墨用的着墨装置 181 19
散墨滚 181 62
散墨滚子 249 51
散墨器 340 22
敬酒的讲话人 267 40
散车 207 52
敞开式设计办公室 248 1-48
敷脸用的毛巾 106 25

片部
片门孔 117 40
片夹 311 24
片场 310 6
片轴 114 8
片轴钮 114 27
片盒 117 45，312 16
片盒的片门 117 30
片路(道) 312 31
版台 340 64
版托 178 41
版夹 178 27，179 8
版面 185 59，342 37
版面标题 342 52
牌楼 337 3
牌照 189 8

斤部
所驯的马 289 3
断层 11 50，12 4，144 51
断层线 12 5
断层落差 12 6
断块山 12 4-11
断纱自停落针 165 37
断条检测滚子 164 4
断线自动停止装置 165 19
断音 321 34
断奏 321 29

断续器 153 55
断路器 152 34，153 51-62
斯坦罕姆人的头颅骨 261 17
斯图卡特天文馆 5 17-28
斯科特尔螺浆 227 20
斯塔斯弗矿层 154 65
斯塔斯弗盐 154 66
新月 4 2
新月丘 13 40
新月形圣体容器 332 36
新月形面包 99 13
新月形冀 229 18
新月旗 253 19
新古典式建筑 336 15
新石器时代 328 10-20
新油油箱 65 46
新闻记者接待室 233 43
新闻照片 342 58
新闻播报员 238 21
新闻摘要 342 50
新郎 332 16
新娘 332 15
新娘之花冠 332 19
新娘花束 332 18
新婚夫妻 332 15-16
新鲜肉柜台 99 51
新鲜空气入口 356 16
新鲜空气入口及控制 191 85
新鲜空气调节器 191 86

爪(爫)部
爪 327 3，362 7
爪形凿子(用) 339 13
爪钩 218 11
采石工人 158 5
采石场 15 87，158 1
采光孔 334 75
采采蝇 81 43
采粉总(蜜蜂的后足) 77 3
采摘路 144 37
受压地下水 12 21
受伤者 21 20
受光管 10 27
受洗之小孩 332 7
受损船 227 2
受料漏斗 147 5
受铁槽 147 22
受理 236 30
受理日瘫 236 29
受款人 250 19
受激状态 1 19
爬虫类围场 356 12
爬行足 357 28
爬行类 364 27-41
爬蝇 273 48，296 19
爬梯 38 4
爱神丘比特 272 20
爱斯基摩人 353 1
爱斯基摩人用的皮舟 353 12
爱斯基摩人所居的雪屋 353 4
爱斯基摩犬 70 22
爱奥尼亚式柱 334 9
爵士小号 324 65
爵士乐队乐器 324 47-78

月部
月台 205 1，14
月台公用电话 205 57
月台天桥 205 3
月台台阶 205 2
月台号码 205 4

月台扩音器

月台扩音器 205 27
月台邮筒 205 56
月台顶篷 205 5
月台钟 205 46
月台座椅 205 54
月台照明设备 205 48
月季花 60 15
月蚀 4 34-35
月相 4 2-7
月亮(球) 4 1-9，31
桂树 377
月球尘埃 6 14
月球轨道 4 1
月球表面 6 13
肋 123 36，230 46
肋木 296 20
肋条 136 24
肋材 283 49
肋板船尾 285 48
肋骨架 222 58
肌力测试 23 26-31
肌肉系统 18 34-64
肝门器肉 20 39
肝叶 20 35
肝的镰状韧带 20 34
肝(脏) 20 10，34-35
肚带 71 18
(肚)脐 16 34
肛门 20 62
肛门括约肌 20 63
肛管 20 61
肘 16 45，72 20
肘甲 329 48
肘机构(部分) 181 16，183 30
肘肉 95 49
肘杆 340 30
肘管接头 126 52
肺 18 13，20 6-7
肺功能检验呼吸描记器 27 36
肺衣 377 7
肺动脉 18 11，20 55
肺动脉瓣 20 50
肺活量测定法 27 36-50
肺静脉 18 12，20 56
肠 20 14-22，77 15
肠胃管 77 15-19
肾上腺 20 29
肾形叶 370 38
肾形盆 23 45
肾盂 20 31
肾盂和胆囊摄影用的压迫带 27 4
肾盂摄影用的X射线装置 27 6
肾盂摄影用照片盒 27 14
肾盂甲片 329 88
肾盏 20 30
肱二头肌 18 37
肱三头肌 18 38
肱骨 17 12
肱桡肌 18 39
肱关节 72 24
肢体连接的电极 23 30
肥皂 49 22
肥皂碟 49 21
肥料散布机 63 39
服务大楼 154 36
服务车 233 22
服务区 207 79
服务台 250 4
服务员 221 110，267 47
服务舱 6 2
服务铃按钮板 267 28
服务窗口 266 66
服装设计 315 39
服装设计师 315 38
服装设计草图 315 40
服装店 315
服装模型 103 6

服装模特儿 103 6
股二头肌 18 61
股动脉 18 19
股神经 18 31
股骨 17 22
股息单 251 18
股息单交换券 251 19
股票 251 11
股票行情表 250 8
股票票面价值 251 12
脊鸡笼 74 19
胚 370 86，382 21，384 22
胚芽 68 16
胚芽植物 68 14
胚轴 370 89
胚珠 58 39，370 63
胚根 370 88
胚盘 74 65
胚囊 74 66，370 64
胃 20 13，41-42，77 16
背 16 22-25
背心 33 4，296 61
背心连裤子的衣服 29 21
背心型短裤 30 16
背心短裤装 32 21
背书 250 27
背书人 250 27
背风处 287 17
背甲 358 31，364 29
背包 86 3，283 65
背包装置 6 20
背对挑战侧面 296 23
背对挑战端 296 25
背向推铅球技术 298 50
背式书包 260 9
背负葡萄窖的搬运夫 78 14
背面 252 9
背(突) 364 21
背甲 71 19，260 11，288 43
背部肥肉 95 40
背脊标签 247 38
背斜层的储油层 12 27
背斜轴 12 17
背椎 17 3
背阔肌 18 59
背景及侧景屏 310 33
背景幕 315 33，316 10
背浪式跳高 298 9
背筐 78 15
背跳越跳马 297 32
背鳍 364 6，367 27
胆 20 11，36
胆囊管 20 38
腕脏 20 44
脉动电线 117 72
脉动发生摄影机 117 71
脉动泵 75 32
脉搏自动计测器 25 42
脉搏定调器视觉监视用的监视器 25 44
脉搏描记器 26 32
胫 16 52
胫前动脉 18 20
胫前神经 18 32
胫骨前肌 18 47
胖女人 308 21
胡萝卜 57 17
胡桃 59 41
胡桃树 59 37-43
胡桃钳 45 49
胡椒树 382 36
胡椒薄荷 380 3
胎环 187 28
胶片容器 170 40
脊瓦 122 3，8
脊柱 17 2-5

脊梁 121 48
脊桁 121 43
脊髓 17 48，18 25
脑干 17 47，18 24
脑下腺 17 43
脑垂(体)腺 17 43
胸 95 4，23
胸甲 329 46
胸压钻 140 58
胸针 36 7
胸轭 71 28
胸轭环 71 27
胸神经 18 26
胸前(口)袋 30 23，33 9，46
胸前 17 8，95 27
胸部抱拖法 21 37
胸(腹)廓 16 28-30，17 8-11，358 29-30
胸盾 358 29
胸梁 166 16
胸梁板 166 16
胸(脯) 72 19
胸锁乳突肌 18 34，19 1
胸椎 17 3
胸罩 32 1
胸墙 329 21
胸鳍 364 7
脆面包 97 50
脆饼(由发酵的面团做的) 99 16
脂肪部分 95 53
胼胝体 17 44，72 27
胜的食物 50 22
胶水 48 4
胶水筒 185 32
胶水滚轮 185 33
胶水槽 184 9
胶合板压力机 133 49
胶合鞋底 101 11
胶布和小器具的配给架 22 64
胶丝溶液准备用的黄酸溶于苛性中 169 10
胶卷 2 13，176 25
胶底滑雪鞋 301 12
胶带 98 47，134 38
胶带分配器 247 27
胶带卷 247 29
胶带架 247 28
胶桶 183 15
胶囊;放入盛釉罐的热水容器 132 13
脱水坩埚 168 18
脱衣舞女 317 27
脱衣舞表演 318 27-32
脱谷圆筒 64 12
脱迷术表演者 308 28
脱脂乳槽 76 17
脱脂棉包 99 28
脱脂棉球包 99 30
脱蜡 145 50
脱圈 167 66
脱圈沉降片片齿 167 52
胯动轴 17 18
胯静脉 18 18
脸部 16 4-17
脸盆架 309 67
脚 16 19，52-63
脚上有蹼的鸟类 359 5-10
脚爪 88 50，368 4
脚手板 122 70
脚手架 122 34
脚手架支柱 118 23
脚手架的角撑 118 25
脚手架横杆 118 20
脚手架横木 118 26
脚灯 316 26

脚尖点地之舞姿 314 19
脚底 19 62
脚环 74 54
脚刮板 123 25
脚轮 50 81，83 61
脚刹车 56 40，188 52
脚刹车飞轮毂 187 63
脚的球状体 19 58
脚注 185 62
脚换挡控制 188 55
脚趾甲 19 57
脚趾节 284 30
脚控制的点熔接机 142 29
脚控制插座 249 66
脚踏联动装置活塞 326 48
脚踏开关 27 21，103 26，66
脚踏发动器 189 38
脚踏式之压纸机 183 18
脚踏杆 100 27
脚踏板 103 11，104 13
脚踏测力器 23 26
脚踏控制 139 27
脚踏缝纫机 309 1
脚踏(凳) 283 47，305 81
脚踏起动器 188 43
脚踏碗 187 79
腓 16 53
腓肚基文 341 14
腓神经 18 33
腓骨 17 24
腓骨长肌 18 64
腓特烈一世金币 252 4
腋斑 88 74
腋窝 16 26
腋窝毛 16 27
腕 19 76
腕木 129 47
腕关节 2 41
腕带 19 77
腕骨 17 15
腌渍小黄瓜 98 29
腌续随子花酱 98 42
腌熏的猪腿肉 96 2
朝北窗 121 21
朝鲜蓟 57 41
脲脏 20 12，27
脲窝 16 51
腿 16 49-54，17 22-25，82 6-8，88 81
腿甲 329 49
腿肉 95 11
腿套筒 304 27
腿部羽毛 362 3
腹 16 36，82 9
腹大动脉 18 16
腹外斜肌 18 43
腹直肌 18 44
腹的下部肉 95 39
腹膜沟 16 51
腹部 16 35-37，95 41
腹滚式跳高 298 23
腹膜 20 58
腹鳍 364 8
腰 16 24，31
腰子附近的肥肉 95 45
腰肉 95 46
腰肉和肋肉 95 3
腰椎 29 55，30 11，31 10，41，32 33，33 23，59
腰带扣 31 12
腰垫 355 69
腰部 88 18，35
腰部纵梁 235 9
腰背部 17 5
腰窝 16 32，88 26
腰椎 17 4

音管盖

音管盖 326 31
音箱 322 18，324 15，63
站牌 205 28
章节标题 185 60
章节符号 342 36
童子军 278 11
童军营地 278 8-11
童蓦 331 29
端箱 211 16
端坡 121 11
端板 229 33
端道 291 7，292 36，293 3-10
端点A 346 17
端点B 346 18
端面铣刀 150 43
端部囊网 90 22

广部

疟蚊 81 44
病人 22 2，24 2
病人卡片 25 5
病人坐凳 27 50
病人的病历表 22 6
病历卡 22 8
病床 25 10
痰盂 23 25
瘦果 58 23

衤部

补角 346 14
补给舰 258 92
补缀缝 102 17
补偿气流 192 4
补整摆子 109 33
补整器杆 112 69
初次轧碎机 158 17
初次显影剂 116 10
初级中学 261 1-45
初镜 113 10
衬布 168 56
衬页 185 49
衬衣 355 5
衬纸 114 21
衬板 123 56
衬衫 30 26
衬衫式上衣 30 40
衬衫钮扣 33 34
(衬衫前装饰用的)绉边 32 44
衬垫紧身上衣 355 30
衬垫鞋口 101 20
衬背纸 128 5
衬裙 309 85，355 37
衫裤相连的工作装 30 21
袜吊 318 28
袜(足球袜) 291 58
袜类、内衣等货品架 99 25
袜类部 271 17
被击倒的失败者 299 40
被单 43 9，50 5
被诱鸟 86 50
被背书人 250 26
被绳索栓住的狗 99 7
被激怒之斗牛 319 28
袖口 30 14，32 45
袖口开叉 30 48
袖口卷边 33 35
袖网 90 16
袖珍小提琴 322 20
袖珍手电筒 127 26
袖珍刻时表 205 45
袖珍型计算器 246 12
袖珍型电子计算器 247 14
袖珍型相机 114 16
裙子 29 52，31 3，24
裙装 31 1
裤沫 32 12
裤脚翻折边 31 40
裤袋 33 47
裤装 30 5
裤裙 29 59，31 48
裤管束带 33 41
褐色 343 5
褐色骆马 366 30
褐虾(属于甲壳动物的褐色小虾) 369 12
褐(鲽)鱼 364 15
裸麦 68 1
裸麦小圆面包 97 16
裸麦穗 68 2
裸体模特儿 338 32
裱糊工具箱 128 33
裱糊刷 128 40
褶边 31 33，34
褶缝线 29 39
襟翼系统 229 37
襟套 43 13

示部

示范图 260 34
示范者 262 6
示范和教学设备 242 45-84
祭坛 334 69
禁止狗进入的标示 99 6
禁区 292 37

石部

石刃柏 57 14
石门 144 31
石头 63 9
石印彩笔 340 26
石灰斗 147 62
石灰坑 13 71
石灰岩层的喀斯特地形 13 71-83
石灰弄 15 86
石灰装入位置 147 56
石匠 158 34
石匠工具 158 35-38
石匠用的榔头 158 35
石园 37 40
石块 63 9，158 8，281 22，302 40
石英 110 15
石松 377 12
石桥 51 17，309 72，331 61
石板瓦 122 85
石板瓦工 122 71
石板瓦工用钉 122 72
石板瓦工用铁件 122 74
石板瓦工用锤 122 73
石板瓦工用鞋 122 75
石板瓦头 122 87
石板瓦尾 122 89
石板瓦背 122 86
石板瓦前缘 122 88
石板瓦屋顶 122 61-89
石版印刷机 340 45
石版印刷机 340 60
石油 12 31，145 41
石油生产 145 22-27
石油产品 145 52-64
石油钻井 145 1-21
石室里的骨灰坛埋葬 328 39
石砌护坡 216 55
石拱桥 215 19
石炭酸 170 14
石南根所制的烟斗 107 39
石南属植物 377 19
石屑 158 23
石瓶 272 35
石桥 15 50
石筍 13 81
石筍和钟乳石的连接部分 13 82
石貂 367 14
石棺 328 17，335 53
石棉防火衣或金属纤维防火衣 270 46
石棉芯纤丝网 350 19
石碑 330 43，334 33
石墓 333 38
石像 272 2
石蜡 145 60
石蜡油 145 60
石榴 384 20
石榴果 384 19
石榴树 384 16
石膏 338 42
石膏库 160 13
石膏粉袋 339 29
石膏像 339 4
石膏模特儿 339 4
石膏碾碎机 160 14
石墙 337 23
石墨坩埚 108 10
石墨和剂 339 4
石时代的崇拜偶像 328 8
石磨 369 16
矿山 15 34
矿井 154 69
矿床 11 31
矿坑换气装置 144 16
矿渣堆 144 19
矽原子 1 14
矽镁层 11 4
码头 222 5，225 64，272 46，283 19
码头台阶 283 22
码头边的马路 225 38
码头边起重机 225 24
码头边铁路 225 21
码头区 225 1
码衣 238 62
码心 148 36
砂包(袋) 210 14，216 50
砂打磨和喷漆 129 28
砂纸 148 4，129 25
砂纸打磨用的木块 128 13
砂纸打磨块 129 26
砂轮 134 23，138 8，140 19
砂垫层 123 8
砂带防护装置 133 12
砂带滚筒 133 18
砂砾过滤层 199 23
砂浆盘 118 39
砂槽 118 20，39，84
砂粒护板 148 40
砂轮 210 15，19
砂模技工 148 30
砂箱 212 59
砂盘 133 35
砂磨吸尘器 133 30
砂磨轮 133 27
砂磨带拉力杆 133 16
砂磨带调节器 133 14
砂磨盘 134 25
砂磨器 129 30
砖厂 15 89
砖工用锤 118 55
砖铺面 123 7
砖堆 118 40
砖墙 118 8，260 45
砖石砌法 118 58-68
砖砌面 123 15
砖铺路面 123 7
砖窑 159 19
研究用火箭范围 7 24
研究显微镜用的万向聚光器 7 21
研钵 349 10
研钵 349 9
研磨轮 100 6
研磨器 129 29
泵 170 31
泵井 199 19
泵水站 146 22
泵压缩弹簧 174 41
泵室 222 33
砌刀坝 217 58
砌成之墙板 120 59
砌面 336 24
砌砖工 118 18
砌砖工用工具 118 50-57
砌砖时留齿缝待砌 118 61
砧木 54 33
砧板 96 57
砧板钉定孔 136 9
砧脚 137 15
破折号 342 23
破冰船 221 50
破碎的瓷器 260 61
硅藻土过滤器 93 4
砼石灰吸收器 27 39
砼性纤维素碎片的成熟 169
砼性柏思麦转炉 147 56-69
硬币 252 1-28
(硬币的)正面 252 8
硬币镶座 36 38
硬木楔 121 96
硬毛刷 105 15
硬化剂测湿度器 130 33
硬玻板 338 24
硬玻板弹壳 87 50
硬底层 123 12
硬质油画纸张 338 22
硬灯丝结结碳化物刀刃 149 50
(硬)钢毛刷 105 16
硬铝 159 20
硬草帽 35 35
硬颈 19 20
硫化氢清洁器 156 22
硫酸生产 156 34
硫酸纸浆厂 172 1-52
硫酸供应 156 33
硫酸铵产品 156 35
硫酸铵溶液 170 26
碎布 103 31
碎砖 158 24
碎石过滤层 199 23
碎石设备 158 18
碎石层 123 12
碎石底基层 200 60
碎石堆 13 29
碎岩 15 30，272 18
碎石撒播机 200 31
碎肉 96 16
碎层云 8 11
碎积云 8 12
碎粒岩 97 43
碰垫桩 222 35
碰碰车 308 63
碰碰车游戏 308 62
碗组 40 6
碑顶之雕刻饰物 334 34
碳纤维竿 89 57
碳原子 242 63
碳素纸之转版机凹版过版机 182

曝光　182 1
合金的触轮滑块　197 24
312 43
20
311 3，312 28
1 63，2 51
312 2
器　311 28
用之配音装置　311 21
230 6
音放音扩大器　311 5
音响台　311 20
242 71
223 6
8 32
7 63，238 5，244 2
243 22
机　249 62
241 57，244 10
242 32
238 6
录音机　309 37，317
8 17
244 9
架　176 34
装置　244 1
199 24
9 10
66，47 33，206 31
80 37

1
369 13
工作台　150 11
14，274 17
14，274 17
7 19，36
4 57
218 16
45 79
2 47，235 7，283 32，
部　279 3
222 49
222 39
9 5

定位转向对准用的车轮镜
钮　112 56
圈　313 7
313 34
216 18
0 17
0 50
267 1，271 44
62 32
117 91
9 8
342 22
人　265 40

省略号　342 29
眉　19 38
眉弓　16 5
盾　218 17，254 5，354 10
盾中心之星标　329 58
盾状火山　11 13
盾状甲　82 5
盾的上部　254 18-19
盾面纵梯六等分　254 18-23
盾章左半边　254 19，21，23
盾章右半边　254 18，20，22
眼肌　19 44
眼角膜　19 47
眼底图表　22 32
眼轮匝肌　19 5
眼点　358 54
眼球　19 45
眼罩　71 26，115 73
眼睛　19，19 38-51，88 15，
33，43，60
眼睛测试　111 43
眼镜　111 9
眼镜架　111 10
眼镜框　111 10-14
眼镜商　111 5
眼镜商工作室　111 20-47
眼镜脚　111 13
眼镜镜片　111 15
瞄准记号　305 56
瞄准具　255 22
瞄准姿势　305 49
瞄准器　87 65，255 45，305 49
瞄准器表尺座　255 36
睫毛　19 41
睡衣　32 16，18
睡莲　51 18
睡觉的洋娃娃　47 11
睡袍　32 35
睡袋　28 17，278 30
睡裤　32 19
瞳孔　19 43
瞬间自转轴　4 25

田部

田　63 3
田边草　69 24
田地　63 4
田鬼　359 21
田间工作　63 1-41
田间守卫者　63 13
田间害虫　80 37-55
田鼠和鼹鼠捕捉机　83 37
由贝壳或鹈鹕石制的装饰　336 13
由木板构成的桶圈　130 6
由毛蚴构成的桶围　169 15
由毛虫产生的虫瘿　80 33
由左而右的直行进路　203 49
由左转右的号志　203 51
由右而左的直行进路　203 50
由右转右的号志　203 52
由基础元件组成的电子线路　242 68-72
由炼焦炉释放的煤气　156 16
由骨头制的投掷矛头　328 2
由纤维胶液转变成固体人造丝的凝固槽　169 15
由蛋白和仿蜡制成的糕饼　97 26
由集合M到集合N上的一对一映射　348 11
由集合M到集合N上的映射　348 10
由集合M到集合N内的映射　348 10
由鹿角所制之鱼叉投掷器　328 5

由琼麻和丝线制的仿男士帽　35 13
由输纸咬爪至给纸滚筒之给纸路线　180 33
由靶垛射猎　86 47-52
电力　22 38
电力机车　211 1
电力系统汇电板　235 55
电力变阻器　152 30
电力起动器　209 13
电力调整可变节矩的发电机　155 46
电工　127 1
电工刀　127 63
电子　1 3，17
电子手表　110 1
电子记分装置　294 32
电子石英表的原理　110 14
电子闪光灯　309 40-41
电子设备柜　177 69
电子自旋　1 4
电子束　240 16
电子码表　238 31
电子壳层　1 6
电子枪　113 37
电子枪组合件　240 24
电子的能阶　1 27
电子闹铃　43 16
电子钟表校正仪　109 25
电子显微镜　113 30
电子琴的构成部分　326 36-52
电子校时器　109 27
电车　268 46
电车轨道　268 23
电车时刻表　268 27
电车线　205 58
电车站　268 25
电车站牌　268 26
电气火车头　205 35
电气烤饼模　40 34
电台选择按钮　309 20
电击昏器　94 7
(电)灯泡　106 8
电灯泡　127 56
电池　65 53，110 7，114 66
电池开关　115 13
电池动力的摩托车电动车的一种　188 20
电池组　65 53
电池供电手提式的电子闪光灯　114 65
电池检验器　25 52
电池装置　115 75
电池箱　211 56
电池槽　115 56
电传印字机　237 61，66，238 12
电动马达　38 59
电动门机构　139 55
电动大种　331 9
电动刈草机　56 31
电动刮胡刀　49 29
电动打字机　249 1
电动卡车　206 2，34
电动冲击钻机　134 43
电动机　138 2，166 18，223 69
电动机房　223 68
电动机底座　164 36
电动收银机　271 2
电动纬纱触杆　166 14
电动咖啡研磨机　39 24
电动和脚踏两用的缝纫机　104 12
电动转数表　191 70
电动转撤　197 37
电动转撤机构　197 43
电动钝剑　294 26

电动理发推子　105 21，106 32
电动推车　205 29
电动脚踏开关　50 2
电动渡船　216 6
电动缘篱修剪机　56 17
电动磨咖啡机　98 69
电动操作信号箱　203 61
电动螺丝起子　195 23
电压计　326 38
电报穿孔纸带　237 68
电报通信　237 69
电报装置　237 65
电位记录仪　23 55
电炉　39 12，46 32
电表　127 32
电表厨　127 31
电话　22 18，41 7，237 6-26，
246 13，248 9
电话——专供紧急使用　233 40
电话、电报和数据转换中心　237 41
电话电缆　198 15
电话电缆管线　198 16
电话号码簿　236 12
电话号码簿架　236 10
电话机壳　237 15
电话交换台　237 27-41
电话交换机盘　238 14
电话收话器　237 7
电话间　237 1，251 10
电话指导用的电话　238 23
电话使用人　237 2
电话亭　268 56
电话接头插座　249 67
电话簿　22 21，237 5
电弧熔接头盖　142 39
电阻器　153 56
电极　25 35，94 8，142 10
电极夹　142 9，20
电极出口点　25 34
电极压圆筒　142 26
电极装置　147 52
电极臂　142 24
电线　94 9，294 31
电线吊杆　195 15
电线挂钩　50 65
电视节目栏　342 64
电视电话　242 21
电视电话幕　242 26
电视声音的红外线发送　242 27
电视机后同步脉冲室　238 27-53
电视机　42 8，46 14，242 28，
243 6
电视机外壳　240 2
电视摄影机　10 67，154 78，
240 16
电钟　191 79
电信　237 30
电钻　56 19，120 21，134 16
电钻附件　134 50-55
电流/电压表　242 77
电流表　191 78，230 18
电瓶舱　257 17
电瓶舱(电瓶装置舱)　257 17
电动机板　56 39
电热水器　126 13
电脑　45 45，174 45，179 3
电脑　177 70，195 1
电脑电线　195 3，38
电脑描绘的设计图样　248 19
电脑自动检查　195 33
电脑控制排板用的照相装置　176 14
电脑数据输入键盘　238 13
电烙铁　127 45
电铃　127 15

电铃按钮 127 2
电唱机 317 19
电梯 271 22，45
电梯升降井 271 51
电梯室 271 46
电梯按钮 271 48
电梯操作人 271 47
电控制盘 168 25，58
电眼 309 18
电插座 127 12，261 12
电灯工 142 2
电灯手套 142 17
电灯台 142 13
电灯夹头把 142 9
电灯枪 134 56
电铸版厂 178 1-6
电缆 152 21，153 41，198 14，326 53
电缆人孔井 198 17
电缆夹 127 40
电缆连接板 239 3
电缆导管 234 29，47，235 61
电缆套 153 37
电缆轴芯 153 36
电缆接线箱 153 33
电缆断路器 23 9
电缆槽 128 32
电源 142 25，155 21
电源开关 132 58，243 16，249 9，64
电源线和通信线用的铰链地面插座 127 23
电源按钮 195 11
电源 237 47
电磁炉 260 63
电磁阻尼器 11 40
电磁阀 139 23
电路连续性测试器 127 55
电熔接条 142 6
电熔接条夹把 142 20
电熔接条盒 142 7
电熔接条臂 142 4
电熔接变压器 125 29
电熔接帽 142 3
电熨槽 142 4
电熨斗 50 6
电熨烫机 50 1
电影广告 268 57
电影观众 312 5
电影放映 312 1-23
电影放映机 117 78，312 24-52
电影制片厂 310 1-13
电影院 312 1
电影院售票亭 312 2
电影配音 311 34，36
电影剧本 310 45
电影票 312 3
电影剪辑人员 311 43
电影照相机可上下左右移动的座头 114 48
电影摄影机 117 1，313 1-39
电影摄影场 310 1
界石 63 2
界埂 63 3
畜底 62 2，75 1
留声机 309 37
留声机箱 309 35
番茄 57 12，99 82
番茄植物 55 44
番茄酱 45 43
畸形人展览 308 19

皿部
罗马人所用之铁笔 341 25

罗马大写字母 341 16
罗马艺术 334 53-60
罗马天主教会 330 31-62
罗马式的装饰图案 335 14-16
罗马式拱形系统 335 17
罗马式建筑艺术 335 1-21
罗马式教堂 335 1-13
罗马妇女 355 7
罗马男人 355 11
罗马数字 344 1
罗经 223 4-11
罗经台 223 4-11
罗盘 224 46-53，227 24，288 12
罗盘卡 224 47
罗盘面(卡) 224 47
罗盘重发器 224 52，53
罗盘碗 224 49
罚出场 291 61
罚球 291 40
罚球区 291 4
罚球线 292 5，38
罚球点 291 6
署名的复印 252 34
置于支架上的梁 120 19
置第一奖的奖券篮 306 11
罩光器 177 8
罩衣工作服 106 2
罩衫 29 8
罩篷 355 10
罩盖 143 80

皿部
监听仪器 311 15
监听扬声器 238 15
监听喇叭 311 13
监视心律和血压的中心控制装置 25 1
监视器 23 27，26 16，33，27 23，238 33
监控扬声器 239 9
监控器 238 1，7，311 8
监控器 117 97
盐水缸 145 33，274 4
盐水槽 146 17，274 3
盐条 97 31
盐矿中的放射性废料的贮藏 154 72
盐饼贮槽 172 36
盐酸羟胺入口 170 21
盐罐和胡椒瓶 266 77
盘子 207 84
盘子温度计 116 13
盘(灰尘盘) 260 60
盘式刹车 192 48-55
盘式录音机 241 56
盘花 375 32
盘(钢盘) 96 54
盘绕的发辫 34 32
盘卷器 148 72
盘海胆 369 19
盘座 288 51
盘腿坐姿 295 11
盘管冷凝器 349 6
盘碟架 39 41
盘磁清水架 39 33
盛行西风带 9 50
盛冰淇淋之锥形蛋卷 308 31
盛烈性甜酒的细颈酒瓶 45 48
盛载基本之圣体架 331 48
盔甲 329 76，353 38
盔顶 329 39
盖子 178 37
盖夹 50 83

盖果 370 95
盖板 163 45，311 10
盖板支承滑轮 163 46
盖板清洁辊滚子 163 44
盖单计数器 2 19
盖单——牟勒计数器 2 19
盥洗台 207 40
盥洗盆 146 29，207 15，278 5，317 31
盥洗室冰箱 126 14

钅(金)部
金币 36 37
金牛座 4 54
金牛座和毕宿五 3 25
金色 254 24
金刚砂盘 24 35
金字塔 333 1
金字塔型的玻璃夹层 5 19
金字塔遗迹 333 6
金龟子 82 1
金龟子的头部 82 2
金龟子蛴螬 82 12
金龟子蛹 82 13
金鸡纳树 380 17
金鱼草 51 32
金饰工(匠) 108 17
金饰店 215 33
金油胶 129 44
金星 4 47
金颈环 328 26
金莺 360 7
金翅 360 1
金翅雀 361 8
金属 254 24-25
金属 301 4
金属开口音管 326 23-30
金属加工厂 140 1-22
金属丝 108 3
金属丝和金属板的滚轧机 108 1
金属丝篮 188 23
金属丝塑型工具 339 11
金属加工工人 140 1
金属夹克 294 15
金属压模装置 111 34
金属网挡板 62 26
金属线 324 77
金属表单切断器 109 19
金属画纸 193 27
金属拖案架 90 15
金属面 303 11
金属衬架 78 9
金属座架 324 76
金属圆盘 309 15
金属框 111 7
金属剪 108 23
金属剪刀 108 23
金属校尖 166 25
金属箔包装的单位货物 225 42
金属箔纸 153 44
金属猫 45 53
金属整流罩 188 50
金属管 326 17-22
金属丝花边细工 102 30
金属链花 374 32
金雀花属树种 374 20
金钱草，珍珠菜 375 26
金箔 129 45，183 5
金箔之切割刀 183 7
金箔之垫板 183 6
金额 250 18
钉 143 51

钉子袋 122 72
钉书铁丝之供应装置 184
钉头 143 52
钉钉 143 51
钉冲头 134 32
钉杆 143 53
钉牢的钉 285 52
钉 151 56
针叶 372 11
针叶树 372 1-71
针叶树林 15 1
针尖附件 151 54
针压调节 241 24
针床 167 55
针床上显示针织的动作
针纵绢镂鲇虫 82 38
针状形衬 370 34
针状锉刀 108 22
针织工厂 167 1-66
针织毛背心 33 53
针织衣服 29 28
针织花边 102 30
针织套头衫 30 4
针织的束紧裤口 29 65
针织衬衫 31 56
针织图案 30 37
针织品 167 48
针织洋装 31 65
针织带状镶边 31 70
针织领 33 31
针垫 104 20
针座 167 21，28
针孔 109 16
针粗大的部分 167 60
针筒 167 8，11
针阀 171 42
针槽 167 15
钓鱼 89 20-94
钓鱼竿 89 49-58
钓具 89 37-94
钓线(丝) 89 63
钓线导架 89 60
钓钩 89 79-87
钓竿 89 49-58
钓竿节 89 54
钓竿状天线 258 60
钓竿扶架 89 23
钓竿杆 89 37
钓罫蠕地迹 89 35
钥匙 140 33-35
钥匙孔 140 40
钥匙架 267 3
钩刀 56 9，85 11
钩叫 362 6
钩状器官的顶部 81 38
钩的弯头 89 81
钩忏 77 12
钩带 270 44
钩拳 299 33
钩竿 270 16
钩眼 89 82
钞票 252 29-39
钟
钟壳 110 26，309 57
钟形杯 328 14
钟形帐篷 278 8
钟形柱头 333 16
钟石 333 16
钟乳饰圆顶 337 17
钟表面的装配工具 109 1
钟表匠 109
钟表匠用钻 109 7
钟表驱动用的变换齿轮装置 10 14
钟表装置 110 36

锚形十字架 332 69
锚状肋 287 32
锚具 223 49-51
锚链 222 75
锚链孔 227 11
锚链筒 222 76，258 54
锚缆 218 18，222 77，223 50，227 12
锦带花 373 23
锦熟黄杨 373 19
锣 299 46
锤子 134 7，340 14
锤子与镰刀旗 253 21
锤打钻 158 11
锤尖头 66 10
锤碎机 158 20，160 2
锡克教庙塔 337 26
锡制士兵 309 52
锡锡纤丝 134 20
锡铅焊料 126 76
锭子 164 46
锭子油 145 61
锭轨 164 50
锭驱动 164 31
锭钩 164 31
锭速度的控制齿轮 164 38
锭翼 164 25
锅 39 29
锅炉 97 69，155 13，210 16
锅炉工场 222 9
锅炉压力计 210 47
锅炉房 38 38-43，55 7，152 1-21
锅炉的膨胀槽 38 24
锅组 40 12-16
锅盖 40 1
锯木厂 144 6，157 1
锯木间 120 3
锯木棚 120 3
锯片 120 62，156 16，260 54
锯开的木材 157 33
锯导板 85 16
锯成木材后的横向链式运送机 157 22
锯条 157 3
锯条的夹紧装置 157 47
锯齿 96 33
锯齿叶 370 44
锯齿式屋顶 121 20
锯齿形图案 335 16
锯齿缘圆盘耙杆 65 85
锯齿磨轮高度调整钮 157 45
锯板机 132 68
锯柄 132 4
锯床用的水平带锯 157 48
锯框 138 25，150 17，157 8
锯框 85 14，120 16
锯链用的润滑油桶 84 35
锯锉 134 6
锥子 136 35，174 17
锥形内螺纹 T 形接头 126 47
锥形轧碎机 172 82
锥形导纱机 165 1
锥形托袋 98 49
锥形帐篷 352 7
锥形树 272 13
锥形绕线机 169 26
锥形浮标 224 76
锥形酒杯 45 85
锥形座 43 46
锥形烧瓶 173 2，350 39
锥形塔顶 335 7
锥形喷嘴 83 23
锥形数轮箱 163 30

锥形精制机 172 27，60，73，83
锥形螺母 187 58
鏊 137 32
镀镍 358 24
镀金工用的刀子 129 51
镀金工用的软垫 129 50
镀金船尾龙 218 55-57
镀铬托架 188 60
镁灰油页岩 154 68
锉 139 26
锉子的各部分 137 26
锉头 137 27，139 12
锉斧 300 37
锉柄 137 30
锉面 137 28
锻后起重机 222 7
锻工炉 137 1-8
锻压机 139 11
锻炉 137 1，138 34
锻炉风咀 137 6
锻带 355 78
锻铁锤 137 23
锻粗块 137 16
锻缩锤 137 33
镊子 22 52，109 14，140 68，174 18
镐 158 31
镐尖 300 33
键 143 73-74，323 32，35
键杆 322 38，49
键盘 174 37，176 2，236 44，237 70，245 27，249 2-6，324 47，325 4-5
键盘式电传打字机 176 31
键盘乐器 326 46
键盘操作者 176 4
键槽 143 66，85
镍 118 52
镜子 49 33，111 4，207 49
镜片磨边机床的样板 111 4
镜头 115 3-8，32，116 32，243 2，52
镜头转座 117 46-49，313 32
镜头转塔 117 46
镜头架 177 27
镜头前镜 115 7
镜头盖 112 18
镜头筒 115 10
镜架展示台 111 5
镜脚与镜片框接合处 111 14
镜筒 113 6
镜筒中心部分 113 9
镜壁 317 28
镇暴盾牌 264 20
镇暴任务 264 16
镰刀 56 8
镰刀刀门 66 13
镰刀柄 66 16
镰刀鞘 66 18
镰形公鸡尾巴 73 25
镰状尾羽 88 68
镶边 323 26
镶边石 272 25
镶边表套 186 23
镶边衣襟 186 22
镶边油口 186 24
镶牙 24 32
镶玻璃用的黄片 124 24
镶嵌纱 171 43
镶嵌物 338 39
镶嵌图 338 37

镶嵌画中的人物像 338 38

矢部

矢车菊 61 1，376 12，380 10
矢车菊属植物 61 1
知更鸟 361 15
矩尺 132 6，134 26
矩形 346 34
矩形取景器 114 14
矫直板 125 3
短大衣 33 63
短上衣 29 51，31 2，221 115
短毛大猎犬 70 43
短斗篷 355 29
短发 34 34
短且硬的胡子 34 23
短传 291 49
短冲程落锤机 139 11
短衫 31 29
短波反射高度 7 26
短波治疗设备 23 39
短波站 237 51
短枝 372 31
短衬裙 32 14
短版胶装机 184 1
短柄冰斧 300 36
短途集材车 85 27
短索 284 19
短烟斗 107 33
短袖上衣 355 12
短袖毛衣(衫) 29 47
短袖运动衫 31 67
短袖夹克 33 26
短袖衬衫 32 38
短袖衬衫 33 33
短袖套头羊毛衫 33 32
短紧身上衣 355 41
短倚音 321 15
短笛 323 7
短笛 323 33，384 32
短粗的胡葡萄 57 18
短窄四轴货车 208 3
短跑选手 298 5
短凿 134 30
短裤 33 25，291 57
短髭 34 13
短翼 232 3
雉鸡 88 77
雉属水仙 60 4
矮干树 52 1，2，16，17，29
矮百合 51 31
矮松 372 21
矮林 84 5
矮牵牛 53 6
矮脚鸡 74 56

禾部

杆，蒿 68 6
秃头部分 34 21
私人保镖 275 16
私人宴会 267 40-43
和声小音阶 320 47
和服 353 40
和服式的抵肩 31 18
和直筒镜联用的活组检查钳 23 17
和弦 321 1-5
秋千台 307 5
秋千吊架 307 6
秋千座位 273 40
秋分点 3 7
秋沙鸭 359 15
秋海棠 53 10

镶嵌画中的人物像 338 38

香水瓶 43 27，105 36
香水喷雾器 43 26，106
香兰 382 46
香兰豆荚 382 48
香芹 57 19
香炉 332 38
香炉钵 332 38
香炉盖 332 40
香炉链 332 39
香肠 96 6-11，98 4，99 54
香肠叉 96 44
香肠夹 308 35
香肠肉 96 41
香肠肉的绞肉机 96 52
香肠的制造 96 31-59
香肠圈 99 55
(香)樱梅 373 33
香烟过滤嘴 107 13
香烟托盘 267 50
香烟贩卖机 268 69
香烟点火器 191 88
香烟烟咀 107 16
香烟盒 107 10
香匙 332 43
香蒲 378 21
香槟水晶杯 45 86
香槟酒水桶 267 59
香槟酒的软木塞 267 58
香槟酒酒杯 45 85-86
香碗 332 42
香菜 99 90，384 33
香焦叶 384 34
香蕉花 384 34
香蕉形状部码头 226 22
香蕉形鞍座 188 59
香蕉树 384 28
种子 54 3，59 8，68 13，15，25，371 20，65 10，15，28，37，54，60 375 25，28，31，34，382 20，35，45，383 15，23 384 21，47
种子漏斗 65 75
种子箱 54 2
种子囊 383 8
科甲拉多甲虫 80 52
科特通气孔 227 21
秒表 129 39
秒指示器 110 21
秘书 209 27
秘书室(厢) 205 37，209 25
秘鲁洋流 14 42
称水果 99 88
称杆放出器 166 62
称重台 22 67
称重装置 170 29
称盘 40 37，349 36
称量瓶 349 24
积木 28 41
积木(块)砖 48 27
积木组件 48 22
积分 345 14
积云 8 1，287 22
积层薄板 301 48
积体电路 110 16
积云 8 17，287 26
移动式果园喷雾机 83 38
移动式养鸡遮棚 74 1
移动式变压器 152 30
移动式柴油引擎空气压缩机 39
移动式监视装置 25 24
移动式起重机 147 41
移动式照明灯廊 316 19
移动式鼓风机 165 2
移动式鼓风机用的导轨 165 3
移动式器具台 26 37

装袋器

装袋器 92 39
装袋嘴 83 55
装煤车 156 6
装煤运送机 144 42
装置于甲板上的货柜 221 22
装填的铲刀 128 35
装熔化玻璃的碗 105 1
装熔化玻璃的套筒 162 50
裂口 13 34
裂纹 373 91-96，375 27
裂钻 24 39
裂幅 288 75，83
裂幅绳 288 76
裂缝 11 52

羊(⺶ 羊)部

羊 73 13
羊毛上装 31 50
羊毛外衣与套头绒线衣成套者 31 49
羊毛帽 29 57
羊头 327 18
羊皮纸膜 324 31
羊皮帽 353 23
羊皮滚轮 130 31
羊肚菌 381 26
羊栏 75 9
养鸡场 74 1-27
养猎鹰者 86 42
养蜂场 77 56
养蜂者 77 57
养蜂面罩 77 58
美人鱼 327 23
美女皇后 306 64
美式四轮单座马车 186 49
美式足球 292 22
美国：1美元=100分 252 33
美洲 14 12-13
美洲石竹 60 6
美洲负子袋鼠 366 2
美洲地锦 374 16

米部

米 98 38
类人猿目 368 14-16
类比控制 242 38
类折谱 7
料斗 200 45
粉红色 343 4
粉红猎装 289 42
粉笔 48 15，260 32
粉笔壁架 260 31
粉盒 43 28，49 35
粉腊笔 338 19
粉碎机 172 5
粘土坑 15 88，159 1
粘土块 161 10
粘土条 159 14，161 8
粘土制面具 260 75
粘土塑像 48 13
粘土箱 339 30
粘合剂 128 27
粘性驱动用的风扇离合器 190 8
粘贴面 260 60
粘结结构注入器 200 53
粘胶工作 260 50-52
粘胶筒 236 5
粘胶辊 260 57
粘着于轨道车 214 1
粗车削用的圆凿 135 15
粗木料 135 21

粗木锉 132 1
粗布帆 353 33
粗刨 132 16
粗纱 164 29
粗纺机操作工 164 24
粗纸（纸坯）173 29
粗体铅字 175 2
粗呢大衣 271 21
粗苯产品 156 41
粗苯槽 156 42
粗制糠麦面包 97 49
粗苯面的木底鞋 101 47
粗绒布帽 35 23
粗削凿 158 37
粗玻璃 124 6
粗烛心纱所编的帽子 35 9
粗积石 269 37
粗调和微调指示器 148 65
粗调整 112 4
粗铅管 118 51
粗脏物专用附件 50 85
粗脏物软管 50 84
粗绳 21 30
粗粒小麦 98 36
粗船帆布 156 40
粗锉 134 9
粗筛 55 13
粗焦油槽 156 32
粗棉布工作服型的童装 29 40
粗混凝土墙 119 7
粗硬橡胶鞋帮 300 45
粗滤器 172 54
粗端离地的树干 85 41
粗磨焦指示器 224 35
粗磨机 160 4
粗磨表面用的粗磨轮 111 36
粪便沟 75 20
粪便桶 221 72
粮食害虫 81 15-30
粮箱 64 23
粮箱木螺钉 64 24
粮箱卸载装置的喂送木螺钻 64 25
精白麦 98 35
精制纤维素或磨木纸浆的出口 172 78
精制细砂糖 98 54
精制结晶糖 98 55
精炼糖 162 4
精制圆弧磨丝 151 66
精密天平 118 35
精密车床 138 20
精密调整(细调)的磨擦驱动装置 116 33
精梳机 163 56
精梳机的原理 163 63
精梳后用卷棉 163 58
精梳棉条 163 72
精浆机 172 84
糊壁纸 128 18-53
糕饼 265 4
糖衣饼 97 43
糖尿病患者病历卡 22 26
糖果 98 75
糖果类 98 75-86
糖果袋 47 32
糖蛾之幼虫 80 44

⺧部

耕耘机 65 51
耕耘机附件 56 21
耕耘器 55 21
耘锄 55 21

耙子 56 4
耙齿杆 64 53
耧斗菜 60 10

老部

老师 260 21
老式的客货轮 223 1-71
老板 266 71
老虎窗(天窗) 37 56，121 6，329 11，336 4
老顾客 266 40
老鳞茎 54 28

耳部

耳朵 16 18，70 2，88 16，32 44，61
耳机 241 66，69，248 35，249 63，261 38，309 24
耳机发 34 37
耳机式发型 34 37
耳机电线 241 71
耳机电线插头 241 70
耳机套 241 72
耳机插座 117 10，249 68
耳坠 36 11
耳状根尊 378 8
耳饰 36 13
耳或膀胱的冲洗注射器 22 54
耳垂 17 57，73 23
耳栓 354 30
耳咽管 17 65
耳廓 17 56
耳蜗 17 63
耳病(羽) 88 78，362 16
耳镜 22 74
取下重锤 167 32
取明钩 89 40
取棉刺滚子 163 53
取景器 114 2
取景器日镜 313 6
取景镜头 114 25
耶路撒冷十字架 332 70
耶稣受难像 330 12，54，331 42，332 33
耻骨 17 20
耻缝 20 65
联合收获机 63 31，64 1-33
联合国旗 253 1-3
联结枕木 202 14
联结轴 148 58
联结装置 65 61
联接式轨枕 202 38
联接挂钩 202 15
联接器螺栓 202 15
联锁瓦 122 7
聚乙烯饲料包 62 43
聚光灯 307 3，318 24
聚光灯开关 195 20
聚光灯桥 310 53
聚光器 112 8，113 32
聚伞花序 370 70
聚合果 370 100，101，384 63
聚焦台 115 86
聚焦组件 240 12
聚焦调整装置 240 30
聚焦望远镜 115 74
聚焦率 177 2
聚焦幕托架 177 3
聚氯乙烯鞋底 101 2
聚酯管 67 26
聚醋胺丝固化 170 43

聚酰胺纤维 170 61
聚酰胺纤维包 170 62
聚酰胺纤维的制造 170 1-
聚酰胺的冷却 170 34
聚酰胺的固化 170 35
聚酰胺筒 170 51

臣部

卧车 207 36
卧式搪铣床 150 25
卧姿 305 29

西(覀)部

西门——马丁平炉 147 21-
西门子低轴电炉 147 51-
西方式跳高 298 16
西风漂流 14 44
西米帽子 383 58
西谷米 98 39
(西服的)上装 33 2
西奈文字 341 13
西点 135 4
西洋双六棋盘 276 22
西洋山茱萸，樱(桃)树 37
西洋骨牌 276 34
西洋跳棋 276 1-16
西洋跳棋子 276 17-19
西洋跳棋盘 276 17
西班牙：1银币=100生丁
西班牙长耳猎狗 70 38
西班牙瓦屋顶 122 56
西特琴 322 21
西(装)裤 33 3
西番莲 53 2
西澳大利亚洋流 14 45
西餐盘 44 7
西藏人 353 27

页部

页 185 53
页边空白处 185 55-58
页码 251 14
页数 185 63
(页数下端)空白处 185 58
顶边腿肉 95 37
顶甲板 146 37
顶灯 210 46
顶尖 135 8
顶尖车床 149 1
顶帆上的小方帆 220 32
顶帆船 220 11-13
顶层 123 41
顶层楼版 315 16
顶杆 325 30
顶芽 370 22
顶饰 254 1，11，30-36
顶环 89 52
顶侧面 36 18
顶标 224 78
顶标浮标 224 80
顶点 87 77，347 28
顶点视力检测器 111 33
顶面涂布器 173 31
顶梁 183 21
顶枪文案 219 13
顶给水盘 210 29
顶瓣 97 4
顶梳 163 67
顶推拖船 221 93，225 60

45
1-29
37 83
149 22，42
221 102
285 12
285 1
285 23
118 63
118 59
43，99 2，18，111 2，
250 6，266 25，271
索引 248 24
代表 248 17
区 207 78
面 64 16
件 139 28
22 3
22 11
器 238 50
238 46
的肉块 96 22
牙根 24 27
294 3
294 33，305 72
箱 232 20
172 21
170 45
版显影机 179 31
圆盘 64 82
165 50
185 30
190 66
212 41
压力计 210 43
器 238 60
97 58
238 54-59
215 58
273 57
1，30-41
19-21，72 15，88 3，364
18 51
5 6，20
28 25
06 27
18 1
19 12
7 2
6 20
16
18 2
精髓) 88 27
57，319 38
31 28
29 43
290 11
奇摩托车 290 12
器 332 2
2 42
41，319 38
36 22
253 23
9
255 30
8
6 8
361 6-7
15
11
电视接收天线 239 4
8 11
75 43

颗粒组织 340 47
额肌 19 4
额动脉 18 5
颌带 71 9
额骨 17 30
额鹿角 88 6
额带 18 6
颜料指示器 127 37
颜料桌 338 25
颜料容器手提盒 315 34
颜料盒 48 6，338 10
颚 16 17
颚托 323 8
颚带 355 22
(颚)颌下腺 19 11
颚动脉 18 3
颚骨 17 33
颚静脉 18 4
颚肌 19 3
颤声金丝雀 360 6
颧骨 16 8，17 37

卢部

虎耳草科醋栗属的植物 58 1-15
虎(老虎) 368 5
虎钳 260 47
虎钳手柄 132 31
虎钳夹住的木块 260 56
虎钳把手 260 48
虎钳螺丝 132 32
虞美人 61 2

虫部

虫孔 58 65
虫卵 80 15，55
虫蛀洞穴 58 63
虫瘿 82 34
虫瘿中的幼虫 82 36
蚊 358 21-22
虹 7 4
虹吸式气压表 10 1
虹吸管 10 43
虹膜 19 42
蚕 358 50
蚋(蚊)，蚊子的一种 358 16
蚜虫 358 13
炸蜢拟饵 89 68
蚯蚓 357 24
蚯蚓拟饵 89 67
蛇行滑道 301 72
蛇足 327 39
蛇形号 322 13
蛇形扣针 328 28
蛇尾 327 31
蛇身 327 2
蛇类 364 38-41
蛇蜥 364 37
蛇腹，暗箱 116 31，177
  10，309 26
蛇腹装置 115 85
蛇舞 297 48
蛋白 74 62，67
蛋白杏仁饼干 97 37
蛋白杏仁糖果 98 32
蛋壳 74 59
蛋形与尖状之反曲线脚 334 42
蛋形姿势 301 33
蛋秤 74 42
蛋黄 74 68
蛋黄囊 74 64
蛋箱 74 45
蛋糕盘 97 25

蛔虫 81 31
蛔虫的头部 81 33
蛛网 358 47
蛀蟆菌 379 10
蛙式 282 33
蛙式姿势 288 61
蛙鞋 279 18
蛹 80 4，25，43，81 3，21，
  24，82 32，358 20
蛹形拟饵 89 66
蝣蟀 358 6
蜗形饼 97 38
蛾 365 7-11
蛾卵 82 19
蛾眉月 4 3
蜂王出巢(房) 77 38
蜂王移动箱 77 44
蜂王巢室 77 47
蜂王隔板 77 47
蜂卵 77 26
蜂房 77 1，4，5
(蜂房的)巢室 77 26-30
蜂房(巢) 77 31-43
蜂虎 360 2
蜂果式火箭发射管 255 71
蜂果织品的平织图 171 29
蜂窝状茅舍 354 28
蜂窝架 77 40
蜂窝隔膜 77 43
蜂群 77 53
蜂蛹 77 30
蜂罩 77 39
蜂蜡 77 67
蜂蜡芯 77 65
蜂蜜抽出器 77 61
蜂蜜瓶 77 63
蜂蜜桶 77 62
蜂刺软膏 77 68
蜻蜒 358 3
蜘蛛 81 9，358 44-46
蜘蛛网 81 10，358 47
蜘蛛网架 273 46
蜘蛛类的节肢动物 358 40-47
蜘蛛蟹 369 15
蜥蜴 364 27，30-37
蜡制品陈列馆 308 68
蜡烛 260 76，330 7
蜡笔 260 6，338 5
蜡像 308 69
蜡像模型 339 26
蝙蝠翅膀 327 4
蝙蝠翼式袖子 31 16
蝮蛇类 364 40-41
蝰蟒类 364 20-22
蝴蝶 365 1-6
蝴蝶花 51 27
蝴蝶结 34 7
蝴蝶领结 32 47，33 11
蝎状聚伞花序 370 77
蝶式 282 34
蝶形花冠植物 57 1
螺骨 17 38
蝶蛹 365 11
蝶宽 17 54
蛇形瓣卵虫 369 9
蟑螂 358 6
整针 77 11
整针器官 77 10-14
整蛹鞘 77 12
螺丝扣 130 4
螺丝攻 140 60
螺丝攻扳手 140 30
螺丝和螺栓 143 13-50
螺丝起子 126 69，127 46，134
  4，140 62
螺丝槽 143 50
螺杆 140 4，143 15，192 59

螺杆扇形齿轮 192 57
螺纹 50 50，67 38，143 16，68
螺纹扳刀 135 14
螺纹切割机 125 27，126 86
螺纹牙 108 15
螺纹套管扳手 126 63
螺纹轴 149 66
螺纹接头 126 42
螺纹模 140 32
螺纹端部 187 75
螺纹座圈 127 59
螺桩 143 22
螺栓 121 98，140 39，143 31，
  202 7，246 23
螺栓头 143 23
螺栓导销 140 41
螺旋刀 168 44
螺旋开布滚轮 168 13
螺旋夹 350 30
螺旋夹钳 120 66
螺旋跳水 282 44
螺旋楼梯 123 76
螺旋扳手 126 67
螺旋独角 327 8
螺旋齿轮 143 85，92-93
螺旋保险栓 300 47
螺旋钻 120 65
螺旋桨 92 46，230 32，288 36
螺旋桨飞机 231 1-6
螺旋桨式高速混合机 79 5
螺旋桨护板 258 40
螺旋桨护板缘饰 258 74
螺旋桨护板毂 258 63
螺旋桨桂 222 71
螺旋桨轴 223 65，232 60，259
  59
螺旋桨螺距指示器 224 20
螺旋盖 83 40，115 11
螺旋弹簧 191 28，192 68
螺旋输送机 92 26
螺旋溜槽 144 28
螺旋舞 297 50
螺旋聚伞花序 370 76
螺帽 119 75
螺模的两半 140 61
蜩 365 10
蝻虫 357 20-26
蝾螈 81 11
鲎鱼 81 14
鲎鱼子 81 13
蟹的一种 358 1

缶部

缸头垫片 190 48
缸盖 190 45
缺边材 120 89
罂粟 380 15
罂粟花 51 30，61 4
罐头 96 26，99 91
罐头盒 96 25，98 15-20
罐形浮标 224 77，94
罐装牛奶 98 15
罐装果汁 99 75
罐装啤酒 93 25，99 73
罐、锅、壶的托垫 39 18

舌部

甜面包 97 40，99 64
甜点盘 45 6
甜酒 98 57
甜菜 68 44
甜菜升降器皮带 64 95
甜菜升降器的拉紧装置 64 94

甜菜叶

甜菜叶 68 47
甜菜收获机 64 85-96
甜菜线虫 80 51
甜菜顶部 68 46
甜菜根 68 45
甜菜清理装置 64 89
甜菜漏斗 64 96
甜菜圈 97 29
甜菜树 384 48
甜椒 57 42
甜旗草(天南星科) 377 22

竹(⺮)部

竹制的越野滑雪雪杖 301 20
竹茎 383 60
竹笔 341 23
竹科 136 31
笔夹 2 18
笔记簿 260 18
笔尖附件 151 55
笛 40 11，224 70，353 47
符头 320 3
符杠 320 6
符尾(棒) 320 4
符钩 320 5
第一打 275 25
第一节火箭 234 3
第一次吹制 162 24
第一压搾机 173 19
第一层 118 67
第一和第二经纱 171 17
第一种独舞 314 1
第一段赛程 285 19
第一湿毛布 173 17
第一键盘 326 42
第二人 300 26
第二个远方信号 203 17
第二节车厢 197 6
第二打 275 26
第二节火箭 234 18
第二列低八度 321 42
第二列高八度 321 47
第二层 118 68
第二级火箭 234 18
第二段赛程 285 20
第二种姿势 314 2
第二姿势交叉接触 294 50
第二趾 19 53
第二湿毛布 173 18
第二键盘 326 43
第三人 300 27
第三打 275 27
第三节火箭 234 33
第三列高八度 321 48
第三次横折装置 185 14
第三层楼座 315 17
第三和第四经纱 171 18
第三种姿势 314 3
第三姿势交叉接触 294 48
第三姿势防守 294 8
第三段赛程 285 21
第三趾 19 54
第三键盘 326 44
第四列高八度 321 49
第四种姿势 314 4，5
第四姿势交叉接触 294 47
第四趾 19 55
第四键盘 326 45
第五列高八度 321 50
第五种姿势 314 6
第五姿势防守 294 24
筛 91 26，118 85，172 57
筛子 340 24

筛网台 168 63
筛网口 168 59
筛网印花操作工人 168 65
筛除物木螺钻 64 21
筛除物排出口 64 22
筛骨 17 39
筛屑 158 22
筛渣槽 172 59
筒子线 104 16
筒子吸尘器 50 68
筒架 165 25
筏横墙壁的水道 283 60
等边三角形 346 26
等日晷线 9 44
等冬温线 9 42
等号键 247 20
等压线 9 4
等雨量线 9 45
等轴晶系 351 1-17
等差级数 345 11
等高线 15 62
等夏温线 9 43
等温线 9 4
等腰三角形 346 27
等震线 11 37
筐 40 42，99 8
筐子 136 16
筐边 136 16
筐底交叉肋 136 21
筑路机械 200 1-54
筋斗 288 1
签字笔 260 14
简讯 342 63
简易四滚子并条机 164 9
简单方程式 345 4
简单分裂式襟翼 229 49
简单比例法 345 8-10
简单凸图形 36 78
简单襟翼 229 46-48
简便牛舍 75 22
简便包装 39 15
简略书名 185 43
筹码 275 12
算术 344 1-26，345 1-24
算术级数 345 11
算命者 308 36
算珠 47 14
算盘 309 77
箍口具 71 53
箕斗升运机 200 49，201 21
箕斗挖泥船 226 41
箕座层 193 11
箕梯 173 18
箕座 193 11
箕链 226 42
箍紧器 130 12
箍桶工 130 1-33
箍桶工人 130 11
箍筋 119 70
管 357 23
管子支承装置 27 47
管子扳手 127 47
管子修理器 126 11
管仓 255 72
管风琴 326 1-52
管风琴正面图 326 1-5
管耳 326 32
管式把手 50 64
管式制图专架 151 37
管式贮墨水装置 151 68
管体 326 29
管层 381 17
管状车胎 290 19
管状金属共鸣器 324 78
管形扳手 134 11
管形织物 167 9

管形撑腿 114 44
管制车架 188 49
管制塔台 287 12
管弦乐队 315 25
管弦乐队席 315 24
管弦乐器 323 1-62
管(板)钳 40 20，126 61，127 47
管虎钳 126 81
管架 22 46，126 53-57，146 4
管座 326 23
管接头 119 53，126 43，350 5
管理大楼 233 16
管理办公室 222 1
管理处 5 17
管帽 260 52
管路 145 65
管路蒸气喷射器 210 41
箭 305 60，352 28
箭手 305 53
箭头 126，305 61，352 29
箭头形叶 370 37
箭扣 305 63
箭杆 305 64
箭杆上所粘的羽毛 305 62
箭杆上涂染的颜色 305 65
箭步挺举 299 4
箭箙 352 27
箱 143 79
箱形进料器 159 7
箱形梁 287 30
箱形桩 217 6
箱形捆扎机 86 20
箱形簧槽 122 83
篮 40 42，292 32
篮子 204 3
篮式滤器 67 12
篮板 292 30
篮板标区 292 34
篮架柱 292 31
篮球 292 28，29
篮球场 292 28
篮圈 288 67，292 33
篑 89 30
篑片 326 19，28
簧风琴 325 43
簧风琴外箱 325 47
簧风琴键盘 325 48
簧管 326 41
篱墙 15 92
篥瓦层 122 49，76
篥垫 121 31
篥缘板 37 8
篥槽 122 92

臼部

臼齿 19 18，35

自部

自己动手做用的工具柜 134 1-34
自己动手做的热衷者 134 61
自由区边界 225 3
自由电子 1 25
自由式 282 37
自由式接力赛 282 24-32
自由式摔角 299 10-12
自由组合键 326 40
自由降落姿势 288 60-62
自由港 291 43
自由港 225 2

自记温度计 10 19
自外撑双杠 296 45
自行车 187 1
自行车气筒 187 48
自行车车轮 187 51
自行车把手 290 18
自行车转动装置 187 35-
自行车竞赛 290 1-23
自行车踏板 187 78
自动飞行控制板 235 23
自动切块锯 157 54
自动切割机 162 19
自动风琴 308 38，309 1
自动计数分级 74 52
自动电压调整器 153 31
自动加油站 196 1-29
自动充水玻璃杯 24 13
自动收片卷盘 117 80
自动光圈控制 117 20
自动饮水钵 74 16
自动步枪 87 23
自动回答与录音组件 22
自动吸管 23 44
自动吸管装置 23 47
自动40或手操作录音选择开关 13
自动制动器 181 47
自动拍摄双杠 115 15
自动拍照器用的调整杆 1
自动表的旋转测试仪器 1
自动表的零件 110 32-43
自动拉索滑轮 301 62
自动金属供应装置 174 4
自动织布机 166 35
自动穿片按钮 117 83
自动通风系统 191 30
自动给水器 181 5
自动影机 116 60
自动起动机和制动装置
自动高速加热板 39 15
自动高射炮 259 34
自动润滑泵 210 42
自动调谐器 241
自动铅笔 151 45
自动盖印机 22 24
自动垃纸机 180 73
自动饲料及排养 74 23-27
自动饲料器 74 23
自动塞焦过载开关 117 1
自动鞋底压型机 100 14
自动横割链锯 100 15
自来水龙头 39 36
自走式草料收割机 64
自走式复砂机 200 41
自附马达的齿轮箱 164 2
自动餐厅 266 45-78
自动餐车厢 207 73
自抛自接 297 33
自附电动机的齿轮箱 164
自给电池电话 224 27，2
9，40
自流井 12 25
自流泉 12 26
自航器 224 18
自数 21 33
(自然)小音阶本位音 320 4
自然色橡皮鞋底 101 38
臭虫 81 39
臭迹 289 49
臭氧层 7 13
臭氧层上限 7 19
鼻 16 10，70 4，364 2
鼻轮舱门 231 24
鼻音符号 342 35
鼻骨 17 41

羽部

系部

紫堇属植物　377 8
紫柳天　377 9
繁分数　344 17

辛部

辣子草　61 31
辣根　57 20
鲜子　34 6
鲜子式假发　34 5
鲜尖　20 48
鲜状袖　355 46

言部

警车　264 38
警犬　264 6
警犬和训练师　264 5
警务　264 1-33
警示十字标　202 41
警示灯　202 46，50
警告灯　230 64
警告牌　280 6
警报器　270 7
警棍　264 22
警察识别证　264 26
警察信号牌　264 14
警徽　264 27

麦部

麦克风　22 15，117 24，74，197
26，209 31，241 49，261 39，
263 7，317 20
麦克风电线　310 32，311 41
麦克风电缆　239 14
麦克风吊杆　310 25
麦克风吊杆操作人员　310 22
麦克风　241 50
麦克风连结导线　117 25
麦克风座　241 51
麦克风插孔　249 65
麦克风插座　249 69
麦克风插座板　238 36
麦芽升降机　92 35
麦芽汁　93 10
麦芽汁冷却器　93 5
麦芽汁的冷却和沉淀物的除去　93
1-5
麦芽汁品质检查用的过滤器具　92
51
麦芽油　98 24
麦芽制造的设备　92 1-41
麦芽浆煮锅(桶)　92 44
麦芽浆槽(桶)　92 43
麦芽啤酒　93 26
麦芽储仓　92 37
麦角病　68 4
麦秆　136 30
麦秆石竹　61 6
麦蚋　80 40

走部

走向　12 2
走步式跳远　298 40
走带计数器　241 64
走钢丝演员　307 40
走廊　5 25，207 11

走梭板　166 42
起毛的织品　168 36
起伏之旋转车床　308 5
起伏滑梯　273 52
起动马达　190 44
起动电动机　212 30
起动电阻　135 3
起动杆　163 17，167 22，178 20
起动杆与停止杆　181 32
起动齿轮圈　192 31
起动停止杆　165 17
起动器开关　241 30
起动器电钮　189 52
起动器和转向角限制器　191 75
起步级　123 18，42
起始位置　89 33
起泡陀螺　309 71
起泡葡萄酒　98 63
起首字母　175 1
起重平台　232 19
起重机　270 48
起重机马达　157 28
起重机轨道　119 27，222 24
起重机架悬构骨架　226 53
起重机驾驶室　119 35，222 16，
226 52
起重机钩　139 45
起重机缆索　222 13
起重机操作浇桶　147 60
起重传动装置　217 73
起重传动装置室　217 71
起重臂　221 25，26
起重的铁臂　255 95
起重起落架　232 18
起重装备　258 88
起重臂　119 36，255 76
起点线和终点线　286 30
起点和终点浮标　285 14
起点柱　292 77
起拱门　336 22
起偏振滤光器　112 19
起落架舱　256 15
超落架液压唧筒　257 41
起跑　298 1-6，3
起跑器　298 1
起跳　298 26，37
起跳板　298 38
起锚绞盘　258 6，259 82
起槽机　132 26
起槽器　140 25
起爆管　87 58
超8型有声电影片盒　117 29
超8型有声摄影机　117 1
超小型底片　114 16
超小型照相机　114 16
超级V型赛车　290 37
超级市场　190 1-96
超级汽油　145 55
超细工表面　151 22
超音波清洗器　109 23
超音速客机　231 15
超高频天线　257 25
越过横杆　298 31
越冬茧　80 31
越位　291 42
越界流体　154 67
越桔　377 23
越野滑雪板　301 42
越野滑雪板　301 14
越野滑雪服　301 17
越野滑雪弹力服　301 43
越野滑雪靴　301 15
越野障碍赛　289 20-22
越野赛　290 33
越野赛装备　301 14-20
越野赛跑道　289 17

越野摩托车(125cc)，
轻型摩托车一种　189 16

赤部

赫雷娄族妇女　354 25

豆部

豆荚　57 6，370 92
豆科植物　57 1-11，8
豆科植物的花　57 9
豆象　81 23
鼓　318 10
鼓手　318 11
鼓风机主管　147 68，148 2
鼓风机　172 4，199 46
鼓风机导轨的上部结构　165 6
鼓风机的吹口　165 5
鼓风机油泵　147 63
鼓风妒设备　147 1-20
鼓风高炉　147 7
鼓风装置　139 56
鼓皮　323 52
鼓形门　245 5
鼓形柱座　335 44
鼓腔　17 60
鼓锤　323 54，56，354 19
鼓膜　17 59
登山用鞋底钉　300 13
登山运动　300 1-57
登山者　300 5
登山绳　214 1-14
登山裤　300 7
登山缆车　214 12
登山鞋　300 30 31-37
登月舱　6 12，234 55
登月制动火箭　6 39
登月舱舱壁　234 54
登机门　233 13
登机走廊　233 12
登记表格本　267 12
登陆艇　258 89，259 46
豌豆　57 1，7
豌豆花　57 2
豌豆卷须　57 4

酉部

配东小丑　307 23
配平片　288 25
配电板　157 67
配有功率输出离合器的有效功率
输出齿轮变速装置　65 40
配有吸入管和压力计的立架
26 29
配字模装置用齿　174 30
配字模的升降牵引转具(托架)
174 22
配字模装置　174 20
配音台　238 29
配音导演　311 38
配音　174 23
配音员　311 36，39
配音架　310 56
配音室微音器(麦克风)　238 34
配重(衡)　119 33，139 34，226
50，241 22，255 78
配密接导管之盖　350 52

配脐室　223 43
酚的氢化产生粗环乙醇
酊载机械手　235 29
酊载舱门　235 14
酊载舱的舱门入口　235 2
酊载舱隔热层　235 13
酪乳槽　76 18
酸化室　159 6
酸轮机　76 42
酸容器　350 62
酸橙　371 46
酵母　97 53
酵母纯粹培养设备　93 6
酿酒厂的酿酒过程　92 42
醋果派　97 22
醋栗　58 9
醋栗尺蠖幼虫　58 5
醋栗花　58 6
醋栗矮灌木　58 1

里部

里昂香肠圈　96 10
里脊　95 13
里程标　216 44
里程碑　15 109
野马　352 4
野马头　328 7
野牛　328 9，367 9
野手(投手)　292 76
野公猪　88 51
野母猪　88 51
野兰花　376 28
野生大麦　61 28
野生萝卜　61 21
野生萝卜花　61 22
野生萝卜叶　61 23
野生燕麦　61 29
野羊　367 6
野芥子　61 18
野芥花　61 19
野苹果　61 20
野莒　57 38
野刺芹　61 32
野兔　86 35，88 59
野兽　307 56
野兽莒　307 49
野猪莒　376 25
野猪　86 32，88 51
野猪皮　88 56
野猪狩猎队　86 31
野腰子豆　69 6
野豌豆　69 18

足(足)部

足　16 54，17 26-29，19
足印　86 8
足尖站立　295 2
足尖鞋(芭蕾舞鞋)　314 30
足床　101 50
足跟　86 8
足底　19 62
足背　19 61
足球　273 10，12，291 17
足球场　291 1-16
足球赛　291 21
足跟　19 63
足跟部自动装置　301 54
距离远方信号灯100米的接近
203 26

信号灯175米的接近标志
信号灯250米的接近标志
环 114 39
和手动焦距调整 117 3
装置 114 28
57
29
26
362 4
5 41
295 2
特体跳水 282 43
3 1，298 6
305 33
292 45，66
导区 292 56
员 292 57
5 15
8 6
路灯 198 18
8 1-5
3 68
197 21
式的桌子 336 14
法国金币 252 5
110
5 8，217 1
车 199 41
1 15
55，268 48
0 59
机 201 1
8 6
4 17
5 14
8 7
7 27
32 25
05 8，305 28
295 20
273 35，307 59
7 1
手翻 297 22
平腾越 296 48
腾越 296 53
282 11
282 5
32 6
80 39
98 37-41
88 37-62
288 50-51
31 53
297 11
32 5-10
簧跳床 297 14
黄跳床上前空翻 297 18
表演者 307 35
171 10
298 7-8
295 12
42
306 52
98 9-27
备用具 298 32
手 298 10
球进攻队员 292 3
273 15，297 42
273 16
马之演员 307 32
脚碰脚之姿势 314 21
和撑杆跳高 298 9-41

跳跃后脚 358 11
跳跃滑水板 286 62
跳圈 297 45
跳棋 276 26-28
跳棋板 276 26
跳越障碍用的马鞍 289 10
跳越障碍的马 289 9
跳越翻蹦旋转 302 8
跳鼠 366 15
跳舞者 317 17，18
跳箱 276 27
踩水 282 39
踢马刺 71 50-51
踪迹 86 8
踏杆 83 34，166 58
踏板 38 27，187 40，305 85，307 36，323 62，325 46
踏板木架 325 42
踏板曲柄 188 25
(踏板)曲柄 187 41
踏板架 187 83
踏板竖琴 323 60
踏板装置 324 54
踏板键 326 51，52
踏板滚子 163 27
踏板滚子的控制杆 163 28
踏脚石 37 64
踏脚板 186 7，13
踏脚栏杆 267 52
踏脚套 290 21
蹄 88 24
蹄骨 17 28
蹲 295 6
蹲踞式起跑 298 4
蹲撑 295 23
蹼足 359 6
蹼足之蹼 359 7

豸部
豹子 368 6
豹式IA3型坦克 255 80
豹猫皮大衣 131 25
貂 86 22
貂皮 131 11
貂皮外衣 131 24
貂皮袄 30 1
貂皮帽 35 17，18，20
貂科 367 14-17
貛 88 48

采部
釉面浮雕瓷砖 333 20
釉粉 260 65
释迦牟尼像 337 20
释放杆 94 6，247 42
释放点 89 34

身部
身历声卡式带放音机座 241 33
身历声麦克风插座 241 65
身高测量器 22 69
身着长袍之讲道人 330 22
躯干 16 22-41，339 7
躺椅 274 13

角部
角 292 18，346 1-23，8

角8之余角 346 15
角8的边 346 3，7
角8的同位角 346 12
角13的对顶角 346 8，13
角尺 140 57
角支柱 120 52
角支撑 120 52
角立树 384 41
角的符号 345 23
角铁 143 1
角钳 137 37
角桩 292 79
角球 291 41
角塔 329 14，17
角落座位 207 58，265 10，266 38
角落装置 39 27
角落餐桌 266 39
角楼 121 62
角锥形树 52 16
角楼 329 14，28
角旗 291 8
角砾石 11 27
角撑 121 57
角镜 177 28
解剖器 110 18
解剖刀 26 43
解剖台 261 22
解答 345 10
触手 357 16，31
触发网 270 62
触角 357 31，358 27，53
触轮 194 42
触版鼓滚 181 18，27，61
触须 82 3，364 13
触摸式按钮 242 25

青部
青少年服装 29 48-68
青虫 80 48
青色双面印刷装置 180 8-9
青色过滤调整装置 116 45
青梅 59 24
青铜水桶 328 34
青铜矛头 328 21
青铜时代和铁器时代 328 21-40
青蝇 358 18
静水池 217 61
静电放电导体 230 51，231 27
静电集尘器 152 13，156 20，172 39
静压轴承 5 10
静物组合 338 27
静脉注射的点滴注管 25 13
静脉注射点滴用的立架 26 9
静索 219 10-19
靛蓝染色和上浆机 165 40

其部
基生叶 375 9，12，15，30，383 2
基本原料 169 1
基本针织组织 171 30-48
基本姿势 295 1
基本算术运算 344 23-26
基本翼形 229 45
基层 198 3
基岩 13 70
基态能阶 1 18
基桩 5 28
基座 177 40，183 25，339 23
基座式手术台 26 5

基座式磨牀 138 7
基座(柱) 44 23，91 33，339 23
基座垫 49 18
基特峰天文太阳塔 5 29-33
基脚 123 2，334 31
基数 344 5
基督教十字架的各种类型 332 55-72
基督教的洗礼 332 1
(基督教)复原教堂 330 1-30
基槽 118 75
期刊架 262 15

雨部
雨 9 32
雨水管 37 13，38 10，122 29
雨斗篷 41 4
雨衣 29 31，228 4
雨伞 41 15，205 12
雨伞架 41 14
雨沟 12 44
雨层云 8 10
雨刮/冲洗器开关和喇叭按钮 191 60
雨披肩 41 4
雨量计 10 38
雨遮 37 67
雨篷(遮) 37 67，196 26
雨燕 359 24
雪 9 34
雪人 304 13
雪水(泥) 304 30
雪冰原 12 48
雪地鞋罩 300 55
雪块 353 5
雪利酒酒杯 45 84
雪花莲(石蒜科) 60 1
雪杖的撑圈 301 8
雪茄 107 2
雪茄切割机 107 9
雪茄烟的外卷叶 107 5
雪茄烟心 107 7
雪茄烟盒 107 1，8
雪桥 300 24
雪履鞋扣 301 56
雪崩 304 1
雪崩走廊 304 3
雪崩林 304 7
雪崩墙 304 2
雪铲 304 23
雪堆 304 5，24
雪犁升起号志 203 34
雪犁号志 203 34-35
雪犁附件 304 9
雪犁放下号志 203 35
雪球 304 15
雪球花 373 10
雪链 304 10
雪貂 86 24
雪蜡 301 21
雪履鼠夹式固定装置 301 15
雪橇驾驶人 303 20
雪橇铃 304 28
雪橇绳 303 4
雪橇绳 35 39
雪覆盖的屋顶 304 20
雪蒸 300 20
雷达天线 223 8，224 104，258 36，259 8，29，48，91
(雷达)天线罩 258 77
雷达设备 224 10-13
雷达图象 224 13
雷达显示装置 224 12

雷达屏幕 224 12
雷达基座 224 10
雷达罩 256 10
雷鸟(鸡) 88 72
雷雨 9 38
雷雨云 7 2
雷射机 242 81
雷射光束 243 53
雷管 87 59，158 28，306 49
零 275 18
零件配件 126 38-52
零点调整(装置) 2 7
零星物品箱 195 31
零度等温线 9 41
零钱兑换机 204 22，236 28
零值双曲线 224 42
雰 9 31
雰灯警示灯 191 63
震央 11 33
震央区 11 38
震动棒 119 89
震波 11 35
震源深度 11 34
霓虹灯广告牌 268 16
霉病 80 20
露天吸入治疗处 274 6
露天咖啡座 272 57
露天剧场 272 6
露天游泳池 282 1-32
露台 37 36
露面头盔 254 9
露背装 31 64
露核果 374 12
露趾无后跟女式拖鞋 101 22
露营用桌上餐具 278 45
露营者 278 46

隹部

隹科 362 1-4
难行之路或尚未铺沙石之路 15 99
集中分离器 172 15
集中式建筑 334 55
集水箱 92 5
集水器 10 40
集市 308 1-69
集电弓开关 211 30
集电器 194 41，197 2，23，211 2
集石器 64 9
集合 348 1，3
集合A的元素 348 2
集合A的余集 348 8
集合A和集合B的交集 348 4
集合A和集合B的联集 348 5-6
集合B的余集 348 7
集尘装置 249 60
集尘器 108 45，199 47
集材车 85 34
集材道 84 3
集汽器 210 21
集拢赌注的耙子 275 5
集草耙 64 44
集料箱 201 20
集蛋系统 74 34
集棉涂油器 163 42
集圈浮线组织 171 44
雅典 252 1
雅典之卫城 334 1-7
雅肉穗花序 383 55，384 4
雄花 371 14，373 21，374 11，378 23，382 13，383 51，384 5，15，44
雄花序 59 39，68 35，371 8，372 17，383 13，384 51

雄花序列 372 24
雄花枝 372 6，44，49，56
雄花枝和雌花球果 372 62，68
雄鸡肉距 73 26
雄狐 88 42
雄荚莱花序 59 45
雄鹿 88 28，367 5
雄鹿茸 87 46
雄蕊 58 45，59 10，370 57，372 7，18，374 3
雄蛐虫 81 34
雄雉 88 77
雄蛾 82 29
雄蜂 77 5
雄蜂巢室 77 36
雉鸡 69 13，376 1
雌花穗花序 384 6
雌花 59 38，371 6，13，373 20，378 6，382 32，383 50，384 7，14，43
雌花序 59 46，68 32，383 11，384 50
雌花枝 372 46，48，384 42
雌花球果 372 4，16，22
雌花球果鳞片 372 34
雌鹿 88 13
雌狐 88 42
雌性马鹿 88 1
雌鹿 378 24
雌鹿 88 34
雌蛐虫 81 32
雌雄同雄花 374 10，382 14
雌雉 88 77
雌蛾 82 30
雌蜂 77 4
雌猪 88 48
雕 36 41
雕刻刀 175 33，340 5，15
雕刻机 177 52
雕刻师 175 32
雕刻家 339 1
雕刻球形部 108 34
雕刻装置 177 66
雕饰物 215 22
雕塑品 339 32
雕塑家 339 6
雕像 272 10，334 5
雕像底座 272 11
雕镂槌 108 41

鱼(鱼)部

鱼刀 89 39
鱼叉 280 40，353 10
鱼市 225 57
(鱼)网 90 8
鱼网声纳电缆 90 14
鱼网声纳装置 90 17
鱼池 89 6
鱼尾 327 25，43，46，49
鱼尾板 202 12
鱼尾板螺栓 202 13
鱼卵 89 12
鱼卵孵化所 89 11-19
鱼饵 89 65-76
鱼类 364 1-18
鱼类养殖 89 1-19
鱼竿引线环 89 58
鱼竿节 89 54
鱼竿环 89 56
鱼钩 89 79-87，79，84
鱼竿形针迹 102 7
鱼梯 89 93
鱼道 89 93
鱼眼镜头 115 44
鱼碟 266 53

鱼雷(发)射管 258 78，259 79
鱼雷快艇 258 69，75
鱼筌 89 25
鱼鳞式图案 335 15
鱼鳞筛 64 17
鱼鳞筛的延长线 64 18
鲁特琴 324 1
鲜乳装瓶和包装设备 76 20
鲜乳槽 76 15
鲤鱼 364 4
鲤鱼池 89 6
鲶鱼 364 12
鲸尾裂片 367 29
鲸油灯 353 7
鲸鱼星座及其变星与蒿增二 3 11
鲸鱼喷水孔 367 26
鲸类 367 23-29
鲛鲤 366 10
鲅鲤 366 10
鲱 364 14
鳃盖 364 5
鳃裂 364 3
鳃膜 364 20
鳃膜 364 5
鳃板 286 43
鳄鱼钩 89 87
鳄鱼化 89 14
鳄鱼苗 89 14
鳄鱼孵化 89 14
鳞片 364 11，372 42
鳞状皮刺真菌 381 24
鳞茎 371 12
鳞翅目 358 48-56

革部

靶 242 84，305 30-33，66
靶场 305 74
靶的飞行路线 305 77
靶球 305 77
靴子 100 57
靴皮剪 100 42
靴刺静脉 72 28
靴面 100 60
鞋(子) 41 16，100 1
鞋子保养工具 50 39-43
鞋内底 291 27
鞋底刀 100 50
鞋匠钳子 100 38
鞋匠铁锤 100 37
鞋扣 100 62，101 52
鞋舌 100 65，101 32
鞋头(头) 100 58，101 16，40
鞋尖拆卸钳 100 52
鞋身(帮) 291 26
鞋楦 41 8
鞋刷 50 41
鞋底 100 66，68
鞋底皮革 100 31
鞋底皮革剃 100 39
鞋底针柱 291 28
鞋底钉护套 300 50
鞋底钉绳钩扣 300 52
鞋底钉缚带 300 51
鞋底修整机 100 5
鞋底修整机 100 26
鞋油罐 50 42
鞋油盒 50 39
鞋油喷雾器 50 40
鞋油海绵 50 43
鞋型 100 32
鞋带 100 64，291 32
鞋带结 101 21
鞋面后部分 100 59
鞋帮后跟的硬皮 291 23
鞋帮的后侧部皮 100 61
鞋锉 100 49

鞋楦 100 34
鞋跟 100 67
鞍马上双腿回旋 296 54
鞍马上的剪式动作 296 5
鞍马式缝线 31 45
鞍头 71 38
鞍管横动用导螺手轮 149 鞍后的弓形部 71 39
鞍形夹 126 53
鞍的护垫 71 40，47
鞍环 296 5
鞍卷 71 48
鞍带 289 11
鞍座 71 37，45，187 22
鞍座支柱 187 24
鞍座弹簧 187 23
鞍座袋 187 25
鞍褥 71 42
毡粗飞弹发射器 258 49
鞘翅 82 10
鞭子 307 53
鞭状天线 258 60
鞭炮 306 51
韁绳 71 25，33，186 31，27

骨部

骨头 70 33
骨灰瓮 331 31
骨灰瓮坟墓 331 30
骨折用的紧急夹板 21 10
骨折的腿 21 11
骨制鱼叉 328 3
骨架 91 3，136 25，149 6，261 14，339 22
骨架雪橇 303 22
骨架雪橇滑雪运动 303 22-24
骨架雪橇滑雪者 303 23
骨架装扮 336 11
骨柑 26 51
骨盘 17 18-21
骨凿 24 49
骨牌游戏 276 33
骨髓 94 19，96 56
骨骼 17 1-29，261 14
骰子 276 29
(骰子上的)点 276 32
骰子杯 47 42，276 30
骰子筒 276 30
骰子游戏 47 19，276 31
髁 72 37
髓线 370 11
骶部 72 32

鬼部

鬼笔鹅膏 379 11
鬼脸天蛾 365 9

彡部

鬓毛 88 73
鬃(毛) 88 52，368 3
鬈发 34 24
髭间涂蜡的范大克式髭 34 13
髭甲 72 17

麻部

麻布捆 206 11
麻花钻头 134 49，140 59

5
二呼吸装置 **26** 24
器械 **26** 1
68 35
290 11
189 21
290 24-38
189 26
灯 **188** 29
士 **288** 34
尤赛 **290** 11-15
尤赛车 **290** 15
条 **189** 22
290 24-28
3 36
4 62
66 19
钢棒 **94** 16
350 31
111 24
172 68
172 53-65
运送带 **172** 79
6 19, **172** 71, **354** 24
版印刷师 **340** 45
91 12
91 20
91 21
装置 **172** 70
91 16
187 8
轮 **187** 9
版 **340** 53
件 **109** 15
100 10, **108** 44
光机 **108** 42
40 18
台 **150** 7
升降杆 **157** 46
身 **150** 6
人 **91** 15
24 36, **137** 19, **150** 4, 43
割机 **125** 16
滑台 **150** 3
111 28
和磨边用的模型 **111** 35
钻 **66** 11
340 46
91 19
襟 **355** 52
152 4
承轴 **163** 41
322 26
306 14
袋形菌 **381** 20
菇 **379** 12

88 28-39
101 30
295 40, **302** 7
88 5-11, 29-31
从下往上数的第三枝 **88** 8
的叉枝 **88** 7
的主干 **88** 11, 30
突出的尖端或叉齿 **88**
, 31
钮扣 **29** 33
根部隆起部分 **88** 5, 29
最上面的叉枝 **88** 9
泪腺 **88** 14
短尾 **88** 19
367 10

麋鹿 **367** 2
麝鼠皮帽 **35** 33

鼠部

鼠李 **380** 13
鼠李粉蝶 **365** 4
鼩鼱 **366** 7
鼹鼠 **366** 4

其他

A大调 **320** 58
A小调 **320** 55, 62
A甲板 **223** 28-30
B大调 **320** 60
B小调 **320** 57
B甲板 **223** 32-42
C大音阶本位音 **320** 45
C大调 **320** 55, 62
C小调 **320** 65
C型框架 **26** 19, **27** 17
CD4录音带四声道解调器 **241** 45
D大调 **320** 57
D小调 **320** 59
E大调 **320** 59
E小调 **320** 56
E层 **7** 27
E型快艇 **258** 69, 75
E型槽钢 **143** 7
F大调 **320** 63
F小调 **320** 66
F孔 **323** 6
F-1发动机 **234** 4
F1层 **7** 28
F2层 **7** 29
F和X触用的闪光灯插座 **115** 14
G大调 **320** 56
G小调 **320** 64
GT小汽车 **193** 32
G3-A3型自动步枪 **255** 16
g_2的垂线(g_4) **346** 6
H型钢梁 **143** 6
H(领港员在船上) **253** 24
I频道电视接收天线 **239** 4
J-2发动机 **234** 19, 34
KR级 **284** 63
K9级模型机棚 **288** 91
L式坐姿 **295** 10
L型手支撑 **295** 16
L(停船,有手事传送) **253** 25
M型万向接头 **67** 29
MG3型机关枪 **255** 32
MP2型机关枪 **255** 8
M113型装甲救护车 **255** 79
O级小艇 **284** 50
P,开航旗 **253** 26
P1型手枪 **255** 1
Rautek氏握法 **21** 18
S型扳手 **126** 66
T字形切口 **54** 32
T型尾翼 **256** 31-32, **287** 10
T型尾翼装置 **229** 29, **256** 31-32
T型姿势 **288** 62
T型铁 **143** 3
T型接头 **126** 44
U型轨道 **214** 22
U型谷 **13** 54
U型急转滑道 **301** 69
U型圆槽 **340** 6
U型管 **349** 2
U型管压力计 **346** 19
V字形照门 **87** 66

V型万向接头 **67** 31
V型手支撑 **295** 17
V型导轨 **132** 61
V型尾翼 **229** 31
V型谷 **13** 53
V型底船 **286** 35-37
V型姿式 **295** 13
V型带转动之护板 **180** 58
V型领 **31** 68
V型槽 **175** 54
W(要求医疗支援) **253** 27
X型十字架 **332** 60
X型圆盘耙片组 **65** 83
X射线头 **27** 18
X射线发生器 **24** 22
X射线技师 **27** 11
X射线胶片盒支架 **27** 2
X射线萤光增倍装置 **27** 16
X射线检查台 **27** 1
X射线装置 **27** 1-35
X照射射下的心脏影像 **25** 39
X射线管 **27** 7
X辐射 **1** 56
Y型十字架 **332** 61
Z长方形旗 **253** 28
Z驱动汽艇 **286** 2
(α)阿伐粒子 **1** 30-31
α粒子的雾室轨迹 **2** 27
(β)贝他粒子 **1** 32
(γ)伽马辐射 **1** 33, 40
"π"键 **247** 24
1,800公斤重铁锤 **90** 21
1~2浬/时 **9** 12
3~7浬/时 **9** 13
8~12浬/时 **9** 14
13~17浬/时 **9** 15
18~22浬/时 **9** 16
23~27浬/时 **9** 17
28~32浬/时 **9** 18
58~9浬/时 **9** 19
.22长步枪弹 **305** 38
.222雷明顿子弹 **305** 39
2.2米左舷望远镜 **113** 1
2.5吨工程车 **255** 75
2×2集圈和浮线组织 **171** 47
3月21日(春分)和9月23日(秋分)太阳的视轨道 **4** 19
"3"字形 **302** 13
"8"字形 **302** 11
5毫米剪切机组 **148** 74
10毫米剪切机组 **148** 75
5.5公尺级 **284** 58
6公尺R级 **284** 59
12瓶缩箔包装 **76** 25
16毫米摄影机 **117** 43
35毫米照相机 **114** 1
24仪器装置 **234** 53
30米远洋游艇 **286** 5
35毫米底壳 **114** 7
110底片 **114** 17
120底片 **114** 19
126底片 **114** 15
135底片壳 **114** 7
40毫米高射炮 **258** 73
40毫米双高射炮 **258** 71
76毫米炮 **258** 70
127毫米多目的炮 **258** 48
100毫米炮塔 **258** 29
44毫米反坦克火箭筒 **255** 25
120毫米AM50型迫击炮 **255** 40
155毫米M109G型自动推进炮 **255** 57
175毫米SFM107型大炮 **255** 49
110SF型火箭炮 **255** 70
42的同伴 **267** 43

43的同伴 **267** 42
42的邻座 **267** 41
50米赛靶 **305** 30
100米赛靶 **305** 32
250公克包装标示的奶油 **76** 37
490公尺的水平坑道 **154** 83
511公尺的水平坑道 **154** 73
12.00m² 帆船 **284** 53
25.00m²统一龙骨船 **284** 62
30.00m²巡航小帆船 **284** 61
30.00m²巡航快艇 **284** 60
I型赛车 **290** 34
II型赛车 **290** 36
II频道的电视接收天线 **239** 5